lonely planet

# Vietnam

**Mason Florence**
**Virginia Jealous**

LONELY PLANET PUBLICATIONS
Melbourne • Oakland • London • Paris

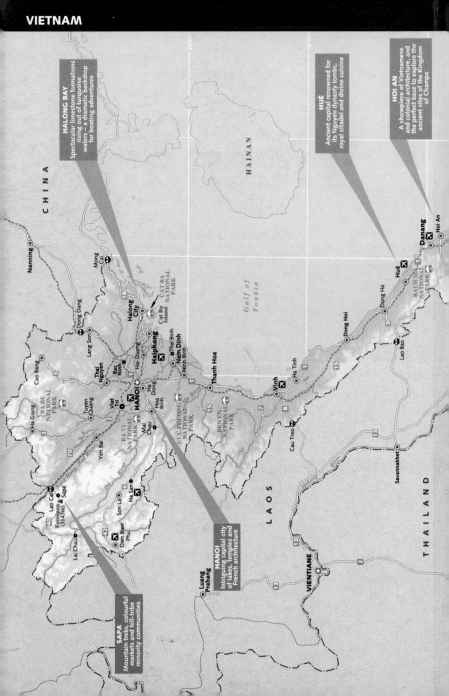

# VIETNAM

**HALONG BAY**
Spectacular limestone formations rising out of turquoise waters – a dramatic backdrop for boating adventures

**HUÉ**
Ancient capital renowned for its Nguyen dynasty tombs, royal citadel and divine cuisine

**HOI AN**
A showpiece of Vietnamese and colonial architecture, and the perfect base to explore the ancient sites of the Kingdom of Champa

**HANOI**
Intriguing capital city of lakes, temples and French architecture

**SAPA**
Mountain treks, colourful markets and hill-tribe minority communities

CHINA

HAINAN

Gulf of Tonkin

LAOS

THAILAND

Nanning

Mong Cai

Dong Dang

Lang Son

Cao Bang

Ha Giang

BA BE NATIONAL PARK

Tuyen Quang

Thai Nguyen

Bac Ninh

Halong City

Cat Ba Island

CAT BA NATIONAL PARK

Haiphong

Hai Duong

Thai Binh

Nam Dinh

Ninh Binh

HANOI

Ha Dong

Viet Tri

Hoa Binh

Thanh Hoa

CUC PHUONG NATIONAL PARK

BEN EN NATIONAL PARK

Mai Chau

BA VI NATIONAL PARK

Yen Bai

Lao Cai

Sapa

Fansipan (3143m)

Son La

Na San

Dien Bien Phu

Lai Chau

Luang Prabang

Mekong River

Cau Treo

Savannakhet

VIENTIANE

Vinh

Ha Tinh

Dong Hoi

Dong Ha

Lao Bao

Hué

Danang

Hoi An

BACH MA NATIONAL PARK

 Red River

Da River

Black River

Me Kong River

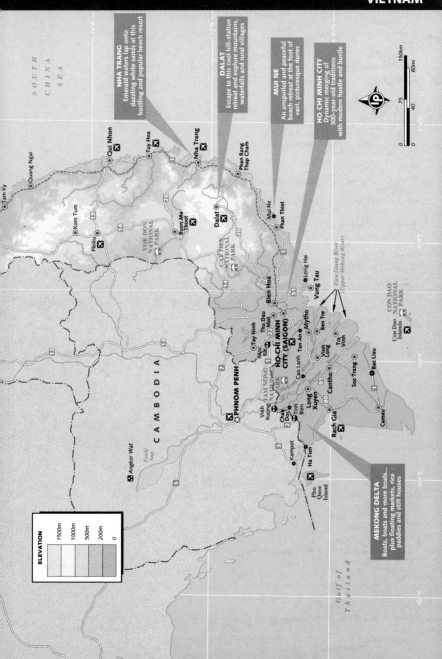

# VIETNAM

**NHA TRANG**
Emerald waters lap onto dazzling white sands at this bustling and popular beach resort

**DALAT**
Escape to this cool hill-station retreat and explore mountains, waterfalls and rural villages

**MUI NE**
An unspoiled and peaceful beach retreat at the foot of vast, picturesque dunes

**HO CHI MINH CITY**
Dynamic merging of 300-year-old traditions with modern hustle and bustle

**MEKONG DELTA**
Boats, boats and more boats... plus floating markets, rice paddies and stilt houses

ELEVATION
1500m
1000m
500m
200m
0

0    75    150km
0    40    80mi

SOUTH CHINA SEA

Tam Ky
Quang Ngai
Qui Nhon
Tuy Hoa
Nha Trang
Kom Tum
Pleiku
Buon Ma Thuot
YOK DON NATIONAL PARK
Phan Rang Thap Cham
CAT TIEN NATIONAL PARK
Dalat
Mui Ne
Phan Thiet
Bien Hoa
Long Hai
Vung Tau
Thieu Giang River (Upper Mekong River)
CON DAO NATIONAL PARK
Con Dao Islands

CAMBODIA
PHNOM PENH
Angkor Wat
Tonle Sap
Tay Ninh
Thu Dau Mot
Hoc Bac
HO CHI MINH CITY (SAIGON)
Tan An
Mytho
Ben Tre
Tra Vinh
Cao Lanh
Vinh Long
Vinh Xuong
Chau Doc
Tinh Bien
Long Xuyen
Bassac River
Cantho
Soc Trang
Bac Lieu
Rach Gia
Camau
Kampot
Ha Tien
Phu Quoc Island

Gulf of Thailand

**Vietnam**
**7th edition** – February 2003
**First published** – February 1991

**Published by**
**Lonely Planet Publications Pty Ltd** ABN 36 005 607 983
90 Maribyrnong St, Footscray, Victoria 3011, Australia

**Lonely Planet offices**
**Australia** Locked Bag 1, Footscray, Victoria 3011
**USA** 150 Linden St, Oakland, CA 94607
**UK** 10a Spring Place, London NW5 3BH
**France** 1 rue du Dahomey, 75011 Paris

**Photographs**
Many of the images in this guide are available for licensing from
Lonely Planet Images.
W www.lonelyplanetimages.com

**Front cover photograph**
Sea salt production, Doc Let (John Banagan)

ISBN 1 74059 355 3

Printed through Colorcraft Ltd, Hong Kong
Printed in China

# Contents – Text

## NORTHEAST VIETNAM                                                                214

## NORTHWEST VIETNAM                                                               243

## NORTH-CENTRAL VIETNAM                                                           272

## CENTRAL VIETNAM                                                                 287

## SOUTH-CENTRAL COAST                                                            358

# Contents – Maps

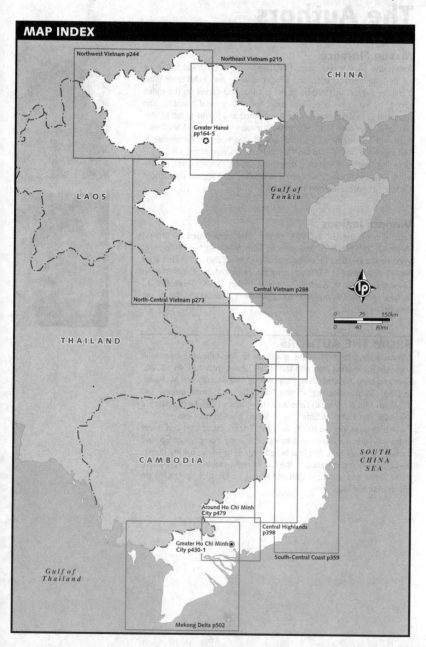

MAP INDEX

Northwest Vietnam p244

Northeast Vietnam p215

CHINA

Greater Hanoi
pp164-5

LAOS

Gulf of
Tonkin

North-Central Vietnam p273

Central Vietnam p288

THAILAND

0    75    150km
0  40   80mi

CAMBODIA

SOUTH
CHINA
SEA

Around Ho Chi Minh
City p479

Central Highlands
p398

Greater Ho Chi Minh
City p430-1

South-Central Coast p359

Gulf of
Thailand

Mekong Delta p502

# The Authors

## Mason Florence

As a native New Yorker, Mason migrated west to Colorado to pursue his life-long dream of becoming a rodeo cowboy and, in his spare time, a college degree. In 1990 he gave up a budding career on the rodeo circuit, traded in his boots and spurs for a Nikon and a laptop, and relocated to Japan. Since then he has worked as a Kyoto-based photo-journalist, spending half the year on the road in Japan and Southeast Asia, and free moments restoring an old thatched-roof farmhouse in Shikoku's Iya Valley. Mason has worked on numerous LP guides including *Southeast Asia on a shoestring*, *Japan*, *Kyoto*, *Hanoi*, *Ho Chi Minh City* and *Rocky Mountains*. His photographs appear throughout Vietnam as *Postcards from the Edge*.

## Virginia Jealous

Since leaving the UK in 1983, Virginia has been based all around Australia, and has lived and worked with NGOs in the Philippines, West Papua and East Timor. Bone-shaken and mildly road-crazed after weeks in a jeep in Vietnam, Virginia retreated to her home on Christmas Island, in Australia's remote Indian Ocean Territories, to recover in a place where you can't drive more than 30 minutes in any direction.

## FROM THE AUTHORS

Mason wishes to express his gratitude to the following people in Vietnam for sharing info and travel tips about their turf. In HCMC, Sinh and Tram, Richard Craik, Paul Levieur, Pete Murray and Mr Hung; in Dalat, Michael Sterling; in Nha Trang, Bu, Jack, Peter, Jeremy and Paolo; in Mui Ne, Pascal, Gino and Hang; and in Qui Nhon, Barbara Dawson. This edition's 'Safe Driver' award goes to Mr Liem.

Thanks from Virginia to My Anh and Thanh, interpreter and driver extraordinaire, for miles and miles of bumpy companionship and endless meals of tofu, fish and boiled vegies; to Fiona, for my home-away-from-home in Hanoi; to the Cat Ba night-clubbers Gary, Darren, Peter, Jackie and Stefan; to Linh and Hoang for logistics; and to Mason for sharing the load.

# This Book

Lonely Planet's first guide to Vietnam started as the Vietnam section of *Vietnam, Laos & Cambodia*, written by Daniel Robinson (Vietnam and Cambodia) and Joe Cummings (Laos). The 2nd edition, dedicated solely to Vietnam, was updated by long-time Lonely Planet author Robert Storey, using material from Daniel's research. Robert also updated the 3rd and 4th editions, while the 5th and 6th editions were updated by Lonely Planet author and Colorado-escapee, Mason Florence.

For this edition, Virginia Jealous updated the Central, North-Central, Northeast and Northwest Vietnam and Hanoi chapters. Mason updated the rest of the book.

## From the Publisher

This book was produced in Lonely Planet's Melbourne office. Victoria Harrison coordinated the editing, and additional editing and proofing was done by David Andrew, Carolyn Boicos, Linda Suttie and Mary Neighbour. Quentin Frayne edited the language chapter. Managing editor Jane Thompson gave plenty of support throughout the project, as did commissioning editor Mary Neighbour.

Chris Thomas coordinated the cartography, with assistance from Nicholas Stebbing, who designed the colour and special sections. Corinne Waddell and Wayne Murphy managed the book's cartography. Designers Vicki Beale and Kate McDonald steered the book through the layout stage, and the book's cover was designed by Margaret Jung and Simon Bracken. Chris Love commissioned the authors and managed the book's production. Thanks to Mark Germanchis for technical support and Pepi Bluck for sourcing illustrations for this book. Illustrations were provided by Simon Borg, Trudi Canavan and Martin Harris.

Special thanks to Brendan Allen of Oxfam CAA, and to Ryan Evans for his courier services.

**THANKS**
Many thanks to the travellers who used the last edition and wrote to us with helpful hints, advice and interesting anecdotes. Your names appear in the back of this book.

# Foreword

## ABOUT LONELY PLANET GUIDEBOOKS

The story begins with a classic travel adventure: Tony and Maureen Wheeler's 1972 journey across Europe and Asia to Australia. There was no useful information about the overland trail then, so Tony and Maureen published the first Lonely Planet guidebook to meet a growing need.

From a kitchen table, Lonely Planet has grown to become the largest independent travel publisher in the world, with offices in Melbourne (Australia), Oakland (USA), London (UK) and Paris (France).

Today Lonely Planet guidebooks cover the globe. There is an ever-growing list of books and information in a variety of media. Some things haven't changed. The main aim is still to make it possible for adventurous travellers to get out there – to explore and better understand the world.

At Lonely Planet we believe travellers can make a positive contribution to the countries they visit – if they respect their host communities and spend their money wisely. Since 1986 a percentage of the income from each book has been donated to aid projects and human rights campaigns, and, more recently, to wildlife conservation.

*Although inclusion in a guidebook usually implies a recommendation we cannot list every good place. Exclusion does not necessarily imply criticism. In fact there are a number of reasons why we might exclude a place – sometimes it is simply inappropriate to encourage an influx of travellers.*

## UPDATES & READER FEEDBACK

Things change – prices go up, schedules change, good places go bad and bad places go bankrupt. Nothing stays the same. So, if you find things better or worse, recently opened or long-since closed, please tell us and help make the next edition even more accurate and useful.

Lonely Planet thoroughly updates each guidebook as often as possible – usually every two years, although for some destinations the gap can be longer. Between editions, up-to-date information is available in our free, quarterly *Planet Talk* newsletter and monthly email bulletin *Comet*. The *Scoop* section of our website covers news and current affairs relevant to travellers. Lastly, the *Thorn Tree* bulletin board and *Postcards* section carry unverified, but fascinating, reports from travellers.

**Tell us about it!** We genuinely value your feedback. A well-travelled team at Lonely Planet reads and acknowledges every email and letter we receive and ensures that every morsel of information finds its way to the relevant authors, editors and cartographers.

Everyone who writes to us will find their name listed in the next edition of the appropriate guidebook, and will receive the latest issue of *Comet* or *Planet Talk*. The very best contributions will be rewarded with a free guidebook.

We may edit, reproduce and incorporate your comments in Lonely Planet products such as guidebooks, websites and digital products, so let us know if you don't want your comments reproduced or your name acknowledged.

**How to contact Lonely Planet:**
Online: e talk2us@lonelyplanet.com.au, w www.lonelyplanet.com
Australia: Locked Bag 1, Footscray, Victoria 3011
UK: 10a Spring Place, London NW5 3BH
USA: 150 Linden St, Oakland, CA 94607

# Introduction

Vietnam has a unique and rich civilisation, spectacular scenery and highly cultured, cordial people. While there is no doubt its long history of war continues to weigh heavily on the consciousness of all who can remember, the Vietnam of today is a country at peace.

Red tape kept foreign tourists and investors out for nearly two decades, but visiting has become considerably easier in recent years and the tourist floodgates have opened wide. Already, the relatively short period of economic liberalisation and openness has brought dramatic changes.

Most visitors to Vietnam are overwhelmed by the sublime beauty of the country's natural setting. The Red River Delta in the north, the Mekong Delta in the south and almost the entire coastal strip are a patchwork of brilliant-green rice paddies tended by peasant women in conical hats. Vietnam's 3451km coastline includes countless unspoiled beaches and a number of stunning lagoons; some sections are shaded by coconut palms and casuarinas, others bounded by seemingly endless expanses of sand dunes or the rugged spurs of the Truong Son Mountain Range.

Between the two deltas, the coast lining the South China Sea gives way to soaring mountains – the slopes of some are cloaked with rich forests. West of the coast, the refreshingly cool plateaus of the central highlands are dotted with waterfalls. To the north you'll not only find stunning mountain scenery but also Vietnam's most prominent hill-tribe communities.

Visitors to Vietnam will have their senses thrilled by all its sights, sounds, tastes and smells. There's nothing quite like grabbing a delicious lunch of local delicacies at a food stall deep inside a marketplace, surrounded by tropical-fruit vendors as well as legions of curious youngsters. Or sitting by a waterfall in the central highlands, sipping soda water with lemon juice and watching honeymooning couples in their 'Sunday finest'. Or being invited by a Buddhist monk to a pagoda to attend prayers, conducted according to Mahayana rites, with chanting, drums and gongs.

Fiercely protective of their independence and sovereignty, the Vietnamese are also graciously welcoming of foreigners who come as guests rather than conquerors. Today the Vietnamese are, almost without exception, extremely friendly to Western visitors (including Americans), and supportive of more contact with the outside world. Visitors to Vietnam play an important role in conveying the value and potential for international friendship and business.

The astonishing pace of development in East Asia has made many countries in the region considerably more polluted and expensive, and less enchanting than they used

to be. The rice paddies have given way to industrial estates belching out black smoke; bicycles have been replaced by tour buses; and thatched huts have been bulldozed to make way for office towers and five-star hotels.

Although Vietnam has not yet reached the level of rampant development found in the region, capitalism is no longer a four-letter word here and private business has mushroomed, adding an atmosphere of hustle and bustle to Ho Chi Minh City, Hanoi and other cities whose resurgent dynamism is reviving the Vietnamese economy. Meanwhile, cities and towns throughout Vietnam are, like the boom towns of old, experiencing rapid alteration as infrastructure development paves the way with new streets, hospitals and attitudes.

Visitors to Vietnam will be intrigued by its dynamic melding of traditional culture, its French-colonial past and communist legacy, and its current transition as a modern Asian power. While conical hats and rice paddies abound, the Vietnam of today is also where you'll find hip city cafés and nightclubs, a thriving art scene and a decided zest for the future.

# Facts about Vietnam

## HISTORY
Visitors to Vietnam will notice that, invariably, the major streets of every city and town bear the same two dozen or so names. These are the names of Vietnam's greatest national heroes who, over the last 2000 years, have led the country in its repeated expulsions of foreign invaders and whose exploits have inspired subsequent generations of patriots.

### Prehistory
The origins of the Vietnamese people are unknown. Recent archaeological finds indicate that the earliest human habitation of northern Vietnam goes back about 500,000 years. Mesolithic and Neolithic cultures existed in northern Vietnam 10,000 years ago, and may have engaged in primitive agriculture as early as 7000 BC. The sophisticated Bronze Age Dong Son culture emerged sometime around the 3rd century BC.

From the 1st to 6th centuries AD, the south of what is now Vietnam was part of the Indianised kingdom of Funan, which produced notably refined art and architecture. The Funanese constructed an elaborate system of canals that were used for both transportation and the irrigation of wet rice agriculture. The principal port city of Funan was Oc-Eo in what is now the Mekong Delta's Kien Giang province. Archaeological excavations have yielded evidence of contact between Funan and China, Indonesia, India, Persia and even the Mediterranean. One of the most extraordinary artefacts found at Oc-Eo was a gold Roman medallion dated AD 152 and bearing the likeness of Antoninus Pius. In the mid-6th century, Funan was attacked by the pre-Angkorian kingdom of Chenla, which gradually absorbed the territory of Funan into its own.

The Hindu kingdom of Champa appeared around present-day Danang in the late 2nd century (see the boxed text 'Kingdom of Champa' in the Central Vietnam chapter). Like Funan, it became Indianised (eg, the Chams adopted Hinduism, used Sanskrit as a sacred language and borrowed heavily from Indian art) through lively commercial relations with India and the immigration of Indian literati and priests. By the 8th century, Champa had expanded southward to include what is now Nha Trang and Phan Rang. The Chams were semipiratic and conducted raids along the entire coast of Indochina; as a result, it was in a constant state of war with the Vietnamese to the north and the Khmers to the west. Some brilliant examples of Cham sculpture can be seen in the Museum of Cham Sculpture in Danang.

### Chinese Rule (circa 200 BC–AD 938)
When the Chinese conquered the Red River Delta in the 2nd century BC, they found a feudally organised society reliant on slash-and-burn agriculture, hunting and fishing; these proto-Vietnamese also carried on trade with other peoples in the area. Over the next few centuries, significant numbers of Chinese settlers, officials and scholars moved to the Red River Delta, taking over large tracts of land. The Chinese tried to impose a centralised state system on the Vietnamese and forcibly Sinocise their culture, but local rulers tenaciously resisted these efforts.

The most famous act of resistance during this period was the rebellion of the Trung Sisters (Hai Ba Trung). In AD 40, the Chinese executed a high-ranking feudal lord. His widow and her sister rallied tribal chieftains, raised an army and led a revolt that compelled the Chinese governor to flee. The sisters then had themselves proclaimed queens of the newly independent Vietnamese entity. In AD 43 the Chinese counterattacked and defeated them; rather than surrender, the Trung Sisters threw themselves into the Hat Giang River.

The early Vietnamese learned a great deal from the Chinese, such as the use of metal ploughs and domesticated beasts of burden, and the construction of dikes and irrigation works. These innovations made possible the establishment of a culture based on rice growing, which remains the basis of the Vietnamese way of life to this day. As food became more plentiful the population grew, forcing the Vietnamese to seek new lands on which to grow rice.

During this era, Vietnam was a key port of call on the sea route between China and India. The Vietnamese were introduced to Confucianism and Taoism by Chinese scholars who came to Vietnam as administrators and refugees. Indians sailing eastward brought Theravada (Hinayana) Buddhism to the Red River Delta while, at the same time, Chinese travellers introduced Mahayana Buddhism. Buddhist monks carried with them the scientific and medical knowledge of the civilisations of India and China; as a result, Vietnamese Buddhists soon counted among their own great doctors, botanists and scholars.

There were numerous major and minor rebellions against Chinese rule, (which was characterised by tyranny, forced labour and insatiable demands for tribute), in the 3rd and 6th centuries, but all were crushed. In 679 the Chinese named the country Annam, which means the 'Pacified South'. Ever since this era, the collective memory of those early attempts to throw off the Chinese yoke has played an important role in shaping Vietnamese identity.

## Independence from China (10th Century)

The Tang dynasty in China collapsed in the early 10th century, and in the aftermath the Vietnamese revolted against Chinese rule. In 938, Ngo Quyen finally vanquished the Chinese armies at a battle on the Bach Dang River, ending 1000 years of Chinese rule. Ngo Quyen established an independent Vietnamese state, but after his death, Vietnam was ruled anarchy until 968, when the powerful and politically astute Dinh Bo Linh ascended the throne as emperor. In the custom of the times, he reached an agreement with China: in return for recognition of the country's de facto independence, the

Vietnamese accepted Chinese sovereignty and agreed to pay triennial tribute.

The dynasty founded by Dinh Bo Linh survived only until 980, when Le Dai Hanh overthrew it, beginning what is known as the Early Le dynasty (980–1009).

## Ly Dynasty (1010–1225)

From the 11th to 13th centuries, the independence of the Vietnamese Kingdom (Dai Viet) was consolidated under the emperors of the Ly dynasty, founded by Ly Thai To. These emperors reorganised the administrative system, founded the nation's first university (the Temple of Literature in Hanoi), promoted agriculture and built the first embankments for flood control along the Red River. Confucian scholars fell out of official favour because of their close cultural links to China; at the same time, the early Ly monarchs, whose dynasty had come to power with Buddhist support, promoted Buddhism.

The Confucian emphasis on educational attainment, ritual performance and government authority reasserted itself with the graduation of the first class from the Temple of Literature in 1075. Following years of classical studies these scholars went into government service, becoming mandarins. The basis for this mandarin system of government, whereby the state was run by a scholar class recruited through civil-service examinations, dates from this era.

During the Ly dynasty the Chinese, Khmers and Chams repeatedly attacked Vietnam, but were repelled, most notably under the renowned strategist and tactician Ly Thuong Kiet (1030–1105), a military mandarin of royal blood who is still revered as a national hero.

Vietnamese conquests of Cham territory, which greatly increased the acreage under rice cultivation, were accompanied by an aggressive policy of colonisation that imposed social structures dominant in the north onto the newly settled territories. Potentially the attackers could have benefited from Cham technological and cultural innovations, but instead the Cham civilisation was destroyed. A chain of homogeneous villages were built in its place and eventually stretched from the Chinese border to the Gulf of Thailand.

## Tran Dynasty (1225–1400)

After years of civil strife, the Tran dynasty overthrew the Ly dynasty. The Tran increased the land under cultivation to feed the growing population and improved the dikes on the Red River.

After Mongol warrior Kublai Khan had completed his conquest of China in the mid-13th century, he demanded the right to cross Vietnamese territory on his way to attack Champa. The Vietnamese refused him, but the Mongols – 500,000 of them – did just that anyway. The outnumbered Vietnamese, under Tran Hung Dao, attacked the invaders and forced them back to China, but the Mongols returned with 300,000 men. Tran Hung Dao lured them deep into Vietnamese territory; at high tide he attacked the Mongol fleet as it sailed on the Bach Dang River, ordering a tactical retreat of his forces to lure the Mongols into staying and fighting. The battle continued for many hours until low tide came, when a surprise Vietnamese counteroffensive forced the Mongol boats back, impaling them on steel-tipped bamboo stakes set in the river bed the night before. The entire fleet was either captured or sunk.

When the Tran dynasty was overthrown in 1400 by Ho Qui Ly, both the Tran loyalists and the Chams (who had sacked Hanoi in 1371) encouraged Chinese intervention. The Chinese readily complied and took control of Vietnam in 1407, imposing a regime characterised by heavy taxation and slave labour; Chinese culture was forced on the population. The Chinese also took the national archives (and some of the country's intellectuals as well) to China, an irrepar-able loss to Vietnamese civilisation. Of this period, poet Nguyen Trai (1380–1442) wrote:

Were the water of the Eastern Sea to be exhausted, the stain of their ignominy could not be washed away; all the bamboo of the Southern Mountains would not suffice to provide the paper for recording all their crimes.

## Later Le Dynasty (1428–1524)

Le Loi was born into a large and prosperous family in the village of Lam Son in Thanh Hoa province, and earned a reputation for using his wealth to aid the poor. The ruling Chinese invited him to join the mandarinate, but he refused. In 1418 Le Loi began to organise what came to be known as the Lam Son Uprising, by travelling around the countryside and rallying the people against the Chinese. Despite several defeats Le Loi persisted, earning the respect of the peasantry by ensuring that even when facing starvation his guerrilla troops did not pillage the land. After his victory in 1428, Le Loi declared himself Emperor Ly Thai To, thus beginning the Later Le dynasty. To this day, Le Loi is revered as one of the country's greatest national heroes.

After Le Loi's victory over the Chinese, Nguyen Trai, a scholar and Le Loi's companion in arms, wrote his famous *Great Proclamation* (Binh Ngo Dai Cao), extraordinary for the compelling voice it gave to Vietnam's fierce spirit of independence:

Our people long ago established Vietnam as an independent nation with its own civilisation. We have our own mountains and our own rivers, our own customs and traditions, and these are different from those of the foreign country to the north…We have sometimes been weak and sometimes powerful, but at no time have we suffered from a lack of heroes.

The Later Le dynasty ruled until 1524 and nominally up until 1788. Le Loi and his successors instituted a vast programme of agrarian reform and land redistribution. They also launched a campaign to take over Cham lands to the south. In the 15th century Laos was forced into the recognition of Vietnamese suzerainty.

Under the Later Le dynasty, an attempt was made to break free from the domination of Chinese civilisation. In the areas of law, religion and literature, indigenous traditions came to into prominence. The Vietnamese language gained favour among scholars, who had preferred Chinese (and treated Vietnamese with disdain), and a number of outstanding works of literature were

## Dynasties of Independent Vietnam

| dynasty | year |
| --- | --- |
| Ngo dynasty | 939–965 |
| Dinh dynasty | 968–980 |
| Early Le dynasty | 980–1009 |
| Ly dynasty | 1010–1225 |
| Tran dynasty | 1225–1400 |
| Ho dynasty | 1400–1407 |
| Post-Tran dynasty | 1407–1413 |
| Chinese Rule | 1414–1427 |
| Later Le dynasty | 1428–1524 |
| | (nominally until 1788) |
| Mac dynasty | 1527–1592 |
| Trinh Lords of the North | 1539–1787 |
| Nguyen Lords of the South | 1558–1778 |
| Tay Son dynasty | 1788–1802 |
| Nguyen dynasty | 1802–1945 |

written. Legal reforms gave women almost-equal rights in the domestic sphere, but two groups were excluded from full civil rights: slaves (many of them prisoners of war) and, oddly, actors. However, in the culture of the elite both Chinese language and traditions continued to dominate; neo-Confucianism remained in the areas of social and political morality.

## Trinh & Nguyen Lords

Throughout the 17th and 18th centuries, Vietnam was divided between the Trinh Lords, who ruled in the North under the titular kingship of the Later Le monarchs, and the Nguyen Lords, who controlled the South and also nominally recognised the Later Le dynasty. The Trinh Lords repeatedly failed in attempts to take over areas under Nguyen control, in part because the Portuguese weaponry used by the Nguyen was far superior to the Dutch armaments supplied to the Trinh. During this period the Nguyen extended Vietnamese control into the Khmer territories of the Mekong Delta, populating the area with Vietnamese settlers. Cambodia was finally forced to

accept Vietnamese suzerainty in the mid-17th century.

Buddhism enjoyed the patronage and support of both the Trinh and the Nguyen Lords, and many pagodas were built throughout the country. However, by this time Vietnamese Buddhism was no longer doctrinally pure, having become diluted by ancestor worship, animism and popularised Taoism.

## Early Contact with the West

According to Chinese records, the first Vietnamese contact with Europeans took place in AD 166 when travellers from the Rome of Marcus Aurelius arrived in the Red River Delta.

The first Portuguese sailors landed in Danang in 1516; they were followed by Dominican missionaries 11 years later. During the next few decades the Portuguese began to trade with Vietnam, setting up a commercial colony alongside those of the Japanese and Chinese at Faifo (present-day Hoi An, near Danang).

Franciscan missionaries from the Philippines settled in central Vietnam in 1580, followed in 1615 by the Jesuits who had just been expelled from Japan. In 1637 the Dutch were authorised to set up trading posts in the North and one Le king even took a Dutch woman as one of his six wives. The first English attempt to break into the Vietnamese market ended with the murder of an agent of the East India Company in Hanoi in 1613.

One of the most illustrious of the early missionaries was the brilliant French Jesuit Alexandre de Rhodes (1591–1660). He is most recognised for his work in devising *quoc ngu*, the Latin-based phonetic alphabet in which Vietnamese is written to this day. Over the course of his long career, de Rhodes flitted back and forth between Hanoi, Macau, Rome and Paris, seeking support and funding for his missionary activities and battling both Portuguese colonial opposition and the intractable Vatican bureaucracy. In 1645, he was sentenced to death for illegally entering Vietnam to proselytise, but was expelled instead; two of the priests with him were beheaded.

By the late 17th century most of the European merchants had left the country as trade with Vietnam had not proved particularly profitable. But the missionaries remained and the Catholic Church eventually had a greater impact on Vietnam than on any country in Asia except the Philippines, which was ruled by the Spanish for 400 years. The Vietnamese, especially in the North, proved highly receptive to Catholicism, but mass conversions were hindered by the church's stand against polygamy and by the Vatican's opposition to ancestor worship. The Catholic emphasis on individual salvation undermined the established Confucian order, and wary mandarins ate often restricted the activities of missionaries and persecuted their followers. However, despite this friction, the imperial court retained a contingent of Jesuit scholars, astronomers, mathematicians and physicians.

The European missionaries did not hesitate to use secular means to help them achieve their goal – the conversion of all of Asia to Catholicism. Towards this end, French missionaries, who had supplanted the Portuguese by the 18th century, actively campaigned for a greater French political and military role in Vietnam.

## Tay Son Rebellion (1771–1802)

In 1765, a rebellion against misgovernment broke out in the town of Tay Son near Qui Nhon. It was led by three brothers from a wealthy merchant family: Nguyen Nhac, Nguyen Hue and Nguyen Lu. By 1773, the Tay Son Rebels (as they came to be known) controlled the whole of central Vietnam and in 1783 they captured Saigon and the rest of the South, killing the reigning prince and his family (as well as 10,000 Chinese residents of Cholon). Nguyen Lu became king of the South, while Nguyen Nhac was crowned king of central Vietnam.

Prince Nguyen Anh, the only survivor of the defeated Nguyen clan, fled to Thailand and requested military assistance from the Thais. He also met the French Jesuit missionary Pigneau de Behaine (the Bishop of Adran), whom he eventually authorised to act as his intermediary in seeking assistance from the French. As a sign of good faith, Nguyen Anh sent his four-year-old son Canh with de Behaine to France. The exotic entourage managed to create quite a sensation when it arrived at Versailles in 1787, prompting Louis XVI to authorise a military expedition to Vietnam. Louis XVI later changed his mind, but the bishop managed to convince French merchants in India to buy him two ships, weapons and supplies. With a force of 400 French deserters he had recruited, de Behaine set sail from Pondicherry, India, in June 1789.

Meanwhile, the Tay Son Rebels had overthrown the Trinh Lords in the North and proclaimed allegiance to the Later Le dynasty. The weak Le emperor, however, proved unable to retain his control of the country and rather than calling on the Tay Son Rebels for help, he turned to the Chinese. Taking advantage of the instability of the situation, China sent 200,000 troops to Vietnam under the pretext of helping the emperor. In 1788, with popular sentiment on his side, one of the Tay Son brothers, Nguyen Hue, proclaimed himself Emperor Quang Trung and set out with his army to expel the Chinese. In 1789, Nguyen Hue's armed forces overwhelmingly defeated the Chinese army at Dong Da (near Hanoi) in one of the most celebrated military achievements in Vietnamese history. However, his victory was to be short-lived as he died soon after in 1792.

In the South, Nguyen Anh (a rare surviving Nguyen lord), whose forces were trained by de Behaine's young French adventurers, gradually pushed back the Tay Son. In 1802, Nguyen Anh proclaimed himself Emperor Gia Long, thus beginning the Nguyen dynasty. When he captured Hanoi, his victory was complete and, for the first time in two centuries, Vietnam was united, with Hué as its new capital city.

## Nguyen Dynasty (1802–1945)

Emperor Gia Long began what historian David G Marr has called 'a policy of massive reassertion of Confucian values and

## Emperors of the Nguyen Dynasty

| emperor | reign |
|---|---|
| Gia Long | 1802–1819 |
| Minh Mang | 1820–1840 |
| Thieu Tri | 1841–1847 |
| Tu Duc | 1848–1883 |
| Duc Duc | 1883 |
| Hiep Hoa | 1883 |
| Kien Phuc | 1883–1884 |
| Ham Nghi | 1884–1885 |
| Dong Khanh | 1885–1889 |
| Thanh Thai | 1889–1907 |
| Duy Tan | 1907–1916 |
| Khai Dinh | 1916–1925 |
| Bao Dai | 1925–1945 |

institutions' in order to consolidate the Nguyen dynasty's shaky position. He appealed to the conservative tendencies of the elite, who had felt threatened by the atmosphere of reform stirred up by the Tay Son Rebels.

Gia Long also commenced a large-scale programme of public works (dikes, canals, roads, ports, bridges and land reclamation) to rehabilitate a country devastated by almost three decades of war. The Mandarin Road, linking Hué to both Hanoi and Saigon, was constructed during this period, as were a string of star-shaped citadels (built according to the principles of the French military architect Vauban) in provincial capitals. All these projects imposed a heavy burden on the population in the form of taxation, military conscription and forced labour.

Gia Long's son, Emperor Minh Mang, worked to consolidate the state and establish a strong central government. Because of his background as a Confucian scholar, he emphasised the importance of traditional Confucian education, which consisted of the memorisation and orthodox interpretation of the Confucian classics and texts of ancient Chinese history. As a result, education, and other spheres of activity that were dependent on it, stagnated.

Minh Mang was profoundly hostile to Catholicism, which he saw as a threat to the Confucian state, and he extended this antipathy to all Western influences. Seven missionaries and an unknown number of Vietnamese Catholics were executed in the 1830s, inflaming passions among French Catholics who demanded that their government intervene in Vietnam.

Serious uprisings broke out in both the North and the South during this period, growing progressively more serious in the 1840s and '50s. To make matters worse, the civil unrest in the deltas was accompanied by smallpox epidemics, tribal uprisings, drought, locusts and – most serious of all – repeated breaches in the Red River dikes, the result of government neglect.

The early Nguyen emperors continued the expansionist policies of the preceding dynasties, pushing into Cambodia and westward into the mountains along a wide front. They seized huge areas of Lao territory and clashed with Thailand over control of the lands of the weak Khmer Empire.

Minh Mang was succeeded by Emperor Thieu Tri, who expelled most of the foreign missionaries. He was followed by Emperor Tu Duc, who continued to rule according to conservative Confucian precepts and in imitation of Qing practices in China. Both responded to rural unrest with repression.

## French Rule (1859–1954)

Ever since de Behaine's patronage of Nguyen Anh in the late 18th century and his son Canh's appearance at Versailles in 1787, certain segments of French society had retained an active interest in Indochina. But it was not until the Revolution of 1848 in France and the advent of the Second Empire that there arose a coalition of interests – Catholic, commercial, patriotic, strategic and idealistic (fans of the *mission civilisatrice*) – with sufficient influence to initiate large-scale, long-term colonial efforts. However, for the next four decades the French colonial venture in Indochina was carried out haphazardly and without any preconceived plan. In fact, it was repeatedly on the verge of being discontinued altogether and at times only the insubordinate and reckless actions of a few adventurers kept it going.

France's military activity in Vietnam began in 1847, when the French Navy attacked Danang harbour in response to Thieu Tri's actions against Catholic missionaries. In 1858, a joint military force of 14 ships from France and the Spanish colony of the Philippines stormed Danang after the killing of several missionaries. As disease began to take a heavy toll and the expected support from Catholic Vietnamese failed to materialise, the force left a small garrison in Danang and followed the monsoon winds southward, seizing Saigon in early 1859. Huge quantities of Vietnamese cannons, firearms, swords, saltpetre, sulphur, shot and copper coins were seized; a fire set ablaze in rice storage granaries is said to have smouldered for three years.

The French victory in the 1861 Battle of Ky Hoa (Chi Hoa) marked the beginning of the end of formal, organised Vietnamese military action against the French in the South and the rise of popular guerrilla resistance led by the local scholar-gentry, who had refused en masse to collaborate with the French administration. This resistance took the form of ambushing French river craft, denying food supplies to French bases and assassinating collaborators.

In 1862, Emperor Tu Duc signed a treaty that gave the French the three eastern provinces of Cochinchina. In addition, missionaries were promised the freedom to proselytise anywhere in the country, several ports were opened to French and Spanish commerce, and Tu Duc undertook to pay a large indemnity. To raise the necessary cash he authorised the sale of opium in the North and sold the monopoly to the Chinese. Additionally, he debased the meritocratic mandarinate by putting the lower-ranking mandarinal posts up for sale.

The French offensive in 1867 broke the morale of the resistance, causing the surviving scholar-gentry to flee the delta. Cochinchina became a French colony and the peasantry assumed a position of non-violent resignation. At the same time, there were voices among the more educated of the Vietnamese classes that began to advocate cooperation with, and subordination to, the French, in the interests of continuing technical and economic development.

During this era, the Vietnamese might have been able to reduce the impact of the arrival of the European maritime powers and to retain their independence, but this would have required a degree of imagination and dynamism lacking in Hué. Indeed, until the mid-19th century, the imperial court at Hué, which was dominated by extreme Confucian conservatism, behaved almost as if Europe did not exist, though events such as the Opium War of 1839 in China should have served as a warning. In addition, resistance to colonialism was severely handicapped by an almost total lack of political and economic intelligence about France and the French.

The next major French action lasted from 1872 to 1874, when Jean Dupuis, a merchant seeking to supply salt and weapons to a Yunnanese general by sailing up the Red River, seized the Hanoi Citadel. Captain Francis Garnier, ostensibly dispatched to reign in Dupuis, instead took over where Dupuis left off. After capturing Hanoi, Garnier's gunboats proceeded to sail around the Red River Delta demanding tribute from provincial fortresses, an activity that ended only when Garnier was killed by the Black Flags (Co Den), a semi-autonomous army of Chinese, Vietnamese and hill-tribe troops who fought mostly for booty but resisted the French in part because of a strong antipathy towards Westerners.

These events threw the North into chaos: the Black Flags continued their piratic activities; local people were organised to take vengeance on the Vietnamese – especially Catholics ones – who had helped the French; Chinese militias in the pay of both the French and the Nguyen emperors sprang up; Le dynasty pretenders began asserting their claims; and the hill tribes revolted. As central government authority collapsed and all established order broke down, Tu Duc went so far as to petition for help from the Chinese and to ask for support from the British and even the Americans.

In 1882, a French force under Captain Henri Rivière seized Hanoi, but any further conquests were stubbornly resisted by both Chinese regulars and the Black Flags, especially the latter. The following year, Black Flags units ambushed Rivière at Cau Giay, killed him and 32 other Frenchmen, and triumphantly paraded his severed head from hamlet to hamlet.

Meanwhile, only a few weeks after the death of Tu Duc in 1883, the French attacked Hué and imposed a Treaty of Protectorate on the imperial court. There then began a tragi-comic struggle for royal succession that was notable for its palace coups, mysteriously dead emperors and heavy-handed French diplomacy. Emperors Duc Duc and Hiep Hoa were succeeded by Kien Phuc, who was followed by 14-year-old Ham Nghi.

By the time Ham Nghi and his advisers decided to relocate the court to the mountains and lead resistance activities from there, the French had rounded up enough mandarin collaborators to give Emperor Dong Khanh, his French-picked successor, a sufficient amount of legitimacy to survive.

Ham Nghi held out against the French until 1888, when he was betrayed, captured by the French and exiled to Algeria. Although the Indochinese Union (Cochinchina, Annam, Tonkin, Cambodia, Laos and the Chinese port of Qinzhouwan) proclaimed by the French in 1887 effectively ended the existence of an independent Vietnamese state, active resistance continued in various parts of the country for the duration of French rule. The establishment of the Indochinese Union ended Vietnamese expansionism and the Vietnamese were forced to give back lands taken from Cambodia and Laos.

Continuing in the tradition of centuries of Vietnamese dynasties, the French colonial authorities carried out ambitious public works, such as the construction of the Saigon–Hanoi railway, as well as ports, extensive irrigation and drainage systems, improved dikes, various public services and research institutes. In order to fund these activities, the government heavily taxed the peasants, devastating the traditional rural economy. The colonial administration also established alcohol, salt and opium monopolies for the purpose of raising revenues. In Saigon, it produced a quick-burning type of opium that helped increase addiction and thus revenue.

And since colonialism was supposed to be a profitable proposition, French capital was invested for quick returns in anthracite coal, tin, tungsten and zinc mines and tea, coffee and rubber plantations. All of these operations became notorious for the abysmal wages paid by the French and their subhuman treatment of Vietnamese workers.

As land, like capital, became concentrated in the hands of a tiny percentage of the population (in Cochinchina, 2.5% of the population came to own 45% of the land), a subproletariat of landless and uprooted peasants was formed. In the countryside these people were reduced to sharecropping, paying up to 60% of their crop in rents.

Whereas the majority of Vietnamese peasants had owned their land before the arrival of the French, by the 1930s about 70% were landless. Because French policies impoverished the people of Indochina, the area never became an important market for French industry.

## Vietnamese Anticolonialism

Throughout the colonial period, the vast majority of Vietnamese retained a strong desire to have their national independence restored. Seething nationalist aspirations often broke out into open defiance of the French, which ranged from the publishing of patriotic periodicals and books to an attempt to poison the French garrison in Hanoi.

The imperial court in Hué, although quite corrupt, was a centre of nationalist feeling, a fact most evident in the game of musical thrones orchestrated by the French. Upon his death the subservient Dong Khanh was replaced by 10-year-old Emperor Thanh Thai, whose rule the French ended when he was discovered to have been plotting against them. Thanh Thai was deported to the Indian Ocean island of Réunion, where he remained until 1947.

His son and successor, Emperor Duy Tan, was only in his teens in 1916 when he and poet Tran Cao Van planned a general uprising in Hué that was discovered the day before it was scheduled to begin; Tran Cao Van was beheaded and Duy Tan was exiled to Réunion. Duy Tan was succeeded by the docile Emperor Khai Dinh. On his death he was followed by his son, Emperor Bao Dai, who at the time of his accession in 1925, was 12 years old and at school in France.

Some Vietnamese nationalists (such as the scholar and patriot Phan Boi Chau, who rejected French rule but not Western ideas and technology) looked to Japan and China for support and political inspiration, especially after Japan's victory in the Russo-Japanese War (1905–4) showed all of Asia that Western powers could be defeated. Sun Yatsen's 1911 revolution in China was also closely followed in nationalist circles.

Viet Nam Quoc Dan Dang (VNQDD), a predominantly middle-class, nationalist party modelled after the Chinese Kuomintang (Nationalist Party), was founded in 1927 by nationalist leaders. One of them, Nguyen Thai Hoc, was later guillotined along with 12 comrades in the savage French retribution for the abortive 1930 Yen Bai uprising.

Another source of nationalist agitation was among those Vietnamese who had spent time in France, where they were not hampered by the restrictions on political activity in force in the colonies. In addition, over 100,000 Vietnamese were sent off to Europe as soldiers during WWI.

Ultimately, the most successful of the anticolonialists were the communists, who were able to relate to the frustrations and aspirations of the population – especially the peasants – and to effectively channel and organise their demands for more equitable land distribution.

The institutional history of Vietnamese communism, which in many ways is also the political biography of Ho Chi Minh (see the boxed text 'Ho Chi Minh' in this chapter), is rather complicated. In brief, the first Marxist grouping in Indochina was the Viet Nam Cach Menh Thanh Nien Dong Chi Hoi (Vietnam Revolutionary Youth League), founded by Ho Chi Minh in Canton, China, in 1925. The Revolutionary Youth League was succeeded in February 1930 by the Dang Cong San Viet Nam (Vietnamese Communist Party), a union of three groups effected by Ho that was renamed the Dang Cong San Dong Duong (Indochinese Communist Party) in October 1930. In 1941, Ho formed the Viet Nam Doc Lap Dong Minh Hoi (League for the Independence of Vietnam), much better known as the Viet Minh, which resisted the Japanese (and thus received Chinese and American aid) and carried out extensive political activities during WWII. Despite its broad nationalist programme and claims to the contrary, the Viet Minh was, from its inception, dominated by Ho's communists.

Communist successes in the late 1920s included major strikes by urban workers. During the Nghe Tinh Uprising (1930–1), revolutionary committees (or soviets) took control of parts of Nghe An and Ha Tinh provinces (thus all the streets named 'Xo Viet Nghe Tinh'), but after an unprecedented wave of terror the French managed to re-establish control. A 1940 uprising in the South was also brutally suppressed, seriously damaging the party's infrastructure. French prisons, filled with arrested cadres, were turned by the captives into revolutionary 'universities' in which Marxist-Leninist theory was taught.

## WWII

When France fell to Nazi Germany in 1940, the Indochinese government of Vichy-appointed Admiral Jean Decoux concluded an agreement to accept the presence of Japanese troops in Vietnam. For their own convenience the Japanese, who sought to exploit the area's strategic location and its natural resources, left the French administration in charge of the daily running of the country. The only group that did anything significant to resist the Japanese occupation was the communist-dominated Viet Minh, which from 1944 received funding and arms

## Ho Chi Minh

Ho Chi Minh (Bringer of Light) is the best known of some 50 aliases assumed by Nguyen Tat Thanh (1890–1969) over the course of his long career. He was founder of the Vietnamese Communist Party and president of the Democratic Republic of Vietnam from 1946 until his death. Born the son of a fiercely nationalistic scholar-official of humble means, he was educated in the Quoc Hoc Secondary School in Hué, before working briefly as a teacher in Phan Thiet. In 1911, he signed on as a cook's apprentice on a French ship, sailing to North America, Africa and Europe. He stopped off in Europe, where, while working as a gardener, snow sweeper, waiter, photo retoucher and stoker, his political consciousness began to develop.

SB

After living briefly in London, Ho Chi Minh moved to Paris, where he adopted the name Nguyen Ai Quoc (Nguyen the Patriot). During this period, he mastered a number of languages (including English, French, German and Mandarin) and began to write about and debate the issue of Indochinese independence. During the 1919 Versailles Peace Conference, he tried to present an independence plan for Vietnam to US President Woodrow Wilson. Ho was a founding member of the French Communist Party, which was established in 1920. In 1923 he was summoned to Moscow for training by Communist International, which later sent him to Guangzhou (Canton), China, where he founded the Revolutionary Youth League of Vietnam, a precursor to the Indochinese Communist Party and the Vietnamese Communist Party.

During the early 1930s the English rulers of Hong Kong obliged the French government by imprisoning Ho for his revolutionary activities in France, Indochina, China and Hong Kong. After his release, he travelled to the USSR and China. In 1941 Ho Chi Minh returned to Vietnam – for the first time in 30 years. That same year, at the age of 51, he helped found the Viet Minh Front, the goal of which was the independence of Vietnam from French colonial rule and Japanese occupation. In 1942 he was arrested and held for a year by the Nationalist Chinese. As Japan prepared to surrender in August 1945, Ho Chi Minh led the August Revolution, which took control of much of Vietnam; and it was he who composed Vietnam's Declaration of Independence (modelled in part on the American Declaration of Independence) and read it publicly. His mausoleum was later built nearby.

The return of the French shortly thereafter forced Ho Chi Minh and the Viet Minh to flee Hanoi and take up armed resistance. Ho spent eight years conducting a guerrilla war until the Viet Minh's victory against the French at Dien Bien Phu in 1954. He led North Vietnam until his death in September 1969 – he never lived to see the North's victory over the South. Ho is affectionately referred to as 'Uncle Ho' (Bac Ho) by his admirers.

The party has worked hard to preserve the image of 'Uncle Ho' who, like his erstwhile nemesis South Vietnamese president Ngo Dinh Diem, never married.

However, a surprise spate of sensationalist stories published in Vietnamese newspapers during the early 1990s alleged that Ho had had numerous lovers, two wives – one French! – and a son born to a Tay minority woman. She later died in mysterious circumstances. Perhaps time will reveal the true story.

The Vietnamese government has so far refused anyone permission to capitalise on Ho Chi Minh's name. A proposed American joint venture called 'Uncle Ho's Hamburgers' flew like a lead balloon, although Kentucky Fried Chicken did managed to enter Vietnam and has successfully been franchised. The Vietnamese joint-venture partner, however, was not amused when the American business rep pointed out that Ho Chi Minh does vaguely resemble Colonel Sanders. 'No' said the frowning Vietnamese, 'Ho Chi Minh was a general.'

from the US Office of Strategic Services (OSS), the predecessor of the CIA. This affiliation offered the Viet Minh the hope of eventual US recognition of their demands for independence; it also proved useful to Ho in that it implied that he had the support of the Americans.

In March 1945, as a Viet Minh offensive was under way and Decoux's government was plotting to resist the Japanese (something they hadn't tried in the preceding 4½ years) the Japanese overthrew Decoux, imprisoning both his troops and his administrators. His administration was replaced with a puppet regime (which was nominally independent within Japan's Greater East Asia Co-Prosperity Sphere) led by Emperor Bao Dai, who abrogated the 1883 treaty that made Annam and Tonkin French protectorates. During this period, Japanese rice requisitions and the Japanese policy of forcing farmers to plant industrial crops, in combination with floods and breaches in the dikes, caused a horrific famine in which two million of North Vietnam's 10 million people starved to death.

By the spring of 1945 the Viet Minh controlled large parts of the country, particularly in the North. In mid-August, after the atomic bombing of Hiroshima and Nagasaki, Ho Chi Minh formed the National Liberation Committee and called for a general uprising, later known as the August Revolution (Cach Mang Thang Tam), to take advantage of the power vacuum. Almost immediately, the Viet Minh assumed complete control of the North. In central Vietnam, Bao Dai abdicated in favour of the new government (which later appointed him its Supreme Adviser, whatever that meant). In the South, the Viet Minh soon held power in a shaky coalition with noncommunist groups. On 2 September 1945, Ho Chi Minh, with American OSS agents at his side and borrowing liberally from the stirring prose of the American Declaration of Independence, declared the Democratic Republic of Vietnam independent at a rally in Hanoi's Ba Dinh Square. Throughout this period, Ho wrote no fewer than eight letters to US president Harry Truman and the State Department asking for US aid, but did not receive replies.

A minor item on the agenda of the Potsdam Conference of 1945 was the procedure for disarming Japanese occupation forces in Vietnam. It was decided at the conference that the Chinese Kuomintang would accept the Japanese surrender north of the 16th Parallel and that the British would do the same south of that line.

When the British arrived in Saigon, chaos reigned with enraged French settlers beginning to take matters into their own hands, and competing Vietnamese groups on the verge of civil war. With only 1800 British, Indian and Ghurka troops at his disposal, British General Gracey ordered the defeated Japanese troops to help him restore order. He also released and armed 1400 imprisoned French paratroopers, who immediately went on a rampage around the city, overthrowing the Committee of the South government, breaking into the homes and shops of the Vietnamese and indiscriminately clubbing men, women and children. The Viet Minh and allied groups responded by calling a general strike and by beginning a guerrilla campaign against the French. On 24 September, French General Jacques Philippe Leclerc arrived in Saigon, with the declaration 'We have come to reclaim our inheritance.'

Meanwhile, in Hué, the imperial library was demolished (priceless documents were being used in the marketplace to wrap fish). In the North, 180,000 Chinese Kuomintang troops were fleeing the Chinese communists and pillaging their way southward towards Hanoi. Ho tried to placate them, but as the months of Chinese occupation dragged on, he decided to accept a temporary return of the French in order to get rid of the anticommunist Kuomintang who, in addition to everything else, were supporting the Viet Minh's nationalist rivals. Most of the Kuomintang soldiers were packed off to Taiwan. The French were to stay for five years in return for recognising Vietnam as a free state within the French Union.

The British wanted out, the French wanted in, Ho Chi Minh wanted the Chinese to go and the Americans under Truman were not as actively opposed to colonialism as they had been under Franklin Roosevelt. So the French managed to regain control of Vietnam, at least in name. But when the French shelled Haiphong in November 1946 after an obscure customs dispute, killing hundreds of civilians, the patience of the Viet Minh ended. Only a few weeks later fighting broke out in Hanoi, marking the start of the Franco–Viet Minh War. Ho Chi Minh and his forces fled to the mountains, where they would remain for the next eight years.

## Franco–Viet Minh War (1946–54)

In the face of Vietnamese determination that their country regain its independence, the French proved unable to reassert their control. Despite massive American aid and the existence of significant indigenous anti-communist elements – which rallied in 1949 to support Bao Dai's 'associated state' within the French Union – it was an unwinnable war. As Ho said to the French at the time, 'You can kill 10 of my men for every one I kill of yours, but even at those odds, you will lose and I will win.'

After eight years of fighting, the Viet Minh controlled much of Vietnam and neighbouring Laos. On 7 May 1954, after a 57-day siege, over 10,000 starving French troops surrendered to the Viet Minh at Dien Bien Phu – a catastrophic defeat that totally shattered France's remaining public support for the war. The following day, the Geneva Conference opened to try to negotiate an end to the conflict; 2½ months later the Geneva Accords were signed. This provided for the following conditions: an exchange of prisoners; the temporary division of Vietnam into two zones at the Ben Hai River (near the 17th Parallel); the free passage of people across the 17th Parallel for a period of 300 days; and the holding of nationwide elections on 20 July 1956. In the course of the Franco–Viet Minh War, more than 35,000 French fighters were killed and 48,000 were wounded; Vietnamese casualties were even greater.

## South Vietnam

After the signing of the Geneva Accords, the South was ruled by a government led by Ngo Dinh Diem, a fiercely anticommunist Catholic whose brother had been killed by the Viet Minh in 1945. His power base was significantly strengthened by some 900,000 refugees – many of them Catholics – who fled the communist North during the 300-day free-passage period.

In 1955 Diem, convinced that Ho Chi Minh would win an election, refused – with US encouragement – to implement the Geneva Accords; instead, he held a referendum on his continued rule. Diem claimed to have won 98.2% of the vote in an election that was by all accounts rigged (in Saigon, he received a third more votes than there were registered voters!). After Diem declared himself president of the Republic of Vietnam, the new regime was recognised by France, the USA, Great Britain, Australia, New Zealand, Italy, Japan, Thailand and South Korea.

During the first few years of his rule, Diem consolidated power fairly effectively, defeating the Binh Xuyen crime syndicate and the private armies of the Hoa Hao and Caodai religious sects. During Diem's 1957 official visit to the USA, President Eisenhower called him the 'miracle man' of Asia. As time went on Diem became increasingly tyrannical in dealing with dissent. Running the government became a family affair (his much-hated sister-in-law became Vietnam's powerful 'first lady' and his father-in-law was appointed as the US ambassador).

Such blatant nepotism was offensive enough, but worse still, Diem's land-reform programme ended up reversing the land redistribution effected by the Viet Minh in the 1940s. The favouritism he showed to Catholics alienated many Buddhists. In the early 1960s, the South was rocked by anti-Diem unrest led by university students and Buddhist clergy, which included several highly publicised self-immolations by monks that shocked the world. When Diem used French contacts to explore negotiations with Hanoi, the USA threw its support behind a military coup; in November 1963,

Diem was overthrown and killed. He was followed by a succession of military rulers who continued his repressive policies.

## North Vietnam

The Geneva Accords allowed the leadership of the Democratic Republic of Vietnam to return to Hanoi and assert control of all territory north of the 17th Parallel. The new government immediately set out to eliminate those elements of the population that threatened its power. A radical land-reform programme was implemented, providing about half a hectare of land each to some 1.5 million peasants. Tens of thousands of 'landlords', some with only tiny holdings, were denounced to 'security committees' by envious neighbours and arrested. Hasty 'trials' resulted in between 10,000 and 15,000 executions and the imprisonment of between 50,000 and 100,000 people. In 1956, the party, faced with serious rural unrest, recognised that the People's Agricultural Reform Tribunals had gotten out of hand and began a Campaign for the Rectification of Errors.

On 12 December 1955, shortly after Diem had declared the South a republic, the USA closed its consulate in Hanoi.

## The North-South War

Although there were communist guerrilla attacks on Diem's government during the mid-1950s, the real campaign to 'liberate' the South began in 1959 when Hanoi, responding to the demands of Southern cadres that they be allowed to resist the Diem regime, changed from a strategy of 'political struggle' to one of 'armed struggle'. Shortly thereafter, the Ho Chi Minh Trail, which had been in existence for several years, was expanded. In April 1960, universal military conscription was implemented in the North. Eight months later, Hanoi announced the formation of the National Liberation Front (NLF), whose political platform called for a neutralisation of Vietnam, the withdrawal of all foreign troops and gradual reunification of the North and South. In the South, the NLF came to be known, derogatorily, as the Viet Cong or just the VC; both are abbreviations

for Viet Nam Cong San, which means Vietnamese communist (today these terms are no longer considered pejorative). American soldiers nicknamed the VC 'Charlie'.

When the NLF campaign got under way, the military situation of the Diem government rapidly deteriorated. To turn things around, the Strategic Hamlets Program (Ap Chien Luoc) began in 1962. Following tactics employed successfully by the British in Malaya during the 1950s, peasants were forcibly moved into fortified 'strategic hamlets' in order to deny the VC bases of support. The programme was widely criticised for incompetence and excessive brutality, and many of the strategic hamlets were infiltrated by the VC and fell under their control. This programme was finally abandoned with the death of Diem, but after the war had ended the VC admitted that it had caused them very serious concern and that they had expended a major effort sabotaging it.

And for the South it was no longer just a battle with the VC. In 1964, Hanoi began infiltrating regular North Vietnamese Army (NVA) units into the South. By early 1965, the Saigon government was in desperate straits; desertions from the Army of the Republic of Vietnam (ARVN), whose command was notorious for corruption and incompetence, had reached 2000 per month. The South was losing 500 men and a district capital each week, yet in 10 years only one senior South Vietnamese army officer had been wounded. The army was getting ready to evacuate Hué and Danang, and the central highlands seemed about to fall. The South Vietnamese army's general staff even prepared a plan to move its headquarters from Saigon to the Vung Tau Peninsula, which was easy to defend and only minutes from ships that could spirit them out of the country. It was at this point that the USA committed its first combat troops.

## Enter the Americans

In the 1870s, Emperor Tu Duc sent a respected scholar, Bui Vien, to Washington in an attempt to garner international support to counter the French. Bui Vien met President Ulysses S Grant, but without the proper documents of accreditation he was sent back to Vietnam empty-handed.

The theory rapidly gaining acceptance in the West was that there was a worldwide communist movement intent on overthrowing one government after another by waging various 'wars of liberation'. Known as the Domino Theory, it gained considerable support after the start of the Korean War in 1950, and the Americans saw France's colonial war in Indochina as an important part of the worldwide struggle to stop communist expansion. By 1954, US military aid to the French war effort topped US$2 billion. In 1950, 35 US soldiers arrived in Vietnam as part of the US Military Assistance Advisory Group (MAAG), ostensibly to instruct the troops receiving US weapons on how to use them; there would be American soldiers on Vietnamese soil for the next 25 years.

In 1950, the People's Republic of China established diplomatic relations with the Democratic Republic of Vietnam; shortly thereafter, the Soviet Union did the same. Only then did Washington recognise Bao Dai's French-backed government. The circumstances of this event are instructive: though Ho's government had been around since 1945, the USSR didn't recognise it until the communist Chinese did and the US State Department, which at the time was reverberating with recriminations over who was to blame for 'losing China' to communism, recognised Bao Dai's government as a reaction to these events. From that point on, US policy in Indochina largely became a knee-jerk reaction against whatever the communists did.

When the last French troops left Vietnam in April 1956, the MAAG, now numbering several hundred men, assumed responsibility for training the South Vietnamese military; the transition couldn't have been neater. The first American troops to die in Vietnam were killed at Bien Hoa in 1959 at a time when about 700 US military personnel were in the country.

As the military position of the South Vietnamese government continued to deteriorate, the Kennedy administration (1961–3) sent even more military advisers to Vietnam.

By the end of 1963, there were 16,300 US military personnel in the country.

Vietnam became a central issue in the 1964 US presidential election. The candidate for the Republican Party, Senator Barry Goldwater, took the more aggressive stance. He warned that if elected he would tell Ho Chi Minh to stop the war 'or there won't be enough left of North Vietnam to grow rice on it'. Many Americans, with bitter memories of how Chinese troops came to the aid of North Korea during the Korean War, feared the same would happen again if the USA invaded North Vietnam. The thought of a possible nuclear confrontation with the USSR could not be ruled out either. With such horrors in mind, voters overwhelmingly supported Lyndon Baines Johnson.

Ironically, it was 'peace candidate' Johnson who rapidly escalated US involvement in the war. A major turning point in US strategy was precipitated by the August 1964 Tonkin Gulf Incidents, in which two US destroyers, the *Maddox* and the *Turner Joy*, claimed to have come under 'unprovoked' attack while sailing off the North Vietnamese coast. Subsequent research indicates that the first attack took place while the *Maddox* was in North Vietnamese territorial waters assisting a secret South Vietnamese commando raid and that the second one simply never took place.

However, on Johnson's orders, carrier-based jets undertook 64 sorties against the North – the first of thousands of such missions that would hit every single road and rail bridge in the country, as well as 4000 of North Vietnam's 5788 villages. Two US aircraft were lost and the pilot of one, Lieutenant Everett Alvarez, became the first American prisoner of war (POW) of the conflict; he would remain in captivity for eight years.

A few days later, an indignant (and misled) US Congress almost unanimously (two senators dissented) passed the Tonkin Gulf Resolution, which gave the president the power to 'take all necessary measures' to 'repel any armed attack against the forces of the United States and to prevent further aggression'. Only later was it established that the Johnson administration had in fact drafted the resolution before the 'attacks' had actually taken place. Until its repeal in 1970, the resolution was treated by US presidents as carte blanche to do whatever they chose in Vietnam without any congressional control.

As the military situation of the Saigon government reached a new nadir, the first US combat troops splashed ashore at Danang in March 1965, ostensibly to defend Danang air base. But once they had 'American boys' fighting and dying, they had to do everything necessary to protect and support them, including sending over more American boys. By December 1965, there were 184,300 US military personnel in Vietnam and 636 Americans had died. Twelve months later, the totals were 385,300 US troops in Vietnam and 6644 dead. By December 1967, there were 485,600 US soldiers in the country and 16,021 had died. In 1967, with South Vietnamese and 'Free World Military Forces' counted in, there were 1.3 million men (one for every 15 people in South Vietnam) under arms for the Saigon government.

By 1966, the failed Strategic Hamlets Program of earlier years was replaced with the policies of 'pacification', 'search and destroy' and 'free-fire zones'. Pacification meant building a pro-government civilian infrastructure of teachers, health-care workers and officials in each village, as well as soldiers to guard them and keep the VC away from the villagers. To protect the villages from VC raids, mobile search and destroy units of soldiers moved around the country (often by helicopter) to hunt bands of VC guerrillas. In some cases, villagers were evacuated so the Americans could use heavy weaponry like napalm, artillery, bombs and tanks in areas that were declared free-fire zones. A relatively little-publicised strategy was dubbed Operation Phoenix, a controversial programme run by the CIA and aimed at eliminating VC cadres by assassination, capture or defection.

These strategies were only partially successful: US forces could only control the countryside by day, while the VC usually controlled it by night. The VC proved adept at infiltrating pacified villages. Although lacking heavy weapons like tanks and aircraft, VC guerrillas continued to inflict heavy casualties on US and ARVN troops in ambushes, and by using mines and booby traps. Although free-fire zones were supposed to prevent civilian casualties, plenty of villagers were nevertheless shelled, bombed, strafed or napalmed to death – their surviving relatives often joined ranks with the VC.

## The Turning Point

In January 1968, North Vietnamese troops launched a major attack at Khe Sanh in the Demilitarised Zone. This battle, the single largest of the war, was in part a massive diversion for what was to follow only a week later: the Tet Offensive.

The Tet Offensive marked a crucial turning point in the war. On the evening of 31 January, as the country celebrated the Lunar New Year, the VC launched a stunning offensive in over 100 cities and towns, including Saigon. As the television cameras rolled, a VC commando team took over the courtyard of the central Saigon US embassy building.

The US forces had long been wanting to engage the VC in an open battle rather than a guerrilla war where the enemy couldn't be seen. The Tet Offensive provided them with this opportunity. Although taken by complete surprise (a major failure of US military intelligence), the South Vietnamese and Americans immediately counterattacked with massive firepower, bombing and shelling heavily populated cities as they had the open jungle. The effect was devastating on the VC, but also on the civilian population. In Ben Tre, a US officer bitterly explained that they 'had to destroy the town in order to save it'.

The Tet Offensive killed about 1000 US soldiers and 2000 ARVN troops, but VC losses were more than 10 times higher at approximately 32,000 deaths. In addition, some 500 American and 10,000 North Vietnamese troops had died at the battle of Khe Sanh a week before. According to American estimates, 165,000 civilians also died in the three weeks following the start of the Tet Offensive; two million more became refugees.

The VC only held the cities for three or four days (with the exception of Hué, which they held for 25 days). The surviving VC then retreated to the jungles. They had hoped the offensive would lead to a popular uprising against the Americans and that ARVN forces would desert or switch sides but this did not happen. General William Westmoreland, commander of US forces in Vietnam, insisted that the uprising had been a failure and a decisive military blow to the communists (and he was right – by their own admission, the VC never recovered from their high casualties). Westmoreland then asked for an additional 206,000 troops – he didn't get them and was replaced in July by General Creighton W Abrams.

Perhaps the VC lost the battle, but they were far from losing the war. After years of hearing that they were winning, many Americans – having watched the killing and chaos in Saigon on their nightly TV news – stopped believing what they were being told by their government. While US generals were proclaiming a great victory, public tolerance of the war and its casualties reached breaking point. For the VC, the Tet Offensive proved to be a big success after all – it made the cost of fighting the war (both in dollars and in lives) unbearable for the Americans.

Antiwar demonstrations rocked American university campuses and spilled onto the streets. Seeing his political popularity plummet in the polls, Johnson decided not to stand for re-election.

Richard Nixon was elected president of the USA, in part because of a promise that he had a 'secret plan' to end the war. Many suspected this would be a military invasion of North Vietnam, but it didn't turn out to be that. The plan, later to be labelled the Nixon Doctrine, was unveiled in July 1969 and called on Asian nations to be more 'self-reliant' in defence matters and not expect the USA to become embroiled in future civil wars. Nixon's strategy called for 'Vietnamisation', which meant making the South's military fight the war without US troops.

Nixon Doctrine or not, the first half of 1969 saw still greater escalation of the conflict. In April, the number of US soldiers in Vietnam reached an all-time high of 543,400. By the end of 1969, US troop levels were down to 475,200; 40,024 Americans had been killed in action, as had 110,176 ARVN troops. While the fighting raged, Nixon's chief negotiator, Henry Kissinger, pursued talks in Paris with his North Vietnamese counterpart Le Duc Tho.

In 1969, the Americans began secretly bombing Cambodia. The following year, American ground forces were sent into Cambodia to extricate ARVN units whose fighting ability was still unable to match the enemy's. This new escalation infuriated previously quiescent elements of the US public, leading to even more bitter antiwar protests. The television screens of America were almost daily filled with scenes of demonstrations, student strikes and even deadly acts of self-immolation. A peace demonstration at Kent State University in Ohio resulted in four protesters being shot dead by National Guard troops.

The rise of organisations like Vietnam Veterans Against the War demonstrated that it wasn't just 'cowardly students fearing military conscription' who wanted the USA out of Vietnam. It was clear that the war was ripping the USA apart. Nor were the protests confined to the USA – huge anti-American demonstrations in Western Europe shook the North Atlantic Treaty Organisation (NATO) alliance. There was even a Vietnamese peace movement – under great risk to themselves, idealistic young students in Saigon protested against the US presence in their country.

In 1971, excerpts from a scandalous top-secret study of American involvement in Indochina were published in the *New York Times* after a legal battle, which went to the US Supreme Court. The study, best known as the Pentagon Papers, was commissioned by the US Defense Department and described how the military and former presidents had systematically lied to Congress and the US public. The Pentagon Papers infuriated Americans and caused antiwar sentiment to reach new heights. The *New York Times* obtained the study from one of its authors, Dr Daniel Ellsberg, who had turned against the war. Ellsberg was subsequently prosecuted for espionage, theft and conspiracy. A judge dismissed the charges after Nixon's notorious White House 'plumbers' (so called because their job was to stop information leaks) burgled the office of Ellsberg's psychiatrist to obtain evidence.

In the spring of 1972, the North Vietnamese launched an offensive across the 17th Parallel; the USA responded with increased bombing of the North and mined seven North Vietnamese harbours. The 'Christmas bombing' of Haiphong and Hanoi at the end of 1972 was meant to wrest concessions from North Vietnam at the negotiating table. Finally, Kissinger and Le Duc Tho reached agreement. The Paris agreements, which were signed by the USA, North Vietnam, South Vietnam and the VC on 27 January 1973, provided for a cease-fire, the establishment of the National Council of Reconciliation and Concord, the total withdrawal of US combat forces and the release of 590 American POWs. The agreement made no mention of approximately 200,000 North Vietnamese troops then in South Vietnam.

Nixon was re-elected president in November 1972, shortly before the Paris peace agreements were signed. By 1973, he became hopelessly mired in the Watergate scandal resulting from the illegal activities of his re-election campaign. The Pentagon Papers and Watergate contributed to such a high level of public distrust in America of the military and presidents that the US Congress passed a resolution which prohibited any further US military involvement in Indochina after 15 August 1973. President Nixon resigned in disgrace in 1974 and was succeeded by Gerald Ford.

In total, 3.14 million Americans (including 7200 women) served in the US armed forces in Vietnam during the war. Officially, 58,183 Americans (including eight women) were killed in action or are listed as missing in action (MIA). The US losses were nearly double those of the Korean War. Pentagon figures indicate that by 1972, 3689 fixed-wing aircraft and 4857 helicopters had been lost and 15 million tonnes of ammunition had been expended. The direct cost of the war was officially put at US$165 billion, though its true cost to the economy was at least twice that. By comparison, the Korean War had cost America US$18 billion.

By the end of 1973, 223,748 South Vietnamese soldiers had been killed in action; North Vietnamese and VC fatalities have been estimated at one million. Approximately four million civilians (or 10% of the Vietnamese population) were injured or killed during the war, many of them in the North as a result of US bombing. At least 300,000 Vietnamese and 2200 Americans are still listed as MIA (see the boxed text 'Missing in Action' in the Central Vietnam chapter).

As far as anyone knows, the Soviet Union and China – who supplied all the weapons to North Vietnam and the VC – did not suffer a single casualty.

## Other Foreign Involvement

Australia, New Zealand, South Korea, the Philippines and Thailand also sent military personnel to South Vietnam as part of what the Americans called the Free World Military Forces, whose purpose was to help internationalise the American war effort and thus confer upon it some legitimacy. The Korean (who numbered nearly 50,000), Thai and Filipino forces were heavily subsidised by the Americans.

Australia's participation in the conflict constituted the most significant commitment of its military forces since the 1940s. At its peak strength, the Australian forces (which included army, navy and air-force units) in Vietnam numbered 8300, two-thirds larger than the Australian contingent in the Korean War. Overall, 46,852 Australian military personnel served in the war, including 17,424 draftees; the Australian casualties totalled 496 dead and 2398 wounded.

Most of New Zealand's contingent, which numbered 548 at its high point in 1968, operated as an integral part of the

Australian Task Force, which was stationed near Baria (just north of Vung Tau).

The Australian foreign affairs establishment decided to commit Australian troops to America's cause in order to encourage US military involvement in Southeast Asia. This, they argued, would further Australia's defence interests by having the Americans play an active role in an area of great importance to Australia's long-term security. The first Australian troops in Vietnam were 30 guerrilla-warfare specialists, with experience in Malaya and Borneo, who were sent to Vietnam in May 1962. Australia announced the commitment of combat units in April 1965, only a few weeks after the first US combat troops arrived in Danang. The last of the Australian combat troops withdrew in December 1971; the last advisers returned home a year later. The Australian and New Zealand forces preferred to operate independently of US units, in part because they felt the Americans took unnecessary risks and were willing to sustain unacceptably high numbers of casualties.

Royal Thai Army troops were stationed in Vietnam from 1967 to 1973; Thailand also allowed the US Air Force to base B-52s and fighter aircraft on its territory. The Philippines sent units for noncombat 'civic action' work. South Korea's soldiers, who operated in the South between 1965 and 1971, were noted for both their exceptional fighting ability and extreme brutality.

Taiwan's brief role was one of the most under-reported facts of the war because it was such an embarrassment. At that time, the USA still recognised Taiwan's ruling Kuomintang as the legitimate government of China. Ever since 1949, when Kuomintang troops were defeated by the communists, Taiwan's president Chiang Kaishek had been promising to 'retake the mainland'. When US president Johnson asked Taiwan to supply around 20,000 troops, Chiang was happy to comply, and some troops were immediately dispatched to Saigon. Chiang then rapidly tried to increase the number to 200,000! It soon became apparent that Chiang was planning to use Vietnam as a stepping stone to invade mainland China and draw the USA into his personal war against the Chinese communists. The USA wanted no part of this and asked Chiang to withdraw his troops from South Vietnam. This was promptly done and the whole incident was hushed up.

It's not generally known that Spain's General Franco, whose regime was regarded by the USA as a bulwark against communism, supplied about 50 military personnel to the war effort. However, their role was noncombatant.

## Fall of the South (1975)

Except for a small contingent of technicians and CIA agents, all US military personnel were out of Vietnam by 1973. The bombing of North Vietnam had ceased and the US POWs were released, but the guerrilla war continued – the only difference was that the fighting had been thoroughly Vietnamised. However, the foreign powers continued to bankroll the war. America supplied the South Vietnamese military with weapons, ammunition and fuel while the USSR and China did the same for the North.

Although the USA had ended its combat role, antiwar organisations such as the Indochina Resource Centre continued to lobby the US government to cut off all financial and military assistance to South Vietnam. They nearly succeeded – the US Senate came within two votes of doing just that. The antiwar lobby did succeed in having funding greatly reduced. In 1975, America gave South Vietnam US$700 million in aid, less than half of what military experts estimated was needed. The South Vietnamese suddenly found they were running desperately low on stocks of ammunition and fuel.

The North Vietnamese were quick to assess the situation. They continued a major military build-up and in January 1975 launched a massive conventional ground attack across the 17th Parallel using tanks and heavy artillery. The invasion – a blatant violation of the Paris agreements – panicked the South Vietnamese army and government, which in the past had always depended on the Americans. In March, the NVA quickly occupied a strategic section of

## Disorderly Departure

One tragic legacy of the American War was the plight of thousands of Amerasians. Marriages, relationships and prostitution between American soldiers and Vietnamese women were common during the war. But when the Americans were rotated home, all too often they abandoned their 'wives' and mistresses, leaving them to raise children who were half-white or half-black in a society not particularly tolerant of such racial integration.

After reunification, the Amerasians – living reminders of the American presence – were often mistreated by Vietnamese and even abandoned by their mothers and other relatives, forcing them to live on the streets. They were also denied educational and vocational opportunities, and were sadly referred to as 'children of the dust'.

At the end of the 1980s, the Orderly Departure Programme (ODP), carried out under the auspices of the United Nations High Commission for Refugees (UNHCR), was designed to allow for the orderly resettlement in the West (mostly in the USA) of Amerasians and political refugees who otherwise might have tried to flee the country by land or sea. Thousands of Vietnamese and their families were flown via Bangkok to the Philippines, where they underwent six months of English instruction before proceeding to the USA.

Unfortunately, many Amerasian children were adopted by Vietnamese eager to emigrate, but were then dumped and left to fend for themselves after the family's arrival in the USA. **Asian American LEAD** (☎ 202-518 6737; Ⓦ www.aalead.org; 1323 Girard St NW, Washington, DC 20009, USA) is an organisation that has been doing good work training and mentoring young Indochinese, especially Amerasian kids and their parents, as they adapt to life in the USA.

The ODP was mainly aimed at the South Vietnamese and failed to stem the flow of refugees from the North. After the Vietnam-China border opened in 1990, many simply took the train to China. From there it was only a short boat ride across the Pearl River to Hong Kong to become 'boat people'.

However, boarding a ramshackle refugee boat, whether it was headed for Hong Kong, Malaysia, the Philippines or Australia, was an enormous risk. With little or no supplies, the boats filled to bursting point, and the craft, ill-equipped for bad-weather conditions, were heinous. Even now many survivors experience psychological trauma stemming from their flight – many boats were attacked by pirates who stole possessions, killed and brutalised passengers and raped the women on board.

As the refugee camps in Hong Kong swelled to bursting point, the public's patience ran out. 'Refugee fatigue' became the buzzword in Hong Kong and the public demanded that something be done.

Since all but a handful of the arrivals were declared to be economic migrants rather than political refugees, the Hong Kong government experimented with forcible repatriation in 1990. This prompted a vehement protest from the USA and the UNHCR. The Hong Kong government backed off temporarily and finally agreed with Vietnam on a programme of combined voluntary and forced repatriation. Those willing to return would not be penalised, would get back their citizenship (the previous policy was to strip all refugees of their citizenship, thus rendering them stateless) and would receive a resettlement allowance of US$30 per month, for several months, from the UNHCR.

The voluntary repatriation didn't go quite as planned; some of the volunteers were back in Hong Kong a few months later seeking another resettlement allowance. In such cases, forcible repatriation swiftly followed. The programme produced results – by the end of 1992 almost no new Vietnamese refugees arrived in Hong Kong.

Among the thousands seeking refuge in Hong Kong was a small hardcore faction of misfits with a criminal past, who the Vietnamese government didn't want back. Hong Kong didn't want them either and no Western countries rolled out the welcome mat. And so these refugees were stuck in camps behind razor wire, preying on each other and staging the occasional violent protest over their grim situation. Finally, major riots broke out in the camps in 1995 and 1996, and some escaped.

the central highlands at Buon Ma Thuot. In the absence of American military support or advice, the South Vietnamese president, Nguyen Van Thieu, decided on a strategy of tactical withdrawal to more defensible positions. This proved to be a spectacular military blunder. Rather than stand and fight as expected, South Vietnamese troops were ordered to retreat from Central Highland bases at Pleiku and Kon Tum. The totally unplanned withdrawal was quite a disaster. Retreating ARVN soldiers were intercepted and attacked by the well-disciplined North Vietnamese troops. The withdrawal became a disaster as panicking ARVN soldiers deserted en masse in order to try to save their families.

Whole brigades of ARVN soldiers disintegrated and fled southward, joining the hundreds of thousands of civilians clogging National Highway 1. City after city – Buon Ma Thuot, Quang Tri, Hué, Danang, Qui Nhon, Tuy Hoa, Nha Trang – was simply abandoned by the defenders with hardly a shot fired. So quickly did the ARVN troops flee that the North Vietnamese army could barely keep up with them. The US Congress, fed up with the war and its drain on the treasury, refused to send emergency aid that Nixon – before his resignation – had promised would be forthcoming in the event of such an invasion.

Nguyen Van Thieu, in power since 1967, resigned on 21 April 1975 and fled the country, allegedly taking with him millions of dollars in ill-gotten wealth. He moved to Britain and bitterly blamed the Americans for 'abandoning' his regime.

Thieu was replaced by Vice President Tran Van Huong, who quit a week later, turning the presidency over to General Duong Van Minh, who surrendered on the morning of 30 April 1975, after only 43 hours in office, in Saigon's Independence Palace (now called Reunification Palace). Minh died in 2001, at the age of 86, while living in exile in California.

The last Americans were evacuated by helicopter from the US embassy roof, to ships stationed just offshore, only a few hours before South Vietnam surrendered.

Thus more than a decade of American military involvement was brought to an end. Throughout the entire episode, the USA had never declared war on North Vietnam.

The Americans weren't the only ones who left. As the South collapsed, 135,000 Vietnamese also fled the country; in the next five years, at least 545,000 of their compatriots would do the same. Those who left by sea would become known to the world as 'boat people'.

## Since Reunification

On the first day of their victory, the communists changed Saigon's name to Ho Chi Minh City (HCMC). That proved to be only the first change of many.

The sudden success of the 1975 North Vietnamese offensive surprised the North almost as much as it did the South. As a result, Hanoi had no specific plans to deal with the integration of the two parts of the country, whose social and economic systems could hardly have been more different.

The North was faced with the legacy of a cruel and protracted war that had literally fractured the country; there were high levels of understandable bitterness (if not hatred) on both sides, and a mind-boggling array of problems. Damage from the fighting extended from the unmarked minefields to war-focused, dysfunctional economies; from vast areas of chemically poisoned countryside to millions of people who had been affected physically or mentally. The country was diplomatically isolated and its old allies were no longer willing or able to provide significant aid. Peace may have arrived, but in many ways the war was far from over.

Until the formal reunification of Vietnam in July 1976, the South was nominally ruled by the Provisional Revolutionary Government. Because the Communist Party did not really trust the Southern urban intelligentsia (even those of its members who had supported the VC) large numbers of Northern cadres were sent southward to manage the transition. This created resentment among Southerners who had worked against the Thieu government and then, after its overthrow, found themselves frozen out of positions of responsibility (even today, a high percentage of the officials and police in HCMC are from the North).

After months of debate, those in Hanoi who wanted to implement a rapid transition to socialism (including the collectivisation of agriculture) in the South gained the upper hand. Great efforts were made to deal with the South's social problems: millions of illiterates and unemployed, several hundred thousand prostitutes and drug addicts, and tens of thousands of people who made their living by criminal activities. Many of these people were encouraged to move to the newly collectivised farms in the country-side. This may have had some benefits, but the results of the transition to socialism were mostly disastrous for the South's economy.

Reunification was accompanied by large-scale political repression. Despite repeated promises to the contrary, hundreds of thousands of people who had ties to the previous regime had their property confiscated and were rounded up and imprisoned without trial in forced-labour camps, euphemistic-ally known as re-education camps. Tens of thousands of businesspeople, intellectuals, artists, journalists, writers, union leaders and many members of the Buddhist, Catholic and Protestant clergy – some of whom had opposed both Thieu and the war – were held in horrendous conditions.

Some were able to buy their way out, but most of the wealthy simply had their bank accounts and property confiscated. While the majority of detainees were released within a few years, some (declared to be 'obstinate and counter-revolutionary elem-ents') were to spend the next decade or more in the camps. The purge and terrible eco-nomic conditions prompted hundreds of thousands of Southerners to flee their home-land by sea or overland through Cambodia (see the boxed text 'Disorderly Departure' earlier in this chapter).

The purge affected not only former op-ponents of the communists, but also their families. Even today, the children of former counter-revolutionaries can be discriminated against. One way this is done is to deny them a *ho khau* permit, which is needed to attend school, seek employment and own farmland, a home or a business.

Relations with China to the north and its Khmer Rouge allies to the west were rapidly deteriorating and war-weary Vietnam seemed beset by enemies.

An anticapitalist campaign was launched in March 1978, during which private prop-erty and businesses were seized. Most of the victims were ethnic Chinese – hundreds of thousands soon became refugees, and rela-tions with China soured further. Meanwhile, repeated attacks on Vietnamese border villages by the Khmer Rouge forced Vietnam to respond. Vietnamese forces entered Cam-bodia at the end of 1978. They succeeded in driving the Khmer Rouge from power in early 1979 and set up a pro-Hanoi regime in Phnom Penh.

China viewed the attack on its Khmer Rouge allies as a serious provocation. In February 1979, Chinese forces invaded Viet-nam and fought a brief, 17-day war before withdrawing.

Khmer Rouge forces, with support from China and Thailand, continued a costly guerrilla war against the Vietnamese on Cambodian soil for the next decade. Viet-nam pulled its forces out of Cambodia in September 1989. The Cambodian civil war was officially settled in 1992 and United Nations peacekeeping forces were called in to monitor the peace agreement. Although Khmer Rouge units continue to violate the terms of the peace plan, Vietnam is no longer involved in the conflict. As a result, Vietnam has enjoyed its first decade of peace since WWII.

## Opening the Door

The relatively recent liberalisation of foreign investment laws and the relaxation of visa regulations for tourists seem to be part of a general opening up of Vietnam to the world.

Sweden was the first Western country, in 1969, to establish diplomatic relations with Hanoi; since then, most Western nations have followed suit.

The USSR began its first cautious open-ing to the West in 1984 with the appointment

## Doi Moi & Beyond

Vietnam surfed the boom transforming much of Southeast Asia in the 1990s and experienced first-hand the stresses and pitfalls of globalisation. Like most nations in the region, Vietnam went from heady growth early in the decade to an equally dramatic slowdown. At the beginning of the new millennium many people were still wondering whether the thrilling ride of the early 1990s had been an illusion and what, if anything, could be done to restart the process.

The groundwork for the reforms that enabled Vietnam's growth spurt were laid in the 1980s, but only took effect in 1990. Foreign investment poured in. Small businesses of all kinds reaped the benefits of liberalisation. The cities in particular were a hive of activity. Many people joined the giddy collective leap from agricultural into post-industrial lifestyles, and the rapidly growing service and tertiary sectors soaked up hundreds of thousands of workers.

Zealot-like converts to the newly-acquired language of market economics were plentiful. People from all walks of life seemed confident their lives would improve. The economy did take off, surpassing most expectations. The World Bank and the International Monetary Fund (IMF) applauded the liberal reforms as Vietnam posted high growth rates typical of tiger-cub economies. The results were seen as the South's vindication, the triumph of the market over Marx and Mao, reversing the Northern-engineered unification of 1975. In a flood of upbeat hype, Vietnam's transition out of communism seemed forsworn.

The lifting of the US embargo on trading with its former enemy in 1994 was heralded as an historic event. When Pepsi and Coca-Cola began their competitive posturing for the huge Vietnamese market, there was a feeling that capitalism had arrived. Yet Vietnam's tide had already turned. The country was full of investors, traders and travellers from Taiwan, South Korea, Hong Kong, Singapore, Indonesia and southern China. No time was wasted in extracting resources at bargain basement prices, flogging off consumer goods, cashing in on cheap labour, sinking capital in quick return ventures and celebrating the good life to be had.

The cultural impacts of Vietnam's regional engagement were significant. In a process better described as 're-Orientalisation' than Westernisation, Vietnam morphed rapidly from East bloc into East Asia. Advertisements for Honda, Daewoo and Cheng Fong brushed aside revolutionary imagery on billboards. Vietnam was quickly overrun with regional popular culture, like the Japanese cartoon 'Doraemon', Canto-pop, karaoke, Korean clothing fashions and Hong Kong martial arts and gangster videos. Television advertisements made in Japan and South Korea for the Thai and Indonesian markets slid between segments of Australian soap operas. When Vietnam joined the Association of Southeast Asian Nations (Asean) in 1995, it diplomatically cemented a process of regional integration that was already taking place in cultural and economic spheres.

Although the upbeat mood was pervasive, there were clear indicators that Vietnam was not immune to problems associated with strong growth. The triumph of a new breed of 'red capitalists' dedicated to getting rich was only one aspect of the transforming social landscape. Pronounced differences in the level of economic activity between country and city resulted in yawning rural-urban differentiation and a flood of migrants to urban centres. With the notable exception of the ethnic Chinese, Vietnam's minorities, mostly located in remote regions, were locked out of the rewards of 'marketisation'. The south and particularly Ho Chi Minh City sucked up the lion's share of investment and remained Vietnam's capitalist frontier, monopolising the best and the worst of what global re-engagement had to offer. As in the north, prostitution re-emerged as a serious problem. While the growth of the sex industry was partly in response to increasing domestic demand, the industry offended the cultural sensibilities of many Vietnamese. Increasingly shrill complaints were voiced about corruption, which only became more entrenched as efforts to eradicate it remained tokenistic. Vietnam's forests, beaches, rivers and fields were ravaged by seemingly unfettered resource extraction and development: a new biological apocalypse visited on a landscape already battered from war.

## Doi Moi & Beyond

In the middle of the decade it became common to hear comments made about the negative impacts of the liberal reforms: complaints about mistreatment of factory workers by foreign bosses; worries about Vietnam's increasingly individualistic, culturally rootless Generation X; anxieties about cultural inundation by 'inappropriate' foreign influences; the resurgence of ritual and popular religious practices denounced in some circles as 'superstitious'; and laments about the relentless commercialisation of the educational and health sectors.

The growing mood of cultural conservatism had political parallels. In 1996 and '97 party conservatives launched campaigns against 'peaceful evolutionism' (the alleged attempt by 'enemies' to subvert socialism) and 'social evils' including prostitution, crime and advertising slogans in foreign languages. Reformists in the Politburo were accused of deviations from the communist path. This reactive mood culminated in the 1996 Party Congress, whose main result was a stalemate on progressing the reforms.

When financial crisis struck the region, Vietnam was already back-peddling. News reports of the flight of capital had been doing the rounds for some time. A number of big companies had their noses bloodied. No longer was Vietnam thought an easy place to make money. Being less integrated into the global economy than Thailand or Indonesia, the regional meltdown hit Vietnam indirectly when its neighbours' capital was withdrawn. Some thought the crisis was a reason to deepen the reforms. Party conservatives saw it as evidence of the superiority of the communist path.

Apart from impasses at the leadership level, the country was experiencing serious internal problems. Riots broke out in Thai Binh and Dong Nai provinces, the people fed up with their corrupt and undemocratic leaders. The government's response, an anticorruption drive, achieved little. The prosecution of several high-flying entrepreneurs only depressed local business. Lowered growth rates, rising unemployment, complaints about excessive taxation, a struggling private sector and a stagnant rural economy were further symptoms of the domestic malaise.

By the late 1990s foreign media reportage on Vietnam was very negative. In a notorious piece in the *Economist* entitled 'Good Night Vietnam', the country was portrayed as a land beyond capitalism. Vietnam also received damaging criticism of its repression of religious groups from the United Nations Rapporteur for Religious Intolerance, Abdelfattah Amor, and from Amnesty International, Human Rights Watch and the US State Department for its mistreatment of dissidents.

Despite the bad publicity and poor figures, the country was changing quickly. Although investors had voted with their feet, Vietnam remained a favoured recipient of bilateral and multilateral development aid. Provincial capitals grew steadily, government offices were refurbished, new markets opened, bridges were built and roads widened. Dedicated industrial regions like Binh Duong province in the south boomed rapidly and continued to receive foreign investment. In urban centres there was much greater choice of consumer goods, lifestyles, services for the growing middle class and a boom in domestic tourism. Internet service providers sprang up like mushrooms, not only in tourist areas but to service an increasingly computer-literate urban population.

With the signing of a trade agreement with the USA in 2000, a more optimistic mood began to creep back into the country. There is no doubt that the country will continue to be drawn into global exchanges; however, equally, communism is not going anywhere fast. Big players like the USA who seek to re-engage Vietnam will have to find ways of coming to terms with its political system and confront the kinds of cultural sensitivities and social rifts that have emerged in the country's engagements with the nonsocialist world.

**Philip Taylor**

Philip Taylor is an anthropologist who has spent over two years in Vietnam. Some of these ideas appear in his book, *Fragments of the Present: Searching for modernity in Vietnam's South*, Allen & Unwin 2001.

of Mikhail Gorbachev as Secretary General of the Communist Party. Vietnam followed suit in 1986 by choosing reform-minded Nguyen Van Linh to be General Secretary of the Vietnamese Communist Party. However, dramatic changes in Eastern Europe and the USSR were not viewed with favour in Hanoi. The Vietnamese Communist Party denounced the participation of noncommunists in Eastern Bloc governments, calling the democratic revolutions 'a counterattack from imperialist circles' against socialism.

General Secretary Linh declared at the end of 1989 that 'we resolutely reject pluralism, a multiparty system and opposition parties'. But in February 1990, the government called for more openness and criticism. The response came swiftly, with an outpouring of news articles, editorials and letters from the public condemning corruption, inept leadership and the high living standards of senior officials while most people lived in extreme poverty. Taken aback by the harsh criticism, official control over literature, the arts and the media were tightened once again in a campaign against 'deviant ideological viewpoints'. An effort was made to blame public dissatisfaction on foreign imperialists. Interior Minister Mai Chi Tho wrote in the army's newspaper:

Through modern communications means and newspapers, letters and video tapes brought to Vietnam, they have conducted virulent attacks against Marxism-Leninism and the party's leadership, blaming all socio-economic difficulties on the Communist Party in order to demand political pluralism, a multiparty system and bourgeois-type democracy.

At age 75, ailing Nguyen Van Linh was replaced as General Secretary in June 1991 by Prime Minister Do Muoi. Regarded as a conservative, Muoi nevertheless vowed to continue the economic reforms started by Linh. At the same time, a major shake-up of the ruling Politburo and Central Committee of the Communist Party saw many members forcibly retired and replaced by younger, more liberal-minded leaders. The sudden collapse of the USSR just two months later caused the government to reiterate its stand

that political pluralism would not be tolerated, but at the same time economic reforms were speeded up.

Muoi and Prime Minister Vo Van Kiet visited Beijing in November 1991 to heal Vietnam's 12-year rift with China. The visit was reciprocated in December 1992 when Chinese prime minister Li Peng visited Hanoi. It was all smiles and warm handshakes in front of the cameras, but relations between the countries remain tense. However, trade across the China-Vietnam border (both legal and otherwise) is booming.

Relations with Vietnam's old nemesis, the USA, have also improved over the last decade. In early 1994, the USA finally lifted its economic embargo, which had been in place since the 1960s. This allowed Vietnam access to loans from the International Monetary Fund (IMF), imported high-tech goods and American companies. Full diplomatic relations with the USA have been restored. (See the boxed text '*Doi Moi & Beyond*' for more on recent history.)

In April-May 2000, mass celebrations were held across Vietnam to commemorate the 25th anniversary of 'liberation' and the end of the American war. Bill Clinton, who didn't fight in the war, helped to mark the occasion later that year by becoming the first US president to visit northern Vietnam and the first in 30 years to visit the country's south. Clinton's November visit lasted four days, and he was accompanied by an entourage of nearly 1500 politicians, journalists and businesspeople, the latter hoping to witness the unlocking of lucrative new investment opportunities.

Throughout 2001 and into 2002, Vietnam pushed ahead with the implementation of its National Tourism Action Programme, a government scheme in which key tourist sites were upgraded.

## GEOGRAPHY

Vietnam stretches over 1600km along the eastern coast of the Indochinese Peninsula (from 8°34' N to 23°22' N). The country's land area is 326,797 sq km, or 329,566 sq km including water. This makes it slightly larger than Italy and a bit smaller than

Japan. Vietnam has 3451km of coastline and 3818km of land borders: 1555km shared with Laos, 1281km with China and 982km with Cambodia.

Vietnamese often describe their country as resembling a bamboo pole supporting a basket of rice on each end. The country is S-shaped, broad in the north and south and very narrow in the centre, where at one point it is only 50km wide.

The country's two main cultivated areas are the Red River Delta (15,000 sq km) in the north and the Mekong Delta (60,000 sq km) in the south. Silt carried by the Red River and its tributaries (confined to their paths by 3000km of dikes) has raised the level of the river beds above that of the surrounding plains. Breaches in the levees result in disastrous flooding.

Three-quarters of the country consists of mountains and hills, the highest of which is 3143m-high Fansipan (or Phan Si Pan) in the Hoang Lien Mountains in the far northwest. The Truong Son Mountain Range (Annamite Cordillera), which forms the central highlands, runs almost the full length of Vietnam along its borders with Laos and Cambodia.

The largest metropolis is HCMC, which many still call Saigon, followed by Hanoi, Haiphong and Danang.

## GEOLOGY

There are several notable geological features in Vietnam, but the most striking by far are the karst formations. Karst consists of irregular limestone in which erosion has produced fissures, sinkholes, caves and underground rivers. The northern part of Vietnam has a spectacular assemblage of these formations, notably around Halong Bay, Bai Tu Long Bay and Tam Coc. At Halong and Bai Tu Long Bays, an enormous limestone plateau has gradually sunk into the ocean – the old mountain tops stick out of the sea like vertical fingers pointing towards the sky. At Tam Coc, the karst formations are similar, except they are all still above sea level. In the south there is a less impressive collection around the Ha Tien area in the Mekong Delta. The Marble

Mountains near Danang in central Vietnam are yet another example.

Not all of Vietnam's mountains are limestone. The coastal ranges near Nha Trang and those at Hai Van Pass (Danang) are composed of granite. The giant boulders littering the hillsides can be quite an impressive sight.

The western part of the central highlands (near Buon Me Thuot and Pleiku) is well known for its red volcanic soil, which is extremely fertile. However, the highlands are just that – high above sea level, but mostly flat and not too scenic.

The Mekong River has produced one of the world's great deltas, composed of fine silt that has washed downstream for millions of years. The silt is fertile and supports lush tropical vegetation. The Mekong Delta continues to expand at a rate of about 100m per year, though global warming and the consequent rise in world sea levels could submerge it.

## CLIMATE

There are no good or bad seasons for visiting Vietnam. When one region is wet, cold or steamy hot, there is always somewhere else that is sunny and pleasantly warm.

Vietnam has a remarkably diverse climate because of its wide range of latitudes and altitudes. Although the entire country lies in the tropics and subtropics, local conditions vary from frosty winters in the far northern hills to year-round, subequatorial warmth in the Mekong Delta. Because about a third of Vietnam is over 500m above sea level, much of the country enjoys a subtropical or – above 2000m – temperate climate.

Vietnam lies in the East Asian monsoon zone. Its weather is determined by two monsoons that set the rhythm of rural life. The winter monsoon comes from the northeast between October and March bringing wet chilly winters to all areas north of Nha Trang, but dry and warm temperatures to the south. From April or May to October, the southwestern monsoon – its winds laden with moisture picked up while crossing the Indian Ocean and the Gulf of Thailand – brings warm, humid weather to the whole

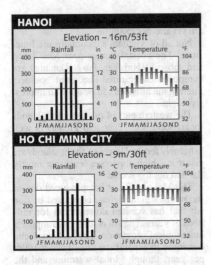

**Central Vietnam**

The coastal lowlands are denied significant rainfall from the southwestern monsoon (April or May to October) by the Truong Son Mountain Range, which is very wet during this period. Much of the coastal strip's precipitation is brought by the northeastern monsoon between December and February. Nha Trang's long dry season lasts from late January to October, while Dalat's dry season is from December to March. Dalat, like the rest of the central highlands, is much cooler than the Mekong Delta and the coastal strip. From November to March, Dalat's daily highs are usually in the low to mid-20s.

The cold and wet winter weather of the north-central coastal lowlands is accompanied by fog and fine drizzle.

**The North**

Areas north of the 18th Parallel have two seasons: winter and summer. Winter is quite cool and wet, and usually lasts from around November to April. February and March are marked by a persistent drizzling rain that the Vietnamese call *crachin*. The hot summers run from May to October. The north is subject to occasional typhoons during the summer months.

**ECOLOGY & ENVIRONMENT**

Vietnam's environment is not in the worst shape, but there are some troubling signs. Because Vietnam is a poor, densely populated agricultural country, humans often compete head-on with native plants and animals for the same resources. The country boasts a vast extent of ecological systems from mountains and wetlands to coral reefs. Deforestation is perhaps the most serious problem. Originally, almost the whole of Vietnam was covered with dense forests. Since the arrival of the first human beings many millennia ago, Vietnam has been progressively denuded of forest cover. While 44% of the original forest cover was extant in 1943, by 1976 only 29% remained, by 1983 only 24% was left and in 1995 it was down to 20%. Fortunately, recent reforestation projects by the Forest Ministry, including banning of unprocessed timber exports

country except for those areas sheltered by mountains (such as the central coastal lowlands and the Red River Delta).

Between July and November, violent and unpredictable typhoons often develop over the ocean east of Vietnam, hitting central and northern Vietnam with devastating results.

Most of Vietnam receives about 2000mm of precipitation annually, although parts of the central highlands get approximately 3300mm.

**The South**

The south, with its subequatorial climate, has two main seasons: the wet and the dry. The wet season lasts from May to November (June to August are the wettest months). During this time, there are heavy but short-lived downpours almost daily, usually in the afternoon. The dry season usually runs from December to April. Late February to May is hot and very humid, but it cools down slightly when the rainy season begins.

In HCMC the average annual temperature is 27°C. In April, daily highs are usually in the low 30s. In January, the daily lows average 21°C. Average humidity is 80% and annual rainfall averages 1979mm. The coldest temperature that has ever been recorded in HCMC is 14°C.

in 1992, have seen a significant rise in forest cover – in early 1998 the coverage was 28%, and by 2000 it was over 30%.

In addition, the Ministry of Education has made the planting and taking care of trees part of school curricula. However, even at this rate, reforestation cannot keep up with forest losses.

Each hectare of land stripped of vegetation contributes to the flooding of areas downstream from catchment areas; irreversible soil erosion (upland soils are very fragile); the silting up of rivers, streams, lakes and reservoirs; the loss of wildlife habitat; and unpredictable climatic changes.

Vietnam has so far suffered little industrial pollution largely because there has been little industry. However, the nation's rapid economic and population growth indicates environmental trouble ahead. The dramatic increase in noisy, smoke-spewing motorbikes in recent years should be taken as a sign of abominations to come.

Ecotourism is increasingly on the rise, with trekking and other outdoor tours being sought out by more and more travellers. The government has been setting aside tens of thousands of square kilometres of forest land with plans to create about a hundred protected areas in the form of national parks and nature reserves. Local ecologists hope that because tropical ecosystems have highly diverse species but low densities of individual species, reserve areas will be large enough to contain viable populations of each species.

However, there are development interests that are not particularly amenable to increasing in the size of Vietnam's national parks and nature reserves. As in the West, even the best-laid plans can sometimes go awry.

Much has been said about the human and economic devastation wrought by the USA during the American War, but it was also the most intensive attempt to destroy a country's natural environment – ecocide. American forces sprayed 72 million litres of herbicides (named Agents Orange, White and Blue after the colour of their canisters), over 16% of South Vietnam to destroy the VC's natural cover.

Another environmentally disastrous method of defoliation involved the use of enormous bulldozers called 'Rome ploughs' to rip up the jungle floor. Large tracts of forest, agricultural land, villages and even cemeteries were bulldozed, removing both the vegetation and topsoil. Flammable melaleuca forests were ignited with napalm. In mountain areas, landslides were deliberately created by bombing and spraying acid on limestone hillsides. Elephants, useful for transport, were attacked from the air with bombs and napalm. By the war's end, extensive areas had been taken over by tough weeds (known locally as 'American grass'). The government estimates that 20,000 sq km of forest and farmland were lost as a direct result of the American War.

Overall, some 13 million tonnes of bombs – equivalent to 450 times the energy of the atomic bomb used on Hiroshima – were dropped on the region. This comes to 265kg for every man, woman and child in Indochina. If the Americans had showered the people of Indochina with the money all those bombs cost (the war cost US$2000 per person in Indochina), it's likely that both the environment and the economy of Vietnam would be in much better shape.

Scientists have yet to conclusively prove a link between the residues of chemicals used by the USA and spontaneous abortions, stillbirths, birth defects and other human health problems. However, the circumstantial evidence is certainly compelling. In 2002, on the heels of a landmark Agent Orange conference in Hanoi, the USA and Vietnam initiated a joint investigation into the health effects of this damaging herbicide. Delegates from Vietnam's National Environmental Agency and the US National Institute of Environmental Health Sciences cosigned a directive for scientists to explore possible links between Agent Orange and various physical illnesses. Research is also being conducted on the cleaning up of dioxin in forests harmed by the chemical.

## FLORA & FAUNA

Despite widespread deforestation, Vietnam's plant growth is what you'd expect to find in a tropical country – abundant and varied. Scientists are only beginning to catalogue the country's flora and fauna, and today the government is showing enthusiasm for ecological protection.

## Flora

Originally Vietnam was virtually covered in forest, from vast mangrove forests fringing the coast to dense rainforest in the mountainous regions. Over millennia the forests have progressively been pushed back: first by the gradual clearing of land for the cultivation of rice and other crops, and then by a rapidly increasing population and the ravages of war.

Although the scars of war can still be seen and much of the damage is irreversible, reforestation programmes have been implemented and today the landscape is showing signs of recovery. Natural forests at higher elevations, such as in the northwest, feature wild rhododendrons, dwarf bamboo and many varieties of orchid; the central coast is drier and features stands of pines; while the river deltas support mangrove forests, which are valuable nurseries for fish and crustaceans as well as feeding sites for many bird species.

The remaining forests of Vietnam are estimated to still contain over 12,000 plant species, only around 7000 of which have been identified and 2300 of which are known to be useful to humans for food, medicines, animal fodder, wood products and other purposes. Recently the islands and caves of Ha Long Bay yielded seven previously unknown types of plant – the largest and most conspicuous of the new flora has been christened the Ha Long Fan Palm.

One controversial development in Vietnam's forestry projects has been the funding of tree plantations by AusAID, a scheme of the Australian government. Most notable is the appearance of large tracts of young eucalyptus trees.

## Fauna

Vietnam has a surprising amount to offer those interested in wildlife, some of which is rapidly disappearing. The main cause is the destruction of wildlife habitats, although hunting, poaching and pollution have all taken their toll too.

Because Vietnam has a wide range of habitats – from equatorial lowlands to high, temperate plateaus and even alpine peaks – its wild fauna is enormously diverse. It is home to over 275 species of mammal, over 800 species of birds (see Books in the Facts for the Visitor chapter for recommended bird-watching guides), 180 species of reptile, 80 species of amphibian, hundreds of species of fish and thousands of species of invertebrates.

Every once in a while, Vietnam reveals a form of life that has otherwise managed to evade scientific classification. Over the past decade or so zoologists have seen previously unknown species of large mammal in Vietnam. In 1998, for example, a new breed of muntjac deer was discovered in the country. The scientific and conservation interest of these recent discoveries has not been lost on authorities, and the Vietnam government has been expanding the size of national parks and nature reserves, while banning logging within their boundaries. As research and conservation efforts continue, the more uncommon and previously undocumented species should be discovered.

Rare and little-known birds previously thought to be extinct are turning up and no doubt more await, particularly in the extensive forests of the Lao border. For example, Edwards' pheasant, a species previously thought to be extinct, was recently discovered; other rare and endangered species recently spotted by scientific expeditions include the white-winged wood duck and white-shouldered ibis.

Even a casual visitor will notice a few birds: swallows and swifts flying over fields and along watercourses; flocks of finches at roadsides and in paddies; and bulbuls and mynas in gardens and patches of forest. Vietnam is on the East Asian flyway and is an important stopover for migratory waders en route from Siberian breeding grounds to their Australian winter quarters. A coastal reserve has been established at the mouth of the Red River for the protection of these birds, and rare species such as the spoon-billed sandpiper and Nordmann's greenshank.

## Endangered Species

Tragically, Vietnam's wildlife has been in precipitous decline as the forest habitats are destroyed and waterways become polluted. In addition, uncontrolled illegal hunting (many people in remote areas have access to weapons left over from the American War) has exterminated local animal populations, in some cases eliminating entire species. Continued habitat destruction and poaching means that many now-rare species are headed for the extinction list. Captive breeding programmes may be the only hope for some.

Officially, the government has recognised 54 species of mammal and 60 species of bird as endangered. The tapir and Sumatran rhinoceros are already extinct in Vietnam, and there are thought to be fewer than 20 koupreys and between 20 and 30 Javan rhinoceroses left in the country. In the early 1990s a small population of the world's rarest rhinoceros, the Javan rhino, was discovered in the Cat Tien National Park, southwest of Dalat.

Larger animals of importance in the country's conservation efforts are the elephant, rhinoceros, tiger, leopard, black bear, honey bear, snub-nosed monkey, douc langur (remarkable for its variegated colours), concolour gibbon, rhesus monkey, serow (a kind of mountain goat), flying squirrel, kouprey (a blackish-brown forest ox), banteng (a kind of wild ox), deer, peacock, pheasant, crocodile, python, cobra and turtle.

It is encouraging that some wildlife seems to be returning to reforested areas. For example, birds, fish and crustaceans have reappeared in replanted mangrove forests. Areas in which large animals were thought to have been wiped out by war and poaching are now 'hot spots' of biodiversity and abundance. Once-extensive forests are still home to spectacular examples, such as the tiger, Asian elephant, clouded leopard and sun bear, although their numbers are dwindling under pressure from hunting and habitat destruction.

## National Parks

Vietnam currently has 13 national parks and an expanding array of nature reserves. Nine of the parks (Ba Be, Ba Vi, Bach Ma, Ben En, Cat Ba, Cat Tien, Cuc Phuong, Tam Dao and Yok Don) are administered by the Ministry of Agriculture and Rural Development (MARD) and Forest Protection Department (FPD). Four others (Con Dao, Tram Chim, Phu Quoc and Bai Tu Long) are under local-government management. There are plans to expand and improve existing parks and nature reserves, and also to establish new ones.

I met the director of Bach Ma National Park. He expressed his desire to see more visitors to the park, used terms like 'ecotourism' and explained that overseas interest in Vietnam's national-parks programme was vital in order to raise the government's commitment. Serious pressures from logging, poaching, agriculture etc, require national and provincial government assistance in overcoming. This will only happen if the park's tourist potential is seen as something worth protecting.

**Tim Weisselbergo**

Most of Vietnam's national parks are seldom visited, as travellers tend to get stuck on the 'must-see' tourist trail, without the time or wanderlust to explore them. Access can be problematic with some parks hidden in remote areas, but others are easy to reach. For those who make the effort to seek them out, national parks reveal a whole other side of Vietnam. They also have the added appeal of being among the few places in Vietnam where tourists are unlikely to be hassled to buy anything.

The most interesting and accessible parks are Cat Ba, Ba Be and Cuc Phuong in the North; Bach Ma in the centre; and Cat Tien and Yok Don in the South (see the National Park Highlights table later for more details).

Cat Ba National Park is a beautiful island and during the summer months it attracts a steady stream of foreign travellers willing to make the boat journey. In 2000, Vietnam also created the Bai Tu Long National Park, a protected reserve situated to the east of Halong Bay, which includes over 15,000 hectares of tropical evergreen forest. Ba Be

## National Park Highlights

| park (park size) | chapter | features | access | best time to visit |
|---|---|---|---|---|
| Cuc Phuong (22,200ha) | North-Central Vietnam | hiking, grottoes, endangered-primate centre, birdlife, Tonkin rare leaf monkeys | car/motorbike | October to March |
| Cat Tien (73,878ha) | Central Highlands | primates, elephants, birdlife, rhinos, tigers | car/motorbike then boat | November to February |
| Ba Be (7610ha) | Northeast Vietnam | lakes, rainforest, waterfalls, towering peaks, bears, monkeys, birdlife | public transport to Cho Ra, then motorbike/4WD | April to November |
| Bach Ma (22,031ha) | Central Vietnam | hiking, waterfalls, birdlife, tigers, primates | car/motorbike | February to September |
| Cat Ba (15,200ha) | Northeast Vietnam | hiking, caves, ethnic groups, monkeys, boars, deer, waterfowl | minibus/ motorbike | April to August |
| Yok Don (115,545ha) | Central Highlands | ethnic groups, elephant rides, stilt houses | 4WD/ motorbike | November to February |

National Park features spectacular waterfalls and is accessible by rented jeep or motorbike from Hanoi. Cuc Phuong National Park is less visited, but easily reached from Hanoi and offers great hiking. Bach Ma National Park near Hué is also seldom visited, but is demonstrating good potential for responsible ecotourism. Cat Tien National Park, in the southern part of the central highlands, is relatively easy to reach from HCMC or Dalat. Cat Tien is very popular with bird-watchers. Also in the central highlands is Yok Don National Park, which is home to many elephants and local minority tribes.

## GOVERNMENT & POLITICS

When it comes to government and politics, Vietnam has a lot of both.

The Socialist Republic of Vietnam (SRV; Cong Hoa Xa Hoi Chu Nghia Viet Nam) came into existence in July 1976 as a unitary state comprising the Democratic Republic of Vietnam (DRV; North Vietnam) and the defeated Republic of Vietnam (RVN; South Vietnam). From April 1975 until the declaration of the SRV, the South had been ruled – at least in name – by a Provisional Revolutionary Government.

Officially, the government espouses a Marxist-Leninist political philosophy. Its political institutions have borrowed a great deal from the Soviet and Chinese models, in particular the ability to create mountains of red tape. Relatively speaking, the policies of the Vietnamese Communist Party have been characterised by a flexible, nondoctrinaire approach.

The national slogan, which appears at the top of every official document, is 'Doc Lap, Tu Do, Hanh Phuc', based on one of Ho Chi

Minh's sayings 'Independence, Freedom, Happiness'.

Vietnam's political system is dominated by the two-million member Communist Party (Dang Cong San Viet Nam), whose influence is felt at every level of the country's social and political life.

The leadership of the Communist Party has been collective in style and structure ever since its founding by Ho Chi Minh in 1930. The party's decentralised structure, though originally necessitated by the difficulty of communications between its headquarters and its branches, has allowed local leaders a considerable amount of leeway for initiative. Unfortunately, this has also allowed the development of localised corruption, which Hanoi has had difficulty controlling.

The official media has described a number of cases. In Thanh Hoa province, local party chief Ha Trong Hoa turned his police force into a band of Mafia-style gangsters and ruled for years before Hanoi finally stepped in and ousted him. Pham Chi Tin, the son of a high-ranking Communist Party official, was arrested by the military in 1994 after his gang (the Nha Trang police force) terrorised local residents for years. Hanoi took action after he kidnapped a tourist from Hong Kong to extort money from the victim's family. There was a similar crackdown in Vung Tau recently.

The most powerful institution in the party is the Politburo, which has about a dozen members. It oversees the party's day-to-day functioning and has the power to issue directives to the government. The Politburo is formally elected by the Central Committee, whose 125 or so full members and about 50 alternate members meet only once or twice a year.

Party Congresses, at which major policy changes are ratified after a long process of behind-the-scenes discussions and consultations, were held in 1935, 1951, 1960, 1976, 1982, 1986, 1991, 1996 and 1997. The last few Party Congresses have reflected intense intra-party disagreements over the path Vietnamese communism should take, with changing coalitions of conservatives and dogmatists squaring off against the more pragmatic elements. The position of Party Chairman has been left vacant since Ho Chi Minh's death in 1969.

Vietnam's unicameral National Assembly (Quoc Hoi) is the highest legislative authority in the country. Its 500 or so deputies, whose terms last five years, each represent around 100,000 voters. The function of the National Assembly is basically to rubber-stamp, in most cases unanimously, Politburo decisions and party-initiated legislation during its biannual sessions, which last about a week.

The Council of State functions as the country's collective presidency. Its members (who numbered 15 at the time of writing) are elected by the National Assembly. The Council of State carries out the duties of the National Assembly when the latter is not in session. The Council of Ministers is another elected by the National Assembly. Its functions are similar to a Western-style cabinet.

During the 1980s and early '90s thousands of party members were expelled to reduce corruption (seen by a fed-up public as endemic) and to make room for more young people and workers. As in China, Vietnam has been ruled by a gerontocracy. Few high-ranking officials ever retire – they just fade away.

There are 25 official government ministries serving under the command of the men in the Council of Ministers. Despite official rhetoric about the equality of women, females are under-represented in the party, especially at the highest levels (there have been no female members of the Politburo since 1945).

Candidates of the National Assembly and local People's Committees are elected to office. Everyone of voting age (18 years) is required to vote, though proxy-voting is allowed (and is very common). This permits the government to boast that elections produce 100% voter participation, thus conferring legitimacy on the process. Only party-approved candidates are permitted to run and opposition parties are prohibited. Some independents have appeared on the slate, but they must also have the government's approval to run.

Theoretically, the military does not seem to have any direct political role, but virtually all Vietnam's high-ranking politicians and officials came from the military.

The government seems to have a hard time deciding how to carve the political turkey. After reunification, the provincial structure of the South was completely reorganised. Then on 1 July 1989, several provinces that were joined after 1975 were separated. Since then there have been even more splits; the last one was in 1996 when eight new provinces were created, bringing the total to 61. Even the Vietnamese have difficulty keeping up with the redrawing of political boundaries.

Vietnam became a member of Association of Southeast Asian Nations (Asean) in July 1995, and in November of the same year the US president, Bill Clinton, officially announced that US–Vietnamese relations were 'normalised'.

In March 2002, the National Assembly convened for the final session of its five-year term, while elections in May 2002 ushered in a new assembly and cabinet.

# ECONOMY

Vietnam is one of the poorest countries in Asia with an estimated per capita income of less than US$300 per year, and hard currency debts of US$1.4 billion (owed mainly to Russia, the IMF and Japan). Unable to repay these loans, Vietnam has been unofficially bankrupt since the 1980s.

An agreement reached in 1996 reduced Vietnam's debt by 50%, with the remainder to be paid off gradually. The country's improving economy increases the possibility that it will meet its obligations to lenders, and that Vietnam will eventually be issuing new bonds overseas.

Despite its hard-working, educated workforce, the country's economy is beset by low wages, poor infrastructure, a trade deficit, unemployment, underemployment and, until the mid-1990s, erratic runaway inflation (700% in 1986, 30% in 1989, 50% in 1991, 3% in 1996 and 8% in 1998).

The economy was hurt by wartime infrastructure damage (not a single bridge in the North survived US air raids, and in the South many were blown up by the VC), but by the government's own admission the present economic conditions are the result of the ideologically driven policies that followed reunification, as well as corruption and the heavy burden of military spending.

Just how the average Vietnamese manages to survive on their salaries is a mystery. Salaries in HCMC are in the range of US$50 to US$90 per month, but elsewhere they're about half that. You simply can't survive on such wages unless you can grow your own food and build your own house (possible in the countryside, but not in HCMC or Hanoi). So people scrounge on the side, finding some odd job they can do. Many women resort to part-time prostitution, while government officials and police often turn to corruption.

Although Vietnam and Russia are still officially as close as lips and teeth, Vietnamese from all parts of the country seem to harbour an unreserved hostility towards the few remaining Russian experts in their country. This bitterness is an outgrowth of the widespread belief that Soviet economic policies are to blame for Vietnam's economy going straight down the toilet after reunification.

The once ubiquitous posters of those two white guys, Marx and Lenin, disappeared almost overnight with the Soviet Union's demise in 1991.

## Economic Reforms

The economy might well have collapsed had it not been for Soviet aid and recent capitalist-style reforms. Vietnam's efforts to restructure the economy really got under way with the Sixth Party Congress held in December 1986. At that time, Nguyen Van Linh (a proponent of reform) was appointed General Secretary of the Communist Party.

Immediately after the legalisation of limited private enterprise, family businesses began popping up all over the country. But it's the south, with its capitalist experience that has had the entrepreneurial skills and managerial dynamism needed to effect the reforms. With 'new thinking' in Hanoi now modelling the economic life of the whole country in the mould of the prereunification South, people have been remarking that, in the end, the South won the war.

As a direct result of these economic reforms, Vietnam moved from being a rice importer in the mid-1980s to become the world's second-largest rice exporter after Thailand in 1997.

Vietnam's economy started growing in the late 1980s, which reversed the trend of the previous decade, when it experienced precipitous negative economic growth. But the official growth figures don't tell the whole story; there is a significant 'black economy' not recorded in the government's statistics. Indeed, the amount of smuggling going on across the Cambodia-Vietnam border easily exceeds the official trade between those two countries.

Another fact that the government doesn't like to admit is that the urban economy is improving much faster than the rural economy, widening the already significant gap in Vietnamese standards of living. The Vietnamese government fears what China is already experiencing – a mass exodus of countryside residents into the already overcrowded cities.

Before 1991, Vietnam's major trading partners were the Soviet Union and other members of the Council for Mutual Economic Assistance (Comecon), the Eastern Bloc equivalent to the European Union. Most of the trade with Comecon was on a barter basis; Vietnam traded crude oil, wood and sugar cane for refined oil, machinery and weapons. Because the value of Vietnam's agricultural products was not nearly enough to pay for the expensive war toys, the Soviet Union had to subsidise the Vietnamese economy, leaving Vietnam with an enormous rouble-denominated debt.

The disintegration of Comecon and the Soviet Union in 1991 could have brought complete economic collapse to Vietnam. Miraculously, this was avoided because Vietnam moved quickly to establish hard-currency trade relations with China, Hong Kong, Japan, Singapore, South Korea, Taiwan, Thailand and Western nations. This explains why Vietnamese officials have suddenly become so anxious to do business with the West. Many former Eastern Bloc countries have not fared as well as Vietnam – their economies collapsed along with the Soviet Union.

The transition from an isolated, socialist barter economy to a free market, hard currency trading economy is not complete and hasn't been easy. Many of Vietnam's manufactured goods (bicycles, shoes and even toothpaste) are of such poor quality that they are practically unsaleable, especially in the face of competition from foreign goods.

One of the first effects of free (or free-ish) trade with capitalist countries was the closure of many of the state-run enterprises, which led to an increase in unemployment. Even Vietnam's sugar-cane growers were hurt. The shoddy equipment used at state-run refineries produced such a low-quality product that imported refined sugar replaced the domestic product for a while.

The Vietnamese government responded with a number of 'temporary import bans'. Such bans theoretically give a boost to struggling domestic industries, but also lead to increased smuggling. Slowly but surely, the country is regaining its ability to compete in foreign markets; low wages and the strong Vietnamese work ethic bodes well for Vietnam's export industries.

The more liberal rules have had a dramatic effect on foreign joint-venture operations – foreign investors have been tripping over themselves to get into the country. Some of the most successful joint ventures to date have involved hotels, though some of these 'investments' are clear cases of real-estate speculation (foreigners cannot buy land, but companies in a joint venture with a local business can). The leading foreign investors are from Korea, Singapore and Taiwan.

Unfortunately, political meddling hasn't stopped completely. The bureaucracy is still plagued by middle-level functionaries with essentially worthless or counterproductive jobs that should be eliminated. However such bureaucrats view the reforms as a serious threat and would like to see them fail. Despite recent successes, the reformers still do not have the upper hand.

The bureaucracy, official incompetence, corruption and the ever-changing rules and regulations continue to irritate foreign investors. On paper, intellectual property rights are protected, but enforcement is lax – patents, copyrights and trademarks are openly pirated. Tax rates and government fees are frequently revised without warning. Some municipalities have forced foreign companies to hire employees from state employment agencies, with the only employees available being the 'spoiled brats' of the cadres.

## Economic Backlash

Recalcitrant bureaucrats or not, the reforms have already gained enough momentum to make it hard to imagine reversing them – putting the toothpaste back in the tube might well be impossible. However, there has been a conservative backlash against the reforms. Joint ventures often come to grief and many foreign investors are becoming disillusioned with Vietnam. In 1996, the number of foreign investment projects actually dropped by 17% from the previous year.

One of the most visible signs of the anti-market backlash was the 'social evils' campaign in late 1995. Borrowing phrases from China's goofy 'spiritual campaign' of the 1980s, the government declared that evil ideas from the West were 'polluting' Vietnamese society. The pollution would have to be 'cleaned up'.

Aside from obvious foreign pollution such as prostitution, drugs and karaoke, one of the major evils identified was the use of English in advertising. Vietnamese police were ordered to destroy English signs – companies like Coca-Cola and Sony watched in disbelief as their multimillion-dollar advertising campaigns were totally destroyed by enthusiastic vigilantes.

Meanwhile, socially evil foreign video tapes, music tapes, magazines and other paraphernalia were burned in public bonfires. Vietnam's official *Moi* newspaper reported that 'thanks to education and propaganda, people voluntarily gave up 27,302 video tapes'.

After foreign investors threatened to pull out of the country, the Vietnamese authorities relaxed the rules somewhat. However, the Vietnamese press still rants periodically about social evils and, even now, every business must have a sign in Vietnamese larger than the English sign.

Tourists were also affected by the social evils campaign. During the first half of 1996, the authorities refused all visa extensions. Then in June 1996 (during the Eighth Party Congress), all tourist visas were refused. This brought about the near collapse of the tourist industry, forcing the government to beat a retreat and ease up on the restrictions. The industry didn't start to recover until nearly the end of the year, but overall 1996 tourist-related revenues declined by an estimated 30%. Since then there has been a gradual increase in the number of tourist arrivals to Vietnam. In 1999 the official government estimate was around 1.7 million, though some question the validity of this figure.

Back in 1995, the government promised to open a capital market by the end of the year, but it just didn't happen and seemed to have been postponed indefinitely. However, in July 2000, Vietnam's first stock market was established in HCMC, a long-awaited prerequisite to future privatisation moves.

Privatisation of large state industries has not yet begun but is being considered. Likely candidates for privatisation would be Vietnam Airlines, the banking industry and telecommunications. Whether or not this generation of socialist leaders can bring themselves to put the state's prime assets on the auction block remains to be seen.

On a more positive note, Vietnam has seen economic growth rates of around 8% to 9% annually in the past few years. Vietnam's joining Asean in 1995 was a step that observers claim should greatly benefit its economy and further spur on reforms.

Hanoi is intent on limiting Vietnam's *doi moi* restructure to economic spheres, keeping ideas such as pluralism and democracy from undermining the present power structure. Whether it's at all possible to have economic liberalisation without substantial changes in the political sphere remains to be seen.

Vietnam's role model at the moment seems to be China, where economic change coupled with harsh political control seems to be at least partially successful in reviving the economy. The role model of the former USSR – where political change preceded economic restructure – is pointed to as an example of the wrong way to reform.

While the war between Vietnam and America is over, the battle for market share is just beginning. And these days everyone wants a piece of the action. Joint-venture capitalists from Japan, Korea, Taiwan, France, Germany, the UK and Australia have been flocking to Vietnam since the start of the 1990s. Prohibited from doing business in Vietnam by the US-imposed embargo (lifted in 1994), US companies are now beating a path to what they hope will be Asia's next economic tiger.

A long awaited commerce pact between Vietnam and the US finally came to fruition in October 2001 with the US Senate's ratification of a bilateral trade agreement. The trade pact completes the normalisation of US–Vietnam relations; this began in 1995 with the establishment of diplomatic ties. Vietnam stands to gain greatly in the manufactured goods export sector (estimated for 2001 to be US$16 billion). Under the new agreement, Vietnamese exports to the USA will enjoy substantially lower tariffs (plummeting from an average of 40% down to just 4%), while the USA will finally gain access to various markets previously under state control. Though some business leaders remain sceptical of the pact's potentiality, other experts foresee a trade turnover between the two countries of over US$1 billion.

American companies have already splashed ashore. Computers sporting the 'Intel Inside' label are on display in newly opened hi-tech electronic shops. Chrysler has formed a joint venture to produce its gas-guzzling Jeep Cherokee in Vietnam. Motorola pagers can be heard beeping in the pockets and handbags of well-to-do Vietnamese people. Pepsi was the first American soft-drink company to return to Vietnam after the war, but Coke was not far behind.

Meanwhile, the Vietnamese Ministry of Foreign Affairs emphatically disapproved of a connection between the recent trade pact and an unrelated Vietnam Human Rights Bill passed by the US House of Representatives, claiming that the bill 'impudently distorts reality'. The bill requires all American humanitarian, educational and business organisations working in Vietnam, to report back to the US government on 'human-rights issues' or face losing US government support. It's possible this will not help diplomatic relations between the two former enemies.

Consumerism is now rampant in Vietnam. Making money is OK and so is spending it. However, foreign investors, for their part, are displeased with the lack of protection for intellectual property rights.

## POPULATION & PEOPLE

In 2001 Vietnam's population reached 78.1 million, making it the 13th most populous country in the world. Vietnam is a young country, with an estimated 65% of the people under the age of 30. Eighty-four per cent of the population is ethnic Vietnamese, 2% is ethnic Chinese, and the rest is made up of Khmers, Chams and members of over 50 ethno-linguistic groups.

Vietnam has an average population density of 225 persons per square kilometre, one of the world's highest for an agricultural country. Much of the Red River Delta has a population density of 1000 people per square kilometre or more. Life expectancy is 66 years and infant mortality is 48 per 1000. The rate of population growth is 2.1% per year and, until recently, ideology prevented any effective family planning.

Unfortunately, the 15 years or so during which Vietnam encouraged large families will be a burden for some time to come. The country's population will likely double in the next century; the task of reducing population growth is daunting. As in most developing countries, low education and low incomes tend to encourage large families.

The government takes a carrot-and-stick approach to family planning. For couples who limit their family to two children, there are promises of benefits in education, housing, health care and employment (though a lack of funding means these promises are often not kept). The stick comes for those who exceed the two-child limit. To begin with, the government has the power to deny the third child household registration (which is necessary to obtain an ID card, admission to school and access to various crucial permits). If the parents have a government job, they can be fired. These inducements have succeeded in urban areas – a two-child family is now the norm in Hanoi and HCMC. However, these family-planning campaigns have had only a minor impact on birth rates in rural areas.

## Ethnic Vietnamese

The Vietnamese people (called Annamites by the French) developed as a distinct ethnic group between 200 BC and AD 200 through the fusion of people of Indonesian stock with Viet and Tai immigrants from the north and the Chinese who arrived, along with Chinese rule (circa 200 BC to AD 938), from the 2nd century BC. Vietnamese civilisation has been profoundly influenced by China and India (via Champa and the Khmers), but the fact that the Vietnamese were never absorbed by China indicates that a strong local culture existed prior to the millennium of Chinese rule.

The Vietnamese have lived for thousands of years by growing rice and, as a result, have historically preferred to settle in lowland areas suitable for rice cultivation. Over the past two millennia, they have slowly pushed southward along the narrow coastal strip, defeating the Chams in the 15th century and taking over the Mekong Delta from the Khmers in the 18th century. The Vietnamese have tended to view highland areas (and their inhabitants) with suspicion.

Vietnamese who have emigrated are known as overseas Vietnamese (or Viet Kieu). They are disliked by many local Vietnamese, who consider them cowardly, arrogant, pampered and privileged. These negative judgments are possibly coloured by jealousy. In the 1990s, returning Viet Kieu were often followed by the police and everyone they spoke to was questioned and harassed by the authorities. This has all changed. Indeed, official policy is to welcome the Viet Kieu and encourage them to resettle in Vietnam. Many Viet Kieu are cynical about this. 'They don't want us back, just our money, professional skills and connections' is a comment you're likely to hear in Viet Kieu communities. That the police still often shake down the Viet Kieu for money is not encouraging. The Vietnamese press frequently writes about the importance to the economy of receiving money from relatives abroad.

## Ethnic Chinese

The Hoa (ethnic Chinese) constitute the largest single minority group in Vietnam. Today, most of them live in the South, especially in and around the Cholon district of HCMC. Although most of Vietnam's ethnic Chinese have lived in Vietnam for generations, historically they have tried to maintain their own Chinese identities, languages, school systems and even citizenship. They have organised themselves into communities, according to their ancestors' province and dialect. Important communities include Fujian (Phuc Kien), Cantonese (Quang Dong; Guangdong in Chinese), Hainan (Hai Nam), Chaozhou (Tieu Chau) and Hakka (Nuoc Hue; Kejia in Mandarin Chinese).

During the 1950s, President Diem tried without much success to forcibly assimilate the South's ethnic-Chinese population. In the North, too, the ethnic Chinese have resisted Vietnamisation.

The Chinese are well known for their entrepreneurial abilities – before the fall of South Vietnam in 1975, the ethnic Chinese controlled nearly half of the economic activity in the country. Historical antipathies between China and Vietnam and the prominence of ethnic Chinese in commerce have generated a great deal of animosity towards them. In March 1978, the Communist Party launched a campaign against the 'bourgeois elements' (a euphemism for ethnic Chinese), which turned into open racial persecution. The campaign influenced China's decision to attack Vietnam in 1979 and caused about a third of Vietnam's ethnic Chinese to flee to China and the West. However, Vietnamese officials have since admitted that the anticapitalist and anti-Chinese campaign was a tragic and costly mistake.

## Other Minorities

Vietnam has one of the most diverse and complex ethno-linguistic mixes in all of Asia. Many of the country's 54 distinct ethnic groups have not-so-distant relations scattered throughout neighbouring Laos, southern China and Cambodia, as well as Thailand and Myanmar (Burma). Most of the Vietnamese ethnic minorities, who are believed to number between six and eight million, reside in the central highlands and the mountainous regions of the northwest, with a smattering along the coastal plains in the South.

See the special section 'Hill Tribes in Vietnam' and the boxed text 'Kingdom of Champa' in the Central Vietnam chapter.

There are about 700,000 Khmers (ethnic Cambodians) in Vietnam, concentrated in the southwestern Mekong Delta. They practise Theravada Buddhism, and many of the temples in the Mekong Delta region resemble those in Cambodia.

Most of South Vietnam's Indian population, whose roots were in southern India, left in 1975. The remaining community in HCMC worships at the Mariamman Hindu temple and the Central Mosque.

Currently, there are only a handful of ethnic Westerners registered in Vietnam, most of whom are American-Vietnamese, French-Vietnamese or French-Chinese.

## EDUCATION

Compared with other developing countries, Vietnam's population is very well educated. Vietnam's literacy rate is estimated at 91%. Before the colonial period, the majority of the population possessed some degree of literacy, but by 1939 only 15% of school-age children were receiving any kind of instruction and 80% of the population was illiterate.

During the late 19th century, one of the few things that French colonial officials and Vietnamese nationalists agreed on was that the traditional Confucian educational system, on which the mandarinal civil service was based, was in desperate need of reform. Mandarinal examinations were held in Tonkin until WWI and in Annam until that war's end.

Many of Indochina's independence leaders were educated in elite French-language secondary schools such as the Lycée Albert Sarraut in Hanoi and the Lycée Chasseloup Laubat in HCMC.

Although the children of foreign residents can theoretically attend Vietnamese schools, the majority of them are educated at expensive private academies.

## ARTS
### Dance

Vietnamese folk dance is usually performed during ceremonies and festivals, though tourism has spurned something of a comeback to the everyday. Of the more interesting and visually stunning traditional dances is the Conical Hat Dance, in which a group of women wearing *ao dai* spin and intermingle, using their elaborate Hué-style hats as props.

Not surprisingly, ethnic minorities have their own dancing traditions, which differ sharply from the Vietnamese majority. While in most hill tribes the majority of the dancers are women, a few hill tribes allow only the men to dance. A great deal of anthropological research has been carried out in recent years in order to preserve and revive indigenous traditions.

### Music

**Traditional** Though heavily influenced by the Chinese and, in the south, the Khmer and Indianised Cham musical traditions, Vietnamese music has a high degree of originality in style and instrumentation. The traditional system of writing down music and the five note (pentatonic) scale are of Chinese origin. Vietnamese choral music is unique in that the melody must correspond to the tones; it cannot rise during a word that has a falling tone.

Vietnamese folk music includes children's songs, love songs, work songs, festival songs, lullabies, lamentations and funeral songs. These are usually sung without any instrumental accompaniment.

Classical, or 'learned music', is rather rigid and formal. It was performed at the imperial court and for the entertainment of the mandarin elite. A traditional orchestra consists of 40 musicians. There are two main types of classical chamber music: *hat a dao* from the north and *ca Hue* from central Vietnam.

Traditional music is played on a wide array of indigenous instruments, dating back to the ancient *do son* drums that are today collected as highly valued works of art. Perhaps the most notable traditional instrument in use is the *dan bau*, a single stringed lute that generates an astounding magnitude of tones. Also common at performances of traditional music is the *dan tranh*, a 16-string zither, and *to rung*, a large bamboo xylophone. Vietnam's myriad wind instruments include water buffalo horns and the peculiar *ken doi*, which is fabricated from two seven-holed bamboo flutes.

Every one of Vietnam's ethno-linguistic minorities has its own musical traditions that often include distinctive costumes and instruments such as reed flutes, lithophones (similar to xylophones), bamboo whistles, gongs and stringed instruments made from gourds.

There are music conservatories teaching traditional Vietnamese and Western classical music in Hanoi, Hué and HCMC.

**Contemporary/Pop** Strange as it seems, much of the world's Vietnamese pop music has been recorded in California by overseas Vietnamese. The reason why few recordings have been made in Vietnam is the high level of music pirating, which deprives the singing stars of the revenue they would receive; works by overseas Vietnamese are protected by copyright. Recently this situation has started to improve and more performers are being produced on Vietnamese soil.

The best known is Khanh Ly, who left Vietnam in 1975 and today resides in the USA. She is enormously popular both in Vietnam and abroad, and her distinctive, angelic voice sends chills. Though her music is widely available in Vietnam, the government takes a deprecating view of her recently composed lyrics that recall the trials of her life as a refugee.

Vietnam's number one domestic heart throb is Hué-born Quang Linh, a former Hanoi banker, whose early popularity among Saigonese shot him up the local pop charts. He is adored by Vietnamese of all ages for his radiant love songs.

Other celebrated local pop singers include sex symbol Phuong Thanh, Vietnam's answer to Madonna or Britney Spears (only without the dirty dancing). Her likeness is plastered on a variety of paraphernalia (from school notebooks to beer glasses). Phuong Thanh's male equivalent would have to be youth idol Lam Truong.

Of the legion of notable Vietnamese composers, the leader of the pack was Trinh Cong Son, who died in HCMC in 2001. A former literature student from Hué, his lyrics touch on themes of love, war and family. Over his long career Trinh Cong Son wrote more than 500 songs, making him perhaps the most prolific Vietnamese composer in history.

Other well-known contemporary composers, whose work you are likely to have heard include Tran Tien and Thanh Tung.

## Literature

There are three types of Vietnamese literature. Traditional oral literature *(truyen khau)* was begun long before recorded history and includes legends, folk songs and proverbs.

Sino-Vietnamese literature was written in Chinese characters *(chu nho)*. It dates from AD 939, when the first independent Vietnamese kingdom was established. Sino-Vietnamese literature became dominated by Confucian and Buddhist texts and was governed by strict rules of metre and verse.

Modern Vietnamese literature *(quoc am)* includes anything recorded in *nom* characters. The earliest extant text written in *nom* is the late-13th-century *Van Te Ca Sau* (Ode to an Alligator). Literature written in *quoc ngu* has played an important role in Vietnamese nationalism.

One of Vietnam's literary masterpieces, *Kim Van Kieu* (The Tale of Kieu) was written during the first half of the 19th century (a period marked by a great deal of literary activity) by Nguyen Du (1765–1820), a poet, scholar, mandarin and diplomat.

## Architecture

The Vietnamese have not been prolific builders like their neighbours the Khmers, who erected the monuments of Angkor in Cambodia, and the Chams, whose graceful brick towers, constructed using sophisticated masonry technology, adorn many parts of the southern half of the country. For more information on Cham architecture, see the boxed text 'Po Klong Garai Cham Towers' in the South-Central Coast chapter and the boxed text 'Kingdom of Champa' in the Central Vietnam chapter.

Traditionally, most Vietnamese constructions are made of wood and other materials that are vulnerable to decay in the tropical climate. This, coupled with the fact that almost all stone structures erected by the Vietnamese have been destroyed in countless feudal wars and invasions, means that very little pre-modern Vietnamese architecture remains.

Plenty of pagodas and temples founded hundreds of years ago are still functioning, but they have usually been rebuilt many times with little concern for making an upgraded structure an exact copy of the original. As a result, many modern elements have been casually introduced into pagoda architecture – the neon haloes for statues of Buddha are glaring examples.

Because of the custom of ancestor worship, many graves from previous centuries survive today. These include temples erected in memory of high-ranking mandarins, royal-family members and emperors.

Memorials for Vietnamese who died in the wars against the Chinese, French and Americans usually contain cement obelisks inscribed with the words *to quoc ghi cong*

('the country will remember their exploits'). Many of the tombstones within the memorials were erected over empty graves; most Viet Minh and Viet Cong dead were buried where they fell.

## Painting

Painting on frame-mounted silk dates from the 13th century. Silk painting was at one time the preserve of scholar-calligraphers, who also painted scenes from nature. Before the advent of photography, realistic portraits for use in ancestor worship were produced. Some of these – usually of former head monks – can still be seen in some of the Buddhist pagodas.

During the past century, Vietnamese painting has been influenced by Western trends. Much recent work has had political rather than aesthetic or artistic motives. According to an official account, the fighting of the French and American forces provided painters with 'rich human material: People's Army combatants facing the jets, peasant and factory women in the militia who handled guns as well as they did their production work, young volunteers who repaired roads in record time...old mothers offering tea to anti-aircraft gunners...' There's lots of this stuff at the Fine Arts Museum in Hanoi.

The recent economic liberalisation has convinced many young artists to abandon the revolutionary themes and concentrate on producing commercial paintings. Some have gone back to the traditional-style silk or lacquer paintings, while others experiment with new subjects. There is a noticeable tendency now to produce paintings of nudes, which might indicate either an attempt to appeal to Western tastes or perhaps an expression of individual-ism rather than collectivism.

To keep up with the latest news in the Vietnamese art world, subscribe to the bimonthly **Asian Art News** (☎ *852-2522 3443, fax 2521 5268;* e *asianart@netvigator.com; G/F 28 Arbuthnot Rd, Central Hong Kong)*, a sleek English-language magazine about contemporary Asian art. It's a great information source and devotes ample attention to Vietnam.

## Sculpture

Traditionally Vietnamese sculpture has centred on religious themes and functioned as an adjunct to architecture, especially within pagodas, temples and tombs. Some examples of inscribed stelae (carved stone slabs or columns), erected hundreds of years ago to commemorate the founding of a pagoda or important national events, can still be seen (eg, Thien Mu Pagoda in Hué and the Temple of Literature in Hanoi).

The Chams produced spectacular carved sandstone figures for their Hindu and Buddhist sanctuaries. Cham sculpture was profoundly influenced by Indian art but over the centuries it managed to also incorporate Indonesian and Vietnamese elements. The largest single collection of Cham sculpture in the world is found at the Museum of Cham Sculpture in Danang.

## Lacquerware

The art of making lacquerware was brought to Vietnam from China in the mid-15th century. Before that time, the Vietnamese used lacquer solely for practical purposes (ie, making things watertight). During the 1930s, the Fine Arts School in Hanoi had several Japanese teachers who introduced new styles and production methods. Their influence is still evident in some Vietnamese lacquerware, especially that made in the north. Although a 1985 government publication declared that 'at present, lacquer painting deals boldly with realistic and revolutionary themes and forges unceasingly ahead', most of the lacquerware for sale is inlaid with mother-of-pearl and appears to be of traditional design.

Lacquer or *cay son*, is made from resin extracted from the rhus tree. It is creamy white in raw form, but is made black or brown by mixing it with pigments in an iron container for 40 hours. After the object (traditionally made of teak) has been treated with a fixative, the requisite 10 coats of lacquer are applied. Each coat must be dried for a week and then thoroughly sanded with pumice and cuttlebone before the next layer can be applied. A specially refined lacquer is used for the 11th and final coat, which is sanded with a fine coal powder and lime wash before the object is decorated. Designs may be added by engraving in low relief, by painting or by inlaying mother-of-pearl, egg shell, silver or even gold.

## Ceramics

The production of ceramics *(gom)* has a long history in Vietnam. In ancient times, ceramic objects were made by coating a wicker mould with clay and baking it. Later, ceramic production became very refined, and each dynastic period is known for its particular techniques and motifs.

It's possible to view ancient ceramics in museums throughout Vietnam. Excavations of archaeological sites are still revealing ancient examples, as are the ongoing discoveries of shipwreck treasures. Hat Bang is famous for its ceramic industry. See Handicraft Villages in the Hanoi chapter for details.

## Cinema

One of Vietnam's first cinematographic efforts was a newsreel of Ho Chi Minh's 1945 Proclamation of Independence. Following this, parts of the battle of Dien Bien Phu were restaged for the benefit of movie cameras.

Prior to reunification, the South Vietnamese movie industry produced mainly sensational, low-budget flicks. Until the early 1990s, most northern Vietnamese film-making efforts were dedicated to 'the mobilisation of the masses for economic reconstruction, the building of socialism and the struggle for national reunification'. Predictable themes include 'workers devoted to socialist industrialisation', 'old mothers who continuously risk their lives to help the people's army' and 'children who are ready to face any danger'.

In recent years Vietnamese cinema has evolved from the realm of propaganda to a world that more closely reflects the lives of modern Vietnamese people and the issues they face. Though strict government control and cultural censorship remain a reality, Vietnamese film makers today operate in a far more tolerant environment, one that has allowed an increase in film production and cinematic achievement.

The relaxation of censorship of the arts has proceeded in fits and starts, but in the last few years the gradual increase in artistic freedoms has affected film-making, as well as many other arts. In the late 1980s and early '90s, paranoia concerning the radical changes in Eastern Europe caused a return to greater government control of the arts. Today, however, film production in Vietnam has taken a notable swing back to more liberal ways, and Vietnamese and overseas-Vietnamese producers, directors and actors are finally beginning to receive due recognition, both in Vietnam and abroad.

For a list of contemporary Vietnamese films (several of which can be rented from your local video store), see Films in the Facts for the Visitor chapter.

## Theatre & Puppetry

These days, the various forms of Vietnamese theatre are performed by dozens of state-funded troupes and companies around the country. Vietnamese theatre integrates music, singing, recitation, declamation, dance and mime into a single artistic whole.

Classical theatre is known as *hat tuong* in the north and *hat boi* in the south. It is based on Chinese opera and was probably brought to Vietnam by the 13th-century Mongol invaders eventually chased out by Tran Hung Dao. Classical theatre is very formalistic, employing gestures and scenery similar to Chinese theatre. The accompanying orchestra, which is dominated by the drum, usually has six musicians. Often, the audience also has a drum so it too can comment on the onstage action.

It has a limited cast of characters, who establish their identities using combinations of make-up and dress that the audience can readily recognise. For instance, red face paint represents courage, loyalty and faithfulness. Traitors and cruel people have white faces. Lowlanders are given green faces; highlanders have black ones. Horizontal eyebrows represent honesty, erect eyebrows symbolise cruelty while lowered ones belong to characters with a cowardly nature. A male character expresses emotions (pensiveness, worry, anger etc) by fingering his beard in various ways.

Popular theatre *(hat cheo)* often engages in social protest through satire. The singing and declamation are in everyday language and include many proverbs and sayings. Many of the melodies are of peasant origin.

Modern theatre *(cai luong)* originated in the South in the early 20th century and shows strong Western influences.

Spoken drama *(kich noi or kich)*, with its Western roots, appeared in the 1920s. It's popular among students and intellectuals.

Conventional puppetry *(roi can)* and that uniquely Vietnamese art form, water puppetry *(roi nuoc)*, draw their plots from the same legendary and historical sources as other forms of traditional theatre. It is thought that water puppetry developed when determined puppeteers in the Red River Delta managed to carry on with the show despite flooding (see the boxed text 'Punch & Judy in a Pool' in the Hanoi chapter). Although water puppetry is performed in HCMC, it's far better staged in Hanoi. See Water Puppets in the Entertainment sections of the Hanoi and Ho Chi Minh City chapters for details on performances.

## SOCIETY & CONDUCT

Try to learn about Vietnamese culture before you arrive and respect cultural differences, rather than trying to change them.

### Traditional Culture

**Face** Having 'big face' is synonymous with prestige, and prestige is particularly important in Vietnam. All families, even poor ones, are expected to have big wedding parties and throw their money around like it's water in order to gain face. This is often ruinously expensive, but the fact that the wedding results in bankruptcy for the young couple is far less important than 'losing' face.

**Beauty Concepts** The Vietnamese consider pale skin to be beautiful. On sunny days trendy Vietnamese women can often be seen strolling under the shade of an umbrella in order to keep from tanning. Women who work in the fields will go to great lengths to preserve their pale skin by wearing long-sleeved shirts, elbow-length silk gloves, a conical hat and by wrapping their face in a towel. To tell a Vietnamese woman that she has white skin is a great compliment; telling her that she has a 'lovely suntan' would be an insult.

**Women in Society** As in most parts of Asia, Vietnamese women are given plenty of hard work to do, but have little authority at the decision-making level. Vietnamese women proved to be highly successful as guerrillas and brought plenty of grief to US soldiers. After the war, their contribution received plenty of lip service, but all the important government posts were given to men. In the countryside, you'll see women doing such jobs as farm labour, crushing rocks at construction sites and carrying baskets weighing 60kg. It's doubtful that most Western men would be capable of such strenuous activity.

The country's two-children-per-family policy appears to benefit women, and more are delaying marriage to get an education. Approximately 50% of university students are female, but their skills don't seem to be put to much use after graduation.

One of the sadder ironies of the recent opening to the West has been the influx of pimps posing as 'talent scouts'. Promises of lucrative jobs in developed countries are being dangled in front of naive Vietnamese women who only discover once abroad that the job really involves prostitution. With no money to return home, they usually have little choice but to submit. Japanese gangsters have been particularly active in this particular form of job recruitment.

**Geomancy** This is the art (or science) of manipulating or judging the environment. The Vietnamese call it *phong thuy* but many Westerners know it by its Chinese name, *feng shui*.

If you want to build a house or find a suitable site for a grave, you call in a geomancer. The orientation of houses, tombs, communal meeting halls *(dinh)*, and pagodas is determined by geomancers, which is why cemeteries have tombstones facing in every possible direction. The location of an ancestor's grave is an especially serious matter – if the grave is in the wrong spot or facing the wrong way, there's no telling what trouble the spirits might cause. Ditto for the location of the family altar, which can be found in every Vietnamese home.

Failing businesses may call in a geomancer. Sometimes the solution is to move a door or a window. If this doesn't do the trick, it might be necessary to move an ancestor's grave. Distraught spirits may have to be placated with payments of cash (donated to a temple), especially if one wishes to erect a building or other structure that blocks the spirits' view. The date on which you begin construction of a new building is also a crucial matter.

The concept of geomancy is believed to have originated with the Chinese. Although both Chinese and Vietnamese communists have disparaged the practice of geomancy as superstition, it still has a large influence on people's behaviour.

**Staring Squads** In urban centres tourists may not rate a second look. But if you're in the hinterlands and doing something unusual, like writing in a diary – or even if you're just standing there! – many curious people, especially children, may gather round you to watch.

Getting used to this can be difficult and stressful for some, but it's best not to worry about it; after all, they are just curious about you. As a tourist you'll probably spend a lot of time just sitting around looking at people and taking snapshots. Being stared at is a good chance to see how it feels to be on the other side of the camera!

**No Knock** Vietnamese don't share Western concepts of privacy and personal space, so don't be surprised if people walk into your room without knocking. For example, you may be sitting starkers in your hotel room when the maid unlocks the door and walks in unannounced. If you'd rather not do nude modelling, check to see if there's a bolt on the door that cannot be opened from the outside with a key. Failing that, prop a chair against the door. Or, just grin and bare it.

**Ong Tay & Ba Tay** The main reason that children shout *ong tay!* (Mr Westerner) and *ba tay!* (Mrs Westerner) at white Westerners is similar to why people tap on aquarium fish tanks or try to catch the attention of primates at the zoo: they want to be recognised by an exotic being and provoke some kind of reaction.

Often, children will unabashedly come up to you and pull the hair on your arms or legs (they want to test if it's real) or dare each other to touch your skin.

In the past, the term *lien xo!* (Soviet Union) was often shouted at Westerners, all of whom were assumed to be the legendary and very unpopular Russians residing in Vietnam. However, Russian tourists and technical advisers are far less common – few of them can afford a holiday in Vietnam any more and their technical skills are considered inferior to those available from the West. Therefore, *lien xo* is going out of fashion as an attention-seeking call.

In the markets, vendors may try to woo you by calling you *dong chi!* (Comrade) on the assumption that you will find this a kindred term of endearment. Depending on your age and how sloppy you look, a more common name you may be called (although not to your face) is *tay balo!* (literally 'Westerner backpack') a relatively recent term for scruffy-looking backpackers.

If you are cycling, you may also hear people call *tay di xe dap* at you, which simply means 'Westerner travelling by bicycle'. While it may seem a strange form of address in the land of bicycles, it's perhaps understandable in a place where locals have only been used to seeing foreigners travelling in Citroëns, followed by Jeeps, then black Volgas and now in white Toyotas.

**Lunar Calendar** The Vietnamese lunar calendar closely resembles the Chinese one, though there are some minor variations. Year one of the Vietnamese lunar calendar corresponds to 2637 BC and each lunar month has 29 or 30 days, resulting in years with 355 days.

Approximately every third year is a leap year; an extra month is added between the

## Vietnamese Zodiac

If you want to know your sign in the Vietnamese zodiac, look up your year of birth in the following chart (future years are included so you can know what's coming). However, because Vietnamese astrology follows the lunar calendar, the Vietnamese New Year usually falls in late January or early February. Therefore if your birthday is in January it will be included in the zodiac year before the calendar year of your birth.

| Rat | 1924 | 1936 | 1948 | 1960 | 1972 | 1984 | 1996 |
| Ox/Cow | 1925 | 1937 | 1949 | 1961 | 1973 | 1985 | 1997 |
| Tiger | 1926 | 1938 | 1950 | 1962 | 1974 | 1986 | 1998 |
| Rabbit | 1927 | 1939 | 1951 | 1963 | 1975 | 1987 | 1999 |
| Dragon | 1928 | 1940 | 1952 | 1964 | 1976 | 1988 | 2000 |
| Snake | 1929 | 1941 | 1953 | 1965 | 1977 | 1989 | 2001 |
| Horse | 1930 | 1942 | 1954 | 1966 | 1978 | 1990 | 2002 |
| Goat | 1931 | 1943 | 1955 | 1967 | 1979 | 1991 | 2003 |
| Monkey | 1932 | 1944 | 1956 | 1968 | 1980 | 1992 | 2004 |
| Rooster | 1933 | 1945 | 1957 | 1969 | 1981 | 1993 | 2005 |
| Dog | 1934 | 1946 | 1958 | 1970 | 1982 | 1994 | 2006 |
| Pig | 1935 | 1947 | 1959 | 1971 | 1983 | 1995 | 2007 |

third and fourth months to keep the lunar year in sync with the solar year. If this were not done, you'd end up having the seasons gradually rotate around the lunar year, playing havoc with all elements of life linked to the agricultural seasons. To find out the Gregorian (solar) date corresponding to a lunar date, check any Vietnamese or Chinese calendar.

Instead of dividing time into centuries, the Vietnamese calendar uses units of 60 years called *hoi*. Each hoi consists of six 10-year cycles *(can)* and five 12-year cycles *(ky)*, which run simultaneously. The name of each year in the cycle consists of the *can* name followed by the *ky* name, a system that never produces the same combination twice. The 10 heavenly stems of the *can* cycle are listed in the following table.

| | |
|---|---|
| giap | water in nature |
| at | water in the home |
| binh | lighted fire |
| dinh | latent fire |
| mau | wood |
| ky | wood prepared to burn |
| canh | metal |
| tan | wrought metal |
| nham | virgin land |
| quy | cultivated land |

The 12 zodiacal stems of the *ky* are listed in the following table.

| | |
|---|---|
| tý | rat |
| suu | water buffalo |
| dan | tiger |
| mao | cat |
| thin | dragon |
| ty | snake |
| ngo | horse |
| mui | goat |
| than | monkey |
| dau | rooster |
| tuat | dog |
| hoi | pig |

Thus in 2003 it's the Vietnamese year of the goat *(quy mui)*, in 2004 the year of the monkey *(giap than)* and in 2005 the year of the rooster *(at dau)*.

## Social Graces

**Clothing** Please respect local dress standards, particularly at religious sites – avoid wearing shorts or sleeveless tops and always remove your shoes before entering a temple. In general, Vietnamese dress standards are conservative, especially in the countryside. Nude and topless sunbathing is considered *totally* inappropriate, even at beaches and hot-spring resorts.

**Greetings** The traditional Vietnamese form of greeting is to press your hands together in front of your body and bow slightly. These days, the Western custom of shaking hands has almost completely taken over, but the traditional greeting is still sometimes used by Buddhist monks and nuns – it is proper to respond in kind.

**Name Cards** Exchanging business cards is an important part of even the smallest transaction or business contact in Vietnam. Get some printed before you arrive in Vietnam and hand them out like confetti. In Bangkok and Hong Kong, machines using the latest laser-printing technology can easily make inexpensive custom-designed business cards in around 20 minutes. You need to put your occupation on your name card; if you don't have one, why not try 'backpacker'?

**Deadly Chopsticks** Leaving a pair of chopsticks sitting vertically in a rice bowl looks very much like the incense sticks that are burned for the dead. This is a powerful sign and is not appreciated anywhere in Asia.

**Mean Feet** Like the Chinese and Japanese, Vietnamese strictly maintain clean floors and it's usual to remove shoes when entering somebody's home; your host will probably provide a pair of slippers. Shoes must be removed inside most Buddhist temples, but this is not universal so look to see what others do. If a bunch of shoes are piled up near the doorway, you should pay heed.

It's rude to point the bottom of your feet towards other people; the only exception may be with close friends. When sitting on the floor, you should fold your legs into the lotus position to avoid pointing your soles at others. Most importantly, never point your feet towards anything sacred, such as figures of Buddhas or the ancestral shrines found in most homes.

In formal situations, do not sit with your legs crossed when sitting on a chair.

**Keep Your Hat in Hand** As a form of respect to elderly or other respected people, such as monks, take off your hat and bow your head politely when addressing them. In Asia, the head is the symbolic highest point – never pat or touch someone on their head.

**Pity the Unmarried** Telling the Vietnamese that you are single or divorced and enjoy a life without children may disturb them greatly. Not having a family is regarded as bad luck and such people are to be pitied, not envied. Many Vietnamese will ask if you are married and have children. If you are young and single, simply say you are 'not yet married' and that will usually be accepted. If you are not so young (over 30) and unmarried, it may just be better to lie.

**Show Some Respect** In face-conscious Asia, foreigners should pay double attention to showing respect.

Vernon Weitzel of the Australian National University sent in these 10 tips for successfully dealing with Vietnamese officials and businesspeople:

- Always smile and be pleasant.
- Don't complain about everything.
- If you want to criticise someone, do it in a joking manner to avoid confrontation.
- Expect delays – build them into your schedule
- Never show anger – ever! Getting visibly upset is not only rude – it will cause you to lose face.
- Don't be competitive. Treating your interaction as a cooperative enterprise works much better.
- If you act as though you deserve service from anyone, you will probably be delayed.
- Don't be too inquisitive about personal matters
- Sitting and sipping tea and the exchange of gifts (sharing cigarettes, for instance) are an important prelude to any business interaction.
- The mentality of officialdom is very Confucian. Expect astounding amounts of red tape.

## RELIGION

Four great philosophies and religions have shaped the spiritual life of the Vietnamese people: Confucianism, Taoism, Buddhism and Christianity. Over the centuries, Confucianism, Taoism and Buddhism have fused with popular Chinese beliefs and ancient Vietnamese animism to form what is known collectively as the Triple Religion, or Tam Giao. Confucianism, more a system of social and political morality than a religion, took on many religious aspects. Taoism, which began as an esoteric philosophy for scholars then mixed with Buddhism, is popular among the peasants, and many Taoist elements became an intrinsic part of popular religion. If asked their religion most Vietnamese people are likely to say that they are Buddhist, but when it comes to family or civic duties they are likely to follow Confucianism and they turn to Taoist conceptions in understanding the nature of the cosmos.

### Pagoda or Temple?

Travelling around Vietnam, one continually encounters the terms 'pagoda' and 'temple'. The Vietnamese use these terms somewhat differently to the Chinese and, as a result, it can be confusing (particularly if you've just come from China).

To the Chinese, a pagoda is usually a tall eight-sided tower built to house the ashes of the deceased. A Chinese temple is an active place of worship.

The Vietnamese regard a pagoda *(chua)* as a place of worship, and it's by no means certain that you'll find a tower to store the ashes of the dearly departed. A Vietnamese temple *(den)* is not really a place of worship, but rather a structure built to honour some great historical figure (Confucius, Tran Hung Dao and even Ho Chi Minh).

The Caodai Temple seems to somehow fall between the cracks. Given the mixture of ideas that is part and parcel of Caodaism, it's hard to say if this is a temple, pagoda, church or mosque.

## Mahayana Buddhism

The predominant religion in Vietnam is Mahayana Buddhism (Dai Thua, or Bac Tong meaning 'From the North', ie, China). The largest Mahayana sect in the country is Zen (Dhyana; Thien), also known as the school of meditation. Dao Trang (the Pure Land school), the second-largest Mahayana sect in Vietnam, is practised mainly in the south.

Mahayana Buddhism differs from Theravada Buddhism in several important ways. Whereas the Theravada Buddhist strives to become one who attains nirvana *(arhat)*, the Mahayanist ideal is that of the Bodhisattva: one who strives to perfect oneself in the necessary virtues (generosity, morality, patience, vigour, concentration and wisdom), but even after attaining this perfection chooses to remain in the world in order to save others.

Mahayanists consider Gautama Buddha to be only one of the innumerable manifestations of the one ultimate Buddha. These countless Buddhas and Bodhisattvas, who are as numberless as the universes to which they minister, gave rise in popular Vietnamese religion – with its countless Taoist divinities and spirits – to a pantheon of deities and helpers whose aid can be sought through invocations and offerings.

Mahayana Buddhist pagodas in Vietnam usually include a number of elements. In front of the pagoda is a white statue of a standing Quan The Am Bo Tat or Avalokiteçvara Bodhisattva (Hindi), Guanyin (Chinese), or Goddess of Mercy (English). A variation of the Goddess of Mercy shows her with multiple arms and sometimes multiple eyes and ears, permitting her to touch, see and hear all. This version of the Goddess of Mercy is called Chuan De or Qianshou Guanyin (Chinese).

Inside the main sanctuary are representations of the three Buddhas: A Di Da, the Buddha of the Past; Thich Ca Mau Ni (Sakyamuni, or Siddhartha Gautama), the historical Buddha; and Di Lac (Maitreya), the Buddha of the Future. Nearby are often statues of the eight Kim Cang (Genies of the Cardinal Directions), the La Han (arhats) and various Bo Tat (Bodhisattvas) such as Van Thu (Manjusri), Quan The Am Bo Tat (Avalokiteçvara) and Dia Tang (Ksitigartha). Sometimes an altar is set aside for Taoist divinities, such as Ngoc Hoang (Jade Emperor) and Thien Hau (Goddess of the Sea or Queen of Heaven). Every pagoda has an altar for funerary tablets commemorating deceased monks (who are often buried in stupas near the pagoda) and lay people.

The function of the Vietnamese Buddhist monk *(bonze)* is to minister to the spiritual needs of the peasantry, but it is largely up to them whether they invoke the lore of Taoism or the philosophy of Buddhism. A monk may live reclusively on a remote hilltop or may manage a pagoda on a busy city street. And they may choose to fulfil any number of functions: telling fortunes, making and selling talismans *(fu)*, geomancy, reciting incantations at funerals or even performing acupuncture *(cham chu)*.

**History**  Theravada Buddhism was brought to Vietnam from India by pilgrims at the end of the 2nd century AD. Simultaneously, Chinese monks introduced Mahayana Buddhism, but this did not become popular with the masses until many centuries later.

Buddhism received royal patronage between the 10th and 13th centuries, including recognition of the Buddhist hierarchy, financial support for the construction of pagodas and other projects, and the active participation of the clergy in ruling the country. By the 11th century, Buddhism had filtered down to the villages and it was proclaimed the official state religion in the mid-12th century.

During the 13th and 14th centuries, Confucian scholars gradually replaced Vietnamese monks as advisers to the Tran dynasty. The Confucians accused the Buddhists of shirking their responsibilities to family and country with their doctrine of withdrawal from worldly matters. The Chinese invasion of 1414 reinvigorated Confucianism while simultaneously resulting in the destruction of many Buddhist pagodas and manuscripts. The Nguyen Lords (1558–1778), who ruled the southern part of the country, reversed this trend.

A revival of Vietnamese Buddhism spread throughout the country in the 1920s with the creation of Buddhist organisations in various parts of the country. In the 1950s and '60s, attempts were made to unite the various streams of Buddhism in Vietnam. During the early 1960s, South Vietnamese Buddhist monks and lay people played an active role in opposing the regime of Ngo Dinh Diem.

Over the centuries, the Buddhist ideals and beliefs held by the educated elite only superficially touched the rural masses (90% of the population), whose traditions were transmitted orally and put to the test by daily observance. The common people were far less concerned with the philosophy of good government than they were with seeking aid from supernatural beings for problems of the here and now.

Gradually, the various Mahayana Buddhas and Bodhisattvas became mixed up with mysticism, animism, polytheism and Hindu Tantrism, as well as the multiple divinities and ranks of deities of the Taoist pantheon. The Triple Religion flourished despite clerical attempts to maintain some semblance of Buddhist orthodoxy and doctrinal purity. Although the majority of the population has only a vague notion of academic Buddhist doctrines, they invite monks to participate in life-cycle ceremonies such as funerals. And Buddhist pagodas have come to be seen by many Vietnamese as a physical and spiritual refuge from an uncertain world.

After 1975, many monks, including some who had actively opposed the South Vietnamese government and the war, were rounded up and sent to re-education camps. Temples were closed and the training of young monks was prohibited. In the last few years, most of these restrictions have been lifted and a religious revival has been taking place.

## Theravada Buddhism

Theravada Buddhism (Tieu Thua, or Nam Tong) is practised mainly in the Mekong Delta region, mostly by ethnic Khmers. The most important Theravada sect in Vietnam is the disciplinary school, Luat Tong.

Basically, the Theravada school of Buddhism is an earlier and, according to its followers, less corrupted form of Buddhism than the Mahayana schools found in most of East Asia and the Himalayan regions. The Theravada school is called the Southern school because it took the southern route from India through Southeast Asia, while the Northern school (Mahayana) proceeded north into Nepal, Tibet, China, Korea, Mongolia, Vietnam and Japan. Because the Southern school tried to preserve or limit the Buddhist doctrines to only those canons codified in the early Buddhist era, the Northern school gave Theravada Buddhism the name Hinayana, or Lesser Vehicle. They considered themselves Greater Vehicle because they built upon the earlier teachings, expanding the doctrine to be more responsive to the needs of lay people.

## Confucianism

While it is more a religious philosophy than an organised religion, Confucianism (Nho Giao or Khong Giao) has been an important force in shaping Vietnam's social system and the everyday lives and beliefs of its people.

Confucius (Khong Tu) was born in China around 550 BC. He saw people as social beings formed by society yet also capable of shaping their society. He believed that the individual exists in and for society and drew up a code of ethics to guide the individual in social interaction. This code laid down a person's obligations to family, society and the state. Confucianism emphasises duty and hierarchy.

According to Confucian philosophy, which was introduced by the Chinese during their 1000-year rule, the emperor alone, governing under the mandate of heaven, can intercede on behalf of the nation with the powers of heaven and earth. Only virtue, as acquired through education, gives one the right (or the mandate of heaven) to wield political power. From this it followed that an absence of virtue would result in the withdrawal of this mandate, sanctioning rebellion against an unjust ruler. Natural disasters or defeat on the battlefield were often interpreted as a sign that the mandate of heaven had been withdrawn.

Confucian philosophy in some senses was democratic: as virtue could be acquired only through learning, education rather than birth made a person virtuous. Therefore, education had to be widespread. Until the beginning of this century, Confucian philosophy and texts formed the basis of Vietnam's education system. Generation after generation of young people – in the villages as well as the cities – were taught their duties to family (including ancestor worship) and community and were told that each person had to know their own place in the social hierarchy and should behave accordingly.

Civil service examinations selected from among the country's best students those who would join the nonhereditary ruling class, the mandarins. As a result, education was prized not only as the path to virtue, but as a means to social and political advancement. This system helped create the respect for intellectual and literary accomplishment for which the Vietnamese are famous to this day.

The political institutions based on Confucianism finally degenerated and became discredited, as they did elsewhere in the Chinese-influenced world. Over the centuries, the philosophy became conservative and backwards looking. This reactionary trend became dominant in Vietnam in the 15th century, suiting despotic rulers who emphasised the divine right of kings rather than their responsibilities under the doctrine of the mandate of heaven.

## Taoism

Taoism (Lao Giao, or Dao Giao) originated in China and is based on the philosophy of Laotse (Thai Thuong Lao Quan). Laotse (literally, The Old One) lived in the 6th century BC. Little is known about Laotse and there is some question as to whether or not he really existed. He is believed to have been the custodian of the imperial archives for the Chinese government and Confucius is supposed to have consulted him.

It is doubtful that Laotse ever intended his philosophy to become a religion. Chang Ling has been credited with formally establishing the religion in 143 BC. Taoism later split into two divisions, the Cult of the Immortals and The Way of the Heavenly Teacher.

Understanding Taoism is not easy. The philosophy emphasises contemplation and simplicity. Its ideal is returning to the Tao (The Way or the essence of which all things are made). Only a small elite in China and Vietnam has ever been able to grasp Taoist philosophy, which is based on various correspondences (eg, the human body represents a microcosm of the earth) and *am* and *duong*, the Vietnamese equivalents of Yin and Yang. As a result, there are very few pure Taoist pagodas in Vietnam, yet much of Taoist ritualism has been absorbed into Chinese and Vietnamese Buddhism. The Taoist influence you are most likely to come across is the use of dragons and demons to decorate temple rooftops.

According to the Taoist cosmology, Ngoc Hoang, the Emperor of Jade, whose abode is in heaven, rules over a world of divinities, genies, spirits and demons in which the forces of nature are incarnated as supernatural beings and great historical personages have become gods. It is this aspect of Taoism that has become assimilated into the daily lives of most Vietnamese as a collection of rituals, and mystical and animistic beliefs. Much of the sorcery and magic that are now part of popular Vietnamese religion have their origins in Taoism.

## Ancestor Worship

Vietnamese ancestor worship, which is the ritual expression of filial piety *(hieu)*, dates from long before the arrival of Confucianism or Buddhism. Some consider it to be a religion in itself.

Ancestor worship is based on the belief that the soul lives on after death and becomes the protector of its descendants. Because of the influence the spirits of one's ancestors exert on the living, it is considered not only shameful for them to be upset or restless, but downright dangerous. A soul that doesn't have descendants is doomed to eternal wandering because it will not receive homage.

Traditionally, the Vietnamese worship and honour the spirits of their ancestors on a regular basis, especially on the anniversary of their death, when sacrifices are offered to both the god of the household and the spirit of the ancestors. To request intercession for success in business or on behalf of a sick child, sacrifices and prayers are offered to the ancestral spirits. The ancestors are informed on occasions of family sorrow or joy, such as death, weddings or examination success. Important worship elements are the family altar, a plot of land whose income is set aside for the support of the ancestors, and the designation of a direct male descendent to assume the obligation of upholding the required rituals.

Many pagodas have altars on which memorial tablets and photographs of the deceased are displayed. Looking at all the young faces in the photographs, you may ponder the tragedy of so many having had their lives cut short. Some visitors wonder if they died as a result of war. The real explanation is less tragic: most had passed on decades after the photos were taken, but rather than use a picture of an aged, infirm parent, survivors chose a more flattering picture of the deceased in their prime.

## Caodaism

Caodaism is a Vietnamese sect that seeks to create the ideal religion by fusing the secular and religious philosophies of both East and West. It was founded in the early 1920s based on messages revealed in seances to Ngo Minh Chieu, the group's founder. At present there are about two million followers of Caodaism in Vietnam. The sect's colourful headquarters is in Tay Ninh, 96km northwest of HCMC (see Tay Ninh in the Around Ho Chi Minh City chapter).

## Hoa Hao Buddhism

The Hoa Hao Buddhist sect (Phat Giao Hoa Hao) was founded in the Mekong Delta in 1939 by Huynh Phu So, a young man who had studied with the most famous of the region's occultists. After he was miraculously cured of an illness, So began preaching a reformed Buddhism based on the common people and embodied in personal faith rather than elaborate rituals. His Buddhist philosophies involve simplicity in worship and exclude the need for intermediaries between humans and the Supreme Being.

In 1940 the French, who called Huynh Phu So the 'mad monk', tried to silence him. When arresting him failed, they committed him to an insane asylum, where he soon converted the Vietnamese psychiatrist assigned to his case. During WWII, the Hoa Hao sect continued to grow and to build up a militia with weapons supplied by the Japanese. In 1947, after clashes between Hoa Hao forces and the Viet Minh, Huynh Phu So was assassinated by the Viet Minh, who thereby earned the animosity of what had by then become a powerful political and military force in the Mekong Delta, especially around Chau Doc. The military power of the Hoa Hao was crushed in 1956 when one of its guerrilla commanders was captured by the Diem government and publicly guillotined. Subsequently, elements of the Hoa Hao army joined the Viet Cong.

Hoa Hao Buddhists are thought to number approximately 1.5 million.

## Catholicism

Catholicism was introduced in the 16th century by Portugese, Spanish and French missionaries. Particularly active during the 16th and 17th centuries were the French Jesuits and Portuguese Dominicans. Pope Alexander VII assigned the first bishops to Vietnam in 1659 and the first Vietnamese priests were ordained nine years later. According to some estimates, there were about 800,000 Catholics in Vietnam by 1685. Over the next three centuries, Catholicism was discouraged and at times outlawed. The first known edict forbidding missionary activity was promulgated in 1533. Missionaries and their followers were severely persecuted during the 17th and 18th centuries.

When the French began colonising Vietnam, the treatment of Catholics was one of their most important pretexts. Under French rule the Catholic Church was given preferential status and Catholicism flourished. Though it incorporated some Vietnamese culture, Catholicism (unlike Buddhism) managed to retain its doctrinal purity.

Today, Vietnam has the highest percentage of Catholics (8% to 10% of the population) in Asia outside the Philippines. Many of the 900,000 refugees who fled from North Vietnam to the South in 1954 were Catholics, as was the then South Vietnamese president Ngo Dinh Diem. Since 1954 in the North and 1975 in the South, Catholics have faced severe restrictions on their religious activities, including strict limits on religious education and the ordination of priests. As happened in the USSR, all churches were viewed as being a capitalist institution and a rival centre of power that could subvert the government.

Since around 1990, the government has taken a more liberal line. There is no question that the Catholic religion is making a comeback, though the old churches have become quite dilapidated and there is a shortage of trained clergy. A lack of funds prevents many churches from doing necessary restoration work, but donations from both locals and overseas Vietnamese are gradually solving this problem.

## Protestantism

Protestantism was introduced to Vietnam in 1911. The majority, who number about 200,000, are Montagnards living in the central highlands. Protestants have been doubly unfortunate in that they were persecuted first by Diem and later by the communists.

Until 1975, the most active Protestant group in South Vietnam was the Christian and Missionary Alliance, whose work went mostly unhindered after Diem's assassination in 1963. After reunification, many clergy members, especially those trained by US missionaries, were imprisoned. Since 1990, the government has ignored them.

## Islam

Muslims, mostly ethnic Khmers and Chams, make up about 0.5% of the population. There were small groups of Malaysian, Indonesian and South Indian Muslims in Saigon until 1975, when most of them fled. Today, the city's 5000 Muslims (including a handful of South Indians) worship in about a dozen mosques, including the Central Mosque.

Arab traders reached China in the 7th century and may have stopped in Vietnam on the way, but the earliest evidence of an Islamic presence in Vietnam is a 10th-century pillar inscribed in Arabic, found near the coastal town of Phan Rang. It appears that Islam spread among Cham refugees who fled to Cambodia after the destruction of their kingdom in 1471, but that these converts had little success in propagating Islam among their fellow Chams still in Vietnam.

The Chams consider themselves Muslims, but in practice they follow a localised adaptation of Islamic theology and law. Their communities have very few copies of the Qur'an and even religious dignitaries can hardly read Arabic. Though Muslims usually pray five times a day, the Chams pray only on Fridays and celebrate Ramadan (a month of dawn-to-dusk fasting) for only three days. Their worship services consist of the recitation of a few Arabic verses from the Qur'an in a localised form. Instead of performing ritual ablutions, they make motions as if they were drawing water from a well. Circumcision is symbolically performed on boys at age 15; when a religious leader makes the gestures of circumcision with a wooden knife. The Chams do not make the pilgrimage to Mecca and although they do not eat pork, they do drink alcohol. In addition, their Islam-based religious rituals coexist with animism and the worship of Hindu deities. The Chams have taken the Arabic words of common Qur'anic expressions and turned them into the names of deities.

Cham religious leaders wear a white robe and an elaborate turban with gold, red or brown tassels. Rank is indicated by the length of the tassels.

## Hinduism

Champa was profoundly influenced by Hinduism and many of the Cham towers, built as Hindu sanctuaries, contain lingas that are still worshipped by ethnic Vietnamese and ethnic Chinese alike. After the fall of Champa in the 15th century, most Chams who remained in Vietnam became Muslims, but continued to practise various Brahmanic (high-caste Hindu) rituals and customs.

# Facts for the Visitor

## HIGHLIGHTS

Vietnam offers a tremendous variety of experiences; enough to suit every taste or preference – it's difficult to say just which places should top your list.

Beach lovers will almost certainly want to check out tranquil Mui Ne Beach, or the bustling party scene further north in Nha Trang. More adventurous beach-goers will appreciate remote Phu Quoc Island.

The splendid rock formations, sea cliffs and grottoes of Halong Bay could easily rate as one of the wonders of the world. Nearby, Cat Ba Island also gets rave reviews from those who make the effort to get there, despite its rapid development. Similar scenery (without the water) can be found at the Perfume Pagoda and in Tam Coc.

Sapa and nearby Bac Ha offer a glimpse of traditional lifestyles in the mountains along the Chinese border. Trekking through Mai Chau and myriad other less-travelled parts of the northern mountains offers the opportunity to visit hill-tribe villages. A motorbike trip through the rugged overland 'northwest loop' passes through some of Vietnam's most scenic high-country landscape; this route ranks among the most memorable for many.

History and architecture buffs will be attracted to Hué and Hoi An, the latter being among the most charming spots in the country. For those fascinated by the American War and all its implications, what better place to explore than the old Demilitarised Zone (DMZ)?

Dalat, with its waterfalls, ethnic minorities and cool mountain climate, is considered the kitsch jewel of the central highlands.

The Mekong Delta is more varied than most people imagine, and growing in popularity with three international land borders now open to travellers. Popular land scenic spots include Cantho, Soc Trang and Chau Doc.

And if you've spent time admiring Vietnam's landscape, perhaps you'd like to see what lies underneath – there are few better places to do this than in Phong Nha Cave.

Finally, don't forget Vietnam's big cities. Freewheeling Ho Chi Minh City (HCMC), with its dilapidated colonial elegance, outstanding food and bustling nightlife, is a laboratory for Vietnam's economic reforms. Hanoi, with its monuments, parks, lakes and tree-lined boulevards, is the beguiling seat of power in a country trying to figure out in which direction to head.

## SUGGESTED ITINERARIES
### One Week

**The North** From Hanoi, make a two-day trip to Halong Bay and/or Mai Chau followed by a day trip to the Perfume Pagoda and/or Tam Coc. Spend the remaining time exploring the delights of the capital.

**The South** From HCMC, it's possible to do a day trip to the Cu Chi Tunnels and a two- or three-day tour of the Mekong Delta. The rest of the time can be spent sightseeing, eating, shopping and carousing in HCMC.

### Two Weeks

Note that highlights of the following two options can also be combined; a typical whirlwind tour means flying into Hanoi, exploring the area (including Halong Bay and/or Sapa) then making a beeline to Hué before heading south to HCMC (or vice-versa). Excursion airline tickets allowing such a routing are common, and recommended to avoid backtracking.

**The North** Follow the above one-week itinerary for the north, then take a spin into the northwest mountains (especially Sapa and Bac Ha) and/or a trip to Cuc Phuong, Ba Be or Cat Ba National Parks.

**The South** A two-week visit to the south will allow for the one-week itinerary, followed by a loop up to Dalat, and back down to the beaches in and around Nha Trang and/or Mui Ne Beach. Time permitting, you could then head to Hoi An and fly back to HCMC from Danang or Hué.

## One Month

A month is enough time to take in most of the major sights. Starting in the south (this itinerary can also be followed in reverse from Hanoi), follow the two-week itinerary as far as Hoi An or Danang before pressing on to Hué. Take a DMZ tour out of Hué, then travel on to Hanoi. Either fly out of Hanoi or continue overland to China.

## Two Months

Two months will allow ample time to see everything in more detail. In addition to our other suggested itineraries, explore the Mekong Delta more thoroughly, with a side trip to lovely Phu Quoc Island. Or spend a few days lingering on the giant sand dunes at Mui Ne Beach (near Phan Thiet), south of Nha Trang. A trip to the western part of the central highlands should include a visit to Dalat. Don't forget Phong Nha Cave to the north of the DMZ. In the far north, you can explore remote areas such as Dien Bien Phu, Cao Bang and Bai Tu Long Bay.

## PLANNING
## When to Go

There is no good or bad time to travel to Vietnam. When one region is wet, cold or steaming hot, there is always somewhere else that is sunny and pleasant.

Visitors should allow for the fact that during Tet, the colourful Lunar New Year in late January or early February, flights into, out of and around Vietnam are likely to be booked solid. The Tet festival continues for at least a week and you are likely to encounter difficulties booking hotels and flights for at least a week before and after. This festival affects the whole of East Asia during this period. See the special section 'Tet Festival' for more information.

## Maps

Almost every bookshop in Vietnam can sell you a map of the entire country. Reasonable tourist maps of HCMC, Hanoi, Danang, Hué and a few other cities are issued within Vietnam in slightly different forms every few years. Unfortunately, maps of smaller towns and cities are practically nonexistent and most Vietnamese have never seen a map of the town they live in.

An oddity found in Vietnam is streets named after momentous historical dates. For example, ĐL 3 Thang 2 (usually written ĐL 3/2) refers to 3 February, the anniversary of the founding of the Vietnamese Communist Party.

Vietnamese street names are preceded with the words Pho, Duong and Dai Lo – on the maps in this book, they appear respectively as P, Đ and ĐL.

Highly detailed topographic maps are produced in Vietnam, but are difficult to find. The government treats them like military secrets – ridiculous in this age of satellite photos.

## What to Bring

Bring as little as possible. Many travellers try to bring everything bar the kitchen sink. Keep in mind that you can and will buy things in Vietnam (especially clothing), so don't burden yourself with lots of unnecessary junk. If you do forget to bring any 'essential' items, it's quite likely they can be bought in Vietnam, at least in the cities.

Backpacks are the easiest type of bag to carry and a frameless or internal-frame pack is the easiest to manage on buses and trains. Packs that close with a zipper can usually be secured with a padlock. Of course, any pack can be slit open with a razor blade, but a padlock will usually prevent pilfering by hotel staff and baggage handlers at airports. A cable lock or loop cable with lock can be used to secure the backpack on buses and trains (pack snatchers are a serious problem).

A day-pack can be handy, so you can leave your main luggage at the hotel or left-luggage room in the train stations. A belt pack is OK for maps, extra film and other miscellanea, but don't use it for valuables such as your travellers cheques and passport, as it's an easy target for pickpockets.

Inside? Lightweight and compact are two words that should be etched in your mind when you're trying to decide on what to bring. Dark-coloured clothing is preferred because it doesn't show the dirt – white clothes will force you to do laundry daily.

Nylon sports shoes are best as they are comfortable, washable and lightweight. Sandals are appropriate footwear in tropical heat – even Ho Chi Minh wore them during public appearances. Rubber thongs are somewhat less appropriate for formal occasions, but are nevertheless commonly worn.

A Swiss army knife or equivalent comes in handy, but you don't need one with 27 separate functions. Basically, you need one small sharp blade, a can opener and a bottle opener – a built-in magnifying glass or backscratcher probably isn't necessary.

The secret of successful packing is plastic bags or nylon 'stuff bags' – they keep things not only separate and clean, but also dry.

Women should bring tampons with them. Also consider bringing name cards; a flashlight; a compass; a camera and accessories; ear plugs; an alarm clock; sunglasses; a hat and sunscreen; a leakproof water bottle; a cup, plate, fork and spoon; rain jacket or poncho; backpack rain cover; sweater (for winter and air-con bus trips); sewing kit; toilet paper; condoms; nail clippers and tweezers; mosquito repellent. See the Health section later in this chapter.

If you'll be cycling, bring all necessary safety equipment (helmet, reflectors, mirrors etc), as well as an inner-tube repair kit. Everything you need to know about cycling in Vietnam is covered in Lonely Planet's *Cycling Vietnam, Laos & Cambodia.*

Hill-climbing boots with 25 eyelets on each side may be great for mountain climbing, but you will soon regret wearing them elsewhere. Etiquette requires the removal of shoes at private homes, temples and even many minihotels. This custom, coupled with predominantly hot weather, means thongs (flip-flops) or sandals are more practical. Just make sure that you have a comfortable pair you can walk in that won't fall off when you ride on a motorbike.

If you have particularly large feet, finding shoes that fit can be difficult in Vietnam, but for most Western tourists this will probably not be a problem.

## RESPONSIBLE TOURISM

Both the positive and negative effects of the arrival of tourism are being felt throughout Vietnam. While positive contributions include dollars flowing into the local economy, the creation of jobs and the growing impact of globalisation, it is important for travellers to recognise and heed the potentially damaging costs of their visit on the country as a whole. The negative effects of tourism, both domestic and international, can be markedly reduced by responsible travel and a general respect for local culture and customs. By minimising negative impact, each visitor can make a difference. Try to be sensitive to local customs and take note of what local people do (see Society & Conduct in the Facts about Vietnam chapter).

The Useful Organisations section later in this chapter lists nongovernment organisations (NGOs) that are working to reduce the impact of tourism on the people, their cultural heritage and the environment of Vietnam.

### Prostitution & Paedophilia

In Asia, the prevalence of a sex-tourism industry is unfortunate but real; however where there is demand, there is usually supply. In Vietnam, the recent liberalisation of government policy has seen prostitution increase to levels not seen since the American War. 'Social evils' campaigns periodically see the government crack down on the sex industry with heavy penalties, but the problem still remains. Avoid patronising bars that offer sex and massage services, such as the 'bar oms', and never buy sexual services.

Vietnam is also among the newest international sites for child prostitution (along with Cambodia, Laos, China and the Dominican Republic). It is quite difficult to find reliable statistics on child prostitution in Vietnam; however, a recent estimate suggested that around 30% of all sex workers were under the age of 16, and police reports show that sex crimes in general are steadily increasing.

The penalties in Vietnam for paedophiles are severe, and other countries around the world also have very strict laws. As a direct response to this child abuse, a number of

## Tread Lightly in the Hills

For the world's indigenous people, tourism is a mixed blessing. The tourism industry (Lonely Planet included) and countries like Vietnam, Thailand and Australia promote images of indigenous people and their distinctive cultures to attract tourists to holiday destinations.

Studies show indigenous cultures are a major drawcard for travellers and attract substantial revenue, yet little of it directly benefits these minority groups, who are often among their country's poorest and most disadvantaged.

Hill-tribe communities in Vietnam have generally not initiated tourist activities, are not the major economic beneficiaries of it, are unable to stop it and have little say in its management.

Studies in Vietnam by the leading aid agency, Oxfam, suggests tourism can bring many benefits to its highland communities. These include cross-cultural understanding; improved infrastructure like roads; cheaper market goods; and tourist dollars supporting handicraft industries and providing employment opportunities for locals as guides and hospitality workers.

However, there are also negative side-effects. Tourism creates or contributes to: overtaxing of natural resources, for instance, agricultural land is turned over to build hotels, and precious water supplies are diverted to tourists taking showers; increased litter and pollutants; dependency on tourist dollars; proliferation of drug use and prostitution; and erosion of local values and practices.

If you travel to these regions, the good news is that you can make a positive contribution and ensure that the benefits of your stay outweigh the costs. We hope you find this guide useful.

### Travel
- Travel in small, less disruptive groups
- Stay, eat and travel with local businesses to ensure your dollar spreads further and stays within the region
- Try to book tours with responsible tourism outlets who employ hill-tribe people (preferably in meaningful work) or contribute to community welfare

### Behaviour
- Be polite and respectful
- Dress modestly – a sarong is acceptable for public bathing and toilet stops
- Minimise your litter – if you trek overnight take out your rubbish with you
- Do not urinate or defecate near villagers' households; bury faeces
- Do not take drugs – young children tend to imitate tourists' behaviour. In neighbouring Thailand drug addiction and HIV infections are decimating hill-tribe populations – similar problems are expected to emerge in Vietnam.

---

countries (including Australia, New Zealand, Germany, Sweden, Norway, France and the USA) now prosecute and punish their citizens for paedophilia offences committed abroad. The fear of contracting HIV/AIDS from mature sex workers has led to increasing exploitation of – supposedly as yet uninfected – children. This is perhaps the most disturbing element of the worldwide growth in the sex trade.

The sexual exploitation of children has become a significant problem throughout Asia so please don't let it get a strong foothold in Vietnam. If you see or suspect anything involving minors, please don't just ignore it; if you have any information, ie, the offenders' name and nationality, speak to their embassy. Any details you have can also be passed on to **End Child Prostitution and Trafficking** (Ecpat; e ecpat@ecpat.org), a global network of organisations that are working to stop child prostitution, child pornography and the trafficking of children for sexual purposes.

## Tread Lightly in the Hills

- Do not engage in sexual relationships with local people, including prostitutes – in recent years a hill-tribe mother and her child, who was born with Western features and skin tone, have been ostracised by their community
- Try to learn something about the community's culture and language and teach something good about yours

### Shopping

- Haggle politely and always pay the agreed (and fair) price for goods and services
- Do not ask to buy a villager's personal household items or the jewellery or clothes they are wearing – they may feel obliged to sell them to please you, but actually need it themselves. There are plenty of items made for tourists that you can buy instead.
- Don't buy village treasures, such as altar pieces (even if offered for sale) – these are valuable to the community and should stay there. Besides, it is illegal to take these items out of Vietnam.

### Photographs

- Do not photograph without first asking permission – this includes children. Some hill tribes (particularly the Dao people) believe the camera will capture their spirit. Don't photograph altars.
- If you take a picture, please do it quickly and avoid using a flash. It is polite to send copies (if possible) – if you promise to do so, keep your word.

### Gifts

- Do not give children sweets or money; it encourages begging and paves the way for prostitution for 'gifts' and money. Sweets also contribute to tooth decay.
- Do not give clothes – communities are self-sufficient; don't create expensive (and unnecessary) consumer desires
- Don't give medicines – it erodes traditional healing practices and the medicine may not be correctly administered
- Individual gifts create jealousy and create expectations. Instead make donations of picture books, basic first-aid equipment or cash to the local school, medical centre or community fund. Other appropriate gifts are pictures you have taken of the community, postcards of your home country and of yourself and/or family.
- No matter how poor they are, villagers are extremely hospitable, however, feeding a guest can result in food shortages. If you accept an invitation to share a meal, be sure to bring a generous contribution, such as rice, tea, or other locally available foodstuffs with you.

**Compiled with assistance from Oxfam Community Aid Abroad**

## The Natural Environment

Vietnam has a low level of environmental awareness and responsibility, and many people remain unaware of the implications of littering. Try and raise awareness of these issues by example, and dispose of all your litter as responsibly as possible.

Vietnam's faunal populations are under considerable threat from domestic consumption and the illegal international trade in animal products (see Flora & Fauna in the Facts about Vietnam chapter). Though it may be 'exotic' to try wild meat such as muntjac, bats, frogs, deer, sea-horses, shark fins and snake (wine) and so on – or to buy products made from endangered plants and animals – it will indicate your support or acceptance of such practices and add to the demand for them.

Forest products such as rattan, orchids and medicinal herbs are under threat and the majority are still collected from the country's dwindling forests. However, some of these products can be cultivated, an industry with potential for local people to earn additional income while protecting natural areas from exploitation and degradation.

When visiting coral reefs and snorkelling or diving, or simply boating, be careful not to touch live coral or anchor boats on it, as this hinders the coral's growth. If your tour operator does this and it's possible to anchor in a sandy area, try to convince the operator to do so and indicate your willingness to swim to the coral. Don't buy coral souvenirs.

Vietnam is home to a large expanse of limestone or Karst landscape. When visiting limestone caves, be aware that touching the formations hinders growth and turns the limestone black. Don't break off the stalactites or stalagmites as they take lifetimes to regrow. Don't carve graffiti onto limestone formations, cave walls or other rock.

Finally do not remove or buy 'souvenirs' that have been taken from historical sites and natural areas.

## Green Travel

Simple acts can make a big difference. While you're in Vietnam you can help to make a positive contribution to the environment. Here are some hints about things you might consider while on holiday (and even when you're at home!):

- Don't buy souvenirs or eat meals produced from endangered wildlife species, including things like turtles and coral
- Think about taking reusable calico shopping bags and refuse plastic bags whenever possible – they end up clogging waterways
- Straws get stuck in dolphin's blowholes – consider reusing your straws or drinking from your own cup
- As an alternative to takeaway food packaging, take a reusable drink bottle and a lightweight aluminium or stainless steel food container (readily available in Western camping stores) – they'll also come in handy on long journeys
- Using rechargeable batteries for your Walkman will cut down on the rubbish you leave behind

## TOURIST OFFICES

Vietnam's tourist offices are not like those found in other countries. If you were to visit a government-run tourist office in Australia, Western Europe or Japan, you'd get lots of free, colourful, glossy brochures, maps and helpful advice on transport, places to stay, where to book tours and so on. Such tourist offices make no profit – indeed, they can lose money.

The tourist offices in Vietnam operate on a different philosophy. They are government-owned enterprises whose primary interests are booking tours and earning a profit. In fact, these 'tourist offices' are little more than travel agencies, but they are among the most profitable hard-currency cash cows the Vietnamese government has. Don't come here looking for freebies; even the colourful brochures and maps, when they have them, are for sale.

Vietnam Tourism and Saigon Tourist are the oldest examples of this genre. However, nowadays every province has at least one such organisation, while larger cities may have dozens of competing government-run 'tourist offices', with each one earning a tidy profit. Many private companies have formed joint ventures with the state-run organisations, thus further diluting any real distinction between these tourist offices and private travel agencies.

Passenger arrivals in Vietnam rose from just 300,000 in 1991 to 1.5 million in 1998, and to 2.2 million in 2001. Many in the travel industry, however, are sceptical about whether Vietnam, which only opened to tourism in the late 1980s, can handle such an increase of tourists. Critics say the country still lacks some important elements of basic tourist infrastructure, including a tourist police force and 'real' tourist information offices. See the Information sections in the destination chapters for further details about tourist offices in Vietnam.

## VISAS & DOCUMENTS
### Passport

A passport is essential. If yours is within a few months of expiration, get a new one – many countries will not issue a visa if your passport has less than six months of validity remaining. Be sure that your passport has at least a few blank pages for visas and entry and exit stamps. It could be very inconvenient to run out of blank pages when you are too far away from an embassy to get a new passport issued or extra pages added.

Losing your passport is very bad news. Getting a new one takes time and money. It's wise to have a driving licence, student card, ID card or something else with your photo on it – some embassies want to see picture ID before issuing a replacement passport. Keeping the original of an old expired passport is also very useful for this purpose.

It certainly helps to keep a separate record of the number and date of issue of your passport as well as a photocopy of either it or your birth certificate. While you're compiling that info, add the serial number of your travellers cheques, travel insurance details and US$300 or so as emergency cash (better hotels have a safe for valuables – that may be a good place to keep this stuff).

In Vietnam, it seems that everyone wants to do something with your passport. You will almost always be required to leave your passport with the hotel reception desk, as well as with a travel agency (to get a local travel permit or visa extension).

## Visas

Tourist visas are stamped *cau cac cua khau quoc te*, which means 'any international border'. This allows you to enter and exit Vietnam at Hanoi, HCMC and Danang airports or at any of its eight land borders (three with Cambodia, two with Laos and three with China).

Arranging the necessary paperwork for a Vietnamese visa has become fairly straightforward – the only problem is that it tends to be quite expensive and unnecessarily time-consuming. In most cases you are better off getting your visa from a travel agent rather than the Vietnamese embassy, mainly for sheer convenience and to avoid queues. The travel agency processing your visa requires a photocopy of your passport and one to three photos (the actual number differs for various countries).

In 2001 the Vietnamese government announced plans to grant French and Japanese travellers free 14-day tourist visas on arrival. But despite persistent lobbying for the plan from the Vietnam National Administration of Tourism (VNAT), the Public Security Ministry, citing a lack in reciprocity with visa exception agreements, has kept the plan on ice.

At the time of writing, the Vietnamese government had plans in the works to grant five-day visas on arrival to *any* international visitors by the end of 2002. Keep an ear to the ground for news of this becoming reality or visit **w** www.lonelyplanet.com for the most up-to-date visa information.

In Asia, Bangkok has always been considered the most convenient place to get visas for Vietnam and most Thai travel agencies offer package deals with a visa and return air ticket included.

**Tourist Visas** Processing a tourist-visa application typically takes four or five working days (two or three days for an express visa). Tourist visas are valid for only a single 30-day stay. To make matters worse, the visa specifies the exact date of arrival and departure. Thus, you must solidify your travel plans well in advance. You cannot arrive even one day earlier than your visa specifies. And if you change your plans and postpone your trip by two weeks, then you'll only have 16 days remaining on your visa instead of 30 days.

If you plan to spend more than a few weeks in Vietnam, or if you plan to exit Vietnam and enter again (say from Cambodia or Laos), try asking for a three-month multiple-entry visa. These cost around US$90 from embassies in Cambodia and Australia, but they are not available from all Vietnamese embassies.

In our experience, personal appearance influences the reception you receive from airport immigration – if you wear shorts or scruffy clothing, look dirty or unshaven, you can expect problems. You don't need to get all dressed up, but try to look 'respectable'.

These days most travellers' visas are stamped or sealed in their passport, but some nationalities may end up with their visa on a separate piece of paper.

**Business Visas** There are advantages to having a business visa: it is usually valid for three or six months; it can be issued for multiple entries; and you are permitted to work.

Getting a business visa has now become fairly easy. Some travel agencies that organise tourist visas can also do business visas. The main drawback is the cost – a business visa costs about four times what you'd pay for a tourist visa. Trying to obtain the visa yourself through a Vietnamese embassy will probably be more trouble than it's worth – it's better to let a travel agent handle it.

It tends to be much easier to apply for a business visa once you are in Vietnam. If it is approved, most people make a short trip abroad to Phnom Penh, Vientiane or Bangkok to pick up the visa from a Vietnamese embassy. It is actually possible to get the visa stamped in Vietnam, but this is far more expensive.

**Student Visas** A student visa is something you usually arrange after your arrival. It's acceptable to enter Vietnam on a tourist visa, enrol in a Vietnamese language course and then apply at the immigration police for a change in status. Of course, students do have to pay tuition and are expected to attend classes for a minimum of 10 hours per week to qualify for student status. A student-visa holder can officially only work up to 10 hours per week.

**Visa Extensions** If you've got the dollars, they've got the rubber stamp. Tourist-visa extensions cost around US$30 but you should probably go to a travel agency to get this taken care of as fronting up at the immigration police in person usually doesn't work. The procedure takes from one or two days. Official policy is that you are permitted one visa extension only, for a maximum of 30 days.

Be alert, however. Sudden and arbitrary changes to the regulations are standard procedure in Vietnam so try not to get caught short in this regard.

In theory, you should be able to extend your visa in any provincial capital. In practice, it goes smoothest in major cities, such as HCMC, Hanoi, Danang and Hué, which cater to mass tourism.

**Re-Entry Visas** It's theoretically possible to enter Cambodia, Laos or any other country from Vietnam and then re-enter without having to apply for another visa. However, you must apply for a re-entry visa *before* you leave Vietnam. You'll be given a receipt and confirmation number to pick up the visa in the country you are headed to. If you do not have a re-entry visa, you will have to go through the whole expensive and time-consuming procedure of applying for a new Vietnamese visa.

One traveller reported that they tried to organise a re-entry visa for Vietnam in HCMC before catching a flight into Cambodia, but were told by immigration officials that a re-entry stamp could be obtained ('no problem') from the Vietnamese embassy in Phnom Penh. However, in Phnom Penh they were told there was no such thing as a re-entry stamp and that they would have to apply for a new visa.

Re-entry visas are easiest to arrange in Hanoi or HCMC, but you will almost certainly have to ask a travel agent to do the paperwork for you. Travel agents charge about US$25 for this service and can complete the procedure in one or two days.

If you already have a valid business visa that allows you multiple entries, you do not need a re-entry visa.

## Travel Permits

Formerly, foreigners had to have internal travel permits to travel anywhere beyond the city in which they arrived. From 1975 to 1988, even citizens of Vietnam needed these permits to travel around their own country (to prevent them from fleeing). The central government changed the rules in 1993 and internal travel permits are no longer needed, although the Vietnamese must carry their ID card at all times.

Although internal travel permits have been abolished, uncertainty still prevails in some remote towns and villages. Unfortunately, the police in some places seem to make up their own rules as they go along, no matter what the Interior Ministry in Hanoi says. In some provinces, such as Ha Giang, you may be asked by the local police to 'pay for a travel permit', but this practice is increasingly becoming the exception rather than the rule.

## Travel Insurance

Although you may have medical insurance in your own country, it is probably not valid while you are in Vietnam. A travel insurance policy to cover theft, loss and medical problems is a good idea. Some policies offer lower and higher medical-expense options; the higher ones are chiefly for countries such as the USA, which has extremely high medical costs. There is a wide variety of policies available, so check the small print.

Some insurance policies specifically exclude such 'dangerous activities' as diving, riding motorbikes and even trekking. A locally acquired motorbike licence is not valid under some policies.

You may prefer a policy that pays doctors or hospitals directly rather than have you pay on the spot and claim later. If you do have to do this, make sure you keep all the documentation. Some policies will ask you to call (reverse charges) a centre in your home country first, where an immediate assessment of your problem is made.

Check that the policy covers ambulances or an emergency flight home.

## Driving Licence & Permits

If you plan to do any driving while you're abroad, get an International Driving Permit (IDP) from your local automobile association or motor vehicle department before you leave. In many countries, these are valid for only one year, so there's no sense getting one too far in advance of your departure. However, some countries will issue IDPs that remain valid for several years – it depends on where you live. Make sure your licence states that it is valid for motorcycles if you plan to ride one.

## Student & Youth Cards

Bona fide full-time students coming from the USA, Australia and Europe can often get some good discounts on international (not domestic) air tickets with the help of an International Student Identity Card (ISIC). To get this card, inquire at your campus.

STA Travel issues STA Youth Cards, which have some of the same benefits, to persons aged between 13 and 26 years. However, these cards are not issued in Vietnam, nor are they of any use within the country.

## International Health Card

An International Health Certificate is useful, though not essential, to record any of the vaccinations you've had. These can be issued in Vietnam.

## Other Documents

If you're travelling with a spouse, a photocopy of your marriage certificate may come in handy should you become involved with the law, hospitals or any other bureaucratic authorities.

If you're planning on working or studying in Vietnam, it could be helpful to bring copies of transcripts, diplomas, letters of reference and other relevant professional qualifications.

A collection of passport photos for visas will be useful if you're planning on visiting several countries or if you need to apply for visa extensions or other documents. Of course, you can get these in Vietnam and elsewhere, but they must have a neutral background.

After arrival in Vietnam it is *very* important that you keep the yellow copy of the customs declaration form that will be stamped when you arrive. Do not lose this. It can be problematic if you do, especially at land borders where the authorities are more prone to extortion and corruption. Consider fixing it in your passport with a paper clip or a rubber band.

## Copies

All important documents (passport data page and visa page, credit cards, travel insurance policy, air/bus/train tickets, driving licence etc) should be photocopied before you actually leave home. Leave one copy with someone there and keep another with you, separate from the originals.

It's also a good idea to store details of your vital travel documents in Lonely Planet's free online Travel Vault in case you lose the photocopies or can't be bothered with them. Your password-protected Travel Vault is accessible online anywhere in the world – create it at **w** www.ekno.lonely planet.com.

During your time in Vietnam, you are almost certain to encounter various people who want to take your valuable documents away from you. This is particularly true of hotel clerks. Some hotels will accept photocopies, but most will not. Once you've handed over your passport, you are left with no documentation at all. At least the photocopies give you something to show to the authorities (the police, the railway ticket office, Vietnam Airlines etc) while the hotel holds your original documents. And if worse comes to worse, photocopies are helpful if you need to replace the documents that the hotel manages to lose.

If police stop you on the street and ask for your passport, give them the photocopy and explain your hotel has the original.

## EMBASSIES & CONSULATES
### Vietnamese Embassies & Consulates

The following are Vietnamese diplomatic representations abroad.

**Australia** (☎ 02-6286 6059, fax 6286 4534)
6 Timbarra Crescent, O'Malley, Canberra, ACT 2603
Consulate: (☎ 02-9327 2539, fax 9328 1653)
489 New South Head Rd, Double Bay, NSW 2028
**Cambodia** (☎ 05-1881 1804, fax 236 2314)
436 Blvd Preach, Monivong, Phnom Penh
**Canada** (☎ 613-232 1957, fax 236 2704) 470 Wilbrod St, Ottawa, Ontario K2P 0L9
**China** (☎ 010-532 1125, fax 532 5720) 32 Guanghua Lu, Jianguomen Wai, Beijing
Consulate: (☎ 020-652 7908, fax 652 7808)
Jin Yanf Hotel, 92 Huanshi Western Rd, Guangzhou

Consulate: (☎ 22-591 4510, fax 591 4524)
15th floor, Great Smart Tower Bldg, 230 Wanchai Rd, Hong Kong
**France** (☎ 01 44 14 64 00, fax 01 45 24 39 48)
62-6 rue Boileau, Paris 75016
**Germany** (☎ 228-357021, fax 351866)
Konstantinstrasse 37, 5300 Bonn 2
**Italy** (☎ 06-854 3223, fax 854 8501)
34 Via Clituno, 00198 Rome
**Japan** (☎ 03-3466 3311, fax 3466 3312) 50-11 Moto Yoyogi-Cho, Shibuya-ku, Tokyo 151
Consulate: (☎ 06-263 1600, fax 263 1770)
10th floor, Estate Bakurocho Bldg, 4-10 Bakurocho, Chuo-ku, Osaka
**Laos** (☎ 214-13409) 1 Thap Luang Rd, Vientiane
Consulate: (☎ 412-12239, fax 12182)
418 Sisavang Vong, Savannakhet
**Philippines** (☎ 2-500 364/508 101)
54 Victor Cruz, Malate, Metro Manila
**Thailand** (☎ 2-251 7201251 5836)
83/1 Wireless Rd, Bangkok
**UK** (☎ 0171-937 1912, fax 937 6108)
12-14 Victoria Rd, London W8 5RD
**USA** (☎ 202-861 0737, fax 861 0917)
1233, 20th St NW, Washington, DC 20036

## Embassies & Consulates in Vietnam

With the exception of those for Laos and Cambodia, Hanoi's embassies and HCMC's consulates do very little visa business for non-Vietnamese. You may, however, have several good reasons to visit your own country's embassy.

It's important to realise what your country's embassy can and can't do to help if you get into trouble. Generally speaking, it won't be much help if the trouble you're in is remotely your own fault. Remember that you are bound by the laws of the country you are in. Your embassy won't be sympathetic if you end up in jail after committing a crime, even if such actions are legal in your own country (though they can intervene to make sure that you're being treated fairly).

In genuine emergencies you might get some assistance, but only if other channels have been exhausted. For example, if you need to get home urgently, a free ticket is exceedingly unlikely – the embassy would expect you to have insurance. If you have all your money and documents stolen, it might assist with getting a new passport, but a loan for onward travel is out of the question.

Some embassies used to keep letters for travellers or have a small reading room with home newspapers, but these days the mail-holding service has mostly stopped and the newspapers tend to be out of date.

If you're staying a long time in Vietnam, you should register your passport at your embassy (this makes it much easier to issue a new one if yours is lost or stolen). Also consider registering with your embassy if you intend on travelling to more remote areas. Your embassy can also help you obtain a ballot for absentee voting or provide forms for filing income-tax returns. Embassies can also advise business people and will sometimes intervene in trade disputes.

However, remember that the people who work at your embassy are busy – please don't bother them with trivial matters.

The following are some of the embassies and consulates found in Vietnam.

**Australia** (☎ 831 7755, fax 831 7711) 8 Đ Dao Tan, Ba Dinh District, Hanoi
*Consulate*: (☎ 829 6035, fax 829 6031) The Landmark, 5B Đ Ton Duc Thang, District 1, HCMC
**Cambodia** (☎ 825 3788, fax 826 5225) 71 Pho Tran Hung Dao, Hanoi
*Consulate*: (☎ 829 2751, fax 829 2744) 41 Đ Phung Khac Khoan, District 1, HCMC
**Canada** (☎ 824 5025, fax 823 5333) 31 Pho Hung Vuong, Hanoi
*Consulate*: (☎ 824 5025, fax 829 4528) 10th floor, Metropolitan Bldg, 235 Đ Dong Khoi, District 1, HCMC
**China** (☎ 845 3736, fax 823 2826) 46 Pho Hoang Dieu, Hanoi
*Consulate*: (☎ 829 2457, fax 829 5009) 39 Đ Nguyen Thi Minh Khai, HCMC
**France** (☎ 825 2719, fax 826 4236) Pho Tran Hung Dao, Hanoi
*Consulate*: (☎ 829 7231, fax 829 1675) 27 Đ Nguyen Thi Minh Khai, District 1, HCMC
**Germany** (☎ 845 3836, fax 845 3838) 29 Pho Tran Phu, Hanoi
*Consulate*: (☎ 829 1967, fax 823 1919) 126 Đ Nguyen Dinh Chieu, District 3, HCMC
**Japan** (☎ 846 3000, fax 846 3043) 27 Pho Lieu Giai, Hanoi

*Consulate*: (☎ 822 5314, fax 822 5316) 13-17 ĐL Nguyen Hue, District 1, HCMC
**Laos** (☎ 825 4576, fax 822 8414) 40 Pho Quang Trung, Hanoi
*Consulate*: (☎ 829 9272) 93 Đ Pasteur, District 1, HCMC
**Netherlands** (☎ 04-831-5650, fax 04-831-5655) Daeha Office Tower, 6th Floor, 360 Kim Ma, Ba Dinh District, Hanoi
*Consulate*: (☎ 823 5932, fax 823 5934) Saigon Tower, 29 ĐL Le Duan, District 1, HCMC
**New Zealand** (☎ 824 1481, fax 824 1480) Level 5, 63 Pho Ly Thai To, Hanoi
*Consulate*: (☎ 822 6907, fax 822 6905) 5th floor, Yoco Bldg, 41 Đ Nguyen Thi Minh Khai, District 1, HCMC
**Philippines** (☎ 825 7948, fax 826 5760) 27B Pho Tran Hung Dao, Hanoi
**Thailand** (☎ 823 5092, fax 823 5088) 63-5 Pho Hoang Dieu, Hanoi
*Consulate*: (☎ 822 2637, fax 829 1002) 77 Đ Tran Quoc Thao, District 3, HCMC
**UK** (☎ 825 2510, fax 826 5762) 31 Pho Hai Ba Trung, Hanoi
*Consulate*: (☎ 829 8433, fax 822 1971) 25 ĐL Le Duan, District 1, HCMC
**USA** (☎ 843 1500, fax 843 1510) 7 Pho Lang Ha, Hanoi
*Consulate*: (☎ 822 9433, fax 822 9434 ) 4 ĐL Le Duan, District 1, HCMC

## CUSTOMS

If you enter Vietnam by air, the customs inspection is usually fast and cursory. Unless the x-ray machine indicates that your backpack is filled with guns or heroin, you should get through the whole procedure in minutes. However, if you enter overland, expect a mild to rigorous search.

You are permitted to bring in a duty-free allowance of 200 cigarettes, 50 cigars or 250g of tobacco; 2L of liquor; gifts worth up to US$50; and a reasonable quantity of luggage and personal effects. Items that you cannot bring into Vietnam include opium, weapons, explosives and 'cultural materials unsuitable to Vietnamese society' (eg, pornographic or seditious publications, film or photography).

Visitors can bring an unlimited amount of foreign currency into Vietnam, but it must be declared on their customs form upon arrival.

Theoretically, when you leave the country you should have exchange receipts for all the foreign currency you have spent, but in practice the authorities really don't care.

On arrival, visitors must also declare all precious metals (especially gold), jewellery, cameras and electronic devices in their possession. Theoretically, declaring your goods means that when you leave, you will have no hassles taking these items out with you. It also means that you could be asked to show these items when leaving so that customs officials know you didn't sell them on the black market. In practice you will seldom be troubled unless you bring in an unreasonable amount of goods or something of great value.

The import and export of Vietnamese currency and live animals is forbidden.

## MONEY
### Currency

The currency of Vietnam is the dong, which is abbreviated to 'd'. The banknotes come in denominations of 200d, 500d, 1000d, 2000d, 5000d, 10,000d, 20,000d, 50,000d and 100,000d. In small towns, it can be difficult to get change for the larger notes, so keep a stack of smaller bills handy.

Now that Ho Chi Minh has been canonised (against his wishes), his picture is on *every* banknote. There are no coins currently in use in Vietnam, though the dong used to be divided into 10 *hao* and 100 *xu*.

The dong has experienced its ups and downs. Past attempts by the government to solve the country's debt problems with the money-printing press led to devastating inflation and frequent devaluations. In 1991 the dong lost close to half its value. A year later it gained 35% against the US dollar, making it one of the best currency investments of the year! This surge in value was due to the shutting down of the printing presses and the turnaround in Vietnam's chronic trade deficit – in 1992 the country experienced its first trade surplus since reunification. The late 1990s Asian economic crisis, which wreaked severe havoc on the Thai, Korean and Indonesian currencies, caused the dong to lose about 15% of its US-dollar value. Since then, the dong has slowly

## Money for Nothing

The dong has certainly had a rocky history. In the days of French Indochina, the local currency was known as the *piastre*. The partitioning of Vietnam in 1954 created separate versions of the dong for North and South Vietnam but the two currencies were valued the same.

In 1975, US$1 was equal to 450d in South Vietnam. In 1976 the Communist Provisional Revolutionary Government (PRG) cancelled the South Vietnamese dong and issued its own PRG dong. The swap rate between the two dong was not set at 1:1, but rather at 500:1 in favour of the PRG dong. Furthermore, southerners were only permitted to exchange a maximum of 200d per family. This sudden demonetarisation of South Vietnam instantly turned much of the affluent population into paupers and caused the swift collapse of the economy. Those with the foresight to have kept their wealth hidden in gold or jewellery escaped some of the hardships.

In 1977 both the north Vietnamese dong and the PRG dong were done away with and swapped for a reunification dong. In the north the swap was 1:1, but in the south the ratio was 1:1.2. This time the southerners got a slightly better deal, though it was small compensation for the 500:1 loss of the previous year.

The last great attempt at currency swapping was in 1985. Realising that inflation was rapidly eroding the value of the dong, the government decided to solve the problem by reissuing a new dong at a swap ratio of 10:1 in favour of the new dong. This time each family was allowed only 2000d of the new banknotes, though on special application more could be allotted. Rather than controlling price increases as the government had hoped, the currency reissue ignited yet another round of hyperinflation. These days, the old 20d notes are not worth the paper they're printed on.

weakened further and at the time of writing, one US dollar was worth roughly 15,000d.

The Americans introduced Western banking practices to South Vietnam – personal cheques were commonly used for large purchases, at least in Saigon before reunification. When the North took over, cheques, credit cards, South Vietnamese banknotes and South Vietnamese bank accounts became instantly worthless. As the Vietnamese dismantled the banking system, telegraphic transfers into Vietnam became practically impossible, though later a company called Cosevina was set up to allow overseas Vietnamese to send money to their relatives.

That was then and this is now. Vietnam is gradually trying to conform to Western-style banking systems so travellers cheques, credit cards, telegraphic transfers and even letters of credit are all experiencing a revival. Domestic personal cheques have still not been reintroduced, but should be coming soon.

Gold is also used extensively, especially for major transactions such as the sale of homes or cars. If you ask someone how much they paid for their house, they will probably tell you how many taels of gold.

Recently the more upmarket hotels and restaurants have been demanding payment in US dollars and will not accept the local currency, even though the government banned this practice in 1994. Officially all businesses in Vietnam must advertise and accept payment in dong only. In reality, many hotels and businesses still quote prices in US dollars and will 'exchange' on the spot.

Where prices are quoted in dong, we quote them in this book in dong. Likewise, when prices are quoted in dollars, we follow suit. While this may seem inconsistent, this is the way it's done in Vietnam and the sooner you get used to thinking comparatively in dong and dollars, the easier your travels will be.

It's advisable to bring a small pocket calculator with you for converting currencies. It's always risky to try to pin down a currency on paper, so try the currency converter at **w** www.oanda.com to give you the most current value of the dong.

## Exchange Rates

| country | unit | | dong |
|---------|------|---|------|
| Australia | A$1 | = | 8907d |
| Canada | C$1 | = | 10,221d |
| China | Y1 | = | 1938d |
| euro | €1 | = | 15,648d |
| Hong Kong | HK$1 | = | 2054d |
| Japan | ¥100 | = | 12,903d |
| New Zealand | NZ$1 | = | 7810d |
| Singapore | S$1 | = | 9028d |
| Taiwan | NT$1 | = | 461d |
| Thailand | B1 | = | 369d |
| UK | UK£ | = | 24,795d |
| USA | US$1 | = | 16,021d |

## Exchanging Money

In theory you can convert major currencies in Vietnam, but the reality is that US dollars are still much preferred. Be sure to bring enough US dollars in cash or travellers cheques for your whole visit and keep them in a safe place, such as a moneybelt. Try not to keep the whole lot in one place (if the moneybelt goes, everything goes with it). Unless you borrow, or get someone to wire money to you, losing your cash could put you in a really bad situation.

Once in Vietnam, beware of counterfeit money, especially the 20,000d and 50,000d notes. These fakes are imported from China. There shouldn't be any problem if you've changed money in a bank, but out on the free market it's a different story.

It's a good idea to check that the dollars and travellers cheques you take do not have anything scribbled on them or look too tatty, lest they be summarily rejected by uptight clerks.

Vietcombank is another name for the state-owned Bank for Foreign Trade of Vietnam (Ngan Hang Ngoai Thuong Viet Nam). Other banks can change foreign currency and travellers cheques, but Vietcombank is the most organised. Banking hours are normally from 8am to 3pm Monday to Friday, and 8am to noon on Saturday; most banks close for 1½ hours during lunch, all day Sunday and on public holidays.

Travellers cheques can be exchanged only at authorised foreign-exchange banks. The problem is that not every city (indeed, not every province) has a foreign-exchange bank. Outrageously, there are no banks at the border crossings with Cambodia and Laos, nor are there any at Lao Cai and Dong Dang (both major border crossings with China). The only way to change money at these places is on the black market. Furthermore, the Vietcombank branches at HCMC and Hanoi airports only operate during banking hours – they are closed when several flights arrive and depart. Therefore, it's imperative that you do not rely entirely on travellers cheques. Keep a reasonable stash of US dollars on hand, in a variety of denominations. It's possible to get travellers cheques replaced in Hanoi and HCMC.

If you only have travellers cheques, stock up on US dollars at foreign-exchange banks, which usually charge anywhere from a 1.25% to 3% commission to change them into US dollars. Vietcombank charges no commission if you exchange travellers cheques for dong (but again, other banks do).

If your travellers cheques are denominated currencies other than US dollars, you may find them difficult to exchange. If you insist, the banks may exchange them for dong, but they will charge a hefty commission (perhaps 10%) to protect themselves against any possible exchange-rate fluctuations – often they do not know the latest exchange rate for anything but US dollars.

You cannot legally take the dong out of Vietnam but you can reconvert reasonable amounts of it into dollars on departure, without an official receipt, though the definition of 'reasonable' is questionable. A 'reasonable' amount would be a few hundred US dollars; a few thousand would attract the attention of officials, who would want to know why you have so many 'leftover' dong. Most visitors have had no problem, but having an official receipt should settle any arguments that arise.

The relatively low value of Vietnamese banknotes means that almost any currency exchange will leave you with piles of banknotes to count; changing US$100 will net you about 1.5 million dong! Smaller notes are usually presented in brick-sized piles

bound with rubber bands; counting them is a slow, but necessary, process.

Visa, MasterCard and JCB cards are now widely acceptable in all major cities and many tourist centres. However, you will usually be charged a 3% commission each time you use a credit card to purchase something or pay a hotel bill; always ask first, as some charge higher commissions than others. Some merchants also accept AmEx, however the surcharge is typically 4%. Better hotels and restaurants do not usually slap on an additional charge.

Getting a cash advance from Visa, Master-Card and JCB is possible at Vietcombank in most cities, as well as at some foreign banks in HCMC and Hanoi. Banks generally charge a 3% commission for this service.

There are several banks in HCMC with automatic teller machines (ATMs) that accept foreign cards, notably ANZ Bank and Hongkong Bank (HSBC). ATM withdrawals can be made in dong only, and there is a daily limit of 2,000,000d (about US$133). Cash advances for larger amounts of dong, as well as US dollars, can be handled during office hours.

Foreigners who plan to spend a lot of time in Vietnam working, doing business or just hanging around, can open an account at Vietcombank. Bank accounts can be in dong or US dollars. Both demand-deposit and time-deposit accounts are available; interest is paid. Vietcombank can arrange letters of credit for those doing import and export business in Vietnam. It is even possible to borrow money from Vietcombank.

Bear in mind that outside major cities it can be very difficult to find banks that cash travellers cheques, so be sure to change sufficient funds before heading out to the countryside. US dollars are far less problem to use, but the exchange rates tend to drop the further away you are from the city.

**Black Market**  The black market is Vietnam's unofficial banking system that is almost everywhere and operates quite openly. Private individuals (eg, taxi drivers) and some shops (eg, jewellery stores, travel agencies) will exchange US dollars for dong and vice versa. While the practice is illegal, law enforcement is virtually nonexistent. However, black market exchange rates are usually *worse* than the official exchange rates, so the only advantage is the convenience of changing money when and where you like. Typically you lose from 1% to 5% on black-market transactions. In some provincial villages (such as Sapa) you can change travellers cheques on the black market but you'll have to pay an exorbitant 10% commission.

One of the most common, convenient and generally safe ways of changing US dollars to dong is at jewellery stores. Most tend to match the going bank rate (with a slightly better rate on higher denominations like US$50 and US$100 notes). Be sure to count the money at the counter before you leave.

If people approach you on the street with offers to change money at rates better than the official one, you can rest assured that you are being set up for a rip-off. Don't even think about trying it! Remember, if an offer seems too good to be true, that's because it probably is.

## Security

Vietnam has its fair share of pickpockets, especially in HCMC, Nha Trang and Hanoi. Rather than lose your precious cash and travellers cheques (not to mention your passport), large amounts of money and other valuables should be kept far from sticky fingers. Various devices that usually thwart pickpockets include pockets sewn on the inside of your trousers, Velcro tabs to seal pocket openings, a moneybelt under your clothes or a pouch under your shirt. A vest (waistcoat) worn under your outer jacket will do very nicely in those rare parts of Vietnam that get cold; however, this isn't feasible during summer or in the south, where it's just too hot to wear an extra layer.

A secret stash of cash for emergencies is a good idea.

## Costs

Vietnam remains one of the best travel bargains in East Asia, and the cost of travel there largely depends on your tastes and susceptibility to luxuries. Ascetics can get by on US$10 a day while a conventional budget traveller can live very well on US$20 to US$25. Transport is likely to be the biggest expense, especially if you rent a car, which many travellers wind up doing. If you opt to travel by bus or train, you can save a considerable sum.

Foreigners are frequently overcharged, particularly when buying souvenirs, and occasionally in restaurants. Rapacious bus and taxi drivers will often bump up their rates to several times the Vietnamese price. However, don't assume that everyone is trying to rip you off. Despite severe poverty, many Vietnamese will only ask the local price for most goods and services.

## Tipping & Bargaining

Tipping is not expected in Vietnam, but it is enormously appreciated. For a person who earns US$50 per month, a US$1 tip is about half a day's wages. Upmarket hotels and some restaurants may slap a 5% service charge on top of the government's 10% value-added tax (VAT). This service charge might be considered a mandatory tip, though it's doubtful that much of it reaches the employees. In general, if you stay a couple of days in the same hotel it's not such a bad idea to tip the staff who clean your room – US$1 should be enough.

You should also consider tipping drivers and guides – after all, the time they spend on the road with you means time away from home and family. Ditto if you take a day tour with a group – the guides and drivers are paid next to nothing. Typically, travellers on minibus tours will pool together to collect a communal tip to be split between the guide and driver. About US$1 per day (per tourist) is standard. Of course, give more if you're feeling generous, but if you find a genuine reason not to tip, don't.

It is considered proper to make a small donation at the end of a visit to a pagoda, especially if the monk has shown you around; most pagodas have contribution boxes for this purpose.

Many visitors just assume that every Vietnamese is out to rip them off. That just isn't true – you needn't bargain for everything. But there are times when bargaining is essential. In touristy areas, postcard vendors have a reputation for charging about five times the going rate. Most cyclo and motorbike drivers also try to grossly overcharge foreigners – find out the correct rate in advance and then bargain accordingly.

Remember that in Asia, 'saving face' is important (see Society & Conduct in the Facts about Vietnam chapter), so bargaining should be good-natured. Smile and don't get angry or argue. Many Westerners seem to take bargaining too seriously and get offended if they don't get the goods for less than half the original asking price. In some cases you will be able to get a 50% discount or more, at other times this may only be 10%, but by no means should you get angry during the bargaining process. And once the money is accepted, the deal is done – if you harbour hard feelings because you later find out that someone else got it cheaper, the only one you are hurting is yourself.

## Taxes

With most goods or services you pay for, the marked or stated price usually includes any relevant taxes. Value-added tax was implemented in 1999, so don't be surprised to find an extra 10% tacked on to your bill. Some hotels and restaurants may also charge an additional 5% service charge, but this should be stated on the rate sheet or menu (ask if you're not sure).

The Vietnamese government is said to be looking at ways to crack down on tax evasion. However if the tax collectors really got their act together, it would be a disaster for the economy.

## POST & COMMUNICATIONS
## Postal Rates

Domestic postal rates are cheap; it only costs 800d to mail a letter.

International postal rates are similar to what you pay in European countries – the exact amount depends on the continent to which you are sending. Postcards cost 7000d to Asia, 8000d to Europe and 9000d to the Americas. While these might not

seem very expensive to you, they are too high for most salaries and locals simply cannot afford to send letters to their friends and relatives abroad. If you would like to correspond with Vietnamese whom you meet during your visit, try leaving them enough stamps to cover postage for several letters, explaining that the stamps were extras you didn't use and would be of no value at home. Or buy a bunch of Vietnamese stamps, take them home with you and when you write to Vietnamese friends include a few stamps for their replies.

## Sending Mail

Post offices all over the country usually keep long hours, about 6am to 8pm including weekends and public holidays (even Tet).

Items mailed from anywhere other than large towns and cities are likely to take over a month to arrive at their international destination. Air-mail service from HCMC and Hanoi takes approximately five to 10 days to get to most Western countries, so long as it readily passes 'security'.

Express-mail service (EMS), available in the larger cities, is perhaps twice as fast as regular air mail. One big advantage is that the letter or small parcel will be registered. There is also a domestic EMS between Hanoi and HCMC (and some smaller cities such as Danang and Nha Trang) that promises next-day delivery.

Foreigners wishing to send parcels out of Vietnam sometimes have to deal with time-consuming inspections of the contents, but this is happening less frequently now. The most important thing is to keep the parcel small. If it's documents only, you should be OK. Sending out video tapes and the like can be problematic.

Private couriers such as FedEx, DHL, Airborne Express and UPS deliver small parcels or documents to both local and international destinations. See the Hanoi and Ho Chi Minh City chapters for listings.

Planning on shipping home Vietnamese furniture or moving an entire household? For this you need the services of an international mover. Check the transport-service listings in the *Guide* or *Time Out* magazines.

## Receiving Mail

Every city, town, village and rural subdistrict in Vietnam has some sort of post office. Post offices are signed 'Buu Dien.'

Mail delivery is mostly reliable and fast. However, this reliability becomes questionable if your envelope or package contains something worth stealing. One reader in HCMC reported that his mail had been opened and newspaper clippings about the Vietnamese economy removed. Normal letters and postcards should be fine.

Poste restante works well in post offices in Hanoi and HCMC. Elsewhere, it's less certain – the smaller the town the less likely the service will exist. Foreigners have to pay a 500d service charge for each letter they pick up from poste restante.

Receiving even a small package from abroad can cause a headache and large ones will produce a migraine. If you're lucky, customs will clear the package and the post-office clerks will let you collect it. If you are unlucky, customs will demand a time-consuming inspection at which you must be present.

If your parcel contains books, documents, video tapes, computer disks or dangerous goods, it's possible that a further inspection will be required. This could take anywhere from a few days to a few weeks. Presumably, you won't have to spend the entire time in the waiting room while this is being done. If you are particularly unlucky, customs may decide that you must pay import duty.

## Telephone

**Useful Phone Numbers** The following phone services are available, but don't be surprised if the person answering only speaks Vietnamese.

| | |
|---|---|
| Ambulance | ☎ 115 |
| Fire | ☎ 114 |
| Police | ☎ 113 |
| Directory Assistance | ☎ 116 |
| International Operator | ☎ 110 |
| Time Information | ☎ 117 |

Every city has a **general information service** (☎ 1080) that provides everything from phone numbers and train and air timetables, to exchange rates and the latest football scores. It even provides marriage counselling or bed time lullabies for your child – no kidding! You can usually be connected to an operator who speaks English or French.

**International Calls** Charges for international calls from Vietnam have fallen significantly in the past few years. Since the introduction of Voice Over Internet Protocol in 2001, international phone services are now available to 50 different countries and territories at a flat rate of just US$1.30/minute, less than half of the previous cheapest rate. The service is easy to use from any phone in the country; just dial ☎ 17100, the country code and the number.

International and domestic long-distance calls can be made at hotels, but it's expensive. A cheaper alternative is to make these calls from the post office.

Another less expensive way to make an International Direct Dial (IDD) call is with a UniphoneKad telephone card, available from larger post offices. UniphoneKads can only be used in special telephones that are mainly found in large cities, sometimes in the lobbies of major hotels. The cards are issued in four amounts: 30,000d, 60,000d, 150,000d and 300,000d. The latter two cards can be used to make both domestic and international calls, while the cheaper cards work for domestic calls only.

If you live in Vietnam, you may be tempted to subscribe to a call-back service, which would greatly reduce your phone bill. However, Vietnam is one of the few countries that has made this illegal and there are draconian penalties if you get caught.

Foreigners are not permitted to make international reverse-charge (collect) calls. However, Vietnamese nationals can. Why? Because the Directorate General of Posts & Telecommunications (DGPT) earns less from a reverse-charge call than from a call paid for in Vietnam. This means that if your credit cards or travellers cheques are stolen, you are unable to make a collect call to report the loss. At best this is a major nuisance but it could prove disastrous if all your cash is stolen and you need to call abroad for help.

## Provincial Area Codes

| no | province | capital | area code (☎) |
|----|----------|---------|---------------|
| 1 | LaiChau | Dien Bien Phu | 023 |
| 2 | Lao Cai | Lao Cai | 020 |
| 3 | Ha Giang | Ha Giang | 019 |
| 4 | Cao Bang | Cao Bang | 026 |
| 5 | Lang Son | Lang Son | 025 |
| 6 | Quang Ninh | Halong City | 033 |
| 7 | Bac Giang | Bac Giang | 0240 |
| 8 | Thai Nguyen | Thai Nguyen | 0280 |
| 9 | Bac Kan | Bac Kan | 0281 |
| 10 | Tuyen Quang | Tuyen Quang | 027 |
| 11 | Yen Bai | Yen Bai | 029 |
| 12 | Son La | Son La | 022 |
| 13 | Phu Tho | Viet Tri | 0210 |
| 14 | Vinh Phuc | Vinh Yen | 0211 |
| 16 | Bac Ninh | Bac Ninh | 0241 |
| 17 | Hai Duong | Hai Duong | 0320 |
| 19 | Thai Binh | Thai Binh | 036 |
| 20 | Hung Yen | Hung Yen | 0321 |
| 21 | Ha Tay | Ha Dong | 034 |
| 22 | Hoa Binh | Hoa Binh | 018 |
| 23 | Ha Nam | Ha Nam | 0351 |
| 24 | Nam Dinh | Nam Dinh | 0350 |
| 25 | Ninh Binh | Ninh Binh | 030 |
| 26 | Thanh Hoa | Thanh Hoa | 037 |
| 27 | Nghe An | Vinh | 038 |
| 28 | Ha Tinh | Ha Tinh | 039 |
| 29 | Quang Binh | Dong Hoi | 052 |
| 30 | Quang Tri | Dong Ha | 053 |
| 31 | Thua Thien-Hué | Hué | 054 |
| 33 | Quang Nam | Tam Ky | 510 |
| 34 | Quang Ngai | Quang Ngai | 055 |
| 35 | Kon Tum | Kon Tum | 060 |
| 36 | Binh Dinh | Qui Nhon | 056 |
| 37 | Gia Lai | Pleiku | 059 |
| 38 | Phu Yen | Tuy Hoa | 057 |
| 39 | Dac Lac | Buon Ma Thuot | 050 |
| 40 | Khanh Hoa | Nha Trang | 058 |
| 41 | Ninh Thuan | Phan Rang | 068 |
| 42 | Lam Dong | Dalat | 063 |
| 43 | Binh Phuoc | Dong Xoai | 0651 |
| 44 | Tay Ninh | Tay Ninh | 066 |
| 45 | Binh Duong | Thu Dau Mot | 0650 |
| 46 | Dong Nai | Bien Hoa | 061 |
| 47 | Binh Thuan | Phan Thiet | 062 |
| 48 | Ba Ria | Vung Tau | 064 |
| 50 | Long An | Tan An | 072 |
| 51 | Tien Giang | Mytho | 073 |
| 52 | Ben Tre | Ben Tre | 075 |
| 53 | Tra Vinh | Tra Vinh | 074 |
| 54 | Vinh Long | Vinh Long | 070 |
| 55 | Dong Thap | Cao Lanh | 067 |
| 56 | An Giang | Long Xuyen | 076 |
| 57 | Kien Giang | Rach Gia | 077 |
| 58 | Cantho | Cantho | 071 |
| 59 | Soc Trang | Soc Trang | 079 |
| 60 | Bac Lieu | Bac Lieu | 0781 |
| 61 | Camau | Camau | 0780 |

| no | municipality | area code (☎) |
|----|--------------|---------------|
| 15 | Hanoi | 04 |
| 18 | Haiphong City | 031 |
| 32 | Danang City | 0511 |
| 49 | Ho Chi Minh City | 08 |

**Domestic Calls** Except for some special numbers (eg, the fire brigade and directory assistance), all phone numbers in Hanoi and HCMC have seven digits. Outside those two cities, phone numbers have six digits.

Telephone area codes are assigned according to province (see the Provincial Area Codes table).

Local calls can usually be made from any hotel or restaurant phone and are often free. You should, however, confirm this with your hotel so you don't receive any unpleasant surprises when you check out.

Domestic long-distance calls are reasonably priced and cheaper if you dial direct.

Any call between Hanoi and HCMC at the full daytime rate will cost approximately 4000d per minute. You can save up to 20% by calling between 10pm and 5am.

**Mobile (Cellular) Phones** As in many developing countries, Vietnam is putting a lot of money into its cellular network. Vietnam uses GSM 900/1800, which is compatible with most of Asia, Europe and Australia but not with the North American GSM 1900 or the totally different system in Japan. If you have a GSM phone, check with your service provider about using it in Vietnam, and beware of calls being routed internationally (very expensive for a 'local' call).

Resident foreigners can apply for a cellular phone in most major cities. Foreign tourists can make a cellular call using their own phones provided they are on the GSM system and acquire a SIM card providing them with a local number to use in Vietnam. SIM cards cost 150,000d, and prepaid calling cards in different denominations are available. Rental mobile phones with prepaid fees are also available.

Rival companies Vina Phone and Mobi Phone have battled it out in the mobile-phone market by price cutting and offering clever promotions to attract new customers. Both of these companies have offices and branches nationwide.

Be aware that mobile-phone numbers in Vietnam start with the prefixes ☎ 0903 or ☎ 0913, and naturally cost more to call than a local number.

**Fax**
Most post offices and hotels offer domestic and international fax, (and telegraph and telex) services. Hotels are likely to charge more than the post office.

**Email & Internet Access**
Today the Internet is widely available in tourist centres such as Hanoi, HCMC, Hoi An, Hué, Danang, Nha Trang and Dalat. You'll find everything from trendy cyber-cafés to computer terminals in the lobbies of hotels and guesthouses. You can also find public Internet access in many Vietnamese post offices.

The cost of Internet access generally ranges from 100d to 500d per minute, depending on where you are and what the competition is like. Printing usually costs around 1000d per page, and scanning about 2000d a page.

Most travellers in Vietnam rely on cyber-cafés and other public-access points to send and check email. In Vietnam, Hotmail tends to download much slower than Yahoo! Mail. However, either can be sluggish, so you may want to bring a book to read while you surf the Net.

If you use cybercafés, you'll need to carry three pieces of information with you to enable you to access your Internet mail account: your incoming (POP or IMAP) mail server name, your account name and your password. Your ISP or network supervisor will be able to give you these. Armed with this information, you should be able to access your email account from any Net-connected machine in Vietnam, provided it runs some kind of email software (remember that Netscape and Internet Explorer both have mail modules). It pays to become familiar with the process for doing this before you leave home. Another option is to open a free **ekno** (Ⓦ *www.ekno.lonelyplanet .com*) email account online. You can then access your mail from anywhere in the world from any Net-connected machine.

Travelling with a portable computer is a great way to stay in touch with life back home, but unless you know what you're doing it's fraught with potential problems.

If you plan to carry your notebook or palm-top computer with you, remember that the power supply voltage in the countries you visit may vary from that at home, risking damage to your equipment. The best investment is a universal AC adapter for your appliance, which will enable you to plug it in anywhere without frying the innards. You'll also need a plug adapter for each country you visit – often it's easiest to buy these before you leave home.

A major boon for laptop travellers is the recent debut of prepaid Internet-access cards that can provide you with nationwide dial up to the Net. **FPT** (☎ 08-821 4160; ⓦ www .hcm.fpt.com) is one of Vietnam's largest ISPs, and its Internet card is sold in most cities (look for the 'FPT' signs). Cards have a scratch-off password and usually come in denominations of 100,000d.

Users of the Internet cards do, however, need to be aware that there is one potential catch. Even though technically they are local calls, when dialling up local access numbers ☎ 1260 and ☎ 1280 from hotels, you will often be charged by the minute. So be *very* sure to check with your hotel – even show them the access number you plan to use – to know how much they charge for the call, and if the charge is a flat rate or per minute. If they charge the latter, you may actually find it cheaper to check your email at an Internet café.

## INTERNET RESOURCES

The World Wide Web is a rich resource for travellers. You can research your trip, hunt down bargain air fares, book hotels, check on weather conditions or chat with locals and other travellers about the best places to visit (or avoid!).

There's no better place to start your Web explorations than at **Lonely Planet** (ⓦ www .lonelyplanet.com). Here you'll find succinct summaries on travelling to most places on earth, postcards from other travellers, and the Thorn Tree bulletin board, where you can ask questions before you go or dispense advice when you get back. You can also find travel news and updates to many of our most popular guidebooks, and the subWWWay

section links you to useful travel resources elsewhere on the Web.

Ironically some of the best online information about Vietnam originates in its old nemesis, the USA. Many online authors are overseas Vietnamese, living in the USA and elsewhere. The Internet changes from day to day, so anything we can say about websites is likely to become dated fast. The following websites are also worth a look.

Everything Vietnam (ⓦ www.everything vietnam.com) is a relatively new site, developed by an American expat living in Hanoi, with tips on where to eat, drink and sleep in Vietnam's big cities.

Jewels of the Mekong Delta (ⓦ www .travelmedia.com/mekong/) features travel information and news about countries along the Mekong River (Vietnam, Cambodia, Laos, Myanmar and Thailand).

Motorbiking Vietnam (ⓦ www.motor bikingvietnam.com), replete with pictures, is the site for two-wheel enthusiasts who are considering a tour of the country.

Things Asian (ⓦ www.thingsasian.com) is brimming with information on the culture of Vietnam, everything from architecture to literature and fashion.

Vietnam Adventures Online (ⓦ www .vietnamadventures.com) is another fine site full of practical travel information that features monthly adventures and special travel deals.

Vietnam Online (ⓦ www.vietnamonline .com) is loaded with useful travel lore and boasts good coverage on employment and business opportunities in Vietnam.

Vietnam Travel (ⓦ www.vietnam-travel .com) is also dedicated to travel in Vietnam, and has an interesting selection of links.

## BOOKS

Take at least a few books with you, since purchasing books within Vietnam is a hit or miss (mostly miss) affair.

Most books are published in different editions by publishers in different countries. As a result, a book might be a hardcover rarity in one country while it's readily available in paperback in another. Fortunately, bookshops and libraries search by title or author, so your local bookshop or library is best placed to advise you on the availability of our recommendations.

There are a number of locally produced English (and some French) guidebooks for sale at bookshops in Vietnam. See Bookshops in the Hanoi and Ho Chi Minh City chapters for details on where to find them.

## Lonely Planet

Lonely Planet's *Vietnamese Phrasebook* is not only educational, but will also give you something to do during those long bus rides.

If you're after the detailed ins and outs of HCMC and Hanoi, there are LP city guides to both *Ho Chi Minh City* and *Hanoi*.

LP's *Southeast Asia on a shoestring* has general travel information for the region.

LP's *World Food Vietnam* is a compact, illustrated guide to eating and drinking your way though Vietnam, and has a handy eating and shopping vocabulary section.

## Travel

*Fragrant Palm Leaves* (Parallax Press, 1998) is a remarkable, poetic collection of journal entries by Zen monk and peace crusader Thich Nhat Hanh. He wrote both in Vietnam and the USA, during the 1960s.

*Sparring with Charlie: Motorbiking down the Ho Chi Minh Trail* by Christopher Hunt is a recent light-hearted travelogue about modern Vietnam.

In a similar vein is *Ten Years After* by Tim Page. This impressive book boasts '12-months worth of photos taken 10 years after the war'. The author also returned to Vietnam to write *Derailed in Uncle Ho's Victory Garden*.

*Vietnam Notebook* is an insightful collection of essays about the country by Murray Hiebert, the Hanoi correspondent for the *Far Eastern Economic Review*.

*A Dragon Apparent* is about author Norman Lewis' fascinating journeys through Vietnam, Laos and Cambodia in 1950.

Karin Muller's *Hitchhiking Vietnam* (1998) is a travelogue detailing a woman's tumultuous seven-month journey through Vietnam. Her story is also online at W www .pbs.com/hitchhikingvietnam/index.html.

Part-memoir and part-travel narrative, *Catfish and Mandala* (1999) is Vietnamese-American Andrew X Pham's fascinating account of his escape from the war-torn Vietnam of 1977 and his subsequent return two decades later, equipped with a bicycle and a need to work out his own mixed-up cultural identity.

In *Yak Pizza To Go! – Travels in an Age of Vanishing Cultures & Extinction* (Minerva Press, 2001) Hanoi resident Phil Karber takes his readers on a wild series of journeys to far flung corners of the Earth, including Vietnam.

## Wildlife

Useful books about Vietnam's wildlife are few and far between, and unfortunately some of the better Vietnamese language books are out of print. *A Guide to the Birds of Thailand* by Philip Round & Boonsong Lakagul (Saha Kam Bhaet Company, 1991) covers the majority if not all of Vietnam's birds. It's particularly relevant to the bird species in the southern and central regions of Vietnam.

*A Field Guide to the Birds of South-East Asia* by Ben King, Martin Woodcock & Edward Dickinson is slightly out of date and difficult to use, but it has thorough coverage of Vietnam. These two books are not available in Vietnam, but you should be able to find them in Bangkok at **Asia Books** (☎ 02-252 7277; Soi 15, 221 Thanon Sukhumvit).

## History & Politics

*Shadows and Wind* by journalist Robert Templer is a snappily written exploration of contemporary Vietnam, from Ho Chi Minh personality cults to Vietnam's rock-and-roll youngsters.

*Vietnam: Politics, Economics and Society* by Melanie Beresford gives a good overview of post-reunification Vietnam.

During Vietnam's colonial period, French researchers wrote quite a number of works on Vietnam's cultural history and archaeology that remain unsurpassed. Several good books on the Chams include: *Les États Hinduisés d'Indochine et d'Indonésie* by Georges Coedes (1928), *L'Art du Champa et*

*Son Evolution* by Philippe Stern (1942) and *Le Royaume du Champa* by Georges Maspero (1928). *Les Arts du Champa: Architecture et Sculpture* by Tran Ky Phuong, curator of the Cham Museum in Danang and Vietnam's foremost Cham scholar, was published in the early 1990s.

*The Birth of Vietnam* by Keith Weller Taylor tackles the country's early history under Chinese rule.

*The Vietnamese Gulag* by Doan Van Toai tells of one man's experiences in the post-reunification re-education camps.

For a very readable account of Vietnamese history from prehistoric times until the fall of HCMC, try Stanley Karnow's *Vietnam: A History*, which was published as a companion volume to the American Public Broadcasting Service (PBS) series *Vietnam: A Television History*.

A number of biographies of Ho Chi Minh have been written, including *Ho Chi Minh: A Political Biography* by Jean Lacouture and *Ho* by David Halberstam.

*Caodai Spiritism: A Study of Religion in Vietnamese Society* by Victor L Oliver is a most scholarly work.

An excellent reference work is *Viet Nam Danh Lam Co Tu* (Vietnam's Famous Ancient Pagodas), which was written in Vietnamese, English, French and Chinese. It's published by the Social Sciences Publishing House and you should be able to find copies in HCMC and Hanoi.

## Fiction

Perhaps the most popular and best known contemporary Vietnamese author is dissident writer Duong Thu Huong, whose books are now banned in Vietnam for their 'subversive' content. *Paradise of the Blind*, the first Vietnamese novel to be published in the USA, is set in a northern village and a Hanoi slum and recalls the lives of three women and the hardships they faced over some 40 years. Huong's *Novel Without a Name* is a captivating story of the horrors and losses of the American War from the perspective of North Vietnamese soldiers. Her latest work, *Memories of a Pure Spring*, tells the powerful tale of a romance between

the leader of a wartime musical troupe and a singer in the group he marries.

Pulitzer Prize–winning author Robert Owen Butler's *A Good Scent from a Strange Mountain* is a captivating series of stories, written from the first person perspective of overseas Vietnamese, living in southern states of the USA. Butler has been widely praised for his astute understanding of Vietnamese people and culture.

*The Sacred Willow* by Duong Van Mai Elliot spans four tumultuous generations of an upper-class Vietnamese family. This enlightening historical memoir traces French colonisation, WWII and the wars with the French and Americans.

*Vietnam: A Traveller's Literary Companion* is an engaging collection of stories by various Vietnamese writers, ranging from folklore and the tragedy of war to love and family ties.

*The Other Side of Heaven* is a unique and well-balanced anthology of postwar fiction, alternating between Vietnamese and US writers.

Two other laudable collections of contemporary fiction from Vietnamese writers are Le Minh Khue's *The Stars, The Earth, The River*, a set of stories on politics and war told from a female perspective, and *Behind the Red Mist* by Ho Anh Thai, one of Vietnam's most important post-war generation authors.

Graham Greene's 1954 novel *The Quiet American*, which is set during the last days of French colonial rule, is probably the most famous Western work of fiction on Vietnam. Much of the action takes place at HCMC's Continental Hotel and at the Caodai complex in Tay Ninh.

*The Lover* is a fictional love story by Marguerite Duras, set in Saigon during the 1930s. It has also been made into a major motion picture.

## Hill Tribes

*Ethnic Minorities of Vietnam* by Dang Nghiem Van presents an English-language ethnographic overview of Vietnam's population and is available in major Hanoi and HCMC bookstores.

For a deeper study, look for Joachim Schliesinger's two-volume *Hill Tribes of Vietnam*. Volume 1 provides an introduction and overview, while Volume 2 introduces detailed profiles of the various hill-tribe groups. Asia Books in Bangkok is a good place to look for these titles.

## Franco–Viet Minh War

Worthwhile books covering this topic include Peter M Dunn's *The First Vietnam War* and two works by Bernard B Fall, *Street Without Joy: Indochina at War 1946–54* (1961) and *Hell in a Very Small Place: The Siege of Dien Bien Phu* (1967).

## American War

What the West calls the Vietnam War, the Vietnamese call the American War. Whatever you call it, there are whole libraries of books on the topic.

The earliest days of US involvement in Indochina – when the US Office of Strategic Services (OSS; predecessor of the Central Intelligence Agency or CIA) was providing funding and weapons to Ho Chi Minh at the end of WWII – are recounted in *Why Vietnam?*, a riveting work by Archimedes L Patti. He was the head of the OSS team in Vietnam and was at Ho Chi Minh's side when he declared Vietnam independent in 1945.

*The Making of a Quagmire* by David Halberstam (1965) is one of the best accounts of America's effort in the war during the early 1960s.

Three of the finest essays on the war are collected in *The Real War* by Jonathan Schell.

An overview of the conflict is provided by George C Herring's *America's Longest War*.

*Fire in the Lake* by Francis Fitzgerald (1972) is a superb history of American involvement in Vietnam; it received the Pulitzer Prize, the National Book Award and the Bancroft Prize for History.

Perhaps the best Vietnamese autobiographical account of the American War is Le Ly Hayslip's captivating *When Heaven and Earth Changed Places*.

A highly acclaimed biographical account of the US war effort is *A Bright Shining Lie: John Paul Vann & America in Vietnam* by Neil Sheehan; it won both the Pulitzer Prize and the National Book Award.

Another fine biography is Tim Bowden's *One Crowded Hour,* which details the life of Australian film journalist Neil Davis. He was responsible for shooting some of the most famous footage of the war, including that of the North Vietnamese tank crashing through the gate of the Presidential Palace in Saigon in 1975.

Two good accounts of the fall of South Vietnam are *The Fall of Saigon* by David Butler and *55 Days: The Fall of South Vietnam* by Alan Dawson.

Perhaps the best book about the fall is *Decent Interval* by Frank Snepp. Except for pirated editions sold in Vietnam itself, it's out of print and for a very interesting reason. The author was the CIA's chief strategy analyst in Vietnam, but he broke his contract with the CIA by publishing this book (CIA agents are prohibited from publishing anything about their work). The US government sued Snepp and all the royalties that he earned from book sales were confiscated. Copies of the book can still be found in some public libraries.

*Brother Enemy* by Nayan Chanda is highly recommended. This is not actually a book about the war, but about its immediate aftermath. Chanda was a correspondent for the *Far Eastern Economic Review* and was in Saigon when it fell.

An oft-cited analysis of where US military strategy in Vietnam went wrong is *On Strategy* by Colonel Harry G Summers Jr.

*The Pentagon Papers*, a massive top-secret history of the US role in Indochina, was commissioned by Defence Secretary Robert McNamara in 1967 and published amid a great furore by the *New York Times* in 1971.

A story mostly neglected by writers is the painful experience of the fatherless Amerasian children left behind in Vietnam after 1975. The whole sordid tale is told in unforgettable detail in *Vietnamerica* by Thomas Bass.

The coffee-table book *Requiem* (1997) features a powerful collection of images shot by combat photographers (both foreign and South and North Vietnamese) who died while on assignment in Vietnam and Indochina.

**Australia** The involvement of Australia in the American War is covered in *Australia's Vietnam*, a collection of essays edited by Peter King; Frank Frost's *Australia's War in Vietnam*; Gregory Pemberton's *All the Way: Australia's Road to Vietnam*; and John J Coe's *Desperate Praise: The Australians in Vietnam*.

**Soldiers' Experiences** One of the finest books about the war is *The Sorrow of War* by Vietnamese writer Bao Ninh. The author fought for North Vietnam, but his book is by no means a piece of anti-US propaganda. On the contrary, he's cynical about the entire war and its avowed goals, and neither side comes out looking very good. The book won a literature prize in Vietnam in 1993, and English-language copies are available in Hanoi and HCMC. However, Vietnamese-language editions of the book are banned in Vietnam!

*Viet Cong Memoir* by Truong Nhu Tang is the autobiography of a Viet Cong cadre who later became disenchanted with post-1975 Vietnam.

Some of the better books about what it was like to be an American soldier in Vietnam include: *Born on the 4th of July* by Ron Kovic; the superb *Dispatches* by Michael Herr; *Chickenhawk* by Robert Mason, a stunning autobiographical account of the helicopter war; *A Rumor of War* by Philip Caputo; and *Nam* by Mark Baker. *A Piece of My Heart* by Keith Walker tells the stories of American women who served in Vietnam.

*Chained Eagle* was written by Everett Alvarez Jr, a US pilot who was imprisoned in North Vietnam for 8½ years. It recounts the horrors endured by American prisoners of war.

*Brothers in Arms* by William Broyles Jr is the story of the 1984 visit to Vietnam by an American journalist who had served as an infantry lieutenant during the war.

## FILMS
### Contemporary Vietnamese

Contemporary films by Vietnamese directors span a wide range of themes, from warfare to modern romance.

In Nguyen Khac's *The Retired General* (1988), the central character copes with adjusting from his life as a soldier during the American War to life as a civilian family man, thus symbolising Vietnam's difficult transition to the post-war era.

*Returning to Ngo Thuy*, a recent production by directors Le Manh Thich and Do Khanh Toan, revisits and pays homage to the women of Ngo Thuy village. In 1971, at the height of the American War, these women were the subject of a widely shown propaganda film aimed at encouraging people to join the war effort.

The period of *doi moi* reform in the 1980s and '90s has had a powerful influence on Vietnamese film, in particular the effects of the new market economy on women. Popular subject-matter includes how Vietnamese women contend with the struggle between traditional duty and modern desires. Vu Xuan Hung's *Misfortunes End* (1996), for example, tells the poignant tale of a Vietnamese silk weaver faced with the reality of being deserted by her two-timing husband for an upwardly mobile business woman.

Dang Nhat Minh is perhaps Vietnam's most prolific film maker. In *The Return* (1993), Minh hones in on the complexities of modern relationships, while *The Girl on the River* (1987) tells the stirring tale of a female journalist who joins an ex-prostitute in the search for her former lover and Viet Cong soldier, whose life she had saved, and whose heart she'd been promised. His tragic films *When the Tenth Morning Comes* (1984) and *Nostalgia for Countryland* (1995) tell of the hardships, suffering and loss the Vietnamese people have endured in the recent past. His latest work (1997), *Hanoi – Winter 1946*, recalls Ho Chi Minh's campaign against the French colonialists.

Though few of Vietnam's domestically produced films ever make it outside the country, young overseas-Vietnamese film directors are steadily carving a niche for themselves in the international film industry and snapping up awards at film festivals worldwide. Sadly, few of these films have been screened in Vietnam.

Tran Anh Hung's touching *The Scent of Green Papaya* (1993), which was filmed in France, celebrates the coming of age of a young peasant girl working as a servant for an affluent Saigon family during the 1950s. *Cyclo*, Tran Anh Hung's visually stunning masterpiece, digs to the core of HCMC's gritty underworld. His latest film, the French-language production *La Verticale de l'été* (2000) tells the story of three Hanoian sisters and the borderless bonds of kinship.

Vietnamese-American Tony Bui made a splash in 1999 with his exquisite feature debut *Three Seasons* (1999). Set in present-day HCMC, this beautifully made film weaves together the lives of four unlikely characters and their interplay with a US war veteran (fleshed out on the screen by Harvey Keitel) who comes to Vietnam in search of his long lost, grown-up daughter.

Lesser-known overseas-Vietnamese film makers include Van Phan Sylvian, whose post-war documentary *Goodbye Vietnam* focuses on the hardships of Vietnam's mixed race 'Amerasian' children left behind by Western soldiers and the discrimination they've had to face at home and abroad.

## Contemporary Western Films

The Americans might have lost the American War, but Hollywood has spent the last 30 years claiming a moral victory on screen. The best offerings reflect the futility of war, but rarely offer a balanced portrayal of the Vietnamese people. Instead, the focus is on American soldiers as multiple victims – of the Viet Cong; the US government, which sent them to war and cheated them of their youth; and their own society, which, sadly, shunned them when they returned – often suffering from extreme mental and physical illnesses.

Director Oliver Stone made the fascinating movie *Heaven and Earth*, adapted from Vietnamese-born American immigrant Le Ly Hayslip's book *When Heaven and Earth Changed Places*. He also directed *Born on the 4th of July* based on Ron Kovic's book.

Some of the most popular war films include *Rambo*, *Full Metal Jacket*, *Platoon*, *The Deer Hunter*, *Good Morning Vietnam* and *Air America*. In 2001 Francis Ford Coppola, the director of *Godfather*, released a new version of his 1979 classic, *Apocalypse Now*. The film, titled *Apocalypse Now Redux,* is the original 153-minute epic as well as nearly an hour of previously unseen footage.

The lead role of Harold G Moore and Joseph L Galloway's action-packed saga *We Were Soldiers* was fleshed out on the big screen in 2002 by Mel Gibson. Written and directed by Randall Wallace, the film hit the top of the charts.

French films include *Indochine* (colonialist nostalgia with Catherine Deneuve) and Pierre Schoendoerffer's *Dien Bien Phu*, which examines the human side of the French–Viet Minh war and the last days of French-colonial rule. Amazingly, it was filmed in Vietnam with the full cooperation of the Vietnamese government.

## CD ROMS

*Passage to Vietnam* was produced by Rick Smolan, who created the famed *Day in the Life* series. It is a collection of beautiful photos and narratives.

## NEWSPAPERS & MAGAZINES

*Vietnam News* (5000d) is a daily English-language newspaper. Despite the name, it contains relatively little news about Vietnam. Most of the stories (including the sports section) cover foreign news. If you are really desperate for some news of the outside world, it will do in a pinch. It's also good for wrapping fish.

The *Saigon Times Daily* (3000d) is also daily English-language paper. Published by the same company, the *Saigon Times* is a weekly magazine heavy on business news, with a few light features.

One of Vietnam's best magazines is the monthly *Vietnam Economic Times (VET)*. It provides a strong, well-rounded monthly news summary and its free insert, the *Guide*, is an excellent source of leisure information. The *Guide* can be picked up in hotels, bars and restaurants in larger cities.

You might also look out for the weekly English-language broadsheet *Vietnam Investment Review (VIR)*. Its free supplement, *Time Out*, may be useful for finding out what's going on in HCMC and Hanoi, but its focus is on the expat scene, which is of little interest to travellers.

Although the Vietnam National Administration of Tourism (VNAT) has yet to open any tourist offices, in 2002 it launched a commendable monthly English-language travel magazine called *Vietnam Discovery*. It costs 15,000d an issue, but free copies can usually be found at popular bars, restaurants and hotels in Hanoi and HCMC.

Imported newspapers and magazines are readily available in HCMC, Hanoi and other large cities. Elsewhere it's slim pickings.

## RADIO

The Voice of Vietnam broadcasts on short wave, AM and FM for about 18 hours a day. The broadcasts consist mostly of music, but there are also news bulletins in Vietnamese, English, French and Russian.

The first broadcast of the Voice of Vietnam took place in 1945. It broadcast a great deal of propaganda to the South during the American War, including special English programmes for American soldiers. From 1968 to 1976, the Voice of Vietnam used the transmitters of Radio Havana Cuba to deliver its message directly to the American people.

The national radio station broadcasts news and music programmes from 7am until 11pm. Visitors wishing to keep up on events in the rest of the world – and in Vietnam itself – may want to bring along a small short-wave receiver. News, music and feature programmes in a multitude of languages are easily picked up, especially at night.

## TV
### Local TV

The first TV programme was broadcast in Vietnam in 1970 and it's fair to say that the

content has improved since then. There are currently five channels broadcasting in Hanoi and HCMC, and two channels elsewhere. News programmes in English, French and Chinese follow the last broadcast (sometime after 10pm). Sometimes soccer or other sports come on at strange hours, for example 3.30am. Each province in Vietnam has a local channel, but you won't find much in English on these.

### Satellite TV

Satellite TV is now widely available, which is a boon for some foreign visitors. You're most likely to find it in an ever-increasing number of hotels, as well as cafés and pubs. Hong Kong's Star TV is one popular station, along with CNN, the Sports Channel, CNBC Asia and MTV. TV5 Asie is a French-language cable station which is usually pumped in where satellite TV is offered.

## VIDEO SYSTEMS

It's hard to know what is Vietnam's official video standard. That's because most new TV sets and video players sold in Vietnam are multistandard: PAL, NTSC and Secam.

Nowadays with the number of cheap (mostly pirated) DVDs and VCDs around, many Vietnamese are abandoning their VCRs for DVD and VCD players. You can pick up decent DVD players in Vietnam (the ones imported from China cost less than two million dong).

## PHOTOGRAPHY & VIDEO
### Film & Equipment

Colour print film (35mm and APS) is widely available, but check the expiry date printed on the box. Avoid buying film from outdoor souvenir stalls – the film may have been cooking in the sun for months. Film prices are reasonable so you really won't save much by bringing film from abroad.

Slide film can be bought in Hanoi and HCMC, but don't count on it elsewhere. Supplies of black-and-white film are rapidly disappearing, so bring a supply with you.

Many tourists travel around Vietnam by van or minibus; the metal floors of these vehicles do get very hot, but you might not notice if it is air-conditioned. Many travellers have roasted their film (as well as food) by placing it in their backpacks and setting the backpack on the floor of the vehicle.

Photo-processing shops have become ubiquitous wherever tourists congregate. Most of these shops are equipped with the latest one-hour, colour-printing equipment. Printing film costs are about US$5 per roll depending on the print size you choose. The quality tends to be quite good. Be sure to specify if you want glossy or mat finish on your prints.

Colour slide film can be developed quickly (three hours) in Hanoi and HCMC, but forget it outside of those two cities. Processing costs about US$5 per roll, but most shops do not mount the slides unless you request (and pay for) it. However, our experiences with processing slides and black-and-white film have been terrible, both in terms of bad development and scratched film, so you really are better off developing them elsewhere.

Cameras are fairly expensive in Vietnam and the selection is limited – bring one from abroad. Happily, lithium batteries (which are needed for many of today's point-and-shoot cameras) and digital-camera memory cards are available in large cities.

## Restrictions

The Vietnamese police usually don't care what you photograph, but on occasion they get pernickety. Obviously, don't photograph sensitive sites such as airports, seaports, military bases and border checkpoints. Photography from aircraft (except on chartered flights) is now permitted. Don't even think of trying to get a snapshot of Ho Chi Minh in his glass sarcophagus!

Perhaps it would be wise to memorise the following message, which appears on signs in various places, *cam chup hinh va quay video*, and means 'No Photography or Video Taping'.

Some touristy sites charge an additional camera or video fee. If the staff refuse to issue a receipt for the camera fee, then you should refuse to pay – the 'fee' in that case is likely to go into their pocket.

## Photographing People

Photographing anyone, particularly hill-tribe people, demands patience and the utmost respect for local customs. The beauty and diversity of the Vietnamese people and the scenery provides ample opportunity, but it is important to remember you are just a visitor and that not only may your actions be interpreted as rude or offensive, but your behaviour will influence the reception of future visitors. That is not to say that taking pictures is bad, but just keep in mind the various effects a camera can have.

Whatever you do, photograph with discretion and manners. It's always polite to ask first and if the person says no, don't take the photo. A gesture, a smile and a nod are all that is usually necessary. Remember, wherever you are in Vietnam, the people are *not* exotic birds of paradise.

The popular weekend market in Sapa is a good example of where a crowd of camera-toting tourists can actually be downright overwhelming to the local folk. While the entrepreneurial Hmong and Red Dzao people do not generally mind being photographed (buying some handicrafts will help facilitate this), others tend to be camera-shy and have had their fair share of 'must-get-this-shot' photographers literally chasing them through the market!

Like their Japanese and Chinese counterparts, Vietnamese people seem to have a near obsession with collecting hundreds (or thousands) of photos of themselves posing in front of something. The pose is always the same: a stiff, frontal shot, hands at the sides etc. The result is that all of their photos look nearly identical. The purpose of the photos seems to be to prove that they've been to a particular place. Since many Vietnamese cannot afford their own camera, most famous tourist sites have a team of local photographers ready to snap pictures. Some photographers will get the film processed and mail it to their customers, while others will shoot a roll and hand it over unprocessed.

Most Vietnamese cannot understand why Westerners shoot dozens of rolls of film without posing in each and every frame.

Furthermore, when Westerners proudly show off their best photographs, Vietnamese look at them and say that the photos are 'boring' because there are seldom any people in them.

## Airport Security

The dreaded x-ray machines at Vietnam's airports are no longer a problem – the old Soviet-made 'microwave ovens' that had a habit of frying your film have been replaced with modern, film-safe equipment from Germany. However, it is hazardous if you attempt to film the airport security procedures (the film will most likely be ripped out of your camera).

Of greater concern are the new-fangled, high-powered x-ray machines that are gradually being installed in airports in other parts of Asia, Europe and the Americas. To avoid possible x-ray damage from these machines, you should always carry your film in your hand luggage, and even if the sign says 'X-ray Safe' insist, politely, on a hand-check.

The authorities seem to be far more sensitive about video-tape material than film. Surprisingly, it's more of a problem when exiting the country than entering (logically you would think the opposite). Fortunately these checks are aimed more at commercial film makers so your holiday footage will probably be excluded.

## TIME

Vietnam, like Thailand, is seven hours ahead of Greenwich Mean Time/Universal Time Coordinated (GMT/UTC). Because of its proximity to the equator, Vietnam does not have daylight-saving or summer time. When it's noon in Vietnam it is 9pm the previous day in Los Angeles, midnight in New York, 5am in London, 1pm in Perth and 3pm in Sydney.

## ELECTRICITY

Electricity in Vietnam mostly runs at 220V (at 50Hz cycles), but often you'll find 110V (also at 50Hz). Unfortunately, looking at the shape of the outlet on the wall gives no clue as to what voltage is flowing through it. In the south, most outlets are US-style flat pins. Despite the American-inspired design, the voltage is still likely to be 220V. In the north, most outlets are the Russian-inspired round pins, which usually carry 220V. If the voltage is not marked on the socket, try finding a light bulb or appliance with the voltage written on it. Electrical sockets are two-prong only.

## WEIGHTS & MEASURES

The Vietnamese use the international metric system (see the metric conversion table at the back of this book). In addition, two weight measurements have been borrowed from the Chinese: the tael and the catty, which equals 0.6kg (1.32lb). There are 16 taels to the catty, so one tael equals 37.5g (1.32oz). Gold is always sold by the tael.

## LAUNDRY

At hotels it is usually easy to get your laundry done for the equivalent of one or two US dollars. There have, however, been a number of reports of gross overcharging at certain hotels, so make sure you ask the price beforehand.

Budget hotels do not have clothes dryers as they rely on the sunshine – so allow at least a day and a half for washing and drying, especially during the wet season.

## TOILETS

The issue of toilets and what to do with used toilet paper has caused some concern. As one traveller wrote:

*We are still not sure about the toilet paper...in two hotels they have been angry with us for flushing down the paper in the toilet. In other places it seems quite OK though.*

In general, if you see a wastepaper basket next to the toilet, that is where you should throw the toilet paper. The problem is that many hotels' sewage systems cannot handle toilet paper. This is especially true in old hotels, where the antiquated plumbing was designed in the pre-toilet-paper era. In rural areas there are no sewage-treatment plants. Toilet waste empties into an underground septic tank and toilet paper will really create a mess in there. For the sake of international relations, be considerate and throw the paper in the wastepaper basket.

Toilet paper is seldom provided in the toilets at bus and train stations or in other public buildings, though hotels usually supply it. You'd be wise to keep a stash of your own with you at all times while travelling.

Another thing you should be mentally prepared for is squat toilets. For the uninitiated, a squat toilet has no seat for you to sit on while reading the morning newspaper; it's a hole in the floor. The only way to flush it is to fill the conveniently placed bucket with water and pour it into the hole. While it may take some practise to get proficient at balancing yourself over a squat toilet, at least you don't need to worry about whether the toilet seat is clean. Furthermore, some experts claim squatting is better for your digestive system.

Better hotels will have Western-style ones, but squat toilets are the norm in cheaper hotels and public places (eg, restaurants).

The scarcity of public toilets seems to be a greater problem for women than for men. Vietnamese men often urinate in public; however, for women this is socially unacceptable. Women might find road-side toilet stops easier if wearing a sarong.

## HEALTH

Travel health depends on your predeparture preparations, your daily health care while travelling and how you handle any medical problem that does develop. While the potential dangers can seem quite frightening, in reality few travellers experience anything more than an upset stomach.

The significant improved in Vietnam's economy has brought with it some major improvements in public health. In the past, people were frequently malnourished and therefore highly prone to disease – this is not such a huge problem any more. In addition to this, immunisation programmes are helping to stop the spread of disease.

Rural areas can still be a problem; although foreigners with cold, hard cash will receive the best treatment available, even bars of gold

cannot buy you blood tests and x-rays when the local health clinic doesn't even have a thermometer or any aspirin. If you become seriously ill in rural Vietnam, get to HCMC or Hanoi as quickly as you can. If you need any type of surgery or other extensive treatment, don't hesitate to fly to Bangkok, Hong Kong or another reasonably developed country as soon as possible.

You can buy plenty of dangerous drugs across the counter in Vietnam without a prescription, but you should exercise restraint. Some drugs, such as steroids, make you feel great and then kill you, especially if you have an infection. Remember that drugs may not be of the same strength as in other countries, or may have deteriorated due to age or poor storage conditions. Check the expiry dates on any medicines you buy. Chinese shops often sell herbal medicines imported from China.

If you need special medication then take it with you.

The addresses and telephone numbers of the best medical facilities in Vietnam can be found under the Information section of the Ho Chi Minh City and Hanoi chapters. These are the only two cities where you are likely to find health facilities that come close to meeting developed-country standards.

## Predeparture Planning

**Immunisations** Plan ahead for getting your vaccinations: some of them require more than one injection, while others should not be given together. Note that some should not be given during pregnancy or to people with allergies – discuss this with your doctor.

It is recommended that you seek medical advice at least six weeks before travel. Be aware that there is often a greater risk of disease with children and during pregnancy. For more details about the diseases themselves, see the individual disease entries later in this section. Although there are currently no mandatory vaccinations for travellers to Vietnam, it is best to carry proof of your vaccinations.

For information on current immunisation recommendations for Vietnam, contact the international team of doctors at the **Family Medical Practice** (e hfmedprac.kot@fmail.vnn.vn; w www.doctorkot.com) in Hanoi and HCMC. They can provide the latest on vaccinations, malaria and dengue fever status (in real time), and offer general medical advice regarding Vietnam.

Discuss your requirements with your doctor, but vaccinations you should consider for this trip include the following:

- cholera
- diphtheria & tetanus
- hepatitis A
- hepatitis B
- Japanese B encephalitis
- polio
- rabies
- tuberculosis
- typhoid
- yellow fever

## Malaria Medication

Antimalarial drugs don't prevent infection, but kill the malaria parasites during their development and significantly reduce the risk of becoming very ill or dying. Expert advice on medication should be sought, as there are many factors to consider, including: the area to be visited; risk of exposure to malaria-carrying mosquitoes; side effects of the medication; your medical history, age

and whether you are pregnant. Travellers to isolated areas in high-risk regions such as Camau and Bac Lieu provinces and the rural south may like to carry a treatment dose of medication for use if symptoms occur.

## Health Insurance

Make sure you have adequate health insurance; see Travel Insurance in the Visas & Documents section earlier in this chapter.

## Travel Health Guides

Lonely Planet's *Healthy Travel Asia* is a handy pocket size and packed with useful information on pretrip planning, emergency first aid, immunisation and disease, plus what to do if you get sick on the road.

Lonely Planet's *Travel with Children* includes advice on travel health for younger children. There are also some excellent travel-health websites on the Internet. **Lonely Planet** (w www.lonelyplanet.com) has links to the World Health Organization (WHO) and the US Centers for Disease Control & Prevention.

## Other Preparations

Make sure you're healthy before you start travelling. If you are going on a long trip make sure your teeth are OK. If you wear glasses take a spare pair and your prescription with you. If you require a particular medication, take an adequate supply because it may not be available locally. Take part of the packaging showing the generic name rather than the brand, which will make getting replacements easier. It's a good idea to have a legible prescription or letter from your doctor to show that you can legally use the medication to avoid any problems.

## Basic Rules

**Food** There is an old colonial adage which says 'If you can cook it, boil it or peel it you can eat it…otherwise forget it.' Vegetables and fruit should be washed with purified water or peeled where possible. Beware of ice cream sold in the street or anywhere it might have melted and been refrozen; if there's any doubt (eg, a power cut in the last day or two), steer well clear.

## Traditional Healing Techniques

There are a number of traditional medical treatments practised in Vietnam. Herbal medicine, much of it imported from China, is widely available and sometimes surprisingly effective. As with Western medicine, self-diagnosis is not advisable – see a doctor. Traditional Chinese doctors are found wherever a large Chinese community exists, including HCMC, Hanoi and Hoi An.

If you visit traditional Chinese doctors, you might be surprised by what they discover about your body. For example, the doctor will almost certainly take your pulse and then may perhaps tell you that you have a 'slippery' or 'thready' pulse. They have identified more than 30 different kinds of pulses. A pulse could be empty, prison, leisurely, bowstring, irregular or even regularly irregular. The doctor may then examine your tongue to see if it is slippery, dry, pale, greasy, has a thick coating or possibly no coating at all. The doctor, having discovered your ailment, eg, wet heat, as evidenced by a slippery pulse and a red greasy tongue, will prescribe the proper herbs for your condition.

Once you have a diagnosis you may be treated by moxibustion, a traditional treatment whereby various types of herbs, rolled into what looks like a ball of fluffy cotton, are held near the skin and ignited. A slight variation of this method is to place the herb on a slice of ginger and then ignite it. The idea is to apply the maximum amount of heat possible without burning the patient. This heat treatment is supposed to be very good for diseases such as arthritis.

It is common to see Vietnamese people with long bands of red welts on their necks, foreheads and backs. Don't worry, this is not some kind of hideous skin disease, but rather a treatment known as *cao gio*, literally 'scrape wind'. In traditional Vietnamese folk medicine, many illnesses are attributed to 'poisonous wind', which can be released by applying eucalyptus oil or tiger balm and scraping the skin with a spoon or coin, thus raising the welts. The results aren't pretty, but the locals say this treatment is good for the common cold, fatigue, headaches and other ailments. Whether the cure hurts less than the disease is something one can only judge from experience.

Another technique to battle bad breezes is called *giac hoi*. This one employs suction cups, typically made of bamboo or glass, which are placed on the patient's skin. A burning piece of alcohol-soaked cotton is briefly put inside the cup to drive out the air before it is applied. As the cup cools, a partial vacuum is produced, leaving a nasty-looking, but harmless, red circular mark on the skin, which goes away in a few days.

Can you cure people by sticking needles into them? The adherents of acupuncture say you can and they have some solid evidence to back them up. For example, some major surgical operations have been performed using acupuncture as the only anaesthetic (this works best on the head). In this case, a small electric current (from batteries) is passed through the needles.

Becoming a human pin cushion might not sound pleasant, but if done properly it doesn't hurt. Knowing where to insert the needle is crucial. Acupuncturists have identified more than 2000 insertion points, but only about 150 are commonly used. The exact mechanism by which it works is not fully understood. Practitioners talk of energy channels or meridians that connect the needle insertion point to the particular organ, gland or joint being treated. The acupuncture point is sometimes quite far from the area of the body being treated.

Non-sterile acupuncture needles pose a genuine health risk in this era of AIDS. You would be wise to purchase your own accupuncture needles if you plan on having this treatment in Vietnam.

LPP

Shellfish, such as mussels, oysters and clams, should be avoided, as well as undercooked meat, particularly in the form of mince. Steaming does not make shellfish safe for eating.

If a place looks clean and well run and the vendor also looks clean and healthy, then the food is probably safe. In general, places that are packed with travellers or locals will be fine, while empty restaurants may be questionable. The food in busy restaurants is cooked and eaten quite quickly, with little standing around and probably without being reheated.

**Water** The number one rule is *be careful of the water*. Ice can be particularly risky; if you don't know for certain that the water is safe, assume the worst. Reputable brands of bottled water or soft drinks are generally fine, although in some places bottles may be refilled with tap water. Only use water from containers with a serrated seal – not tops or corks. Take care with fruit juice, particularly if water may have been added. Milk should be treated with suspicion as it is often unpasteurised, though boiled milk is fine if it is kept hygienically. Tea or coffee should also be OK, since the water should have been boiled.

The simplest way of purifying water is to boil it thoroughly. Vigorous boiling should be satisfactory; however, at high altitude water boils at a lower temperature, so germs are less likely to be killed. Make sure you boil it for longer in these environments.

Consider purchasing a water filter for a long trip. There are two main kinds of filter. Total filters take out all parasites, bacteria and viruses and make water safe to drink. They are often expensive, but they can be more cost effective than buying bottled water. Simple filters, (which can even be a nylon mesh bag), take out dirt and larger foreign bodies from the water so that chemical solutions work much more effectively; if water is dirty, chemical solutions may not work at all.

It's very important when buying a filter to read the specifications, so that you know exactly what it removes from the water and what it doesn't. Simple filtering will not remove all dangerous organisms, so if you cannot boil water, it should be treated chemically. Chlorine tablets will kill many pathogens, but not some parasites, such as giardia and amoebic cysts. Iodine is more effective in purifying water and is available in tablet form. Follow the directions carefully and remember that too much iodine can be harmful.

## Medical Problems & Treatment

Self-diagnosis and treatment can be risky, so you should always seek medical help. An embassy, consulate or hotel can usually recommend a local doctor or clinic. Although we do give drug dosages in this section, they

## Nutrition

If your diet is poor or limited in variety, if you're travelling hard and fast and therefore missing meals or if you simply lose your appetite, you can soon start to lose weight and place your health at risk.

Make sure your diet is well balanced. Cooked eggs, tofu, beans, lentils (dhal in India) and nuts are all safe ways to get protein. Fruit you can peel (bananas, oranges or mandarins, for example) is usually safe and a good source of vitamins. Melons can harbour bacteria in their flesh and are best avoided. Try to eat plenty of grains (including rice) and bread. Remember that although food is generally safer if it is cooked well, overcooked food loses much of its nutritional value. If your diet isn't well balanced or if your food intake is insufficient, it's a good idea to take vitamin and iron pills.

In hot climates make sure you drink enough – don't rely on feeling thirsty to indicate when you should drink. Not needing to urinate or voiding small amounts of very dark yellow urine is a danger sign. Always carry a water bottle with you on long trips. Excessive sweating can lead to loss of salt and therefore muscle cramping. Salt tablets are not a good idea as a preventative, but in places where salt is not used much, adding salt to food can help.

are for emergency use only. Correct diagnosis from a qualified physician is vital. In this section we have used the generic names for medications – check with a pharmacist for brands available locally.

Note that antibiotics should ideally be administered only under medical supervision. Take only the recommended dose at the prescribed intervals and use the whole course, even if the illness seems to be cured earlier. Stop immediately if there are any serious reactions and don't use the antibiotic at all if you are unsure that you have the correct one. Some people are allergic to commonly prescribed antibiotics such as penicillin; carry this information (eg, on a bracelet) when travelling.

## Environmental Hazards

**Heat Exhaustion** Dehydration and salt deficiency can cause heat exhaustion. Take time to acclimatise to high temperatures, drink sufficient liquids and do not do anything too physically demanding.

Salt deficiency is characterised by fatigue, lethargy, headaches, giddiness and muscle cramps; salt tablets may help, but adding extra salt to your food is better.

Anhidrotic heat exhaustion is a rare form of heat exhaustion that is caused by an inability to sweat. It tends to affect people who have been in a hot climate for some time, rather than newcomers. It can progress to heatstroke. Treatment involves removal to a cooler climate.

**Heatstroke** This serious, occasionally fatal condition can occur if the body's heat-regulating mechanism breaks down and the body temperature rises to dangerous levels. Long, continuous periods of exposure to high temperatures and insufficient fluids can leave you vulnerable to heatstroke.

The symptoms are not sweating very much (or at all) and a high body temperature (39°C to 41°C or 102°F to 106°F). Where sweating has ceased, the skin becomes flushed and red. Severe, throbbing headaches and lack of coordination will also occur, and the sufferer may be confused or aggressive. Eventually the sufferer will become delirious or convulse. Hospitalisation is essential, but in the interim get victims out of the sun, remove their clothing, cover them with a wet sheet or towel

### Medical Kit Check List

You should consider including the following in your medical kit – consult your pharmacist for brands available in your country.

☐ **Aspirin or paracetamol (acetaminophen in the USA)** – for pain or fever

☐ **Antihistamine** – for allergies, eg, hay fever; to ease the itch from insect bites or stings; and to prevent motion sickness

☐ **Cold and flu tablets, throat lozenges and nasal decongestant**

☐ **Multivitamins** – consider for long trips, when your dietary vitamin intake may be inadequate

☐ **Antibiotics** – consider including these if you're travelling well off the beaten track; see your doctor, as they must be prescribed, and carry the prescription with you

☐ **Loperamide or diphenoxylate** – 'blockers' for diarrhoea

☐ **Prochlorperazine or metaclopramide** – for nausea and vomiting

☐ **Rehydration mixture** – to prevent dehydration, which may occur, for example, during bouts of diarrhoea; particularly important when travelling with children

☐ **Insect repellent, sunscreen, lip balm and eye drops**

☐ **Calamine lotion, sting relief spray or aloe vera** – to ease irritation from sunburn and insect bites or stings

☐ **Antifungal cream or powder** – for fungal skin infections and thrush

☐ **Antiseptic (such as povidone-iodine)** – for cuts and grazes

☐ **Bandages, Band-Aids (plasters) and other wound dressings**

☐ **Water purification tablets or iodine**

☐ **Scissors, tweezers and a thermometer** – note that mercury thermometers are prohibited by airlines

☐ **Sterile kit** – in case you need injections in a country with medical hygiene problems; discuss with your doctor

and then fan continually. Give fluids if they are conscious.

**Jet Lag** When a person flies across more than three time zones (each time zone usually represents a one-hour time difference), jet lag is experienced. It occurs because many of the human body's functions (such as temperature, pulse rate and emptying of the bladder and bowels) are regulated by internal 24-hour cycles. When we travel long distances rapidly, our bodies take time to adjust to the 'new time' of our destination, and we may experience fatigue, disorientation, insomnia, anxiety, impaired concentration and loss of appetite. These effects will usually be gone within three days of arrival, but to minimise the impact of jet lag:

- Rest for a couple of days prior to departure
- Try to select flight schedules that minimise sleep deprivation; arriving late in the day means you can go to sleep soon after you arrive. For very long flights, try to organise a stopover.
- Avoid excessive eating (which bloats the stomach) and alcohol (which causes dehydration) during the flight. Instead, drink plenty of noncarbonated, nonalcoholic drinks such as fruit juice or water.
- Avoid smoking
- Make yourself comfortable by wearing loose-fitting clothes and perhaps bringing an eye mask and ear plugs to help you sleep
- Try to sleep at the appropriate time for the time zone you are travelling to

**Motion Sickness** Eating lightly before and during a trip will reduce your chances of getting motion sickness. If you are prone to it, try to find a place that minimises movement: near the wing on aircraft; close to midship on boats; near the centre on buses. Fresh air usually helps; reading and cigarette smoke don't. Commercial motion-sickness preparations, which can cause drowsiness, have to be taken before the trip commences. Ginger (available in capsule form) and peppermint (including mint-flavoured sweets) are natural preventatives.

**Prickly Heat** Excessive perspiration, trapped under the skin, can cause an itchy rash called prickly heat. It usually strikes people who have just arrived in a hot climate. Keeping cool, bathing often, drying the skin and using a mild talcum or prickly heat powder, or resorting to the sanctuary of air-con may help.

**Sunburn** In the tropics, the desert or at high altitude your skin can burn surprisingly quickly, even through cloud. Use a sunscreen, a hat, and a barrier cream for your nose and lips. Calamine lotion or a commercial after-sun preparation are both good for mild sunburn. Protect your eyes with good quality sunglasses, particularly if you will be near water, sand or snow.

## Infectious Diseases

**Diarrhoea** Simple things like a change of water, food or climate can all cause a mild bout of diarrhoea, but a few rushed toilet trips with no other symptoms is not indicative of a major problem.

Dehydration is the main danger with any diarrhoea, particularly in children or the elderly, where dehydration can occur quite quickly. Under all circumstances, *fluid replacement* is the most important thing to remember. Weak black tea with a little sugar, soda water, or soft drinks allowed to go flat and diluted 50% with clean water are all good for this. With severe diarrhoea, a rehydrating solution is preferable to replace lost minerals and salt. Commercial oral-rehydration salts (ORS) are very useful; add them to boiled or bottled water. In an emergency, make up a solution of six teaspoons of sugar and a half teaspoon of salt to a litre of boiled or bottled water. You need to drink at least the same volume of fluid that you are losing in bowel movements and vomiting. Urine is the best guide to the adequacy of replacement – if you have small amounts of concentrated urine, you need to drink more. Keep drinking small amounts often. Stick to a bland diet as you recover.

Gut-paralysing drugs such as loperamide or diphenoxylate can be used to bring relief from the symptoms, although they don't really cure the problem. Only use these drugs if you do not have access to toilets or if you *must* travel. Note that these drugs are not recommended for children under 12 years.

In certain situations antibiotics may be required: diarrhoea with blood or mucus (dysentery), any diarrhoea with fever, profuse watery diarrhoea, persistent diarrhoea not improving after 48 hours and severe diarrhoea. These suggest a more serious cause of diarrhoea, and in these situations gut-paralysing drugs should be avoided.

In these situations, a stool test may be necessary to diagnose what bug is causing your diarrhoea, so you should seek medical help urgently. Where this is not possible, the recommended drugs for bacterial diarrhoea (the most likely cause of severe diarrhoea in travellers) are norfloxacin (400mg twice daily for three days) or ciprofloxacin (500mg twice daily for five days). These are not recommended for children or pregnant women. The drug of choice for children is co-trimoxazole with dosage dependent on weight. A five-day course is given. Ampicillin or amoxycillin may be given during pregnancy, but medical care is necessary.

Two other causes of persistent diarrhoea in travellers are giardiasis and amoebic dysentery. Giardiasis is caused by a common parasite, *Giardia lamblia*. Symptoms include stomach cramps, nausea, a bloated stomach, watery, foul-smelling diarrhoea and frequent gas. Giardiasis can appear several weeks after you have been exposed to the parasite. The symptoms may disappear for a few days and then return; this can go on for several weeks.

Amoebic dysentery, caused by the protozoan *Entamoeba histolytica*, is characterised by a gradual onset of low-grade diarrhoea, often with blood and mucus. Cramping abdominal pain and vomiting are less likely than in other types of diarrhoea, and fever may not be present. It will persist until treated and can recur and cause other health problems.

You should seek medical advice if you think you have giardiasis or amoebic dysentery, but where this is not possible, tinidazole (2g single dose) or metronidazole (250mg three times daily for five to 10 days) are the recommended drugs.

**Fungal Infections** Fungal infections occur more commonly in hot weather and are usually found on the scalp, between the toes (athlete's foot) or fingers, in the groin and on the body (ringworm). You get ringworm (which is a fungal infection, not a worm) from infected animals or other people. Moisture encourages these infections.

To prevent fungal infections wear loose, comfortable clothes, avoid artificial fibres, wash frequently and dry yourself carefully. If you do get an infection, wash the infected area at least daily with a disinfectant or medicated soap and water, and rinse and dry well. Apply an antifungal cream or powder such as tolnaftate. Try to expose the infected area to air or sunlight as much as possible and wash all towels and underwear in hot water, change them often and let them dry in the sun.

For women, antibiotic use, wearing synthetic underwear sweating and contraceptive pills can lead to fungal vaginal infections, especially when travelling in hot climates.

For both men and women, maintaining good personal hygiene and wearing loose-fitting clothes and cotton underwear may help prevent these infections.

**Hepatitis** This is a general term for inflammation of the liver, which is a common disease worldwide. There are several different viruses that cause hepatitis, and they differ in the way that they are transmitted. The symptoms are similar in all forms of the illness, and include fever, chills, headache, fatigue, feelings of weakness and aches and pains, followed by loss of appetite, nausea, vomiting, abdominal pain, dark urine, light-coloured faeces, jaundiced (yellow) skin and yellowing of the whites of the eyes. People who have had hepatitis should avoid alcohol for some time after the illness, as the liver usually needs time to recover.

Hepatitis A is transmitted by contaminated food and drinking water. You should seek medical advice, but there is not much you can do apart from resting, drinking lots of fluids, eating lightly and avoiding fatty foods. Hepatitis E is transmitted in the same way as hepatitis A; it can be particularly serious in pregnant women.

There are almost 300 million chronic carriers of hepatitis B in the world. It is spread through contact with infected blood, blood products or body fluids, for example, through sexual contact, unsterilised needles and blood transfusions, or contact with blood via small breaks in the skin. Other risk situations include shaving, tattooing or body piercing with contaminated equipment. The symptoms of hepatitis B may be more severe than type A and the disease can lead to long-term problems such as chronic liver damage, liver cancer or a long-term carrier state. Hepatitis C and D are spread in the same way as hepatitis B and can also lead to long-term complications.

There are vaccines against hepatitis A and B, but there are currently no vaccines against the other types. Follow the basic rules about food and water (hepatitis A and E) and avoid risk situations (hepatitis B, C and D) as important preventative measures.

**HIV & AIDS** Infection with the human immunodeficiency virus (HIV) may lead to acquired immune deficiency syndrome (AIDS), which is a fatal disease. Any exposure to blood, blood products or body fluids may put the individual at risk. The disease is often transmitted through sexual contact or used needles – vaccinations, acupuncture, tattooing and body piercing can be potentially as dangerous as intravenous drug use. HIV/AIDS can also be spread through infected blood transfusions.

If you do need an injection, ask to see the syringe unwrapped in front of you, or take a needle and syringe pack with you.

The official figures on the number of people with HIV/AIDS in Vietnam are vague. Though health-education messages relating to HIV/AIDS can be seen all over the countryside, the official line is that infection is largely limited to sex workers and drug users. Condoms are widely available throughout Vietnam.

**Intestinal Worms** These parasites are most common in rural, tropical areas. The different worms have different ways of infecting people. Some may be ingested on food such as undercooked meat (eg, tapeworms) and some enter through your skin (eg, hookworms). Infestations may not show up for some time, and although they are generally not serious, if left untreated some can cause severe health problems later. Consider having a stool test when you return home to check for these and determine the appropriate treatment.

**Schistosomiasis** Also known as bilharzia, this disease is transmitted by minute worms. They infect certain varieties of freshwater snails found in rivers, streams, lakes and particularly behind dams. The worms multiply and are eventually discharged into the water systems.

The worm enters through the skin and attaches itself to your intestines or bladder. The first symptom may be a general feeling of being unwell, or a tingling and sometimes a light rash around the area where it entered. Weeks later a high fever may develop. Once the disease is established, abdominal pain and blood in the urine are other signs. The infection often causes no symptoms until it is well established (several months to years after exposure) and damage to the internal organs irreversible.

Avoid swimming or bathing in fresh water where bilharzia is present. Even deep water can be infected. If you do get wet, dry off quickly and dry your clothes as well.

A blood test is the most reliable way to diagnose the disease, but the test will not show positive until a number of weeks after exposure.

**Sexually Transmitted Infections (STIs)** As discussed earlier, HIV/AIDS and hepatitis B can be transmitted through sexual contact. Other STIs include gonorrhoea, herpes and syphilis; sores, blisters or rashes around the genitals, and discharges or pain when urinating are common symptoms. In some STIs, such as wart virus or chlamydia, the symptoms may be less marked or not observed at all, especially in women. A chlamydia infection can cause infertility in men and women before any symptoms have been noticed.

Syphilis symptoms eventually disappear completely, but the disease continues and can cause severe problems in later years. The treatment of gonorrhoea and syphilis is with antibiotics. The different sexually transmitted diseases each require specific antibiotics.

While abstinence from sexual contact is the only 100% effective prevention, using condoms is also effective. Condoms are widely available throughout Vietnam, but when purchasing, ensure the package hasn't been stored in the sun as the rubber could have deteriorated.

**Typhoid** This dangerous gut infection is caused by contaminated water and food. Medical help must be sought.

During its early stages sufferers may feel as if they have a bad cold or flu on the way. Early symptoms include a headache, body aches and a fever that rises a little each day until it is around 40°C (104°F) or more. The victim's pulse is usually slow, relative to the degree of fever present – unlike a normal fever where the pulse increases. There may also be vomiting, abdominal pain, diarrhoea or constipation.

In the second week the high fever and slow pulse continue and a few pink spots may appear on the body; trembling, delirium, weakness, weight loss and dehydration may occur. Complications such as pneumonia, perforated bowel or meningitis may occur.

## Insect-Borne Diseases

Filariasis, Lyme disease and typhus are all insect-borne diseases, but they do not pose a great risk to travellers. For more information on these diseases, see Less Common Diseases at the end of this section.

**Malaria** This serious and potentially fatal disease is spread by mosquito bites. If you are travelling in endemic areas it is extremely important to avoid mosquito bites and to take tablets to prevent this disease. Symptoms range from fever, chills and sweating, headache, diarrhoea and abdominal pains to a vague feeling of ill-health. Seek medical help immediately if malaria is suspected. Without treatment malaria can rapidly become more serious and can be fatal.

There is a variety of medications such as mefloquine, Fansidar and Malarone. You should seek medical advice, before travelling, on the right medication and dosage for you. If medical care is not available, malaria tablets can be used for treatment. You need to take a malaria tablet that is different from the one you were taking when you contracted malaria.

Travellers are advised to prevent mosquito bites at all times. The main messages are:

- Wear light-coloured clothing, long trousers and long-sleeved shirts
- Use mosquito repellents containing the compound DEET on exposed areas (prolonged overuse of DEET may be harmful, especially to children, but its use is considered preferable to being bitten by disease-transmitting mosquitoes)
- Avoid perfumes or aftershave
- Use a mosquito net that's impregnated with mosquito repellent (permethrin) – it may be worth taking your own
- Impregnating your clothes with permethrin effectively deters mosquitoes and other insects

**Dengue Fever** This viral disease is transmitted by mosquitoes and is fast becoming one of the top public-health problems in the tropical world. Unlike the malaria mosquito, the *Aedes aegypti* mosquito, which transmits the dengue virus, is most active during the day, and is found mainly in urban areas, in and around human dwellings.

Signs and symptoms of dengue fever include a sudden onset of high fever, headache, joint and muscle pains (hence its old name, 'breakbone fever') and nausea and vomiting. A rash of small red spots sometimes appears three to four days after the onset of fever. In the early phase of the illness, dengue may be mistaken for other infectious diseases, including malaria and influenza. Minor bleeding such as nose bleeds may occur in the course of the illness, but this does not necessarily mean that you have progressed to the potentially fatal dengue haemorrhagic fever (DHF). This is a severe illness, characterised by heavy bleeding, which is thought to be a result of a second infection by a different strain (there are four major strains) and it usually affects residents of the country rather than travellers. Recovery even from simple dengue fever may be prolonged, with tiredness lasting for several weeks.

You should seek medical attention as soon as possible if you think you may be infected. A blood test can exclude malaria and indicate the possibility of dengue fever. There is no specific treatment for dengue. Aspirin should be avoided, as it increases the risk of haemorrhaging. There's no vaccine against dengue fever. The best prevention is to avoid mosquito bites at all times by covering up, using insect repellents containing the compound DEET and mosquito nets (see the Malaria section earlier for more advice on avoiding mosquito bites).

**Japanese B Encephalitis** This viral infection of the brain is also transmitted by mosquitoes. Most cases occur in rural areas, as the virus exists in pigs and wading birds. Symptoms include fever, headache and alteration in consciousness. Hospitalisation is needed for correct diagnosis and treatment. There is a high mortality rate among those who have symptoms; of those who survive, many are intellectually disabled.

## Cuts, Bites & Stings

See Less Common Diseases, later in this section, for information about rabies, which is contracted through animal bites.

**Cuts & Scratches** Wash well and treat any cut with an antiseptic such as povidone-iodine. Apply a breathable waterproof dressing such as Cutifilm or Tegaderm. Coral cuts are notoriously slow to heal and if they are not adequately cleaned, small pieces of coral can remain embedded in the wound. Consider using antibiotics such as Bactrim if a wound appears to be getting infected.

**Bedbugs & Lice** Bedbugs live in various places, but particularly in dirty mattresses and bedding, evidenced by spots of blood on bedclothes or on the wall. Bedbugs leave itchy bites in neat rows. Calamine lotion or a sting relief spray may help.

All lice cause itching and discomfort. They make themselves at home in your hair (head lice), your clothing (body lice) or in your pubic hair (crabs). You catch lice through direct contact with infected people or by sharing combs, clothing and the like. Powder or shampoo treatment will kill the lice and infected clothing should then be washed in very hot, soapy water and left in the sun to dry.

**Bites & Stings** Bee and wasp stings are usually painful rather than dangerous. However, in people who are allergic to them, severe breathing difficulties may occur and require urgent medical care. Calamine lotion or a sting relief spray will give relief and ice packs will reduce the pain and swelling. There are some spiders with dangerous bites but usually antivenins are available. Scorpion stings are notoriously painful and in some parts of Asia can actually be fatal. Scorpions often shelter in shoes or clothing.

There are various fish and other sea creatures that can sting or bite, or that are dangerous to eat – seek local advice.

**Jellyfish** Avoid contact with these sea creatures, which have stinging tentacles. Stings from most jellyfish are rather painful. Dousing in vinegar will deactivate any stingers that have not 'fired'. Calamine lotion, antihistamines and analgesics may reduce the reaction and relieve the pain; you can also apply an ice pack, but be careful not to get any water on the wound as it will definitely sting.

**Leeches & Ticks** Leeches may be present in damp rainforest conditions; they attach themselves to the skin to suck blood. Trekkers often get them on their legs or in their boots. Salt or a lighted cigarette end will make them fall off. Do not pull them off, as the bite is then more likely to become infected. Clean and apply pressure if the point of attachment is bleeding. An insect repellent may keep them away.

You should always check all over your body if you have been walking through a potentially tick-infested area as ticks can cause skin infections and other more serious diseases. If a tick is found attached, press down around the tick's head with a pair of tweezers, grab the head and gently pull upwards. Avoid pulling the rear of the body as this may squeeze the tick's gut contents through the attached mouth parts into the skin, increasing the risk of infection and disease. Smearing chemicals on the tick will not make it let go and is not recommended.

**Snakes** To minimise your chances of being bitten, always wear boots, socks and long trousers when walking through undergrowth. Don't put your hands into holes and crevices, where snakes may be present, and be careful when collecting firewood.

Snake bites do not cause instantaneous death and antivenins are usually available. Immediately wrap the bitten limb tightly, as you would for a sprained ankle, and then attach a splint to immobilise it. Keep the victim still and seek medical help, if possible with the dead snake for identification. But don't attempt to catch the snake if there is a possibility of being bitten again. Tourniquets and sucking out the poison are now comprehensively discredited.

## Less Common Diseases
The following diseases pose a small risk to travellers, and so are only mentioned in passing. Seek medical advice if you think you may have any of these diseases.

**Cholera** This is the worst of the watery diarrhoeas and medical help should be sought. Outbreaks of cholera are generally widely reported, so you can avoid such problem areas. Fluid replacement is the most vital treatment – the risk of dehydration is severe as you may lose up to 20L a day. If there is a delay in getting to hospital, then begin taking tetracycline. The adult dose is 250mg four times daily. It is not recommended for children under nine years or for pregnant

women. Tetracycline may help shorten the illness, but adequate fluids are required to save lives.

**Filariasis** This is a mosquito-transmitted parasitic infection found in parts of Asia. Possible symptoms include fever, pain and swelling of the lymph glands; inflammation of lymph drainage areas; swelling of a limb or the scrotum; skin rashes; and blindness. Treatment is available to eliminate the parasites from the body, but some of the damage may not be reversible. Medical advice should be obtained promptly if the infection is suspected.

**Rabies** This fatal viral infection is found in many countries. Many animals can be infected (such as dogs, cats, bats and monkeys) and it is their saliva which is infectious. Any bite, scratch or even lick from an animal should be cleaned immediately and thoroughly. Scrub with soap and running water, and then apply alcohol or iodine solution. Medical help should be sought promptly to receive a course of injections to prevent the onset of symptoms and death.

**Tetanus** This disease is caused by a germ that lives in soil and in the faeces of horses and other animals. It enters the body via breaks in the skin. The first symptom may be discomfort in swallowing, or stiffening of the jaw and neck; this is followed by painful convulsions of the jaw and whole body. The disease can be fatal. It can be prevented by vaccination.

**Tuberculosis (TB)** This bacterial infection is usually transmitted from person to person by coughing but it may also be transmitted through consumption of unpasteurised milk. Boiled milk is safe to drink, and the souring of milk to make yoghurt or cheese also kills the bacilli. Travellers are usually not at great risk as close household contact with the infected person is usually required before the disease is passed on. You may need to have a TB test before you travel as this can help diagnose the disease later if you become ill.

**Typhus** This disease is spread by ticks, mites or lice. It begins with fever, chills, headache and muscle pains followed a few days later by a body rash. There is often a large painful sore at the site of the bite and nearby lymph nodes are swollen and painful. Typhus can be treated under medical supervision. Seek local advice on areas where ticks pose a danger and always check your skin carefully for ticks after walking in a danger area such as a tropical forest. An insect repellent can help, and walkers in tick-infested areas should consider having their boots and trousers impregnated with benzyl benzoate and dibutylphthalate.

## WOMEN TRAVELLERS

Like Thailand and other predominantly Buddhist countries, Vietnam is relatively free of serious hassles for Western women. But it is a different story for some Asian women, particularly those who are young. It is not uncommon for an Asian woman accompanied by a Western male to be mistaken for a Vietnamese prostitute. The fact that the couple could be married (or friends) might not occur to everyone, nor does the fact that the woman may not be Vietnamese at all. Asian women travelling in Vietnam with a Western male companion have occasionally reported verbal abuse.

However, there's no need to be overly paranoid, as locals are becoming more accustomed to seeing Asian women. Things have improved as more Vietnamese people are exposed to foreigner visitors.

Sanitary napkins are widely available in larger cities, though tampons are nearly impossible to find.

## GAY & LESBIAN TRAVELLERS

Vietnam is a relatively hassle-free place for homosexuals. There are no official laws on same-sex relationships in Vietnam, nor much in the way of official harassment.

However, the government is still notorious for closing down gay venues, and places that get written up in the mass media have a mysterious tendency to be raided soon after. As such, most gay venues keep a fairly low profile. There is, however, a healthy gay scene in Vietnam, especially in Hanoi and HCMC, evident by unabashed cruising around certain lakes in Hanoi and the thriving café scene in HCMC.

Common local attitudes suggest a general social prohibition, though the lack of any laws make things fairly safe (even if the authorities do break up a party on occasion). Major headlines were made in 1997 with Vietnam's first gay marriage, and again in 1998 at the country's first lesbian wedding, in the Mekong Delta. However, displaying peculiar double standards, two weeks later government officials broke up the women's marriage and the couple signed an agreement promising not to live together again.

With the vast number of same-sex travel partners – gay or otherwise – checking into hotels throughout Vietnam, it is fair to say there is little scrutiny over how travelling foreigners are related. However, it would be prudent not to flaunt your sexuality. As with heterosexual couples, passionate public displays of affection are considered a basic no-no. Vietnamese of the same sex, friends and otherwise, can be frequently seen walking hand in hand, so theoretically there is no reason same-sex foreign couples couldn't do the same.

**Utopia** (W www.utopia-asia.com) features gay travel information and contacts, including detailed sections on the legality of homosexuality in Vietnam and some local gay terminology.

## DISABLED TRAVELLERS

Vietnam is not a particularly good place for disabled travellers, despite the fact that many Vietnamese are disabled as a result of war injuries. Tactical problems include the crazy traffic, a lack of pedestrian footpaths, a lack of lifts in the buildings and the ubiquitous squat toilets.

Potential travellers might try asking for tips or travel suggestions at relevant action groups in their home town (some Vietnam-veteran groups which organise reunion tours to Vietnam might have some good ideas). The **Royal Association for Disability and Rehabilitation** (Radar; W www.radar.org.uk) and the **Society for Accessible Travel &**

Hospitality (SATH; w www.sath.org) both provide practical tips for disabled travel.

Lonely Planet's **Thorn Tree** (w www .lonelyplanet.com) is a good place to seek the advice of other travellers.

## SENIOR TRAVELLERS

As in many Asian countries there is a deep and definite sense of respect for the elderly in Vietnam, though seniors are likely to encounter some mobility problems. That said, senior travellers may want to avoid public transportation (the toilets on most trains, for example, are squat only).

There are no 'senior citizen' discounts for pensioners nor are any international cards officially recognised, but it may be worth flashing your card and seeing what you can get.

## TRAVEL WITH CHILDREN

In general, children have a good time in Vietnam, mainly because of the overwhelming amount of attention they attract (the Vietnamese are big on family) and the fact that almost everybody wants to play with them!

There is plenty to do in big cities to keep kids interested, though in most smaller towns and rural areas you will probably encounter the boredom factor. The zoos, parks and some of the best ice-cream shops in Southeast Asia are recommended. Kids visiting the south should not miss one of HCMC's water parks, while Hanoi's two must-sees are the circus and water-puppet performances.

Nature lovers with children can hike in one of Vietnam's expansive national parks or nature reserves. Cuc Phuong National Park (see the North-Central Vietnam chapter) in particular is home to the interesting Endangered Primate Rescue Centre, where you can have a look at efforts to protect and breed endangered species of monkeys. This is a good place to learn first hand about the pressures on the environment and the plight of our furry friends.

Babies can present their own peculiar problems. In larger cities baby food, diapers and children's clothing are widely available, but this is not the case in the countryside.

For kids who are too young to handle chopsticks, forks and knives can be found at most restaurants.

Lonely Planet's *Travel with Children* by Cathy Lanigan gives a rundown on health precautions for kids and advice on travel during pregnancy.

## USEFUL ORGANISATIONS

In both Hanoi and HCMC international associations such as the Alliance Française, Goethe Institute, British Council and American Club can be found. See the Hanoi and HCMC chapters for details.

### Chamber of Commerce

The aim of Vietcochamber (*Chamber of Commerce and Industry;* w www.vcci.com.vn) is to initiate and facilitate contacts between foreign businesses and Vietnamese companies. It may also be able to help with obtaining and extending business visas. Vietcochamber publishes a listing of government companies and its contact details.

### Nongovernment Organisations

Nongovernment organisations (NGOs) in Vietnam include churches and humanitarian-aid organisations. Since opening its doors to the world in the late 1980s, Vietnam has welcomed hundreds of local and international NGOs, whose aim is to provide support to its people, animals and natural environment. Many of these organisations seek volunteers and/or donations, but you should always contact them before visiting. The following are some notable NGOs that do good work in Vietnam, in particular for disadvantaged children.

The best place to begin is at the **NGO Resource Centre** (☎ 04-832 8570, fax 832 8611; e ngocentr@netnam.org.vn; Hotel La Thanh, 218 Pho Doi Can, Hanoi), which keeps extensive files on all of the NGOs operating in Vietnam.

**Christina Noble Children's Foundation** (CNCF; ☎ 08-822 2276, fax 822 2276; e cncf sponsorvn@hcm.vnn.vn, w www.cncf.org; 38 Đ Tu Xuong, District 3, HCMC) helps those at risk of exploitation and in need of emergency and long-term medical care, nutritional rehabilitation, educational opportunities, vocational training and job placement.

**East Meets West** (☎ *0511-829 110, fax 821 850;* e *emwfvn@dng.vnn.vn,* w *www .eastmeetswest.org; 56 Đ Pasteur, Danang)* assists with the education and health of children by building and renovating vital institutions such as schools, hospitals and medical and dental clinics, and providing clean and safe water systems. It was founded in 1988 by Le Ly Hayslip, whose life story was chronicled in two autobiographies, and became the subject material for Oliver Stone's film *Heaven and Earth.*

**Education for Development** (EFD; ☎/fax *08-837 6799;* e *efd-vn@hcm.vnn.vn; 245 Đ Nguyen Trai, District 1, HCMC)* works with street children and working children.

**Green Bamboo Shelter** (☎ *08-821 0199;* e *gbwarmshelter@hcm.fpt.vn; 40/34 Đ Cal-mette, District 1, HCMC)* provides shelter, food, clothing and protection for street kids, as well as facilitating access to education programmes.

**Koto** (☎ *04-747 0337, fax 747 0339;* w *www .streetvoices.com.au; 61 Pho Van Mieu, Hanoi)* is a restaurant that provides career training and guidance to former street kids. Travellers can also help out by eating here.

**Saigon Children's Charity** (SCC; e *scc@ hcmc.netnam.vn,* w *www.saigonchildren.com)* provides education and development programmes for disadvantaged children.

**Carry for Kids** (☎ *618-8238 4525, fax 8211 7393;* e *carryforkids@telstra.com;* w *www .carryforkids.org; 101 Currie St, Adelaide, SA 5000, Australia)* is a laudable Aussie organ-isation that helps Australian visitors to Vietnam donate goods to worthy causes, such as orphanages.

**World Wildlife Fund** (w *www.wwf.org)* and **Birdlife International** (w *www.birdlife .net)* are two eco-NGOs with offices in Hanoi. **Unicef** (☎ *04-826 1170, fax 826 2641; 72 Ly Thuong Kiet, Hanoi)* also has an office in the capital.

## DANGERS & ANNOYANCES
### Culture Shock

The most dangerous thing in Vietnam is your own psyche. As one traveller noted:

My first day on landing in HCMC was one of shock and horror. For the first couple of days I thought the whole idea of Vietnam was a terrible mistake. No matter how much reading and research you do prior to arriving, nothing prepares you for the sights, sounds and smells of this place. Three days after arriving I was OK, had settled down and was having a fantastic time.

**Craig McGrath**

Another traveller had this to say:

Some extremely upsetting sights, sounds and smells in HCMC were a shock, but that was over-come because of the wonderful people. The street kids were an absolute joy. The smiling people, the most hard working and industrious anyone could ever meet…facing their everyday hardships with laughter and companionship – just great.

**Audrey Snoddon**

This is not to say that nothing can go wrong. There are some things you should definitely be concerned about. Just remember, though, that worrying about all the 'problems' you will encounter can do more to ruin your trip than the problems themselves. Just take the necessary precautions to guard yourself against the minority of schemers and thieves so you can focus on connecting with the other 99.9% of the population who are genu-inely honest and delightful. After all, you're here to have fun!

### Theft

The Vietnamese are convinced that their cities are very dangerous and full of crimi-nals. Before reunification, street crime was rampant in the south, especially in Saigon. Motorbike-borne thieves (called cowboys by the Americans) would speed down major thoroughfares, ripping pedestrians' watches off their wrists. Pickpockets and confidence tricks were also common. Even after the fall of Saigon, a few bold criminals managed to swindle some newly arrived North Viet-namese troops. When a few such outlaws were summarily shot, street crime almost disappeared overnight.

Well, it seems to have reappeared with a vengeance. We have had countless reports of street crime, particularly in HCMC and Nha Trang, and regardless of how safe it may seem, you should always exercise common sense and caution. One strong suggestion is simply not to have anything dangling off your body that you are not ready to part with. This includes bags and any jewellery, even of the costume variety, which might tempt a robber.

Especially watch out for drive-by thieves on motorbikes – they specialise in snatching handbags and cameras from tourists on foot and riding cyclos in the city. Some have become proficient at grabbing valuables from the open window of a car and speeding away with the loot. Foreigners have occasionally reported having their eyeglasses and hats snatched too.

Pickpocketing, which often involves kids, women with babies and newspaper vendors, is also a serious problem, especially in the tourist areas of HCMC, such as Đ Dong Khoi and the Pham Ngu Lao area. Many of the street kids, adorable as they may be, are very skilled at liberating people from their wallets or whatever else may be in pockets or handbags. You need to watch very carefully (beware of large groups of children) and in some cases you may have to physically keep the kids at arm's length.

Of course they're not all bad – there are heaps of kids trying to survive by selling postcards and souvenirs – but some know exactly how to prey on people's weaknesses for cute kids.

Letters from travellers such as the following are common:

We didn't have trouble with pickpockets except in HCMC. The children selling postcards will place a postcard-filled hand over your fanny pack while expertly unzipping the thing with their free hand. We luckily noticed what was going on before the pack was fully unzipped and contents stolen. However, I recommend fannypack (moneybelt) locks or, better yet, steering clear of children selling postcards.

**Dee Mahan**

In HCMC another one of our fellow travellers lost his camera while trying to take a picture. The thieves were two young guys on a motorcycle.

The idea is to get close enough to the tourist so the passenger can grab anything not properly secured, ie handbags, cameras, sunglasses and even hats! Another thing to watch are crowds of lovely little children who try and sell postcards, etc. These children work in groups and while the older kids are keeping your attention diverted, the smaller kids are able to open the zips on bumbags (moneybelts) and empty their contents. These kids are very touchy feely and after a while you become impervious to them touching your arms or rubbing your skin, but keep an eye on them as they are able to steal your watch with amazing ease. As terrible as all this sounds, as long as you are careful then you should be safe. My trip to Vietnam was one of the greatest trips of my life, and with a certain amount of wariness there are few problems to be encountered.

**Matthew Ford**

Avoid putting things down while you're eating or at least take the precaution of fastening these items to your seat with a strap or chain. Remember, any luggage that you leave unattended for even a moment may grow legs and vanish.

There are also 'taxi girls' (sometimes transvestites), who approach Western men, give them a big hug and ask if they'd like 'a good time'. Then they suddenly change their mind and depart, along with a wristwatch and wallet.

We have also had reports of people being drugged and robbed on long-distance buses. It usually starts with a friendly passenger offering you a free Coke, which turns out to be a chloral-hydrate cocktail. You wake up hours later to find your valuables and newfound 'friend' gone.

Despite all this, don't be overly paranoid. Although crime certainly exists and you need to be aware of it, theft in Vietnam does not seem to be any worse than what you'd expect anywhere else. Don't assume that everyone's a thief – most Vietnamese are poor, but honest.

And finally, there is the problem of your fellow travellers. It's a disgusting reality that a number of backpackers subsidise their journey by ripping off whoever they can, including other backpackers. This is most likely to happen if you stay in a dormitory, though dorms are rare in Vietnam. Perhaps most disturbing are attempts by foreigners to rip off the Vietnamese. We've heard reports of backpackers slipping out of restaurants without paying their bills and cheating their guides out of promised pay. We know of one fellow who deliberately short-changed his driver US$40 because the car's air-con broke down on the last day of the trip. This is a pretty sick thing to do.

To avoid theft, probably the best advice you can follow is to not bring anything valuable that you don't really need. Expensive watches, jewellery and electronic gadgets invite theft – do you really need these things while travelling?

## Beggar Fatigue

Just as you're about to dig into the scrumptious Vietnamese meal you've ordered, you feel someone gently tugging on your shirt sleeve. You turn around to deal with this latest 'annoyance' only to find it's a bony, eight-year-old boy holding his three-year-old sister in his arms. The little girl has a distended stomach, her palm is stretched out to you and her hungry eyes are fixed on your plate of steaming chicken, vegetables and rice.

This is the face of poverty. How do you deal with these situations? If you're like most of us, not very well. All of the children and people on the streets selling or begging have found themselves in such a position due to circumstance. It certainly wasn't a choice. These people deserve a chance and respect, and it helps to gain a better understanding of the life these people lead and have led.

So what can you do to help these street people, many of whom are malnourished, illiterate and with no future? It is a difficult question with no simple answer, but if you would like to do something to help, please think before acting.

Many people become overcome with guilt when seeing so much blatant poverty, and desperation tends to bring out people's charitable side.

Taking the matter into your own hands by giving out money or gifts to people on the streets can prove to cause more damage than

good. The more people are given hand-outs, the more reliant and attracted to life on the streets they become . When money becomes too difficult to acquire, people recognise that life on the streets is no longer so fruitful. This will hopefully discourage parents and 'leaders' forcing children and beggars onto the streets and gradually reduce the growing problems.

One way to contribute and help improve the situation is to invest just a few hours to find out about local organisations that work with disadvantaged people; these groups are far more likely to make sure contributions are used in the most effective way possible to help those who need it. If you want to give, the most effective way is to seek out those who will use it wisely in your absence. For a list of reputable organisations that accept donations, see the Useful Organisations section earlier in this chapter.

However, if you want to do something on the spot, at least avoid giving money or anything that can be sold. The elderly and, in particular, young children begging will almost always have a parent or leader only a few steps behind them to take away whatever is given or earned. The elderly and the young are easily controlled and are ideal begging tools; people know how much they can make by pushing them into these unfair conditions. Small children are often forced to beg for money, with the cash going towards their parents' drinking and gambling habits rather than food or schooling for the children. Of course, that's if the kids have parents, which many of them don't.

So, if you are going to give something directly to a beggar, it's better to give food than money; take them to a market or stall and buy them a nutritious meal or some fruit to be sure they are the only beneficiaries and no harm is done. Even something not so good for their teeth is better than money, as one traveller realised:

I will always remember the beam of delight that came over the face of a hard-bitten child beggar when I offered him a cake similar to the one I was eating.

**Gordon Balderston**

## Violence

Unlike it is in many Western countries, recreational homicide is not a popular sport in Vietnam. The country is virtually free of terrorists who harbour a political agendas.

Violence against foreigners is extremely rare and is not something you should waste much time worrying about. In general theft is not life-threatening – like most thieves in the world, they are simply after your valuables.

### Tuan

Tuan (his name has been changed for the purpose of this book) was a bright 18-year-old boy who had worked on the streets of Hanoi selling postcards for about four years. He had become a well-known face in the area he worked, particularly with a number of expats. Tuan had a physical deformity that attracted a great deal of attention and sympathy over the years. The problem was a treatable one, something that is easily resolved in the West but in Vietnam is almost impossible to fix for someone in the circumstances of a street child.

Like many postcard sellers, Tuan spoke very good English and could easily interact with and charm foreign tourists. Many street children become great storytellers, realising that hard-luck tales (often exaggerated, though based on reality) are a good way to get money. It's also a way of attracting the sympathy, attention and affection the children obviously lack and yearn for.

Over the years, a number of foreigners were very taken by Tuan and his problems. While they could do little to solve the underlying social problems that lead to homelessness, in Tuan's case it was clear that some of his problems could be solved with a straightforward trip to the doctor. Consequently, many people gave money to him without hesitation. People would hand over $100 or more and either take him along to a doctor to plan an operation or they would trust him to make the visit himself. The majority of people who assisted Tuan over the years were only visiting the area for a short period of time, so they were unable to follow up their support, or assist Tuan in his treatment.

Children like Tuan have no idea how to be responsible for large amounts of money. They don't get paid large pay packets – they rely on the goodwill of tourists to pay for overpriced postcards to make enough cash to get through the day. Overcharging foreigners is justified by the belief that all foreigners are rich – what's an extra $5 to them? The problem is that they become totally dependent on tourists as a source of income.

So what happened to the money? In Tuan's case it sadly led him into a life of drugs. He became a heroin addict. Like other addicts, he was supported through drug rehabilitation, and went through five detoxification programmes. Why? The donor helping Tuan was usually unable to go through the programme with him and give the support and encouragement he desperately needed. If someone had paid in advance, Tuan would go along for the treatment – although he was addicted, some tiny piece of will seemed to remind him he must stop to survive. But, if Tuan was given the money and responsibility to take himself along to the hospital, as was so often the case, then the money was inevitably used for his next fix.

The problem with most addicts is that after going through the gruelling and lonely ordeal of detoxification, they leave the programme and end up back on the streets – exposed to the same street life and drug culture as before. Without proper counselling, guidance or support, these youngsters do not have the strength to walk away and begin their lives over without drugs.

People want to help, but what they don't realise is that sometimes they are actually making the situation far worse, and in Tuan's case creating even bigger problems that did not exist in the first place. If all of those people who had helped Tuan over the years had instead focused their time on seeking out people or local organisations who could have helped, perhaps Tuan would be alive today. Instead Tuan no longer has that chance, as his drug use resulted in him contracting AIDS. In the end, Tuan lost his battle.

You do see a lot of street arguments between locals. Usually this takes the form of two young macho types threatening and pushing each other while their girlfriends try to separate them. The whole point of the threats and chest thumping is to save face and there is seldom any bloodshed. Money is usually the cause of these arguments; for example, a minor motor-vehicle accident and the heated issue of who should pay for the broken headlight or squashed chicken. Such macho posturing is likely to exclude foreigners.

As a good general rule do not get into fights with Vietnamese. Social incorrectness aside, these fights often boil down to strength in numbers and many a macho foreigner has wound up in the hospital after the one little guy he squared off with whistled for his friends who were nearby. If you become embroiled in one of these situations, swallow your pride and find a safer way to vent your frustration.

## Scams

Con artists and thieves are, of course, always seeking new tricks to separate naive tourists from their money and are becoming more savvy in their ways. We can't warn you about every trick you might encounter, so perhaps the best advice we can give is to maintain a healthy scepticism (as you would any where else in the world) and be prepared to argue when unnecessary demands are made for your money.

One sound piece of advice is *never* to take up with prostitutes who may chat you up in a bar or on the street – period. Beside the fundamental objections to this (the illegality of it and the obvious health risks involved), there are other serious dangers at hand (like getting ripped off, for one). The chances of a man 'getting lucky' with a Vietnamese woman who is not a prostitute without a long and proper period of courtship are virtually zero. Vietnamese women willing to sleep with a man they hardly know are doing it for the money – don't let your ego get in the way.

Beware of a motorbike-rental scam that some travellers have encountered in HCMC.

What happens is that you rent a motorbike and the owner supplies you with an excellent lock and suggests you use it. What he doesn't tell you is that he, too, has a key and that somebody will follow you and 'steal' the bike at the first opportunity. You then have to pay for a new bike or forfeit your passport, visa, deposit or whatever security you left with him.

More common is when your motorbike won't start after you parked it in a 'safe' area with a guard. But yes, the guard knows somebody who can repair your bike. The mechanic shows up and quickly goes about reinstalling the parts they removed earlier and now the bike works fine. That will be US$10 please.

Despite an array of scams, however, it is important to keep in mind the Vietnamese are not always out to get you. One concerning trend we're noticing in Vietnam, relative to neighbouring countries such as Thailand and Laos, is a general lack of trust in the locals on the part of foreigners. Some may blame guidebooks, in part, for trying to make people aware of all the potential dangers and annoyances they might encounter while travelling; the key is trying to differentiate between who is good and bad and not close yourself off to every person you encounter.

This is not always an easy thing to do. Even one of the original authors of this book, a veteran travel writer and Vietnam hand, was duped by a long-time Vietnamese friend who, unbeknown to him, had tried to collect fees from hotels and restaurants that wished to be included in this guide!

One final word of advice (this may sound strange coming from the people who write these books): we're seeing an awful lot of travellers in Vietnam with their noses dug too deep inside guidebooks. The paranoia people develop from being hassled so much seems to result in many refusing to believe anyone if it's 'not in the book'. For both better or worse, often it's not. Try to keep an open mind, be aware of what can happen and what things 'should' cost, and then use this information in conjunction with your own better judgment.

## Undetonated Explosives

Four armies expended untold energy and resources for over three decades mining, booby-trapping, rocketing, strafing, mortaring and bombarding wide areas of Vietnam. When the fighting stopped most of this ordnance remained exactly where it had landed or been laid; American estimates at the end of the war placed the quantity of unexploded ordnance at 150,000 tonnes.

Since 1975, about 40,000 Vietnamese have been maimed or killed by this leftover ordnance while clearing land for cultivation or ploughing their fields. While cities, cultivated areas and well-travelled rural roads and paths are safe for travel, straying from these areas could land you in the middle of a minefield that, though known to the locals, may be completely unmarked.

In 1997 several children were killed by a bomb blast in a school yard in Nghe An province. More recent tragedies include the deaths of six children, in August 2000, who were killed when a leftover shell detonated in Binh Dinh, central Vietnam. And again in 2002, two young schoolboys perished when a US-made cluster bomb, which they had fished out of a canal near Hanoi, detonated.

The moral of the story is *never* touch any rockets, artillery shells, mortars, mines or other relics of war you may come across. Such objects can remain lethal for decades. In Europe, people are still occasionally injured by ordnance leftover from WWII, and even WWI, and every few years you read about city blocks in London or Rotterdam being evacuated after an old bomb is discovered in someone's backyard. Finally, don't climb inside bomb craters – you never know what undetonated explosive device is at the bottom.

One US-based organisation worth a mention is **Peace Trees Vietnam** (☎ 202-842 8451; ⓦ www.peacetreesvietnam.org; PO Box 10697, Bainbridge, WA 98110, USA), which trains Vietnamese military personnel to clear old mine fields; once the bombs are removed, it sends teams of former US soldiers to replant these areas with hundreds of new trees. This helps to restore the environment and contributes to improving relations between the two former enemies. You can learn more about landmines from the Nobel Peace Prize–winner **International Campaign to Ban Landmines** (ICBL; ⓦ www.icbl.org).

## Sea Creatures

If you plan to spend your time swimming, snorkelling and scuba diving, you should be aware of various hazards. The list of dangerous creatures that are found in seas off Vietnam is extensive and includes sharks, jellyfish, stonefish, scorpion fish, sea snakes and stingrays, to name a few. However, there is little cause for alarm as most of these creatures avoid humans, or humans avoid them, so the actual number of people injured or killed is fairly small. Nonetheless, it is strongly advised that you exercise a certain degree of common sense in this regard.

Jellyfish tend to travel in groups, so as long as you look before you leap into the sea, avoiding them should not be too hard. Make local inquiries – many places have a 'jellyfish season' (usually summer). Stings from most jellyfish are simply painful (see Cuts, Bites & Stings in the Health section of this chapter).

Stonefish, scorpion fish and stingrays tend to hang out in shallow water along the ocean floor and can be very difficult to see. One way to protect yourself against these nasties is to wear shoes in the sea. To treat a sting by a stonefish or scorpion fish, immerse the affected area in hot water and seek medical treatment.

All sea snakes are poisonous but are usually nonaggressive. Furthermore, their small fangs are placed towards the rear of the mouth so it's difficult for them to bite large creatures like humans.

## Noise

One annoyance that can be insidiously draining on your energy during a trip to Vietnam is noise. At night, there is often a competing cacophony from motorbikes, dance halls, cafés, video parlours, karaoke lounges, restaurants and so on; if your hotel is near any of these (and it's unlikely to be in a totally noise-free zone), it may be difficult to sleep. In some places, even the ice cream and snack vendors' carts have a booming, distorted portable cassette player attached.

The Vietnamese themselves seem to be immune to the noise. Indeed, a café that doesn't have an eardrum-splitting clamour emanating from a loudspeaker will have difficulty attracting customers; that is to say, Vietnamese customers. The foreigners will flee as soon as the sound system is turned on. Those who stay long enough to finish a meal or a cup of coffee will walk away with their heads literally pounding.

Fortunately, most noise subsides around 10pm or 11pm, as few places stay open much later than that. Unfortunately, however, the Vietnamese are very early risers; most are up and about from around 5am onwards. This not only means that traffic noise starts early, but you may be woken up by the crackle of café speakers, followed by very loud (and usually atrocious) karaoke music. It's worth trying to get a room at the back of a hotel, or wherever else the street noise looks likely to be minimal. Other than that, consider bringing a set of earplugs.

## LEGAL MATTERS
### Civil Law

The French gave the Vietnamese the Napoleonic Code, much of which has still to be repealed, although these laws may conflict with later statutes. From about 1960 to 1975, South Vietnam modified much of its commercial code to resemble that of the USA. Since reunification, Soviet-style laws have been applied to the whole country with devastating consequences for private property owners. The recent economic reforms have seen a flood of new property legislation, much of it the result of advice from the United Nations, the International Monetary Fund and other international organisations. The rapid speed at which legislation is being enacted is a challenge for those who must interpret and enforce the law.

On paper, it all looks good. In practice, the rule of law barely exists in Vietnam these days. Local officials interpret the law any way it suits them, often against the wishes of Hanoi. This poses serious problems for joint ventures – foreigners who have gone to court in Vietnam to settle civil disputes have generally fared pretty badly. It's particularly difficult to sue a state-run company, even if that company committed obvious fraud. The government has a reputation for suddenly cancelling permits, revoking licences and basically tearing up written contracts. There is no independent judiciary.

Not surprisingly, most legal disputes are settled out of court. In general, you can accomplish more with a carton of cigarettes and a bottle of good cognac than you can with a lawyer.

### Drugs

During the American War, US troops were known to consume large quantities of potent weed, hashish and other stronger recreational chemicals. After 1975, the loss of American customers, plus the sophisticated police-state apparatus and the country's extreme poverty, suppressed the domestic demand for drugs. However, the recent influx of foreign tourists along with economic progress has revived the drug trade. Vietnam has a very serious problem with heroin these days and the authorities are taking serious steps. In 2001 alone, the government executed 55 people for their drug offences; in 2002 a Vietnamese-American bought himself 20 years' jail back in his homeland for dealing methamphetamine pills to nightclubs.

You may well be approached with offers to buy marijuana and occasionally opium. Giving in to this temptation is risky at best. There are many plain clothes police in Vietnam and just because you don't see them, doesn't mean they aren't there. If arrested, you could be subjected to a long prison term and/or a large fine.

Vietnam's proximity to the Golden Triangle means you can expect vigorous luggage searches by customs officials when you leave and arrive at your next destination. In short, drug use in Vietnam is still a very perilous activity and taking any out is even riskier. Nearby Thailand, Malaysia and Indonesia impose life-time prison sentences and the death penalty for drug use and trafficking.

## The Police

The problem of police corruption has been acknowledged in official newspapers. The same problems that plague the police forces in many developing countries (eg, very low pay and low levels of education and training) certainly exist in Vietnam. If something does go wrong, or if something is stolen, the police often can't do much more than write a report for your insurance company.

Hanoi has warned all provincial governments that any police caught shaking down foreign tourists will be fired and arrested. The crackdown has dented the enthusiasm of the police to confront foreigners directly with demands for bribes. However, it has not eliminated the problem altogether. You may be stopped, for no apparent reason, while riding a motorcycle (or even just riding as a passenger in a car) and have a fine imposed.

All this said, there is really no need for paranoia. The Vietnamese police can be a nuisance and you (or more likely your driver or guide) may have to occasionally pay, but this will rarely cost a lot. To avoid getting upset, you have to do as the Vietnamese do – think of 'fines' as a 'tax'. Remember too that you are not being targeted because you are a foreigner; in fact, most cops prefer preying on locals, who are easier to extort money from.

Foreigners who stay in Vietnam attempting to do business can expect periodic visits from the police collecting 'taxes' and 'donations'. Often they will direct their requests towards the Vietnamese employees rather than confront a foreign manager directly. The issue is further complicated by the fact that most Vietnamese police (perhaps 75%) don't wear uniforms – so are those police really who they say they are? It's just one of those things that makes doing business in Vietnam so exciting. Good luck.

## BUSINESS HOURS

Vietnamese people rise early and consider sleeping in to be a sure indication of illness. Offices, museums and many shops open between 7am and 8am (a tad earlier in the summer) and close between 4pm and 5pm. Lunch is taken very seriously and virtually everything shuts down between noon and 1.30pm. Government workers tend to take longer breaks, so figure on getting nothing done between 11.30am and 2pm.

Most government offices are open on Saturday until noon but closed on Sunday. Most museums are closed on Monday while temples are usually open all day every day.

The Vietnamese tend to eat their meals by the clock, and disrupting someone's meal schedule is considered very rude. What this effectively means is that you shouldn't visit people during lunch unless you have been invited to do so. It also means that if you hire somebody for the whole day (eg, a cyclo driver or guide), you must take a lunch break by noon and dinner by 5pm. Delaying the lunch or dinner break, by even an hour, will earn you a reputation as a sadistic employer.

Many of the small privately owned shops, restaurants and street stalls stay open seven days a week, often until late at night.

## PUBLIC HOLIDAYS & SPECIAL EVENTS

Politics affects everything, including public holidays. After a 15-year lapse, Christmas, New Year's Day, Tet (Lunar New Year) and Buddha's Birthday were re-established as holidays in 1990. The following are public holidays in Vietnam:

**New Year's Day (Tet Duong Lich)** 1 January

**Anniversary of the Founding of the Vietnamese Communist Party (Thanh Lap Dang CSVN)** 3 February – the Vietnamese Communist Party was founded on this date in 1930

**Liberation Day (Saigon Giai Phong)** 30 April – the date on which Saigon surrendered is commemorated nationwide as Liberation Day. Many cities and provinces also commemorate the anniversary of the date in March or April of 1975 when they were 'liberated' by the North Vietnamese Army.

**International Workers' Day (Quoc Te Lao Dong)** 1 May – also known as May Day, this falls back-to-back with Liberation Day, giving everyone a two-day holiday.

**Ho Chi Minh's Birthday (Sinh Nhat Bac Ho)** 19 May

**Buddha's Birthday (Phat Dan)** Eighth day of the fourth moon (usually June)

**National Day (Quoc Khanh)** 2 September – commemorates the proclamation of the Declaration of Independence of the Democratic Republic of Vietnam in Hanoi, by Ho Chi Minh in 1945

**Christmas (Giang Sinh)** 25 December

Special prayers are held at Vietnamese and Chinese pagodas when the moon is full or just the thinnest sliver. Many Buddhists eat only vegetarian food on these days, which, according to the Chinese lunar calendar, fall on the 14th and 15th days of the month and from the last (29th or 30th) day of the month to the first day of the next month.

The following major religious festivals have lunar dates (check against any Vietnamese calendar for the Gregorian dates):

**Tet (Tet Nguyen Dan)** First to seventh days of the first moon – the Vietnamese Lunar New Year is the most important festival of the year and falls in late January or early February. This public holiday is officially three days, but many people take an entire week off work and few businesses are open.

**Holiday of the Dead (Thanh Minh)** Fifth day of the third moon – people pay solemn visits to graves of deceased relatives, which are specially tidied up a few days before, and make offerings of food, flowers, joss sticks and votive papers.

**Buddha's Birth, Enlightenment and Death** Eighth day of the fourth moon – this day is celebrated at pagodas and temples which, like many private homes, are festooned with lanterns. Processions are held during the evening. This festival has been redesignated a public holiday.

**Summer Solstice Day (Tiet Doan Ngo)** Fifth day of the fifth moon – offerings are made to spirits, ghosts and the God of Death to ward off epidemics. Human effigies are burned to satisfy the requirements of the God of Death for souls to staff his army.

**Wandering Souls Day (Trung Nguyen)** Fifteenth day of the seventh moon – this is the second largest Vietnamese festival of the year. Offerings of food and gifts are made in homes and pagodas for the wandering souls of the forgotten dead.

**Mid-Autumn Festival (Trung Thu)** Fifteenth day of the eighth moon – this festival is celebrated with moon cakes of sticky rice filled with lotus seeds, watermelon seeds, peanuts, the yolks of duck eggs, raisins, sugar and other such things. For this festival children carry colourful lanterns in the form of boats, unicorns, dragons, lobsters, carp, hares and toads in an evening procession accompanied by the banging of drums and cymbals.

**Confucius' Birthday** Twenty-eighth day of the ninth moon.

## ACTIVITIES
### Cycling
For short and long distances, cycling is an excellent way to experience Vietnam. A bicycle can be rented in most tourist centres for around US$1 a day. See the Bicycle section in the Getting Around chapter for details.

### Trekking
Vietnam offers some excellent trekking opportunities, notably in its growing array of national parks and nature reserves. You aren't likely to do much long-distance walking in the steamy, tropical lowlands, which are dominated by dense vegetation. However, there are plenty of chances to hike to minority villages in the northwest, northeast and central highlands regions. Tour operators in Hanoi and HCMC offer a variety of programmes that feature hiking and trekking.

Remember that you may need to arrange special permits, especially if you want to spend the night in remote mountain villages where there are no hotels.

One thing to be aware of in the south is that in equatorial regions there is very little twilight: night comes on quickly and without warning. Therefore, you can't readily judge how many hours of daylight remain unless you have a watch. Do pay attention to how much time you'll need to get back to civilisation; otherwise, be prepared for an impromptu camping trip.

### Swimming
With 3451km of mostly tropical coastline, you would imagine Vietnam to be Asia's answer to coastal beaches of Queensland, Florida or Spain. Indeed, there are some excellent beaches, though perhaps not quite as many as you'd expect. Part of the reason

is that the southern part of the country, which has the best tropical climate and highest population, is dominated by the huge Mekong Delta. While this region is lush, green and lovely, it's also very muddy and the 'beaches' tend to be mangrove swamps. One of the few beach areas in the delta region is Hon Chong, which faces the Gulf of Thailand. Other good beaches can be found on nearby Phu Quoc Island, also in the Gulf of Thailand.

The southernmost sandy beach on the east coast is Vung Tau, a very popular place close to HCMC, which is unfortunately plagued by crowds and polluted water. Fortunately there are other considerably cleaner beaches in the area, such as Long Hai and Ho Coc. Farther north, Mui Ne Beach is even more beautiful, and travel time from HCMC is now just three hours. If you're planning to beach-hop up the coast, consider stopping at Ca Na, about halfway between Phan Thiet and Nha Trang. Nha Trang has emerged as Vietnam's premier beach resort, in part because of its offshore islands and scuba diving, and vast accommodation, eating and nightlife offerings.

Heading north towards Danang other good beaches include isolated Doc Let and the fine sands of Cua Dai, near Hoi An. There are plenty of other beaches to explore along this stretch, mostly undeveloped, but the weather here becomes more seasonal – May to July is the best time, while during the winter powerful rip tides can make swimming dangerous.

The Danang area is blessed with a 30km white sand beach consisting of a variety of Vietnamese names, but known collectively as 'China Beach' in English.

Hué has truly awful winter weather and it just gets worse the further north you go. During the summer though, the beaches are thick with sun-tanned locals, though few foreigners go there. The best-known of the northern beaches are at Cua Lo (near Vinh), Sam Son (near Thanh Hoa) and Do Son (near Haiphong), though these pale in comparison with beaches further south.

Most Vietnamese people love the beach, but have a respectful fear of the sea – they like to wade up to their knees, but seldom dive in and go for a proper swim. They are more likely to swim in rivers and public swimming pools. Many mid-range and upmarket hotels in Vietnam have swimming pools, and there are also numerous water parks in places like HCMC, Nha Trang and Hanoi.

## Gambling
The Vietnamese government recently lifted its 14-year ban on gambling. Consequently, that most bourgeois of capitalist activities is staging a comeback. Once again, horse racing is popular in HCMC. Vietnam's first casino, since liberation, opened in 1994 at Do Son Beach near Haiphong. In the back alleys of large cities, slot machines have popped up inside karaoke clubs and are now legal as 'entertainment devices'.

It's easy to ignore the horse racing, casinos and slot machines if you don't want to play, but you'll have a hard time escaping the state lottery (xo so). Touts (mostly children and elderly folks) selling lottery tickets will approach you anytime, anywhere, and they are usually persistent.

While your chances of winning are minuscule, hitting the jackpot in the state lottery can make you a dong multimillionaire. The smallest denomination of lottery ticket is 2000d, while the largest prize is about 50 million dong.

The official state lottery has to compete against danh de, which is an illegal numbers game, reputed to offer better odds. Two of the most popular forms of illegal gambling are dominoes (tu sat) and cock fighting (choi ga).

Some of the ethnic-Chinese living in the Cholon district of HCMC are said to be keen mah jong players.

## Surfing & Windsurfing
Surfing and windsurfing have only recently arrived on the scene, but they are quickly catching on. The best place to look into these pursuits is at Mui Ne Beach on the south-central Coast, followed by Nha Trang (further north) and Phu Quoc Island in the Mekong Delta.

## Diving & Snorkelling

The best scuba-diving area in Vietnam is around Nha Trang. There are several excellent dive operators here, whose equipment and training is up to international standards. It is also possible to hire snorkelling gear and scuba equipment at several beach resorts, such as Vietnam Scuba near Ca Na, and the Furama Resort near Danang. Phu Quoc Island shows good potential for underwater exploration, but at the time of writing there were still no dive operators on the island. See the relevant chapters for more information.

## Martial Arts

Vietnam has a long history of martial arts, logical if you consider its proximity to China. Unfortunately, however, there is very little access to martial arts for the short-term visitor. If you're sticking around Vietnam for a while and want to get involved, ask around about some of the dojos in Hanoi or HCMC.

One martial art, however, that can be easily tried is slow-motion shadow boxing *(thai cuc quyen)*. In recent years this ancient form of exercise has become quite trendy in Western countries. It is basically a form of exercise, but is also considered to be an art and a form of martial arts related to kung fu, although the latter is performed at a much higher speed and with the intention of doing bodily harm. Kung fu also often employs weapons. *Thai cuc quyen* is not a form of self-defence, but it does employ similar movements to kung fu. There are also different styles, and it's very popular among old people and young women, who believe it will help keep their bodies beautiful. The movements develop breathing muscles, promote digestion and improve muscle tone. A modern innovation is to perform *thai cuc quyen* movements to the thump of disco music!

*Thai cuc quyen* and all manner of exercises are customarily done just as the sun rises, which means that if you want to see or participate in them, you have to get up early. You can find it being practised all over Vietnam, particularly around lakes, parks and on beaches.

## Golf

Mark Twain once said that playing golf was 'a waste of a good walk' and apparently Ho Chi Minh agreed with him. When the French departed Vietnam, Ho's advisers declared golf to be a 'bourgeois practice'. In 1975, after the fall of South Vietnam, golf was banned and all courses were shut down and turned into farming cooperatives. However, times have changed – golf was revived in 1992 and now even government officials can often be seen riding around in electric carts in hot pursuit of a little white ball.

All over East Asia, playing golf can win you considerable points in the 'face game' even if you never hit the ball. For maximum snob value, you need to join a country club, and the fees are outrageously high. In Vietnam, golf memberships start at around US$20,000. Of course Japanese visitors always comment on how incredibly cheap this is.

Most golf clubs will allow you to simply pay a guest fee for attacking a golf ball with a No 5 iron. The best two golf courses in Vietnam are located in Dalat (central highlands) and Phan Thiet (south-central coast). See the destination chapters for details on individual clubs and courses.

For information about golf package deals, visit w www.vietnamgolfresorts.com.

## Fitness Clubs

The Vietnamese government has put a lot of energy into the promotion of gymnastics, which is also a mandatory subject from elementary school to university – a Soviet and Chinese influence.

Unless you're working at a school with such facilities, your best bet is to try the exercise clubs at major hotels. Some hotels open their exercise facilities to nonguests for a fee. Depending on the particular hotel, you may be charged a single day's use or monthly membership.

Some hotels also have tennis courts that can be rented by the hour. If you're interested in badminton, it's easy to pick up a game on the street, especially with local kids.

[Continued on page 125]

## Tastes of Vietnam

JOHN HAY

GARRETT CULHANE

OLIVER STREWE

GARRETT CULHANE

JOHN BANAGAN

GARRETT CULHANE

**Title Page:** A wide choice of vegetables from the central market in Dalat (Photograph by Noboru Komine)

**Top:** Soup made with local fish, tomato and Asian celery

**Middle:** (Clockwise from top left) Green prawns on ice; chillies, onions and dried mushrooms for sale; fish at a market in Hoi An; longan fruit peeled and ready to go

**Bottom:** The inner sanctum – a restaurant kitchen in Ho Chi Minh City

One of the delights of visiting Vietnam is the amazing cuisine – there are said to be nearly 500 traditional Vietnamese dishes. Food is generally superbly prepared and very reasonably priced. Eating is such an integral part of the culture that a time-honoured Vietnamese proverb, 'hoc an, hoc noi', dictates that people should 'learn to eat before learning to speak…'

Vietnam is almost completely self-sufficient when it comes to tasty ingredients, and although its cuisine has been subject to colonial influences from the French and Chinese, it retains a unique flavour. This is largely due to the use of the uniquely Vietnamese fermented fish sauce, *nuoc mam*, an abundance of fresh vegetables and herbs, and the dominance of rice. The proximity of Vietnam to the sea, and having two major deltas within its borders, has ensured the use of fish and seafood in many dishes.

For the full scoop on Vietnamese cuisine, snap up a copy of Lonely Planet's *World Food Vietnam*, a compact yet exhaustive guide to the culinary pleasures of Vietnam.

## Utensils

Traditionally Vietnamese cooking was done over the hearth, which was considered to be the most important part of a house. There were no ovens as such, so food was prepared by boiling, steaming, grilling or frying. Thus a traditional kitchen would be equipped with terracotta cooking pots, woks, bamboo chopsticks and utensils, and a rice cooker. A pestle and mortar would also be used to finely grind herbs and spices.

Most of these utensils are still regularly used in Vietnamese kitchens, although these days gas burners have replaced the hearths. Some restaurants serve food in traditional terracotta pots that resemble samovars with their tops cut off, and put live coals in the centre to keep the food hot while it is being served.

## Eating Etiquette

Eating plays a huge role in Vietnamese society and there's a certain etiquette involved in the dining experience. Although your hosts will be too polite to actually point out your faux pas, it is worth abiding by certain customs. When invited out to dine, it is polite to bring along a small gift – flowers are suitable but should never be white as this signifies death.

Unlike the Western practice of each person ordering their own plate of food, dining in most Asian countries is a communal affair: a selection of dishes are put on the table to be shared. Sharing with three or four people ensures that you get to sample several dishes, and it is a fun and very sociable way to eat – many visitors come to prefer it over the Western style of individualism. If you eat with a group of Vietnamese, you may find that some of your fellow diners pick out the

**Inset:** Photograph by Noboru Komine

best-looking pieces of food with their chopsticks and put them into your rice bowl – a way of honouring you as a distinguished guest.

No-one will be offended if you ask for a knife and fork, although in some places this may not be an option. Fortunately spoons will usually be provided alongside chopsticks – although it's worth noting that the Vietnamese sip their food from the spoon and never place it directly into their mouth.

The proper way to eat Vietnamese food is to take rice from the large shared dish and put it in your rice bowl, then use your ceramic spoon to take meat, fish or vegetables from the serving dishes (never pour dipping sauces directly into your bowl). Transfer all food to your rice bowl before eating it and never use the chopsticks to pierce food on communal plates. Holding the rice bowl near your mouth, use your chopsticks to eat. Leaving the rice bowl on the table and conveying your food, precariously perched between chopsticks, all the way from the table to your mouth strikes Vietnamese as odd, though they will be more amused than offended. When passing or taking something always use both hands and acknowledge the transaction with a small nod.

It is polite for the host to offer more food than the guests can eat, and it is polite for the guests not to eat everything in sight!

If you want to deliver a 'delicious' compliment to the chef, just say *long num* or *ngoc hoa*.

# Dining Out

You'll never have to look very far for food in Vietnam – restaurants *(nha hang)* of one sort or another seem to be in every nook and cranny. Unless you eat in exclusive hotels or restaurants, Vietnamese food is very cheap. The best bargains can be found at street stalls, most of which are limited to the amount of ingredients they can carry, so tend to specialise in a couple of dishes. Wander around until something takes your fancy – a bowl of noodles costs around 8000d.

Basic restaurants with bamboo and cardboard walls have rice, meat and vegetable meals costing around 15,000d. Most cafés and decent restaurants can fill your stomach for 30,000d to 70,000d. There has been a recent surge of classier Vietnamese restaurants popping up in the cities. Traditional Vietnamese dishes taste all the better for being consumed in ambient French-style courtyards or riverside terraces. However, the bill can add up fast; be aware that the small snacks that appear on the table may cost you, if you indulge.

Although most serve exclusively Vietnamese food, many cafés can rustle up something Western, but the Vietnamese are much better at producing their food than the Western stuff – the Vietnamese pizza is particularly notorious. However, Western restaurants are increasing in number, and the cooks are slowly learning to accommodate Western tastes. Plus, there is a growing wave of expat chefs, notably Italians and French, offering up savoury delights from their home countries.

There are no set hours of business for places to eat, but as a general rule of thumb, cafés (especially travellers cafés) are open most of the day and into the night. Street stalls are open from very early in the morning till late at night. Restaurants will usually open for lunch, from about 11 am to 2 pm, and for dinner, from 5 to 10 pm.

## Exotic Meat

It is disturbing to most animal lovers that Fido can wind up on the menu, however, most Vietnamese don't eat dog – it's a speciality. Dog meat is most popular in the north, where its consumption is believed to bring good fortune (as long as it is only eaten during the second half of the lunar month). To find (or avoid) a restaurant serving dog meat, look for a sign saying *thit cho*, in the north, or *thit cay*, in the south.

Though it may be exotic to try wild meat such as muntjac, bat, frog, deer, sea horse, shark fin and snake, many of these are endangered; eating it will indicate your support and acceptance of such practices and add to the demand for these products.

Laws regarding the capture and sale of snakes have made snake meat a rarity. However, you are still likely to see it around, since it is believed to have some medicinal properties and widely touted as being an aphrodisiac. The more poisonous the snake, the worthier its reputation (and the higher the price charged). Cobras are a favourite, though pythons have a lot more meat. Feasting on such delicacies is not cheap and be aware that eating undercooked snake meat can prove dangerous.

One nonendangered animal eaten in the countryside is *chuot dong*, a rice-paddy dwelling rodent that tastes 'just like chicken'. Do not confuse these creatures with *chuot cong*, the larger and nastier urban rats similar to those found in cities around the world.

## The Bill

Many visitors are surprised to find that many local Vietnamese restaurants do not display prices on the menu at all. This is normal. Vietnamese typically eat out in groups and are charged by the amount ordered to feed the whole group. In the case of no-price menus, you should definitely ask the total price when you place your order. To get the bill, politely catch the attention of the waiting staff and write in the air as if with a pen on an imaginary piece of paper. Once you have it, check it carefully – overcharging or simple human error is not uncommon when more than one person orders food, or when many items are listed on the bill.

The moist hand towels, sealed in plastic, that you are given at most restaurants are sometimes free, but other times you'll be charged from 500d to 3000d for the pleasure of using them (a small price to pay depending on how dirty your hands are). It is advisable not to wipe your face with these – people have complained of eye irritation, though it's hard to say if this is from bacteria or the chemicals used to clean the towels.

# Typical Vietnamese Dishes

On menus, dishes are usually listed according to their main ingredient. For instance, all the chicken dishes appear together, as do all the beef dishes and so on. Basic culinary words to learn include the following:

*com* – rice
*pho* – noodle soup
*sup* – soup
*ga* – chicken
*bo* – beef
*heo* – pork
*tom* – shrimp
*ca* – fish

One of the most popular dishes is Vietnamese spring rolls *(nem)*, which are known as *cha gio* (pronounced, chow yau) in the south and *nem Sai Gon* or *nem ran* in the north. They are made of rice paper, and are filled with minced pork, crab, vermicelli, an edible fungus known as *moc nhi*, onion, mushroom and eggs, and then fried until the rice paper turns a crispy brown. *Nem rau* are vegetable spring rolls.

A variation on the theme are the delicious larger 'fresh' spring rolls called *banh trang* in the south and *banh da* in the north. With these you put the ingredients together yourself and roll your own. The outer shell is a translucent rice crepe. These are excellent, and are typically eaten with a kind of shrimp paste called *mam tep* or *mam tom* (the latter smells stronger).

Other popular dishes available throughout Vietnam include:

*banh cuon* – a steamed rice dumpling into which minced pork and *moc nhi* is rolled, and served with ca cuong, a special type of *nuoc mam* dipping sauce containing a filtered extract from insect semen, which gives the sauce its flowery aroma and pear taste
*bo bay mon* – sugar-beef dishes
*bun cha* – rice vermicelli with roasted pork and vegetables, served with a mixture of vinegar, chilli and sugar
*cha* – pork paste fried in fat or broiled over hot coals
*cha ca* – filleted fish slices broiled over charcoal, often served with noodles, green salad, roasted peanuts and a sauce made from *nuoc mam*, lemon and a special volatile oil
*cha que* – *cha* prepared with cinnamon
*chao tom* – grilled sugar cane rolled in spiced shrimp paste
*com tay cam* – rice with mushrooms, chicken and finely sliced pork flavoured with ginger
*dua chua* – bean-sprout salad that tastes vaguely like Korean *kimchi*
*ech tam bot ran* – frog meat soaked in a thin batter and fried in oil, usually served with *nuoc mam cham* and pepper
*gio* – lean, seasoned pork pounded into a paste before being packed into banana leaves and boiled

*lau* – Vietnamese hot pot, popular served with fish *(lau ca)* or goat *(lau de)* or vegetables only *(lau rau)*

*oc nhoi* – snail meat, pork, chopped green onion, *nuoc mam* and pepper rolled up in ginger leaves and cooked in snail shells

There is also a wide variety of Western-style foods available. Excellent French bread is sold everywhere – it's best in the morning when it's warm and fresh (a baguette costs about 1000d). Imported French cheese spread can be bought from street stalls for around 20,000d per pack, and some kind of salami or pâté is available.

## Hué Cuisine

The historic city of Hué, on the banks of the Perfume River in central Vietnam, is home to a remarkable tradition of Vietnamese *haute cuisine*. As the former Nguyen emperors' capital, it is the place where intricate and delicious dishes were developed and prepared. Emperor Tu Duc, who reigned from 1848 to 1883, demanded that his tea be made from dew that had accumulated on leaves overnight. He also expected 50 dishes prepared by 50 cooks to be served by 50 servants at each meal. Ironically, as the size of the servings declined, the time taken to prepare them rose in direct proportion.

His cooks obediently learned sophisticated techniques and presentation skills to keep the king happy. Recipes were passed down from generation to generation, and are the source of some of the delicate combinations of flavours found today.

Typical Hué-style dishes include the following:

*banh bo* – steamed rice-flour cake with ground shrimp
*banh khoai* – an omelet with bean sprouts, considered an aphrodisiac
*banh nan* – ground shrimp and pork steamed with rice flour and wrapped in banana leaves
*nem lui* – roll-em-yourself spring-roll kebabs with peanut sauce
*banh bot let* – shrimp, pork and tropical starch flour wrapped in banana leaves
*bun bo hue* – rice vermicelli and vegetables served dry, or usually with beef soup
*bun cha cua* – crab-paste noodle soup
*banh canh cua* – shrimp, crab meat, sliced pork with special rice noodle soup
*com ben* – clams with rice
*bun ben* – clams with rice noodles

One excellent place in Hué to sample haute cuisine inspired by these creative traditions is **Tinh Gia Vien** *(☎ 522243; 20/3 Đ Le Thanh Ton)* on the North Bank. See Hué in the Central Vietnam chapter. In Ho Chi Minh City (HCMC), look for a Hué-style restaurant near the Ben Thanh market called **Nam Giao**.

# Rice

The staple of Vietnamese cuisine is plain white rice *(com)* dressed up with a plethora of vegetables, meat, fish and spices. Rice is also used to make wine and noodles.

SB

The most common style of Vietnamese restaurant, found throughout the country, is known as *com pho*, which means rice-and-noodle shop. You will see signs reading *com pho* everywhere in your travels.

Another common type of rice restaurant, *com binh dan*, are inexpensive places that offer an array of fresh meat and vegetables served with steamed rice; there are no menus, just point to order. Most dishes are under 20,000d.

## Nuoc Mam

*Nuoc mam* is a type of fermented fish sauce – instantly identifiable by its distinctive smell – without which no Vietnamese meal is complete. Though *nuoc mam* is to Vietnamese cuisine what soy sauce is to Japanese food, many hotel restaurants won't serve it to foreigners, knowing that the odour may drive away their Western customers.

The sauce is made by fermenting highly salted fish in large ceramic vats for four to 12 months. Famous places for *nuoc mam* production include Phu Quoc Island in the Mekong Delta, and Phan Thiet on the south central coast. The price of *nuoc mam* varies considerably according to the quality. Connoisseurs insist the high-grade rocket fuel has a much milder aroma than the cheaper variety, though most foreigners will find it hard to tell the difference.

A more palatable version of fish sauce served in eateries throughout Vietnam is *nuoc mam cham*. This is basically *nuoc mam* with lime, vinegar, sugar, water, chilli and garlic added, which makes it much more agreeable to Western taste buds.

*Nuoc mam* actually isn't bad once you get used to it, and in the past some people even took a few bottles home with them in their luggage (God help you if the bottle leaked). However, in accordance with international aviation regulations against taking strong-smelling and corrosive substances on board, *nuoc mam* recently joined the nasally obnoxious durian fruit among the food substances banned on Vietnam Airlines flights. The ban apparently resulted from an incident in which a bottle of the sauce broke during a flight, causing angry protests from perturbed foreign passengers sensitive to its smell.

If *nuoc mam* isn't strong enough for you, try *mam tom*, a powerful shrimp paste that American soldiers sometimes called 'Viet Cong tear gas'. It's often served with dog meat – foreigners generally find it far more revolting than the dog itself.

# Noodles

Vietnamese noodles are eaten at all hours of the day, but are a breakfast favourite. Most Westerners prefer their noodles at lunch and fortunately you can also get bread, cheese and eggs in the morning. Most noodles are usually eaten as a soup rather than 'dry' like spaghetti.

There are three types of noodles served with soups: white-rice noodles *(banh pho)*; clear noodles made from rice mixed with manioc powder *(mien);* and yellow, wheat noodles *(mi)*. Noodles are available either with broth *(nuoc leo)* or dry *(kho)*. Some of the more popular dishes include:

**bun thang** – rice noodles and shredded chicken with fried egg and prawns on top, served with a broth made by boiling chicken, dried prawns and pig bones
**canh kho hoa** – a bitter soup (said to be especially good for the health of people who have spent a lot of time in the sun)
**mi ga** – chicken soup with dry noodles
**mien luon** – vermicelli soup with eel, seasoned with mushrooms, shallots, fried eggs and chicken
**pho bo** – beef noodle soup
**pho ga** – chicken noodle soup

Noodle stalls and shops start serving *pho* (Vietnam's 'breakfast of champions') to hungry customers from around 5am or 6am, and usually close up before lunch, though some keep longer hours. A bowl of *pho* typically costs between 7000d and 15,000d.

# Vegetarian Food

Buddhist monks of the Mahayana tradition are strict vegetarians (at least they are supposed to be) so vegetarian cooking *(an chay)* has a long history in Vietnam and is an integral part of the cuisine. Because it does not include many expensive ingredients, vegetarian food is unbelievably cheap, especially at vegetarian street stalls signposted *com chay*. In some speciality restaurants, chefs prepare vegetarian dishes (mostly tofu-based) that bear a remarkable resemblance to common meat dishes.

On full-moon (the 15th day of the lunar month) or new-moon days (the last day of the lunar month), many Vietnamese and Chinese avoid eating meat or even *nuoc mam*. On such days, some food stalls, especially in the markets, serve vegetarian meals. To find out when the next new or full moon is, consult any Vietnamese calendar.

Common vegetarian selections include:

**rau xao hon hop** – fried vegetables
**xao thap cam** – stir-fried mixed vegetables
**com xao thap cam** – fried rice with mixed vegetables
**hu tieu xao** – fried rice noodles
**xup rau** – vegetable soup
**tau hu kho** – braised soya cake

# Desserts & Cakes

Vietnamese sweets *(do ngot)* and desserts *(do trang mieng)* are popular everywhere, and are especially prevalent during festivals when traditional cakes *(danh)* come in a wide variety of shapes and flavours.

In addition to the delicious European-style pastries and ice cream found in Vietnam, try to find an opportunity to sample one or more of the following traditional delicacies:

*banh bao* – sweet, doughy Chinese pastry with a red dot on top and filled with meat, onions and vegetables and dunked in soy sauce
*banh chung* – square cake made from sticky rice and filled with beans, onion and pork, boiled in leaves for 10 hours – a traditional Tet favourite
*banh dau xanh* – mung-bean cake that 'melts on your tongue' and is usually served with hot tea
*banh deo* – cake made of dried sticky-rice flour mixed with a boiled sugar solution and filled with candied fruit, sesame seeds and fat, and eaten during the mid-autumn festival
*banh it nhan dau* – a traditional pastry made of pulverised sticky rice, beans and sugar that's steamed (and sold) in a banana leaf folded into a triangular pyramid and usually on sale at Mekong Delta ferry crossings
*banh it nhan dua* – a variation of *banh it nhan dau* but made with coconut instead of beans
*che* – highly popular with Hanoians, this is served in a tall ice-cream sundae glass, and typically contains beans, fruit, coconut and sugar; an interesting variety made with pomelo flower is called *che buoi*
*kem dua, kem trai dua* – delicious mix of ice cream, candied fruit and the jellylike flesh of young coconut, served in a baby coconut shell
*mut* – candied fruit or vegetables, made with carrot, coconut, kumquat, gourd, ginger root, lotus seeds and tomato
*yaourt* – little jars or plastic cups of sweetened frozen yoghurt that are usually available from ice-cream stalls

---

## Ice Cream

*Kem*, or ice cream, was introduced on a large scale by the Americans, who made a reliable supply of the stuff a top wartime priority. The US army hired two American companies, Foremost Dairy and Meadowgold Dairies, to build dozens of ice-cream factories around the country. Inevitably, the locals developed a taste for the product. Even 15 years after bona fide Foremost products ceased to be available, the company's orange-and-white logo was prominently on display in shops selling ice cream. Foremost did in fact return to Vietnam in 1994 to set up a new dairy, and was soon followed by two American ice-cream giants, Baskin Robbins and Carvel.

Proving more popular than the American stuff, however, is the laudable, French-run Fanny Ice Cream, which whips up delicious home-made flavors using fresh local fruit and even young sticky rice! Fanny has branches in Hanoi and Ho Chi Minh City.

# Fruit

Fruit *(qua* or *trai)* is available in Vietnam year-round, but many of the country's most interesting specialties have short seasons.

*avocado* – often eaten in a glass with ice and sweetened with either sugar or condensed milk

*cinnamon apple* – also known as custard apple, sugar apple and sweetsop, it is ripe when it's very soft and the area around the stem turns blackish

*coconut* – in their mature state, coconuts are eaten only by children or as jam. For snacking, Vietnamese prefer the soft jellylike flesh and fresher milk of young coconuts. The coconuts grown around the Ha Tien area in the Mekong Delta are a special variety with delicious coconut flesh, but no milk.

*durian* – a large fruit (about football size) covered in big sharp spikes, with pale flesh. Despite being considered the 'king of fruit,' and also the most expensive tropical fruit in Vietnam, durian is often said to 'taste like heaven, but smell like hell.' It is so smelly that some hotels post signs saying not to eat it in their rooms!

*green banana* – sold in markets and usually ripe enough to eat (in fact, they taste better than the yellow ones)

*jackfruit* – an enormous watermelon-sized fruit, with bright yellow segments and a slightly rubbery texture

*longan* – small and juicy brown-skinned balls grown all over the Mekong Delta region

*lychee* – these are larger and sweeter that longans

*papaya or pawpaw* – has bright orange flesh that tastes like a melon and the black seeds are said to act as a contraceptive

*pomelo* – looks like a huge orange or grapefruit; the skin is greenish and the flesh often has a purple tinge

## Dragon Fruit

Vietnam is well known for its astounding array of tropical fruits, and one of the most exotic treats is green dragon fruit *(thanh long)*. This fruit, which is the size and shape of a small pineapple and has a smooth magenta skin, grows mainly in the Mekong Delta and coastal areas south of Nha Trang.

A large dragon fruit can weigh up to 800g. Its delicious white flesh is speckled with black seeds, and tastes a bit like kiwi fruit. Green dragon fruit grows on a kind of creeping cactus – said to resemble a green dragon – that climbs up the trunks and branches of trees and flourishes on parched hillsides that get little water. *Thanh long* is in season from May to November and can be purchased at nearly any local market in the areas where it's grown. The fruit is sold around Vietnam, and even exported (it fetches a high price in Taiwan), but it is cheapest and freshest at the source. Locals often make a refreshing drink out of crushed green dragon fruit, ice, sugar and sweetened condensed milk. It's also used to make jam.

# Drinks
## Coffee

Vietnamese coffee is fine stuff. Particularly notable are the beans grown in the central highlands around Buon Ma Thuot. There is, however, one qualifier – you'll probably need to dilute it with hot water. The Vietnamese prefer their coffee so strong and so sweet that it will turn your teeth inside out. Ordering 'white coffee' *(ca phe sua da)* usually results in a coffee with about 30% to 40% sweet condensed milk. Ovaltine and Milo, which are regarded as desserts rather than drinks, will also be served this way. Restaurants used to foreigners will be prepared with a flask of hot water so you can dilute your coffee as you wish. However, restaurants that deal with mainly Vietnamese people will probably be dumbfounded by your request for hot water. You'll also need to communicate the fact that you need a large glass – ultra-sweet coffee is traditionally served in a tiny shot glass, leaving you no room to add any water.

Instant coffee *(ca phe tan* or *ca phe bot)* made its debut in 1996 – a disaster! Many cafés assume Westerners prefer instant coffee because it's 'modern' and comes from the West. You need to communicate the fact that you want fresh-brewed Vietnamese coffee *(ca phe phin)*, not imported instant powder.

Rather than prepare coffee in a pot, the Vietnamese prefer to brew it right at the table, French-style – a dripper with coffee grounds is placed over the cup and hot water poured in. If you prefer iced coffee, the same method is applied, but with a glass of ice under the dripper. Both the drippers and packaged coffee make inexpensive souvenirs. In cafés, Vietnamese tea in doll-house sized tea cups is usually served (free) after you've finished your coffee.

Perhaps the highest-grade Vietnamese coffee *(chon)* is made of beans that are fed to a certain species of weasel and later collected from the weasel's excrement. One place you can try a cup of this stuff (for about 10,000d) is Trung Nguyen, a popular chain of coffee shops found in Hanoi and Ho Chi Minh City (HCMC). Trung Nguyen, Vietnam's answer to Starbucks, means 'Central Highlands'.

## Tea

In the south, Vietnamese tea is cheap but disappointing – the aroma is perfume-like, but the taste sometimes resembles the glue found on postal envelopes. Guests are always served tea (local green tea or Lipton) when visiting a Vietnamese home or business. In restaurants, a cheap and delicious choice is local iced tea *(tra da);* it usually costs just 1000d.

Tea from the north is much better but also stronger so be prepared for a caffeine jolt. Northern tea is similar to Chinese green tea and is almost always sold in loose form rather than teabags. The locals never put milk or sugar into green tea and will think you're a loony if you do.

Imported tea (in teabag form) can be bought in major cities, but is still rare in rural areas. The price is perfectly reasonable so there's no need to bring it from abroad. Most restaurants can dig up some lemon and sugar for your tea, although milk is not always available.

## Mineral Water

The selection of mineral water *(nuoc suoi)* has been expanding rapidly ever since the Vietnamese realised that tourists were willing to pay good money for water sealed in plastic bottles. See the 'C'est La Vie' boxed text. If you prefer your mineral water with fizzy bubbles, look for Vinh Hao carbonated water (available in the south only). It's normally mixed with ice, lemon and sugar (outstanding!), which is called *so-da chanh*.

## Coconut Milk

There is nothing more refreshing on a hot day than fresh coconut milk *(nuoc dua)*. The Vietnamese believe that coconut milk, like hot milk in Western culture, makes you tired. Athletes would never drink it before a competition.

The coconuts grown around the Ha Tien area in the Mekong Delta are a special variety with delicious coconut flesh, but no milk.

## Soft Drinks

These days nearly all of Vietnam's domestic carbonated soft drinks have been replaced by Coca-Cola and Pepsi.

One excellent domestic soft drink with a pleasant fruit flavour is *nuoc khoang kim boi*; a bottle costs 5000d.

In addition, various flavours of fresh fruit juices *(sinh to)*, including delicious sugar-cane juice, are available throughout Vietnam.

## Beer

Saigon Export (yes, they do really export it) and Saigon Lager are two local brands of beer. Other Vietnamese brands include Castel, Huda (from Hué), Halida, Bia Hanoi and 333 (pronounced ba-ba-ba). Dozens of locally produced regional beers, though watery and often flat, are available in bottles for less than the name brands. One traveller described some of these as being a cross between light beer and iced tea. There are a number of foreign brands that are brewed in Vietnam under licence. These include BGI, Carlsberg, Heineken and Tiger.

Memorise the words *bia hoi*, which mean 'draught beer'. There are signs advertising it everywhere and most cafés have it on the menu. The quality varies, but it is generally OK and very cheap (about 3000d per litre). Places that serve *bia hoi* usually also have good, cheap food. 'Fresh beer' *(bia tuoi)* is similar to draught beer.

## Wine

Vietnam produces over 50 varieties of wine *(ruou)*, many of them made from rice. The cheapest rice wines *(ruou de)* are used for cooking so drink them at your peril.

Another Vietnamese speciality is snake wine *(ruou ran)*. This is basically rice wine with a pickled snake floating in it. This elixir is considered a tonic and allegedly cures everything from night blindness to impotence.

A variation on the theme is to have the snake killed right at your table and the blood poured into a cup. To get the full health benefits, the Vietnamese recommend that you drink the snake's blood mixed with rice wine and eat the gall bladder raw (delicious!). Connoisseurs of this cuisine also recommend that you put the snake's still-beating heart into a glass of rice wine and 'bottoms up'. This cocktail is believed to work as an aphrodisiac.

A superb place to sample a wide variety of high-grade Vietnamese rice wine is Highway 4, in the Old Quarter of Hanoi. See Entertainment in the Hanoi chapter.

For the less adventurous, there is plenty of good Italian, French, Australian and US wine available.

## Hard Liquor

Alcoholic beverages *(ruou manh)* from China are very cheap, taste like paint thinner and smell like diesel fuel. Russian vodka is one of the few things the former Soviet Union has left to export. Locally produced Hanoi Vodka is also available. *Nep moi* is a smooth vodka made from sticky rice.

As in the rest of Asia, the Vietnamese nouveaux riches prefer foreign-name brands such as Johnny Walker Black. You can sit in almost any high-class Vietnamese restaurant and watch groups of rosy-cheeked businessmen or government officials polish off bottles of the stuff in no time flat.

*[Continued from page 112]*

## COURSES
### Language
If you'd like to learn Vietnamese, there are courses offered in HCMC, Hanoi and elsewhere. To qualify for student-visa status, you need be enrolled to study at a bona fide university (as opposed to a private language centre or with a tutor). Universities require that you attend classes for at least 10 hours per week. Lessons usually last for two hours per day, and cost from US$2.80 to US$4 per hour.

You should establish early on whether you want to study Vietnamese in Hanoi or HCMC, as the northern and southern dialects differ. Many have been dismayed to discover that if they studied in one city that they cannot communicate in the other. But (get ready for this) the majority of the teachers at universities in the south have been imported from the north and will tell you that the northern dialect is the 'correct one'! So even if you study at a university in HCMC, you may find that you need to hire a local private tutor (cheap at any rate) to help rid you of a northern accent.

For further information see the Language Courses sections in the Hanoi and Ho Chi Minh City chapters.

### Cooking
Interesting Vietnamese cooking classes are offered in Hoi An and HCMC. Courses range from a few hours to several days. For more information, refer to these chapters of the book.

## WORK
From 1975 to about 1990, Vietnam's foreign workers were basically technical specialists and military advisers from Eastern Europe and the now-defunct Soviet Union, whose declining fortunes have meant that most of these advisers have been withdrawn.

Vietnam's opening up to capitalist countries has suddenly created all sorts of work opportunities for Westerners. However, don't go there looking to make big money. The best-paid Westerners living in Vietnam are those working for international organisations, such as the UN and embassies, or those hired by foreign companies. People with specialist technology skills may also find themselves in demand and may be able to secure high salaries and cushy benefits.

It's nice work if you can get it, but such plum jobs are thin on the ground. Foreigners who look like Rambo have occasionally been approached by Vietnamese talent scouts wanting to recruit them to work as extras in war movies, but for most travellers, the main work opportunities will be teaching a foreign language.

English is by far the most popular foreign language with Vietnamese students, and about 10% of foreign-language students in Vietnam also want to learn French. Many also want to learn Chinese, but there is a large ethnic-Chinese community in Vietnam so there is little need to import foreign teachers. There is also a limited demand for teachers of Japanese, German, Spanish and Korean.

Government-run universities in Vietnam hire some foreign teachers. Pay is generally around US$5 per hour, but benefits such as free housing and unlimited visa renewals are usually thrown in. Teaching at a university requires some commitment (eg, you may have to sign a one-year contract).

There is also a budding free market in private language centres and home tutoring; this is where most newly arrived foreigners seek work. Pay in the private sector is slightly better – expect about US$6 to US$10 per hour depending on where you teach. However, it is likely that these private schools won't be able to offer the same benefits as a government-run school. You will also need a business visa and in some cases the school may not be able to help you acquire one. A possible way around the visa hurdles is to sign up for Vietnamese language lessons at a university, but be aware that you may actually be expected to attend class and study.

Private tutoring usually pays even better – around US$10 to US$15 per hour. In this case, you are in business for yourself. The authorities may or may not turn a blind eye to such activities.

Finding teaching jobs is quite easy in places such as HCMC and Hanoi, and is sometimes possible in towns that have universities. Pay in the smaller towns tends to be lower and work opportunities are fewer.

Looking for employment is a matter of asking around – jobs are rarely advertised. The longer you stay, the easier it is to find work – travellers hoping to land a quick job and depart two months later will probably be disappointed.

## Volunteer Work

For information on volunteer work opportunities, you may wish to contact the NGO Resource Centre. See the Useful Organisations section earlier in this chapter for full details.

## ACCOMMODATION

The tourist boom initially created a shortage of hotels, but overbuilding has now produced a glut.

In larger cities there is a plentiful supply of international-standard hotel rooms, and prices are competitive. This applies across the board, from guesthouses to top-notch hotels. What this means is that travellers are in a better negotiating position. During our last visit rooms could be found in posh four-star hotels (many of which were operating with as low as a 20% occupancy rate) for as little as US$80! In the high seasons, however, you may have to search around, especially in popular places like Hoi An, where there are still not enough rooms to accommodate its large number of visitors.

At most government-run hotels foreigners are charged more than Vietnamese (usually double). The theory is that foreigners are richer than local Vietnamese and therefore can afford to pay a premium.

Remember that some hotels levy a room tax of 10%. Ask in advance if the room rate includes tax or not. Top end hotels often work on the 'plus plus' (++) concept, adding 10% value added tax (VAT) and another 5% service charge. At upmarket places, for example, a lunch buffet at a five-star hotel might be quoted at US$10++, but the total price is really US$11.50.

There are regulations requiring hotels and guesthouses to maintain 'acceptable standards' before they can be approved to receive foreign guests (you'd never know it by some of the dumps around). So it is possible that you will front up to what seems like a perfectly serviceable hotel and be refused a room even if the place is empty. In that case, there is little point arguing. The hotel staff won't risk trouble with the police just to accommodate you, though they may refer you elsewhere.

Theoretically, these regulations are meant to protect foreign tourists from staying in dirty and dangerous places. Though a highly unlikely scenario, if all of the approved hotels were booked out, and you couldn't stay in the unapproved ones, your only choice would be to sleep in the street. The Vietnamese have an expression for sleeping out in the street – it's called staying in a 'thousand-star hotel'.

## Reservations

A 'reservation' means next to nothing unless you've paid for the room in advance. It's possible to arrange this through some travel agencies, but don't expect much at the budget end of the spectrum. However, there is seldom much need for reservations as you can almost always find a place to stay in cities. An important exception is during the Tet Festival and the 10-day period that immediately follows it: at that time reservations are recommended.

## Camping

Perhaps because so many millions of Vietnamese spent much of the war years living in tents (often either as soldiers or refugees), camping is not the popular pastime it is in the West. Even in Dalat, where youth groups often go for outdoor holidays, very little proper equipment can be hired.

The younger generation, however, seems to have discovered a taste for sleeping in tents (just so long as there is karaoke nearby). At beach resorts such as Mui Ne Beach (near Phan Thiet), beachfront camping has become all the rage, and is more affordable than a private bungalow.

Some innovative private travel agencies in HCMC and Hanoi offer organised camping trips, especially to national parks. See the Travel Agencies sections in the Hanoi and Ho Chi Minh City chapters.

## Dormitories

While there are Vietnamese dormitories *(nha tro)* all over Vietnam (especially around train and bus stations), most of these are officially off-limits to foreigners. In this case, the government's motives are not about charging you more money. There is a significant chance of getting robbed while sleeping in a Vietnamese dorm, and by Western standards many of these places are considered substandard (beds generally consist of a wooden platform and straw mat). Even though budget travellers do like to complain about this policy, it's one case where the Vietnamese government is really trying to protect them.

The concept of the relatively upmarket, foreigner-only dorm (furnished with real mattresses) is continuing to catch on. Some of these 'dormitories' are actually rooms with just two beds – you share the room with only one other person and still pay only US$2 to US$4 each. You are most likely to find these in private minihotels in areas frequented by budget travellers. HCMC's Pham Ngu Lao area pioneered the concept, but there are dorm-style rooms found in guesthouses and minihotels in Hanoi, Nha Trang and other backpacker centres. Expect to see more of these places in the future.

## Hotels

Many of the large hotels *(khach san)* and guesthouses *(nha khach* or *nha nghi)* are government-owned or joint ventures. There is also a rapidly increasing number of small private hotels, usually referred to as minihotels.

There is some confusion over the terms 'singles', 'doubles', 'double occupancy' and 'twins', so let's set the record straight here. A single is a room containing one bed, even if two people sleep in it. If there are two beds in the room, that is a twin, even if only one person occupies it. If two people stay in the same room, that is double occupancy – in most cases, there is no extra charge for this. There is considerable confusion over the term 'doubles' – in some hotels this means twin beds, while in others it means double occupancy. More than a few travellers have paid extra for twin beds when what they really wanted was a bed for two people. It's always a good idea to take a look at the room to make sure that you're getting what you wanted and are not paying extra for something you don't need.

Most hotels now offer rooms that have a private bathroom – ask first or take a look at the room to be sure. Some hotels have a private bath, but the toilet is outside (a peculiar arrangement).

A few hotels might try to charge the foreigners' price for your Vietnamese guide and/or driver if they know that you're paying the bill. Don't accept this nonsense from anyone.

It's a good idea to ask for a receipt when you pay (and save it), especially if you'll be staying for more than a few days. Confusion can arise over how many days you have paid for and how much you still owe. A few hotels are guilty of chaotic book-keeping (sometimes deliberate), and one shift at the front desk might have no clue about what other shifts have and have not done.

It's important to realise that many hotels have both a new upmarket wing and an old squalid wing, with a wide variation in prices between the two. Furthermore, many Vietnamese hotels offer a wide range of prices within the same building! For example, one hotel in Hanoi we checked into had rooms from around US$6 to US$60! The cheaper rooms are almost always on the top floor because few hotels have lifts and guests paying US$60 are not keen on having to walk up seven storeys or more.

Even at the biggest and most expensive hotels, it's possible to get discounts if you're staying long term. For definition's sake, long term can mean three days or more. Booking through some foreign or domestic travel agencies can also net you a discount.

Don't forget that most of the smaller hotels shut their doors early, usually around

11pm. This does *not*, however, mean there is a curfew, nor that you've been locked out. If you get back after hours, just ring the bell and someone will let you in; it may take a couple of rings, however, to wake them up.

The following are some of the more common hotel names and their translations:

| hotel name | English translation |
| --- | --- |
| Binh Minh | Sunrise |
| Bong Sen | Lotus |
| Cuu Long | Nine Dragons |
| Doc Lap | Descending Dragon |
| Hoa Binh | Peace |
| Huong Sen | Lotus Fragrance |
| Huu Nghi | Friendship |
| Thang Long | Ascending Dragon |
| Thong Nhat | Reunification |
| Tu Do | Freedom |

**Hotel Security** Many hotels post a small sign warning you not to leave cameras, passports and other valuables in your room. Most places have a safety deposit system of some kind, but if you are leaving cash (not recommended) or travellers cheques, be sure to seal the loot in an envelope and have it signed for by the staff.

Some hotel rooms come equipped with a closet that can be locked – if so, use it and take the key with you. You would be very wise to bring a chain with a padlock – this can be used to lock the closet and then you won't have to worry about the employees having keys. If your room or the hotel has a safe, make use of it. A few hotels have doors that you can attach a padlock to the outside of, rather than using a lock built into the door itself. The hotel will provide you with a padlock, but you'd be wise to bring your own. A combination lock might be more convenient, but make sure it's one that is not easily broken (cheaper ones can be pried apart with a screwdriver).

Beware of hotel rooms with windows or balconies that might allow a thief to enter while you are out. We have heard several reports of theft in this fashion, so when you do go out, be sure to lock all windows and doors.

The government no longer requires police registration of hotel guests. The bad news is that provincial governments sometimes make up their own rules. Though technically you do not need to leave your passport with hotel reception, most hotels will request it anyway as 'security' (ie, to make sure you don't run away without paying).

The regulations are as clear as mud. Each city you visit may have its own arbitrary rules and these can change at the drop of a hat. There's no question that most foreigners don't like to see their valuable documents passing through so many hands with the chance that something could get lost.

When you check out of a hotel, you must check your documents very carefully. Be sure that the yellow customs declaration paper is still together with the passport.

## Homestays

It's possible to arrange to stay in the homes of local people, but depending on the local government, the family may have to register all foreign guests, including relatives, with the police. The police can, and often do, arbitrarily deny such registration requests and will force you to stay in a hotel or guesthouse licensed to accept foreigners.

Popular places to homestay are the fruit-orchard islands near Vinh Long; see the Mekong Delta chapter for details.

## Rental Accommodation

Renting a medium-size house in HCMC or Hanoi costs anywhere from around US$200 to US$500 per month. Higher-priced villas or expensive luxury flats rent for anywhere from around US$500 to US$3000.

Many expats wind up living in minihotels. Big discounts can be negotiated for long-term stays. It's wise to first live in the hotel for at least one night before agreeing to anything. You'll want to be sure that the place really is clean and quiet with functional plumbing before you hand over a month's rent.

## FOOD & DRINKS

Vietnamese cuisine has become a favourite throughout the Western world – but what can you expect when you arrive there? For the full story on Vietnamese cuisine, see the special section 'Tastes of Vietnam' earlier in this chapter.

## ENTERTAINMENT
### Pubs

Vietnamese-style pubs tend to be karaoke lounges – you know you've assimilated when you start enjoying these places. However, the increasing number of tourists and expats (especially in Hanoi and HCMC) has caused a boom in Western-style pubs. Many of these are husband-and-wife joint ventures (typically a Western husband and Vietnamese wife). In spite of the Tiger beer, many of these places seem almost indistinguishable from their counterparts over in London, Berlin, New York or Melbourne. Features such as Darts, Mexican food, rock music, oak furniture and CNN can make you forget where you are.

### Discos

Following reunification, ballrooms and discos were denounced as imperialist dens of iniquity and shut down by the authorities. Since 1990 they have reopened, though some forms of dancing (such as Brazil's erotic dance, the lambada) technically remain banned. Hanoi and HCMC are the hot beds for nightclubs – the 'in' place to go seems to change by the week.

### Karaoke

Most Westerners find karaoke about as appealing as roasted gecko with shrimp paste. Nonetheless, karaoke has taken over Asia and you'll have a hard time avoiding it.

For those unfamiliar with karaoke, it's simply a system where you are supposed to sing along with a video. The words to the song are flashed on the bottom of the screen (a number of languages are possible) and participants are supplied with a microphone. Really fancy karaoke bars have superb audio systems and big-screen video, but no matter how good the equipment, it's not going to sound any better than the ability of the singer. And with a few exceptions, it sounds truly awful. The Vietnamese only enjoy karaoke if it's played at over 150 decibels.

---

### C'est la Vie

The Vietnamese are notorious copycats, and the prevailing trend in business is to imitate thy neighbour, rather than create an original niche. This tendency is displayed by hotels, restaurants, street names and tour programmes, but perhaps the best example is the bottled-water market.

In 1989 La Vie, the famed French mineral-water maker, was the first foreign outfit to set up bottling plants in Vietnam. Since then, strikingly close variations on the trademark red, white and blue label design, as well as variations on the name La Vie, have appeared in all corners of the country.

At last count there were over 25 different spin-offs, including those with nonsense names like La Viei, La Vu, La Vi and La Ve. The best, perhaps, are the those that have meaning in French: slurp down a cold bottle of La Vif (The Lively); La Vide (The Empty); or, brace yourself, La Viole (The Rape). If you're in Hanoi and visit the rice-wine bar Highway 4 (see Entertainment in the Hanoi chapter), look for the diverse collection of copycat La Vie labels framed on the bathroom wall.

---

A big warning – many karaoke places have hidden charges, in particular at *karaoke om* joints where young women are provided to 'hold' while you sing. It is best to avoid these type of places. Even at regular karaoke places, the beers might only be US$1 apiece, but there can be a hefty charge for use of the microphone and video tapes. Get this all worked out in advance.

### Cinemas

Movie theatres are common in nearly all major towns and cities. Many urban maps have cinemas *(rap)*.

Films from the former Soviet Union have been replaced with Western movies that are either subtitled or dubbed. The dubbed ones are a kick, as most voice-overs are handled by just one person (who by nature can only be either male *or* female). Watching Arnold Schwarzenegger speaking in Vietnamese is hard enough to swallow, but try to imagine what it's like when he has a dainty woman's voice!

Regional imports are popular, but Vietnam now produces its own kung fu movies rather than importing them from China, Hong Kong and Taiwan. Love stories are also popular, but while Vietnamese censors take a dim view of nudity and sex, murder and mayhem are OK.

## SPECTATOR SPORTS

Football (soccer) is Vietnam's number-one spectator sport and the country has gone hog-wild for the game. During the World Cup or any major European championship game, half of the country stays up all night to watch live games in different time zones around the world. Post-game fun includes hazardous high-speed motorbike cruising in the streets of Hanoi and HCMC.

Tennis has considerable snob appeal – trendy Vietnamese like to both watch and play. The Vietnamese are incredibly skilled at badminton. Other favourite sports include volleyball and table tennis.

## SHOPPING

As a general principal, items sold in touristy areas, with no visible price tags, must be bargained for – expect the vendor to start the bidding at two to five times the real price. Tagged items may be negotiable, but more often than not the prices are fixed.

Please don't buy souvenirs taken from historical sites, or made from endangered wildlife such as turtle shells.

### Art & Antiques

There are several good shops to hunt for art and antiques, but Vietnam has strict regulations on the export of real antiques, so be sure that what you buy can be taken out of the country legally.

Both traditional and modern paintings are a popular item. The cheaper mass-produced stuff (US$5 to US$20 per piece) is sent mostly to souvenir shops and street vendors. Works of a higher standard are displayed in art galleries. Prices for paintings range from US$50 to US$500, but some of the hottest

Vietnamese artists now fetch up to 10 times that. It's important to know that there are quite a few forgeries around – just because you spot a painting by a 'famous Vietnamese artist' does not mean that it's an original, though it may still be an attractive work of art.

A Vietnamese speciality is the 'instant antique', such as a teapot or ceramic dinner plate, with a price tag of around US$2. Of course, it's OK to buy fake antiques as long as you aren't paying genuine antique prices. However, a problem occurs if you've bought an antique (or something that looks antique) and didn't get an official export certificate:

When I was in the airport in Hanoi, a customs officer eyed out two porcelain vases I had bought and told me that I should go to the Department of Culture in Hanoi to have them assessed or pay a fine of US$20. Of course, there was no representative of the Department of Culture at the airport...so getting them assessed would require me to miss my flight.

**Anna Crawford Pinnerup**

Most reputable shops can either provide the necessary paperwork or advise on where to get it. Just what happens to the confiscated 'antiques' is a good question. Some say that the authorities sell them back to the souvenir shops. You might call it recycling.

### Clothing

*Ao dai* (**ow**-zai in the north, **ow**-yai in the south) is the national of dress of both Vietnamese women and men and is a popular item, especially for women. Ready-made *ao dai* cost from US$10 to US$20, while the custom-tailored sets are notably more. Prices vary by the store and material used. If you want to buy custom-made clothing for your friends, you'll need their measurements: neck diameter, breast, waist, hip and length (from waist to hem). As a general rule, you get best results when you're right there and are measured by the tailor or seamstress. There are *ao dai* tailors nationwide, but the ones in places like HCMC, Hoi An and Hanoi are more accustomed to dealing with foreigners.

Women all over the country wear conical hats to keep the sun off their faces, though they also function as umbrellas in the rain. If you hold a well-made conical hat up to the light, you'll be able to see that between the layers of straw material are fine paper cuts. The best-quality conical hats are produced in the Hué area.

Hanoi and HCMC are good places to pick up contemporary fashion items: from beaded slippers and bags to original-design silk pieces.

T-shirts are ever popular items with travellers. A printed shirt costs around 20,000d while an embroidered design will cost maybe 50,000d. However, 'large' in Asia is often equivalent to 'medium' in the West. If you are really large, forget it unless you want to have your shirts individually tailored.

These days more and more hill-tribe garb is finding its way to shops in Hanoi and HCMC. It is indeed colourful, but you may need to set the dyes yourself, so those colours don't bleed all over the rest of your clothes.

## Electronics

Electronic goods sold in Vietnam are actually not such a great bargain. You'd be better off purchasing these in duty-free ports such as Hong Kong and Singapore. However, the prices charged in Vietnam are not bad, mainly due to the black market (smuggling), which also results in 'duty-free' goods.

## Gems

Vietnam produces some good gems, but there are plenty of fakes and flawed ones around. This doesn't mean that you can't buy something if you think it's beautiful, but don't think that you'll find a cut diamond or polished ruby for a fraction of what you'd pay at home. Some travellers have actually thought that they could buy gems in Vietnam and sell these at home for a profit. Such business requires considerable expertise and good connections in the mining industry.

## Handicrafts

Hot items on the tourist market include lacquerware, boxes and wooden screens with mother-of-pearl inlay, ceramics (check out the elephants), colourful embroidered items (hangings, tablecloths, pillow cases, pyjamas and robes), greeting cards with silk paintings on the front, wood-block prints, oil paintings, watercolours, blinds made of hanging bamboo beads (many travellers like the ones that have a replica of the Mona Lisa), reed mats, carpets, jewellery and leatherwork.

## Music

Across Vietnam, especially in larger cities, you'll find an astounding collection of CDs, VCDs, DVDs and audio tapes for sale, 99% of which are pirated. The official word is that this illegal practice will be 'cleaned up' by the authorities, but don't hold your breath waiting.

There are also plenty of opportunities to purchase Vietnamese musical instruments throughout the country. You can find hill-tribe instruments in their local markets.

## Stamps

Postage stamps, already set in a collector's book, are readily available either inside or near the post office in major cities or at some hotel gift shops and bookshops. You can even find stamps from the now-extinct South Vietnamese regime.

## War Souvenirs

In places frequented by tourists, it's easy to buy what looks like equipment left over from the American War. However, almost all of these items are reproductions and your chances of finding anything original are slim. Enterprising back-alley tailors turn out US military uniforms, while metalcraft shops have learned how to make helmets, bayonets and dog tags.

The fake Zippo lighters engraved with 'soldier poetry' are still one of the hottest-selling items. You can pay extra to get one that's been beat up to look like a war relic, or just buy a brand-new shiny one for less.

One thing you should think twice about purchasing are weapons and ammunition *even if fake*. It's illegal to carry real or fake ammunition and weapons on airlines and many countries will arrest you if any such goods are found in your luggage.

# Getting There & Away

## AIR

### Airports

Tan Son Nhat Airport in Ho Chi Minh City (HCMC) is Vietnam's busiest international air hub, followed by Hanoi's Noi Bai Airport. A handful of international flights also serve Danang.

### Airlines

**Vietnam Airlines** (*Hang Khong Viet Nam;* w *www.vietnamairlines.com.vn*) is the state-owned flag carrier, and the majority of flights into and out of Vietnam are joint operations between Vietnam Airlines and foreign airlines. The air ticket you purchase might have the words 'Vietnam Airlines' printed on it, but you could actually find yourself flying with Cathay Pacific or Thai (Thai Airways International).

Although most of Vietnam Airlines' aging fleet aircraft have been upgraded to modern French Airbuses and American Boeings, the airline still has some improving to do. Among its problems are frequent delays and the cancellation of domestic flights (more often than not because not enough seats were sold!).

The government is gradually adjusting the different airfares for foreigners and Vietnamese so that they will soon be the same. The dual-ticketing system could be phased out as early as late 2003.

While discounted flights can be taken into Vietnam, these airfares must be purchased outside the country. Vietnam Airlines will not allow foreign carriers to sell airfares in Vietnam that might undercut theirs. For example, a ticket from Bangkok to Hanoi or HCMC costs almost half the price of a Vietnam Airlines' flight, if it's purchased in Bangkok.

A large number of international flights leaving Hanoi connect through HCMC, but instead of allowing passengers to check in for their international flight in Hanoi, Vietnam Airlines requires passengers to first pay a domestic departure tax, fly to HCMC,

claim their bags, wait in line (again) to recheck your bags, then pay an international departure tax before boarding the international flight. Ugh.

Be aware that most international flights within Asia enforce a strict 20kg check-in baggage limit; ditto for domestic flights within Vietnam. Keep your baggage locked. Travellers have reported things being pilfered from their luggage on departure.

Bicycles can travel by air. You *can* take them to pieces and put them in a bike bag or box, but it's much easier simply to wheel your bike to the check-in desk, where it should be treated as a piece of baggage. You may have to remove the pedals and turn the handlebars sideways so that it takes up less space in the aircraft's hold; check all this with the airline well in advance, preferably before you pay for your ticket.

In an apparent attempt to give Vietnam Airlines some much-needed competition, **Pacific Airlines** (w *www.pacificairlines.com .vn*) commenced operations in 1992. Its domestic and international flight schedule,

### Warning

The information in this chapter is particularly vulnerable to change: prices for international travel are volatile, routes are introduced and cancelled, schedules change, special deals come and go, and rules and visa requirements are amended. You should check directly with the airline or a travel agent to make sure you understand how a fare (and ticket you may buy) works and be aware of the security requirements for international travel.

The upshot of this is that you should get opinions, quotes and advice from as many airlines and travel agents as possible before you part with your hard-earned cash. The details given in this chapter should be regarded as pointers and are not a substitute for your own careful, up-to-date research.

however, is restricted to flights between HCMC and Hanoi, Danang. Taipei, Kahsiung and Hong Kong.

## Tickets

With a bit of research – ringing around travel agents, checking Internet sites, perusing the travel ads in newspapers – you can often get yourself a good travel deal. Start early as some of the cheapest tickets need to be bought well in advance and popular flights can sell out.

Full-time students and people under 26 years (under 30 in some countries) have access to better deals than other travellers. You have to show a document proving your date of birth or a valid International Student Identity Card (ISIC) when buying your ticket and boarding the plane.

Generally, there is nothing to be gained by buying a ticket direct from the airline. Discounted tickets are released to selected travel agents and discount-travel agencies, and these are usually the cheapest deals going.

One exception is booking on the Internet. Many airlines, full-service and no-frills, offer some excellent fares. They may sell seats by auction or simply cut prices to reflect the reduced cost of electronic selling.

Many travel agencies around the world have websites, which can make the Internet a quick and easy way to compare prices. There is also an increasing number of agents that operate only on the Internet.

Online ticket sales work well if you are doing a simple one-way or return trip on specified dates. However, online super-fast fare generators are no substitute for a travel agent who knows all about special deals, has strategies for avoiding layovers and can offer advice on everything from which airline has the best vegetarian food to the best travel insurance to bundle with your ticket.

You may find the cheapest flights are advertised by obscure agencies. Most such firms are honest and solvent, but there are some rogue fly-by-night outfits around. Paying by credit card generally offers protection, as most card issuers provide refunds if you can prove you didn't get what you paid for. Agents who accept only cash should hand

over the tickets straight away and not tell you to 'come back tomorrow'. After you have made a booking or paid your deposit, call the airline and confirm that the booking was made. It's generally not advisable to send money (even cheques) through the post unless the agent is very well established – some travellers have reported being ripped off by fly-by-night mail-order ticket agents.

If you purchase a ticket and later want to make changes to your route or get a refund, you need to contact the original travel agent. Airlines issue refunds only to the purchaser of a ticket – usually the travel agent who bought the ticket on your behalf. Many travellers change their routes halfway through their trips, so think carefully before you buy a ticket that cannot easily be refunded.

It is really difficult to get reservations for flights to/from Vietnam during and around holidays, especially the Tet Festival, which falls roughly between late January and mid-February. If you will be in Vietnam during this period (a favourite time for family visits by overseas Vietnamese), make reservations well in advance or you may find yourself marooned in Bangkok on the way in or stranded in HCMC on the way out. During other times it shouldn't be too difficult to get a flight out of the country, but it's wise to book your departure at least a few days in advance.

Be aware that Vietnam is not the only country to celebrate the Lunar New Year – it's also *the* major holiday in Singapore, Macau, China, Taiwan and Korea, and is celebrated by sizeable Chinese minorities in Thailand and Malaysia. Many people hit the road at this time, resulting in overbooked airlines, trains and hotels all over Asia. The chaos begins about a week before Tet and can last for about two weeks after it.

**Frequent Fliers** Most airlines (including Vietnam Airlines) offer frequent-flier deals that can earn you a free air ticket or other goodies. To qualify, you have to accumulate sufficient mileage with the same airline or airline alliance. Many airlines have 'blackout periods', or times when you cannot fly for free on your frequent-flier points (Christmas and Tet, for example). The worst thing about frequent-flier programmes is that they tend to lock you into one airline, and that airline may not always have the cheapest fares or most convenient flight schedule.

**Courier Flights** If you are interested in saving money and travelling as a courier, there are only a few possible ways to do it. Courier flights are occasionally advertised in newspapers, or you could contact air-freight companies listed in the phone book. You may even have to go to the air-freight company to get an answer – the companies aren't always keen to give out information over the phone. For more information, contact the **International Association of Air Travel Couriers** (IAATC; w www.courier.org). Joining IAATC does not guarantee that you'll get a courier flight. This association may be able to assist with courier passage to Hong Kong, Taipei and Bangkok.

**Second-hand Tickets** You'll occasionally see advertisements for 'second-hand tickets' on youth-hostel bulletin boards and sometimes in newspapers. That is, somebody jas purchased a return ticket or a ticket with multiple stopovers and now wants to sell the unused portion of the ticket.

The prices offered look very attractive indeed. Unfortunately, these tickets, if used for international travel, are usually worthless, as the name on the ticket must match the name on the passport of the person checking in. Some people think that the ticket holder can check you in with their passport, and then give you the boarding pass – wrong again! The immigration people usually want to see your boarding pass, and if it doesn't match the name in your passport, then you won't be able to board your flight.

**Ticketless Travel** Although it isn't as common in Vietnam as it is in the West, ticketless travel is becoming more common throughout Asia. On simple return trips the absence of a ticket can be a benefit – it's one less thing to worry about. However, if you are planning a complicated itinerary that

you may wish to amend en route, there is no substitute for the good old paper version.

## Travellers with Special Needs
Most international airlines cater to people with special needs, eg, travellers with disabilities, people with young children and even children travelling alone.

Travellers with special dietary preferences (vegetarian, kosher etc) can enjoy appropriate meals with advance notice. If you are travelling in a wheelchair, most international airports can provide an escort from the check-in desk to the plane if needed, and ramps, lifts, toilets and phones are generally available.

Airlines usually allow babies of up to two years of age to fly for 10% of the adult fare, although a few airlines may allow them to travel free of charge. Reputable international airlines usually provide nappies (diapers), tissues, talcum powder and all the other paraphernalia needed to keep babies clean, dry and half-happy. For children between the ages of two and 12, the fare on international flights is usually either 50% of the regular fare or 67% of a discounted fare.

## Departure Tax
The departure tax for international flights from Vietnam is US$12, which can be paid in dong or US dollars. Children under two years of age are exempt.

## The USA
Discount travel agents in the USA are known as consolidators (although you won't see a sign on the door saying 'Consolidator'). San Francisco is the ticket-consolidator capital of America, although some good deals can be found in Los Angeles, New York and other big cities.

**Council Travel** (☎ 800-226 8624; w www .counciltravel.com), America's largest student travel organisation, has around 60 offices in the USA. **STA Travel** (☎ 800-777 0112; w www.statravel.com) has offices in Boston, Chicago, Miami, New York, Philadelphia, San Francisco and other major cities.

At the time of writing, no US air carriers were flying directly into Vietnam, however, several have established code-sharing agreements with Vietnam Airlines and other Asian airlines.

Low-season San Francisco–HCMC one-way/return tickets are priced at around US$600/800; while New York–HCMC costs around US$700/950.

Other airlines with routes between the USA and Vietnam include Cathay Pacific (via Hong Kong), Singapore Airlines (via Singapore), Thai (via Bangkok), Japan Airlines (via Tokyo or Osaka), China Airways and Eva Air (via Taipei) and Asiana Airlines (via Seoul).

## Canada

Canadian discount air-ticket sellers are also known as consolidators, but their fares tend to be about 10% higher than those sold in the USA.

**Travel Cuts** (☎ 800-667 2887; W www .travelcuts.com) is Canada's national student-travel agency and has offices in all major cities.

Typical fares for return low-/high-season tickets to Vietnam from Toronto are C$2000/3500, or C$1500/2500 from Vancouver.

## Australia

Fares between Australia and Asia are relatively expensive considering the distances flown. Ethnic-Vietnamese people living in Australia are known to have the inside scoop on ticket discounts. Most flights between Australia and Vietnam involve stopovers at Kuala Lumpur, Bangkok or Singapore.

Two well-known agents for cheap fares are **STA Travel** (☎ 131776, ☎ 03-9349 2411; W www.statravel.com.au; 222 Faraday St, Carlton, Melbourne), which has offices in all major cities and some on university campuses; and **Flight Centre** (☎ 131600; W www .flightcentre.com.au; 82 Elizabeth St, Sydney), which has dozens of offices throughout Australia. Some travel agents, particularly smaller ones, advertise cheap air fares in the travel sections of weekend newspapers.

Qantas and Vietnam Airlines offer a nine-hour joint service from Melbourne and Sydney to HCMC. Rock-bottom excursion fares from Melbourne usually hover around

A$700/1000 one way/return, or A$800/1200 from Sydney. Most flights to Hanoi involve a change of plane in HCMC.

## New Zealand

**Flight Centre** (☎ 09-309 6171; W www .flightcentre.com.au; National Bank Towers, cnr Queen & Darby Sts, Auckland) has many branches throughout the country, while **STA Travel** (☎ 09-309 0458; W www.statravel .co.nz; 10 High St, Auckland) has branches in Hamilton, Palmerston North, Wellington, Christchurch and Dunedin.

Low-season return fares from Auckland to either HCMC or Hanoi, flying with Malaysian Airlines or Thai, start from around NZ$1500. In the high season, fares start from around NZ$1800.

## The UK

Discount air travel is big business in London. Many advertisements for travel agencies appear in the travel pages of the weekend broadsheet newspapers, in *Time Out*, the daily *Evening Standard* and in the free magazine *TNT*.

For students or travellers under 26 years, a popular travel agency in the UK is **STA Travel** (☎ 020-7361 6262; W www.statravel .co.uk; 86 Old Brompton Rd, London SW7), which also caters to all types of traveller.

Other recommended agencies include **Trailfinders** (☎ 020-7937 1234, ☎ 020-7938 3939; W www.trailfinders.co.uk; 194 Kensington High St, London W8), **Bridge the World** (☎ 020-7734 7447, ☎ 020-7916 0990; W www.b-t-w.co.uk), **Flightbookers** (☎ 020-7757 2000; W www.ebookers.com; 177-8 Tottenham Court Rd, London W1), **Quest Travel** (☎ 020-8547 3123; W www.questtravel .co.uk; 10 Richmond Rd, Kingston-upon-Thames, Surrey KY2 5HL) and **Flight Centre** (☎ 020-8543 9070; W www.flightcentre.com; 112-34 The Broadway, London SW19 1RL). **North-South Travel** (☎ 012-4560 8291; W www.nstravel.demon.co.uk; Moulsham Hill, Parkway, Chelmsford, Essex CM2 7PX) donates part of its profits to projects in the developing world.

There are no direct flights between the UK and Vietnam, but there are relatively cheap tickets are available via Hong Kong, Bangkok or Kuala Lumpur. Fares from London to HCMC/Hanoi on Thai (via Bangkok) average UK£500 in the low season (April to June) and UK£700 in the high season (July to August). These fares allow for an open-jaw option, flying into Hanoi and out of HCMC or vice versa.

## Continental Europe

Although London is known as the discount-travel capital of Europe, there are other cities where you will find a range of good deals. Generally, there is not much variation in air fares for departures from the main European cities. All the major airlines are usually offering some sort of deal, and travel agents generally have a number of deals on offer, so shop around.

In France, recommended travel agencies include **OTU Voyages** (☎ 01 40 29 12 12; **W** www.otu.fr; 39 ave Georges-Bernanos, 75005 Paris), **Voyageurs du Monde** (☎ 01 42 86 16 00; 55 rue Ste-Anne, 75002 Paris) and **Nouvelles Frontières** (☎ 08 25 00 08 25, ☎ 01 45 68 70 00; **W** www.nouvelles-frontieres.fr; 87 blvd de Grenelle, 75015 Paris). These agencies have branches across the country.

In Spain, recommended agencies include **Usit Unlimited** (☎ 91-225 2575; **W** www.usitunlimited.es; 3 Plaza de Callao, 28013 Madrid), **Barcelo Viajes** (☎ 91-559 1819; Princesa 3, 28008 Madrid) and **Nouvelles Frontières** (☎ 91-547 4200; **W** www.nouvelles-frontieres.es; Plaza de España 18, 28008 Madrid), which all have branches in the major cities.

In Italy, recommended travel agents include **CTS Viaggi** (☎ 06-462 0431; 16 Via Genova, Rome), a student- and youth-travel specialist with branches in major cities, and **Passagi** (☎ 06-474 0923; Stazione Termini FS, Galleria Di Tesla, Rome).

In Switzerland, recommended agencies include **SSR** (☎ 022-818 0202; **W** www.ssr.ch; 8 rue de la Rive, Geneva), which has branches throughout the country, and **Nouvelles Frontières** (☎ 022-906 8080; 10 rue Chante Poulet, Geneva).

In the Netherlands, recommended agencies include **NBBS Reizen** (☎ 020-620 5071; **W** www.nbbs.nl; 66 Rokin, Amsterdam), which has branches in most cities, and **Budget Air** (☎ 020-627 1251; **W** www.nbbs.nl; 34 Rokin, Amsterdam). Another agency, **Holland International** (☎ 070-307 6307), has offices in most cities.

In Germany, recommended agencies include **STA Travel** (☎ 030-311 0950; Goethest-trasse 73, 10625 Berlin), which has branches in major cities across the country. Recommended online agencies include **Just Travel** (**W** www.justtravel.de) and **W** www.last minute.de, useful for checking last-minute fares.

## Asia

Although most Asian countries now offer fairly competitive air fare deals, Bangkok, Singapore and Hong Kong are still the best places to shop around for discount tickets. Hong Kong's travel market can be unpredictable, but some excellent bargains are available if you are lucky.

**Cambodia** There are daily flights between Phnom Penh and HCMC (US$115/215 one way/return) on either Siem Reap Air or Vietnam Airlines. A boon for Angkor Wat visitors, there are now daily direct flights between HCMC and Siem Reap, Cambodia. There is a US$5 airport tax to fly out of Cambodia. One-month visas for Cambodia are available upon arrival at Phnom Penh airport for US$20.

**China** Both China Southern Airlines and Vietnam Airlines fly China–Vietnam routes. The only direct flight between HCMC and mainland China is to Guangzhou (Canton). All other flights, such as Beijing and Shanghai, are via Hanoi.

**Hong Kong** After Bangkok, Hong Kong is the second most popular point for departures to Vietnam. The 2½-hour flights between Hong Kong and HCMC run daily. Hanoi–Hong Kong flights also operate daily and take 1¾ hours.

Hong Kong's flag carrier, Cathay Pacific, and Vietnam Airlines offer a joint service between Hong Kong and HCMC and offers one-way/return fares for US$300/550. There are also direct flights between Hong Kong and Hanoi (US$275/500 one way/return). The most popular ticket is an open-jaw deal for US$525 – this allows you to fly from Hong Kong to HCMC and on the return trip depart from Hanoi (or vice versa).

Hong Kong has a number of excellent, reliable travel agencies and some not-so-reliable ones. A good way to check on a travel agent is to look it up in the phone book: fly-by-night operators don't usually stay around long enough to get listed. **Phoenix Services** (☎ 2722 7378, fax 2369 8884; Room B, 6th floor, Milton Mansion, 96 Nathan Rd, Tsimshatsui) is recommended. Other agencies to try are **Shoestring Travel** (☎ 2723 2306; Flat A, 4th floor, Alpha House, 27-33 Nathan Rd, Tsimshatsui) and **Traveller Services** (☎ 2375 2222; Room 1012, Silvercord Tower 1, 30 Canton Rd, Tsimshatsui).

**Japan** The cheapest round-trip tickets from Tokyo or Osaka are usually available with Korean Air (via Seoul) or Thai (via Bangkok). A 60-day fixed-date return ticket can go for as little as ¥40,000.

Vietnam Airlines shares a daily direct route with Japan Airlines between Osaka and HCMC or Hanoi. Flights take approximately 5½ hours and return fares cost around ¥55,000 for a 10-day fixed ticket. ANA also has direct flights.

Arranging visas in Japan is expensive and time-consuming, and Japanese travel agents charge high prices to process visa applications; consider taking care of your visa somewhere else, like Bangkok.

**South Korea** Asiana Airlines, Korean Air and Vietnam Airlines all fly the Seoul–HCMC route, so there's at least one flight offered per day. There are also direct Seoul–Hanoi flights at least three times weekly. Flying time between HCMC and Seoul is 4¾ hours.

A good travel agency for discount tickets, **Joy Travel Service** (☎ 02-776 9871, fax 756 5342; 10th floor, 24-2 Mukyo-dong, Chung-gu, Seoul) is directly behind Seoul's City Hall.

**Laos** There is a joint service offered by Lao Aviation and Vietnam Airlines between Vientiane and Hanoi or HCMC.

**Malaysia** There's a joint service offered by Malaysia Airlines and Vietnam Airlines between Kuala Lumpur and HCMC. There are also flights from Kuala Lumpur to Hanoi.

**The Philippines** There's a joint service by Philippine Airlines and Vietnam Airlines from Manila to HCMC (2½ hours).

**Singapore** A daily joint service is offered by Singapore Airlines and Vietnam Airlines on the HCMC–Singapore route (two hours). Most flights from Singapore continue on to Hanoi.

In Singapore **STA Travel** (☎ 65-737 7188; W www.statravel.com.sg; 35a Cuppage Rd, Cuppage Terrace) offers competitive fares for Asian destinations and beyond. Singapore, like Bangkok, has hundreds of travel agents, so you can compare prices on flights. Chinatown Point shopping centre, on New Bridge Rd has a good selection of travel agents.

**Taiwan** The large numbers of Taiwanese who visit Vietnam have made Taiwan a good embarkation point for Vietnam, with frequent flights now offered by four competing airlines. The flight time between Vietnam and Taiwan is around three hours.

A long-running discount travel agent with a good reputation is **Jenny Su Travel** (☎ 02-2594 7733, ☎ 2596 2263, fax 2592 0068; 10th floor, 27 Chungshan N Rd, Section 3, Taipei).

**Thailand** Bangkok, only 80 minutes' flying time from HCMC, has emerged as the main port of embarkation for air travel to Vietnam.

Thai, Air France and Vietnam Airlines offer daily Bangkok–HCMC services for around B4200 one way; return tickets cost about double. There are also direct flights between Bangkok and Hanoi for approximately the same price.

Many choose an open-jaw ticket (around B9500) that flies you into either HCMC or Hanoi, from where you travel overland, before flying back to Bangkok from the other city.

Khao San Rd in Bangkok is the budget-travellers headquarters. While Bangkok has a number of excellent travel agents, there are also some suspect ones; ask the advice of other travellers before handing over your cash. **STA Travel** (☎ 02-236 0262; 33 Surawong Rd, Bangkok) is a good and reliable place to start.

## LAND
## Border Crossings

Tourist visas allow you to enter and exit Vietnam at any of the official international borders. There are currently eight international land borders: with Cambodia (3), Laos (2) and China (3).

There are very few legal money-changing facilities on the Vietnamese side of these crossings, so be sure to have some US dollars handy (preferably in small denominations). The black market is also an option, and will exchange local currencies – Vietnamese dong, Chinese renminbi, Lao kip and Cambodian riel. Still, try to find a bank or legal moneychanger – black marketeers have a well-deserved reputation for short-changing and outright theft.

Vietnamese police at the land-border crossings, especially the Lao borders, are known to be particularly problematic. Most travellers find that it's much easier to exit Vietnam overland than it is to enter that way. Travellers at the border crossings are occasionally asked for an 'immigration fee' and/or a 'customs fee' of some kind. Though of course they know this is illegal, the Vietnamese border guards are accustomed to collecting tourists' money.

**Cambodia** The most popular border crossing between Cambodia and Vietnam is Moc Bai, which connects Vietnam's Tay Ninh province with Cambodia's Svay Rieng province. Buses run every day between Phnom Penh and HCMC (via Moc Bai). The cheapest tickets are sold at the travellers cafés in HCMC's Pham Ngu Lao area. Daily departures in either direction are at around 8.30am, and tickets cost just US$6 – cheap!

Buses departing from HCMC arrive at the border around 11.30am and ffter clearing customs you switch to a different bus on the Cambodian side for the final six- to seven-hour ride to Phnom Penh.

Another way to get to/from the Moc Bai border is share taxi; these run directly from HCMC to Moc Bai border crossing and cost around US$20 for up to four people. Check at travel agencies or cafés in the Pham Ngu Lao area of HCMC for the latest.

Another cheap, if more complicated and time-consuming way, is to board one of the many bus tours heading for the Caodai Great Temple at Tay Ninh. But instead of going to Tay Ninh, get off at Go Dau where the highway forks. There will be motorbike taxis waiting here, and for as little as 5000d you can get a ride to the Moc Bai border crossing. You have to walk across the border but you will find air-con share taxis waiting on the Cambodian side to take you to Phnom Penh for about US$5 per person.

A highly popular alternative to the Moc Bai border is Vinh Xuong border near Chau Doc, in the Mekong Delta. One major plus of entry or exit via Vinh Xuong is that you can take in a trip through the Mekong Delta en route, and on the Cambodian side of the border a spectacular boat ride up the Mekong River is part of the trip. A good place to inquire about this trip in HCMC is Delta Adventure Tours (see the Information section in the Ho Chi Minh City chapter).

At the time of writing a third international border between Cambodia and Vietnam had been opened at Tinh Bien, about 25km west of Chau Doc, along the road to Ha Tien.

To cross overland into Vietnam or Cambodia, you *must* prearrange a visa for either country; visas on arrival are *not* available. If you plan to exit Vietnam and return to Vietnam again, try applying for a multiple-entry Vietnam tourist visa.

**Laos** There are two points where you can cross overland between Laos and Vietnam – Lao Bao and the Keo Nua Pass. We have received scores of letters complaining about immigration and local transport hassles on the Vietnamese side of both of these borders, but the situation does seem to be improving.

Keep your ears open for news on the Tay Trang border near Dien Bien Phu (northwestern Vietnam) opening up to foreigners.

Visas for entering Laos must be prearranged, and you can only obtain them in HCMC, Hanoi or Danang.

**Lao Bao**  The tiny Vietnamese village of Lao Bao is on National Hwy 9, 80km west of Dong Ha and 3km east of Laos. Just across the border is the southern Lao province of Savannakhet, but there is no town on that side of the border. An international bus runs between Danang (Vietnam) and Savannakhet via Dong Ha and Lao Bao. In Laos, the only place you are likely to board is Savannakhet. Local buses from Lao Bao go only as far as Dong Ha, and not to Hué, in spite of what drivers say.

There are also local buses that just go to the border from either side. While it's cheaper to get a local bus, rather than the cross-border express, it also involves more hassle. For one thing, there is a 1km walk between the Vietnamese and Laotian border checkpoints. Furthermore, the bus from Dong Ha terminates at Lao Bao, about 3km from the actual border checkpoint (although you can cover this by motorbike). Departure times are irregular and the buses won't leave until they're completely full.

**Keo Nua Pass**  Vietnam's National Hwy 8 crosses the border at Keo Nua Pass (734m), known as Cau Treo in Vietnamese.

The nearest Vietnamese city of any importance is Vinh, about 80km from the border and accessible via National Hwy 8. On the Lao side it's about 200km from the border to Tha Khaek, just opposite Kakhon Phanom in Thailand. There is at least one international bus daily, plus local buses that approach the border checkpoint from either side but do not cross.

**China**  The Vietnam-China border-crossing hours are from 7am to 4pm (Vietnam time). Set your watch when you cross the border as the time in China is one hour behind. Neither country observes daylight-saving time (summer time).

There are currently three border checkpoints where foreigners are permitted to cross between Vietnam and China: Friendship Pass, Lao Cai and Mong Cai.

**Friendship Pass**  The busiest border crossing is at the Vietnamese town of Dong Dang, 164km northeast of Hanoi. The closest town on the Chinese side of the border is Pinxiang (about 10km north of the border gate). The crossing point (Friendship Pass) is known as Huu Nghi Quan (Vietnamese) or Youyi Guan (Chinese).

Dong Dang is an obscure town. The nearest city is Lang Son (see the Northeast Vietnam chapter), 18km to the south. Buses and minibuses on the Hanoi–Lang Son route are frequent. The cheapest way to cover the 18km between Dong Dang and Lang Son is to hire a motorbike for about 20,000d. There are also minibuses cruising the streets looking for passengers. Just make sure they take you to Huu Nghi Quan – there is another checkpoint, but Huu Nghi Quan is the only point where foreigners can cross. There is a customs checkpoint between Lang Son and Dong Dang, and sometimes there are long delays while the officials thoroughly search the luggage of Vietnamese and Chinese travellers. For this reason, a motorbike might prove faster than a van, since you won't have to wait for your fellow passengers to be searched. Note that this is only a problem when you're heading south towards Lang Son, not the other way.

On the Chinese side, it's a 20-minute drive from the border to Pinxiang by bus or a shared taxi – the latter costs around US$3. Pinxiang is connected by train and bus to Nanning, the capital of China's Guangxi province.

There is a 600m walk between the Vietnamese and Chinese border posts.

There is a twice-weekly international train between Beijing and Hanoi that stops at Friendship Pass. You can board or get off at numerous stations in China. The entire Beijing–Hanoi run is about 2951km and takes approximately 55 hours, including a three-hour delay (if you are lucky) at the border checkpoint. Schedules change.

A word of advice – because train tickets to China are more expensive in Hanoi, some travellers prefer to buy a ticket to Dong Dang, walk across the border and then buy a Chinese train ticket on the Chinese side. However, the Friendship Pass is several kilometres from Dong Dang and you will have to hire someone to take you there by motorbike. It's a better idea to buy a ticket from Hanoi to Pinxiang, and then purchase another ticket to Nanning or beyond once you're in Pinxiang.

**Lao Cai–Hekou**  There's a 762km metre-gauge railway, inaugurated in 1910, linking Hanoi with Kunming in China's Yunnan province. The border town on the Vietnamese side is Lao Cai (294km from Hanoi). On the Chinese side, the border town is Hekou (468km from Kunming).

Vietnamese and Chinese authorities have started a direct train service between Hanoi and Kunming. Make inquiries for the latest schedule. Domestic trains also run daily on both sides of the border. On the Chinese side, the Hekou–Kunming trip takes approximately 17 hours.

**Mong Cai–Dongxing**  Vietnam's third (but seldom-used) border crossing to China can be found at Mong Cai, in the northeastern corner of the country, just opposite the Chinese city of Dongxing. See the Mong Cai section in the Northeast Vietnam chapter for details on this border crossing.

## Car & Motorbike

Drivers of cars and riders of motorbikes will need the vehicle's registration papers, liability insurance and an International Driving Permit (IDP) in addition to your domestic licence. You also need a *carnet de passage en douane*, which is like a passport for the vehicle and acts as a temporary waiver of import duty. The *carnet* may also need to specify any expensive spare parts that you're planning to carry with you (eg a gearbox). This is designed to prevent car-import rackets. For details about all the necessary

documentation, contact your local automobile association .

Liability insurance cannot be purchased in advance for many Asian countries but has to be bought when crossing the border. The cost and quality of such local insurance varies wildly, and you will find in some countries that you are effectively travelling uninsured.

Anyone who is planning to take their own vehicle should check in advance what spare parts and petrol are likely to be available.

## Bicycle

Cycling is a cheap, environmentally sound, convenient, healthy and above all fun way of travelling. With the loosening of the borders in Southeast Asia, more and more people are planning overland trips by bicycle. All you need to know about bicycle travel in Vietnam's region is contained in Lonely Planet's *Cycling Vietnam, Laos & Cambodia*.

One note of caution: before you leave home, go over your bike with a fine-toothed comb and fill your repair kit with every imaginable spare part. As with cars and motorbikes, you won't necessarily be able to buy that crucial gizmo for your machine when it breaks down somewhere in the back of beyond as the sun sets.

See the Organised Tours section at the end of this chapter for information about cycling tours.

## SEA

For visitors, there are few options for legal arrival or departure by sea. However, a growing number of luxury cruise ships dock at Vietnamese ports, notably HCMC, Danang and Haiphong.

**Star Cruises** (W www.starcruises.com) travels between Bangkok and Phu Quoc Island in the Mekong Delta, as well as between Hong Kong and Halong Bay. Seattle-based **Zegram Expeditions** (W www.zeco.com) organises sensational upmarket sea voyages to Vietnam.

## ORGANISED TOURS

Package tours to Vietnam are offered by travel agencies worldwide. Nearly all these tours follow one of a dozen or so set itineraries. Tours booked outside Vietnam are not a total rip-off, given what you get (air tickets, accommodation, food, transport, a guide etc), but then again they're not cheap.

It's quite easy to fly into Vietnam and make all of your travel arrangements after arrival (see Organised Tours in the Getting Around chapter). The main thing you gain by booking before arrival is time, and if your time is more precious than money, a pre-booked package tour could be right for you.

Almost any reputable travel agency can book you onto a standard mad-dash minibus tour around Vietnam. More noteworthy are the adventure tours arranged for people with a particular passion. These include speciality tours for cyclists, trekkers, bird-watchers, war veterans, 4WD enthusiasts and Vietnamese cuisine buffs. If you have an interest in one of these and want to organise a group tour, try surfing and advertising your interest on the Internet.

Consider contacting the following speciality travel outfits.

### Australia

**Community Aid Abroad (CAA), Oxfam Australia** (☎ 08-8232 2727, ☎ 1800 814 848, fax 8232 2808, e info@tours.caa.org.au, W www.caa.org.au/travel) Specialises in sustainable, responsible tourism tours – a percentage of proceeds supports local CAA aid projects.

**Griswalds Vietnamese Vacations** (☎ 02-9564 5040, fax 9550 0246, e griswalds@vietnamvacations.com.au, W www.vietnamvacations.com.au) PO Box 501, Leichhardt, NSW 2040

**Intrepid Travel** (☎ 1300 360 667, fax 9419 5878, W www.intrepidtravel.com.au) 11 Spring St, Fitzroy, Vic 3065

**Obitours** (☎ 02-9954 1399, fax 9954 1655) 3rd floor, 73 Walker St, North Sydney, NSW 2059

**Peregrine** Sydney: (☎ 02-9290 2770, W www.peregrine.net.au) 5/38 York St, NSW 2000
Melbourne: (☎ 03-9662 2800, fax 9663 8618) 258 Lonsdale St, Vic 3000

**Travel Indochina** (☎ 02-9244 2133, fax 9244 2233, e travindo@concorde.com.au, W www.travelindochina.com.au) 403 George St, Sydney, NSW 2000

### Canada

**Global Adventures** (☎ 640-947 2263, W www.globaladventures.bc.ca/) Runs 12-day sea-kayaking trips in Halong Bay.

### New Zealand

**Adventure World** (☎ 649-524 5118, fax 520 6629) 101 Great South Rd, Auckland

**Go Orient Holidays** (☎ 649-379 5520, fax 377 0111) 151 Victoria St West, Auckland

### Thailand

**Asian Trails** (☎ 02-658 6080, fax 02-658 6099, e asiantrails@asiantrails.org, W www.asiantrails.net) 15th floor, Mercury Tower, 540 Ploenchit Rd, Bangkok 10330

### UK

**Asian Journeys** (☎ 1604-234855, fax 234866) 32 Semilong Rd, Northampton NN2 6BT

**Bales Worldwide** (☎ 0870-241 3208; fax 01306-876904, e enquiries@balesworldwide.com, W www.balesworldwide.com) Bales House, Junction Rd, Dorking, Surrey RH4 4HL

### USA

**Asia Transpacific Journeys** (☎ 800-642 2742, W www.southeastasia.com) PO Box 1279, Boulder, CO 80306

**Asian Pacific Adventures** (☎ 800-825 1680, ☎ 323-935 3156) 826 South Sierra Bonita Ave, Los Angeles, CA 90036

**Geographic Expeditions** (☎ 800-777 8183, ☎ 415-922 0448, fax 346 5535, e info@geoex.com, W www.geoex.com) 2627 Lombard St, San Francisco CA 94123

**Global Spectrum** (☎ 800-419 4446; e gspectrum@gspectrum.com, W www.asianpassages.com/) Suite 204, 1901 Pennsylvania Ave NW, Washington, DC 20006

**Sea Canoe International Adventures** (☎ 800-444 1043, fax 888-824 5621, W www.seacanoe.com)

**Velo-Asia Cycling Adventures** (☎ 415-282 3788, e info@veloasia.com, W www.veloasia.com)

**Wild Card Adventures** (☎ 800-590 3776, fax 360-387 9816, e swild7@juno.com, W www.awildcard.com/) 751 Maple Grove Rd, Camano Island, WA 98292

**Zolo Trips** (☎ 800-657 2694, ☎ 415-255 9520, fax 680 1522, e info@zolotrips.com, W www.zolotrips.com) 101 Baker St, San Francisco, CA 94117

## Vietnam

The following Vietnam-based travel agencies offer premium tours throughout Vietnam and Indochina.

**Destination Asia** (☎ 08-844 8071, fax 844 7885; 📧 destinations@hcm.fpt.vn, 🌐 www .destination-asia.com) 143 Đ Nguyen Van Troi, Phu Nhuan district, HCMC

**Elephant Guide** (🌐 www.elephantguide.com)

**Exotissimo** *Hanoi:* (☎ 04-828 2150, fax 828 2146; 📧 vietnam@exotissimo.com, 🌐 www.exotissimo.com) 26 Tran Nhat Duat *HCMC:* (☎ 08-825 1723, fax 829 5800) Saigon Trade Center, 37 Đ Ton Duc Thang

**Phoenix Vietnam** *Hanoi:* (☎ 04-716 1956, fax 716 1958; 📧 phoenix.vn@fpt.vn, 🌐 www.phoenixvietnam.com) 52 Pho Nguyen Khac Hieu, Truc Bach, Ba Dinh District *HCMC:* (☎ 08-824 4282, fax 824 4286; 📧 phoenixvietnam@hcm.fpt.vn, 🌐 www .phoenixvietnam.com) 4 Đ Chu Manh Trinh

**Sinhbalo Adventures** (☎ 08-837 6766, ☎/fax 836 7682; 📧 sinhbalo@hcm .vnn.vn, 🌐 www.sinhbalo.com) 283/20 Đ Pham Ngu Lao, District 1

**Vidotour** (☎ 08-933 0457, fax 933 0470; 📧 info@vidotourtravel.com) 145 Đ Nam Ky Khoi Nghia, HCMC

**Visit Mekong** (🌐 www.visit-mekong.com)

# Getting Around

## AIR

**Vietnam Airlines** (W *www.vietnamairlines .com.vn*) has a virtual monopoly on domestic flights, though **Pacific Airlines** (W *www .pacificairlines.com.vn*) also flies the Hanoi–Ho Chi Minh City (HCMC) route and the HCMC–Danang route.

Most travel agents do not charge any more than if you book direct with the airline as the airline pays a commission to them. You'll need your passport to make a booking on all domestic flights, and you'll have to show it at the check-in counter and yet again at the security checkpoint.

Vietnam Airlines is gradually getting its act together and many (but not all) branch offices accept travellers cheques and credit cards for ticket purchases. The airline has retired its ancient Soviet-built fleet (thank heavens!) and purchased new Western-made aircraft. When landing at Hanoi's Noi Bai airport, you may still see a handful of the old Tupolev 72s rusting out on the tarmac. Good riddance.

Most aircraft return to their point of origin on the same day as their departure. See the Air Routes map and boxed text 'Domestic Airline Schedules' in this chapter. These cover all the possible routes available within Vietnam.

Vietnam Airlines charges US$30 if you want to refund an unused domestic air ticket.

There's a helicopter charter service from Hanoi to Halong Bay. See Halong Bay in the Northeast Vietnam chapter.

### Domestic Departure Tax

The domestic departure tax is currently 50,000d, payable in local currency only. Children under the age of two are exempt.

## BUS

Vietnam has an extensive network of dirt-cheap buses and other passenger vehicles that reach virtually every far-flung corner of the country. However, few foreign travellers use them because of safety reasons.

Road safety is definitely not one of the country's strong points. Vietnam's intercity road network of two-lane highways is becoming more and more dangerous due to the rapid increase in the number of motor vehicles that now travel on it. High-speed, head-on collisions between buses, trucks and other smaller vehicles (including motorbikes and bicycles) have become a sickeningly familiar sight on National Hwy 1. Vietnam does not have an efficient emergency-rescue system, so if something happens to you out on the road, you could be hours from even rudimentary medical treatment.

If possible, try to travel during daylight hours only. Indeed, many drivers generally refuse to drive after dark in rural areas because the unlit highways tend to have gaping potholes and lots of bicycles and

**AIR ROUTES**

CHINA

Dien Bien Phu
Na San
HANOI
Haiphong
LAOS
VIENTIANE
Vinh
Hué
Danang
THAILAND
Pleiku
Qui Nhon
Tuy Hoa
CAMBODIA
Buon Ma Thuot
Dalat
Nha Trang
PHNOM PENH
HO CHI MINH CITY (SAIGON)
Phu Quoc Island
Rach Gia
Con Son Island

## Domestic Airline Schedules

### Vietnam Airlines

| from | to | frequency | economy (d) | 1st class (d) |
|------|-----|-----------|-------------|---------------|
| Danang | Buon Ma Thuot | 5 weekly | 530,000 | – |
| | Haiphong | 3 weekly | 950,000 | 1,200,000 |
| | Nha Trang | 1 daily | 550,000 | – |
| | Pleiku | 5 weekly | 520,000 | – |
| | Vinh | 2 weekly | 670,000 | – |
| Hanoi | Danang | 2-3 daily | 950,000 | 1,200,000 |
| | Dien Bien Phu | 5 weekly | 620,000 | – |
| | Ho Chi Minh City | 7 daily | 1,800,000 | 2,400,000 |
| | Hué | 2 daily | 950,000 | 1,200,000 |
| | Nha Trang | 1-2 daily | 1,400,000 | – |
| | Son La | 4 weekly | 520,000 | – |
| Ho Chi Minh City | Buon Ma Thuot | 1 daily | 620,000 | – |
| | Dalat | 1-2 daily | 430,000 | – |
| | Danang | 5-6 daily | 950,000 | 1,200,000 |
| | Haiphong | 1 daily | 1,800,000 | 2,400,000 |
| | Hanoi | 7 daily | 1,800,000 | 2,400,000 |
| | Hué | 1-2 daily | 950,000 | 1,200,000 |
| | Nha Trang | 2-3 daily | 630,000 | – |
| | Phu Quoc | 1-2 daily | 670,000 | – |
| | Pleiku | 5 weekly | 670,000 | – |
| | Qui Nhon | 1 daily | 670,000 | – |
| | Rach Gia | 5 weekly | 670,000 | – |
| | Vinh | 5 weekly | 1,200,000 | – |
| Phu Quoc | Rach Gia | 3 weekly | 1,200,000 | – |

### Pacific Airlines

| from | to | frequency | economy (d) | 1st class |
|------|-----|-----------|-------------|-----------|
| Ho Chi Minh City | Danang | 1 daily | 950,000 | – |
| Ho Chi Minh City | Hanoi | 3 daily | 1,800,000 | – |

pedestrians (including dogs and chickens), who seem oblivious to the traffic. However, if you like living dangerously, there are some overnight buses.

Package-tour groups tend to travel on modern, Japanese- and Korean-made buses, which have both air-con and cushy seats. However, public bus companies rarely use these types of vehicle because they're too expensive.

Buses usually come in four flavours: Korean (relatively new), Russian (c. 1970), US (c. 1965) and French (antique). The most comfortable are the Korean-made (usually Hyundai) buses. Many of these have air-con and the seats are reasonably comfortable. You will find these buses almost exclusively on very-long-distance routes such as HCMC–Hanoi (a two-day, nonstop drive!). However the bad news is that most of them are equipped with video-tape players and evil karaoke machines. You can ignore the blood-splattered kung fu videos by closing your eyes (or wearing a blindfold), but you would need to be deaf to sleep through the karaoke sessions – ear plugs are recommended!

A toddler from the Dao hill tribe in Sapa, Lao Cai province

Children playing in Hoi An, central Vietnam

A game of Chinese checkers in Nha Trang

Near Nha Trang, a rice-paddy worker holds a scythe, which is used during harvest

The ubiquitous conical hat is traditional wear for Vietnamese women and also provides shade and shelter during the sweltering summers experienced throughout most of the country

The majority of Vietnam's public buses are Russian or American. The Vietnamese have modified the vehicles with fancy paint jobs – a nice touch. Not so nice is the fact that the bus companies have installed many additional seats – you can expect little leg room and much discomfort. Many buses are standing room only – if you drop dead, you'll never hit the floor. Luggage is stacked wherever it fits, which in many cases means that it gets tied onto the roof. Mechanical breakdowns occur far too frequently.

The French-made buses are becoming rare, which is not surprising since they are about 50 years old. How the Vietnamese keep the old bangers running is anybody's guess. These museums-on-wheels sputter, creep and crawl along at around 30km/h – don't expect to get anywhere fast. As with the Russian- and US-made buses, you can expect overloading, extreme discomfort and frequent breakdowns. After an eight-hour ride, one traveller put it succinctly when she said 'I feel like a million dong'.

It's fair to say that riding the buses will give you ample opportunity to have 'personal contact' with the Vietnamese people. If you're looking to meet locals, what better way than to have a few sitting on your lap! As one reader said:

I enjoyed the bus-riding scene, the scenery and the conversations (gesturing) with people. Although I'd rate the conditions as terrible, the riding community suffered, slept and ate together.

Figuring out the bus system is anything but easy. Many cities have several bus stations, and responsibilities are divided according to the location of the destination (whether it is north or south of the city) and the type of service being offered (local or long distance, express or nonexpress).

Most long-distance buses depart in the early morning. Often, half a dozen vehicles heading for the same destination will leave at the same time, usually around 5.30am. The first thing they always seem do after departure is look for a petrol station – just why they don't fill the tank the night before has always mystified us.

## Passing Water

The engines of many older trucks and buses are equipped with an ingenious gravity-powered heat-dissipation system. This is designed to supplement the radiator, which cannot cope when these ancient vehicles are heavily over-loaded (a frequent occurrence), and helps prevent overheating.

A drum attached to the roof of the cab is connected to the engine by a hose. This hose passes by the driver's window, where a stop-cock allows the driver to control the water flow. Cold water in the rooftop drum slowly drains into the engine; hot water squirts out the radiator overflow tank. When the drum is empty, the driver simply stops at any of the numerous water-filling stations that line major highways and tops it up.

Overnight buses began once curfews were relaxed in 1989, but neither passengers nor drivers are especially fond of travelling all night. Short-distance buses, like mini-buses, depart when full (ie, jam-packed with people and luggage). They often operate throughout the day, but don't count on many leaving after about 4pm.

Be aware that your luggage can easily be pilfered at toilet stops unless you have a trusted friend watching it or you take it to the toilet with you. When tied to the rooftop it should theoretically be safe from pilfering, but we've heard a number of reports to the contrary, so try keeping your bags in sight. A distinct disadvantage of having your gear on top is that it will be exposed to constant road dust and sometimes heavy rain.

No matter how honest your fellow passengers might seem, *never* accept drinks from them, as there is a chance you may be drugged and robbed.

## Reservations & Costs

Buses normally leave early in the morning, so if you don't plan to bargain with the bus driver, you might show up at the bus station the day before departure and at least *try* to purchase a ticket.

Costs are negligible, though foreigners are typically charged anywhere from twice to 10 times the going rate. Outside of the Mekong Delta and major cities, most ticket offices won't even sell foreigners a normal ticket; rather, they leave you to battle it out with the bus driver. It is helpful to determine the cost of the ticket for Vietnamese before starting these negotiations.

## Open Tours

In backpacker haunts throughout Vietnam, you'll see lots of signs advertising 'Open Tour', 'Open Date Ticket' or 'Open Ticket'. This is a bus service catering mostly to foreign budget travellers, not to Vietnamese. These air-con buses run between HCMC and Hanoi and you may get on and off the bus at any major city along the route. You are not obliged to follow a fixed schedule.

Competition has driven the price of these tours so low that it would practically only be cheaper if you walked. At the time of writing you could purchase the following open-tour bus tickets in HCMC.

| route | price (US$) |
| --- | --- |
| Ho Chi Minh City–Dalat | 5 |
| Ho Chi Minh City–Mui Ne | 6 |
| Ho Chi Minh City–Nha Trang | 7 |
| Ho Chi Minh City–Hoi An | 13 |
| Ho Chi Minh City–Hué | 14 |
| Ho Chi Minh City–Hanoi | 21 |

Although we've been saying the same thing for years, and one of these days the numbers will hit rock bottom, don't be surprised to find that these prices keep dropping. What we really wish they would do is *raise* the cost of the tickets, and in turn, by actually making money off the bus fare, allow passengers to simply get off and wander freely when the bus arrives at its destination. Rather, they depend on kickbacks from a very elaborate and well-established network of sister hotels, restaurants etc all along the coast.

However, bear in mind that if they weren't collecting commissions by delivering you to selected hotels or restaurants, the ticket you buy could never be so cheap. So if you do go this route, it's not worth complaining when they do. Trying to avoid the commission circus will not only waste time that you've gained by using these relatively speedy buses, but it can make your hair turn grey (or fall out!).

As cheap and popular as it is, we are not overly keen on the open-tour deal. Once you've bought the ticket, you're stuck with it. If you're dissatisfied with the service provided, that's too bad. Also, it really isolates you from Vietnam – you should try to have at least some contact with the locals (other than the bus driver). Buying minibus tickets or shorter point-to-point tickets on the open-tour buses, all along the way, costs a bit more but you achieve maximum flexibility.

Nevertheless, cheap open-tour tickets are a temptation and many people go for them. A couple of shorter routes we might suggest using the open tours for are HCMC–Dalat and HCMC–Mui Ne Beach, two places that are not serviced by train. Ditto for travelling between HCMC and Phnom Penh (Cambodia) via the Moc Bai border (this costs just US$6). If you're not in a rush, however, we recommend the boat trip between Chau Doc (in the Mekong Delta) and Phnom Penh. It's far more scenic along the Mekong River, and you can check out some of the delta along the way.

Otherwise, if you want to avoid feeling like you're in a herd of a sheep, take the train, take public buses or minibuses. Ultimately, you might consider splurging a bit by hiring a private car (so you can actually tell the driver where to take you), or cycle/motorbike there yourself.

If you want open-tour tickets, look for them at budget cafés in HCMC and Hanoi.

## MINIBUS

Public minibuses (which are actually privately owned) run like the bus services: they depart when full. Minibuses, with anywhere from eight to 15 seats, congregate near bus stations, though you can sometimes arrange to have one pick you up at your hotel.

Nonexpress minibuses will drop off and pick up as many passengers as possible along the route, so try to avoid these. They usually become ridiculously crowded as the journey progresses and are not comfortable at all. The frequent stops to pick up and drop off (and arrange luggage and chickens) can make for a slow journey.

Express minibuses, on the contrary, generally make a beeline from place to place. This is the deluxe class – air-con is standard and you can usually be certain of there being enough space to sit comfortably. Such luxury, of course, is something you must pay a premium for. Nevertheless, it's still very cheap by most standards.

Budget hotels and cafés are the best places to inquire about these vehicles. However, there are some unscrupulous cafés that will tell you anything to sell you one of their tours, or, equally as bad, sell you a tourist-priced ticket and then stick you on a malfunctioning local bus.

It is also perfectly feasible (and highly recommended) to kick in with some fellow travellers and charter your own minibus. See the Car & Motorbike section later in this chapter for details.

## TRAIN

The 2600km Vietnamese railway system, operated by **Vietnam Railways** (Duong Sat Viet Nam; ☎ 04-747 0308; ⓦ www.vr.com.vn), runs along the coast between HCMC and Hanoi, and links the capital with Haiphong and northern towns. While sometimes even slower than buses, trains offer a more relaxing way to get around and more leg and body room than the jam-packed buses. Dilapidated as the tracks, rolling stock and engines may appear, the trains are much safer than the country's kamikaze bus fleet. One reader wrote:

The trains are a great way to meet 'normal' Vietnamese people. One thing that worries me a lot about the tourist buses is that many of the people who use them are just conveyed from the door of one guesthouse to another in the company of other foreign tourists, and probably never have any significant contact with locals who are not working in (or preying on) the tourist industry in one way or another.

**Alan Davies**

Furthermore, Vietnam's railway authority has been rapidly upgrading trains and facilities (with air-con sleeping berths and dining cars available now on express trains), as well as lowering the price for foreigners. In February 2002 prices on all train routes in Vietnam were significantly slashed for non-Vietnamese travellers. The move was part of an ongoing effort to bring ticket prices into line for locals and foreigners; it's said that by the end of 2003, following several more gradual cuts, all passengers will pay the same fare.

One key factor to take into account, when deciding whether to go by train or bus, is the hour at which the train gets to where you want to go – trying to find a place to stay at 3am is likely to be very frustrating.

Even the express trains in Vietnam are slow by developed-country standards, but conditions are improving as the tracks and equipment are upgraded. The quickest rail journey between Hanoi and HCMC takes 30 hours. The slowest express train on this route takes 41 hours.

There are also local trains that only cover short routes like HCMC to Nha Trang. These local trains can crawl along at 15km/h. There are several reasons for the excruciating slowness. There is only one track running between HCMC and Hanoi. Trains can pass each other only at those few points where a siding has been constructed. Each time trains go by each other, one of them has to stop on the prearranged sidetrack and wait for the oncoming train to pass. If one is late, so is the other. Subsequent trains going in both directions may also be delayed.

Petty crime is a problem on Vietnamese trains, especially if you travel in budget class, where your fellow passengers are likely to be poorer. While there doesn't seem to be organised pack-napping gangs, such as those in India, the Vietnamese seem convinced that the young men and boys you see hanging out in the stations and on trains have only larceny on their minds. Thieves have become proficient at grabbing packs through the windows as trains pull out of stations. To protect your belongings, always keep your bag near you and lock or tie it to something, especially at night. If you are riding in a sleeper car, try to secure the bottom berth; bags can be stowed underneath and the only way a thief can get to your stuff is by literally lifting you up. If you must leave your pack for a moment, ask someone who looks responsible to keep an eye on it.

Another hazard is children throwing rocks at the train. Passengers have been severely injured this way and many conductors insist that you keep down the metal window shield for this reason. Unfortunately, however, these shields also obstruct the view.

There is supposedly a 20kg luggage limit on trains in Vietnam. Enforcement isn't really strict, but if you have too much stuff you might have to send it in the freight car (hopefully on the same train) and pay a small extra charge. This is a hassle that you'll probably want to avoid. Bicycles and motorbikes can also travel in the freight car. Just make sure that the train you are on has a freight car (most have) or your luggage will arrive later than you do.

Eating is no problem as there are vendors at every station who board the train and practically stuff food, drinks, lottery tickets and cigarettes into your pockets. However, the food supplied by the railway company (free, as part of the cost of the ticket for some long journeys) could be better. It's a good idea to stock up on your favourite munchies before taking a long trip.

## The *Reunification Express*

Construction of the 1726km-long Hanoi–Saigon railway, the Transindochinois, began in 1899 (under Governor General Paul Doumer) and was completed in 1936. In the late 1930s, the trip from Hanoi to Saigon took 40 hours and 20 minutes at an average speed of 43km/h. During WWII, the Japanese made extensive use of the rail system, resulting in Viet Minh sabotage on the ground and US bombing from the air. After WWII, efforts were made to repair the Transindochinois, major parts of which were either damaged or had become overgrown.

During the Franco–Viet Minh War, the Viet Minh engaged in massive sabotage against the rail system. Sometimes they would pry up and carry off several kilometres of track in a single night. In 1948 the French responded by introducing two armoured trains that were equipped with turret-mounted cannon, anti-aircraft machine guns, grenade launchers and mortars (similar trains are used in Cambodia today on the Phnom Penh–Battambang line). The Viet Minh used their bounty to create a 300km network of tracks (between Ninh Hoa and Danang) in an area wholly under their control – the French quickly responded with their own sabotage.

In the late 1950s, the South, with US funding, reconstructed the track between Saigon and Hué, a distance of 1041km. But between 1961 and 1964 alone, 795 Viet Cong attacks were launched on the rail system, forcing the abandonment of large sections of track (including the Dalat spur). A major reconstruction effort was carried out between 1967 and 1969, and three sections of track were put back into operation: one in the immediate vicinity of Saigon, another between Nha Trang and Qui Nhon, and a third between Danang and Hué.

By 1960 the North had repaired 1000km of track, mostly between Hanoi and China. During the US air war against the North, the northern rail network was repeatedly bombed. Even now clusters of bomb craters can be seen around virtually every rail bridge and train station in the north.

After reunification, the government immediately set about re-establishing the Hanoi–Ho Chi Minh City (HCMC) rail link as a symbol of Vietnamese unity. By the time the *Reunification Express* trains were inaugurated on 31 December 1976, 1334 bridges, 27 tunnels, 158 stations and 1370 shunts (switches) had been repaired.

Today the *Reunification Express* chugs along slightly faster than the trains did in the 1930s; at an average of 48km/h, it takes between 30 and 41 hours to get from Hanoi to HCMC, depending on which train you catch.

## Schedules

Odd-numbered trains travel south and even-numbered ones travel north. The fastest train service is provided by the *Reunification Express*, which runs between HCMC and Hanoi, making only a few short stops en route. If you want to stop at some obscure point between the major towns, you'll have to use one of the slower local trains.

Aside from the main HCMC–Hanoi run, three rail-spur lines link Hanoi with the other parts of northern Vietnam. One takes you east to the port city of Haiphong. A second heads northeast to Lang Son, crosses the border and continues to Nanning, China. A third goes northwest to Lao Cai and onwards to Kunming, China; the new soft-sleeper carriages were recently installed on the Hanoi–Lao Cai route.

Four *Reunification Express* trains depart HCMC's Saigon station between 9am and 10.30pm every day. The same number of trains depart Hanoi between 5am and 6.40pm daily. In addition, there are local trains, for example between HCMC and Nha Trang or Hué.

The train schedules change frequently (about every six months). The timetables for all trains are posted on the Vietnam Railway website and at major stations so you can copy them down. Most travel agents and some hotels keep a copy of the latest schedule on hand. In HCMC, call or visit the **Saigon Railways Tourist Service** (☎ 08-836 7640, fax 836 9031; 275C Đ Pham Ngu Lao, District 1) in the Pham Ngu Lao area.

It's important to realise that the train schedule is 'bare-bones' during the Tet festival. For example, the *Reunification Express* is suspended for nine days, beginning four days before Tet and continuing for four days afterwards.

At the time of writing, there were plans to discontinue the practice of checking tickets on arrival. It's no longer necessary to hang on to your ticket, in order to exit the platform at your destination.

## Classes

There are five classes of train travel in Vietnam: hard seat; soft seat; hard sleeper; soft sleeper (normal); and soft sleeper (air-con). Since it's all that many Vietnamese can afford, hard-seat class is usually packed. Hard seat is tolerable for day travel, but overnight it can be even less comfortable than the bus, where at least you are hemmed in and thus propped upright.

Soft-seat carriages have vinyl-covered seats rather than the uncomfortable hard benches.

A hard sleeper has three tiers of beds (six beds per compartment). Because the Vietnamese don't seem to like climbing up, the upper berth is cheapest, followed by the middle berth and finally the lower berth. The best bunk is the one in the middle because the bottom berth is invaded by seatless travellers during the day. There is no door to separate the compartment from the corridor.

Soft sleeper has two tiers (four beds per compartment) and all bunks are priced the same. These compartments have a door. The best trains have two categories of soft sleeper, one with air-con and one without. At present, air-con is only available on the very fastest express trains.

## Reservations

The supply of train seats is often insufficient to meet demand. Reservations for all trips should be made at least one day in advance. For sleeping berths, you may have to book passage several days before the date of travel. Bring your passport when buying train tickets. Though such documents are never checked at bus stations, train personnel may ask to have a look at them.

You do not necessarily need to go to the train station to get your ticket. Many travel agencies, hotels and cafés sell train tickets for a small commission (in most cases, well worth the time and trouble you'll save buying the tickets on your own). It's a good idea to make reservations for onward travel as soon as you arrive in a city.

If you are travelling by train with a bicycle or motorbike (for which there is usually a nominal surcharge), it may be possible to get it out of checked baggage only at certain stations.

## *Reunification Express* Fares from Ho Chi Minh City (d)

### Ho Chi Minh City–Hanoi (S4/S6/S8 Trains); 41 hours

| station | hard seat | soft seat | A/C seat | top berth | middle berth | bottom berth | soft sleeper (4 berth) |
|---|---|---|---|---|---|---|---|
| Muong Man | 38,000 | 42,000 | 45,000 | 45,000 | 53,000 | 60,000 | 73,000 |
| Thap Cham | 69,000 | 76,000 | 82,000 | 82,000 | 97,000 | 109,000 | 133,000 |
| Nha Trang | 88,000 | 98,000 | 105,000 | 105,000 | 124,000 | 141,000 | 171,000 |
| Tuy Hoa | 118,000 | 131,000 | 140,000 | 140,000 | 166,000 | 188,000 | 228,000 |
| Dieu Tri | 143,000 | 159,000 | 170,000 | 170,000 | 201,000 | 227,000 | 276,000 |
| Quang Ngai | 179,000 | 199,000 | 213,000 | 213,000 | 251,000 | 285,000 | 346,000 |
| Tam Ky | 192,000 | 214,000 | 229,000 | 229,000 | 270,000 | 306,000 | 372,000 |
| Danang | 208,000 | 231,000 | 248,000 | 248,000 | 292,000 | 331,000 | 403,000 |
| Hué | 230,000 | 256,000 | 274,000 | 274,000 | 323,000 | 366,000 | 446,000 |
| Dong Ha | 245,000 | 273,000 | 292,000 | 292,000 | 345,000 | 391,000 | 475,000 |
| Dong Hoi | 267,000 | 297,000 | 318,000 | 318,000 | 375,000 | 425,000 | 517,000 |
| Vinh | 339,000 | 377,000 | 403,000 | 403,000 | 476,000 | 539,000 | 656,000 |
| Thanh Hoa | 350,000 | 389,000 | 416,000 | 416,000 | 491,000 | 557,000 | 677,000 |
| Ninh Binh | 357,000 | 397,000 | 426,000 | 426,000 | 502,000 | 569,000 | 692,000 |
| Nam Dinh | 363,000 | 404,000 | 433,000 | 433,000 | 511,000 | 578,000 | 704,000 |
| Hanoi | 370,000 | 411,000 | 441,000 | 441,000 | 520,000 | 589,000 | 717,000 |

### Ho Chi Minh City–Hanoi (S2 Express Train); 33 hours; all cars air-con

| station | soft seat | top hard berth | middle hard berth | bottom hard berth | soft sleeper (4 berth) |
|---|---|---|---|---|---|
| Thap Cham | 94,000 | 107,000 | 126,000 | 138,000 | 143,000 |
| Nha Trang | 121,000 | 138,000 | 162,000 | 178,000 | 185,000 |
| Tuy Hoa | 161,000 | 184,000 | 217,000 | 238,000 | 246,000 |
| Dieu Tri | 195,000 | 223,000 | 263,000 | 288,000 | 298,000 |
| Quang Ngai | 244,000 | 280,000 | 329,000 | 360,000 | 374,000 |
| Tam Ky | 262,000 | 301,000 | 354,000 | 388,000 | 402,000 |
| Danang | 284,000 | 325,000 | 383,000 | 420,000 | 435,000 |
| Hué | 314,000 | 360,000 | 423,000 | 464,000 | 481,000 |
| Dong Ha | 335,000 | 384,000 | 451,000 | 495,000 | 513,000 |
| Dong Hoi | 364,000 | 417,000 | 491,000 | 538,000 | 558,000 |
| Vinh | 462,000 | 530,000 | 623,000 | 683,000 | 708,000 |
| Thanh Hoa | 477,000 | 547,000 | 643,000 | 705,000 | 736,000 |
| Nam Dinh | 495,000 | 568,000 | 668,000 | 733,000 | 760,000 |
| Hanoi | 504,000 | 579,000 | 681,000 | 746,000 | 774,000 |

## Reunification Express Fares from Ho Chi Minh City (d)

Ho Chi Minh City–Hanoi (E2 Express Train); 30 hours; all cars air-con

| station | soft seat | top hard berth | middle hard berth | bottom hard berth | soft sleeper (4 berth) |
|---|---|---|---|---|---|
| Nha Trang | 124,000 | 142,000 | 167,000 | 183,000 | 190,000 |
| Dieu Tri | 200,000 | 229,000 | 270,000 | 296,000 | 307,000 |
| Danang | 292,000 | 334,000 | 393,000 | 432,000 | 448,000 |
| Hué | 322,000 | 370,000 | 435,000 | 478,000 | 495,000 |
| Dong Hoi | 374,000 | 428,000 | 504,000 | 554,000 | 574,000 |
| Vinh | 475,000 | 544,000 | 640,000 | 704,000 | 729,000 |
| Hanoi | 518,000 | 594,000 | 700,000 | 769,000 | 796,000 |

Fares are the same as those shown above from Hanoi to Ho Chi Minh City on trains E1 (30 hours), S1 (33 hours) and S3/S5S7 (41 hours).

## Costs

Until quite recently foreign train travellers were required to pay a surcharge of around 400% over and above what Vietnamese paid, which made spending a little more than that for an air ticket seem all the more appealing. All of this has changed, luckily, and prices have dropped tremendously in the past few years. However, non-Vietnamese still do pay more for any ticket.

Some foreigners have managed to pay local prices, but this is almost impossible to do unless you have Asian features. Even with Asian features, you are supposed to show ID when the ticket is purchased, though a Vietnamese person could buy the ticket for you. The ticket clearly indicates whether you paid foreign or local prices, and the name of the purchaser is also written on the ticket. Most conductors enforce the rules – if you have blond hair and a big nose, don't think that you're going to fool the conductors into believing you're Vietnamese, even if you do happen to be under a conical hat.

The price for a ticket depends on which train you take: the HCMC–Hanoi run takes 30, 32, 37, 39 or 41 hours – the fastest trains are naturally the most expensive. See the boxed text 'Reunification Express Fares from Ho Chi Minh City' in this chapter.

## CAR & MOTORBIKE

The discomfort and unreliability of Vietnam's public transport combined with the relative affordability of vehicle hire makes the latter a popular option. Having your own set of wheels gives you maximum flexibility to visit remote regions and stop where and when you please.

The major considerations are safety, the mechanical condition of the vehicle, reliability of the rental agency and your budget. We strongly recommend that you not consider driving a car yourself in Vietnam; a motorbike is challenging enough, and moreover, experienced Vietnamese drivers can be hired for around US$5 per day. As one reader has commented:

I have visited about 50 countries and driven in over half of them. Nowhere have I seen worse drivers than in Vietnam. We saw four fatal traffic accidents, and several additional less serious ones, all within a two-week period. I think it is sheer lunacy for anyone who lacks substantial experience driving in similar countries to attempt to do so here.

**John Findling**

In general, the major highways are hard surfaced and reasonably well maintained, but seasonal flooding can be a problem. A big typhoon can create potholes the size of bomb craters. In remote areas roads are not surfaced and will become a sea of mud if the weather turns bad – such roads are best tackled with a 4WD vehicle or motorbike. Mountain roads are particularly dangerous; those landslides, falling rocks and runaway vehicles can add unwelcome excitement to your journey. The occasional roadside cemetery often indicates where a bus plunged over the edge.

The pumps in petrol stations may say something like 'regular' or 'super-unleaded'. Basically this means nothing except that the petrol pump was purchased from abroad. However, petrol does have an octane rating – 86 would be low and 95 would be top-end. There can also be several gradations of strength in between.

Black-market petrol *(xang)* and oil *(dau)* is sold in soft-drink bottles at little stalls along major roads and highways. In rural areas you'll see the bottles stacked by the roadside next to a stall. In HCMC, it's not permitted to stack bottles of petrol by the roadside, so the vendor places a couple of

## On the Plate

You can learn a great deal about a vehicle by examining its licence plate. Whether you are in a confusing bus station looking for the right bus or hitchhiking and trying to avoid accidentally flagging down an army truck, the following information should prove useful.

First, there are the several types of licence plates. Privately owned vehicles have black digits on a white background. Vehicles with white numbers on a green field are owned by the government, while white on blue are police-owned. Diplomatic cars have the letters NG in red, before green numbers on a white field. Other cars owned by foreigners begin with the letters NN and are green-on-white. Military plates have white numbers on red.

The first two numbers on a number plate are the two-digit code assigned to the vehicle's province of origin. For a comprehensive list of Vietnam's 61 provinces and municipalities, see the boxed text 'Provincial Area Codes' in the Facts for the Visitor chapter.

Some of the more common two-digit codes to look for on licence plate are, from north to south, listed here.

### Licence Plate Codes

| code | province | capital | code | province | capital |
|------|----------|---------|------|----------|---------|
| 21 | Lao Cai | Lao Cai | 47 | Quang Ngai | Quang Ngai |
| 20 | Thai Nguyen | Thai Nguyen | 47 | Dac Lac | Buon Ma Thuot |
| 13 | Bac Ninh | Bac Ninh | 48 | Binh Thuan | Phan Thiet |
| 15 | Haiphong City* | | 49 | Lam Dong | Dalat |
| 17 | Thai Binh | Thai Binh | 50 | HCMC (govt)* | |
| 18 | Ninh Binh | Ninh Binh | 51 & 55 | HCMC (pvt)* | |
| 29–32 | Hanoi* | | 63 | Tien Giang | Mytho |
| 36 | Thanh Hoa | Thanh Hoa | 64 | Vinh Long | Vinh Long |
| 37 | Nghe An | Vinh | 65 | Cantho | Cantho |
| 39 & 40 | Thua Thien | Hué | 66 | Dong Thap | Cao Lanh |
| 43 | Danang City* | | 67 | An Giang | Long Xuyen |
| 44 | Binh Dinh | Qui Nhon | 69 | Camau | Camau |
| 45 | Khanh Hoa | Nha Trang | 70 | Tay Ninh | Tay Ninh |
| 46 | Kon Tum | Kon Tum | 78 | Ba Ria | Vung Tau |

*indicates a municipality

bricks with a rolled-up newspaper stuck vertically in between. In cities, this is the universal sign indicating petrol for sale. Be forewarned that black-market petrol is often mixed with kerosene (it's cheaper), which is likely to cause engine problems – use in emergencies only.

Leaving an unattended vehicle parked out on the street overnight is not wise. If travelling by motorbike you can usually bring it inside the hotel. If travelling by car, it's necessary to find a hotel with a garage or fenced-in compound (many hotels are so equipped). There are also commercial non-hotel garages, but your driver will be able to figure this one out.

If you're on a motorbike, serious sunburn is a major risk and something you should take care to prevent. The cooling breeze prevents you from realising how badly you are burning until it's too late. Cover up exposed skin or wear sunscreen. Bikers also must consider the opposite problem – occasional heavy rains. Rainsuits and ponchos should be carried – especially during the monsoon season. Sun block is somewhat hard to find in Vietnam, but rain gear is readily available.

## Road Rules

Basically, there aren't any. The biggest vehicle wins, by default. Be particularly careful about children on the road – you'll find kids playing hopscotch in the middle of a major highway. Many young boys seem to enjoy playing a game of 'chicken', in which they deliberately stick their arms and legs in front of fast-approaching vehicles then withdraw them (hopefully) at the last possible moment. Other children try to entertain themselves by throwing rocks at passing vehicles so make sure you wear a helmet if you're on a motorbike. Livestock on the road are also a menace; hit a cow on a motorbike and you'll both be hamburger.

In cities there is a rule that you cannot turn right on a red light. It's easy to run afoul of this law in Vietnam and the police will fine you for this offence.

When the locals have an accident, the usual response is for the two drivers to stand in the street and argue with each other for 30 minutes about whose fault it was. Whoever tires of the argument first hands over some money to pay for damages and it's all settled. As a foreigner, you're at a disadvantage in these negotiations. Perhaps it's best to offer to pay for the other driver's minor damages. If none of this works and you are being asked to pay excessive damages, you should contact the nearest police station.

**Car** Although the police frequently stop drivers and fine them for all sorts of real and imagined offences, we have never seen anybody stopped for speeding. Driving is normally performed Grand Prix–style, as if there were some sort of prize for the first car to cross the finish line.

Honking at all pedestrians and bicycles (to warn them of your approach) is considered a basic element of safe driving – larger trucks and buses might as well have a permanent siren attached.

There is no national seat-belt law and the locals often laugh at foreigners who insist on using seat belts.

The law says that you are supposed to turn on your headlights at night. That seems elementary enough, but many people drive at night without lights because they believe that this saves petrol (it doesn't).

**Motorbike** The legal definition of a moped is any motor-driven, two-wheeled vehicle that's 50cc or less. Motorbikes are two-wheeled vehicles with engines over 50cc. You don't need an International Driving Permit (IDP) for a moped, but you'll need one with motorbike endorsement to drive a motorbike. Expats remaining in the country over six months are expected to obtain a Vietnamese driving licence. A Vietnamese licence will be valid only for the length of your visa! If you extend your visa, you need to extend your driving licence too.

Technically, the maximum legal size of a motorbike is 125cc. There are indeed larger bikes around and these are classified as motorcycles.

The major cities have parking lots *(giu xe)* for bicycles and motorbikes that are usually just a roped-off section of sidewalk.

They charge around 2000d to guard your vehicle (bike theft is a major problem). Always use these unless you want your bike to disappear. When you pull up, a number will be chalked on the seat or stapled to the handlebars and you'll be handed a reclaim chit. Without it, getting your wheels back may be a real hassle, especially if you come back after the workers have changed shifts. Outside of the designated parking lots, some travellers simply ask a stranger to watch their bikes – this is not such a good idea. As one traveller wrote:

We asked some locals to watch our motorbike while we went to explore a beach in a nearby cove. When we returned, we found that our new 'friends' had removed some vital engine components and we had to buy these back from the very people who stole them.

Locals are required to have liability insurance on their motorbikes, but foreigners are not covered and there is currently no way to arrange this. If you want to insure yourself against injury, disfigurement or death, you'll need some sort of travel insurance with a foreign company – be sure that motorbike accidents are not excluded from your policy! Travel insurance is something that must be arranged before you come to Vietnam. As for liability insurance, consider burning some incense at a local temple.

With more than eight million motorbikes on the road today in Vietnam (more than 15 times the number of just a decade ago!), it's not surprising that over half of the road fatalities in Vietnam are suffered by motorbike drivers. These horrific statistics have caused the government to take action: the current laws require motorbike riders and passengers to wear helmets (known locally as 'rice cookers') while they're swerving along the majority of the country's national highways. Judging by the overwhelming majority who still do not, the law is clearly not being enforced.

You can purchase high-quality safety helmets in HCMC and Hanoi for around US$40, or else buy a low-quality 'eggshell' helmet for US$20. For the serious biker,

bringing a helmet from abroad is the best idea, but make sure it's something that you can tolerate wearing in hot weather. As a last resort, you might consider purchasing a slightly battered US army helmet from the War Surplus Market in HCMC – the bullet holes provide ventilation!

The law says that a motorbike can carry only two persons, but we've seen up to seven on one vehicle (and they had luggage). This law is occasionally enforced in cities, but mostly ignored in rural areas.

## Rental

**Car & Minibus**   Drive-yourself rental cars have yet to make their debut in Vietnam, but cars with drivers can be hired from various outlets. Given the low cost of labour, renting a vehicle with a driver and guide is a realistic option even if you're a budget traveller. Split between several people, the cost per day can be surprisingly reasonable.

Hanoi and HCMC have an especially wide selection of travel agencies that rent out vehicles. The service is also offered by various competing parties, including many provincial tourism authorities and private companies. Bargaining is possible and, when you've completed negotiations, a contract should be signed to prevent any later disputes.

For sightseeing trips around HCMC or Hanoi, a car with driver can also be rented by the day or by the hour (renting by the day is cheaper). For definition purposes, a 'day' is eight hours or less with a total distance travelled of less than 100km. Based on this formula, it costs about US$25 per day (or US$4 per hour) for a Russian car; US$35 per day (US$5 per hour) for a small Japanese car, and US$40 per day (US$6 per hour) for a larger, late-model Japanese car.

Renting a minibus (van) is worth considering for larger groups. Vans usually hold between eight to 15 passengers, so the cost per person works out less than a car. One advantage of vans is that they have high clearance, a consideration on some of Vietnam's dismal unsurfaced roads.

For the really bad roads of northwest Vietnam, the only reasonably safe vehicle is a 4WD. Without one, the muddy mountain roads can be deadly. In Vietnam, 4WDs come in different varieties – the cheapest (and least comfortable) are Russian-made, while more cushy Korean and Japanese vehicles are about twice the price.

With the exception of Russian-built or really old vehicles, most are equipped with air-con. Since these often cost more to rent, make your preferences known early when negotiating a price.

Many travellers have rented cars from individuals – some have been satisfied and some havn't. Some of these self-proclaimed guides with cars offer very low prices, but they have no insurance and by law are not permitted to transport tourists. There have been reports of reckless driving, vehicles in lousy mechanical condition and trouble with the police. It's often better to find companions and rent a car and driver from a reliable company.

Most cars are equipped with a cassette-tape player. Bring some music tapes or buy them from the local markets and hope your driver, guide and fellow passengers have the same taste in music as you do!

**Motorbike** You can rent a motorbike from a variety of outlets (eg, cafés, travel agencies, motorbike shops and hotels). If you don't want to drive yourself, there are plenty of local drivers who are also willing to act as your personal motorbike chauffeur and guide for around US$6 to US$10 per day. However, take care to find someone who you feel is competent and easy to get along with.

How much you end up paying for a motorbike depends on the engine size. Renting a 50cc moped (the most popular model) is cheap at around US$6 per day, usually with unlimited mileage.

The **Saigon Scooter Centre** (☎ 0903-845819, fax 511 3491; e ssc@hcm.vnn.vn, w www.saigonscootercentre.com; 174 Đ Bui Thi Xuan, Tan Binh district) in HCMC hires out various motorbikes and can arrange one-way/drop-off rental options.

Complications can occur if a deposit or some other form of security is required.

Since new motorbikes cost about US$2000, a deposit to cover its value would not be a trivial lump of cash. Others prefer to hold your passport until you return the bike. There have not been any problems with rental companies losing or refusing to return these, though you are placing yourself in their hands and you really do need your passport on the road for checking into hotels.

You should definitely sign some sort of agreement (preferably in English or a language you understand) clearly stating what you are renting, how much it costs, the extent of compensation you must pay if the bike is stolen etc. People in the business of renting out motorbikes are usually equipped with a standard rental agreement.

Most bikes' rear-view mirrors are removed or turned around so that they don't get broken in the handlebar-to-handlebar traffic. This might make sense in HCMC or Hanoi, with the continuous close encounters, but have the mirrors properly installed if you're going out on the highway. It's rather important to know if a big truck is bearing down on you from behind.

## Purchase

**Car** Foreigners with resident certificates can purchase a car, but unless you're staying long-term it does not make much sense to do so. Foreign companies can also purchase cars, though companies that do so also usually hire a Vietnamese driver rather than let their foreign employees drive themselves. Special licence plates are affixed to foreign-owned vehicles.

**Motorbike** Except for bona fide foreign residents, buying a motorbike for touring in Vietnam is technically illegal. However so far the authorities have largely turned a blind eye to the practice. Apparently, you buy a bike but register it in the name of a trusted Vietnamese friend. Some shops that sell motorbikes will let you keep the bike registered in the shop's name. This requires that you trust the shopkeepers, but in most cases this seems to work out OK.

The big issue is what to do with the bike when you're finished with it. If you return to the city where you originally purchased the bike, you can simply sell it back to the shop you bought it from (at a discount, of course). Another possible solution is to sell it to another foreigner travelling in the opposite direction – notice boards at the cafés in HCMC and Hanoi can be useful in this regard. If you're unlucky, you might have to simply scrap the bike. Given this possibility, it's best not to buy a very expensive motorbike in the first place. Remember however that buying a motorbike is illegal and a crackdown may come at any time.

Japanese-made motorbikes are the best available, but by far the most expensive. Honda Dream is everyone's favourite for the lowlands – and the most likely to get stolen. A new Dream goes for about US$2000.

The best alternative for the mountains is to buy a used 125cc Russian-made Minsk, for around US$400 to US$450, and brand new for around US$600. It is a powerful bike and it's very easy to find spare parts and mechanics who can do repairs. The Minsk handles particularly well on muddy roads, a significant point in its favour.

A compromise is the Taiwanese-made Bonus. This 125cc bike costs around US$1800 new, and its quality is somewhere halfway between a Minsk and a Honda Dream. The bike handles well on paved roads, but poorly in the mud – the Minsk is better for mud-slogging.

There are some other cheap bikes from Eastern Europe, but basically they are junk.

## BICYCLE

A great way to get around Vietnam's towns and cities is to do as the locals do: ride a bicycle. During rush hours, urban thoroughfares approach gridlock, as rushing streams of cyclists force their way through intersections, without the benefit of traffic lights. Riders are always crashing into each other and getting knocked down, but because bicycle traffic is so heavy, they are rarely going fast enough to be injured. In the countryside, Westerners on bicycles are often greeted enthusiastically by locals, who may never have seen a foreigner pedalling around before.

Bicycles are utility vehicles in much of rural Vietnam. To see a bike carrying three pigs or 300kg of vegetables is not unusual. One has to marvel at how people manage to load all these items on the bike and ride it without the whole thing tipping over.

Long-distance cycling is also a possibility in Vietnam: much of the country is flat or only moderately hilly, and the major roads are of a serviceable standard. Safety, however, is a considerable concern. Bicycles can be transported around the country on the top of buses or in train baggage compartments. Lonely Planet's *Cycling Vietnam, Laos & Cambodia* gives the low-down on cycling through Vietnam.

The flatlands of the Mekong Delta region are a logical place for long-distance riding. The entire coastal route along National Hwy 1 is feasible, but the insane traffic makes it unpleasant and dangerous.

North of the old Demilitarised Zone (DMZ), cycling is probably not a good idea in the winter months, particularly if heading from south to north. This is because of monsoonal winds, which blow from the north. Nothing is more depressing than constantly riding into a cold headwind. Doing it from north to south means you'll have the wind to your back (although it's still cold).

Mountain bikes and 10-speed bikes can be bought at a few speciality shops in Hanoi and HCMC, but it's probably better to bring your own if you plan to travel long distances by pedal power. Mountain bikes are the preferable option as the occasional large pothole or unsealed road can be rough on a set of delicate rims. Basic cycling safety equipment is not available in Vietnam: bring helmets, night lights, front and rear reflectors, leg reflectors and rear-view mirrors. For long-distance riding, pack spare parts such as spokes, tubes, a pump, cables and a water bottle. Take some tools: a spoke wrench, a chain tool, a multifunction tool and a small bottle of chain lube. A bell is mandatory – the louder the better. Padded gloves ease the shock of rough roads. A pocket-size inner-tube repair kit is necessary. Don't forget to deflate your tyres before boarding planes, as your bike will probably travel in an unpressurised cabin, which can result in exploded tubes.

Hotels and some travel agencies are starting to get into the business of renting out bicycles. The cost varies, but is around US$1 per day. Although you will often see two Vietnamese riding on a single bike, this is generally *not* a good idea for Westerners. Local bikes are not built to carry the extra weight.

There are innumerable bicycle-repair stands along the side of the roads in every city and town in Vietnam. Usually, they consist of no more than a pump, an upturned military helmet and a metal ammunition box filled with oily bolts and a few wrenches.

Pumping up a tyre costs 500d. Fixing a punctured inner tube should only cost about 5000d, depending on the size of the patch. The common practice is to use 'hot patches', which have to be burned into place – this is more time-consuming than using glue, but it makes for a good seal.

Many travellers buy a cheap bicycle, use it during their visit and, at the end, either sell it or give it to a Vietnamese friend. Locally produced bicycles are available, starting at about US$30, but are of a truly inferior quality. A fairly decent one-speed, Chinese-made bicycle costs about US$60 to US$80. A Taiwanese-made mountain bike usually goes for about US$200 and Japanese-made bikes for about US$300 each.

Groups of foreign cyclists have begun touring Vietnam, and there are even tour companies that specialise in bicycling trips. See the Organised Tours section in the Getting There & Away chapter for details.

## HITCHING

Hitching is never entirely safe in any country in the world, and we don't recommend it. Travellers who decide to hitch should understand that they are taking a potentially serious risk. People who do choose to hitch will be safer if they travel in pairs and let someone know where they are planning to go.

In Vietnam, locals do flag down private and public vehicles for a lift, but a small fee is usually paid. Of course for foreigners this would be more.

## BOAT

Vietnam has an enormous number of rivers that are at least partly navigable, but the most important by far is the multibranched Mekong River. Scenic day trips by boat are also possible on rivers in Hoi An, Danang, Hué, Tam Coc and even HCMC, but only in the Mekong Delta are boats used as a practical means of transport.

Hydrofoils run to Cat Ba Island (near Halong Bay), and between HCMC and the beach resort of Vung Tao.

Boat trips are also possible on the sea – a cruise to the islands off the coast of Nha Trang is a particularly popular trip. Ferries are a practical means of getting from the Mekong Delta to Phu Quoc Island, as well as from Vung Tao to the Con Dao Islands. If you visit Halong Bay, a cruise to the islands located in that region is practically mandatory.

Pay attention to the condition of the boats. Small boats with small engines (or no engines) are going to be slow. If the water is rough, small boats will bounce around like a cork. Many people enjoy this, but it's not much fun if you're prone to seasickness. Some of the smaller river craft can only accommodate two or three people and you can easily get splashed. Whenever you take such a small boat, it's wise to keep your camera in a plastic bag (when not actually in use) to protect it from splashes.

In some parts of Vietnam (particularly the Mekong Delta) you'll have to make some ferry crossings. This is no big deal, but a few precautions are called for. Passengers are sometimes required to get out of their vehicles before these are driven onto the ferries – be sure that your luggage is secure. Don't stand between parked vehicles on the ferry as they can roll and you could wind up as the meat in the sandwich. Be sure you buy a passenger ticket before boarding – at some ferry crossings, you buy the ticket on one side of the river and have to give it to the gatekeeper on the other side. But on some very small ferries (the ones that do not carry cars) you buy the tickets on board – confusing.

## LOCAL TRANSPORT

### Bus

Vietnam has some of the worst local inner-city bus transport in Asia. The bus systems in Hanoi and HCMC have improved in the past few years but are light years behind Hong Kong and Bangkok, and in general, bus is not a practical way to get around town. Fortunately, there are many other fast and economical options such as meter taxis, cyclos and motorbike taxis.

### Taxi

Western-style taxis with meters were introduced to HCMC in 1994 and have spread quickly to most major cities.

For details on exactly what is available in each city, see the Getting There & Away and Getting Around sections of each chapter.

### Cyclo

The cyclo *(xich lo)*, from the French *cyclo-pousse*, is the best invention since sliced bread. Cyclos, or pedicabs, offer easy, cheap and aesthetic transportation around Vietnam's confusing, sprawling cities. Riding these clever contraptions will also give you the moral superiority that comes with the knowledge you are being kind to the local environment – more so than all those drivers on whining, smoke-spewing motorbikes.

Groups of cyclo drivers always hang out near major hotels and markets, and many speak at least broken English. Those who do speak English charge a little more than those who don't, but avoiding the language problem may be worth the minor added expense. To make sure the driver understands where you want to go, it's useful to bring a city map with you.

All cyclo drivers are male, although they vary in age from around 15 to perhaps 60 years old. Many of the younger ones are transients from the countryside and are in HCMC and Hanoi to seek their fortune. With no place to live, they may even sleep in their cyclo (see the boxed text 'Life on the Streets' in the Ho Chi Minh City chapter). Since 1995 the government has required cyclo drivers to obtain a licence, which requires passing an exam on traffic-safety laws.

Most cyclo drivers rent their vehicles for about 15,000d per day. The more affluent cyclo drivers buy their own vehicle for about US$200, but to do so the owner must have a residence permit for the place where the cyclo is to be driven – the transients from rural areas are thus excluded from vehicle ownership. Operating a cyclo can often be a family business – a father and son take turns so the vehicle gets used 18 hours a day.

Bargaining is almost always necessary. If the cyclo drivers waiting outside your hotel want too much, flag down someone else less used to spendthrift tourists. Settle on a fare *before* going anywhere or you're likely to be asked for some outrageous quantity of dong at the trip's end.

I had a fingers bargaining session with a cyclo driver, only to discover at the end of the ride that he was bargaining dollars and I was bargaining dong! He got 10,000d not US$10 – much to his disappointment – but I had to be very forceful to get away with it.

**Mike Conrad**

We should point out that sometimes these misunderstandings are sincere, not always attempts to cheat you. We know one traveller who had a vociferous argument when he tried to pay his cyclo driver 1000d rather than US$1. In fact, no-one, not even a Vietnamese, can hire a cyclo for 1000d and the price really should have been about US$1. Bargaining solely by sign language is not such a good idea as you cannot possibly hold up 10,000 fingers. Probably the best solution is to write things down, or ideally learn to say the basic Vietnamese numbers (this can help immensely in keeping the price under control).

As a basic rule, short rides around town should cost about 5000d. For a long ride, say over 2km, you can expect to pay a bit more, but rarely over 10,000d. Cyclo drivers will almost certainly try to demand more, but in most cases politely refusing them and walking away will bring a change of heart. It's also a good idea to have your money counted out and ready before getting on a cyclo. It pays to have the exact change as drivers may claim they cannot change a 10,000d note.

Cyclos are cheaper by time rather than distance. A typical price is US$1 per hour. If this works out well, don't be surprised if the driver comes around to your hotel the next morning to see if you want to hire him again.

We found the best friends we made were the incredibly loyal cyclo drivers in Nha Trang and Hanoi, who would wait outside your hotel all day to take you anywhere as a 'regular' customer. They were all charming and we were sad to say goodbye to them.

**Meriel Rule**

There have been some reports of travellers being mugged by their cyclo drivers in HCMC, so as a general rule of thumb, hire cyclos only during the day. Especially if you are coming home from a bar late at night, take a meter taxi; it will not cost much more than a cyclo – sometimes it can even be cheaper – and it is much safer.

### Motorbike Taxi

The *xe om* (say-**ohm**) is an ordinary motorbike on which you ride seated behind the driver. *Xe* means motorbike, and *om* means hug (or hold), so you probably get the picture. In other words, it's a motorbike taxi. Getting around by *xe om* is quite respectable, if a bit dangerous, as long as you don't have a lot of luggage with you.

Don't expect to find one with a meter – negotiate the price beforehand. The fare is typically comparable with a cyclo, but this all depends on what you can negotiate with the driver. As with cyclos, if the driver will not take you for the price you want, politely say 'no thank you' and walk away; chances are he'll come to see things your way, so long as what you're asking for is not too little.

You'll find plenty of *xe om* drivers hanging around street corners, markets, hotels and bus stations. They make themselves pretty conspicuous, so they're not hard to find. However, it can be difficult to find one when you're just walking down a street: stand by the road and try to flag someone down, or ask a local to find one for you.

### Xe Lam

*Xe lam* are tiny, three-wheeled trucks used for short-haul passenger and freight transport (similar to the Indonesian *bajaj*). They tend to have whining two-stroke 'lawn mower' engines with no mufflers, and emit copious quantities of blue exhaust smoke, but they get the job done.

### Xe Dap Loi & Xe Loi

The two forms of transport used mostly in the Mekong Delta are the *xe dap loi*, which is a wagon pulled by a bicycle, and the *xe loi*, a wagon pulled by a motorbike.

### WALKING

If you don't want to wind up like a bug on a windshield, you need to pay close attention to a few pedestrian survival rules, especially on the streets of motorbike-crazed HCMC and Hanoi. Foreigners frequently make the mistake of thinking that the best way to cross a busy street in Vietnam is to run quickly across it. This does not always work, and sometimes it can get you creamed. Most Vietnamese cross the street slowly – very slowly – giving the motorbike drivers sufficient time to judge their position so they can pass on either side of you. They won't stop or even slow down, but they will try to avoid hitting you. Just don't make any sudden moves. Good luck.

Crossing the street in Saigon is an art. Move slowly and deliberately, never be indecisive or hesitant, unless you see a bus coming, then the above does not apply...RUN!

**Ron Settle**

### ORGANISED TOURS

We get an awful lot of letters complaining about the quality of bottom-end budget tours being peddled in HCMC and Hanoi. Some are better than others, but you must always remember that you usually get what you pay for. Tour operator gimmicks like 'one free beer', 'one free breakfast', 'ten minutes of Internet' and 'a free CD' are usually not a good sign.

If you decide to rent a car with driver and guide, you'll have the opportunity to design

## Urban Orienteering

Urban orienteering is very easy in Vietnam. Vietnamese is written with a Latin-based alphabet. You can at least read the street signs and maps, even if the pronunciation is incomprehensible! In addition, finding out where you are is easy: street signs are plentiful, and almost every shop and restaurant has the street name and number on its sign. Street names are sometimes abbreviated on street signs with just the initials; for example, 'DBP' for 'Dien Bien Phu', 'CMT8' for 'Cach Mang Thang Tam' (*tam* means 'eight') etc.

Most street numbers are sequential, with odd and even numbers on opposite sides of the street, but there are confusing exceptions. In some places, consecutive buildings are numbered 15A, 15B, 15C and so forth, while elsewhere, consecutive addresses read 15D, 17D, 19D etc. Sometimes, especially in Danang and Ho Chi Minh City (HCMC), two numbering systems – the old confusing one and the new, even-more-confusing one – are in use simultaneously, so that an address may read '1743/697'. In some cases (such as Duong Lac Long Quan, where Giac Lam Pagoda is in HCMC) several streets, originally numbered separately, have been run together under one name, so that as you walk along the numbers go from one into the hundreds (or thousands) and then start all over again.

The Vietnamese post office is comfortable with the English words and abbreviations for street (St), road (Rd) and boulevard (Blvd), but this is not what you'll see on street signs around Vietnam. There are several words for 'street', the main ones used in HCMC being *dai lo* (ĐL) and *duong* (Đ). In Vietnamese, the word 'street' comes before the name, so Le Duan Blvd becomes Dai Lo Le Duan (or abbreviated ĐL Le Duan). In Hanoi and other cities in northern Vietnam, street names are commonly prefaced with *pho*. Though less and less these days, you may occasionally see street names carrying the French prefix 'Bis', a fading remnant of colonial days.

A few tips: many restaurants are named after their street addresses. For instance, 'Nha Hang 51 Nguyen Hue' (*nha hang* means restaurant) is at 51 Đ Nguyen Hue. If you are travelling by bus or car, a good way to get oriented is to look for the post office – the words following Buu Dien (Post Office) on the sign are the name of the district, town or village you're in.

On maps in this book, Pho is shortened to 'P', Dai Lo to 'ĐL' and Duong to 'Đ'.

---

your own itinerary for what amounts to a private tour for you and your companions. Seeing the country this way is almost like independent travel, except that it's more luxurious, you can cover more ground in a shorter period of time, and it also offers the advantage of stopping anywhere you like along the route for that once-in-a-lifetime photo.

The cost varies considerably. On the high end are tours booked through government travel agencies like Saigon Tourist and up-market tour companies, while budget and mid-range companies can usually arrange something good for a cheaper price.

The price typically includes accommodation at a tourist-class hotel, a guide who will accompany you everywhere, a driver and a car. Insist that your guides are fluent

in a language you know well. The cost of the car depends largely on the type of vehicle you choose.

When you settle on your itinerary, make sure to get a written copy from the travel agency. If you later find that your guide feels like deviating from what you paid for, that piece of paper is your most effective leverage. If your guide asks for the itinerary, keep the original and give them a photocopy, as there have been reports of guides taking tourists' itineraries and then running the tour their way.

A good guide can be your translator and travelling companion, and can usually save you as much money as they cost you (by helping you save money along the way). A bad guide can ruin your trip. If possible, you should meet and interview your guide before starting out – make sure that this is someone you can travel with.

Agree on the price before beginning the journey. Good, experienced private guides typically range from US$10 to US$30 per day. Less-experienced guides (especially students working part-time) can be hired for around US$5 to US$10 per day. It's proper to throw in a bonus at the end of your trip if your guide proved particularly helpful.

You are usually responsible for private guides' travel expenses, but this varies from operator to operator, so you'll need to check. If you can gather up a small group of travellers, the cost of hiring a guide can be shared among all of you. If you are travelling solo, your guide may be able to drive you around on a motorbike, but you should pay for the petrol and parking fees.

For trips in and around big cities like HCMC and Hanoi, you'll often find women working as guides. However, it seems relatively few women are employed as guides on long-distance trips.

# Hanoi

☎ 04 • pop 3,500,000

Welcome to a city of lakes, shaded boulevards and verdant public parks – where young jeans-clad lovers stroll beside their venerable elders as they practise elegant, slow-motion shadow boxing. While the prosperous shop owners of Hanoi exemplify Vietnam's new economic reforms, traditional trading continues along the merchant guild streets in the Old Quarter as a reminder of the city's rich cultural heritage.

Hanoi, capital of the Socialist Republic of Vietnam (SRV), is different things to different people. Most foreigners on a short visit find Hanoi to be relatively slow paced, pleasant and even charming. Physically, it's a more attractive city than Ho Chi Minh City (HCMC) – there is less traffic, noise and pollution – with more trees and open spaces. Hanoi's centre is an architectural museum piece and its blocks of ochre buildings retain the air of a provincial town in 1930s France. Some have called it the Paris of the Orient, but it's more like catching fleeting impressions of Paris with the smell of warm baguettes permeating street corners where the bread sellers congregate, the occasional view of the Opera House, and often being greeted with a 'bonjour' rather than 'good morning'.

Hanoi's past reputation for harassment of foreigners and resisting economic reform has historically caused most foreign investment to flow into HCMC and other places in the south. Resistance to reform is strongest among ageing officials, but the younger generation – with no romantic or political attachment to the past – is more interested in the side of the bread that is buttered. Attitudes have changed fast and the Hanoi of today is dramatically different from just a few years ago. Foreigners have returned in the form of tourists, business travellers, students and expatriates. Foreign investors are now looking at Hanoi with the same enthusiasm that only a few years ago was reserved exclusively for HCMC.

## Highlights

- Take a walking tour through the historical streets of the bustling Old Quarter
- Explore Hanoi's intriguing museums, pagodas and the spectacular Temple of Literature
- Enjoy a performance of the city's famed water puppets
- See 'Uncle Ho' in the flesh at Ho Chi Minh's Mausoleum
- Sample the flourishing culinary delights, cafés and nightlife of modern Hanoi
- Take a trip to the excellent Museum of Ethnology, devoted to the culture of Vietnam's ethnic minorities

Greater Hanoi p164-5
Central Hanoi p168-9
Old Quarter p178
Old Quarter Walking Tour p182
Around Hanoi p209

The first beneficiaries of the city's recent economic resurgence have been the shop and restaurant owners. Colour and liveliness has returned to the streets and unfortunately, so has the traffic – though the roads are still less frenzied than they are in Bangkok or Manila or Jakarta. Buildings are being repaired and foreign companies are now investing in everything from joint-venture hotels to telecommunications and banks. Hanoi, as well as the rest of the north, has a great potential to develop export-oriented manufacturing industries – a potential now only beginning to be realised.

The people of Hanoi are known for being more reserved – and at the same time more traditionally hospitable to visitors – than their southern compatriots. And, thankfully, for a big city Hanoi is comparatively safe. Of course travellers need to be aware of personal security, but you're unlikely to be robbed and even less likely to be physically assaulted. There's a bit of a hassle factor with street vendors but it's nothing compared with, say, Kuta in Bali.

## HISTORY

The site where Hanoi now stands has been inhabited since the Neolithic period. Emperor Ly Thai To moved his capital here in AD 1010, renaming the site Thang Long (City of the Soaring Dragon). Hanoi served as the capital of the Later Le dynasty, founded by Le Loi, from its establishment in 1428 until 1788 when it was overthrown by Nguyen Hué, the founder of the Tay Son dynasty. The decision by Emperor Gia Long, founder of the Nguyen dynasty, to rule from Hué relegated Hanoi the status of a regional capital.

Over the centuries Hanoi has been called a variety of names, including Dong Kinh (Eastern Capital), from which the Europeans derived the name they eventually applied to all of northern Vietnam – Tonkin. The city was named Hanoi (The City in a Bend of the River) by Emperor Tu Duc in 1831. From 1902 to 1953, Hanoi served as the capital of French Indochina.

Hanoi was proclaimed the capital of Vietnam after the August Revolution of 1945, but it was not until the Geneva Accords of 1954 that the Viet Minh, driven from the city by the French in 1946, were able to return.

During the American War, US bombing destroyed parts of Hanoi and killed many hundreds of civilians; almost all the damage has since been repaired. One of the prime targets was the 1682m-long Long Bien Bridge, originally built from 1888 to 1902, under the direction of the same architect who designed the Eiffel Tower in Paris. It was once named after French governor general of Indochina Paul Doumer (1857–1932). US aircraft repeatedly bombed the strategic bridge, yet after each attack the Vietnamese somehow managed to improvise replacement spans and return it to road and rail service. It is said that when US prisoners of war (POWs) were put to work repairing the bridge, the US military, fearing for their safety, ended the attacks.

In Hanoi, and much of the north, Ho Chi Minh created a very effective police state. For four decades locals suffered under a regime characterised by ruthless police power; anonymous denunciations by a huge network of secret informers; detention without trial of monks, priests, landowners and anyone seen as a potential threat to the government; and the blacklisting of dissidents and their children and their children's children. The combined legacy of economic turmoil and human-rights violations produced a steady haemorrhage of refugees to other countries, even into China, despite that country's less-than-impressive human-rights record. Ironically, the political and economic situation turned around so sharply in the 1990s that Vietnamese officials now worry about an invasion of refugees from China.

## ORIENTATION

Hanoi sprawls along the banks of the Song Hong (Red River), which is spanned by two bridges – the Long Bien Bridge (now used only by nonmotorised vehicles and pedestrians), and, 600m south, the newer Chuong Đ Bridge.

The attractive centre of Hanoi is built around Hoan Kiem Lake. Just north of this lake is the Old Quarter (known to the French as the Cité Indigène), which is characterised by narrow streets whose names change every one or two blocks. Tourists mostly like to base themselves in this part of town.

Along the western periphery of the Old Quarter is the ancient Hanoi Citadel, which was originally constructed by Emperor Gia

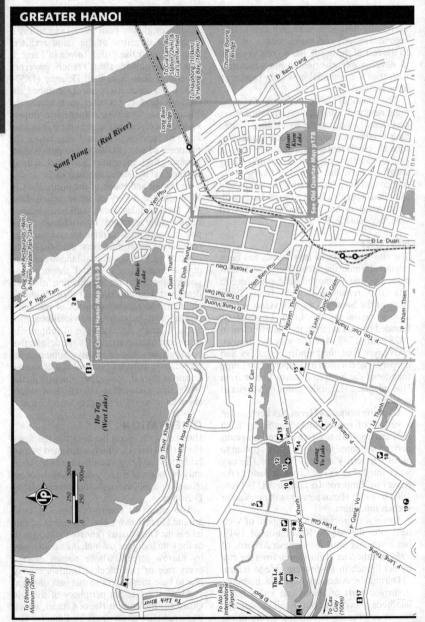

# GREATER HANOI

To Dog-Meat Restaurants (4km) & Hanoi Water Park (2km)

Song Hong (Red River)

Ho Tay (West Lake)

To Ethnology Museum (2km)

To Lich River

To Noi Bai International Airport

To Cau Giay (100m)

Thu Le Park

Chuong Duong Bridge

Đ Bach Dang

Long Bien Bridge

To Gia Lam Bus Station (2km) & Gia Lam Airfield

To Haiphong (103km) & Halong Bay (165km)

Old Quarter

Hoan Kiem Lake

See Old Quarter Map p178

See Central Hanoi Map p168-9

Đ Yen Phu

Đ Le Duan

Truc Bach Lake

P Quan Thanh

P Phan Dinh Phung

P Hoang Dieu

Đ Điện Biên Phủ

Đ Tôn Thất Đàm

Đ Hùng Vương

Nguyen Thai Hoc

Cat Linh

Quoc Tu Giam

P Ton Duc Thang

P Kham Thien

P Doi Can

Đ Thuy Khue

Đ Hoang Hoa Tham

P Giang Vo

P La Thanh

Giang Vo Lake

P Kim Ma

P Ngoc Khanh

P Lieu Giai

P Giang Vo

Đ Lang Trung

P Nghi Tam

P Buoi

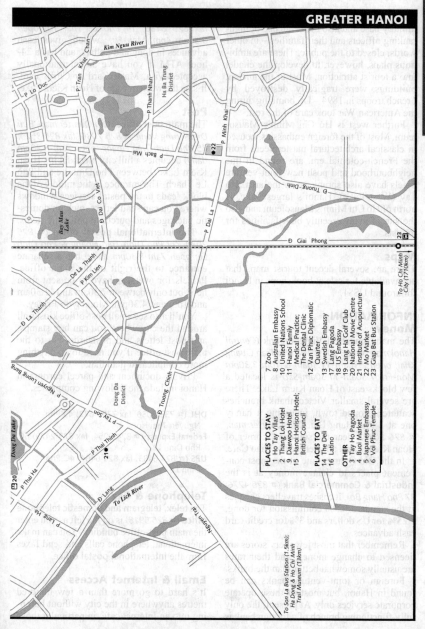

**GREATER HANOI**

PLACES TO STAY
1 Ho Tay Villas
9 Thang Loi Hotel
9 Daewoo Hotel
15 Hanoi Horison Hotel;
British Council

PLACES TO EAT
14 The Deli
16 Latino

OTHER
3 Tay Ho Pagoda
4 Buoi Market
5 Japanese Embassy
6 Voi Phuc Temple
7 Zoo
8 Australian Embassy
10 United Nations School
11 Hanoi Family
Medical Practice;
The Dental Clinic
12 Van Phuc Diplomatic
Quarter
13 Swedish Embassy
17 Lang Pagoda
18 US Embassy
19 Lang Ha Golf Club
20 National Movie Centre
21 Institute of Acupuncture
22 Mo Market
23 Giap Bat Bus Station

HANOI

Long. Unfortunately, the Citadel is now a military base and also the residence of high-ranking officers and their families – in other words, closed to the public. There are ambitious plans, however, to develop the citadel into a tourist attraction. Most of the ancient buildings were tragically destroyed by French troops in 1894 – US bombing during the American War took care of the rest.

Further west is Ho Chi Minh's Mausoleum. Most of the foreign embassies, housed in classical architectural masterpieces from the French-colonial era, are found in this neighbourhood and posh new joint-venture hotels have also sprung up in the area. Ho Tay (West Lake), Hanoi's largest lake, is north of Ho Chi Minh's Mausoleum and also the site of many recently built facilities for tourists.

### Maps

There are several decent tourist maps that are available for sale at bookshops in Hanoi for around US$1.

## INFORMATION
### Money

The main branch of **Vietcombank** (Central Hanoi map; ☎ 826 8045; 198 Pho Tran Quang Khai; open 7.30am-11.30am & 1pm-3.30pm Mon-Fri, 7.30am-11.30am Sat) is located a few blocks east of Hoan Kiem Lake. There are several smaller Vietcombank branches scattered around town, including a handy one at 2 Pho Hang Bai (Old Quarter map; ☎ 826 8031), near the southeast corner of Hoan Kiem Lake, adjacent to the Ciao Cafe.

In the Old Quarter, one of the most convenient places to change money at is the **Industrial & Commercial Bank** (☎ 825 4276; 37 Pho Hang Bo). It cashes travellers cheques at the standard 0.5% commission for dong, 1.25% for US dollars and 3% for credit-card cash advances.

Remember that most jewellery stores are licensed to change money, and their rates are usually somewhat better than the banks.

Foreign or joint-venture banks can be found in Hanoi, but most of these operate corporate services only. At present, the only fully-functioning branch of a foreign bank is

the **ANZ Bank** (Old Quarter map; ☎ 825 8190, fax 825 8188; 14 Pho Le Thai To; open 8.30am-4pm Mon-Fri), which gives cash advances in dong and dollars, and has a 24-hour ATM if you have an internationally accepted Visa, MasterCard or Cirrus card. It's on the western edge of Hoan Kiem Lake.

### Post

The **main post office** (Old Quarter map; Buu Dien Trung Vong; ☎ 825 7036, fax 825 3525; 75 Pho Dinh Tien Hoang; open 7am-8.30pm daily) occupies a full city block facing Hoan Kiem Lake, between Pho Dinh Le and Pho Le Thach. The entrance in the middle of the block leads to the postal-services windows where you can send letters, pick up domestic packages and purchase philatelic items.

The **international postal office** (☎ 825 2030; cnr Pho Dinh Tien Hoang & Pho Dinh Le; open 7am-8.30pm daily) has a separate entrance to the right of the main office. Parcels for overseas have to be sent from here, but only between 7.30am and 11.30am and 1pm and 4.30pm, Monday to Friday.

You'll also see small post-office kiosks all around the city where you can buy stamps, and post letters and postcards. Go to the main post office if you need to do anything more complicated than that.

Private document and parcel carriers in Hanoi include the following companies.

**DHL** (☎ 733 2086, fax 775 4672) 49 Pho Nguyen Thai Hoc
**Federal Express** (☎ 824 9054, fax 825 2479) 6C Pho Dinh Le
**UPS** (☎ 824 6483, fax 824 6464) 4C Pho Dinh Le

### Telephone & Fax

The **telex, telegram and domestic telephone office** (☎ 825 5918) is on the left as you enter the main post-office building. You can make international telephone calls and send faxes from the **international postal office**.

### Email & Internet Access

It's hard to go more than a few hundred metres anywhere in the city without bumping into an Internet café, in particular those at backpacker cafés and travel agents in the Old Quarter.

The going rate for online access in Hanoi is somewhere between 100d and 200d per minute. Cheap! 'Ten free minutes online' is the latest tour-operator gimmick to attract customers – it beats 'one free Chinese beer'!

## Travel Agencies

There are plenty of travel agencies in Hanoi, both government ones and those privately owned, which can book tours, provide cars and guides, issue air tickets and arrange visa extensions.

A lot of the budget agencies also double as restaurant-cafés, which offer cheap eats, rooms for rent and Internet access. The mighty alliance between HCMC's Sinh Café and state-run Hanoi Toserco captures a large share of the local 'fast-food' tourist market, in particular the dirt-cheap 'open tours', which shuttle travellers in buses along Hwy 1, between Hanoi and HCMC. The proliferation, however, of 'fake' Sinh cafés in Hanoi has confused more than a few travellers.

The majority of Hanoi's hotels also pedal tours (most of which are farmed out to the agencies listed in this chapter), however it is not advisable to book trips through hotels. Though the prices are roughly the same (the hotels collecting a sales commission from the agents), booking directly with the tour operators will give a much better idea of what you'll get for your money, who it is you'll be travelling with, and also with how many other people.

There has been a stream of complaints lately about some budget tour operators in Hanoi. The biggest issue seems to be the gap between what they promise and what they actually deliver. Competition is fierce, and cut-throat price cutting among various tour operators has driven the cost of tours so low that in some cases it has become difficult to provide a satisfactory product. Sometimes the profit margin for the tour operator is so slim the only way for them to make any money is to increase the number of customers, and in doing so, lower the quality of the tour. You can do the maths for yourself. Usually these customers have booked the same tour from a variety of outlets for different prices (usually within a few dollars of each other).

You can indeed buy a two-day/one-night, all-inclusive excursion to Halong Bay for as little as US$16, but do you really care to travel on a 45-seat bus and be herded en masse onto a boat to tour the bay and grottoes? In the long run, the dollars saved will probably not be remembered as much as the quality of the trip itself. It's your choice of course, but if you buy the cheapest thing out there, you'll have to share the blame if you don't come away satisfied.

We suggest seeking out tour operators who stick to small groups, and use their own vehicles and guides. At the time of writing, the following companies were getting good raves from travellers in terms of group size and quality for price. In the Old Quarter **Handspan Adventure Travel** (☎ 926 0444, fax 926 0445; e operator@handspan.com; w www.handspan.com; 80 Pho Ma May) receives consistently good reviews, as does **Kangaroo Café** (☎ 828 9931; e kangaroo@hn.vnn.vn; 18 Pho Bao Khanh). The newer **Fansipan Tours** (☎/fax 926 0910; 24a Pho Hang Bac) has also been recommended by travellers. Also worth a plug in the upmarket bracket is **Buffalo Tours** (☎ 828 0702, fax 826 9370; w www.buffalotours.com; 11 Pho Hang Muoi), which runs innovative ecotours throughout Vietnam.

New places open all the time, and existing places change, so the suggestions here are not exhaustive. With that caveat in mind, shop around and consider the following places. All of the following agencies are found on the Old Quarter map.

**A to Z Queen Cafe** (☎ 826 0860, fax 826 0300, e queenaz@fpt.vn) 13 Pho Hang Bac & 50 Pho Hang Be

**ET Pumpkin** (☎ 926 0739) 85 Pho Ma May

**Explorer Tours** (☎ 923 0713, fax 923 0835) 75 Pho Hang Bo

**Footprint Travel** (☎/fax 826 0879, e footprint travel@yahoo.com) 16 Pho Hang Bac

**Kim's Café** (☎ 824 9049, e kimscafe@hotmail.com) 79 Pho Hang Bac

**Lotus Guesthouse & Café** (☎ 826 8642) 42V Pho Ly Thuong Kiet

HANOI

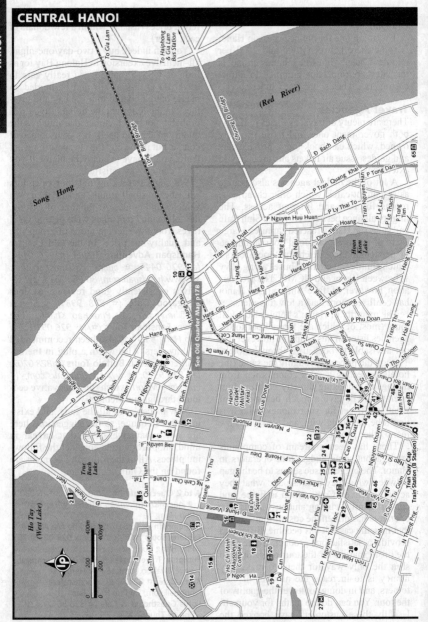

# CENTRAL HANOI

To Gia Lam

To Haiphong & Gia Lam Bus Station

(Red River)

Long Bien Bridge

Chuong D Bridge

Song Hong

Đ Bach Dang

P Tran Quang Khai

P Tong Dan

P Nguyen Huu Huan

P Ly Thai To

P Tran Nguyen Han

P Le Lai

P Le Thach

P Trang Tien

Tran Nhat Duat

P Hang Chieu

P Hang Bac

Gia Ngu

Đ Dinh Tien Hoang

Hang Dau

P Hang Buom

Hang Giay

Huan Kiem Lake

Hang Trong

Hang Dao

Hang Can

Hang Gai

Hang Trong

Hang Khay

Hang Luoc

Hang Gai

P Nha Chung

P Phu Doan

Hang Than

Phu

Hang Cot

Bat Dan

Hang Non

Đ Thanh

Hang Ca

P Ly Nam De

P Hai Ba Trung

P Tho Nhuom

P Trang Thi

P Quan Su

See Old Quarter Map p178

Hanoi Citadel (Military Area)

P Cua Dong

P Cua Bac

Đ Phung Hung

Cam Chi

P Hang Bong

P Phan Boi Chau

Nam Ngu

Pham Hong Thai

Nguyen Truong To

Yen Phu

P Đ Đuc

Đ Nguyen Bieu

P Nguyen Tri Phuong

P Hoang Dieu

Nguyen Khuyen

Đ Ly Nam De

Đ Đang Dung

Đ Chau Long

Đ Quan Thanh

P Cua Dong

Ngo Si Lien

Truc Bach Lake

P Nguyen Bieu

Hoang Van Thu

Đ Bac Son

Ba Dinh Square

Dien Bien Phu

Khuc Hao

Le Hong Phong

P Cao Ba Quat

Nguyen Thai Hoc

Đ Tran Phu

Văn Miều

P Quoc Tu Giam

Tran Quy Cap Train Station (B Station)

Thanh Nien

Ho Tay (West Lake)

Đ Thuy Khue

Ngu Xa

Le Canh Chan

Đ Đang

Tat

Hung Vuong

Ong Ich Khiem

Ho Chi Minh Mausoleum Complex

Ngoc Ha

Đ Doi Can

N Thong Phg

Tran Hoai Duc

Nguyen Thai Hoc

P Cat Linh

400m

400yd

200

200

0

0

# CENTRAL HANOI

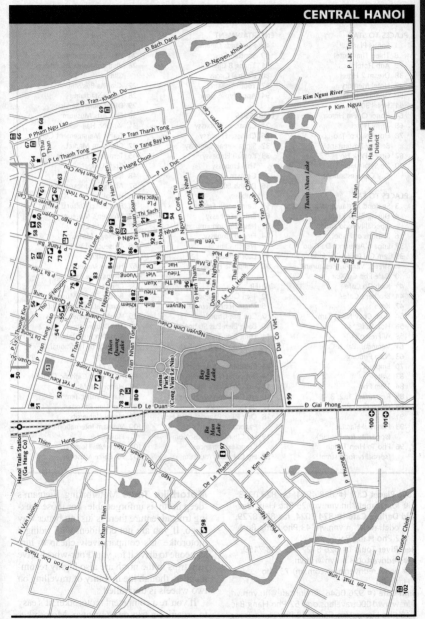

## CENTRAL HANOI

**PLACES TO STAY**
1  Sofitel Plaza
8  Thien Thai Hotel
9  Anh Hotel II
38  Dream 2 Hotel
43  Hotel Memory
50  Guoman Hotel
51  Hotel 30/4
64  Hanoi Opera Hilton
68  Army Hotel
78  Hotel Nikko; Tao-Li;
    Benkay Restaurant
82  Green Park Hotel
90  De Syloia Hotel;
    Cay Cau Restaurant

**PLACES TO EAT**
3  Seafood Restaurants
4  Đuong Thuy Khue
    (speciality food street)
6  Seasons of Hanoi
37  Luna d'Autunno; Da Gino
39  Cam Chi (speciality food
    street); Van An Restaurant
40  Café Pho Cu Xua
41  Kinh Do Cafe
44  Brother's Cafe
47  Koto
54  Com Chay Nang Tam
56  Hoa Sua
58  Al Fresco's
61  Verandah Bar & Café
63  Nam Phuong
70  Emperor
83  Soho
84  Tiem Pho
85  Restaurant 1, 2, 3
88  Quan Com Pho
91  Ky Y
93  Pho Mai Hac De
    (speciality food street)
96  Pho To Hien Thanh
    (speciality food street)

**ENTERTAINMENT**
49  Fanslands Cinema
59  Spotted Cow
71  Thang 8 Cinema
80  Central Circus
87  Youth Theatre
94  Apocalypse Now

**EMBASSIES**
21  Canadian Embassy
25  Chinese Embassy
32  Singaporean Embassy
33  Korean Embassy;
    Thai Embassy
35  German Embassy
36  Danish Embassy; Swiss
    Embassy
55  Cambodian Embassy
62  British Embassy
72  New Zealand Embassy
74  French Embassy;
    French Clinic
77  Laos Embassy
98  Philippine Embassy

**OTHER**
2  Tran Quoc Pagoda
5  Quan Thanh Temple
7  Cua Bac Church
10  Long Bien Bus Station
11  Long Bien Train Station
12  Cua Bac (Northern Gate of
    Old Citadel)
13  Presidential Palace
14  Botanical Gardens
15  Ho Chi Minh's Stilt House
16  Ho Chi Minh's Mausoleum
17  Ba Dinh Square
18  One Pillar Pagoda; Dien Huu
    Pagoda
19  Ho Chi Minh Mausoleum
    Complex Entrance
20  Ho Chi Minh Museum

22  Flag Tower
23  Army Museum
24  Lenin Monument
26  Vietnam-Korea Friendship
    Clinic
27  Kim Ma Bus Station
28  Hanoi Stadium
29  DHL Courier Service
30  Fine Arts Museum
31  Vu Doo Hair Salon
34  Traffic Management Centre
42  Cua Nam Market
45  Temple of Literature
46  Craft Link
48  Ipa-Nima
52  Alliance Française de
    Hanoi
53  Friendship Cultural Hall
57  Women's Museum
60  American Club
65  Geology Museum
66  Museum of Vietnamese
    Revolution
67  History Museum;
    Vietnamese Language
    Centre
69  Border Guard Museum
73  Immigration Police Office
75  Western Canned Foods
76  The Bookworm
79  Kim Lien Bus Station
81  Institute of Traditional
    Medicine
86  Hom Market
89  Ham Long Catholic Church
92  Hanoi Star Mart
95  Hai Ba Trung Temple
97  Kim Lien Pagoda
99  Hanoi University
100  Vietnam International
    Hospital
101  Bach Mai Hospital
102  Air Force Museum

**Love Planet Café** (☎ 828 4864, fax 828 0913, e loveplanet@hn.vnn.vn) 25 Pho Hang Bac
**Old Darling Café** (☎ 824 3024, fax 828 8729, e odctravel@hn.vnn.vn) 43 Pho Hang Bo & 142 Pho Hang Bac
**Red River Tours** (☎ 826 8427, fax 828 7159, e redrivertours.hn.vn@fpt.vn, w www.redrivertours.com.vn) 73 Pho Hang Bo
**Sinh Café** (☎ 926 0646, e sinhcafe@hn.vnn.vn, w www.1000traveltips.org) 52 Pho Hang Bac, 18 Pho Luong Van Can & 98 Pho Hang Trong

**Motorbike Tours** Motorbiking Vietnam's 'deep north' is unforgettable. For those seeking true adventure there is just no better way to go. If you are not confident with riding a motorbike, it's comparatively cheap to hire someone to drive it for you. Four-wheel-drive jeep trips in the north are also highly recommended, though the mobility of travelling on two wheels is unrivalled.

If you're a competent motorbiker, it's easy to organise a trip on your own. Motorbikes can be hired in Hanoi. For information about motorbike rental in Hanoi, see the Getting There & Away section later in this chapter.

There are a handful of companies in Hanoi running motorbike tours, with a growing contingent of freewheeling guides who can make your trip run smoothly, find secret road routes, and open doors you could never touch from the cursory scan of a map. Foreign guides charge considerably more than local Vietnamese guides, but if you're not a Vietnamese speaker, readers' reports suggest they are worth every dong. Based on a group of four people, you can expect to pay around US$50 per day per person for an all-inclusive tour providing motorbike rental, tour guide, food, drinks and accommodation.

One such outfit is **Free Wheelin Tours** (☎ 747 0545, fax 747 0557; e info@free wheelin-tours.com, w www.freewheelin-tours.com), run by Fredo (Binh in Vietnamese), a French-Vietnamese expat who speaks French, English and Vietnamese. He also has Vietnamese guides on call.

Other guides well worth tracking down are **Digby & Dan** (☎ 0913-524658; w www.motorbikingvietnam.com). These two biking connoisseurs hail from Oz and the UK, respectively. Ask for them at Highway 4, a bar on Pho Hang Tre.

## Bookshops
If you're out of reading material, Hanoi's good chance to stock up. Far and away the best selection of English-language books, primarily fiction, is found at **The Bookworm** (☎ 943 7226; e bookworm@fpt.vn; 15a Ngo Van So; open 10am-7pm Tues-Sun). There are new and second-hand books available, and if you return books previously bought there, you'll get a third off the price of the next one you buy. There are plans to make newspapers and coffee available in a reading room at the back.

In the Old Quarter, the **Thang Long Bookshop** (☎ 825 7043; 53-55 Pho Trang Tien), just a short walk from Hoan Kiem Lake, has a good selection of English and French non-fiction books on Vietnam, and carries some international newspapers and magazines.

The **Foreign Language Bookshop** (☎ 825 7376; 64 Pho Trang Tien) carries much the same, plus some German-language guide-books, a selection of English literature classics and also some good regional maps.

A couple of blocks away, the **Hanoi Bookstore** (Hieu Sach Hanoi; ☎ 824 1616; 34 Pho Trang Tien) is similar, and also stocks some beautiful coffee-table souvenir books.

Many of the budget hotels and travellers cafés in the Old Quarter have small book exchanges. There's also a large used-book shop with a wide selection of mostly English paperbacks, but some in French and other languages, on the 2nd floor of the **Love Planet Café** (☎ 828 4864; 25 Pho Hang Bac).

## Libraries
The **National Library and Archives** (☎ 825 3357; 31 Pho Trang Thi) is in the Old Quarter.

## Cultural Centres
Activities ranging from the sporting to the culinary are held at the following cultural centres in Hanoi.

**Alliance Française de Hanoi** (Central Hanoi map; ☎ 942 2970) Pho Yet Kieu (moving to Pho Trang Tien, opposite Dan Chu Hotel)
**The American Club** (Central Hanoi map; ☎ 824 1850, e amclub@fpt.vn) 19/21 Pho Hai Ba Trung
**British Council** (Greater Hanoi map; ☎ 843 6780, w www.britishcouncil.org.vietnam) 40 Pho Cat Linh (next to the Hanoi Horison Hotel)
**Goethe Institute** (Old Quarter map; ☎ 923 0035, e goethe@fpt.vn) 54-56 Hang Đ

## Medical Services
The **Hanoi Family Medical Practice** (Greater Hanoi map; ☎ 843 0748, 24-hr emergency service ☎ 0903-401919, ☎ 0913-234911, fax 846 1750; e hfmedprac.kot@fmail.vnn.vn, w www.doctorkot.com; Van Phuc Diplomatic Compound, Building A1, Suite 109-112, Pho Kim Ma) has a team of well-respected international physicians. It's pricey so make sure your medical insurance is up to date.

For tooth problems, contact **The Dental Clinic** (☎ 846 2864, ☎ 0903-401919, fax 823 0281), adjacent to the Hanoi Family Medical Practice and run by the same crew.

In central Hanoi, the **Vietnam International Hospital** (Central Hanoi map; ☎ 574 0740, 24-hr emergency service ☎ 547 1111; Đ Giai Phong) is staffed by French doctors. Just next door is the **Bach Mai Hospital** (Benh Vien Bach Mai; Central Hanoi map; ☎ 869 3731). It has an international department, where doctors speak English.

Resident foreigners can contact the **International SOS Clinic** (Old Quarter map; ☎ 934 0555, fax 934 0556; 31 Pho Hai Ba Trung) for information about a long-term medical and emergency-evacuation plan. Many international travel-insurance companies also use SOS as their medical counterpart.

The **French embassy** (Central Hanoi map; ☎ 825 2719; 49 Pho Ba Trieu) operates a 24-hour clinic for French nationals.

In the Old Quarter, **Viet Duc Hospital** (Benh Vien Viet Duc; ☎ 825 3531; 40 Pho Trang Thi; open 24hrs) does emergency surgery; the doctors here speak English, French and German.

If you don't have insurance, the **Vietnam-Korea Friendship clinic** (☎ 843 7231; 12 Chu Van An; open 9am-noon & 2pm-5pm Mon-Fri) is a nonprofit clinic, reputed to be the least expensive in Hanoi, with a high international standard; initial consultations cost US$5. It's on the corner of Đ Tran Phu.

For traditional Vietnamese medicine, see the Massage section later this chapter.

## THE OLD QUARTER

Hanoi's Old Quarter, with over a thousand years of history, remains one of Vietnam's most lively and unusual places. The city's commercial quarter evolved alongside the Red River and the smaller To Lich River, which once flowed through the city centre in an intricate network of canals and waterways teeming with boats. As the waters could rise as high as 8m during the monsoon, dikes, which can still be seen along Tran Quang Khai, were constructed to protect the city.

In the 13th century, Hanoi's 36 guilds established themselves here with each taking a different street, hence the original name 36 Streets, although there are around 50 streets in today's Old Quarter. *Hang* means 'merchandise' and is usually followed by the name of the product that was traditionally sold in that street. Thus, Pho Hang Gai translates as 'Silk Street' (see the boxed text 'Meaning of the 36 Streets', later in this chapter, for the rest); these days the street name may not indicate what's sold there.

Exploring the maze of back streets can be fascinating; some streets open up while others narrow into a warren of alleys. The area is known for its tunnel (or tube) houses – so called because of their narrow frontages and long rooms. These tunnel houses were developed to avoid taxes based on the width of their street frontage. By feudal law, houses were also limited to two storeys and, out of respect for the king, could not be taller than the Royal Palace. These days there are taller buildings (six- to eight-storeys high) but no real high-rise buildings.

Opportunities to lighten your load of dong are almost endless. As you wander around you'll find wool clothes, cosmetics, fake Ray Ban sunglasses, luxury food, printed T-shirts, musical instruments, plumbing supplies, herbal medicines, gold and silver jewellery, religious offerings, spices, woven mats and much, much more (see the Shopping section in this chapter).

Some of the more specialised streets include Pho Hang Quat, with its red candlesticks, funeral boxes, flags and temple items; and the more glamorous Pho Hang Gai, with its silk, embroidery, lacquerware, paintings and water puppets (silk sleeping-bag liners and elegant *ao dai* are very popular here). Finally, no trip to the Old Quarter would be complete without a visit to **Dong Xuan Market** (cnr Pho Hong Khoai & Pho Dong Xuan), which was rebuilt after a fire in 1994.

A stroll through the historic Old Quarter can last anywhere from a few minutes to the better part of a day, depending on your pace and how well you navigate the increasing motor traffic plaguing the streets. However long, or whatever detours you might take, the suggested route in the boxed text 'Old Quarter Walking Tour' will provide you with a good dose of Vietnamese culture, and some insight into the country's long history.

[Continued on page 177]

# TET FESTIVAL

The Tet Nguyen Dan (Festival of the First Day) announces the Lunar New Year, and is the most important date in the Vietnamese festival calendar. Commonly known as Tet, it is much more than your average Gregorian New Year's celebration; it's a time when families reunite in the hope of good fortune for the coming year and ancestral spirits are welcomed back into the family home. And Tet is everybody's birthday; on this day everyone becomes one year older.

The festival falls some time between 19 January and 20 February on the Western calendar. The exact dates vary from year to year due to differences between the lunar and solar calendars. The first three days after New Year's Day are the official holidays but many people take the whole week off, particularly in the south.

Tet rites begin seven days before New Year's Day. This is when the Tao Quan – the three Spirits of the Hearth, found in the kitchen of every home – ascend to the heavens to report on the past year's events to the Jade Emperor. Often these kitchen gods are described as a single person and may be called Ong Tao, Ong Lo or Ong Vua Bep. The Tao Quan ride fish on their journey to heaven, so on this day people all over Vietnam release live carp into rivers and lakes. Altars, laden with offerings of food, fresh water, flowers, betel and more live carp for celestial transport, are assembled in preparation for the gods' departure, all in the hope of receiving a favourable report and ensuring good luck for the family in the coming year.

## Spirits of the Hearth

One legend behind the Tao Quan is based on the story of a woodcutter and his wife. The couple lived happily together until the man was driven to drink, through the worry of being unable to provide enough food for them both. He became violent towards his wife and eventually she could no longer bear it and left him. After some time she met and married a local hunter, forgetting the terrors of her previous marriage.

A few days before the Vietnamese New Year, the woman received a beggar at the front door while the hunter was searching for game. She offered the beggar a meal and soon realised that he was her former husband. Panicked by the sound of her current husband returning, she hid the beggar under a pile of hay. The hungry hunter promptly set the hay alight and placed his recently caught game on it to roast, unaware that there was someone there. Fearing that the hunter might kill the woman if he cried out, the beggar remained silent. The poor woman was torn with grief, realising that her former husband was dying for her sake. With little hesitation, she threw herself onto the fire to die with him. The confused hunter thought that he must have driven her to such desperation, so he too jumped into the fire, unable to contemplate life without her.

All three perished, an act of devotion which so deeply touched the Jade Emperor that he made them gods. In their new role, they were to look out for the wellbeing of the Vietnamese people from the vantage point of the hearth.

**Inset:** Photograph by Mason Florence

Other rituals performed during the week before Tet include visiting cemeteries and inviting the spirits of dead relatives home for the celebrations. Absent family members start to make their way home, so that the whole family can celebrate Tet under the same roof. All loose ends are tied up so that the new year can be started with a clean slate; debts are paid and everything is cleaned, including ancestors' graves.

Much like the tradition of Christmas trees in the West, Vietnamese homes are decorated with trees at this time. A New Year's tree *(cay neu)* is constructed to ward off evil spirits. Kumquat trees are popular throughout the country, while branches of pink peach blossoms *(dao)* grace houses in the north, and yellow apricot blossoms *(mai)* can be found in southern and central Vietnamese homes.

For a spectacular sight, go to ĐL Nguyen Hue in Ho Chi Minh City (HCMC), much of which is taken over by the annual Tet flower market at this time of year. In Hanoi, the area around Pho Hang Dau and Pho Hang Ma is transformed into a massive peach-blossom and kumquat-tree market. Or be dazzled by the blocked-off streets near the Dong Xuan market, ablaze with red and gold decorations for sale. A few days before the New Year is heralded in, the excitement at these markets is almost palpable, as people rush to buy their food and decorations, and motorbikes laden with blossoms and two or three kumquat trees jam the streets.

This is an expensive time of year for most families with so much to buy (the kumquat trees alone cost around US$20). In addition, children are given red envelopes containing substantial amounts of *li xi*, or lucky money. The Vietnamese see all this expense as being necessary to gain favour with the gods for the coming year.

Like special events anywhere, a large part of the celebrations revolve around food. A Tet staple is *banh chung*. These intriguing square parcels are made of fatty pork and bean paste, sandwiched between two layers of glutinous *nep* rice. They're wrapped in green dong, a leaf resembling that of a banana tree, and tied with bamboo twine, giving them the appearance of a present. You'll see mountains of them everywhere and will no doubt be invited to taste one. A similar food which is round in shape, *banh day*, is served in the south.

Banh chung is often accompanied by *mang*, a dish made with boiled bamboo shoots and fried pork marinated in fish sauce *(nuoc mam)*. Many visitors don't appreciate these dishes but they have a symbolic significance for Vietnamese people: their simple ingredients are reminders of past hard times. Popular sweets include *mut*, which is candied fruit (such as sugared apples, plums and even tomatoes). Fresh fruit is another essential element of Tet: red dragon fruit and watermelons are big favourites.

On New Year's Eve, the Tao Quan return to earth. At the stroke of midnight, all problems from the previous year are left behind and jubilant celebrations ensue. The goal seems to be to make as much noise as possible: drums and percussion are popular, and so were firecrackers, until they were banned in 1995 (although you might still hear

## Banh Chung

The fable behind *banh chung* cakes originated with King Hung Vuong the Sixth, who fathered 22 sons, all worthy heirs. In order to select his successor, the king instructed them to search the globe for delicacies unknown to him. Whoever returned with the best dish would rule the kingdom. Twenty-one of them did as they were told, but one young prince, Lang Lieu, remained in the palace with no idea of where to start looking. He was filled with gloom until one night a genie appeared in his dreams. 'Man cannot live without rice', she said, and told him the recipe for *banh chung*. When the time came for the king to taste the 22 dishes, he was bitterly disappointed with the 21 from the princes who had travelled abroad. Finally he tasted the rice creations of Lang Lieu and was amazed at how delicious they were. When told of the genie's assistance with the recipe, the king was impressed with this divine support and named Lang Lieu his successor.

recordings of exploding firecrackers blaring from cassette players). Any noise will do really, as long as it provides a suitable welcome back for the gods, while scaring off any evil spirits that may be loitering.

The events of New Year's Day are very important as it's believed they affect the course of life in the year ahead. People take extra care not to be rude or show anger. Other activities to avoid include sewing, sweeping, swearing and breaking things, which may attract bad spirits.

Similarly, it's crucial that the first visitor of the year to each household is suitable. They're usually male – best of all is a wealthy married man with several children. Foreigners are sometimes welcomed as the first to enter the house, although not always, so it's wise not to visit any Vietnamese house on the first day of Tet, unless you are explicitly invited (and make sure you confirm the time they want you to arrive). Those blacklisted as first visitors include single middle-aged women, and anyone who has lost their job, had an accident or lost a family member during the previous year – all signs of bad luck. Such unfortunates and their families can be ostracised from their community and sometimes stay home during the whole Tet period.

Unique to the south is the Unicorn Dance – a procession led by people carrying brightly coloured square flags followed by the unicorn itself (several men dressed up in tight uniforms) and then another mythical creature called Ong Dia (a man with a moonlike face mask). At the tail end come the drums and cymbals. The procession begins early on the first morning of Tet, and systematically visits every home and shop in its area, looking for donations. The Vietnamese are generous in their gifts, as the unicorn is regarded as a symbol of wealth, peace and prosperity. However, they make the unicorn work for its rewards: homeowners or shopkeepers often present their donations tied to a pole, suspended from the first-floor balcony or window. To reach the gifts, the unicorn is elevated through a human pyramid until it can swallow the prize in its mouth.

In Hanoi, a popular activity during the weeks that follow Tet is *co nghoi*, or human chess. All the human chess pieces come from the same village, Lien Xa, in the northern province of Ha Tay. They're chosen because they're attractive, young, unmarried and have had no recent deaths in their families or other signs of bad luck. The form of chess played is Chinese. Although the pieces and moves are different from Western chess, the objective remains the same: to capture the opposing leader, in this case the 'general'.

Apart from New Year's Eve itself, Tet is not a particularly boisterous celebration. It's like Christmas Day: a quiet family affair. Difficulty in booking transport and accommodation aside, this is an excellent time to visit the country, especially to witness the contrasting frenzied activity before the New Year and the calm (and quiet streets!) afterwards. Wherever you're staying, it's more than likely you'll be invited to join in the celebrations.

New Year's Day will fall on the following dates: 1 February 2003, 22 January 2004 and 9 February 2005.

If you are visiting Vietnam during Tet, be sure you learn this phrase: *chúc mùng nam mói* – Happy New Year!

Locals celebrate the annual Tet Festival with woven masks, lucky money (placed on trees as an offering to appease ancestors), and kumquat trees, which are decorated in Vietnamese homes

Blue-and-white ceramics for sale in Hoi An

Motorbike – the coolest way to get around town

Water puppets in Hanoi

Chaos rules the streets of Vietnam's major cities

[Continued from page 172]

# LAKES, TEMPLES & PAGODAS

## Hoan Kiem Lake

Hoan Kiem Lake is an enchanting body of water right in the heart of Hanoi. Legend has it that, in the mid-15th century, Heaven gave Emperor Ly Thai To (Le Loi) a magical sword, which he used to drive the Chinese out of Vietnam. One day after the war, while out boating, he came upon a giant golden tortoise swimming on the surface of the water; the creature grabbed the sword and disappeared into the depths of the lake. Since that time, the lake has been known as Ho Hoan Kiem (Lake of the Restored Sword) because the tortoise restored the sword to its divine owners.

The forlorn Thap Rua (Tortoise Tower), topped with a red star, on an islet in the middle of the lake, is often used as an emblem of Hanoi. Every morning around 6am, local residents can be seen doing their traditional morning exercises, jogging and playing badminton around this lake.

## Ngoc Son Temple

Founded in the 18th century, Ngoc Son Temple *(Old Quarter map; Jade Mountain Temple; admission 2000d; open 8am-5pm daily)* is on an island in the northern part of Hoan Kiem Lake. Surrounded by water and shaded by trees, it is a delightfully quiet place to rest. The temple is dedicated to the scholar Van Xuong, General Tran Hung Dao, who defeated the Mongols in the 13th century, and La To, who was deemed the patron saint of physicians.

Ngoc Son Temple is reached via the red-painted, wooden The Huc (Rising Sun) Bridge, which was constructed in 1885. To the left of the gate stands an obelisk, whose top is shaped like a paintbrush.

## Temple of Literature

The Temple of Literature *(Central Hanoi map; Van Mieu; Pho Quoc Tu Giam; admission 20,000d; open 8am-5pm daily)* is a pleasant retreat from the streets of Hanoi, around 2km west of Hoan Kiem Lake. This temple is a rare example of well-preserved

---

## The Tortoises of Hoan Kiem Lake: Fact or Fiction?

Astonishingly there *are* tortoises in the somewhat less than clear waters of Hoan Kiem Lake.

Surfacing on rare occasions, and bringing luck to anyone fortunate enough to see one, the Sword Lake Tortoise *Rafetus leloii* is not just your common garden-variety tortoise – it is a huge animal. A specimen that died in 1968 weighed in at 250kg and was 2.10m long! Its preserved remains are on show in the Ngoc Son Temple complex, together with a photo taken of a tortoise that appeared in the lake in 2000. No-one is sure how many there still are, or how they have survived in this urban setting.

Rumours abound. Are these really the lake-dwelling descendants of the golden tortoise of Le Loi? Or are they safeguarded in enclosures elsewhere and transported to the lake from time to time, where their occasional appearance is simply an orchestrated ploy to keep the legend of the lake alive?

Those ripples on the lake surface will never seem so innocent again.

---

traditional Vietnamese architecture and is well worth a visit.

It was founded in 1070 by Emperor Ly Thanh Tong, who dedicated it to Confucius (Khong Tu) in order to honour scholars and men of literary accomplishment. Vietnam's first university was established here in 1076 to educate the sons of mandarins. In 1484 Emperor Le Thanh Tong ordered that stelae be erected, on the temple premises, recording the names, places of birth and achievements of men who received doctorates in each triennial examination from 1442. Though 116 examinations were held between 1442 and 1778, when the practice was discontinued, only 82 stelae are extant. In 1802 Emperor Gia Long transferred the National University to his new capital, Hué. Major renovations were carried out here in 1920 and 1956.

The Temple of Literature is made up of five separate courtyards. The central pathways and gates between them were reserved

HANOI

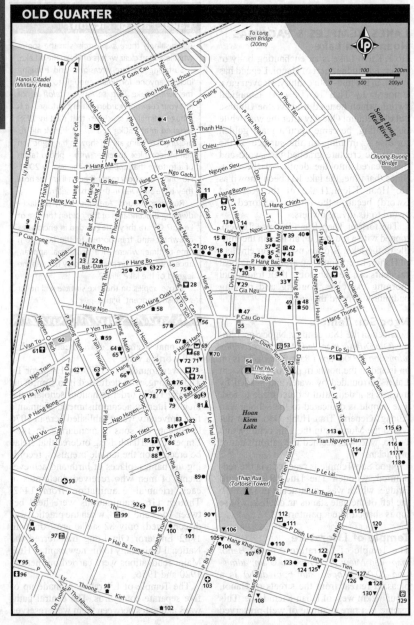

OLD QUARTER

To Long
Bien Bridge
(200m)

Hanoi Citadel
(Military Area)

Song Hong
(Red River)

Chuong Duong
Bridge

Hoan Kiem
Lake

The Huc
Bridge

Thap Rua
(Tortoise Tower)

## OLD QUARTER

**PLACES TO STAY**
1 Chains First Eden Hotel
2 Galaxy Hotel
9 Viet Anh Hotel
15 Prince Hotel (1)
16 Thuy Nga Guesthouse;
Prince Cafe
17 Van Minh Hotel
21 Old Darling Café
22 Quoc Hoa Hotel
23 Stars Hotel
32 A to Z Queen Cafe 1
38 Camellia Hotel
47 Mai Son Guesthouse
48 Classic Street Hotel
49 A to Z Queen Café 2
50 Anh Sinh Hotel
57 Trang An Hotel
58 Real Darling Cafe
59 Thu Giang Guesthouse;
Manh Dung Guesthouse
64 Hong Ngoc Hotel 1
67 Win Hotel
76 Tu Do (Freedom) Hotel
79 Ho Guom Hotel
88 Spring Hotel;
Hotel Tien Trang;
Nam Phuong Hotel (1)
94 Hanoi Towers; Somerset
Grand Hanoi; Jacc's;
Citimart; Cathay Pacific
Airline
98 Melia Hotel;
Thai Airways
102 Lotus Guesthouse
& Café
116 New Tong Dan Hotel
119 Sofital Metropole;
Le Beaulieu Restaurant;
Met Pub; Malaysia
Airlines
124 Trang Tien Hotel
128 Dan Chu Hotel

**PLACES TO EAT**
6 Thang Long
7 Baan Thai Restaurant
8 Cha Ca La Vong
14 Little Hanoi (1)
24 Cha Ca 66
29 Restaurant-Café
Linh Phung
30 The Whole Earth
Restaurant
33 Tandoor
34 Love Planet
39 69 Bar-Restaurant
43 Ily Café

45 Trung Nguyen
56 Little Hanoi (2)
62 Cyclo Bar & Restaurant
65 Hanoi Garden
66 Pho Bo Dac Biet
70 Thuy Ta Cafe
71 Mama Rosa
72 Café des Arts
77 Puku
78 Pepperonis Pizza & Cafe
82 Café Le Malraux
84 La Brique
86 Mediterraneo Restaurant;
La Salsa
87 No Noodles
90 Fanny Ice Cream
95 San Ho Restaurant
101 Saigon Sakura
105 Restaurant Bobby Chinn
106 Dak Linh Cafe
108 Al Fresco's
114 Revival
117 Le Restaurant D'Arthur
120 Diva; Au Lac;
The Deli & The Restaurant
(Press Club); Club Opera
125 Kem Trang Tien Ice Cream
130 Paris Deli

**ENTERTAINMENT**
12 Bar Le Maquis
28 Jazz Club Quyen
Van Minh
46 Highway 4
51 R&R Tavern
53 Municipal Water Puppet
Theatre
68 Funky Monkey
73 Polite Pub
74 GC
91 New Century Nightclub
129 Opera House

**OTHER**
3 Mosque
4 Dong Xuan Market
5 Cua O Quan Chuong
(Old East Gate)
10 Goethe Institute
11 Bac Ma Temple
13 Furniture Gallery
18 Vietnamese House
19 Footprint Travel
20 Hanoi Gallery
25 Red River Tours
26 Explorer Tours
27 Industrial &
Commercial Bank

31 Kim's Café;
Prince 79 Hotel
35 Fansipan Tours
36 Sinh Café
37 Handspan Adventure
Travel; Tamarind Café &
Fruit Juice Bar
40 Handspan Adventure
Travel HQ & Bookings
41 Buffalo Tours
42 Memorial House
44 ET Pumpkin
52 Martyrs' Monument;
Shoe Market
54 Ngoc Son Temple
55 Trung Tam Thuong Mai
Supermarket
60 Hang Da Market
61 Protestant Church
63 Khai Silk
69 Post Office
75 Kangaroo Café;
Nam Phuong Hotel (2)
80 ANZ Bank
81 Le Thai To Statue
83 La Boutique and the Silk
85 St Joseph Cathedral
89 Intimex
92 Credit Lyonnais
93 Viet Duc Hospital
96 Ambassadors' Pagoda
97 Hoa Lo Prison
Museum
99 National Library and
Archives
100 Vietnam Airlines &
Airport Minibus
103 International SOS Clinic
104 Air France
107 Vietcombank
109 Thang Long Bookshop
110 Foreign Language
Bookshop
111 Fed Ex & UPS Courier
Services
112 Main Post Office
113 Hanoi Star Mart
115 Vietcombank
118 Fivimart
121 Hanoi Bookstore;
Singapore Airlines
122 A Gallery; Gallery
Huong Xuyen; Hanoi
Contemporary Art
Gallery
123 Nam Song Gallery
126 Van Gallery
127 Hanoi Studio

HANOI

for the king. The walkways on one side were solely for the use of administrative mandarins, while those on the other side were for military mandarins.

The main entrance is preceded by a gate, on which an inscription requests that visitors dismount their horses before entering. Khué Van Pavilion, at the far side of the second courtyard, was constructed in 1802 and is a fine example of Vietnamese architecture. The 82 stelae, considered the most precious artefacts in the temple, are arrayed to either side of the third enclosure; each one sits on a stone tortoise.

## Ho Tay (West Lake)

Two legends explain the origins of Ho Tay, also known as the Lake of Mist and the Big Lake. According to one legend, Ho Tay was created when the Dragon King drowned an evil nine-tailed fox in his lair, which was in a forest on this site. Another legend relates that in the 11th century, a Vietnamese Buddhist monk, Khong Lo, rendered a great service to the emperor of China, who rewarded him with a vast quantity of bronze from which he cast a huge bell. The sound of the bell could be heard all the way to China, where the Golden Buffalo Calf, mistaking the ringing

## Meaning of the 36 Streets

| street name | description | street name | description |
| --- | --- | --- | --- |
| Bat Dan | Wooden Bowls | Hang Giay | Paper |
| Bat Su | China Bowls | Hang Giay | Shoes |
| Cha Ca | Roasted Fish | Hang Hanh | Onions |
| Chan Cam | String Instruments | Hang Hom | Cases |
| Cho Gao | Rice Market | Hang Huong | Incense |
| Gia Ngu | Fishermen | Hang Khay | Trays |
| Hai Tuong | Sandals | Hang Khoai | Sweet Potato |
| Hang Bac | Silversmiths | Hang Luoc | Comb |
| Hang Be | Rafts | Hang Ma | Votive Papers |
| Hang Bo | Basket | Hang Mam | Pickled Fish |
| Hang Bong | Cotton | Hang Manh | Bamboo Screens |
| Hang Buom | Sails | Hang Muoi | Salt |
| Hang But | Brushes | Hang Ngang | Transversal Street |
| Hang Ca | Fish | Hang Non | Hats |
| Hang Can | Scales | Hang Phen | Alum |
| Hang Chai | Bottles | Hang Quat | Fans |
| Hang Chi | Threads | Hang Ruoi | Clam Worms |
| Hang Chieu | Mats | Hang Than | Charcoal |
| Hang Chinh | Jars | Hang Thiec | Tin |
| Hang Cot | Bamboo Lattices | Hang Thung | Barrel |
| Hang Da | Leather | Hang Tre | Bamboo |
| Hang Dao | (Silk) Dyer | Hang Trong | Drum |
| Hang Dau | Beans | Hang Vai | Cloth |
| Hang Dau | Oils | Lo Ren | Blacksmiths |
| Hang Dieu | Pipes | Lo Su | Coffins |
| Hang Dong | Copper | Ma May | Rattan |
| Hang Duong | Sugar | Ngo Gach | Bricks |
| Hang Ga | Chicken | Thuoc Bac | Herbal Medicine |
| Hang Gai | Hemp | | |

for its mother's call, ran southward, trampling on the site of Ho Tay and turning it into a lake.

In scientific terms, the lake was created when the Song Hong (Red River) overflowed its banks. Indeed, Song Hong has changed its course numerous times, alternately flooding some lands and creating new ones through silt build up. The flood problem has been partially controlled by building dikes. The highway along the eastern side of Ho Tay is built upon one.

The lake was once ringed by magnificent palaces and pavilions that were destroyed throughout the course of various feudal wars. The circumference of West Lake is around 13km.

On the southern side of the lake is a popular strip of **outdoor seafood restaurants** (see Places to Eat later in this chapter), while the northern side has been earmarked for a development of luxurious villas and hotels.

### Tran Quoc Pagoda (Chua Tran Quoc)

One of the oldest pagodas in Vietnam, Tran Quoc Pagoda is on the eastern shore of Ho Tay, just off Đ Thanh Nien, which divides Ho Tay from Truc Bach Lake. A stele here, dating from 1639, tells the history of this site, during which the pagoda was rebuilt in the 15th century, and again in 1842. There are a number of monks' funerary monuments in the garden.

### Tay Ho Pagoda

The most popular spot for worship in Hanoi is at Tay Ho Pagoda (Greater Hanoi map; Chua Tay Ho; Pho Tay Ho; open 6am-7pm daily). Throngs of people come here on the first and 15th day of each lunar month with the hope of decreasing risk and receiving good fortune. The walk in is along a lively and colourful lane of stalls selling temple offerings and food, and a line of good fresh seafood restaurants fronts the lake. It's a great place to watch the world go by.

### Truc Bach Lake

Truc Bach Lake (Ho Truc Bach) is separated from Ho Tay by Đ Thanh Nien, which is lined with flame trees. During the 18th century, the Trinh lords built a palace on this site; it was later transformed into a reformatory for deviant royal concubines, who were condemned to spend their days weaving a very fine white silk.

### Quan Thanh Temple (Den Quan Thanh)

Quan Thanh Temple (Central Hanoi map) is on the shore of Truc Bach Lake, near the intersection of Đ Thanh Nein and Pho Quan Thanh.

The temple, shaded by huge trees, was established during the Ly dynasty (1010–1225) and was dedicated to Tran Vo (God of the North), whose symbols of power were the tortoise and the snake. A bronze statue and bell here date from 1677.

### Ambassadors' Pagoda (Chua Quan Su)

This pagoda (Old Quarter map; ☎ 825 2427; 73 Pho Quan Su; open 7.30am-11.30am & 1.30pm-5.30pm daily) is the official centre of Buddhism in Hanoi, attracting quite a crowd – mostly old women – on holidays. During the 17th century, there was a guesthouse here for the ambassadors of Buddhist countries. Today, there are about a dozen monks and nuns based at the Ambassadors' Pagoda. Next to the pagoda is a store selling Buddhist ritual objects.

The Ambassadors' Pagoda is located between Pho Ly Thuong Kiet and Pho Tran Hung Dao.

### Hai Ba Trung Temple (Den Hai Ba Trung)

This temple (Central Hanoi map; Pho Tho Lao), founded in 1142, is 2km south of Hoan Kiem Lake. A statue located here shows the two Trung sisters (1st century AD) kneeling with their arms raised in the air, as if they are addressing a crowd. Some people say the statue shows the sisters, who had been proclaimed the queens of the Vietnamese, about to dive into a river. They are said to have drowned themselves rather than surrender, following their defeat at the hands of the Chinese.

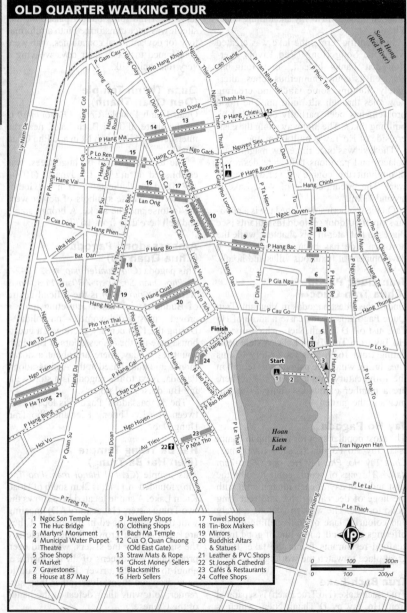

# OLD QUARTER WALKING TOUR

| | | |
|---|---|---|
| 1 Ngoc Son Temple | 9 Jewellery Shops | 17 Towel Shops |
| 2 The Huc Bridge | 10 Clothing Shops | 18 Tin-Box Makers |
| 3 Martyrs' Monument | 11 Bach Ma Temple | 19 Mirrors |
| 4 Municipal Water Puppet | 12 Cua O Quan Chuong | 20 Buddhist Altars |
| Theatre | (Old East Gate) | & Statues |
| 5 Shoe Shops | 13 Straw Mats & Rope | 21 Leather & PVC Shops |
| 6 Market | 14 'Ghost Money' Sellers | 22 St Joseph Cathedral |
| 7 Gravestones | 15 Blacksmiths | 23 Cafés & Restaurants |
| 8 House at 87 May | 16 Herb Sellers | 24 Coffee Shops |

## Old Quarter Walking Tour

Start at the **Ngoc Son Temple** (1) in the northern end of **Hoan Kiem Lake** (2) – see the Lakes, Temples & Pagodas section in this chapter. After crossing back over the bright-red **Huc Bridge** (3), stop for a quick look at the **Martyrs' Monument**, erected to those who died fighting for Vietnam's independence. Head north on Pho Hang Dau, after walking past the **Water Puppet Theatre** (4) (see the boxed text 'Punch & Judy in a Pool' in this chapter), on So Lau, and you'll soon be surrounded by **shoe shops** (5) selling every shape, size and style, demonstrating how serious Hanoians are about their footwear. Crossing over Pho Cau Go to Pho Hang Be, pop into the colourful **market** (6), which occupies the narrow eastern terminus of Pho Gia Ngu.

Back on Pho Hang Be, continue north to the 'T' intersection with Pho Hang Bac. Near here are several shops, where artisans carve intricate **gravestones** (7) (most bearing an image of the deceased) by hand. A short detour north on Pho Ma May will lead you to the **Memorial House** (8) at number 87, an exquisite Chinese merchant's home that was recently restored and opened as a museum (see Museums later in this chapter).

Return to Pho Hang Bac and head west past a strip of snazzy **jewellery shops** (9), then right onto Pho Hang Ngang past a row of **clothing shops** (10), and right again onto Pho Hang Buom; this will take you past the small **Bach Ma Temple** (11). As you pass the pagoda, with its red funeral palanquin, look for its white-bearded guards, who spend their days sipping tea. Legend has it that Ly King used the pagoda to pray for assistance in building the city walls because they persistently collapsed, no matter how many times he rebuilt them. His prayers were finally answered when a white horse appeared out of the temple and guided him to the site where he could safely build his walls. Evidence of his success is still visible at **Cua O Quan Chuong** (12), the quarter's well-preserved Old East Gate at the eastern end of Pho Hang Chieu, near the intersection with Pho Tran Nhat Duat.

Head west, back along Pho Hang Chieu past a handful of shops selling **straw mats and rope** (13) to reach one of the most interesting streets, Pho Hang Ma (Counterfeit Street), where imitation **'ghost money'** (14) is sold for burning in Buddhist ceremonies – it even has US$5000 bills! Loop around and follow your ears to the sounds of skilful **blacksmiths** (15) pounding away on metal on the corner of Pho Lo Ren and Pho Thuoc Bac. Moving south on Pho Hang Duong, head right past the **towel shops** (16) onto Pho Lan Ong, a fantastic row of **herb sellers** (17) filling the street with succulent aromas.

Finally, head south past the **tin-box makers** (18), opposite the **mirror shops** (19) on Pho Hang Thiec, then left toward the interesting shops selling **Buddhist altars and statues** (20) along Pho Hang Quat. Time permitting, loop around and zigzag west over to check out the **leather and PVC shops** (21) along Pho Ha Trung, then head east again to the superb, neo-Gothic **St Joseph Cathedral** (22) (see the Lakes, Temples & Pagodas section in this chapter). If you're feeling a bit knackered from the walk, a few steps from the church, along Pho Nha Tho, there is an alluring cluster of stylish **restaurants and cafés** (23). If you're looking for something a bit more local in flavour, turn left, then right at the end of Pho Nha Tho and swing left again onto Pho Hang Trong, right onto Pho Bao Khanh and Pho Hang Hanh. This street is chock-a-block with **Vietnamese coffee shops** (24) and is a good place to stop, rest your weary legs, and watch the world go by.

## Thu Le Park & Zoo (Bach Thu Le)

Thu Le Park and Zoo *(Greater Hanoi map; admission 2000d; open 4am-10pm daily)*, with its vast expanses of shaded grass and ponds, is located about 4km west of Hoan Kiem Lake.

## St Joseph Cathedral

Stepping inside the Old Quarter's neo-Gothic St Joseph Cathedral *(Pho Nha Tho; main gate open 5am-7am & 5pm-7pm daily)* is like being instantly transported to medieval Europe. The cathedral, inaugurated in 1886, is noteworthy for its square towers, elaborate altar and stained-glass windows. The first Catholic mission in Hanoi was founded in 1679. The cathedral stands facing the western end of Pho Nha Tho, which has developed into a fashionable strip of restaurants, cafés and boutiques.

The main gate to St Joseph Cathedral is open when Mass is held. Guests are welcome at other times of the day, but must enter the cathedral via the compound of the Diocese of Hanoi, the entrance to which is a block away at 40 Pho Nha Chung. After walking through the main gate, go straight and then turn right. When you reach the side door to the cathedral, ring the small bell high up to the right-hand side of the door so the priest can let you in.

## HO CHI MINH MAUSOLEUM COMPLEX

To the west of the Old Quarter is the Ho Chi Minh mausoleum complex *(Central Hanoi map)*, a traffic-free area of parks, monuments, memorials and pagodas. This important place of pilgrimage for many Vietnamese combines the secular and the spiritual, and it's usually crowded with groups of all ages, who have come to pay their respects.

The entrance to the mausoleum complex is on the corner of Pho Ngoc Ha and Pho Doi Can. Photography is permitted outside the building but not inside, and visitors must leave their bags at a counter just inside the entrance. There's no charge for this service. The soundtrack for a 20-minute video about Ho Chi Minh is available in Vietnamese, French, English, Khmer, Lao, Russian and Spanish.

### Ho Chi Minh's Mausoleum

In the tradition of Lenin and Stalin before him, and Mao after, the final resting place of Ho Chi Minh *(admission free; open 8am-11am Tues-Thur, Sat & Sun, Dec-Sept)* is a glass sarcophagus set deep in the bowels of a monumental edifice that has become a site of pilgrimage. Ho Chi Minh's Mausoleum – built despite the fact that his will requested cremation – was constructed, between 1973 and 1975, of native materials gathered from all over Vietnam. The roof and peristyle are said to evoke either a traditional communal house or a lotus flower, though to many tourists it looks like a concrete cubicle with columns. It's closed for about three months each year while Ho Chi Minh's embalmed corpse goes to Russia for maintenance.

The queue, moving quite quickly, usually snakes for several hundred metres to the mausoleum entrance itself. Inside, more guards, regaled in snowy-white military uniforms, are posted at intervals of five paces, giving an eerily authoritarian aspect to the macabre spectacle of the embalmed body with its wispy white hair. The whole place has a 'sanitised for your protection' atmosphere.

The following rules are strictly applied to all visitors to the mausoleum:

- People wearing shorts, tank tops etc will not be admitted
- Nothing (including day packs and cameras) may be taken into the mausoleum
- A respectful demeanour must be maintained at all times
- For obvious reasons of decorum, photography is absolutely prohibited inside the mausoleum
- It is forbidden to put your hands in your pockets
- Hats must be taken off inside the mausoleum building

Most of the visitors are Vietnamese, and it's interesting to watch their reactions. Most show deep respect and admiration for Ho Chi Minh, who is honoured for his role as the liberator of the Vietnamese people from colonialism, as much as for his communist ideology. This view is reinforced by Vietnam's educational system, which emphasises Ho's deeds and accomplishments.

If you're lucky, you'll catch the changing of the guard outside Ho's mausoleum – the pomp and ceremony displayed here rivals the British equivalent at Buckingham Palace.

### Ho Chi Minh's Stilt House & the Presidential Palace

Behind Ho Chi Minh's Mausoleum is a stilt house, Nha San Bac Ho, where Ho lived on and off from 1958 to 1969. The house is built in the style of Vietnam's ethnic minorities, and has been preserved just as Ho left it. It's set in a well-tended garden next to a carp-filled pond. Just how much time he would have actually spent here is questionable – the house would have been a tempting target for US bombers had it been suspected that Ho could be found here.

Near the stilt house is the Presidential Palace *(admission 5000d; open 8am-11am & 2pm-4pm)*, a beautifully restored colonial building constructed in 1906 as the Palace of the Governor General of Indochina. It is now used for official receptions and isn't open to the public. There is a combined entrance gate to the stilt house and Presidential Palace grounds on Pho Ong Ich Kiem, inside the mausoleum complex; when the main mausoleum entrance is closed, enter from Ð Hung Vuong near the palace building.

## Ho Chi Minh Museum

The Ho Chi Minh Museum *(Bao Tang Ho Chi Minh; admission 5000d; open 8am-11am & 1.30pm-4.30pm Tues-Thur, Sat & Sun)* is divided into two sections: Past and Future. You start in the past and move to the future by walking in a clockwise direction downwards through the museum, starting from the right-hand side of the top of the stairs. The modern displays all have messages, eg, 'peace', 'happiness' and 'freedom'.

It's probably worth taking an English-speaking guide, since some of the symbolism is hard to figure out. The 1958 Ford Edsel bursting through the wall (a US commercial failure to symbolise their military failure) is a knockout.

The museum is the huge cement structure next to Ho Chi Minh's Mausoleum. Photography is forbidden and upon entry, you must leave bags and cameras at reception.

## One Pillar Pagoda

Hanoi's famous One Pillar Pagoda *(Chua Mot Cot; Pho Ong Ich Kiem)* was built by the Emperor Ly Thai Tong, who ruled from 1028 to 1054. According to the annals, the heirless emperor dreamed that he had met Quan The Am Bo Tat, the Goddess of Mercy, who, while seated on a lotus flower, handed him a male child. Ly Thai Tong then married a young peasant girl he met by chance and had a son and heir by her. As a way of express his gratitude for this event, he constructed this pagoda in 1049.

The One Pillar Pagoda, built of wood on a single stone pillar, 1.25m in diameter, is designed to resemble a lotus blossom, symbol of purity, rising out of a sea of sorrow. One of the last acts of the French, before quitting Hanoi in 1954, was to destroy the One Pillar Pagoda; the structure was rebuilt by the new government. The pagoda is between the mausoleum and the museum.

## Dien Huu Pagoda

The entrance to Dien Huu Pagoda is a few metres from the staircase of the One Pillar Pagoda. This small pagoda, which surrounds a garden courtyard, is one of the most delightful in Hanoi. The old wood and ceramic statues on the altar are distinctively northern. An elderly monk can sometimes be found performing acupuncture on the front porch.

## MUSEUMS

In addition to the usual two-hour lunch break, it's worth noting that many of Hanoi's museums are closed on Monday.

## Vietnam Museum of Ethnology

The wonderful Vietnam Museum of Ethnology *(Around Hanoi map; ☎ 756 2193; Ð Nguyen Van Huyen; admission 10,000d; open 8.30am-5.30pm Tues-Sun)* was designed with the help of the Musée de l'Homme in Paris. It features a fascinating collection of art and everyday objects gathered from throughout Vietnam and its diverse tribal people.

It has excellent maps and the displays are well labelled in Vietnamese, French and English. Interesting dioramas portray a typical village market, the making of conical hats and a Tay shamanic ceremony, while videos show the real life contexts. There are fabulous displays of weaving and fabric motifs. Visitors can also enter a traditional Black Thai house reconstructed within the museum, and there are outdoor exhibits in the landscaped grounds. There is also a centre for research and conservation where the staff collaborate regularly with international ethnographers and scholars. A craft shop here – affiliated with Craft Link, which is a fair trade organisation – sells books, beautiful postcards, and arts and crafts from ethnic communities.

The museum is a little outside Hanoi, but it shouldn't be missed.

**Getting There & Away** The museum is in the Cau Giay district, about 7km from the city centre. A good way to get there is by rented bicycle (30 minutes). If you're short of time or energy, a motorbike taxi should cost around 20,000d or 50,000d round-trip, including waiting time. An air-con meter taxi costs around 40,000d each way.

## Memorial House

This delightful house *(87 Pho Ma May; admission 5000d; open 9am-11.30am & 2pm-5pm daily)*, north of Hoan Kiem Lake in the Old Quarter, is definitely worth visiting. This thoughtfully restored traditional Chinese-style dwelling is sparsely but beautifully decorated, and gives an excellent idea of how local merchants used to live in the Old Quarter. The restoration of the house was carried out in 1999 in cooperation with the city of Toulouse, France. While there are many such houses open to the public in Hoi An, there is little, if anything, else like it in Hanoi.

## History Museum

Once the museum of the École Française d'Extrême Orient, the History Museum *(Bao Tang Lich Su; Central Hanoi map; 1 Pho Pham Ngu Lao; admission 15,000d; open 8am-11.30am & 1.30pm-4.30pm Tues-Sun)* is an elegant, ochre-coloured structure and was built between 1925 and 1932. French architect Ernest Hebrard was among the first in Vietnam to incorporate a blend of Chinese and French design elements in his creations, and this particular building remains one of Hanoi's most stunning architectural showpieces.

Exhibited here are some artefacts from the country's turbulent past, including: prehistory (Palaeolithic and Neolithic periods); proto-Vietnamese civilisations (1st and 2nd

millennia BC); the Dong Son culture (3rd century BC to 3rd century AD); the Oc-Eo (Funan) culture of the Mekong Delta (1st to 6th century AD); the Kingdom of Champa (2nd to 15th century); the Khmer kingdoms; various Vietnamese dynasties and their resistance to Chinese attempts at domination; the struggle against the French; and the history of the Communist Party.

## Museum of Vietnamese Revolution

This museum *(Bao Tang Cach Mang; Central Hanoi map; 25 Pho Tong Dan; admission 10,000d; open 8am-11.45am & 1.30pm-4.15pm Tues-Sun)* creatively presents the history of the Vietnamese Revolution. It's diagonally across the road from the History Museum.

## Geology Museum

The Geology Museum *(Bao Tang Dia Chat; Central Hanoi map; 6 Pho Pham Ngu Lao; admission free; open 8.30am-11.30am & 1.30pm-4.30pm Mon-Fri)* tells the story of the geologic processes that created such breathtaking spots as Halong Bay; however, most of the explanations are in Vietnamese. It's close to the History Museum, but the opening hours seem to be a bit erratic.

## Fine Arts Museum

The Fine Arts Museum *(Bao Tang My Thuat; Central Hanoi map; 66 Pho Nguyen Thai Hoc; admission 10,000d; open 9.15am-5pm Tues-Sun)* is housed in the former French Ministry of Information. Here you can see some very intricate sculptures, paintings, lacquerware, ceramics and other traditional Vietnamese fine arts. Reproductions of antiques are on sale here, but be sure to ask for a certificate to clear these goods through customs when you leave Vietnam.

The Fine Arts Museum is on the corner with Pho Cao Ba Quat, across the street from the back wall of the Temple of Literature.

## Women's Museum

The excellent Women's Museum *(Bao Tang Phu Nu; Central Hanoi map; 36 Pho Ly Thuong Kiet; admission 10,000d; open 8am-4pm daily)* has some terrific displays. There is the inevitable tribute to women soldiers, balanced by some great exhibits from the international women's movement protesting the American War. And there's much more in terms of cultural and political information. On the 4th floor you can see different costumes worn by the women of the ethnic-minority groups, and examples of tribal basketware and fabric motifs. This is one place where many of the exhibits have Vietnamese, French and English explanations.

## Army Museum

Outside the Army Museum (Bao Tang Quan Doi; Central Hanoi map; Pho Dien Bien Phu; admission 10,000d; open 8am-11.30am & 1.30pm-4.30pm Tues-Sun), Soviet and Chinese weaponry supplied to the North are displayed alongside French- and US–made weapons captured in the Franco–Viet Minh and American Wars. The centrepiece is a Soviet-built MiG-21 jet fighter, triumphant amid the wreckage of French aircraft downed at Dien Bien Phu, and a US F-111. The displays include scale models of various epic battles from the long military history of Vietnam, including Dien Bien Phu and the capture of Saigon.

Next to the Army Museum is the hexagonal Flag Tower, which has become one of the symbols of Hanoi.

## Hoa Lo Prison Museum

This provocative site is all that remains of the former Hoa Lo Prison (Old Quarter map; 1 Pho Hoa Lo, cnr Pho Hai Ba Trung; admission 10,000d; open 8am-11.30am & 1.30pm-4.30pm Tues-Sun), ironically nicknamed the 'Hanoi Hilton' by US POWs during the American War. Those incarcerated at Hoa Lo included Pete Peterson, who would later become the first US Ambassador to Vietnam following the re-establishment of diplomatic ties between the two countries in 1995.

The vast prison complex was built by the French in 1896. Originally intended to house around 450 inmates, records indicate that by the 1930s there were close to 2000 prisoners inside! Much of the prison was recently razed to make room for a modern skyscraper,

though the section at the front of the site has been thoughtfully preserved and restored as a museum (look for the sign over the gate reading 'Maison Centrale'). There are some English and French labels corresponding with the displays, and you may be able to find an English-speaking guide on site.

The bulk of the exhibits relate to the prison's use up to the mid-1950s, focusing on the Vietnamese struggle for independence from France. Notable tools of torture on display in the dark chambers include an ominous French guillotine that was used to behead Vietnamese revolutionaries during the colonial period, and the fetters with which prisoners were chained to the bunks. It has to be said that, even allowing for the propaganda, it looks like the treatment of Americans by the Vietnamese was infinitely better than that of Vietnamese nationalists by the French.

There are also mug shots on display of Americans and Vietnamese who served time at Hoa Lo. Propaganda photos of cheerful-looking American prisoners (showing how well the Vietnamese hosts treated their guests) are shown with a placard reading:

From August 5, 1964 to January 24, 1973, US government carried out two destruction wars by air and navy against Northern Vietnam. The Northern Army and people brought down thousands of aircrafts and captured hundreds of American pilots. Part of these pilots were detained in Hoa Lo Prison by our Ministry of Interior. Though having committed untold crimes on our people, but American pilots suffered no revenge once they were captured and detained. Instead they were well treated with adequate food, clothing and shelter. According to the provisions of Paris Agreement, our government had in March 1973 returned all captured pilots to the US government.

## Air Force Museum

This is one of the larger museums in the country and, though seldom visited by foreigners, it's very worthwhile if you are a war history or aircraft buff.

The Air Force Museum (Bao Tang Khong Quan; Central Hanoi map; Ð Truong Chinh; admission 10,000d, video-camera fee 10,000d, still-camera fee 2000d; open 8am-11am & 1pm-4.30pm Tues-Sat) has many of exhibits outdoors. These include a number of Soviet-built MiG fighters, reconnaissance planes, helicopters and anti-aircraft equipment. Inside the hall are other weapons, including mortars, machine guns and some US–made bombs. There is a partially truncated MiG with a ladder so that you can climb up into the cockpit and have your photo taken. The museum has other war memorabilia, including paintings of obvious Soviet design and portraits of Ho Chi Minh.

The Air Force Museum is in the Dong Da district, in the far southwest.

### Border Guard Museum

The Border Guard Museum (Bao Tang Bien Phong; Central Hanoi map; 2 Pho Tran Hung Dao; admission free; open 8am-11am Mon-Sat) is dedicated to those friendly boys in uniform you encountered at the airport or border crossing. Theoretically, it has official opening times but it's often shut.

## SWIMMING

Several upmarket hotels have swimming pools, but most are for hotel guests and members only. For the general public, the **Army Hotel** (Central Hanoi map; Pho Pham Ngu Lao), near the History Museum, charges 40,000d or US$3 for day use of their pool which is big enough to do laps and is open all year. Just about big enough to do laps – but a much nicer place to lounge around afterwards – is the pool at the **Melia Hotel** (Old Quarter map; Pho Ly Thuong Kiet), where 'walk-in-members' pay US$5 to swim, or US$10 to swim and use the gym. Some other hotels charge a US$10 day-use fee (see Places to Stay later in this chapter).

Out by Ho Tay (West Lake), the **Ho Tay Villas** (Greater Hanoi map; ☎ 825 8241) charges 30,000d per day to swim. Also by Ho Tay is the **Thang Loi Hotel**, which has a swimming pool in a nicer location that's open to the public for the same price. These two pools are only open in summer months, from about May to October.

Following in the footsteps of HCMC, the recently completed **Hanoi Water Park**

(Greater Hanoi map; ☎ 753 2757) is about 5km from the city centre and offers the usual variety of pools, slides and splashing opportunities. Entry costs 50,000d for those over 110cm-tall, or 30,000d for shorter people. Go figure. It's open daily from April 15 to November.

## FITNESS CLUBS

A number of international hotels open their exercise centres to the public for a fee. Among these is the top-of-the-market **Clark**

---

### A Walk in the Park

If you want to join Hanoians at their most relaxed and informal, take an early morning walk in Lenin Park. Early means early, from first light (about 5am in summer) to 7am.

People of all ages are out and about, wearing an extraordinary array of leisure garments from floppy cotton pyjamas to high-tech skin-tight Lycra. Young men play football, old women practise flag dancing, all ages and sexes perform aerobics to loud and crackly cover versions of such gems as Love Story, the aged gracefully perform t'ai chi, a few solitary figures meditate cross-legged beside the water. Some brave souls occasionally swim. The path around the lake's edge is jam-packed with runners and walkers, moving in an organised chaos that functions more smoothly than the traffic starting up outside the park boundary.

Obstacles on the path include second-hand clothes sellers; rice-porridge, sweet-corn, potato and soy-milk sellers; fruit vendors; weighing-machine owners (so you can check how much weight you lost this morning); sweepers; and gardeners. Not to mention the fact that you have to dodge the shuttlecocks of the many groups of friends and families, who string badminton nets from trees and poles across the path and play loud and lively matches for an hour or so.

By 7.30am it's over. Most people have headed off to begin their working day, and the park quiets down until the evening strollers return. It's a great way to start the day.

Hatch Fitness Centre in the Sofitel Metropole Hotel and Sofitel Plaza (☎ 826 6919 ext 8881), which has a day-use fee of US$12 for the gym. Similar is the **Daewoo Hotel Fitness Centre** (☎ 835 1000), which has a day-use fee of US$20 for all facilities including the pool.

## GOLF

**King's Island** is an 18-hole golf course 45km west of Hanoi, close to the base of Ba Vi Mountain. Membership is a whopping US$5000, but the club is open to visitors.

On the western side of Hanoi, but still within the city limits, is the **Lang Ha Golf Club** (Greater Hanoi map; ☎ 835 0909; 16A Pho Lang Ha; nonmembers fee US$20; open 6am-10pm daily), opposite the TV tower. Basically, this is just a driving range – you'll have to go to King's Island if you want to pursue a white ball over hills and fields.

## MASSAGE

The government has severely restricted the number of places licensed to give massages because of the concern that naughty 'extra services' might be offered (as indeed they are at most places). At present, you can get a good legitimate massage at the Hoa Binh Hotel, Dan Chu Hotel and Thang Loi Hotel for about US$4 to US$6 per hour. The upmarket Guoman, Sofitel Metropole Hotel and Nikko Hotels charge around US$10 or US$20 per hour for this service.

You might also see what's on offer at the **Institute of Traditional Medicine** (Central Hanoi map; ☎ 943 1018; 26-29 Pho Nguyen Binh Khiem) or the **Institute of Acupuncture** (Greater Hanoi map; ☎ 853 3881; H3 Pho Vinh Ho & 49 Pho Thai Thinh).

## BEAUTY SALONS

Many of Hanoi's beauty salons offer – ahem – 'extra services' as standard. If you feel in need of sprucing, a good, legitimate hairdresser is **Vu Doo Salon** (☎ 823 3439; 32c Pho Cao Ba Quat). It's run by a friendly, English-speaking stylist named Vu who has earned a steady following among Hanoi's expat community.

His salon maintains a high international standard and hairdressing prices are quite reasonable at US$9/10 for men/women (including a wash, head massage, cut, blow dry and finish). Manicures and pedicures cost about US$4.

## LANGUAGE COURSES

**Vietnamese Language Centre** (Central Hanoi map; ☎ 826 2468; Hanoi Foreign Language College, 1 Pho Pham Ngu Lao; open 8am-11.30am & 1.30pm-5pm Mon-Fri) offers professionally taught courses at this college, which is a branch of Hanoi National University. This small campus is in the History Museum compound.

Tuition varies depending on class size, but individual tutoring should be no more than US$7 per session. There is a dormitory for foreign students and they can stay for around US$200 per month. The Vietnamese embassy in your home country should be able to provide you with more detailed information about these options.

## SPECIAL EVENTS

Tet, the Vietnamese Lunar New Year, falls in late January or early February (see 'The Tet Festival' special section in the Facts for the Visitor chapter). A flower market is held during the week preceding Tet on Pho Hang Luoc. A two-week flower exhibition and competition, beginning on the first day of the new year, takes place in Lenin Park. On the 13th day of the first lunar month boys and girls in Lim village (Ha Bac province) engage in hat doi, a traditional game in which groups conduct a sung dialogue with each other; other cultural activities include human chess games and cock fighting. Wrestling matches are held on the 15th day of the first lunar month at Dong Da Mound, site of the uprising against Chinese invaders led by Emperor Quang Trung (Nguyen Hue) in 1788.

Vietnam's National Day, 2 September, is celebrated in Hanoi at Ba Dinh Square (the expanse of grass in front of Ho Chi Minh's Mausoleum) with a rally and a display of fireworks; also boat races are usually held on Hoan Kiem Lake.

## PLACES TO STAY

The majority of Hanoi's budget accommodation is within 1km of Hoan Kiem Lake. Unlike HCMC's Pham Ngu Lao district, where the cheapies are lined up wall-to-wall, lodgings here are more scattered, though they're mostly in and around the traditional Old Quarter.

There are several budget places around with both dorm beds (around US$3) and cheap rooms (under US$10), but for between US$10 and US$15 you can choose from a wide selection of 'minihotels', which offer clean, air-con rooms and many even have satellite TV.

In the US$20 to US$50 range there is usually little to justify the price difference between the cheaper minihotels in town, though there are a few exceptions.

If you are willing and able to shell out between US$50 and US$100, however, it is possible to stay in posh four-star hotels that in cities like Hong Kong or Bangkok would cost around double. Keep an eye out in *Vietnam News*, the *Guide* and *Time Out* for the latest deals, and always ask about current 'promotions' – ie, reduced room rates – at reception.

## PLACES TO STAY – BUDGET
## Old Quarter

**Thu Giang Guesthouse** (☎ 828 5734; e thuy han00@hotmail.com; 5A Pho Tam Thuong; singles/doubles with bath US$6/7) is quite a friendly place that is popular with budget travellers. It's tucked away in a narrow alley between Pho Yen Thai and Pho Hang Gai. The rooms are modest and have air-con.

**Manh Dung Guesthouse** (☎ 826 7201, fax 824 8118; e manhdung@vista.gov.vn; 2 Pho Tam Thuong; singles/doubles US$6/7) is a family-run place that is worth a try if the nearby Thu Giang Guesthouse is full. It charges the same and has Internet facilities.

**Thuy Nga Guesthouse** (☎ 826 6053; e thuy ngahotel@hotmail.com; 24C Pho Ta Hien; rooms with/without balcony US$10/9) is a bright, airy family-run place with six tiny, spotless rooms.

**Stars Hotel** (☎ 828 1911, ☎ 828 1928; 26 Pho Bat Su; rooms with/without balcony US$15/10) has received a steady stream of positive reports for its clean, comfortable rooms and friendly service. Rooms are air-con; nicer rooms have balconies.

**A to Z Queen Café 1** (☎ 826 0860, fax 825 0000; e queenaz@fpt.vn; 65 Pho Hang Bac; twins US$5) has very basic – we mean very basic – fan rooms with shared bath.

**A to Z Queen Café 2** (☎ 826 7356; e queen az@fpt.vn; 50 Pho Hang Be; dorm beds US$3, doubles with fan/air-con US$6/12) is getting seriously tatty and is a bit grubby, but there's a busy Internet café on the 1st floor, and a popular bar downstairs.

**Camellia Hotel** (☎ 828 3583, fax 824 4277; 13 Pho Luong Ngoc Quyen; air-con rooms US$12-20) is a popular hotel where rates include breakfast and satellite TV. It's getting a bit tatty, but is in a good location.

**Mai Son Guesthouse** (☎ 926 0863; 66 Pho Cau Go; approx US$8) is a small, centrally located guesthouse run by a very nice woman, and offers pleasant accommodation in rooms decorated with antiques.

**Anh Sinh Hotel** (☎/fax 824 2229; e ahnsinh tour@hotmail.com; 49 Pho Hang Be; air-con rooms US$15-40, dorm beds US$3), just across the street from Queen 2, is good value for the price.

**Real Darling Cafe** (☎ 826 9386, fax 825 6562; e darling_cafe@hotmail.com; 33 Pho Hang Quat; dorm beds US$3, singles/doubles US$5/10) has pretty basic rooms on offer, but it is clean and has staff who speak good English.

**Prince Hotel (1)** (☎ 828 0155, fax 828 0156; e ngodzung@hn.vnn.vn; 51 Pho Luong Ngoc Quyen; small/large rooms US$15/20) is still recommended. The clean, spacious doubles here are decorated with Chinese-style furniture and have balconies. Breakfast and Internet access are included in the room rate.

**Prince Cafe** (☎ 828 1893; 53 Pho Luong Ngoc Quyen; rooms with/without balcony US$10/8), just next door to Prince Hotel, has tiny, but clean, budget rooms.

**Van Minh Hotel** (the hotel formerly known as Prince (2); ☎ 926 0150; e nngoc minh@fpt.vn; 88 Pho Hang Bac; all rooms air-con US$15-30) is around the block from the

Prince. This one is also good; its clean rooms come with bath and satellite TV. Some of the cheaper rooms have no windows, though.

**New Tong Dan Hotel** *(Nam Phuong Hotel; ☎ 825 2219, fax 825 5354; e tongdanhotel@hn.vnn.vn; 210 Pho Tran Quang Khai or 17 Pho Tong Dan; single/double rooms US$10/20)* is a friendly place that gets good comments from travellers. It's east of Hoan Kiem Lake near the Red River. Their motto is 'More than a hotel, it's a home!' Rooms are well appointed. You can enter the hotel on Pho Tran Quang Khai or Pho Tong Dan.

There's a cluster of cheap hotels in a good location in the artsy quarter near the cathedral on Pho Nha Chung. **Spring Hotel** *(☎ 826 8500, fax 826 0083; e spring.hotel@fpt.vn; 8a Pho Nha Chung; rooms US$10-18)* has small, simple rooms and a good feel to it. It's run by a helpful family that speaks fluent English.

Close by, at number 24, **Hotel Thien Trang** *(☎ 826 9823, fax 828 6717; e thientranghotel24@hotmail.com; rooms US$10-15)* is on the border of OK for the price but definitely go for rooms upstairs; they're the ones with windows.

**Nam Phuong Hotel (1)** *(☎ 824 6894; 26 Pho Nha Chung; rooms with fan/air-con from US$7/8)* was being refurbished when we visited, so should be clean and bright when it reopens.

**Lotus Guesthouse** *(☎ 934 4197, fax 826 8642; e lotus-travel@hn.vnn.vn; 42V Pho Ly Thuong Kiet; rooms US$6-15)* is quiet and clean but small and with low ceilings; it might be a bit cramped for claustrophobes or big people. There's also an in-house café.

**Trang Tien Hotel** *(☎ 825 6115, fax 825 1416; 35 Pho Trang Tien; doubles US$15-20)* is an eccentrically sprawling hotel worth considering – it's decent value for the location, between Hoan Kiem Lake and the Opera House.

## Central Hanoi
**Dream 2 Hotel** *(☎ 828 7045, fax 828 7472; 3B Pho Tong Duy Tan; doubles with/without balcony US$15/12)* is a six-room, standard minihotel, but it's clean with air-con rooms

and on a quiet street between the Old Quarter and the mausoleum complex.

**Hotel Memory** *(☎ 934 9909; e memoryhotel@fpt.vn; 25 Pho Nguyen Thai Hoc; all rooms air-con US$12-18)* is good value. Room rates include breakfast and satellite TV and it's near the train station, Cam Chi, the speciality-food street, and a short walk from the Old Quarter.

**Hotel 30/4** *(☎ 826 0807, fax 822 1818; 115 Pho Tran Hung Dao; rooms without bath US$7-10, with bath US$15)*, opposite the Hanoi train station, is named after 30 April 1975, the date when the North Vietnamese entered Saigon. Not surprisingly, it's state-owned. Rooms are large echo chambers.

## PLACES TO STAY – MID-RANGE
### Old Quarter
**Hong Ngoc Hotel 1** *(☎ 828 5053; e hongngochotel@hn.vnn.vn; 34 Pho Hang Manh; singles/doubles US$25/35)*, a short stroll northwest from Hoan Kiem Lake, is pleasant enough; the more expensive rooms are spacious, but some of the cheaper rooms have no windows. Breakfast is included.

**Quoc Hoa Hotel** *(☎ 828 4528, fax 826 7424; Pho Bat Dan; e quochoa@hn.vnn.vn; standard/deluxe rooms US$20/35)* is a good find: a small business hotel that is quiet, spotlessly clean and well maintained, and with all mod-cons. Internet use is outrageously expensive though, at US$1 for 10 minutes; use the Internet café across the road.

**Classic Street Hotel** *(☎ 825 2421; e hohoa@hn.vnn.vn; 41 Pho Hang Be; standard rooms US$18, deluxe singles/doubles with breakfast US$25/35)* is an attractive, new place within the stylish milieu of old Hanoi. All rooms have air-con and satellite TV and some have fantastic views of the quarter's higgledy-piggledy rooftops.

**Tu Do Hotel** *(Freedom Hotel; ☎ 826 7119, fax 824 3918; e freedomhotel@hn.vnn.vn; 45 Pho Hang Trong; rooms US$18-30)* is a smaller hotel with 12 decent, if small, rooms with air-con and satellite TV.

**Ho Guom Hotel** *(☎ 825 2225, fax 824 3564; e hoguomtjc@hn.vnn.vn; 76 Pho Hang Trong; standard/deluxe rooms US$20/35)* is that rarity: a state-run hotel that's clean and quiet, with pleasant staff and in a good location. The rooms with balconies overlooking the inner courtyard are very good value for the price.

**Trang An Hotel** (☎ 826 8992, fax 825 8511; e trangan@camellia-hotels.com; w www .camellia-hotels.com; 58 Pho Hang Gai; rooms US$12-25) gets the thumbs up for its location, helpful staff and great-value rooms. They're a bit tatty but spotless, and for the higher rates you can get a two-room suite with balcony, air-con and satellite TV. It's popular, so you might want to book ahead and yes, you really do walk through a silk shop to reach reception.

**Win Hotel** (☎ 826 7150; e esm-ntb@ hn.vnn.vn; 34 Pho Hang Hanh; air-con rooms US$20-30) is a friendly place, bright as a new pin, with good rooms set amid a slew of busy and fun local **cafés** on 'coffee street'. The single rooms are pretty small though.

**Dan Chu Hotel** (☎ 825 4937, fax 826 6786; e danchu@hn.vnn.vn; 29 Pho Trang Tien; standard rooms from US$40) was built in the late 19th century and has a pleasant air of slightly decaying grandeur. It's well located between the opera house and the lake. The well-respected massage service is open to nonguests for 80,000d per hour.

**Chains First Eden Hotel** (☎ 828 3896, fax 828 4066; e cfeden@hn.vnn.vn; 3A Pho Phan Dinh Phung; standard/deluxe rooms US$30/89) is near the Hanoi Citadel. This large business hotel has a health club, sauna, business centre, satellite TV, and Chinese-Vietnamese **restaurant**. Deluxe rooms are pleasant; the cheaper rooms are pricey for the size.

**Galaxy Hotel** (☎ 828 2888, fax 828 2466; e galaxyhtl@netnam.org.vn; 1 Pho Phan Dinh Phung; standard rooms from US$45) is a clean and well-equipped lodging, popular with European tour groups. Based around the original 1918 building, it has a business centre, an attractive **café-restaurant** and satellite TV in all rooms.

**Viet Anh Hotel** (☎ 846 8525, fax 824 3198; 22 Pho Cua Dong; singles/doubles US$20/22) is an attractive minihotel northwest of the Old Quarter, near the Hanoi Citadel. Rooms at the back cost less, but are

dark and windowless; front rooms with balconies are a much better deal.

## Central Hanoi

**Thien Thai Hotel** (Paradise Hotel; ☎ 823 7126, fax 823 6917; 45 Pho Ngyuen Truong To; standard/deluxe rooms US$35/50) is a new, spiffy-looking place with a colonial motif. All rooms have balconies and include breakfast, and are of a good standard as you'd expect for the price.

**Anh Hotel II** (☎ 843 5141, fax 843 0618; 43 Pho Nguyen Truong To; singles/doubles from US$18/20) is a smaller place next to Thien Thai Hotel, and has rooms of all different shapes and sizes, including some with alcoves and raised platforms. Ask to see a few before checking in.

**Army Hotel** (Khach San Quan Doi; ☎ 825 2896, fax 825 9276; 33C Pho Pham Ngu Lao; singles/doubles US$35/50) is indeed owned by the army but looks nothing like barracks; it is a rather splendid, old colonial building. A popular place for tour groups, Army Hotel has its own gym and salt-water swimming pool. You can use the decent-sized pool for US$3 per day.

**Green Park Hotel** (☎ 822 7725, fax 822 5977; e greenpark@hn.vnn.vn; 48 Pho Tan Nhan Tong; standard rooms US$45), a short walk from Lenin Park, is, well, big and green. If you can handle the colour scheme, it is not a bad place to stay. There are good views from the top-floor **restaurant**. Primarily a business hotel, a 30% discount on the rack rates is usually offered depending on availability.

## Greater Hanoi

**Thang Loi Hotel** (Cuban Hotel; ☎ 829 4211; e thangloihtl@hn.vnn.vn; Duong Yen Phu; standard rooms US$40) was nicknamed so because it was built, in the mid-1970s, with Cuban assistance. The floor plan of each level is said to have been copied from a one-storey Cuban building, which explains the doors that lead nowhere. Around the main building are bungalows. The hotel is built on pylons over the water at Ho Tay (West Lake), and is surrounded by attractive landscaping and a swimming pool, which is open only in the summer months (May to September). The hotel also boasts tennis courts, a sauna and a massage service. With the exception of the massage, all this cushy comfort is included in the rates. The hotel is 3.5km from the city centre.

**Ho Tay Villas** *(Khuy Biet Thu Ho Tay;* ☎ *804 7772;* e *hotayvillas@fmail.vnn.vn; standard/suite rooms US$24/120)* was previously known as the Communist Party Guesthouse but is now just a tourist hotel. These spacious villas, set on Ho Tay, were once the exclusive preserve of top party officials; but now visitors with US dollars are welcome to use the once-splendid facilities. Even if you don't stay, it's instructive to visit to see how the 'people's representatives' lived in one of Asia's poorest countries. The hotel is often full with government delegations and conferences. The hotel is 5.5km north of central Hanoi.

## PLACES TO STAY – TOP END
### Old Quarter

**Sofitel Metropole Hotel** *(*☎ *826 6919, fax 826 6920;* e *sofitelhanoi@hn.vnn.vn; 15 Pho Ngo Quyen; rooms from US$200)* is a giant property that is one of Vietnam's great luxury hotels. This place has a French motif that just won't quit – close the curtains and you'll think you're in Paris. Facilities include a small swimming pool, fitness centre, sauna and beauty parlour.

**Melia Hotel** *(*☎ *934 3343,* ☎ *934 3344;* e *solmelia@meliahanoi.com.vn; 44B Pho Ly Thuong Kiet; rooms US$88++)* is one of the ugliest modern skyscrapers in Hanoi but once you are inside the place is blissfully tasteful. The lobby deli sells good rye breads.

### Central Hanoi

**De Syloia Hotel** *(*☎ *824 5346, fax 824 1083; 17A Pho Tran Hung Dao; standard/deluxe rooms US$50/70)* is a small and elegant boutique hotel with a French theme. There is a fitness centre and sauna here, and the in-house Vietnamese restaurant, Cay Cau, is recommended.

**Guoman Hotel** *(*☎ *822 2800, fax 822 2822;* e *guomanhn@hn.vnn.vn; 83A Pho Ly Thuong Kiet; standard/deluxe rooms US$70/120)* is a

stately place that maintains an international four-star standard and often offers special deals on the rates quoted here. It's located about 1km southwest of Hoan Kiem Lake. Facilities include a sleek health club; a café and fine dining; two good bars and staff who remember your name.

**Hotel Nikko** *(*☎ *822 3535; 84 Tran Nhan Tong; rooms from US$180++)* is in a good location on the edge of Lenin Park and there's often a 50% discount offered on the rack rates.

**Hanoi Opera Hilton** *(*☎ *933 0500, fax 933 0530;* w *www.hilton.com; 1 Le Thanh Tong; rooms US$120++)*, in a prime location beside Hanoi's grand Opera House, looks dazzling from the outside, and is everything you'd expect from a Hilton in terms of facilities, service and food. You can treat yourself to day-use of the luxurious health club and pool for US$11.

**Sofitel Plaza** *(*☎ *823 8888, fax 829 388; 1 Đ Thanh Nien; rooms from US$180++, presidential suite US$1000)*, formerly the Meritus Westlake, is a gigantic Singaporean joint venture boasting every possible amenity, including Southeast Asia's first ever indoor-outdoor swimming pool with a retractable roof. The **Summit Lounge Bar** on the 20th floor has a daily happy hour from 4.30pm to 8pm, with great sunset views across West Lake and the city.

### Greater Hanoi

**Hanoi Horison Hotel** *(*☎ *733 0808;* e *hhh_sale@netnam.org.vn; 40 Pho Cat Linh; rooms US$90-170)* is a snazzy hotel featuring a heritage brick smokestack in front, which was preserved from an old brick factory that once stood on the site. It also has an excellent health club and swimming pool, with a US$7 day-use fee.

**Daewoo Hotel** *(*☎ *831 5000;* e *info@daewoohotel.com.vn; standard rooms US$199++, suites from US$319++)* is in the Daeha Centre (western Hanoi) and is the city's largest and most expensive hotel. The style at this South-Korean joint venture is most definitely *not* French colonial. The hotel is a 15-storey behemoth and offers everything you could want in life, including a vast landscaped

**HANOI**

swimming pool, nightclub, health club, business centre and three restaurants. You can use the pool only for US$10 per day or all the health-club facilities for US$20.

## PLACES TO STAY – RENTAL

As elsewhere in Vietnam, the budget end of the rental market is served by minihotels. Look around for the best deal and don't be afraid to negotiate.

There are around 5000 expats living in Hanoi (about three times the number living in HCMC). Well-heeled foreigners with big budgets typically live in fancy apartments that command high rents. A typical luxury two-bedroom flat leases from US$800 to US$3000 per month. Those of us who are more budget constrained can find a good private air-con room in a local guesthouse or minihotel for around US$200 to US$300 a month.

**Somerset Grand Hanoi** (☎ 934 2342, fax 822 1968; w www.somerset.com; 49 Pho Hai Ba Trung; 1-/2-/3-bedroom flats US$110/ 135/220 per night, with reduced long-stay rates) is found in the Hanoi Towers building, a modern skyscraper built on the site of the former Hoa Lu POW prison. The apartments are very good value, good-sized and self-contained down to the washing machine and kitchen cutlery. A stay at the hotel also means access to a pool, health club and sauna, **Jacc's restaurant** is on the fourth floor, and there's a good supermarket at ground level. Discounts off the published rates are often given, and the longer you stay at the Somerset, the cheaper it is.

## PLACES TO EAT

In recent years Hanoi has undergone a miraculous transformation from a culinary wasteland to a premier city for eating and drinking. The city boasts everything from cheap backpacker joints (yes, *more* banana pancakes) to exquisite Vietnamese restaurants and a growing legion of chic cafés.

You can combine food for the body with food for the soul at Hoa Sua restaurant and Koto (later in this section). Both are recommended for their good food and vocational training programmes for street kids.

Restaurants, bars and cafés have a strong tendency to change names, location, management and just about everything else, so ask around and keep an eye out in for current listings the *Guide* and *Time Out*.

### Vietnamese

**Old Quarter** There are plenty of Vietnamese restaurants to choose from in the Old Quarter.

**Little Hanoi (1)** (☎ 926 0168; 25 Pho Ta Hien; meals from 15,000d; open 11am-11pm) is a cosy eatery that's worth seeking out. It's remained cheap and friendly, and is popular with backpackers and locals for both lunch and dinner.

**Hanoi Garden** (☎ 824 3402; 36 Pho Hang Manh; set menu from US$5.50, á la carte from 40,000d; open 10am-2pm & 5pm-10pm daily) is a fine choice for lunch or dinner. It serves southern Vietnamese and spicy Chinese meals in an elegant building with indoor and courtyard seating.

One of Hanoi's most famous food specialities is *cha ca*, perhaps best thought of as sumptuous little fish burgers. **Cha Ca La Vong** (☎ 825 3929; 14 Pho Cha Ca), the best known *cha ca* restaurant in town, has been family-run for five generations. Other worthy (and cheaper) places to try this local delicacy at include **Cha Ca 66** (☎ 826 7881; 66 Pho Hang Ga) and **Thang Long** (☎ 824 5115; 40 Pho Hang Ma).

**Pho Bo Dac Biet** (2B Pho Ly Quoc Su) is a good place to go to for a bowl of beef noodle soup *(pho bo)*, but pretty much any of the restaurants or street stalls are fine for *pho* as long as you can see that the soup pot's boiling.

**The Whole Earth Restaurant** (☎ 926 0696, ☎ 926 0349; 7 Pho Dinh Liet; set menus from 25,000d; open 8am-11pm) offers a wide choice of vegetarian 'meat' dishes.

**Central Hanoi** All of the following restaurants and eateries can be found on the Central Hanoi map.

**Soho** (☎ 826 6555; 57 Pho Ba Trieu) is a stylish but casual Vietnamese restaurant about 1km south of Hoan Kiem Lake. Try out their signature dish, Franco-Vietnamese bouillabaisse, or check the daily specials board. You can sit indoors or outside on the pleasant verandah.

**Quan Com Pho** (☎ 943 2356; 29 Pho Le Van Huu; dishes from 25,000d; open 10.30am-2pm & 4.30pm-10pm daily) serves terrific food and has big clean dining rooms on several levels. The honey-barbecued squid is delicious. Lunchtime is particularly busy with Vietnamese and expat office workers. (And 10 out of 10 for the toilets.)

**Tiem Pho** (48-50 Pho Hué) serves up great chicken noodle soup (pho ga), and keeps late hours. Diagonally across from the corner is **Restaurant 1,2,3** (☎ 822 9100; 55 Pho Hué; meals 30,000d), a kind of upmarket fast-food restaurant. The barbecued fish, and 'fish porridge' (chao), are terrific.

### Gourmet Vietnamese

**Old Quarter** Just across from the Sofitel Metropole Hotel, **Club Opera** (☎ 824 6950; 59 Pho Ly Thai To; mains from US$6; open 11am-2pm & 5.30pm-10.30pm) serves delicious Vietnamese fare in an elegant European atmosphere, and the menu changes seasonally.

**Central Hanoi** The remarkable eatery, **Brother's Cafe** (☎ 733 3866; 26 Pho Nguyen Thai Hoc; lunch/dinner buffet US$5/10; open 11am-2pm Mon-Sat & 6.30pm-10.30pm daily) is set in the courtyard of an elegantly restored, 250-year-old Buddhist temple. The nightly dinner buffet is very reasonable and includes one drink; their lunch special is a bargain. The 'one with nature' atmosphere created by owner Khai (founder of the trendy boutique Khai Silk) is simply serene, even when it's busy.

**Emperor** (☎ 826 8801; 18B Pho Le Thanh Tong; main courses from US$5; open 11am-2pm & 5.30pm-10pm), also indoor-outdoor, serves great Vietnamese cuisine, and there's a stylish bar with a pool table. This is a great place for live **traditional music** from 7.30pm to 9.30pm, Wednesday and Saturday, and Latino music from 8pm to 10pm on Tuesday and Friday.

**Seasons of Hanoi** (☎ 843 5444; 95B Pho Quan Thanh) is yet another excellent choice

for Vietnamese haute cuisine. It is housed in a classic French villa and quite tastefully decorated with an eclectic collection of Vietnamese and colonial-era antiques.

**Nam Phuong** (☎ 824 0926; 19 Pho Phan Chu Trinh; main courses 60,000d; open 11am-2pm & 5.30pm-10pm daily) is an elegant setting for authentic and delicious Vietnamese food, and occupies a charming villa. **Traditional music** is played for a couple of hours from 7.30pm daily, and there's also an impressive wine list.

### Other Asian

Good Chinese and Japanese food in Hanoi tends to be pricey, and the best stuff is usually at upmarket hotels. Sofitel Plaza Hotel does a fantastic daily all-you-can-eat dim sum lunch for US$10, as does the Melia Hotel for US$6.

**Old Quarter** Almost every kind of Asian cuisine, from Thai to Indian, can be found in the Old Quarter.

**Baan Thai Restaurant** (☎ 828 1120; 3B Pho Cha Ca; 30,000-60,000d; open lunch & dinner) is centrally located, and has a handy photo-illustrated menu at the door.

For Indian food, try **Revival** (☎ 824 1166; 41B Pho Ly Thai To), which does good Indian food in a pleasant atmosphere, and will deliver. **Tandoor** (☎ 824 5359; 24 Pho Hang Be; set lunch 52,000d; open lunch & dinner Mon-Sat) makes up for a lack of atmosphere with its food.

**Saigon Sakura** (☎ 825 7565; 17 Pho Trang Thi), despite the cheesy name, dishes up good Japanese fare. Expect to pay around US$10-15 for sushi and miso soup.

**Central Hanoi** One of Hotel Nikko's restaurants, **Tao-Li** (☎ 822 3535; 84 Tran Nhan Tong; dishes from US$6; open 11.30am-2pm & 6pm-10pm daily), specialises in Schezuan-style cooking.

For Japanese fare, **Benkay Restaurant** (☎ 822 3535; 84 Tran Nhan Tong; set lunches from US$7; open 11.30am-2pm & 6pm-10pm daily) can't be beaten (according to Hanoi's resident Japanese). It's on the 2nd floor of the Hotel Nikko.

**Ky Y** (☎ 978 1386; 29 Phu Dong Thien Vuong; open for lunch & dinner Mon-Sat) is a less expensive, but excellent Japanese option that serves fresh sushi and sashimi. It was closed for renovation when we visited; hopefully the standard will remain high.

**Van Anh** (☎ 928 5163; 5a Pho Tong Duy Tan) is a Thai restaurant with a Thai chef, in the middle of the gaggle of Vietnamese restaurants in Pho Cam Chi.

## European

**Old Quarter** For budget Western food, try some of the travellers cafés listed under Travel Agencies earlier in this chapter. Among them is the popular **Kangaroo Cafe** (☎ 828 9931; e kangaroo@hn.vnn.vn; 18 Pho Bao Khanh), just off the west shore of Hoan Kiem Lake, which is a friendly place run by an Australian couple and serving good Western food at Vietnamese prices. See Travel Agencies earlier for details about its tours.

**Restaurant-Café Linh Phung** (☎ 926 0592; 7 Pho Dinh Liet; dishes from 20,000d) serves a mix of reasonably priced Vietnamese and Western food.

**Café des Arts** (☎ 828 7207; 11B Pho Bao Khanh; set menus US$7-10; open 9am-late), in the Old Quarter, is a casual place with good ambience and modelled on a Parisian brasserie. There's a rotating series of art exhibitions and cultural events held here.

**Cyclo Bar & Restaurant** (☎ 828 6844; 38 Pho Duong Thanh; set lunch US$4) is worthy of a plug for creative design alone. It serves up respectable Vietnamese and French food to customers seated in actual cyclos that have been cleverly transformed into tables. The set lunch is good value.

**La Salsa** (☎ 828 9052; 25 Pho Nha Tho; open 10.30am-midnight daily) is a French Canadian–run tapas bar on the trendy strip opposite St Joseph Cathedral. It's proving to be very popular with both tourists and local expats. Thursday is paella day, at 110,000d.

**The Restaurant** (The Press Club; ☎ 934 0888; 59a P Ly Thai To; mains around US$15) is regarded by many as the city's premier fine-dining experience, with stylish surroundings and utilising a mix of fine local and imported foods. Try the famed signature

sauce of black bean and cabernet sauvignon for seafood.

**Le Restaurant d'Arthur** (☎ 934 5238; e moreaux.d@fpt.vn; 17 Pho Ton Dan; 4-course set menu 100,000d; open 8am-10pm Mon-Sat & 9am-7pm Sun) is a casual, intimate French restaurant, well located between the Opera House and the Old Quarter. The fabulous deli downstairs can whip up a filled baguette for your picnic lunch.

**Le Beaulieu Restaurant** (☎ 826 6919 ext 8028; 15 Pho Ngo Quyen), at the elegant Sofitel Metropole Hotel, is probably Hanoi's best upmarket French restaurant. It offers savoury, authentic French cooking and a romantic atmosphere.

**Restaurant Bobby Chinn** (☎ 934 8577; 1 Pho Ba Trieu; main dishes US$6-10; open 10am-late) offers fusion cuisine (great ingredients with a blend of Western and Asian culinary influences) in a very classy setting. Try the superb salads and *anything* on the menu with salmon; when it's time for coffee move through silk drapes to the comfortable sofas and floor cushions at the back of the restaurant.

There are several Italian restaurants in the Old Quarter to choose from. **Pepperonis Pizza & Cafe** (☎ 928 5246; 29 Pho Ly Quoc Su; open daily from lunch; pizzas US$1.25-4, pasta dishes US$1.60) does decent pasta and salad, and can deliver.

**Mama Rosa** (☎ 825 8057; 6 Pho Le Thai To; pasta & pizza from 50,000d) is just across from Hoan Kiem Lake. It looks more formal (wait staff with bow ties and all) than it needs to.

**Mediterraneo Restaurant** (☎ 826 6288; 23 Pho Nha Tho; mains US$5-7; open 10.30am-10.30pm daily) offers good pasta, pizza and salads but in some of the smallest servings we've ever seen; be prepared to order more.

**Jacc's** (☎ 934 8325; 4th floor Hanoi Towers, 49 Hai Ba Trung; Sunday recovery brunch US$8; open 6.30am-midnight) is a busy bar and restaurant, catering mostly to expats, with a creative à la carte menu as well as bar snacks. There's a bright indoor/outdoor patio, and it's the place to be to watch all of the international – especially Australian – sporting events on TV.

**Central Hanoi** A popular Aussie-run eatery, **Al Fresco's** (☎ 826 7782; 23L Pho Hai Ba Trung; meals US$5-15; open from lunch) does fantastic pizza, juicy Tex-Mex ribs and salads. The fish fajitas are good.

**Verandah Bar & Café** (☎ 825 7220; 9 Pho Nguyen Khac Can; mains from US$5; open 11am-2pm & 5.30pm-late) is located in a stylish French villa. The menu includes chicken enchiladas, smoked salmon and quiche; or else you can just swing by for a relaxed drink. There's comfortable seating near the bar and tables upstairs and out on the verandah.

**Luna d'Autunno** (Autumn Moon; ☎ 823 7338; 11B Dien Bien Phu; pizza from 55,000d, fresh pasta from 80,000d; salads from 30,000d; open lunch & dinner daily) is an artsy, indoor-outdoor place. The food is eclectic and authentic Italian, with good home-made antipasto and fresh pasta. Pizzas from the wood-fired oven can be delivered. Associated with the restaurant is the next-door wine bar **Da Gino**, with changing art exhibitions upstairs, and a small Italian-language library.

**Hoa Sua** (☎ 824 0448; 81 Pho Tho Nhuom; Vietnamese/French set lunch 25,000/65,000d; open 8am-10pm) is recommended for lunch and is well worth supporting. This open-air eatery is a successful goodwill project that takes in and trains a steady stream of disadvantaged kids for culinary careers. They serve good French and Vietnamese food and pastries, there's a takeaway bakery on-site, and live classical music on Saturday evening and Sunday lunchtime.

## Seafood

**Old Quarter** Along the trendy strip opposite St Joseph Cathedral, **La Brique** (☎ 928 5638; 6 Pho Nha Tho; filled baguettes 20,000d, fish dishes 60,000d; open 9am-midnight) is a cool and relaxed restaurant. It serves a simple but excellent selection of local seafood. The cha ca barbecued fish, and fish wrapped in banana leaf, are still delicious. The exposed brick walls of this one-time wholesale fish market give the place its name, and the music selection is pleasantly mellow European.

**San Ho Restaurant** (☎ 822 2184; 58 Pho Ly Thuong Kiet; open lunch & dinner daily), set in an attractive villa, is known as one of the best seafood restaurants in Hanoi. It sells seafood at market prices; expect to pay around 100,000d per person.

**Central Hanoi** This giant fish-market-cum-restaurant, **Sam Son Seafood Market** (☎ 825 0780; 77 Pho Doc Bac), is on the banks of Song Hong (Red River) with delicious food. Choose your live fish and eat it several minutes later – that's fresh!

## Vegetarian

The following places are the few strictly vegetarian restaurants in Hanoi.

**Tamarind Cafe & Fruit Juice Bar** (Old Quarter map; ☎ 926 0580; 80 Pho Ma May; meals US$2-4; open 6am-midnight), a bright, comfortable café in the heart of the Old Quarter, serves Asian-style vegetarian dishes and fresh fruit juices and smoothies.

**Com Chay Nang Tam** (Central Hanoi map; ☎ 826 6140; 79A Pho Tran Hung Dao; set meals from 20,000d; open 11am-1.30pm & 5pm-10pm daily), about 1km southwest of Hoan Kiem Lake, is a smoke-free Hanoi institution. It is famed for delicious vegetarian creations, some of which are named after, and look remarkably like, meat dishes. Some vegetarians may find this confronting, but it's an ancient Buddhist tradition that is designed to make meat-eating guests feel at home. Yes, it really is down that unlikely looking alleyway and behind those buildings. There's also a smaller branch of **Com Chay Nang Tam** (79 Pho Hang Bac) in the Old Quarter.

## Cafés, Coffee Shops & Ice Cream

**Old Quarter** Near the northwest corner of Hoan Kiem Lake, **Little Hanoi (2)** (☎ 928 5333; 21 Pho Hang Gai; sandwiches around 30,000d; open 7.30am-11pm daily) is unrelated to Little Hanoi (1). This one is more of a buzzy café, serving some Vietnamese food and deli-type sandwiches.

**Ily Café** (☎ 826 0247; 97 Pho Ma May; soups & salads 25,000-30,000d; open 10am-11pm *daily)* is a good venue, especially if you can persuade someone to play the piano.

**69 Bar-Restaurant** (☎ 926 0452; 69 Pho Ma May; meals from 30,000d; open 10am-midnight daily) has opened in a beautifully restored old Vietnamese house; it's open later than many places and is the perfect place for a nightcap.

**Thuy Ta Cafe** (☎ 825 1907; 1 Pho Le Thai To; pastries 5000d, meals 40,000d; open 6am-11pm) is usually bustling, and has shady garden seating right on the edge of Hoan Kiem Lake.

**Dak Linh Cafe** (☎ 828 7043) offers a prime patio setting for drinks, at the other end of Hoan Kiem Lake.

**Puku** (☎ 928 5244; upstairs 60 Pho Hang Trong; breakfasts 25,000-35,000d; open 7am-10pm) is an eccentrically decorated café with good vibes, good food and a tiny balcony.

**No Noodles** (☎ 928 5969; 20 Pho Nha Chung; sandwiches from 25,000d) is a sandwich and fresh-juice bar, with a creative selection to eat there or take away.

**Café Le Malraux** (☎ 928 6203; 6 Nha Tho; French breakfast 55,000d; open all day) is a funky and stylish French-run bar and café serving all sorts of food from pastries to full meals. It's run in conjunction with a rattan furniture shop so the seating's varied and comfortable, and the music is laid-back French melodic.

**Trung Nguyen** (☎ 926 0473; 20 Pho Hang Mam) is one of a popular HCMC café chain that serves real Vietnamese coffee from the central highlands. The 2nd- and 3rd-floor balconies are a good place to watch the world go by.

There is a fun, busy and chaotic gaggle of Vietnamese **coffee shops** on Pho Hang Hanh; relax on one of the upstairs balconies and watch the bustle below.

**Fanny Ice Cream** (☎ 828 5656; 48 Pho Le Thai To) is the best ice cream joint in town. It's across the lake from the main post office and serves great 'Franco-Vietnamese' ice cream and crepes. If you are there in the right season don't miss the *com*, a delightful local flavour extracted from young sticky rice.

Close to the opera house is a cluster of classy cafés. **Au Lac** (☎ 825 7807; 57 Pho Ly Thai To), set in the pleasant front courtyard of a French villa, opposite the Sofitel Hotel, serves excellent light food and the coffee is among Hanoi's best.

**Diva** (☎ 934 4088; breakfasts 15,000d, light meals from 35,000d; open 7am-midnight daily), a few steps away from Au Lac, is another lovely French-style place, and offers relaxed indoor and outdoor seating.

**The Deli** (The Press Club Deli; ☎ 934 0888; 59A Pho Ly Thai To; gourmet sandwiches from US$3, set lunch from US$5), at the Press Club, is a first-rate bakery-deli, with both an eat-in and takeaway service.

**Paris Deli** (☎ 934 5269; 2 Pho Phan Chu Trinh; light meals from 30,000d; open 7.30am-11pm) is a Parisian-style café-restaurant that's opposite the Opera House. It serves excellent baguette sandwiches and pastries, and also delivers.

**Kem Trang Tien** (54 Pho Trang Tien), between the Opera House and Hoan Kiem Lake, is the most popular ice-cream shop with Hanoians. Just look for the mob on the sidewalk lined up for sticks of the tasty treat. There is also an attached indoor café here, where you can relax in air-con comfort.

**Central Hanoi** It's popular with young Vietnamese professionals but **Café Pho Cu Xua** (☎ 928 5749; 195 Pho Hang Bong; open 11am-7pm) has a very ordinary shop front. Walk through to the back where there's a pretty, quiet garden café serving coffee, ice cream and cocktails.

**Kinh Do Cafe** (☎ 825 0216; 252 Pho Hang Bong; light meals 20,000d; open 7am-10pm daily), near the city centre, serves some of the best yogurt in Vietnam, French pastries and coffee in Vietnam. For movie buffs, this was the simple setting where Catherine Deneuve had her morning cuppa during the making of the film *Indochine,* and the owner speaks good French.

**Koto** (☎ 747 0338; W www.streetvoices .com.au; 61 Pho Van Mieu; juices from 20,000d; open 6.30am-4pm daily) is a grass-roots project providing career training and guidance to former street kids. Koto stands for 'Know One, Teach One'. They make delicious sandwiches and cakes, real coffees, fruit shakes and other healthy dishes in a relaxed and comfortable space. It's located just around the corner from the Temple of Literature, a handy place to recharge your batteries before or after you tour the site.

Out of town, **The Deli** (*Greater Hanoi map; ☎ 846 0007; 18 Pho Tran Huy Lieu*), near Giang Vo Lake, whips up tasty sandwiches for about US$1.20.

## Speciality Food Streets

If you would like to combine eating with exploration, the following food streets can be found on the Central Hanoi map.

**Cam Chi** This street is about 500m northeast of Hanoi train station. Cam Chi is a very small street – basically an alley – crammed full of lively **street stalls** serving budget-priced, delicious food. Forget about English menus and don't expect comfortable seating. Still, where else can you have a small banquet for US$2? The derivation of 'Cam Chi' (meaning forbidden to point) dates from centuries ago. It is said that the street was named as a reminder for the local residents to keep their curious fingers in their pockets when the king and his entourage went through the neighbourhood.

**Pho Mai Hac De & Pho To Hien Thanh** Located in the south-central area, Pho Mai Hac De has several blocks of **restaurants**, running south from the northern terminus at Pho Tran Nhan Tong. It intersects with a street that specialises in **seafood**, Pho To Hien Thanh.

**Duong Thuy Khue** On the south bank of Ho Tay, Đ Thuy Khue features a strip of 30-odd **outdoor seafood restaurants** with pleasant lakeside seating. These places are on the lane to the Ho Tay Pagoda and are popular with locals. The level of competition is evident by the daredevil touts who literally throw themselves in front of oncoming traffic to steer people to their tables. You can eat well here for about US$6 per person.

**Pho Nghi Tam** About 10km north of central Hanoi, Pho Nghi Tam has a 1km-long stretch

of about 60 **dog-meat restaurants** (*Around Hanoi map; meals from 30,000d*). The street runs along the embankment between Ho Tay (West Lake) and Song Hong (Red River). Even if you have no interest in eating dog meat, it's interesting to cruise this stretch of road on the last evening of the lunar month. Hanoians believe that eating dog meat in the first half of the lunar month brings bad luck. As a consequence, these restaurants are deserted at that time and most of them shut down. Business picks up in the second half of the lunar month and the last day is particularly auspicious so the restaurants are packed. Cruise by in the evening and you'll see thousands of motorbikes parked here. As you drive along, hawkers practically leap out in front of you to extol the virtues of their particular canine specialities.

## Self-Catering

**Old Quarter** One of the best ranges of Western supermarket supplies in the city is found at **Fivimart** (*210 Tran Quang Khai; open 8am-9pm daily*).

**Intimex** supermarket is pretty good too. It's on the western side of Hoan Kiem Lake, almost opposite the main post office, and the entrance is tucked down a driveway behind the Clinique beauty shop.

**Trung Tam Thuong Mai** (*7 Pho Dinh Tien Hoang; open 8am-noon & 1.30pm-7pm daily*) is a well-located grocery shop with some imported Western junk food and drinks. You can enter by the lake or in back.

**Citimart** (*ground floor Hanoi Towers, 49 Hai Ba Trung*) is a supermarket with a decent range of imported goods.

**Central Hanoi** For a quick shop, **Hanoi Star Mart** (*☎ 822 5999; 60 Pho Ngo Thi Nham*) is one of the best minisupermarkets in town. There is a smaller branch next to the Energy Hotel at 30 Pho Ly Thai To.

**Western Canned Foods** (*Pho Ba Trieu*) carries a good range of exactly what it sounds like, plus other dry and refrigerated goods.

More determined self-caterers can buy fresh vegetables at the **Hom Market**, just

HANOI

south of the city centre near the intersection of Pho Hué and Pho Tran Xuan Soan.

## ENTERTAINMENT
### Pubs & Bars

Unless otherwise indicated, the following venues can be found on the Old Quarter map.

**Highway 4** (☎ 926 0639; 5 Pho Hang Tre) is a popular gathering point for members of Hanoi's notorious Minsk Club. This is the place to discover the mystical, medicinal (and intoxicating) qualities of Vietnamese rice wine *(ruou)* – consider sampling the fragrant, fruit-flavoured varieties. The bar boasts a rugged mountain decor and a rooftop terrace, and is an excellent place to find information on motorbiking Vietnam.

**Bar Le Maquis** (☎ 828 2598; 2A Pho Ta Hien) is a cosy little bar and bistro tucked away in the Old Quarter. It's one of the few places you'll find in the area that stays open after 11pm.

**Funky Monkey** (☎ 928 6113; 15b Pho Hang Hanh) is the current alternative hangout for broad-minded adults. It's a bar with pool table, loud music, serious cocktails and is especially lively late on Friday and Saturday.

**GC** (☎ 825 0499; 5 Pho Bao Khanh) and **Polite Pub** (☎ 825 0959) are both next door to each other, and are popular pubs known for their late hours. Pho Bao Khanh is near the northwest corner of Hoan Kiem Lake.

**R&R Tavern** (☎ 971 0498; 47 Pho Lo Su) is run by a mellow American and his Vietnamese wife, who can regale you with friendly conversation and Southeast Asia's best selection of Grateful Dead classics. They also serve up home-cooked meals and if you're stumbling home in the wee hours, or just an early riser, try the *real* buttermilk pancakes for breakfast.

**Met Pub** (☎ 826 6919 ext 8857) is in the new annexe of the Sofitel Metropole Hotel. It's a lovely place with fine food and Hanoi's best beer selection, but it's also expensive.

**Spotted Cow** (Central Hanoi map; ☎ 824 1028; 23C Pho Hai Ba Trung) is a popular Aussie-run pub and is often the gathering point for Hash House Harrier runs.

### Nightclubs

If you want to see how fashionable Vietnamese yuppies 'do the hustle', there are several local discos to check out. These places have a strong tendency to change with the wind, so ask around for what's hot or not during your visit. Most clubs have a cover charge of around US$4.

**New Century Nightclub** (☎ 928 5285; 10 Pho Trang Thi), in the Old Quarter, is all the rage. This club is right out of New York, London or Paris.

**Apocalypse Now** (Central Area map; ☎ 971 2783; 5C Pho Hoa Ma; open 9pm-late) is a legendary bar run by the same family as the one in HCMC. It's best on weekends and is known for its loud and raucous music and street-wise clientele. Apocalypse closes when the last customers trickle away.

### Jazz

**Jazz Club By Quyen Van Minh** (Old Quarter map; Cau Lac Bo; ☎ 825 7655; 31-33 Pho Luong Van Can; performances 8.30pm-11.30pm nightly) is *the* place in Hanoi to catch hot, live jazz (well, mostly jazz). Bar owner Minh teaches saxophone at the Hanoi Conservatory and moonlights here, jamming with a variety of musicians from his students and his talented son to top-notch international jazz players.

### Traditional Music

Some of the best places to catch live traditional music at are upmarket Vietnamese restaurants in central Hanoi, like **Club Opera**, **Nam Phuong** or **Cay Cau** (in the De Syloia Hotel).

There is also live music performed daily at the **Temple of Literature**.

### Classical Music

**Hanoi Opera House** (Nha Hat Lon; Old Quarter map; ☎ 825 4312; Pho Trang Tien) is a magnificent 900-seat venue that faces east up Pho Bao Khanh. It was built in 1911, and its painstaking three-year renovation was recently completed. It was from a balcony on this building that the Viet Minh–run citizens committee announced, on 16 August 1945, that it had taken over the city. Performances of classical music are periodically held here in the evenings in a wonderful atmosphere of decaying grandeur. The theatre's Vietnamese name appropriately translates to 'House Sing Big'. Check the listings in the *Guide* or *Time Out* to find out if anything is happening here during your stay.

## Cinemas

**National Movie Centre** *(Greater Hanoi map; ☎ 514 1114; 87 Pho Lang Ha)* is the newest and best venue to catch foreign films in Hanoi. **Fanslands Cinema** *(Central Hanoi map; ☎ 825 7484; 84 Pho Ly Thuong Kiet)* also screens Western movies.

**Alliance Française de Hanoi** *(☎ 826 6970; 42 Pho Yet Kieu)* screens French films. It's due to move to Pho Trang Tien in 2003.

**Thang 8 Cinema** *(Central Hanoi map; Pho Hang Bai)*, opposite the Immigration Police Office, sometimes shows foreign films.

## Circus Troupes

**Central Circus** *(Rap Xiec Trung Uong; Central Area map; admission US$2.50; shows 8pm-10pm Tues-Sun, 9am Sun)* has performances in a huge tent near the northern entrance to Lenin Park (Cong Vien Le Nin). There is a special show staged for children on Sunday mornings. The circus is one Russian entertainment tradition that has survived and thrived in Vietnam. Performers – gymnasts, jugglers, animal trainers – were originally trained in Eastern Europe, though today's new recruits learn their skills from their Vietnamese elders.

## Water Puppets

This fantastic art form (see the boxed text 'Punch & Judy in a Pool') originated in northern Vietnam, and Hanoi is the best place to see it.

**Municipal Water Puppet Theatre** *(Roi Nuoc Thang Long; Old Quarter map; ☎ 825 5450; 57B Pho Dinh Tien Hoang; admission 40,000-10,000d/US60¢-$2.60, still-camera fee 10,000d, video fee 50,000d; performances at 6.30pm & 8pm daily, 9.30am Sun)* is just near the shore of Hoan Kiem Lake. The higher admission price will get you the best seats and a take-home cassette of the music;

fans and multilingual programmes are free and it helps to read the title of each vignette in the programme as it's performed. Check out the faces of enthralled Vietnamese kids in the audience, they're magic!

## SHOPPING

Whether or not you wish to buy anything, your first encounter will likely be with the children who sell postcards and maps. Of course, they are found all over the country, but in Hanoi many are orphans who have a special card to prove it, which they will immediately show to foreigners. They are also the most notorious overchargers, asking about triple the going price. A reasonable amount of bargaining is called for.

### Markets

In the Old Quarter, the three-storey **Dong Xuan Market** is 900m north of Hoan Kiem Lake. The market burned down in 1994, killing five people (all of whom had entered the building after the fire started, to either rescue goods or steal them). The market has now been rebuilt and is a tourist attraction in its own right. There are hundreds of stalls here, employing around 3000 people.

**Hang Da Market** is a relatively small one, but it is good for imported foods, wine, beer and flowers. The 2nd floor is good for fabric and ready-made clothing. The market is located very close to the Protestant Church.

**Hom Market** *(Central Hanoi map)* is on the northeast corner of Pho Hué and Pho Tran Xuan Soan. It is a good general-purpose market with lots of imported food items and a good place to buy fabric if you plan to have clothes made.

**Cua Nam Market** is a few blocks north of the Hanoi train station. The market itself is of no great interest (except maybe for the flowers), but Đ Le Duan between the market and the train station is a treasure trove of household goods, such as electronics and plasticware. It's a particularly good shopping area if you're setting up a residence in Hanoi.

A couple of kilometres out of town, on the road to the airport, is the **Flower Market** (Cho Hoa). It's at its busiest around 5am,

## Punch & Judy in a Pool

The ancient art of water puppetry *(roi nuoc)* was virtually unknown outside of northern Vietnam until the 1960s. Depending on which story you believe, it originated with rice farmers who spent much of their time in flooded fields and either saw the potential of the water surface as a dynamic stage or adapted conventional puppetry during a massive flood of the Red River Delta. Whatever the true history, it is at least 1000 years old.

The farmers carved the puppets from water-resistant fig-tree timber *(sung)* in forms modelled on the villagers themselves, animals from their daily lives and more fanciful mythical creatures such as the dragon, phoenix and unicorn. Performances were usually staged in ponds, lakes or flooded paddy fields.

Ancient scholarly references to water puppetry indicate that during the Ly and Tran dynasties (1010–1400) water puppetry moved from being a simple pastime of villagers to formal courtly entertainment. The art form then all but disappeared, until interest was rekindled by the opening of the Municipal Water Puppet Theatre in Hanoi.

Contemporary performances use a square tank of waist-deep water for the 'stage'; the water is murky to conceal the mechanisms that operate the puppets. The wooden puppets can be up to 50cm long and weigh as much as 15kg; they're painted with a glossy vegetable-based paint. Each lasts only about three to four months if used continually, so puppet production provides several villages outside Hanoi with a full-time industry.

Eleven puppeteers, trained for a minimum of three years, are involved in each performance. They stand in the water behind a bamboo screen and have traditionally suffered from a host of water-borne diseases – these days they wear waders to avoid this nasty occupational hazard.

Some puppets are simply attached to a long pole, while others are set on a floating base, which in turn is attached to a pole. Most have articulated limbs and heads, some also have rudders to help guide them. There can be as many as three poles attached to one puppet, and in the darkened auditorium it looks as if they are literally walking on water.

The considerable skills required to operate the puppets were traditionally kept secret and passed only from father to son; never to daughters through fear that they would marry outside the village and take the secrets with them.

The music, which is provided by a band, is as important as the action on stage. The band includes wooden flutes *(sao)*, gongs *(cong)*, cylindrical drums *(trong com)*, bamboo xylophones and the fascinating single-stringed *dan bau*. The body of the *dan bau* is made of the hard rind of the *bau*, a Chinese cucumber, and produces a range of haunting notes through the use of a 'whammy bar', a flexible bamboo stem attached to one end of the soundbox, which alters the tension on the string.

The performance consists of a number of vignettes depicting pastoral scenes and legends that explain the origins of various natural and social phenomena from the formation of lakes to the formation of nation states. One memorable scene is a wetly balletic depiction of rice farming in which the rice growing looks like accelerated film footage and the harvesting scenes are frantic and graceful. Another tells of the battle between a fisherman and his prey which is so realistic it appears as if a live fish is being used. There are also fire-breathing dragons (complete with fireworks), a slapstick cat-and-mouse game between a jaguar, a flock of ducks and the ducks' keeper, and a flute-playing boy riding a buffalo.

The performance is unquestionably entertaining. The water puppets are both curiously amusing and graceful, and the water greatly enhances the drama by allowing the puppets to appear and disappear as if by magic. Spectators in the front row seats can expect a bit of splashing.

but if you get there before 7am you can enjoy the frenzy of colours and scents. There's an astonishing skill to stacking and piling masses of bunches of flowers on the back of bicycles and motorbikes, so that they almost totally obscure the driver but still just leave room to see! It's a great photo-opportunity.

In the greater Hanoi region, **Mo Market** is far to the south of the central area, on Pho Bac Mai and Pho Minh Khai. It's not a place for tourists, as the main products are fresh meat, fish and vegetables, but may be of interest to expats who prefer to do their own cooking.

**Buoi Market,** out in the far northwest, is notable for live animals (chickens, ducks, pigs and so on), but also features ornamental plants. You can probably find better-quality ornamental plants for sale at the gardens in front of the Temple of Literature.

## Shops

Around Pho Hang Bong and Pho Hang Gai, just northwest of Hoan Kiem Lake, are plenty of shops selling souvenir T-shirts and Viet Cong (VC) headgear. T-shirts are either printed or embroidered. It might be worth noting, however, that neither Ho Chi Minh T-shirts nor VC headgear are very popular apparel with Vietnamese refugees and certain war veterans living in the West. Wearing such souvenirs while walking down a street in Los Angeles or Melbourne might offend someone and possibly endanger your relationship with the local overseas-Vietnamese community, as well as your dental work.

Pho Hang Gai and its continuation, Pho Hang Bong, are a good place to look for embroidered tablecloths, T-shirts and wall hangings. Pho Hang Gai is also a good place to have clothes custom-made. Take a look along Pho Hang Dao (just north of Hoa Kiem Lake) for souvenir Russian-made watches.

If you don't make it up to Sapa, there is a wide selection of **ethnic-minority garb and handicrafts** available in Hanoi; a stroll along Pho Hang Bac or Pho To Tich will turn up close to a dozen places. **Craft Link** (Central Hanoi map; ☎ 843 7710; 43 Pho Van

Mieu) is a not-for-profit organisation that buys good quality tribal handcrafts and weavings at fair-trade prices, and funds community development initiatives for the artisans.

There is an outstanding **shoe market** (Pho Hang Dau) at the northeast corner of Hoan Kiem Lake; however, it's difficult to find large sizes for big Western feet.

For the best in **CDs and DVDs** (usually about US$2), there are several shops along Pho Hang Bong and Pho Trang Tien. Be aware that they're bootleg, though, so not strictly legal.

On Pho Trang Tien you'll also find many shops willing to make dirt-cheap **eyeglasses** in a mere 10 minutes.

## Designer Boutiques

**La Boutique and the Silk** (Old Quarter map; ☎ 928 5368; 6 Pho Nha Tho), near St Joseph Cathedral, is well worth stopping by. The original designs are inspired by Vietnamese ethnic-minority costumes and made from high-quality Lao silk.

**Khai Silk** (Old Quarter map; ☎ 825 4237; [e] khaisilk@fpt.vn; 96 Pho Hang Gai) is another place in vogue for silk clothing. The proprietor, Khai, is fluent in both French and English, and the clothes are modern and Western in design. There are also Khai Silk branches in the posh Sofitel Metropole and Nikko Hotels.

**Ipa-Nima** (☎ 942 1872; 59G Pho Hai Ba Trung) has a fabulous collection of clothes and what can only be described as designer-kitsch beaded tops and accessories.

Several beautiful **furnishings shops** are located on Pho Nha Tho.

## Galleries

Aspiring young artists display their works in Hanoi's private art galleries in the hope of attracting a buyer. The highest concentration of upmarket galleries is on Pho Trang Tien, between Hoan Kiem Lake and the Opera House – just stroll down the strip. Most art galleries have some English-speaking staff, and are open daily until 8pm or 9pm. Prices range from a few dollars into the thousands, and polite bargaining is the norm.

In a cluster around the Old Quarter corner of Pho Trang Tien and Pho Ngo Quyen are **Gallery Huong Xuyen** (W *www.huong xuyengallery.com)*, which also stocks some beautiful greetings cards; **A Gallery** (W *www .vietnamesepainting.com)*, with both permanent and visiting exhibitions; and **Hanoi Contemporary Art Gallery** (W *www.han oi-artgallery.com)*, with some ceramics as well as paintings. Just about opposite these is **Nam Son Art Gallery** (e *namson@fpt.vn)*, another interesting contemporary exhibition gallery.

Close to the Dan Chu Hotel is the well-established **Hanoi Studio** and **Van Gallery** (W *www.vangallery.com)*.

**Hanoi Gallery** (*110 Hang Bac; open 9am-8pm daily)*, in the Old Quarter, stocks a great selection of old propaganda posters, with translations of the slogans, and mailing tubes for easy carrying or mailing.

## Handicrafts & Antiques

There are quite a number of stores in Hanoi offering new and antique Vietnamese handicrafts (lacquerware, mother-of-pearl inlaid furniture, ceramics, sandalwood statuettes etc), as well as watercolours, oil paintings, prints and assorted antiques (real and fake). Pho Hang Gai, Pho To Tich, Pho Hang Khai and Pho Cau Go are good areas for souvenir hunting.

**Furniture Gallery** (*Old Quarter map; ☎ 826 9769; 8B Pho Ta Hien)* is an enormous warehouse of antiques, paintings, furniture and handicrafts.

**Vietnamese House** (*☎ 826 2455; 92 Hang Bac)*, not far from Furniture Gallery, is a small but attractive shop dealing in a hodgepodge of old and new treasures.

There is a strip of **antique shops** on Duong Le Duan, across from the Nikko Hotel (see Central Area map), but most tend to be overpriced.

## GETTING THERE & AWAY
### Air

Hanoi has fewer direct international flights than HCMC, but with a change of aircraft in Hong Kong or Bangkok you can get to almost anywhere. For further information

about international flights, see the Getting There & Away chapter.

International airlines that have booking offices in Hanoi are listed here. Map references are given for those with specific airline offices and that are likely to be most useful to travellers; contact details are given for other agents that handle several airlines.

**Air France** (Old Quarter map; ☎ 825 3484/824 7066, fax 826 6694) 1 Pho Ba Trieu

**All Nippon Airways** (☎ 934 7237, fax 934 7299) 25 Pho Ly Thuong Kiet

**British Airways** (☎ 934 7239, fax 934 7242) 25 Pho Ly Thuong Kiet

**Cathay Pacific** (Old Quarter map; ☎ 826 7298, fax 826 7709) Hanoi Towers, 49 Hai Ba Trung

**China Airlines** (☎ 824 2688, fax 824 2588) 18 Pho Tran Hung Dao

**China Southern Airlines** (☎ 771 6611, fax 771 6600) 360 Kim Ma

**Emirates Airline** (☎ 934 7240, fax 934 7242) 25 Pho Ly Thuong Kiet

**Japan Airlines** (☎ 826 6693, fax 826 6698) 63 Pho Ly Thai To

**Korean Air** (☎ 934 7236, fax 934 7235) 25 Pho Ly Thuong Kiet

**Malaysia Airlines** (Old Quarter map; ☎ 826 8820, fax 824 2388) Sofitel Metropole Hotel, 15 Pho Ngo Quyen

**Qantas Airways** (☎ 974 7238, fax 974 7242) 25 Ly Thuong Kiet

**Singapore Airlines** (Old Quarter Map; ☎ 826 8888, fax 826 8666) 17 Pho Ngo Quyen

**Thai Airways** (Old Quarter Map; ☎ 826 6893, fax 826 7934) Melia Hotel, 44B Pho Ly Thuong Kiet

**Vasco** (☎ 827 1707, fax 827 2705) Gia Lam Airport

**Vietnam Airlines** (Old Quarter map; ☎ 942 0848, fax 942 0846) 94 Pho Quang Trung

### Bus

Hanoi has several main long-distance bus stations and each one serves a particular area. They are fairly well organised with ticket offices and printed schedules and prices. You'd be well advised to check information and buy tickets the day before you plan to travel.

In central Hanoi, **Kim Ma bus station** (*Ben Xe Kim Ma; Central Hanoi map; cnr Pho Nguyen Thai Hoc & Pho Giang Vo)* is where you get buses to the northwestern part of

Vietnam, including Lao Cai, Sapa and Dien Bien Phu.

**Gia Lam bus station** (Ben Xe Gia Lam) is where you catch buses to points northeast of Hanoi. These include Halong Bay, Haiphong and Lang Son (near the China border). The bus station is 2km northeast of the centre – you have to cross the Red River to get there. Cyclos won't cross the bridge so you need to get there by motorbike or taxi.

**Giap Bat bus station** (Ben Xe Giap Bat; Greater Hanoi map) serves points south of Hanoi, including HCMC. The station is 7km south of the Hanoi train station on Đ Giai Phong.

**Son La bus station** (Ben Xe Son La; Km8, Pho Nguyen Trai), southwest of Hanoi (near Hanoi University), is also a departure point for buses to the northwest (Hoa Binh, Mai Chau, Son La, Tuan Giao, Dien Bien Phu and Lai Chau). Most travellers will find the Kim Ma station more convenient for these destinations.

## Minibus
Tourist-style minibuses can be booked through most hotels and cafés. Popular destinations include Halong Bay and Sapa.

There are frequent minibuses throughout the day to Haiphong (25,000d; two hours) from Gia Lam bus station. Services begin around 5am and the last bus leaves Hanoi at about 6pm. These minibuses depart when full (and they really mean 'full'). In Haiphong, you catch minibuses at the Tam Bac bus station.

## Train
The main **Hanoi train station** (Ga Hang Co; ☎ 825 3949; 120 Đ Le Duan; ticket office open 7.30am-12.30am & 1.30pm-7.30pm) is at the western end of Pho Tran Hung Dao; trains from here go to destinations south. Foreigners can buy tickets for southbound trains at counter two where the staff usually speaks English. It's often best to buy tickets at least one day before departure to ensure a seat or sleeper.

To the right of the main entrance of the train station is a separate ticket office for northbound trains to Lao Cai (for Sapa) and

China. Tickets to China must be bought from counter 13.

However, where you purchase the ticket is not necessarily where the train departs! Just behind the main 'A Station' on Đ Le Duan is **Tran Quy Cap station** (B Station; Pho Tran Qui Cap; ☎ 825 2628) and all northbound trains leave from there.

To make things even more complicated – some northbound (Viet Tri, Yen Bai, Lao Cai, Lang Son) and eastbound (Haiphong) trains depart from **Gia Lam** on the east side of the Red River, and **Long Bien** (☎ 826 8280) on the western (city) side of the river. Be sure to ask just where you need to go to catch your train; you can try phoning for information, but don't expect much English-language help. You can buy tickets at the main station until about two hours before departure; if it's any closer to the departure time, you need to go to the relevant station and buy tickets there.

Check with **Vietnam Rail** (Duong Sat Viet Nam; ⓦ www.vr.com.vn) for the current timetables. For more information on trains see the Getting Around chapter. For information on trains to Haiphong, see the Haiphong section in the Northeast Vietnam chapter.

## Car & Motorbike
To hire a car with a driver, contact a hotel, travellers café or travel agency. The main roads in the northeast are generally OK, but in parts of the northwest they can be awful. For this reason, you may need a high clearance vehicle or a 4WD.

The average cost for a six-day trip in a Russian jeep is US$180, including the jeep, a driver and petrol. These old jeeps fit only two passengers and are truly uncomfortable: they're dusty and hot, or damp and cold, depending on the weather. For a fancier Japanese or Korean air-con 4WD you are looking at paying around double the cost, but if you can afford the comfort, why not have it? You should inquire about who is responsible for the driver's room and board – usually the price will include the driver's expenses, but it's a good idea to clarify this.

Land distances from Hanoi are as follows:

| destination | distance (km) |
| --- | --- |
| Ba Be National Park | 240 |
| Bac Giang | 51 |
| Bac Ninh | 29 |
| Bach Thong (Bac Can) | 162 |
| Cam Pha | 190 |
| Cao Bang | 272 |
| Da Bac (Cho Bo) | 104 |
| Danang | 763 |
| Dien Bien Phu | 420 |
| Ha Dong | 11 |
| Ha Giang | 343 |
| Hai Duong | 58 |
| Haiphong | 103 |
| Halong City | 165 |
| Hoa Binh | 74 |
| HCMC | 1710 |
| Hué | 658 |
| Lai Chau | 490 |
| Lang Son | 146 |
| Lao Cai | 294 |
| Ninh Binh | 93 |
| Sapa | 324 |
| Son La | 308 |
| Tam Dao | 85 |
| Thai Binh | 109 |
| Thai Nguyen | 73 |
| Thanh Hoa | 175 |
| Tuyen Quang | 165 |
| Viet Tri | 73 |
| Vinh | 319 |
| Yen Bai | 155 |

A long-distance journey from Hanoi into the mountainous hinterland of the north is exciting, though slightly risky in terms of traffic accidents, and definitely tiring. You probably wouldn't want to do it during the coldest months (January and February), and in midsummer you have to contend with occasionally heavy rains. Despite such annoyances, many travellers prefer motorbike travel to all other forms of transport.

If you plan to tour the north by bike, see the Motorbike Tours section under Travel Agencies earlier in this chapter. There are several good outfits that can arrange guides, rentals and help with itinerary planning.

The 125cc Russian-made Minsk is the best overall bike for touring the north – you will need that kind of power for the mountainous

regions, and all mechanics know how to fix them. Quality of rental motorbikes can be extremely variable, so try to find a reputable dealer, especially if you're planning long trips. Hanoi's expat community seems to agree that Phung Duc Cuong has got the best bikes in Hanoi; to contact him inquire at Highway 4 (*Old Quarter map;* ☎ *926 0639; 5 Pho Hang Tre*). Cuong rents out, repairs, buys and sells Minsks.

The daily rental cost of a Minsk is around US$5; you may be able to find them for a dollar or so cheaper, but beware of the quality. If you intend to buy a Minsk, remember that it is not necessarily better to buy a new one. Used bikes have been tested, and a well-maintained second-hand bike is often more reliable, and definitely cheaper, than purchasing something new.

There are dozens of motorbike shops along Pho Hué where you can inquire about purchasing a machine. These shops also sell good-quality helmets.

## GETTING AROUND
## To/From the Airport

Hanoi's Noi Bai airport is about 35km north of the city and the journey can take from 45 minutes to an hour. The airport freeway is one of the most modern roads in Vietnam, although you'll see oxen herded by farmers dressed in rags crossing it. The freeway suddenly terminates in the suburbs north of Hanoi.

Vietnam Airlines minibuses between Hanoi and Noi Bai airport charge US$2 a seat. There are few information signs inside the new terminal building; you need to go outside and look for the signs for taxis and minibuses. Coming from the airport, the driver will drop you at the office of Vietnam Airlines at Pho Quang Trung. From here it is a short walk north into the Old Quarter, or you can hire one of the countless cyclo or motorbike drivers to deliver you to your hotel. A ride from here to any place in the city centre should not cost more than 5000d per person; if you can't agree on the fare, just start to walk away – the drivers will likely have a change of heart. Be prepared to pay a bit more if you have heavy bags that the driver needs to balance on the bike.

The airport minibus service works OK but there are a few scams, especially at the airport. Occasionally local touts (well dressed and posing as employees of Vietnam Airlines) board the official minibuses. They are skilled at befriending newly arrived passengers, and by the time you reach the city will offer to recommend a 'good, cheap hotel'. If you want to avoid the sales pitch, just tell them that you've already got a hotel reservation, even if you don't.

To get to the airport from town, you can take one of the minibuses that depart roughly every half-hour from opposite the same Vietnam Airlines office on Pho Quang Trung. It's best – though not essential – to book the day before. Tickets are sold inside the booking office.

**Airport Taxi** (☎ 873 3333) charges US$10 for a taxi ride door-to-door to or from Noi Bai airport. They do *not* require that you pay the toll for the bridge you cross en route. Some other taxi drivers require that you pay the toll, so ask first.

Inside the terminal, touts will offer taxi services. The 'official' taxi rank is outside the concourse and you buy tickets from the seller at the head of the taxi line. There is presently no booking desk as such in the new terminal building, but this may change.

In central Hanoi, there is always a collection of taxi drivers just outside the Vietnam Airlines office – it doesn't take much effort to find one. Don't pay more than US$10, including the toll.

There are share cabs/private minibuses from travellers' cafés for about US$2.

The Hanoi public bus company has started a service from the airport, which stops at the Daewoo Hotel and then goes onto the Opera House. Line No 7 (2500d) departs every 15 or 20 minutes, between 5am and 9pm daily. It's worth considering as it's cheaper than the taxi.

### Bus

There are 31 public bus lines in Hanoi. Figuring out exactly where the buses go can be a challenge, and service on some of the lines

is infrequent. Still, when it comes to economy, only walking is cheaper. Bus fares are typically 1000d depending on the route.

A long-awaited city bus-route guide was published in 2001. Presently, the only place to get a copy is from the **Traffic Management Center** (16 Cao Ba Quat; ☎ 747 0403; e hncauduong@fpt.vn). The guide also shows interprovincial routes and bus interchanges.

### Motorbike

Though many travellers have rented motorbikes and scooters to tour Hanoi, it is *not* recommended that you drive in the city. It's extremely dangerous for someone who isn't accustomed to Vietnamese driving style, not to mention dealing with the hassles of traffic, parking, and so on. It's also easy to unknowingly violate road rules, which the police will happily remind you of.

If you are set on exploring Hanoi on two wheels, do it on a bicycle.

### Taxi

There are several companies in Hanoi offering metered taxi services. All charge similar rates. Flag fall is about 2500d, which takes you 2km; every kilometre thereafter costs about 5000d. Competitors in this business include the following companies.

| | |
|---|---|
| Airport Taxi | ☎ 873 3333 |
| City Taxi | ☎ 822 2222 |
| Red Taxi | ☎ 856 8686 |
| Taxi PT | ☎ 856 5656 |
| Viet Phuong Taxi | ☎ 828 2828 |

### Bicycle

A good way to get around Hanoi is by bicycle. Many hotels and cafés offer these for rent for about US$1 per day.

If you want to purchase your own set of wheels, Pho Ba Trieu and Pho Hué are the best places to look for bicycle shops (see the Central Hanoi map).

### Cyclo

The cyclos in Hanoi are wider than the HCMC variety, making it possible for two people to fit in one vehicle and share the fare. One common cyclo driver's ploy when carrying two passengers is to agree on a price, and then *double* it upon arrival gesturing 'no, no, no...that was per person'.

In any case, you should pay around 5000d per person for a journey in the city centre. Longer rides (for example from the Old Quarter to Ho Chi Minh's Mausoleum) can be as much as double that. Try to negotiate in dong, not dollars. You'll also find that a little bit of Vietnamese goes a long way when talking about prices.

The cyclo drivers in Hanoi are even less likely to speak English than in HCMC, so take a map of the city with you. A notebook and pencil to write your destination and to negotiate prices is useful! It's a thankless job, so don't agonise too much about giving a cyclo driver that extra thousand dong or so.

### Motorbike Taxi
You won't have any trouble finding a *xe om* in Hanoi. Just stroll along any major street and you'll get an offer from a driver almost every 10 seconds.

The official cost for a *xe om* is 1000d per kilometre. In reality, tourists are expected to pay around 5000d per person for rides in the city centre, or 10,000d for longer rides.

# Around Hanoi

## HO CHI MINH TRAIL MUSEUM
The Ho Chi Minh Trail Museum (*Bao Tang Duong Ho Chi Minh; Hwy 6; admission 10,000d; open 7.30am-11am & 1.30pm-4pm Tues-Sun*) is about 13km southwest of Hanoi. It can be combined with a visit to Van Phuc handicraft village, or visited on the way to the Perfume Pagoda (see later in this section).

## PERFUME PAGODA
The Perfume Pagoda (*Chua Huong; admission 17,000d plus 8000d return boat trip*) is about 60km southwest of Hanoi by road. It is a complex of pagodas and Buddhist shrines built into the limestone cliffs of Huong Tich Mountain (Mountain of the Fragrant Traces). Among the better known sites here are Thien Chu (Pagoda Leading to Heaven); Giai Oan Chu (Purgatorial Pagoda), where the faithful believe deities purify souls, cure sufferings and grant offspring to childless families; and Huong Tich Chu (Pagoda of the Perfumed Vestige).

The fun boat trip along the scenic waterways between limestone cliffs takes about two-hours return, and allow yourself an additional two or three hours return to climb to the top. A word of warning: bring good walking shoes! The path to the top is steep in places and if it's raining the ground can get *very* slippery.

Great numbers of Buddhist pilgrims come here during a festival that begins in the middle of the second lunar month and lasts until the last week of the third lunar month (usually corresponding to March and April). It's *very* busy during this period, especially on the even dates of the lunar month; you'll have a much easier time if you establish the lunar date, and plan to go on an odd date. In 2002, on the particularly auspicious sixth day of the first lunar month, 3000 boats crammed the waterway and there was a boat jam that lasted from noon until 9pm! Weekends tend to draw crowds all year, when pilgrims and other visitors spend their time boating, hiking and exploring the caves. Litter and noisy stalls and hawkers are part and parcel of the visit; you have been warned.

### Getting There & Away
Getting to the pagoda requires a journey first by road, then by river, then by foot.

First, you will need to travel from Hanoi by car for two hours to the township of My Duc. Vehicles usually drop you about a 15-minute walk from the boat ramp, or hop on a *xe om* for 2000d. Then take a small boat, usually rowed by women, for one to 1½ hours to the foot of the mountain.

The main pagoda area is about a 4km steep hike up from where the boat lets you off. Allow yourself at least two hours to make the return trip, longer if it's been raining and is slippery. The combined fee for the boat journey and general admission ticket is 28,000d; if you want to charter a boat to go

Ho Chi Minh's Mausoleum, in Hanoi, is a place of pilgrimage for many

Passing traffic near Hoan Kiem Lake in Hanoi

Hanoi's Temple of Literature

A boatman near the Perfume Pagoda outside Hanoi

Pottery from Bat Trang, Hanoi

The lotus is a symbol of purity

One of Hanoi's many pagodas

The carp-filled pond of the Presidential Palace in Hanoi

up and back at your convenience, it will cost you an extra 45,000d. Negotiate this while still at the boat ramp itself – the ticket office at the main entrance tries to charge 200,000d! The return trip to your vehicle is also by rowboat.

Most of the travellers' cafés in Hanoi offer inexpensive tours to the pagoda. You can find day trips as cheap as US$9 or US$10, inclusive of transport, guide and lunch. For a better quality tour (ie, a smaller group as well as a more comfortable vehicle) expect to spend around US$14 to US$16. Take a tour! Unless you charter a

vehicle, it's a real pain trying to do this trip by public transport.

## HANDICRAFT VILLAGES

There are numerous villages surrounding Hanoi that specialise in particular cottage industries. Visiting these villages can make for a rewarding day trip, though you will need a good guide to make the journey worthwhile.

**Bat Trang** is known as the 'ceramic village'. You can see artisans mass-produce ceramic vases and other pieces in their kilns. It's hot sweaty work, but the results are

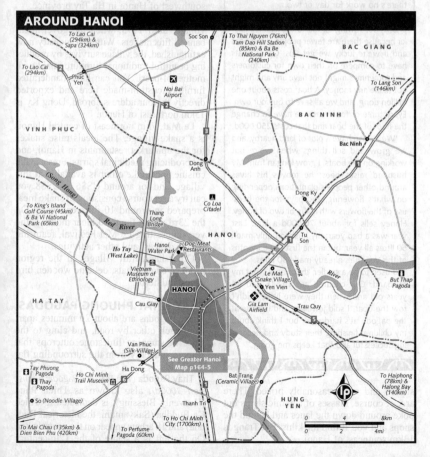

**AROUND HANOI**

To Lao Cai (294km) & Sapa (324km)

Soc Son

To Thai Nguyen (76km); Tam Dao Hill Station (85km) & Ba Be National Park (240km)

BAC GIANG

To Lao Cai (294km)

Phúc Yen

Noi Bai Airport

To Lang Son (146km)

VINH PHUC

BAC NINH

Bac Ninh

Dong Anh

Dong Ky

(Song Hong)

To King's Island Golf Course (45km) & Ba Vi National Park (65km)

Red River

Thang Long Bridge

Co Loa Citadel

HANOI

Tu Son

Ho Tay (West Lake)

Hanoi Water Park

Dog-Meat Restaurants

Vietnam Museum of Ethnology

HANOI

Duong River

Le Mat (Snake Village)

Yen Vien

But Thap Pagoda

HA TAY

Cau Giay

Gia Lam Airfield

Trau Quy

Van Phuc (Silk Village)

See Greater Hanoi Map p164-5

Tay Phuong Pagoda

Thay Pagoda

Ho Chi Minh Trail Museum

Ha Dong

Bat Trang (Ceramic Village)

To Haiphong (78km) & Halong Bay (140km)

So (Noodle Village)

Thanh Tri

HUNG YEN

To Mai Chau (135km) & Dien Bien Phu (420km)

To Perfume Pagoda (60km)

To Ho Chi Minh City (1700km)

0        4        8km
0    2    4mi

**HANOI**

## Mrs Thuyen, Boat Woman

'I've rowed tourists to the Perfume Pagoda for about two years now. Our boat group is made up of 27 boats rowed by women who all belong to martyr's families – our husbands or fathers or children were killed or injured in the war. There are more than 100 of us in the same group, but only 27 of us are allowed to work at one time, so there's an annual lottery to establish which of us will row each year. So I may not work every year, but when I do it's consistent and I get paid 15,000d every day, regardless of how many trips I do, or even if there's no work for day or two.

'You see our group of martyrs' families has priority for rowing all the foreigners. It's easier because there are fewer people in the boat and if we're lucky we get tips. Other boats have to compete on their own for customers and sometimes might not have any and might not make any money. A boat costs about one million dong, and we all save to buy our own. Every three or four years we have to change the floor of the boat and that costs 250,000d.

'We all also have a plot of land nearby, and we grow and sell things when we're not working on the boats. I grow longan fruit. My husband raises bees; he moves his hives around other people's plantations depending on what's flowering, and pays for the bees' use of the flowers with a litre or two of honey. Honey sells for about 70,000d a litre. Last year was a bad year; my husband only made 50 litres all year, but in the first three months of this year he's already made 30 litres.

'I used to be a soldier, that's how I met my husband. Our children are 19, 16 and 14 years old and when they were little I didn't row the boat, I sold jewellery and incense at the pagoda. It's hard work but I think about my children finishing their study and becoming successful and that keeps me going.'

superb and very reasonably priced. There are, of course, masses of ceramic shops but poke around down the lanes and behind the shops and you'll find the kilns. Bat Trang is 13km southeast of Hanoi.

**So** is known for its delicate noodles. The village even produces the flour from which the noodles are made. The flour is made from yams and cassava (manioc) rather than wheat. So is in Ha Tay province, about 25km southwest of Hanoi.

**Van Phuc** is a silk village. You can see silk cloth being produced on a loom, and buy or order custom-made clothes. Many of the fine silk items you see on sale in Hanoi's Pho Hang Gai originate here. There's a small daily fruit-and-vegetable market here in the morning, and a village pagoda with a lily pond. Van Phuc is 8km southwest of Hanoi in Ha Tay province.

**Dong Ky** was known as the 'firecracker village' until 1995, when the government banned firecrackers. With that industry now extinguished, the village survives by producing beautiful traditional furniture inlaid with mother-of-pearl. You can have handcrafted furniture custom-made here and exported directly to your address abroad. Dong Ky is 15km northeast of Hanoi.

**Le Mat**, 7km northeast of central Hanoi, is a snake village. The locals raise snakes for the upmarket restaurants in Hanoi, and for producing medicinal spirits. Fresh snake cuisine and snake elixir is available at this village, and for around US$6 or US$8 you can try a set course consisting of snake meat prepared in around 10 different ways. On the 23rd day of the third lunar month is the very interesting Le Mat Festival, featuring 'snake dances' and other activities.

Other handicraft villages in the region produce conical hats, delicate wooden bird cages and herbs.

## THAY & TAY PHUONG PAGODAS

These pagodas are about 20 minutes apart from each other by road, and cling to the sides of stunning limestone outcrops that emerge suddenly from the surrounding flat rice fields.

**Thay Pagoda** (The Master's Pagoda; admission 3000d), also known as Thien Phuc (Heavenly Blessing), is dedicated to Thich Ca Buddha (Sakyamuni, the historical Buddha) and 18 arhats appear on the central altar. On the left is a statue of the 12th-century monk Tu Dao Hanh, the master after whom the pagoda is named; on the right is a statue of King Ly Nhan Tong, who is believed to have been a reincarnation of Tu Dao Hanh. In front of the pagoda is a small stage built on stilts in the middle of a pond; the water-puppet shows are staged here for festivals. Follow the path around the outside of the main pagoda building, and take a steep 10-minute climb up to a beautiful smaller pagoda perched high on the rock. Thay Pagoda is a big and confusing complex for non-Buddhists – you may want to hire a pagoda guide to get the most from a visit.

The pagoda's annual festival is held from the fifth to the seventh days of the third lunar month. Pilgrims and other visitors enjoy watching water-puppet shows, hiking and exploring caves in the area.

Tay Phuong Pagoda (Pagoda of the West; admission 3000d), also known as Sung Phuc Pagoda, consists of three single-level structures built in descending order, on a hillock said to resemble a buffalo. The figures representing 'the conditions of man' are carved from jackfruit wood, many dating from the 18th century, and are the pagoda's most celebrated feature. The earliest construction here dates from the 8th century. Take the steep steps up to the main pagoda building, then find a path at the back that loops down past the other two pagodas and wanders through the hillside village that surrounds the complex. At the base, return to the car park a couple of hundred metres to your right.

## Getting There & Away

The pagodas are about 30km southwest of Hanoi in Ha Tay province. Hanoi's cafés catering to budget travellers can arrange combined day tours of the Thay and Tay Phuong Pagodas. Alternatively, you could hire a car and driver for US$30, and make a good day tour combining the pagodas and Ba Vi National Park.

## BA VI NATIONAL PARK
☎ 034

Ba Vi National Park (☎ 881205; admission 6000d) is centred on scenic Ba Vi Mountain

(Nui Ba Vi) and attracts Hanoians looking for a weekend escape from the city. The park has several rare and endangered plants in its protected forest, and its mammals include two species of rare 'flying' squirrel. Human encroachment on the area has made the chances of seeing any of them pretty rare.

There's an orchid garden and a bird garden, and hiking opportunities through the forested slopes of the mountain. There's also a temple to Uncle Ho at the mountain's summit (1276m) – it's a hard but beautiful 30-minute climb up 1229 steps through the forest – with spectacular views of the Red River valley and Hanoi in the distance. At least there are views between April and December when the air is clear; at other times it's damp and misty but eerily atmospheric. The road to the summit car park is scarily steep, slippery and narrow, but road widening was due for completion by 2003.

Ba Vi Guesthouse (☎ 881197; rooms with fan/air-con US$8/10) in the park rents rooms with bath. Prices go up about US$2 per room on weekends, and there's a big swimming pool used in the summer months. Ask for one of the less-noisy guesthouses away from the pool and restaurant area if you're there on a weekend. You must have your passport with you to check into the guesthouse here; one traveller we know of was sent back to Hanoi because he had forgotten to bring it along. Even if you don't stay here, check out the fantastic, creative English-language version of the guesthouse rules in the guest rooms!

Despite its unpromising appearance, the park restaurant serves good, cheap, fresh-cooked food; a tasty meal for three costs around 35,000d so make this your lunch stop if you're on a day tour, combining the park with Thay and Tay Phuong Pagodas. The toilets are disgusting – pee behind a tree.

Ba Vi National Park is about 65km west of Hanoi, and presently the only practical option for visiting is by hired vehicle (see the Thay & Tay Phuong Pagodas section). You could check with the travel cafés in Hanoi to see if any day tours are operating.

There has been some confusion between attractions near Ba Vi town, which is well away from the park boundaries, and Ba Vi National Park. The waterfall at Ao Vua (King's Pond) is near Ba Vi town, and about 14km further north are Suoi Mo cold springs. These are more developed and very busy at weekends, so make sure your driver knows which destination you want.

## CO LOA CITADEL

Co Loa Citadel *(Co Loa Thanh; admission 2000d per person, 5000d per car; open 8am-5pm daily)*, the first fortified citadel ever recorded in Vietnamese history, dates from the 3rd century BC and became the national capital during the reign of Ngo Quyen (AD 939–44). Only vestiges of the massive ancient ramparts, which enclosed an area of about 5 sq km, remain. In the centre of the citadel are temples dedicated to the rule of King An Duong Vuong (257–208 BC), who founded the legendary Thuc dynasty, and his daughter My Nuong (Mi Chau). When My Nuong showed her father's magic crossbow trigger (which made the Vietnamese king invincible in battle) to her husband (who was the son of a Chinese general), he stole it and gave it to his father. With its help, the Chinese were then able to defeat An Duong Vuong and his forces, thus depriving Vietnam of its independence.

Co Loa Citadel is 16km north of central Hanoi in Dong Anh district, and can be visited as a short detour while on the way to or from Tam Dao.

## TAM DAO HILL STATION

☎ 0211 • elevation 930m

Tam Dao Hill Station was founded by the French in 1907. It was a popular place of escape from the heat of the Red River Delta, and became known to them as the Cascade d'Argent (Silver Waterfall, or Thac Bac). Most of the grand old colonial villas were destroyed during the war in the 1950s and the ruins have since been replaced by Soviet-inspired, concrete-box architecture. A somewhat belated effort to restore some of the colonial villas is now under way.

Hanoi residents sometimes call Tam Dao 'the Dalat of the north'. This has more to do with its high elevation and cool climate than

any resemblance to Dalat. If you're living in Hanoi and would like to find a summer weekend retreat, it's worth heading up for the cool weather and a change of pace. However, unless you plan to do some serious hiking or bird-watching, there really isn't that much to see and do here. Except, that is, to spend hours listening to loud karaoke ricochet around the valley from the bars. If you are planning to visit the mountains elsewhere in Vietnam, you won't miss much by passing up Tam Dao.

**Tam Dao National Park** was designated in 1996 and covers much of the area. Tam Dao means 'Three Islands', and the three summits of Tam Dao Mountain, all about 1400m in height, are sometimes visible to the northeast of the hill station, floating like islands in the mist. The relative dampness and altitude makes the area particularly rich in rainforest and associated animals. There are at least 64 mammal species – including langurs – and 239 bird species in the park, but you'll need a good local guide, and be prepared to do some hiking to look for them. Illegal hunting remains a big problem. Many of the bars in Tam Dao offer rice wines with, variously, whole birds, reptiles or small mammals from the park pickled in it; it's not uncommon for tourists to be offered live wildlife for sale. Logging, both legal and otherwise, has also had a serious impact on the environment. Some hill-tribe people live in the Tam Dao region, though the communities are less prominent than they used to be.

Remember that it is cool up in Tam Dao and that this part of Vietnam has a distinct winter. Don't be caught unprepared. Hikes vary from half an hour return to the waterfall, to eight hours into primary rainforest. A guide is essential for the longer treks and can be hired for about 50,000d; inquire about these at the Mela Hotel. Generally the best time to visit is between late April and mid-October, when the mist sometimes lifts and the weather can be fine. As with other popular sites in Vietnam, weekends can be packed with Vietnamese tour groups, so try to make your visit during the week if possible.

## Places to Stay & Eat

There are many hotels and guesthouses in Tam Dao, charging anything from 80,000d to US$65. You can walk around the town in less than ten minutes, so look around, negotiate, and watch out for neighbouring karaoke bars.

**Mela Hotel** *(☎/fax 824352; rooms US$45-65)* is as stylish and elegant as the price suggests, and is a favoured haunt for Hanoi expats. In fact it's the only stylish and elegant place in town.

**Anh Dao Hotel** *(☎ 824309; rooms 120,000-150,000d)* is tatty but fine for the price. The rooms are good-sized and some have balconies.

**Nha Nghi Suoi Bac** *(☎ 824275; rooms 80,000-100,000d)* is a tiny, basic, three-room guesthouse next to a small spring. It's

included here as one of the few lodgings that, at time of writing, doesn't have a karaoke machine.

There are **hotel restaurants** and **com pho** places in town. Try to avoid eating the local wildlife if you can.

## Getting There & Away

Tam Dao National Park is 85km northwest of Hanoi in Vinh Phuc province. Buses run from **Kim Ma bus station** in Hanoi to Vinh Yen (one hour). From there you can hire a motorbike (about 30,000d) to travel the 24km single-lane road that leads to the national park.

Hiring a car and driver for the day from Hanoi will cost about US$40. If you rent a motorbike in Hanoi, the journey time is about two hours.

# Northeast Vietnam

Dominated by the Red River basin and the sea, the fertile northeast is the cradle of Vietnamese civilisation. Much of Vietnamese history, not all of it happy, was made here. In particular, Vietnam had less than cordial relations with the Chinese, who invaded in the 2nd century BC and stayed for about 1000 years. Indeed, the last invasion took place as recently as 1979 (see the boxed text 'Playing for High Stakes' in this chapter).

On a more positive note, this part of Vietnam is showing real economic potential. Much investor interest centres on Haiphong, Vietnam's largest seaport. However, it's the scenery, not the history, politics or economics, that is the major tourist drawcard here. In particular, the spectacular coastline of Halong Bay, Bai Tu Long Bay and Cat Ba Island offer some of nature's more bizarre and beautiful geologic displays. Add to that the Ba Be Lakes, the mountains around Cao Bang, the region's Montagnard inhabitants and its accessibility to China, and it's not hard to see why Vietnam's northeast is a major magnet for visitors.

## CON SON & DEN KIEP BAC
These places are perhaps of more interest to domestic travellers than foreigners, but make good stops for a couple of hours en route to Haiphong or Halong City.

Con Son was home to Nguyen Trai (1380–1442), the famed Vietnamese poet, writer and general. Nguyen Trai assisted Emperor Le Loi in his successful battle against the Chinese Ming dynasty in the 13th century. Con Son pagoda complex *(admission 3000d per person & 5000d per vehicle)* has a temple honouring Nguyen Trai atop a nearby mountain. It's a 600-step climb to reach it, so you'll get some exercise if you visit. Alternatively, you can take the loop walk past a spring, heading up through pine woods, and return down the steps. It's a lovely walk if you keep your eyes above the litter on the ground.

## Highlights

- Cruise the emerald waters of Halong Bay and explore some of the 3000-plus islets and grottoes of this magnificent Unesco World Heritage site
- Relax on the beaches of Cat Ba Island, or trek through its scenic and untamed national park
- Discover the lakes, rivers, waterfalls and caves in Ba Be National Park from the comfort of a boat
- Explore the beautiful, remote and little-visited waterfalls, caves and historical sites around Cao Bang on the Chinese border

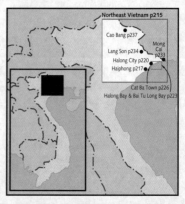

Northeast Vietnam p215
Cao Bang p237
Mong Cai p233
Lang Son p234
Halong City p220
Haiphong p217
Cat Ba Town p226
Halong Bay & Bai Tu Long Bay p223

Several kilometres away, Den Kiep Bac *(Kiep Bac Temple; admission 2000d per person & 5000d per vehicle)* is dedicated to Tran Hung Dao (1228–1300). He was an outstanding general of renowned bravery, whose armies defeated 300,000 Mongol invaders in the mid-1280s. Perhaps second only to Ho Chi Minh, he is a revered Vietnamese folk hero.

This beautiful temple was founded in 1300 and built on the site where Tran Hung

Dao is said to have died. The temple was built not only for the general, but also to honour other notable members of his family. One was the general's daughter, Quyen Thanh, who married Tran Nhat Ton, the person credited with founding the Vietnamese sect of Buddhism called Truc Lam.

Within the temple complex there's a small exhibition on Tran Hung Dao's exploits, but you'll need someone who speaks Vietnamese to translate the information. The **Tran Hung Dao Festival** is held at Den Kiep Bac every year from the 18th to the 20th day of the eighth lunar month.

Den Kiep Bac and Con Son are in Hai Duong province, about 80km from Hanoi. If you have your own transport, you can easily visit on the way to Haiphong or Halong Bay. There are several **hotels** and **guesthouses** in the immediate area.

## HAIPHONG
☎ 031 • pop 1,667,600
By expanding its city limits, Haiphong has become Vietnam's third-most-populous city. It is the north's main industrial centre and one of the country's most important seaports.

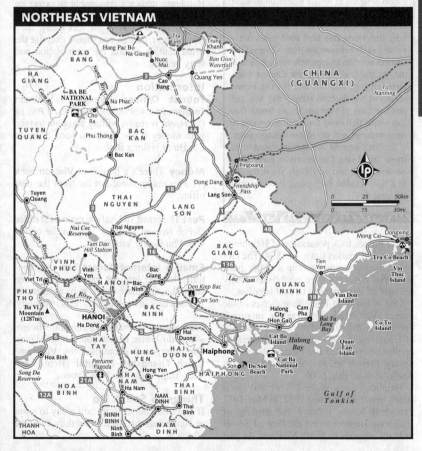

**NORTHEAST VIETNAM**

## Playing for High Stakes

A military general and one of Vietnam's greatest heroes, Tran Hung Dao (1226–1300) three times defeated the Mongol warriors of the Chinese army as they attempted to invade Vietnam.

His most famous victory was at the Bach Dang River in northeastern Vietnam in 1288 where, copying the military strategy of Ngo Quyen (who had regained Vietnam's independence in 939, after 1000 years of Chinese rule), he retained that independence.

After dark, sharpened bamboo poles – of a length designed to remain hidden underwater at high tide – were set vertically in the river, near the bank where it was shallow. On high tide, Tran Hung Dao sent small boats out – passing easily between the posts – to goad the Chinese warships to approach, which they duly did. As the tide receded, the Chinese boats were left high and dry, and flaming arrows destroyed the fleet. In Halong Bay you can visit the Cave of Wooden Stakes (Hang Dau Go) where Tran Hung Dao's forces are said to have prepared and stored the bamboo poles.

So that's why he is commemorated in all those Tran Hung Dao streets in every Vietnamese town, and why every street parallel to a river is called Bach Dang, in memory of the victory.

---

The French took possession of Haiphong, then a small market town, in 1874. The city soon developed and became a major port; industrial concerns were established partly because of its proximity to coal supplies.

One of the most immediate causes of the Franco–Viet Minh War was the infamous French bombardment of the 'native quarters' of Haiphong in 1946, in which hundreds of civilians were killed and injured. A contemporary French account estimated civilian deaths at more than 6000.

Haiphong came under US air and naval attack between 1965 and 1972. In May 1972 President Nixon ordered the mining of Haiphong Harbour to cut the flow of Soviet military supplies to North Vietnam. As part of the Paris cease-fire accords of 1973, the USA agreed to help clear the mines from Haiphong Harbour – 10 US navy minesweepers were involved in the effort.

Since the late 1970s Haiphong has experienced a massive exodus, including many ethnic-Chinese refugees, who have taken much of the city's fishing fleet with them.

Despite being a major port and one of Vietnam's largest cities, Haiphong today is a relatively sleepy place with little traffic and many beautiful French-colonial buildings. It's clean, and there's an air of prosperity. While it may not be worth a special trip, Haiphong makes a reasonable stopover en route to/from Cat Ba Island or Halong Bay. In general, the city is far less hassle than many others, though you should exercise the usual caution around the train station and ferry landing.

### Information

**Tourist Offices** Haiphong's **Vietnam Tourism** (☎ 842957, fax 842974; 20 Pho Le Dai Hanh) is ready, willing and able to take your money if you'd like to book a trip to Cat Ba or Halong Bay.

**Money** There's a branch of **Vietcombank** (11 Pho Hoang Dieu) not far from the post office.

**Post** The grand, old, yellow **main post office** (3 Pho Nguyen Tri Phuong) is on the corner with Pho Hoang Van Thu.

**Email & Internet Access** There are centrally located **Internet cafés** on Pho Dien Bien Phu, and there seems to be at least one Internet café in most other streets in the city.

**Emergency** If you need medical treatment, you'd do better to get yourself to Hanoi. For emergency situations, the **Vietnam-Czech Friendship Hospital** (Benh Vien Viet–Tiep) is on Pho Nha Thuong.

### Things to See & Do

If you find yourself with half a day to spare in Haiphong, there are a few things to take a look at.

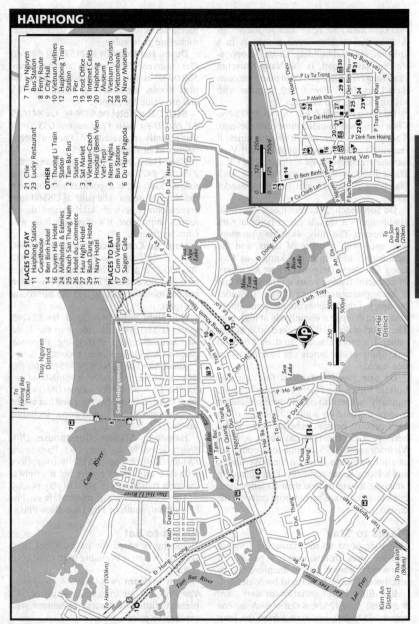

# HAIPHONG

**PLACES TO STAY**
11  Haiphong Station Guesthouse
14  Ben Binh Hotel
16  Duyen Hai Hotel
24  Minihotels & Eateries
25  Khach San Thang Nam
26  Hotel du Commerce
27  Huu Nghi Hotel
29  Bach Dang Hotel
31  Navy Hotel

**PLACES TO EAT**
17  Com Vietnam
19  Saigon Cafe
21  Chie
23  Lucky Restaurant

**OTHER**
1  Thuong Li Train Station
2  Tam Bac Bus Station
3  Sat Market
4  Vietnam-Czech Hospital (Benh Vien Viet-Tiep)
5  Niem Nghia
6  Du Hang Pagoda
7  Thuy Nguyen Bus Station Ferry Route
8  City Hall
9  Haiphong
10  Vietnam Airlines
12  Haiphong Train Station
13  Pier
15  Post Office
18  Internet Cafés
20  Haiphong Museum
22  Vietnam Tourism
28  Vietcombank
30  Navy Museum

**NORTHEAST VIETNAM**

**Haiphong Museum** *(Bao Tang Hai Phong; Pho Dien Bien Phu; open 8am-10.30am Tues & Thur, 8pm-9.30pm Wed & Sun)* is in a splendid colonial building. Close by, opposite the Navy Hotel, is the **Navy Museum** *(Bao Tang Hai Quan; Pho Dien Bien Phu; open 8am-11am Tues, Thur & Sat)*, popular with visiting sailors and veterans.

**Du Hang Pagoda** *(Chua Du Hang; 121 Pho Chua Hang)* was founded three centuries ago. Though it has been rebuilt several times, it remains a good example of traditional Vietnamese architecture and sculpture. Pho Chua Hang itself is narrow and bustling with Haiphong street life, and is fun to wander along.

**Do Son Beach**, 21km southeast of central Haiphong, is a seaside resort popular with Vietnamese. The hilly, 4km-long promontory ends with a string of islets, and the peninsula's nine hills are known as Cuu Long Son (Nine Dragons). There are plenty of colourful fishing boats on the water, and a long promenade lined with oleander bushes, but the beaches are disappointingly small and disappear completely at high tide. The resort is not all it's cracked up to be (or, rather, it's more cracked up than it used to be). Many of the hotels are looking rather dog-eared.

**Do Son town** is famous for its ritual **buffalo fights**, the finals of which are held annually on the 10th day of the eighth lunar month, the date on which the leader of an 18th-century peasant rebellion was killed here. In 1994 the first **casino** to open in Vietnam since 1975 commenced operation as a joint venture between the government and a Hong Kong company. Foreigners are welcome to win or lose their fortunes here, but Vietnamese are barred from entering the casino.

## Places to Stay

Haiphong hosts up to a thousand Chinese tourists – bus groups, mostly – per day. If you want to stay in one of the more expensive hotels, you'd be wise to book ahead.

**Ben Binh Hotel** *(Nha Khach Ben Binh; ☎ 842260, fax 842524; 6 Đ Ben Binh; air-con rooms US$15-25)*, just across from the ferry station, is an enormous place. The cheaper rooms are scruffy, though the larger US$25 rooms are good value.

**Duyen Hai Hotel** *(☎ 842157, fax 841140; Pho Nguyen Tri Phuong; air-con rooms 150,000d)* is a five-minute walk from the pier. Rooms are small but clean, have TV and are value for money.

**Bach Dang Hotel** *(☎ 842444, fax 841625; 42 Pho Dien Bien Phu; rooms US$20-35)* was recently renovated and is now a decent, international-standard hotel.

**Navy Hotel** *(Khach San Hai Quan; ☎ 823 713, fax 842278; 27C Pho Dien Bien Phu; rooms US$20-60)* is a spacious hotel opposite the Navy Museum. The palatial US$60 suite comes complete with kitchen and dining room – impressive. It's often *very* busy with Chinese groups.

**Hotel du Commerce** *(☎ 842706, fax 842 560; 62 Pho Dien Bien Phu; rooms 150,000-300,000d)* is a French-era hotel. There's a nice 2nd-floor shared balcony at this place, but the rooms are stuffy and the bathrooms are grim.

**Huu Nghi Hotel** *(☎ 823310, fax 823245; rooms US$50-300)*, next door to the Hotel du Commerce, is a snazzy, big, three-star place with well-appointed rooms.

**Khach San Thang Nam** *(☎ 745432, fax 745 674; ℮ vntourism.hp@bdvn.vnmail.vnd.net; 55 Pho Dien Bien Phu; rooms 170,000d)* is great value. It opened in 2002 and has bright, clean rooms and all mod cons, including satellite TV.

**Haiphong Station Guesthouse** *(Nha Khach Ga Hai Phong; ☎ 855391; 75 Đ Luong Khanh Thien; rooms US$15)* is overpriced with its musty, dingy rooms, but it's right at the train station, if you need to stay nearby.

There are masses of **minihotels** on Pho Minh Khai, south of Pho Dien Bien Phu.

## Places to Eat

Haiphong is noted for its excellent fresh seafood, which is available from most hotel restaurants.

**Com Vietnam** *(☎ 841698; 4 Pho Hoang Van Thu)*, not far from the post office, is a pleasant little Vietnamese restaurant with reasonable prices.

**Lucky Restaurant** *(☎ 842009; 22-B2 Pho Minh Khai)* is much the same, and is in the middle of a swag of **cheap eateries** on Pho Minh Khai.

**Chie** *(☎ 823327; 64 Pho Dien Bien Phu; meals around US$10)* has great Japanese food that's worth treating yourself to, if you're hanging out for sushi and the like.

**Saigon Cafe** *(cnr Pho Dien Bien Phu & Pho Dinh Tien Hoang)* is a loungey café with live music some evenings.

## Getting There & Away

**Air** Only **Vietnam Airlines** *(☒ www.vietnam air.com.vn; near cnr Pho Tran Phu & Pho Pham Ngu Lao)* flies the Haiphong– Ho Chi Minh City (HCMC) and Haiphong– Danang routes; check current schedules.

**Bus** Haiphong has three long-distance bus stations.

Buses to Hanoi (25,000d, two hours) leave from **Tam Bac bus station**, about every 10 minutes between 4.50am and 7pm. Buses to Vinh (45,000d, seven hours), the junction town for Cau Treo on the Lao border, leave several times a day.

Buses to HCMC (193,000d, 42 hours) via Nha Trang and other southern points leave from **Niem Nghia bus station**. Two buses leave daily at 6am and 8.30am.

The station for buses to Bai Chay (in Halong City), and for Mong Cai on the Chinese border, is in the Thuy Nguyen district, on the northern bank of the Cam River. To reach it, you must take a ferry, and then, as it's tucked in a back street, you'd be wise to get a *xe om* to take you there. It's much easier, quicker and more comfortable to access both these cities by boat.

**Train** Haiphong is not on the main line between Hanoi and HCMC, but there is a spur line connecting it to Hanoi. There's one express train daily to Hanoi's B Station (22,000d, two hours) at 6.10pm and several others to Hanoi's Long Bien station (22,000d, 2½ hours), on the eastern side of the Red River.

There are two train stations within the Haiphong city limits. The **Thuong Li train station** is in the far western part of the city. The **Haiphong train station** is right in the city centre; this is the last stop for the train coming from Hanoi, and is where you should get off.

**Car & Motorbike** Haiphong is 103km from Hanoi on Hwy 5. This expressway (Vietnam's first) between the two cities was completed in 1999.

**Boat** All boats leave from the pier at the end of Đ Ben Binh, 10 minutes' walk from the centre of town.

Hydrofoils leave for Cat Ba (90,000d, 75 minutes) at 6.30am, 9am and 1pm.

Slow boats to Mong Cai via Cat Ba (70,000d) also leave from there at 6.30am, 9am and 1pm.

Hydrofoils to Hong Gai in Halong City (90,000d, 75 minutes) leave at 7am, 10.30am and 4.30pm.

## Getting Around

Haiphong is serviced by several companies that use metered, air-con taxis. Try **Haiphong Taxi** *(☎ 838383)*. There are also plenty of cyclos and *xe om* cruising around town.

## HALONG CITY
☎ 033 ● pop 149,900

The majority of food, accommodation and other life-support systems for Halong Bay are to be found in Halong City, the capital of Quang Ninh province and Vietnam's latest sin city (the number of signs advertising 'Thai Massage' gives a good indication of the size of the prostitution market). In more recent years this once-peaceful outpost has developed into a pleasure den for package tourists, both domestic and international, with a large following of border-hopping Chinese.

There's little reason to stay in Halong City itself, although you'll probably transit the city on the way to Halong Bay. This is one place where you'll be thankful for arriving on a group tour: you'll miss the significant hassle from young men wanting to sell you trips to the bay. Consider a tour on which you can sleep aboard a boat in the

NORTHEAST VIETNAM

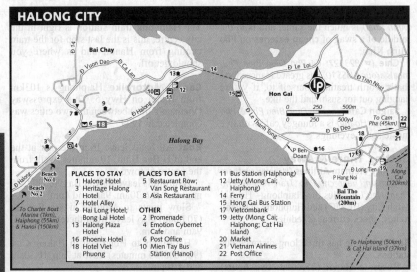

**HALONG CITY**

Bai Chay

Đ Vuon Dao

Đ Ca Lan

Đ 14

13

14

10

11

12

Đ Halong

8

9

7

6

18

5

3

4

2

1

Beach No 1

Beach No 2

Đ Halong

To Charter Boat Marina (1km); Haiphong (55km) & Hanoi (150km)

*Halong Bay*

Đ Le Loi

15

Đ Tran Nhat

Hon Gai

0      250      500m

0      250      500yd

To Cam Pha (45km)

22

Đ Le Thanh Tong

Đ Ba Deo

18

P Ben Doan

16

17

Đ Long Tien

P Hang Noi

Bai Tho Mountain (200m)

20

21

19

To Mong Cai (120km)

To Haiphong (50km) & Cat Hai Island (37km)

| PLACES TO STAY | PLACES TO EAT | 11 Bus Station (Haiphong) |
|---|---|---|
| 1 Halong Hotel | 5 Restaurant Row; | 12 Jetty (Mong Cai; |
| 3 Heritage Halong | Van Song Restaurant | Haiphong) |
| Hotel | 8 Asia Restaurant | 14 Ferry |
| 7 Hotel Alley | | 15 Hong Gai Bus Station |
| 9 Hai Long Hotel; | **OTHER** | 17 Vietcombank |
| Bong Lai Hotel | 2 Promenade | 19 Jetty (Mong Cai; |
| 13 Halong Plaza | 4 Emotion Cybernet | Haiphong; Cat Hai |
| Hotel | Cafe | Island) |
| 16 Phoenix Hotel | 6 Post Office | 20 Market |
| 18 Hotel Viet | 10 Mien Tay Bus | 21 Vietnam Airlines |
| Phuong | Station (Hanoi) | 22 Post Office |

bay, rather than in the city. If you are travelling independently to Halong Bay from Hanoi, it is advisable to give Halong City a miss and make a beeline via Haiphong to less hassle-ridden Cat Ba Island (see the Halong Bay section later in this chapter), where you can also arrange an independent itinerary.

## Orientation

Halong City is bisected by a bay, and the most important district for travellers is called Bai Chay. Accommodation can be found on both sides of the bay, but Bai Chay, on the western side, is more scenic, closer to Hanoi and much better endowed with hotels and restaurants. Bai Chay is also where the majority of tourist boats are moored.

A short ferry ride (500d) across the bay takes you to the Hon Gai district. Hon Gai is the main port district and exports coal (a major product of this province), which means this area is a bit dirty, but at least there is some local flavour. The ferry from Haiphong docks in Hon Gai, so if you arrive late, you may find it easier to spend the night there before crossing to Bai Chay the next morning.

District names are important: most long-distance buses will be marked 'Bai Chay' or 'Hon Gai' rather than 'Halong City'.

## Information

**Money** There's a branch of **Vietcombank** in Hon Gai, which is somewhat inconvenient, as most tourists stay in Bai Chay on the other side of the bay.

**Email & Internet Access** Internet access is available at the **Emotion Cybernet Cafe**, right on the main drag in Bai Chay. The cost is 400d per minute. There are also several Internet cafés on 'hotel alley'.

## Beaches

The 'beaches' around Halong City are basically mud and rock – a problem the authorities are trying to 'correct'. A Taiwanese company has built two beaches in Bai Chay with imported sand, but they are not at all attractive for swimming.

## Places to Stay

The majority of visitors stay in Bai Chay. There are more than 100 hotels here, and keen competition keeps prices down, especially if you can avoid the commission-seeking touts. You will probably have to pay more in the peak season (summer) or during Tet. There are also accommodation options in Hong Gai, which is handy for late or early bus and boat journeys.

**Bai Chay** The heaviest concentration of hotels is in town, in the aptly named 'hotel alley'. This is where you'll find countless minihotels, most of them nearly identical. Expect to pay something between US$8 and US$12 for a double room with private bath and air-con.

A couple of hillside hotels with views of the bay provide an interesting alternative. **Bong Lai Hotel** (☎ 845658; rooms with/without balcony US$12/10) is simple, clean, cheap and friendly. The views are fantastic.

**Hai Long Hotel** (☎ 846378; fax 846171; air-con rooms US$12) is next door to Bong Lai. It's a bit bigger, and there are fine rooftop views. Renovations were underway when we visited.

**Halong Plaza Hotel** (☎ 845810, fax 846867; e plaza.qn@hn.vnn.vn; rooms from US$140++) is a good hotel right by the car-ferry landing, with all the facilities you would expect for the price. Discounts of around 40% of the published price are usually offered.

The majority of the other hotels are strung out for 2km along the main road heading west of town (towards Hanoi). Most accommodation here consists of large, expensive, state-run hotels.

**Heritage Halong Hotel** (☎ 846888, fax 846718; e heritagehl.qn@hn.vnn.vn; rooms US$110-250) is a glitzy place – a huge upmarket Singaporean joint venture. The rooms are pleasant, with fine views, and it's popular with international tour groups.

**Halong Hotel** (☎ 846320; fax 846318; air-con rooms US$15-110) is a huge complex divided into four buildings of differing standards, reflected in the prices.

**Hon Gai** There are fewer places to stay here, but the demand is low (and there are fewer touts) so prices remain cheap. The hotels are clustered mainly along Đ Le Thanh Tong, which runs on an east-west axis, as well as tucked away on Pho Hang Noi, just about directly opposite the bank. The hotels range from very ordinary to really grotty, and the road is very noisy, very early.

**Hotel Viet Phuong** (☎ 826197; Đ Le Thanh Tong; air-con rooms 120,000d) is one of the cleanest, and it's next to good **com binh dan restaurants** and **fresh-bread shops** for breakfast.

**Phoenix Hotel** (☎ 827236; 169 Đ Le Thanh Tong; rooms with fan/air-con 150,000/200,000d) is just about OK.

## Places to Eat
Except for minihotels, most hotels have restaurants. If you're on a tour, it's likely that meals will be included.

For independent travellers, the area just west of central Bai Chay contains a solid row of cheap **restaurants**, all of which are OK. The owner of the **Van Song Restaurant** speaks fluent French.

**Asia Restaurant** (☎ 846927), on the 'hotel alley' slope, remains popular. The owner used to run a restaurant in East Berlin and speaks excellent German and some English. The Vietnamese food here is very good and prices are reasonable.

In Hong Gai, check out the string of **local eateries** along Pho Ben Doan, and clustered around the Hotel Viet Phuong.

## Getting There & Away
**Bus** In Halong City, you can catch Hanoi-bound buses (35,000d, 3½ hours) from **Mien Tay bus station** in Bai Chay, close to the public ferry pier, every 15 minutes.

Buses to Haiphong (18,000d, two hours) leave every 20 minutes from a bus station across the road from Mien Tay.

Buses to northeastern destinations leave from the **Hon Gai bus station**. Buses for Mong Cai (35,000d, six hours) and Cua Ong (9000d, two hours) for Van Don Island depart regularly during daylight hours.

**Car & Motorbike** Halong City is 160km from Hanoi, 55km from Haiphong and 45km from Cam Pha. The one-way trip from Hanoi to Halong City takes about three hours by car.

**Boat** There are daily slow boats connecting Hon Gai with Haiphong (30,000d, three hours). Boats depart Hon Gai at 6.30am, 11am and 4pm. Hydrofoils leave Hon Gai for Haiphong (60,000d, 75 minutes) at 8am and 1pm.

There's a daily boat connecting Hon Gai to Cat Hai Island (30,000d, two hours), but its departure times depend on the season and the number of visitors. This trip offers decent views of Halong Bay. From Cat Hai you can hop on another small ferry to get to Cat Ba Island (30,000d, two hours): see the Cat Ba Island section later in this chapter. There are occasional direct boats from Hong Gai to Cat Ba Island.

There are also services from Hong Gai to Mong Cai. A hydrofoil (170,000d, three hours) leaves daily at 6am, and there's a ferry (70,000d, seven hours) daily at 9pm.

From Bai Chay there are also hydrofoil services to Mong Cai (US$12; three hours) leaving at 8am and 1pm. There's also a hydrofoil from Bai Chay to Haiphong (US$5; 50 minutes) at 9.10am and 1.10pm.

As always, be prepared for changes to these schedules.

## HALONG BAY

Magnificent Halong Bay, with its 3000-plus islands rising from the emerald waters of the Gulf of Tonkin and covering an area of 1500 sq km, is one of the natural marvels of Vietnam. In 1994 it was designated Vietnam's second World Heritage site. Visitors have compared the area's magical landscape of limestone islets to Guilin in China and Krabi in southern Thailand. These tiny islands are dotted with beaches and grottoes created by wind and waves, and have sparsely forested slopes ringing with birdsong.

Besides the breathtaking vistas, visitors to Halong Bay come to explore the caves – some of which are beautifully illuminated for the sake of tourists – and to hike in Cat Ba National Park. There are few 'proper' beaches in Halong Bay itself, except for on Cat Ba Island, but in Lan Ha Bay (off Cat Ba Island) the opposite is true. Lan Ha boasts over 100 beaches, but almost no caves at all.

As the number-one tourist attraction in the northeast, Halong Bay draws a steady stream of visitors year-round. From February to April, the weather in this region is often cool and drizzly. The ensuing fog can make visibility low, although the temperature rarely falls below 10°C. During the summer months tropical storms are frequent, and tourist boats may have to alter their itineraries, depending on the weather.

*Ha long* translates as 'where the dragon descends into the sea'. Legend has it that the islands of Halong Bay were created by a great dragon that lived in the mountains. As it ran towards the coast, its flailing tail gouged out valleys and crevasses; as it plunged into the sea, the areas dug up by the tail became filled with water, leaving only the high land visible.

The dragon may be legend, but sailors in the Halong Bay region have often reported sightings of a mysterious marine creature of gargantuan proportions known as the Tarasque. The more paranoid elements of the military suspect it's an imperialist spy submarine, while eccentric travellers believe they have discovered Vietnam's version of the Loch Ness monster. Meanwhile, the monster – or whatever it is – continues to haunt Halong Bay, unfettered by the marine police, Vietnam Tourism and the immigration authorities. Enterprising Vietnamese boat owners have made a cottage industry out of the creature, offering cash-laden tourists the chance to rent a junk and pursue the Tarasque before it gets fed up and swims away.

Dragons aside, the biggest threat to the bay may be from souvenir-hunting tourists. Rare corals and seashells are rapidly being stripped from the sea floor, and stalactites and stalagmites are being broken off from the caves. These items get turned into key rings, paperweights and ashtrays, which are on sale in the local souvenir shops. Obviously the fewer people buy, the less the local people will take to sell: so please don't!

There's an excellent map of Halong Bay, shown together with neighbouring Bai Tu Long Bay, published in 1998 by the Management Department of Ha Long Bay. Look for

# HALONG BAY & BAI TU LONG BAY

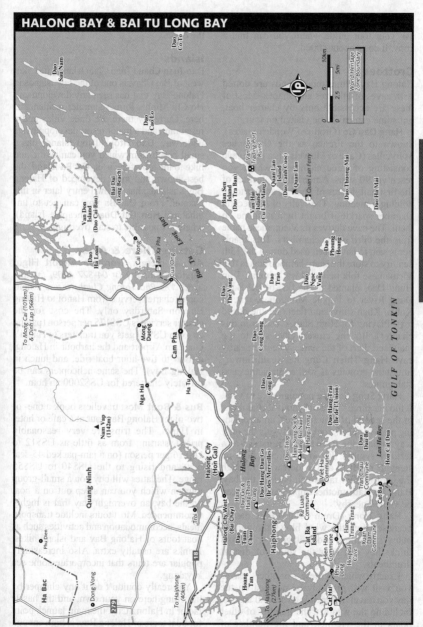

NORTHEAST VIETNAM

it at the souvenir stalls at the cave sites, or ask your tour guide where you can find a copy. It costs about 8000d.

## Grottoes

Halong Bay's limestone islands are dotted with caves of all sizes and shapes. Most of these are accessible only by charter boat, but some can easily be visited on tour.

**Hang Dau Go** (Grotto of Wooden Stakes), known to the French as the Grotte des Merveilles (Cave of Marvels), is a huge cave consisting of three chambers, which you reach via 90 steps. Among the stalactites of the first hall, scores of gnomes appear to be holding a meeting. The walls of the second chamber sparkle if bright light is shone on them. The cave derives its Vietnamese name from the third of the chambers. This chamber is said to have been used during the 13th century to store the sharp bamboo stakes that Vietnamese folk hero and war general, Tran Hung Dao, planted in the bed of the Bach Dang River to impale Mongolian general Kublai Khan's invasion fleet (see the boxed text 'Playing for High Stakes' earlier in this chapter). It's the closest cave site to the mainland. Part of the same system, a nearby cave **Hang Thien Cung** has 'cauliflower' limestone growths as well as stalactites and stalagmites.

**Hang Sung Sot** is a popular cave to visit. It too has three vast and beautiful chambers, in the second of which there's an astonishing pink-lit 'penis rock' (really, it's the only way to describe it), which is regarded as a fertility symbol. It too requires a hike up steps to reach it, and a loop walk through the cool interior takes you back to the bay. **Hang Bo Nau**, another impressive cave, can be visited nearby.

**Hang Trong** (Drum Grotto) is so named because when the wind blows through its many stalactites and stalagmites, visitors think they can hear the sound of distant drumbeats.

Exactly which of these – or other – caves you visit will probably be decided on the day you travel. It depends on several factors, including the weather, the number of other boats in the vicinity, and the number of people putting environmental pressure on the caves.

## Islands

**Dao Tuan Chau** (Tuan Chau Island), just 5km west of Bai Chay, is one of the few islands in Halong Bay that has seen any development. Ho Chi Minh's former summer residence is here. Currently there are three villas and a restaurant, and a major resort development is underway. **Dao Titop** (Titop Island) has a small beach from which you can swim, and hike to the top of the islet. **Cat Ba Island**, the best-known and most developed of Halong Bay's islands, has its own entry later in this chapter. From Cat Ba you can get to uninhabited **Hon Cat Dua** (Pineapple Island), where it's possible to stay overnight.

## Getting There & Away

**Air** At present, **Northern Airport Flight Service Company** (☎ 04-827 4409, fax 827 2780; 173 Pho Truong Chinh) offers a helicopter charter service from Hanoi to Halong Bay on Saturday only. The cost for the charter service is US$175 per person (paying an extra US$20 gets you transfers to Hanoi's Gia Lam Airport and the harbour in Halong, a four- to five-hour boat ride, and lunch in Halong Bay). The same helicopters can be privately chartered for US$2000 an hour.

**Bus & Boat** Most travellers book a one- or two-night Halong Bay tour at a café or hotel in Hanoi. The trips are very reasonably priced, starting from as little as US$12 to US$16 per person (on a jam-packed 45-seat bus), and rising to the US$40 to US$55 range. The latter will buy you a small-group tour on which you can sleep out on a boat on the bay, an overnight stay that is highly recommended. Most tours include transport, meals, accommodation and activities such as boat tours of Halong Bay and island hikes. Drinks are usually extra. Also increasingly popular are tours that incorporate some sea kayaking.

You really couldn't do it any cheaper by travelling here on your own, and the hassle factor in Halong City, the main launch point for boat tours of Halong Bay, is high enough

The magical landscape of Halong Bay: not only are there innumerable beaches and islands to explore; there are also reports of a mysterious dragon-like marine creature called the Tarasque

Stilted farmhouse, Hoa Binh

Hill-tribe children from northwestern Vietnam

A farmer plants rice along the terraces in Lai Chau province

H'mong boys playing near Sapa in Lao Cai

Rice fields in Hoa Binh

in peak season to make your hair turn grey. But for those who prefer independent travel, there are buses direct from Hanoi to Halong City and Haiphong, from where you can organise transport to Halong Bay. (For further information see the Halong City and Haiphong sections earlier in this chapter.) A better independent travel option is to get to Cat Ba Island (see Getting There & Away in the Cat Ba Island section later), from where you can also include Halong Bay on a chartered boat trip.

If you book a tour, there is always a small chance that the boat-trip part may be cancelled due to bad weather. This may entitle you to a partial refund, but remember that the boat trip is only a small portion of the cost of the journey (it's the hotels, food and transport along the way that really add up). Depending on the number of people in your group, you probably won't get back more than US$5 to US$10 if the boats don't sail.

## Getting Around

**Boat** You won't see much unless you take a boat tour of the islands and their grottoes. If you do end up travelling independently to Halong City, cruises are offered by private boat owners, travel agencies and hotels in Bai Chay. Competition is fierce, and overcharging and high-pressure sales tactics are still the norm.

Since the area is large, it's advisable to take a fast boat in order to see more. The rare but romantic junks are very photogenic (indeed, videogenic) and can be hired as well. However, junks are so slow on a calm day that they hardly seem to be moving at all.

You don't have to rent a whole boat for yourself – there are plenty of other travellers, Vietnamese and foreign, to share with. A small boat can hold six to 12 people and costs around US$6 per hour. Mid-sized boats (the most popular ones) take around 20 passengers and cost US$15 per hour. Larger boats can hold 50 to 100 people and cost US$25 per hour.

All tourist boats are located at a marina about 2km west of central Bai Chay.

Be careful, of course, with your valuables. Sleep-over boats have lockable cabins, but

you'll need to ask someone to keep an eye on your things if you're swimming off a day-tour boat.

## CAT BA ISLAND
☎ 031 • pop 7,000

Cat Ba is the largest island in the vicinity of Halong Bay. **Lan Ha Bay**, off the eastern side of the island, is especially scenic and offers numerous beaches to explore. While the vast majority of Halong Bay's islands are uninhabited vertical rocks, Cat Ba has a few tiny **fishing and farming villages** as well as a fast-growing town. Except for a few fertile pockets, the terrain is too rocky for serious agriculture: most residents earn their living from the sea, while others cater to the tourist trade. Life has always been hard here and many Cat Ba residents joined the exodus of Vietnamese 'boat people' in the 1970s and '80s. Although the island lost much of its fishing fleet this way, overseas Vietnamese have sent back large amounts of money to relatives on the island, thus financing the new hotels and restaurants that you'll see. Cat Ba is still relatively laid-back, despite about a 20-fold increase in hotel rooms (and karaoke machines!) since 1996.

About half of Cat Ba Island (which has a total area of 354 sq km) and 90 sq km of the adjacent waters were declared a national park in 1986, to protect the island's diverse ecosystems. These include subtropical evergreen forests on the hills, freshwater swamp forests at the base of the hills, coastal mangrove forests, small freshwater lakes and coral reefs. Most of the coastline consists of rocky cliffs, but there are a few sandy beaches tucked into small coves.

There are numerous lakes, waterfalls and grottoes in the spectacular limestone hills, the highest of which rises 331m above sea level. The growth of the vegetation is stunted near the summits because of high winds. The largest permanent body of water on the island is **Ech Lake**, which covers an area of three hectares. Almost all of the surface streams are seasonal; most of the island's rainwater flows into caves and follows under-ground streams to the sea, creating a shortage of fresh water during the dry

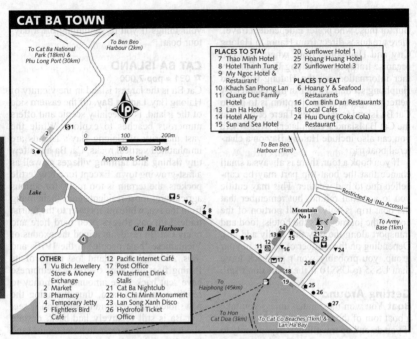

## CAT BA TOWN

To Cat Ba National
Park (18km) &
Phu Long Port (30km)

To Ben Beo
Harbour (2km)

| PLACES TO STAY | 20 Sunflower Hotel 1 |
| --- | --- |
| 7 Thao Minh Hotel | 25 Hoang Huang Hotel |
| 8 Hotel Thanh Tung | 27 Sunflower Hotel 3 |
| 9 My Ngoc Hotel & Restaurant | **PLACES TO EAT** |
| 10 Khach San Phong Lan | 6 Hoang Y & Seafood Restaurants |
| 11 Quang Duc Family Hotel | 16 Com Binh Dan Restaurants |
| 13 Lan Ha Hotel | 18 Local Cafés |
| 14 Hotel Alley | 24 Huu Dung (Coka Cola) Restaurant |
| 15 Sun and Sea Hotel | |

0    100    200m
0    100    200yd
Approximate Scale

Lake

To Ben Beo
Harbour (1km)

Restricted Rd (No Access)

Cat Ba Harbour

Mountain
No 1

To Army
Base (1km)

To
Haiphong (45km)

| OTHER | 12 Pacific Internet Café |
| --- | --- |
| 1 Vu Bich Jewellery Store & Money Exchange | 17 Post Office |
| | 19 Waterfront Drink Stalls |
| 2 Market | 21 Cat Ba Nightclub |
| 3 Pharmacy | 22 Ho Chi Minh Monument |
| 4 Temporary Jetty | 23 Lan Song Xanh Disco |
| 5 Flightless Bird Café | 26 Hydrofoil Ticket Office |

To Hon
Cat Dua (3km)

To Cat Co Beaches (1km) &
Lan Ha Bay

season. Although parts of the interior of the island are below sea level, most of the island is between 50m and 200m in elevation.

The waters off Cat Ba Island are home to 200 species of fish, 500 species of molluscs and 400 species of arthropods. Larger marine animals in the area include seals and three species of dolphins.

Stone tools and bones left by humans who lived here between 6000 and 7000 years ago have been found at 17 sites on the island.

Ho Chi Minh himself paid a visit to Cat Ba Island on 1 April 1951, and there is a large annual festival on the island to commemorate the day. A **monument** to Uncle Ho stands on Mountain No 1, the hillock across from the pier in Cat Ba town.

The best weather on Cat Ba Island is from late September to November, particularly the latter, when the air and water temperature is mild and skies are mostly clear. December to February is cooler, but still pleasant. From February to April, rain is common, while the

summer months, from June through August, are hot and humid.

## Cat Ba National Park

Cat Ba National Park *(admission 25,000d, guide fee US$5 per day per person or group)* is home to 32 types of mammals – including François monkeys, wild boar, deer, squirrels and hedgehogs – and over 70 species of birds have been sighted, including hawks, hornbills and cuckoos. Cat Ba lies on a major migration route for waterfowl (ducks, geese and shore birds) which feed and roost on the beaches in the mangrove forests. There are 745 species of plants recorded on Cat Ba including 118 timber species and 160 plants with medicinal value. The park is home to a species of tree called Cay Kim Gao (for aspiring horticulturists the Latin name is *Podocarpus fleuryi hickel*). In ancient days, kings and nobles would eat only with chopsticks made from this timber; anything poisonous it touches is reputed to turn the light-coloured wood to black! It's also found in Cuc Phuong National Park.

A guide is not mandatory, but is definitely recommended if you want to go walking – otherwise, all you are likely to see is a canopy of trees. **Camping** is also allowed in the park, but you'll need to bring your own gear or hire it from Cat Ba town.

Two caves in the national park are open to visitors. **Hospital Cave** has lots of historical significance – it served as a secret, bomb-proof hospital during the American War. **Trung Trang Cave** (Hang Trung Trang) is easily accessible, however, you will need a torch (flashlight) if you want to see anything. The cave is just south of the park entrance along the main drag, and there's a small entry fee.

There is a *very* challenging 18km (five to six hour) hike through the park and up to one of the mountain summits that many people enjoy. You need a guide, plus bus or boat transport to the trailhead and a boat to return. All of this can be easily arranged at the hotels in Cat Ba if you're travelling independently, and is usually included if you're on a group tour. Many hikes end at Viet Hai, a remote minority village just outside the park boundary, from where you can catch a boat back to Cat Ba town. If you're planning on doing this hike, equip yourself with proper hiking shoes, a raincoat and a generous supply of water (at least 3L) plus some food. Independent hikers can buy basic snacks at the kiosks in Viet Hai, which is where many hiking groups stop for lunch. This is *not* an easy walk, and is made harder and more slippery after rain. There are shorter hiking options that are less hard-core.

To reach the national park headquarters at Trung Trang, take a minibus from one of the hotels in Cat Ba (8000d, 30 minutes). All restaurants and hotels should be able to sell you minibus tickets. Another option is to hire a motorbike for about 20,000d one way.

## Beaches

The white-sand Cat Co beaches (simply called **Cat Co 1** and **Cat Co 2**) make a great place to lounge around for the day. They are about 1km southeast from Cat Ba town over

a steep headland, and can be reached on foot or by motorbike (about 3000d). There is a 7000d entry fee to the beaches.

The two beaches are separated by a small hillock that can be climbed over in about 20 minutes. Most, however, take the easier route along a new, 700m, wooden seaside walkway around the mountain. Cat Co 2 is the less busy and more attractive of the two, and also offers simple accommodation and camping.

On weekends the beaches fill up with Vietnamese tourists and become messy with litter, but during the week the crowds diminish.

The main beaches, apart from those at Cat Ba town itself, are Cai Vieng, Hong Xoai Be and Hong Xoai Lon.

## Places to Stay

Over the past few years the number of accommodation offerings in Cat Ba has risen dramatically, while development continues apace, feeding an expanding tourist market. Look around, as the quality of budget hotels varies widely. A good rule of thumb is to avoid the hotels where reception consists of rude young men lounging around listening to loud music, and go for the family-run joints where women and children are in evi-dence; these will usually be cleaner, quieter, and have less-aggressive vibes. Since being 'discovered' by Hanoi residents, Cat Ba has turned into a highly popular summer getaway, filling up on weekends and holidays, when the town is jumping.

In May 1998 the island was finally hooked up to the national power grid, which brings with it such modern amenities as air-con, satellite TV and hot water. The good news is the departure of the noisy generators, which used to rattle so loudly that having a conversation over dinner was a challenge. The bad news is that the clamour of the generators has been replaced with off-tune melodies flowing from a plethora of open-air karaoke joints and thumping discos.

Few hotels have Internet access, but **Pacific Internet Café** on 'hotel alley' has several terminals with access, costing 200d per minute.

## Places to Stay – Budget & Mid-Range

Most of Cat Ba Island's hotels are situated on the waterfront in Cat Ba town. The ones to the east (ie, the ones not built right up against the hillside) tend to offer better cross breezes and less of the seedy, karaoke call-girl scene. Most hotels have at least one staff member who speaks English, but you may have to wait around if that person isn't there at the time.

Room rates fluctuate greatly. In the high-season summer months (May to September) you can expect to pay a minimum of US$15 for a room. During the slower winter months (October to April) you can find decent rooms for between US$5 and US$10. The rates given here are for winter, when there's usually the opportunity for negotiation. The hotels are listed here geographically, starting from the eastern end of the waterfront, and there are plenty of others to choose from if these are full.

**Sunflower Hotel 3** (☎ 888215, fax 888451; e sunflowerhotel@hn.vnn.vn; fan rooms US$8-13) is the waterfront budget version of the three family-run Sunflower hotels in town. It's fine, but add US$2 if you want to use the air-con.

**Hoang Huong Hotel** (☎ 888274; fan/air-con rooms US$7/12) has decent clean rooms; the front rooms have virtually glass walls and a shared balcony, bang over the water.

**Quang Duc Family Hotel** (☎ 888231, fax 888423; air-con rooms US$10) is Cat Ba's original 'family hotel'. Rooms come with satellite TV. You can book tours here, and hire kayaks from US$10 per day.

**Lan Ha Hotel** (☎ 888999, fax 888299; lower-/upper-floor fan rooms US$4/5) is basic, but good value for the price. It's one of the better cheapies on this 'hotel alley', but look around though; some of the hotels here have decidedly seedy vibes.

**Khach San Phong Lan** (☎ 888605; air-con rooms US$10) is in a good location, and the front rooms, although pretty basic, have balconies overlooking the harbour.

**My Ngoc Hotel Restaurant** (☎ 888199, fax 888422; rooms US$10-15) has simple, clean rooms and a restaurant spilling out onto the waterfront pathway. You can get tour information here, and kayaks are available for US$6 per day.

**Thao Minh Hotel** (☎/fax 888630; rooms US$10-15) has fine waterfront rooms with balconies. Next door, **Hotel Thang Tung** (☎ 888364; fan rooms US$6) is basic, as you'd expect for the price, but it's clean and in a good waterfront location. There are several hotels on the waterfront west of these two; they're OK but are flanked by a row of karaoke bars and massage joints, which means it's not the quietest part of town.

**Sun and Sea Hotel** (☎ 888315, fax 888475; air-con rooms US$15) has fine rooms, but they're small for the price (although that does include breakfast). It's just off the waterfront.

**Sunflower Hotel 1** (☎ 888215, fax 888451, e sunflowerhotel@hn.vnn.vn; rooms US$18) is the upmarket version of the Sunflower family of hotels, complete with satellite TV and comfortable rooms. **Sunflower Hotel 2** was under construction when we visited.

To avoid the hoopla in town, spend a night at the simple two-room **guesthouse** (rooms 50,000d) over on Cat Co Hai (Cat Co 2). The manager also rents out tents for guests to **camp** on the beach.

If you really want to get away from it all, the national parks department recently built a basic four-room **beach guesthouse** (rooms US$10) on the nearby island of **Hon Cat Dua** (Pineapple Island). It is also possible to camp on the beach, provided you bring your own gear. Except for the local park rangers, the island is uninhabited (unless you count the wild deer, monkeys and snakes!). Come prepared to be self-sufficient for the night. Cat Dua is about 30 minutes by boat from Cat Ba town; there is no public ferry, so you must arrange a private boat to take you over and pick you up. A boat, able to carry about 15 people, should cost about US$6 one way. To make arrangements, ask at My Ngoc Hotel or Quang Duc Family Hotel.

## Places to Eat

Seafood is, of course, fresh and delicious in Cat Ba town, and there are restaurants along the length of the waterfront.

**Hoang Y**, towards the western end of the waterfront, serves the most fantastic selection of seafood dishes. Fresh grilled shrimp or squid with garlic costs around 50,000d for a huge helping. There are also good vegetarian dishes on offer. The potatoey-tomatoey dish is really tasty. It's a simple, no-frills restaurant and is always packed.

**Huu Dung Restaurant** continues to be popular, but eat early; two discos have opened nearby and you'll find yourself shouting to be heard once the music starts. The restaurant was formerly known as the Coka Cola Restaurant, when the red-tile roof of the open-air wooden building was painted like a Coke billboard. It's still known locally by that name. The house special is whole steamed fish.

There are plenty of cheap **com binh dan** restaurants on 'hotel alley'.

**Floating Restaurants**  There are numerous 'floating' seafood restaurants just offshore in Cat Ba Harbour. There have been several reports of overcharging, so be sure to work out the price, as well as the cost of a boat to get you out there and back, in advance. Locals advise heading around the bay to the couple of floating restaurants in Ben Beo Harbour; the water's cleaner and it's less touristy. A boat ride there and back, including waiting time, should cost around 15,000d. Ask your hotel to recommend a boatman.

One of these restaurants is **Xuan Hong** (☎ 888485), a fish-farm-cum-restaurant at Ben Beo Pier, just next to the passenger jetty, where you can tread on the edges of the large fish cages and get a close look at the workings of the 'farm'. You will know that the fish is fresh when it is plucked from the cages *after* you've ordered. Fresh char-grilled prawns, a dipping sauce, and rice: simple and delicious. Prices simply go by weight and type of seafood; you can eat your fill of a selection of fish for around 100,000d.

## Entertainment

One of the most enjoyable ways to spend time in the evening is to sit at the tables on the waterfront towards the eastern end of the harbour, order a drink from one of the stalls, and watch the world and the water go by.

If you want to do something a bit more social, the **Flightless Bird Café** (☎ 888517; open from 6.30pm) continues to be popular with foreign tourists. Run by a congenial expat New Zealander, who's a good source of local information, this stylish café-bar is a good place for drinks (Australian wine at 20,000d a glass), darts, music and movies. There is a pleasant 2nd-floor balcony overlooking the harbour. It's open at night but if you're going boating or hiking, the owner will make packed lunches to order. There's a small book exchange here.

There are presently two seriously loud discos on the slope behind town. **Cat Ba Nightclub** is in an enormous purple building, and has the rather interesting sales technique, on quiet nights, of refusing to put the music on until you buy a drink. Next door is **Lan Song Xanh Disco**, which plays music for its customers regardless.

The **Seaview Bar** on the 8th floor is open in the evenings; there's a billiard table and great views, but no lift!

## Getting There & Away

Cat Ba Island is 40km east of Haiphong and 20km south of Halong City. Be aware that there is more than one pier on Cat Ba Island. One is called Ben Bao, near Cat Ba town, (which is where most travellers want to go) and the other is at Phu Long, some 30km away, where boats from Cat Hai dock. At Phu Long, motorbike drivers will be waiting to whisk you away for the 30km ride to the centre of town (or the 15km to the Cat Ba National Park) for about 50,000d. There is also a public bus that meets the boats, but this takes considerably longer to get you to your hotel.

At the time of writing, a temporary jetty at the western end of town had been in use for some months, though there were plans to return to the permanent jetty near the post office; check out the current location when you arrive.

A great innovation are the 75-seat and 108-seat Russian-built hydrofoils. These air-con water rockets reduce the Cat Ba–Halong City and Cat Ba–Haiphong journeys to just 45 minutes and 75 minutes respectively. Both hydrofoils currently run to Haiphong once a day at 3pm (90,000d). Why they leave at the same time, and do not stagger the departures, is a true mystery. Hydrofoils depart from Cat Ba, for Haiphong, at 6.30am, 9am and 1pm. Be aware, however, that the schedule is highly subject to change. In general, but especially on peak-season summer weekends, you should book tickets in advance and be at the wharf early, as boats tend to run as often as they fill up.

Slow boats take about 2½ hours and cost 70,000d per person. Schedules are in a constant state of flux, so make inquiries locally. An alternative way to reach Cat Ba town is via the island of Cat Hai, which is closer to Haiphong. A boat departs Haiphong and makes a brief stop in Cat Hai on the way to the port of Phu Long on Cat Ba Island. There is also a 12.30pm slow boat from Hon Gai (Halong City), which takes about two hours to get to Cat Hai, from where it's possible to catch another boat across to Phu Long port (10,000d, 20 minutes). News is filtering out that a car ferry now operates this run. It *may* be possible to drive a motorbike or car to Haiphong, from where you can get the ferry to Cat Hai, then drive 15 minutes across the island to a pier from where you take a ferry to Phu Long on Cat Ba. Ask locally if you're feeling intrepid.

There are plenty of slow, chartered tourist boats making the run from Halong City to Cat Ba Island. Check with the cafés and travel agencies in Hanoi about tour options. Such trips generally include all transport, accommodation, food and a guide, but ask to make sure.

### Getting Around
Rented bicycles are a great way to explore the island. Several of the hotels can find you a cheap Chinese bike, or inquire at the Flightless Bird Café about decent mountain-bike rentals.

Minibuses (always with a driver) are easily arranged. Motorbike rentals (either with or without a driver) are available from most of the hotels. If you are heading out to

the beaches or national park, pay the 2000d parking fee to make sure your vehicle is still there when you return: there have been reports of theft and vandalism.

You'll get plenty of offers to tour Cat Ba fishing harbour in a small rowboat (around 20,000d), or hire a kayak from one of the hotels for around US$2 per hour.

Tours of the island and national park, boat trips around Halong Bay, and fishing trips are being peddled by nearly every hotel and restaurant in Cat Ba town. The cost depends on the number of people, but typical prices are US$8 for day trips and US$20 for two-day, one-night trips.

Among the consistently reputable tour operators, we can recommend **My Ngoc Hotel Restaurant** (☎ 888199) and **Quang Duc Family** Hotel (☎ 888231).

## BAI TU LONG BAY
☎ 033

There's more to northeastern Vietnam than Halong Bay. The sinking limestone plateau, which gave birth to the bay's spectacular islands, continues some 100km to the Chinese border. The area immediately northeast of Halong Bay is known as Bai Tu Long Bay.

Bai Tu Long Bay is every bit as beautiful as its famous neighbour. Indeed, you could say it's more beautiful, since it has scarcely seen any tourist development. This has its positives and negatives. The bay is unpolluted and undeveloped; however, as yet there's no tourism infrastructure. It's pretty hard travelling around and staying here, and unless you speak Vietnamese, it's difficult to get information.

Charter boats can take you to Bai Tu Long Bay from Halong Bay; a boat suitable for 20 passengers costs US$10 per hour and the one-way journey takes about five hours. A much cheaper alternative is to travel overland to Cua Ong pier, catch a public ferry to Van Don Island and visit some of the remote outlying islands, or charter a boat from the island's Cai Rong pier.

### Van Don Island (Dao Cai Bau)
Van Don is the largest and most populated and developed island in the archipelago.

However, there is no tourism development here yet.

**Cai Rong** is the main town on the island, which is about 30km in length and 15km across at the widest point. Bai Dai (Long Beach) runs along much of the southern side of the island and is hard-packed sand with some mangroves. Just offshore, almost touching distance away, there are stunning **rock formations** similar to those in Halong Bay. At the time of writing, a hotel was being constructed right on Long Beach, and should be open by the time you read this; presently this is the only planned beach-frontage accommodation.

**Places to Stay & Eat** The only hotels are at Cai Rong pier, about 8km from Tai Xa Pha, which is where ferries from the mainland dock. Cai Rong is a colourful, busy area, with lots of fishing boats and passenger vessels, and a backdrop of limestone mountains in the bay. It's also full of karaoke bars and motorbikes; the racket starts about 5am and you might want to get a room with air-con to block out some of the noise. There's no beach.

**Hung Toan Hotel** (☎ 874220; fan rooms 60,000d) is about 100m before the pier. The three rooms on the top floor are best – they share a huge balcony – but they're small and fairly grubby.

**Duyen Huong Guesthouse** (☎ 874113; rooms with/without air-con, 100,000/60,000d) is a clean little place. Its decent-sized rooms have attached bath and hot water, and some have balconies.

**Nha Nghi Nhu Hoa** (air-con rooms 80,000d) is next door and pretty much the same in style. It's fine, but keep away from the excruciatingly loud karaoke room on the 2nd floor.

**Khach San Sy Long** (☎ 874854; fan rooms 70,000d) is situated in a nice location, right on the corner of the pier, but the rooms are small and facilities more basic than some of the other hotels. It's clean though, and that's a plus.

There are a couple of other guesthouses, and some reasonable **restaurants** at which to eat, in the same street.

**Getting There & Away** For the moment, the island's inhabitants mostly rely on ferries that run between Cua Ong Pha (Cua Ong Pier) on the mainland and Tai Xa Pha (Tai Xa Pier) on Van Don Island. The passenger ferry (which also carries bicycles, motorbikes and chickens) runs every 30 minutes (1000d, 20 minutes) from 6am to 5pm. The car ferry (15,000d per car; 15 minutes) leaves Cua Ong every two hours between 6.30am and 4.30pm (1 October–31 March) and between 5am and 5pm (1 April to 30 September).

There's also a daily hydrofoil between Van Don Island and Halong City (US$6, 70 minutes) leaving at 3.50pm, and between Van Don Island and Mon Cai (US$12, 2½ hours) leaving at 8.30am.

A warning – these boat schedules may change and are, of course, dependent on the weather. Be prepared to hang around there a day or so.

Frequent buses run between Hon Gai (Halong City) and Cua Ong bus station, 1km from the pier on the mainland. You'll pass plenty of coal mines en route – your face (and lungs) will receive a fine coating of black coal dust before the journey is completed. Just pity the folks who live here and have to breathe this in every day.

You can get a motorbike to take you the 8km between Tai Xa Pier and Cai Rong town (10,000d).

**Other Islands** Cai Rong Pier (Cai Rong Pha) is just on the edge of Cai Rong town. This is where you catch boats to the outlying islands. You can charter a boat from here to Hon Gai or Bai Chay for around US$10 per hour (the one-way journey takes five hours).

You can also charter a tourist boat (du lich) at Cai Rong to cruise the nearby islands for a few hours. Ask at the pier. The hourly rate is between 70,000d and 80,000d.

## Quan Lan Island (Dao Canh Cuoc)

The main attraction here is a beautiful, 1km-long **white-sand beach** shaped like a crescent moon. The water is clear blue and the waves are suitable for surfing. The best time to play in the water is from about May to October – winter is too chilly. However, at present there are no tourist facilities.

The rowing-boat festival **Hoi Cheo Boi** is held here from the 16th to the 18th day of the sixth lunar month. It's the biggest festival in the bay area, and thousands of people turn out to see it.

The northeastern part of the island has some battered **ruins** of the old Van Don Trading Port. There is little to show that this was once part of a major trading route between Vietnam and China. Deep-water ports, such as Haiphong and Hon Gai, long ago superseded these islands in importance.

A ferry service between Quan Lan and Van Don Islands runs daily (17,000d, two hours), departing Van Don at 2pm and Quan Lan at 7am; in other words, a trip to the island requires an overnight stay. As there are no hotels, you'll have to camp and bring all your own gear and supplies.

### Van Hai Island (Cu Lao Mang)
Ancient Chinese graves have been found here, indicating that this region has seen considerable maritime trade. There are many good beaches, but a sand-mining pit (used to make glass) is destroying the place. There are boats to and from Van Don Island at 7am and 2pm (17,000d, 80 minutes).

### Ban Sen Island (Dao Tra Ban)
Also known as Tra Ban Island, this is the closest major island to Van Don Island, making it easy to visit. However, there are no tourist facilities and as a visit will mean an overnight stay, be prepared to be self-sufficient.

Boats depart from Van Don Island at 2pm and arrive on the northern side of Ban Sen Island between 3pm and 3.30pm (10,000d). Going the other way, boats leave Ban Sen Island daily at 7am and arrive at Van Don between 8am and 8.30am.

### Co To Island (Dao Co To)
In the northeast, Co To Island is the farthest inhabited island from the mainland. Its highest peak reaches a respectable 170m. There are numerous other hills, and a large

lighthouse atop one of them. The coastline is mostly cliffs or large rocks, but there's at least one fine sandy **beach**. Fishing boats usually anchor just off here, and you can walk to some of them during low tide. There is a small and very basic **guesthouse** on the island.

Ferries bound for Co To Island depart Van Don Island on Monday, Wednesday and Friday at unspecified times – check the schedule in Cai Rong. They return from Co To Island on Tuesday, Thursday and Friday. There are no boats on Sunday. The one-way fare is 30,000d and the journey takes about five hours, depending on the wind.

## MONG CAI & CHINESE BORDER
☎ 033 • pop 48,100

Mong Cai is located on the Chinese border in the extreme northeastern corner of Vietnam. Previously the border gate (Cua Khau Quoc Te Mong Cai) was only open to Vietnamese and Chinese, but today it is one of the official international overland border crossings in Vietnam. It's open from 7.30am to 4.30pm daily. However, your Chinese visa *must* be issued in Hanoi only (or your Vietnam visa issued by the embassy in Beijing only, if you're going the other way). At least, that's what we were assured by the Vietnamese border control; with no travellers in evidence it was a bit difficult to confirm.

One would be hard-pressed to say that Mong Cai is an attractive place. For the Vietnamese, the big attraction here is a chance to purchase low-priced (and low-quality) Chinese-made consumer goods. Some of the Chinese tourists come across for the low-cost Vietnamese food, booze and prostitutes.

If you've been learning to speak Chinese, you'll find plenty of opportunity to practice in Mong Cai. Many hotels, restaurants and shops are staffed by Vietnamese who can speak at least basic Chinese. Furthermore, about 70% of the stalls are run by Chinese, who cross the border daily to flog their wares. This explains why the market shuts so early – the Chinese have to head across the border before it closes at 4.30pm. It also means you won't have any problem spending Chinese yuan if you have them.

Other than the prospect of crossing the border, Mong Cai has little of interest for tourists. The town is dusty, the buildings are ramshackle, and there's construction-site chaos everywhere. Dongxing (on the Chinese side) is apparently even worse.

## Information

There's a branch of **Vietcombank** in the centre of town; travellers cheques can be cashed here.

**Internet access** is available in several places on Pho Hung Vuong.

## Places to Stay & Eat

The hotels in Mong Cai aren't the best. There are masses of them, in varying degrees of average. Look around, or try these.

**Nha Nghi Hai Dang** (☎ 881555; 107 Pho Tran Phu; rooms with fan/air-con 80,000/120,000đ) is just about OK, and hey, it's cheap and in the centre of town.

**Nha Nghi Hai Van** (☎ 886479; Thang Loi; air-con rooms 150,000đ) is the newest and cleanest of the hotels we visited, with helpful reception staff.

**Truong Minh Hotel** (☎ 883368; 202 Trieu Đ; rooms 135,000-150,000đ) is marginally quieter than others on the main drag.

There is a gaggle of hotels opposite the bus station. Among them, **Nha Nghi Cao Son** (☎ 883883; air-con rooms 120,000-150,000đ) is fine, but get a room at the back, off the noisy road.

There are **food stalls** around town, and a couple of **restaurants** at the roundabout.

## Getting There & Away

**Bus** Mong Cai is 360km from Hanoi. Buses to/from Hanoi (42,000đ to 62,000đ, 10 hours) leave five times a day between 5.30am and 7.30am. Many buses and minibuses connect Mong Cai and Hong Gai (Halong City) (25,000đ to 35,000đ, six hours) between 5.30am and 4.30pm.

Mong Cai to Lang Son is a five-hour journey. However, buses on this route leave only once or twice a day, early, if at all, and you'll have to change at Tien Yen. Much of the road is unpaved – expect plenty of dust or mud.

**Boat** High-speed hydrofoils run daily between Mong Cai and Bai Chay (170,000đ,

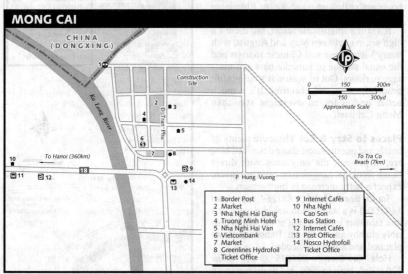

## MONG CAI

CHINA (DONGXING)

Construction Site

Ka Long River

To Hanoi (360km)

Đ Tran Phu

P Hung Vuong

To Tra Co Beach (7km)

0   150   300m
0   150   300yd
Approximate Scale

1  Border Post
2  Market
3  Nha Nghi Hai Dang
4  Truong Minh Hotel
5  Nha Nghi Hai Van
6  Vietcombank
7  Market
8  Greenlines Hydrofoil Ticket Office
9  Internet Cafés
10 Nha Nghi Cao Son
11 Bus Station
12 Internet Cafés
13 Post Office
14 Nosco Hydrofoil Ticket Office

NORTHEAST VIETNAM

three hours) in Halong City at 12.30pm and Haiphong also at 12.30pm (230,000d, 4½ hours). From Mong Cai, shuttle vans leave the hydrofoil ticket offices in town, for the pier at Dan Tien Port, about 15km away.

There are several hydrofoil ticket offices in town. Try **Greenlines Fast Ferry Booking Service** (43 Pho Tran Phu) or **Northern Shipping Company** (Nosco; Pho Hung Vuong). Both are only open before the daily hydrofoil departures at 12.30pm.

There is also a daily slow ferry between Hon Gai and Mong Cai (about 12 hours); check schedules locally.

It's also possible to charter a boat from Van Don Island to Mong Cai; captains in Van Don ask about US$150/200 one way/ return. The one-way trip takes six hours.

## AROUND MONG CAI
### Tra Co Beach
Seven kilometres to the southeast of Mong Cai is Tra Co, an oddly shaped peninsula widely touted as a beach resort. It's a fine beach of hard-packed sand with shallow water, and, at 17km in length, it's one of the longest stretches of sandy beachfront real estate in Vietnam. Painted wooden fishing boats are pulled up on shore, or illuminate the water during night-fishing excursions.

It's still a small-scale resort, but there's a high season between May and August, with many Vietnamese and Chinese tourists and the usual swathe of karaoke bars and massage parlours. Out of season it's delightful: peaceful, clean and beautiful. It's a much better option for an overnight stay than Mong Cai itself.

**Places to Stay & Eat** There are plenty of hotels and guesthouses; those described here are, at present, the only ones with direct beach frontage. Low-season rates are given; expect a hefty increase in high season.

**Tra Co Beach Hotel** (☎ 881264; twins from 140,000d) is a state-run motel-like place. It's in a fabulous location, but at present is horribly shabby and rundown. Renovations are planned and are much-needed.

**Hotel Gio Bien** (☎ 881635; air-con rooms 120,000d), built in 2001, is family-run (with

no call-girls allowed on the premises) and is still bright and clean. The rooms at the top have shared balconies and wonderful eagle-eye vistas along the beach.

**Sao Bien Hotel** (☎ 881243; air-con rooms 140,000-180,000d) is lovely, but during our visit an enormous pool and park were being constructed ocean-side and completely blocked the view!

Opposite the Tra Co Beach Hotel, on the edge of the beach, is a good cheap **restaurant** serving fresh seafood. The steamed ginger fish is great.

## LANG SON
☎ 025 • pop 62,300 • elevation 270m
The capital of the mountainous Lang Son province, Lang Son is in an area populated largely by Tho, Nung, Man and Dzao Montagnards, many of whom continue living their traditional way of life.

Lang Son was partially destroyed in February 1979 by invading Chinese forces (see

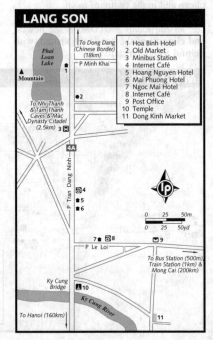

**LANG SON**

To Dong Dang
(Chinese Border)
(18km)

Phai Loan Lake

P Minh Khai

▲ Mountain

To Nhi Thanh & Tam Thanh Caves & Mac Dynasty Citadel (2.5km)

4A

P Tran Dang Ninh

P Le Loi

To Bus Station (500m)
Train Station (1km) & Mong Cai (200km)

Ky Cung Bridge

Ky Cung River

To Hanoi (160km)

1  Hoa Binh Hotel
2  Old Market
3  Minibus Station
4  Internet Café
5  Hoang Nguyen Hotel
6  Mai Phuong Hotel
7  Ngoc Mai Hotel
8  Internet Café
9  Post Office
10 Temple
11 Dong Kinh Market

0    25    50m
0    25    50yd

the boxed text 'Neighbouring Tensions' in this chapter); the ruins of the town and the devastated frontier village of Dong Dang were often shown to foreign journalists as evidence of Chinese aggression. Although the border is still heavily fortified, Sino-Vietnamese trade appears to have resumed

and to be in full swing again; both towns have been rebuilt.

Close to Lang Son, there are a couple of impressive caves in the surrounding limestone hills, and remnants of the ruined 16th-century Mac Dynasty Citadel. Most travellers come to Lang Son because of its role as a

## Neighbouring Tensions

Mong Cai is a free-trade zone with plenty of frenetic activity in the city's booming markets. It wasn't always so. From 1978 to 1990, the border was virtually sealed. How two former friends became such bitter enemies and 'friends' again is an interesting story.

China was on good terms with North Vietnam from 1954 (when the French left) until the late 1970s. But relations began to sour shortly after reunification, as the Vietnamese government became more and more friendly with China's rival, the USSR. There's good reason to believe that Vietnam was simply playing them off against each other, while receiving aid from both.

In March 1978 the Vietnamese government launched a campaign in the south against 'commercial opportunists', seizing private property in order to complete the country's 'socialist transformation'.

The campaign hit the ethnic Chinese particularly hard. It was widely assumed that the Marxist-Leninist rhetoric veiled ancient Vietnamese antipathy towards the Chinese.

The anticapitalist and anti-Chinese campaign caused up to 500,000 of Vietnam's 1.8 million ethnic Chinese to flee the country. Those in the north fled overland to China, while those in the south left by sea. The creation of Chinese refugees in the south proved to be lucrative for the government – to leave, refugees typically had to pay up to US$5000 each in 'exit fees'. Chinese entrepreneurs in Ho Chi Minh City (HCMC), had that kind of money, but refugees in the north were mostly dirt poor.

In response, China cut all aid to Vietnam, cancelled dozens of development projects and withdrew 800 technicians. Vietnam's invasion of Cambodia in late 1978 was the final straw: Beijing – alarmed because the Khmer Rouge was its close ally, and worried by the huge build-up of Soviet military forces on the Chinese-Soviet border – became convinced that Vietnam had fallen into the Russian camp, which was trying to encircle China with hostile forces.

In February 1979 China invaded northern Vietnam at Lang Son 'to teach the Vietnamese a lesson'. Just what lesson the Vietnamese learned is not clear, but the Chinese learned that Vietnam's troops – hardened by many years of fighting the USA – were no pushovers. Although China's forces were withdrawn after 17 days, and the operation was officially declared a 'great success', most observers soon realised that China's People's Liberation Army (PLA) had been badly mauled by the Vietnamese. It is believed to have suffered 20,000 casualties in 2½ weeks of fighting. Ironically, China's aid to Vietnam was partially responsible for China's humiliation.

Officially, these 'misunderstandings' are considered ancient history – trade across the Chinese-Vietnamese border is booming and both countries publicly profess to be 'good neighbours'. In practice, China and Vietnam remain highly suspicious of each other's intentions. Continued conflicts over who owns oil-drilling rights in the South China Sea is an especially sore point. The border area remains militarily sensitive, though the most likely future battleground is at sea.

If you visit China and discuss this border war, you will almost certainly be told that China acted in self-defence because the Vietnamese were launching raids across the border and murdering innocent Chinese villagers. Virtually all Western observers, from the US government's Central Intelligence Agency to historians, consider China's version of events to be nonsense. The Chinese also claim they won this war – nobody outside of China believes that, either.

trading post and crossing point into China: the border is actually just outside Dong Dang, a township 18km to the north. It's not a town to linger in, but if you find yourself with a few hours to spare there's quite a bit to explore.

## Things to See & Do

There are two large and beautiful **caves** (admission 5000d; open 6am-6pm daily) just 2.5km from the centre of Lang Son. Both are illuminated, which makes for easy exploration, and both have Buddhist altars inside.

**Tam Thanh Cave** is vast and beautiful. There's an internal pool and a viewing point (a natural 'window') presenting a sweeping view of the surrounding rice fields. A 100m walk away, up a stone staircase, are the ruins of the **Mac Dynasty Citadel**. It's a deserted and lovely spot, with stunning views across the country.

The Ngoc Tuyen River flows through **Nhi Thanh Cave**, 700m beyond Tam Thanh. The cave entrance has a series of carved poems written by the cave's discoverer, a soldier called Ngo Thi San, in the 18th century. There's also a carved stone plaque commemorating an early French resident of Lang Son, complete with his silhouette in European clothing.

## Places to Stay & Eat

There are no hotels to write home about in Lang Son.

**Hoang Nguyen Hotel** (☎ 870349; 84 Pho Tran Dang Ninh; singles/twins US$10/15) is friendly, privately owned and just about clean enough. Take a room at the back overlooking the rice fields. There's an Internet café a couple of doors away.

**Hoa Binh Hotel** (☎ 870807; 127 Pho Tran Dang Ninh; air-con rooms US$12) is a relatively new place. It's OK.

**Mai Phuong Hotel** (☎ 870458; 82 Pho Tran Dang Ninh; rooms 120,000-150,000d) is next to the Hoang Nguyen Hotel. Rooms are OK, if you can get past the smell of the lobby.

**Ngoc Mai Hotel** (☎ 871837; 25 Pho Le Loi; air-con rooms 180,000d) has big, bright, musty rooms. There's also an Internet café next door.

There are plenty of other hotels and guesthouses in town, of much the same standard. Few have restaurants, but there are some **com pho** places in town and a couple of cheap restaurants near the bus station.

## Shopping

The **Dong Kinh Market** and the **Old Market** are dens of cheap goods (that break easily) from China.

## Getting There & Away

Buses heading to Hanoi's Long Bien (30,000d, five hours) depart regularly from the **long-distance bus station**. A daily bus leaves Lang Son for Cao Bang (30,000d, five hours) at 4.30am. Minibuses heading to Cao Bang via That Khe and Dong Khe leave regularly from the minibus station on Pho Tran Dang Ninh.

Three daily trains run between Lang Son and Hanoi (71,000d, five hours) at 2.21am, 6.40am and 2.10pm.

## Getting Around

The usual xe om can be found almost anywhere, but are especially abundant around the post office and the market.

On Pho Tran Dang Ninh you'll see minibuses looking for passengers who are heading to the border at Dong Dang.

## DONG DANG & FRIENDSHIP PASS (CHINESE BORDER)

There is nothing in Dong Dang to hold the traveller's interest, except its position as a border town. The border post itself is at Huu Nghi Quan, 3km north of town; a xe om will take you there for 5000d. The border is open from 7am to 5pm daily, and there's a 500m walk between the Vietnamese and Chinese frontiers. There's a train from Hanoi to Dong Dang, via Lang Son, three times a day, if you want to make your own way across the border.

There was also, at the time of writing, a train on Tuesday and Friday from Hanoi to Beijing via Friendship Pass, a 55-hour journey that involves a three-hour stop for border formalities. This may change; check the schedule when you arrive.

## CAO BANG
☎ 026 • pop 45,500

The dusty capital of Cao Bang province, Cao Bang town is high above sea level and has a pleasant climate. The main reason to for coming here is to go on excursions into the surrounding scenic countryside. This is the most beautiful mountain area in the northeast and is worth exploring.

While in Cao Bang town, climb the hill leading up to the **War Memorial**; head up the second laneway off Đ Pac Bo, go under the entrance to a primary school, and you'll see the steps. There are great 360-degree views from the summit, and it's very peaceful (not to mention good aerobic exercise).

### Information
The **Bank for Foreign Investment and Development** will change US dollars but it's a major exercise, undertaken by lethargic and rude staff. Try to arrive with enough cash to cover your stay.

When we visited there was no public Internet access in Cao Bang.

### Places to Stay & Eat
**Thanh Loan Hotel** (Khach San Thanh Loan; ☎ 857026, fax 857028; 159 Pho Vuon Cam; air-con rooms US$15) is bright and clean with pleasant staff. Shame about the stuffed eagle in the lobby. All rooms are the same price, irrespective of size; the ones at the front and back are much lighter and bigger than the ones in the middle of the building. Rates include breakfast.

**Huong Thom Hotel** (☎ 855888; Đ Kim Dong; air-con rooms 180,000d), near the market, is fine too. Some of the rooms have river views, and rates include breakfast and TV.

**Bang Giang Hotel** (☎ 853431; air-con rooms 150,000-200,000d), near the bridge in the north of town, is an enormous state-run hotel that's better than some. Rooms on the upper floors in the rear of the building have sweeping views overlooking the river.

**Duc Trung Mini-Hotel** (☎ 853424; rooms 180,000-200,000d) is a small, privately owned place on a quiet street at the southern edge of town. Try to ignore the stuffed black bear in the lobby.

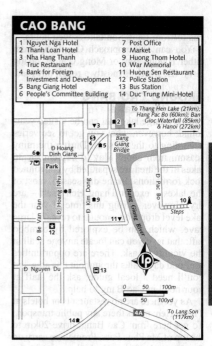

**CAO BANG**

1 Nguyet Nga Hotel
2 Thanh Loan Hotel
3 Nha Hang Thanh Truc Restaurant
4 Bank for Foreign Investment and Development
5 Bang Giang Hotel
6 People's Committee Building
7 Post Office
8 Market
9 Huong Thom Hotel
10 War Memorial
11 Huong Sen Restaurant
12 Police Station
13 Bus Station
14 Duc Trung Mini-Hotel

To Thang Hen Lake (21km); Hang Pac Bo (60km); Ban Gioc Waterfall (85km) & Hanoi (272km)

Đ Hoang Dinh Giang
Đ Hoang Nhu
Đ Kim Dong
Đ Pac Bo
Đ Be Van Dan
Đ Nguyen Du
Bang Giang Bridge
Bang Giang River
Park
Steps

To Lang Son (117km)

**Nguyet Nga Hotel** (☎ 856445; fan/air-con rooms 100,000/140,000d) is diagonally opposite the Bang Giang Hotel, across the bridge. It's the best of the cheaper hotels. There are several other **guesthouses** in town too.

Besides the hotel restaurants, there are plenty of good **food stalls** near the market, and **Huong Sen Restaurant** is a decent *com binh dan* place on the riverbank. Opposite the bank, **Nha Hang Thanh Truc Restaurant** serves good, cheap local food; if you don't have someone who speaks Vietnamese with you, the staff will take you into the kitchen to show you what's on the menu and you can use the 'point and nod' technique. Eat early: most food places are closed by 8pm.

### Getting There & Away
Cao Bang is 272km north of Hanoi, along Hwy 3. This is a sealed road, but due to the mountainous terrain, it's a full day's drive. There are several direct buses daily from

Hanoi (10 hours) and Thai Nguyen. A daily bus to/from Lang Son takes seven hours.

You can also approach Cao Bang from either Halong Bay or Mong Cai, by taking Hwy 4B, which is mostly a rough dirt road.

## AROUND CAO BANG
### Thang Hen Lake

This is a large lake that can be visited year-round; however, what you get to see varies according to the seasons. During the rainy season, from about May to September, 36 lakes in the area are separated by convoluted rock formations. In the dry season, most of the lakes – except Thang Hen itself – are dry. However, during this time of the year the lake level drops low enough to reveal a large **cave**, which can be explored by bamboo raft; that is, if you can locate anyone at all in the vicinity to ask. There are opportunities for good day **walks** throughout this area, but you'll need a local guide; ask the staff at your hotel in Cao Bang to help.

As yet there are no restaurants or hotels at Thang Hen; nor is there any public transport. To get here from Cao Bang, drive 20km to the top of Ma Phuc Pass. From there carry on for 1km to the fork in the highway – take the left branch and go another 4km.

### Hang Pac Bo

Hang Pac Bo (Water-Wheel Cave) is just 3km from the Chinese border. The cave and the surrounding area is sacred ground for Vietnamese revolutionaries. Here, on 28 January 1941, Ho Chi Minh re-entered Vietnam after living abroad for 30 years. His purpose in returning was to lead the revolution that he had long been planning.

Ho Chi Minh lived in this cave, writing poetry while waiting for WWII to end. The reason for remaining so close to China was to allow him to flee across the border if French soldiers discovered his hiding place. He named the stream in front of his cave Lenin Creek and a nearby mountain Karl Marx Peak.

There's an Uncle Ho **museum** (admission free; open 7.30am-11.30am & 1.30pm-4.30pm daily) at the entrance to the Pac Bo area. About 2km beyond this is a parking area.

---

### The Legend of the Lakes

The charming setting of Thang Hen wouldn't be complete without a depressing legend to go along with it. It seems that there was a very handsome and clever young man named Chang Sung. His mother adored him and deemed that he should become a mandarin and then marry a beautiful girl.

Under Confucian tradition, the only way to become a mandarin was to pass a competitive examination – Chang Sung, being a clever boy, sat the exam and passed. He received an official letter bearing the good news and ordering him to report to the royal palace just one week later.

With her son virtually guaranteed admission to mandarinhood, Chang Sung's mother completed her plan – a beautiful girl, Biooc Luong (Yellow Flower), was chosen to marry Chang Sung and a big wedding was hastily arranged.

Chang Sung couldn't have been happier, in fact, he and Biooc were having such a great time on their honeymoon that he forgot all about his crucial appointment at the royal palace until the night before the deadline.

Knowing how disappointed his mother would be if he missed his chance to be a mandarin, Chang Sung summoned magical forces to help him hop in great leaps and bounds to the palace. Unfortunately, he messed up the aerodynamics and leapt 36 times, with no control over his direction or velocity, and wound up creating 36 craters, finally landing at the top of Ma Phuc Pass, where he died of exhaustion and became a rock. The craters filled up with water during the rainy season and became the 36 Lakes of Thang Hen.

---

The cave is a 10-minute walk away, and a **jungle hut**, which was another of Ho's hideouts, is about 15 minutes' walk in the opposite direction, across a paddy field and in a patch of forest. On the way to the hut is a rock outcrop used as a 'dead-letter box', where he would leave and pick up messages. It's a lovely, quiet spot and presently almost wholly undeveloped.

Hang Pac Bo is about 60km northwest of Cao Bang; allow three hours to make the return trip by road, plus 11/2 hours to poke around. To do this as a return half-day trip by *xe om*, expect to pay around US$10. No permits are currently needed, despite the proximity to the Chinese border.

## Ban Gioc Waterfall

This scenic spot, on the border with China, sees very few visitors. The name Ban Gioc is derived from the Montagnard languages spoken in the area, and is sometimes spelt Ban Doc.

The waterfall is the largest, although not the highest, in the country. The vertical drop is 53m, but it has an impressive 300m span; one end of the falls is in China, the other is in Vietnam. The water volume varies considerably between the dry and rainy seasons: the falls are most impressive from May to September, but swimming during this period in the waterholes below may be difficult due to turbulence. The falls have three levels, creating a sort of giant staircase, and there's enough water any time, most years, to make the trip worthwhile. Half the pleasure of the visit is walking across paddy fields to reach the base of the falls.

The falls are fed by the Quay Son River. An invisible line halfway across the river marks the border, and **rafts** *(30,000d)* pole out the few metres to exactly the halfway mark – and no further! – from each side. There's been some development of tourist facilities on the Chinese side in recent years, as you'll see, but almost nothing except a bamboo footbridge and a couple of bamboo rafts on the Vietnamese side.

There is no official border checkpoint there, but a police permit is needed to visit – you cannot simply rent a motorbike and go there on your own. The permit is officially US$10, but hotels in Cao Bang will do the paperwork for between 100,000d and 200,000d. Let them do it – it's much less hassle than doing it yourself at the Cao Bang police station. About 10km before the falls you show your permit – and leave your passport – at a roadside checkpoint. When you arrive at the parking area at the falls, you

leave your permit with an official there. You collect each from the same place on return. It was all very straightforward at the time of writing, but be prepared for changes to the regulations.

**Nguom Ngao Cave** The main entrance to this cave *(admission & guide 50,000d)* is 2km from Ban Gioc Waterfall, just off the road to Cao Bang. The cave is enormous (about 3km long) and one branch reaches almost all the way to the waterfalls, where there is a 'secret' entrance. Normally a guided tour will take about an hour and will only go about 400m into the cave; ask if you want to see more. The price remains the same, and a full tour takes about two hours. Mains electricity is due to be installed, but it's probably sensible to take a torch (flashlight).

**Places to Stay & Eat** At the time of writing, there were no hotels on the Vietnamese side of the border. Cao Bang is the nearest real option for accommodation, though it may be possible to get a very basic bed at the **People's Committee Guesthouse** (Nha Khach UBND) in Trung Khanh.

There is limited food available in Trung Khanh, and nothing at all in Ban Gioc. You'd be wise to prepare at least a picnic lunch for the trip to the waterfall and caves.

**Getting There & Away** The road between Cao Bang and Ban Gioc via Quang Yen is in good nick, and is presently fine for 2WD. The 87km trip will take you about 2½ hours each way; it's mountainous and winding and very beautiful. If you take the loop route to and from the falls, the section between Tra Linh and Trung Khanh is still very bumpy, and 4WD is recommended for this stretch, especially after rain. There is public transport between Cao Bang and Trung Khanh but nothing beyond that; you may be able to negotiate for a *xe om* (in Trung Khanh) to take you to the falls.

## Montagnard Markets

In Cao Bang province, Kinh (ethnic Vietnamese) are a distinct minority. The largest ethnic groups are the Tay (46%), Nung

(32%), H'mong (8%), Dzao (7%), Kinh (5%) and Lolo (1%). Intermarriage, mass education and 'modern' clothing is gradually eroding tribal and cultural distinctions. Check out Tim Doling's book *Mountains and Ethnic Minorities: North East Vietnam* for detailed accounts of tribal people in the region. It's available from the Vietnam Museum of Ethnology and most bookshops in Hanoi.

Most of Cao Bang's Montagnards remain blissfully naive about the ways of the outside world. Cheating in the marketplace, for example, is virtually unknown and even tourists are charged the same price as locals without bargaining. Whether or not this innocence can withstand the onslaught of even limited tourism remains to be seen.

The following big Montagnard markets in Cao Bang province are held every five days, according to lunar calendar dates.

**Trung Khanh** 5th, 10th, 15th, 20th, 25th and 30th day of each lunar month

**Tra Linh** 4th, 9th, 14th, 19th, 24th and 29th day of each lunar month

**Nuoc Hai** 1st, 6th, 11th, 16th, 21st and 26th day of each lunar month

**Na Giang** 1st, 6th, 11th, 16th, 21st and 26th day of each lunar month. Held 20km from Hang Pac Bo in the direction of Cao Bang, and attracting Tay, Nung and H'mong, this is one of the best and busiest markets in the provinces.

## BA BE NATIONAL PARK
☎ 0281 • elevation 145m

Ba Be National Park *(Vuon Quoc Gia Ba Be; ☎ 894014, fax 894026; admission 10,000d per person, plus 1000d insurance fee, plus 10,000d per car)* is sometimes referred to as Ba Be Lakes. It is in Bac Kan province and was established in 1992 as Vietnam's eighth national park. It's a beautiful region that covers more than 23,000 hectares and boasts waterfalls, rivers, deep valleys, lakes and caves set amid towering peaks. The surrounding area is home to members of the Tay minority, who live in stilt homes.

The park is a tropical-rainforest area with over 550 named plant species, and the government subsidises the villagers not to cut down the trees. The 300 or so wildlife species in the forest include 65 (mostly rarely seen) mammals, 214 bird species, butterflies and other insects. Hunting is forbidden, but villagers are permitted to fish.

The park is surrounded by steep mountains, up to 1554m in height. The 1939 *Madrolle Guide to Indochina* suggested getting around Ba Be Lakes 'in a car, on horseback, or, for ladies, in a chair', meaning, of course, a sedan chair.

Ba Be (Three Bays) is in fact three linked lakes, which have a total length of 8km and a width of about 400m. The deepest point in the lakes is 35m, and there are nearly 50 species of freshwater fish.

Two of the lakes are separated by a 100m-wide strip of water called Be Kam, sandwiched between high walls of chalk rock. The **Thac Dau Dang** (Dau Dang or Ta Ken Waterfall) consists of a series of spectacular cascades between sheer walls of rock, and is accessible by boat and on foot during a day trip. Just 200m below the rapids is a small Tay village called Hua Tang.

**Hang Puong** (Puong Cave) is another place that is visited on day tours. It's about 30m high and 300m long, and completely passes through a mountain. A navigable river flows through the cave, making for an interesting boat trip.

Renting a boat is *de rigueur*, and costs 40,000d per hour. The boats carry about eight people (but it's the same price if there are just two), and you should allow at least seven hours to take in most sights. Enjoy the ride: it's lovely despite the noisy engines. An optional guide (recommended) costs US$10 per day. The boat dock is about 2km from park headquarters.

The park staff can organise several **tours**. Costs depend on the number of people, but expect to pay at least US$25 per day if you're travelling alone. It will cost less per person with more people in a group. There's the option of a one-day tour by boat; a one-day tour combining motorboat, a 3km or 4km walk, and a trip by dugout canoe; and there are also combination cycling, boating and walking possibilities. Homestays can be arranged at several of the villages in the park, and longer treks can also be arranged.

The park entrance fee is payable at a checkpoint on the road into the park, about 15km before the park headquarters, just after leaving Cho Ra.

## Places to Stay & Eat

Not far from the park headquarters are two accommodation options. Rooms in the newly built **guesthouses** *(US$20)* are fine, if a bit pricey. There are also pleasant air-con two-room **cottages** *(rooms US$25)*. Negotiate as the price in dong may be cheaper. There's an OK **restaurant** on-site, and you need to place your order an hour or so before you want to eat. Internet access is available for 10,000d per hour.

**Ba Be Hotel** *(☎ 876115; fan rooms US$12-15)* is in Cho Ra, 18km from the lakes. It's

### The Legend of Widow's Island

A tiny islet in the middle of Ba Be Lakes is the source of a local legend. The Tay people believe that what is a lake today was once farmland, and in the middle was a village called Nam Mau.

One day, the Nam Mau residents found a buffalo wandering in the nearby forest. They caught it, butchered it and shared the meat. However, they didn't share any with a certain lonely old widow.

Unfortunately for the villagers, this wasn't just any old buffalo. It belonged to the river ghost. When the buffalo failed to return home, the ghost went to the village disguised as a beggar. He asked the villagers for something to eat, but they refused to share their buffalo buffet and ran the poor beggar off. Only the widow was kind to him and gave him some food and a place to stay for the night.

That night the beggar told the widow to take some rice husks and sprinkle them on the ground around her house. Later in the evening, it started to rain, and then a flood came. The villagers all drowned, and the flood washed away their homes and farms, thus creating Ba Be Lakes. Only the widow's house remained: it's now Po Gia Mai (Widow's Island).

pretty grotty for the price; you're better off staying in the park.

It's also possible to stay in **stilt houses** at a couple of hamlets in the park. The park office can organise this for about US$3 per person. Food is available at the homestays, including fresh fish from the lake, and prices are reasonable.

Take enough cash for your visit – there are no money-exchange facilities.

## Getting There & Away

Ba Be National Park is in Bac Kan province not far from the borders of Cao Bang province and Tuyen Quang province. The lakes are 240km from Hanoi, 61km from Bac Kan (also known as Bach Thong) and 18km from Cho Ra.

Most visitors to the national park get there by chartered vehicle from Hanoi. Since the 2000 opening of a new road into the park, 4WD is no longer necessary. The one-way journey from Hanoi takes about six hours; most travellers allow three days and two nights for the entire excursion.

Reaching the park by public transport is possible, but not easy. Take a bus from Hanoi to Phu Thong (30,000d, six hours) via Thai Nguyen and/or Bac Kan, and from there take another bus to Cho Ra (10,000d, two hours). In Cho Ra you will have to get a motorbike (about 30,000d) to take you the last 18km, unless you are willing to walk it.

## THAI NGUYEN

☎ 028 • pop 171,400 • elevation 300m

There isn't a whole lot in Thai Nguyen to hold your interest, but the **Museum of the Cultures of Vietnam's Ethnic Groups** *(Bao Tang Van Hoa Cac Dan Toc; admission 10,000d; open 7am-11am & 2pm-5.30pm Tues-Sun, last admission at 5pm)* is worthwhile seeing on the way to Ba Be Lakes. It is the largest Montagnard museum in Vietnam. The giant pastel-pink building houses a wide array of colourful exhibits representing the 50-odd hill tribes residing in Vietnam.

There is an interesting English booklet about the displays for US$2.

## Getting There & Away

Thai Nguyen is 76km north of Hanoi, and the road there is in good nick.

Buses and minibuses to Thai Nguyen (15,000d, three hours) depart from Hanoi's Gia Lam station regularly between 5am and 5pm.

## AROUND THAI NGUYEN
### Phuong Hoang Cave

Phuong Hoang Cave is one of the largest and most accessible caverns in northern Vietnam. There are four main chambers, two of which are illuminated by the sun when the angle is correct. Most of the stalactites and stalagmites are still in place, although quite a few have been broken off by thoughtless souvenir hunters. Like many caves in Vietnam, this one served as a hospital and ammunition depot during the American War. If you want to see anything, you'd best bring a good torch (flashlight).

The cave is a 40km motorbike ride over a bumpy road from Thai Nguyen.

### Nui Coc Reservoir

A scenic spot popular with locals, Nui Coc Reservoir (admission 6000d; hotel rooms 80,000-250,000d) is 25km west of Thai Nguyen. It's a pretty stretch of water, and is a major drawcard for city-bound Hanoi residents looking to get away from it all. On summer weekends it can get particularly crowded. A one-hour, circular motorboat tour of the lake is the thing to do and costs about 180,000d. You can use the water park's swimming pool for 20,000d, and also rent rowboats. It might be worth a visit if you're on route to Ba Be Lakes, with your own transport, and want to cool off.

# Northwest Vietnam

Northwest Vietnam offers travellers some of the country's most spectacular scenery. The mountainous areas are also home to many distinct hill tribes, often still living as they have for generations despite increasing outside influences.

Hwy 6 winds through beautiful mountains and high plains, which are inhabited by Montagnards, notably the Black Thai, White Thai, Dao and H'mong. The Thai live mostly in the lower lands, where they cultivate tea and fruit and live in attractive stilt houses. The Dao and H'mong live in the bleaker highlands over 1000m.

The road is mostly surfaced with bitumen from Hanoi to Dien Bien Phu – but even so, it's a thrill! Even more exciting is Hwy 12 (between Dien Bien Phu and Lai Chau), a dangerous cliffhanger still regularly wiped out by landslides. Although it's mostly sealed, stretches of this road are so rough it can jar the fillings out of your teeth. The ensuing stretch from Lai Chau into Sapa is bumpy in places, but offers some of the best mountain vistas in Southeast Asia.

The northwestern roads improve annually. However, if you suffer from vertigo, backache or (God forbid) haemorrhoids, you might want to stick to the shorter trips. Many travel only as far as Mai Chau or Son La, or Sapa in the other direction, before turning back.

The most interesting journey in this area is the 'northwest loop'. Head for Mai Chau, followed by Son La and Dien Bien Phu, then north to Lai Chau or Tam Duong, Sapa, Lao Cai and back to Hanoi. The loop is best driven by 4WD or motorbike, in case the raods are cut and you need to do some bushbashing. It is also possible – if you've got lots of time and stamina – to travel the loop by public transport. You should allow at least a week for this journey, and considerably more time if you're braving the local buses. And three cheers and more for the hardy cyclists who pump up and down these roads.

## Highlights

- Hit the 'northwest loop' by jeep, motorbike or bicycle to take in some of Southeast Asia's most exhilarating mountain scenery
- Trek to highland villages and spend time with hill-tribe communities
- Enjoy the sights and sounds of vibrant Montagnard markets
- Explore the foothills – or make the challenging ascent – of Fansipan, Vietnam's highest mountain

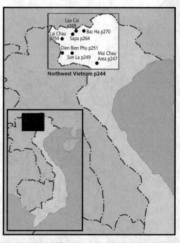

Lao Cai p269
Lai Chau p254 • Bac Ha p270
Sapa p264
Dien Bien Phu p251
Son La p249 • Mai Chau Area p247

**Northwest Vietnam p244**

## Warning

In the entire northwest of Vietnam, there are very few places to cash travellers cheques, and credit cards are of little use. You can cash travellers cheques at some hotels in Sapa, but you will be charged a steep 10% commission. It's easier to swap US dollars for Vietnamese dong, but the rate is not great; you'd be wise to complete all your money-changing transactions before you leave Hanoi.

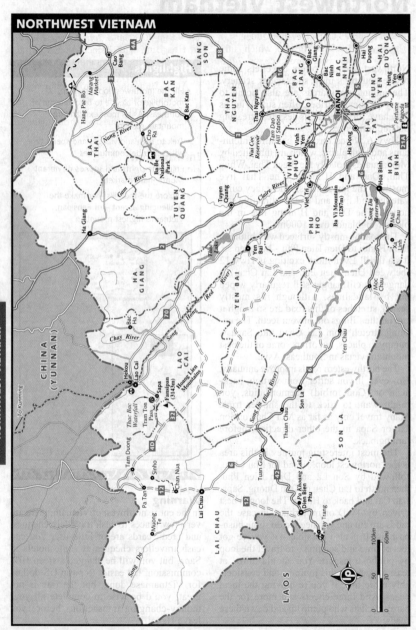

**NORTHWEST VIETNAM**

243

## HOA BINH

☎ 008 • pop 75,000 • elevation 200m

The city of Hoa Binh (Peace), which is the capital of Hoa Binh province, is 74km southwest of Hanoi. This area is home to many hill-tribe people, such as the H'mong and Thai. Hoa Binh is a stop on the long drive towards Dien Bien Phu via Mai Chau.

The town is situated on the flats at the base of the mountains. The locals have adopted modern Vietnamese garb, but a selection of Montagnard clothing, together with crossbows, opium pipes and lots of other Montagnard paraphernalia, can be bought at the **souvenir shop** in the Hoa Binh Hotel I.

There's a small **museum** (admission free; open 8am-10.30am & 2pm-4.30pm Mon-Fri) in Hoa Binh with French–Viet Minh and American Wars memorabilia – including a rusty French amphibious vehicle.

About 200m along the road to the right of the museum, the **dam wall** of a vast and impressive hydroelectric station is visible; across the river is a massive shrine to the 161 workers who died during its construction.

### Information

**Hoa Binh Tourism Company** (☎ 854374, fax 854372) does not have a walk-in office, but staff at the company's Hoa Binh Hotels I and II can help with information.

---

## The Roads Well-Travelled: Conversations with Jeep Drivers

'I didn't plan to be a tourist driver. In the early 1980s I went to Moscow on a scholarship, to take a degree in civil engineering, and hoped to make that my career. Many of us Vietnamese went to study in Russia during that time. I learned to speak Russian, too, of course. That lasted three years, but by the time I came back the political climate here had changed, a Russian education was not highly valued and my degree didn't count for much.'

'My extended family pooled our money and bought this 4WD. It's a 1993 model and we bought it secondhand in a shipment that came from the US. It registers miles, not kilometres, which was a bit confusing for me at first!'

'Me, I don't work for any travel agency in particular, but there are one or two that give me most work. Sometimes customers call you directly, maybe ex-pats or tourists who've heard of you through other friends. That's good because then you can negotiate the trip yourself, you know exactly what people want, and they pay you directly rather than go through the agents. It doesn't happen often though. I drive all over the country, but the northwest is the area that tourists want most to see and I go there most often, I suppose at least 30 times a year. Yes, they're long days, but as long as I can have an hour at lunch to eat and rest that's fine. And the tourists usually bring snacks to share during the journey; I really like those M&Ms.'

'Mostly when I drive foreigners there's a guide/interpreter with them, so I don't need to speak another language. You can understand a lot, just by gestures and tone of voice and expressions. But I know it would be sensible to learn more English. I can understand some, but I'm not good at speaking it. My last passenger and I had fun learning to say things from the phrase book; I taught her how to pronounce the Vietnamese and she taught me how to pronounce the English, then we'd test each other on the longer road trips. Foreigners always find it really hard to pronounce Vietnamese though, too many tones. She left the book with me, so I must keep practicing.'

'I'm usually home in Hanoi for one night and one day a week if I'm lucky. My wife works full-time in an office, but our children are almost teenagers so they can pretty well look after themselves when we're busy. We spend a lot on mobile phone calls though!'

Internet access is available at the **post office**.

## Places to Stay & Eat

**Hoa Binh Hotels I & II** (☎ 852537, fax 854372; singles/doubles US$28/33) are in Montagnard stilt-house style with comfortable nontraditional amenities like hot water and TV. They're on the road heading out of town towards Mai Chau, and are two of the better hotels found in northwestern Vietnam. There are cheaper **guesthouses** and many **com pho places** lining Hwy 6 in the centre of town.

## SONG DA RESERVOIR

Stretching west of Hoa Binh is the Song Da Reservoir (Ho Song Da), Vietnam's largest. The flooding of the Da River has displaced a large number of farmers for about 200km upstream, and is part of a major hydroelectric scheme that generates power for northern Vietnam. In 1994, a 500kV power line was extended from this area to the south, freeing Ho Chi Minh City (HCMC) from the seasonal power shortages that often blacked out the city for up to three days at a time.

Easiest access to the reservoir is by taking a spur road that cuts off from Hwy 6 at Dong Bang Junction (60km west of Hoa Binh and just outside Mai Chau). From Dong Bang Junction it's about a 5km drive to Bai San Pier. There's no obvious jetty here – hang around and someone will come out from one of the houses and ask where you want to go. You'll need a Vietnamese speaker to help make arrangements.

One of the trips you can take is to the **Ba Khan Islands**. The islands are the tops of submerged mountains and the visual effect is like a freshwater version of Halong Bay. The return trip to the islands takes three hours and costs 150,000d per boat (each boat can seat 10 passengers).

Another possible boat trip is to Than Nhan village, home to members of the Dao tribe. The two-hour return trip costs about 100,000d. The boat leaves you at a pier from where it's a steep 4km uphill walk to the village. If you'd like to stay in the village, you can take the boat one way for 50,000d and get a return boat to Bai San Pier the next day.

The last option is to charter a boat from Bai San Pier to Hoa Binh (400,000d, six hours).

## MAI CHAU

☎ 018 • pop 47,500 • elevation 300m

This is one of the closest places to Hanoi where you can visit a 'real' **Montagnard village**. Mai Chau is rural with no town centre as such – rather, it's a collection of villages, farms and huts spread out through a large valley. It's a beautiful area, and most people here are ethnic White Thai, said to be distantly related to tribes in Thailand, Laos and China.

Things to do here include staying overnight in one of the Thai stilt houses, **walking** across the beautiful valley through the rice fields and **trekking** to minority villages. A typical walk farther afield covers 7km to 8km; a local guide can be hired for about US$5.

Although most local people no longer wear traditional dress, the Thai women are masterful weavers who ensure that there is plenty of traditional-style clothing to buy in the village centre or when strolling through the pleasant lanes. You will probably see women weaving on looms under or inside their houses in the village. Refreshingly, the Thai of Mai Chau are far less likely to employ strong-arm sales tactics than their H'mong counterparts in Sapa: polite bargaining is the norm.

If you'd like more adventure, there is a popular 18km trek from **Lac village** (Ban Lac) in Mai Chau, to **Xa Linh village**, near a mountain pass (elevation 1000m) on Hwy 6. Lac village is home to the White Thai people, while the inhabitants of Xa Linh are H'mong. The trek is too strenuous to be done as a day hike, so you'll have to spend the night in a small village along the way. You'll need a local guide but, as part of the deal, a pre-arranged car will pick you up at the mountain pass and bring you back to Mai Chau. Be forewarned that you climb 600m in altitude on this route and the trail can be dangerously slippery in the rain.

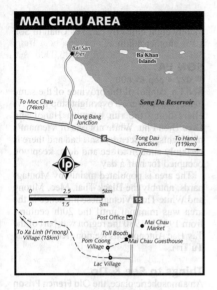

**MAI CHAU AREA**

Bai San Pier

Ba Khan Islands

Song Da Reservoir

To Moc Chau (74km)

Dong Bang Junction

Tong Dau Junction

To Hanoi (119km)

0    2.5    5km
0    1.5    3mi

Post Office

Mai Chau Market

To Xa Linh (H'mong) Village (18km)

Toll Booth

Pom Coong Village

Mai Chau Guesthouse

Lac Village

Longer treks of three to seven days are possible. Try contacting **Hoa Binh Tourism Company** (☎ 008-854374, fax 854372) at the Hoa Binh Hotel I to make arrangements, or simply ask around in the Mai Chau villages of Lac or Pom Coong.

Many cafés and travel agencies in Hanoi run inexpensive trips to Mai Chau. These include all transport, food and accommodation.

## Places to Stay & Eat

**Mai Chau Guesthouse** (☎ 851812; rooms from 120,000d) is a decent, if basic, state-run guesthouse on the main road through the valley. Rooms at the back have balconies and views across the rice fields to the mountains.

However, most travellers choose to walk a few hundred metres back from the 'main' roadside and stay in the **Thai stilt houses** (50,000d per person) of Lac or Pom Coong village. Lac is the busier of the two, and villagers will sometimes organise (for a fee) traditional song-and-dance performances in the evenings.

If you are anticipating an exotic Indiana Jones encounter (sharing a bowl of eyeball soup, taking part in some ancient fertility ritual and so on), think again. Spending a night in one of Mai Chau's minority villages is a very 'civilised' experience: the local authorities have made sure that the villages are up to tourist standards, so electricity flows, modern amenities abound and there are hygienic Western-style toilets. Mattresses and mosquito nets are provided. While this is not a bad thing per se, it may not live up to your rustic hill-tribe trekking expectations. Tour operators are not helping the situation: somehow they cannot seem to resist slapping up their oversized advertisement stickers wherever their groups stop to eat or drink, even if that happens to be on these lovely wooden stilt houses.

Despite (or perhaps because of) modern amenities, most people come away pleased with the experience. The Thai villages are exceedingly friendly and, when it's all said and done, even with TV and the hum of the refrigerator, it *is* a peaceful place and you're still sleeping in a thatched-roof stilt house on split-bamboo floors.

Reservations are not necessary; you can just show up, but it's advisable to arrive before dark (preferably by mid-afternoon). You can book a meal at the house where you're staying for around 20,000d, depending on what you require. The women here have learned to cook everything from fried eggs to French fries, but try to eat the local food – it's more interesting.

## Getting There & Away

Mai Chau is 135km from Hanoi and just 5km south of Tong Dau junction on Hwy 6 (the Hanoi–Dien Bien Phu route).

There's no direct public transport to Mai Chau from Hanoi; however, buses to nearby Hoa Binh (12,000d, two hours) are plentiful. From Hoa Binh there are scheduled buses to Mai Chau (20,000d, two hours) at 6am, noon, 1pm and 4pm daily. Usually these stop at Tong Dau junction; a *xe om* from there to Mai Chau proper will cost about 5000d.

Theoretically, foreigners must pay a 5000d entry fee to Mai Chau; there's a toll booth at the state-run guesthouse on the 'main' road. Sometimes it's staffed, sometimes not.

NORTHWEST VIETNAM

## MOC CHAU
☎ 022 • pop 113,100 • elevation 1500m
This highland town produces some of Vietnam's best tea and is a good place to stock up. The surrounding area is also home to several ethnic minorities, including Green H'mong, Dao, Thai and Muong.

Moc Chau boasts a pioneer dairy industry that started in the late 1970s with Australian and, later, UN assistance. The dairy provides Hanoi with such delectable luxuries as fresh milk, sweetened condensed milk and little tooth-rotting sweet bars called *banh sua*. Not surprisingly, Moc Chau is a good place to sample some fresh milk and yogurt. You should indulge yourself at one of the dairy shops that line Hwy 6 as it passes through Moc Chau.

**Duc Dung Guesthouse** (☎ 866181; rooms 120,000d), about 100m off Hwy 6 – turn left at the post office in the middle of town – is the place to stay if you're planning to overnight here.

Moc Chau is 200km from Hanoi, and the journey takes roughly six hours by private car. The road is in good condition. It's another 120km from Moc Chau to Son La. (See Son La later in this chapter.)

## YEN CHAU
☎ 022 • pop 50,800
This small agricultural district is well known for its fruit-growing industry. Apart from bananas, the different kinds of fruit grown here are seasonal – mangoes, plums and peaches are harvested from April to June, longans in July and August, and custard apples in August and September.

The mangoes, in particular, are considered to be some of the best in Vietnam, although overseas travellers may find them disappointing at first. This is because they are small and green rather than big, yellow and juicy as in the tropical south. However, many Vietnamese prefer the somewhat tart taste and aroma of the green ones, especially dipped in fish sauce *(nuoc mam)* and sugar. The colour doesn't give a clue as to when the fruit is ripe, so you may need to ask one of the locals for advice on the ripeness of the mangoes.

Yen Chau is 260km from Hanoi, approximately eight hours by car. Yen Chau to Son La is another 60km.

## SON LA
☎ 022 • pop 61,600
Son La, capital of the province of the same name, makes a good overnight stop for travellers doing the run between Hanoi and Dien Bien Phu. While not one of Vietnam's highlights, the scenery isn't bad and there is certainly enough to see and do to keep you occupied for half a day.

The area is populated mainly by Montagnards, notably the Black Thai, Meo, Muong and White Thai. Vietnamese influence in the area was minimal until the 20th century; from 1959 to 1980 the region was part of the Tay Bac Autonomous Region (Khu Tay Bac Tu Tri).

### Things to See & Do
An atmospheric place, the **Old French Prison & Museum** (Nha Tu Cu Cua Phap; admission 10,000d; open 7.30am-11am & 1.30pm-5pm daily) in Son La was once the site of a French penal colony where anticolonial revolutionaries were incarcerated. It was destroyed by the infamous 'off-loading' of unused ammunition by US warplanes returning to their bases after bombing raids on Hanoi and Haiphong, and has been partially restored. Rebuilt turrets and watchtowers stand guard over the remains of cells, fetters, inner walls and a famous lone surviving peach tree. The tree, which blooms with traditional Tet flowers, was planted in the compound by To Hieu, a former inmate from the 1940s. To Hieu has subsequently been immortalised, with various landmarks about town named after him.

A narrow road leads uphill to the prison, off the main highway. At the end of a road is a People's Committee office with a small **museum** on the top floor where there are some interesting hill-tribe displays and a good bird's-eye view of the prison ruins. The prison itself is at the back, entered beneath a faded sign marked 'Penitencier'.

Perched above the town, a **lookout tower** offers a sweeping overview of Son La and the surrounding area. The climb is steep and takes about 20 minutes, but the view from the top is well worth it. Photography of the scenery is permitted, but the guards will get uptight if you try to photograph the installations, which serve both telecommunications and military purposes. They may also offer you rice-wine and conversation. The stone steps leading up to the tower are immediately to the left of the Trade Union Hotel.

You can find a small selection of colourful woven shoulder bags, scarves, silver buttons and necklaces, clothing and other Montagnard crafts at Son La's **market**.

Unfortunately, **Tam Ta Toong Caves** (formerly a minor tourist attraction just outside town) remain closed because of fears that people will contaminate the waters: the caves are the main water source for Son La. Inquire as to whether they have been reopened at your hotel.

A few kilometres south of town are the **Suoi Nuoc Nong hot springs**. They won't be everyone's cup of tea: there's a rather soupy small communal pool (admission free), and several privately run concrete cubicles (admission 5000d) where water is pumped into a private bathtub. To get here, start opposite

the museum road. The road leads past the party headquarters building, after which there's 1km or so of bumpy track before the road is sealed for the 5km to the springs.

## Places to Stay

Almost all travellers journeying between Hanoi and Dien Bien Phu spend the night in Son La. There are plenty of hotels in town, many of which are truly grotty and/or double as brothels; those listed here are currently exceptions.

**Ngoc Hoa Guesthouse** (Nha Nghi Ngoc Hoa; ☎ 853993; bed in 6-bed dorm US$3, doubles with bath US$12) is the cheapest OK place in town.

**Nha Nghi Long Phuong** and **Nha Nghi Thanh Loan** are two cheap, basic, but OK guesthouses at the main junction in town. Rooms are around US$5.

**Trade Union Hotel** (Khach San Cong Doan; ☎ 852244, fax 855312; air-con twins US$15) remains, for a state-run place, a rare gem. The staff is exceedingly friendly and prices are reasonable. Large rooms come with hot water and breakfast.

**People's Committee Guesthouse** (Nha Khach Uy Ban Nhan Dan Tinh Son La; ☎ 852080;

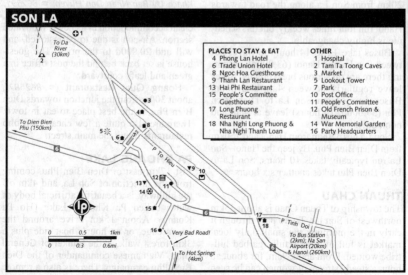

**SON LA**

| PLACES TO STAY & EAT | OTHER |
| --- | --- |
| 4 Phong Lan Hotel | 1 Hospital |
| 6 Trade Union Hotel | 2 Tam Ta Toong Caves |
| 8 Ngoc Hoa Guesthouse | 3 Market |
| 9 Thanh Lan Restaurant | 5 Lookout Tower |
| 13 Hai Phi Restaurant | 7 Park |
| 15 People's Committee | 10 Post Office |
| Guesthouse | 11 People's Committee |
| 17 Long Phuong | 12 Old French Prison & |
| Restaurant | Museum |
| 18 Nha Nghi Long Phuong & | 14 War Memorial Garden |
| Nha Nghi Thanh Loan | 16 Party Headquarters |

To Da River (30km)

To Dien Bien Phu (150km)

P To Hieu

P Tinh Doi

To Bus Station (2km); Na San Airport (20km) & Hanoi (260km)

Very Bad Road!

To Hot Springs (4km)

0 0.5 1km
0 0.3 0.6mi

*air-con rooms 150,000d)* has an enormous extension underway, which should be open by the time you read this. These new rooms will probably be worth a look.

**Phong Lan Hotel** *(☎ 853516, fax 852318; rooms with fan US$15, air-con twins US$18-20)* includes breakfast in its rates and is just opposite the market.

## Places to Eat

At the main junction, **Long Phuong Restaurant** *(☎ 852339)* offers a good, interesting menu. Try the sour *mang dang* (bamboo shoots) soup, a speciality of the Thai minority people; and sticky rice dipped in sesame seed salt.

**Hai Phi Restaurant** dishes up Son La's speciality – *lau* (goat meat). Try the highly prized *tiet canh*, a bowl of goat's-blood curd dressed with a sprinkling of peanuts and veggies. Or go for the more conventional, but tasty, goat-meat steamboat.

For good, standard Vietnamese food try **Thanh Lan Restaurant**, along from the post office.

## Getting There & Away

Son La's airport is called Na San and is 20km from Son La along the road towards Hanoi. At time of writing, flights to/from Hanoi run four times weekly, but this schedule is highly changeable.

Buses take 12 to 14 hours to travel between Son La and Hanoi (63,000d), assuming there are no serious breakdowns. Buses leave regularly between 4am and noon. Buses going from Son La to Dien Bien Phu (39,000d, 10 hours) leave at 4am and noon also.

Son La lies 320km from Hanoi and 150km from Dien Bien Phu. By jeep the Hanoi–Son La run typically takes 10 hours. Son La to Dien Bien Phu takes another six hours.

## THUAN CHAU

The township of Thuan Chau is about 35km northwest of Son La. Try to pass through it early in the morning; the small daily local **market** is full of wonderfully garbed hill-tribe women. From about 9am, for about an hour, a steady stream of women can be seen walking, cycling and motorbiking home to their villages along the main road.

## TUAN GIAO

**☎ 023 • pop 94,900 • elevation 600m**

This remote town is at the junction of Hwy 42 to Dien Bien Phu (three hours, 80km) and Hwy 6 to Lai Chau (four hours, 98km). Most travellers approach from Son La (three hours, 75km) or Hanoi (13 hours, 406km). The driving times quoted here assume that you are travelling by car or motorbike – for public buses, multiply the travel time by at least 1.5.

Not many people spend the night unless they are running behind schedule and can't make it to Dien Bien Phu, though if you are taking your time through the northwest it is a logical place to stop for the night.

## Places to Stay & Eat

**Tuan Giao Hotel** *(Khach San Tuan Giao; ☎ 862613; rooms with/without bath 120,000/ 60,000d)* is a relatively new place with fan rooms. It's fine, and the staff are welcoming. It's about 150m from the main junction in the direction of Lai Chau.

**People's Committee Guesthouse** *(Nha Khach Uy Ban Nhan Dan Huyen; ☎ 862391; new-wing rooms 120,000d)* offers good, clean accommodation in its newly renovated section. Air-con is due to be installed, and will add 20,000d to the price. The guesthouse is set back behind the post office in a green and leafy courtyard.

**Hoang Quat Restaurant** *(☎ 862582)*, about 300m from the junction towards Dien Bien Phu, is the best place to eat in town. There are also quite a few cheap **com pho restaurants** lining the main street.

## PA KHOANG LAKE

Just 17km east of Dien Bien Phu, coming from the direction of Son La, and 4km off the highway, is a beautiful artificial body of water called Pa Khoang Lake (Ho Pa Koang). About 15km drive around the lake's edge, or an hour's boat ride plus a 3km forest walk, is the **bunker of General Giap**, Vietnamese commander of the Dien Bien Phu campaign. There is also a remote

**Thai and Sa village** that can be visited across the lake.

There is accommodation at Pa Khoang, in the 1997 built, but rapidly disintegrating, **Pa Khoang Hotel** (☎ 926552; fan rooms US$10-12); it's in a gorgeous setting, but the cobwebby and musty rooms are falling apart. While the hotel might not cry out for overnight guests, it's a good venue in which to spend a few hours en route to or from Dien Bien Phu; hire a motor boat (US$10 return) to the bunker or villages, and stay for lunch. If she's still around, a splendid elderly woman with blackened teeth will probably embrace and kiss you before she cooks for you.

## DIEN BIEN PHU
☎ 023 • pop 22,400

Dien Bien Phu, the capital of Dien Bien District of Lai Chau Province, is in one of the most remote parts of Vietnam. The town is 34km from the Lao border in the flat, heart-shaped Muong Thanh Valley, which is about 20km long and 5km wide and surrounded by steep, heavily forested hills.

For centuries, Dien Bien Phu was a transit stop on the caravan route from Myanmar and China to northern Vietnam. The town itself was established in 1841 by the Nguyen dynasty to prevent raids on the Red River Delta by bandits. More recently, Dien Bien Phu was the site of that rarest of military events – a battle that can be called truly decisive. On 6 May 1954, the day before the Geneva Conference on Indochina was set to begin half a world away, Viet Minh forces overran the beleaguered French garrison at Dien Bien Phu after a 57-day siege. This shattered French morale and forced the French government to abandon its attempts to re-establish colonial control of Indochina.

History is the main attraction here and the scenery – though pleasant enough – is just a sideshow enjoyed during arrival and departure overland. Not surprisingly, the majority of travellers who come here now are French – Dien Bien Phu seems to hold the same sort of fascination for them as the Demilitarised Zone (DMZ) does for North Americans.

The area is inhabited by Montagnards, most notably the Thai and H'mong. For greater detail on northwestern hill tribes, Tim Doling's *Mountains and Ethnic Minorities: North West Vietnam*, available in most Hanoi bookshops, makes a good companion on a tour of the region. The government has been encouraging ethnic Vietnamese to settle in the region and populate the relatively new provincial capital. They currently make up about a third of the Muong Thanh Valley's total population of 60,000.

Tourism is having quite an impact on Dien Bien Phu – most of the buildings you

## DIEN BIEN PHU

| PLACES TO STAY | OTHER |
| --- | --- |
| 3  May Hong Hotel | 1  Airport |
| 4  Airport Hotel; | 2  Bus Station |
|      Vietnam Airlines & | 6  Market |
|      Nga Luan Restaurant | 7  Internet Café |
| 5  Construction Hotel | 9  Radio-TV Tower |
| 8  Binh Long Hotel | 12  Main Post Office |
| 11  Lottery Hotel | 13  Bunker of Chief Artillery |
| 19  Dien Bien Phu Hotel |       Commander Pirot |
| 22  Beer Factory | 14  Muong Thanh Bridge |
|      Guesthouse | 15  Surrender Site |
|  |       (Bunker de Castries) |
| PLACES TO EAT | 16  Tank |
| 10  Com-Pho | 17  French War Memorial |
|      Restaurants | 18  Dien Bien Phu Museum |
| 21  Lien Tuoi Restaurant | 20  Cemetery |

0    150    300m
0    150    300yd
Approximate Scale

To Lai Chau (102km)

To Muong Thanh Hotel (500m); Pa Khoang Lake (21km) & Hanoi (470km)

Old Artillery

Ron River

A1 Hill

To Lao Border (34km)

NORTHWEST VIETNAM

see are very new. Another reason for the construction boom is that Dien Bien Phu was made the capital of Lai Chau Province in 1993. This honour was bestowed upon it mainly because the old capital (Lai Chau) may be submerged under water in a few years (see the Lai Chau section later in this chapter for details). The size and look of the city is surprising considering the remote location (especially if you survived getting here overland). There's even Internet access for 10,000d per hour at a café about 300m towards town from the Muong Thanh Hotel.

## Things to See & Do

The site of the battle is now marked by the **Dien Bien Phu Museum** (☎ 824971). The bunker headquarters of the French commander, Colonel Christian de Castries, has been re-created, and there are old French tanks and artillery pieces nearby. There is a monument to Viet Minh casualties on the site of the former French position, known to the French as Eliane and to the Vietnamese as **A1 Hill**, where bitter fighting took place. Each of these sites charges 5000d admission, and is open 7.30am to 11am and 1.30pm to 4.30pm daily.

The old **Muong Thanh Bridge** is preserved and closed to motorised traffic. Near the southern end of the bridge – though not much more than a crater in the ground overgrown with weeds – is the **bunker** where Chief Artillery Commander Pirot committed suicide.

A **memorial** to the 3000 French troops buried under the rice paddies was erected in 1984 on the 30th anniversary of the battle. The stylishly-designed **Dien Bien Phu Cemetery** commemorates the Vietnamese dead, and you can catch a good view over it by climbing the stairs inside the main entry gate.

## Places to Stay & Eat

The cheaper accommodation in town comes care of the local airline, lottery commission, construction ministry and – get this – the beer brewery!

**Dien Bien Phu Airport Hotel** (☎ 825052; air-con rooms 150,000d) is above the Vietnam Airlines office. The higher floors have bigger, lighter rooms but it's pretty ordinary and on a noisy street.

The **Lottery Hotel** (rooms with bath 120,000d), close to the post office, has basic rooms and is in a quiet location.

**Construction Hotel** (☎ 824386; rooms 80,000d) is right by the river and is as basic as you'd expect for the price.

## The Siege of Dien Bien Phu

In early 1954 General Henri Navarre, commander of the French forces in Indochina, sent 12 battalions to occupy the Muong Thanh Valley to prevent the Viet Minh from crossing into Laos and threatening the former Lao capital of Luang Prabang. The French units, of which about 30% were ethnic Vietnamese, were soon surrounded by a Viet Minh force under General Vo Nguyen Giap that consisted of 33 infantry battalions, six artillery regiments and a regiment of engineers. The Viet Minh force, which outnumbered the French by five to one, was equipped with 105mm artillery pieces and anti-aircraft guns, carried by porters through jungles and across rivers in an unbelievable feat of logistics. The guns were emplaced in carefully camouflaged positions dug deep into the hills that overlooked the French positions.

A failed Viet Minh human-wave assault against the French was followed by weeks of intense artillery bombardments. Six battalions of French paratroopers were parachuted into Dien Bien Phu as the situation worsened, but bad weather and the Viet Minh artillery, impervious to French air and artillery attacks, prevented sufficient French reinforcements and supplies from arriving. An elaborate system of trenches and tunnels allowed Viet Minh soldiers to reach French positions without coming under fire. The trenches and bunkers were overrun by the Viet Minh after the French decided against the use of US conventional bombers – and the Pentagon proposal to use tactical atomic bombs. All 13,000 men in the French garrison were either killed or taken prisoner; Viet Minh casualties were estimated at 25,000.

**Beer Factory Guesthouse** *(Nha May Bia;* ☎ *824635; rooms 100,000-120,000d)* has basic rooms popular with beer afficionados, as there's an *bia hoi* pub attached.

**Muong Thanh Hotel** *(☎ 826719, fax 826720; twins with bath US$15-18)* is the nicest place in town, but it's often full with tour groups so you may want to book ahead. Get a room in the new wing – the standard is much better for the same price. There's a decent-sized swimming pool (not so clean though, so it's a good idea to wear earplugs and goggles), large restaurant, karaoke and 'Thai Massage'. Rates include breakfast.

**Binh Long Hotel** *(☎ 824345; 429 Đ Muong Thanh; air-con rooms US$12)* is run by a friendly family and has clean, if tiny, twin-bedded rooms with bathrooms. Rates include breakfast.

**May Hong Hotel** *(☎ 826300; twins 100,000d)*, near the bus station, is a mini-hotel that's just about OK for the price if you can get past the snapping, barking guard dog chained up in the courtyard.

**Dien Bien Phu Hotel** *(☎ 825103, fax 825467; Đ 7.5; air-con rooms US$12)* is a large, state-run hotel that is centrally located but with fairly grotty, musty rooms. Some serious maintenance work is needed.

As far as eating goes, **Lien Tuoi Restaurant** *(☎ 824919; Đ Hoang Van Thai; mains around 30,000d)* is the best eatery in town and is about 400m from the Dien Bien Phu Museum. The menu is in English and French with some wacky translations. Ever wanted to try boiled wild boor? Now's your chance. There are private dining rooms on the 2nd floor.

**Nga Luan Restaurant**, next to the Dien Ben Phu Airport Hotel, serves a good mix of standard Vietnamese fare.

Beside the restaurants in some hotels, there are a couple of decent local **com pho joints** on Đ 7.5.

## Getting There & Away

The overland trip to Dien Bien Phu can be more intriguing than the actual battlefield sites for which the town is so famous. Of course, you miss out on this if you fly.

**Air** Vietnam Airlines presently runs flights between Dien Bien Phu and Hanoi four times a week. The schedule varies according to demand, with the majority of the flights during July and August.

**Vietnam Airlines** *(☎ 824692, fax 826060; open 7.30am-11.30am & 1.30pm-4.30pm daily)* has a booking desk at the Airport Hotel.

The airport is 1.5km from the town centre, along the road towards Lai Chau.

**Bus** There is a direct bus service that runs from Hanoi to Dien Bien Phu (100,000d, 16 hours) and it leaves at 4.30am, 8.30am and 10.30am.

Buses to Lai Chau (25,000d, three hours) leave at 8am, 9am, 10am, 11am and 1.30pm. The daily bus to Son La (38,000d, five hours) leaves at – ouch – 4.30am.

Although the bus is cheap, it's not really much fun. Buses are so packed that the only scenery you get to admire is the armpit of the person sitting next to you. If overloaded vehicles, bad roads and bad brakes worry you, consider flying or travelling overland by 4WD or motorbike.

**Car & Motorbike** The 470km drive from Hanoi to Dien Bien Phu on Hwys 6 and 42 takes 16 hours (if you're lucky). Conceivably it could be done in a single direct journey, but almost everyone stays overnight in Son La. You certainly wouldn't want to attempt this road in the dark!

**Tay Trang (Lao Border)** The Lao border is only 34km from Dien Bien Phu and there is much speculation about this crossing being opened to foreign tourists. We spoke with the border guards in mid-2002 and their information was that authorisation has been given to upgrade the crossing to an open international border, and that the final paperwork should be completed by 2004 at the latest. So keep your ear to the ground!

## LAI CHAU

☎ 023 • pop 19,600 • elevation 600m

This small town is nestled in a beautiful valley carved from spectacular mountains by the Da River, and, with Tam Duong, is

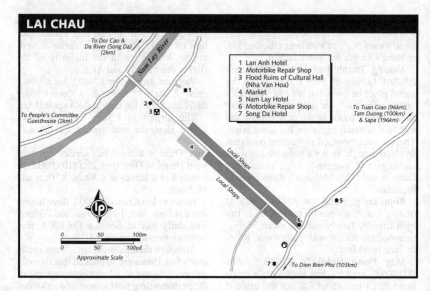

**LAI CHAU**

To Doi Cao &
Da River (Song Da)
(2km)

Nam Lay River

1  Lan Anh Hotel
2  Motorbike Repair Shop
3  Flood Ruins of Cultural Hall
   (Nha Van Hoa)
4  Market
5  Nam Lay Hotel
6  Motorbike Repair Shop
7  Song Da Hotel

To People's Committee
Guesthouse (2km)

To Tuan Giao (96km),
Tam Duong (100km)
& Sapa (196km)

Local Shops

Local Shops

0      50      100m
0      50      100yd
Approximate Scale

To Dien Bien Phu (103km)

one of the lunch and/or overnight stops for people travelling between Dien Bien Phu and Sapa.

Beneath Lai Chau's beauty lies a difficult existence for locals. Despite a marked increase in tourist numbers, for most of the local people it's a hard living. Far from busy trade routes, normal commerce is limited and the town has only been really successful in harvesting particularly valuable cash crops. These include opium and timber. Needless to say, opium harvesting does not find favour with the central government, which has been trying to discourage the Montagnards from producing opium poppies.

If the opium business is falling on hard times, the same must be said for the timber industry. In recent years the forest cover has been reduced and flooding has increased dramatically. Around 140 people lost their lives in 1990 in a devastating flood on the Da River that swept through the narrow valley. An even worse flood in 1996 killed 100 people and cut all roads into town for two months; the ruins of the flooded former cultural hall can be seen in town.

It seems that this kind of flooding could become a permanent feature of Lai Chau.

There are government plans to place a dam just above the current Song Da Reservoir, and this will fill the Lai Chau valley with water. (This is the reason that the provincial capital was transferred from Lai Chau to Dien Bien Phu in 1993.) If and when this comes to pass (not before 2010), this will be the largest hydroelectric station in Southeast Asia. It also could mean that in the future the only way to visit Lai Chau will be by submarine.

Being underwater, however, would at least keep things cooler. Odd as it might seem, in summer Lai Chau is one of the hottest places in Vietnam. June and July temperatures can soar as high as 40°C. This has something to do with the southeast summer monsoon blasting in from the Indian Ocean, and the surrounding mountains enclosing the heat. It's an interesting phenomenon for budding climatologists.

### Places to Stay & Eat

**Lan Anh Hotel** (☎/fax 852370; twins in concrete wing or basic stilt house US$8, in stilt houses US$10-20) is the best of Lai Chau's hotels. The wooden Thai-style stilt houses are pretty, with wide fan-cooled verandas. There is a good **restaurant** here and the hotel owners can provide travel advice and arrange boat trips and private tours.

**Song Da Hotel** (☎ 852527; twins 150,000d) is another decent option with basic rooms but with hot water and air-con. It's on the road to Dien Bien Phu.

**Nam Lay Hotel** (☎ 852346; rooms 100,000d), on the way to Lai Chau, is set slightly above the main road and is very basic.

### Getting There & Away

Most travellers will arrive from Dien Bien Phu (three hours, 103km), although there's also the road option of Hwy 6 from Tuan Giao (four hours, 96km). The road from Lai Chau to Sapa and Lao Cai (eight hours, 180km) is one of the most beautiful drives in Vietnam, but it's bumpy. Remember that all of the travel times listed here are pretty much hypothetical – it only takes a single landslide to cause considerable delays.

Public buses make the run to/from Hanoi, as well as to points in the northwest like Dien Bien Phu, Son La and Sapa, and if you're bent on the thrill, the folks at the **Lan Anh Hotel** (☎/fax 852370) will happily provide destination and schedule information.

## MUONG TE

☎ 023 • pop 43,900 • elevation 900m

Muong Te is one of Vietnam's most remote outposts. It's 98km northwest of Lai Chau along the scenic Da River, towards the junction of the borders of Vietnam, China and Laos. The majority of the population here is ethnic Thai, though they have assimilated and are nearly indistinguishable from the Vietnamese. Other minority groups found in the area include the Lahu (Khau Xung), Si La and Ha Nhi.

Apart from a small Sunday **market** and some nearby **villages**, there is not much to see or do in Muong Te. There are also few visitors, which, for some, makes it more of an appealing place to be. The only accommodation available in town is the shabby **People's Committee Guesthouse**, which also has a small **restaurant**.

Even if you're not planning to visit, you might take the Muong Te turn-off along

Hwy 12 (about 7km outside of Lai Chau). Almost immediately you'll reach a rickety wooden suspension bridge worth a look or even a crossing for Indiana Jones wannabes, though crossing on anything much heavier than a motorbike looks like a decided risk. If you continue for about 8km beyond this bridge, you'll see a peculiar historical relic: an ancient **poem carved in stone** by 15th-century Emperor Le Loi, who had succeeded in expelling the Chinese from the region. The poem was left as a warning for any other potential invaders not to mess with Le Loi. The translation from Chinese reads:

Hey! The humble, coward and frantic rebels, I come here to counter-attack for the sake of the border inhabitants. There existed the betrayed subjects since the beginning of the human's history. The land is no longer dangerous. The plants' figures, the whisper of the wind, and even the singing of the songbirds startle the mean enemy. The nation is now integrated and this carved poem – an amulet for Eastern peace of the country.

*An Auspicious Day of December,*
*The Year of the Pigs (1432)*

To find this vestige, look for the narrow flight of steps marked by a small stone placard reading 'Di Tich Lich Su – Bia Le Loi' on the roadside overlooking the river.

## SINHO

☎ 023 • pop 56,200 • elevation 1054m

Sinho is a scenic mountain village that is home to a large number of ethnic minorities. There is a colourful Sunday **market** here, although the dingy **People's Committee Guesthouse** is the only hotel in town.

Sinho is a 38km climb on an abysmal dirt road off Hwy 12; it will take about 1½ hours each way. The turn-off is about 1km north of the village of Chan Nua, on the road from Lao Cai. Sinho can also be reached by a challenging trek from the town of Tam Duong.

## TAM DUONG

☎ 023 • pop 94,400

This remote town lies between Sapa and Lai Chau. While the town is nothing special, along with Lai Chau it's one of the possible lunch/overnight stops between Dien Bien Phu and Sapa.

The local **market**, about midway through the town on Hwy 12, is worth a visit. The majority of people are Montagnards from nearby villages, although the ethnic Vietnamese is still the largest single group. If you're not in a rush to get to Sapa or Lai Chau, you could base yourself in Tam Duong for a day or so and explore the surrounding areas.

The drive from Tam Duong to Sapa along Hwy 4D, threading the Fansipan Mountain Range and the Chinese border, is a beautiful stretch of road.

## Places to Stay & Eat

**Phuong Thanh Hotel** (☎ 875158; rooms with bath US$10) is a popular place with good, clean, newish fan rooms. The rooms at the back offer nice views and a veranda; there's also an annexe across the road. Breakfast is included in the rates.

**Tam Duong Hotel** (☎ 875288; rooms 120,000d) is a friendly hotel with clean, if a bit musty, fan rooms. Rates include breakfast.

**Tuan Anh Restaurant** offers the best food in town. Other nearby **com-pho spots** like Phuong Thanh are OK too. Be aware that **Kieu Trinh** is known for its canine fare.

## SAPA

☎ 020 • pop 36,200 • elevation 1650m

The premier destination of northwest Vietnam, Sapa is a former hill station built in 1922. It lies in a beautiful valley close to the Chinese border. The whole area has spectacular scenery frequently shrouded in mist, and is home to diverse hill-tribe communities.

In the past, getting to Sapa from Hanoi was not easy, owing to the bad roads. Other historical reasons that prevented Sapa from becoming a slick tourist resort include: WWII; the guerrilla war against the French; the war with the USA; and the border skirmish with China in 1979; not to mention Vietnam's severe economic decline in the 1980s. The old hotels built by the French were allowed to fall into disrepair, and Sapa was pretty much forgotten.

Recently, the place has been rediscovered, and the subsequent tourist boom has caused a sea change in Sapa's fortunes. The bad roads are being upgraded, countless new hotels are appearing, the electricity supply is now pretty reliable and the food has improved immeasurably. The authorities are even preparing to assign street names in the town! Inherent in all of this prosperity is cultural change for the Montagnards, many of whom are now well-versed in the ways of the cash economy and are reaping the financial rewards of the tourism influx.

One inconvenience that will not change is the weather. If you visit off-season, don't forget your winter woollies. Not only is it cold (0°C), but winter brings fog and drizzle. The chilly climate does have a few advantages, though – the area boasts temperate-zone fruit trees bearing fruit such as peaches and plums, and gardens for raising medicinal herbs. The dry season in Sapa lasts from around January to June; afternoon showers in the mountains are quite frequent.

January and February are the coldest (and foggiest) months. From March to May the weather is often excellent, and the summer is warm despite the rains between June and August. The window from September to mid-December is a pleasant time to be in Sapa, though there is a bit of lingering rain at the start and the temperature rapidly cools down towards the end of the year.

If possible, try to go during the week, when prices are cheaper and Sapa is less crowded and generally more pleasant. Crowds flock to Sapa for the Saturday market, but a smaller **market** is held every day. There is plenty to see on weekdays, and there are many interesting villages within walking distance of the centre.

Sapa would be of considerably less interest without the H'mong and Dzao people, the largest ethnic groups in the region. They are mostly very poor, but are rapidly learning about free enterprise. Most of the Montagnards have had no formal education and are illiterate, yet many of the youngsters have a good command of English and French.

[Continued on page 263]

# Hill Tribes in Vietnam

ALISON WRIGHT

KRAIG LIEB

**Title Page:** Large silver hoop earrings, worn by many of the ethnic minorities in Vietnam, are here worn by a H'mong woman in Sapa, Lao Cai (Photograph by Liz Thompson)

**Top:** A young H'mong girl near Sapa in Lao Cai

**Bottom:** A Dao girl in traditional dress, Lao Cai

While the ethnic Vietnamese and ethnic Chinese live mainly in urban centres and coastal areas, the remaining people, an estimated 10% of Vietnam's total population, live primarily in the high country. While several of these groupings represent about a million people, others are feared to have dwindled to as few as 100.

The most prominent of these communities reside in the northwest, in the plush mountain territory along the Lao and Chinese borders, while most of the tribes in the central highlands and the south can be quite difficult to distinguish, at least for foreign visitors, from other Vietnamese.

The French dubbed the hill-tribe peoples 'Montagnards' (highlanders or mountain people) and this name is still used when speaking in French or English. The Vietnamese generally refer to them as *moi*, a derogatory term that means 'savages', which unfortunately reflects all-too-common popular attitudes. The present government, however, prefers to use the term 'national minorities'. Some have lived in Vietnam for thousands of years, while others have migrated into the region over the past few centuries. The areas inhabited by each community are often delimited by altitude, with more recent arrivals settling at higher elevations.

Historically, the highland areas were allowed to remain independent as long as their leaders recognised Vietnamese sovereignty and paid tribute and taxes. The 1980 Constitution abolished two such regions established in the northern mountains in 1959.

Over the last century, the Montagnards have been pushed into increasingly smaller territories; under French rule, many found themselves dispossessed by French plantations that sprang up all over the highlands. Surrounded by plantations, denied access to their traditional hunting and agricultural grounds, many found themselves forced into plantation labour. Plantation owners also 'imported' lowlander Vietnamese labourers – further displacing the Montagnards.

Attempts by the ethnic Vietnamese to subjugate the highlanders were met with active resistance (see the boxed text 'Fulro' in the Central Highlands chapter). During the American War the Montagnards occupied the strategic position of what became known as the Ho Chi Minh Trail. Consequently, both the Communists and the USA actively recruited Montagnard fighters from the central highlands. Familiarity with the territory meant Montagnards were particularly adept at guerrilla war techniques. US officials estimate that around 200,000 Montagnards died during the American War. After the North Vietnamese took over, many who had fought beside the South Vietnamese and US forces were punished, imprisoned or executed. The Vietnamese government only recently lifted special restrictions against US tourists wanting to visit hill-tribe areas around the central highlands, out of paranoia that the US Central Intelligence Agency (CIA) could *still* be trying to recruit locals.

**Inset:** Photograph by Liz Thompson

Most hill-tribe communities share a rural, agricultural lifestyle with similar architecture and traditional rituals alongside a long history of intertribal warfare. Many are seminomadic, cultivating crops such as 'dry' rice and using slash-and-burn methods, which have taken a heavy toll on the environment. Because such practices destroy the ever-dwindling forests, the government has been trying to encourage the hill tribes to adopt more settled agriculture techniques, often at lower altitudes, with wet (paddy) rice and cash crops such as tea, coffee and cinnamon. Still, some see this as yet another attempt by the government to 'integrate' the Montagnards into mainstream society. Despite the allure of benefits like subsidised irrigation, better education and health care, a long history of independence coupled with a general distrust of the ethnic-Vietnamese majority keeps many away from the lowlands.

As in other parts of Asia, the culture of many of Vietnam's ethnic minorities is gradually giving way to a variety of outside influences. Symbolic is the fact that few still dress in traditional clothing. Most who do are found in the remote villages of the far north, and even there it is often only the women who do so, while the men more typically have switched over to Vietnamese or Western-style clothes. While factors such as the introduction of electricity, modern medicine and education do create advantages, unfortunately it has also contributed to the abandonment of many age-old traditions.

A more recent, and perhaps equally threatening, outside influence is tourism. With further exposure to lowlanders, a developing trend towards commercialism, and growing numbers of visitors travelling to see hill-tribe regions, the situation will likely worsen. The influence of tourism, in Sapa for instance, has resulted in some children expecting hand-outs of money or sweets.

Montagnard-watching seems to be a favourite 'sport' of travellers on 'snap-shot safari'. Please remember to treat the locals with respect. Some travellers seem to think that the hill-tribe people are running around in 'costumes' for the benefit of photographers – this, of course, is not the case.

Vietnam's minorities have substantial autonomy and, though the official national language is Vietnamese, children still learn their local languages (see the Language chapter for useful phrases). Taxes are supposed to be paid, but Hanoi is far away and it seems that if they don't interfere with the political agenda, the Montagnards can live as they please. Police officers and members of the army in minority areas are often members of local tribal groups, and the National Assembly in Hanoi has representation by a good number of ethnic minorities.

While there may be no official discrimination system, cultural preju-dice against hill-tribe people helps ensure they remain at the bottom of the educational and economic ladder. Despite improvements in rural schooling, there are few employment opportunities. Life expectancy is low and child mortality rates are high. Those who live closer to urban centres and the coast fare better, thanks to better access to medical and education facilities.

## Tay

**Population** 1.2 million
**Provinces** Bac Can, Bac Giang, Cao Bang, Lang Son, Quang Ninh, Thai Nguyen

The Tay, the most populous of the hill tribes, live at low elevations and valleys in the northern provinces. They adhere closely to Vietnamese beliefs in Buddhism, Confucianism and Taoism, but also worship genies and local spirits. Since they developed their own script in the 16th century, Tay literature and arts, including music, folk songs, poems and dance, have gained substantial renown. The Tay are known for their abilities in cultivating wet rice, tobacco, fruit, herbs and spices.

They traditionally live in wooden stilt houses, though a long history of proximity to ethnic Vietnamese has seen a gradual change to brick-and-earthen housing. Tay people wear distinctive indigo-blue and black clothes, and often don head wraps of the same colours. They sometimes carry machine-like farming tools in belt sheaths.

## Thai

**Population** 1 million+
**Provinces** Hoa Binh, Lai Chau, Nghe An, Son La

Like the Tay, the Thai originated in southern China before settling along fertile riverbeds, once used for irrigation purposes. Theories vary on the Thai's relationship to the Thais of Siam (Thailand), as do references to colours in the subgroups, such as the Red, Black and White Thai. Some contend that the colours correspond to those of the women's skirts, while others believe the names come from the nearby Black and Red Rivers. The Black Thai are predominant in Son La, while the White Thai are concentrated in Hoa Binh. Black Thai women usually wear vibrantly coloured blouses and headgear, while the White Thai tend to dress in less colourful or modern clothing. Most Thai men dress as the ethnic Vietnamese do.

Villages typically have 40 to 50 bamboo-stilt households. The Thai, using a script developed in the 5th century, have produced literature ranging from poetry and love songs to folk tales. Travellers staying overnight in the village of Lac (see the Mai Chau section in the North-west Vietnam chapter) should be able to catch a performance of some of the Thai's renowned music and dance.

## Muong

**Population** 900,000+
**Provinces** Hoa Binh, Thanh Hoa

Found predominantly in Hoa Binh province, the male-dominated Muong live in small stilt-house hamlets called *quel*, grouped into *muong*. Each *muong* is overseen by *lang*, a hereditary noble family. Though their origins lie close to the ethnic Vietnamese and nowadays they are difficult to distinguish, the Muong have a culture similar to the Thai.

They are known for producing folk literature, poems and songs, much of which has been translated into Vietnamese. Musical instruments such as the gong, drums, pan pipes, flutes and two-stringed violin are popular with the Muong. Like the ethnic Vietnamese, they too cultivate rice in paddies; in the past, sticky rice was a staple part of their diet.

Muong women wear long skirts and short vest-like blouses, while the men traditionally wear indigo tops and trousers.

# Nung

**Population** 700,000
**Provinces** Bac Thai, Cao Bang, Ha Bac, Lang Son, Tuyen Quang

Concentrated into small villages, Nung homes are typically divided into two sections, one to serve as living quarters and the other for work and worship. From their deep ancestral worship to traditional festivities, the Nung are spiritually and socially similar to the Tay. Nung brides traditionally command high dowries from prospective grooms and tradition dictates inheritance from father to son, a sign of Chinese influences.

Most Nung villages still have medicine men, who are called upon to help get rid of evil spirits and cure the ill. Their astute gardening skills are known to reap a wide range of crops like vegetables, fruit, spices and bamboo. The Nung are also known for their handicrafts such as bamboo furniture, basketry, silverwork and paper making. The Nung wear primarily black and indigo clothing with head dresses.

# H'mong

**Population** 550,000+
**Provinces** Cao Bang, Ha Giang, Lai Chau, Lao Cai, Nghe An, Tuyen Quang, Son La, Yen Bai

Since migrating from China in the 19th century, the H'mong have grown to become one of the largest and most underprivileged of the ethnic groups in Vietnam.

The H'mong live at high altitudes and cultivate dry rice, vegetables, fruit and medicinal plants (including opium), and raise pigs, cows, chickens and horses. The H'mong are found throughout Southeast Asia and many have also fled Vietnam to Western countries as refugees.

There are several groups within the H'mong, including Black, White, Red, Green and Flower, each of which bears its own subtle variation on traditional dress. One of the easiest to recognise are the Black H'mong, who wear indigo-dyed linen clothing (which gives off an almost metallic shine) with women typically wearing skirts, aprons, wrap-on leggings and a cylindrical hat. The Flower H'mong men wear dark black and blue. The women wear slightly more elaborate outfits than the Black H'mong, usually with a plaid wool headdress. H'mong women typically wear large silver necklaces and clusters of silver bracelets and earrings.

# Jarai

**Population** 190,000+
**Provinces** Dac Lac, Gia Lai, Khanh Hoa, Phu Yen

The Jarai are the most populous minority in the central highlands, especially around Pleiku. Villages are often named for a nearby river, stream or tribal chief; a large stilt house that's a kind of community centre *(nha-rong)* is usually found in the centre. Jarai women typically propose marriage to men through a matchmaker, who delivers the prospective groom a copper bracelet. Animistic beliefs and rituals still abound, and the Jarai pay respect to their ancestors and nature through a host of genie *(yang)*. Popular spirits include Po Teo Pui (King of Fire) and Po Teo La (King of Water), who are summoned to bring forth rain.

Perhaps more than any of Vietnam's other hill tribes, the Jarai are renowned for their indigenous musical instruments, from stringed 'gongs' to bamboo tubes, which act as wind flutes and percussion. Jarai women typically wear sleeveless indigo blouses and long skirts.

# Bahnar

**Population** 135,000
**Provinces** Kon Tum, Binh Dinh, Phu Yen

The Bahnar are believed to have migrated long ago to the central highlands from the coast. They are animists and worship trees such as the banyan and ficus. The Bahnar keep their own traditional calendar, which calls for 10 months of cultivation, with the remaining two months set aside for social and personal duties, such as marriage, weaving, buying and selling food and wares, ceremonies and festivals.

A traditional ceremony was held when babies were one month old; their ears were blown into and their lobes pierced, thus making the child a village member. It was believed that those who died without these rites would be taken to a land of monkeys, by a black-eared goddess, Duydai. The Bahnar are renowned for their wood carvings, especially those used to decorate funeral homes. They wear similar dress to the Jarai.

# Sedang

**Population** 95,000+
**Provinces** Kon Tum, Quang Ngai, Quang Nam

Native to the central highlands, the Sedang have relations stretching as far as Cambodia. Like many of their neighbours, the Sedang have been adversely affected by centuries of war and outside invasion. The Sedang do not carry family names, and there is said to be complete equality between the sexes. The children of one's siblings are also given the same treatment as one's own, creating a strong fraternal tradition. Although most Sedang spiritual and cultural ceremonies relate to agriculture, they still practice unique customs, such as grave abandonment, sharing of property with the deceased and giving birth at the forest's edge. Sedang women traditionally wear long skirts and a sarong-like top wrap.

# Dao

**Population** 470,000+
**Provinces** Chinese and Lao border areas, Sapa

The Dao (or Zao) are one of Vietnam's largest ethnic groups and they live predominantly in the northwestern provinces along the borders with China and Laos. The Dao practise ancestor worship of spirits known as 'Ban Ho' and hold elaborate rituals with sacrifices of pigs and chickens. The Dao's close proximity to China explains the common use of traditional Chinese-influenced medicine and the similarity of the Nom Dao script to Chinese characters.

The Dao are famous for their elaborate dress; women's clothing typically features elaborate weaving and silver-coloured beads and coins (the wealth of a woman is said to be in the weight of coins she carries). Long locks of hair are tied up into a large red or embroidered turban.

# Ede

**Population** 24,000+
**Provinces** Gia Lai, Kon Tum, Dac Lac

The polytheist Ede live communally in beamless, boat-shaped longhouses on stilts. About a third of these homes, which frequently accommodate large extended families, are for communal use, with the rest partitioned into smaller quarters to give privacy to married couples. The Ede people are matrilineal, like the Jarai: the families of Ede girls make proposals of marriage to men and, once wed, the couple resides with the wife's family. Children bear the mother's family name. Inheritance is also reserved solely for women, particularly the youngest daughter of the family. Ede women generally wear colourfully embroidered vests with copper and silver jewellery, and beads.

[Continued from page 256]

Lots of the women and young girls have gone into the souvenir business; the older women in particular are known for their strong-armed sales tactics. One frequent Sapa sight is a frenzy of elderly H'mong women clamouring around hapless backpackers to hawk their goods, which range from colourful ethnic garb to little pouches of opium stashed away in matchboxes. When negotiating prices, you do need to hold your ground, but go easy when it comes to bargaining. They may be persistent, but are not nearly as rapacious as many other vendors. Besides, with the government cracking down on opium crops, and increasing pressure on land, few other employment opportunities exist.

A word of warning on the clothes: as beautiful and cheap as they are, the dyes used are natural and are not set. Much of the stuff sold has the potential to turn anything it touches (including your skin) an unusual blue/green colour – check out the hands and arms of the H'mong for an indication. Wash the fabric separately in cold salt water – it helps stop the dye from running. Wrap anything you buy in plastic bags before stuffing it in your luggage.

## Information

There is a small **bank** in Sapa, but it does not handle foreign-currency exchange. You can use or change US dollars at most hotels, but don't expect to be given the same exchange rate as in Hanoi.

**Internet access** is available in many hotels around town, usually for 500d per minute.

## Sapa Market

Montagnards from surrounding villages don their best clothes and head to the market most days. Saturday is the busiest day, but the town becomes so crowded with tourists that it's a much more pleasant experience on other days of the week.

The market is a big magnet for organised-tour groups from Hanoi, many of which arrive here on Friday night. If you'd rather

---

### Out of the Mouths of Children

Exchange in English, overheard, between a small shoeshine boy, an even smaller postcard-selling boy, and a tourist:

Shoeshine boy: 'I clean your shoes?'

Tourist: 'No thanks, I've cleaned them myself.'

Postcard boy: 'Well you can't make postcards yourself, can you? So you'd better buy some of mine.'

Tourist (after a moment's stunned silence): 'Well I can't argue with that. Let me see your cards!'

---

enjoy Sapa at a more sedate pace, avoid the Saturday market.

## Trekking to Local Villages

The nearest village within walking distance is **Cat Cat**, 3km south of Sapa. Like everywhere in this area, it's a steep and very beautiful hike down; if you're too exhausted or unfit to hike back up, there are plenty of *xe om* ready and willing to cart you back to your hotel.

Another popular hike is to **Ta Phin village**, about 10km from Sapa. Most people take a *xe om* to a starting point about 8km from Sapa, and then make a 14km loop walk of the area. Most hotels offer guided day and half-day treks; depending on the number of people and what, if any, vehicles are needed, expect to pay somewhere between US$4 and US$10.

Long-standing (and still recommended) places to ask about guided treks include **Auberge Hotel** (☎ 871243), **Mountain View Hotel** (☎ 871334) and the **Friendly Cafe** (*Royal Hotel*). There are also several tour-booking offices on the main street.

## Fansipan

Surrounding Sapa are the Hoang Lien Mountains, nicknamed the Tonkinese Alps by the French. These mountains include Fansipan, which at 3143m is Vietnam's highest. The summit towers above Sapa, although it is

NORTHWEST VIETNAM

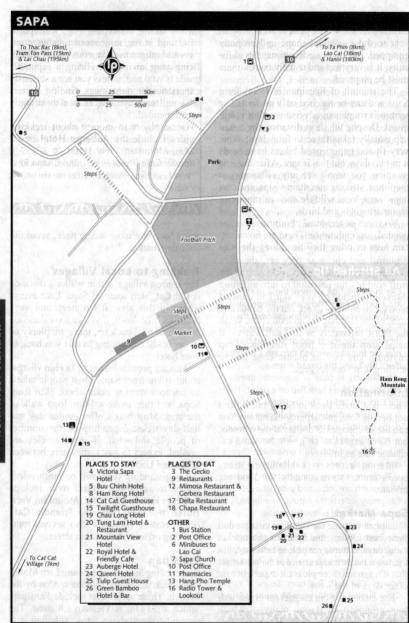

# SAPA

To Thac Bac (8km),
Tram Ton Pass (15km)
& Lai Chau (195km)

To Ta Phin (8km),
Lao Cai (38km)
& Hanoi (380km)

0    25    50m
0    25    50yd

Steps

Park

Steps

Football Pitch

Steps

Steps

Steps

Market

Steps

Ham Rong
Mountain

Steps

To Cat Cat
Village (3km)

**PLACES TO STAY**
4  Victoria Sapa
   Hotel
5  Buu Chinh Hotel
8  Ham Rong Hotel
14 Cat Cat Guesthouse
15 Twilight Guesthouse
19 Chau Long Hotel
20 Tung Lam Hotel &
   Restaurant
21 Mountain View
   Hotel
22 Royal Hotel &
   Friendly Cafe
23 Auberge Hotel
24 Queen Hotel
25 Tulip Guest House
26 Green Bamboo
   Hotel & Bar

**PLACES TO EAT**
3  The Gecko
9  Restaurants
12 Mimosa Restaurant &
   Gerbera Restaurant
17 Delta Restaurant
18 Chapa Restaurant

**OTHER**
1  Bus Station
2  Post Office
6  Minibuses to
   Lao Cai
7  Sapa Church
10 Post Office
11 Pharmacies
13 Hang Pho Temple
16 Radio Tower &
   Lookout

often obscured by clouds and is occasionally dusted with snow. The peak is accessible all year to those in good shape and properly equipped, but don't underestimate its difficulty. It is very wet and usually cold, so you must be prepared.

The summit of Fansipan is 19km from Sapa and can be reached only on foot. The terrain is rough and adverse weather is frequent. Despite the short distance, the round trip usually takes three to four days; some very fit and experienced hikers have made it in two days, but this is rare. After the first morning you won't see any villages; just the forest, striking mountain vistas, and perhaps some local **wildlife** such as monkeys, mountain goats and birds.

No ropes or technical climbing skills are needed, just endurance. There are no mountain huts or other facilities along the way

(yet), so you need to be self-sufficient. This means taking a sleeping bag, waterproof tent, food, stove, raincoat or poncho, compass and other miscellaneous survival gear. Bring your own gear. Hiring a reputable guide is vital and, unless you are a seriously experienced mountaineer, finding porters who will carry your gear is also strongly recommended.

Good places to inquire about trekking guides include the **Auberge Hotel** (☎ 87 1243), **Mountain View Hotel** (☎ 871334), **Friendly Cafe** (Royal Hotel), and **Chapa Restaurant** (☎ 871245). If you organise the climb through a local operator, you'll find yourself paying an all-inclusive rate of around US$60 per person for a couple, US$50 per person for a group of four and US$45 per person for the sensible maximum group size of six.

## All Stitched Up

Like many hill-tribe women, those of the Yao of Ta Phin – a community about 10km from Sapa – are expert at embroidery, an art handed down through generations. Traditionally, only silk thread is used. Unprocessed silk is bought from the market, boiled to make it smooth, and then dyed with natural colours extracted from plants that include turmeric and tea leaves. Three strands of silk are then twisted together and drawn taut by the sewer, who pins one end to the knee of her trousers, runs the thread down and through a bracelet held on one toe, then pulls it back up to her knee. A quick twist, and the thread is ready.

Embroidery is done in segments. Items of everyday clothing include the *luy khia*, a densely embroidered lower back flap on a jacket. The smaller *luy tan* is a rectangle of pattern that decorates the back of a jacket. The *luy leng* is a band of decoration at the front opening of a jacket. Trousers, *la peng*, are decorated with distinctive stripes of colour rather than blocks of pattern. *La peng pe* are cloths used to bind the lower legs. *La sin* is a belt used to hoist up the back flap of the jacket when women work in the fields. *Chap hoong* is the bib of red cotton behind the opening of a jacket, and may be studded with silver ornaments. The red head-covering worn by Yao women is called a *hong*, and is usually made up of at least seven layers of cotton scarves.

There are many recurring motifs in Yao embroidery, although their symbolism, if any, is unknown. Most motifs are associated with nature, from gibbon hands to cabbages to thunder deities. Maybe this simply reflects the natural surroundings; maybe it also reflects a Taoist appreciation of balance between wild and cultivated nature.

Like all cultures, Yao culture is dynamic and constantly changing. Women say they 'borrow' or copy motifs from other tribal groups and incorporate them with their own; H'mong flower motifs are common. It may not be long before recognisably Western images, such as hiking boots and cats' paws, make their appearance in the market place.

Source: 'Our Craft Traditions' Series: *A Yao Community in Sapa, Vietnam* by Vo Mai Phuong & Claire Burkert, The Vietnam Museum of Ethnology, 2001.

Fansipan's summit is accessible year-round, though weather-wise the best time for making the ascent is from mid-October to mid-December, and again in March, when wildflowers are in bloom.

## Tram Ton Pass

If you travel along the Sapa–Lai Chau road, you will cross Tram Ton Pass on the north side of Fansipan, 15km from Sapa. At 1900m, this is the highest mountain pass in Vietnam. Aside from magnificent views, the climate changes dramatically. On the Sapa side of the mountain you can often expect cold, foggy and generally nasty weather. Drop down a few hundred metres below the pass on the Lai Chau side and it will often be sunny and warm. Ferocious winds come ripping over the pass, which is not surprising given the temperature differences – Sapa is the coldest place in Vietnam while Lai Chau is the warmest. Tram Ton Pass is the dividing line between two great weather fronts – who says you can't see air? (The day we passed by, there was fog and cloud on the Lau Chai side and blazing sun towards Sapa, but hey, you just can't pick the weather.)

Alongside the road, about 5km towards Sapa, is **Thac Bac**, the Silver Waterfall. With a height of 100m, it's a big one, and the loop track *(admission 3000d)* that takes you up steps and across a bridge halfway up is steep and spectacular.

## Places to Stay

If you're on a tour booked through a café or travel agency in Hanoi, your accommodation presumably will be pre-arranged for you. However, self-propelled travellers need to know that prices can fluctuate wildly according to the volume of tourist traffic. On weekends, prices can skyrocket, with a US$8 room going for at least double the price. Look around and negotiate. Needless to say, it's wise to avoid the Friday/Saturday rush; midweek there should be no problem, especially during the icy winter.

Beware of hotels using old-style charcoal burners for heat – the fumes can cause severe breathing problems if your room's not well ventilated. Many hotels now offer electric heaters instead, or open fireplaces during the winter.

There are now roughly 50 accommodation options, from a solid string of cheap guest-houses to a luxury resort. The majority of Sapa's villa-hotels are owned and run by the government, and, unfortunately, restoration efforts have fallen short of their potential; still, the hotels are atmospheric. Worse are the characterless new minihotels popping up and plaguing the town with karaoke. Construction is continuing full bore.

The hotels named here offer rooms and/or balconies with views; the scenery is, after all, one of the main reasons for visiting Sapa. It's not an exhaustive list: there are *plenty* of other hotels in town that are also good value, especially along the main street, but simply lack the scenic location.

## Places to Stay – Budget

**Auberge Hotel** *(☎ 871243, fax 871666; e auberge@sapadiscovery.com; w www.sapa discovery.com; singles/doubles US$6/28)* is notable for its town and valley views and bonsai garden. Some upper-floor rooms have fireplaces; cheaper rooms are in an older section of the hotel and lost their mountain views during the building boom. The restaurant is recommended and it's a good place to find travel and trekking information.

**Queen Hotel** *(☎ 871301, fax 871282; twins US$4-10)*, just next door to the Auberge, is a friendly place offering good-value rooms with great views and some fireplaces.

**Tulip Guest House** *(☎ 871914; singles/ doubles US$4/7)*, which was built in 2001, is small, simple, very clean and also has some terrific views.

**Green Bamboo Hotel** *(☎ 871214; rooms US$8-25)* is in French-villa style with fine views, a small garden and a popular bar. The more expensive rooms are pretty basic for the price though, with nowhere to sit and no tables.

**Mountain View Hotel** *(☎ 871334; e ninh hongsapa@hn.vnn.vn; rooms US$6-15)*, formerly Ninh Hong Guesthouse, has relocated to a prime spot on the edge of town; corner rooms have views to die for. The owner, Mrs Hong, speaks fluent English, and was one of the first female trekking guides in Sapa. She now has a small team of local women working with her as guides.

**Tung Lam Hotel & Restaurant** (☎ 871404, fax 871081; rooms US$15) offers fine, well-maintained rooms, and also a decent terrace **restaurant**, perched over the valley.

**Cat Cat Guesthouse** (☎ 871387; e catcat@ fpt.vn; rooms US$7-20) is a multilevel guesthouse that gets top marks for its sweeping views from the terraces and some of the rooms. But housekeeping is not a strong point here; check the state of the bed linen and the bathroom before you check in.

**Twilight Guesthouse** (Nha Nghi Hoang Hon; ☎ 871601, fax 871318; rooms from US$8), built in 2001, is small and quiet, and has spotless rooms with bath. US$12 buys you a corner room with a view, and there are shared balconies for all.

## Places to Stay – Mid-Range

**Royal Hotel** (☎/fax 871313; e royalhotel _sapa@yahoo.com; rooms US$18-30) is well located, with only a few rooftops obscuring the view from the more expensive rooms. Rooms are of good standard, and the long-standing **Friendly Cafe**, known for touring information, has relocated here.

**Chau Long Hotel** (☎ 871245, fax 871844; e chapatour@hn.vnn.vn; w www.chaulong hotel.com; rooms US$28-51) opened in 2001 and has good standard rooms, as you would expect for the price. The location is magnificent, and the Internet café and bar on the 3rd floor is very pleasant.

**Buu Chinh Hotel** (☎ 871389, fax 871332; rooms US$20) is owned by the postal service and is situated in a Swiss chalet–style building. A little way out of the town centre, it's popular with tour groups. The rooms are clean and all have balconies with gorgeous views.

## Places to Stay – Top End

**Victoria Sapa Hotel** (☎ 871522, fax 871539; e victoriasapa@fpt.vn; w www.victoriaho tels-asia.com; superior/deluxe rooms US$85/ 103, 6-bed family studios US$147, luxury suites US$180) offers a delightful lodging experience. This hotel has it all – tastefully

decorated rooms, sweeping views from the restaurant, two bars, a heated indoor swimming pool, fitness centre and tennis court. Rates include breakfast, tax and service. Non-guests can treat themselves to a swim for US$5.

As part of a package, hotel guests can travel between Hanoi and Lao Cai in the resort's **Victoria Express** (☎ 04-933 0318, fax 933 0319; e victoria@fpt.vn), with luxurious, private train carriages (with private dining car) attached to the regular train.

## Places to Eat

**Mimosa Restaurant** and **Gerbera Restaurant** (mains from 20,000d) are next-door to each other. Both have terraces and are family-run eateries, with good and reasonably-priced barbecue beef, wild boar and venison, as well as pasta, salad and a variety of Vietnamese dishes.

**The Gecko** (☎ 871504; packed lunch 40,000d) is a good French-run restaurant where you can drink an espresso, pick up picnic lunches, have a light lunch or treat yourself to a splendid set menu for 150,000d. If that breaks the budget, the bar offers reasonably priced drinks and is a good meeting place.

**Delta Restaurant** (☎ 871799), Sapa's first (and still the town's only) mainly Italian restaurant, does good pizzas and pastas.

**Chapa Restaurant** (☎ 871245; e chapa tour@fpt.vn) is a true travellers' café, with the usual banana pancakes and spring rolls. If you peek in the front door, the place may appear full but there are more tables in the room upstairs.

**Auberge Hotel** has a popular terrace restaurant with some vegetarian dishes. Most of the busier hotels also have reasonably priced cafés.

There's a string of popular **restaurants** worth checking out near the bottom of the main drag (south of the stairs leading down to the market), and below the market as you head in the direction of Cat Cat village.

## Entertainment

Considering the number of travellers to Sapa, organised entertainment is relatively scarce. Mostly it's a cosy café scene at the various guesthouses.

**Bamboo Bar** *(Green Bamboo Hotel)* was the first Western-style watering hole to open in Sapa. There's a free traditional hill-tribe music-and-dance show from 8.30pm to 10pm Friday and Saturday.

**Ham Rong Hotel** also offers a nicely low-key outdoor hill-tribe show (admission 25,000d including one free drink) with an authentic feel, from 8.30pm to 10pm Friday and Saturday.

**The Gecko** has a decent bar and a good, laid-back music selection.

**Victoria Sapa Hotel** offers two cosy bars and a terrace for a more 'civilised' drink in this stylish hotel. Drinks cost a bit more than elsewhere in town, but the atmosphere is hard to beat.

## Getting There & Away
**Bus, Minibus & Motorbike** Sapa's proximity to the border region makes it a possible first or last stop for travellers crossing the border between Vietnam and China.

The gateway to Sapa is Lao Cai, 38km away on the Chinese border. Minibuses make the trip regularly between 5am and 5pm (25,000d, one to two hours depending on roadwork). In Sapa, minibuses wait in front of the church but do not run on any particular schedule. However, the minibuses do wait in Lao Cai for the train that arrives from Hanoi.

The advertised rate of hotel minibus services to Bac Ha (110km) for the Sunday market is around US$10 per person; departure from Sapa is at 6am and from Bac Ha at 1pm. You can also go to Bac Ha by public minibus, if youe change vehicles at Lao Cai.

Public buses from Sapa to Hanoi (about 12 hours) leave around 5am.

Driving a motorbike from Hanoi to Sapa is feasible, but it's a very long trip, so start early. The total distance between Hanoi and Sapa is 380km. The last 38km are straight uphill – unless you've been training for the Olympics, it's hell on a bicycle.

Cafés in Hanoi offer weekend trips to Sapa for around US$40, usually combining train and minibus transport. This is probably the most hassle-free way to do the journey, but many prefer to do it on their own. See Travel Agencies in the Hanoi chapter for more information.

**Train** The train trip to and from Hanoi has become much more comfortable with the opening of a public soft-sleeper class. At the moment, a sleeper ticket from Hanoi to Sapa can be booked only through hotels and agencies; it's expected that by the time you read this you'll be able to book this service directly at the station.

Ticket prices vary from around 62,000d for a hard seat to around 130,000d for a soft sleeper. The day train leaves Lao Cai at 10.20am; the night train at 6.45pm. The journey takes about 10 hours. Both trains leave Hanoi around 10pm. Purchasing tickets from agents in Sapa costs a bit more than at the station in Lao Cai, but ensures you a seat or a sleeper on the train. It also ensures that you can book a seat on a Sapa–Lao Cai minibus timed to coincide with train departures.

## Getting Around
The best way to get around Sapa is to walk, and almost everywhere it's steep! If you've got only an hour or so to kill, it is worthwhile following the steps up to the Sapa radio tower; the views of the valley from here are breathtaking.

For excursions further out, you can hire a self-drive motorbike for about US$6 a day, or take one with a driver for about US$10.

## LAO CAI
☎ 020 • pop 35,100 • elevation 650m
Lao Cai, the major town at the northwestern end of the train line, is right on the Vietnam-China border. The town was razed in the Chinese invasion of 1979, so most of its buildings are new. Needless to say, the border crossing here slammed shut during the 1979 war – it reopened in 1993.

Today, Lao Cai is a major destination for travellers journeying between Hanoi or Sapa and Kunming in China. But Lao Cai is no place to linger – don't bother spending the night if you don't have to.

## Orientation & Information

The border town on the Chinese side is called Hekou – you would have to be an enthusiast of Chinese border towns to want to hang out here.

There is a **bank** on the Lao Cai side of the river, opposite Song Hong Guesthouse, that will handle foreign exchange, but it's cash transactions only. It's best to have a ready supply of US dollars handy just in case. Be wary of black marketeers, especially on the Chinese side – they frequently short-change tourists. If you do black-market dealings, it's best to change only small amounts.

## Places to Stay & Eat

**Song Hong Guesthouse** (☎ 830004; rooms US$10) is closest to the border gate. Some of the 14 fairly grubby rooms have air-con. Ask for a room upstairs for a good view of the river and China.

**Binh Minh Hotel** (☎ 830085; 39 Pho Nguyen Hué; rooms 100,000-150,000d) is a standard state-run place with surprisingly friendly staff. Some rooms were being upgraded when we visited, and will probably be fine for the price.

**Huyen Trang Guesthouse** (☎ 832199; 27 Pho Nguyen Hué; rooms 120,000d) is near Binh Minh. It's tatty, but OK. Go for a room on a high floor, away from the loudspeakers and music in the lobby.

**Gia Nga Guest House** (☎ 830459; rooms 80,000-120,000d) opened in late 2001 and it's still looking clean and new. The enthusiastic owner, who doesn't speak a word of English, has sensibly set aside a shower (15,000d with towel and soap) and luggage room behind reception, for travellers who want to freshen up after the night train from Hanoi.

**Viet Hoa Restaurant** (Pho Nguyen Hué), clean and with an English menu, is the best restaurant. It's close to the border crossing.

## Getting There & Away

Minibuses to Sapa (25,000d, one to two hours depending on roadworks) leave regularly until mid-afternoon. Minibuses to Bac Ha (40,000d, two hours) leave three times daily; the last service is around noon.

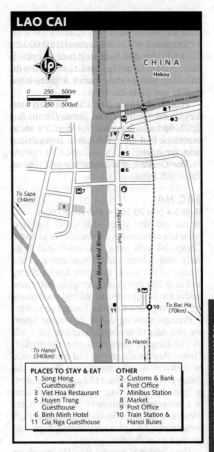

**LAO CAI**

CHINA
Hekou

Song Hong (Red River)

P Nguyen Hue

To Sapa (34km)

To Bac Ha (70km)

To Hanoi (340km)

To Hanoi

0    250    500m
0    250    500yd

**PLACES TO STAY & EAT**
1  Song Hong Guesthouse
3  Viet Hoa Restaurant
5  Huyen Trang Guesthouse
6  Binh Minh Hotel
11 Gia Nga Guesthouse

**OTHER**
2  Customs & Bank
4  Post Office
7  Minibus Station
8  Market
9  Post Office
10 Train Station & Hanoi Buses

Lao Cai is 340km from Hanoi. Buses make the run (53,000d, 10 hours), leaving from the train station (yes, the train station) at 4.30am and 5am, but most travellers prefer to do the journey by train.

See Getting There & Away in the Sapa section for details on train travel between Hanoi and Lao Cai.

**Chinese Border** The border is open daily between 7am and 5pm. China is separated from Vietnam by a road bridge and also a separate rail bridge over the Red River. Pedestrians pay a toll of 3000d to cross.

NORTHWEST VIETNAM

The border is about 3km from Lao Cai train station. This journey is easily done on a motorbike, which costs around 10,000d.

The Friday and Sunday Hanoi–Kunming train, No LC1, leaves Lao Cai at 9.40am on Saturday and Monday after a three-hour stop to complete border formalities.

There is also a separate Lao Cai–Kunming service on Saturday and Sunday, train No 5121, that also leaves at 9.40am. For some inexplicable reason, the Lao Cai–Kunming fares are quoted in Swiss francs! At current exchange rates, this amount works out at about 300,000d.

## BAC HA
☎ 020 • pop 70,200 • elevation 700m
In the last few years, this small highland town has emerged as an alternative to Sapa. Compared with Sapa, tourism is still in its early stages here and, if you arrive in the middle of the week, the town has an empty feel to it. But things are changing fast – new hotels are being constructed and restaurants are learning how to make banana pancakes.

Perhaps slowing down the tourist boom are two sets of loudspeakers; one on a hill overlooking the town and one at the market. These relay the clamorous and crackly Voice of Vietnam, which reverberates through the valley from 5am to 6am and again from 6pm to 7pm every day. Take your earplugs. There is a movement underway by some hotel owners to get these loudspeakers turned off completely; it's a plea we can only hope will triumph over the din.

The highlands around Bac Ha are about 900m above sea level, making it somewhat warmer than Sapa. There are 10 Montagnard groups that live around Bac Ha: Flower H'mong, Dzao, Giay (Nhang), Han (Hoa), Xa Fang, Lachi, Nung, Phula, Thai and Thulao, plus the Kinh (ethnic Vietnamese).

One of Bac Ha's main industries is the manufacture of alcoholic brews (rice wine, cassava wine and corn liquor). The corn stuff produced by the Flower H'mong is so potent it can ignite! Bac Ha is the only place in Vietnam where you'll find this particular ferment; there's an entire area devoted to it at the Sunday market.

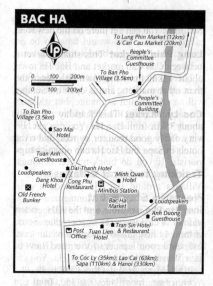

Harvesting opium used to be a major source of revenue, but the government put a stop to that several years ago.

Keep a torch (flashlight) handy if wandering around town in the evening. Bac Ha's electric power supply isn't very stable and sudden blackouts are a common occurrence.

## Montagnard Markets
There are several interesting markets around Bac Ha, most within about 20km of each other.

**Bac Ha Market** This lively and crowded concrete bazaar is the main market in Bac Ha proper. You'll see plenty of Flower H'-mong – so-named because the women embroider flowers on their colourful skirts. Items on sale include water buffaloes, pigs, horses and chickens. Tourists, however, seem to stick to buying handicrafts and local wine. The market operates on Sunday.

**Can Cau Market** This is one of the most fascinating open-air markets. It's 20km north of Bac Ha and just 9km south of the Chinese border. Can Cau attracts a large number of Chinese traders, evidenced by the booming dog trade here. The market is only open on Saturday. You can get there on the new road.

**Lung Phin Market** This small market is between Can Cau market and Bac Ha town, about 12km from the town. It's less busy than other markets, and is open on Sunday.

**Coc Ly Market** This Tuesday market is about 35km from Bac Ha. You can get here via a fairly good road, or by road and river; hotels in Sapa and Bac Ha can organise trips.

### Trekking to Local Villages
Villages around Bac Ha provide a good opportunity to see how Montagnard people live. **Ban Pho** is nearest, and the villagers live simply. The Flower H'mong villagers are extremely hospitable and some of the kindest people you'll meet in Vietnam. Ban Pho is a 7km return trip from Bac Ha. You can take a loop route to get there and back.

Other nearby villages include: **Trieu Cai**, an 8km return walk; **Na Ang**, a 6km return walk; and **Na Hoi**, a 4km walk. Ask at your hotel for directions.

### Plum Blossoms
There are many plum trees in and around Bac Ha and in spring (March) the countryside is white with blossoms. May and June produce some of the best plums.

### Places to Stay & Eat
Because of the loudspeakers, it's fair to say that, for now, there is no quiet place to stay in Bac Ha. As in Sapa, room rates tend to increase on weekends, when tourists come to town for the Sunday market. On weekends it's hard to find a room, and there's also no air-con accommodation. Be prepared for the masses of (mostly) friendly flea-bitten dogs that wander into restaurants looking for scraps.

**Sao Mai Hotel** (☎ 880288; fax 880285; rooms in old/newish/newest sections US$10/15/20) is popular with groups, and the rooms are clean and pleasant, with an older concrete building and two recently built wooden houses. However, the staff we met could do with a lesson in good manners.

**Tuan Anh Guesthouse** (☎ 880377; rooms 100,000d) is a family-run place that is no-frills and fine for the price.

**Dai Thanh Hotel** (☎ 880448; rooms 80,000-150,000d) was being refurbished when we visited; check out the new standard when you visit.

**Dang Khoa Hotel** (☎ 880290; rooms 120,000-150,000d) is a bit run-down, but the adjacent restaurant has a decent menu.

**Minh Quan Hotel** (☎ 880222; rooms 120,000-150,000d) is a good hotel, with comfortable rooms, and balconies with views over the Bac Ha market and mountains.

**Anh Duong Guesthouse** (☎ 880329; rooms 80,000-100,000d) is a friendly place that overlooks the market. Rooms are small, but are bright and were renovated in 2002.

**Tran Sin Hotel** (☎ 880240; rooms US$7-10,) overlooking the market, has balconies and mountain views from some rooms, and its **restaurant** is one of the few in town.

**Tuan Lien** (☎ 880261; rooms 70,000-80,000d), just next door to the Tran Sin, has small and grubby rooms and should be a last resort. It had just changed hands when we visited, so hopefully standards will improve.

Apart from hotel restaurants, the best option is **Cong Phu Restaurant** (☎ 880254; open lunch & dinner, closes about 9pm) for tasty, low-priced meals on an English menu.

### Getting There & Away
Minibuses depart from Lao Cai for Bac Ha (40,000d, two hours) around 6.30am, 11am and 1pm daily. Buses from Bac Ha leave for Lao Cai around 5.30am, 11.30am and 1pm. The road is well maintained and the rural scenery is lovely.

Locals on motorbikes will do the Lao Cai–Bac Ha run for about US$5, or even Sapa–Bac Ha (110km) for US$12. Sunday minibus tours from Sapa to Bac Ha cost around US$10, including transportation, guide and trekking to a minority village. On the way back to Sapa it's possible stop in Lao Cai and catch the night train back to Hanoi.

Bac Ha is about 330km (10 hours) from Hanoi. Some cafés in Hanoi offer four-day bus trips to Bac Ha for around US$60, usually with a visit to Sapa included.

# North-Central Vietnam

The north-central region is one of the poorest areas of Vietnam, and perhaps the least visited by foreign tourists. Most travellers make a beeline between Hué and Hanoi by bus, train or air, choosing to spend more time in places like Hoi An, Hué and points in the far south or north.

However, there are several interesting sites just a couple of hours from Hanoi, with the option of visiting on day or overnight trips from the capital. Tam Coc is an area of extraordinary beauty, where limestone pinnacles sit bang in the middle of rice paddies, while nearby the ancient capital of Hoa Lu is impressively atmospheric. The floating village of Kenh Ga gives a glimpse of life on the water, and the cathedral at Phat Diem brings European and Vietnamese religious architecture together in a unique blend. Cuc Phuong National Park offers the opportunity to get close to nature at its best.

The beaches of north-central Vietnam, though popular with domestic tourists, pale in comparison to those in the centre and along the south-central coast.

## History

The region's historical importance dates back to the 10th century, when the country's capital was at Hoa Lu, with its magnificent temples set amid a beautiful rural landscape of limestone cliffs and rice paddies.

In the 13th and 14th centuries, the Tran dynasty kings ruled from the capital of Thang Long, present-day Hanoi. This was the only period in Vietnamese history when the heirs to the throne partially succeeded their fathers, taking over the official role of king, while the older generation shared power in a second unofficial capital in Tuc Mac, about 5km from Nam Dinh. This prevented the traditional practice of feuding brothers killing each other off for the throne, making the Tran dynasty one of the most politically stable and prosperous periods in Vietnamese history.

## Highlights

- Visit Tam Coc, the beautiful 'Halong Bay on the rice fields' near Ninh Binh, and the floating village of Kenh Ga
- Make a forest trek and visit the Endangered Primate Rescue Center at Cuc Phuong National Park
- Go temple-hopping in the ancient capital of Hoa Lu
- Visit the impressive Sino-Vietnamese Phat Diem Cathedral

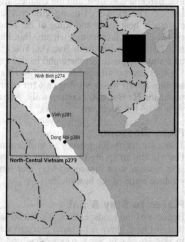

Ninh Binh p274

Vinh p281

Dong Hoi p284

North-Central Vietnam p273

During the American War, north-central Vietnam suffered great damage from US bombing, notably in Thanh Hoa.

## THAI BINH
☎ 036 • pop 135,000

Few travellers visit Thai Binh, because it's not on Hwy 1. You're only likely to come here if you're following the spur route that connects Ninh Binh to Haiphong. The only sight of interest around here is nearby Keo Pagoda.

## Keo Pagoda

Keo Pagoda (Chua Keo) was founded in the 12th century to honour Buddha and the monk Khong Minh Khong, who miraculously cured Emperor Ly Thanh Ton (r. 1128–38) of leprosy. The finely carved wooden bell tower is considered a masterpiece of traditional Vietnamese architecture. The nearby dike is a good place to get a general view of the pagoda complex.

Keo Pagoda is in Thai Binh province, 9.5km from Thai Binh. It's easy to catch a motorbike taxi (10,000d) from Thai Binh to the pagoda.

## NINH BINH
☎ 030 • pop 53,000

Ninh Binh has evolved into a major travel centre in recent years. Its sudden transformation from sleepy hamlet to tourist magnet has little to do with Ninh Binh itself, but rather with its proximity to nearby Tam Coc (9km), Hoa Lu (12km), Kenh Ga (21km) and Cuc Phuong National Park (45km).

Although it is certainly possible to visit these sights as a day trip from Hanoi, many travellers chose to overnight in Ninh Binh or the national park to appreciate the scenery at a more leisurely pace.

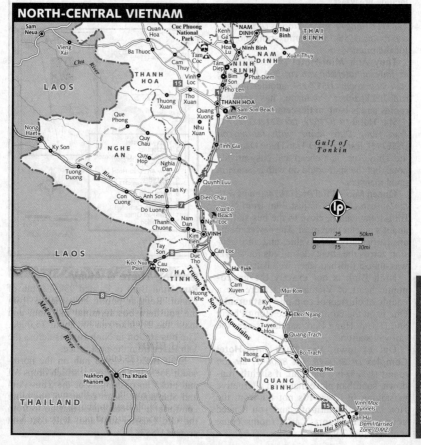

**NORTH-CENTRAL VIETNAM**

## Places to Stay & Eat

The hotels in Ninh Binh are considerably cleaner and better maintained than is the norm in rural Vietnam. They all offer Internet access for around 500d per minute, make tour and transport bookings, and offer motorbikes and bikes for hire. Most places also offer basic food. The following hotels are listed by location, travelling north to south along Hwy 1.

**Viet Hung Hotel** (☎ 872002; e viethunghotel-nb@hn.vnn.vn; 2 Đ Tran Hung Dao; aircon rooms US$10-35) was built in 2001. It's clean and bright, good value, and the prices include breakfast.

**Thanh Thuy's Guesthouse** (☎ 871811; 128 Đ Le Hong Phong; fan rooms US$4-6, aircon rooms US$8-15) is family-run, and fine for the price.

**Thuy Anh Mini-Hotel** (☎/fax 871602; e thuyanhhotel@hn.vnn.vn; 55A Đ Truong Han Sieu; rooms US$7-25), another family-run backpacker favourite, has spotless rooms and is bang in the centre of town.

**Star Hotel** (☎ 871522, fax 871200; 267 Đ Tran Hung Dao; rooms with fan/air-con US$6/15), just across Đ Tran Hung Dao from the Thuy Anh, is a cheap and busy private hotel, but the staff could do with a lesson in good manners.

**Queen Mini-Hotel** (☎ 871874; rooms with fan/air-con US$6/8) is just 30m from Ninh Binh train station, close to the bus station, and it's quieter than most. The newer rooms are particularly good value, and an extension across the street (dorm beds for US$1) was almost finished when we visited.

Ninh Binh is not exactly the gastronomic heart of Vietnam, but there are a couple of clusters of **com pho restaurants**. One is on the corner of Đ Le Hong Phong and Đ Tran Hung Dao; another is near the railway station.

Out of town, **Van Xuan Inter-Hotel Complex** (☎ 860648, fax 860647; air-con rooms US$25) is a pleasant, if slightly run-down, suburban place that is an alternative to staying in town. It's not far from the Hoa Lu citadel turn-off, and you'll need your own transport. Large rooms come with satellite TV.

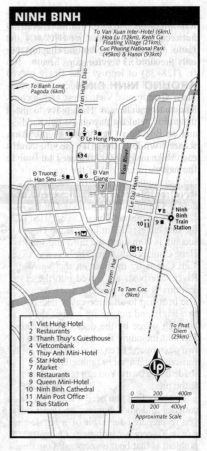

**NINH BINH**

To Van Xuan Inter-Hotel (6km),
Hoa Lu (12km), Kenh Ga
Floating Village (21km),
Cuc Phuong National Park
(45km) & Hanoi (93km)

To Banh Long
Pagoda (6km)

Đ Tran Hung Dao

Đ Le Hong Phong

Van River

Đ Truong
Han Sieu

Đ Van
Giang

Đ Le Dai Hanh

Ninh
Binh
Train
Station

Đ Nguyen Hue

To Tam Coc
(9km)

1 Viet Hung Hotel
2 Restaurants
3 Thanh Thuy's Guesthouse
4 Vietcombank
5 Thuy Anh Mini-Hotel
6 Star Hotel
7 Market
8 Restaurants
9 Queen Mini-Hotel
10 Ninh Binh Cathedral
11 Main Post Office
12 Bus Station

To Phat
Diem
(29km)

0      200      400m
0      200      400yd
Approximate Scale

## Getting There & Away

**Bus** Ninh Binh is located 93km south of Hanoi. Regular public buses leave from the **southern bus terminal** in Hanoi and make the 2½ hour run for about 25,000d. The **bus station** in Ninh Binh is across the Van River from the post office.

Ninh Binh is also a hub on the north-south open-tour bus route, which drops off and picks up passengers at the Thuy Anh and Star hotels. Seats on one of the more comfortable air-con buses that go to/from the Old Quarter in Hanoi will cost you around US$3.

**Train** Ninh Binh is a scheduled stop for the *Reunification Express* trains travelling between Ho Chi Minh City (HCMC) and Hanoi (see the Getting Around chapter), but only the slow S3 service stops here.

## AROUND NINH BINH

### Tam Coc

Known to travellers as 'Halong Bay without the water', 'Halong Bay on the rice paddies' and so on, Tam Coc boasts breathtaking scenery. While Halong Bay (see the Northeast Vietnam chapter) features huge rock formations jutting out of the sea, Tam Coc has them jutting out of its rice paddies. Some travellers will notice a striking resemblance here to Guilin and Yangshuo in China.

Tam Coc means 'Three Caves'. Hang Ca, the first cave, is 127m long; Hang Giua, the second, is 70m long; the third and smallest, Hang Cuoi, is only 40m. The best way to see Tam Coc is by rowboat on the Ngo Dong River. The boats are rowed into the caves, and this is a very peaceful and scenic trip. The boat trip to all three caves takes about two hours and tickets are sold at the small booking office by the docks. A boat costs 55,000d including the entry fee, and seats two passengers. Even on cloudy days, bring sunscreen and a hat or umbrella – there's no shade in the boats. You can rent an umbrella at the pier.

You may find you need a healthy dose of patience and good humour at Tam Coc; if you're prepared for a bit of a hassle then it won't seem so irritating. One reported problem is that boat owners ask you almost constantly to buy embroidery – if you don't want it, just say no. There are also boat vendors who paddle up alongside your boat and try to sell drinks; if you don't want any, they will 'suggest' (rather strongly) that you buy a Coke for the person rowing your boat. Many travellers do this and then later find that the oarsperson simply sells the Coke back to the drink vendors for half the price.

The area behind the Tam Coc restaurants is **Van Lan village**, which is famous for its embroidery. Here you can watch the local artisans make napkins, tablecloths, pillowcases and T-shirts. A lot of these items wind up being sold on Hanoi's Pho Hang Gai, but it's cheaper to buy them here directly from the artisan. The village has a better selection and slightly lower prices than those available from the boat vendors.

**Getting There & Away** Tam Coc is 9km southwest of Ninh Binh. Follow Hwy 1 south and turn west at the Tam Coc turn-off. Budget cafés in Hanoi book day trips to Tam Coc; the fast-food version goes for about US$12, or it's closer to US$20 with a smaller group, comfortable vehicle and professional guide. Ninh Binh hotels also run day tours, and rent motorbikes and bicycles if you're staying in town and want to make your own way there.

### Hoa Lu

The scenery here resembles nearby Tam Coc, though Hoa Lu has an interesting historical twist. Hoa Lu was the capital of Vietnam during the Dinh (968–80) and early Le (980–1009) dynasties. The site was a suitable choice for a capital city due to its proximity to China and the natural protection afforded by the region's bizarre landscape.

The **ancient citadel of Hoa Lu** *(admission 30,000d)*, most of which has been destroyed, covered an area of about 3 sq km. The outer ramparts encompassed temples, shrines and the king's palace. The royal family lived in the inner citadel.

Yen Ngua mountain provides a scenic backdrop for Hoa Lu's two remaining temples. The first temple, **Dinh Tien Hoang**, was restored in the 17th century and is dedicated to the Dinh dynasty. Out the front is the stone pedestal of a royal throne; inside are bronze bells and a statue of Emperor Dinh Tien Hoang with his three sons. The second temple, **Le Dai Hanh** (or Duong Van Nga), commemorates the rulers of the early Le dynasty. Inside the main hall are an assortment of drums, gongs, incense burners, candle holders and weapons. On the hillside above the temples is the tomb of Dinh Tien Hoang. It's a good climb up 207 steps, but your efforts will be rewarded with great views.

In 1998, archaeologists unearthed a 'new' section of the old citadel, which has been dated to the 10th century. This, and some associated artefacts, have been preserved on site and are on show in a display room built around them.

There are guides at the temples who work for free (offer a tip if you use their services) or you can wander around alone. Once you've got through the hassle of persistent sellers on the way in, it's very peaceful inside the complex, especially in the late afternoon when you miss the crowds.

**Getting There & Away** Hoa Lu is 12km north of Ninh Binh. There is no public transport, so most travellers get there by bicycle (US$1 per day from Ninh Binh), motorbike or car.

## Banh Long Pagoda

While not spectacular, this Buddhist pagoda is only 6km from Ninh Binh and worth at least a quick look. From Hwy 1 (Đ Tran Hung Dao in Ninh Binh), turn west on the road beyond the Viet Hung Hotel.

## Kenh Ga Floating Village

Kenh Ga (Chicken Canal) apparently gets its name from the number of wild chickens that used to live in the area. Well, that's the story told by our boat driver's father, who remembers them from his youth, though you're unlikely to see any now. Kenh Ga is essentially a floating village on the Hoang Long River, with just a few permanent buildings on the riverbanks. About the only other place in Vietnam where you can see anything like this is in the Mekong Delta. On the other hand, nowhere in the Mekong Delta will you find as stunning a mountain backdrop as the one at Kenh Ga. Another difference; people in Kenh Ga row boats with their feet, leaning back and watching the world go by.

It's a lovely area, and one of the best places in northern Vietnam to see river life. People here seem to spend most of their lives floating on water, either at their floating fish-breeding pens, harvesting river grass to feed the fish, trawling in the muddy shallows for shellfish, or selling vegies boat-to-boat. Even the children commute to school by boat.

From the pier, you can hire a motorboat to take you for an hour or so touring around the village for 80,000d per boat. The boat trips have been organised through the local government tourism agency since 2000 and, thankfully, so far they've managed to keep the operation low-key and hassle-free. How long can it last?

The locals are very friendly. The children gleefully shout 'tay oi' (Westerner) at every tourist they see, even Vietnamese tourists!

**Getting There & Away** The Kenh Ga floating village is 21km from Ninh Binh. Follow Hwy 1 north for 11km, then it's a 10km drive west to reach the boat pier. There are some fantastic, apparently un-mapped back roads, through wonderful scenery, which also lead to the pier, but you'll need a local to draw a mud map for you. Alternatively, try to locate **Mr Cao**, a well-travelled, English-speaking Kenh Ga local who has been guiding and training tour guides in the area for many years. **ET Pumpkin Tours** (☎ 9260739; 85 Pho Ma May, Hanoi) should be able to contact him.

## PHAT DIEM

Phat Diem (sometimes called its former name, Kim Son) is the site of a **cathedral** remarkable for its vast dimensions and unique Sino-Vietnamese architecture with a European flavour. During the French era, the cathedral was an important centre of Catholicism in the north, and there was a seminary here. The 1954 division of Vietnam caused Catholics to flee to the south en masse, and the cathedral was closed. It is now functional again, and there are also several dozen other churches in the Phat Diem district. Current estimates are that about 120,000 Catholics live in the area.

The vaulted ceiling is supported by massive wooden columns that are almost 1m in diameter and 10m tall. In the lateral naves, there are a number of curious wood and stone sculptures. The main altar is made of a single block of granite. The outside of the church reaches a height of 16m.

The cathedral complex comprises a number of buildings; the main one was completed in 1891. The whole project was founded by a Vietnamese priest named Six, whose tomb is in the square fronting the cathedral. Behind the main building is a large pile of limestone boulders – Father Six piled them up to test whether the boggy ground would support his planned empire. Apparently the test was a success.

Opposite the main entrance at the back of the cathedral is the bell tower. At its base lie two enormous stone slabs, one atop the other. Their sole purpose was to provide a perch for the mandarins to sit and observe (no doubt with great amusement) the rituals of the Catholics at mass. All the big carved stones here were transported from some 200km away with only very rudimentary equipment.

Atop the cathedral's highest tower is such an enormous bell that Quasimodo's famous chimer at Notre Dame pales in comparison. This bell, and all the other heavy metal, was pushed and pulled to the cathedral's top via an enormous earth ramp. After construction was completed, the earth was used to raise the whole site about 1m higher than the surrounding terrain. This has, no doubt, offered important protection against floods.

Near the main cathedral is a small chapel built of large carved stone blocks, and inside it's as cool as a cave. Also not far from this cathedral is a covered bridge dating from the late 19th century.

Hordes of Vietnamese tourists come to this place. Few of them are Catholic, but many are extremely curious about churches and Christianity in general. Admission to the complex is free, but you may have to negotiate hordes of sellers and beggars at busy times. The church is usually locked – if you want to go inside, ask at the guide kiosk just outside the main entrance. Daily mass is celebrated at 5am and 5pm.

## Getting There & Away

Phat Diem is 121km south of Hanoi and 29km southeast of Ninh Binh. There are direct buses from Ninh Binh to Phat Diem, or you can go by motorbike.

There are no regular tours to Phat Diem, though any of the budget agents in Hanoi should be able to offer a customised day trip by private car, with or without a guide.

## CUC PHUONG NATIONAL PARK
☎ 030 • elevation 648m

Cuc Phuong National Park (☎ 846006; Nho Quan district, Ninh Binh province; admission 40,000d • ☎ 04-829 2604; 1 Pho Doc Tan Ap, Hanoi), established in 1962, is one of Vietnam's most important nature reserves. Ho Chi Minh personally took time off from the war in 1963 to dedicate this, Vietnam's first national park. He offered a short dedication speech:

Forest is gold. If we know how to conserve it well, it will be very precious. Destruction of the forest will lead to serious effects on both life and productivity.

This national park is 70km from the coast and covers an area about 25km in length and 11km in width in the provinces of Ninh Binh, Hoa Binh and Thanh Hoa. The elevation of the park's highest peak, Dinh May Bac (Silver Cloud Peak) is 648m. At the park's lower elevations, the climate is subtropical. The stone tools of prehistoric humans have been discovered in Con Moong Cave, one of the park's many grottoes. The park is home to the excellent **Endangered Primate Rescue Center** – see the boxed text in this chapter for details.

Though wildlife has suffered a precipitous decline in Vietnam in recent decades, the park's 222 sq km of primary tropical forest remains home to an amazing variety of animal and plant life. There are 320 species of bird, 97 species of mammal including bats, and 36 species of reptile identified so far. Of the 1983 known plant species, 433 have medicinal properties and 299 are food sources. The park is also home to a species of tree called Cay Kim Gao (for aspiring horticulturists, the Latin name is *Podocarpus fleuryi hickel* and it's also found in Cat Ba National Park). In ancient days, kings and noble people would only eat with chopsticks made from this lumber – it was said that anything poisonous it touches turns the light coloured wood to black! These chopsticks make a nice souvenir.

Poaching and habitat destruction is a constant headache for the park rangers. Many native species, such as the black bear, wild cats, birds and reptiles, have perished in the park as a result of human impact. Episodes of violence have erupted between the Muong and park rangers who have tried to stop logging in the park. The government has responded by relocating the villagers further from the park's boundary. Hopefully the park authorities will be able to create opportunities for local people to participate in the eco-tourism ventures, thereby giving conservation an economic value that will benefit the environment. A highway has recently been scheduled to bisect the park and this, of course, will have a huge impact on the growth, movement and conservation of plants and animals.

The best time of year to visit the park is in the dry months from October to March. From April to June it becomes increasingly hot and wet, and from July to September the rains arrive, bringing *lots* of leeches. Visitors in April and May should be lucky enough to see literally millions of butterflies that breed here.

There is a low-key, informative visitor centre a few hundred metres before the park entrance.

## Hiking in Cuc Phuong

Excellent hiking opportunities abound in the park and you could spend several days trekking through the forest here.

Short walks include a large, enclosed **botanical garden** near the park headquarters where some native animals – deer, civets, gibbons and langurs – have been released. Another short trail leads to a steep stairway up to the archaeologically significant **Cave of Prehistoric Man**.

Popular day-trails include an 8km return walk to the massive 1000 year-old Big Tree *(Tetrameles nudiflora)*, and a longer hike to Silver Cloudy Top Mountain.

There's also a strenuous five-hour hike to Kanh, a Muong village. You can overnight here, and raft on the Buoi river.

Park staff can provide you with basic maps to find the well-marked trail heads, but a guide is recommended for day trips and is mandatory for longer treks. A guide will cost a minimum of US$5 per day for up to five people, plus US$1 for each extra person.

## Places to Stay & Eat

There are two accommodation areas in the park, with a complicated range of prices and options.

You can stay in the centre of the park, 18km from the gate, which is the best place to be if you want to do an early morning walk or bird-watching. Here there are basic **rooms** *(US$6 per person)* in a pillar house, or a couple of self-contained **bungalows** *(one person/two people US$15/25)*. There's also an enormous river-fed swimming pool.

At park headquarters, and along the quiet park access road, there are self-contained **bungalows and guesthouse rooms** *(US$15/ 20 for one/two people)*. There are also **rooms in a pillar house** *(US$5 per person)*. You can **camp** *(US$2 per person)*, but need to bring your own gear. You can order food from reception, including a vegetarian option.

It can get *very* busy here at weekends and during Vietnamese school holidays; you may want to avoid these times of the year. Reservations can be made by contacting the national park office.

## Getting There & Away

Cuc Phuong National Park is 45km from Ninh Binh. The turn-off from Hwy 1 is north of Ninh Binh, and follows the road that goes past the Kenh Ga floating village. There is no public transport on this route.

## THANH HOA
☎ 037

Thanh Hoa is the capital of Thanh Hoa province. The only feature of real interest is a large and attractive church on the northern outskirts of town, and you will pass through the town on the way to Sam Son Beach.

Thanh Hoa province was the site of the Lam Son Uprising (1418–28), in which Vietnamese forces, led by Le Loi (who later became Emperor Ly Thai To) expelled the

Chinese and re-established the country's independence. Muong and Red Tai (Thai) hill tribes live in the western part of the province.

**Places to Stay & Eat**

**Thanh Hoa Hotel** (☎ 852517, fax 853963; 25A Đ Quang Trung; rooms US$10-35) is on the western side of the highway in the centre

## Endangered Primate Rescue Center

One of the highlights of a visit to Cuc Phuong is the Endangered Primate Rescue Center (**W** www .primatecenter.org; admission free; open 9am-11am & 1pm-4pm daily). The facility, run by German biologists and local Vietnamese, is a laudable endeavour to improve the wellbeing of Vietnam's primates.

What started out as a small-scale operation in 1995, with just a handful of animals, has grown into a highly productive centre, where today about 85 creatures are cared for, studied and bred. There are around 14 species of gibbons and langurs on site. The langur is a long-tailed, tree-dwelling monkey; the gibbon is a long-armed, fruit-eating ape. There are also lorises (smaller nocturnal primates) at the centre.

There are estimated to be only about 20 species of primates remaining in the wild in Vietnam, most of which are threatened by hunters and/or habitat destruction. Some people attempt to keep these animals as pets, which is almost impossible. Langurs survive exclusively on fresh-cut leaves, and their digestive systems will not tolerate anything else. By feeding them incorrectly, people usually discover they've murdered their new 'pet' before they can even show it off to their friends. All the animals in the centre were rescued either from cages or from illegal traders, who transport them mostly to China to become medicine ingredients. Such rare animals can fetch anywhere between US$200 and US$1000 from buyers looking to cash in on their 'medicinal worth', be it for gallstone relief or as an aphrodisiac. Thankfully, steps are being taken to curb the illegal trading and to protect the langurs that still exist.

In cooperation with the Vietnamese authorities, the centre has had some major recovery and breeding successes. When we visited, we saw a world-first: a week-old grey-shanked Douc langur, the first ever bred in captivity. (The proud new father did the protective male thing by sticking his neck out and frowning fiercely at observers while exposing a long erect pink penis!) The red-shanked Douc langurs are breeding fantastically and are fascinating animals that look as though they are wearing red shorts (their Vietnamese name translates as 'monkeys wearing shorts'). It's a treat to be able to see these remarkable – and seriously cute – animals. Some southern species of langur at the centre even have heated sleeping quarters in winter, which is more than can be said for the human residents.

One of the larger aims of the centre is to re-introduce these primates into their natural habitat. Currently hunting pressures are still too high, but as a preliminary step, some gibbons and a group of Hatinh langurs have been released into a 2-hectare, semi-wild area adjacent to the centre, and a group of Douc langurs are in a second, 4-hectare, semi-wild enclosure. If you're keen to look for langurs in the wild, ask at the centre about the best places to spot them; for obvious reasons we won't publicise their possible locations here.

The centre is about 500m before the national park reception centre and is open to visitors at the specified times only. You can't wander around the centre alone, so if you're travelling independently you need first to go to the national park reception area and arrange a guide. If you're going to take a guided tour from Ninh Binh, be aware that the centre welcomes the tour guides used by Thuy Anh Hotel and Thanh Thuy's Guesthouse, but has banned several others from entering!

Entry is free, but you might consider purchasing some postcards or a poster, or making a donation. Biologists and other relevant professionals may want to email ahead to see if any supplies are needed from abroad.

of town. It's expensive for what it is – the rooms are small and in need of refurbishing.

**Loi Linh Hotel** (☎ 851667; 22 Đ Tran Phu; rooms US$10) is a family-run hotel, rather oddly designed above a sort of massive entry hall. Rooms are small and dark, but they're clean and have air-con.

**Soup shops**, **cafés** and a few **restaurants** can be found along Hwy 1, especially near the southern entrance to town.

### Getting There & Away

Thanh Hoa is a stop for the *Reunification Express* trains (see the Getting Around chapter). The city is 502km from Hué, 139km from Vinh and 153km from Hanoi by road.

## SAM SON BEACH
☎ 037

Sam Son is possibly the most popular beach resort in the north. It's too far from Hanoi for day-trippers, but during summer (May to September) the place is chock-a-block with weekenders escaping the oven-hot capital. During winter, Sam Son is pretty much deserted and only a few hotels bother to stay open.

There are in fact two beaches here, separated by a rocky headland. The main beach, which is beautiful out of season, is on the north side of the headland and is where you'll find a concrete jungle of hotels, karaoke bars and massage parlours. It's not to everyone's taste, but is probably fine for an out-of-season day trip, if you've got your own transport. The southern beach is mostly undeveloped, but it can still fill up with picnickers. The headland itself offers some decent **hiking** and scenic views, though the promontory has a military base and a sign (in English) telling you to keep out. The rest of the headland is a park and is open to the public.

The area is notable for its **pine forests**, enormous granite boulders, sweeping views and long stretches of white sand.

### Places to Stay

Most of Sam Son's ugly state-run hotels offer luxury hotel prices without the luxury.

Be aware that prices tend to go up between June and August (high season for domestic tourists). It's possible to negotiate discounts in winter, though there's not much point visiting at that time.

Most hotels are state-run but **Hoa Dang Hotel** (☎ 821288; 3-bed rooms low/high season 100,000/350,000d) is a smaller private hotel. Don't expect too much for the price, but at least you can sit on the balcony overlooking the beach and escape the room.

There is a crowd of **hotels** (rooms low/high season US$15/30) along the beach.

### Getting There & Away

Access to Sam Son is from the Thanh Hoa road and railway junction. It's only 16km to Sam Son, a short enough trip by motorbike.

## VINH
☎ 038 • pop 201,900

The port city of Vinh is the capital of Nghe An province. Apart from lashings of dreary Soviet-style architecture, there's nothing of interest there, though there are a few sights in the surrounding area. Recently Vinh's economic fortunes have greatly improved by the sharp increase in traffic on Hwy 1. For travellers, the town is a convenient place to stop for the night, if you are on the overland route between Hué and Hanoi. Vinh is also an essential transit point if you're heading overland to/from Tha Khaek in Laos via the Cau Treo border crossing.

Nghe An and neighbouring Ha Tinh provinces have been lumped with poor soil and some of the worst weather in Vietnam; the area frequently suffers from severe floods and devastating typhoons. The locals say, 'The typhoon was born here and comes back often to visit'. The summers are very hot and dry, while in winter the cold and rain are made all the more unpleasant by biting winds from the north.

As a result of the poor climate and many years of ill-managed collectivised farming policies, Nghe An and Ha Tinh provinces are among the most destitute regions in Vietnam. The recent economic reforms have greatly improved things, but nobody has yet figured out a way to reform the lousy weather.

## History

Vinh's more recent history has not been the happiest. It was a pleasant citadel city during its colonial days, but was destroyed in the early 1950s as a result of French aerial bombing and the Viet Minh's scorched-earth policy. Vinh was later devastated by a huge fire.

The Ho Chi Minh Trail began in Nghe An province, and much of the war *matériel* transported on the Ho Chi Minh Trail was shipped via the port of Vinh. Not too surprisingly, the US military obliterated the city in hundreds of air attacks and naval

artillery bombardments from 1964 to 1972, which left only two buildings intact. The Americans paid a high price for the bombings – more US aircraft and pilots were shot down over Nghe An and Ha Tinh provinces than over any other part of North Vietnam. The heavy loss of planes and pilots was one reason why the USA later brought in battleships to pound North Vietnam from offshore.

## Orientation & Information

As Hwy 1 enters Vinh from the south, it crosses over the mouth of the Lam River

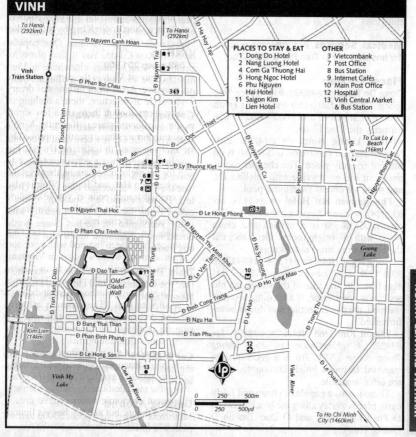

**VINH**

To Hanoi (292km)
To Hanoi (292km)
Đ Nguyen Canh Hoan
Đ Ha Huy Tap
Vinh Train Station
Đ Phan Boi Chau
Đ Nguyen Trai
Đ Truong Chinh
Doc Thiet
Đ Chu Van An
Đ Le Loi
Đ Ly Thuong Kiet
Đ Nguyen Van Cu
Đ Hecman
Đ Nguyen Phong Sac
To Cua Lo Beach (16km)
ĐT 3 - 2
Đ Nguyen Thai Hoc
Đ Le Hong Phong
Đ Nguyen Thi Minh Khai
Đ Ho Sy Doung
Đ Phan Chu Trinh
Quang Trung
Goong Lake
Đ Dao Tan
Old Citadel Wall
Đ Le Van Tam
Đ Ho Tung Mau
Đ Tran Hung Dao
Đ Dinh Cong Trang
Đ Le Mao
Đ Dang Thai Than
Đ Ngu Hai
To Kim Lien (14km)
Đ Phan Dinh Phung
Đ Tran Phu
Đ Le Hong Son
Cua Tien River
Vinh My Lake
Vinh River
Đ Le Duan
Đ Trong Thi
To Ho Chi Minh City (1460km)

**PLACES TO STAY & EAT**
1 Dong Do Hotel
2 Nang Luong Hotel
4 Com Ga Thuong Hai
5 Hong Ngoc Hotel
6 Phu Nguyen Hai Hotel
11 Saigon Kim Lien Hotel

**OTHER**
3 Vietcombank
7 Post Office
8 Bus Station
9 Internet Cafés
10 Main Post Office
12 Hospital
13 Vinh Central Market & Bus Station

0    250    500m
0    250    500yd

**NORTH-CENTRAL VIETNAM**

(Ca River), also known as Cua Hoi Estuary. Street address numbers are often not used in Vinh. There are several **Internet cafés** on Đ Le Hong Phong.

**Money** The **Vietcombank** (Ngan Hang Ngoai Thuong Viet Nam) is close to the roundabout at which Đ Le Loi becomes Đ Nguyen Trai.

**Post** The **main post office** (Đ Nguyen Thi Minh Khai; open 6.30am-9pm daily) is near the corner of Đ Dinh Cong Trang. It was being rebuilt at the time of writing, but the renovations were almost over. There's a small post-office **kiosk** next to Phu Nguyen Hai Hotel.

**Medical Services** For emergencies, try the **hospital** (cnr Đ Tran Phu & Đ Le Mao).

## Places to Stay

**Dong Do Hotel** (☎ 846989; 9 Đ Nguyen Trai; rooms 100,000-120,000đ) has rooms (with bath) that are clean and good value. It was formerly the Vina Hotel.

**Nang Luong Hotel** (☎ 844788; 2 Đ Nguyen Trai; air-con rooms US$15-34) is an old but friendly place. The cheaper rooms are clean and great value with satellite TV, and there's a decent swimming pool.

**Phu Nguyen Hai Hotel** (☎ 848429, fax 832014; e ctpnh@hn.vnn.vn; 81 Đ Le Loi; rooms US$18-35) is a newish and clean place, with big bright rooms. Get a room at the back as the street side is noisy.

**Hong Ngoc Hotel** (☎ 841314, fax 841229; 99 & 13 Đ Le Loi; air-con rooms US$15-25) is also fine. On one side of the street, the old section is good value, if a bit dingy. Across the road, the newer section was due to be re-furbished.

**Saigon Kim Lien Hotel** (☎ 838899, fax 838898; e sgklna@hn.vnn.vn; 25 Đ Quang Trung; rooms US$30-70) is a good quality, standard business hotel. Discounted rates are often available.

There is also a gaggle of cheap and fairly nasty places to stay along the block between Đ Phan Chu Trinh and Đ Dao Tan on Đ Quang Trung.

## Places to Eat

**Vinh Central Market** (Cho Vinh) carries the usual plethora of household goods, and there are food stalls around the back, heading towards the bus station. The market is at the end of Đ Cao Thang, which is the southern continuation of Đ Quang Trung.

**Com Ga Thuong Hai** (99 Đ Le Loi) has good Chinese-style dishes. It's connected to the old wing of Hong Ngoc Hotel. The restaurant's name means 'Rice Chicken Shanghai' (which is also the good house speciality) and the menu has some wild and wacky translations into English, particularly of the frog and snake dishes.

If you poke around town, you'll notice the peanut candies that are on sale almost everywhere. There are at least three different kinds, each one outstanding. One popular brand is Keo Cu-do. You'll find plenty of similar-looking candies elsewhere in Vietnam, but the Vinh varieties are far and away the best.

## Getting There & Away

**Bus** There are two **bus stations** in Vinh. The station on Đ Le Loi is where most Hanoi and HCMC buses leave and arrive. The bus station behind the market is where to go for buses to Tay Son, and on to the Lao border (see the Cau Treo section later in this chapter). Be aware that Tay Son was formerly called Trung Tam, and this is usually what you'll see signed on the bus. Some northbound and southbound buses also use this bus station.

**Train** The *Reunification Express* stops here (see the Getting Around chapter). The **Vinh train station** (Ga Vinh; ☎ 824924) is 1km west of the intersection of Đ Le Loi and Đ Phan Boi Chau and about 1.5km north of Vinh Market.

**Car & Motorbike** From Vinh it's 87km to the Lao border, 139km to Thanh Hoa, 96km to Dong Hoi and 319km to Hanoi.

## Getting Around

Motorbike taxis charge about 5000đ to most places in town.

## Betel Nut

One thing you'll undoubtedly see for sale at street stalls everywhere in Vietnam is betel nut. This is not a food – swallow it and you'll be sorry! The betel nut is the seed of the betel palm (a beautiful tree, by the way) and is meant to be chewed. The seed usually has a slit in it and is mixed with lime and wrapped in a leaf. Like tobacco, it's strong stuff that you can barely tolerate at first, but eventually become addicted to.

The first time you bite into betel nut, your whole face gets hot – chewers say it gives them a buzz. Like chewing tobacco, betel nut causes excessive salivation and betel chewers must constantly spit. The reddish-brown stains you see on footpaths are not blood, but betel-saliva juice. Years of constant chewing cause the teeth to become stained progressively browner, eventually becoming nearly black.

Despite its small size, Vinh has three taxi companies: **Phu Nguyen Taxi** (☎ 833333), **Quynh Ha Taxi** (☎ 858585) and **Viet Anh Taxi** (☎ 843999).

## AROUND VINH
☎ 038

### Cua Lo Beach
This is one of the three major beach resorts in the northern half of the country. The other two are at Sam Son and Do Son. It's designed to Vietnamese taste, and may not suit many travellers' style.

The beach here is beautiful, with white sand, clean water and a shady grove of pine trees along the shore, but in high season (May to September) there's lots of litter. Nevertheless, if you're in the area and the weather is suitably warm and dry, Cua Lo could be worth a visit to cool off – at least as a half-day trip from Vinh – and to eat a good seafood lunch at one of the restaurants on the beach.

**Places to Stay** There are masses of **hotels** (rooms US$5) along the waterfront, **guesthouses** (rooms US$30) to huge government

enterprises. Most offer 'massage' and karaoke, and most have prostitutes hanging around outside, even in low season. Hotel rates drop considerably during the winter months – the name of the game is negotiation if for some reason you really want to stay here.

**Getting There & Away** Cua Lo is 16km northeast of Vinh and can be reached easily by motorbike or taxi.

### Kim Lien
Just 14km northwest of Vinh is **Ho Chi Minh's birthplace** in the village of Hoang Tru. The house in which he was born in 1890 is maintained as a sacred shrine, and it is a favourite pilgrimage spot for Vietnamese tourists. Ho Chi Minh's childhood home is a simple farmhouse that's made of bamboo and palm leaves, reflecting his humble beginnings. He was raised in this house until 1895, when the family sold it and moved to Hué so that his father could study.

In 1901, Ho Chi Minh's family returned to a **house in Kim Lien**, about 2km from Hoang Tru. Not far from this house, there is a **museum**.

Admission to all the sites (open 7.30am-11am & 1.30pm-5pm daily) is free. However you are obliged to buy three bouquets of flowers (10,000d each) from the reception desk and place one by each of the three altars. No English-language information is available.

At the car park by the museum are quite a few vendors plugging the peanut candies for which Vinh is famous.

There is no public transport to Kim Lien, but it is easy enough to hire a motorbike or taxi in Vinh.

### CAU TREO (LAO BORDER)
This border post is 96km west of Vinh, and the last 25km or so climb through some spectacular steep and forested country. The border is open from 7am-5pm daily, and there is absolutely nothing there except the border post itself, so stock up on water and snacks in Tay Son as you pass through.

From the Vietnamese side it's 1.5km to the Laos border. You can walk this, or if a motorbike has brought you up from Tay Son, it's permitted to take you through the 'no-man's land' between the border posts.

### Getting There & Away

Vinh is the junction for transport to the border. Buses leave from the central market bus station, ten times a day between 6am and 2pm (10,000d). The bus takes you as far as the town of Tay Son (formerly Trung Tam), from where it's 26km to the border. You can wait for a local bus to take you the last stretch, or hire a motorbike to take you there directly. The cost (50,000d) is the same for both. These are prices for locals, and you may need to negotiate.

## DEO NGANG

Deo Ngang (Ngang Pass) is a mountainous coastal area that constitutes the easternmost section of the Hoanh Son Mountains (Transversal Range), which stretches from the Lao border to the sea along the 18th parallel. Until the 11th century, the range formed Vietnam's frontier with the Kingdom of Champa. Later, the French used it as the border between their protectorates of Annam and Tonkin; Annam Gate (Porte d'Annam) is still visible at Ngang Deo from Hwy 1.

## DONG HOI

☎ 052 • pop 93,500

The pretty fishing port of Dong Hoi is the capital of Quang Binh province, and some important archaeological finds from the Neolithic period have been made in its vicinity. During the American War, the city suffered extensive damage from US bombing. When you travel along Hwy 1, north of the DMZ, note the old French bunkers and US bomb craters lining the route; they're especially prolific near road and rail bridges.

The Vietnam-Cuba Hospital is 1km north of town and the Nhat Le River flows along the eastern side of town. If you're staying overnight, head 200m or so east of Hwy 1 to the river and its fishing harbour – it's

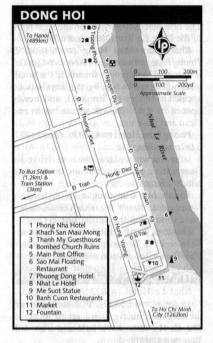

**DONG HOI**

To Hanoi (489km)

D Thuong Phap

D Nguyen Du

D Ly Thuong Kiet

Nhat Le River

To Bus Station (1.2km) & Train Station (3km)

D Tran

Hung Dao

D Quach

Xuan Ky

D Hung Vuong

D N Trai

To Ho Chi Minh City (1263km)

0      100      200m
0      100      200yd
Approximate Scale

1  Phong Nha Hotel
2  Khach San Mau Mong
3  Thanh My Guesthouse
4  Bombed Church Ruins
5  Main Post Office
6  Sao Mai Floating Restaurant
7  Phuong Dong Hotel
8  Nhat Le Hotel
9  Me Suot Statue
10  Banh Cuon Restaurants
11  Market
12  Fountain

picture-postcard pretty and there are plenty of hotels and guesthouses along the water.

Usually travellers spend the night in Dong Hoi only if they wish to visit Phong Nha Cave (see the Phong Nha Cave section in this chapter). The cave is 55km from Dong Hoi, so it can be visited as a day trip. Some hotels in Dong Hoi book trips to the cave.

### Beaches

Most of Quang Binh province is lined with sand dunes and beaches. These spread for dozens of kilometres north of town and on a long spit of sand south of town. **Nhat Le Beach** is at the mouth of the Nhat Le River, about 2.5km from central Dong Hoi. Another bathing site in the region is **Ly Hoa Beach**.

If you're heading north along Hwy 1 from Dong Hoi, it's possible to follow the beautiful coast road for a few kilometres, and then branch left to rejoin the highway.

## Places to Stay & Eat
The best places to stay are on the west bank of the Nhat Le River, just east of Hwy 1.

**Khach San Mau Hong** (☎ 821804; Đ Truong Phap; 3-bed rooms 100,000-140,000d) is the best option we found. It's a small guesthouse, run by a delightful family (who speak absolutely no English), and newly opened in 2002. The rooms are bright and clean and it's quiet.

**Phong Nha Hotel** (☎ 824971, fax 824973; 5 Đ Truong Phap; air-con rooms US$15-40) is a large, newish place close to Nhat Le Beach. It's a fair hike from the town centre and restaurants.

**Thanh My Guesthouse** (☎ 821026; Đ Nguyen Du; rooms 90,000-100,000d) has basic rooms, but the setting's lovely.

**Phuong Dong Hotel** (☎ 822276, fax 822404; 20 Đ Quach Xuan Ky; air-con rooms US$10-35) has several standards of room with varying prices. It's a state-run monolith and is very grubby.

**Nhat Le Hotel** (☎ 822180; 16 Đ Quach Xuan Ky; rooms US$10-20) is the largest of the riverside hotels. It's a grand location, and front rooms have balconies, but it's state-run and run-down.

There are plenty of other hotels and guesthouses along the waterfront, as well as along Hwy 1.

**Sao Mai Floating Restaurant** offers good seafood at reasonable prices. Moored on the Nhat Le River, it makes for an atmospheric dining choice.

For something a bit more casual, there is a cluster of good local **restaurants** near the market specialising in pancake-like *banh cuon*. Delicious! A good meal for two will cost around 30,000d.

## Getting There & Away
**Bus** Dong Hoi is on Hwy 1 and is serviced by regular bus traffic.

**Train** Dong Hoi is a stop for the *Reunification Express* train (see the Getting Around chapter).

**Car & Motorbike** Dong Hoi is about 166km from Hué, 94km from Dong Ha, 197km from Vinh and 489km from Hanoi.

## PHONG NHA CAVE
Formed approximately 250 million years ago, Phong Nha Cave (☎ 823424; admission 20,000d, charter boat 60,000d; open 6am-4pm daily) is the largest and most beautiful known cave in Vietnam. Located in the village of Son Trach, 55km northwest of Dong Hoi, it was designated a Unesco World Heritage site in 2000. It's remarkable for its thousands of metres of **underground passageways** and **river caves** filled with abundant stalactites and stalagmites. In November and December, the river is prone to flooding; the underground cave may be closed, though it's possible – but also may be dangerous – to visit the dry cave.

In 1990, a British caving expedition explored 35km of the cave and made the first reliable map of Phong Nha's underground (and underwater) passageways. They discovered that the main cavern is nearly 8km long, with 14 other caves nearby.

Phong Nha means 'Cave of Teeth', but, unfortunately, the 'teeth' (or stalagmites) that were by the entrance are no longer there. Once you get further into the cave, it's mostly unspoiled. There's also a dry cave in the mountainside just above Phong Nha Cave. You can walk to it from the entrance to Phong Nha Cave (10 minutes) – look for the sign to Tien Son at the foot of the stairs.

The Chams used the cave's grottoes as Buddhist sanctuaries in the 9th and 10th centuries; the remains of their altars and inscriptions are still there. Vietnamese Buddhists continue to venerate these sanctuaries, as they do other Cham religious sites.

More recently, this cave was used as a hospital and ammunition depot during the American War. The entrance shows evidence of fighter aircraft attacks. That US warplanes spent considerable time bombing and strafing the Phong Nha area is not surprising: this was one of the key entrance points to the Ho Chi Minh Trail. Some overgrown remains of the trail are still visible, though you'll need a guide to point them out to you.

You should be aware that Phong Nga is heavily visited. The cave itself is fantastic, the experience less so. That is unless you like your World Heritage sites to incorporate

**NORTH-CENTRAL VIETNAM**

litter, noise, people climbing on stalagmites, and cigarette smoke in the underground caverns. Of course these things are prohibited, but enforcement appears to be lax to say the least. Presumably these distractions can be avoided if you arrive early in the morning. The toilets might be less putrid then, too.

The Phong Nha Reception Department, an enormous complex in **Son Trach village**, organises tourist access to the cave. You buy your admission ticket here and organise a boat to take you to the cave. Boats seat about 10, so it's cheaper to share. The cave system is electrically lit, but you may want to bring a torch (flashlight); some of the cavern's walking track is not well-lit.

### Places to Stay & Eat

There's a bare-bones guesthouse in Son Trach, but the cave is an easy day trip from Hwy 1 and other accommodation options.

In Son Trach itself, there are plenty of cheap **com pho places**. Don't expect *haute cuisine*.

### Getting There & Away

Some hotels in Dong Hoi (20km south of Bo Trach) offer pricey tours to Phong Nga. There is no public transport to Son Trach. You can travel by public bus from Dong Hoi to Bo Trach, where you will find motorbikes at the bus station. You should be able to negotiate a trip to Son Trach for around US$5 and the driver will wait for you while you visit the cave.

The actual cave entrance is 3km by river from Son Trach. The one-way ride takes about 30 minutes, and gives a great glimpse of the life of river people. Overall, you'll probably spend about two hours if you go just to the river cave, about four hours if you explore the dry cave too.

# Central Vietnam

Central Vietnam is home to some of the most interesting sights the country has to offer. There are moving memorials to, and reminders of, the recent American War and remnants of French-colonial influence. From earlier times there were merchants' houses in formerly wealthy trading ports and, earlier still, monumental remains from some of the most ancient cultures in the country. All these are set in swathes of beautiful landscape that stretch from ocean beaches to the mountainous Lao border country.

From 1954 to 1975, the Ben Hai River served as the demarcation line between the Republic of Vietnam (RVN; South Vietnam) and the Democratic Republic of Vietnam (DRV; North Vietnam). On either side of the river was an area 5km wide that was known as the Demilitarised Zone (DMZ).

The DMZ itself and areas to the south saw plenty of action and experienced a strong military presence during the American War.

Heading south from the DMZ you reach the historic towns of Hué and Hoi An, two of the most relaxed places you'll find and both World Heritage–listed sites. Hué, probably the most historically interesting city in Vietnam, served as Vietnam's political capital from 1802 to 1945 under the 13 emperors of the Nguyen dynasty. The old port of Hoi An, formerly known as Faifo, has a great deal of rustic charm and is an ideal spot to relax and appreciate what life must have been like in past centuries.

The province of Quang Nam, bordering the municipality of Danang, contains Vietnam's most important Cham sites, including My Son and Tra Kieu (Simhapura) – both have become popular tourist destinations. Side trips to places like the Marble Mountains and China Beach also continue to draw a steady trickle of travellers. While the once bustling city of Danang is rather quiet these days, its Museum of Cham Sculpture is top-notch and, a short journey inland, the beautiful Bach Ma National Park offers a chance to catch up with nature at its best.

## Highlights

- Make a day-long visit to the former battlefields of the Demilitarised Zone (DMZ)

- Take a dragon-boat cruise along the scenic Perfume River in Hué and soak in the atmosphere of one of the majestic Royal Tombs

- Wander along nature walks and explore old French-villa ruins in spectacular Bach Ma National Park

- Linger in the old-world atmosphere of charming Hoi An

- Make a sunrise excursion to the extra-ordinary Cham ruins at My Son

- Take in Vietnam's pre-eminent collection of Cham statues at the Museum of Cham Sculpture in Danang

- Catch some rays on famous China Beach and explore the canyons and caves of the mystical Marble Mountains

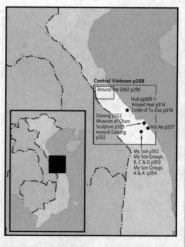

Central Vietnam p288
Around the DMZ p290
Hué pp300-1
Around Hué p314
Tomb of Tu Duc p316
Danang p322
Museum of Cham
Sculpture p325
Around Danang
p332
Hoi An p337
My Son p352
My Son Groups
B, C & D p353
My Son Groups
A & A' p354

CENTRAL VIETNAM

## DMZ

The idea of partitioning Vietnam had its origins in a series of agreements concluded between the USA, UK and the USSR at the Potsdam Conference, held in Berlin in July 1945. For logistical and political reasons, the Allies decided that the Japanese occupation forces to the south of the 16th Parallel would surrender to the British while those to the north would surrender to the Kuomintang (Nationalist) Chinese army led by Chiang Kaishek.

In April 1954 at Geneva, Ho Chi Minh's government and the French agreed to an armistice; among the provisions was the creation of a demilitarised zone at the Ben Hai River. The agreement stated explicitly that the division of Vietnam into two zones was merely temporary and that the demarcation line did not constitute a political boundary. But when nationwide general elections planned for July 1956 were not held, Vietnam found itself divided into two states with the Ben Hai River, which is almost exactly at the 17th Parallel, as their de facto border.

During the American War, the area just south of the DMZ was the scene of some of the bloodiest battles of the conflict. Quang

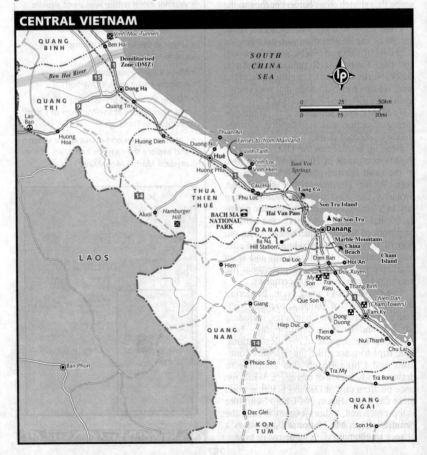

## CENTRAL VIETNAM

Tri, The Rockpile, Khe Sanh, Lang Vay and Hamburger Hill became household names in the USA as, year after year, TV pictures and casualty figures provided Americans with their evening dose of war.

Since 1975, 5000 people have been injured or killed in and around the DMZ by mines and ordnance left over from the war. Despite the risk, impoverished peasants still dig for chunks of leftover metal to sell as scrap, for which they are paid a pittance.

## Orientation

The old DMZ extends from the coast westward to the Lao border; National Hwy 9 (Quoc Lo 9) runs more or less parallel to the DMZ, about 10km south. The Ho Chi Minh Trail (Duong Truong Son) – actually a series of roads, trails and paths – ran between North and South Vietnam (perpendicular to National Hwy 9) through the Truong Son Mountain Range and western Laos; it was used by the Viet Cong (VC) to transport troops and equipment.

To disrupt the flow of troops and supplies along the Ho Chi Minh Trail, the Americans established a line of bases along National Hwy 9, including (from east to west) Cua Viet, Gio Linh, Dong Ha, Con Thien, Cam Lo, Camp Carroll, The Rockpile, Ca Lu (now called Dakrong Town), Khe Sanh and Lang Vay.

The old bases along National Hwy 9 can be visited as a long day trip from Hué, or as a long half-day trip from Dong Ha. The road leading southeast from the Dakrong Bridge on National Hwy 9 goes to the Ashau Valley (site of the infamous Hamburger Hill) and Aluoi. With a 4WD it is possible to drive the entire 60 rough kilometres from Aluoi to Hué, but an experienced driver, who'd driven the track in 2001, said the journey had taken a whole day!

The DMZ sites of significance along National Hwy 1 are more easily accessed, and somewhat easier to find.

## Information

In you want an in-depth tour of the DMZ, you will require the services of a good guide, both to fully appreciate the history and,

### Warning

The war may be over, but death and injury are still fairly easy to come by in the old Demilitarised Zone (DMZ). At many of the places listed in this section there may be live mortar rounds, artillery projectiles and mines strewn about. Watch where you step and don't leave the marked paths. As tempted as you might be to collect souvenirs, *never* touch any leftover ordnance. If the locals have not carted it off for scrap it means that even they are afraid to disturb it. White phosphorus shells – whose contents burn fiercely when exposed to air – are remarkably impervious to the effects of prolonged exposure and are likely to remain extremely dangerous for many more years.

critically, to actually find some of the sites. Many are unmarked, and it's easy to get lost in the labyrinth of dirt tracks.

Day tours are most readily available in Hué, and the same tours will also pick up passengers as they pass through Dong Ha. You can make bookings at almost any hotel or café in town. There are actually only a few agencies running the tours, so no matter where you sign up you'll still wind up as part of a group.

Expect to pay around US$11 to US$15 for a day-long outing into the DMZ. Most of these tours have English-speaking guides, but some speak French. You should make your linguistic preferences known when you book.

## MILITARY SITES ON NATIONAL HIGHWAY 1
### Vinh Moc Tunnels

The remarkable tunnels of Vinh Moc (*admission plus guided tour 25,000d*) are yet another monument to the determination of the North Vietnamese to persevere and triumph – at all costs and despite some incredible sacrifices – in the American War. A visit to the tunnels can be combined with bathing at the beautiful beaches that extend for many kilometres to the north and south of Vinh Moc.

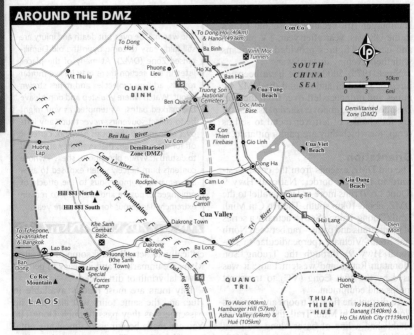

# AROUND THE DMZ

The 2.8km of tunnels here, all of which can be visited, are the real thing and unadulterated for viewing by tourists, unlike the tunnels at Cu Chi near Ho Chi Minh City (HCMC). Vinh Moc's underground passageways are also larger and taller than those at Cu Chi, which makes for an easier and less claustrophobic visit.

There are lights installed inside the tunnels, but you may also want to bring a torch (flashlight) just in case.

**History** In 1966 the USA began a massive aerial and artillery bombardment of North Vietnam. Just north of the DMZ, the villagers of Vinh Moc found themselves living in one of the most heavily bombed and shelled pieces of land on the planet. Small family shelters could not withstand this onslaught and villagers either fled or began tunnelling by hand into the red-clay earth.

Of course, the Viet Cong (VC) found it useful to have a base here and encouraged the villagers to stay. After 18 months of work (during which the excavated earth was camouflaged to prevent its detection from the air), an enormous VC base was established underground. Civilians were employed in the digging and were accommodated in new underground homes. Whole families lived here and 17 babies were born in the underground delivery room.

Later, the civilians and VC were joined by North Vietnamese soldiers, whose mission was to keep communications and supply lines to nearby Con Co Island open. A total of 11,500 tonnes of military supplies reached Con Co Island and a further 300 tonnes were shipped to the South, thanks to the Vinh Moc Tunnels.

Other villages north of the DMZ also built tunnel systems, but none were as elaborate as Vinh Moc. The poorly constructed tunnels of Vinh Quang village (at the mouth of the Ben Hai River) collapsed after repeated bombing, killing everyone inside.

The tunnel network at Vinh Moc remains essentially as it looked in 1966, though some of the 12 entrances – seven of which open onto the palm-lined beach – have been retimbered and others have become overgrown. The tunnels were built on three levels ranging from 15m to 26m below the crest of the bluff.

The tunnels were repeatedly hit by American bombs, but the only ordnance that posed a real threat was the feared 'drilling bomb'. Only once did such a bomb score a direct hit, but it failed to explode and no-one was injured; the inhabitants adapted the bomb hole for use as an air shaft. Occasionally the mouths of the tunnel complex, which faced the sea, were struck by naval gunfire.

**Getting There & Away** The turn-off to Vinh Moc from National Hwy 1 is 6.5km north of the Ben Hai River in the village of Ho Xa. Vinh Moc is another 13km east from Hwy 1.

Offshore is Con Co Island, which during the war was an important supply depot. Today the island, which is ringed by rocky beaches, houses a small military base.

## Missing in Action

An issue that continues to plague relations between the USA and Vietnam is that of US military personnel officially listed as 'missing in action' (MIA). There are still over 2000 American soldiers officially 'unaccounted for' and many of their families are adamant that their loved ones are prisoners of war (POWs) in secret prison camps deep in the jungles of Vietnam. POW–MIA groups in the USA continue to lobby Congress to 'do something'. It remains a highly emotive issue.

Others believe the POW–MIA groups are flogging a dead horse. The figure of 2265 MIAs is almost certainly too high. About 400 flight personnel were killed when their planes crashed into the sea off the coast of Vietnam, others died when their aircraft went down in flames or in ground combat – the tropical jungle quickly reclaims a human corpse. However, when Vietnam returned the last 590 American POWs, 37 soldiers believed to have been captured were not among them. The Vietnamese government adamantly denies that there are MIAs still in Vietnam; it would make no logical sense for Vietnam to continue holding US POWs.

Not much is said about the 300,000 Vietnamese who are also MIAs – they are difficult to identify because they didn't wear ID tags. However, the Vietnamese do feel just as strongly about their MIAs, particularly as they consider it their duty to perform ancestor worship – a difficult task without a corpse.

In the meantime, MIA teams continue to comb the Vietnamese countryside – at an ongoing cost of millions of dollars to American taxpayers. Investigative crews carry out assessments, based on wartime records and interviews with local villagers; once they have enough evidence to warrant a search, a recovery team conducts an on-site excavation. Any remains discovered are flown to the Central Identification Laboratory, Hawaii (Cilha) for forensic identification analysis based on dental records and DNA.

Many Vietnamese are also employed in the search teams, with 75% of their salaries going to the government. Not surprisingly, the Vietnamese government is in no hurry to see the MIA teams leave, despite the Americans raising this issue in diplomatic negotiations. The fact that the MIA teams have been digging through Vietnamese cemeteries looking for American bones has also irritated many locals who would prefer to see their dead rest in peace.

Meanwhile, the sad saga continues to play itself out. When private POW–MIA groups started circulating photographs showing US soldiers being held prisoner in a Vietnamese camp, there was a flurry of official investigations. The photos proved to be fakes but groups such as the National League of Families of American Prisoners and Missing in Southeast Asia were very effective at stalling the US government's attempts to forge diplomatic relations with Vietnam. Despite protests, diplomatic relations were finally established in 1995, and serving US President Bill Clinton visited in 2000.

## Cua Tung Beach

This long, secluded stretch of sand, where Vietnam's last emperor, Bao Dai, used to vacation, is just north of the mouth of the Ben Hai. There are beaches on the southern side of the Ben Hai River as well. Every bit of land in the area not levelled for planting is pockmarked with bomb craters of all sizes.

There are no buses to Cua Tung Beach, which can be reached by turning right (east) off National Hwy 1 at a point 1.2km north of the Ben Hai River. Cua Tung Beach is about 7km south of Vinh Moc via the dirt road that runs along the coast.

## Doc Mieu Base

Doc Mieu Base, next to National Hwy 1 on a low rise 8km south of the Ben Hai River, was once part of an elaborate electronic system (McNamara's Wall, named after the US Secretary of Defence 1961–68) intended to prevent infiltration across the DMZ. Today, it is a lunar landscape of bunkers, craters, shrapnel and live mortar rounds. Bits of cloth and decaying military boots are strewn about on the red earth. This devastation was created not by the war, but by scrap-metal hunters, who have found excavations at this site particularly rewarding.

## Ben Hai River

Twenty-two kilometres north of Dong Ha, National Hwy 1 crosses the Ben Hai River, once the demarcation line between North and South Vietnam. Beside the new crossing is the old bridge, used during the war. Until 1967 (when it was bombed by the Americans), the northern half of the bridge that stood on this site was painted red, while the southern half was yellow. Following the signing of the Paris cease-fire agreements in 1973, the present bridge and the two flag towers were built. A typhoon knocked over the flagpole on the northern bank of the river in 1985.

## Truong Son National Cemetery

Truong Son National Cemetery is a memorial to tens of thousands of North Vietnamese soldiers from transport, construction and anti-aircraft units who were killed in the Truong Son Mountain Range (Annamite Cordillera) along the Ho Chi Minh Trail. Row after row of white tombstones stretch across the hillsides and the cemetery is maintained by disabled war veterans.

The soldiers are buried in five zones, according to the part of Vietnam they came from; each zone is further subdivided into provinces. The gravestones of five colonels and seven decorated heroes (Trung Ta and Dai Ta represent the ranks of the martyrs), including one woman, are in a separate area. Each headstone bears the inscription 'Liet Si', which means 'Martyr'. The remains of soldiers interred here were originally buried near the spot where they were killed and were brought here after reunification. Many graves are empty, simply bearing the names of a small number of Vietnam's 300,000 MIAs.

On the hilltop above the sculpture garden is a three-sided stele. One face has engraved tributes from high-ranking Vietnamese leaders to the people who worked on the Ho Chi Minh Trail. At the bottom is a poem by the poet To Huu. Another side tells the history of the May 1959 Army Corps (Doang 5.59), which is said to have been founded on Ho Chi Minh's birthday in 1959 with a mission to construct and maintain a supply line to the South. The third side lists the constituent units of the May 1959 Army Corps, which eventually included five divisions. The site where the cemetery now stands was used as a base by the May 1959 Army Corps from 1972 to 1975.

The road to Truong Son National Cemetery intersects National Hwy 1 13km north of Dong Ha and 9km south of the Ben Hai River; the distance from the highway to the cemetery is 17km.

A rocky cart path that is passable by motorbike links Cam Lo (on National Hwy 9) with Truong Son National Cemetery (18km). This track passes rubber plantations and also the homes of the Bru people, who cultivate, among other crops, black pepper.

## Con Thien Firebase

In September 1967, North Vietnamese forces, backed by long-range artillery and rockets, crossed the DMZ and besieged the US Marine Corps base of Con Thien, which was established in attempt to stop infiltrations across the DMZ and to form part of McNamara's Wall.

The USA responded with 4000 bombing sorties (including 800 by B-52s), during which more than 40,000 tonnes of bombs were dropped on the North Vietnamese forces around Con Thien, transforming the gently sloping brush-covered hills that surrounded the base into a smoking moonscape of craters and ashes. The siege was lifted, but the battle had accomplished its real purpose: to divert US attention from South Vietnam's cities in preparation for the Tet Offensive. The area around the base is still considered too dangerous, even for scrap-metal hunters, to approach.

Con Thien Firebase is 10km west of National Hwy 1 and 7km south of Truong Son National Cemetery along the road that links National Hwy 1 with the cemetery. Concrete bunkers mark the spot a few hundred metres to the south of the road where the base once stood.

Six kilometres towards National Hwy 1 from Con Thien (and 4km off the highway) is another US base, C-3, the rectangular ramparts of which are still visible just north of the road. It is inaccessible because of mines.

## MILITARY SITES ON NATIONAL HIGHWAY 9
### Huong Hoa (Khe Sanh)

Set amid beautiful hills, valleys and fields at an elevation of about 600m, the town of Khe Sanh is a pleasant district capital. The town is known for its coffee plantations, which were originally cultivated by the French.

Many of the inhabitants are Bru (Van Kieu) tribal people, who have moved here from the surrounding hills. You'll notice their different clothing, with women wearing sarong-like skirts, and woven baskets taking the place of plastic bags.

The town has now been officially renamed Huong Hoa, but the Western world will forever remember it as Khe Sanh.

**Places to Stay** About the only reason for staying here is if you're planning to hit the road to Laos the next morning. At the time of writing the **People's Committee Guesthouse** (☎ 053-880563; rooms around US$10) was the sole option.

**Getting There & Away** About 600m southwest (towards the Lao frontier) of the triangular intersection, where the road to Khe Sanh Combat Base branches off, is **Khe Sanh bus station** (National Hwy 9). Buses to Dong Ha (10,000d, 1½ hours) and Lao Bao (10,000d, one hour) depart regularly. Change at Dong Ha for all other destinations.

## Khe Sanh Combat Base

This is the site of the most famous siege (and one of the most controversial battles) of the American War in Vietnam. Khe Sanh sits silently on a barren plateau, surrounded by vegetation-covered hills that are often obscured by mist and fog. It is hard to imagine as you stand in this peaceful, verdant land – with the neat homes and vegetable plots of local people all around – that in early 1968 the bloodiest battle of the war took place here. About 500 Americans (the official figure of 205 was arrived at by statistical sleight of hand), 10,000 North Vietnamese troops and uncounted civilian bystanders died amid the din of machine guns and the fiery explosions of 1000kg bombs, white-phosphorus shells, napalm, mortars and artillery rounds of all sorts.

The site (admission 25,000d) has been cleared in preparation for the opening of a memorial museum. A couple of bunkers have been recreated and some photos and other memorabilia are on show. Behind the main site, the outline of the airfield remains distinct – to this day nothing will grow on it. Some of the comments in the visitors' book – especially those written by visiting war veterans – can make for emotional reading.

The MIA team still visits the area regularly to search for the bodies of Americans who disappeared during the fierce battles in the surrounding hills. Most remains they find are Vietnamese.

**History** Despite opposition from marine corps brass to the attrition strategy of the commander of US forces in Vietnam, General William Westmoreland (they thought it futile), the small US Army Special Forces (Green Beret) base at Khe Sanh, built to recruit and train local tribespeople, was turned into a marines stronghold in late 1966. In April 1967 there began a series of 'hill fights' between US forces and the well dug-in North Vietnamese infantry, who held the surrounding hills. In only a few weeks, 155 marines and perhaps thousands of North Vietnamese were killed. The fighting centred on hills 881 South and 881 North, both of which are about 8km northwest of Khe Sanh Combat Base.

In late 1967, American intelligence detected the movement of tens of thousands of North Vietnamese regulars armed with mortars, rockets and artillery into the hills around Khe Sanh. General Westmoreland became convinced that the North Vietnamese were planning another Dien Bien Phu (the decisive battle in the Franco–Viet Minh War in 1954). This was an illogical analogy given American firepower and the proximity of Khe Sanh to supply lines and other US bases. President Johnson himself became obsessed by the spectre of Dien Bien Phu. To follow the course of the battle, he had a sand table model of the Khe Sanh plateau constructed in the White House situation room and took the unprecedented step of requiring a written guarantee from the Joint Chiefs of Staff that Khe Sanh could be held.

Westmoreland, determined to avoid another Dien Bien Phu at all costs, assembled an armada of 5000 planes and helicopters and increased the number of troops at Khe Sanh to 6000. He even ordered his staff to study the feasibility of using tactical nuclear weapons.

The 75-day siege of Khe Sanh began on 21 January 1968 with a small-scale assault on the base perimeter. As the Marines and the South Vietnamese Rangers braced for a full-scale ground attack, Khe Sanh became the focus of global media attention. It was the cover story for both *Newsweek* and *Life* magazines and appeared on the front pages of countless newspapers around the world. During the next two months, the base was subject to continuous ground attacks and artillery fire. US aircraft dropped 100,000 tonnes of explosives on the immediate vicinity of Khe Sanh Combat Base. The expected attempt to overrun the base never came and, on 7 April 1968 after heavy fighting, US troops reopened National Hwy 9 and linked up with the Marines to end the siege.

It now seems clear that the siege of Khe Sanh, in which an estimated 10,000 North Vietnamese died, was merely an enormous diversion intended to draw US forces and the attention of their commanders away from the South Vietnamese population centres, in preparation for the Tet Offensive, which began a week after the siege started. However, at the time Westmoreland considered the entire Tet Offensive to be a 'diversionary effort' to distract attention from Khe Sanh!

A few days after Westmoreland's tour of duty in Vietnam ended in July 1968, US forces in the area were redeployed. Policy, it seemed, had been reassessed and holding Khe Sanh, for which so many men had died, was deemed unnecessary. After everything at Khe Sanh was buried, trucked out or blown up – nothing recognisable that could be used in a North Vietnamese propaganda film was to remain – US forces upped and left Khe Sanh Combat Base under a curtain of secrecy. The American command had finally realised what a marine officer had expressed long before: 'When you're at Khe Sanh, you're not really anywhere. You could lose it and you really haven't lost a damn thing.'

**Getting There & Away** To get to Khe Sanh Combat Base from Khe Sanh bus station, head 600m towards Dong Ha then turn northwest at the triangular intersection; there's a small sign. The base is 2.5km further, 500m off the right-hand (east) side of the road.

## Lang Vay Special Forces Camp

In February 1968, Lang Vay (Lang Vei) Special Forces Camp, established in 1962, was attacked and overrun by North Vietnamese infantry backed by nine tanks. Of the base's 500 South Vietnamese, Bru and Montagnard defenders, 316 were killed. Ten of the 24 Americans at the base were killed and 11 were wounded.

All that remains of dog bone–shaped Lang Vay base are the overgrown remains of numerous concrete bunkers, and a rusty tank memorial.

The base is on a ridge southwest of National Hwy 9, between Khe Sanh bus station (9.2km) and Lao Bao (7.3km).

## Camp Carroll

Established in 1966, Camp Carroll was named after a Marine Corps captain, who was killed while trying to seize a nearby ridge. The gargantuan 175mm cannons at Camp Carroll were used to shell targets as far away as Khe Sanh. In 1972 the South Vietnamese commander of the camp, Lieutenant Colonel Ton That Dinh, surrendered and joined the North Vietnamese Army.

These days there is not that much to see at Camp Carroll, except for a Vietnamese memorial marker, a few overgrown trenches and the remains of their timber roofs. Bits of military hardware and rusty shell casings can still be found. The concrete bunkers were destroyed by local people seeking to extract the steel reinforcing rods to sell as scrap; concrete chunks from the bunkers were hauled off for use in construction.

The area around Camp Carroll now belongs to the State Pepper Enterprises (Xi Nghiep Ho Tieu Tan Lam). On the road in, you'll see pepper plants trained so that they climb up the trunks of jackfruit trees. There are also rubber plantations nearby.

The turn-off to Camp Carroll is 10km west of Cam Lo and 23km northeast of Dakrong Bridge. The base is 3km from National Hwy 9.

## The Rockpile

The Rockpile was named after what can only be described as a 230m-high pile of rocks. There was a US Marine Corps lookout on top of The Rockpile and a base for American long-range artillery was nearby.

Today there isn't much left of The Rockpile and you will probably need a guide to point it out to you.

The Rockpile is 26km west of Dong Ha on National Hwy 9.

## Dakrong Bridge

Dakrong Bridge, crossing the Dakrong River (also known as the Ta Rin River) 13km east of the Khe Sanh bus station, was rebuilt during 2001.

The road that heads southeast from the bridge to Aluoi passes by the stilted homes of the Brus and was once a branch of the Ho Chi Minh Trail.

## Aluoi

Aluoi is located approximately 65km southeast of Dakrong Bridge and 60km southwest of Hué. There are a number of waterfalls and cascades in the surrounding area. Tribes living in the mountainous Aluoi area include the Ba Co, Ba Hy, Ca Tu and Taoi. US Army Special Forces bases in Aluoi and Ashau were overrun and abandoned in 1966; the area then became an important transhipment centre for supplies coming down the Ho Chi Minh Trail.

Among the better known military sites in the vicinity of Aluoi are landing zones Cunningham, Erskine and Razor, as well as Hill 1175 (west of the valley) and Hill 521 (in Laos). Further south in the Ashau Valley is Hamburger Hill (Apbia Mountain). In May 1969, US forces on a search-and-destroy operation near the Lao border fought in one of the fiercest battles of the war, suffering many terrible casualties (hence the name). In less than a week of fighting, 241 US soldiers died at Hamburger Hill – a fact that was very well-publicised in the American media. A month later, after the US forces withdrew from the area to continue operations elsewhere, the hill was reoccupied by the North Vietnamese Army.

## DONG HA
☎ 053 • pop 65,200

Dong Ha, the capital of the recently reconstituted Quang Tri province, is at the busy intersection of National Hwys 1 and 9. Dong

Ha served as a US Marine Corps command and logistics centre from 1968 to '69. In the spring of '68, a division of North Vietnamese troops crossed the DMZ and attacked Dong Ha. The city was later the site of a South Vietnamese army base. Today, there is no conceivable reason to visit it, except as a stopover on the way to the DMZ and/or the Lao border. National Hwy 1 thunders through town, dust blowing and horns blaring, and almost all the hotels are beside it. The public loudspeakers start their broadcasting at 5am.

## Orientation

National Hwy 1 is called Đ Le Duan as it passes through Dong Ha. National Hwy 9, signposted as going to Lao Bao, intersects National Hwy 1 next to the bus station. Đ Tran Phu (which is the old National Hwy 9) intersects Đ Le Duan 600m north of the bus station (towards the river). Đ Tran Phu then runs south for 400m before turning west.

There is a market area along National Hwy 1 between Đ Tran Phu and the river.

## Information

About a kilometre north of the bridge heading out of town, **Dong Que Restaurant** (**e** *dongqueqt@dng.vnn.vn; 159 Đ Le Duan*) can book DMZ tours, and bus and train tickets. The family there is charming and helpful and the teenage children speak very good English, so try to get there out of school hours. **DMZ Tours** (☎ *852927, fax 851617; 66 Đ Le Duan*), inside the Dong Ha Hotel, and **Trung Tam Quan Restaurant** (*Đ Le Duan, about 200m south of Dong Ha Hotel*), the local agent for Sinh Café, can also help.

Motorbike tours of the DMZ cost US$12-15 per person and bus tours cost around US$10 per person (you'll probably be added to a tour group coming from Hué). If this happens, you could conceivably hitch a ride to Hué at the end of the tour with them if you're heading in that direction anyway.

## Places to Stay

**Dong Ha Hotel** (☎ *852262; National Hwy 1; single/double rooms US$6/15*), just north of the bus station, is old and dirty but has the cheapest budget rooms in town. The double rooms here have air-con.

**Nha Khach Buu Dien Tinh Quang Tri** (☎ *854418; National Hwy 1; air-con singles/doubles US$15/20*) is a better choice than Dong Ha Hotel, but still very ordinary for the price. The hotel is about 1km from the bus station towards the southern part of town, and is the post-office guesthouse.

**Thanh Tinh Hotel** (☎ *852236, fax 852850; 220 Đ Le Duan; doubles/triples US$15/20*) rents basic rooms with air-con and hot water. Be sure to ask for a room on the 2nd or 3rd storey and at the back – they are cleaner, newer and quieter.

**Khach San Phung Hoang** (☎ *854567; Đ Le Duan; air-con rooms US$15-20*) is newish with good-sized rooms, but get one at the back, off the road.

**Nha Nghi Du Lich Cong Doan** (☎ *852744; 4 Đ Le Loi; rooms with cold water & fan 70,000d, with hot water & air-con 170,000-210,000d*) is 500m west of the bus station. This is the state-run trade-union guesthouse and it's probably the best of a bad lot, even though the bathrooms are dismal; it's certainly the quietest, being off the main road.

**Hieu Giang Hotel** (☎ *855036, fax 856859; 183 Đ Le Duan; rooms US$25-40*) is a new place, and the snazziest accommodation in Dong Ha (though that's not saying a lot). It is located right where National Hwy 9 intersects National Hwy 1.

**Dong Que Restaurant** is planning to add some accommodation rooms in the near future, and these will be worth checking out.

## Places to Eat

Besides the dining rooms in Dong Ha's hotels, there's a slew of roadside **com pho restaurants** along National Hwy 1, particularly in the vicinity of the bus station and the intersection of National Hwy 9.

**Trung Tan Quan Restaurant**, in the centre of town, does good food. The 'Vietnamese Food' – as it's written on the menu – is a good, freshly cooked meal of fish or meat, vegies, rice and condiments for 20,000d. There's an Internet terminal here too.

**Dong Que Restaurant** also does tasty fresh food, and the toilets are good.

## Getting There & Away

**Bus** Near the intersection of National Hwys 1 and 9, you'll find the **Dong Ha bus station** *(Ben Xe Khach Dong Ha; 122 Đ Le Duan)*. Vehicles to Hué (5,000d, two hours), and to Khe Sanh (10,000d, 1½ hours) and Lao Bao (15,000d, two hours), leave regularly. You may have to change buses in Khe Sanh for Lao Bao. These are prices for locals to ride the bus and they should be the same for tourists, but you may find yourself paying a bit more. Buses also link Dong Ha with Ho Xa, along National Hwy 1, about 13km west of Vinh Moc.

Buses between Hué and Dong Ha depart from and arrive at the **An Hoa bus station** in Hué.

**Train** *Reunification Express* trains stop in Dong Ha (see the Train section in the Getting Around chapter).

To get to the **Dong Ha train station** (Ga Dong Ha) from the bus station, head 1km southeast on National Hwy 1 to a big guesthouse called Nha Khach 261. Turn right here and you'll see the back of the train station about 150m along a track.

**Car & Motorbike** You can expect to pay about US$10 for a *xe om* to/from Dong Ha and the Lao border at Lao Bao. The following are road distances from Dong Ha.

| | |
|---|---|
| Ben Hai River | 22km |
| Danang | 190km |
| Dong Hoi | 94km |
| Hanoi | 617km |
| Ho Chi Minh City | 1169km |
| Hué | 72km |
| Khe Sanh | 65km |
| Lao Bao (Lao border) | 80km |
| Savannakhet, Laos | 327km |
| Truong Son National Cemetery | 30km |
| Vinh | 294km |
| Vinh Moc | 41km |

## LAO BAO (LAO BORDER)

☎ 053

As more and more travellers enter and exit Vietnam overland, Lao Bao is becoming an important border crossing for trade and tourism between Laos, Thailand and central Vietnam. The Lao Bao border is open for crossing, in either direction, from 7am to 5pm daily, provided you have the relevant visa. Many travellers walk across, and report that formalities are straightforward.

Lao Bao is on the Tchepone River (Song Xe Pon), which marks the Vietnam-Laos border. Towering above Lao Bao on the Lao side of the border is Co Roc Mountain, once a North Vietnamese artillery stronghold.

Two kilometres from the border post is Lao Bao Market, where Thai goods smuggled through the bush from Laos are readily available. Merchants accept either Vietnamese dong or Lao kip. Don't change your US dollars at the border unless you have to; the rate can be about 50% less than the banks!

There's absolutely no reason to linger in Lao Bao, but if you miss the border opening hours and need to stay, there are a few **guesthouses** and **com pho places**. And, a couple of kilometres out of the town, there are the ruins of a French colonial **prison** *(Nha Tu Lao Bao)* to visit.

## Getting There & Away

The town of Lao Bao is 18km west of Khe Sanh, 80km from Dong Ha, 152km from Hué, 46km east of Tchepone (Laos), 250km east of Savannakhet (also in Laos, on the Thai frontier) and 950km from Bangkok (Thailand, via Ubon Ratchathani).

**Bus & Motorbike** Dong Ha is the junction town for Lao Bao. Regular public buses go from Dong Ha to Khe Sanh (10,000d, 1½ hours) and Lao Bao (15,000d, two hours). You may need to change buses in Khe Sanh for Lao Bao.

The border post is 2km from Lao Bao town. The local price for a *xe om* to the border is 5,000d (foreigners pay about 10,000d) or you can walk for about 20 minutes to the crossing. The distance from the Vietnam border post to the Laos border post is another kilometre, which you will have to walk.

If you're travelling by tourist bus through to Savannakhet, expect a wait at the border while documents are checked. Be aware that some through buses arrive at Lao Bao around 2am – this means that you may have a fun five-hour wait until the border post opens at 7am.

Independent motorbike travellers coming through from Laos have reported no problems clearing customs and immigration at this crossing.

Travellers coming from Laos should be aware that no public buses go directly to Hué, despite what drivers may tell you! Buses only go as far as Dong Ha.

## QUANG TRI
☎ 053 • pop 15,400

The town of Quang Tri, 59km north of Hué and 12.5km south of Dong Ha, was once an important citadel city. In the spring of 1972, four divisions of North Vietnamese regulars, backed by tanks, artillery and rockets, poured across the DMZ into Quang Tri province in what became known as the Eastertide Offensive. They laid siege to the city of Quang Tri, shelling it heavily before capturing it along with the rest of the province. During the next four months, the city was almost completely obliterated by South Vietnamese artillery and massive carpet bombing by US fighter-bombers and B-52s. The South Vietnamese army suffered 5000 casualties in the rubble-to-rubble fighting to retake the city.

Today, there is little to see in the town of Quang Tri except a **memorial** and a few remains of the moat, ramparts and gates of the **citadel**, which once served as a South Vietnamese army headquarters. The remnants of the citadel are 1.6km north from National Hwy 1. A pockmarked, ruined two-storey building between the highway and the bus station used to be a Buddhist high school and is preserved as a memorial. Along National Hwy 1, just on the Hué side of Quang Tri, is the skeleton of a church scarred chillingly with bullet holes and mortar shells.

Cua Viet Beach, which was once the site of an important US landing dock, is an OK swimming beach, 16km northeast of Quang Tri. There are plans to build a major port here to handle import and export materials from Laos and northern Thailand. Another beach called Gia Dang is 13km east of town, but neither of these, in fact, is worth going out of

your way to find. Most travellers wait to get a bit further south to Thuan An Beach (near Hué) or China Beach (near Danang).

## Getting There & Away
The **bus station** (Ð Tran Hung Dao) is about 1km from National Hwy 1. However, locals suggest that rather than wait at the bus station for north, or southbound buses, stand on the highway and flag them down.

The daily bus to Khe Sanh leaves the bus station at about 8am; be there early.

## HUÉ
☎ 054 • pop 286,400

Traditionally, Hué has been one of Vietnam's main cultural, religious and educational centres. Today, its main attractions are the splendid tombs of the Nguyen emperors (see the Around Hué section), several notable pagodas and the remains of the Citadel. In May 2001 the first Festival of Hué was celebrated, with local and international cultural performers at locations throughout the city. This was such a success that it was being repeated in 2002 and there are hopes that it will become an international event. Hotel accommodation is at a premium at this time, so book ahead if you can.

Tourism may just have saved Hué's cultural sites from oblivion. Between 1975 and 1990, all the old buildings were regarded as politically incorrect, signs of the 'feudal Nguyen dynasty'. Everything was left to decay. It was only in 1990 that the local government recognised the tourist potential of the place and declared these sites 'national treasures'. In 1993 Unesco designated the complex of monuments in Hué a World Heritage site, and restoration and preservation work continues.

Most of the city's major sights have an admission charge of 55,000d; often there is an additional charge for video cameras.

## History
The citadel city of Phu Xuan was originally built in 1687 at Bao Vinh Village, 5km northeast of present-day Hué. In 1744 Phu Xuan became the capital of the southern part of Vietnam, which was under the rule of the

Nguyen lords. The Tay Son Rebels occupied the city from 1786 until 1802, when it fell to Nguyen Anh. He crowned himself Emperor Gia Long, thus founding the Nguyen dynasty, which ruled the country – at least in name – until 1945.

In 1885, when the advisers of 13-year-old Emperor Ham Nghi objected to French activities in Tonkin, French forces encircled the city. Unwisely, the outnumbered Vietnamese forces launched an attack; the French responded mercilessly. According to a contemporary French account, the French forces took three days to burn the imperial library and remove from the palace every single object of value, including everything from gold and silver ornaments to mosquito nets and toothpicks. Ham Nghi fled to Laos, but he was eventually captured and exiled to Algeria. The French replaced him with the more pliable Dong Khanh, thus ending any pretence of genuine independence for Vietnam.

The city's present name probably evolved from its former name, Thanh Hoa. The word *hoa* means 'peace' or 'harmony' in Vietnamese. The city has been called Hué for over two centuries now.

Hué was the site of the bloodiest battles of the 1968 Tet Offensive and was the only city in South Vietnam to be held by the communists for more than a few days. While the American command was concentrating its energies on relieving the siege of Khe Sanh, North Vietnamese and VC troops skirted the American stronghold and walked right into Hué, South Vietnam's third-largest city. When the communists arrived, they hoisted their flag from the Citadel's Flag Tower, where it flew for the next 25 days; the local South Vietnamese governmental apparatus completely collapsed.

Immediately upon taking Hué, communist political cadres implemented detailed plans to liquidate Hué's 'uncooperative' elements. Thousands of people were rounded up in extensive house-to-house searches, conducted according to lists of names meticulously prepared months before. During the 3½ weeks Hué remained under communist control, approximately 3000 civilians, including merchants, Buddhist monks, Catholic priests, intellectuals, and a number of travellers, as well as people with ties to the South Vietnamese government – were summarily shot, clubbed to death or buried alive. The victims were buried in shallow mass graves that were discovered at various spots around the city over the next few years.

When South Vietnamese army units proved unable to dislodge the occupying North Vietnamese and VC forces, General Westmoreland ordered US troops to recapture the city. During the next few weeks, whole neighbourhoods were levelled by VC rockets and US bombs. In 10 days of bitter combat, the VC were slowly forced into a retreat from the 'New City'. Over the next two weeks, most of the area inside the Citadel (where two-thirds of the population lived) was battered by the South Vietnamese air force, US artillery and brutal house-to-house fighting. Approximately 10,000 people died in Hué during the Tet Offensive. Thousands of VC troops, 400 South Vietnamese soldiers and 150 US marines were among the dead, but most of those killed were civilians.

Long after the American War ended, one American veteran is said to have returned to Hué and, upon meeting a former VC officer, commented that the USA never lost a single major battle during the entire war. 'You are absolutely correct', the VC officer agreed, 'but that is irrelevant, is it not?' Journalist Gavin Young's 1997 memoir *A Wavering Grace* is a moving account of his 30-year relationship with a family from Hué – and with the city itself – during and beyond the American War. It makes a good reading companion for a stay in the city.

## Orientation

The city of Hué lies along either side of the Perfume River. The north side of the river has the Citadel and a few places to stay, making for a pleasant and quiet stop. However, it is the south side that has most facilities and a greater selection of hotels and restaurants. The island on which Phu Cat and Phu Hiep subdistricts

# HUÉ

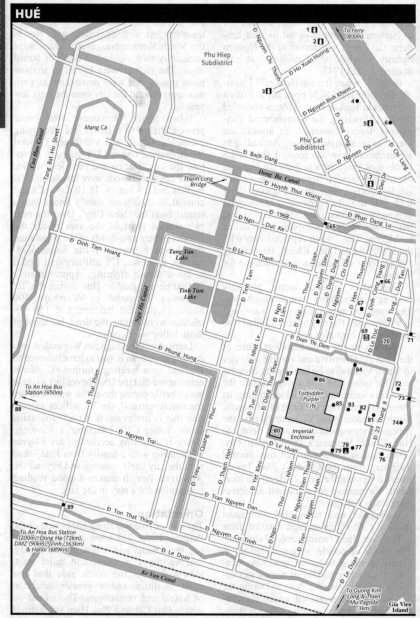

To Ferry
(800m)

Phu Hiep
Subdistrict

Đ Nguyen Chi Thanh

Đ Ho Xuan Huong

Đ Nguyen Binh Khiem

Đ Chua Ong

Đ Nguyen Du

Phu Cat
Subdistrict

Đ Chi Lang

Đ Dieu De

Mang Ca

Cua Hau Canal

Tang Bat Ho Street

Đ Bach Dang

Thanh Long
Bridge

Dong Ba Canal

Đ Huynh Thuc Khang

Đ Phan Dang Lu

Đ 1968

Đ Ngo
Duc Ke

Đ Dinh Tien Hoang

Tang Tau
Lake

Đ Le
Thanh
Ton

Đ Nguyen Dieu

Đ Dang Dung

Đ Chi Dieu

Đ Nguyen

Đ Han

Đ Thuyen

Đ Dinh Cong Trang

Duy Tan

Đ Khai Dinh

Tinh Tam
Lake

Đ Tinh Tam

Đ Mai Thuc Loan

Đ Ngo Si Liem

Đ Doan Thi Diem

Đ Tong

Đ Le Truc

Nga Ha Canal

Đ Phung Hung

Đ Nhat Le

Đ Tue Tinh

Đ Dang Thai Than

Đ Thai Phien

To An Hoa Bus
Station (650m)

Forbidden
Purple City

Imperial
Enclosure

Đ Thai Phien

Đ Nguyen Trai

Đ Quang
Phuc

Đ Le Huan

Đ Trieu

Đ Thach Han

Đ Yet Kieu

Đ Nhiem

Đ Nguyen Thien Thuat

Đ L Han

Đ 23 Thang 8

Đ Tran Nguyen Dan

Đ Ton That Thiep

Đ Thoi

Đ Tran

To An Hoa Bus Station
(200m), Dong Ha (72km),
DMZ (90km), Vinh (363km)
& Hanoi (689km)

Đ Nguyen Cu Trinh

Đ Ngo

Đ Le Duan

Đ Le Duan

Ke Van Canal

To Duong Kim
Long & Thien
Mu Pagoda
(3km)

Gia Vien
Island

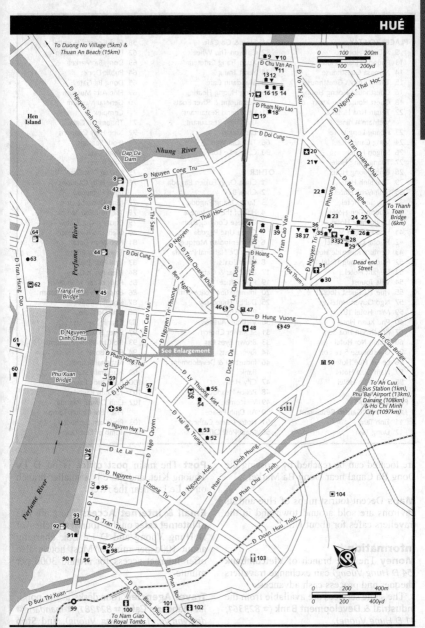

# HUÉ

To Duong No Village (5km) &
Thuan An Beach (15km)

Đ Nguyen Sinh Cung

Hen Island

Nhung River

Dap Da Dam

Đ Nguyen Cong Tru

Perfume River

Trang Tien Bridge

Đ Tran Hung Dao

Đ Vo Thi Sau

Đ Chu Van An

Đ Pham Ngu Lao

Đ Doi Cung

Đ Nguyen

Đ Tran Quang Khai

Đ Ben Nghe

Đ Nguyen - Thai Hoc

Thai Hoc

Đ Doi Cung

Đ Tran Quang Khai

Đ Ben Nghe

To Thanh Toan Bridge (6km)

Phuong

Đ Tran Cao Van

Đ Nguyen Tri

Dead end Street

Đ Hoang

Hoa Tham

Đ Truong Dinh

Đ Nguyen Tri - Phuong

Đ Tran Cao Van

Đ Le Quy Don

Đ Dong Da

Đ Hung Vuong

An Cuu Bridge

Đ Nguyen Dinh Chieu

Phu Xuan Bridge

Đ Le Loi

Đ Hanoi

Đ Pham Hong Thai

Đ Nguyen Huy Tu

Perfume River

Đ Le Loi

Đ Le Lai

Ngo Quyen

Đ Ly Thuong Kiet

Đ Hai Ba Trung

Truong Tu

Đ Nguyen Hue

Đ Phan

Đ Phan Chu Trinh

Dinh Phung

To An Cuu
Bus Station (1km),
Phu Bai Airport (13km),
Danang (108km)
& Ho Chi Minh
City (1097km)

Đ Nguyen

Đ Tran Thuc

Đ Doan Huu Trinh

Đ Bưu Thi Xuan

Đ Dien Bien Phu

Chau

Đ Phan Boi

To Nam Giao
& Royal Tombs

0     100     200m
0     100     200yd

0     200     400m
0     200     400yd

## HUÉ

**PLACES TO STAY**
9  A Dong Hotel
13  Phuong Hoang Hotel
14  Mimosa Guesthouse
15  Thanh Thuy's Guesthouse
16  Guesthouse Hoang Huong
18  Guest House Van Xuan
22  Thuan Hoa Hotel &
     Vietnam Airlines
23  Hoang Long Hotel
24  Vong Canh Hotel
26  Saigon Hotel
27  Thang Long Hotel
28  Binh Duong Hotel
29  Thai Binh Hotel
35  Binh Minh Hotel
37  Duy Tan Hotel
39  Truong Tien Hotel
40  L'Indochine Hotel
41  Hotel Saigon Morin
42  Huong Giang Hotel
43  Century Riverside Hotel
52  Huong Duong Hotel
53  Elegant Hotel
54  Villa Tourist
55  Hue TU Guest House
57  Ngo Quyen Hotel
59  Mini Hotel 18
60  Phu Xuan Hotel
67  Khach San Hoa Sen
68  Thanh Noi Hotel
91  Guesthouse 5 Le Loi
96  Le Loi Hué Hotel
97  Nam Giao Hotel
98  Dien Bien Hotel

**PLACES TO EAT**
10  Tropical Garden Restaurant
11  Tinh Tam
12  Dong Tam

21  Stop & Go Cafe
32  Cafe on Thu Wheels
34  Xuan Trang Cafeteria
36  Xuan Trang 2
38  Mandarin Café
45  Song Huong Floating
     Restaurant & River Boats
61  Lac Thanh Restaurant;
     Lac Thien Restaurant;
     Lac Thuan
66  Tinh Gia Vien
90  Cafe 3 Le Loi

**OTHER**
1  Chua Ong; Fukien Pagoda
2  Chua Ba
3  Tang Quang Pagoda
4  Hall of the Cantonese
    Chinese Congregation
5  Chieu Ung Pagoda
6  Former Indian Mosque
7  Dieu De National Pagoda
8  River Boats
17  DMZ Bar & Cafe
19  Post Office
20  Immigration Police Office
25  Dai Ly Thuoc Tay
     Pharmacy
30  Vietnam Airlines
31  St Xavier Church
33  Brown Eyes Bar
44  River Boats
46  Industrial & Development
     Bank
47  City Hall
48  Police Headquarters
49  Vietcombank
50  An Dinh Palace
51  Notre Dame Cathedral
56  Main Post Office

58  Hué General Hospital
62  Dong Ba Bus Station
63  Dong Ba Market
64  Public Dock
65  Dong Ba Gate
69  Fine Arts Museum
70  General Museum
     Complex
71  Thuong Tu Gate
72  Nine Holy Cannons
     (Four Seasons)
73  Ngan Gate
74  Flag Tower
75  Quang Duc Gate
76  Nine Holy Cannons
     (Five Elements)
77  Nine Dynastic Urns
78  The To Mieu Temple
79  Chuong Duc Gate
80  Dien Tho Residence
81  Ngo Mon Gate
82  Trung Dao Bridge
83  Thai Hoa Palace
84  Hien Nhon Gate
85  Halls of the Mandarins
86  Emperor's Reading Room
87  Hoa Binh Gate
88  Nha Do Gate
89  Chanh Tay Gate
92  River Boats
93  Ho Chi Minh Museum
94  River Boats
95  National School
99  Hué Train Station
100  Bao Quoc Pagoda
101  Tu Dam Pagoda
102  Linh Quang Pagoda;
      Phan Boi Chau's Tomb
103  Phu Cam Cathedral
104  Tomb of Duc Duc

are located can be reached by crossing the Dong Ba Canal near Dong Ba Market.

**Maps** Decent tourist maps of Hué and its environs are sold around town and in the travellers cafés for about US$1.

## Information

**Money** The Hué branch of **Vietcombank** (54 Đ Hung Vuong) can exchange travellers cheques and process cash advances.

The same services are available from the **Industrial & Development Bank** (☎ 823361; 41 Đ Hung Vuong).

**Post** The main **post office** is on Đ Ly Thuong Kiet, and there is a smaller branch on Đ Le Loi near the river.

**Email & Internet Access** There are lots of **Internet cafés** on the 'tourist stretches' of Đ Hung Vuong and Đ Le Loi, charging about 100d per minute. Most hotels also offer Internet access for around 300d per minute.

**Travel Agencies** Tour desks at the popular **Mandarin Café** (☎ 821281; ⓔ mandarin@ dng.vnn.vn; 12 Đ Hung Vuong), and **Stop**

and Go Café (☎ 889106; 4 Ben Nghe St) are as good a place as any to book transportation, and DMZ and Perfume River tours. Mr Cu at the first, and Mr Do at the second, are good sources of local travel information. The travel centre at **Le Loi Hué Hotel** (☎ 824668; 2 Le Loi) offers a range of booking services too.

**Medical Services** For medical treatment, head for **Hué General Hospital** (Benh Vien Trung Uong Hué; ☎ 822325; 16 Ð Le Loi), which is close to Phu Xuan Bridge.

**Dai Ly Thuoc Tay** (☎ 823361; 33 Ð Hung Vuong), near the junction of Ð Ben Nghe, is a good pharmacy.

**Visas** There's an office of the **immigration police** (Ð Ben Nghe) in Hué, where you can try to get visa extensions processed.

## Citadel

Construction of the moated Citadel (Kinh Thanh), which has a 10km perimeter, was begun in 1804 on a site chosen by Emperor Gia Long's geomancers. The Citadel was originally made of earth, but tens of thousands of workers laboured to cover the ramparts, built in the style of the French military architect Vauban, with a layer of bricks 2m thick.

The emperor's official functions were carried out in the Imperial Enclosure (Dai Noi or Hoang Thanh), a citadel-within-a-citadel with 6m-high walls that are 2.5km in length. The Imperial Enclosure has four gates, the most famous of which is Ngo Mon Gate. Within the Imperial Enclosure you'll find the Forbidden Purple City, which was reserved as the private residence of the emperor.

Three sides of the Citadel are straight; the fourth is rounded slightly to follow the curve of the river. The ramparts are encircled by a zigzag moat, which is 30m across and about 4m deep. In the northern corner of the Citadel is Mang Ca Fortress, once known as the French Concession, which is still used as a military base. The Citadel has 10 fortified gates, each reached via a bridge across the moat.

Wide areas within the Citadel are now devoted to agriculture, a legacy of the destruction of 1968.

**Flag Tower** The 37m-high Flag Tower (Cot Co), also known as the King's Knight, is Vietnam's tallest flagpole. Erected in 1809 and extended in 1831, a terrific typhoon, which devastated the whole city, knocked it down in 1904. The tower was rebuilt in 1915, only to be destroyed again in 1947. It was erected once again, in its present form, in 1949. During the VC occupation of Hué in 1968, the National Liberation Front flag flew defiantly from the tower for 3½ weeks.

**Nine Holy Cannons** Located just inside the Citadel ramparts near the gates to either side of the Flag Tower, the Nine Holy Cannons, symbolic protectors of the palace and kingdom, were cast from brass articles captured from the Tay Son Rebels. The cannons, which were cast on the orders of Emperor Gia Long in 1804, were never intended to be fired. Each is 5m long, has a bore of 23cm and weighs about 10 tonnes. The four cannons near Ngan Gate represent the four seasons, while the five cannons next to Quang Duc Gate represent the five elements: metal, wood, water, fire and earth.

## The Imperial Enclosure

**Ngo Mon Gate** The principal entrance to the Imperial Enclosure is Ngo Mon Gate (Noontime Gate; admission 55,000d; open 6.30am-5.30pm daily), which faces the Flag Tower.

The central passageway with its yellow doors was reserved for the use of the emperor, as was the bridge across the lotus pond. Others had to use the gates to either side and the paths around the lotus pond.

On top of the gate is Ngu Phung (Belvedere of the Five Phoenixes), where the emperor appeared on important occasions, most notably for the promulgation of the lunar calendar. On 30 August 1945, Emperor Bao Dai ended the Nguyen dynasty here when he abdicated to a delegation sent by Ho Chi Minh's Provisional Revolutionary Government. The middle section of the roof is covered with yellow tiles; the roofs to either side are green.

**Thai Hoa Palace** Built in 1803 and moved to its present site in 1833, Thai Hoa Palace (Palace of Supreme Harmony) is a spacious hall with an ornate roof of huge timbers supported by 80 carved and lacquered columns. Accessible from Ngo Mon Gate via Trung Dao Bridge, it was used for the emperor's official receptions and other important court ceremonies, such as anniversaries and coronations. During state occasions, the king sat on his elevated throne and received homage from the mandarins. Nine stelae divide the two-level courtyard into separate areas for officials in each of the nine ranks of the mandarinate; administrative mandarins stood to one side while the military mandarins stood to the other.

**Halls of the Mandarins** The buildings in which the mandarins prepared for court ceremonies, held in Can Chanh Reception Hall, were restored in 1977. The structures are directly behind Thai Hoa Palace on either side of a courtyard, where there are two gargantuan bronze cauldrons *(vac dong)*, dating from the 17th century.

**Nine Dynastic Urns** These urns *(dinh)* were cast between 1835 and 1836. Traditional ornamentation was chiselled into the sides of the urns, each dedicated to a different Nguyen sovereign. The designs, some of which are of Chinese origin and date back 4000 years, include the sun, moon, meteors, clouds, mountains, rivers and various landscapes. About 2m in height and weighing 1900kg to 2600kg each, the urns symbolise the power and stability of the Nguyen throne. The central urn, which is the largest and most ornate, is dedicated to Gia Long.

**Forbidden Purple City** Reserved solely for the personal use of the emperor, the only servants allowed into this compound were eunuchs, who would pose no threat to the royal concubines.

The Forbidden Purple City (Tu Cam Thanh) was almost entirely destroyed during the Tet Offensive. The area is now given over to vegetable plots, between which touchsensitive mimosa plants flourish. The twostorey **Emperor's Reading Room** (Thai Binh Lau) has been partially restored in its landscaped surrounds and now houses a small photographic exhibition. The foundations of the **Royal Theatre** (Duyen Thi Duong), begun in 1826 and later home of the National Conservatory of Music, can also be seen nearby.

**Dien Tho Residence** In the western corner of the Imperial Enclosure is the stunning Dien Tho Residence. This comprises the apartments and audience hall of the Queen Mothers of the Nguyen dynasty. The audience hall now houses an exhibition of photos showing its former use, and there is a beautiful display of original and copied embroidered royal garments. Just outside is their Highnesses' enchanting pleasure pavilion, a carved wooden building set above a lily pond.

**The To Mieu Temple** Close to Chuong Duc Gate is The To Mieu Temple and its associated buildings, constructed in 1821. It's dedicated to the Nguyen emperors, and restoration work on the wooden structures was completed in 1998.

**Tinh Tam Lake** In the middle of Tinh Tam Lake, which is 500m north of the Imperial Enclosure, are two islands connected by bridges. The emperors used to come here with their retinues to relax.

**Tang Tau Lake** An island in Tang Tau Lake, which is north of Tinh Tam Lake, was once the site of a royal library. It is now occupied by a small Hinayana (Theravada, or Nam Tong) pagoda, called Ngoc Huong Pagoda.

## Museums

**Fine Arts Museum** The beautiful hall that houses the Fine Arts Museum *(3 Đ Le Truc; admission 22,000d; open 7am-5pm daily)* was built in 1845 and restored when the museum was founded in 1923. The walls are inscribed with poems written in Vietnamese script *(nom)*. The most precious artefacts were lost during the American War, but the ceramics, furniture and royal clothing that remain are well worth a look.

On the left side of the hall is a royal sedan chair, a gong and a musical instrument consisting of stones hung on a two-level rack. On the other side of the hall is the equipment for a favourite game of the emperors – the idea was to bounce a stick off a wooden platform into a tall, thin jug.

**General Museum Complex** The equally lovely building across the street was once a school for princes and the sons of high-ranking mandarins. It's now a gallery, and forms part of a complex that seems to be known as the **General Museum** *(admission*

*free; open 7.30am-5pm Fri-Wed)*. It combines, in an odd juxtaposition, the **Military Museum**, with its usual assortment of American- and Soviet-made weapons, and a small **Natural History Museum**. The complex can be entered from either Đ Le Truc or Đ 23 Thang 8.

**Ho Chi Minh Museum** On display at this museum *(Bao Tang Ho Chi Minh; 9 Đ Le Loi)* are photographs, some of Ho's personal effects, and documents relating to his life and accomplishments.

## Pagodas, Temples & Churches
**Thien Mu Pagoda** Built on a hillock overlooking the Perfume River, this pagoda *(Linh Mu Pagoda; admission free)* is one of the most

---

### Thien Mu Pagoda

The Thien Mu Pagoda just outside Hué was a hotbed of antigovernment protest during the early 1960s. Surprisingly, it also became a focus of protest in the 1980s when someone was murdered near the pagoda and anticommunist demonstrations started here, closing traffic around Phu Xuan Bridge. Monks were arrested and accused of disturbing the traffic and public order. Things calmed down and a small group of monks, novices and nuns now live at the pagoda.

Behind the main sanctuary of the Thien Mu Pagoda is the Austin motorcar that transported the monk Thich Quang Duc to the site of his 1963 self-immolation.

Thich Quang Duc travelled to Saigon and publicly burned himself to death to protest the policies of President Ngo Dinh Diem. A famous photograph of his act was printed on the front pages of newspapers around the world. His death soon inspired a number of other self-immolations.

Many Westerners were shocked less by the suicides than by the reaction of Tran Le Xuan (Madame Nhu, the president's notorious sister-in-law), who happily proclaimed the self-immolations a 'barbecue party' and said, 'Let them burn and we shall clap our hands'. Her statements greatly added to the already substantial public disgust with Diem's regime; the US press labelled Madame Nhu the 'Iron Butterfly' and 'Dragon Lady'. In November, both President Diem and his brother Ngo Dinh Nhu (Madame Nhu's husband) were assassinated by Diem's own military. Madame Nhu was outside the country at the time.

A memorial to Thich Quang Duc (Dai Ky Niem Thuong Toa Thich Quang Duc) can be found at the intersection of Đ Nguyen Dinh Chieu and Đ Cach Mang Thang Tam, around the corner from the Xa Loi Pagoda, in Ho Chi Minh City.

famous structures in Vietnam. The existing 21m-high octagonal tower, the seven-storey Thap Phuoc Duyen, was constructed under the reign of Emperor Thieu Tri in 1844 and has become the unofficial symbol of the city of Hué. Each of the seven storeys is dedicated to a *manushi-buddha*, which is a Buddha that appeared in the human form. See the boxed text 'Thien Mu Pagoda'.

Thien Mu Pagoda was originally founded in 1601 by the Nguyen lord Nguyen Hoang, governor of Thuan Hoa province. According to legend, a Fairy Woman (Thien Mu) appeared and told the people that a lord would come to build a pagoda for the country's prosperity. On hearing that, Nguyen Hoang ordered a pagoda to be constructed here. Over the centuries, its buildings have been destroyed and rebuilt several times.

To the right of the tower is a pavilion containing a stele dating from 1715. It is set on the back of a massive marble turtle, a symbol of longevity. To the left of the tower is another six-sided pavilion, this one sheltering an enormous bell, Dai Hong Chung, which was cast in 1710 and weighs 2052kg; it is said to be audible 10km away. In the main sanctuary, in a case behind the bronze laughing Buddha, are three statues: A Di Da, the Buddha of the Past; Thich Ca, the historical Buddha (Sakyamuni); and Di Lac Buddha, the Buddha of the Future.

Thien Mu Pagoda is on the banks of the Perfume River, 4km southwest of the Citadel. To get there (a nice bicycle ride), head southwest (parallel to the river) on riverside Ð Tran Hung Dao, which turns into Ð Le Duan after you pass Phu Xuan Bridge. Cross the railway tracks and keep going on Ð Kim Long. Thien Mu Pagoda can also be reached by rowing boat.

**Bao Quoc Pagoda** Last renovated in 1957, Bao Quoc Pagoda (Pagoda Which Serves the Country) was founded in 1670 by Giac Phong, a Buddhist monk from China. It was given its present name in 1824 by Emperor Minh Mang, who later celebrated his 40th birthday here in 1830. A school for training monks was opened here in 1940 and the orchid-lined courtyard behind the

sanctuary is still a quiet place where students gather to study.

The central altar in the main sanctuary contains three identical Buddha statues, which represent (from left to right) Di Lac, Thich Ca and A Di Da, and behind these is a memorial room for deceased monks. Around the main building are monks' tombs, including a three-storey, red-and-grey stupa built for the pagoda's founder.

Bao Quoc Pagoda is on Ham Long Hill in Phuong Duc District. To get there, head south from Ð Le Loi on Ð Dien Bien Phu and turn right immediately after crossing the railway tracks.

**Tu Dam Pagoda** This pagoda *(cnr Ð Dien Bien Phu and Ð Tu Dam)*, which is about 400m south of Bao Quoc Pagoda, is one of Vietnam's best known pagodas. Unfortunately, the present buildings are recent additions that date from 1936.

Tu Dam Pagoda was founded around 1695 by Minh Hoang Tu Dung, a Chinese monk. It was given its present name by Emperor Thieu Tri in 1841. It was here that the Unified Vietnamese Buddhist Association was established at a meeting in 1951. During the early 1960s, Tu Dam was a major centre of the Buddhist anti-Diem and antiwar movements, and in 1968 it became the scene of heavy fighting, scars of which remain.

Today, Tu Dam Pagoda, home to a handful of monks, is the seat of the provincial Buddhist Association. The peculiar bronze Thich Ca Buddha in the sanctuary was cast locally in 1966.

Just east of the pagoda down Ð Tu Dam is **Linh Quang Pagoda** and the **tomb** of the scholar and anticolonialist revolutionary Phan Boi Chau (1867–1940).

**Notre Dame Cathedral** This cathedral *(Dong Chua Cuu The; 80 Ð Nguyen Hué)* is an impressive modern building that combines the functional aspects of a European cathedral with traditional Vietnamese elements, including a distinctly Asian spire. At present, the huge cathedral, which was constructed between 1959 and 1962, has 1600 members. Two French-speaking priests hold daily masses at 5am and 5pm with an extra 7am service on Sunday; children's catechism classes are also conducted on Sunday mornings. Visitors who find the front gate locked should ring the bell of the yellow building next door.

**Phu Cam Cathedral** Construction of the cathedral *(20 Đ Doan Huu Trinh)* began in 1963 and was halted in 1975, before the completion of the bell tower. It is the eighth church to be built on this site since 1682 and the Hué diocese, which is based here, hopes eventually to find the funds to complete the structure. Phu Cam Cathedral is at the southern end of Đ Nguyen Truong Tu. Masses are held at 5am and 6.45pm from Monday to Saturday and at 5am, 7am, 2pm and 7pm on Sunday.

**St Xavier Church** This Catholic church *(Đ Nguyen Tri Phuong)* was built around 1915. From the outside it looks derelict, but the inside is well maintained and it has a functioning electric organ. There is no admission charge, but you might want to make a small donation to help maintain the place.

St Xavier Church is southwest of the Binh Minh Hotel. You can ask to be let in through the building at the rear. Some of the caretakers speak French, but not much English.

**Dieu De National Pagoda** The entrance to Dieu De National Pagoda *(Quoc Tu Dieu De; 102 Đ Bach Dang)*, built under Emperor Thieu Tri's rule (1841–47), is along Dong Ba Canal. It is one of the city's three 'national pagodas', which were once under the direct patronage of the emperor. Dieu De is famous for its four low towers, one to either side of the gate and two flanking the sanctuary. There are bells in two of the towers; the others contain a drum and a stele dedicated to the pagoda's founder.

During the regime of Ngo Dinh Diem (1955–63) and through the mid-1960s, Dieu De National Pagoda was a stronghold of Buddhist and student opposition to the South Vietnamese government and the war. In 1966 the pagoda was stormed by police, who confiscated the opposition movement's

radio equipment and arrested many monks, Buddhist laypeople and students. Today, a handful of monks live at the pagoda.

The pavilions on either side of the main sanctuary entrance contain the 18 La Ha, whose rank is just below that of Bodhisattva, and the eight Kim Cang, protectors of Buddha. In the back row of the main dais is Thich Ca Buddha flanked by two assistants, Pho Hien Bo Tat (to his right) and Van Thu Bo Tat (to his left).

**Former Indian Mosque** Hué's Muslim-Indian community constructed this mosque *(120 Đ Chi Lang)* in 1932. The structure was used as a house of worship until 1975, when the Indian community fled. It is now a private residence and you need to peer between the adjoining buildings to make out its distinctive silhouette.

**Chieu Ung Pagoda** This pagoda *(Chieu Ung Tu; opposite 138 Đ Chi Lang)* was founded by the Hainan Chinese Congregation in the mid-19th century and rebuilt in 1908. It was last repaired in 1940. The pagoda's sanctuary retains its original ornamentation, which is becoming faded but has been mercifully unaffected by the third-rate modernistic renovations that have marred other such structures. The pagoda was built as a memorial to 108 Hainan merchants, who were mistaken for pirates and killed in Vietnam in 1851.

**Tang Quang Pagoda** Down the alley opposite 80 Đ Nguyen Chi Thanh, Tang Quang Pagoda (Tang Quang Tu) is the largest of the three Hinayana pagodas in Hué. Built in 1957, it owes its distinctive architecture to Hinayana Buddhism's historical links to Sri Lanka and India (rather than China). The pagoda's Pali name, Sangharansyarama (Light Coming from the Buddha), is inscribed on the front of the building.

## Assembly Halls
### Hall of the Cantonese Chinese Congregation
This hall *(Chua Quang Dong; opposite 154 Đ Chi Lang)* was founded almost a century ago. Against the right-hand wall is

a small altar holding a statue of Confucius (Khong Tu) with a gold beard. On the main altar is red-faced Quan Cong (in Chinese, Guangong) flanked by Trung Phi (left) and Luu Bi (right). On the altar to the left is Laotse with disciples to either side. On the altar to the right is Phat Ba, a female Buddha.

**Chua Ba** Founded by the Hainan Chinese Congregation almost a century ago, Chua Ba *(across the street from 216 Đ Chi Lang)* was damaged in the Tet Offensive and subsequently reconstructed. On the central altar is Thien Hau Thanh Mau, the Goddess of the Sea and Protector of Fishermen and Sailors. To the right is a glass case in which Quan Cong sits flanked by his usual companions, the mandarin general Chau Xuong (to his right) and the administrative mandarin Quang Binh (to his left).

**Chua Ong** This large pagoda *(opposite 224 Đ Chi Lang)* was founded by Hué's Fujian Chinese Congregation during the reign of Vietnamese emperor Tu Duc (1848–83). This building was severely damaged during the Tet Offensive, when a nearby ammunition ship blew up. A gold Buddha sits in a glass case opposite the main doors of the sanctuary. The left-hand altar is dedicated to Thien Hau Thanh Mau, who is flanked by her two assistants, 1000-eyed Thien Ly Nhan and red-faced Thuan Phong Nhi, who can hear for 1000 miles. On the altar to the right is Quan Cong.

Next door is a pagoda of the Fukien Chinese Congregation (Tieu Chau Tu).

## National School

One of the most famous secondary schools in Vietnam, the National School *(Quoc Hoc; 10 Đ Le Loi; open after 3pm)* was founded in 1896 and run by Ngo Dinh Kha, the father of South Vietnamese president Ngo Dinh Diem, and many of the school's pupils later rose to prominence in both North and South Vietnam. Numbered among the National School's former students is General Vo Nguyen Giap, strategist of the Viet Minh victory at Dien Bien Phu and North Vietnam's long-serving deputy premier, defence minister and commander-in-chief. Pham Van Dong, North Vietnam's prime minister for over a quarter of a century, and the secretary-general and former prime minister Do Muoi also studied here. Even Ho Chi Minh attended the school briefly in 1908.

The school was given a major renovation in 1996 to celebrate its 100th anniversary and a statue of Ho Chi Minh was erected. The National School and the neighbouring Hai Ba Trung Secondary School cannot be visited until after classes finish at about 3pm.

## Thanh Toan Bridge

If you miss the famous Japanese bridge in Hoi An, or prefer the less beaten track, there is another classic covered footbridge about 7km east of central Hué well worth seeking out. Thanh Toan Bridge is architecturally similar to its cousin in Hoi An, though it receives far less visitors (it's mostly used by local villagers for naps in the shady walkway).

The bridge is best reached by motorbike or bicycle. Finding it is a bit tricky, but tolerable if you consider getting lost part of the excursion. Head north for a few hundred metres on Đ Ba Trieu until you see a sign to the Citadel Hotel. Turn right here and follow the delightful (and bumpy) dirt road for another 6km past villages, rice paddies and several pagodas until you reach the bridge.

## Places to Stay – Budget

**East Đ Le Loi Area** A good place to find basic, cheap rooms near the river is in the narrow alley off Đ Le Loi between Đ Pham Ngu Lao and Đ Chu Van An. Many budget hotels offer pick-ups from the airport if you book in advance.

**Guesthouse Hoang Huong** *(☎ 828509; 46/2 Đ Le Loi; dorm beds US$2, singles $4-6, air-con rooms US$7-10)* has dorms and private rooms. It's basic but usually full, which is a good sign.

**Mimosa Guesthouse** *(☎ 828068, fax 823858; e tvhoang4@hotmail.com; 46/6 Đ Le Loi; air-con rooms US$10-12)* is a good place run by Mr Tran Van Hoang, a former French teacher and author of several books written in French. It's quiet and has pleasant common balconies. And it's popular – get there early in the day or book ahead.

**Thanh Thuy's Guesthouse** (☎ 824585; 46/4 Đ Le Loi; singles/doubles from US$6/7) is a small, family-run guesthouse with air-con rooms. Book ahead here too, if you can.

**Phuong Hoang Hotel** (Phoenix Hotel; ☎ 826736, fax 828999; e phoenixhotel@ dng.vnn.vn; 48/3 Đ Le Loi; air-con rooms US$10-25) has good-value, good-sized rooms with satellite TV. There's a decent **vegetarian restaurant** attached.

**A Dong Hotel** (☎ 824148; e adongcoltd@ dng.vnn.vn; 18 Chu Van An; singles/twins US$12/15) is a pleasant small hotel, but it's on the roadside so take your earplugs.

**Guesthouse Van Xuan** (☎ 826567; 4 Pham Ngu Lao; singles/twins US$5/7) is a fine budget place that's low-key, low-rise and with a pleasant shared balcony.

**Đ Hung Vuong Area** There's another cluster of budget hotels located around the junction of Đ Nguyen Tri Phuong and Đ Hung Vuong.

**Binh Duong Hotel** (☎/fax 833298; e binh duong@dng.vnn.vn; 10/4 Đ Nguyen Tri Phuong; dorm beds US$3, singles with fan/ air-con US$5/6, doubles with fan/air-con US$8/10, rooms with bath US$15), tucked into a quiet narrow alley in the city centre, is usually chock-full and especially popular with Japanese backpackers. It's terrific – good value and clean, with pleasant public sitting areas. All rooms have satellite TV, and there's Internet access. At the time of writing **Binh Duong 2** was due to open near the main post office.

**Thai Binh Hotel** (☎ 828058, fax 832867; e ksthaibinh@dng.vnn.vn; 10/9 Đ Nguyen Tri Phuong; standard rooms US$8-15, deluxe rooms with balconies US$20-30), just across the alley, is a popular hotel with a new and an old wing. The old wing is at the back, and is quieter. All rooms have satellite TV and there's Internet access in the lobby.

**Binh Minh Hotel** (☎ 825526, fax 828362; e binhminhhue@dng.vnn.vn; 12 Đ Nguyen Tri Phuong; air-con rooms US$8-35) is another pleasant family-run place that gets very good reviews from travellers. It has a

good range of rooms, but as it's on the main road, ask for one at the back.

**Hoang Long Hotel** (☎ 828235, fax 823858; e hoanglong-hue@dng.vnn.vn; 20 Đ Nguyen Tri Phuong; air-con budget rooms US$7-10) is a strange hodge-podge of concrete, marble and tile and some rooms have balconies. It's OK.

**Thang Long Hotel** (☎ 826462, fax 826464; 16 Đ Hung Vuong; e thuhuong@dng.vnn.vn; fan rooms US$7, air-con rooms US$10) is not overly friendly but is often full, so it must be doing something right.

**Duy Tan Hotel** (☎ 825001, fax 826477; e duytancoecco@dng.vnn.vn; 12 Đ Hung Vuong; air-con rooms US$12-30) is in a good central location with plenty of parking available. Rates are reasonable and the more expensive ones buy you large, bright rooms with balconies.

**Truong Tien Hotel** (☎ 823127, fax 847225; e truongtien@dng.vnn.vn; 8 Đ Hung Vuong; dorms US$3, rooms US$8-20), is a no-frills, motel-style place. The three-bed dorms with bath are good value, especially if you find yourself the only one in the room.

**Vong Canh Hotel** (☎ 824130, fax 826798; 25 Đ Hung Vuong; fan rooms US$8, air-con rooms US$12-30) has recently been refurbished and the more expensive rooms are very green; the cheap rooms are tiny and windowless.

**Saigon Hotel** (☎ 821007; 32b Đ Hung Vuong; air-con rooms US$12-20) has rates that include breakfast, and the cheaper rooms at the back are fine and quiet.

**L'Indochine Hotel** (Dong Duong Hotel; ☎ 823866, fax 825910; e indochinehotel@ dng.vnn.vn; 2 Đ Hung Vuong; rooms US$12-30) is centrally located and set back off the main road; the cheaper rooms in the old wing are fine.

**Other Areas** There are a couple of interestingly different places, centrally located on Đ Ly Thuong Kiet.

**Villa Tourist** (☎ 825461; 14 Đ Ly Thuong Kiet; 3 rooms only US$10, US$15 & US$20) offers rooms in a family home in a small colonial villa. It has a kind of decaying grandeur – the bathrooms are bigger than most hotel rooms! It's usually full, so book if you can.

**Hué Trade Union Guest House** *(Nha Khach Cong Doan;* ☎ *823064; 13 Đ Ly Thuong Kiet; rooms 100,000d-150,000d)* is across the road. The union office is downstairs in this elegant but tired colonial building; upstairs are four enormous, high-ceiling air-con rooms that have from two to four beds.

Towards the railway station there's another area with budget hotels.

**Le Loi Hué Hotel** *(Khach San Le Loi;* ☎ *822153, fax 824527; 2 Đ Le Loi; rooms US$7-30)* is enormous. It's also been enormously successful at attracting backpackers, thanks to low prices, good rooms – budget rooms are tiny and tatty but fine – and its location (only a 100m walk from the train station). Satellite TV is on tap, there's Internet access, and it's also a good place for booking cars, taxis and tours.

**Nam Giao Hotel** *(☎ 825736; 3b Đ Dien Bien Phu; rooms 200,000d)* is OK if you need to be near the train station and Le Loi is full. Next door, **Dien Bien Hotel** *(☎ 821678, fax 821676; 3 Đ Dien Bien Phu; singles/doubles with fan US$8/10, with air-con US$15/20)* is much the same.

Budget hotels in other parts of town include the following.

**Huong Duong Hotel** *(☎ 821550; 3b Đ Hai Ba Trung; rooms US$8-15)* is a little further from the centre, and the US$12 rooms are much better value than the cheaper ones.

**Mini Hotel 18** *(☎ 823720, fax 825814;* ⓔ *huetc@dng.vnn.vn; 18 Đ Le Loi; twins US$12-13)* is a small place near the river, with reasonable, light, air-con rooms that have been recently repainted.

**Ngo Quyen Hotel** *(☎ 823278, fax 823502; 11 Đ Ngo Quyen; doubles US$12-25)* has a seen-better-days appearance from the outside, but the US$25 rooms are of a good standard and it's fairly central.

## Places to Stay – Mid-Range & Top End
**North Bank** There are three mid-range hotels near the Citadel, on the northern bank of the river.

**Thanh Noi Hotel** *(☎ 522478, fax 527211;* ⓔ *thanhnoi@dng.vnn.vn; 3 Đ Dang Dung; air-con rooms US$12-30)* is a popular hotel that boasts an ideal location. The quiet, tree-shaded compound has its own restaurant, ample parking and a decent-sized swimming pool with water jets. Be aware that while the US$15-plus rooms are good value, the US$12 rooms vary enormously; ask to see several. There's Internet access in the lobby.

**Khach San Hoa Sen** *(Lotus Hotel;* ☎ *525997; 33 Đ Dinh Cong Trang; air-con rooms US$15-25)*, further in on the north bank, is among trees in a very quiet residential street and has good-sized rooms.

**Phu Xuan Hotel** *(☎ 527512; 27 Đ Tran Hung Dao; air-con rooms US$16-19)* is an older place near Phu Xuan Bridge; it's in a good, but noisy, location.

**South Bank** There are several options in the more luxurious range to consider.

**Guesthouse 5 Le Loi** *(☎ 822155, fax 828816;* ⓔ *5leloihotel@dng.vnn.vn; 5 Đ Le Loi; air-con rooms US$40-80)*, housed in a stately old villa, has some nice river views and lovely gardens. The more expensive rooms are fine, but many of the others need serious refurbishment, especially at these prices.

**Thuan Hoa Hotel** *(☎ 822553, fax 822470;* ⓔ *t_hoahtl@dng.vnn.vn; 7 Đ Nguyen Tri Phuong; air-con rooms US$25-50)* looks like a large bank, but the US$25 rooms are good value, with clean new furnishings and most mod cons.

**Elegant Hotel** *(Thanh Lich Hotel;* ☎ *825973, fax 825972;* ⓔ *thanhlichks@dng.vnn.vn; 33 Đ Hai Ba Trung; singles/doubles US$30/35)* is a bit away from the river. It's well-appointed with nothing special about it.

**Century Riverside Hotel** *(☎ 823390, fax 823399; 49 Đ Le Loi; rooms US$65-170)* is a grand place on the shore of the Perfume River. Luxury like this comes at a price, of course, but discounts of between 15% and 30% may be offered to walk-ins depending on the season and availability. There's a US$5 fee to use the pool for the day.

**Huong Giang Hotel** *(☎ 822122, fax 823102;* ⓔ *hghotel@dng.vnn.vn; 51 Đ Le Loi; rooms US$50-230)*, is another giant place on the river. The riverside terrace is lovely, and you can use the landscaped pool for a reasonable US$2 per day.

**Hotel Saigon Morin** (☎ 823526, fax 825155; e sgmorin@dng.vnn.vn; 30 Ð Le Loi; standard rooms US$50-60, deluxe rooms US$80-100, suites US$180-300) is a luxurious historic hotel that occupies an entire city block near the south bank of the Perfume River. The hotel offers all the trimmings, and features three restaurants, a lovely courtyard café-bar (with a very reasonably priced bar-food menu) and a swimming pool in the shape of a gourd.

## Places to Eat
Hué is a famed culinary city and has set the trends for central Vietnamese cooking. See the special section 'Tastes of Vietnam' for leads on what to try.

**South Bank** There is a solid string of popular budget cafés worth checking out along Ð Hung Vuong. The competition is fierce and the prices low. The cafés are good places to meet people and swap travellers tales.

**Mandarin Café** (☎ 821281; e mandarin@ dng.vnn.vn; 12 Ð Hung Vuong; breakfasts around 10,000d; open 6.30am-10.30pm) is a magnet for travellers. The BLTs, potato salad and trademark banana pancakes are recommended. The cheerful owner Mr Cu speaks English well and is full of useful travel advice; he's also been consistently improving his services since the first LP mention, and that doesn't often happen.

**Stop & Go Cafe** (☎ 889106; 4 Ð Ben Nghe; Hué specialties around 8,000d; open 6.30am-late), is an indoor-outdoor café run by Mr Do, a silver-haired painter and freelance tour guide, who ensures the café's slightly eccentric air. The house specialties are a savoury rice pancake, banh khoai, and nem lui, delicious grilled kebabs that you roll yourself in rice paper with lettuce and cucumber and dip into peanut sauce. Yum.

**Xuan Trang Cafeteria** (☎ 832480; 14A Ð Hung Vuong; main dishes around 12,000d) is recommended for cheap and excellent food. There's a good vegetarian selection.

**Tropical Garden Restaurant** (☎ 847143; 5 Ð Chu Van An; dishes around US$2, open for dinner from 6.30pm) is pleasant. You can dine in the attractive main building, or outdoors in a delightful, shaded garden. It specialises in central Vietnamese cuisine, and is presently the only place in Hué with low-key and unobtrusive traditional music performed live, nightly, between 7pm and 9pm.

**Song Huong Floating Restaurant** (☎ 823 738; open 8am-9pm) is a pleasant spot on the bank of the Perfume River, just north of Trang Tien Bridge. The food is OK, but you can just come for a drink, and enjoy the river breeze and atmosphere.

There is a **café** in the grounds of Le Loi Hué Hotel, and **Cafe 3 Le Loi**, just across the street, also dishes up fine food at reasonable prices. They're near the train station and especially handy if you want to eat before travelling.

Vegetarian food has a long tradition in Hué. Stalls in the **markets** serve vegetarian food on the first and 15th days of the lunar month.

**Dong Tam** (☎ 828403; 48/7 Ð Le Loi; set lunch or dinner 25,000d), down a narrow alley and in a garden setting, has some of the best Vietnamese vegetarian fare in town and prices are cheap.

Next door, **Phuong Hoang Restaurant** (48/3 Ð Le Loi) in the hotel of the same name, is another good strictly vegie place, as is the **Tinh Tam** (4 Ð Chu Van An), just around the block. Tinh Tam's 'deer' with black pepper and lemongrass, and 'tuna' with tomato, are delicious.

You'll find several vegie options on most menus in town, many using soya-bean 'mock meat'.

**North Bank** A fashionable gathering spot for travellers is **Lac Thanh Restaurant** (☎ 524674; 6A Ð Dinh Tien Hoang; dishes from 7000d). Its congenial owner, Mr Lac, is deaf and mute so everything is communicated with sign language. However, his daughter, Lan Anh, speaks English well. Don't be put off by the grubby entrance, or the equally grubby stairs at the back; there's a pleasant upstairs room and balcony.

**Lac Thien Restaurant**, right next door to Lac Thanh, has cloned Lac Thanh's motif. Deaf people working here also produce fine food, plus an entertaining atmosphere. In true Vietnamese fashion, yet a *third* clone called **Lac Thuan** recently appeared on the other side of Lac Thanh.

**Tinh Gia Vien** (☎ 522243; 20/3 Đ Le Thanh Ton; set-course meals US$10-15) has a beautiful garden setting, and is known for serving dishes in the traditional style of Hué's imperial court. The artistic presentation of the food is more interesting than its taste, but it's a fun experience, if a bit like a conveyor-belt when tour groups are eating. (And yes, it really is down that unlikely looking lane.)

Backpackers on a tight budget might explore the **Dong Ba Market**. Food here is so cheap, they might as well give it away. Nevertheless, it's good quality. The only real problem will be finding comfortable chairs (or, for that matter, any chairs) so you can sit down and enjoy your meal.

## Entertainment

**DMZ Bar & Cafe** (44 Đ Le Loi) is a popular eating, drinking, and pool-shooting spot in the evening for expats and travellers.

**Brown Eyes Bar** (Đ Nguyen Tri Phuong), is next to **Cafe on Thu Wheels**. It's copied the style, but is more bar and pool table than café. Both these places are lively after 9pm, and stay open with music until late. The walls make great reading.

## Shopping

Hué is known for producing the finest conical hats in Vietnam. The city's speciality is 'poem hats' which, when held up to the light, reveal black cut-out scenes that are sandwiched between the layers of translucent palm leaves.

Hué is also home to one of the largest and most beautiful selections of rice-paper and silk paintings available in Vietnam, but the prices quoted are usually inflated to about four times the real price. You can often negotiate a 50% discount simply by starting to walk away from a souvenir stall.

**Dong Ba Market**, on the north bank of the Perfume River a few hundred metres north of Trang Tien Bridge, is Hué's largest market – where anything and everything can be bought. It was rebuilt after much of the structure was destroyed by a typhoon in 1986.

## Getting There & Away

**Air** The booking office of **Vietnam Airlines** (☎ 823249; 12 Đ Hanoi; open 7am-11am & 1.30pm-5pm Mon-Sat) handles reservations. There is also a **booking office** (☎ 824709) in the Thuan Hoa Hotel. Several flights a day connect Hué to HCMC and Hanoi.

**Bus** Hué has three main bus stations. **An Cuu bus station**, which is behind the Mobil garage, 1km south of the An Cuu bridge at the southeastern end of Đ Hung Vuong, serves southern destinations. Public buses leave from this bus station, for HCMC, at 6am (100,000d), for Dalat at 5am (95,000d) and for Danang every half-hour between 6am and 4.30pm (20,000d).

**An Hoa bus station**, northwest of the Citadel on National Hwy 1, serves northern destinations.

**Dong Ba bus station**, for short-haul bus trips, is next to Dong Ba Market.

**Minibus** Hué is a major target for tourist minibus companies and most backpackers travel this way. A popular run is the Hué–Hoi An minibus, which also stops in Danang. Tickets for the minibuses are sold at some hotels or the Sinh Café booking desk at the Mandarin Café – staff will tell you where the minibuses pick up from. Departure from either end is twice daily at 8am and 1pm, and there is usually a scenic, 10-minute stop at Lang Co Beach and Hai Van Pass. Hué–Hoi An or Hué–Danang tickets cost around US$3.

**Train** The *Reunification Express* trains stop in Hué. For information on ticket prices and schedules, see the Train section in the Getting Around chapter.

**Hué train station** (Ga Hué; ☎ 822175; ticket office open 7.30am-5pm) is on the south bank, at the southwestern section of Đ Le Loi.

**Car & Motorbike** The following are road distances from Hué.

| | |
|---|---|
| Ben Hai River | 94km |
| Danang | 108km |
| Dong Ha | 72km |
| Dong Hoi | 166km |
| Hanoi | 689km |
| Ho Chi Minh City | 1097km |
| Lao Bao (Lao border) | 152km |
| Quang Tri | 56km |
| Savannakhet, Laos | 400km |
| Vinh | 368km |

## Getting Around

**To/From the Airport** Hué is served by Phu Bai Airport, once an important US air base, which is 14km south of the city centre. Taxi fares there are typically US$8. Share taxis to the airport cost as little as US$2 – inquire at hotels to find these vehicles. Vietnam Airlines runs its own minibus from its office to the airport, a couple of hours before flight times (20,000d).

**Taxi** There are four metered taxi companies in Hué.

| | |
|---|---|
| Co Do Taxi | ☎ 830830 |
| Gili | ☎ 828282 |
| Mai Linh | ☎ 898989 |
| Thanh Do | ☎ 858585 |

**Cyclo & Motorbike** A typical scene in Hué is a foreigner walking down the street with two cyclos and a motorbike in hot pursuit, the drivers yelling 'hello cyclo' and 'hello motorbike' and the foreigner yelling 'no, thank you, no!'. There's a pretty standard fare for both of 15,000d per kilometre, then negotiate.

Self-drive motorbikes can be hired from some hotels, particularly around the tourist 'enclaves' in Le Loi and Hung Vuong. A 70cc to 100cc bike costs from 50,000d to 70,000d per day.

There have been good reports of motorbike tours in the Hué area offered by **Ms Thu Cafe On Thu Wheels** (☎ 832241; 10/2 Đ Nguyen Tri Phuong). Nice play on words! Rates are around US$7 a day, including a guide.

**Bicycle** If it's not raining and you can cope with the traffic, a pleasant way to tour Hué and the nearest royal tombs is by two-wheeled pedal power. Many hotels rent out bicycles for about US$1 per day.

**Boat** A boat ride down the Perfume River is recommended. Tours typically take in the tombs of Tu Duc, Thieu Tri, Minh Mang (see the Around Hué section) and Thien Mu Pagoda; any hotel or travellers café can make bookings. Prices vary, but are generally around US$2 per person. The journey takes about six hours, usually runs from 8am to 2pm, and includes lunch.

Many sights in the vicinity of Hué, including Thuan An Beach, Thien Mu Pagoda and several of the Royal Tombs, can be reached by river. Rates for chartering a boat are around 60,000d for an hour's sightseeing on the river; a half-day charter to one or more sites will cost around 150,000d. Ask directly at any of the four main river-boat moorings; it's cheaper than chartering through an agency and you can negotiate your own route.

## AROUND HUÉ
☎ 054

## Duong No Village

The peaceful village of Duong No makes for a refreshing short excursion from Hué. The main attraction here is the well-preserved, modest, and beautiful **Ho Chi Minh's House** (Nha Bac Ho; admission free; open daily) where Uncle Ho lived from 1898 to 1900. Walk a few metres further along the riverbank to **Ben Da**, the steps down to the water where Ho bathed. Another 300m or so beyond them, over a quaint bridge, is **Am Ba**, or 'female spirit' temple. It's in some disrepair, but it's quiet and contemplative, with ceramic mosaic work decorating the walls.

Duong No, 6km northeast of Hué, can easily be reached by rented bicycle or motorbike. Look for a small wooden sign on the left at a bridge off the main road; cross over the bridge and turn immediately right. The house is a few hundred metres along the riverbank. A nice loop can be made by

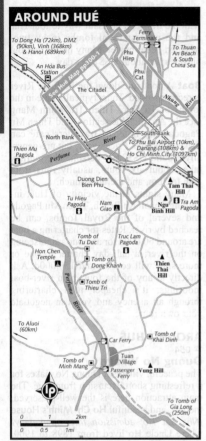

AROUND HUÉ

To Dong Ha (72km), DMZ (90km), Vinh (368km) & Hanoi (689km)

Ferry Terminals

To Thuan An Beach & South China Sea

An Hòa Bus Station

Phu Hiep

Phu Cat

See Hué Map pp300-1

The Citadel

Nhung River

North Bank

River

South Bank

To Phu Bai Airport (10km), Danang (108km) & Ho Chi Minh City (1097km)

Thien Mu Pagoda

Perfume

Duong Dien Bien Phu

Tam Thai Hill

Tu Hieu Pagoda

Nam Giao

Ngu Binh Hill

Tra Am Pagoda

Tomb of Tu Duc

Truc Lam Pagoda

Hon Chen Temple

Tomb of Dong Khanh

Thien Thai Hill

Perfume River

Tomb of Thieu Tri

To Aluoi (60km)

Tomb of Khai Dinh

Car Ferry

Tuan Village

Tomb of Minh Mang

Passenger Ferry

Vung Hill

To Tomb of Gia Long (250m)

0    1    2km
0   0.5  1mi

following the path beside Uncle Ho's house to a road at the end; turn left and continue through a pretty rural village for a couple of kilometres. Turn left again, and the road rejoins the bridge to the main road.

## Thuan An to Vinh Hien

Thuan An Beach (Bai Tam Thuan An), 15km northeast of Hué, is on a splendid lagoon near the mouth of the Perfume River, at the tip of a long, thin island. It's lovely for walking along, and quite undeveloped except for a few kiosks; but the water's often too rough to swim in from September to April.

It is joined to the mainland by a short bridge, and beyond the beach a 50km scenic road (actually National Hwy 49, though you'd never guess) stretches the length of the undeveloped island – no-one could tell us its name – from Thuan An to Vinh Hien. This makes a great day trip by motorbike or hire car from Hué. It also offers an alternative route to or from Hué by travellers making their way by motorbike or bike along the coast road.

Coming from Thuan An the island is skinny, and the road winds along the lagoon with fishing activity on one side and the ocean on the other. There are several villages on the way with stacks of enormous *nuoc mam* jars lining the outer walls of many houses, and miles of fertile raised vegetable gardens. But most extraordinary are the vast, colourful and opulent graves and family temples lining the ocean side of the road. Thousands upon thousands of them. The area is known in Vietnam as the **'city of tombs'**, with families vying to outdo their neighbours' ancestral monuments. There was a huge outflow of boat people from this area (it was, and remains, comparatively easy to at least get to the open sea from here) and the overseas Vietnamese now provide the funds to construct these astonishing buildings.

**Getting There & Away** There are at least three options for driving this road, two if you're making a day tour from Hué, and one for through travellers.

Day visitors can, of course, drive as far as they like and then return to Thuan An. An alternative is to drive to Vinh Tanh, about halfway along the road, turn right and head to a wharf where a ferry runs back and forth across the lagoon until about 4pm. The 20-minute crossing costs about 5000d for motorbikes, around 30,000d for cars, and drops you 13km from National Hwy 1, a little south of Hué airport.

An option for through travellers – on motorbikes and bicycles only – is to make their way to Vinh Hien and, from there, catch a public boat to Cau Hai on the mainland, close to the Bach Ma National Park access road. The cost for two people and a motorbike is 5000d, and the journey takes an hour or so.

The road from Thuan An is unsealed, a bit bumpy, and very slow for the first 15km. It's then sealed to Vinh Hien. Be aware that weather conditions affect the running of the boats, and be prepared to backtrack if necessary.

## Royal Tombs

The tombs *(Lang Tam; admission 55,000d per tomb; open 6.30am-5.30pm daily, in winter 7am-5pm daily)* of the rulers of the Nguyen dynasty (1802–1945) are extravagant mausoleums that were constructed along the banks of the Perfume River. They are situated between 2km and 16km south of Hué.

**Nam Giao** This temple *(Temple of Heaven; admission free)* was once the most important religious site in all Vietnam. It was here that, every three years, the emperor solemnly offered elaborate sacrifices to the All-Highest Emperor of the August Heaven (Thuong De). The topmost esplanade,which represents heaven, is round; the middle terrace, representing earth, is square, as is the lowest terrace.

After reunification, the provincial government erected (on the site where the sacrificial altar had once stood) an obelisk in memory of soldiers killed in the war against the South Vietnamese government and the Americans. There was strong public sentiment in Hué against the obelisk and the Hué Municipal People's Committee finally tore it down in 1993. Nam Giao remains unrestored and crumbling.

**Tomb of Tu Duc** The majestic and serene tomb of Emperor Tu Duc is set amid frangipani trees and a grove of pines. Tu Duc designed the exquisitely harmonious tomb, which was constructed between 1864 and 1867, for use both before and after his death. The enormous expense of the tomb and the forced labour used in its construction spawned a coup plot that was discovered and suppressed in 1866.

It is said that Tu Duc, who had the longest reign of any Nguyen monarch (1848–83), lived a life of truly imperial luxury (see the special section 'Tastes of Vietnam'). Though Tu Duc had 104 wives and countless concubines, he had no offspring. One theory has it that he became sterile after contracting smallpox.

Tu Duc's tomb, which is surrounded by a solid octagonal wall, is entered from the southeast via Vu Khiem Gate. A path paved with *bat trang* tiles leads to Du Khiem Boat Landing, which is on the shore of Luu Khiem Lake. From the boat landing, Tinh Khiem Island, where Tu Duc used to hunt small game, is to the right. Across the water to the left is Xung Khiem Pavilion, where the emperor would sit among the columns with his concubines, composing or reciting poetry. The pavilion, built over the water on piles, was restored in 1986.

Across Khiem Cung Courtyard from Du Khiem Boat Landing are steps leading through Khiem Cung Gate to Hoa Khiem Temple, where Emperor Tu Duc and Empress Hoang Le Thien Anh are worshipped. Before his death, Tu Duc used Hoa Khiem Temple as a palace, staying here during his long visits to the complex.

The temple contains a number of interesting items, including a mirror used by the emperor's concubines; a clock and other objects given to Tu Duc by the French; the funerary tablets of the emperor and empress; and two thrones, the larger of which was for the empress (Tu Duc was only 153cm tall).

Minh Khiem Chamber, just to the right behind Hoa Khiem Temple, was originally built for use as a theatre. Tu Duc's mother, the Queen Mother Tu Du, is worshipped in Luong Khiem Temple, directly behind Hoa Khiem Temple.

At the bottom of the stairway, the brick path continues along the shore of the lake to the Honour Courtyard. Across the lake from there are the tombs of Tu Duc's adopted son, Emperor Kien Phuc, who ruled for only seven months (1883–84), and Empress Le Thien Anh, Tu Duc's wife. After walking between the honour guard of elephants, horses and diminutive civil and military

## TOMB OF TU DUC

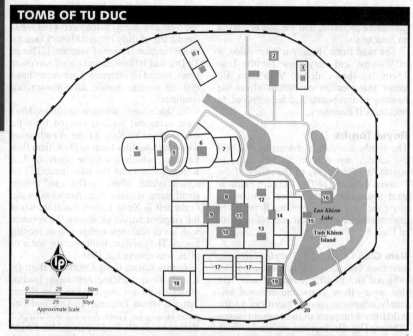

## TOMB OF TU DUC

| | | | | | |
|---|---|---|---|---|---|
| 1 | Le Thien Anh Tomb | 8 | Minh Khiem Chamber | 15 | Du Khiem Boat |
| 2 | Chap Khiem Temple | 9 | Luong Khiem Temple | | Landing |
| 3 | Kien Phuc's Tomb | 10 | On Khiem Palace | 16 | Xung Khiem Pavilion |
| 4 | Tu Duc's Tomb | 11 | Hoa Khiem Temple | 17 | Harems |
| 5 | Half Moon Lake | 12 | Le Khiem House | 18 | Deer Raising Garden |
| 6 | Stele Pavilion | 13 | Phap Khiem House | 19 | Chi Khiem Temple |
| 7 | Honour Courtyard | 14 | Khiem Cung Gate | 20 | Vu Khiem Gate |

mandarins (the stone mandarins were made even shorter than the emperor), you reach the masonry Stele Pavilion, which shelters a massive stone tablet weighing about 20 tonnes. It took four years to transport the stele, the largest in Vietnam, from the area of Thanh Hoa, 500km to the north. Tu Duc drafted the inscriptions on the stele himself in order to clarify certain aspects of his reign. He freely admitted that he had made mistakes and chose to name his tomb Khiem, which means 'modest'. The two nearby towers symbolise the emperor's power.

Tu Duc's sepulchre, enclosed by a wall, is on the other side of a half-moon-shaped lake. In fact, Tu Duc was never actually interred here. The site where his remains were buried (along with great treasure) is not known. Because of the danger of grave robbers, some extreme measures were taken to keep the location secret – every one of the 200 servants who buried the king was beheaded.

Tu Duc's tomb is about 5km south of Hué on Van Nien Hill in Duong Xuan Thuong Village.

**Tomb of Dong Khanh** Emperor Dong Khanh was the nephew and adopted son of Tu Duc, and was placed on the throne by the French after they captured his predecessor, Ham Nghi. Predictably, Dong Khanh proved docile; he ruled from 1885 until his death three years later.

Dong Khanh's mausoleum (admission 22,000d), the smallest of the Royal Tombs, was built in 1889. It's low-key, very beautiful and seems to be rarely visited. It is about 5km from the city, 500m or so behind the Tomb of Tu Duc.

**Tomb of Thieu Tri** Construction of the tomb of Thieu Tri, who ruled from 1841 to 1847, was completed in 1848. It is the only Royal Tomb not enclosed by a wall. Thieu Tri's tomb (admission free) has a similar layout to Minh Mang's tomb, but is smaller (see the Tomb of Minh Mang section). Thieu Tri's tomb is about 7km from Hué, in a peaceful rural landscape, and seems to be off the tour-bus trail. If you're walking, cycling, or on a motorbike, there's a pretty 2km or so cross-country track that leads here from the tomb of Dong Khanh.

**Tomb of Khai Dinh** The hillside tomb of Emperor Khai Dinh, who ruled from 1916 to 1925, is perhaps symptomatic of the decline of Vietnamese culture during the colonial era. Begun in 1920 and completed in 1931, the grandiose concrete structure is completely unlike Hué's other tombs, being a synthesis of Vietnamese and European elements. Even the stone faces of the mandarin honour guards are endowed with a mixture of Vietnamese and European features.

After climbing 36 steps between four dragon banisters, you reach the first courtyard, flanked by two pavilions. The Honour Courtyard, with its rows of elephants, horses and civil and military mandarins, is 26 steps further up the hillside. In the centre of the courtyard is an octagonal Stele Pavilion.

Up three more flights of stairs is the main building, Thien Dinh, which is divided into three halls. The walls and ceiling are decorated with murals of the Four Seasons, Eight Precious Objects and Eight Fairies; other designs are made from colourful bits of broken porcelain and glass embedded in cement. Under a graceless, one-tonne concrete canopy is a gilt bronze statue of Khai Dinh in regalia. Behind the statue is the symbol of the sun. The emperor's remains are interred 18m below the statue. Khai Dinh is worshipped in the last hall.

The tomb of Khai Dinh is 10km from Hué in Chau Chu Village.

**Tomb of Minh Mang** Perhaps the most majestic of the Royal Tombs is that of Minh Mang, who ruled from 1820 to 1840. Renowned for its architecture, which harmoniously blends into the natural surroundings, the tomb was planned during Minh Mang's lifetime and built between 1841 and 1843 by his successor.

The Honour Courtyard is reached via three gates on the eastern side of the wall: Dai Hong Mon (Great Red Gate; centre), Ta Hong Mon (Left Red Gate; left); and Huu Hong Mon (Right Red Gate; right). Three granite staircases lead from the courtyard to the square Stele Pavilion, Dinh Vuong. Nearby there once stood an altar on which buffaloes, horses and pigs were sacrificed.

Sung An Temple, dedicated to Minh Mang and his empress, is reached via three terraces and Hien Duc Gate. On the other side of the temple, three stone bridges span Trung Minh Ho (Lake of Impeccable Clarity). The central bridge, Cau Trung Dao, constructed of marble, could be used by the emperor only. Minh Lau Pavilion stands on the top of three superimposed terraces representing the 'three powers': the heavens, the earth and water. Visible to the left is the Fresh Air Pavilion; the Angling Pavilion is to the right.

From a stone bridge across crescent-shaped Tan Nguyet Lake (Lake of the New Moon), a monumental staircase with dragon banisters leads to the sepulchre, which is surrounded by a circular wall symbolising the sun. In the middle of the enclosure, reached through a bronze door, is the emperor's burial place: a mound of earth covered with mature pine trees and dense shrubbery.

The tomb of Minh Mang, which is on Cam Ke Hill in An Bang village, is on the west bank of the Perfume River, about 12km from Hué. Take a boat across the river from a point about 1.5km west of Khai Dinh's tomb and south of the village. Expect to pay about US$1 for the return trip, but you'll have to wait until about 20 people arrive – it won't take long – for it to leave. You may be able to negotiate a one-way charter for about 50,000d but do just that – negotiate!

**Tomb of Gia Long** Emperor Gia Long, who founded the Nguyen dynasty in 1802 and ruled until 1819, ordered the construction of his tomb in 1814. According to royal annals, the emperor himself chose the site after scouting the area on the back of an elephant. The rarely visited tomb, which is presently in a state of ruin, is 14km south of Hué and 3km from the river on the west bank of the Perfume River. You can take a motorbike across with you on the boat for about US$1 but, again, be prepared to negotiate.

## BACH MA NATIONAL PARK
☎ 054 ● elevation 1200m

Bach Ma (*Vuon Quoc Gia Bach Ma;* ☎ 871330, fax 871299; e bamaecot@dng .vnn.vn; admission 10,500d), a French-era hill station known for its cool weather, is 1200m above sea level, but only 20km from Canh Duong Beach. It's simply gorgeous. The French started building villas here in 1930; by 1937 the number of holiday homes had reached 139 and it became known as the 'Dalat of central Vietnam'. Most of the visitors were high-ranking French VIPs. Not surprisingly the Viet Minh tried hard to spoil the holiday – the area saw some heavy fighting in the early 1950s. After independence from the French, Bach Ma was soon forgotten and the villas abandoned; today they are in total ruin – only a few stone walls remain.

Bach Ma has some stunning views across the coastline near Hai Van Pass, which the Americans used to their advantage – during the war, US troops turned the area into a fortified bunker. The VC did their best to

## Tombs Fit for Kings

Although all are unique in structure and design, most of the mausoleums consist of five parts:

- A stele pavilion in which the accomplishments, exploits and virtues of the deceased emperor are engraved on a marble tablet. The testaments were usually written by the dead ruler's successor (though Tu Duc chose to compose his own).
- A temple for the worship of the emperor and empress. In front of each altar, where the deceased ruler's funerary tablets were placed, is an ornate dais that once held items the emperor used every day (eg, his tea and betel nut trays and cigarette cases), most of which have disappeared.
- A sepulchre, usually inside a square or circular enclosure, where the emperor's remains are buried
- An honour courtyard paved with dark-brown *bat trang* bricks, along the sides of which stand stone elephants, horses, and civil and military mandarins. The civil mandarins wear square hats and hold the symbol of their authority, an ivory sceptre; the military mandarins wear round hats and hold swords.
- A lotus pond surrounded by frangipani and pine trees

Almost all the tombs, which are in walled compounds, were planned by the Nguyen emperors during their lifetimes. Many of the precious ornaments that were once reposited in the tombs disappeared during Vietnam's wars.

harass the Americans, but couldn't dislodge them. Between the eerie remains, and memories of the American War, spooky stories abound among locals, who maintain that the park is a ghost town (it may well be!)

In 1991, 22,000 hectares of land were set aside as a nature preserve and designated Bach Ma National Park. Efforts are now fast under way to regenerate patches of forest that were destroyed by clear-felling and defoliation during the American War.

Ninety-three species of mammal have been recorded within the boundaries of the park, including tigers, bears and several species of primate. A recent victory in the wildlife stakes came with the discovery in 1992 of evidence of a previously unknown antelope-like creature *(sao la)*, whose footprints and horns were found in the Bach Ma domain. Two other animals were discovered in the late 1990s, the deer-like Truong Son muntjac and the giant muntjac. And with enforced protection from poachers, there is some hope that wild elephants, currently restricted to the Lao side of the border, will return to seek the sanctuary of Bach Ma.

As most of the park's resident mammals are nocturnal, sightings demand a great deal of effort and patience. Bird-watching is fantastic here, but of course you need to be up at dawn to get the best sightings. Of the 800-odd species of bird known to inhabit Vietnam, the park is home to some 330 including the fabulous crested argus pheasant and the tenacious Edwards' pheasant (unseen and thought to be extinct for 70 years, it was recently discovered in the park's buffer zone).

More than 1150 species of plant have also been discovered in the park, though this figure is estimated to be just half of the actual number. Among these, at least 338 species are medicinal plants, 33 produce essential oils, 26 are used for weaving and 22 bear edible fruit.

It was not until March 1998 that Bach Ma National Park began receiving visitors. Despite its newness, the efforts of the park's staff are laudable and they are hard at work protecting the area, working on community development with the ethnic minorities in

## Walking Tracks in Bach Ma National Park

There are several hiking opportunities through this beautiful forest. The national park's map describes several nature trails, but you'd be wise to check with the rangers on the current condition of each track.

**Pheasant Trail** is named after the rare and beautiful crested argus pheasant; you're more likely to hear the birds calling than see them, unless you have lots of time and patience. The 2.5km track starts 5km along the summit-access road, and leads through forest to a series of waterfalls and pools. You can cool off here before the return hike.

**Five Lakes Cascade Trail** starts 1km beyond the national-park guesthouse. A 2km walk takes you through forest and follows a series of cascades. The water is so cold that not much is living in it – just a recently discovered species of frog.

**Rhododendron Trail** can be walked as an extension of the Five Lakes Cascade Trail, or can be reached by a separate track from km16 on the summit-access road. Spring is the best time to walk this trail, when the rhododendrons are in bloom. At the end of the trail is a waterfall, and you can get to the bottom if you're fit enough to climb the 650 steps that lead down! The water here eventually makes its way down to join up with the Perfume River in Hué.

**Summit Trail** is a steep but short 500m walk to Hai Vong Dai, the 1450m summit of Bach Ma. Today visitors simply enjoy the stunning views, but in 1968 a helicopter base was maintained at this strategic spot. The white streams of cloud *(bach ma)* often seen at the summit are thought to look like the hair of a white horse and inspired the park's name.

These trails and others are described more fully in the national park's map, which you get with your ticket; further information is available in a bi-lingual booklet called simply *Bach Ma National Park* and available for 12,000d at the park entrance.

the area and promoting sustainable eco-tourism. Several young rangers here speak English well and there is an interesting display in the visitor centre: as well as plenty of natural-history information, it includes a huge crate of confiscated hunting and cutting tools, weaponry and the remains of a crashed helicopter.

Bach Ma is very foggy and wet from July to February, and the rains in October and November bring plenty of leeches. Still, these winter months are not out of the question for visiting. The best time to visit Bach Ma is from February to September, particularly between March and June, for what's likely to be the best weather.

## Places to Stay & Eat

**National Park Guesthouse** (*☎/fax 871330; campsites 3000d, 6-person tents 80,000d, rooms with/without bath 100,000/150,000d*) is a pleasant spot, rebuilt from one of the French ruins (actually one of Emperor Bao Dai's) that sits towards the summit of the park. The more expensive rooms are in a separate building and are a better bet for views and facilities. You need to give at least four hours notice for meal requirements as fresh food is brought up to the park from the market on demand.

Several private companies have built, or are building, small accommodation units in the park. Near the summit trail **Morin-Bach Ma Hotel** (*rooms US$20*) has already opened. All accommodation is being constructed under the watchful eye of the park authorities, so hopefully a low-key eco-friendly standard will be maintained.

There is a **canteen** near the visitor centre.

## Getting There & Away

Bach Ma is 28km west of Lang Co and 45km southwest of Hué. The narrow road into the park was originally built by the French in 1932, was rebuilt in 1993 and is now sealed nearly all the way to the summit.

The entrance and visitors centre is at km3 on the summit road, which starts at the town of Cau Hai on National Hwy 1. It's another steep and meandering 16km from the gate to the summit, and unless you have your own vehicle or are willing to walk it, you'll need to hire private transport from the park. Four-seater jeeps rent for around 250,000d per same-day return, 300,000d next-day return, or 150,000d one way. Be aware that motorbikes are no longer allowed on the summit road.

If you choose to walk down, it will take about three to four hours, so take plenty of water and wear a hat; you'll be walking in full sunlight on much of the lower part of the road.

## Getting Around

Your visit will be much easier if you can hire a vehicle to stay with you for your time in the park, especially if you plan to walk some of the trails, as they are spread along the 16km of the summit access road.

## SUOI VOI SPRINGS

About 15km north of Lang Co Beach is the inland turn-off to Suoi Voi Springs (*Elephant Springs; admission 10,000d per person plus 10,000/5000d per car/motorbike*). This is a secluded recreation area, where you could easily spend a half-day traipsing through the forest and swimming in cool, crystal-clear streams. It's a pleasant detour and recommended for motorbikers and cyclists who are braving their way north or south along National Hwy 1.

The main springs are a short walk from the parking area. This is a bumpy 1.5km from the entry gate, which is 2.3km from the main road. The springs feature huge boulders (one vaguely in the shape of an elephant's head, and cosmetically enhanced to look more like it!) and the stunning backdrop of the Bach Ma National Park in the distance. Further exploration will lead to less-populated swimming holes, including the **Vung Do Pool**, about 200m beyond the main area.

Foreign visitors here are scarce (most seem to be rushing in one direction or another along the coast), and on weekdays you may have the whole place to yourself. Weekends, however, are jam-packed with Vietnamese, notably young couples exploring the birds and bees.

To reach the springs from National Hwy 1, look for a large faded sign reading 'Suoi Voi' about 15km north of Lang Co Beach. You will see the 19th-century Thua Lau Church just ahead of you, after making a turn-off to the west. From there, follow the dirt road for 2.3km to the entry gate.

You'll need to buy an entry ticket here. Hold onto your ticket as you may be asked to show it more than once. There are some basic **food stalls** near the springs, but you're better off bringing a picnic.

About another 15km north of this turn-off is the village of Cau Hai, and the turn-off to reach Bach Ma National Park.

## LANG CO BEACH
☎ 054

Lang Co is a pretty, island-like stretch of palm-shaded sand with a crystal-clear, turquoise-blue lagoon on one side and many kilometres of beachfront facing the South China Sea on the other. It's a tranquil spot where lots of travellers make a lunch stop and some spend the night. If you're travelling on one of the 'open tours' along the coast, this makes a fine place to hop off for a night or two, depending, of course, on the weather and season.

The beach here is best enjoyed between April and July. From late August till November, rains are frequent, and during the chilly months, from December to February, it may serve best as just a lunch stop.

There are spectacular views of Lang Co, just north of Hai Van Pass, from both National Hwy 1 and from the trains linking Danang and Hué.

### Places to Stay & Eat
**Lang Co Hotel** (☎ 874426; doubles with/ without bath US$8/6, triples/quads without bath US$10/12, doubles/triples with bath, hot water & air-con US$12/15), in a shaded, garden-like compound close to the beach, is a large hotel run by the government trade union. It's fine and friendly if a bit tatty (but renovations are planned) and is recommended. Bicycles can be hired for 10,000d a day, and you can take a private boat trip around the lagoon for 150,000d; boats take up to 15 people – if you want to share costs. There is a reasonably priced, good beachfront seafood restaurant called **Hai Duong** on site.

**Thanh Tam Seaside Resort** (☎ 874456; fan rooms US$10-15) is about 1km north of Lang Co Hotel and has basic beachfront cottages for US$10; strangely, the more expensive rooms look onto a very attractive patch of concrete that's been designated a garage. The outdoor terrace restaurant has great views and the menu is OK.

**Lang Co Beach Resort** (☎ 973555; e langco@dng.vnn.vn; air-con rooms from US$60) is a stylish beachfront resort with a pool and simple, elegant rooms.

### Getting There & Away
**Bus** Buses pass through daily, en route for Hué (noon, US$3), Danang (10am, US$3), Hoi An (4pm, US$3), and Hanoi (4.30pm, US$14).

**Train** Served by nonexpress trains, **Lang Co train station** is 3km from the beach. Finding someone to take you from the train station to the beach by motorbike shouldn't be difficult.

**Car & Motorbike** Lang Co is 35km north of Danang over the Hai Van Pass.

## DANANG
☎ 0511 ● pop 1,100,000

Back in the heady days of the American War, Danang was often referred to as the 'Saigon of the North'. This held a note of both praise and condemnation – like its big sister to the south, Danang was notable for its booming economy, fine restaurants, busy traffic and glittering shops. Entertaining the military was also a profitable business – bars and prostitution were major industries, and that legacy lingers. As in Saigon, corruption also ran rampant. Liberation arrived in 1975, promptly putting a sizeable dent in the city's economy. Vietnam's recent economic liberalisation has helped Danang get back on its feet and the city is undergoing a huge programme of renovation and infrastructure development. At present it rather

CENTRAL VIETNAM

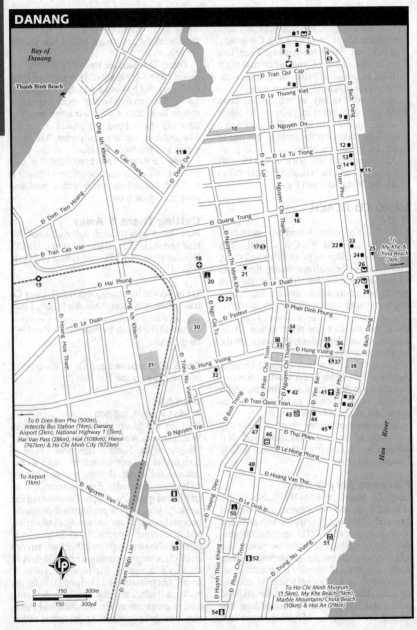

# DANANG

Bay of
Danang

Thanh Binh Beach

Đ Ong Ich Khiem

Đ Cao Thang

Đ Dong Da

Đ Tran Qui Cap

Đ Ly Thuong Kiet

Đ Nguyen Du

Đ Ly Tu Trong

Đ Le Loi

Đ Nguyen Chi Thanh

Đ Bach Dang

Đ Tran Phu

Đ Dinh Tien Hoang

Đ Tran Cao Van

Đ Quang Trung

Đ Nguyen Thi Minh Khai

Đ Hai Phong

Đ Le Duan

Đ Hoang Hoa Tham

Đ Le Duan

Đ Ong Ich Khiem

Đ Ngo Gia Tu

Đ Pasteur

Đ Hung Vuong

Đ Trieu Nu Vuong

Đ Binh Trong

Đ Phan Chu Trinh

Đ Nguyen Chi Thanh

Đ Yen Bai

Đ Tran Phu

Đ Bach Dang

Đ Phan Dinh Phung

Đ Hung Vuong

Đ Tran Quoc Toan

Đ Nguyen Trai

Đ Thai Phien

Đ Le Hong Phong

Đ Nguyen Van Linh

Đ Hoang Dieu

Đ Hoang Van Thu

Đ Le Dinh

Đ Pham Ngu Lao

Đ Huynh Thuc Khang

Đ Phan Chu Trinh

Đ Trung Nu Vuong

Han River

To My Khe &
China Beach
(2km)

To Đ Dien Bien Phu (500m),
Intercity Bus Station (1km), Danang
Airport (2km), National Highway 1 (3km),
Hai Van Pass (28km), Huế (108km), Hanoi
(767km) & Ho Chi Minh City (972km)

To Airport
(1km)

To Ho Chi Minh Museum
(1.5km), My Khe Beach (5km),
Marble Mountains/China Beach
(10km) & Hoi An (29km)

0    150    300m
0    150    300yd

## DANANG

resembles a massive construction site. Hopefully most of the public works will be finished by the time you read this.

Danang is Vietnam's fourth-largest city. It also marks the northern limits of Vietnam's tropical zone and boasts a pleasant climate all year round: nearby Hué is much colder in winter. Travellers pass through Danang when they visit the Museum of Cham Sculpture and also to make transport connections. Most people prefer to stay in Hoi An or out at nearby China Beach, though if all the hotels in Hoi An are full you may need to stay in Danang.

### History
Danang, known during the French-colonial rule as Tourane, succeeded Hoi An as the most important port in central Vietnam during the 19th century.

In late March 1975, Danang, which is the second-largest city in South Vietnam, was the scene of utter chaos. Saigon government forces were ordered to abandon Hué, while Quang Ngai had fallen to the communists, cutting South Vietnam in two. Desperate civilians tried to flee the city, as soldiers of the disintegrating South Vietnamese army engaged in an orgy of looting, pillage and rape. On 29 March 1975, two truckloads of communist guerrillas, more than half of them women, drove into what had been the most heavily defended city in South Vietnam and, without firing a shot, declared Danang 'liberated'.

Almost the only fighting that took place as Danang fell was between South Vietnamese soldiers and civilians battling for space on flights and ships out of the city. On 27 March, the president of World Airways, Ed Daly, ignored explicit US government orders and sent two 727s from Saigon to Danang to evacuate refugees. When the first plane landed, about a thousand desperate and panicked people mobbed the tarmac. Soldiers fired assault rifles at each other and at the plane as they tried to shove their way through the rear door. As the aircraft taxied down the runway trying to take off, people climbed up into the landing-gear wells and someone threw a hand grenade, damaging the right wing.

Those who managed to fight their way aboard, kicking and punching aside anyone in their way, included over 200 soldiers, mostly members of the elite (Vietnamese) Black Panthers company. The only civilians on board were two women and one baby – and the baby was only there after being thrown aboard by its desperate mother, who was left on the tarmac. Several of the stowaways in the wheel wells couldn't hold on and, as the plane flew southward, TV cameras on the second 727 filmed them falling into the South China Sea.

## Orientation

Danang is on the western bank of the Han River. The eastern bank is accessible via the new Song Han Bridge or Nguyen Van Troi Bridge further south. The city is part of a long, thin peninsula, at the northern tip of which is Nui Son Tra (called Monkey Mountain by US soldiers). A newish road is gradually circling Nui Son Tra, and it's slowly opening to tourism. China Beach and the Marble Mountains lie south of the city and Hai Van Pass overlooks Danang from the north.

## Information

**Money** There's a branch of **Vietcombank** (*140 Đ Le Loi*) near the corner of Đ Hai Phong. It's the only place in town that will change travellers cheques. The **VID Public Bank** (*2 Đ Tran Phu*) and the **Danang Commercial Joint Stock Bank**, just across Đ Hung Vuong from Dana Tours, will also change money.

**Email & Internet Access** There is plenty of Internet access in Danang, including a gaggle of **Internet cafés** on Đ Tran Quoc Toan, between Đ Yen Bai and Đ Nguyen Chi Thanh.

**Travel Agencies** If you need to organise tours, transport and tickets head for **Dana Tours** (*☎ 822516, fax 821312;* **e** *danamarle@ dng.vnn.vn; 76 Đ Hung Vuong*), Danang's main tour agency. It has an enlightened attitude compared with most of the state-run agencies and so is a good place to ask about tours. It will also organise car rentals, boat trips, visa extensions and treks to the nearby Ba Na hill station or further afield to Bach Ma National Park.

**Truong Van Trong's Tour** (*☎ 0903-597971;* **e** *trongn59@yahoo.com*) offers sightseeing with a difference. Trong conducts tours of the central highlands by motorbike, one-way

motorbike tours to Hanoi or HCMC, or day tours from Danang. He and his co-bikers between them speak good English, French, Japanese, German and Italian and they get good raves from travellers.

**Medical Services** There are four hospitals in town. **Hospital C** (*Benh Vien C; ☎ 822480; 35 Đ Hai Phong*) is Danang's most advanced medical facility.

**Visas** There is a **Lao consulate** (*12 Đ Tran Qui Cap; open 8am-11.30am & 2pm-4.30pm Mon-Fri*) at the northern end of town.

There is talk of a **Thai consulate** opening when the direct Vietnam-Laos-Thailand road link is finished; check current details when you're in town.

## Museum of Cham Sculpture

The best sight in Danang city has to be the Museum of Cham Sculpture (*Cham Museum, Bao Tang Cham; cnr Đ Trung Nu Vuong & Đ Bach Dang; admission 20,000d; open 7am-5pm daily*). Founded in 1915 by the École Française d'Extrême Orient, this collection of Cham sculpture is the finest in the world. Many of the sandstone carvings (altars, lingas, *garudas*, *ganeshas*, and images of Shiva, Brahma and Vishnu) are exquisitely detailed; take time to look closely.

A trilingual guidebook about the museum, *Bao Tang Dieu Khac Cham Da Nang* (Museum of Cham Sculpture – Danang), was written by its director, Tran Ky Phuong, Vietnam's most eminent scholar of Cham civilization. The book provides excellent background on the art of Champa; it also includes details on the museum's exhibits. The book is usually on sale at the entrance. Guides wait at the entrance to offer their services. If you do decide to take a guide, agree on a price before you begin.

The museum's artefacts, which date from the 7th to 15th centuries, were discovered at Dong Duong (Indrapura), Khuong My, My Son, Tra Kieu (Simhapura), Thap Mam (Binh Dinh) and other sites, mostly in Quang Nam and Danang provinces. The museum's rooms are named after the localities in which the objects displayed in them were found.

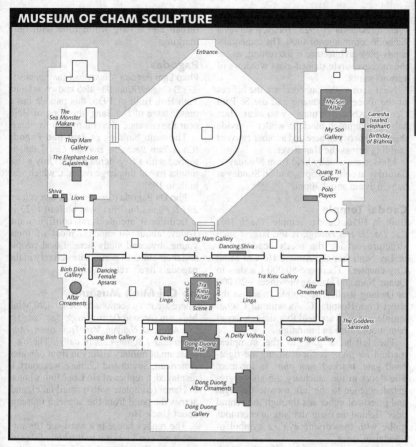

**MUSEUM OF CHAM SCULPTURE**

*Entrance*

My Son Altar

Ganesha (seated elephant)

The Sea Monster Makara

Thap Mam Gallery

My Son Gallery

Birthday of Brahma

The Elephant-Lion Gajasimha

Shiva

Lions

Quang Tri Gallery

Polo Players

Quang Nam Gallery

Dancing Shiva

Binh Dinh Gallery

Dancing Female Apsaras

Altar Ornaments

Linga

Scene C

Scene D

Tra Kieu Altar

Scene A

Scene B

Tra Kieu Gallery

Linga

Altar Ornaments

The Goddess Sarasvati

Quang Binh Gallery

A Deity

Dong Duong Altar

A Deity Vishnu

Quang Ngai Gallery

Dong Duong Altar Ornaments

Dong Duong Gallery

The four scenes carved around the base of the 7th-century Tra Kieu Altar tell parts of the Ramayana epic and are influenced by the Amaravati style of South India. Scene A (16 characters) tells the story of Prince Rama, who broke the sacred bow (Rudra) at the citadel of Videha, thus winning the right to wed King Janak's daughter, Princess Sita.

Scene B (16 characters) shows the ambassadors sent by King Janak to Prince Rama's father, King Dasaratha, at Ayodhya. The emissaries inform King Dasaratha of his son's exploits, present him with gifts and invite him to Videha to celebrate the wedding.

Scene C (18 characters) shows the royal wedding ceremony (including three of Prince Rama's brothers, who are marrying three of Princess Sita's cousins).

In Scene D, 11 heavenly maidens *(apsaras)* dance and present flowers to the newlyweds under the guidance of the two *gandhara* musicians who appear at the beginning of Scene A.

**Danang Cathedral**

Known to locals as Con Ga Church (Rooster Church) because of the weathercock on top of the steeple, Danang Cathedral *(Chinh Toa*

Da Nang; Đ Tran Phu) was built for the city's French residents in 1923. Today, it serves a Catholic community of 4000. The cathedral's candy-pink architecture is interesting, as are the medieval-style stained-glass windows of various saints.

Next door to the cathedral are the offices of the diocese of Danang and the St Paul Convent. About 100 nuns – who wear white habits in summer, black in winter – divide their time between here and another convent building across the Han River.

Masses are usually held from Monday to Saturday at 5am and 5pm, and on Sunday at 5am, 6.30am and 4.30pm.

## Caodai Temple

Built in 1956, Caodai Temple (Thanh That Cao Dai; Đ Hai Phong), is the largest such structure outside the sect's headquarters in Tay Ninh (see the Around Ho Chi Minh City chapter). There are 50,000 Caodais in Quang Nam and Danang provinces – 20,000 in Danang itself. The temple is across the street from Hospital C. As with all Caodai temples, prayers are held four times a day at 6am, noon, 6pm and midnight.

The left-hand gate to the complex, marked nu phai, is for women; the right-hand gate, marked nam phai, is for men. The doors to the sanctuary are also segregated: women to the left, men to the right and priests of either sex through the central door. Behind the main altar sits an enormous globe with the 'divine eye', a symbol of Caodaism, on it.

A sign reading van giao nhat ly, which means 'All religions have the same reason', hangs from the ceiling in front of the altar. Behind the gilded letters is a picture of the founders of five of the world's great religions. From left to right they are: Mohammed; Laotse (wearing blue robes cut in the style of the Greek Orthodox); Jesus (portrayed as he is in French icons); Buddha (who has a distinctly Southeast Asian appearance); and Confucius (looking as Chinese as could be).

Portraits of early Caodai leaders, dressed in turbans and white robes, are displayed in the building behind the main sanctuary. Ngo Van Chieu, the founder of Caodaism, is

shown standing, wearing a pointed white turban and a long white robe with blue markings.

## Pagodas

**Phap Lam Pagoda** (Chua Phap Lam; opposite 373 Đ Ong Ich Khiem) is also known as Chua Tinh Hoi. Built in 1936, this pagoda has a brass statue of Dia Tang, the King of Hell, near the entrance. Several monks live here.

The main building of **Tam Bao Pagoda** (Chua Tam Bao; 253 Đ Phan Chu Trinh) is topped with a five-tiered tower. Only a few monks live at this large pagoda, which was built in 1953.

**Pho Da Pagoda** (Chua Pho Da; across from 293 Đ Phan Chu Trinh) was built in 1923 in a traditional architectural configuration. Today, about 40 monks, most of them young, live and study here. Local people and their children participate actively in the pagoda's lively religious life.

## Ho Chi Minh Museum

There are three sections to the Ho Chi Minh Museum (Around Danang map; Bao Tang Ho Chi Minh; Đ Nguyen Van Troi; open 7am-11am and 1.30pm-4.30pm daily). There's a museum of military history in front of which American, Soviet and Chinese weaponry is displayed; a replica of Ho Chi Minh's house in Hanoi (complete with a small lake); and, across the pond from the house, a museum about Uncle Ho.

The replica house is a must-see for anyone who won't make it to the bona fide stilt house in Hanoi (or to one of the other many reproductions scattered throughout the country).

The museum is 250m west of Đ Nui Thanh.

## Boating

The Thuy Tu River north of Danang (near Hai Van Pass) has clean water and is good for boating. Some boats leave from the village of Nam O, which is famous for nuoc mam. There is another local speciality here called goi ca, which is fresh, raw fish fillets marinated in a special sauce and coated in a spicy powder – something like Vietnamese

## 'Mad Jack' Percival in Danang

In May 1845, Captain John 'Mad Jack' Percival sailed the USS *Constitution* into Turon Bay (Danang) and dropped anchor. He was a full year from Boston on a goodwill tour to show the American flag and look for coal. The ageing ship was in dire need of provisions.

At the time, a fort commanded both the harbour entrance and the mouth of the Han River. Percival's first order of business was to bury a seaman cook – dead from dysentery – in a pristine cove beside the hill fort.

On the third day Percival saluted the fort with six cannon shots and received a single shot in return. He dispatched a longboat into the town to make arrangements for reprovision. The exchanges were curt. The Americans found the emperor's representatives evasive.

Emperor Thieu Tri had reason to be cautious. China had been forced by British gunboats to open its ports three years earlier. Thieu Tri knew that France was anxious to join its rivals in the China trade. Vietnam, with its splendid harbour at Danang, would be a perfect platform. An armed frigate in the harbour was a cause for concern no matter whose flag the French flew.

On the fourth day, during a return visit to the ship by local authorities, a Chinese interpreter smuggled aboard a note. It was a plea for help from an imprisoned French missionary named LeFevre, who was under sentence of death for plotting against the emperor.

That was enough to get Mad Jack out of his cabin: a Christian prelate was held by 'barbarians'. Interpreting his benign brief rather broadly, Percival led an armed column back to town and delivered a withering note to the Mandarins, demanding the release of LeFevre. To show his resolve, he took three hostages and returned to the ship. He gave the Vietnamese a 24-hour ultimatum: release the missionary or he would seize the harbour forts and snatch all the shipping he could lay his hands on.

Anchored off the fort were three armed junks. Percival sent a party of longboats to capture them. During the night, soldiers from the fort boarded the junks – not to free them, but to punish the captains for dereliction. The unlucky commanders were flogged, yoked and tied to the mast. One had his eyes shut with pitch, with the emperor's seal stamped on the tar.

The Vietnamese ignored Percival's ultimatums. So Mad Jack raged against the inner harbour. He sent his longboats chasing deep up the Han, spilling Vietnamese sailors into the river. American marines, armed with muskets and cutlasses, went ashore against soldiers and civilians alike.

But Percival still needed to reprovision. Knowing this, the mandarins countered his ultimatums with a deal of their own: release the three officials and you may continue to take on stores. Then we will give you LeFevre.

The approaches to the forts were patiently reinforced. Vietnamese soldiers marched beneath colourful battle pennants along the riverbanks in ever increasing numbers. More ships – armed and fitted – appeared in the harbour. The USS *Constitution* was outgunned and outmanoeuvred. Neither Percival's reckless posturing nor the threat of two decks of cannon had made an impression on the Vietnamese.

Finally, Percival pulled anchor before dawn on 26 May and sailed from Danang. He fired a final salvo at a harbour island and the rounds fell short. He never saw LeFevre, but left with his stores fully replenished.

In 1849 President Taylor sent a note of apology to Thieu Tri. He deplored the incident and prayed that 'no more blood be spilled between our two peoples'.

Percival – rebuked by the navy – retired to Massachusetts. His 16 days in Danang slipped from sight. The next hostile Americans who ventured into Danang, 120 years later, could have profited from Mad Jack's experience.

**Peter Kneisel**

sushi. There are also sandy river beaches here that are fine for swimming. See Nam O Beach in the Around Danang section.

You might also ask about night cruises on the Han River in Danang; there's a cruising restaurant moored opposite the Museum of Cham Sculpture.

## Swimming

An enormous **water park** (admission 5000d open 9am-9pm Wed-Mon) opened in early 2002 and it's on the riverbank, 1km beyond the Ho Chi Minh Museum.

Don't even think about swimming in the run-down public pool by the Danang stadium unless you can protect every orifice in your body and have the constitution of an ox.

## Places to Stay

The following places are clustered around central and northern Danang. They range from standard-for-the-price, to very ordinary, to extremely-dumpy-for-the-price. If you don't like what you're being offered, shop around; the list given here is quite extensive. At busy times in Hoi An, Danang becomes the overflow accommodation centre and you may have no choice but to stay here.

For information on accommodation at My Khe and China Beaches, see the Around Danang section.

## Places to Stay – Budget & Mid-Range

There's a group of budget hotels located at the northern tip of the Danang Peninsula. The adjacent cargo shipping terminal is a bit of an eyesore, but it's quieter than the traffic-clogged city centre about 2km to the south. It's also a fair old hike into town, or to the waterfront to eat. The town is noisy, but traffic dies right off from about 9pm to 6am; it is possible to sleep if you're not next to one of the zillion karaoke bars in town.

**Danang Hotel – Old Wing** (☎ 823258; 3 Ð Dong Da; rooms with fan/air-con US$5/7) remains a total dump. The building was built in the late 1960s to house US military personnel and it hasn't seen much improvement since. Rooms are spartan and grubby.

**Danang Hotel – New Wing** (☎ 834662, fax 823431; air-con rooms US$16-40) hasn't aged well, but it is slightly better than the old wing. Both are slated for refurbishment, so fingers crossed.

**Harmony Hotel** (☎ 829146, fax 829145; 20 Ð Dong Da; air-con rooms from US$15) is just about OK. You'll need earplugs.

More towards town, **Bank's Guest House** (Nha Khach Ngan Hang; ☎ 821090; 195 Ð Dong Da; fan rooms from US$5) is a decent enough budget place for the price.

**Guest House 34** (Nha Nghi 34; ☎ 822732; 34 Ð Bach Dang; fan/air-con rooms US$5/7) is the best value in town. A few basic, clean rooms are set around a quiet garden courtyard on the waterfront; air-con rooms have hot water, fan ones have cold.

**Dai A Hotel** (☎ 827532, fax 825760; 27 Ð Yen Bai; rooms from US$15) is an all air-con place; it's fine, but there are newer, quieter places for the same price.

**Binh Duong Mini-Hotel** (☎ 821930, fax 827666; 30-32 Ð Tran Phu; air-con rooms US$15-30) is a standard minihotel that has good-sized rooms. It's on a relatively central and quiet road.

**Hoa Sen Hotel** (☎ 824505, fax 829001; 101-105 Ð Hung Vuong; rooms US$15-40), relatively close to the train station, is just a few blocks from Con Market (Cho Con). It's a newer minihotel but the cheaper rooms are windowless and gloomy. The lobby walls are decorated with provocative quotations.

**Song Han Hotel** (☎ 822540, fax 821109; 36 Ð Bach Dang; rooms US$16-55), right on the Han River, offers good views. It's OK for the cheaper price.

**Bach Dang Hotel** (☎ 823649, fax 821659; e bdhotel@dng.vnn.vn; 50 Ð Bach Dang; rear/river-view rooms US$18/50) is a large place that boasts river views from the upper-floor rooms. The huge, cheaper rooms are at the back, where it's quieter.

**Thu Bon Hotel** (☎ 821101, fax 822854; 10 Ð Ly Thuong Kiet; air-con rooms US$20-30) is an OK older place. There are some quiet rooms with small balconies at the back, and prices include satellite TV and breakfast.

**Elegant Hotel** (☎ 892893, fax 835179; e elegant@dng.vnn.vn; 22A Ð Bach Dang;

*rooms from US$60)* lives up to its name and many rooms have river views. You can expect 30% off the rack rates, when there's availability.

**Saigon Tourane Hotel** *(☎ 821021, fax 895285; e sgtouran@dng.vnn.vn; 14A Đ Tran Qui Cap & 5 Đ Dong Da; rooms US$60-150)*, close to the top of top-end accommodation in Danang, is a stylish place. Rates for well-appointed rooms include tax, service and breakfast; walk-in room rates can drop to as little as US$28, which is a great deal. There is a pleasant roof-top terrace restaurant overlooking the river.

**Royal Hotel** *(☎ 823295, fax 827279; e royalhotel@dng.vnn.vn; 17 Đ Quang Trung; rooms from US$55)* is a three-star, stylish hotel with an in-house Japanese restaurant. It's on a quietish road.

**Bamboo Green Riverside** *(☎ 832591, fax 832593; e riversidets@dng.vnn.vn; 68 Đ Bach Dang; rooms US$55-120)*, also with river views, is good, and offers a standard 30% discounts off the rack rates.

**Bamboo Green Harbourside** *(☎ 822722, fax 824165; e bamboogreen@dng.vnn.vn; 177 Đ Tran Phu; singles/doubles US$35/40)* is a new place conveniently located near the centre of town, across the road from Danang Cathedral. It's good value if you're offered the walk-in rate of US$25.

**Daesco Hotel** *(☎ 892807, fax 892988; e daescohotel@dng.vnn.vn; 155 Đ Tran Phu; rooms US$35-70)*, a standard business hotel, has facilities such as a fitness centre with sauna (and steam bath), bar and restaurant.

## Places to Eat

**Christie's Restaurant** *(☎ 824040, fax 829323, fax 826645; e christies@hotmail.com; 112 Đ Tran Phu; pasta from 20,000d; open 10am-10pm daily)* is a 2nd-storey bar-restaurant that serves passable burgers, pizza, pasta, and Japanese and Vietnamese food. There is a small, mostly Japanese, book exchange.

**Hong Ngoc Restaurant** *(193 Đ Nguyen Chi Thanh)* is a fine and busy Chinese restaurant.

As is **Phi Lu Restaurant** *(225 Đ Nguyen Chi Thanh; meals from 20,000d; open lunch & dinner)*, which doesn't have a great atmosphere, but it does excellent Chinese food.

**Hanakim Dinh Restaurant** *(15 Đ Bach Dang; dishes around 40,000d)*, a Japanese joint venture, is a riverside restaurant and bar with an extensive food and cocktail menu, and pleasant outdoor seating.

**Mi Quang Restaurant** *(1A Đ Hai Phong)*, near the Caodai Temple, is a popular lunch place serving filling and good bowls of *mi quang* – yellow-noodle soup with salad greens stirred through it.

**Com Chay Chua Tinh Hoi** *(500 Đ Ong Ich Khiem; dishes around 3000d; open 6am-10pm daily)* is cited by locals as the best vegetarian food in town; it's just inside the entrance gate to the Phap Lam Pagoda. There are more vegie places in the streets outside the pagoda.

**Bamboo Bar** *(☎ 837175; e bamboo_dn@dng.vnn.vn; 5 Đ Bach Dang)* is a rustic riverside place that is a good spot to enjoy drinks, a game of pool or some pub grub on the outdoor terrace. The friendly owners here speak English, French and German, and can help organise boat tours and motorbike rentals.

Near the Bamboo Bar, two other places serving Vietnamese, Chinese and Western dishes in a great location on the river are **Mien Trung** *(9 Đ Bach Dang)* and **Thoi Dai** *(☎ 826404; 5 Đ Bach Dang)*.

## Entertainment

Traditional Vietnamese music and dance is performed at the **Nguyen Hien Dinh Theatre** *(cnr Đ Le Hong Phong & Đ Phan Chu Trinh; admission 20,000d; 7.30pm Fri, Sat & Sun)* a new-in-2002 venture.

**The Cool Spot Bar** is below Christie's Restaurant. It's comfortable and has air-con, but is decidedly lacking in atmosphere and service.

## Shopping

**Han Market** *(Cho Han; cnr Đ Hung Vuong & Đ Tran Phu)* usually stays open late and is a fine place for a casual stroll or to shop in the evenings.

The **Con Market** *(Cho Con)* is Danang's largest, but functions mostly during the day. This huge, colourful market has a selection of just about everything sold in Vietnam including household items, ceramics, fresh vegetables, stationery, cutlery, fruit, flowers and polyester clothes.

## Getting There & Away

**Air** During the American War, Danang had one of the busiest airports in the world. It still distinguishes itself by having one of Vietnam's three international airports. Recently direct flights from Bangkok, Hong Kong and Singapore were re-established. Most international flights from Danang fly via HCMC so you can complete your immigration and customs formalities in Danang.

**Vietnam Airlines** (☎ 821130; 35 Đ Tran Phu) has an extensive schedule to/from Danang (see the boxed text 'Domestic Airline Schedules' in the Getting Around chapter).

**Pacific Airlines** (☎ 583583; 35 Nguyen Van Linh; open 9am-5pm daily) flies from Danang to Hong Kong.

**Bus** The **Danang intercity bus station** (Around Danang map; Ben Xe Khach Da Nang; open 7am-11am & 1pm-5pm) is about 3km from the city centre on the thoroughfare known, at various points along its length, as Đ Hung Vuong, Đ Ly Thai To and Đ Dien Bien Phu. There is an efficient ticket office for long-distance services, just inside the bus station, with prices clearly marked.

First/last services leave for Hanoi at 6am and 8am (87,000d); for Saigon at 5.30am and 2pm (104,000d); for Hué at 5.30am and 5pm (22,000d).

You can book and board buses here for Savannakhet in Laos, via Dong Ha and the Lao Bao border crossing (see Border Crossings in the Getting There & Away chapter). Presently buses leave the interchange Monday, Wednesday, Friday and Sunday at 7pm (120,000d) but this may change.

Hoi An buses (10,000d) go from a **local bus station** 200m away from the bus interchange, and leave regularly in daylight hours.

**Minibus** Most travellers prefer to stay in Hoi An rather than Danang, so Hoi An has better minibus services. Nevertheless, it is possible to get a seat on an upmarket minibus in Danang. Check at the Bamboo

Bar for information on the minibuses to Hué and Nha Trang.

There is also a daily minibus service between Danang and Hoi An. The bus leaves Danang at 8am and returns at 5pm (US$3/5.50 one way/return) depending on the demand (it always requires a minimum of four passengers).

**Train** Danang is, of course, served by all *Reunification Express* trains (see the Train section in the Getting Around chapter) and there are several trains daily to HCMC, Hanoi and points between.

The **Danang train station** (Ga Da Nang) is about 1.5km from the city centre on Đ Hai Phong, at the northern end of Đ Hoang Hoa Tham. The train ride to Hué (20,000d) is one of the nicest in the country (although the drive up and over Hai Van Pass is also spectacular).

Northbound, the quickest train takes about 3¼ hours to reach Hué and leaves at 6.15am; the local train leaves at 2.20pm and take about six hours. Watch your belongings as you pass through the pitch-black tunnels.

**Car & Motorbike** The simplest way to get to Hoi An is to hire a car for around US$10 from a local travel agency, or a motorbike for around US$8 from one of the guys on the street corners. For a slightly higher fee you can ask the driver to stop off and wait for you, while you visit the Marble Mountains and China Beach. You can also reach My Son by motorbike (US$12) or car (US$35), with the option of being dropped off in Hoi An on the way back if you don't wish to return to Danang.

The following are road distances from Danang.

| Hanoi | 764km |
| Ho Chi Minh City | 972km |
| Hoi An | 30km |
| Hué | 108km |
| Lao Bao | 350km |
| Nha Trang | 541km |
| Quang Ngai | 130km |
| Qui Nhon | 303km |
| Savannakhet, Laos | 500km |

## Getting Around

**To/From the Airport** Danang's airport is just 2km west of the city centre, close enough to reach by cyclo in 15 minutes.

**Cyclo & Motorbike** Danang has plenty of motorbike taxis and cyclo drivers; take the usual caution and be prepared to bargain the fare.

Self-drive motorbikes can be rented at the Bamboo Bar.

**Taxi** Both **Airport Taxi** (☎ 825555) and **Dana Taxi** (☎ 815815) provide modern vehicles with air-con and meters.

**Boat** Inquire at the Bamboo Bar about chartered boat trips in the area.

## AROUND DANANG

☎ 0511

### Nui Son Tra

Much of Son Tra peninsula is a military and naval base, and is therefore off limits. However there's a nice rural road partway around the coast, a very low-key beach area and a memorial to an episode of colonial history that aren't.

Spanish-led Filipino and French troops attacked Danang in August 1858, ostensibly to end Emperor Tu Duc's mistreatment of Vietnamese Catholics and Catholic missionaries. The city quickly fell, but the invaders had to contend with cholera, dysentery, scurvy, typhus and mysterious fevers. By the summer of 1859, the number of invaders that had died of illness was 20 times the number that had been killed in combat. Many of the tombs of the Spanish and French soldiers are below a **chapel** *(Bai Mo Phap Va Ta Ban Nha; Around Danang map)* about 15km north of the city. The names of the dead are written on the walls.

To get there, cross the Song Han Bridge and turn left onto Đ Ngo Quyen. Continue north to Tien Sa Port (Cang Tien Sa). The ossuary, a small white building, stands on the right on a low hill, about 500m before the gate of the port and below the chapel.

The sheltered **Tien Sa Beach**, behind the port and the chapel, is quiet and calm and

with clear water. It's nice for a swim if you can ignore the picnic litter on the sand, and there are great views across to the Hai Van Pass. Several tourist bungalows were being built when we visited, and more are planned; hopefully it won't become overdeveloped.

Heading east around the coast you'll notice the *nuoc mam* factories: you might not see them, but you'll certainly smell them! After a few bumpy kilometres you come to the beachside settlement of **Bai But**. It's a rather strange place of low-key, tiny **bungalows** *(50,000-100,000d)* that dot the hillside above the beach and look great, but are basic inside – take a sleeping mat if you choose to stay – and a few ugly **restaurants**, set in a placid and gorgeous bay. It's a nice spot to while away an hour or so.

### Nam O Beach

Nam O Beach is on the Bay of Danang about 15km northwest of the city. The small community of Nam O has supported itself for years by producing firecrackers. Unfortunately, since the ban on firecrackers by the government in 1995, the community has fallen on hard times. However, the resourceful locals have recently gone into making *nuoc mam* instead – and while it's not as profitable as firecrackers, it's better than nothing.

### China Beach

Made famous in the American TV series of the same name, China Beach stretches for many kilometres north and south of the Marble Mountains. During the American War, US soldiers were airlifted here for rest and relaxation (R&R), which often included a picnic on the beach. For some, it was their last meal before their return to combat by helicopter.

The jumbo beach stretches some 30km south from Son Tra almost all the way to Hoi An. It has become a very popular seaside escape for both domestic and foreign tourists, and is now home to one of Vietnam's plushest resort hotels.

Though the entire stretch of oceanfront here is collectively known as China Beach, it is worth noting that the name is a recent creation. The beachfront is, in fact, divided into sections, each with its own local name.

The most populated areas are My Khe Beach (Bai Tam My Khe), where the Americans did most of their R&R, and the tract of seashore by the Non Nuoc Seaside Resort. Expect an onslaught of vendors flogging 'China Beach' baseball caps, woodcarvings of Buddha, jade bracelets, new antiques and other tourist paraphernalia, but there are plenty of other peaceful, secluded areas to explore along the coastline.

Many people insist that My Khe Beach was the real China Beach of wartime fame

and that the present China Beach is a fake. My Khe is about 6km by road from central Danang. The beach has a dangerous undertow, especially in winter. However, it is safer than the rest of China Beach – the bulk of Son Tra Mountain protects it from winds that cause rough surf.

The best time for swimming along Danang's beaches is from May to July, when the sea is at its calmest. During other times the water can get rough; lifeguards patrol only Non Nuoc, My An and sometimes My Khe Beaches. Ironically, the dangerous winter conditions go hand-in-hand with

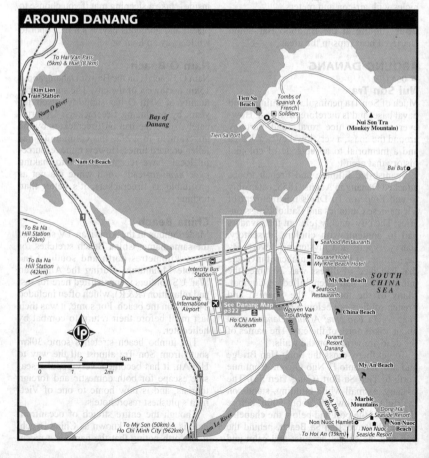

large breakers, which are ideal for surfing – assuming that you know what you're doing. The surf can be very good from around mid-September to December, particularly in the morning when wind conditions are right. In December 1992, China Beach was the site of the first international surfing competition to be held in Vietnam.

**Places to Stay & Eat** A cavernous Soviet-built place, **Non Nuoc Seaside Resort** (☎ 836214, fax 836335; singles/doubles with fan US$6/12, rooms with air-con US$11-18) is essentially an old concrete block. Rooms are nothing to write home about, but it's cheap and within crawling distance of the beach. It's quite surreal – and nice – to rattle around the enormous property when it's quiet, but check that there isn't a busy conference on while you're there. There's a vast, ocean-view **restaurant** there, too.

**Dong Hai Seaside Resort** (☎ 961009; cottages US$7) is on the way to the Non Nuoc Seaside Resort. It has very basic rooms in cute little brick cottages, and you can eat at restaurants on the beach or on the nearby laneway.

**My Khe Beach Hotel** (☎ 836125, fax 836123; singles/doubles from US$10/12) is another cheap spot right on the beach, although it is ageing and badly needs refurbishing. At the time of writing a new wing was almost complete. There's a good **restaurant** here as well, which offers friendly service, and donates 10% of its proceeds to a local charity.

**Tourane Hotel** (☎ 932666, fax 844328; ℮ touranehotel@dng.vnn.vn; rooms US$25-40), absolutely no relation to the plush Saigon Tourane in town, is just across the road from the beach and has aged quickly and become tatty. At the time of writing, however, it was due for major renovations.

**Furama Resort Danang** (☎ 847333, fax 847666; ℮ furamadn@hn.vnn.vn; rooms US$140-400++) is Danang's luxury hotel. In fact, it's Vietnam's luxury hotel. Perched on its own private slice of China Beach, this stylish resort features a diving facility, a putt-putt golf range and two landscaped swimming pools. If you can't afford more

than a taste of luxury, day-use of the stunning grounds, pools and fitness centre is available for US$10++.

My Khe Beach is the place to go for seafood. A short walk north of Tourane Hotel, and south of My Khe Beach Hotel, are two strings of **seafood restaurants** with open decks overlooking the ocean.

**Getting There & Away** To get to My Khe Beach from central Danang, cross the Song Han Bridge and head toward the sea. A xe om can take you, and wait for a couple of hours or so, for about US$2.

To reach the Non Nuoc Seaside Resort by private transport, head towards the Marble Mountains and turn left into Non Nuoc Hamlet. Follow the road and look for the signs to Non Nuoc Seaside Resort. Then take the track through the casuarina trees.

## Marble Mountains
These mountains (admission 10,000d) consist of five sizeable rock outcrops that are made of…marble.

Each is said to represent a natural element and is named accordingly: Thuy Son (Water), Moc Son (Wood), Hoa Son (Fire), Kim So (Metal or Gold) and Tho Son (Earth). The largest and most famous, Thuy Son, has a number of natural caves in which first Hindu, and later Buddhist, sanctuaries have been built over the centuries. Thuy Son is a popular pilgrimage site, especially on days of the full and sliver moons and during Tet, when it's a very beautiful place to visit.

A torch (flashlight) is useful inside the caves. Local children have learned that foreigners buy souvenirs and leave tips for unsolicited guided tours, so you are not likely to begin your visit alone. And watch your wallets! The local government adopted a regulation (which it sternly enforces) that the children cannot take tips, but can sell you souvenirs. This seems counterproductive; most travellers would rather tip the kids for the guided tours than buy the crappy souvenirs. In general, the kids are good-natured, if extremely persistent, and some of the caves are difficult to find without their assistance.

Of the two paths leading up Thuy Son, the one closer to the beach (at the end of the village) makes for a better circuit once you get up the top. So, unless you want to walk the following route in reverse, don't go up the staircase with concrete kiosks. The admission fee is collected at either entrance.

At the top of the staircase (from where Cham Island is visible) is a gate, Ong Chon, which is pockmarked with bullet holes. Behind Ong Chon is Linh Ong Pagoda. As you enter the sanctuary, look to the left to see a fantastic figure with a huge tongue. To the right of Linh Ong are monks' quarters and a small orchid garden.

Behind Linh Ong, a path leads left through two short tunnels to several caverns known as Tang Chon Dong. There are several concrete Buddhas and blocks of carved stone of Cham origin in these caves. Near one of the altars is a flight of steps leading up to another cave, partially open to the sky, with two seated Buddhas in it.

To the left of the small building left of Linh Ong (ie, immediately to the left as you enter Ong Chon Gate) is the main path to the rest of Thuy Son. Stairs off the main pathway lead to Vong Hai Da, a viewpoint for a brilliant panorama of China Beach and the South China Sea.

The stone-paved path continues to the right and into a canyon. On the left is Van Thong Cave. Opposite the entrance is a cement Buddha and behind that, there is a narrow passage, which leads up to a natural chimney open to the sky.

Exit the canyon and pass through a battle-scarred masonry gate. There's a rocky path to the right, which goes to Linh Nham, a tall chimney-shaped cave with a small altar inside. Nearby, another path leads to Hoa Nghiem, a shallow cave with a Buddha inside. If you go down the passageway to the left of the Buddha, you come to cathedral-like Huyen Khong Cave, lit by an opening to the sky. The entrance to this spectacular chamber is guarded by two administrative mandarins (to the left of the doorway) and two military mandarins (to the right).

Scattered about the cave are Buddhist and Confucian shrines; note the inscriptions carved into the stone walls. On the right, a door leads to two stalactites, dripping water that local legend describes as coming from heaven. Actually, only one stalactite drips; the other one supposedly ran dry when Emperor Tu Duc touched it. During the American War, this chamber was used by the VC as a field hospital. Inside is a plaque dedicated to the Women's Artillery Group, which destroyed 19 US aircraft as they sat at a base below the mountains in 1972.

Just to the left of the battle-scarred masonry gate is Tam Thai Tu, a pagoda restored by Emperor Minh Mang in 1826. A path heading obliquely to the right goes to the monks' residence, beyond which are two shrines. From there, a red dirt path leads to five small pagodas. Before you arrive at the monks' residence, stairs on the left-hand side of the path lead to Vong Giang Dai, which offers a fantastic 180-degree view of the other Marble Mountains and the surrounding countryside. To get to the stairway down, follow the path straight on from the masonry gate.

### Non Nuoc Hamlet
Non Nuoc Hamlet is on the southern side of Thuy Son and is a few hundred metres west of My An Beach. The marble carvings made here by skilled (and not-so-skilled) artisans would make great gifts if they didn't weigh so much. It's fun to watch the carvers at work, and there are some tiny carved figures that make nice gifts.

The town has been spruced up for tourism. During the war, the Americans referred to the shantytown near here as 'Dogpatch', after a derelict town in the comic strip *L'il Abner*. Most of the residents living there at the time were refugees fleeing the fighting in the surrounding countryside.

### Getting There & Away
**Car & Motorbike** The 11km route from Danang to the Marble Mountains passes by the remains of a huge 2km-long complex of former US military bases; aircraft revetments are still visible.

The Marble Mountains are 19km north of Hoi An along the 'Korean Hwy'.

**Boat** It is possible to get to the Marble Mountains from Danang by chartered boat. The 8.5km trip up the Han and Vinh Diem Rivers takes about 1¼ hours.

## HAI VAN PASS

Hai Van (Sea Cloud) Pass crosses over a spur of the Truong Son Mountain Range that juts into the South China Sea. About 30km north of Danang, National Hwy 1 climbs on an elevation of 496m, passing south of the Ai Van Son peak (1172m). It's an incredibly mountainous stretch of highway with spectacular views. The railway track, with its many tunnels, goes around the peninsula, following the shoreline to avoid the hills.

In the 15th century, Hai Van Pass formed the boundary between Vietnam and the Kingdom of Champa. Until the American War, the pass was heavily forested. At the summit is an old French fort, later used as a bunker by the South Vietnamese and US armies.

If you visit it in winter, you will probably find that the pass serves almost as a visible dividing line between the climates of the north and south. Acting as a virtual wall, the pass protects the area to the south of it from the fierce 'Chinese winds' that sweep in from the northeast. From about November to March the exposed side on the north of the pass (including Lang Co Beach) can be uncomfortably wet and chilly, while just to the south (on the beaches around Danang and Hoi An) it's warm and dry. Of course, variations in this weather pattern occur but, in general, when the winter weather is lousy in Hué, it is usually good in Danang.

Most buses make a 10-minute rest stop at the top of the pass. You'll have to fight off a rather large crowd of very persistent souvenir vendors. You would be wise not to agree to change money with anyone on the pass as you're more likely to get short-changed.

In June 2000, construction began on a US$150 million tunnel under Hai Van Pass to facilitate traffic flow. The project is estimated to take four years.

## BA NA HILL STATION

☎ 0511 ● elevation 1485m

Ba Na (admission 10,000d, 5000/10,000d per motorbike/car), optimistically called 'the Dalat of Danang province' by the provincial government, is a former French hill station along the crest of Mt Ba Na (Nui Chua). The 360-degree view is truly spectacular and the air is fresh and cool. When it's 36°C on the coast, it's likely to be between 15°C and 26°C at Ba Na. Rain often falls between 700m and 1200m above sea level, but around the hill station itself, the sky is usually clear. Mountain tracks in the area lead to a variety of waterfalls and viewpoints.

Ba Na was founded in 1919 and, until WWII, the French were carried up the last 20km of rough mountain road by sedan chair! Of the 200-odd villas that originally stood, a few tattered – but photogenic and atmospheric – ruins remain. The provincial government has high hopes of once again making Ba Na a magnet for tourists, and is redeveloping the site to suit domestic visitors. This means a variety of accommodation and restaurants (which is good) but also lots of karaoke, constant loud piped music and litter, which are maybe not quite so good.

Views from Le Nim restaurant balcony are fantastic – eat lunch there. The Ba Na By Night Resort (don't be fooled by the name, it's open all day too) has preserved an old French wine cellar in its foundations – walk in and feel the remarkable coolness. You can also walk along a marked track, just behind the plushest accommodation section, to the atmospheric ruins of one of the French villas. An enormous Buddha that's visible for miles around is also being constructed on site.

### Places to Stay & Eat

Each resort has an extraordinarily complex system of different room standards and prices, depending on season, day of the week, number of people, length of stay and so on. Rates given below are very general guidelines. More resorts are under construction at time of writing.

**Ba Na Resort** (☎ 818055, ☎ 746447, fax 712307; e banatourist@dng.vnn.vn; hotel rooms US$15-30, bungalows, with/without bath 70,000/50,000d) consists of a 30-room hotel and 40 teeny-weeny bungalows, that just accommodate two. There is also a large **restaurant** located here.

**Le Nim** (☎ 670026; rooms 50,000-200,000d) is on a pathway directly below Ba Na Resort. All rooms are around an open courtyard where karaoke campfires take place of a weekend – you have been warned. The **restaurant** serves up terrific fresh seafood dishes and has an unsurpassed daytime view.

**Ba Na By Night Resort** (☎ 671016; e bana night@dng.vnn.vn; rooms 200,000-700,000d) is a nice setup, but misses out on the views. The remnants of a colonial-era wine cellar and French villa at this place are interesting to check out.

### Getting There & Away
Ba Na is 42km west of Danang along a beautiful, if somewhat narrow and scary, winding road.

Pay the entry fee at bottom of the access road. If you arrive by public bus from Danang, shuttle buses take passengers up the mountain for another 15,000d.

If you don't want to drive all the way – or if you want the thrill – there is a cable car that whisks visitors up from a free parking lot a few kilometres below the hill station. Tickets cost 35,000d return. You can also drive right up to the top.

### SUOI MO
A pleasant detour for an hour or so on the way to Ba Na, is via the waterfall at Suoi Mo (Dream Springs; admission 3000d). To get there, turn right just before the Ba Na access-road entry gate. There's another entry gate here, where you pay the entry fee. Continue up the bumpy track for 2km or so and look for a small arrowed sign 'Suoi Mo' on the left. Park here, and walk along the track that leads off to the right, beside a few houses. A 20-minute climb – slippery when wet – takes you past some clear swimming holes and up to the waterfall. It's a pretty, undeveloped spot, if you can ignore the litter; and go on a weekday to avoid the crowds.

## HOI AN
☎ 0510 • pop 75,800

Hoi An is a picturesque riverside town, 30km south of Danang. Most visitors agree it is the most enchanting place along the coast and one spot worth lingering in.

Known as Faifo to early Western traders, it was one of Southeast Asia's major international ports during the 17th, 18th and 19th centuries. In its heyday, Hoi An, a contemporary of Macau and Melaka, was an important port of call for Dutch, Portuguese, Chinese, Japanese and other trading vessels. Vietnamese ships and sailors based in Hoi An sailed to all sections of Vietnam, as well as Thailand and Indonesia. Perhaps more than any other place in Vietnam, Hoi An retains a sense of history that envelopes you as you explore the town.

Every year during the rainy season, particularly in October and November, Hoi An has problems with flooding, especially in areas close to the waterfront. The greatest flood ever recorded in Hoi An took place in 1964, when the water reached all the way up to the roof beams of the houses.

Declared a Unesco World Heritage site, Hoi An Old Town (w www.hoianworldher itage.org; admission 50,000d) is governed by preservation laws that are well up to par. Several buildings of historical and cultural significance are open for public viewing, a number of streets in the centre of town are off-limits to cars, and building alterations and height restrictions are well enforced. If only Hanoi would follow suit in its historic Old Quarter.

The admission fee goes towards funding all this conservation work. This ticket gives you a rather complicated choice of heritage attractions to visit. You can visit all the old streets, and one each of the five types of places: museums; assembly halls; old houses; 'intangible culture', such as a traditional music concert or handicraft workshop; and 'other' (which means Quan Cong's Temple or the temple within the Japanese Covered Bridge). If you want to visit more buildings than this you should buy another ticket; there are ticket offices dotted around the town.

# HOI AN

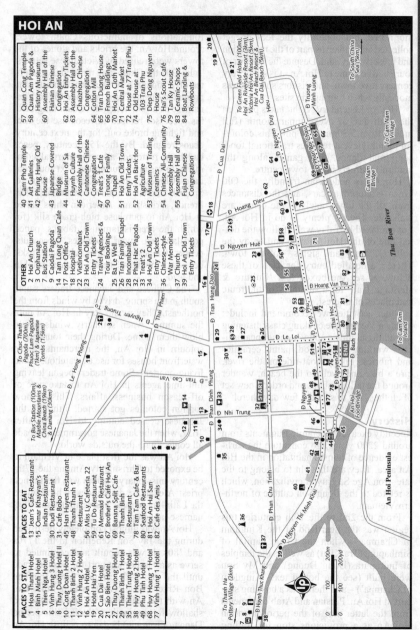

**PLACES TO STAY**
1 Hoai Thanh Hotel
4 Binh Minh Hotel
5 Thien Nga Hotel
6 Vinh Hung 3 Hotel
8 Thuy Duong Hotel II
10 Cong Doan Hotel
11 Thanh Binh 2 Hotel
12 Vinh Hung 2 Hotel
16 Hoi An Hotel
19 Hotel Hai Yen
20 Cua Dai Hotel
21 Sao Bien Hotel
27 Thanh Binh 1 Hotel
29 Thanh Binh 1 Hotel
35 Thien Trung Hotel
38 Huy Hoang 2 Hotel
49 Phu Tinh Hotel
68 Huy Hoang 1 Hotel
77 Vinh Hung 1 Hotel

**PLACES TO EAT**
13 Jean's Cafe Restaurant
15 Omar Khayyam's Indian Restaurant
30 Dudi Restaurant
31 Cafe Bobo
45 Han Huyen Restaurant
48 Thanh Thanh 1 Restaurant
56 Miss Ly Cafeteria 22
59 Tu Do Restaurant
61 Mermaid Restaurant
67 Brother's Café Hoi An
69 Banana Split Cafe
73 Thanh Binh Restaurant
78 Tam Tam Cafe & Bar
80 Seafood Restaurants
81 Hoi An Hai San
82 Cafe des Amis

**OTHER**
2 Hoi An Church
3 Orphanage
7 Bus Station
9 Caodai Pagoda
14 Tam Long Quan Cafe
17 Post Office
18 Hospital
22 Vietincombank
23 Hoi An Old Town Entry Tickets
24 Travel Agencies & Tour Bookings
25 Ba Le Well
26 Tran Family Chapel
28 Incombank
32 Phat Hac Pagoda
33 Treat's 2
34 Hoi An Old Town Entry Tickets
36 Chinese-style Church
37 Hoi An Old Town Entry Tickets
39 Hoi An Old Town Entry Tickets
40 Cam Pho Temple
41 Art Galleries
42 Phung Hung Old House
43 Japanese Covered Bridge
44 Museum of Sa Huynh Culture
46 Assembly Hall of the Cantonese Chinese Congregation
47 Treat's 1 Cafe
50 Truong Family Chapel
51 Hoi An Old Town Entry Tickets
52 Hoi An Bank for Agriculture
53 Museum of Trading Ceramics
54 Chinese All-Community Assembly Hall
55 Assembly Hall of the Fujian Chinese Congregation
57 Quan Cong Temple
58 Quan Am Pagoda & History Museum
60 Assembly Hall of the Hainan Chinese Congregation
62 Hoi An Entry Tickets
63 Assembly Hall of the Chaozhou Chinese Congregation
64 Cotton Mill
65 Tran Duong House
66 French Buildings
70 Hoi An Cloth Market
71 Central Market
72 House at 77 Tran Phu
74 Old House at 103 Tran Phu
75 Diep Dong Nguyen House
76 Hai's Scout Café
79 Tan Ky House
83 Ceramic Shops
84 Boat Landing & Rowboats

The system doesn't seem to be well-monitored, but hopefully the fees do get collected and end up as part of the restoration and preservation fund. Despite the number of tourists who come to Hoi An, it is still a very conservative town, and visitors should dress modestly when touring the sites.

'Hoi An Legendary Night' takes place on the 14th day of every lunar month (full moon) from 5.30pm to 10pm. This colourful monthly event features traditional food, song and dance, and games along the lantern-lit streets in the town centre.

Hoi An is pedestrian-friendly: the Old Town is closed to cars, and the distances from all the town hotels to the centre are walkable. There's plenty to do in Hoi An. For a relaxed half-day walk, follow the dotted line on the Hoi An map and enjoy the cultural sites – and sights – of the town. There's a detailed entry for each of these below, or see the boxed text 'Culture & Heritage Trail' for a summary of the route and places of interest.

Other activities we recommend include: taking a Vietnamese cooking class; listening to traditional music and watching local artisans working with wood, paint, ceramics and fabrics. Take a boat-ride on the river, hire a bike and cycle to the beach; wander around the tailors' shops and order a new set of clothes. Try to spend a few days here!

## History

Recently excavated ceramic fragments from around 2200 years ago constitute the earliest evidence of human habitation in the Hoi An area. They are thought to belong to the late-Iron Age Sa Huynh civilization, which is related to the Dong Son culture of northern Vietnam.

From the 2nd to the 10th centuries this region was the heartland of the Kingdom of Champa – when the Cham capital of Simhapura (Tra Kieu) as well as the temples of Indrapura (Dong Duong) and My Son were built (see the boxed text 'Kingdom of Champa') – and there was a bustling seaport at Hoi An. Persian and Arab documents from the latter part of the period mention Hoi An as a provisions stop for trading ships. Archaeologists have uncovered the foundations of numerous Cham towers around Hoi An: the bricks and stones of the towers were reused by Vietnamese settlers.

In 1307 the Cham king married the daughter of a monarch of the Tran dynasty and presented Quang Nam province to the Vietnamese as a gift. When the Cham king died, his successor refused to recognise the deal and fighting broke out; for the next century, chaos reigned. By the 15th century, peace had been restored, allowing normal commerce to resume. During the next four centuries, Chinese, Japanese, Dutch, Portuguese, Spanish, Indian, Filipino, Indonesian, Thai, French, British and American ships called at Hoi An to purchase high-grade silk (for which the area is famous), fabrics, paper, porcelain, tea, sugar, molasses, areca nuts, pepper, Chinese medicines, elephant tusks, beeswax, mother-of-pearl, lacquer, sulphur and lead.

The Chinese and Japanese traders sailed south in the spring, driven by winds from the northeast. They would stay in Hoi An until the summer, when southerly winds would blow them home. During their four-month sojourn in Hoi An, the merchants rented waterfront houses for use as warehouses and living quarters. Some traders began leaving full-time agents in Hoi An to take care of off-season business affairs. This is how foreign colonies got started, although the Japanese ceased coming to Hoi An after 1637, when the Japanese government forbade all contact with the outside world.

Hoi An was the first place in Vietnam to be exposed to Christianity. Among the 17th-century missionary visitors was the French priest Alexandre de Rhodes, who devised the Latin-based *quoc ngu* script for the Vietnamese language.

Hoi An was almost completely destroyed during the Tay Son Rebellion in the 1770s and '80s. It was rebuilt and continued to serve as an important port for foreign trade until the late 19th century, when the Thu Bon River (Cai River), which links Hoi An with the sea, silted up and became too shallow for navigation. During this period Danang (Tourane) began to eclipse Hoi An

## Architecture of Hoi An

A number of Hoi An's wooden buildings date from the early 19th century or before that. Imaginative visitors feel that they have been transported back a couple of centuries to a time when the wharf was crowded with sailing ships, the streets teemed with porters transporting goods to and from warehouses, and traders from a dozen countries haggled in a babble of different languages.

Because Hoi An was relatively untouched by the American War, it serves as a museum piece of Vietnamese history. At the time of writing, over 800 structures of historical significance have been officially identified in Hoi An. These structures can be categorised into nine types:

- houses and shops
- wells
- family chapels for ancestor worship
- pagodas
- Vietnamese and Chinese temples
- bridges
- communal buildings
- assembly halls of various Chinese congregations
- tombs (Vietnamese, Chinese and Japanese; no original European tombs survive)

Many of Hoi An's older structures exhibit features of traditional architecture rarely seen today. As they have for centuries, some shopfronts (which are open during the day to display their wares) are shuttered at night by the shopkeepers inserting horizontal planks into grooves that cut into the columns, which support the roof. Some of the buildings' roofs are made up of thousands of brick-coloured Yin-Yang (am-duong) roof tiles – so called because of the way the alternating rows of concave and convex tiles fit snugly together. During the rainy season, the lichens and moss that live on the tiles spring to life, turning entire rooftops bright green.

A number of Hoi An's houses have round pieces of wood with an am and duong symbol in the middle surrounded by a spiral design over the doorway. These 'watchful eyes' (mat cua) are supposed to protect the residents of the house from coming to any harm.

Hoi An's historic structures are gradually being restored and there is a sincere effort being made to preserve the unique character of the city. The local government has put some thought into this: old houses must be licensed for restoration work, which must be done in a tasteful manner.

Many of the house owners also charge for the invasion of their privacy – as much as US$3 for a guided tour of the building – but this is negotiable. The government permits this on the basis that the funds will be used for renovation of the homes.

Assistance in historical preservation is being provided to local authorities by the Archaeological Institute in Hanoi, the Japan-Vietnam Friendship Association, and experts from Europe and Japan.

as a port and centre of commerce. In 1916 a rail line linking Danang with Hoi An was destroyed by a terrible storm; it was never rebuilt.

During French colonisation Hoi An served as an administrative centre. During the American War the city, luckily, remained almost completely undamaged.

Hoi An was the site of the first Chinese settlement in southern Vietnam. The town's Chinese congregational assembly halls (hoi quan) still play a special role among southern Vietnam's ethnic-Chinese, some of whom come to Hoi An from all over to participate in congregation-wide celebrations. Today, 1300 of Hoi An's population of 75,800 are ethnic Chinese. Relations between ethnic Vietnamese and ethnic Chinese in Hoi An are excellent, partly because the Chinese here have become assimilated to the point where they even speak Vietnamese among themselves.

## Information

**Money** Theree's a local branch of **Vietincombank** (Đ Hoang Dieu), which can exchange both cash and travellers cheques. Cash advances on credit cards are also given here. **Incombank** (Đ Le Loi) and **Hoi An Bank for Agriculture** (Đ Tran Phu) will also exchange cash.

**Post** The **post office** is located on the northwest corner of Đ Ngo Gia Tu and Đ Tran Hung Dao.

**Email & Internet Access** You will fall over **Internet cafés** on every street in Hoi An. Most charge around 300d per minute, with a minimum 10-minute charge.

**Travel Agencies** Check out the strip of agencies opposite the Hoi An Hotel on Đ Tran Hung Dao. It's difficult to recommend one over the other; typically most of them offer the same services (including tours to My Son, bus and plane ticketing, and visa extensions) for the same costs. Competition around here is pretty fierce, so if you want to book something expensive or complicated, it's probably worth checking out a few options and negotiating.

**Medical Services** The **hospital** (10 Đ Tran Hung Dao) is opposite the post office.

## Phac Hat Pagoda

This newish pagoda (map item 32) has a colourful facade of ceramics and murals and is an active place of worship.

## Truong Family Chapel

The Truong Family Chapel (Nha Tho Toc Truong; map item 50), founded about two centuries ago, is a shrine dedicated to the ancestors of the ethnic-Chinese Truong family. A number of the memorial plaques were presented by emperors of Vietnam to honour members of the Truong family, who served as local officials and also as mandarins at the imperial court. To get

there, turn into the alley next to 69 Đ Phan Chu Trinh.

## Tran Family Chapel

The Tran Family Chapel (map item 26; 21 Đ Le Loi) is at the northeast corner of Đ Phan Chu Trinh at the intersection of Đ Le Loi. This house for worshipping ancestors was built about 200 years ago with donations from family members. The Tran family moved from China to Vietnam around 1700. The architecture of the building reflects the influence of Chinese and Japanese styles. The wooden boxes on the altar contain the Tran ancestors' stone tablets, and feature chiselled Chinese characters.

## Museum of Trading Ceramics

Showcasing a collection of blue and white ceramics of the Dai Viet period, this simply restored house (map item 53) is delightful. In particular, notice the great ceramic mosaic that's set above the pond in the inner courtyard.

## House at 77 Đ Tran Phu

This private house (map item 72) is about three centuries old. There is some especially fine carving on the wooden walls of the rooms around the courtyard, on the roof beams and under the crab-shell roof (in the salon next to the courtyard). Note the green ceramic tiles built into the railing around the courtyard balcony. The house is open to visitors for a small fee.

## Chinese All-Community Assembly Hall

The Chinese All-Community Assembly Hall (Chua Ba; map item 54) was founded here in 1773 and was used by all of the five different Chinese congregations in Hoi An: Fujian, Cantonese, Hainan, Chaozhou and Hakka. The pavilions off the main courtyard incorporate elements of 19th-century French architecture.

The main entrance to the assembly hall is located on Đ Tran Phu, opposite Đ Hoang Van Thu. However the only way to get inside these days is to enter from around the back at 31 Đ Phan Chu Trinh.

## Assembly Hall of the Fujian Chinese Congregation

This assembly hall *(map item 55; opposite 35 Đ Tran Phu; open 7.30am-noon & 2pm-5.30pm daily)* was founded as a place to hold community meetings. Later, it was transformed into a temple for the worship of Thien Hau, the deity who was born in Fujian province. The triple gate to the complex was built in 1975.

The mural near the entrance to the main hall, on the right-hand wall, depicts Thien Hau, her way lit by lantern light, crossing a stormy sea to rescue a foundering ship. On the wall opposite is a mural of the heads of the six Fujian families, who fled from China to Hoi An in the 17th century, following the overthrow of the Ming dynasty.

The second-to-last chamber contains a statue of Thien Hau. To either side of the entrance stand red-skinned Thuan Phong Nhi and green-skinned Thien Ly Nhan. When either sees or hears sailors in distress, they inform Thien Hau, who sets off to effect a rescue. The replica of a Chinese boat along the right-hand wall is in 1:20 scale. The four sets of triple beams that support the roof are typically Japanese.

The central altar in the last chamber contains seated figures of the heads of the six Fujian families. The smaller figures below them represent their successors as clan leaders. In a 30cm-high glass dome is a figurine of Le Huu Trac, a Vietnamese physician renowned in both Vietnam and China for his curative abilities.

Behind the altar on the left is the God of Prosperity. On the right are three fairies and smaller figures representing the 12 'midwives' *(ba mu)*, each of whom teaches newborns a different skill necessary for the first year of life: smiling, sucking, lying on their stomachs and so forth. Childless couples often come here to pray for offspring. The three groups of figures in this chamber represent the elements most central to life: ancestors, children and financial wellbeing.

The middle altar of the room to the right of the courtyard commemorates deceased leaders of the Fujian congregation. On either side are lists of contributors – women on the left and men on the right. The wall panels represent the four seasons.

The Fujian assembly hall is fairly well-lit and can be visited after dark. Shoes should be removed upon mounting the platform just past the naves.

## Quan Cong Temple

Founded in 1653, Quan Cong Temple *(Chua Ong; map item 57; 24 Đ Tran Phu)* is a Chinese temple that is dedicated to Quan Cong, whose partially gilt statue, made of papier-mache on a wooden frame, is in the central altar at the back of the sanctuary. On the left is a statue of General Chau Xuong, one of Quan Cong's guardians, striking a tough-guy pose. On the right is the rather plump administrative mandarin Quan Binh. The life-size white horse recalls a mount ridden by Quan Cong, until he was given a red horse of extraordinary endurance, representations of which are common in Chinese pagodas.

Stone plaques on the walls list contributors to the construction and repair of the temple. Check out the carp-shaped rain spouts on the roof surrounding the courtyard. The carp is a symbol of patience in Chinese mythology and is popular in Hoi An.

Shoes should be removed when mounting the platform in front of the statue of Quan Cong. Note that according to the old numbering system, the address is 168 Đ Tran Phu.

## Quan Am Pagoda & History Museum

This comparatively austere building *(map item 58)* houses a small collection of bronze temple bells, gongs and cannon. There's also a display of Cham artefacts.

## Assembly Hall of the Hainan Chinese Congregation

This assembly hall *(map item 60; Đ Tran Phu)* was built in 1883 as a memorial to the 108 merchants from Hainan Island, who were mistaken for pirates and killed in Quang Nam province during the reign of Emperor Tu Duc. The elaborate dais contains plaques in their memory. In front of the central altar is a fine gilded woodcarving of Chinese court life.

The Hainan congregation hall is at the east end of Đ Tran Phu, near the corner of Đ Hoang Dieu.

## Assembly Hall of the Chaozhou Chinese Congregation

The Chaozhou Chinese in Hoi An built their congregational hall *(map item 63; opposite 157 Đ Nguyen Duy Hieu)* in 1776. Some outstanding woodcarvings are on the beams, walls and altar. On the doors in front of the altar are carvings of two Chinese girls wearing their hair in a Japanese style.

The assembly hall is near the corner of Đ Hoang Dieu.

## Tran Duong House

There is a whole city block of colonnaded French-colonial buildings on Đ Phan Boi Chau, between Nos 22 and 73, among them the 19th-century home of Mr Tran Duong *(map item 65; 25 Đ Phan Boi Chau)*. Mr Duong, a friendly retired mathematics teacher, speaks English and French, and is happy to explain the history of its 62m-long house and its contents to visitors. There is no entrance fee, but contributions are welcomed by the owner.

## Old House at 103 Tran Phu

The wooden frontage and shutters make a good photographic backdrop to this eclectic shop *(map item 74)*, where women make silk lanterns, ornamental aquarium fish are for sale and you can buy shampoo.

## Assembly Hall of the Cantonese Chinese Congregation

Founded in 1786, this assembly hall *(map item 46; 176 Đ Tran Phu; open 6am-7.30am & 1pm-5.30pm daily)* has a main altar that is dedicated to Quan Cong. Note the long-handled brass 'fans' to either side of the altar. The lintel and door posts of the main entrance and a number of the columns supporting the roof are made of single blocks of granite. The other columns were carved out of the durable wood of the jackfruit tree. There are some interesting carvings on the

wooden beams that support the roof in front of the main entrance.

## Museum of Sa Huynh Culture

Artefacts from the early Dong Son civilisation of Sa Hunynh are displayed at this museum *(map item 44)*. The building itself is not as interesting as many others but you should go visit the museum for the collection of objects it houses, rather than for its setting.

## Japanese Covered Bridge

This famed bridge *(Cau Nhat Ban or Lai Vien Kieu; map item 43)* connects 155 Đ Tran Phu with 1 Đ Nguyen Thi Minh Khai. The first bridge on this site was constructed in 1593. It was built by the Japanese community of Hoi An in order to link them with the Chinese quarters across the stream. The bridge was constructed with a roof so that it could be used as a shelter from both the rain and sun.

The Japanese Covered Bridge is very solidly constructed; apparently the original builders were concerned about the threat of earthquakes. Over the centuries, the ornamentation of the bridge has remained relatively faithful to the original Japanese design. Its understatement contrasts greatly with the Vietnamese and Chinese penchant for wild decoration. The French flattened out the roadway to make it more suitable for their motor vehicles, but the original arched shape was restored during major renovation work carried out in 1986.

Built into the northern side of the bridge is a small **temple**, Chua Cau. The writing over the door of the temple is the name given to the bridge in 1719 to replace the name meaning Japanese Covered Bridge. However the new name, Lai Vien Kieu (Bridge for Passers-By from Afar), never quite caught on.

According to legend, there once lived an enormous monster called Cu, who had its head in India, its tail in Japan and its body in Vietnam. Whenever the monster moved, terrible disasters such as floods and earthquakes befell Vietnam. This bridge was built on the monster's weakest point and killed it, but the people of Hoi An took pity on the slain monster and built this temple to pray for its soul.

The entrances of the bridge are guarded by a pair of monkeys on one side and a pair of dogs on the other. According to one story, these animals were popularly revered because many of Japan's emperors were born in years of the dog and monkey. Another tale relates that construction of the bridge started in the year of the monkey and didn't finish until the year of the dog.

The stelae, listing all the Vietnamese and Chinese contributors to a subsequent restoration of the bridge, are written in Chinese characters *(chu nho)* – the *nom* script had not yet become popular in these parts.

### Phung Hung Old House

In a lane full of beautiful buildings, this old house *(map item 42)* stands out. At present it houses a bookshop and showcases designer ceramics; wander through and enjoy the ambience.

### Cam Pho Temple

This less-ornate, newish building *(map item 40)* is not often open, and is notable mainly for its ceramic dragon roof-line.

### Caodai Pagoda

Serving Hoi An's Caodai community, many of whom live along the path out to the Japanese tombs, is the small Caodai Pagoda *(map item 9)*, between Nos 64 and 70 Đ Huynh Thuc Khang (near the bus station). Only one priest, who grows sugar and corn in the front yard to make some extra cash, lives here. It was built in 1952.

### Tan Ky House

Built two centuries ago as the home of a well-to-do ethnic-Vietnamese merchant, the Tan Ky House *(map item 79; ☎ 861474; 101 Đ Nguyen Thai Hoc; open 8am-noon and 2pm-4.30pm daily)* has been lovingly preserved and today looks almost exactly as it did in the early 19th century.

The design of Tan Ky House shows some evidence of the Japanese and Chinese influence on local architecture. Japanese elements

include the ceiling (in the area immediately before the courtyard), which is supported by three progressively shorter beams one on top of the other. There are similar beams in the salon. Under the crab-shell ceiling there are carvings of crossed sabres wrapped in silk ribbon. The sabres symbolise force; the silk represents flexibility.

Chinese poems written in inlaid mother-of-pearl are hung from a number of the columns that hold up the roof. The Chinese characters on these 150-year-old panels are formed entirely of birds gracefully portrayed in various positions of flight.

The courtyard here has four functions: to let in light; to provide ventilation; to bring a glimpse of nature into the home; and to collect rainwater and provide drainage. The stone tiles covering the patio floor were brought from Thanh Hoa province in north-central Vietnam. The carved, wooden balcony supports around the courtyard are decorated with grape leaves, which are a European import and further evidence of the unique mingling of cultures that took place in Hoi An.

The back of the house faces the river. In the past, this section of the building was rented out to foreign merchants. That the house was a place of commerce, as well as a residence, is indicated by the two pulleys attached to a beam in the storage loft just inside the front door.

The exterior of the roof is made of tiles; inside, the ceiling consists of wood. This design keeps the house cool in summer and warm in winter. The floor tiles were brought from near Hanoi.

Tan Ky House is a private home, but is one of the choices on your Hoi An entrance ticket. The owner, whose family has lived here for seven generations, speaks fluent French and English.

### Diep Dong Nguyen House

This house *(map item 75; 58 Đ Nguyen Thai Hoc; open 8am-noon & 2pm-4.30pm daily)* was built for a Chinese merchant, an ancestor of the current inhabitants of the house, in the late 19th century. The front room on the ground floor was once a dispensary for Chinese medicine *(thuoc bac)*; the medicines were stored in the glass-enclosed cases lining the walls. The owner's private collection of antiques, which includes photographs, porcelain and furniture, is on display upstairs. The objects are not for sale! Two of the chairs were once lent by the family to Emperor Bao Dai.

The house is at 58 Đ Nguyen Thai Hoc, by the old numbering system.

## Other Sites of Significance

**Hoi An Church** The only tombs of Europeans in Hoi An are found in the yard of this church *(cnr Đ Nguyen Truong To & Đ Le Hong Phong)*. This modern building was built to replace an earlier structure at another site. Several 18th-century missionaries were exhumed from tombs at the original site and reburied here.

**Chuc Thanh Pagoda** Founded in 1454 by Minh Hai, a Buddhist monk from China, Chuc Thanh Pagoda is the oldest pagoda in Hoi An. Among the antique ritual objects still in use are several bells, a stone gong two centuries old and a carp-shaped wooden gong said to be even older. Today, several elderly monks live here.

In the main sanctuary, the gilt Chinese characters inscribed on a red roof beam give details of the pagoda's construction. An A Di Da Buddha flanked by two Thich Ca Buddhas sits under a wooden canopy on the central dais. In front of them is a statue of a boyhood Thich Ca flanked by his servants.

To get to Chuc Thanh Pagoda, go all the way to the end of Đ Nguyen Truong To and turn left. Follow the sandy path for 500m.

**Phuoc Lam Pagoda** This pagoda was founded in the mid-17th century. The head monk at the end of that century was An Thiem, a Vietnamese prodigy who had become a monk at the age of eight. When he was 18, the king drafted An Thiem's brothers into his army to put down a rebellion. An Thiem volunteered to take the places of the other men in his family and eventually rose to the rank of general. After the war, he returned to the monkhood, but felt guilty

about the many people he had slain. To atone for his sins, he volunteered to clean the Hoi An Market for 20 years. When that time was up, he was asked to come to Phuoc Lam Pagoda as head monk.

To reach Phuoc Lam Pagoda, continue past Chuc Thanh Pagoda for 350m. The path passes an obelisk that was erected over the tomb of 13 ethnic Chinese, who had been decapitated by the Japanese during WWII for resistance activities.

**Japanese Tombs** The tombstone of the Japanese merchant Yajirobei, who died in 1647, is clearly inscribed with Japanese characters. The stele, which faces northeast towards Japan, is held in place by the tomb's original covering, made from an especially hard kind of cement, the ingredients of which include powdered seashells, the leaves of the boi loi tree (which are used to make incense) and cane sugar. Yajirobei may have been a Christian who came to Vietnam to escape persecution in his native land.

To get to Yajirobei's tomb, head north to the end of Đ Nguyen Truong To and follow the sand path around to the left (west) for 40m, until you get to a fork. The path that continues straight on leads to Chuc Thanh Pagoda, but you should turn right (north). Keep going for just over 1km, turning left (north) at the first fork and left (northwest) at the second fork. When you arrive at open fields, keep going until you cross the irrigation channel. Just on the other side of the channel turn right (southeast) onto a raised path. After 150m, turn left (northeast) into the paddies and walk another 100m. The tomb, which is on a platform bounded by a low stone wall, stands surrounded by rice paddies.

The tombstone of a Japanese named Masai, who died in 1629, is a few hundred metres back towards Hoi An. To get there, turn left (southeast) at a point about 100m towards town from the edge of the rice fields. The tombstone is on the right-hand side of the trail about 30m from the main path.

For help in finding the Japanese tombs, show the locals the words *ma nhat* or *mo nhat*, which mean 'Japanese tombs'.

## Culture & Heritage Trail

Follow this trail to see Hoi An's main sights in a half-day walk. All the sights are described in detail in the main text, and the dotted line on the map shows the route.

The trail starts at **Phac Hat Pagoda**. Heading east along Ð Phan Chu Trinh, turn right into the alley next to street number 69. Here you'll find the **Truong Family Chapel**. Back on the main road, look out for the **Tran Family Chapel** at the northeast corner of Ð Phan Chu Trinh. Head south now on Ð Le Loi and turn left at the next junction onto Ð Tran Phu. Visit the **Museum of Trading Ceramics**. Opposite the museum is the **House at 77 Tran Phu**. Continuing along Ð Tran Phu there is a cluster of interesting buildings on the left side of the road, including the **Chinese All-Community Assembly Hall**. Next door is the **Assembly Hall of the Fujian Chinese Congregation**. Back on the road, keep heading east and at the next junction you'll see the **Quan Cong Temple**. Take a short detour north on Ð Nguyen Hué to the **Quan Am Pagoda & History Museum**. Back on Ð Tran Phu, still walking east, the **Assembly Hall of the Hainan Chinese Congregation**, is on your left. Cross the next junction and the road becomes Ð Nguyen Duy Hieu. On your left is the **Assembly Hall of the Chaozhou Chinese Congregation**.

Take the next right and turn right again onto Ð Phan Boi Chau. There is a whole city block of colonnaded French buildings here between Nos 22 and 73, among them the 19th-century **Tran Duong House**. Wander along Ð Phan Boi Chau, take the fourth street on your right, turn left into Ð Nguyen Thai Hoc and enjoy the ambience of this street. Turn right onto Ð Le Loi then left onto Ð Tran Phu. Almost immediately on your left is the **Old House at 103 Tran Phu**. Keep heading west now, and you'll pass the **Assembly Hall of the Cantonese Chinese Congregation**. A little further along on the left is the **Museum of Sa Huynh Culture**. Beyond the museum is the famed **Japanese Covered Bridge**, connecting Ð Tran Phu with Ð Nguyen Thi Minh Khai. Continue along Ð Nguyen Thi Minh Khai and notice **Phung Hung Old House**. Pause at **Cam Pho Temple**.

From here you can either retrace your steps, or continue on to the **Caodai Pagoda**. Then, back across the Japanese bridge, turn right and follow the road onto Ð Nguyen Thai Hoc, where you'll see the **Tan Ky House** at No 101. On the left before the next junction is the **Diep Dong Nguyen House**.

There are more Japanese tombs in Duy Xuyen district, across the delta of the Thu Bon River.

## Places to Stay

Tiny Hoi An gets packed in the peak travel seasons – August to October and December to February. Unlike much of the rest of Vietnam, where the overbuilding of hotels has caused mass vacancies and cheaper prices, Hoi An is the one spot that still faces shortages. During the high season, hundreds of Hoi An visitors typically have to head up to Danang just to find a room. New hotels are springing up around town, but if you have your heart set on a particular hotel, you should probably book ahead.

Most travellers want to find a room right in the town centre, so not surprisingly these fill up quickly. Yet the quieter and more spacious hotels tend to be on the outskirts of town. Considering how small Hoi An is, and how easily you can walk around, there should be no great compulsion to find a place in the bustling heart of town.

Rates listed here are 'standard' rates; expect most of these to skyrocket during the busy months, especially November to January. Alternatively – it's unusual, but it does happen – if you walk in without a booking, when a hotel's not full, you may well be offered a discount.

Near to and in the town centre there is a range of accommodation options.

**Thanh Binh 1 Hotel** (☎ 861740, fax 864192; e vothihong@dng.vnn.vn; 1 Ð Le Loi; twins with fan US$8, with air-con US$12-20) is a family-run hotel close to the town centre and rooms are a good size; try to get one that looks over the small park beside the hotel.

**Thien Nga Hotel** (☎ 916330; Đ Nhi Trung; air-con rooms US$10) is a small, bright hotel a few minutes' walk from the centre that looks over rice fields, from the balcony at the back.

**Phu Tinh Hotel** (☎ 861297, fax 861757; 144 Đ Tran Phu; rooms with bath US$8-15) is a bit tatty but it's central and has a pleasant garden forecourt.

**Hoai Thanh Hotel** (☎ 861242, fax 861135; 23 Đ Le Hong Phong; rooms with fan/air-con from US$8/10, with satellite TV US$28/35), on the northern outskirts of town, is a huge, state-run place. The budget rooms in the old section are tatty, but clean and quiet.

**Huy Hoang 1** (☎ 861453, fax 863722; 73 Đ Phan Boi Chau; rooms with fan US$10-15, with air-con US$15-20, river-view rooms US$30) is a pleasant place by Cam Nam Bridge. Breakfast on the balcony, which overlooks the river, is included.

**Thien Trung Hotel** (☎ 861720, fax 863799; e thientrungha@dng.vnn.vn; 63 Đ Phan Dinh Phung; rooms US$10-15) is an older, motel-style place. The rooms and bathrooms are good, though it's on the main road and a bit noisy. If you're travelling by car or motor-bike, it has ample parking.

**Thuy Duong Hotel I** (☎ 861574; e thuy duongco@dng.vnn.vn; 11 Đ Le Loi; rooms from US$10-18) has fairly tatty rooms and a busy Internet area.

**Binh Minh Hotel** (☎ 861943; e binhminh hotel@dng.vnn.vn; 12 Đ Thai Phien; twins with fan US$8-10) has parking, if you have your own transport; otherwise it's fairly ordinary but fine if other hotels are full.

**Vinh Hung 1 Hotel** (☎ 861621, fax 861893; e vinhhung.ha@dng.vnn.vn; 143 Đ Tran Phu; downstairs/upstairs rooms US$15/ 20, deluxe rooms US$30-45) is an atmospheric hotel that's housed in a classic Chinese trading house. For a little more you can stay in one of two rooms used by Michael Caine when filming The Quiet American; each is deco-rated with antiques and a beautiful canopy bed. Unless you're a heavy sleeper, try to avoid the one directly above reception. Rates include breakfast.

**Vinh Hung 2 Hotel** (☎ 863717, fax 864094; e quanghuy.ha@dng.vnn.vn; Đ Nhi Trung;

fan rooms US$15, air-con rooms US$20-35) is an attractive, larger, new hotel featuring a swimming pool in the central courtyard.

**Vinh Hung 3** (☎ 863717) was opening the day we visited. It's near Vinh Hung 2, of a similar standard, and also has a great roof-top pool.

**Cong Doan Hotel** (Trade Union Hotel; ☎ 826370, fax 861899; e hatradeunion@dng .vnn.vn; 50 Đ Phan Dinh Phung) was being renovated when we visited and was close to reopening. It's near Vinh Hung 2.

**Thanh Binh 2 Hotel** (☎ 863715, fax 864192; e vothihong@dng.vnn.vn; Đ Nhi Trung; rooms US$15-30) is a new place that's larger and smarter than Thanh Binh 1; rates in-clude breakfast.

**Hoi An Hotel** (☎ 861373, fax 861636; 6 Đ Tran Hung Dao; rooms US$45-100) is in a grand, modern, colonial-style building and is government-owned. It is one of the largest hotels in Vietnam. Room rates range widely and there's a good-sized swimming pool. Many tour groups stay here.

On the eastern edge of town, on the way to Cua Dai Beach, there's a gaggle of decent mid-range hotels. A small cluster of restaur-ants, Internet cafés and travel agencies has sprung up nearby. From the following hotels, it's a 10-minute stroll to the Old Town.

**Sao Bien Hotel** (Sea Star Hotel; ☎ 861589, fax 861382; 15 Đ Cua Dai; twins US$8-15) is tatty but fine for the price. The budget rooms at the top have fine views over Hoi An's red-brick roofs.

**Green Field Hotel** (Dong Xanh Hotel; ☎ 863484; e greenfield@dng.vnn.vn; air-con rooms US$10-25) is the furthest away from town. Rooms are fine; a new annexe and pool were about to open.

**Cua Dai Hotel** (☎ 862231, fax 862232; e cuadaihotel@dng.vnn.vn; 18 Đ Cua Dai; singles/twins US$20/25) is an elegant place. It's an attractive option as it's semirural, yet still walking distance to the town centre. There are comfy rattan chairs doted around and a good balcony. Rooms are air-con with satellite TV, and rates include breakfast. Book ahead if you can.

**Hotel Hai Yen** (☎ 862445, fax 862443; e kshaiyen@dng.vnn.vn; 22A Đ Cua Dai;

rooms US$25, suites US$50), near Cua Dai, is a friendly place. The standard rooms are equipped with air-con, satellite TV and bath tubs, and there's a pleasant quiet garden.

There is also a cluster of decent hotels near the bus station, about 10 minutes' walk from town.

**Thuy Duong Hotel II** (☎ 861394, fax 86 1330; 68 Đ Huynh Thuc Khang; fan rooms from US$7, air-con rooms US$15), right between the bus station and a small Caodai pagoda, is a pleasant-enough cheapie. Ask for one of the rooms overlooking the pagoda gardens.

**Huy Hoang 2 Hotel** (☎ 916234; e kshuy hoang@dng.vnn.vn; 87 Đ Huynh Thuc Khang; rooms from US$10) is good value with big clean rooms with satellite TV and a garden restaurant. It's opposite the bus station, about 10 minutes' walk from the Old Town.

Towards and on Cua Dai Beach are some splendid (and splendidly expensive) resorts.

**Hoi An Riverside Resort** (☎ 864800; e hoianriver@dng.vnn.vn; Đ Cua Dai; rooms from US$109) is an elegant hotel in a fabulous rural setting, overlooking the river and rice fields. It's only a couple of kilometres from the beach and there's a huge pool. Discounted rates are often available.

**Victoria Hoi An Resort** (☎ 04-933 0318; Cua Dai Beach; e victoria@fpt.vn; rooms from US$120++), at Cua Dai Beach itself, about 5km east of town, has a fabulous private-beach frontage and all the stylish facilities you'd expect for the price. The rooms are gorgeous, and you may get a 30% discount if there are available rooms. For US$10++ you can have day-use of the facilities.

**Hoi An Beach Resort** (☎ 927011; e hoian beachresort@dng.vnn.vn; Cua Dai Beach; rooms from US$80) has fantastic big, airy rooms that have balconies, but avoid those on the noisy beachfront road. There are two swimming pools here.

## Places to Eat

Hoi An's contribution to Vietnamese cuisine is cao lau, which are doughy flat noodles mixed with croutons, bean sprouts and greens and topped off with pork slices. It is mixed with crumbled, crispy rice paper immediately before eating. You'll see cao lau listed on menus all over Hoi An, which is the only place genuine cao lau can be made because the water used in its preparation must come from the Ba Le Well. (The well itself, which is said to date from Cham times, is square in shape. To get there, turn down the alley opposite 35 Đ Phan Chu Trinh and hang a right before reaching number 45/17. You might need to ask someone for directions.)

Other Hoi An specialities are fried won ton and the delicate 'white rose' (steamed shrimp wrapped in rice paper). You can find these in most local eateries.

There are heaps of restaurants on Đ Nguyen Hué, Đ Tran Phu and, on the waterfront, along Đ Bach Dang where you can enjoy a leisurely meal or linger over drinks. Many types of cuisine are available, including Western (eg, banana pancakes, pasta, pizza), Vietnamese, Chinese and vegetarian. Unless otherwise stated, you can expect to get a filling plate of food for around 15,000d. Around 50,000d will buy a good three-course set menu in many of the restaurants.

**Miss Ly Cafeteria 22** (☎ 861603; 22 Đ Nguyen Hué; open from 6.30am), a true Hoi An institution, has some of the best won tons and white roses in town. The restaurant closes when empty (and that's usually late) and is nearly always crowded.

**Mermaid Restaurant** (☎ 861527; 2 Đ Tran Phu) serves good food all day and sensational, three-course set menus during the evening.

**Brother's Cafe Hoi An** (☎ 914150; 27 Phan Boi Chau; set lunch US$6; open 10am-10pm) is within a complex of restored French-colonial buildings and a garden that runs down to the river, at the eastern end of town. It's a gorgeous setting and the attention to designer detail is perfect; you can just drop by for coffee or a drink.

**Cafe des Amis** (☎ 861616; 52 Đ Bach Dang; 4-course vegetarian menus 50,000d, seafood menus 60,000d; open from 5pm) continues to get good reviews for its 'surprise' dinners – the set menu is whatever the chef, Kim, feels like cooking that day.

**Hoi An Hai San** (☎ 861652; D64 Đ Bach Dang; main meals around 50,000d; open from breakfast) is a seafood restaurant serving innovative Vietnamese and international meals.

Heading west beyond the previous two restaurants, the Đ Bach Dang riverfront is a virtual eating arcade. Cruise the next few hundred metres and check out the line of waterfront **seafood restaurants** and their daily specials.

**Han Huyen Restaurant** (Floating Restaurant; ☎ 861462; meals from 30,000d; open from breakfast) is moored on the banks of the river. It's in a great setting and has OK food.

Chinese-style places include the **Thanh Thanh 1 Restaurant** and **Tu Do Restaurant**, both on Đ Tran Phu, and the **Thanh Binh Restaurant** (Đ Le Loi).

Some other popular spots for traditional and good backpacker cuisine include **Cafe Bobo** and the excellent **Dudi Restaurant**, both on Đ Le Loi.

**Banana Split Cafe** (☎ 861136; 53 Đ Hoang Dieu), cloned direct from the beaches of Nha Trang, is where sweet-tooths can relieve any sudden cravings for ice cream, fresh fruit juices and, of course, banana splits.

**Omar Khayyam's Indian Restaurant** (☎ 910245; 14 Đ Phan Dinh Phung; veg/non-veg thalis 39,000d/49,000d) has good-value and filling, if unimaginative, curries.

On the fringe of the Hoi An Old Town, on the corners of D Nhi Trung and D Phan Dinh Phung, a gaggle of lively cafés and bars has sprung up. **Treat's Café 2**, a popular bar-café, has opened a second one here ('same same not different'), and **Jean's Cafe Restaurant** is popular with travellers.

## Entertainment

**Tam Tam Cafe & Bar** (☎ 862212, fax 862207; e tamtam.ha@dng.vnn.vn; 110 Đ Nguyen Thai Hoc) is located upstairs in a thoughtfully restored tea warehouse. Started by an expat, this most unexpected retreat has a good menu of French and Italian food, a wide range of wine, salads, an airy billiard table and bar area, a balcony for summer dining and a collection of over 400 CDs. The Aussie steaks (90,000d upwards)

washed down with a frosty draught beer are popular. There is also a simple bar menu for light bites, and coffee and cake on offer.

**Treat's 1 Café** (☎ 861125; 158 Đ Tran Phu) is another watering hole that gets good reports. It is a spacious place with a pleasant restaurant-café on the 2nd storey. The congenial young owner Treat is known for his generous happy hour. **Treat's 2 Café** is near the corner of Đ Phan Dinh Phung and Đ Nhi Trung and is the same style.

**Hai's Scout Cafe** (☎ 863210; 98 Đ Nguyen Thai Hoc; sandwiches around 30,000d; open all day) is a dimly lit local café with a pleasant courtyard. It serves sandwiches, light meals, real cappuccinos and lattes, and cocktails. You can enter the café on Đ Nguyen Thai Hoc or Đ Tran Phu.

**Tam Long Quan Cafe** (☎ 862113; 48/10 Đ Tran Cao Van) is an interesting little Chinese-style coffee shop that is worth seeking out. It is tucked into a narrow alley near the Vinh Hung 2 Hotel. It is run by Mr Ngo Thi Hai, a local kung-fu master, who has decorated the place with various weapons and an impressive collection of hand-carved wooden sculptures.

## Cooking Classes

Several cafés offer an early evening cooking class, where over a couple of hours you learn informally how to make two or three dishes and then – of course! – sit down to enjoy them. At present, **Hai's Scout Cafe** (☎ 863210) offers classes most evenings, and **Mermaid Restaurant** also does, when the owner isn't too busy in the restaurant. A small group class costs about US$5 per person; ask around town when you arrive, as other places plan to follow suit.

## Shopping

Hoi An is a shoppers' haven, and though the air of commercialism has increasingly taken a toll on the mellowed charm of the town, it is nowhere near as overwhelming as many other tourist centres in Vietnam.

Hoi An is known for its production of **cotton cloth**. All over the city there are cotton mills with rows of fantastic wooden looms that make a rhythmic 'clackety-clack, clackety-clack' sound as a whirring, cycloidal drive wheel shoots the shuttle back and forth under the watchful eyes of the machine attendant. The elegant technology used in building these domestically produced machines dates from the Industrial Revolution. This is probably what mills in Victorian England must have looked like.

Tailor-made clothing is one of Hoi An's specialities and in the space of just a few years the number of tailor shops has grown from a handful to over 200! (See the boxed text 'Sewing up a Storm'.) Recommending one tailor over another is a difficult proposition, and with so many tailors competing for limited tourist dollars, touts are out in full force (most of them cute young girls who use the 'What's your name? Where are you from? Would you like to come and see my auntie's shop?' approach). In fact, the tailors are all rather similar, and most of them should be fine, whether you're looking for alterations or a whole new wardrobe. They're very good at copying, so take any favourite clothes you want replicated. Leave yourself time for adjustments to be made, and for a final fitting. For a look at the various materials available locally, take a peek at the **Hoi An Cloth Market** on Đ Tran Phu.

The presence of numerous tourists has turned the fake antique business into a major growth industry for Hoi An. Theoretically you could find something here that is really old, but it's hard to believe that all the genuine stuff wasn't scooped up long ago.

On the other hand, there is some really elegant artwork around, even if it was made only yesterday. Paintings are generally the

## Sewing Up a Storm

From dawn until dusk, the whirring of sewing machines resounds through historic Hoi An. The town itself is a virtual treasure trove with fabric of every type to be found all over – in some places stacked to the ceilings of the various cloth shops.

Spending a morning being pampered in any of the dressmakers' shops in and around the market is a great experience. Choose your new wardrobe from endless rolls of material and, for a little over the cost of the cloth, you'll soon have tailor-made shirts, trousers, dresses and skirts.

A completely new wardrobe, including material, can cost as little as US$100: an evening dress starts at around US$15, a summer dress at US$8 and a suit at US$20.

Incredibly, the master tailors here can whip together anything from slinky silk pyjamas to a formal Japanese kimono, and are even able to copy designs straight out of fashion magazines – anything from a copy of a designer ball gown to a top city-slicker suit in less than a couple of hours. Whether silk, cotton, linen or synthetic, people rave about the clothes they had made in Hoi An.

When buying silk it is important to ascertain that the material is real silk and not 'Vietnamese silk' – a term often used to describe polyester and other synthetic fabrics that look and feel like silk. The only real test is with a cigarette or match (synthetic fibres melt and silk burns), but be careful not to set the shop on fire! Ask for a cut-off sample of the material you are thinking of buying and go outside to test it if you're concerned about its authenticity.

It is also important to check the seams of the finished garment, a single set of stitching along the inside edges will soon cause fraying and, in many cases, great big gaping holes. All well-tailored garments have a second set of stitches (known in the trade as blanket stitching), which binds the edge, oversewing the fabric so fraying is impossible. Ask the person tailoring the outfit to use the same colour cotton as the material – otherwise they will use white cotton throughout. Where possible, also insist on the clothes being lined, as it helps them move and fall in the right direction.

A few hours after your initial consultation, when you will be measured from every angle, you can return for your final fitting session and adjustments. Your only concern will be whether to carry your new gear around or make a dash to the post office to send it home.

**Juliet Coombe**

mass-produced kind of stuff, but are still hand painted; for a few US dollars you can't complain. A row of **art galleries** inside the gorgeous old buildings on Đ Nguyen Thi Minh Khai, just across from the Japanese Covered Bridge, are great to browse through.

**Woodcarvings** are also a local speciality. Cross Cam Nam Bridge to **Cam Nam village**, a lovely spot where woodcarvings are made. Across the An Hoi footbridge is the An Hoi Peninsula, which is known for both its **boat** and **mat-weaving factories**.

There are lovely blue-and-white **ceramic goods** for sale at a strip of small shops along the Đ Bach Dang riverfront.

## Getting There & Away
**Bus** The main **Hoi An bus station** (*74 Đ Huynh Thuc Khang*) is 1km west of the centre of town. Buses from here go to Dai Loc (Ai Nghia), Danang, Quang Ngai, Que Son, Tam Ky and Tra My. More frequent services to Danang leave from the **northern bus station** on Đ Le Hong Phong. The cost is about 20,000d and services begin at 5am; the last Danang bus departs in the late afternoon.

**Minibus** Virtually every hotel in Hoi An can sell you a minibus ticket to either Nha Trang or Hué. The Hoi An–Hué minibus (US$4) goes through Danang (US$2) and you can be dropped off there if you like. Or you can get out at Nha Trang (US$8) or My Lai (US$6). Most minibuses leave from the cafés on the corner of Đ Phan Dinh Phung and Đ Nhi Trung at around 8am; there's often a mid-afternoon service too.

**Car & Motorbike** There are two land routes from Danang to Hoi An. The shorter way is via the Marble Mountains (11km), from where you continue south for another 19km. Alternatively, head south on National Hwy 1 and, at the signposted intersection 27km from the city, turn left and Hoi An is 10km to the east.

The going rate for a motorbike taxi between Danang and Hoi An is about 30,000d. A taxi will cost from US$8 to US$10.

**Boat** Small, motorised ferries leave Hoi An for nearby districts and Cham Island from the landing at the end of Đ Hoang Van Thu. There are daily boats to Cham Island (usually departing between 7am and 8am), weather-dependent, and foreigners need permits to make this trip on a public boat. There is also frequent service to Cam Kim Island.

## Getting Around
Anywhere within town can be reached on foot. To go further afield, rent a bicycle from 5000d per day, but spend about US$1 if you want a more comfortable bike. A motorbike will cost around US$5/10 per day without/with a driver. Hire places are located all over town.

**Boat** A paddle-boat trip on the Thu Bon River (Cai River) – the largest in Quang Nam province – is recommended. A simple rowing boat with someone to row it costs something like US$2 per hour, and one hour is probably long enough for most travellers. Some My Son tours offer the return trip to Hoi An by boat, which is a fun way to travel.

Boats that carry up to five people can also be hired to visit handicraft and fishing villages in the area; expect to pay around US$4 per hour. Look for the boats near the rowboat dock.

## AROUND HOI AN
### Cua Dai Beach
The fine sands of palm-lined Cua Dai Beach (Bai Tam Cua Dai) are popular at weekends, but can often be deserted at other times. Safe swimming is usually only possible between April and October, but it's nice to walk or just hang out here. During the full moon, people wander around until late at night. Fresh seafood and refreshments are sold at a line of kiosks that lead to the beachfront.

Cua Dai Beach is 5km east of Hoi An on Đ Cua Dai, which is the continuation of Đ Tran Hung Dao and Đ Phan Dinh Phung. The road passes shrimp-hatching pools built with Australian assistance.

For information about accommodation at Cua Dai Beach, see Places to Stay in the Hoi An section.

## Cam Kim Island

The master woodcarvers, who in previous centuries produced the fine carvings that graced the homes of Hoi An's merchants and the town's public buildings, came from Kim Bong Village on Cam Kim Island. These days, most of the woodcarvings on sale in Hoi An are produced here. Some of the villagers also build wooden boats.

To reach the island, catch one of the frequent boats that leave from the Đ Hoang Van Thu Dock.

## Cham Island

Also known as Culao Cham, Cham Island is 21km from Hoi An in the South China Sea. The island is famous as a source of swiftlet nests, which are exported to Hong Kong, Singapore and elsewhere for use in bird's-nest soup.

Permits are needed to visit Cham Island, and the weather determines when boats run there. Public boats leave at around 7am and the one-way journey takes three hours, but it's difficult for foreigners to organise the paperwork to travel on one of these. Some tours run to the island; ask for information at Son My Son Tour, among the agencies opposite the Hoi An Hotel.

## Thanh Ha

Sometimes called the 'pottery village', Thanh Ha is 3km west of Hoi An. In the recent past, there were many pottery factories here, but the pottery industry has been in decline. Still, some artisans are employed in this hot, sweaty work. The locals don't mind if you visit their factories to watch them at work, though they'd be happier if you bought something in exchange for showing you around. Many tours to My Son make a stop here on the way back to Hoi An.

## MY SON

One of the most stunning sights to see in the Hoi An area is My Son (admission 50,000d, open 6.30am-4.30pm daily), Vietnam's most important site of the ancient kingdom of Champa, and, as of 2000, a Unesco World Heritage site.

During the centuries when Tra Kieu (then known as Simhapura) served as the political capital of the kingdom of Champa, My Son was the site of the most important Cham intellectual and religious centre, and also may have served as a burial place for Cham monarchs. My Son is considered to be Champa's smaller counterpart to the grand cities of Southeast Asia's other Indian-influenced civilisations: Angkor (Cambodia); Bagan (Myanmar); Ayuthaya (Thailand); and Borobudur (Java).

The monuments are set in a verdant valley surrounded by hills and overlooked by the massive Cat's Tooth Mountain (Hon Quap). Clear streams run between the structures and past nearby coffee plantations.

## History

My Son became a religious centre under King Bhadravarman in the late 4th century and was occupied until the 13th century – the longest period of development of any monument in Southeast Asia (by comparison, Angkor's period of development lasted only three centuries, as did that of Bagan). Most of the temples were dedicated to Cham kings associated with divinities, especially Shiva, who was regarded as the founder and protector of Champa's dynasties.

Champa's contact with Java was extensive. Cham scholars were sent to Java to study and there was a great deal of commerce between the two empires – Cham pottery has been found on Java and, in the 12th century, the Cham king wed a Javanese woman.

Because some of the ornamentation work at My Son was never finished, archaeologists know that the Chams first built their structures and only then carved decorations into the brickwork. Researchers have yet to figure out for certain how the Chams managed to get the baked bricks to stick together. According to one theory, they used a paste prepared with a botanical oil that is indigenous to central Vietnam. During one period in their history, the summits of some of the towers were completely covered with a layer of gold.

During the American War, this region was completely devastated and depopulated in extended bitter fighting. Finding it to be a convenient staging ground, the VC used My Son as a base; in response the Americans bombed the monuments. Traces of 68 structures have been found, of which 25 survived repeated pillaging in previous centuries by the Chinese, Khmer and Vietnamese. The American bombings spared about 20 of these, some of which sustained extensive damage. These days, Vietnamese authorities

are attempting to restore as much as possible of the remaining sites.

## Information

The entry fee includes local transport from the parking area to the sites, about 2km away. By departing from Hoi An at about 5am, you will arrive to wake up the gods (and the guards) for the sunrise and could be leaving just as the tour groups reach the area! It gets very busy at My Son; if you can go early or late do so, and soak up the scenery and atmosphere in relative peace and quiet.

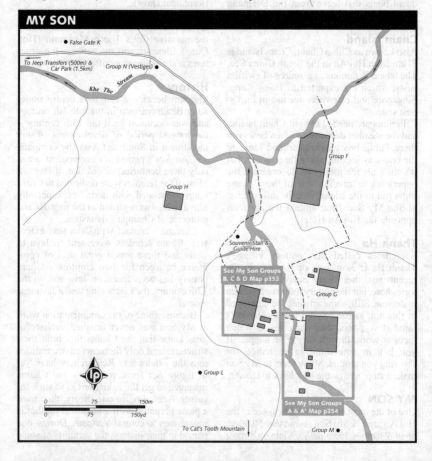

MY SON

False Gate K

To Jeep Transfers (500m) & Car Park (1.5km)

Group N (Vestiges)

Khe  The  Stream

Group F

Group H

Souvenir Stall & Guide Hire

See My Son Groups B, C & D Map p353

Group G

Group L

See My Son Groups A & A' Map p354

0        75        150m
0        75        150yd

To Cat's Tooth Mountain

Group M

OLIVER STREWE

THOMAS DOWNS

GREG ELMS

CRAIG PERSHOUSE

North-central Vietnam is one of the country's poorest regions but boasts breathtaking scenery around Tam Coc, known as 'Halong Bay on the rice paddies'

THOMAS BOEHM

Birds in cages are a sign of the Chinese influence in Hoi An

SARA-JANE CLELAND

Perfume River, Hué

NOBORU KOMINE

Stone guards in front of the Tomb of Emperor Khai Dinh near Hué

NOBORU KOMINE

Minh Mang Tomb, near Hué

## The Site

Archaeologists have divided My Son's monuments into 10 main groups, lettered A, A', B, C, D, E, F, G, H and K. Each structure has been given a name consisting of a letter followed by a number.

The first structure you encounter along the trail is the false gate K, which dates from the 11th century. Between K and the other groups is a coffee plantation begun in 1986; peanuts and beans are also grown among the bushes.

**Group B** The main sanctuary *(kalan)*, **B1**, was dedicated to Bhadresvara, which is a contraction of the name of King Bhadravarman, who built the first temple at My Son, combined with '-esvara', which means Shiva. The first building on this site was erected in the 4th century, destroyed in the 6th century and rebuilt in the 7th century. Only the 11th-century base, made of large sandstone blocks, remains; the brickwork

walls have disappeared. The niches in the wall were used to hold lamps (Cham sanctuaries had no windows). The linga inside was discovered during excavations in 1985, 1m below its current position.

**B5**, built in the 10th century, was used for storing sacred books and precious objects (some made of gold), which were used in ceremonies performed in B1. The boat-shaped roof (the 'bow' and 'stern' have fallen off) demonstrates the influence of Malayo-Polynesian architecture. Unlike the sanctuaries, this building has windows and the fine Cham masonry inside is original. Over the window on the wall facing B4 is a brick bas-relief of two elephants under a tree with two birds in it.

The ornamentation on the exterior walls of **B4** is an excellent example of a Cham decorative style, typical of the 9th century, said to resemble worms. This style is unlike anything found in other Southeast Asian cultures.

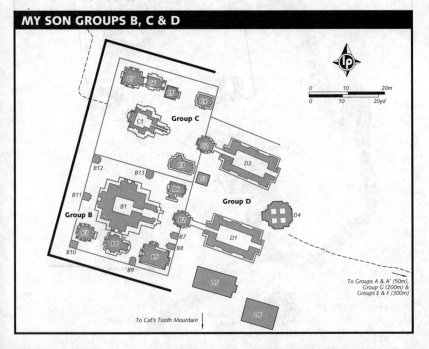

**MY SON GROUPS B, C & D**

**B3** has an Indian-influenced pyramidal roof typical of Cham towers. Inside **B6** is a bath-shaped basin for keeping sacred water that was poured over the linga in B1; this is the only known example of a Cham basin. **B2** is a gate.

Around the perimeter of Group B are small temples, **B7-13**, dedicated to the gods of the directions of the compass *(dikpalaka)*.

**Group C** The 8th-century **C1** was used to worship Shiva, portrayed in human form (rather than in the form of a linga, as in B1). Inside is an altar where a statue of Shiva,

now in the Museum of Cham Sculpture in Danang, used to stand. On either side of the stone doorway it's possible to see, bored into the lintel and the floor, the holes in which two wooden doors once swung. Note the motifs, characteristic of the 8th century, carved into the brickwork of the exterior walls.

**Group D** Buildings **D1** and **D2**, once meditation halls, now house small displays of Cham sculpture.

**Group A** The path from Groups B, C and D to Group A leads eastward from near D4.

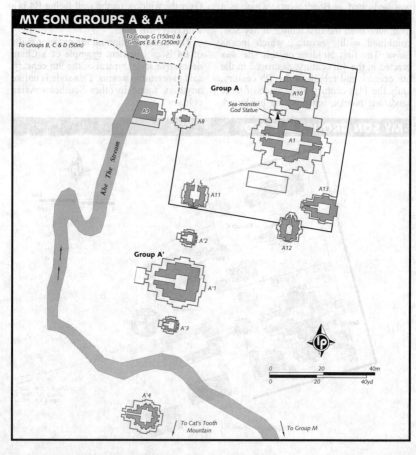

**MY SON GROUPS A & A'**

## Kingdom of Champa

The kingdom of Champa flourished from the 2nd to the 15th centuries. It first appeared around present-day Danang and later spread south to what is now Nha Trang and Phan Rang. Champa became Indianised through commercial relations with India: the Chams adopted Hinduism, employed Sanskrit as a sacred language and borrowed from Indian art.

The Chams, who lacked enough land for agriculture along the mountainous coast, were semipiratic and conducted attacks on passing trade ships. As a result, they were in a constant state of war with the Vietnamese to the north and the Khmers to the west. The Chams successfully threw off Khmer rule in the 12th century, but were entirely absorbed by Vietnam in the 17th century.

The Chams are best known for the many brick sanctuaries (Cham towers) they constructed throughout the south. The greatest collection of Cham art is in the Museum of Cham Sculpture in Danang. The major Cham site is at My Son (near Hoi An), and other Cham ruins can be found in Nha Trang, Phan Rang and Thap Cham (see the South-Central Coast chapter). These more-southern Cham ruins belonged to a slightly different group of Chams who followed Muslim doctrines.

Elements of Cham civilisation can still be seen in the life of the people of Quang Nam, Danang and Quang Ngai provinces, whose forebears assimilated many Cham innovations into their daily lives. These include techniques for pottery, fishing, sugar production, rice farming, irrigation, silk production and construction.

Group A was almost completely destroyed by US attacks. According to locals, massive **A1**, considered the most important monument at My Son, remained impervious to aerial bombing and was finally finished off by a helicopter-borne sapper team. All that remains today is a pile of collapsed brick walls. After the destruction of A1, Philippe Stern, an expert on Cham art and curator of the Guimet Museum in Paris, wrote a letter of protest to the US president, Nixon, who ordered US forces to continue killing the VC, but not to do any further damage to Cham monuments.

A1 was the only Cham sanctuary with two doors. One faced east, in the direction of the Hindu gods; the other faced west towards Groups B, C and D and the spirits of the ancestor kings that may have been buried there. Inside A1 is a stone altar pieced together in 1988. Among the ruins, some of the brilliant brickwork, which is of a typical 10th-century style, is still visible. At the base of A1 on the side facing A10 (decorated in 9th-century style) is a carving of a worshipping figure, flanked by round columns, with a Javanese sea-monster god *(kala-makara)* above. There may be some connection between the presence of this Javanese motif and the studies in Java of a great 10th-century Cham scholar. There are plans to partially restore A1 and A10 as soon as possible.

**Other Groups** Dating from the 8th century, **Group A'** is at present overgrown and inaccessible. **Group E** was built from the 8th to 11th centuries, while **Group F** dates to the 8th century. **Group G**, which has been damaged by time rather than war, dates to the 12th century. There are long-term plans to restore these monuments.

### Places to Stay

The nearest hotels are in Hoi An and Danang.

### Getting There & Away

**Minibus** Numerous hotels in Hoi An can book a day trip to My Son that includes a stop-off at Tra Kieu. At US$2 to US$3 per person, you could hardly do it cheaper unless you walked. The minibuses depart from Hoi An at 8am and return at 2pm. Some agencies offer the option of returning to Hoi An by boat.

**Car** A hire car with driver will get you to My Son for around US$20. Going under your own steam gives you the option of arriving before or after the tour groups, and My Son is quite spectacular and atmospheric when you're one of only a few people there.

**Motorbike** It's possible to get to the sites by rented motorbike. We have had numerous complaints from travellers that their rented motorbikes were vandalised by the locals at My Son, who then asked about US$25 to repair the damage they caused. The police are supposed to have cracked down on this, but we suggest caution nonetheless. It may be better to get somebody else to drive you on their motorbike and then ask them to wait for you.

## TRA KIEU (SIMHAPURA)

Formerly called Simhapura (Lion Citadel), Tra Kieu was the first capital city of Champa, serving in that capacity from the 4th through to the 8th centuries. Today, nothing remains of the ancient city except the rectangular ramparts. A large number of artefacts, including some of the finest carvings in the Museum of Cham Sculpture in Danang, were found here.

## Mountain Church

You can get a good view of the city's outlines from the Mountain Church (Nha Tho Nui), on the top of Buu Chau Hill in Tra Kieu. This modern, open-air structure was built in 1970 to replace an earlier church destroyed by time and war. A Cham tower once stood on this spot.

The Mountain Church is 6.5km from National Hwy 1 and 19.5km from the start of the footpath to My Son. Within Tra Kieu, it is 200m from the morning market, Cho Tra Kieu, and 550m from Tra Kieu Church.

## Tra Kieu Church

This church (Dia So Tra Kieu), which serves the town's Catholic population of 3000, was built a century ago. There's a fantastic ceramic mosaic dragon on the external stairs. A priest working here, who died in 1989, was interested in Cham civilization and amassed a collection of Cham artefacts found by local people. A 2nd-floor room in the building to the right of the church opened as a museum in 1990. The round ceramic objects that have faces on them, which date to between the 8th and 10th centuries, were affixed to the ends of tiled roofs. The face is of Kala, the God of Time. Tra Kieu Church is 7km from National Hwy 1 and 19km from the trail to My Son. It is 150m down an alley opposite the town's **Clinic of Western Medicine** (Quay Thuoc Tay Y), 350m from the morning market and 550m from the Mountain Church.

## Getting There & Away

Most day trips to My Son from Hoi An include a stop-off at Tra Kieu. Otherwise you'll need to rent a bike or a car (with driver). See the Getting There & Away section for My Son.

## TAM KY
☎ 0510

Tam Ky, the capital of Quang Nam province, is a nondescript town on the highway between Chu Lai and Danang. However, travellers are drawn to the **Cham towers** at nearby Chien Dan (Chien Dan Cham), which is located 5km north of Tam Ky, 69km north of Quang Ngai and 62km south of Danang.

The three towers are enclosed by a wall, and a broken stele here dates from the 13th-century reign of King Harivarman. Many of the Cham statues you can see on display at Chien Dan were collected from other parts of the country after the American War and show signs of war-related damage. Expect to have to make a donation to the site's insistent custodian; there were no tickets or price lists when we visited, but around 5,000d per person is probably a fair amount to give.

## Dong Duong

The Cham religious centre of Dong Duong (formerly called Indrapura) was the site of the Monastery of Lakshmindra-Lokeshvara, an important Mahayana Buddhist monastery that was founded in AD 875. Dong Duong also served as the capital of Champa from AD 860 to AD 986, until the capital was transferred to Cha Ban (near Qui Nhon). Tragically, as a result of the devastation wrought by wars with the French and Americans, only part of the gate to Dong Duong remains.

## Places to Stay

**Tam Ky Hotel** *(Khach San Tam Ky; National Hwy 1)* is a big pink place in the centre of town. This is the only hotel in Tam Ky that can accommodate travellers; you're better off staying in Hoi An.

## CHU LAI

About 30km north of Quang Ngai, the buildings and concrete aircraft revetments of the huge American base at Chu Lai stretch along several kilometres of sand to the east of National Hwy 1.

Dung Quat oil refinery, the first refinery in Vietnam, is being developed at Chu Lai. An airport to service it was due to open at the time of writing; this will provide another point of entry (by air) to central Vietnam. Check scheduled services on offer when you arrive.

# South-Central Coast

This section covers the littoral provinces of Binh Thuan, Ninh Thuan, Khanh Hoa, Phu Yen, Binh Dinh and Quang Ngai. The cities, towns, beaches and historical sites in this region, most of which are along National Highway 1, referred to by many foreign tourists as the 'Ho Chi Minh Trail' (the real one is actually farther inland), appear in this chapter from north to south.

Some of Vietnam's most beautiful beaches are scattered along the coast, and there are many ruins of Cham culture. If you are heading north, be sure to visit the Museum of Cham Sculpture in Danang, which has an extensive and fine collection of Cham statuary (see the Central Vietnam chapter).

The south-central coast is logically best known for its excellent seafood. Another regional treat is green dragon fruit *(thanh long)*, grown widely around Phan Rang. The southernmost province, Binh Thuan, is one of the most arid regions of Vietnam (particularly north of Phan Thiet). The nearby plains, dominated by rocky, roundish mountains, support some marginal irrigated rice farms.

There is also easy access in and out of the mountainous regions inland from several points along the coast (see the Central Highlands chapter).

## QUANG NGAI
**☎ 055 • pop 108,200**

Quang Ngai, the capital of Quang Ngai province, offers very little to see or do, but makes a convenient stopover spot for travellers along National Hwy 1.

Built on the southern bank of the Tra Khuc River (known for its oversized water wheels), the city is about 15km from the coast. The city and province of Quang Ngai are also known as Quang Nghia; the name is sometimes abbreviated to Quangai.

Even before WWII, Quang Ngai was an important centre of resistance to the French. During the Franco–Viet Minh War, the area was a Viet Minh stronghold. In 1962, the

## Highlights

- Soak up the sun and enjoy the sea on peaceful Mui Ne Beach, near Phan Thiet
- Visit some of the area's impressive Cham ruins around Phan Rang, Thap Cham and Qui Nhon
- Go island hopping or scuba diving in the turquoise waters off Nha Trang

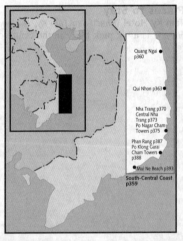

Quang Ngai p360

Qui Nhon p363

Nha Trang p370
Central Nha
Trang p373
Po Nagar Cham
Towers p375

Phan Rang p387
Po Klong Garai
Cham Towers
p388

Mui Ne Beach p393

South-Central Coast
p359

South Vietnamese government introduced its ill-fated Strategic Hamlets Program to the area. Villagers were forcibly removed from their homes and resettled in fortified hamlets, infuriating and alienating the local population and increasing popular support for the Viet Cong (VC). Some of the bitterest fighting of the American War took place in Quang Ngai province.

Son My subdistrict, 14km north of Quang Ngai, was the scene of the infamous My Lai Massacre of 1968, in which hundreds of civilians were slaughtered by US soldiers. A memorial has been erected on the site of the killings.

As a result of these wars, very few of the older bridges in Quang Ngai province remain intact. At many river crossings, the rust-streaked concrete pylons of the old French-built bridges, probably destroyed by the Viet Minh, stand next to the ruins of their replacements, blown up by the VC.

## Orientation

National Hwy 1 is called Đ Quang Trung as it passes through Quang Ngai. The train station is 1.5km west of the town centre, on Đ Hung Vuong.

## Information

The **main post office** (cnr Đ Hung Vuong & Đ Phan Dinh Phung) is 150m west of Đ Quang Trung.

## Places to Stay

**Hotel 502** (☎ 822656; 28 Đ Hung Vuong; fan rooms from US$6, air-con rooms US$10) is worth a try if you're looking for a peaceful night's sleep; it's in a courtyard down a quiet alley. The rooms are clean.

**Kim Thanh Hotel** (☎ 823471; 19 Đ Hung Vuong; doubles US$10-15) seems fairly well attuned to the backpacker market.

**Dong Hung Hotel** (☎ 821704; rooms with fan & cold water US$4, air-con rooms US$7-10) is on the busy central artery of town.

**Central Hotel** (☎ 829999, fax 822460; e cen tral@dng.vnn.vn; 784 Đ Quang Trung; doubles US$35-65), one of the classiest accommodation options in Quang Ngai, is located at the southern end of town. This fancy pleasure palace includes facilities such as a tennis court and swimming pool.

**My Tra Hotel** (☎ 842985, fax 842980; rooms US$25-40) is another upmarket place, although it is not as good value as the Central Hotel. Rates include breakfast. It's on the northern outskirts of town, just across the Tra Khuc River.

## Places to Eat

Quang Ngai province is famous for a local delicacy called *com ga*, which actually originates further north at Tam Ky. It consists of boiled chicken over yellow rice (the colour comes from being steamed with

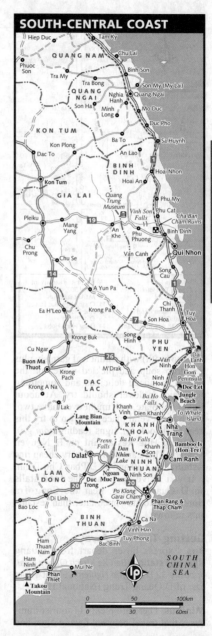

SOUTH-CENTRAL COAST

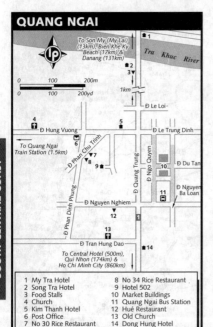

**QUANG NGAI**

To Son My (My Lai)
(13km), Bien Khe Ky
Beach (17km) &
Danang (131km)

Tra Khuc River

0    100    200m
0    100    200yd

1km

Ð Le Loi

Ð Hung Vuong

To Quang Ngai
Train Station (1.5km)

Ð Le Trung Dinh

Ð Phan Chu Trinh

Ð Ngo Nguyen

Ð Quang Trung

Ð Du Tan

Ð Phan Dinh Phung

Ð Nguyen Nghiem

Ð Nguyen
Ba Loan

Ð Tran Hung Dao

To Central Hotel (500m),
Qui Nhon (174km) &
Ho Chi Minh City (860km)

| 1 My Tra Hotel | 8 No 34 Rice Restaurant |
| 2 Song Tra Hotel | 9 Hotel 502 |
| 3 Food Stalls | 10 Market Buildings |
| 4 Church | 11 Quang Ngai Bus Station |
| 5 Kim Thanh Hotel | 12 Hue Restaurant |
| 6 Post Office | 13 Old Church |
| 7 No 30 Rice Restaurant | 14 Dong Hung Hotel |

chicken broth) with a mint leaf garnish, plus egg-drop soup and pickled vegies on the side. It is indeed delicious and something any chicken lover should try. At about 7000d per plate, you might even have two. There are several places in town to try this treat (just look for signs reading *com ga*), including **Hue Restaurant** on Ð Nguyen Nghiem. There are also two very cheap **rice restaurants** at 30 and 34 Ð Phan Chu Trinh.

If you arrive after dark, the **food stalls** on Ð Quang Trung, near the Song Tra Hotel, tend to stay open later than restaurants in town.

### Getting There & Away

**Bus** Express buses depart from **Quang Ngai bus station** (*Ben Xe Khach Quang Ngai; opposite 32 Ð Nguyen Nghiem*), about 100m east of Ð Quang Trung (National Hwy 1).

**Minibus** There are plenty of tourist minibuses that travel between Quang Ngai and

Hoi An for around US$5. Quang Ngai is about 100km from Hoi An; the ride takes about two hours.

**Train** *Reunification Express* trains stop at Quang Ngai – see the Train section in the Getting Around chapter.

The **Quang Ngai train station** (*Ga Quang Nghia, Ga Quang Ngai*) is 1.5km west of the centre of town.

**Car & Motorbike** From Quang Ngai road distances are: 131km to Danang; 860km to Ho Chi Minh City (HCMC); 412km to Nha Trang; and 174km to Qui Nhon.

## AROUND QUANG NGAI
### Son My (My Lai)

The site of the My Lai Massacre is located 14km from central Quang Ngai. To get there from town, head north (towards Danang) on Ð Quang Trung (National Hwy 1) and cross the long bridge over the Tra Khuc River. Metres from the northern end of the bridge, you will come to a triangular concrete stele indicating the way to the Son My Memorial. Turn right (eastward, parallel to the river) on the dirt road and continue for 12km. The road to Son My passes through particularly beautiful countryside: rice paddies, manioc patches and vegetable gardens shaded by casuarinas and eucalyptus trees.

The Son My Memorial is set in a park where the Xom Lang subhamlet once stood (see the boxed text 'My Lai Massacre'). Around it, among the trees and rice paddies, are the graves of some of the victims, buried in family groups. Near the memorial is a **museum** (*admission 10,000d*), which opened in 1992.

If you don't have a car, the best way to get to Son My district from Quang Ngai is to hire a *xe om* near the bus station or along Ð Quang Trung.

### Bien Khe Ky Beach

Bien Khe Ky Beach (*Bai Bien Khe Ky*) is a long, secluded beach of fine sand 17km from Quang Ngai and several kilometres east of the Son My Memorial. The beach stretches for many kilometres along a long, thin casuarina-lined spit of sand. It is separated from the mainland by Song Kinh Giang, a body of water about 150m inland from the beach.

## SA HUYNH
☎ 055

Sa Huynh is a little seaside town with a beautiful semicircular beach bordered by rice paddies and coconut palms. The town

## My Lai Massacre

Son My subdistrict was the site of the most horrific war crimes committed by US troops during the American War. The My Lai Massacre consisted of a series of atrocities carried out all over Son My subdistrict, which is divided into four hamlets, only one of which is named My Lai. The largest mass killing took place in Xom Lang (Thuan Yen) subhamlet, where the Son My Memorial was later erected.

Son My subdistrict was a known Viet Cong (VC) stronghold, and it was widely believed that villagers in the area were providing food and shelter to the VC (if true, the villagers would have had little choice – the VC was known for taking cruel revenge on those who didn't 'cooperate'). Just whose idea it was to 'teach the villagers a lesson' has never been determined. What is known is that several US soldiers had been killed and wounded in the area in the days preceding the 'search-and-destroy operation' that began on the morning of 16 March 1968.

The operation was carried out by Task Force Barker – three companies of US infantry. At about 7.30am – after the area around Xom Lang had been bombarded with artillery, and the landing zone raked with rocket and machine-gun fire from helicopter gunships – Charlie Company (commanded by Captain Ernest Medina) landed by helicopter. They encountered no resistance during the 'combat-assault', nor did they come under fire at any time during the entire operation; but as soon as their sweep eastward began, so did the atrocities.

As Lieutenant William Calley's 1st Platoon moved through Xom Lang, they shot and bayoneted fleeing villagers, threw hand grenades into houses and bomb shelters, slaughtered livestock and burned dwellings. Somewhere between 75 and 150 unarmed villagers were rounded up and herded to a ditch, where they were mowed down by machine-gun fire.

In the next few hours, as command helicopters circled overhead and American navy boats patrolled offshore, the 2nd Platoon (under Lieutenant Stephen Brooks), the 3rd platoon (under Lieutenant Jeffrey La Cross) and the company headquarters group also committed unspeakable crimes. At least half a dozen groups of civilians, including women and children, were assembled and executed. Villagers fleeing towards Quang Ngai along the road were machine-gunned, and wounded civilians (including young children) were summarily shot. As these massacres were taking place, at least four girls and women were raped or gang-raped by groups of soldiers.

One soldier is reported to have shot himself in the foot to get himself out of the slaughter; he was the only American casualty in the entire operation. Troops who participated were ordered to keep their mouths shut, but several disobeyed orders and went public with the story after returning to the USA. When it broke in the newspapers, it had a devastating effect on the military's morale and fuelled further public protests against the war. Unlike WWII veterans, who returned home to parades and glory, soldiers coming home from Vietnam often found themselves ostracised by their fellow citizens and taunted as 'baby killers'.

A cover-up of the atrocities was undertaken at all levels of the US army command, eventually leading to several investigations. Lieutenant Calley was made chief ogre and was court-martialled and found guilty of the murders of 22 unarmed civilians. He was sentenced to life imprisonment in 1971 and spent three years under house arrest at Fort Benning, Georgia, while appealing his conviction. Calley was paroled in 1974 after the US Supreme Court refused to hear his case. Calley's case still causes controversy – many claim that he was made a scapegoat because of his low rank, and that officers much higher up ordered the massacres. What is certain is that he didn't act alone.

is also known for its salt marshes and salt-evaporation ponds.

Archaeologists have unearthed remains of the Dong Son Civilisation dating from the 1st century AD in the vicinity of Sa Huynh.

## Places to Stay & Eat

**Sa Huynh Hotel** (☎ 860311, fax 822836; singles with fan US$8, doubles with fan/air-con US$10/15), the only place to stay in town, is a crumbling concrete hotel right on the beach. Other than the pleasant beachside setting, there's little to recommend the place.

The state-run restaurant on the hotel grounds is depressing and the service is poor. Fortunately, there are a number of small roadside **restaurant-cafés** a few hundred metres away, out on National Hwy 1. One of the best is called **Vinh**.

## Getting There & Away

**Train** Some nonexpress trains stop at the Sa Huynh train station (Ga Sa Huynh), but it will be slow going.

**Car & Motorbike** Sa Huynh is on National Hwy 1, about 114km north of Qui Nhon and 60km south of Quang Ngai.

## QUI NHON

☎ 056 • pop 260,000

Qui Nhon (Quy Nhon) is the capital of Binh Dinh province and one of Vietnam's more active second-string seaports. It's a pleasant enough place to break the long journey from Nha Trang to Danang, and a great spot to sample some fresh local seafood.

The beaches in the immediate vicinity of the city are nothing special, but south of Qui Nhon there are some nice beaches to explore, notably on the newly-built coastal road to Song Cau.

On the outskirts of Qui Nhon there are numerous **Cham towers** to visit, including some along National Hwy 1, about 10km north of the Qui Nhon turn-off.

During the American War, there was considerable South Vietnamese, US, VC and South Korean military activity in the Qui Nhon area. Refugees dislocated by fighting and counter-insurgency programmes built whole slums of tin and thatch shacks around the city. During this period, the mayor of Qui Nhon, hoping to cash in on the presence of US troops, turned his official residence into a large massage parlour.

There is an obscure historical connection between Qui Nhon and New Zealand dating back to the early 1960s, when funds from New Zealand were provided to build the provincial hospital and later to aid refugees. The New Zealand connection continues with volunteers working on development projects in the province.

## Orientation

Qui Nhon is on the coast, 10km east of National Hwy 1. The highway junction where you turn off to Qui Nhon is called Phu Tai.

Qui Nhon proper is located on an east-west orientated peninsula, shaped like an anteater's nose. The tip of the nose (the port area) is closed to the public. The municipal beach is on the peninsula's southern coast.

From the municipal beach, Cu Lao Xanh Island is visible offshore, as is a rusting US Army tank lying half submerged closer to the shore. Due east of the beach you can see, in the distance, an oversize statue of Tran Hung Dao, erected on a promontory over-looking the fishing village of Hai Minh.

The streets around Lon Market constitute Qui Nhon's town centre.

## Information

**Money** There's a branch of **Vietcombank** (☎ 822266; 148 Đ Le Loi) on the corner of Đ Tran Hung Dao.

**Email & Internet Access** Check your email at **Binh Dinh Internet** (245 Đ Le Hong Phong) for just 100d per minute.

**Travel Agencies** For tours to the Cham ruins of Thap Doi, Cha Ban and Duong Long, contact **Binh Dinh Tourist** (☎ 892953, fax 892963; e biditravel@dng.vnn.vn; 25 Đ Nguyen Hue).

**Barbara's Backpackers** (☎ 892921; e nz barb@yahoo.com; 18 Đ Nguyen Hue) is a budget travellers hostel that also organises unique regional tours and boat trips.

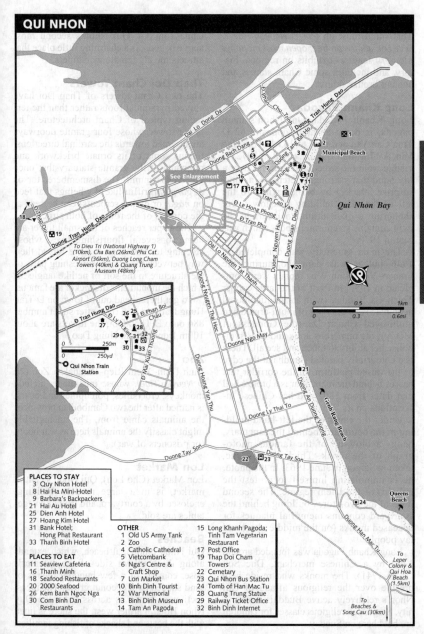

# QUI NHON

*See Enlargement*

To Dieu Tri (National Highway 1)
(10km), Cha Ban (26km), Phu Cat
Airport (36km), Duong Long Cham
Towers (40km) & Quang Trung
Museum (48km)

*Qui Nhon Bay*

*Qui Nhon Bay*

Ghenh Rang Beach

Municipal Beach

*Queens
Beach*

To
Leper
Colony &
Qui Hoa
Beach
(1.5km)

To
Beaches &
Song Cau (30km)

Đ Tran Hung Đạo
Đ Ly Th Kiet
Đ Phan Boi
Chau
Qui Nhon Train
Station

Duong Tran Hung Dao
Dai Lo Dong Da
Đ. Phan Chu Trinh
Duong Tran Hung Dao
Duong Bach Dang
Duong Tang Bat Ho
Ba Trung
Tran Cao Van
Đ Le Hong Phong
Đ Tran Phu
Dai Lo Nguyen Tat Thanh
Duong Nguyen Hue
Duong Xuan Dieu
Duong Nguyen Thai Hoc
Duong Ngo May
Duong Hoang Van Thu
Duong Ly Thai To
Duong An Duong Vuong
Duong Tay Son
Duong Tay Son
Duong Han Mac Tu

SOUTH-CENTRAL COAST

## PLACES TO STAY
3   Quy Nhon Hotel
8   Hai Ha Mini-Hotel
9   Barbara's Backpackers
21  Hai Au Hotel
25  Dien Anh Hotel
27  Hoang Kim Hotel
31  Bank Hotel;
    Hong Phat Restaurant
33  Thanh Binh Hotel

## PLACES TO EAT
11  Seaview Cafeteria
16  Thanh Minh
18  Seafood Restaurants
20  2000 Seafood
26  Kem Banh Ngoc Nga
30  Com Binh Dan
    Restaurants

## OTHER
1   Old US Army Tank
2   Zoo
4   Catholic Cathedral
5   Vietcombank
6   Nga's Centre &
    Craft Shop
7   Lon Market
10  Binh Dinh Tourist
12  War Memorial
13  Binh Dinh Museum
14  Tam An Pagoda

15  Long Khanh Pagoda;
    Tinh Tam Vegetarian
    Restaurant
17  Post Office
19  Thap Doi Cham Towers
22  Cemetery
23  Qui Nhon Bus Station
24  Tomb of Han Mac Tu
28  Quang Trung Statue
29  Railway Ticket Office
32  Binh Dinh Internet

## Binh Dinh Museum

This small museum *(cnr Đ Nguyen Hue & Đ Le Loi; admission free; open most mornings Mon-Fri)* features exhibits on regional history, and includes some Cham statues and ancient bronze drums.

## Long Khanh Pagoda

Long Khanh Pagoda, Qui Nhon's main pagoda, is down an alley opposite 62 Đ Tran Cao Van and next to 143 Đ Tran Cao Van. A 17m-high Buddha (built in 1972) is visible from the street, and presides over a lily pond that's strongly defended (against surprise attack?) by barbed wire. To the left of the main building is a low tower sheltering a giant drum; to the right, its twin contains an enormous bell, which was cast in 1970.

The main sanctuary was completed in 1946 but it was damaged during the Franco–Viet Minh War; repairs were completed in 1957. In front of the large copper Thich Ca Buddha (with its multicoloured neon halo) is a drawing of multi-armed and multi-eyed Chuan De (the Goddess of Mercy); the numerous arms and eyes symbolise her ability to touch and see all. There is a colourfully painted Buddha at the edge of the raised platform. In the corridor that passes behind the main altar is a bronze bell that dates from 1805 and has Chinese inscriptions on it.

Under the eaves of the left-hand building in the courtyard, behind the sanctuary, hangs a blow-up of the famous photograph of the monk, Thich Quang Duc, taken in Saigon in June 1963. In the photo, he is immolating himself to protest the policies of the Diem regime. The second level of the two-storey building behind the courtyard contains memorial plaques for deceased monks (on the middle altar) and lay people.

Long Khanh Pagoda was founded around 1700 by a Chinese merchant, Duc Son (1679–1741). The monks who reside here preside over the religious affairs of Qui Nhon's relatively active Buddhist community. Single-sex religious classes for children are held here on Sunday.

## Tam An Pagoda

Chua Tam An, Qui Nhon's second most active pagoda, is a charming little place that attracts mostly female worshipers.

## Thap Doi Cham Towers

The two Cham towers of Thap Doi have curved pyramidal roofs rather than the terracing typical of Cham architecture. The larger tower, whose four granite doorways are oriented towards the cardinal directions, retains some of its ornate brickwork and remnants of the granite statuary that once graced its summit. The dismembered torsos of *garuda (*griffin-like sky beings that feed on *naga*, or divine serpents) can be seen at the corners of the roofs of both structures.

The upper reaches of the small tower are home to several flourishing trees, whose creeping tendrilous roots have forced their way between the bricks, enmeshing parts of the structure in the sort of netlike tangle for which the monuments of Angkor are famous.

To get there, head out of town on Đ Tran Hung Dao and turn right after street number 886 onto Đ Thap Doi; the towers are about 100m from Đ Tran Hung Dao.

## Zoo

Binh Dinh–Xiem Riep–Ratanakiri Zoo *(2B Đ Nguyen Hue)*, whose inhabitants include monkeys, crocodiles, porcupines and bears, is named after the two Cambodian provinces the animals came from. The uncharitable might classify the animals here as war booty (or prisoners of war).

## Lon Market

Lon Market (Cho Lon), Qui Nhon's central market, is in a large modern building, enclosed by a courtyard, and fruit and vegetables are sold.

## Beaches

Qui Nhon municipal beach, which extends along the southern side of the anteater's nose, consists of a few hundred metres of sand shaded by a coconut grove. The nicest section of beach is across from the Quy Nhon Hotel. Farther west, the shore is lined with the boats and shacks of fishing families.

The longer, quieter Queen's Beach begins about 2km southwest of the municipal beach. To get there, follow Đ Nguyen Hue away from the tip of the peninsula westward. Further south there are several good beaches on the recently completed coastal road to Song Cau.

## Qui Hoa Leper Colony & Queen's Beach

This is a tourist attraction and visitors are welcome, for a small entrance fee, to enjoy the beach. As leper colonies go, this one is highly unusual. Rather than being a depressing place, it's a sort of model village near the seafront, where treated patients live together with their families in small well-kept houses. According to their abilities, the patients work in the rice fields, in fishing, and in repair-oriented businesses or small craft shops (one supported by Handicap International produces prosthetic limbs).

The grounds of the **hospital** (☎ 646343; admission 3000d; open 8am-11.30am & 1.30pm-4pm daily) are so well maintained that it looks a bit like a resort, complete with numerous busts of distinguished and historically important doctors (both Vietnamese and foreign) scattered around the property.

Fronting the leper colony is **Queen's Beach**, one of the nicer stretches of sand around Qui Nhon and a popular weekend hang-out of the city's expat community.

The leper colony and beach are at the western end of An Đ Huong, about 1.5km off the main road. En route to the beach, consider making a detour to visit the hillside **Tomb of Han Mac Tu**.

Qui Hoa is alos accessible from the new road to Song Cua – turn left (down to the village) at the top of the first hill, if coming from Qui Nhon. There is a sign for the hospital at the junction.

## Places to Stay

**Barbara's Backpackers** (☎ 892921; e nz barb@yahoo.com; 18 Đ Nguyen Hue; dorm beds US$2, fan rooms US$5-7), a venerable travellers' favourite, is run by Qui Nhon's local foreign travel expert, a congenial Kiwi named Barbara. The hotel is directly across

from the beach and boasts a certain antiquated charm. All rooms have en suite bathrooms. Various types of tours and transport can be also arranged here, and the in-house **Kiwi Cafe** features cheap home-style international food (the only Western food menu in town!).

**Hai Ha Mini-Hotel** (☎ 891295, ☎ 892300; 5 Đ Tran Binh Trong; rooms US$15-30), one block from the city beach, is a friendly place with decent air-con rooms.

The ageing **Bank Hotel** (☎ 823591, fax 821013; 257 Đ Le Hong Phong; fan rooms US$12, air-con rooms US$13-18) is central and accustomed to hosting foreign guests.

**Thanh Binh Hotel** (☎ 822041, fax 827569; e thanhbinhhotel@dng.vnn.vn; 6 Đ Ly Thuong Kiet; old-wing rooms US$8-18, new-wing rooms US$20-40), just around the block from the Bank Hotel, has a somewhat derelict old wing, and a fancier new wing.

**Dien Anh Hotel** (☎ 822876, fax 822869; 298 Đ Phan Boi Chau; singles/doubles with fan US$9/10, with air-con US$13/15), just across from the town square, is owned by the local movie studio and attracts aspiring actors.

**Hoang Kim Hotel** (Golden Age Hotel; ☎ 828768, fax 823826; 369 Đ Le Hong Phong; air-con rooms US$10-17) is another older place that is also centrally located.

**Hai Au Hotel** (Seagull Hotel; ☎ 846473, fax 846926; e ks.haiau@dng.vnn.vn; 489 Đ An Duong Vuong; rooms US$20-45), southwest of the town centre, is popular with foreign tour groups and right on the beach, but the rooms smell a bit musty. A simple breakfast is included in the rates.

**Quy Nhon Hotel** (☎ 822401, fax 821162; e hotelquynhon@dng.vnn.vn; 8 Đ Nguyen Hue; rooms US$27-60) is directly opposite the city beach. Judging from the hotel's brochures, it seems that the management believes the Qui Nhon municipal beach and Quy Nhon Hotel are Vietnam's answer to the French Riviera and Club Med. However, Club Med is not exactly shaking in its boots.

## Places to Eat

**Seaview Cafeteria** (☎ 892953; Đ Nguyen Hue) is a pleasant and friendly beachfront place that's outdoors and next to the local tourist office. There's a wide selection of dishes on the menu, and it's also good for a cold drink or a coffee.

**2000 Seafood** (☎ 814503; 1 Đ Tran Doc) is among the most popular seafood restaurants in Qui Nhon and tends to be packed with locals. Recommended is its seafood hotpot (lau).

**Hong Phat** (☎ 811550; 261 Đ Le Hong Phong), just beside the Bank Hotel, does respectable Thai and Vietnamese dishes.

**Thanh Minh** (151 Đ Phan Boi Chau) and **Tinh Tam** (141 Đ Tran Cao Van), right next to Long Khanh Pagoda, both serve amazingly good (and cheap!) vegetarian dishes.

In the town centre, look for the local point-and-eat **com binh dan restaurants** near the Bank Hotel. Nearby, check out the tasty bakery items and excellent ice cream at **Kem Banh Ngoc Nga**.

## Shopping
**Nga's Centre & Craft Shop** (100 Đ Phan Boi Chau), a workshop for disabled women and orphans, is well worth stopping in for a look. They sell lovely Bahnar weavings, cushion covers and the like.

## Getting There & Away
**Air** Vietnam Airlines flights link HCMC with Qui Nhon six times weekly.

In Qui Nhon, the **Vietnam Airlines' booking office** (☎ 822953) is near the town end of the old airstrip.

Phu Cat airport is 36km north of Qui Nhon. For airline passengers, transport to and from Phu Cat is provided by Vietnam Airlines minibus (25,000d).

**Bus** There are express buses to Buon Ma Thuot, Dalat, Danang, Dong Hoi, Hanoi, Hué, Nha Trang, Ninh Binh, Quang Tri, HCMC, Thanh Hoa and Vinh.

**Qui Nhon bus station** (Ben Xe Khach Qui Nhon; ☎ 822246; opposite 543 Đ Tran Hung Dao) is across from the corner with Đ Le Hong Phong.

**Train** The nearest the Reunification Express trains get to Qui Nhon is Dieu Tri, 10km from the city. **Qui Nhon train station** (Ga Qui Nhon; ☎ 822036) is at the end of a 10km spur line off the main north-south track. Only very slow local trains stop at Qui Nhon train station and they are not worth bothering with. It's better to get to/from Dieu Tri by taxi or xe om for around 50,000d.

Tickets for trains departing from Dieu Tri can be purchased at the Qui Nhon train station, though if you arrive in Dieu Tri by train, your best bet is to purchase an onward ticket before leaving the station. There is also a ticket office near the Bank Hotel. For ticket prices, see the Train section in the Getting Around chapter.

**Car & Motorbike** Road distances from Qui Nhon are: 677km to HCMC; 238km to Nha Trang; 186km to Pleiku; 198km to Kon Tum; 174km to Quang Ngai; and 303km to Danang.

## AROUND QUI NHON
There are half a dozen or so groups of Cham structures in the vicinity of Qui Nhon.

## Cha Ban
The ruins of the former Cham capital of Cha Ban (also known at various times as Vijaya and Qui Nhon) are 26km north of Qui Nhon and 5km from Binh Dinh. The city was built within a rectangular wall measuring 1400m by 1100m. Canh Tien Tower (Tower of Brass) stands in the centre of the enclosure. The tomb of General Vu Tinh is nearby.

Cha Ban, which served as the seat of the royal government of Champa from the year 1000 (after the loss of Indrapura, also known as Dong Duong) until 1471, was attacked and plundered repeatedly by the Vietnamese, Khmer and Chinese.

In 1044, the Vietnamese prince Phat Ma occupied the city and carried off a great deal of booty as well as the Cham king's wives, harem and female dancers, musicians and singers. Cha Ban was under the control of a Khmer overseer from 1190 to 1220.

In 1377, the Vietnamese were defeated and their king was killed in an attempt to capture Cha Ban. The Vietnamese emperor Le Thanh Ton breached the eastern gate of the city in 1471 and captured the Cham king and 50 members of the royal family. During this, the last great battle fought by the Cham, 60,000 Cham were killed and 30,000 more were taken prisoner by the Vietnamese.

During the Tay Son Rebellion, Cha Ban served as the capital of the central Vietnam region, and was ruled by the eldest of the three Tay Son brothers. The capital was attacked in 1793 by the forces of Nguyen Anh (later Emperor Gia Long), but the assault failed. In 1799, the forces of Nguyen Anh, under the command of General Vu Tinh, laid siege to the city and captured it. The Tay Son soon reoccupied the port of Thi Nai (modern-day Qui Nhon) and then lay siege to Cha Ban themselves. The siege continued for over a year, and by June 1801, Vu Tinh's provisions were gone. Food was in short supply; all the horses and elephants had long before been eaten. Refusing to consider the ignominy of surrender, Vu Tinh had an octagonal wooden tower constructed. He filled it with gunpowder and, arrayed in his ceremonial robes, went inside and blew himself up. Upon hearing the news of the death of his dedicated general, Nguyen Anh wept.

## Duong Long Cham Towers

The Duong Long Cham towers (Thap Duong Long, meaning Towers of Ivory) are about 15km from Cha Ban. The largest of the three brick towers is embellished with granite ornamentation representing *naga* and elephants. Over the doors are bas-reliefs of women, dancers, standing lions, monsters and various other animals. The corners of the structure are formed by enormous dragon heads.

## Quang Trung Museum

Quang Trung Museum is dedicated to the second-oldest of the three brothers, Nguyen Hue, who led the Tay Son Rebellion, and who crowned himself Emperor Quang Trung in 1788. In 1789 Quang Trung led the campaign that overwhelmingly defeated a Chinese invasion of 200,000 troops near Hanoi. This epic battle is still celebrated as one of the greatest triumphs in Vietnamese

history. Quang Trung died in 1792 at the age of 40.

During his reign, Quang Trung was something of a social reformer. He encouraged land reform, revised the system of taxation, improved the army and emphasised education, opening many schools and encouraging the development of Vietnamese poetry and literature. Indeed, communist literature often portrays him as the leader of a peasant revolution whose progressive policies were crushed by the reactionary Nguyen dynasty, which came to power in 1802 and was overthrown by Ho Chi Minh in 1945.

The Quang Trung Museum (*admission 10,000d*), 48km from Qui Nhon, displays various statues, costumes, documents and artefacts from the 18th century, most of them labelled in English. Especially notable are the elephant skin–wrapped battle drums and gongs from the Bahnar tribal people in Gia Lai province. The museum is also known for its demonstrations of *vo binh dinh*, a traditional martial art that is performed with a bamboo stick.

**Getting There & Away** To get there, take National Hwy 19 west towards Pleiku. The museum is about 5km off the highway – the turn-off is sign posted) in the Tay Son district, known for the production of a wine made from sticky rice.

## Vinh Son Falls

Vinh Son Falls is 18km off National Hwy 19, which links Binh Dinh and Pleiku.

## SONG CAU
☎ 057

The village of Song Cau is an obscure place that you could easily drive past without ever noticing, but it's worth stopping if you have the time. Near the village is an immense bay, a beautiful rest stop that attracts both foreign and domestic tourists.

Tourists doing the Nha Trang–Hoi An run often make a stopoff for brunch in Song Cau, and some visitors decide to spend the night. Song Cau is along a notorious stretch of National Hwy 1 dubbed the 'Happy 16 Kilometres' by long-distance truck drivers.

SOUTH-CENTRAL COAST

It was so named for the vast number of 'taxi girls', who ply their trade by the roadside along this stretch.

An amusing thing to do here is to take a boat trip around the bay. The **Bai Tien Restaurant-Hotel** can help arrange a boat for six people that costs about 30,000d per hour. There are some lovely secluded beaches in the area, including Bai Tro (Tro Beach), which can be reached by boat, or a scenic drive south of Song Cau through rice fields, fish farms and over rickety wooden bridges. Ask for directions at the restaurant.

### Places to Stay & Eat
**Bai Tien Restaurant-Hotel** (☎ 870207; *doubles US$12*) has rooms with hot water. This privately run hotel and restaurant complex is built on stilts over a fish farm on the bay, which makes for an attractive setting.

About 100m south of here is another **seafood restaurant** also worth trying.

### Getting There & Away
Song Cau is 170km north of Nha Trang and 43km south of Qui Nhon. Highway buses can drop off and pick up here (with luck), but most travellers will probably arrive by chartered minibus.

If travelling with your own wheels, consider taking the newly completed coastal road between Song Cau and Qui Nhon; the scenery is stunning, and there are several good beaches en route.

### TUY HOA
☎ 057 • pop 185,700
Tuy Hoa, the capital of Phu Yen province, is a nondescript little town on the coast between Dai Lanh Beach and Qui Nhon. The navigable river justifies Tuy Hoa's existence: there isn't much else to the place, not even a good beach. One minor attraction is the **Nhan Cham Tower**, perched on a hill in the southern part of town, just off National Hwy 1.

The main appeal of Tuy Hoa for travellers is that it has decent accommodation, which could be useful if you have a late start heading north or south along National Hwy 1.

### Places to Stay & Eat
**Huong Sen Hotel** (☎ 823775, fax 823460; *fan rooms US$10, air-con rooms US$12-15*) and attached **restaurant** is a large place near the centre of town.

**Hong Phu Hotel** (☎ 824349; *fan rooms 50,000d, air-con rooms 100,000d*) is an old state-run place that is a cheaper option than Huong Sen. It's about 500m north of the bus station.

### Getting There & Away
Vietnam Airlines operates two flights weekly between Tuy Hoa and HCMC.

You can also reach Tuy Hoa by bus or local train.

### BEACHES NORTH OF NHA TRANG
☎ 058
There are four noteworthy beach spots north of Nha Trang. Dai Lanh Beach and Doc Let Beach are two popular places, though both are largely geared toward Vietnamese holiday makers. If you're not into crowds, try to avoid visiting on weekends.

Of considerably more interest than these, however, and definitely worth finding your way to, are Jungle Beach and Whale Island, two of Vietnam's most secluded and peaceful beach venues.

### Dai Lanh Beach
Semicircular, casuarina-shaded Dai Lanh Beach is a beautiful spot 83km north of Nha Trang and 150km south of Qui Nhon, right on National Hwy 1.

About 1km south of Dai Lanh Beach is a vast sand-dune causeway worth exploring; it connects the mainland to Hon Gom, a mountainous peninsula almost 30km in length. The main village on Hon Gom is Dam Mon (known to the French as Port Dayot), which is on a sheltered bay facing the island of Hon Lon.

At the northern end of Dai Lanh Beach is Dai Lanh Promontory (Mui Dai Lanh), which was named Cap Varella by the French.

Keep a close eye on your gear if you're overnighting at Dai Lanh Beach; we've heard a few reports of theft.

**Places to Stay & Eat** Mid-way down the beach, **Thuy Ta Restaurant** (☎ 842117; tents 15,000d, fan rooms 70,000-120,000d) has tents for rent, as well some ultra-simple straw-roof beach bungalows with brick floors and fans. Toilets are shared, and for non-guests there's a charge of 3000d for the use of cold showers.

**Getting There & Away** Dai Lanh Beach runs along National Hwy 1, so any vehicle travelling along the coast between Nha Trang and Tuy Hoa (or Qui Nhon) will get you there. The coastal scenery is stunning, in particular north of Dai Lanh Beach.

Local trains stop directly across from the beach.

## Doc Let Beach
Doc Let Beach is long and wide, with chalk-white sand and shallow water. Domestic tourists have gradually claimed this one away from foreign backpackers, who once had free range of this lovely stretch of beachfront. Still, Doc Let is easily accessible from Nha Trang, and worth considering as a day trip or overnight stop.

The 3000d beach-entry fee is waived for resort guests.

**Places to Stay** Access to the beach is via **Doc Let Beach Resort** (☎ 849663, fax 849506; e docletresort@dng.vnn.vn; double/triple/quad bungalows with fan & cold water 150,000/170,000/190,000d; double/triple/quad bungalows with air-con & hot water 280,000/300,000/320,000d), which has 28 concrete beach bungalows, each with private toilet and fridge, and close to the beach. Other facilities include tennis courts (30,000d per hour), two restaurants, a bar and, of course, karaoke and massage facilities. Internet access costs 500d per minute.

**Getting There & Away** Doc Let Beach is on a peninsula to the north of Nha Trang. There is no public transport to this spot. Some people take day tours from Nha Trang (US$6) – inquire at Mr Vu's Tour Adventures – while others hire a vehicle or drive themselves. Doc Let is 30km north of Nha Trang on National Hwy 1; just north of the Hyundai Shipyards take the right fork (east) and continue for 10km past photogenic **salt fields** until you reach the beach. A sign in English marks the turn-off.

## Whale Island
Whale Island Resort (☎/fax 840501; e de couvrirvn@dng.vnn.vn; w www.whaleisland resort.com; US$35 per person per day) is a lovely and secluded French-run beach retreat on Whale Island (Port Dayot). Electricity is supplied by generator, thankfully out of ear shot of the simple wooden beachfront bungalows. Rates include accommodation, all meals and boat transfers.

Scuba-diving season on the island ends in mid-October, starting up again in mid-February. The best season for diving is from April to September. Despite the damaging affects of dynamite fishing, environmental-protection efforts (including the planting of sea coral) around the resort bay have brought about a marked increase in the number of marine species from 40 to over 170.

To reach Whale Island, follow National Hwy 1 to Van Ninh, 60km north of Nha Trang and 64km south of Tuy Hoa. From there, it's a two-hour **boat trip** (in Hanoi ☎ 08-8458096, fax 8440205) to the island.

## Jungle Beach
Jungle Beach Resort (☎ 811350, ☎ 0913-429144; w www.lotusvietnam.com; bunga-lows US$10-25) sits on an enchanting three-hectare tract of land where jungle clad mountains converge with 550m of pristine beach front.

The brainchild of an eco-friendly French-Canadian-Vietnamese couple, this peaceful retreat features bungalows that are invisible to each other, spread out amid an astounding array of fruit trees, herb, flower and vegetable gardens – all part of a working organic farm. Solar and wind power supply much of the energy, and all of the tasty food is MSG-free.

In addition to the bungalows, basic dome-tent camping, as well as deluxe sleep outs (four-posters under mosquito nets!), are also possible here.

Behind the resort is superb for trekking, while out front there are top notch sea-kayaking opportunities, as well as the chance for rock climbing (boat access only). Surf's up around Jungle Beach from December until late March.

Jungle Beach is about half way between Doc Let Beach and Nha Trang, 59km by road from Nha Trang via National Hwy 1, but just 15km as the crow flies (or by boat). Motorbike drivers from Dalat know the place, or if you're taking an open-tour bus, ask the driver to drop you at the turn off to Jungle Beach on National Hwy 1.

## NHA TRANG
☎ 058 • pop 315,200

Nha Trang, the capital of Khanh Hoa province, has one of the most popular municipal beaches in all of Vietnam. Club Med hasn't arrived yet, and there are still no Monte Carlo–style casinos, but the resort town has rapidly developed into a bustling destination for sun and fun.

Nha Trang is a place to come and party, and the service on the beach is incredible – massage, lunch, cold beer, manicure, beauty treatments, etc. If you are after something more tranquil, however, consider heading for Mui Ne Beach (see later in this chapter) further south or, north of Nha Trang, to beautiful Jungle Beach or Whale Island (see earlier sections).

The clear turquoise waters around Nha Trang make for excellent fishing, snorkelling and scuba diving. However, you aren't likely to enjoy these pursuits in the off-season months of November and December, when the rains come. During heavy rains, water levels rise in the two rivers at either end of the 6km beach; runoff carried by the fresh water flows into the bay, which can turn a murky brown. Most of the year, however, the water is as it appears in the tourist brochures.

The combined fishing fleet of Khanh Hoa province and neighbouring Phu Yen prov-ince numbers about 10,000 trawlers and junks; they are able to fish during the 250 days of calm seas per year. The area's seafood products include abalone, lobster,

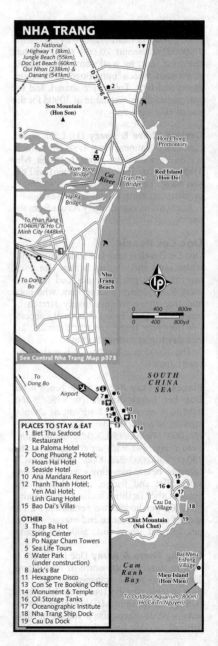

**NHA TRANG**

To National
Highway 1 (8km),
Jungle Beach (55km),
Doc Let Beach (60km),
Qui Nhon (238km) &
Danang (541km)

Son Mountain
(Hon Son)

Hon Chong
Promontory

Xom Bong
Bridge

Cai
River

Tran Phu
Bridge

Red Island
(Hon Do)

Ha Ra
Bridge

To Phan Rang
(104km) & Ho Chi
Minh City (448km)

To Dong
Bo

Nha
Trang
Beach

0    400    800m
0    400    800yd

See Central Nha Trang Map p373

To
Dong Bo

Airport

SOUTH
CHINA
SEA

Cau Da
Village

Chut Mountain
(Nui Chut)

Bai Mieu
Fishing
Village

Cam
Ranh
Bay

Mieu Island
(Hon Mieu)

To Outdoor Aquarium (800m)
(Ho Cá Tri Nguyen)

**PLACES TO STAY & EAT**
1 Biet Thu Seafood Restaurant
2 La Paloma Hotel
7 Dong Phuong 2 Hotel; Hoan Hai Hotel
9 Seaside Hotel
10 Ana Mandara Resort
12 Thanh Thanh Hotel; Yen Mai Hotel; Linh Giang Hotel
15 Bao Dai's Villas

**OTHER**
3 Thap Ba Hot Spring Center
4 Po Nagar Cham Towers
5 Sea Life Tours
6 Water Park (under construction)
8 Jack's Bar
11 Hexagone Disco
13 Con Se Tre Booking Office
14 Monument & Temple
16 Oil Storage Tanks
17 Oceanographic Institute
18 Nha Trang Ship Dock
19 Cau Da Dock

prawns, cuttlefish, mackerel, pomfret, scallops, shrimps, snapper and tuna. Nha Trang's fishing fleet operates mostly at night, using the days in port for rest and equipment repair. Agricultural products exported from the area include cashew nuts, coconuts, coffee and sesame seeds. Salt production is also large, employing over 4000 people – a good place to observe some photogenic **salt fields** is on the access road leading to Doc Let Beach (see that section earlier).

Nha Trang's dry season, unlike that of HCMC, runs from June to October. The wettest months are October and November, but rain usually falls only at night or in the morning. Weather patterns vary greatly from year to year, but in general the best season is from late January to late October. November typically brings the worst weather and December is not much better. The best beach weather is generally before 1pm; the afternoon sea breezes can make things unpleasant until the wind dies back down around 8pm. Although well within the tropics, Nha Trang has cool evenings.

Boat trips are a real highlight of Nha Trang (see The Islands & Boat Tours in the Around Nha Trang section).

Warning: we continue to hear reports of theft on the beach, as well as a proliferation of 'motorbike cowboy' thieves along Ð Tran Phu, the street running parallel to the beach.

## Information

**Money** There's a branch of **Vietcombank** (☎ 822720; 17 Ð Quang Trung; open 7.30am-11am & 1.30pm-4pm Mon-Fri), where you can change travellers cheques and get cash advances.

**Post** The **main post office** (cnr Ð Le Loi & Ð Pasteur; open 6.30am-8pm daily) is near the northern end of Nha Trang Beach.

For night owls, there's another **post office** (50 Ð Le Thanh Ton) that's open 24 hours.

**Email & Internet Access** There is plenty of Internet access available at **La Fregate Internet** (☎ 829011; 4 Ð Pasteur; open 8am-noon & 2pm-midnight daily) for a mere 100d per minute.

**Thanh's Family Booking Office** (2 Ð Hung Vuong) in the town centre charges about the same.

Many hotels also offer Internet access, as do the travellers cafés mentioned earlier.

**Travel Agencies** The provincial tourism authority, **Khanh Hoa Tourist** (☎ 822753, fax 824206; 1 Ð Tran Hung Dao) is beside the Vien Dong Hotel. It offers various tour programmes, but you'll likely find it cheaper and more interesting to book elsewhere.

The following are a few of Nha Trang's budget-traveller cafés-cum-travel-agencies (all of which sell bottom of the barrel 'fast food' tours).

**Hanh Cafe** (☎ 814227, e hanhcafe@dng.vnn.vn) 26 Ð Tran Hung Dao
**Sinh Cafe** (☎ 811981, e sinhcafent@dng.vnn.vn) 10 Ð Biet Thu
**TM Brothers Cafe** (☎ 814556, fax 815366, e hoanhaont@dng.vnn.vn) 22 Ð Tran Hung Dao)

**Lotus Tourist** (☎ 811350, ☎ 0913-429144; w www.lotusvietnam.com, w www.aseansail andpaddle.com) is worthy of a plug for its outdoor activities such as kayaking, surfing, sailing, trekking and camping. It's run out of the tranquil Jungle Beach Resort, north of Nha Trang.

**Wave Killer** (☎ 512308, ☎ 0903-572106; e oceane@dng.vnn.vn), found at the Louisiane Cafe, is a good place in town to hire water-sports equipment.

**Con Se Tre** (☎/fax 811163; 1006 Ð Tran Phu) offers interesting boat tours to peaceful Hon Tre (Bamboo Island). Full day tours cost US$5/10 with/without lunch, and their popular dinner trips (US$8) are also worth looking into. For more information (including about camping on the island) visit the booking office across from the Ana Mandara Resort.

**Mama Linh's Boat Tours** (☎ 826693, fax 815365; 2A Ð Hung Vuong) runs a fleet of island-hopping party boats. Daily trips last from 8.45am until 4.30pm, and typically include stops on Hon Mun (Salangane Island), Hon Mot, Hon Tam and Hon Mieu – see the

Around Nha Trang section later for more information on these islands. Tickets (US$5) are sold at this office, but you can easily book at your hotel for a dollar or two more.

**Sea Life Tours** (☎ 827528; W *www.sealife tours.com; 96A/4 Đ Tran Phu*) peddles three-hour glass-bottom boat tours (145,000d per person) in Nha Trang Bay.

**Mr Vu's Tour Adventures** (☎ 813009, fax 828996; e *tranvuvn@hotmail.com*), attached to Cafe des Amis, can be recommended for inland excursions to the central highlands. One reader wrote:

If you're in Nha Trang, heading north or south, an interesting alternative to the Sinh Cafe tourist bus trail is to take a tour of the Central Highlands en route to Hoi An, Hué, HCMC or Dalat. You can trek or raft to minority villages, ride elephants, see waterfalls and more.

**Caprice Olsthoorn**

Nha Trang is Vietnam's number one **scuba-diving** destination; for a list of local dive operators, see the Activities section later.

**Bookshops & Photo Processing** Outdoors, near the War Memorial, is **Mr. Lang's Book Exchange** (*Đ Tran Phu*), which stocks a good collection of used books in a variety of languages.

**Hung Hara** (☎ 828030; *2C Đ Biet Thu*) is a reliable local photo lab to have your film developed at.

**Dangers & Annoyances** Although Nha Trang is generally a safe place, be very careful at night, especially on the beach and along Đ Tran Phu. The best advice, in fact, is to stay off the beach after dark. We've heard countless stories of thievery and rip-offs, mostly instigated by quick-witted prostitutes who canvass the area.

## Beaches
Coconut palms provide shelter for both bathers and strollers along most of Nha Trang's 6km of beachfront. Beach chairs are available for rent – you can just sit and enjoy the drinks and light food that the beach vendors have on offer. About the only

time you need to move is to use the toilet or when the tide comes up.

Hon Chong Beach (Bai Tam Hon Chong) is a series of beaches that begin just north of Hon Chong Promontory; fishing families live here among the coconut palms, but the refuse makes the place unsuitable for swimming or sunbathing. Behind the beaches are steep mountains, whose lower reaches support crops that include mangoes and bananas.

About 300m south of Hon Chong (ie, towards Nha Trang) and a few dozen metres from the beach is tiny Hon Do (Red Island), which has a Buddhist temple on top.

## Louisiane Cafe
Louisiane Cafe (☎ 812948, fax 814722; e *loui sianecafe@hotmail.com*) is a large and pleasant beachfront place that resembles a Western-style beach club. This attractive, thoughtfully landscaped facility has been done in a stylish Mediterranean blue motif. In the daytime, vendors are not permitted on the private beach, a restriction you'll come to appreciate with time.

The best thing about Louisiane Cafe is that it is free – well, almost. Guests can indulge themselves in use of the swimming pool and beach chairs here in exchange simply for patronising the restaurant, bakery or bar. Their cakes and pastries are superb!

Also at the café, Wave Killer rents out surfing, windsurfing and kite-sail gear, plus catamarans.

## Pasteur Institute
Nha Trang's Pasteur Institute (☎ 822406, fax 824058; *10 Đ Tran Phu*) was founded in 1895 by Dr Alexandre Yersin (1863–1943), who was, from among the tens of thousands of colonists who spent time in Vietnam, probably the Frenchman most loved by the Vietnamese. Vietnam's two other Pasteur Institutes are in HCMC and Dalat.

Born in Switzerland, of French and Swiss parents, Dr Yersin came to Vietnam in 1889 after working under Louis Pasteur in Paris. He learned to speak Vietnamese fluently, and spent the next few years travelling throughout the central highlands and recording his

# CENTRAL NHA TRANG

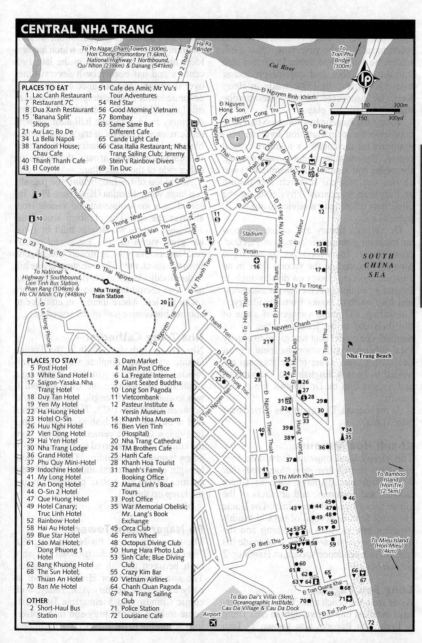

To Po Nagar Cham Towers (300m),
Hon Chong Promontory (1.6km),
National Highway 1 Northbound,
Qui Nhon (238km) & Danang (541km)

Ha Ra
Bridge

To
Tran Phu
Bridge
(300m)

Cai River

0    150    300m
0    150    300yd

SOUTH
CHINA
SEA

Nha Trang Beach

To Bamboo
Island
(Hon Tre)
(2.5km)

To Mieu Island
(Hon Mieu)
(4km)

**PLACES TO EAT**
1  Lac Canh Restaurant
7  Restaurant 7C
8  Dua Xanh Restaurant
15  'Banana Split'
    Shops
21  Au Lac; Bo De
34  La Bella Napoli
38  Tandoori House;
    Chau Cafe
40  Thanh Thanh Cafe
43  El Coyote
51  Cafe des Amis; Mr Vu's
    Tour Adventures
54  Red Star
56  Good Morning Vietnam
57  Bombay
63  Same Same But
    Different Cafe
65  Cande Light Cafe
66  Casa Italia Restaurant; Nha
    Trang Sailing Club; Jeremy
    Stein's Rainbow Divers
69  Tin Duc

**PLACES TO STAY**
5  Post Hotel
13  White Sand Hotel I
17  Saigon-Yasaka Nha
    Trang Hotel
18  Duy Tan Hotel
19  Yen My Hotel
22  Ha Huong Hotel
23  Hotel O-Sin
26  Huu Nghi Hotel
27  Vien Dong Hotel
29  Hai Yen Hotel
30  Nha Trang Lodge
36  Grand Hotel
37  Phu Quy Mini-Hotel
41  My Long Hotel
42  An Dong Hotel
44  O-Sin 2 Hotel
47  Que Huong Hotel
49  Hotel Canary;
    Truc Linh Hotel
52  Rainbow Hotel
58  Hai Au Hotel
59  Blue Star Hotel
61  Sao Mai Hotel;
    Dong Phuong 1
    Hotel
62  Bang Khuong Hotel
68  The Sun Hotel;
    Thuan An Hotel
70  Ban Me Hotel

**OTHER**
2  Short-Haul Bus
   Station
3  Dam Market
4  Main Post Office
6  La Fregate Internet
9  Giant Seated Buddha
10  Long Son Pagoda
11  Vietcombank
12  Pasteur Institute &
    Yersin Museum
14  Khanh Hoa Museum
16  Bien Vien Tinh
    (Hospital)
20  Nha Trang Cathedral
24  TM Brothers Cafe
25  Hanh Cafe
28  Khanh Hoa Tourist
31  Thanh's Family
    Booking Office
32  Mama Linh's Boat
    Tours
33  Post Office
35  War Memorial Obelisk;
    Mr. Lang's Book
    Exchange
45  Orca Club
46  Ferris Wheel
48  Octopus Diving Club
50  Hung Hara Photo Lab
53  Sinh Cafe; Blue Diving
    Club
55  Crazy Kim Bar
60  Vietnam Airlines
64  Chanh Quan Pagoda
67  Nha Trang Sailing
    Club
71  Police Station
72  Louisiane Café

To Tran Phu Bridge
(300m)

Đ 2 Thang 4
Đ Nguyen Binh Khiem
Đ Nguyen
Hong Son
Đ Nguyen Cong Tru
Đ Ngo Quyen
Đ Hang
Ca
Đ Nguyen Thai Hoc
Đ Phan Boi Chau
Đ Dinh Phong
Đ Le Loi
Đ Tran Qui Cap
Đ Phan Chu Trinh
Đ Ti trang Nu Vuong
Đ Quang Trung
Đ Thong Nhat
Đ Yet Kieu
Đ Hoang Van Thu
Đ Le Thanh Phuong
Stadium
Đ Yersin
Đ Pasteur
Đ 23 Thang 10
Đ Thai Nguyen
Đ Ly Thanh Ton
Đ Hoang Hoa Tham
Đ Ly Tu Trong
Đ Le Thanh Ton
Đ To Hien Thanh
Đ Nguyen Chanh
Đ Tran Hung Dao
Đ Nguyen Trai
Đ Le Hong Phong
Nha Trang
Train Station
Đ Le Qui Don
Đ Nguyen Tung Truc
Đ Nguyen Trung Truc
Đ Hung Vuong
Đ Nguyen Thien Thuat
Đ Tran Nguyen Han
Đ Thi Minh Khai
Đ Biet Thu
Đ Tran Quang Khai
Đ Tui Tinh

To National
Highway 1 Southbound,
Lien Tinh Bus Station,
Phan Rang (104km) &
Ho Chi Minh City (448km)

To Bao Dai's Villas (3km),
Oceanographic Institute,
Cau Da Village & Cau Da Dock

Airport

observations. During this period, he came upon the site of what is now Dalat and recommended to the government that a hill station be established there. Dr Yersin also introduced rubber and quinine-producing trees to Vietnam. In 1894, while in Hong Kong, he discovered the rat-borne microbe that causes bubonic plague.

Today, the Pasteur Institute in Nha Trang coordinates vaccination and hygiene programmes for the country's southern coastal region. The institute produces vaccines (eg, for rabies and Japanese B encephalitis) and carries out medical research and testing at European standards. Physicians at the clinic here offer medical advice to around 70 patients a day.

Dr Yersin's library and office are now an interesting museum (admission 26,000d; open 7am-11.15am Mon-Sat, 2pm-4.30pm Mon-Fri), located on the second floor in an adjacent building. Items on display include laboratory equipment (such as his astronomical instruments), books from his library, a fascinating 3-D photo viewer and some of the thousand or so letters written to his mother! The model boat was given to him by local fishermen with whom he spent a great deal of his time. Tours of the museum are guided in French, English and Vietnamese, and a short film on Dr Yersin's life is also shown.

At his request, Dr Yersin was buried near Nha Trang.

## Khanh Hoa Museum

This sleepy local museum (admission free; open 8am-10am & 2pm-4pm Mon, Wed, Thur & Sun) features displays such as Cham statutes and costumes, and artefacts of the ethnic minorities in the province. The Uncle Ho room features several of Ho Chi Minh's personal effects, such as clothing and the actual microphone with which he made his famous independence speech in Hanoi on 2 September 1945.

## Long Son Pagoda

Aside from the beach and Cham towers, perhaps the most impressive sight in Nha Trang is Long Son Pagoda, also known as Tinh Hoi Khanh Hoa Pagoda and An Nam Phat Hoc Hoi Pagoda. It's about 500m west of the train station. The pagoda, which has resident monks, was founded in the late 19th century and has been rebuilt several times over the years. The entrance and roofs are decorated with mosaic dragons constructed of glass and bits of ceramic tile. The main sanctuary is an attractive hall adorned with modern interpretations of traditional motifs. Note the ferocious nose hairs on the colourful dragons wrapped around the pillars on either side of the main altar.

At the top of the hill, behind the pagoda, is a huge white Buddha (Kim Than Phat To) seated on a lotus blossom and visible from all over the city. The platform around the 14m-high figure, which was built in 1963, has great views of Nha Trang and nearby rural areas. As you approach the pagoda from the street, the 152 stone steps up the hill to the Buddha begin to the right of the structure. You should take some time to explore off to the left, where there's an entrance to another impressive hall of the pagoda.

## Nha Trang Cathedral

Nha Trang Cathedral, built in the French Gothic style and complete with medieval-looking stained glass windows, stands on a small hill overlooking the train station. It was constructed of simple cement blocks between 1928 and 1933. Today, the cathedral is the seat of the bishop of Nha Trang. In 1988, a Catholic cemetery not far from the church was disinterred to make room for a new train-station building. The ashes were brought to the cathedral and reburied in the cavities behind the wall of plaques that line the ramp up the hill.

Masses are held daily.

## Po Nagar Cham Towers

The Cham towers of Po Nagar (Thap Ba, The Lady of the City; admission 3000d) were built between the 7th and 12th centuries. The site was used for Hindu worship as early as the 2nd century AD. Today, both ethnic Chinese and Vietnamese Buddhists come to Po Nagar to pray and make offerings according to their respective traditions.

# PO NAGAR CHAM TOWERS

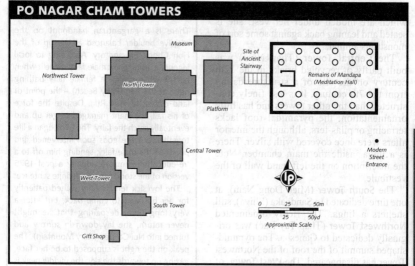

Museum

Site of Ancient Stairway

Remains of Mandapa (Meditation Hall)

Northwest Tower

North Tower

Platform

Central Tower

Modern Street Entrance

West Tower

South Tower

Gift Shop

0        25        50m
0        25        50yd
Approximate Scale

This site has a continuing religious significance, so do remember to remove your shoes before entering.

The towers serve as the Holy See, honouring Goddess Yang Ino Po Nagar, the Goddess of the Dua (Liu) clan, which ruled over the southern part of the Cham Kingdom covering Kauthara and Pan Duranga (present day Khanh Hoa and Thuan Hai provinces). The original wooden structure was razed to the ground by attacking Javanese in AD 774 but was replaced by a stone and brick temple (the first of its kind) in 784. There are many stone slabs scattered throughout the complex, most of which relate to history or religion, and provide great insight into the spiritual life and social structure of the Chams.

Originally the complex covered an area of 500 sq metres and there were seven or eight towers, four of which remain. All of the temples face east, as did the original entrance to the complex, which is to the right as you ascend the hillock. In centuries past, a person coming to pray passed through the pillared **meditation hall**, 10 pillars of which can still be seen, before proceeding up the staircase to the towers.

The 28m-high **North Tower** (Thap Chinh), with its terraced pyramidal roof, vaulted interior masonry and vestibule, is a superb example of Cham architecture. One of the tallest Cham towers, it was built in AD 817 by Pangro, a minister of King Harivarman I, after the original temples here were sacked and burned. The raiders also carried off a linga made of precious metal. In AD 918 King Indravarman III placed a gold *mukha-linga* in the North Tower, but it too was taken, this time by the Khmers. This pattern of statues being destroyed or stolen and then replaced continued for some time until 965, when King Jaya Indravarman I replaced the gold *mukha-linga* with the stone figure, Uma (*shakti*, or a feminine manifestation of Shiva), which remains to this day.

Above the entrance to the North Tower, two musicians flank a dancing four-armed Shiva, one of whose feet is on the head of the bull Nandin. The sandstone doorposts are covered with inscriptions, as are parts of the walls of the vestibule. A gong and a drum stand under the pyramid-shaped ceiling of the antechamber. In the 28m-high pyramidal main chamber, there is a black stone statue of the goddess Uma (in the shape of Bhagavati) with 10 arms, two of which are hidden under her vest; she is seated and leaning back against some sort of monstrous animal.

The **Central Tower** (Thap Nam) was built partly of recycled bricks in the 12th century on the site of a structure dating from the 7th century. It is less finely constructed than the other towers and has little ornamentation; the pyramidal roof lacks terracing or pilas-ters, although the interior altars were once covered with silver. There is a linga inside the main chamber. Note the inscription on the left-hand wall of the vestibule.

The **South Tower** (Mieu Dong Nam), at one time dedicated to Sandhaka (Shiva), still shelters a linga. The richly ornamented **Northwest Tower** (Thap Tay Bac) was originally dedicated to Ganesha. The pyramid-shaped summit of the roof of the Northwest Tower has disappeared. The **West Tower**, of which almost nothing remains, was constructed by King Vikrantavarman during the first half of the 9th century. Near the North Tower is a small **museum** with a few mediocre examples of Cham stone-work; the explanatory signs are in Vietnam-ese only. At one time there was a small temple on this site.

The towers of Po Nagar stand on a granite knoll, 2km north of central Nha Trang and on the banks of the Cai River. To get there from central Nha Trang, take Đ Quang Trung (which becomes Đ 2 Thang 4) north across Ha Ra Bridge and Xom Bong Bridge, which span the mouth of the Cai River. Po Nagar can also be reached via the new Tran Phu bridge along the beach-front road.

## Hon Chong Promontory

Hon Chong is a narrow granite promontory that juts out into the turquoise waters of the South China Sea. The views of the mountainous coastline north of Nha Trang and nearby islands are certainly fine, and the beach here offers a more local flavour than the main beach in the town centre.

To the northwest is Nui Co Tien (Fairy Mountain) with three summits believed to

### Fairy Romance

There is a gargantuan handprint on the massive boulder balanced at the tip of the Hon Chong Promontory. According to local legend, a drunk giant male fairy made it when he fell while spying a female fairy bathing nude at Bai Tien (Fairy Beach) – the point of land closest to Hon Rua. Despite the force of his fall, the giant managed to get up and eventually catch the fairy. The two began a life together, but the gods soon intervened and punished the male fairy, sending him off to a 're-education camp' (evidently a post-1975 version of the story) for an indefinite sentence.

The lovesick female fairy waited patiently for her husband to come back, but after a very long time, despairing that he might never return, she lay down in sorrow and turned into Nui Co Tien (Fairy Mountain). The peak on the right is supposed to be her face, gazing up towards the sky; the middle peak is her breasts; and the summit on the left (the highest) forms her crossed legs.

When the male fairy finally returned and saw what had become of his wife, he prostrated himself in grief next to a boulder, leaving his handprint on it. He, too, turned to stone and can be seen to this day.

resemble a reclining female fairy (see the boxed text 'Fairy Romance').

To the northeast is Hon Rua (Tortoise Island), which really does resemble a tortoise. The two islands of Hon Yen are off in the distance to the east.

## Thap Ba Hot Spring Center

Thap Ba Hot Spring Center (☎ 514099, fax 514278; e saomaitk21@dng.vnn.vn; open 8am-8pm Mon-Fri, 7am-9pm Sat, Sun & public holidays) is an outdoor leisure complex on the northern outskirts of Nha Trang, near the Po Nagar Cham Towers. The big attraction here is the chance to soak your bones in soothing pools of hot, mineral-rich mud.

Facilities at this suburban oasis include swimming and bathing pools (both private and public), a massage service, a butterfly garden, a waterfall, a restaurant and a café. You can also rent simple **bungalows** here.

Ticket prices are 15,000d for use of the mineral-water swimming pools, 25,000d for a regular hot-spring water bath, and 50,000d for a bath in mineral mud. Kids get a 50% discount. Towels and bathing costumes are provided free of charge.

To get there, follow Đ 2 Thang 4 north from the centre of town. Cross the Ha Ra Bridge and the Xom Bong Bridge, after which you will see the Po Nagar Cham Towers on your left. The turn-off (signposted) to the springs is on the same side of the street, just beyond the pagoda. Turn and follow the bumpy road for 2.5km.

## Oceanographic Institute

The Oceanographic Institute (Vien Nghiem Cuu Bien; ☎ 590036; admission 5000d; open 7.30am-noon & 1pm-4.30pm daily), founded in 1923, is housed in a grand French-colonial building 6km south of Nha Trang's main post office in the port district of Cau Da (also called Cau Be). It has an aquarium (ho ca) and specimen room open to the public; it also has a library. The 23 tanks on the ground floor are home to a variety of colourful live specimens of local marine life, including seahorses.

Behind the main building and across the volleyball court is a large hall filled with 60,000 dead specimens of sea life, including stuffed seabirds and fish, corals and the corporeal remains of other marine creatures preserved in glass jars.

As nice as the Oceanographic Institute is, if you really want to see an aquarium, you should take a boat across to nearby Mieu Island (see Around Nha Trang later in this chapter).

## Bao Dai's Villas

These are the former retreats of Bao Dai, Vietnam's own 'last emperor' (he abdicated in 1945). Between the mid-1950s and 1975, Bao Dai's Villas (Biet Thu Cau Da) were used by the high-ranking officials of the South Vietnamese government, including President Thieu. This all changed in 1975, when the villas were taken over for use by

high-ranking communist officials, including the prime minister, Pham Van Dong. Today, low-ranking 'capitalist tourists' can rent a room in the villas (see Places to Stay).

Bao Dai's five villas, built in the 1920s, are set on three hills south of town, and have brilliant views of the South China Sea, Nha Trang Bay (to the north) and Cau Da dock (to the south). Between the buildings are winding paths lined with tropical bushes and trees. Most of the villas' furnishings have not been changed in decades.

There's a 2000d charge to enter the grounds of the villas, but if you're heading for the **restaurant**, there is usually no need to pay the entry fee.

To get to Bao Dai's Villas from Nha Trang, turn left off Đ Tran Phu, just past the white-cement oil storage tanks (but before reaching Cau Da village). These villas are several hundred metres north of the Oceanographic Institute.

## Scuba Diving

Nha Trang is Vietnam's premier scuba-diving locale. Visibility averages 15m, but can be as much as 30m depending on the season (late October to early January is the worst time of year).

There are around 25 dive sites in the area, both shallow and deep. There are no wrecks to dive on (yet), but some sites have good drop-offs and there are a few small underwater caves to explore. The waters support a good variety of soft and hard corals, and a reasonable number of small reef fish. There are a few resident sharks, including grey-nurse sharks and a white-tip shark named 'Eric'. Whale sharks have also been known to pass through and stingrays are a common sight.

A full-day outing including boat transport, two dives and lunch typically costs between US$40 and US$60. Most dive operators also offer a range of dive courses, including a 'discover diving' programme for uncertified, first-time divers to experience the thrill under the supervision of a qualified dive master.

It is difficult to recommend one dive operator over another, so our best advice is to shop around, speak to a few different operators and use your better judgement. With that caveat in mind, consider the following outfits.

**Blue Diving Club** (☎ 825390, fax 816088; e bluedivingclub@hotmail.com, w www .vietnamdivers.com; Ð Biet Thu) is French-British owned and operated.

**Coco Dive Center** (☎ 812900, fax 810444; e cocodive@dng.vnn.vn, w www.cocodive center.com; 2E Ð Biet Thu) was opened by Ms Minh Xuan, Vietnam's first and only PADI Instructor, and consequently a champion swimmer and local karate champion!

**Jeremy Stein's Rainbow Divers** (☎ 829946, fax 811223; e rainbowdivers@hotmail.com, w www.divevietnam.com) is located at the Sailing Club and is run by Briton Jeremy Stein (who also just happens to be a dead ringer for Chuck Norris).

**Octopus Diving Club** (☎ 810629, fax 827436; e haison.aaa@dng.vnn.vn; 62 Ð Tran Phu) is a French-run dive shop right across from the beach.

**Orca Club** (☎ 811375, fax 811374; e vie travel.diving@dng.vnn.vn; 58 Ð Tran Phu) is Vietnamese-run, and part of a company called Vietravel.

## Places to Stay

Nha Trang is a trendy place for both domestic and foreign tourists, with the result that there are around 100 hotels to choose from. Several of the state-run hotels occupying prime beachfront property have become markedly run-down, and most are not worth considering. For the same money, you can do much better at one of the countless private minihotels, which even if not on the beach, will be within a few minutes' walk.

### Considerations for Responsible Diving

The popularity of diving is placing immense pressure on many sites. Please consider the following tips when diving and help preserve the ecology and beauty of reefs.

- Do not use anchors on the reef, and take care not to ground boats on coral. Encourage dive operators and regulatory bodies to establish permanent moorings at popular dive sites.
- Avoid touching living marine organisms with your body or dragging equipment across the reef. Polyps can be damaged by even the gentlest contact. Never stand on corals, even if they look solid and robust. If you must hold on to the reef, only touch exposed rock or dead coral.
- Be conscious of your fins. Even without contact, the surge from heavy fin strokes near the reef can damage delicate organisms. When treading water in shallow reef areas, take care not to kick up clouds of sand. Settling sand can easily smother the delicate organisms of the reef.
- Practise and maintain proper buoyancy control. Major damage can be done by divers descending too fast and colliding with the reef. Make sure you are correctly weighted and that your weight belt is positioned so that you stay horizontal. If you have not dived for a while, have a practice dive in a pool before taking to the reef. Be aware that buoyancy can change over the period of an extended trip: initially you may breathe harder and need more weight; a few days later you may breathe more easily and need less weight.
- Resist the temptation to collect or buy coral or shells. Aside from the ecological damage, taking home marine souvenirs depletes the beauty of a site and spoils the enjoyment of others. The same goes for marine archaeological sites (mainly shipwrecks). Respect their integrity; some sites are even protected from looting by law.
- Ensure that you take home all your rubbish and any litter you may find as well. Plastics in particular are a serious threat to marine life. Turtles can mistake plastic for jellyfish and eat it.
- Resist the temptation to feed fish. You may disturb their normal eating habits, encourage aggressive behaviour or feed them food that is detrimental to their health.
- Minimise your disturbance of marine animals

For two secluded-beach accommodation alternatives outside of Nha Trang, see the Whale Island and Jungle Beach sections earlier in this chapter.

## Places to Stay – Budget

**Hotel O-Sin** (☎ 825064, fax 824991; e osin hotel@hotmail.com; 4 Đ Nguyen Thien Thuat; dorm beds US$2, fan rooms US$5-7, air-con rooms US$8-9) has earned itself a steady following with backpackers for its good, cheap rooms.

**O-Sin 2 Hotel** (☎ 822902; 15 Đ Hung Vuong) charges similar rates.

**Sao Mai Hotel** (☎ 827412; 99 Đ Nguyen Thien Thuat; dorm beds US$3, fan rooms US$5-7, air-con rooms US$9-11) is another budget place with a dorm.

**Bang Khuong Hotel** (☎ 813516; 1 Đ Quan Tran; air-con rooms US$7-10) is a nice new place tucked into a quiet alley near the Chanh Quan Pagoda on Đ Hung Vuong.

**Yen My Hotel** (☎ 829064; e yenmyhotel@ hotmail.com; 22 Đ Hoang Hoa Tham; fan rooms US$5-8, air-con rooms US$8-12) is a good budget place run by a friendly man named Mr Duan.

**Thuan An Hotel** (☎ 815577; e thuanan hotel@dng.vnn.vn; 1A Đ Tran Quang Khai; fan rooms US$5-7, air-con rooms US$8-12) is a friendly place offering Internet access in the lobby. Next door, **The Sun Hotel** (☎ 814428; e kshoangvan@dng.vnn.vn; 1 Đ Tran Quang Khai; fan rooms US$7-9, air-con rooms US$10-15) provides a welcoming reception, satellite TV and bathtubs in most rooms. Both of these places are very close to the beach.

**Blue Star Hotel** (☎ 826447; 1B Đ Biet Thu; fan rooms US$7, air-con rooms US$10-12), also close to the beach, has received good reports from travellers.

**My Long Hotel** (☎/fax 814451; e my longhotel@yahoo.com; 26A Đ Nguyen Thien Thuat; fan rooms US$7-10, air-con rooms US$10-15) is a centrally located, clean and friendly choice.

**Hotel Canary** (Kim Tuoc; ☎ 828679; 27C Đ Hung Vuong; rooms US$10-12) and **Truc Linh Hotel** (☎ 815201; e internet_bt@yahoo.com; 27B Đ Hung Vuong; rooms US$8-20) are two flashy, new, jumbo minihotels located side by side. Some rooms feature large balconies.

**Dong Phuong 1 Hotel** (☎ 828247, fax 825986; 103 Đ Nguyen Thien Thuat; old-wing rooms US$4-8, new-wing rooms US$8-20) is older than Dong Phuong 2, but has spacious rooms featuring the thickest mattresses in Nha Trang. The new-wing minihotel next door features an elevator and sea views from the upper-floor rooms.

**An Dong Hotel** (☎ 828905; 31 Đ Nguyen Thien Thuat; fan rooms US$6, air-con rooms US$10) has clean and comfortable rooms.

**Huu Nghi Hotel** (☎ 826703, fax 827416; 3 Đ Tran Hung Dao; singles with fan/ air-con 80,000/170,000d, doubles 100,000/ 200,000d, triples 120,000/220,000d) is a time-honoured backpackers haunt. Air-con rooms also have satellite TV.

**Ha Huong Hotel** (☎ 512069; e hahuong nt@dng.vnn.vn; 26 Đ Nguyen Trung Truc; fan rooms US$6, air-con rooms US$8-15) is a friendly hotel on a quiet street about five minutes' walk from the beach. Rooms are clean and the air-con rooms have satellite TV and a balcony.

**White Sand Hotel I** (☎ 825861, fax 810449; 14 Đ Tran Phu; rooms US$12-14) is a motel-style place near the beach with basic air-con doubles.

**Post Hotel** (☎ 821250, fax 824205; e post hotel@dng.vnn.vn; 2 Đ Le Loi; rooms with shared toilet US$8, rooms with private toilet US$18-22) is in a good location near the beachfront. The better rooms provide a view of the sea.

**Phu Quy Mini-Hotel** (☎ 810609, fax 812954; e phuquyhotel@dng.vnn.vn; 54 Đ Hung Vuong; fan rooms US$10, with air-con US$15-18) receives good reports.

**Grand Hotel** (Nha Khach 44; ☎ 822445, fax 825395; 44 Đ Tran Phu; fan rooms from US$4, air-con rooms US$10-20) is a huge beachfront place housed in a stately (but faded and crying out to be restored) French colonial-style building. The cheaper prison cells with fan only are in a separate wing.

There's a strip of fine oceanfront mini-hotels along the southern part of Đ Tran Phu; some rooms feature balconies overlooking the sea. Worth checking out are the

Thanh Thanh Hotel (☎ 824657, fax 823031; e thanhthanhhotel@dng.vnn.vn; 98A Đ Tran Phu; air-con rooms US$7-15), the **Seaside Hotel** (☎ 821178, fax 828038; 96B Đ Tran Phu; rooms US$10-20) next door and the **Yen Mai Hotel**.

Last but not least, **La Paloma Hotel** (Nha Trang map; ☎ 831216; e datle@dng.vnn.vn; 1 Đ Hon Chong; rooms US$8-25) is a commendable little family-run oasis on the northern outskirts of town, near the Hon Chong Promontory. Fronting the hotel is a pleasant outdoor café situated in a palm-tree garden. The friendly owner Mr Bu offers guests free jeep shuttles to/from the train station and airport, as well as between the hotel and downtown. There's a small beach nearby with good local flavour.

## Places to Stay – Mid-Range

**Rainbow Hotel** (☎ 810501, fax 810030; e rainbowhotel@dng.vnn.vn; Đ 8 Biet Thu; rooms US$15-25) has an elevator and satellite TV, and is in a pastel-green building not far from the beach – it's hard to miss.

**Indochine Hotel** (☎ 815333, fax 821515; 14 Đ Hung Vuong; rooms US$12-25) keeps a similar standard as the Rainbow.

**Linh Giang Hotel** (☎ 816454; e linhgianghotelkh@dng.vnn.vn; 98A Đ Tran Phu; rooms US$15-20) is a good spot right across from the beach.

**Dong Phuong 2 Hotel** (☎ 814580, fax 825986; e dongphuongnt@dng.vnn.vn; 96A 6/1 Đ Tran Phu; air-con rooms US$15-25) is a large and quiet place set back off the main road. Rates vary depending on what floor you are on and the size of the balcony. Nearly attached is the squeaky-clean **Hoan Hai Hotel** (☎ 821262, fax 813123; e hoanhai96tp@dng.vnn.vn; 96 Đ Tran Phu; rooms US$20-30), offering satellite TV, an elevator and minibars.

**Que Huong Hotel** (☎ 825047, fax 825344; 60 Đ Tran Phu; rooms US$40-60) boasts a swimming pool and a tennis court. It looks a bit better on the outside than it does on the inside. Air-con rooms also come with satellite TV.

**Duy Tan Hotel** (☎ 822671, fax 825034; 24 Đ Tran Phu; singles/doubles with air-con from US$15/20) is a large seafront place that is OK for a state-run hotel.

**Vien Dong Hotel** (☎ 821606, fax 821912; e viendonghtl@dng.vnn.vn; 1 Đ Tran Hung Dao; singles/doubles/triples from US$24/28/32) is a large old place that has long been a travellers favourite. It has a swimming pool, photo-processing facilities and bicycle rentals (US$5 per day). According to the hotel's pamphlet, 'Weapons and objects with offensive smell should be kept at the reception desk'.

**Hai Yen Hotel** (☎ 822828, fax 821902; 40 Đ Tran Phu; rooms US$10-52) is notable for its swimming pool and balcony sea views. Its name means 'sea swift'. All rooms have air-con, hot water and satellite TV, and rates include breakfast.

**Ban Me Hotel** (☎ 829500, fax 810035; 3/3 Đ Tran Quang Khai; singles/doubles/triples/ quads 253,000/275,000/319,000/418,000d) is a large place just a few hundred metres from the beach. All rooms have air-con and satellite TV. Rates include breakfast.

**Bao Dai's Villas** (☎ 590148, fax 590146; e baodai@dng.vnn.vn; standard rooms US$25-50, deluxe rooms US$70-80), furthest from the town centre, is near Cau Da on the coast, 6km south of the train station. The spacious top-end rooms are classic, with high ceilings, huge bathrooms and prime views of the bay, though it's questionable if they're worth the price tag. This is where Vietnam's ruling elite has rested itself since the days of French rule. Rates include breakfast. There is a private beach below the hotel with a good restaurant and another restaurant up top with fine views of the bay.

## Places to Stay – Top End

**Ana Mandara Resort** (☎ 829829, fax 829629; e resvana@dng.vnn.vn; rooms US$166-330++) is a gorgeous set of open timber-roofed beach villas south of town. This exquisite resort offers every possible luxury and is hands-down Nha Trang's classiest accommodation offering.

**Nha Trang Lodge** (☎ 810500, fax 828800; e nt-lodge@dng.vnn.vn; 42 Đ Tran Phu; rooms US$45-150), with 13 floors, is one of Nha Trang's tallest and fanciest high-rises.

Another snazzy skyscraper, **Saigon-Yasaka Nha Trang Hotel** (☎ 810500, fax 828800; e nt-lodge@dng.vnn.vn; 42 Đ Tran Phu; rooms US$98-198++) is a glitzy joint venture between Saigon Tourist and the Japanese. Facilities include a health club and swimming pool.

At the time of writing, plans were in the works for **Ruaka**, a five-star mega-resort north of the city. It is questionable whether it will be open by the time you read this, but when it does, Ruaka promises to be Vietnam's most exclusive and elegant beach resort.

## Places to Eat

Nha Trang is naturally a seafood haven, and there is a wide variety of excellent eateries. If you've been enjoying the fresh baguettes in Vietnam, you're in for a treat. Nha Trang has its own unique variety of French bread, a heavier loaf, which is closer in consistency (and taste) to a New York City hot pretzel. Proud locals say the bread is more filling for Nha Trang's hard-working fishermen.

**Beach Area** Serving up excellent Italian food, **La Bella Napoli** (☎ 829621; Đ Tran Phu) is found in a delightful terrace setting, overlooking the beach. The congenial owners Marinella and Gigi specialise in home-cooked southern Italian dishes and great brick-oven pizzas. Inquire (the day before) about their special fish dishes (the sea bass cooked in salt crust is divine!).

**Casa Italia Restaurant** (☎ 826528; 72-4 Đ Tran Phu), yet another authentic Italian ristorante, serves excellent pasta and fine wine. You can choose a selection of fresh seafood from a traditional Vietnamese boat and have it cooked in front of you. Attached is the **Nha Trang Sailing Club** (☎ 826528), a popular bar-restaurant that serves a variety of cuisines from Vietnamese and European to Indian and Japanese.

**Good Morning Vietnam** (☎ 815071; 19B Đ Biet Thu; mains 20,000-50,000đ), also Italian-run, does good and reasonably priced pizza, pasta and salads, plus a bit of Thai and Vietnamese to spice things up. Upstairs you can kick back on cosy Thai cushions to eat or watch movies (shown daily at 5pm and 8pm).

**Cafe des Amis** (☎ 813009; 2D Đ Biet Thu) is a popular spot with excellent vegetarian fare. The walls here are covered with an interesting collection of works by Vietnamese painters. Attached to the café, Mr Vu's Tour Adventures is a recommended place to inquire about jeep/motorbike tours into the Central Highlands.

**Tin Duc** (☎ 827030; 16 Đ Tran Quang Khai; most mains 25,000đ) is a reliable choice for breakfast, lunch or dinner. This place has received good marks from many travellers.

**Same Same But Different Cafe** (☎ 524079; 4 Đ Tran Quang Khai) is another good spot run by cool people, who prepare Vietnamese and Western food (including vegie dishes and tasty muesli for breakfast) at reasonable prices. There's a similar setup down the road at the **Candle Light Cafe** (6Đ Tran Quang Khai).

**Red Star** (☎ 812790; 14 Đ Biet Thu) is a no-frills place with excellent seafood. Try the crab or clams with ginger, lemongrass and chilli, or the fish hotpot.

**El Coyote** (☎ 820202; 76 Đ Hung Vuong; mains 40,000-60,000đ) does authentic Tex-Mex food like *chili con carne* and *pato con coca* – duck leg with coca sauce. The owner has perhaps the most curious ethnic roots in town: he's a mixture of French, Vietnamese, Lao and Cheyenne Indian.

**Bombay** (15 Đ Biet Thu) does Indian food that is worth a try. Ditto for **Tandoori House** (Đ Hung Vuong). Just next door is the **Chau Cafe**.

**Thanh Thanh Cafe** (☎ 824413; 10 Đ Nguyen Thien Thuat) is a travellers café serving pizza, Vietnamese dishes and other standard backpacker fare.

**Central Area** A Nha Trang institution, **Lac Canh Restaurant** (☎ 828189; 44 Đ Nguyen Binh Khiem) is one of the busiest local eateries in town. Here, on the street level or upstairs, beef, squid, giant shrimps, lobsters and the like are grilled right at your table.

**Restaurant 7C** (☎ 828243; 7C Đ Le Loi; mains 20,000-25,000đ) is *the* place to head if you're craving an authentic German sausage.

This expat-run place serves up excellent bratwurst and schnitzel, plus home-baked brown bread and fresh shark. Prices are reasonable, including the good local Viet Duc beer on tap (12,000d). Restaurant 7C is a short walk from the beach, near the main post office.

**Au Lac** (28C Đ Hoang Hoa Tham) has cheap and excellent vegetarian food. This tiny place is near the corner of Đ Nguyen Chanh. **Bo De** (28B Đ Hoang Hoa Tham) next door is also good.

Then there's **Dam Market** itself, which has a colourful collection of stalls in the covered semicircular food pavilion. Vegetarian food (com chay) can also be found here.

**Dua Xanh Restaurant** (☎ 823687; 23 Đ Le Loi) is a nice spot with many seafood dishes. There are outdoor garden tables and more tables indoors. Leave room for dessert.

For some great ice cream, try one of the remarkable little **Banana Split Cafés** near the roundabout where Đ Quang Trung meets Đ Ly Thanh Ton. Both are long time rivals, evidenced by their strong-arm tactics for luring customers inside.

**Hon Chong Area** A noteworthy local seafood restaurant that is well off the beaten track, **Biet Thu** (Nha Trang map; ☎ 828441) is worth seeking out. Fresh seafood and shellfish are plucked right out of an open-air aquarium near the tables.

## Entertainment

**Jack's Bar** (☎ 813862; 96A Đ Tran Phu; food 10,000-30,000d; open late) is a fine place to get the night started. Run by a congenial young Brit named, you guessed it, Jack, the bar boasts a roof terrace overlooking Nha Trang Bay, two pool tables, good music and cheap cold beer (happy hour lasts from 6pm until 10pm!). A full menu is offered from 8am to 10pm, and you can be sure there will be no hawkers to disturb your meal.

**Crazy Kim Bar** (Kim Dien Bar; ☎ 816072; 19 Đ Biet Thu; open 10am-1am daily) is a funky pub run by a Vietnamese-Canadian woman named Kimmy. She opened the bar as a vehicle in her commendable 'Hands off the Kids!' campaign, which is working to thwart the growing problem of paedophilia in Nha Trang. Proceeds from the sale of food, booze (try the killer cocktail buckets!) and T-shirts go towards the cause. Inquire at the bar if you're interested in volunteering to teach English to local street kids.

**Nha Trang Sailing Club** (☎ 826528; 72 Đ Tran Phu; open early till late) is a highly popular open-air beach bar. Aussie-run, the Sailing Club is where most of the hard-core party crowd ends up at some point in the evening. It's best known for thumping music, wild dancing, flowing shots, pool and general mayhem. You can escape the madness (sort of) outside on the large beachside terrace.

**Hexagone Disco** is a long running dance spot, right on the beach near the Ana Mandara Resort.

**Vien Dong Hotel** (☎ 821606; 1 Đ Tran Hung Dao; shows 7.30pm nightly) offers free ethnic-minority song and dance performances.

## Shopping

Along with Hanoi, HCMC and Hoi An, Nha Trang has emerged as a reasonable place to look for art. Though actual galleries are scant, there are several local painters and photographers who display their work on the walls of Nha Trang's resorts, restaurants, cafés and bars.

There are quite a number of shops selling beautiful seashells (and items made from seashells) near the Oceanographic Institute in Cau Da village. As a glossy tourist brochure put it, 'Before leaving Nha Trang, tourists had better call at Cau Da to get some souvenirs of the sea…for their dears at home'. The environmentally conscious may choose to resist the temptation and take photos instead.

**Bambou Company** (☎ 0903-573602; e bambou_company@hotmail.com), run by a French expat, produces high quality T-shirts (from 75,000d to 100,000d) featuring cool original designs (a rarity in Vietnam!). You can find them for sale at local bars and restaurants like La Bella Napoli.

Also worth checking out are the hand-painted T-shirts done by a friendly local painter named Kim Quang (☎ 0913-416513). Quang works every night from his wheelchair at the Sailing Club.

## Getting There & Away
**Air** There are regular flights by **Vietnam Airlines** (☎ 826768, fax 825956; 91 Đ Nguyen Thien Thuat), connecting Nha Trang with HCMC, Hanoi and Danang.

**Bus** Express and regular buses depart from Mien Dong bus station in HCMC to Nha Trang. The express bus trip takes 11 to 12 hours.

**Lien Tinh bus station** (Ben Xe Lien Tinh; ☎ 822192; Đ 23/10) is Nha Trang's main intercity bus terminal, and is 500m west of the train station. The short-haul bus station is for local routes only.

**Minibus** The preferred option, chartered minibuses are easy to book at most places where travellers congregate.

**Train** Hotels and travellers cafés all book train tickets, and it's worth paying the small commission to use these booking services.

The **Nha Trang train station** (Ga Nha Trang; ☎ 822113; opposite 26 Đ Thai Nguyen; ticket office open 7am-2pm) is overlooked by the nearby cathedral.

Nha Trang is well served by express trains connecting Hanoi and HCMC, and a daily local train between HCMC and Nha Trang (see the Train section in the Getting Around chapter).

**Car & Motorbike** Road distances from Nha Trang are: 205km to Buon Ma Thuot;

## Long Thanh – Photographer

Of the 500-odd members of the National Association of Photographers, most are based in Hanoi or Ho Chi Minh City (HCMC), and in this day and age, most choose colour film as their medium. Long Thanh, a photographer born in Nha Trang in 1951, is a rare exception.

A family man, Long Thanh has managed, with limited resources and a geographical disadvantage, to establish himself as Nha Trang's most acclaimed local shutterbug. He has been taking pictures since the 1960s, when at the age of 13 he learned to use a camera while working in a local photo shop. Since then he has not stopped shooting, nor has he abandoned his home town of Nha Trang to seek big-city stardom.

A purist, Long Thanh religiously uses black-and-white film, and laments the fact that so many great photographers prefer to shoot in colour. He works out of a makeshift darkroom in his simple kitchen, mixes his own chemicals, and awaits the day when professional quality black-and-white photographic paper will be sold in Vietnam (for now, he relies on friends from abroad to keep him stocked).

Long Thanh's powerful images capture the heart and soul of Vietnam. Among his most compelling works, Under Rain is a perfectly timed shot of two young girls caught in a sudden downpour, with a mysterious beam of sunlight streaming down on them. Afternoon Countryside is another rare scene – a boy dashing across the backs of a herd of water buffalos submerged in a lake outside Nha Trang. Perhaps his most striking image of all is Young Mother, Young Son, which portrays a bare-breasted elderly woman, her wrinkled skin like leather, sharing a moment of peace with her tiny grandson.

Though he has shown his photos in group exhibitions abroad nearly 50 times, and had his first international solo exhibition in Hamburg, Germany in 1999, Long Thanh's talents remain relatively undiscovered outside Vietnam. Visitors to Nha Trang, however, can view Long Thanh's photos on the walls of his favourite watering hole, the Nha Trang Sailing Club (the bar features an ongoing exhibition of his work).

If you've got the time, it may be possible to visit Long Thanh's home-studio and talk photography; that is, however, if he is not out on the road looking to capture the next great shot. Long Thanh is an incurable traveller, and has been known to happily accompany new friends on excursions into the Vietnamese countryside. For fellow photographers, who could be a better travel companion?

541km to Danang; 448km to HCMC; 104km to Phan Rang; 424km to Pleiku; 412km to Quang Ngai; and 238km to Qui Nhon.

A series of roughly parallel roads heads inland from near Nha Trang, linking Vietnam's deltas and coastal regions with the central highlands.

## Getting Around

**To/From the Airport** The airport is on the southern side of town and is so close to many of the hotels that you can actually walk.

Cyclos can get you to the airport for about US$1. They're good for around town, but limit your cyclo riding to the daytime.

**Nha Trang Taxi** (☎ 824000) and **Khanh Hoa Taxi** (☎ 810810) have air-con cars with meters.

**Bicycle** Most major hotels have bicycle rentals. The cost is around US$1 per day.

## AROUND NHA TRANG
## The Islands & Boat Tours

Khanh Hoa province's 71 offshore islands are renowned for the remarkably clear water surrounding them. A trip to these islands is one of the best reasons for visiting Nha Trang, so try to schedule at least one day for a boat journey. If you're interested in overnighting offshore, consider Whale Island or Hon Tre.

In the interests of environmental preservation, when booking a boat tour you might consider asking if the captain anchors his boat to a buoy, as opposed to dropping anchor directly on the coral. Of course, when booking a tour through a hotel or tourist operator it's hard to know if you'll get a truthful or informed answer to this question. If you do take a tour and it looks as though the captain is about to drop anchor on the coral, then very politely suggest he attaches the boat to a buoy instead. You can also take it up with the actual boat operators.

Mama Linh's boat trips (see Travel Agencies in the Nha Trang section) are now the hottest ticket for island hopping, guzzling fruit wine at the impromptu 'floating bar' and deck-side dancing. Of course all of this fun in the sun, let's just say, might not be the best environment for families with children (or recovering alcoholics). If the cultural fanfare of the Mama Linh experience does not sound up your alley, there are other more orthodox boat tours around.

Virtually every hotel in town books island boat tours. You can also pay more for a less-crowded and more luxurious boat that takes you to more islands. Indeed, you'll have to do this if you want to get in much snorkelling. The place to charter boats is at the Cau Da dock, south of Nha Trang. If you're not with an organised group, you'd better book the day before or go to Cau Da dock early in the morning – by 10am all the boats are gone. One attractive alternative is joining up with one of the local dive boats, most will take nondivers along for a discounted rate.

At some of the fishing villages on the islands, shallow water prevents the boats from reaching shore. In this case, you must walk perhaps several hundred metres across floats – a careful balancing act. The floats were designed for Vietnamese and weightier Westerners might get wet – take care with your camera. Nevertheless, it's all good fun and a visit to these fishing villages is highly recommended.

**Hon Mieu** Also called Tri Nguyen Island, Hon Mieu is touted in all the tourist literature as the site of an outdoor aquarium (Ho Ca Tri Nguyen). In fact, the 'aquarium' is an important fish-breeding farm, where over 40 species of fish, crustacean and other marine creatures are raised in three separate compartments. There is also a **café** built on stilts over the water. Ask around for canoe rentals.

The main village on Hon Mieu is Tri Nguyen. Bai Soai is a gravel beach on the far side of Hon Mieu from Cau Da. There are a few rustic **bungalows** on the island, which you can rent for US$6.

Most people will take some sort of boat tour booked through a hotel, café or Khanh Hoa Tourist. Impoverished and less-hurried travellers might catch one of the regular ferries that go to Tri Nguyen village from Cau Da dock.

Hawkers night market – Dalat, Lam Dong

GREG ELMS

The town of Tuy Hoa at the mouth of the Da Rang River, Phu Yen

NOBORU KOMINE

Steps at the Po Nagar Cham towers

TOM SMALLMAN

Colourful fishing boats in the bay off Dai Lanh Beach

ANDERS BLOMQVIST

Duong Tran Phu – a boulevard in Nha Trang

Nha Trang is the best municipal beach in Vietnam

Nhan Cham Tower near Darong River

French-Gothic Nha Trang Cathedral

**Bamboo Island (Hom Tre)** Several kilometres from the southern part of Nha Trang Beach is Bamboo Island, the largest island in the Nha Trang area. Tru Beach (Bai Tru) is at the northern end of the island. Boats can be hired to take you there, and we can also recommend the day and overnight trips offered by Con Se Tre (see Travel Agencies in the Nha Trang section).

**Hon Mun** Also called Ebony Island, Hon Mun is just southeast of Bamboo Island and is known for its snorkelling. To get here, you'll probably have to hire a boat.

**Hon Tam** Southwest of Bamboo Island, this island is close to shore and costs just 2000d to get to, but the beach is dirty and there's not much else to see.

**Hon Mot** This tiny island is sandwiched neatly between Ebony Island and Hon Tam. This is another great place for snorkelling.

**Monkey Island** Called Hon Lao in Vietnamese, Monkey Island is named after its large contingent of resident monkeys, and has become a big hit with tourists. Most of the monkeys have grown quite accustomed to receiving food handouts from the tourists, providing ample opportunity to take a memorable photo. However, these are wild monkeys, not zoo animals – you should not make any attempt to pet them, shake hands or pick them up. Some travellers have been scratched and bitten, while attempting to embrace their new-found friends; monkey bites are a fairly reliable source of rabies.

Aside from being unwilling to cuddle, the monkeys are materialistic. They will grab the sunglasses off your face or snatch a pen from your shirt pocket and run off. So far, we haven't heard of monkeys slitting open travellers' handbags with a razor blade, but you do need to be almost as careful with your valuables here as you do on the streets of HCMC!

Monkey Island is 12km north of Bamboo Island, and one-day boat tours can easily be arranged in Nha Trang. A faster way to get here is to take a motorbike or car 15km north of Nha Trang on National Hwy 1 – near a pagoda and the pleasant **Nha Trang Restaurant,** from where boats will ferry you to the island in fifteen minutes for 50,000d. Other destinations from here include Hoa Lan Springs on Hon Heo (40,000d, 45 minutes), and Hon Thi (20,000d, 20 minutes).

**Bird's-Nest Island** Salangane Island (Hon Yen or Dao Yen) is the name applied to two lump-shaped islands visible from Nha Trang Beach. These and other islands off Khanh Hoa province are the source of Vietnam's finest swiftlet *(salangane)* nests. The nests are used in bird's-nest soup as well as in traditional medicine, and are considered an aphrodisiac. It is said that the extraordinary virility of Emperor Minh Mang, who ruled Vietnam from 1820 to 1840, was derived from the consumption of swiftlet nests.

The nests, which the swiflets build out of their silklike salivary secretions, are semioval and about 5cm to 8cm in diameter. They are usually harvested twice a year. Red nests are the most highly prized. Annual production in Khanh Hoa and Phu Yen provinces is about 1000kg. At present, swiftlet nests fetch US$2000 per kilogram in the international marketplace!

There is a small, secluded beach at Salangane Island. The 17km trip out to the islands takes three to four hours by small boat from Nha Trang.

### Dien Khanh Citadel
The citadel dates from the 17th-century Trinh dynasty. It was rebuilt by Prince Nguyen Anh (later Emperor Gia Long) in 1793 during his successful offensive against the Tay Son Rebels. Only a few sections of the walls and gates are extant. Dien Khanh Citadel is 11km west of Nha Trang near the villages of Dien Toan and Dien Khanh.

### Ba Ho Falls
Ba Ho Falls (Suoi Ba Ho), with its three waterfalls and pools, is in a forested area about 20km north of Nha Trang and about 2km west of Phu Huu Village. Turn off National Hwy 1 just north of Quyen restaurant.

## Fairy Spring

The enchanting little Fairy Spring (Suoi Tien) seems to pop out of nowhere as you approach it. Like a small oasis, the spring is decorated with its own natural garden of tropical vegetation and smooth boulders.

You'll need to rent a motorbike or car to reach the spring. Driving south on National Hwy 1, you come to a spot 17km from Nha Trang, where there is a signpost to your left (the east side of the highway). Turn off the highway here and go through the village.

The road twists and winds its way for 8km through the hills until it reaches a valley. Just as the road starts to get bad, you come upon the spring. You'll probably see some other vehicles parked here as it's a popular spot with locals.

## PHAN RANG & THAP CHAM

☎ 068 • pop 143,700

The twin cities of Phan Rang and Thap Cham, which are famous for their production of table grapes, are in a semi-arid region.

---

### Cam Ranh Bay

Cam Ranh Bay is a gorgeous natural harbour 56km north of Phan Rang and Thap Cham, in Khanh Hoa province. The strategic naval base here has long been considered one of Asia's prime deep-water anchorages.

The Russian fleet of Admiral Rodjestvenski used it in 1905 at the end of the Russo-Japanese War, as did the Japanese during WWII, when the area was still considered an excellent place for tiger hunting. In the mid-1960s, the Americans constructed a vast base here, including an extensive port, ship-repair facilities and an airstrip.

After reunification, the Russians and their fleet came back, enjoying far better facilities than they had found seven decades before. For a while this became the largest Soviet naval installation outside the USSR.

Despite repeated requests from the Russians, the Vietnamese refused to grant them permanent rights to the base. Then in 1988 Mikhail Gorbachev offered to abandon the installation if the Americans promised to do the same with their six bases across the South China Sea in the Philippines. The Soviet presence at Cam Ranh Bay was significantly reduced in 1990 as part of the Kremlin's cost-cutting measures.

With the collapse of the Soviet Union in 1991 and the end of the Cold War, the USA did close its bases in the Philippines in 1991 (or, more accurately, the Filipino senate unceremoniously told the Americans to leave). Subsequent economic problems forced the Russians to vastly cut back on their overseas military facilities, including one of their chief Cold War bases in Cuba. Although the initial contract on Cam Ranh Bay was due to expire in 2004, the Russian military agreed to vacate their position, a last hurrah for the Russian navy in Asia, by the end of 2002.

As for the future of Cam Ranh Bay, just because the USA and former USSR no longer compete for turf does not mean that there is no need for a military base at Cam Ranh Bay. The Vietnamese are growing increasingly nervous about China's intentions. The Chinese have been rapidly and relentlessly building up their naval facilities in the South China Sea – in 1988, and again in 1992, China seized several islands claimed by Vietnam. In 1995 the Chinese navy seized some more islands claimed by the Philippines.

Although the Vietnamese will likely want the facilities at Cam Ranh Bay for their own military use, there has been recent talk of the bay being earmarked for tourism. There are beautiful beaches around Cam Ranh Bay – indeed, Americans stationed here during the war sometimes called this gorgeous harbour Vietnam's Hawaii. Meanwhile, the United States proposed an open-port arrangement after the Russians leave, while Vietnam Airlines has expressed interest in developing an international airport at Cam Ranh Bay to help serve the beach resort town of Nha Trang. Only time will reveal the ultimate fate of Cam Ranh Bay.

The sandy soil supports scrubby vegetation; local flora includes poinciana trees and prickly-pear cacti with vicious thorns. Many of the houses on the outskirts of town are decorated with Greek-style grape trellises.

The area's best known sight (and a common stop on the Dalat-Nha Trang route) is the group of Cham towers known as Po Klong Garai, from which Thap Cham (Cham Tower) derives its name (see the boxed text 'Po Klong Garai Cham Towers'). You can see Cham towers dotted about the countryside 20km north of Phan Rang.

Ninh Thuan province is home to tens of thousands of descendants of the Cham people, many of whom live in and around Phan Rang and Thap Cham. There are also three or four thousand Chinese descendants in the area, many of whom come to worship at the 135-year old **Chua Quang Cong**, a colourful Chinese temple in the town centre.

## Orientation

National Hwy 1 is Phan Rang's main commercial street (called Đ Thong Nhat). Thap Cham, about 7km from Phan Rang, is strung out along National Hwy 20, which heads west from Phan Rang towards Ninh Son and Dalat.

## Information

The main **post office** is in the north of town. Internet access is available for 500d per minute from 7am to 5pm Monday to Friday.

## Po Ro Me Cham Tower

Po Ro Me Cham Tower (Thap Po Ro Me), among the newest of Vietnam's Cham towers, is about 15km south of Phan Rang on a rocky hill 5km west of National Hwy 1. The ruins are very interesting, but are also very difficult to reach. The 'road' is a dirt track that can only be negotiated by motorbike or on foot. As one reader advised:

The road to take is between km1566 and km1567 from National Hwy 1. We did cross small Cham hamlets, which were nice to go through. Following the image of a small distant tower, we took a road that became a path, and then less than that. Even the motorbike almost did not make it. And after about 2km of the hill, that was it – not even

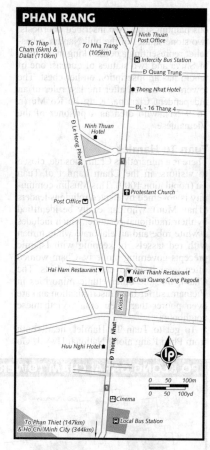

**PHAN RANG**

To Thap Cham (6km) & Dalat (110km)

To Nha Trang (105km)

Ninh Thuan Post Office

Intercity Bus Station

Đ Quang Trung

Thong Nhat Hotel

ĐL - 16 Thang 4

Đ Le Hong Phong

Ninh Thuan Hotel

Protestant Church

Post Office

Hai Nam Restaurant

Nam Thanh Restaurant

Chua Quang Cong Pagoda

Kiosks

Đ Thong Nhat

Huu Nghi Hotel

0    50    100m
0    50    100yd

Cinema

To Phan Thiet (147km) & Ho Chi Minh City (344km)

Local Bus Station

SOUTH-CENTRAL COAST

a tiny path to follow. Our poor old bike could not survive the rocks and cactus and died (again!). We finally walked up the hill (great snakes!). That was magic. The feeling of being completely alone on that small hill, with only the distant sound of bells around a cow's neck and nobody around for many kilometres (amazing after weeks in Saigon), was indescribable. At the bottom of the tower are long stairs. The single tower was closed, but still worth the hill climb to get there. It is decorated with beautiful stone statues and there are two Nandin statues, just before the entrance. Thank you for at least mentioning its existence, even if we were probably the only foreigners to reach it this year.

**Genevieve Mayers**

The *kalan*, which is decorated with numerous paintings, has two inscribed doorposts, two stone statues of the bull Nandin, a bas-relief representing a deified king in the form of Shiva and two statues of queens, one of whom has an inscription on her chest. The towers are named after the last ruler of an independent Champa, King Po Ro Me (r. 1629–51), who died as a prisoner of the Vietnamese.

## Tuan Tu Hamlet

There is a minaretless Cham mosque, closed to visitors, in the Cham hamlet of Tuan Tu (population 1000). This Muslim community is governed by elected religious leaders (Thay Mun), who can easily be identified by their traditional costume, which includes a white robe and an elaborate white turban with red tassels. In keeping with Islamic precepts governing modesty, Cham women often wear head coverings and skirts. The Cham, like the other ethnic minorities in Vietnam, suffer from discrimination and are even poorer than their ethnic-Vietnamese neighbours.

To get to Tuan Tu Hamlet, head south from Phan Rang along National Hwy 1. Go 250m south of the large bridge to a small bridge. Cross it and turn left (to the southeast) onto a dirt track. At the market (just past the Buddhist pagoda on the right), turn right and follow the road, part of which is lined with cacti, for about 2km, crossing two white concrete footbridges. Ask villagers for directions along the way. Tuan Tu is 3km from National Hwy 1.

## Places to Stay

**Huu Nghi Hotel** (☎ 822606; 354 Đ Thong Nhat; rooms US$10-18) is certainly the cheapest and dumpiest hotel in Phan Rang. It's in the centre of town and therefore noisy, but at least the bus station is within walking distance. There is air-con available but no hot water. A sign in the lobby reads: Not to carry weapons, explosives, toxic drugs, inflammables, radioactive substances and animals in the hotel.

**Ninh Thuan Hotel** (☎ 827100, fax 822142; 1 Đ Le Hong Phong; rooms US$22-35) is a pleasant place that boasts air-con and satellite TV. The hotel is on the north side of town opposite a small park.

**Thong Nhat Hotel** (☎ 827201, fax 827343; 99 Đ Thong Nhat; doubles US$22-32) is a

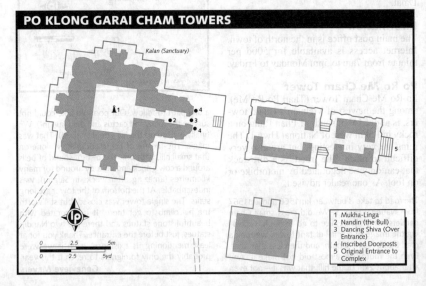

**PO KLONG GARAI CHAM TOWERS**

Kalan (Sanctuary)

1 Mukha-Linga
2 Nandin (the Bull)
3 Dancing Shiva (Over Entrance)
4 Inscribed Doorposts
5 Original Entrance to Complex

0    2.5    5m
0    2.5    5yd

## Po Klong Garai Cham Towers

Phan Rang and Thap Cham's most famous landmark is Po Klong Garai *(admission 5000d)*, also known as Po Klong Girai – *girai* means dragon. The four brick towers were constructed at the end of the 13th century, during the reign of the Cham monarch Jaya Simhavarman III. The towers were built as Hindu temples and stand on a brick platform at the top of Cho'k Hala, a crumbly granite hill covered with some of the most ornery cacti this side of the Rio Grande.

Over the entrance to the largest tower (the *kalan,* or sanctuary) is a carving of a dancing Shiva with six arms. This bas-relief is known locally as Po Klaun Tri – the Guardian of the Temple Tower – and is famous for its beauty. Note the inscriptions in the ancient Cham language on the doorposts. These tell of past restoration efforts and offerings of sacrifices and slaves made to the temple towers.

Inside the vestibule is a statue of the bull Nandin (also known as the Kapil Ox), symbol of the agricultural productivity of the countryside. To ensure a good crop, farmers would place an offering of fresh greens, herbs and areca nuts in front of Nandin's muzzle.

Under the main tower is a *mukha-linga*, a linga with a human face painted on it. A wooden pyramid has been constructed above the *mukha-linga*.

Inside the tower, opposite the entrance to the *kalan*, you can get a good look at some of the Cham's sophisticated building technology; the wooden columns that support the lightweight roof are visible. The structure attached to it was originally the main entrance to the complex.

On a nearby hill is a rock with an inscription from the year 1050, commemorating the erection of a linga by a Cham prince.

On the hill directly south of Cho'k Hala is a concrete water tank built by the Americans in 1965. It is encircled by French pillboxes, built during the Franco–Viet Minh War to protect the nearby rail yards. To the north of Cho'k Hala, you can see the concrete revetments of Thanh Son Airbase, used since 1975 by the Vietnamese Air Force.

The Cham New Year *(kate)* is celebrated at the towers in the seventh month of the Cham calendar (around October in the Gregorian calendar). The festival commemorates ancestors, Cham national heroes and deities such as the goddess Po Ino Nagar, who assisted the Chams with their farming.

On the eve of the festival, a procession guarded by the mountain people of Tay Nguyen carries King Po Kloong Garai's clothing to the accompaniment of traditional music. The procession lasts until midnight. The following morning the garments are carried to the tower, once again accompanied by music along with banners, flags, singing and dancing. Notables, dignitaries and village elders follow behind. This colourful ceremony continues into the afternoon.

The celebrations then carry on for the rest of the month, as the Cham attend parties and visit friends and relatives. They also use this time to pray for good fortune.

Po Klong Garai is located several hundred metres north of National Hwy 20, at a point 6km from Phan Rang towards Dalat. The towers are on the opposite side of the tracks to Thap Cham train station. Keep in mind that if you're travelling between Dalat and Nha Trang or Mui Ne, you will pass the site en route, which is a logical time to visit. Most of the open-tour buses shuttling people between Dalat and the coast make a requisite pit stop here.

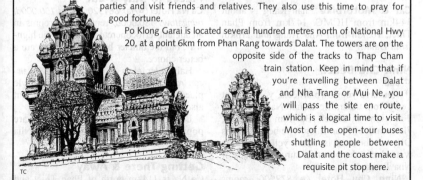

TC

four-storey building with two stars. All rooms have air-con, bathtubs, satellite TV and minibars.

## Places to Eat

One of the local delicacy here is roasted or baked gecko *(ky nhong)*, served with fresh green mango. If you prefer self-catering and have fast reflexes, you could consider catching your own gecko from the ceiling in your hotel room!

Some good, centrally located places to eat Vietnamese dishes include **Hai Nam** and **Nam Thanh**.

Phan Rang is the grape capital of Vietnam. **Stalls** alongside National Hwy 1 on the south side of town sell fresh grapes, grape juice and dried grapes (too juicy to be called raisins).

## Getting There & Away

**Bus** Buses from HCMC to Phan Rang and Thap Cham depart from Mien Dong bus station.

**Phan Rang intercity bus station** *(Ben Xe Phan Rang; opposite 64 Đ Thong Nhat)* is on the northern outskirts of town.

The **local bus station** *(opposite 426 Đ Thong Nhat)* is located at the southern end of town.

**Train** The Thap Cham train station is about 6km west of National Hwy 1, within sight of Po Klong Garai Cham towers.

**Car & Motorbike** Phan Rang is about 344km from HCMC, 147km from Phan Thiet, 105km from Nha Trang and 110km from Dalat.

## Ninh Chu Beach
☎ 068

If you have your own wheels, you can get away from the traffic around National Hwy 1 at Ninh Chu Beach (Bai Tam Ninh Chu), 7km south of Phan Rang. The beach here is OK, but the sand is a dark yellow and the water lacks the beautiful turquoise hues of Nha Trang.

**Ninh Chu Hotel** *(☎ 873900; rooms US$10-20)* is situated near the beach.

## CA NA
☎ 068

During the 16th century, princes of the Cham royal family would fish and hunt tigers, elephants and rhinoceroses here. Today, Ca Na is better known for its white-sand beaches dotted with huge granite boulders – it's a beautiful and relaxing spot, but lacks the isolated tropical-beach feeling further south at Mui Ne (it's tough to ignore the rumble of trucks drifting over from nearby National Hwy 1). Most continue on to Mui Ne (south) or Nha Trang (north), but it's not a bad place to stay.

The terrain is studded with magnificent prickly-pear cacti. A small pagoda on the hillside makes for an interesting, but steep, climb over the boulders (see the boxed text 'Lizard Fishing').

Rau Cau Island is visible offshore, and there is a well-outfitted scuba-diving centre a few kilometres south of Ca Na in Vinh Hao.

Farther afield is Tra Cang Temple, located about midway between Ca Na and Phan Rang. Unfortunately, you have to sidetrack over an abysmal dirt road in order to reach it. Many ethnic Chinese from Cholon visit the temple.

Ca Na's high season runs from December till August, while rain and cooler weather are common from September through November (hotels offer discounts in the low season).

## Places to Stay & Eat

**Ca Na Hotel** *(☎/fax 861320; rooms 150,000d, bungalows 180,000d)* rents crusty rooms in an ancient ferroconcrete hotel near the highway, but the quieter beach bungalows are a better choice.

**Haison Hotel** *(☎ 861312, fax 861339; air-con rooms US$15)* is a decent motel-style place, across from the Lac Son Pagoda, but also close to the highway.

Both hotels have **restaurants** that are popular lunch spots on the HCMC–Nha Trang route.

## Getting There & Away

Ca Na is 114km north of Phan Thiet and 32km south of Phan Rang. Many long-haul

## Lizard Fishing

When most people think of fishing in the mountains they conjure up images of hooking river trout or lake bass. But in the arid foothills of the south-central coast (notably around places like Ca Na, Phan Rang, Phan Thiet and Mui Ne) there is whole other kind of angling, and a walk in these hills can yield one of the strangest sights in Vietnam – lizard fishing!

These lizards, called *than lan nui*, are members of the gecko family and good for eating – some say they taste like chicken. The traditional way of catching the lizards is by setting a hook on a long bamboo fishing pole and dangling bait from the top of a boulder until the spunky little reptiles strike.

In local restaurants lizards could be served grilled, roasted or fried, and are often made up into a pate (complete with their finely chopped bones) and used as a dip for rice-paper crackers. Yum.

buses cruising National Hwy 1 can drop you here. No train service is available.

## VINH HAO
☎ 062

Vinh Hao is an obscure town just off National Hwy 1 between Phan Thiet and Phan Rang. The town's claim to fame is its celebrated mineral waters, which are bottled and sold all over Vietnam. If you spend any length of time in the country, you are almost certain to sip water from a bottle of Vinh Hao.

### Scuba Diving
**Vietnam Scuba** (☎ 853919, fax 853918 • *in HCMC* ☎ 08-925 4301, fax 839654; ⓔ *viet namdive@hanmail.net*, ⓦ *www.vietnamscuba .com*) is an attractive and well-appointed Korean-run dive centre on a private beach about 3.5km south of Ca Na. The resort is simple to spot on the sea side of National Hwy 1.

Vietnam Scuba is very much a by-Koreans for-Koreans resort, but serious scuba divers (and *kimchi* lovers) will appreciate the set-up and some of the best diving in Vietnam.

Marine life includes big fish, manta rays, barracuda and sharks.

Daily dive packages (US$130, non-divers US$50) include accommodation in nice beachfront villas, boat trips and guides, and three meals a day. A PC and regulator can be rented for an extra US$50 a day. All dive sites are offshore, anywhere from 30 to 90 minutes from the resort's private jetty.

## PHAN THIET
☎ 062 • pop 168,400

Phan Thiet is traditionally known for its *nuoc mam*, though today tourism is playing an increasingly larger role in the local economy. The population includes descendants of the Cham, who controlled this area until 1692. During the colonial period, the Europeans lived in their own segregated ghetto stretching along the northern bank of the Phan Thiet River, while the Vietnamese, Cham, Southern Chinese, Malays and Indonesians lived along the southern bank.

Besides the excellent golfing and a relatively nice beach, there is little to do in Phan Thiet itself. Most travellers head for nearby Mui Ne Beach, 11km away.

### Orientation
Phan Thiet is built along both banks of the Phan Thiet River, also known as the Ca Ti River and the Muong Man River. National Hwy 1 runs right through town; south of the river, it is known as Ð Tran Hung Dao, while north of the river it is called Ð Le Hong Phong.

### Information
Hotel 19-4 (see Places to Stay) offers tours of the area – you can also book cars and arrange guides here.

### Phan Thiet Beach
To get to Phan Thiet's beachfront, turn east at Victory Monument, an arrow-shaped concrete tower with victorious cement people at the base.

### Fishing Harbour
The river flowing through the centre of town creates a small fishing harbour, which

SOUTH-CENTRAL COAST

is always chock-a-block with boats. It makes for charming photos.

## Golf

The **Ocean Dunes Golf Club** (☎ 823366, fax 821511; e odgc@hcm.vnn.vn; 1 Đ Ton Duc Thang) is a top notch 18-hole golf course near the beachfront at the Novotel (see Places to Stay).

To drum up business, very reasonably priced golf package tours are available if you book from HCMC. Per golfer deals are as inexpensive as US$76/82 weekdays/ weekends, including one round of golf, a night at the stylish Novotel and breakfast. There is a minibus shuttle service between the golf course and HCMC.

For information, contact the resort's HCMC **marketing office** (☎ 08-910 1457, fax 910 1458; e dpodgc@hcm.fpt.vn, w www .vietnamgolfresorts.com, Saigon Trade Centre, #710A, 37 Ton Duc Thang).

## Places to Stay

Unless you are bypassing Mui Ne Beach and just looking for a place to sleep, or golfing, don't bother staying in Phan Thiet. Hotels here are not too cheap, and tend to be noisy.

**Phan Thiet Hotel** (☎/fax 815930; 40 Đ Tran Hung Dao; doubles 230,000-250,000d) is right in the centre of town. It a bit old and musty, and the on-the-highway location is anything but aesthetic. However, all the rooms have air-con and the rates include breakfast.

**Hotel 19-4** (☎ 825216, fax 825184; 1 Đ Tu Van Tu; air-con rooms from 190,000d) is an enormous old concrete place on the north side of town.

**Thanh Cong Hotel** (☎ 825016, fax 823905; 49-51 Đ Tran Hung Dao; rooms with fan & cold bath 70,000d, with air-con & hot water from 120,000d), opposite Hotel 19-4, is a newer minihotel.

**Novotel Ocean Dunes Resort** (☎ 822393, fax 825682; e novpht@hcm.vnn.vn; 1 Đ Ton Tuc Thang; rooms US$110-156++) is another luxurious option. To get to the hotel, turn towards the sea (east) at the Victory Monument. Facilities include a golf course, several restaurants, a swimming pool, a private

beach, tennis courts and a fitness centre. Rack rates are usually heavily discounted.

Near the Novotel are two relatively new hotels: **Doi Duong Hotel** (☎ 822108, fax 825858; e doiduonghotel@hcm.vnn.vn; 403 Đ Vo Thi Sau; rooms US$30-55) and the cheaper **Binh Minh Hotel** (☎ 823344, fax 823354; 405 Đ Vo Thi Sau; fan rooms 136,000d, air-con rooms from 220,000d).

## Places to Eat

**Hoang Yen Restaurant** (☎ 821614; 51 Đ Tran Hung Dao) is a good eatery about midway through Phan Thiet. It is very popular with tour groups passing through town.

## Getting There & Away

**Bus** The buses from HCMC to Phan Thiet depart from Mien Dong bus station.

**Phan Thiet bus station** (Ben Xe Binh Thuan; Đ Tu Van Tu; open 5.30am-3.30pm) is on the northern outskirts of town, just past 217 Đ Le Hong Phong (National Hwy 1).

**Train** The nearest train station to Phan Thiet is 12km west of town in dusty little Muong Man. The *Reunification Express* train between Hanoi and HCMC stops here (see the Train section in the Getting Around chapter).

**Car & Motorbike** Phan Thiet is on National Hwy 1, 198km east of HCMC, 250km from Nha Trang and 247km from Dalat.

When driving, be careful of the fishsauce trucks – hit one of these and the odour may follow you for life.

## Getting Around

Phan Thiet has a few cyclos, some of which always seem to be at the bus station.

## MUI NE BEACH
☎ 062

Peaceful Mui Ne Beach is a long and beautiful stretch of white sand 22km east of Phan Thiet on Route 706, near a fishing village at the tip of Mui Ne Peninsula. It's a lovely spot with swaying palm trees, and for traffic-weary travellers, as well as residents of HCMC, Mui Ne offers a relaxed and welcome change of pace.

Mui Ne is famous for its enormous sand dunes. These have been a favourite subject matter for many a Vietnamese photographer, including some who sit like camels on the blazing hot sand for hours, waiting for the winds to sculpt the dunes into that perfect 'Kodak moment'.

Also of interest is the **Fairy Spring** (Suoi Tien), which is really a stream that flows through a patch of dunes with interesting sand and rock formations. It's a beautiful trek to follow from the sea to its source, though it might be wise to hire a local guide. You can do the trek barefoot, but if you're heading out into the big sand dunes, this is out of the question unless you have leather soles on your feet; sandals are even questionable during the midday sun.

Further afield there are some lovely **lakes** to explore. There is a small **Cham tower** called Thap Poshaknu about 5km out of Phan Thiet on the way to Mui Ne. The tranquil Ta Ku Pagoda is 25km south from Mui Ne.

Mui Ne sees only about half the rainfall of nearby Phan Thiet. The sand dunes help protect Mui Ne's unique microclimate, and even during the wet season (from June to September) rains tend to be fairly light and sporadic.

There is no scuba diving in Mui Ne, but when Nha Trang and Hoi An get the rains, Mui Ne gets the waves. Surf's up from August to December. For windsurfers, the gales howl as well, especially from late October to late April, when swells stir over from the Philippine typhoons. In 2001, there were reportedly 240 days with a minimum wind speed of 12 knots.

## Orientation

A narrow palm-lined road runs for about 10km along the Mui Ne seafront. Local addresses are designated by a kilometre mark measuring the distance along Rte 706 from National Hwy 1 in Phan Thiet.

## Information

**Hanh Cafe/Ha Phuong Tourist** (☎ 847347; km13) caters mainly to backpackers, with cheap transportation, fast food and Internet access (1000d per minute). There's a similar setup just down the road at **TM Brothers Cafe** (☎ 847359; km13). If you arrive by open tour it's likely you'll be delivered to one of these places.

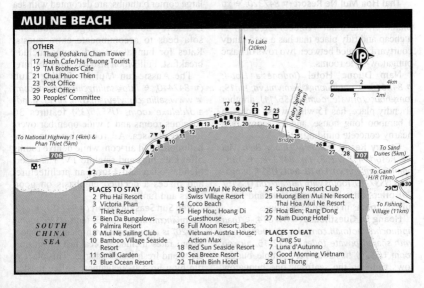

## MUI NE BEACH

**OTHER**
1 Thap Poshaknu Cham Tower
17 Hanh Cafe/Ha Phuong Tourist
19 TM Brothers Cafe
21 Chua Phuoc Thien
23 Post Office
29 Post Office
30 Peoples' Committee

To Lake (20km)

To National Highway 1 (4km) & Phan Thiet (5km)

Fairy Spring (Suoi Tien)

Bridge

To Sand Dunes (5km)

To Ganh H/R (1km)

To Fishing Village (11km)

SOUTH CHINA SEA

**PLACES TO STAY**
2 Phu Hai Resort
3 Victoria Phan Thiet Resort
5 Bien Da Bungalows
6 Palmira Resort
8 Mui Ne Sailing Club
10 Bamboo Village Seaside Resort
11 Small Garden
12 Blue Ocean Resort
13 Saigon Mui Ne Resort; Swiss Village Resort
14 Coco Beach
15 Hiep Hoa; Hoang Di Guesthouse
16 Full Moon Resort; Jibes; Vietnam-Austria House; Action Max
18 Red Sun Seaside Resort
20 Sea Breeze Resort
22 Thanh Binh Hotel

24 Sanctuary Resort Club
25 Huong Bien Mui Ne Resort; Thai Hoa Mui Ne Resort
26 Hoa Bien; Rang Dong
27 Nam Duong Hotel

**PLACES TO EAT**
4 Dung Su
7 Luna d'Autunno
9 Good Morning Vietnam
28 Dai Thong

## Places to Stay

Although Mui Ne has seen an extraordinary increase in the number of beach resorts, it has yet to suffer the commercialisation and social ills of Nha Trang. Another distinct advantage to Mui Ne over Nha Trang is that nearly all local accommodation is right on the beachfront.

For budget travellers, there are several cheap places to stay, some of which hire out tents for around US$5 (including use of shared toilet and shower facilities). In the mid-range, nice bungalows can be found for between US$15 and US$45. At Mui Ne's pricier resorts you can expect all the trimmings, including satellite TV, IDD phones and minibars, plus breakfast included in the room rate.

High-/low-season dates vary from resort to resort, and rates are typically higher on weekends.

## Places to Stay – Budget

**Rang Dong** (☎ 848645; km19; tents 50,000-60,000d, doubles/quads with fan US$7/10, air-con rooms US$15-18) is a good budget place with friendly staff and a commendable on-site restaurant.

**Thai Hoa Mui Ne Resort** (☎ 847320; e xu antrangdt@hcm.fpt.vn; km18; bungalows with shared/private toilet 120,000/150,000d) is a cheap and tidy place that has a nice sandy courtyard situated between two rows of basic bungalow-style rooms.

**Nam Duong Hotel** (Indonesia Hotel; ☎ 848646; e namduong@hcm.vnn.vn; km19; long-house/private rooms US$5/11), another friendly place, has 15 windowless rooms in a bamboo long house, and 11 rooms in a nearby concrete building.

**Canary Resort** (formerly Huong Bien Mui Ne Resort ☎ 847258, fax 847338; e ntd_hbmn@hcm.vnn.vn; km18; tents US$4, bungalows US$7-10, rooms with fan/air-con US$15/20) offers ultra-basic bungalows and basic air-con rooms in concrete buildings.

**Hoang Di Guesthouse** (☎ 847014; e than hphuochd@hotmail.com; km13; bungalows with shared/private toilet US$12/15, air-con room US$20) has four very simple bungalows right on the seafront, one bungalow

with private bath (cold water only) and one air-con room in a concrete box.

**Small Garden** (Vuon Nho; ☎ 847012, fax 847377; e smallgarden@hcm.vnn.vn; km11; rooms US$7-10, triple bungalows US$10-20; 6-8 person bungalow US$40) is run by a Swiss-Vietnamese couple. Guests can sleep in a communal house, bungalows, in the open-air gazebo, or on the beach for a per person rate. Bungalows have private bath.

**Hiep Hoa** (☎ 847262; e hiephoatourism@ yahoo.com; km13.3; rooms US$10, bungalows with sea views US$12-15) is fairly reasonable for the price.

**Bien Da** (☎ 847282; km12; bungalows US$10) is better known for its open-air restaurant, but also rents out simple bamboo bungalows with fan and cold shower. It's cheap, but the beach in front is not the cleanest.

## Places to Stay – Mid-Range

**Full Moon Resort** (Trang Tron; ☎ 847008, fax 847160; e fullmoon@windsurf-vietnam.com; km13; tents US$5, bungalows US$20-40, rooms US$45) is a popular place run by Phuong and her windsurfing French husband Pascal. Simple bungalows, some with large corner bathtubs, are decorated with sea shells and split coconuts. Rooms in the new two-storey house have huge bathtubs and sofa beds to accommodate extra guests. Rates for bungalows and rooms include breakfast. Full Moon also has tents for hire.

The Aussie-run **Mui Ne Sailing Club** (☎ 847440; e info@sailingclubvietnam.com, w www.sailingclubvietnam.com; km13; standard/deluxe rooms US$25/35) features 36 spacious rooms and a wide open bar overlooking the sea. All rooms have en suite bathrooms and air-con, while deluxe rooms offer bath tubs and satellite TV. The resort blends Asian and European architecture, and places a decided emphasis on good times and funky music.

**Red Sun Seaside Resort** (☎ 847387; e cafe loumi@hcm.vnn.vn; km13; tents US$5, rooms US$20) is a quiet spot with plenty of shade. Room rates include a breakfast of an omelette and fresh-baked pastries. This place is run by a French-Vietnamese coffee roaster, so you can be sure the java is good. At the time we visited there was a French artist-in-residence here.

**Mai Khanh** (Paradise Huts; ☎ 847177; e cheznina@vnn.vn; fan rooms US$15-20, air-con rooms US$20, bungalows US$25), next door to Full Moon Resort, has very basic fan rooms as well as bungalows and air-con rooms.

**Vietnam-Austria House** (☎ 847047; km13.5; e ngothikimhong@hotmail.com; rooms US$10, bungalows US$15-20), next door to Mai Khanh, offers squeaky-clean rooms in a modern villa or wooden bungalows; there's also a small swimming pool.

**Bamboo Village Seaside Resort** (☎ 847007, fax 847095; e dephan@netnam2.org.vn, w www.vietnamtourism.com/muine; km11.8; low-season bungalows US$41-57, bungalows 21 Dec–1 May US$49-69), close to Bien Da, this is a beautifully landscaped resort with attractive bungalows. There is also a swimming pool and a good **restaurant** on the premises.

**Palmira Resort** (☎ 847004, fax 847006; e cocogarden@palmiraresort.com, w www.palmiraresort.com; km11; singles/doubles from US$39/49) offers large ferroconcrete villas with air-con, either in the garden or on the beachfront. All rooms have satellite TV and rates include breakfast. Facilities include two **restaurants**, four bars, a huge swimming pool, tennis courts, a sauna, a fitness room, billiards, table soccer and a kiddy's play area.

**Sea Breeze Resort** (☎ 847373, fax 847430; e seabreeze-lanno@hcm.vnn.vn; km13.7; double rooms/bungalows US$30/35) is a cosy place with finely manicured gardens. Comfy rooms and A-frame bungalows feature terracotta floors and air-con. The beach, however, disappears under high tide in the afternoon.

**Thanh Binh Hotel** (☎ 847450; km15; air-con room 250,000d) is a lime green motel-style place; OK at a pinch, if you can't book elsewhere.

## Places to Stay – Top End
Run by a German-French couple, **Coco Beach** (Hai Duong Resort; ☎ 847111, fax 847115; e paradise@cocobeach.net, w www.cocobeach.net; km12.5; early May–late Oct bungalows/villas US$65/130, Nov–early May US$80/160) is was the first proper resort in Mui Ne. There are pleasant thatched-roof bungalows and villas, and activities include windsurfing, sailing, water-skiing, fishing and snorkelling.

**Victoria Phan Thiet Resort** (☎ 847170, fax 847174; km9; e victoriapt@hcm.vnn.vn, w www.victoriahotels-asia.com; US$120-170++, Internet rates US$80-95++), is a stylish resort with sea-view cottages that are furnished to a 'T'. There's a nice terrace **restaurant**, two bars, a swimming pool, a fitness club, a massage room, a sauna and an indoor-outdoor Jacuzzi. Excursions from the hotel can be arranged by jeep, classic sidecar or Minsk motorbike.

**Swiss Village Resort** (☎ 847399, fax 847491; e swissvil@hcm.vnn.vn, w www.phamch.com; km12; standard/sea-view rooms US$40/50, bungalows US$60, suites US$90) has 70 well-appointed rooms modelled on a traditional Vietnamese design. Facilities include a tennis court, a Jacuzzi and a pool with the Swiss flag emblazoned on the floor tile. From mid-December to mid-June, rates increase by US$10.

**Blue Ocean Resort** (Bien Xanh; ☎ 847322, fax 847351; e blueocean@hcm.vnn.vn, w www.blueoceanresort.com; km12.2; bungalows US$55) is another stylish choice with thatched-roof cottages, a bar in the swimming pool and an **Irish pub**.

**Saigon Mui Ne Resort** (☎ 847303, 847307; km12.2; bungalows US$50, villas US$65) is a snazzy place set in a large, well-manicured compound decorated in a somewhat Balinese style.

**Phu Hai Resort** (☎ 812799, fax 812797; e phuhairesort@hcm.vnn.vn, w www.phuhairesort.com; km8; early May–mid-Nov rooms US$55 villas from US$65, mid-Nov–early May rooms US$65 villas from $75) could be described as Mui Ne's first 'mega resort'. Swiss-Vietnamese run, this palatial spread has 19 villas and 38 rooms, and offers tennis courts, a fitness centre, a game room, a beauty salon, massage and sauna rooms, a 600-sq-metre swimming pool and jet skis for rent. The **Geneva Restaurant** offers Vietnamese and European fare, while the wall of the Phu Hai Bar is modelled after Cambodia's Angkor Wat.

The antithesis of Phua Hai Resort is **Sanctuary Resort Club** (☎ 847232; e *sanctuaryresort@hotmail.com, km19; rooms US$80-160*). Entry is via a long driveway and this secluded boutique resort has just two luxurious villas and one bungalow, each with its own private dipping pool. Appropriately named, it's got a decidedly 'away from it all' feel, albeit for the wealthy recluse (as opposed to resort types).

## Places to Eat
Beside the ubiquitous in-house restaurants at the beach resorts, there are a handful of interesting eateries in Mui Ne.

**Dai Thong** (☎ 848968; *km19; most dishes 25,000-35,000d*) is a low-key seafront place near the eastern end of the beach. Most people go there for the cheap seafood, but the restaurant also serves 'special wild food' like wild boar, deer, pigeon, rabbit and frog.

**Dung Su** (☎ 847310; *km10*) near the western end of the beach is raised on stilts, and sits over the water. Highly popular with Vietnamese, tasty seafood is sold by the kilo here, plucked fresh from tanks across the back wall.

Wherever tourists congregate, it's only a matter of time before the Italians arrive to fatten everyone up. **Luna d'Autunno** (*Autumn Moon;* ☎ 847330; *km12; salads from 30,000d, pizza from 50,000d, fresh pasta from 70,000d; open lunch & dinner daily*) is an unexpected retreat serving authentic Italian fare like antipasto, salads, fresh pasta and great wood-fired pizza. Meanwhile, **Good Morning Vietnam** (☎ 847342), the popular Italian chain with eateries in Nha Trang, Hoi An and HCMC, have set up shop at the Mui Ne Sailing Club.

## Entertainment
Beach bars that get hopping at night include the **Mui Ne Sailing Club** and **Jibes**. Both of these places also serve food. If you're craving a Guinness, **Sheridan's Irish House** is at the Blue Ocean Resort.

## Activities
**Jibes** (☎ 847405, fax 847160; e *jibe@windsurf-vietnam.com,* w *www.windsurf-vietnam.com; km13*) is a surf water-sports haven near the Full Moon Resort. Run by an expat Frenchman, it rents state-of-the-art gear like windsurfers (30min/1hour/half-day/full-day US$5/10/25/40), surfboards (US$5 per hour) and kite-surfing boards (US$10 per hour). Check out its website for package deals. Jibes works in conjunction with **Action Max** (☎ 0913-929137; e *actionmax@hcm.vnn.vn*), an ecotourism and adventure-sports outfit that organises trekking, canyoning and rock-climbing trips in the area.

## Getting There & Away
Mui Ne is 200km from HCMC (three hours' drive). Many of the open-tour buses cruising National Hwy 1 make a detour to Mui Ne. The cost from HCMC or Nha Trang is US$6. From Tuesday to Sunday there's a comfortable shuttle service (one-way/return US$9/16) by Mercedes van between the Blue Ocean Resort and Sheridan's Irish Pub in HCMC.

To best way to reach the beach from the highway in Phan Thiet is by *xe om* (50,000d) or you can rent your own bike for around US$6 a day (ask at the Hoang Yen Restaurant). A local bus makes trips between Phan Thiet bus station and Mui Ne, but it is irregular and slow.

## Getting Around
Mui Ne is small enough to get around on foot or you canrent a bicycle from most hotels.

## TAKOU MOUNTAIN
The highlight here is the white reclining Buddha (Tuong Phat Nam). At 49m, it's the largest in Vietnam. The pagoda was constructed in 1861 (Nguyen dynasty) but the Buddha is much more recent (1972). It has become an important pilgrimage centre for Buddhists, who stay overnight in the pagoda's dormitory. Foreigners can't do this without police permission – not easy to get.

The mountain is just off National Hwy 1, 28km south from Phan Thiet, from which the Buddha is a beautiful two-hour trek.

# Central Highlands

The central highlands cover the southern part of the Truong Son Mountain Range (Annamite Cordillera) and include the provinces of Lam Dong, Dac Lac (Dak Lak), Gia Lai and Kon Tum. The region, which is home to many hill-tribe minority groups, or Montagnards (French for highlanders), is renowned for its cool climate, mountain scenery, and innumerable streams, lakes and waterfalls.

Although the population of the central highlands is only around four million, the area has always been considered strategically important: during the American War, considerable fighting took place around Buon Ma Thuot, Pleiku and Kon Tum.

The western region of the central highlands along the border with Cambodia and Laos is a vast, fertile plateau with red volcanic soil. The good soil and sparse population has not gone unnoticed – the government has targeted the area for a massive resettlement programme. Most of the new settlers are farmers from the crowded Red River Delta area in the north of the country and the government-financed scheme is mostly successful, although the local hill tribes have been less than thrilled by the sudden influx of northern Vietnamese.

The western highlands area has lost much of its natural beauty. Some remnant forests remain, but most of the trees were either destroyed by Agent Orange during the American War or have been stripped to make way for agriculture. The only thing that really adds a bit of colour to this part of Vietnam are the Montagnards, though they are nowhere near as colourful as the tribes in the deep north of Vietnam.

With the exception of Lam Dong province (where Dalat is), the central highlands was closed to foreigners, until 1992. Even Westerners with legitimate business in the area were arrested and sent back to Ho Chi Minh City (HCMC). This extreme sensitivity stemmed partly from the limited nature of central government control in remote areas,

## Highlights

- Explore the old French hill station of Dalat, where pine-forested hills, cultivated valleys, lakes and waterfalls meet Vietnamese kitsch

- Visit the Bahnar and Jarai hill-tribe villages around Buon Ma Thuot, Pleiku and Kon Tum

- Get off the beaten track and into the wilds of Yok Don or Cat Tien National Parks

- Hit the road on two wheels and follow the rugged and historic 'Ho Chi Minh Trail'

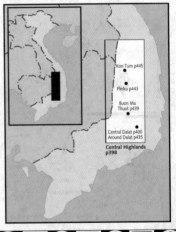

Kon Tum p445
Pleiku p443
Buon Ma Thuot p439
Central Dalat p400
Around Dalat p435
Central Highlands p398

but also from a concern that secret re-education camps (rumoured to be hidden in the region) would be discovered and publicised. The situation has changed and almost all of the central highlands is now open to foreign visitors.

According to news reports in February 2001, the government had forbidden travellers from visiting the central highlands because of local uprisings over land distribution. By early June some 900 local minority

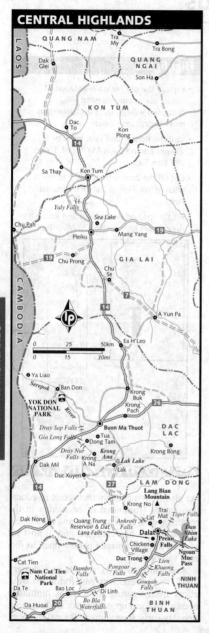

**CENTRAL HIGHLANDS**

people who had fled to Cambodia, were granted refugee status and relocated to the USA, much to the chagrin of the Vietnamese authorities. At the time of writing the situation had cooled down, but before heading to the hills make local inquires to confirm that the areas you plan to visit are accessible.

For outdoor types, Yok Don National Park, near Buon Ma Thuot, boasts many minority villages and lots of elephants. Cat Tien National Park (an excellent place for bird-watching and hiking) is also accessible from the central highlands (see the Around HCMC chapter for details).

### Getting There & Away

The central highlands is easily approached from the south, as well as points along the eastern coast. From HCMC and Nha Trang, private open-tour buses to Dalat are cheap and frequent, but to reach places further afield such as Buon Ma Thuot, Pleiku and Kon Tum, you'll either have to depend on rattletrap public buses, or arrange some form of private transport.

The central highlands is one area where having the right guide and vehicle can make all the difference, especially for visiting national parks and hill-tribe villages. **Sinh-balo Adventures** (w www.sinhbalo.com) in HCMC and **Mr Vu's Tour Adventures** (e tran vuvn@hotmail.com) in Nha Trang both know the region very well and can be recommended for customised trips into the highlands. Another interesting option is to hire one of the popular motorbike drivers , who work in Dalat (see the boxed text 'Easy Riders' in the Dalat section).

### DALAT

☎ 063 • pop 130,000 • elevation 1475m

The jewel of the central highlands, Dalat is in a temperate region dotted with lakes, waterfalls, evergreen forests and gardens. The cool climate and the park-like environment make this one of the most delightful places in all of Vietnam.

The city was once called Le Petit Paris and to this day there is a miniature replica of the Eiffel Tower behind the main post office. Dalat is also the favourite haunt of

Vietnamese artists and avant-garde types, many of whom have made it their permanent home. It is also the country's most popular honeymoon spot, and although the locals are thankfully scaling back on circus-style 'tourist attractions', Dalat still remains the final word in Vietnamese kitsch.

Local industries include growing garden vegetables and flowers (especially beautiful hydrangeas), which are sold all over southern Vietnam. But the biggest contribution to the economy of Dalat is tourism: more than 800,000 domestic tourists and another 80,000 or so foreign tourists visit here every year.

The Dalat area was once famous for its big-game hunting and a 1950s brochure boasted that 'a two-hour drive from the town leads to several game-rich areas abounding in deer, roe, peacocks, pheasants, wild boar, black bear, wild caws, panthers, tigers, gaurs and elephants'. So successful were the hunters that all of the big game is now extinct. However, you will get a whiff of Dalat's former glory by viewing some of the 'souvenirs' about town:

What will stick in my mind most is the appalling stuffed animals they seem so fond of in Dalat. These seem to have spread all over Vietnam, but the citizens of Dalat in particular have taken taxidermy to new lows. We had a terrible fit of the giggles as we left the Ho Chi Minh Mausoleum in Hanoi, when the thought surfaced of what the Dalat animal stuffers could have done with Ho Chi Minh, if the stuffing contract hadn't been given to the Russians.

**Tony Wheeler**

The city's population includes about 5000 members of hill tribes, of which there are said to be some 33 distinct communities in Lam Dong province. Members of these hill tribes, who still refer to themselves as Montagnards, can occasionally be seen in the market places in their traditional dress. Hill-tribe women of this area carry their infants on their backs in a long piece of cloth worn over one shoulder and tied in the front.

Dalat is often called the City of Eternal Spring. The average maximum daily temperature here is a cool 24°C and the average minimum daily temperature is 15°C. The dry season runs from December to March and even during the rainy season, which lasts more or less from April to November, it is sunny most of the time.

## History

The local area has been home to various Montagnard groups for centuries. In the local Lat language, 'Da Lat' means 'River of the Lat Tribe'.

In 1893, the first European to claim the 'discovery' of Dalat was Dr Alexandre Yersin, a protégé of Louis Pasteur and the first person to identify the plague bacillus. The city itself was established in 1912 and quickly became popular with Europeans as a cool retreat from the sweltering heat of the coastal plains and the Mekong Delta. At one point during the French colonial period some 20% of Dalat's population was foreign, as evidenced by the 2500-odd chalet-style villas scattered around the city.

During the American War Dalat was, by the tacit agreement of all parties concerned, largely spared the ravages of war. Indeed, it seems that while South Vietnamese soldiers were being trained at the city's military academy and affluent officials of the Saigon regime were relaxing in their villas, Viet Cong (VC) cadres were doing the same thing not far away in *their* villas. Dalat fell to North Vietnamese forces without a fight on 3 April 1975. There is no problem with leftover mines and ordnance in the Dalat area.

Dalat was the first city in Vietnam to introduce a city water purification system that provides potable water from the tap (an 80% Danish government–funded project).

## Orientation

Dalat's sights are very spread out, and the terrain in and around the city is hilly. Still, trekking around in Dalat is made easier by the cool temperatures. The city centre is around Rap 3/4 cinema (named after the date on which Dalat was liberated in 1975), which is up the hill from the central-market building.

Xuan Huong Lake is a prominent landmark on the southern side of town. A delight-ful walk (or jog) around the 7km lake road provides an excellent city orientation and a very nice overview of Dalat, including the French influence. Along the way are the Dalat Flower Gardens, views of the golf course and the grand old villas on Ð Tran Hung Dao. A stroll up the steps to the Hotel Sofitel Dalat Palace garden provides spectacular views. From there, head up to the post office and the higher quality buildings of old and new along Ð Tran Phu.

The best way to enjoy the forests, sites and cultivated countryside around Dalat is by foot, motorbike or bicycle. Some suggested routes include:

- Heading out on Ð 3 Thang 4, which becomes National Hwy 20, to the pine forests of Prenn Pass and Quang Trung Reservoir
- Going via the Governor-General's Residence and up Ð Khe Sanh to Thien Vuong Pagoda
- Taking Ð Phu Dong Thien Vuong from Dalat University to the Valley of Love
- Going out to Bao Dai's Summer Palace and from there, after stopping at Lam Ty Ni Pagoda, heading via Ð Thien My and Ð Huyen Tran Cong Chua to Du Sinh Church

See the Around Dalat section later in this chapter for attractions that are located on the outskirts of Dalat.

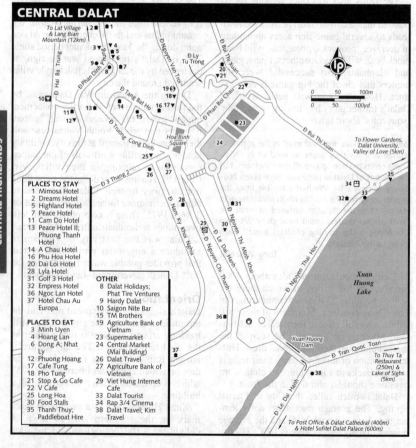

**CENTRAL DALAT**

To Lat Village & Lang Bian Mountain (12km)

Ð Hai Ba Trung
Ð Phan Dinh Phung
Ð Nguyen Van Troi
Ð Bui Thi Xuan
Ð Ly Tu Trong
Ð Tang Bat Ho
Ð Phan Boi Chau
Ð Truong Cong Dinh
Ð Bui Thi Xuan
Ð 3 Thang 2
Ð Nam Ky Khoi Nghia
Ð Le Dai Hanh
Ð Nguyen Thi Minh Khai
Ð Nguyen Chi Thanh
Ð Nguyen Thai Hoc
Ð Tran Quoc Toan

Hoa Binh Square

To Flower Gardens, Dalat University, Valley of Love (5km)

Xuan Huong Lake

Xuan Huong Dam

To Thuy Ta Restaurant (250m) & Lake of Sighs (5km)

To Post Office & Dalat Cathedral (400m) & Hotel Sofitel Dalat Palace (600m)

0    50    100m
0    50    100yd

**PLACES TO STAY**
1 Mimosa Hotel
2 Dreams Hotel
5 Highland Hotel
7 Peace Hotel
11 Cam Do Hotel
13 Peace Hotel II; Phuong Thanh Hotel
14 A Chau Hotel
16 Phu Hoa Hotel
20 Dai Loi Hotel
28 Lyla Hotel
31 Golf 3 Hotel
32 Empress Hotel
36 Ngoc Lan Hotel
37 Hotel Chau Au Europa

**PLACES TO EAT**
3 Minh Uyen
4 Hoang Lan
6 Dong A; Nhat Ly
12 Phuong Hoang
17 Cafe Tung
18 Pho Tung
21 Stop & Go Cafe
22 V Cafe
25 Long Hoa
30 Food Stalls
35 Thanh Thuy; Paddleboat Hire

**OTHER**
8 Dalat Holidays; Phat Tire Ventures
9 Hardy Dalat
10 Saigon Nite Bar
15 TM Brothers
19 Agriculture Bank of Vietnam
23 Supermarket
24 Central Market (Mai Building)
26 Dalat Travel
27 Agriculture Bank of Vietnam
29 Viet Hung Internet Cafe
33 Dalat Tourist
34 Rap 3/4 Cinema
38 Dalat Travel; Kim Travel

## Information

**Travel Agencies** Dalat's state-run travel agency is **Dalat Tourist** (☎ 822520, fax 834144; e dalatour@hcm.vnn.vn, w www .dalattourist.com; 2 Nguyen Thai Hoc). For booking tours or vehicle rentals, visit its booking office, **Dalat Travel** (☎ 822125, fax 828330; e ttdhhd@hcm.vnn.vn; 7 Đ 3 Thang 2) near the city centre.

**Dalat Travel/Kim Travel** (☎/fax 822479; e dltoseco@hcm.vnn.vn; 9 Đ Le Dai Hanh) is another government travel agency.

**TM Brothers** (☎ 828383; e dalat_tm brother@yahoo.com; 9 Đ Tang Bat Ho) is a smaller outfit selling open-tour bus tickets and fast-food tours.

For chauffeured tours by motorbike, see the boxed text 'Easy Riders'.

**Money** A convenient place to exchange money and travellers cheques, or to do Visa cash advances, is the **Agriculture Bank of Vietnam** (Ngan Hang Nong Nghiep Vietnam; ☎ 822535; 6 Đ Nguyen Van Troi & 22 Khu Hoa Binh Square; 7.30am-11.30am & 1pm-4pm Mon-Fri, 7.30am-11.30am Sat). Both banks are located right in the centre of town.

**Post & Communications** The **main post office** (14 Đ Tran Phu), across the street from the Novotel Dalat, also has international telephone, fax and email facilities.

A convenient place to check email (150d per minute) is the **Viet Hung Internet Cafe** (☎ 835737; e dhoaithu@hcm.vnn.vn; 7 Đ Nguyen Chi Thanh).

## Xuan Huong Lake

Created by a dam in 1919, Xuan Huong Lake is in the centre of Dalat. It is named after a 17th-century Vietnamese poet known for her daring attacks on the hypocrisy of social conventions, and the foibles of scholars, monks, mandarins, feudal lords and kings. The lake can be circumnavigated along a 7km sealed path.

Paddle boats that look like giant swans can be rented near Thanh Thuy Restaurant,

---

### Easy Riders

Dalat's notorious Easy Riders are a witty crew of freelance motorbike guides who were truly born to be wild. Most of the 30-odd members carry their clients on the back of vintage Russian and East German motorcycles, and their popularity is reaching cult proportions among travellers seeking an exciting alternative to being herded around on the Sinh Café tourist trail.

The Easy Riders can be hired for fun day trips around Dalat, and the cost is very reasonable (about US$8 a day around the city, or US$10 a day around the outskirts). You can also make arrangements with them for longer trips around the central highlands (Lak Lake is a popular spot) or down to the coast. Some have even adopted their drivers and ridden with them all the way north to Hanoi!

We've received countless letters recommending these guys. One reader had this to say:

The best part of my trip to Vietnam was the day I spent with an independent guide in Dalat. The guides approached my friends and I at our hotel, and we were hesitant at first to ride behind strangers on motorbikes. Luckily they were able to convince us to go with them. We had a fantastic day seeing the sites around Dalat. They ended up being careful drivers who provided an insight into Vietnam that we couldn't get on the guided bus tours.

**Laura Schubert**

Travelling with the Easy Riders is a great way to explore the region, and having a friendly and articulate guide along can really help put things into perspective. You can usually find the Easy Riders hanging around the hotels in Dalat, but don't worry about looking; they'll find you. All of them speak English, and some can speak French and German. Most of the Easy Riders carry portable guestbooks containing raving testimonials from past clients.

CENTRAL HIGHLANDS

and the Dalat Sailing and Fishing Club rents a wide selection of water craft, from kayaks and two-person sail boats to electric motor-boats. The fishing club has netted off an area of the lake and stocked it with fish; it also rents equipment, and has a per-kilo catch rate, as well as catch-and-release rules for sport. Shade umbrellas are supplied.

The Dalat Palace Golf Club occupies 50 hectares on the northern side of the lake near the Dalat Flower Gardens. The majestic hilltop Hotel Sofitel Dalat Palace overlooks Xuan Huong Lake from the south.

## Crémaillère Railway

About 500m east of Xuan Huong Lake is a cog-railway station (☎ 834409) and, although you aren't likely to arrive in Dalat by train, the station is worth a visit. There is an old Russian steam train on display here.

The *crémaillère* linked Dalat and Thap Cham from 1928 to 1964, when it was closed because of VC attacks. The line has been partially repaired and is now operated as a tourist attraction. You can't get to anywhere useful (like HCMC) on this train, but you can ride 8km (30 minutes) down the tracks to Trai Mat village and back again.

Departures are at 8am, 9.30am, 2pm and 3.30pm; and the return trip costs US$5.

Once in Trai Mat, most travellers make a requisite stroll over to visit the ornate **Linh Phuoc Pagoda**. This colourful pagoda was originally built between 1949 and 1952, and recent renovations included the installation of an 8½-tonne bell (cast in 1999) in a seven-tiered tower. You must remove your shoes when entering the main temple building, where an amusement-park dragon guards the gate. Once inside, visitors are greeted by a 5m high Buddha statue seated under a Bodhi Tree painting – this Buddha even sports a five-ringed neon halo! The statue is flanked by Pho Hien riding an elephant, and Van Thu riding a tiger. From the ground floor, take the left-hand staircase up to the 2nd-level balcony area for great views! In a small room here another Buddha statue with multiple heads and arms sits surrounded by 108 Bodhisattvas painted on the wall.

## Lam Dong Museum

This hill-top museum (☎ 822339; 4 Đ Hung Vuong; admission 10,000d; open 7.30am-11.30am & 1.30pm-4.30pm Tue-Sat) displays stone artefacts and pottery excavated from an ancient Oc-Eo archaeological site, costumes and musical instruments of local ethnic minorities, and displays relating to the struggles against the French and Americans.

The museum is housed in a lovely French-style villa, once the abode of Nguyen Huu Hao, father of Empress Nam Phuong, Bao Dai's wife. Nguyen Huu Hao, who died in 1939, was the richest person in the Go Cong district of the Mekong Delta. His tomb lies on a hilltop near Dalat, 400m west of Cam Ly Falls. Walk around the valley side of the villa to discover an interesting fusion of Chinese-style longevity symbols on the side of the building.

## Hang Nga Guesthouse & Art Gallery

Nicknamed the 'Crazy House' by locals, this guesthouse, café and art gallery (☎ 822070; 3 Đ Huynh Thuc Khang; admission 5000d) is about 1km southwest of Xuan Huong Lake. The architecture is something straight out of *Alice in Wonderland* and cannot easily be described: there are caves, giant spider webs made of wire, concrete 'tree trunks', a nude female statue (a rarity in Vietnam), a concrete giraffe (with a tearoom built inside) and so on. Yes it's tacky, and exceedingly commercialised, but many are astounded to find such a countercultural construction in Dalat.

The gallery's designer, Mrs Dang Viet Nga, is from Hanoi and lived in Moscow for 14 years, where she earned a PhD in architecture. She dresses in pure 1960s hippie garb, burns incense and has something of an air of mystery about her. Hang Nga has designed a number of other buildings, which dot the landscape around Dalat, including the Children's Cultural Palace and the Catholic church in Lien Khuong.

The Dalat People's Committee has not always appreciated such innovative designs. An earlier Dalat architectural masterpiece, the 'House with 100 Roofs', was torn down as a 'fire hazard' because the People's Committee thought it looked 'antisocialist'. However, there is little chance that Hang Nga will have such trouble with the authorities – her father, Truong Chinh, was Ho Chi Minh's successor. He served as Vietnam's second president from 1981 until his death in 1988.

All this said, there have been a large number of negative reports recently, and we received a shockingly rude reception on our last visit here. If you feel like you *have* to see this place, you might just do a drive-by and sneak a peek inside from the gate. Rather than cough up the entry fee, however, we recommend spending your time and money elsewhere. Have a coffee at the delightful Stop & Go Cafe (see under Cafés later in this section), an old Dalat institution that is still – thousands of tourists later – as pleasant as ever to visit.

## Governor-General's Residence

Built in 1933, the French Governor-General's Residence *(Dinh Toan Quyen or Dinh 2; Đ Tran Hung Dao; ☎ 822092)* is a dignified building of modernist design. It is today used as a guesthouse and for official receptions, and the original style of furnishing has been retained in most of its 25 rooms. At the time of writing it was closed to the public, and plans for renovation were in the works (inquire locally).

The Governor-General's Residence is about 2km east of the centre of town, up the hill from the intersection of Đ Tran Hung Dao and Đ Khoi Nghia Bac Son.

## Bao Dai's Summer Palace

Emperor Bao Dai's Summer Palace *(Biet Dien Quoc Truong or Dinh 3; admission 5000d; open 7am-11am & 1.30pm-4pm)* is a 25-room villa constructed in 1933. The decor has not changed in decades, except for the addition of Ho Chi Minh's portrait over the fireplace, but the palace is filled with artefacts from decades and governments past and is extremely interesting.

For instance, the engraved-glass map of Vietnam was given to Emperor Bao Dai in 1942 by Vietnamese students in France.

In Bao Dai's office, the life-sized white bust above the bookcase is of Bao Dai himself; the smaller gold and brown busts are of his father, Emperor Khai Dinh. Note the heavy brass royal seal (on the right) and military seal (on the left). The photographs over the fireplace are of (from left to right) Bao Dai, his eldest son; Bao Long (in uniform); and Empress Nam Phuong, who died in 1963.

Upstairs are the royal living quarters. The room of Bao Long, who now lives in England, is decorated in yellow, the royal colour. The huge semicircular couch was used by the emperor and empress for family meetings, during which their three daughters were seated in the yellow chairs and their two sons tan in the pink chairs. Check out the ancient tan Rouathermique infrared sauna machine near the top of the stairs.

Bao Dai's Summer Palace is set in a pine grove 500m southeast of the Pasteur Institute, which is on Đ Le Hong Phong, 2km southwest of the city centre. The palace is open to the public and shoes must be removed at the door. There is an extra charge for cameras and videos.

## Dalat Flower Gardens

These beautiful gardens *(Vuon Hoa Dalat; ☎ 822151; 2 Đ Phu Dong Thien Vuong; admission 4000d; open 7.30am-4pm daily)* were established in 1966 by the South Vietnamese Agricultural Service, renovated in 1985, and have been greatly refined in recent years.

Flowers here include hydrangeas, fuchsias and orchids *(hoa lan)*. Most of the latter are in special shaded buildings to the right of the entrance. The orchids are grown in blocks of coconut-palm trunk and in terracotta pots with lots of ventilation holes.

Hasfarm, a local Dutch-run nursery, has chipped in with some displays. All in all, it's a very nice and well-kept cross section of Dalat foliage. The plants still have a lot of space in which to grow, and before long they may be calling it a botanic garden. Travellers have described them as 'a marvel!'

A few monkeys live in cages on the grounds of the Dalat Flower Gardens, and a warning to any feeble-minded tourists who might enjoy tormenting the monkeys by throwing things – these clever monkeys have learned to throw back!

Near the gate you can buy *cu ly*, which are reddish-brown animal-shaped pieces of fern stems, whose fibres are used to stop bleeding in traditional medicine. Plants and flowers are also for sale.

The Dalat Flower Gardens front Xuan Huong Lake, on the road that leads from the lake to Dalat University.

## Dalat University

Dalat is actually something of an education centre. The reason for this is its climate: before air-con, it was one of the few places in Vietnam where it was possibly to study without working up a sweat. Therefore, a number of educational institutions were located in town, with Dalat University *(1 Đ Phu Dong Thien Vuong)* being the most famous.

Dalat University was founded as a Catholic university in 1957 by Hué Archbishop Ngo Dinh Thuc, the older brother of President Ngo Dinh Diem (assassinated in 1963), with the help of Cardinal Spelman of New York. The university was seized from the church in 1975 and closed, but it reopened two years later as a state-run institution.

There are presently more than 12,000 students studying here, although they all live in off-campus boarding houses. The university library contains 10,000 books, including some in English and European languages.

The 38-hectare campus can easily be identified by the triangular tower topped by a red star, which was stuck over the cross originally erected by the church. The fact that the cross was never actually removed has led some to speculate that the church may some day get the campus returned to it.

Foreign visitors are generally welcome to visit the campus.

## Petit Lycée Yersin

The former school is now a **cultural centre** (☎ 822511; 1 Đ Hoang Van Thu) run by the provincial government. Music lessons in electric and acoustic musical instruments are held here, making this a good place to meet local musicians. This building's older sister, the former Grand Lycée Yersin, is located east of Xuan Huong Lake.

## Valley of Love

Named the Valley of Peace by Emperor Bao Dai, this area *(Thung Lung Tinh Yeu, or Vallée d'Amour; Đ Phu Dong Thien Vuong; admission US$0.40)* had its name changed in 1972 (the year Da Thien Lake was created) by romantically minded students from Dalat University.

Today this ever-tacky place has taken on a carnival atmosphere and now local tour guides call it the Valley of Shops! Tourist buses line up to regurgitate visitors and boats line up to accommodate them. Get into the spirit with some aquatic activities: paddle boats, 15-person canoes and obnoxious noise-making motorboats can be hired to tour the lake.

This is a good place to see the 'Dalat cowboys', Vietnamese guides dressed as American cowboys – come back in another year and they'll have the Montagnards dressed up as Indians. We've also seen locals dressed as bears; can Mickey Mouse and Donald Duck costumes be far behind? The cowboys rent horses to tourists and can take you on a guided tour around the lake. The Dalat cowboys and bears expect cash if you take their picture – they want about 5000d per photo!

Refreshments and local delicacies (such as jams and candied fruits) are on sale at the lookout near where the buses disgorge tourists.

The Valley of Love is 5km north of Xuan Huong Lake.

## Pagodas & Churches

**Lam Ty Ni Pagoda** This pagoda *(Quan Am Tu; 2 Đ Thien My)* was founded in 1961. The decorative front gate was constructed by the pagoda's only monk, Vien Thuc, an industrious man who learned English, French, Khmer and Thai at Dalat University. During his time here, he has built flowerbeds and gardens in several different styles, including a miniature Japanese garden complete with a bridge. Nearby are trellis-shaded paths decorated with hanging plants. Signs list the

Chinese name of each garden. Vien Thuc also built much of the pagoda's wooden furniture.

But more than the pagoda and its gardens the attraction here is Mr Thuc himself and his mind-boggling collection of self-brushed art works. It would be a gross understatement to call him prolific. By his own estimates he has churned out more than 100,000 works of art, piles and piles of which hang in and around the pagoda – even out in the rain!

So industrious is this eccentric local celebrity, that since he began selling his paintings to tourists he has become, some say, the wealthiest person in Dalat. Judging by the astounding number of 'instant paintings' he sells, you could believe it. The one-time hermit monk has today earned himself the esteemed title of 'the business monk' by local motorbike guides (many of whom resent his financial success, not to mention having to wait for hours, while their customers linger at the pagoda).

Paintings sell anywhere from a dollar or two to whatever smooth-talking Mr Thuc can take you for. These days the monk is saving those dollars while waiting for his long-awaited around-the-globe journey. His plans include visiting travellers who have been to see him (and the homes where his paintings hang).

Mr Thuc's status has already made him the subject of much rumour and myth. Not long ago we received a sorrowful letter to inform us of his untimely death – he got a good chuckle out of this one! Commercial or not, he is certainly a interesting man and provides a most unusual encounter. Be aware that the monk's popularity has sailed to such heights that these days there is a steady stream of visitors at the pagoda, so many that he often needs to lock the pagoda gate just to have time to eat!

Lam Ty Ni Pagoda is about 500m north of the Pasteur Institute. A visit here can easily be combined with a stop at Bao Dai's Summer Palace.

**Linh Son Pagoda** Built in 1938, this pagoda (Chua Linh Son; 120 Đ Nguyen Van Troi) is a lovely ochre-coloured building that fuses French and Chinese architecture.

The giant bell is said to be made of bronze mixed with gold, its great weight making it too heavy for thieves to carry off. Behind the pagoda are coffee and tea plants tended by 20 monks, who range in age from 20 to 80, and half a dozen novices.

Linh Son Pagoda is about 1km from the town centre, near the corner of Đ Phan Dinh Phung. The sign on the front gate reads 'Phat Giao Viet-Nam' (Vietnam Buddhist Association).

**Dalat Cathedral** Next to the Novotel Dalat, this cathedral (Đ Tran Phu) was built between 1931 and 1942 for use by French residents and holiday-makers. The cross on the spire is 47m above the ground. Inside, the stained-glass windows bring a hint of medieval Europe to Dalat. The first church built on this site (in the 1920s) is to the left of the cathedral; it has a light-blue arched door.

There are three priests here, and masses are held daily.

**Vietnamese Evangelical Church** Dalat's pink Evangelical Church (72 Đ Nguyen Van Troi), the main Protestant church in the city, was built in 1940. Until 1975, it was affiliated with The Christian and Missionary Alliance.

Since reunification, Vietnam's Protestants have been persecuted even more than the Catholics, in part because many Protestant clergymen were trained by US missionaries. Although religious activities at this church are still restricted by the government, Sunday is a busy day with Bible study, worship and a youth service.

Most of the 25,000 Protestants in Lam Dong province, who are served by more than 100 churches, are hill-tribe people. Dalat's Vietnamese Evangelical Church is one of only six churches in the province whose membership is ethnic Vietnamese.

The Vietnamese Evangelical Church is 300m north of Rap 3/4.

**Domaine de Marie Convent** The pink tile–roofed structures of the hill-top Domaine de Marie Convent (Nha Tho Domaine; 6 Đ Ngo Quyen), constructed between 1940 and

**CENTRAL HIGHLANDS**

1942, were once home to 300 nuns. Today, the remaining nuns support themselves by making ginger candies and selling the fruit grown in the orchard out the back.

Suzanne Humbert, wife of Admiral Jean Decoux (French Governor-General of Indochina from 1940 to 1945) is buried at the base of the outside back wall of the chapel. A benefactor of the chapel, she was killed in a car accident in 1944.

The French-speaking nuns are pleased to show visitors around and explain the work they do for orphans, the homeless and handicapped children. The shop sells handicrafts made by the children and nuns.

Masses are held in the large chapel Monday to Friday, and on Sunday.

**Du Sinh Church** This church was built in 1955 by Catholic refugees from the north. The four-post, Sino-Vietnamese steeple was constructed at the insistence of a Hué-born priest of royal lineage. The church is on a hilltop with beautiful views in all directions, making this a great place for a picnic.

To get to Du Sinh Church, walk 500m southwest along Đ Huyen Tran Cong Chua from the former Couvent des Oiseaux, which is now a teachers' training high school.

**Thien Vuong Pagoda** This pagoda *(Chua Tau or Chinese pagoda; Đ Khe Sanh)* is popular with domestic tourists, especially ethnic Chinese. Set on a hilltop amid pine trees, the pagoda was built by the Chaozhou Chinese Congregation. Tho Da, the monk who initiated the construction of the pagoda in 1958, emigrated to the USA; there are pictures of his 1988 visit on display. The stalls are the front are a good place to buy local candied fruit and preserves.

The pagoda itself consists of three yellow buildings made of wood. In the first building is a gilded, wooden statue of Ho Phap, one of the Buddha's protectors. On the other side of the glass case is a gilded wooden statue of Pho Hien, a helper of A Di Da Buddha (Buddha of the Past). Remove your shoes before entering the third building, in which there are three 4m-high standing Buddhas, donated by a British Buddhist and

brought from Hong Kong in 1960. Made of gilded sandalwood and weighing 1400kg each, the figures (which is said to be the largest sandalwood statues in Vietnam) represent Thich Ca Buddha (the historical Buddha Sakyamuni; in the centre); Quan The Am Bo Tat (Avalokiteçvara, the Goddess of Mercy; on the right); and Dai The Chi Bo Tat (an assistant of A Di Da; on the left).

Thien Vuong Pagoda is about 5km southeast of the centre of town.

**Minh Nguyet Cu Sy Lam Pagoda** A second Chinese Buddhist pagoda, Minh Nguyet Cu Sy Lam Pagoda is reached by a path beginning across the road from the gate of Thien Vuong Pagoda. It was built by the Cantonese Chinese Congregation in 1962. The main sanctuary of the pagoda is a round structure constructed on a platform representing a lotus blossom.

Inside the pagoda (remove shoes before entering) is a painted cement statue of Quan The Am Bo Tat flanked by two other figures. Notice the repetition of the lotus motif in the window bars, railings and gateposts. There is a giant, red, gourd-shaped incense-burning oven near the main sanctuary.

**Su Nu Pagoda** Built in 1952, this pagoda *(Chua Linh Phong; 72 Đ Hoang Hoa Tham)* is a Buddhist nunnery. The nuns here – who, in accordance with Buddhist regulations, are bald – wear grey or brown robes, except when praying, at which time they wear saffron attire. Men are allowed to visit, but only women live here. The nunnery is open all day, but it is considered impolite to come around lunch time, when the nuns sing their prayers a cappella before eating. Across the driveway from the main buildings, and set among tea plants, is the grave marker of head nun Thich Nu Dieu Huong.

Su Nu Pagoda is about 1km south of Đ Le Thai To.

### Adventure Tours
Nature lovers looking for their outdoor-adventure fix should check out the activities offered by **Dalat Holidays** (☎ 829422, fax 821122; e langbian@hcm.vnn.vn; 73 Đ

*Truong Cong Dinh; open 7.30am-8.30pm daily).* Unlike many operators in Vietnam, who cluelessly throw the terms 'eco' and 'environment' around for the sake of profit, these folks take the term ecotourism seriously. Dalat Holidays employs knowledgeable English- and French-speaking guides, all of whom are Red Cross certified.

It offers canyoning, abseiling and treks to the minority villages in the mountains surrounding Dalat. Treks range from half-day low-impact hikes to multiday nature outings to national parks. Dalat Holidays also offers technical rock climbing and mountain biking (see the following section). Trips range in price from US$10-100.

**Hardy Dalat** *(☎ 836840; e hardydl@ hcm.vnn.vn; 133 Đ Phan Dinh Phung)* is another contender in the adventure-tour game.

**Action Max** *(☎ 0913-929137; e actionmax@ hcm.vnn.vn),* based in HCMC, runs occasional team-building outdoor trips to Dalat.

## Mountain-Bike Tours

Working in conjunction with Dalat Holidays, **Phat Tire Ventures** *(☎ 829422; e kim@phattireventures.com, w www.phat tireventures.com; 73 Đ Truong Cong Dinh)* is an ass-kicking mountain-bike outfit that guides praiseworthy 'fat tire' tours of the Dalat area. Phat Tire is headed up by a pair of hip American mountain bikers, Kim and Brian, who maintain a fleet of high quality imported mountain bikes, as well as rappelling equipment from Europe and the US. They offer a wide range of two-wheeled adventures around Dalat, or you might even consider biking with them all the way to the coast, 120km *downhill* to the sand dunes at Mui Ne Beach.

## Golf

The **Dalat Palace Golf Club** *(☎ 821201, fax 824325; e dpgc@hcm.vnn.vn; Đ Phu Dong Thien Vuong),* established in 1922, was once used by Bao Dai, the last Vietnamese emperor. Visitors can play 18-hole rounds here for US$65, but the more affordable 'twilight gold specials' practically make golfing an option for budget travellers! These rates are just US$35 after 2.30pm, or

US$25 after 3.30pm, including play until sundown, caddie fees, rental clubs, rental shoes and six used golf balls.

Happy hour at the club house is from 4pm to 7pm and worth checking out just for the guacamole and home-baked tortilla chips!

To lure the customers up to Dalat, very reasonably priced golf-package tours are available if you book from HCMC. Per golfer deals are as inexpensive as US$62/70 on a weekday/weekend, including a round of golf, a night at the elegant Novotel Dalat and breakfast. Tack on around US$30 to these rates and you can upgrade to the Sofitel Dalat Palace.

For information, contact the golf club's HCMC **marketing office** *(☎ 08-910 1457, fax 910 1458; e dpodgc@hcm.fpt.vn, w www .vietnamgolfresorts.com).*

## Places to Stay

Owing to its popularity with domestic tourists, Dalat has an extensive network of excellent lodgings, from backpacker dives and private villas to elegant luxury hotels.

Few hotels in cool Dalat have air-con and it's hard to imagine why anyone would want it!

## Places to Stay – Budget

**Phuong Thanh Hotel** *(☎ 825097; 65 Đ Truong Cong Dinh; singles US$3-4, doubles US$5-6, triples & quads US$10)* is a friendly attractive villa-style place with wooden floors. The cheapest rooms are in the basement.

Next door is another attractive villa, **Peace Hotel II** *(☎ 822982, fax 836153; e peace12@ hcm.vnn.vn; 67 Đ Truong Cong Dinh; singles/ doubles US$5/7),* but rooms are on the small side. **Peace Hotel** *(Khach San Hoa Binh; ☎ 822787; e peace12@hcm.vnn.vn; 64 Đ Truong Cong Dinh)* is a long-time favourite with backpackers and charges similar rates.

**Cam Do Hotel** *(☎ 822482, fax 830273; 81 Đ Phan Dinh Phung; dorm beds US$3, singles US$5-8, doubles US$8-12)* is another backpackers special.

**Highland Hotel** *(☎ 823738, fax 832275; 90 Đ Phan Dinh Phung; singles US$4, doubles US$5-6)* is a rather run-down budget choice near the city centre.

**Phu Hoa Hotel** (☎ 822194, fax 833956; 16 Đ Tang Bat Ho; singles US$4-5, doubles US$7-12) is also old, but still reasonably pleasant and in the centre.

**Mimosa Hotel** (☎ 822656, fax 832275; 170 Đ Phan Dinh Phung; singles US$6-8, twins US$8-12) is another old Dalat budget institution, but slightly away from the centre.

**Lam Son Hotel** (☎ 822362, fax 833956; 5 Đ Hai Thuong; rooms US$10-15) is 500m west of the centre of town in an old French villa. This large, quiet place is decent value if you don't mind the 10-minute walk to the town centre. The attached **Sapa Restaurant** does good barbecued ribs.

**Lyla Hotel** (☎ 834540, fax 835940; e lylahotel@hcm.vnn.vn; 18A Đ Nguyen Chi Thanh; rooms 200,000-300,000d) is a stylish place with an in-house **restaurant** serving Vietnamese and European fare.

**A Chau Hotel** (☎ 823974; 13 Đ Tang Bat Ho; doubles/triples US$10/15) is centrally located and modelled after a Swiss chalet, with big airy rooms.

**Dreams Hotel** (☎ 833748, fax 837108; e dreams@hcm.vnn.vn; 151 Đ Phan Dinh Phung; single rooms US$8, doubles US$10-12) has received a steady stream of good reports and wins hands-down when it comes to value for dollar. This friendly place offers tidy rooms (some with balconies) and Internet access; musical instruments (in the lobby) are available for use, and breakfast is included. It even accepts credit cards.

**Hotel Chau Au Europa** (☎ 822870, fax 824488; e europa@hcm.vnn.vn; 76 Đ Nguyen Chi Thanh; rooms US$10-15) is another friendly, family-run place. The in-house **restaurant** is also good.

There is a camping site on the park-like grounds of the peaceful **Stop & Go Cafe** (☎ 828458; 2A Đ Ly Tu Trong). At the time of writing, plans were in the works for bungalows.

## Places to Stay – Mid-Range

**Ngoc Lan Hotel** (☎ 822136, fax 824032; e ctcpdlngoclan@hcm.vnn.vn; 42 Đ Nguyen Chi Thanh; rooms US$15-30) is a big old place overlooking the lake. Rooms with views start at US$25. All rates include breakfast.

**Dai Loi Hotel** (Fortune Hotel; ☎ 837333, fax 837474; 3A Đ Bui Thi Xuan; rooms US$14-25) is one of the newest hotels in Dalat. Rooms are spacious and comfortable.

**Golf 3 Hotel** (☎ 826042, fax 830396; e golf3hot@hcm.vnn.vn, w www.vietnam golfhotel.com; 4 Đ Nguyen Thi Minh Khai; rooms US$35-70) is centrally located property and the **rooftop café** commands great views of Dalat. The steam bath facilities are the best in town. This is the best of the three Golf Hotels in Dalat, the others being **Golf 1 Hotel** and **Golf 2 Hotel**.

**Empress Hotel** (☎ 833888, fax 829399; e empress@hcm.vnn.vn; 5 Đ Nguyen Thai Hoc; rooms US$60-80, suites US$110-190) is an elegant hotel set on Xuan Huong Lake – the views are great. This hotel has some of the most beautiful rooms in Dalat and discounts can usually be negotiated. Rates include a buffet breakfast.

**Villa Hotel 28 Tran Hung Dao** (☎ 822764, fax 835639; 28 Đ Tran Hung Dao; rooms US$20, annexe rooms US$15) is a charming place resembling a British country inn. Rooms feature wooden trim and brick floors. The 'family room' has a fireplace and can sleep up to six (US$5 per person).

**Minh Tam Villas** (☎ 822447, fax 824420; 20A Đ Khe Sanh; twins US$18, cottages US$15) is 3km out of town, set amid lovely **flower gardens** (admission nonguests 4000d). There are good views of the surrounding landscape from here. The house originally belonged to a French architect, who sold it to a well-to-do Vietnamese family in 1954. It underwent several major renovations and in 1975 was 'donated' to the victorious communist government. There are rooms available in the main house, and cosy A-frame cottages; both, however, are looking a bit worse for the wear.

## Places to Stay – Top End

**Hotel Sofitel Dalat Palace** (☎ 825444, fax 825666; e sofitel@bdvn.vnd.vn, w www .sofitel.com; 12 Đ Tran Phu; rooms US$149-414) is a grand old place built between 1916 and 1922. Major renovation work has turned this into Dalat's premier luxury accommodation: panoramic views of Xuan

Huong Lake can be enjoyed in the expansive ground-floor public areas, where one can sit in a rattan chair, sip tea or soda and gaze out through a wall of windows. The nearby tennis courts are owned by the hotel.

**Novotel Dalat** *(☎ 825777, fax 825888; 7 Đ Tran Phu; rooms US$99-189)*, another vintage hotel, is a large place nearly opposite the Sofitel. It was constructed in 1932 as the Du Parc Hotel and has undergone extensive renovation work. Today it too retains much of the original French-colonial air.

Discounted rates can usually be negotiated at both of these glorious hotels. If you golf, it's well worth looking into their reasonably priced package deals (see the Golf section earlier).

## Places to Eat – Local Specialities

Dalat is a paradise for lovers of fresh garden vegetables, which are grown locally and sold all over the south. The abundance of just-picked peas, carrots, radishes, tomatoes, cucumbers, avocados, green peppers, lettuce, Chinese cabbages, bean sprouts, beets, green beans, potatoes, corn, bamboo shoots, garlic, spinach, squash and yams makes for meals unavailable elsewhere in the country.

The Dalat area is justifiably famous for its strawberry jam, dried blackcurrants and candied plums, persimmons and peaches, all of which can be purchased from **food stalls** in the market area just west of the lake. Other local delicacies include avocado ice cream, sweet beans *(mut dao)* and strawberry, blackberry and artichoke extracts (for making drinks). The strawberry extract is great in tea. The region also produces grape, mulberry and strawberry wines. Vang Dalat, a brand of local wine, is not bad tasting and it's cheap at around 45,000d a bottle. Artichoke tea, another local speciality, is made from the root of the artichoke plant. Most of these can be purchased at the **central market** and at **stalls** in front of Thien Vuong Pagoda.

*Dau hu*, a type of pudding made from soy milk, sugar and a slice of ginger, is one of Dalat's specialities, as is hot soy milk *(sua dau nanh)*. Both are sold by itinerant female **vendors**, who walk around carrying a large bowl of the stuff and a small

stand suspended from either end of a bamboo pole.

The stairway down to Đ Nguyen Thi Minh Khai turns into a big **food stall** area in the late afternoon and early evening. Women sell all sorts of precooked homemade dishes or prepare them on a portable charcoal stove. The prices are amazingly cheap. Of course, other vendors with more permanent stalls in the market sell similar things, but at higher prices.

## Places to Eat – Restaurants

**V Cafe** *(☎ 837576; 1 Đ Bui Thi Xuan; mains 15,000-30,000d; open 10am-10pm)* is a fine place to begin a culinary exploration of Dalat. It's white table-cloth dining at very reasonable prices. The friendly proprietor Vy (with her American husband singing back-up) dishes up great home-style Vietnamese food, as well as respectable soups, salads, burgers, tacos and quesadillas with home-made flour tortillas. The roasted pork loin with mashed potatoes and gravy is divine. Top it all off with Vy's home-made lemon meringue – yum! V Cafe is also an excellent place to pick brains for travel tips.

**Trong Dong** *(☎ 821889; 220 Đ Phan Dinh Phung; mains 20,000-45,000d)* is another good choice to sample superb Vietnamese food served on white tablecloths. House specialities include grilled shrimp paste on sugar cane, fish in a clay pot and minced beef wrapped in lalot leaves. Trong Dong a bit outside the centre, but it's well worth walking over to.

**Long Hoa** *(☎ 822934; 6 Đ 3 Thang 2; open 10.30am-9.30pm; mains 15,000-30,000d)* has long been in vogue with travellers, and proves to be consistent. It does great sautéed dishes and hotpot. You might opt for the rear seating, away from the street noise.

**Hoang Lan Restaurant, Dong A Restaurant** and **Nhat Ly Restaurant** are three neighbouring budget places on Đ Phan Dinh Phung, all dishing up inexpensive Vietnamese, Chinese, Western and vegetarian cuisine.

For something more local, head across the street to Dalat's best budget hole-in-the-wall,

**Minh Uyen** (meals 10,000d). Its com thap cam, a mixture of rice, chicken, beef, pork, egg and vegies, is a guaranteed filler!

**Quan Diem Tam** (☎ 820104; 217 Đ Phan Dinh Phung; noodle soup 7000d) is a long running Chinese-style soup shop serving up delicious yellow-noodle won ton soup (mi hoanh thanh).

**Pho Tung**, near the Rap 3/4 cinema, has an outstanding bakery. It's difficult to resist all those delectable pastries and cakes in the windows.

**Phuong Hoang** (☎ 822773; 81 Đ Phan Dinh Phung), near the Cam Do Hotel, is a new place with good food and an attractive decor.

**Thuy Ta Restaurant** (☎ 822288, 1 Đ Yersin) is built on pilings over Xuan Huong Lake. The views are definitely better than the food and service.

For fine dining, **Le Rabelais** in the Hotel Sofitel cannot be beat, but bring a credit card or a wheelbarrow full of dong. Downstairs, **Larry's Bar** serves respectable pub grub and the best pizza in town. Across from the hotel, **Le Cafe de La Poste** is a casual bistro serving good light meals and baked goods.

## Places to Eat – Vegetarian
There are vegetarian **food stalls** (signposted com chay) in the market area, west of Xuan Huong Dam. All serve up delicious 100% vegetarian food, some prepared to resemble and taste like traditional Vietnamese meat dishes.

## Places to Eat – Cafés
Coffee and cake in Dalat is some of the best in Vietnam and a visit to any of the town's finer cafés should make you an instant addict of both.

**Stop & Go Cafe** (☎ 828458; 2A Đ Ly Tu Trong) has long been Dalat's avant-garde hang-out and is well worth finding your way to. This little bohemian oasis is run by a delightful former journalist named Duy Viet. He speaks English and French, and always sports a French beret and a smile. Duy Viet is a notable poet, and judging by the gorgeous bonsai and orchids in the gardens outside the villa, a man with a green thumb. Check out the book of poems and the paintings for

sale, or read the comments in the guestbooks that date back to 1989.

**Cafe Tung** (6 Khu Hoa Binh Square) was a famous hang-out of Saigonese intellectuals during the 1950s. Old-timers swear that the place remains exactly as it was when they were young. As it did then, Cafe Tung serves only tea, coffee, hot cocoa, lemon soda and orange soda to the accompaniment of mellow French music. This is a marvellous place to warm up and unwind on a chilly evening.

## Entertainment
Dalat has an interesting variety of watering holes, and more happy hours per capita than any other place in Vietnam!

**Saigon Nite Bar** (☎ 820 007; 11A Đ Hai Ba Trung) is run by zany Mr Dung and his friendly daughter. This lively little place has a billiards table and happy hour is from 5pm to 8pm.

**Larry's Bar**, in the basement of the Hotel Sofitel Dalat Palace, is a cosy little tavern with exposed wooden rafters and stone walls. Happy hour lasts from 5pm to 7pm, and also applies to food on the bar menu.

The busy **market area**, just to the west of Xuan Huong Dam, provides another form of entertainment. Here you can hang out drinking coffee and chatting with the locals at a strip of **local cafés** near the Viet Hung Internet Cafe.

## Shopping
In the past few years, the Dalat tourist-kitsch market has really come into its own. Without any effort at all, you'll be able to find that special something for your loved ones at home – perhaps a battery-powered stuffed koala that sings 'Waltzing Matilda' or a lacquered alligator with a light bulb in its mouth.

In addition to these useful items, Dalat is known for its kim mao cau tich, a kind of fern, whose fibres are used to stop bleeding in traditional Chinese medicine. The stuff is also known as cu ly because the fibrous matter is sold attached to reddish-brown branches pruned to resemble hairy animals.

The hill tribes of Lam Dong province make handicrafts. Lat products include dyed rush mats and rice baskets that roll up when empty. Koho and Chill people produce the split-bamboo baskets used by all the Montagnards in this area to carry things on their backs. The Chill also weave cloth, including the dark blue cotton shawls worn by some of the Montagnard women. The hill-tribe people carry water in a hollow gourd, with a corn-cob stopper that is sometimes wrapped in a leaf for a tighter fit. If you are interested in Montagnard handicrafts, try Chicken village or Lat village.

Hoa Binh Square (and the central-market building that's adjacent to it) is one big buy and sell, and a good place to pick up clothing at a reasonable price.

## Getting There & Away

**Air** A short walk from the Hotel Sofitel Dalat Palace, **Vietnam Airlines** (*☎ 822895; 40 Đ Ho Tung Mao*) has daily services connecting Dalat and HCMC (see the Getting Around chapter). Dalat's Lien Khuong Airport is 30km south of the city.

**Bus & Minibus** Although there are plenty of public buses to/from Dalat, it's nearly as cheap (and far more comfortable and convenient) to use the private tourist buses and minibuses. Another thing to take into consideration is that the long distance public bus station is 1km south of Xuan Huong Lake, while most private services will (if asked) pick up and drop off at the hotel of your choice.

Prices for HCMC–Dalat and Nha Trang–Dalat have come down to about $5. Most of the private buses and minibuses travelling between Dalat and Nha Trang /Mui Ne make a stop at the impressive Po Klong Garai Cham towers in Thap Cham, a few kilometres from the junction of National Hwys 1 and 20 (see the boxed text 'Po Klong Garai Cham Towers' in the South-Central Coast chapter).

**Car & Motorbike** From HCMC, taking the inland route to Dalat via Bao Loc and Di Linh is faster than the coastal route via Ngoan Muc Pass. The following are road distances from Dalat.

| | |
|---|---|
| Danang | 746km |
| Di Linh | 82km |
| Nha Trang | 205km |
| Phan Rang & Thap Cham | 101km |
| Phan Thiet | 247km |
| HCMC | 308km |

There are roads connecting Dalat to Buon Ma Thuot and other parts of the central highlands.

## Getting Around

**To/From the Airport** The Vietnam Airlines shuttle bus between Lien Khuong airport and Dalat cost US$3 per person, including door-to-door drop off at your hotel. Private taxis can be hired to make the trip for around US$10, while a motorbike taxi should cost from US$3 to US$5.

**Motorbike** Dalat is much too hilly for cyclos, but motorbike is a popular way of touring the environs. For short point-to-point trips around town, *xe om* drivers can be flagged down around the central market area for around 5000d.

Self-drive motorbikes can be rented for around US$6 to US$8 a day, but for a dollar or two more we highly recommend hiring one with a driver, and leave the navigation to someone else. Countless motorbike drivers in Dalat offer their services, though you'd be better off finding an Easy Rider (see the boxed text 'Easy Riders' earlier in this chapter).

**Taxi & Car** Dalat Tourist now has a reliable fleet of taxis. One way, to just about anywhere in Dalat, costs $2 or less. Daily rentals (with driver) cost around US$25.

**Bicycle** Pedal power is a great way of seeing Dalat, but the hilly terrain and long distances between the sights make it both time and energy consuming. Still, if you're not in a rush and have the stamina, it's a good option.

Several hotels around town rent out bicycles to tourists. It's also well worth looking into the cycling tours offered by Phat Tire Ventures (see Adventure Tours earlier in this chapter).

## AROUND DALAT
### Lake of Sighs
The Lake of Sighs (Ho Than Tho; admission 5000d) is a natural lake enlarged by a French-built dam; the forests in the area are hardly Dalat's finest.

According to legend, Mai Nuong and Hoang Tung met here in 1788 while he was hunting and she was picking mushrooms. They fell in love and sought their parents' permission to marry. But at that time Vietnam was threatened by a Chinese invasion and Hoang Tung, heeding Emperor Quang Trung's call to arms, joined the army without waiting to tell Mai Nuong. Unaware of this and afraid that his absence meant that he no longer loved her, Mai Nuong sent word for him to meet her at the lake. When he did not come she was overcome with sorrow and, to prove her love, threw herself into the lake and drowned. Thereafter, the lake has been known as the Lake of Sighs.

There are several small **restaurants** up the hill from the dam. Horses can be hired for 80,000d an hour, while a ride in a horse-drawn carriage costs 140,000d per hour.

The Lake of Sighs is 6km northeast of the centre of Dalat via Đ Phan Chu Trinh.

### Tiger Falls
These falls (Thac Hang Cop; admission 4000d) is named from the local legend of a ferocious tiger living in a nearby cave. This helps explain the huge ceramic tiger statue, as well as the nearby statue of a hill-tribe hunter. The falls themselves are set in a quiet pine forest, and are very photogenic. There are also good hiking trails in the area.

Tiger Falls is about 14km east of Dalat and can be easily reached by bicycle or motorbike. Follow Đ Hung Vuong to Trai Mat village and from the train station there, continue for another 3.5km to the left-hand turn (signposted). From here it's another

## National Highway 20: Roadside Attractions

The HCMC–Dalat road (National Hwy 20) spans **Langa Lake**, a reservoir which is crossed by a bridge (see the Around HCMC map). Lots of **floating houses**, where families harvest the fish underneath, can be seen here. It's a very scenic spot for photography, and most tourist vehicles on the HCMC–Dalat road make a short pit-stop here.

The town of **Bao Loc** is a convenient place to break the trip between HCMC and Dalat as there are several local hotels. Tea, mulberry leaves (for the silkworms) and silk are the major local industries, and free samples of the **local tea** can be had at a couple of roadside rest stops in town.

There are **volcanic craters** near Dinh Quan on National Hwy 20 (see the Around HCMC map). All three volcanoes are now extinct, but are nonetheless very impressive. The craters date from the late Jurassic period, about 150 million years ago. You can't see many of the craters from the highway – you have to do a little walking. One crater is on the left-hand side of the road, about 2km south of Dinh Quan, and another on the right-hand side about 8km beyond Dinh Quan, towards Dalat.

A bit beyond the volcanic craters in the direction of Dalat are underground **lava tubes**. These rare caves were formed as the surface lava cooled and solidified, while the hotter underground lava continued to flow, leaving a hollow space. Lava tubes differ sharply in appearance from limestone caves (the latter are formed by underground springs). While limestone caves have abundant stalactites and stalagmites, the walls of lava caves are smooth.

The easiest way to find the lava tubes is to first find the **teak forest** on National Hwy 20 between the km120 and km124 markers. The children who live around the forest can point you to the entrance of the lava tubes. However, you are strongly advised not to go into the tubes by yourself. It's best to have a guide and, furthermore, inform someone responsible where you are going. You definitely need to take a torch (flashlight).

For more information on the waterfalls and other attractions along National Hwy 20, see the Around Dalat section.

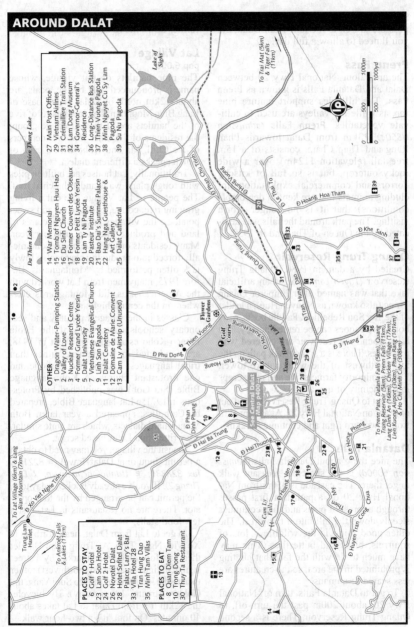

# AROUND DALAT

**OTHER**
1 Dragon Water-Pumping Station
2 Valley of Love
3 Nuclear Research Centre
4 Former Grand Lycée Yersin
5 Dalat University
9 Linh Son Pagoda
11 Dalat Cemetery
12 Domaine de Marie Convent
13 Cam Ly Airstrip (Unused)
14 War Memorial
15 Tomb of Nguyen Huu Hao
16 Du Sinh Church
17 Former Couvent des Oiseaux
18 Former Petit Lycée Yersin
19 Lam Ty Ni Pagoda
20 Pasteur Institute
21 Bao Dai's Summer Palace
22 Hang Nga Guesthouse & Art Gallery
25 Dalat Cathedral
27 Main Post Office
29 Vietnam Airlines
31 Crémaillère Train Station
32 Lam Dong Museum
34 Governor-General's Residence
36 Long-Distance Bus Station
37 Thien Vuong Pagoda
38 Minh Nguyet Cu Sy Lam Pagoda
39 Su Nu Pagoda

**PLACES TO STAY**
6 Golf 1 Hotel
23 Lam Son Hotel
24 Golf 2 Hotel
26 Novotel Dalat
28 Hotel Sofitel Dalat Palace; Larry's Bar
33 Villa Hotel 28
35 Minh Tam Villas

**PLACES TO EAT**
8 Quan Diem Tam
10 Trong Dong
30 Thuy Ta Restaurant

To Lat Village (6km) & Lang Bian Mountain (7km)

To Ankroet Falls & Lakes (11km)

Trung Lam Hamlet

To Trai Mat (5km) & Tiger Falls (11km)

Lake of Sighs

Chien Thang Lake

Da Thien Lake

Flower Gardens

Golf Course

Xuan Huong Lake

See Central Dalat Map p400

To Prem Pass, Datanla Falls (5km), Quang Trung Reservoir (5km), Prenn Falls (11km), Lang An (19km), Chicken Village (17km), Lien Kuong Airport (30km), Phan Rang (101km) & Ho Chi Minh City (308km)

**CENTRAL HIGHLANDS**

3km along a dirt road to the falls. It is also possible to trek to the falls from Dalat, but you'll need to allow a full day.

## Prenn Pass

The area along National Hwy 20 between Dalat and Datanla Falls is known as Prenn Pass. The hillsides support mature pine forests while the valleys are used to cultivate vegetables. **Prenn Falls** (admission US50¢), 13km from Dalat towards Phan Rang and Thap Cham, consists of a 15m free fall (elevation 1124m) over a wide rocky outcrop, but is so full of kitschy horrors and commercial exploitation (including animals that are kept in deplorable conditions) that it is no longer worth visiting. The park around the falls was dedicated by the Queen of Thailand in 1959.

## Quang Trung Reservoir

Created by a dam in 1980, Quang Trung Reservoir (Tuyen Lam Lake) is an artificial lake that was named after Emperor Quang Trung (also known as Nguyen Hué), a leader of the Tay Son Rebellion. Paddle boats, rowboats and canoes can be rented nearby. The hills around the reservoir are covered with pine trees. There is a switchback path up the hill southwest of the water-intake tower. Ethnic-minority farmers live and raise crops in the vicinity of the lake.

To get to Quang Trung Reservoir, head out of Dalat on National Hwy 20. At a point 5km from town turn right and continue for 2km.

## Datanla Falls

The nice thing about Datanla Falls (admission 5000d) is the short but pleasant walk to get there. The cascade is 350m from National Hwy 20 on a path that first passes through a forest of pines and then continues steeply down the hill into a rainforest. The other good thing is the wildlife – lots of squirrels, birds and butterflies. This may have much to do with the fact that hunting is prohibited in the area, so the creatures are less scared of humans.

To get to Datanla Falls, turn off National Hwy 20, about 200m past the turn-off, to Quang Trung Reservoir. There is a second entrance to the falls several hundred metres further down the road.

## Lat Village

pop 6,000

The nine hamlets of Lat village, whose name is pronounced 'lak' by the locals, are about 12km north of Dalat at the base of Lang Bian Mountain. The inhabitants of five of the hamlets are of the Lat ethnic group; the residents of the other four are members of the Chill, Ma and Koho tribes, each of which speaks a different dialect.

Traditionally, Lat houses are built on piles with rough plank walls and a thatched roof. The people of Lat Village eke out a living growing rice, coffee, black beans and sweet potatoes; the villages have 300 hectares of land and produce one rice crop per year. Many residents of Lat have been economically forced into producing charcoal, a lowly task often performed by Montagnards. Before 1975, many men from Lat worked with the Americans, as did Montagnards elsewhere in the central highlands.

Classes in the village's primary and secondary schools, successors of the École Franco-Koho established in Dalat in 1948, are conducted in Vietnamese rather than tribal languages. Lat has one Catholic and one Protestant church. A Koho-language Bible (Sra Goh) was published by Protestants in 1971; a Lat-language Bible, prepared by Catholics, appeared a year later. Both Montagnard dialects, which are quite similar, are written in a Latin-based script.

To visit the village, you may need to obtain a permit. Inquire at **Dalat Travel** (☎ 822125, fax 828330; e ttdhhd@hcmvnn.vn; 7 Đ 3 Thang 2). If you've already booked a day tour, the permit can be arranged by the tour operator. There are no restaurants in Lat, just a few **food stalls**.

To get to Lat from Dalat, head north on Đ Xo Viet Nghe Tinh. At Trung Lam Hamlet there is a fork in the road marked by a street sign. Continue straight on (northwest) rather than to the left (which leads to Suoi Vang, the Golden Stream, 14km away). By bicycle, the 12km trip from Dalat to Lat takes about 40 minutes. On foot, it's a two-hour walk.

## Lang Bian Mountain

Lang Bian Mountain (also called Lam Vien Mountain) has five volcanic peaks ranging in altitude from 2100m to 2400m. Of the two highest peaks, the eastern one is known to locals by the woman's name K'Lang; the western one bears a man's name, K'Biang. The upper reaches of the mountain are forested. Only half a century ago, the verdant foothills of Lang Bian Mountain, now defoliated, sheltered wild oxen, deer, boars, elephants, rhinoceroses and tigers.

The hike up to the top of Lang Bian Mountain, from where the views are truly spectacular, takes three to four hours from Lat village. The path begins due north of Lat and is easily recognisable as a red gash in the green mountainside.

You do not need a permit to visit Lang Bian Mountain, though taking a guide along will certainly make the trip more interesting. Consider contacting Dalat Holidays (see the earlier Dalat section) to see what outdoor programmes they are offering to Lang Bian.

## Ankroët Falls & Lakes

The two Ankroët Lakes were created as part of a hydroelectric project. The waterfall, Thac Ankroët, is about 15m high. The Ankroët Lakes are 18km northwest of Dalat in an area inhabited by hill tribes.

## Chicken Village

This village has become very popular with travellers because it's conveniently situated on the Dalat–Nha Trang highway, 17km from Dalat.

This village is home to the Koho minority, who, to a certain extent, have been assimilated into Vietnamese society. For example, most no longer live in stilt houses and they wear Vietnamese-style clothing. Nevertheless, they have a lifestyle all of their own and it could be worth a stopover if you're heading to Nha Trang anyway.

This place takes its name from a huge concrete statue of a chicken, which sits squarely in the centre of the village. We questioned the villagers extensively to learn the history behind this unusual statue and were surprised

to find that most had no idea or else refused to discuss when the statue was built or why. It certainly has no religious significance to the villagers. Finally we heard this story from a local woman:

When a couple gets married here, it's the bride's family who must pay for the engagement ring and wedding party. Her family is also supposed to present the groom's family with a gift. We had a sad case many years ago where the man's family demanded a special gift, a chicken with nine fingers. No one had ever seen such a chicken, but there were rumours that these could be found in the mountains. So the girl went to the mountains to search for one. Unfortunately, her effort was in vain and she died in the wilderness. The villagers were stricken with grief by this senseless tragedy and the girl was made into a hero.

There was fighting in this area during the war and after liberation the government wanted to give the locals some sort of gift. The villagers asked if they could commemorate the brave young girl who died for love. The government officials were touched by this tragic story and complied with the wishes of the villagers. So the concrete chicken was built.

The story does sound a bit far-fetched and one local man had a somewhat different tale to tell. He claims that after the communist victory in 1975, the villagers retreated to the woods and adopted nomadic slash-and-burn agriculture because of attempts to enforce farm collectivisation. Many of the men went into the illegal timber harvesting, which did quite a bit of damage to the region's forests.

The government then granted them several redeeming concessions to entice them to relocate to their permanent village site. After they returned, the government thought of building some sort of memorial, possibly a statue of Ho Chi Minh. It was finally decided that the huge concrete chicken would be most appropriate because it would commemorate the hard-working peasants. After all, what better way to symbolise the chicken farmers than to build a statue of a chicken?

The residents of Chicken village are extremely poor, but we were surprised to find no beggars there at all. This is particularly remarkable given the large number of

CENTRAL HIGHLANDS

tourists who stop here. We'd like to suggest that you do *not* give sweets or money to the children – if you want to help the villagers, there are a couple of shops where you can buy simple things like drinks, biscuits and such. There are also beautiful weavings for sale near the highway.

## DAMBRI FALLS

This is one of the highest (90m) and most magnificent and easily accessible waterfalls *(admission 10,000d)* in Vietnam. The views are positively breathtaking – the steep walk up the path to the top of the falls will almost certainly take your breath away (unless you opt to ride the new cable car for US40¢).

If you continue walking upstream from the top of the falls you reach 'Monkey Island', a mini-zoo filled with monkeys and reindeer.

Dambri Falls is close to Bao Loc in an area populated chiefly by Montagnards. Near Bao Loc, you have to turn off the main highway and follow the road for 18km. As you're driving towards the falls you can see plentiful tea and mulberry plantations; the high peak off to your right is May Bay Mountain.

The **Dambri Restaurant**, which adjoins the car park, is cheap and good.

## DI LINH

The town of Di Linh (**zee**-ling), also known as Djiring, is 1010m above sea level. The area's main product is tea, which is grown on giant plantations founded by the French. The Di Linh Plateau, sometimes compared to the Cameron Highlands of Malaysia, is a great place for day hikes. Only a few decades ago, the region was famous for its tiger hunting.

### Bo Bla Waterfall

The 32m-high Bo Bla Waterfall is 7km southwest of Di Linh, close to National Hwy 20.

### Getting There & Away

Di Linh is 226km northeast of HCMC and 82km southwest of Dalat on the main HCMC–Dalat highway. The town is 96km from Phan Thiet by a secondary road.

## PONGOUR FALLS

Pongour Falls *(admission 5000d)*, the largest in the Dalat area, is about 55km towards HCMC from Dalat and 7km off the highway. During the rainy season, the falls form a full semicircle.

## GOUGAH FALLS

Gougah Falls *(admission 4000d)* is approximately 40km from Dalat towards HCMC. It is only 500m from the highway so it's easy to get to.

## LIEN KHUONG FALLS

At Lien Khuong Falls, the Dan Nhim River, 100m wide at this point, drops 15m over an outcrop of volcanic rock. The site, which can be seen from the highway, is 25km towards HCMC from Dalat. Lien Khuong Falls is not far from Lien Khuong airport.

Lien Khuong Falls is not just one, but a number of falls close to the road, which are very nice to climb around in. There is a waterfall where you can crawl under the rocky outcrop. The falls are not commercialised – there's not even a sign by the road.

**Per Arenmo**

## DAN NHIM LAKE

**elevation 1042m**

Dan Nhim Lake was created by a dam built between 1962 and 1964 by Japan as part of its war reparations. The huge Dan Nhim hydroelectric project supplies electricity to much of the south.

The lake is often used by HCMC movie studios for filming romantic lake scenes. The lake's surface area is 9.3 sq km.

The power station is at the western edge of the coastal plain. Water drawn from Dan Nhim Lake gathers speed as it rushes almost a vertical kilometre down from Ngoan Muc Pass in two enormous pipes.

It is said that the forested hills around Dan Nhim Lake are fine for hiking and that there is good fishing in the area.

## Getting There & Away

Dan Nhim Lake is about 38km from Dalat in the Don Duong district of Lam Dong province. As you head towards Phan Rang and Thap Cham, the dam is about a kilometre to the left of the Dalat–Phan Rang highway. The power station is at the base of Ngoan Muc Pass near the town of Ninh Son.

## NGOAN MUC PASS

Ngoan Muc Pass (altitude 980m), known to the French as Bellevue Pass, is about 5km towards Phan Rang and Thap Cham from Dan Nhim Lake and 64km west of Phan Rang. On a clear day, you can see all the way across the coastal plain to the Pacific Ocean, an aerial distance of 55km. As the highway winds down the mountain in a series of switchbacks, it passes under two gargantuan water pipes (still guarded by armed troops in concrete fortifications) that link Dan Nhim Lake with the hydroelectric power station.

To the south of the road (to the right as you face the ocean) you can see the steep tracks of the *crémaillère* linking Thap Cham with Dalat (see the Dalat section earlier).

Sites of interest at the top of Ngoan Muc Pass include a waterfall next to the highway, pine forests and the old Bellevue train station.

## BUON MA THUOT

☎ 050 • pop 186,600 • elevation 451m

Buon Ma Thuot (or Ban Me Thuot), is the capital of Dac Lac province and the largest town in the western highlands. Before WWII, the city was a centre for big-game hunting, but the animals have all but disappeared (along with most of the region's rainforest).

The region's main crop is coffee, and it's the coffee industry that accounts for Buon Ma Thuot's current prosperity. Some local plantations are run by German managers, who are said to be as imperiously demanding as their French predecessors. If you can find a good guide, visiting the coffee plantations and processing plants could be interesting.

A large percentage of the area's population is made up of Montagnards. The government's policy of assimilation has been effective: nearly all of them now speak Vietnamese fluently.

The rainy season around Buon Ma Thuot lasts from May to October, though downpours are usually short. Because of its lower elevation, Buon Ma Thuot is warmer and more humid than Dalat; it is also very windy.

Buon Ma Thuot is the gateway to Yok Don National Park and even a possible back door to Cat Tien National Park (see the Around HCMC chapter). However, most travellers approach Cat Tien from the Dalat side.

## Information

**Money** The local branch of the **Agriculture & Rural Development Bank** (☎ 853930; 37 Đ Phan Boi Chau) can make foreign-currency exchanges.

**Email & Internet Access** Both **Nhip Song Net** (35 Đ Hoang Dieu; ☎ 851136; e nhipsong@dng.vnn.vn; open 8am-10pm) and **Internet Service** (48 Đ Hung Vuong) are two good places to catch up on email for around 5000d per hour.

**Travel Agencies** The provincial tourism authority, **Dak Lak Tourist** (☎ 852108, fax 852865; e daklaktour@dng.vnn.vn; 3 Đ Phan Chu Trinh; open 7.30am-11am & 1.30pm-5pm daily), is next to the Thang Loi Hotel.

**Dam San Tourist** (212-214 Đ Nguyen Cong Tru; ☎ 851234, fax 852309; e damsantour@dng.vnn.vn) is a private company based at the excellent Dam San Hotel. It specialises in tours to the waterfalls at Gia Long and Dray Nur.

Local English-speaking motorbike guides can be hired for trips outside the city, notably to Yok Don National Park. **Nguyen Van Mui** (☎ 856085, ☎ 0914-010411) is one such guide worth tracking down.

**Travel Permits** These may still be required to visit certain minority villages in the area surrounding Buon Ma Thuot. Contact Dak Lak Tourist to get these valuable bits of paper.

## Victory Monument

You can hardly miss this one, as it dominates the square in the centre of town. The victory monument commemorates the events of 10 March 1975, when VC and North Vietnamese troops 'liberated' the city. It was this battle that triggered the complete collapse of South Vietnam.

As an interesting footnote, there was formerly a real army tank here facing south, but when it was later replaced with a concrete replica, it was turned north (toward Pleiku), to indicate the correct direction during Ho Chi Minh's campaign to 'liberate' Saigon.

## Museum of Dak Lak Province

The Dak Lak Province Museum (Bao Tang Tinh Dak Lak) is in fact two separate museums, the Ethnographic Museum and the Revolution Museum. The latter is possibly of less interest to foreign tourists.

There are said to be 31 distinct ethnic groups in Dac Lac province, and the **Ethnographic Museum** (☎ 850426; cnr Đ Nguyen Du & Đ Le Duan; admission 10,000d; open 7.30am-11am & 1.30pm-5pm) is one place to get some understanding of these disparate groups. Displays at the museum feature traditional Montagnard dress, as well as agricultural implements, fishing gear, bows and arrows, weaving looms and musical instruments. There is a photo collection with accompanying explanations about the

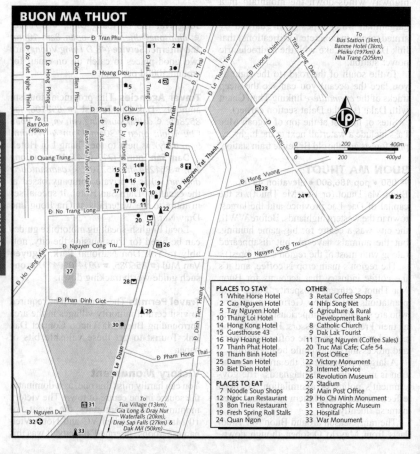

**BUON MA THUOT**

To
Bus Station (3km),
Banme Hotel (3km),
Pleiku (197km) &
Nha Trang (205km)

0        200       400m
0        200       400yd

PLACES TO STAY
1  White Horse Hotel
2  Cao Nguyen Hotel
5  Tay Nguyen Hotel
10 Thang Loi Hotel
14 Hong Kong Hotel
15 Guesthouse 43
16 Huy Hoang Hotel
17 Thanh Phat Hotel
18 Thanh Binh Hotel
25 Dam San Hotel
30 Biet Dien Hotel

PLACES TO EAT
7  Noodle Soup Shops
12 Ngoc Lan Restaurant
13 Bon Trieu Restaurant
19 Fresh Spring Roll Stalls
24 Quan Ngon

OTHER
3  Retail Coffee Shops
4  Nhip Song Net
6  Agriculture & Rural
   Development Bank
8  Catholic Church
9  Dak Lak Tourist
11 Trung Nguyen (Coffee Sales)
20 Truc Mai Cafe; Cafe 54
21 Post Office
22 Victory Monument
23 Internet Service
26 Revolution Museum
27 Stadium
28 Main Post Office
29 Ho Chi Minh Monument
31 Ethnographic Museum
32 Hospital
33 War Monument

To
Tua Village (13km),
Gia Long & Dray Nur
Waterfalls (20km),
Dray Sap Falls (27km) &
Dak Mil (50km)

To
Ban Don
(45km)

historical contacts between the Montagnards and the rest of Vietnam – some of the history is plausible, some is pure fiction.

The Ethnographic Museum is in the former reception of the Bao Dai Villa, a grand French colonial building. A local guide can show you around the exhibits for around 5000d.

The **Buon Ma Thuot Revolution Museum** (☎ 852527; 1 Đ Le Duan; admission 10,000d; open 7.30am-11am & 2pm-5pm) focuses on the city's role during the American War.

## Places to Stay – Budget

**Guesthouse 43** (☎ 853921; 43 Đ Ly Thuong Kiet; rooms with/without private toilet 100,000/60,000d) has old and fairly run-down fan rooms.

**Hong Kong Hotel** (☎ 852630; 35 Đ Hai Ba Trung; rooms with fan/air-con US$8/10) is another cheapie, but likewise is definitely showing its age.

Better budget choices include the **Thanh Phat Hotel** (☎ 854857, fax 813366; e ksthanhphat@pmail.vnn.vn; 41 Đ Ly Thuong Kiet; rooms with fan & shared toilet 80,000d, with air-con & private bath 120,000-180,000d); the all air-con **Thanh Binh Hotel** (☎ 853812, fax 811511; 24 Đ Ly Thuong Kiet; rooms 120,000-150,000d); and the **Huy Hoang Hotel** (☎ 858020; 30 Đ Ly Thuong Kiet; rooms with fan & shared toilet 50,000d, with air-con & private toilet 150,000-170,000d).

**Biet Dien Hotel** (☎ 852177; 12 Đ Le Duan; rooms 140,000-160,000d) rents some grotty-looking rooms near the roadside, but the nicer rooms in the large A-frame house, set back from the road, are much better value.

**Banme Hotel** (☎ 851001; rooms with fan & hot water US$6-10, rooms with air-con US$15), about 3km north of the centre, but within walking distance of the bus station, is a large motel. From the centre, you can catch a motorbike to the hotel for around 5000d. Air-con rates include breakfast.

## Places to Stay – Mid-Range

**Dam San Hotel** (212-214 Đ Nguyen Cong Tru; ☎ 851234, fax 852309; e damsantour@dng.vnn.vn; rooms with air-con US$25/30) is

the best mid-range value in town. This quiet, attractive hotel features clean rooms with wooden floors and satellite TV, plus a good **restaurant**. Rooms at the back of the building overlook the swimming pool, tennis court and neighbouring coffee plantations.

**White Horse Hotel** (☎ 853963, fax 852121; 50-54 Đ Hai Ba Trung; rooms US$26-36) is a decent private hotel with air-con rooms and satellite TV. Best of all are the bonsai and birds at the top-floor garden **café**.

**Thang Loi Hotel** (☎ 857615, fax 857622; 3 Đ Phan Chu Trinh; rooms US$35-45) is one of the big government-run tourist hotels in town. *Thang loi* means 'victory', so it's not surprising that the hotel faces the local Victory Monument. You can find most modern amenities here, including satellite TV.

**Tay Nguyen Hotel** (☎ 851009, fax 852250; 110 Đ Ly Thuong Kiet; singles/doubles US$20/22) is another decent place with satellite TV and room fridges. There is a large **restaurant** on the ground floor.

**Cao Nguyen Hotel** (☎ 851913, fax 851912; e daklaktour@dng.vnn.vn; 65 Đ Phan Chu Trinh; doubles/triples US$40/45) is operated by Dak Lak Tourist. It's a few years old now, but still fairly luxurious and is known for its dance hall, karaoke and massage service. Rates include breakfast.

## Places to Eat

**Quan Ngon** (☎ 851909; 72-74 Đ Ba Trieu) is Buon Ma Thuot's most remarkable eatery. This large indoor-outdoor place offers seating in a pleasant courtyard garden, or in a wooden stilt house. It has an extensive menu with a wide range of Vietnamese dishes, and to add to the flavour is an astonishing display of home-made rice wine. Large wine bottles lining the walls inside the restaurant contain everything from snakes, geckos, and birds to large reptiles. There is even a small wild cat in a fish tank filled with rice wine!

If Quan Ngon doesn't sound like your cup of tea, **Bon Trieu Restaurant** (33 Đ Hai Ba Trung) is known for its delicious beef dishes.

**Ngoc Lan Restaurant** (24 Đ Hai Ba Trung) is also popular with locals and worthy of depositing your dong.

For excellent *nem ninh hoa* – grilled pork wrapped in dried rice paper – head for the bustling fresh **spring-roll stalls** *(20-22-26 Đ Ly Thuong Kiet)* near the Victory Monument. There are also good **noodle-soup shops** on Đ Hai Ba Trung.

## Cafés

Buon Ma Thuot is justifiably famous for its coffee, which is the best in Vietnam. As usual, the Vietnamese serve it so strong it will make your hair stand on end, and typically in a very tiny cup that allows you no room to add water or milk. Most coffee shops in Buon Ma Thuot also throw in a free pot of tea – be sure you don't mistake it for water and use it to dilute your coffee!

Try the side-by-side cafés, **Truc Mai** *(54B Đ Trang Long)* and **Cafe 54** *(54 Đ Trang Long)*, near the Victory Monument. Both serve good coffee, blare bad Vietnamese pop music and have chairs facing the street.

## Shopping

If you like the coffee enough to take some home, be sure to pick up a bag here because the price is higher and quality is lower in HCMC or Hanoi. You can buy whole beans or coffee already ground to a fine powder. Coffee is for sale everywhere in Buon Ma Thuot, and prices average around 14,000d to 16,000d per 500g. Good places to buy coffee beans include **Thanh Bao** *(☎ 854164; 32 Đ Hoang Dieu)*, **Nam Nguyen** *(☎ 852248; 26 Đ Hoang Dieu)* and nearby **An Thuy**.

**Trung Nguyen** *(☎ 855529; 5 Đ Hai Ba Trung)*, Vietnam's answer to Starbucks, is more expensive, but not necessarily better.

## Getting There & Away

**Air** There are **Vietnam Airlines** flights between Buon Ma Thuot and HCMC, as well as Danang.(See the Getting Around chapter.)

**Bus** There are bus services to Buon Ma Thuot from HCMC, Danang, Nha Trang, Dalat, Pleiku and Kon Tum. The Buon Ma Thuot–HCMC buses take 20 hours.

**Car & Motorbike** The road linking the coast with Buon Ma Thuot town, intersects National Hwy 1 at Ninh Hoa (160km from Buon Ma Thuot), which is only 34km north of Nha Trang (see the South-Central Coast map). The road is surfaced and in good condition, though a bit steep. Buon Ma Thuot to Pleiku is 197km on an excellent highway.

There is a scenic road connecting Buon Ma Thuot with Dalat (via Lak Lake), but parts of it are in rough condition and you can expect a quagmire if it's been raining. It's recommended for sturdy motorbikes or 4WDs only.

## AROUND BUON MA THUOT
### Dray Sap Falls

Dray Sap Falls *(admission 10,000d)*, about 27km from Buon Ma Thuot, is in the middle of a hardwood rainforest.

### Gia Long & Dray Nur Falls

Both of these waterfalls, 3km apart on the Krong Ana River, are stunning and offer good riverside trekking opportunities. Ruins of ramparts ordered by the French during the colonial period can be seen near the falls.

Both can be done as day trips, but you can also consider camping out. Entry to Gia Long Falls *(admission US$2)* includes the right to **camp** *(tents US$5)*. Simple **food** (noodle soup, rice etc) is also available.

To reach the falls, follow National Hwy 14 south from Buon Ma Thuot to a fork about 8km south of town; bear left there and continue for 6.5km to the small village of Dong Tam; turn right at the village centre, and continue another 10.5km to a lonely dirt crossroads; turn left here and travel the final 300m to a gate. Although it was once a thick jungle, the landscape viewed from the road, these days, is largely a product of slashing and burning to make way for the coffee plantations.

In Buon Ma Thuot **Dam San Tourist** *(212-214 Đ Nguyen Cong Tru; ☎ 851234, fax 852309; e damsantour@dng.vnn.vn)* is the place to inquire about information and tours to Gia Long and Dray Nur.

### Tua Village

The Rhade (or Ede) hamlet of Tua is 13km south from Buon Ma Thuot. The people raise animals and grow cassava (manioc), sweet potatoes and maize. This village has become one of the most heavily 'Vietnamised' in the region, but along with the loss of cultural identity, it has earned a higher standard of living.

Rhade society is matrilineal and matrilocal (centred on the household of the wife's family). Extended families live in longhouses – each section of which houses a nuclear family. Each longhouse is presided over by a man, often the husband of the senior woman of the family. The property of the extended family is owned and controlled by the oldest woman in the group.

The religion of the Rhade is animistic. In the past century many Rhade have converted to Christianity.

## Yok Don National Park
☎ 050

The largest of Vietnam's nature preserves, Yok Don National Park *(Vuon Quoc Gia Yok Don;* ☎ *783049, fax 783056, fax 783022;* e *yokdon@dng.vnn.vn)* has been gradually expanded and today encompasses 115,545 hectares. There is excellent forest trekking in Yok Don and the beautiful **Serepok River** flows through the park and has several waterfalls and good fishing holes.

Yok Don is home to 63 mammal species, 38 of which are listed as endangered in Indochina, and 17 of those endangered worldwide. The park habitat accommodates elephants, tigers and leopards, as well as nearly 200 different species of bird, including peacocks. Other common wildlife in the park includes deer, monkeys and snakes. In recent years previously unknown animals like the *Canisauvus*, a species of wild dog, have been discovered in the park. In case you don't spot any mammals in the wild, you can always peek at the captive souls in the enclosure behind the Yok Don Guesthouse.

There are 17 ethnic groups in the region, including a significant number that have recently migrated from northern Vietnam. The locals are mostly M'nong, a matrilineal tribe so the family name is passed down through the mother and children are considered members of their mother's family. The

M'nong are known for their fiercely belligerent attitude towards other tribes in the area, as well as towards ethnic Vietnamese.

The M'nong are known for their astute skills in capturing wild elephants, dozens of which live in the area (see the boxed text 'The Elephant Man'). Traditional elephant-racing festivals are put on from time to time. Visitors can arrange elephant rides through some beautiful forests. Elephants typically carry three people, but for heavier Westerners, two is usually the limit. Elephant rides can be arranged through Dak Lak Tourist in Buon Ma Thuot, but you can also simply turn up and make arrangements. Booking direct costs from 100,000 to 200,000d per hour.

Most of the domestic tourist action in the area centres on **Ban Don village** in Ea Sup district, 45km northwest of Buon Ma Thuot. The village, 5km beyond the turn-off into the national park, has unfortunately become overrun with bus loads of tourists.

Traditional activities around Yok Don involve gong performances and drinking wine from a communal jug. Everybody gathers around the wine jug and drinks at the same time through very long straws – it makes for good photos.

There are the neglected ruins of a 13th-century Cham tower called Yang Prong 50km north of Ban Don at Ya Liao, near the Cambodia border. A permit and guide are necessary to visit this spot.

There's no public transport to Yok Don National Park, but it's easily reached by car or motorbike. Local motorbike guides in Buon Ma Thuot can take you to the park for around US$7 one way, or US$10 round trip. **Nguyen Van Mui** (☎ *856085,* ☎ *0914-010411)* is one such guide who speaks English.

Elephants can be hired overnight for 600,000d per day.

**Places to Stay** In the national park, **Yok Don Guesthouse** (☎ *853110; rooms 100,000d)* has four basic rooms (cold water only), each with two beds.

**Camping** *(tents 50,000d)* in the park is possible, but you must have a guide with you in order to do so. You'll need to bring your own sleeping bag.

In Ban Don contact **Banmeco Travel Agency** or **Ban Don Tourist** (☎ 798119) about overnighting in minority **stilt houses** (US$5 per person). Another option is the **bungalows** (US$12) out on nearby Aino Island, reached via a rickety series of bamboo suspension bridges.

## Lak Lake

Emperor Bao Dai built a small palace at Lak Lake (Ho Lak), but it is now a ruin. Nevertheless, the lake views are fantastic and the climb up the adjacent hills is well worthwhile. The nearby M'nong village is a unique experience.

Lak Lake is 50km south of Buon Ma Thuot, along a sealed and relatively flat road. The hillier stretch of road from the lake to Dalat, 154km on Rte 27, is breathtaking in spots, with some nice forest patches and jungle. There's a good deal of evidence of slashing and burning, and clearcutting. The road is only partially paved, and

outside of the dry season you will most likely need a 4WD or motorbike to pass this way. There is little in the way of facilities en route. Krong No has a couple of **com pho restaurants**; it's a small town 41km from Lak Lake in the direction of Dalat.

**Places to Stay** In a peaceful lake setting, **Khu Duclich Ho Lak** (☎ 864144; fan rooms in concrete longhouse with shared/private toilet US$7/10, beds in rattan longhouse US$5) was built a under the shade of jackfruit trees. There's a **floating restaurant** nearby that does decent food.

A more authentic accommodation alternative is the **stilt houses** (☎ 886268, fax 886343; US$5 per person) in the pleasant lakeside village of the Ede minority group. Jun village (admission US$1) is surrounded by plush green rice paddies and the Ede-style stilt longhouses are indeed atmospheric. There is a small **restaurant** here and some souvenir shops selling hill-tribe handicrafts.

---

## The Elephant Man

Throughout history, kings from Thailand, Vietnam, Cambodia and Laos have come to the area around present-day Yok Don National Park in search of elephants. To this day the tradition of elephant trapping continues, and no-one else knows more about it than local legend Yprong Eban.

Yprong Eban, a gentle 86-year-old, is Vietnam's greatest living elephant hunter. Born of a M'nong father and Lao mother, Yprong Eban spent his childhood years riding on the backs of elephants with his uncle, the late Khun Su Nop. Also known as Y'thu, Khun Su Nop was so renowned that he is hailed as Kuru or King of the Elephant Hunters. Khun Su Nop's old tribal house still stands in the village of Ban Don, and his grave is also nearby.

Yprong Eban spend most of his life in the forest, and by the time he retired in 1996 he had captured more than 300 elephants. Typically hunters use two domesticated elephants in order to catch one wild calf. Only elephants under the age of three are targeted, otherwise they are too wild, hard to train, and run a higher risk of returning to the jungle.

One interesting local custom is that men must abstain from sex for a week or more before preparing for the hunt. The hunts involve a series of quick attacks and retreats, and their energy needs to be saved in case they are chased down by a herd of stampeding elephants! Unlike the evil elephant poachers in Africa, the elephant hunters of Ban Don never cause physical harm to the parents when capturing their young. Otherwise they face severe punishment.

Despite his desire to head back into the forest in search of elephants, these days Yprong Eban spends his time hanging around the park headquarters chatting with curious tourists and sharing his stories of love and respect for these intelligent and faithful creatures. He still dresses in traditional M'nong garb and enjoys blowing the old buffalo horn he used to alert the village with when an elephant had been caught. Yprong Eban speaks French, Vietnamese, Lao and several hill-tribe languages, and is happy to entertain visitors to the park with elephant hunting stories.

Two-hour elephant rides can be arranged in Jun for around US$30.

## PLEIKU

☎ 059 • pop 141,700 • elevation 785m

Pleiku (or Playcu) is the major market town of the western highlands, but as a tourist destination most call it 'a hole'. More than 140,000 souls live here now and the population is rapidly growing. The city is 785m above sea level, which makes the climate cool. It's warmer than Dalat, but windier.

In February 1965 the VC shelled a US compound in Pleiku, killing eight Americans. Although the USA already had more than 23,000 military advisers in Vietnam, their role was supposed to be noncombative at the time. The attack on Pleiku was used as a justification by President Johnson to begin a relentless bombing campaign against North Vietnam and the rapid build-up of US troops.

When US troops departed in 1973, the South Vietnamese kept Pleiku as their main combat base in the area. When these troops fled the advancing VC, the whole civilian population of Pleiku and nearby Kon Tum fled with them. The stampede to the coastline

involved over 100,000 people, but tens of thousands died along the way.

The departing soldiers torched Pleiku, but the city was rebuilt in the 1980s with assistance from the Soviet Union. As a result, the city has a large collection of ugly, Soviet-style buildings and lacks much of the colour and antiquity you find elsewhere in Vietnamese towns. Hopefully, the recent inflow of tourist dollars will bring some badly needed improvements to the architecture, as well as the local economy, but for now Pleiku is a monotonous town.

The Jarai minority live in the Pleiku area and have an unusual burial custom: each deceased gets a portrait carved from wood and for years relatives bring them food. The grave is set up as a miniature village with several people buried in one graveyard. After seven years, the grave is abandoned.

### Information

**Travel Agencies** Located beside the beside the Hung Vuong Hotel, **Gia Lai Tourist** (☎/fax 824891; 215 Đ Hung Vuong) offers a wide variety of tours including trekking, elephant riding and programmes catering to war veterans.

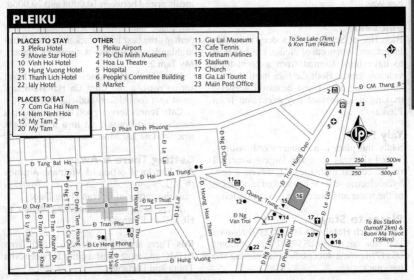

## PLEIKU

| PLACES TO STAY | OTHER |
|---|---|
| 3 Pleiku Hotel | 1 Pleiku Airport |
| 9 Movie Star Hotel | 2 Ho Chi Minh Museum |
| 10 Vinh Hoi Hotel | 4 Hoa Lu Theatre |
| 19 Hung Vuong Hotel | 5 Hospital |
| 21 Thanh Lich Hotel | 6 People's Committee Building |
| 22 Ialy Hotel | 8 Market |

| PLACES TO EAT |
|---|
| 7 Com Ga Hai Nam |
| 14 Nem Ninh Hoa |
| 15 My Tam 2 |
| 20 My Tam |

11 Gia Lai Museum
12 Cafe Tennis
13 Vietnam Airlines
16 Stadium
17 Church
18 Gia Lai Tourist
23 Main Post Office

To Sea Lake (7km) & Kon Tum (46km)

To Bus Station (turnoff 2km) & Buon Ma Thuot (199km)

CENTRAL HIGHLANDS

**Travel Permits** You don't need a permit to stay overnight in Pleiku itself, or to travel the major highways, but you are likely to need one to visit villages in Gia Lai province. The permits cost money and you may be forced to hire a guide, car and driver in Pleiku, even if you have your own vehicle. This puts off many travellers, who usually just skip Pleiku entirely and head north to Kon Tum, where the authorities are more hospitable. Gia Lai Tourist can arrange the permit.

## Museums

Pleiku has two museums, neither of them remarkable and both often closed.

The **Ho Chi Minh Museum** (☎ 824276; 1 Phan Dinh Phuong; admission free; open 8am-11am & 1pm-4.30pm Mon-Fri) displays documents and photos to demonstrate Uncle Ho's affinity for hill-tribe people, and their love for Uncle Ho. There are also displays about a Bahnar hero named Nup who led the hill tribes through wars with both the French and the USA. Nup died in 2001.

The **Gia Lai Museum** (☎ 824520; 28 Ð Quang Trung; admission 10,000d) features hill-tribe artefacts and photographs that memorialise Pleiku's role during the American War.

## Sea Lake

Bien Ho, or Sea Lake, is a deep mountain lake about 7km north of Pleiku. It is believed to have been formed from a prehistoric volcanic crater. Both the lake itself and the surrounding area boast beautiful scenery, making it a pleasant day excursion from Pleiku.

## Yaly Falls

Sadly, this place is no longer worth visiting. Yaly Falls was once the largest waterfall in the central highlands. However, a new hydroelectric scheme has sucked away most of the water and there is only a trickle left.

## Places to Stay

**Thanh Lich Hotel** (☎ 824 674; 86 Ð Nguyen Van Troi; fan rooms US$7-10, air-con rooms US$17) is most successful at attracting the backpacker set.

**Vinh Hoi Hotel** (☎ 824644, fax 871637; 39 Ð Tran Phu; rooms with fan & cold water US$7, with air-con & hot water US$22-24) is one of Pleiku's nicest accommodation offerings.

**Ialy Hotel** (☎ 824843, fax 827619; 89 Ð Hung Vuong; rooms 180,000-350,000d) has bright and airy rooms with air-con and hot water. It's a good choice.

**Movie Star Hotel** (Khach San Dien Anh; ☎ 823855, fax 823700; 6 Ð Vo Thi Sau; fan rooms US$10, air-con rooms US$18-29) is a bit dumpy and is notable for its 1970s decor. Rooms with air-con come in three standards; try to avoid the blaring TV noise on the 1st floor.

**Hung Vuong Hotel** (☎ 824270, fax 827170; 2 Ð Le Loi; twins US$11-24) is a large hotel with an attractive lobby and satellite TV. However, it's close to a busy and noisy intersection.

**Pleiku Hotel** (☎ 824628, fax 822151; Ð Le Loi; fan rooms US$11, air-con rooms with hot water US$27-37) is a big old state-run monolith that has impressive Stalinesque architecture.

## Places to Eat

Most of the place recommended here serve meals priced between 10,000d and 20,000d.

**My Tam Restaurant** is a Chinese family-run place that is a hit with locals. It has perhaps the best fried chicken in the central highlands. Also good is its other branch, **My Tam 2**.

**Nem Ninh Hoa** does tasty and fresh spring rolls, while **Com Ga Hai Nam** is a good spot for chicken-and-rice dishes.

**Cafe Tennis** serves good local coffee in a bamboo stilt house next to a tennis court near the Gia Lai Museum.

## Getting There & Away

**Air** The local office of **Vietnam Airlines** (☎ 823058, ☎ 825893; 55 Ð Quang Trung) is near the corner of Ð Tran Hung Dao.

There are flights connecting Pleiku to HCMC and Danang.

**Bus** There are bus services to Pleiku from HCMC and most coastal cities between Nha Trang and Danang.

**Car & Motorbike** Pleiku is linked by road to Buon Ma Thuot (197km), Qui Nhon (166km) and Kon Tum (49km). There is a particularly barren stretch of land on the road from Buon Ma Thuot, probably the result of Agent Orange use and overlogging.

Road distances from Pleiku are 550km to HCMC and 424km to Nha Trang.

## KON TUM
☎ 060 • pop 89,800 • elevation 525m

This sleepy mountain town is the capital of Kon Tum province, the northernmost region of the central highlands. It's a region inhabited primarily by Montagnards, including the Bahnar, Jarai, Rengao and Sedang communities. Relatively little English is spoken in Kon Tum and the relative lack of foreign tourists also means that overcharging is equally uncommon.

So far, Kon Tum remains largely unspoiled and the authorities remain blessedly invisible. Some may argue that Dalat offers more things to see and do, but Dalat is very touristy and if you're trying to avoid the beaten track, this is one place to do it.

Kon Tum is on the original (and seldomtravelled) 'Ho Chi Minh Trail'.

There are plenty of minority villages in the area, though the hill tribes in the central highlands are nowhere near as colourful as those in the north of Vietnam. One interesting aspect of village life that you will not see in the north are the communal *rong* houses: tall and impressive thatched-roof buildings on stilts. If your timing is right, you may be able to catch a local festival with gong playing and rice-wine drinking from ceramic jars.

Like elsewhere in the highlands, Kon Tum saw its share of combat during the war. A major battle between South Vietnamese forces and the North Vietnamese took place in and around Kon Tum in the spring of 1972 – the area was devastated by hundreds of American B-52 raids.

### Information
**Money** There is no place to cash travellers cheques in Kon Tum. The nearest place to accomplish this is in Pleiku. US dollars can be exchanged for dong at the **National Bank** and **Investment & Development Bank**.

---

## Fulro

Front Unifié de Lutte des Races Opprimées (Fulro), or the United Front for the Struggle of the Oppressed Races, was for decades a thorn in the side of successive Vietnamese regimes. Fulro, a band of well-organised guerrillas, drew recruits mainly from the Montagnards, who had no love for the Vietnamese majority. While the old South Vietnamese government suppressed the Montagnards, the US military exploited their valuable skills in jungle survival during the American War.

When the communists took over in 1975, they sought retribution against Fulro rather than attempting to make peace. The guerrillas continued their insurrection for years, but by the mid-1980s, they were considered a spent force, with most of their guerrilla bands either dead, captured, living abroad or having given up the fight. In 1992 the surrender of a lone band of Fulro adherents, conducting raids from the remote northeastern corner of Cambodia, appeared to confirm this appraisal.

The insurrection issue would seem to be dead and buried, but the Vietnamese government is still very sensitive about Fulro. Government guides will not answer any questions about the organisation other than to assure travellers that it's 'perfectly safe' to visit former Fulro areas.

In contrast to the far north, where minorities are mostly left alone, the government keeps a very tight grip on the Montagnards of the central highlands. Hanoi's policies in this region include:

• populating the highlands with ethnic-Vietnamese settlers, especially in New Economic zones

• encouraging the replacement of traditional slash-and-burn agriculture with sedentary farming

• promoting Vietnamese language and culture (Vietnamisation).

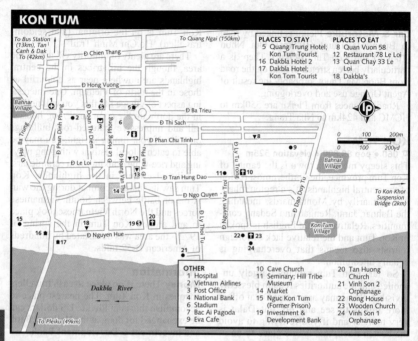

# KON TUM

To Bus Station
(13km), Tan
Canh & Dak
To (42km)

To Quang Ngai (150km)

Đ Chien Thang

Đ Hong Vuong

Bahnar
Village

Đ Doan Thi Diem

Đ Phan Dinh Phung

Đ Le Hong Phong

Đ Ha Ba Trung

Đ Ba Trieu

Đ Thi Sach

Đ Phan Chu Trinh

Đ Le Loi

Đ Hoang Van Thu

Đ Tran Phu

Đ Ly Tu Trong

Đ Tran Hung Dao

Đ Ngo Quyen

Đ Nguyen Van Troi

Đ Ly Thoi Tu

Đ Dao Duy Tu

Đ Nguyen Hue

Dakbla   River

To Pleiku (49km)

To Kon Khor
Suspension
Bridge (2km)

Bahnar
Village

KonTum
Village

0    100    200m
0    100    200yd

## PLACES TO STAY
5  Quang Trung Hotel;
   Kon Tum Tourist
16 Dakbla Hotel 2
17 Dakbla Hotel;
   Kon Tom Tourist

## PLACES TO EAT
8  Quan Vuon 58
12 Restaurant 78 Le Loi
13 Quan Chay 33 Le
   Loi
18 Dakbla's

## OTHER
1  Hospital
2  Vietnam Airlines
3  Post Office
4  National Bank
6  Stadium
7  Bac Ai Pagoda
9  Eva Cafe
10 Cave Church
11 Seminary; Hill Tribe
   Museum
14 Market
15 Nguc Kon Tum
   (Former Prison)
19 Investment &
   Development Bank
20 Tan Huong
   Church
21 Vinh Son 2
   Orphanage
22 Rong House
23 Wooden Church
24 Vinh Son 1
   Orphanage

**Travel Agencies** The provincial tourism authority, **Kon Tum Tourist** (☎ 861626, fax 863336; 2 Đ Phan Dinh Phung), has its main booking office at the Dakbla Hotel. Staff here can help answer queries, and arrange trekking tours, overnight stays in villages, and boating trips on Yaly Lake and the Dakbla River. One of their star guides, Mr Huyen, speaks the local Bahnar language.

**Vietnam Airlines** (☎ 862282, 129 Đ Ba Trieu) can handle air-travel bookings.

## Montagnard Villages
There are quite a few Montagnard villages around Kon Tum. In general, the local tribes welcome tourists, but only if you are not too intrusive with regard to their lifestyle.

Some of the small villages (or perhaps we should say 'neighbourhoods') are on the periphery of Kon Tum and you can even walk to them from the centre. There are two Bahnar villages, simply called Lang Bana in Vietnamese: one is on the east side of town, the other on the west side.

On the east side of Kon Tum is Kon Tum village (Lang Kon Tum). This is, in fact, the original Kon Tum before it grew up to become a small Vietnamese city.

At the time of writing, the Kon Tum police were allowing tourists to visit minority villages without a permit. Let us hope that this enlightened attitude continues.

## *Rong* House
Kon Tum's *rong* house is the scene of important local events such as meetings, weddings, festivals, prayer sessions and so on. If you happen to arrive on the day of an auspicious occasion and stumble upon one of these activities in progress, it could indeed be interesting.

*Rong* houses are type of a thatched-roof community house built on tall stilts. The original idea of building these on stilts was for protection from elephants, tigers and other overly-assertive animals.

There's an attractive old **wooden church** next to the *rong* house.

## Seminary & Hill-Tribe Museum

Kon Tum is home to a lovely old Catholic seminary that looks as if it was beamed here from a provincial French village. The residents are generally welcoming of visitors, and the **hill-tribe museum** on the second floor is worth stopping to see.

Near the gate to the seminary is a curious little **cave church**.

## Orphanages

A short walk from the town centre, these delightful sister orphanages are well-worth spending a few hours at. Staff at both the **Vinh Son 1** and **Vinh Son 2** orphanages are welcoming of visitors who come to share some time with the adorable and multi-ethnic resident children.

If you plan to visit, please make a donation to the orphanage; they are very much in need of support. Canned food, clothing or toys for the kids would be appropriate, and monetary contributions are of course appreciated.

Vinh Son 1 is just behind the wooden church on Đ Nguyen Hué. From here, you can continue east to visit nearby minority villages. Vinh Son 2, south of there and beyond a small Bahnar village, is less visited and more populous (with around 175 children) so is usually in need of more help.

## Nguc Kon Tum

This former prison compound, near the western edge of Kon Tum, is today a quiet park on the banks of the Dakbla River. The prisoners incarcerated here were VC and all were freed in 1975 when the war ended. This was one of the more famous prisons run by the South Vietnamese; VC who survived their internment here were made into heroes after liberation.

## Dak To & Charlie Hill

This obscure outpost, 42km north of Kon Tum, was a major battlefield during the American War. In 1972, it was the scene of intense fighting and one of the last big battles before American troops pulled out.

Dak To has become popular with visiting groups of US veterans, so you probably won't find much of interest if you're not a war buff. More intriguingly, those few VC veterans with sufficient free time and money also like to come here to stir their memories.

About 5km south of Dak To is Charlie Hill. The hill was a fortified South Vietnamese stronghold before the VC tried to overrun it. The South Vietnamese officer in charge, Colonel Ngoc Minh, decided that he would neither surrender nor retreat and the battle became a fierce fight to the death. Unusually for a guerrilla war, this was a prolonged battle. The VC laid siege to the hill for 1½ months before they managed to kill Colonel Minh and 150 South Vietnamese troops, who had made their last stand here.

Although largely forgotten in the West, the battle is well known, even now, in Vietnam. The reason for this is largely because the fight was commemorated by a popular song, 'Nguoi O Lai Charlie' ('The People Stayed in Charlie').

Not surprisingly, the hill was heavily mined during the war and is still considered unsafe to climb.

There's a **rong house** in Dak To that is worth seeking out.

## Places to Stay

Our biggest gripe with Kon Tum is the low standard and high price of the local accommodation. All three of Kon Tum's hotels are owned and managed by Kon Tum Tourist.

**Dakbla Hotel** (☎ 863333, fax 863336; e ktourist@dng.vnn.vn; 2 Đ Phan Dinh Phung; air-con rooms US$23-30) is near the river, and most travellers prefer to stay here. Rates include breakfast. **Dakbla Hotel 2** (☎ 863335, fax 863336; e ktourist@dng.vnn.vn; 163 Đ Nguyen Hué; fan rooms US$10), a budget hotel across the road, has large but very basic fan rooms.

**Quang Trung Hotel** (☎ 862249, fax 862122; e ktourist@dng.vnn.vn; 168 Đ Ba Trieu; rooms with fan/air-con US$19/25) is another oldie. For hardcore backpackers there are a few $5 fan rooms that are like prison cells.

## Places to Eat

**Dakbla's** (☎ 862584; 168 Đ Nguyen Huế) has good food and reasonable prices, so it tends to draw the most travellers. They prepare Vietnamese standards, as well as exotic fare such as wild boar and frog. The owner displays his impressive collection of hill-tribe artefacts on the walls. Yes, some are for sale.

**Restaurant 78 Le Loi** (78 Đ Le Loi) is crowded with locals eating hotpot *(lau)* and drinking beer. Across the road there is good vegetarian food at **Quan Chay 33 Le Loi** (33 Đ Le Loi).

**Quan Vuon 58** is an indoor-outdoor goat-meat specialty restaurant. Goat *(de)* can be ordered over a dozen ways among them: steamed *(de hap)*, grilled *(de nuong)*, sautéed *(de xao lan)*, curried *(de cari)*, and the ever-popular hotpot *(de lau)*.

## Entertainment

**Eva Cafe** (☎ 862944; 1 Đ Phan Chu Trinh) is a good place for a coffee or cold beer in the evening. This unique-looking, three-story building resembles a local hill-tribe house. Vietnamese poetry and stained glass adorns the wooden walls. Outside there is a pleasant courtyard garden.

## Getting There & Away

**Bus** There's a convenient bus service from Kon Tum to HCMC via the scenic National Hwy 14 (12 hours). Buses connect Kon Tum to Danang, Pleiku and Buon Ma Thuot. Kon Tum's **bus station** is inconveniently located about 13km north of the town centre, although many long-distance buses still pass through town, so you can hop off then. One traveller, however, had this to say:

A trip to the highlands town of Kon Tum is definitely worth it, if only to escape the Sinh Cafe tourist trail on the coast. However, travellers should be aware of the sign at the bus station that clearly states that foreigners can't be sold tickets. This of course means that on the bus the fare is as high as the conductor wants it to be.

**Todd Griffin**

**Car & Motorbike** The fastest approach to Kon Tum from the coast is on National Hwy 19 between Qui Nhon and Pleiku. National Hwy 14 between Kon Tum and Buon Ma Thuot is also in good nick. The road that connects Quang Ngai with Kon Tum is particularly scenic.

Looking at a map, it might seem feasible to drive between Kon Tum and Danang on National Hwy 14. Although this is a beautiful drive, the road is still in poor condition and only motorbikes or 4WDs can get through. If you've got the right form of transport, this challenging ride on the Ho Chi Minh Trail is surely a great option. It is logical to break the trip, however, in Phuoc Son (see the Central Vietnam map).

# Ho Chi Minh City

☎ 08 • pop 5,500,000

In this, the largest of Vietnam's cities, you'll see the hustle and bustle of Vietnamese life everywhere, and there is something invigorating about it all. Contrasting images of the exotic and mundane abound. There are street markets, where bargains are struck and deals done; the pavement cafés, where stereo speakers fill the surrounding streets with a melodious thumping beat; and the sleek new cafés and pubs, where tourists chat over beer, peanuts, coffee and croissants. A young office worker manoeuvres her Honda Dream through rush-hour traffic, long hair flowing, high heels working the brake pedal. The sweating Chinese businessman chats on his cellular phone, cursing his necktie in the tropical heat. A desperate beggar suddenly grabs your arm, a rude reminder that this is still a developing city, despite the trimmings.

The city churns, ferments, bubbles and fumes. Yet within this teeming 300-year-old metropolis are timeless traditions and the beauty of an ancient culture. In the pagodas monks pray and incense burns. Artists create masterpieces on canvas or in carved wood. Puppeteers entertain children in the parks, while in the back alleys, where tourists seldom venture, acupuncturists treat patients and students learn to play the violin. A seamstress carefully creates an *ao dai*, the graceful Vietnamese costume that could make the fashion designers of Paris envious.

Actually, Ho Chi Minh City (HCMC) is not so much a city as a small province covering an area of 2029 sq km stretching from the South China Sea almost to the Cambodian border. Rural regions make up about 90% of the land area of HCMC and hold around 25% of the municipality's population; the other 75% is crammed into the remaining 10% of land, which constitutes the urban centre.

Unofficially the city is still called 'Saigon'. But officially, Saigon refers only to District 1, which is one small piece of the municipal

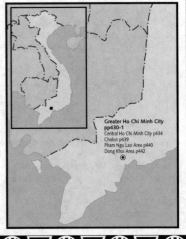

pie. Southerners certainly prefer the name Saigon, but if you have to deal with government officials, it's best to use HCMC.

To the west of the city centre is District 5, the huge Chinese neighbourhood called Cholon, which means Big Market. However, it is decidedly less Chinese than it used to be, largely thanks to the anticapitalist and anti-Chinese campaign from 1978 to 1979, which caused many ethnic Chinese to flee the country – taking with them their money and entrepreneurial skills. Many of these

# GREATER HO CHI MINH CITY

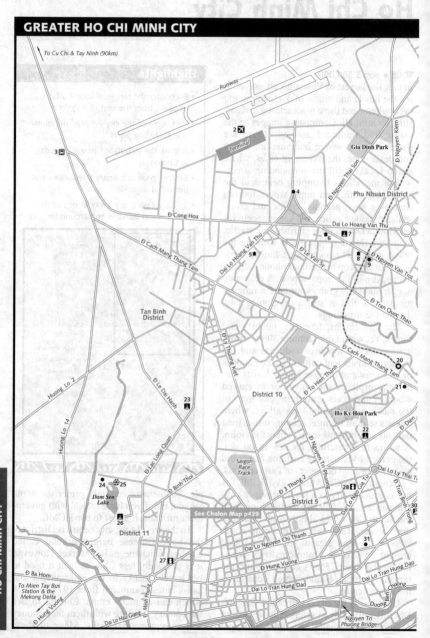

To Cu Chi & Tay Ninh (90km)

Runway

Terminal

Gia Dinh Park

Phu Nhuan District

Đ Nguyen Kiem

Đ Nguyen Thai Son

Đ Cong Hoa

Đ Cach Mang Thang Tam

Dai Lo Hoang Van Thu

Dai Lo Hoang Van Thu

Đ Le Van Sy

Đ Nguyen Van Troi

Đ Tran Quoc Thao

Tan Binh District

Đ Ly Thuong Kiet

Đ Le Dai Hanh

Đ Cach Mang Thang Tam

Đ To Hien Thanh

District 10

Ho Ky Hoa Park

Đ Dien

Huong Lo 2

Huong Lo 14

Đ Lac Long Quan

Saigon Race Track

Đ Nguyen Tri Phuong

Dai Lo Ly Thai T

Đ Binh Thoi

Dam Sen Lake

District 11

See Cholon Map p439

District 5

District 3 Thang 2

Dai Lo Ngo Gia Tu

Đ Tran Binh Trong

Đ Tan Hoa

Dai Lo Nguyen Chi Thanh

Đ Hung Vuong

To Mien Tay Bus Station & the Mekong Delta

Đ Ba Hom

Đ Hung Vuong

Đ Minh Phung

Dai Lo Hau Giang

Dai Lo Tran Hung Dao

Ben Chuong Duong

Dai Lo Tran Hung Dao

Nguyen Tri Phuong Bridge

# GREATER HO CHI MINH CITY

To Saigon Water Park (3km) & Thu Dau Mot (23km)

Binh Quoi Tourist Village (2.5km)

Go Vap District

Đ No Trang Long

Quoc Lo 13

Đ Nguyen Van Luong

Đ Le

Quang Dinh

Binh Thanh District

Dai Lo Phan Dang Luu

Đ Bach Dang

Đ Xo Viet Nghe Tinh

Đ Dien Bien Phu

To Points North & Vietnam Water World (20km), Artex Saigon Orchid Farm & Bien Hoa (30km), Vung Tau (125km)

0     500     1000m
0     500     1000yd

Đ Dinh Tien Hoang

Đ Phan Dinh Phung

Đ Dien Bien Phu

Thi Nghe Channel

Đ Nguyen Binh Khiem

Saigon River

Ly Chinh Thang

Đ Vo Thi Sau

Dai Lo Hai Ba Trung

Đ Dinh Tien Hoang

District 3

Đ Nam Ky Khoi Nghia

Dai Lo Le Duan

Dai Lo Le Loi

District 2

Nguyen Dinh Chieu

Đ Nguyen Thi Minh Khai

Dai Lo Ham Nghi

Ben Nghe Channel

District 1

Đ Le Lai

Đ Nguyen Thai Hoc

Đ Doan Van Bo

Đ Nguyen Tat Thanh

Dai Lo Nguyen Van Cu

See Central Ho Chi Minh City Map p434

Đ Ben Chuong Duong

District 4

Đ Ton That Thuyet

Đ Tran Xuan Soan

District 7

To Can Gio (50km)

**PLACES TO STAY**
5   Chains First Hotel
6   Novotel
8   Omni Hotel

**TEMPLES, PAGODAS & CHURCHES**
7   Dai Giac Pagoda
10  Le Van Duyet Temple
15  Jade Emperor Pagoda
16  Tran Hung Dao Temple
17  Tan Dinh Church
19  Vinh Nghiem Pagoda
22  Vietnam Quoc Tu Pagoda
23  Giac Lam Pagoda
26  Giac Vien Pagoda
27  Phung Son Pagoda
28  An Quang Pagoda
32  Cho Quan Church

**OTHER**
1   Mien Dong Bus Station
2   Tan Son Nhat Airport
3   Tay Ninh Bus Station
4   Airport Tollgate
9   Destination Asia
11  Ba Chieu Market
12  History Museum
13  Saigon Zoo
14  Military Museum
18  Binh Soup Shop
20  Saigon Train Station
21  International Club
24  Dam Sen Water Park
25  Dam Sen Park
29  General University of HCMC
30  Lam Son Pool
31  Andong Market

refugees are now returning (with foreign passports) to explore investment possibilities and Cholon's hotels are once again packed with Chinese-speaking businesspeople.

Officially, greater HCMC claims a population of 5½ million, although seven to eight million may be the real figure: the government census counts only those who have official residence permits and probably a third of the population lives here illegally. Many of these illegal residents actually lived in the city before 1975, but their residence

## War of the Names

One of the primary battlegrounds for the hearts and minds of the Vietnamese people during the last four decades has been the naming of Vietnam's provinces, districts, cities, towns, streets and institutions. Some places have been known by three or more names since WWII and, in many cases, more than one name is still used.

Urban locations have borne: French names (often of the generals, administrators and martyrs who made French colonialism possible); names commemorating the historical figures chosen for veneration by the South Vietnamese government; and the alternative set of heroes selected by the Hanoi government. Buddhist pagodas have formal names as well as one or more popular monikers. Chinese pagodas bear various Chinese appellations (most of which also have Vietnamese equivalents) based on the titles and celestial ranks of those to whom they are consecrated. In the highlands, both Montagnard and Vietnamese names for mountains, villages and so on are in use. The differences in vocabulary and pronunciation between the north, centre and south sometimes result in the use of different words and spellings (such as 'Pleiku' and 'Playcu').

When French control of Vietnam ended in 1954, almost all French names were replaced in both the North and the South. For example, Cap St Jacques became Vung Tao, Tourane was rechristened Danang and Rue Catinat in Saigon was renamed Đ Tu Do (Freedom) – since reunification it has been known as Đ Dong Khoi (Uprising). In 1956, the names of some of the provinces and towns in the South were changed as part of an effort to erase from popular memory the Viet Minh's anti-French exploits, which were often known by the places in which they took place. The village-based southern communists, who by this time had gone underground, continued to use the old designations and boundaries in running their regional, district and village organisations. The peasants quickly adapted to this situation, using one set of names for where they lived when dealing with the communists and a different set of names when talking to representatives of the South Vietnamese government.

Later, US soldiers in Vietnam gave nicknames (such as China Beach near Danang) to places whose Vietnamese names they found inconvenient or difficult to remember or pronounce. This helped to make a very foreign land seem a bit more familiar.

After reunification, the first order of Saigon's provisional municipal Military Management Committee was to change the name of the city to Ho Chi Minh City (HCMC), a decision confirmed in Hanoi a year later. The new government immediately began changing street names considered inappropriate – an ongoing process – and renamed almost all the city's hotels, dropping English and French names in favour of Vietnamese ones. The only French names still in use are those of Albert Calmette (1893–1934), developer of a tuberculosis vaccine; Marie Curie (1867–1934), who won the Nobel Prize for her research into radioactivity; Louis Pasteur (1822–95), chemist and bacteriologist; and Alexandre Yersin (1863–1943) discoverer of the plague bacillus.

All this renaming has had mixed results. Streets, districts and provinces are usually known by their new names. As if navigating your way around HCMC wasn't confusing enough, in 2000, when the municipal Peoples' Committee set out to name 25 new city streets, they also decided to *rename* another 152! This makes using anything but the latest street maps a risky proposition, though fortunately most important streets in the city centre have not changed name, and tourist maps of the city are also updated annually.

permits were transferred to rural re-education camps after reunification. Not surprisingly, they (and their children and grandchildren) have simply sneaked back into the city, although without a residence permit they cannot own property or a business. They are being joined by an increasing number of rural peasants who come to seek their fortune – many end up sleeping on the pavement.

Still, the city accommodates them all. This is the industrial and commercial heart of Vietnam, accounting for 30% of the country's manufacturing output and 25% of its retail trade. Incomes here are three times the national average. It is to HCMC that the vast majority of foreign businesspeople come to invest and trade. It is here that ambitious young people and bureaucrats – from the north and south – gravitate, in order to 'make a go of it'.

Explosive growth is making its mark with new high-rise buildings, joint-venture hotels and colourful shops. The downside is the sharp increase in traffic, pollution and other urban ills. Still, the city's neoclassical and international-style buildings, and pavement kiosks selling French rolls and croissants, give neighbourhoods such as District 3 an attractive, vaguely French atmosphere. The Americans left their mark on the city too, at least in the form of some heavily fortified apartment blocks and government buildings.

HCMC hums and buzzes with the tenacious will of human beings to survive and improve their lot. It is here that the economic changes sweeping Vietnam (and their negative social implications) are most evident.

## HISTORY

Saigon was captured by the French in 1859, becoming the capital of the French colony of Cochinchina a few years later. In 1950, the author Norman Lewis described Saigon as follows: 'Its inspiration has been purely commercial and it is therefore without folly, fervour or much ostentation…a pleasant, colourless and characterless French provincial city'. The city served as the capital of the Republic of Vietnam from 1956 until 1975, when it fell to advancing North Vietnamese forces.

Cholon rose to prominence after Chinese merchants began settling there in 1778 and, despite the mass migrations after 1975, it still constitutes the largest ethnic-Chinese community in Vietnam.

## ORIENTATION

HCMC is divided into 16 urban districts *(quan,* derived from the French *quartier)* and five rural districts *(huyen).* District 1 is known as Saigon and District 5, HCMC's Chinatown, is called Cholon.

The majority of places aand sights described in this chapter are located in District 1, unless otherwise indicated.

## INFORMATION

If you arrive in HCMC in need of some grooming, head for **Tony & Guy Beauty Salon** *(Central HCMC map;* ☎ *925 0664;* e *tonyguy68@yahoo.com; 89c Cach Mang Thang Tam; 8.30am-8pm Mon-Sat, 8.30am-5pm Sun)* is run by a friendly Vietnamese-American stylist, Tony, who trained in Hollywood and New York before moving back to his homeland. The salon (not one of the Toni & Guy group) maintains an international standard and prices are reasonable: US$7/10 men/women for a wash, head massage, cut, blow dry and finish. It also offers beauty treatments.

### Tourist Offices

The closest thing Vietnam has to an official tourist office is the **information counter** in the international arrivals terminal at HCMC's Tan Son Nhat Airport. It's run by the **Southern Airports Services Company** *(Sasco;* ☎ *848 6711, fax 848 6712;* e *sasco @hcm.vnn.vn,* w *www.saigonairport.com; open 9 am-11 pm daily).* Just beyond the baggage carousels, Sasco's Visitors Information & Services counter offers free city maps' tourist literature and an airport timetable, and can also help with transportation, accommodation and tour bookings (handy if you just haven't got the time to shop around in town, but by no means the last word in local tour companies). See Travel Agencies later in this section for information about private companies.

## Money

Just outside the airport exit, there is an exchange counter run by **Vietindebank-Sasco** (☎ 844 0740), which gives the official exchange rate. Opening hours are irregular, so carry sufficient US notes in small denominations to get yourself into the city, in case the bank is closed.

**Vietcombank** (*Central HCMC map;* ☎ *829 7245, fax 823 0310; open 7am-11.30am & 1.30pm-3.30pm Mon-Fri, 7am-11.30am Sat, closed last day of the month*) occupies two adjacent buildings at the intersection of Đ Ben Chuong and Đ Pasteur. The eastern

building is for foreign exchange only but it is also worth a visit just to see the stunningly ornate interior. The bank will accept a wide range of foreign currencies. Travellers cheques in US dollars can be changed into cash for about 1.5% or 2% commission; 3% is the going rate for cash advances with Visa or MasterCard.

Banks with 24-hour ATMs include ANZ Bank, Hongkong Bank (HSBC), Vietcombank and Sacombank. You can only make dong withdrawals, to a maximum amount of 2,000,000d per day. Visa or MasterCard cash advances for larger amounts of dong, as well

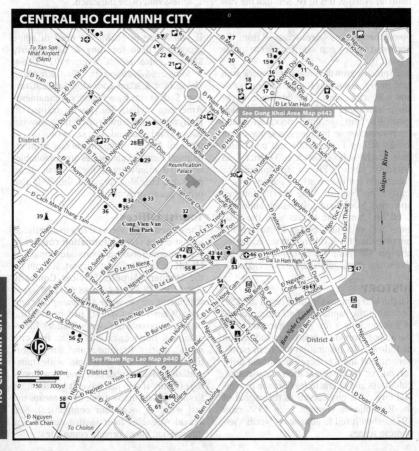

CENTRAL HO CHI MINH CITY

as US dollars, can be handled at the bank counters during banking hours. All of these banks can also exchange travellers cheques.

**ANZ Bank** *(Dong Khoi Area map; ☎ 829 9319, fax 829 9316; 11 Me Linh Square)* is located near the end of ĐL Hai Ba Trung, near the Saigon River.

**Hongkong Bank** *(Dong Khoi Area map; HSBC; ☎ 829 2288, fax 823 0530; 235 Đ Dong Khoi)* is on the ground floor of the Metropolitan Building, across from Notre Dame Cathedral.

**Sacombank** *(Pham Ngu Lao Area map; ☎ 836 4231; [W] www.sacombank.com; 211 Đ Nguyen Thai Hoc)* is located right in the centre of the budget-traveller zone, on the corner of Đ Pham Ngu Lao.

**Fiditourist** *(Pham Ngu Lao Area map; ☎ 835 3018; 195 Đ Pham Ngu Lao; open 8 am -10pm daily)* is a nearby travel agency that exchanges money and keeps late hours.

## Post

HCMC's French-style **main post office** *(Dong Khoi Area map; Buu Dien Thanh Pho Ho Chi Minh; ☎ 829 6555; 2 Cong Xa Paris;*

*open 6am-10pm daily)*, with its glass canopy and iron frame, is right next to Notre Dame Cathedral. Built between 1886 and 1891, it is the largest post office in Vietnam, and worth visiting just for its architecture.

Customers conduct their post and tele-communications business here under the benevolent gaze of Ho Chi Minh. To your right as you enter the building is the poste restante counter. Pens, envelopes, aerograms, postcards and stamp collections are sold at the counter to the right of the entrance and outside the post office along Đ Nguyen Du.

Countless other post-office branches are scattered around town (several of them are marked on maps in this chapter). Like the main post office, many of these also keep late hours.

The following private carriers operate near the main post office and can be found on the Dong Khoi Area map.

**Airborne Express** (☎ 829 2976, fax 829 2961)
  80C Đ Nguyen Du
**DHL** (☎ 823 1525, fax 845 6841) Metropolitan
  Building, 235 Đ Dong Khoi

## CENTRAL HO CHI MINH CITY

**PLACES TO STAY**
14 Hotel Sofitel Plaza Saigon
29 International Hotel
34 Chancery Saigon Hotel
35 Saigon Star Hotel
43 Tan Hai Long Hotel
55 New World Hotel
59 Metropole Hotel
60 Miss Loi's Guesthouse
61 Guesthouse District

**PLACES TO EAT**
1 Pho Hoa
4 Tib Restaurant;
  Spa Tropic
5 L'Etoile
7 Hoa Vien
20 AQ Cafe
23 A'Manoir du Khai
26 ABC Restaurant
31 Nam Giao
37 Tandoor
44 Pho 2000
54 Tin Nghia Vegetarian
  Restaurant

**TEMPLES & PAGODAS**
38 Xa Loi Pagoda
42 Mariamman Hindu Temple
51 Phung Son Tu Pagoda

**OTHER**
2 Pasteur Institute
3 Ao Dai Si Hoang
6 Cambodian Consulate
8 Zoo & Botanic Garden
9 No 5 Ly Tu Trong
10 Phoenix Voyages
11 Saigon Trade Center;
  Exotissimo
12 Oriental Home
13 Nguyen Freres; Oriental
  Home
15 Viet My Bookshop
16 UK Consulate; British Council
17 Saigon Tower; Nederlands
  Consulate; Singapore Airlines
18 US Consulate
19 French Consulate
21 German Consulate
22 Lao Aviation

24 Chinese Consulate; New
  Zealand Consulate
25 Vidotour
27 Thai Consulate
28 War Remnants Museum
30 Lao Consulate
32 Conservatory of Music
33 Worker's Club
36 Vinh Loi Gallery
39 Thich Quang Duc Memorial
40 Tony & Guy Beauty Salon
45 Bicycle Shops
45 Ben Thanh Market
46 Emergency Centre
47 Ferries Across Saigon River &
  Cargo Boats to Mekong Delta
48 Ho Chi Minh Museum
49 Vietcombank
50 Fine Arts Museum; Blue
  Space Gallery
52 Dan Sinh Market
53 Tran Nguyen Han Statue
56 Co-op Mart
57 Hanoi Mart
58 Immigration Police Office

HO CHI MINH CITY

**Federal Express** (☎ 829 0995, fax 829 0477)
146 Đ Pasteur
**UPS** (☎ 824 3597, fax 824 3596; W www.ups
.com) 80 Đ Nguyen Du

## Telephone

International as well as domestic phone
calls can be made from post offices and
better hotels. At the post office local calls
cost 2000d; hotel prices for local calls vary,
so be sure to ask the price beforehand.

## Fax

It's possible to have faxes sent to you at the
**main post office** (fax 84-8-829 8540);
there's a 2200d charge to pick up, and these
can also be delivered to your hotel for a
small charge. The fax should clearly indicate your name, hotel phone number and
the address (including your room number).

## Email & Internet Access

Internet access is widely available in
HCMC. The largest concentration of **Internet cafés** is in the Pham Ngu Lao area, with
around 30 places along Đ Pham Ngu Lao, Đ
De Tham and Đ Bui Vien; just stroll around
and take your pick. Most places charge
peanuts – just 100d to 200d per minute.

A couple of convenient options in the
Dong Khoi area are **Internet World** (☎ 822
0091; e itsnetcafe@yahoo.com; 170 Đ
Pasteur; open 8am-midnight daily), which
charges 400d per minute, and **VNV Internet**
(☎ 822 6874; e vnv@hcm.vnn.vn; 24 Đ Le
Thanh Ton; open 7.30am-10.30pm daily),
which charges 150d per minute.

## Travel Agencies

HCMC's official government-run travel
agency is **Saigon Tourist**. It owns, or is a
joint-venture partner in, more than 70 hotels
and numerous restaurants around town, plus
a car-rental agency, golf clubs and tourist
traps like Binh Quoi Tourist Village.

There are plenty of other travel agencies
in town, virtually all of them joint ventures
between government agencies and private
companies. These places can provide cars,
book air tickets and extend your visa. Competition between the private agencies is
keen, and you can often undercut Saigon

Tourist's tariffs by 50% if you shop around.
Many agencies have multilingual guides
that speak English, French, Japanese etc.

Most of the guides around are excellent
and standards are ever-improving. Many of
the 'old school' guides are veterans who
fought along side the Americans during the
war. These guys make for interesting conversation, and many have kept their distinct
breed of 'GI English'. The new generation of
tour guides, most of them born after the
American War, offers a different perspective.

Young or old, most tour guides and
drivers are paid poorly, so if you're happy
with their service, consider tipping them.
Many travellers on minibus or bus tours to
Cu Chi or the Mekong Delta, for example,
collect a kitty (say US$1 or US$2 per person), and give it to the guide and driver at the
end of the trip.

We recommend visiting several tour
operators to see what's being offered to suit
your taste and budget. There are plenty of
cheap tours sold, especially in the Pham
Ngu Lao backpackers area. One good way
to find out the latest is to speak with other
travellers who have just arrived back from a
tour. Another appealing option to consider is
arranging a customised private tour with
your own car, driver and guide. Travelling
this way provides maximum flexibility, and
split between a few people can be surprisingly affordable.

There are two tour operator outfits in the
Pham Ngu Lao area that are worthy of a spe-
cial mention. For budget travellers, **Delta Ad-
venture Tours** (☎ 836 8542, 836 7535; W www
.deltaadventuretour.com; 187A Đ Pham Ngu
Lao) is a reliable outfit. It's run by Kim and
Steven, an overseas-Vietnamese couple,
who returned from the US several years ago.
It specialises in boat tours of the Mekong
Delta, including trips to/from Cambodia via
the Vinh Xuong border crossing near Chau
Doc.

For customised tours, **Sinhbalo Adventures**
(☎ 837 6766, ☎/fax 836 7682; e sinhbalo@
hcm.vnn.vn, W www.sinhbalo.com; 283/20
Đ Pham Ngu Lao) is one of the best in Vietnam. The brainchild of Vietnam travel guru
Le Van Sinh, Sinhbalo specialises in cycling

trips, but also arranges innovative special interest journeys to the Mekong Delta, central highlands and further afield. Their programmes range from remote hill-tribe trekking and bird-watching in national parks to motorbiking the Ho Chi Minh Trail. We've been using them for more than 10 years and have yet to hit a snag.

**Action Max** (☎ 0913-929137; e action max@hcm.vnn.vn) is an ecotourism and adventure sports outfit run by a French expat, Didier. It organises trekking, canyoning and rock climbing trips to Buu Long Mountain, Dalat, Mui Ne Beach and Nha Trang.

The following agencies (found in the Pham Ngu Lao area unless otherwise stated) can be used as a starting point. See also the Organised Tours section in the Getting There and Away chapter.

### Budget Agencies

**Fiditourist** (☎ 835 3018) 195 Đ Pham Ngu Lao
**Kim Travel** ( ☎/fax 835 9859, e cafekim@hcm .vnn.vn, w www.kimtravel.com) 270 Đ De Tham
**Linh Cafe** (☎ 836 0643, fax 836 7016, e linh travel@hcm.vnn.vn) 291 Đ Pham Ngu Lao
**Mekong Tours** (☎ 837 6429, e mekongtours@ hotmail.com) 272 Đ De Tham
**Sinh Cafe** (☎ 836 7338, fax 836 9322, e sin hcafe@yahoo.com) 248 Đ De Tham
**TM Brothers II** (☎ 837 8394, e nguyenvantuan@ yahoo.com) 269 Đ De Tham
**Tometeco/Pro Tour** (☎/fax 837 3716, e pro _tours@yahoo.com) 40 Đ Bui Vien
**Tropic Tour** (☎ 837 0082, e vietnam@tropic tour.com) 203 Đ Pham Ngu Lao

### Mid-Range & Top-End Agencies

**Ann Tours** (☎ 833 2564, fax 832 3866, e ann tours@yahoo.com, w www.anntours.com) 58 Đ Ton That Tung
**Diethelm Travel** (Dong Khoi Area map; ☎ 829 4932, fax 829 4747, e dtvlsgn@hcm.vnn.vn, w www.diethelm-travel.com) 1A Me Linh Square
**Saigon Tourist** (Dong Khoi Area map; ☎ 829 8129, fax 822 4987) 49 Đ Le Thanh Ton
**Travel Indochina** (Dong Khoi Area map; ☎ 845 5080, fax 845 5079) 1A Me Linh Square

**Ben Thanh Tourist** (Pham Ngu Lao Area map; ☎ 886 0365, fax 836 1953; w www .benthanhtour.com; 45 Đ Bui Vien) is a good place to look for domestic and international air tickets. Ditto for **Saigon Logistics** (Pham Ngu Lao Area map; ☎ 836 9630, fax 836 9632; 213 Đ Pham Ngu Lao; open 8am-5.30pm Mon-Sat), which also deals in freight forwarding, if you've out-shopped yourself.

## Bookshops

The best area to look for maps, books and stationery is along the north side of ĐL Le Loi, between the Rex Hotel and Đ Nam Ky Khoi Nghia, in the Dong Khoi area. There are many small, privately run shops, and the large government-run **Saigon Bookstore** (☎ 829 6438; 60-62 ĐL Le Loi) is just a stone's throw from the Rex Hotel.

**Viet My Bookshop** (Central HCMC map; ☎ 822 9650; 2A ĐL Le Duan; open 8am-9.30pm daily) has a number of imported books and magazines published in English, French and Chinese.

**Fahasa Bookshop** (Dong Khoi Area map; ☎ 822 4670; 185 Đ Dong Khoi • ☎ 822 5446; 40 ĐL Nguyen Hué) are two of the better government-run bookshops. You should at least manage to find a good dictionary or some maps here, as well as general books in English and French.

The cosy **Tiem Sach Bookshop** (Dong Khoi Area map; 20 Đ Ho Huan Nghiep; open 8.30am-10pm daily) has a massive library of mostly used English and French titles. The shop doubles as the **Bo Gio** café.

On Đ De Tham, in the Pham Ngu Lao area, there is a handful of shops dealing in used paperbacks and bootleg CDs. Here you can also swap books.

## Medical Services

There are several doctors in HCMC providing excellent medical and surgical services.

The **International Medical Center** (Dong Khoi Area map; ☎ 827 2366, 24-hr emergency ☎ 865 4025, fax 827 2365; e fac@ hcm.vnn.vn; 1 Đ Han Tuyen) is a nonprofit organisation that bills itself as the least expensive Western health-care centre in the country. All doctors are French, but English is spoken. Consultations cost US$40 (US$80 for emergency or after hours).

The **HCMC Family Medical Practice** (Dong Khoi Area map; ☎ 822 7848, 24-hr

HO CHI MINH CITY

*emergency* ☎ *0913-234911;* e *hcmfmed prac_kot@hcm.vnn.vn,* w *www.doctorkot.com; Diamond Plaza, 34 ĐL Le Duan)* is run by the well-respected Dr Rafi Kot.

**SOS International** *(Dong Khoi Area map;* ☎ *829 8424, 24-hr emergency* ☎ *829 8520, fax 829 8551; 65 Đ Nguyen Du)* has a medical services programme (including dental treatment) for resident expats.

The **Emergency Centre** *(Central HCMC map;* ☎ *829 2071; 125 ĐL Le Loi)* is open 24 hours a day and has doctors that speak English and French.

The **Pasteur Institute** *(Central HCMC map;* ☎ *820 0739; 167 Đ Pasteur, District 3)* has good facilities for medical tests. You must be referred here by a doctor.

**Cho Ray Hospital** *(Cholon map; Benh Vien Cho Ray;* ☎ *855 4137, fax 855 7267; 201 ĐL Nguyen Chi Thanh, District 5)*, with 1000 beds, is one of the largest medical facilities in Vietnam. There is a section for foreigners on the 10th floor. About a third of the 200 doctors speak English and there are 24-hour emergency facilities.

Dental care is available in the Dong Khoi area at the **Dental Clinic Starlight** *(*☎ *822 2433, 24-hour emergency* ☎ *0903-834901; 10C Đ Thai Van Lung)* and **Grand Dentistry** *(*☎ *824 5772; 10 Đ Ngo Duc Ke)*.

## Photo Processing

HCMC is well endowed with modern labs which can process colour print film in about an hour. These are easy to spot (look for the Fuji and Kodak signage), with several good ones in the Dong Khoi area along ĐL Nguyen Hué between the Rex Hotel and the Saigon River, as well as in the Pham Ngu Lao area.

## Visas

In order to get their visa extensions, most people would head for the **Immigration Police Office** *(Central HCMC map; Phong Quan Ly Nguoi Nuoc Ngoai;* ☎ *839 2221; 254 Đ Nguyen Trai; open 8am-11am & 1pm-4pm)*. However if you do, you will most likely be told to use the services of a travel agency, most of which can arrange visa extensions.

## Dangers & Annoyances

HCMC is the most theft-ridden city in Vietnam; don't become a statistic. See Dangers & Annoyances in the Facts for the Visitor chapter for advice on how to avoid street crime. Be especially careful in the Dong Khoi area, where motorbike 'cowboys' operate.

## MUSEUMS

HCMC has several excellent museums, the best of which can be visited on foot. You might also consider renting a bicycle and pedalling around, or perhaps hiring a cyclo (for a half or full day) to do the pedalling for you.

## War Remnants Museum

Once known as the Museum of Chinese and American War Crimes, the museum's name was changed to avoid offending Chinese and American tourists. However, the pamphlet, *Some Pictures of US Imperialists Aggressive War Crimes in Vietnam,* handed out at reception pulls no punches.

The War Remnants Museum *(Bao Tang Chung Tich Chien Tranh;* ☎ *930 5587; 28 Đ Vo Van Tan; admission 10,000d; open 7.30am-11.45am & 1.30pm-5.15pm daily)* is now the most popular museum in HCMC with Western tourists. Many of the atrocities documented here were well publicised in the West, but rarely do Westerners have the opportunity to hear the victims of US military action tell their own story.

US armoured vehicles, artillery pieces, bombs and infantry weapons are on display outside. There's also a guillotine – used by theFrench on Viet Minh 'troublemakers'. Many photographs illustrating US atrocities are from US sources, including photos of the infamous My Lai Massacre. There is a model of the notorious tiger cages used by the South Vietnamese military to house Viet Cong (VC) prisoners on Con Son Island. There are also pictures of deformed babies, their defects attributed to the USA's widespread use of chemical herbicides. An adjacent room has exhibits of 'counter-revolutionary warcrimes' that were committed after 1975 by saboteurs within Vietnam. Counter-revolutionaries are portrayed as being allied with both the US and Chinese imperialists.

# CHOLON

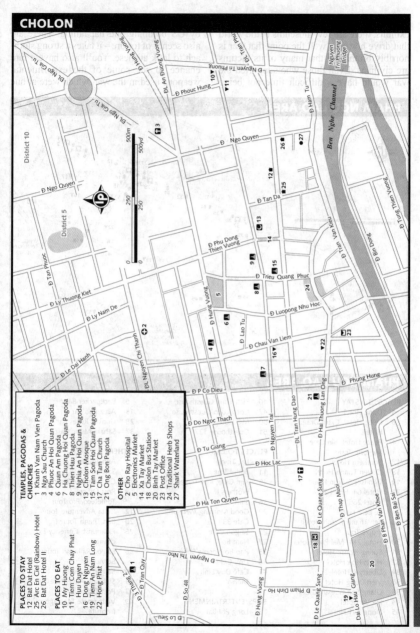

**PLACES TO STAY**
12 Bat Dat Hotel
25 Arc En Ciel (Rainbow) Hotel
26 Bat Dat Hotel II

**PLACES TO EAT**
10 My Huong
11 Tiem Com Chay Phat
    Huu Duyen
16 Dong Nguyen
19 Tiem An Nam Long
22 Hong Phat

**TEMPLES, PAGODAS &
CHURCHES**
1 Khanh Van Nam Vien Pagoda
3 Nga Sau Church
4 Phuoc An Hoi Quan Pagoda
6 Quan Am Pagoda
7 Ha Chuong Hoi Quan Pagoda
8 Thien Hau Pagoda
9 Nghia An Hoi Quan Pagoda
13 Cholon Mosque
15 Tam Son Hoi Quan Pagoda
17 Cha Tam Church
21 Ong Bon Pagoda

**OTHER**
2 Cho Ray Hospital
5 Electronics Market
14 Xa Tay Market
18 Cholon Bus Station
20 Binh Tay Market
23 Post Office
24 Traditional Herb Shops
27 Shark Waterland

District 10

District 5

Đ Ngo Quyen

Đ Tan Phuoc

Đ Ly Thuong Kiet

Đ Ly Nam De

Đ Le Dai Hanh

DL Ngo Gia Tu

Đ Hung Vuong

DL An Duong Vuong

Đ Phuoc Hung

Đ Nguyen Tri Phuong

Đ Ham Tu

Ben Nghe Channel

Nguyen Tri Phuong Bridge

Đ Ngo Quyen

Đ Tan Da

Đ Phu Dong Thien Vuong

Đ Tri eu Quang Phuc

Đ Luopong Nhu Hoc

Đ Lao Tu

Đ Chau Van Liem

Đ Hung Vuong

DL Nguyen Chi Thanh

Đ Phung Hung

Đ P Co Dieu

Đ Do Ngoc Thach

Đ Nguyen Trai

DL Tran Hung Dao

Đ Hai Thuong Lan Ong

Đ Tu Giang

Đ Hoc Lac

Đ Ha Ton Quyen

Đ Le Quang Sung

Đ Thap Muoi

Đ Phan Van Khoe

Đ B Ben Bai Sai

Đ Nguyen Tri Nho

Đ Pham Dinh Ho

Đ Hung Vuong

Đ Le Quang Sung

Dai Lo Hau Giang

Đ So 48

Đ Tran Quy

Tỉnh 2

Đ Lo Sieu

Đ Tran Van Kieu

Đ Tung Thien Vuong

Đ Bin Dong

Despite the relative one-sidedness of the exhibits, there are few museums in the world that drive home so well the point that war is horribly brutal and that many of its victims are civilians. Even those who supported the war would have a difficult time not being horrified by the photos of children mangled by US bombing and napalming. There are also scenes of torture – it takes a strong stomach to look at these. You'll also have a rare chance to see some of the experimental weapons used in the war, which were at one

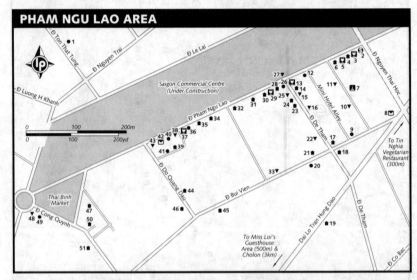

# PHAM NGU LAO AREA

**PLACES TO STAY**
4  Duna Hotel
6  Le Le Hotel; Giant Dragon Hotel
14  Peace Hotel; Bin Café; Mekong Tours
17  Southern Hotel
18  Quyen Thanh Hotel
19  Windsor Saigon Hotel
21  Hotel 64; Hotel 70
23  Hotel 265
24  Le Le 2 Hotel
28  Tan Thanh Thanh Hotel; Tropic Tour
30  Hotel 211; Mai Phai Hotel
31  Spring House Hotel
32  Hanh Hoa Hotel
34  Liberty 4 Hotel
35  Vien Dong Hotel
39  Giang Son Guesthouse
44  Ha Vy Hotel
45  Dong A-1 Hotel

46  Bich Thuy Guesthouse
47  Coco Loco Guesthouse
50  MC Hotel
51  Guesthouse 127

**PLACES TO EAT**
10  Lac Thien
11  Bodhi Tree
15  Kim Cafe; Kim Travel; Tm Brothers II
16  Sinh Cafe
22  Good Morning Vietnam; Cafe 333
25  Saigon Cafe
27  Nam Bo
33  Pho Bo Noodle Shop
38  Linh Cafe
43  Café Duy Linh
48  Dinh Y

**BARS/ENTERTAINMENT**
3  Long Phi Bar

5  Backpacker Bar
13  Allez Boo Bar
28  Guns & Roses Bar
37  Sahara Music Cafe

**OTHER**
1  Ann Tours
2  Sacombank
7  Chua An Lac Temple
8  Post Office
9  Tometeco/Pro Tour
12  Delta Adventure Tours
20  Ben Thanh Tourist
26  Fiditourist; Currency Exchange
36  Saigon Railways Tourist Services
40  Saigon Logistics
41  Sinhbalo Adventures
42  Post Office
49  Vietnamese Massage Institute

HO CHI MINH CITY

time military secrets, such as the fléchette (an artillery shell filled with thousands of tiny darts).

The War Remnants Museum is in the former US Information Service building, at the intersection with Đ Le Qui Don. Explanations are in Vietnamese, English and Chinese. Though a bit incongruous with the museum's theme, **water-puppet theatre** is staged in a tent on the museum grounds.

## Museum of Ho Chi Minh City

Housed in a grey, neoclassical structure built in 1886 and once known as Gia Long Palace (later, the Revolutionary Museum), the Museum of Ho Chi Minh City *(Dong Khoi Area map; Bao Tang Thanh Pho Ho Chi Minh, ☎ 829 9741; 65 Đ Ly Tu Trong; admission US$1; open 8am-4pm daily)* is a singularly beautiful and amazing building.

The museum displays artefacts from the various periods of the communist struggle for power in Vietnam. The photographs of anticolonial activists executed by the French appear out of place in the gilded, 19th-century ballrooms, but then again the contrast gives a sense of the immense power and complacency of the colonial French. There are photos of Vietnamese peace demonstrators in Saigon demanding that US troops get out; and a dramatic photo of Thich Quang Duc, the monk who made headlines worldwide, when he burned himself to death in 1963 to protest against the policies of President Ngo Dinh Diem, (also see the boxed text 'Thien Mu Pagoda' in the Central Vietnam chapter).

The information plaques are in Vietnamese only, but some of the exhibits include documents in French or English, and many others are self-explanatory if you know some basic Vietnamese history (see History in the Facts about Vietnam chapter). The exhibitions cover the various periods in the city's 300-year history.

Among the most interesting artefacts on display is a long, narrow rowing boat *(ghe)*, with a false bottom in which arms were smuggled. Nearby is a small diorama of the Cu Chi Tunnels. The adjoining room has examples of infantry weapons used by the VC and various South Vietnamese and US

medals, hats and plaques. A map shows communist advances during the dramatic collapse of South Vietnam in early 1975. There are also photographs of the liberation of Saigon.

Deep beneath the building is a network of reinforced concrete bunkers and fortified corridors. The system, branches of which stretch all the way to Reunification Palace, included living areas, a kitchen and a large meeting hall. In 1963, President Diem and his brother hid here before fleeing to Cha Tam Church. The network is not currently open to the public because most of the tunnels are flooded, but if you want to bring a torch (flashlight), a museum guard might show you around.

In the garden behind the museum is a Soviet tank and a US Huey UH-1 helicopter and anti-aircraft gun. In the garden fronting Đ Nam Ky Khoi Nghia is more military hardware, including the American-built F-5E jet used by a renegade South Vietnamese pilot to bomb the Presidential Palace (now Reunification Palace) on 8 April 1975.

The museum is located a block east of Reunification Palace.

## History Museum

The stunning Sino-French style building, which houses the History Museum *(Greater HCMC map; Bao Tang Lich Su; ☎ 829 8146; Đ Nguyen Binh Khiem; admission 10,000d; open 8am-11am & 1.30pm-4pm)* was built in 1929 by the Société des Études Indochinoises. It's worth a visit just to view the architecture!

The museum has an excellent collection of artefacts illustrating the evolution of the cultures of Vietnam, from the Bronze-age Dong Son civilization (13th century BC to 1st century AD) and the Oc-Eo (Funan) civilization (1st to 6th centuries AD), to the Chams, Khmers and Vietnamese. There are many valuable relics taken from Cambodia's Angkor Wat.

At the back of the building on the 3rd floor is a **research library** *(☎ 829 0268; open Mon-Sat)* with numerous books, from the French-colonial period, about Indochina.

Across from the entrance to the museum you'll see the elaborate **Temple of King**

**Hung Vuong**. The Hung kings are said to be the first rulers of the Vietnamese nation, having established their rule in the Red River region before it was invaded by the Chinese.

The museum is located just inside the main gate to the city zoo and botanic gardens, where the east end of ĐL Le Duan meets Đ Nguyen Binh Khiem.

Just across Đ Nguyen Binh Khiem is a small **military museum** (☎ 822 9387; 2 ĐL Le Duan) devoted to Ho Chi Minh's campaign to liberate the south. Inside is of minor interest, but some US, Chinese and Soviet war material is on display outdoors,

including a Cessna A-37 of the South Vietnamese Air Force and a US–built F-5E Tiger with the 20mm nose gun still loaded. The tank on display is one of the tanks that broke into the grounds of Reunification Palace on 30 April 1975.

### Fine Arts Museum

The museum (*Central HCMC map; Bao Tang My Thuat;* ☎ 822 2441; 97A Đ Pho Duc Chinh; admission 10,000d; open 9am-4.30pm Mon-Sat), in this classic yellow-and-white building with its modest Chinese influence, houses one of the more interesting collections

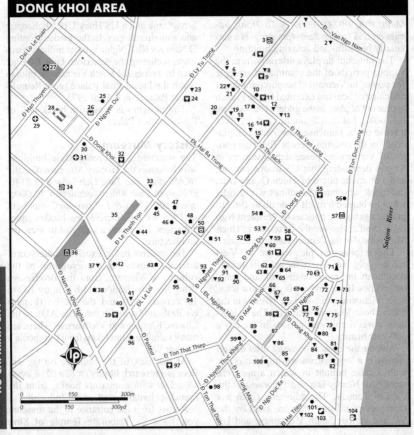

in Vietnam. If you're not interested in that, just go to see the huge hall with its Art Nouveau windows and floors. On the 1st floor is a display of officially accepted contemporary art: most of it is just kitsch or desperate attempts to master abstract art, but occasionally something brilliant is displayed here. Most of the recent art is for sale and prices are fair.

The 2nd floor has older politically correct art. Some of it is pretty crude: pictures of heroic figures waving red flags, children with rifles, a wounded soldier joining the Communist Party, innumerable tanks and weaponry, grotesque Americans and Godlike reverence for Ho Chi Minh. However, it's worth seeing because Vietnamese artists managed not to be as dull and conformist as their counterparts in Eastern Europe. Once you've passed several paintings and sculptures of Uncle Ho, you will see that those

## DONG KHOI AREA

**PLACES TO STAY**
17 Orchid Hotel
20 Spring Hotel
38 Norfolk Hotel
43 Rex Hotel
47 Asian Hotel
48 Continental Hotel; Malaysia Airlines
51 Caravelle Hotel
54 Bong Sen Annexe
62 Thang Long Hotel
63 Kim Long Hotel
64 Bach Dang Hotel; Dong Do Hotel
73 Renaissance Riverside Hotel
78 Grand Hotel
79 Riverside Hotel
82 Majestic Hotel
90 Bong Sen Hotel & Mondial Hotel
94 Kim Do Hotel
100 Saigon Prince Hotel

**PLACES TO EAT**
1 Hoi An
2 Mandarine
5 Why Not?
6 Chao Thai
7 Indian Heritage
8 Ashoka
12 Skewers
13 Bibi's
15 Camargue; Vascos Bar
16 Mogambo's Cafe; Thy 4 Two
18 Sawadeee
19 Hakata
22 Le Jardin
23 Bo Tung Xeo
33 Chi Lang Cafe
37 Miss Saigon
40 Kem Bach Dang
41 Kem Bach Dang
49 Givral
53 Tan Nam

59 Cafe Latin & Billabong Restaurant; Indochine House Antiques
60 Dong Du Cafe
65 Annie's Pizza
67 Gartenstadt; Cool
68 Paloma Cafe
74 La Fourchette
75 Restaurants 19 & 13
83 Maxim's Dinner Theatre
84 Paris Deli
85 Santa Lucia
86 Nam An
91 Brodard Café
92 Encore Angkor
93 Lemon Grass; Globo Cafe; Augustin
102 Urvashi

**ENTERTAINMENT**
4 Tex-Mex Cantina
9 Sheridan's Irish House
11 Wild Horse Bar
14 Maya
24 Blue Gecko Bar
32 Chu
39 Sam Son
50 Municipal Theatre; Q Bar
55 Apocalypse Now
58 Wild West Saloon
61 Hard Rock Cafe
77 Shark
88 Underground
97 Temple Club; Fanny

**OTHER**
3 VNV Internet
10 Dental Clinic Starlight
21 IDECAF
25 UPS; EMS; Airborne Express
26 Main Post Office
27 Diamond Department Store; Diamond Superbowl; HCMC Family Medical Practice

28 Notre Dame Cathedral
29 International Medical Centre
30 Metropolitan Building; HSBC Bank; DHL; Canada Consulate
31 SOS International; Thai Airways International
34 Internet World
35 Former Hôtel de Ville (People's Committee Building)
36 Museum of Ho Chi Minh City
42 Federal Express
44 Vietnam Airlines
45 Saigon Tourist
46 Fahasa Bookshop
52 Saigon Central Mosque; Indian Canteen
56 Landmark Building; Le Caprice; Australian Consulate
57 Ton Duc Thang Museum
66 Cathay Pacific Airways
69 Tiem Sach Bookshop; Bo Gio Café (ice cream)
70 ANZ Bank
71 Me Linh Square & Tran Hung Dao Statue
72 Me Linh Square Point Building; Travel Indochina; Diethelm Travel
76 Grand Dentistry
80 Authentique Interiors
81 Pacific Airlines
87 Pedestrian Mall
89 Fahasa Bookshop
95 Tax Department Store
96 Saigon Centre; Paris Deli; Post Office
98 Huynh Thuc Khang Street Market
99 Sun Wah Tower
101 Harbour View Tower
103 Japanese Consulate
104 Bach Dang Jetty (Hydrofoils to Vung Tao; Boats for hire)

**HO CHI MINH CITY**

artists who studied before 1975, managed to somehow transfer their own aesthetics onto the world of their prescribed subjects. Most impressive are some drawings of prison riots in 1973 and some remarkable abstract paintings.

The 3rd floor has a good collection of older art, mainly Oc-Eo (Funan) sculptures strongly resembling styles of ancient Greece and Egypt. You will also find here the best Cham pieces outside of Danang. Also interesting are the many pieces of Indian art, such as stone statues of elephant heads. Some pieces clearly originated in Angkor culture.

The garden café in front of the museum is a preferred spot for elderly gentlemen to exchange stamp collections and sip iced tea.

## Ton Duc Thang Museum

This small, seldom-visited museum (Dong Khoi Area map; Bao Tang Ton Duc Thang; ☎ 829 7542; 5 Đ Ton Duc Thang; admission US$1; open 7.30am-11.30am & 1.30pm-5pm Tues-Fri) is dedicated to Ton Duc Thang, Ho Chi Minh's successor as president of Vietnam, who was born in Long Xuyen, An Giang province, in 1888. He died in office in 1980. Photos and displays illustrate his role in the Vietnamese Revolution, including a couple of very lifelike exhibits representing the time he spent imprisoned on Con Dao Island (see the Around Ho Chi Minh City chapter).

The museum is on the waterfront, half a block north of the Tran Hung Dao statue.

## Ho Chi Minh Museum

This museum (Central HCMC map; Khu Luu Niem Bac Ho; ☎ 840 0647; 1 Đ Nguyen Tat Thanh; admission 5000d; open 7.30am-11.30am & 1.30pm-5pm daily) is in the old customs house in District 4, just across Ben Nghe Channel from the quayside end of ĐL Ham Nghi. Nicknamed the 'Dragon House' (Nha Rong), it was built in 1863. The tie between Ho Chi Minh and the museum building is tenuous: 21-year-old Ho, having signed on as a stoker and galley boy on a French freighter, left Vietnam from here in 1911, beginning 30 years of

exile in France, the Soviet Union, China and elsewhere.

The museum houses many of Ho's personal effects, including some of his clothing (he was a man of informal dress), sandals, his beloved US–made Zenith radio and other memorabilia. The explanatory signs in the museum are in Vietnamese, but if you know something about Uncle Ho (see the boxed text 'Ho Chi Minh' in the Facts about Vietnam chapter) you should be able to follow most of the photographs and exhibits.

## REUNIFICATION PALACE

It was towards this building – then known as Independence Palace, or the Presidential Palace – that the first communist tanks to arrive in Saigon charged on the morning of 30 April 1975. After crashing through the wrought-iron gates – in a dramatic scene recorded by photojournalists and shown around the world – a soldier ran into the building and up the stairs to unfurl a VC flag from the 4th-floor balcony. In an ornate 2nd-floor reception chamber, General Minh, who had become head of state only 43 hours before, waited with his improvised cabinet. 'I have been waiting since early this morning to transfer power to you,' Minh said to the VC officer who entered the room. 'There is no question of your transferring power,' replied the officer. 'You cannot give up what you do not have'.

Reunification Palace (Central HCMC map; Hoi Truong Thong Nhat; ☎ 829 4117; 106 Đ Nguyen Du; admission 15,000d; open 7.30am-11am & 1pm-4pm daily) is one of the most fascinating sights in HCMC, both because of its striking modern architecture and the eerie feeling you get as you walk through the deserted halls. The building, once the symbol of the South Vietnamese government, is preserved almost as it was on that day in April 1975 when the Republic of Vietnam, which hundreds of thousands of Vietnamese and 58,183 Americans had died trying to save, ceased to exist. Some recent additions include a statue of Ho Chi Minh and a viewing room where you can watch a video of Vietnamese history in a variety of languages. The national anthem is played at the end of the tape and you are expected to stand up – it would be rude not to.

In 1868 a residence was built on this site for the French governor-general of Cochinchina and gradually it expanded to become **Norodom Palace**. When the French departed, the palace became home for South Vietnamese president Ngo Dinh Diem. So hated was Diem that his own air force bombed the palace in 1962 in an unsuccessful attempt to kill him. The president ordered a new residence to be built on the same site, this time with a sizeable bomb shelter in the basement. Work was completed in 1966, but Diem did not get to see his dream house because he was murdered by his own troops in 1963. The new building was named Independence Palace and was home to South Vietnamese president Nguyen Van Thieu until his hasty departure in 1975.

Norodom Palace, designed by Paris-trained Vietnamese architect Ngo Viet Thu, is an outstanding example of 1960s architecture. It has an airy and open atmosphere and its spacious chambers are tastefully decorated with the finest modern Vietnamese art and crafts. In its grandeur, the building feels worthy of a head of state.

The ground-floor room with the boat-shaped table was often used for conferences. Upstairs, in the Presidential Receiving Room (Phu Dau Rong, or the Dragon's Head Room), which is the one with the red chairs in it, the South Vietnamese president received foreign delegations. He sat behind the desk; the chairs with dragons carved into the arms were used by his assistants. The chair facing the desk was reserved for foreign ambassadors. Next door is a meeting room. The room with gold-coloured chairs and curtains was used by the vice president. You can sit in the former president's chair and have your photo taken.

In the back of the structure is the president's living quarters. Check out the model boats, horse tails and severed elephants' feet. On the 3rd floor there is a card-playing room with a bar and a movie-screening chamber. This floor also boasts a terrace with a heliport – there is still a moribund helicopter parked here. The 4th floor has a dance hall and casino.

Perhaps most interesting of all is the basement with its network of tunnels, tele-communications centre and war room (with the best map of Vietnam you'll ever see pasted on the wall).

Reunification Palace is not open to visitors when official receptions or meetings are taking place. English- and French-speaking guides are on duty during opening hours.

## PEOPLE'S COMMITTEE BUILDING

HCMC's gingerbread Hôtel de Ville, one of the city's most prominent landmarks, is now the somewhat incongruous home of the Ho Chi Minh City People's Committee. It was built between 1901 and 1908 after years of the sort of architectural controversy peculiar to the French. Situated at the northwestern end of ĐL Nguyen Hué and facing towards the river (see the Dong Khoi Area map), the former hotel is notable for its gardens, ornate facade and elegant interior, lit with crystal chandeliers. It's easily the most photographed building in Vietnam. At night, the exterior is usually covered with thousands of geckos feasting on insects.

Unfortunately, you'll have to content yourself with admiring the exterior only. The building is not open to the public and requests by tourists to visit the interior are rudely rebuffed.

## ZOO & BOTANICAL GARDENS

The Zoo and Botanical Gardens (*Central HCMC map; Thao Cam Vien; ☎ 829 3901; 2 Đ Nguyen Binh Khiem; admission 8000d; open 7am-8pm daily*) is a pleasant place for a relaxing stroll under the giant tropical trees that thrive amid lakes, lawns and flowerbeds. Unfortunately, the zoo facilities are a bit run-down, but they are gradually improving.

The gardens, founded in 1864, was one of the first projects undertaken by the French after they established Cochinchina as a colony. It was once one of the finest such gardens in Asia, but this is certainly no longer true. The emphasis now is on the fun fair, with kids rides, a fun house, miniature train, house of mirrors etc.

The zoo's main entrance is on Đ Nguyen Binh Khiem on the eastern end of ĐL Le Duan. Standing just inside the main zoo gate you'll be flanked by two striking architectural gems, the impressive **Temple of King Hung Vuong** and the History Museum.

## PAGODAS, TEMPLES & CHURCHES
### Greater Ho Chi Minh City

**Giac Lam Pagoda** Believed to be the oldest pagoda in greater HCMC, Giac Lam Pagoda *(118 Đ Lac Long Quan; open 6am-9pm)* dates from 1744. The last reconstruction here was in 1900, so the architecture, layout and ornamentation remain almost unaltered by the modernist renovations that have transformed so many of Vietnam's religious structures. Ten monks live at this Vietnamese Buddhist pagoda, which also incorporates aspects of Taoism and Confucianism. It is well worth the trip out here from the city centre, as one couple observed:

It's incredibly beautiful and best of all we met Dat Le Tan, a caretaker who worked as an interpreter for the US Army between 1968 and 1975. While we were at Giac Lam, it began pouring down rain. He invited us to stay until the rain had stopped, made us tea and sat down to talk to us. We were also joined by some students, who are attracted to the compound because of the peace and quiet – they can settle down there to do some serious study without distraction. For us, Giac Lam was one of the highlights of HCMC.

**Debbie Hanlon & Paul Fewster**

To the right of the gate to the pagoda compound are the ornate tombs of venerated monks. The Bodhi, or pipal tree *(bo de)*, in the front garden, was the gift of a monk from Sri Lanka. Next to the tree is a regular feature seen in Vietnamese Buddhist temples, a gleaming white statue of Quan The Am Bo Tat (Avalokiteçvara, Guanyin in Chinese, the Goddess of Mercy) standing on a lotus blossom, a symbol of purity.

The roof line of the main building is decorated both inside and outside with unusual blue-and-white porcelain plates. Through the main entrance is a reception hall lined with funeral tablets and photos of the deceased. Roughly in the centre of the hall, near an old French chandelier, is a figure of the 18-armed Chuan De, another form of the Goddess of Mercy. Note the carved hardwood columns which bear gilded Vietnamese inscriptions written in *nom* characters. The wall to the left is covered with portraits of great monks from previous generations. Their names and other biographical information are recorded on the vertical red tablets in gold *nom* characters. A box for donations sits nearby. Shoes should be removed when passing from the rough red floor tiles to the smaller, white-black-grey tiles.

On the other side of the wall from the monks' funeral tablets is the main sanctuary, which is filled with countless gilded figures. On the dais in the centre of the back row sits A Di Da, the Buddha of the Past (Amitabha). To his right is Kasyape and to his left Anand; both are disciples of the Thich Ca Buddha (the historical Buddha Sakyamuni, whose real name was Siddhartha Gautama). Directly in front of A Di Da is a statue of the Thich Ca Buddha, flanked by two guardians. In front is a tiny figure of the Thich Ca Buddha as a child. As always, he is clothed in a yellow robe.

The fat laughing fellow, seated with five children climbing all over him, is Ameda. To his left is Ngoc Hoang, the Taoist Jade Emperor, who presides over a world of innumerable supernatural beings. In the front row is a statue of the Thich Ca Buddha with two Bodhisattvas on each side. On the altars along the side walls of the sanctuary are various Bodhisattvas and the Judges of the 10 Regions of Hell. Each of the judges is holding a scroll resembling the handle of a fork.

The red-and-gold Christmas tree–shaped object is a wooden altar bearing 49 lamps and 49 miniature statues of Bodhisattvas. People pray for sick relatives or ask for happiness by contributing kerosene for use in the lamps. Petitioners' names and those of ill family members are written on slips of paper, which are attached to the branches of the 'tree'.

The frame of the large bronze bell in the corner looks like a university bulletin board because petitioners have attached to it lists of names: those of people seeking happiness and those of the sick and the dead, placed there by relatives. It is believed that when the bell is rung, the sound will resonate to the heavens above and the underground heavens, carrying with it the attached supplications.

Prayers here consist of chanting to the accompaniment of drums, bells and gongs and they follow a traditional rite seldom performed these days. Prayers are held daily from 4am to 5am, 11am to noon, 4pm to 5pm and 7pm to 9pm.

Giac Lam Pagoda is about 3km from Cholon in the Tan Binh district. Beware: the numbering of Đ Lac Long Quan is extremely confusing, starting over from '1' several times and at one point jumping to four digits. In many places, odd and even numbers are on the same side of the street. The best way to get to Giac Lam from Cholon is to take ĐL Nguyen Chi Thanh or ĐL 3 Thang 2 to Đ Le Dai Hanh. Head northwest on Đ Le Dai Hanh and turn right onto Đ Lac Long Quan. Walk 100m and the pagoda gate will be on your left.

**Giac Vien Pagoda** This pagoda *(Đ Lac Long Quan; open 7am-7pm daily)* is architecturally similar to Giac Lam. Both share an atmosphere of scholarly serenity, though Giac Vien, which is right next to Dam Sen Lake in District 11, is in a more rural setting. Giac Vien Pagoda was founded by Hai Tinh Giac Vien about 200 years ago. It is said that Emperor Gia Long, who died in 1819, used to worship at Giac Vien. Today, 10 monks live here.

The pagoda is in a relatively poor part of the city. Because of the confusing numbering on Đ Lac Long Quan, the best way to get there from Cholon is to take ĐL Nguyen Chi Thanh or ĐL 3 Thang 2 to Đ Le Dai Hanh. Turn left (southwest) off Đ Le Dai Hanh onto Đ Binh Thoi and turn right (north) at Đ Lac Long Quan. The gate leading to the pagoda is at 247 Đ Lac Long Quan.

Pass through the gate and go several hundred metres down a potholed, dirt road,

turning left at the 'T' and right at the fork. You will pass several impressive tombs of monks on the right before arriving at the pagoda itself.

The first chamber as you enter the pagoda is lined with funeral tablets. At the back of the second chamber is a statue of Hai Tinh Giac Vien, holding a horse-tail switch. The nearby portraits are of his disciples and successors as head monk. A donation box sits to the left of the statue. Opposite Hai Tinh Giac Vien is a representation of 18-armed Chuan De, who is flanked by two guardians.

The main sanctuary is on the other side of the wall behind the Hai Tinh Giac Vien statue. A Di Da is at the back of the dais. Directly in front of him is the Thich Ca Buddha, flanked by his disciples Anand (on the left) and Kasyape (on the right). To the right of Kasyape is the Ti Lu Buddha; to the left of Anand is the Nhien Dang Buddha. At the foot of the Thich Ca Buddha is a small figure of Thich Ca as a child. Fat, laughing Ameda is seated with children climbing all over him; on either side of him stand guardians. In the front row of the dais is Thich Ca with two Bodhisattvas sitting on each side.

In front of the dais is a fantastic brass incense basin with fierce dragon heads emerging from each side. On the altar to the left of the dais is Dai The Chi Bo Tat, on the altar to the right is Quan The Am Bo Tat. The Guardian of the Pagoda is against the wall opposite the dais. Nearby is a 'Christmas tree' similar to the one in Giac Lam Pagoda. Lining the side walls are the Judges of the 10 Regions of Hell (holding scrolls) and 18 Bodhisattvas.

Giac Vien Pagoda is open during the hours listed, but go before dark as the electricity is often out in the evening. Prayers are held daily from 4am to 5am, 8am to 10am, 2pm to 3pm, 4pm to 5pm and 7pm to 9pm.

**Jade Emperor Pagoda** Built in 1909 by the Cantonese (Quang Dong) Congregation, the Jade Emperor Pagoda *(Phuoc Hai Tu or Chua Ngoc Hoang; 73 Đ Mai Thi Luu)* is truly a gem of a Chinese temple. It is one of the most spectacularly colourful pagodas in HCMC, filled with statues of phantasmal divinities and grotesque heroes. The pungent smoke of burning joss sticks fills the air, obscuring the exquisite woodcarvings decor-ated with gilded Chinese characters. The roof is covered with elaborate tile work. The statues, which represent characters from both the Buddhist and Taoist traditions, are made of reinforced papier-mache.

As you enter the main doors of the building, Mon Quan, the God of the Gate, stands to the right in an elaborately carved wooden case. Opposite him, in a similar case, is Tho Than (Tho Dia), the God of the Land. Straight on is an altar on which are placed, from left to right, figures of: Phat Mau Chuan De, mother of the five Buddhas of the cardinal directions; Dia Tang Vuong Bo Tat (Ksitigartha), the King of Hell; the Di Lac Buddha (Maitreya), the Buddha of the Future; Quan The Am Bo Tat; and a bas-relief portrait of the Thich Ca Buddha. Behind the altar, in a glass case, is the Duoc Su Buddha, also known as the Nhu Lai Buddha. The figure is said to be made of sandalwood.

To either side of the altar, against the walls, are two especially fierce and menacing figures. On the right (as you face the altar) is a 4m-high statue of the general who defeated the Green Dragon. He is stepping on the vanquished dragon. On the left is the general who defeated the White Tiger, which is also being stepped on.

The Taoist Jade Emperor, Ngoc Hoang, draped in luxurious robes, presides over the main sanctuary. He is flanked by his guardians, the Four Big Diamonds (Tu Dai Kim Cuong), so named because they are said to be as hard as diamonds. In front of the Jade Emperor stand six figures, three to each side. On the left is Bac Dau, the Taoist God of the Northern Polar Star and God of Longevity, flanked by his two guardians; and on the right is Nam Tao, the Taoist God of the Southern Polar Star and God of Happiness, also flanked by two guardians.

In the case to the right of the Jade Emperor is 18-armed Phat Mau Chuan De. Two faces, affixed to her head behind each ear, look to either side. On the wall to her right, at a height of about 4m, is Dai Minh Vuong Quang, who was reincarnated as Sakyamuni,

riding on the back of a phoenix. Below are the Tien Nhan, literally the 'god persons'.

In the case to the left of the Jade Emperor sits Ong Bac De, a reincarnation of the Jade Emperor, holding a sword. One of his feet is resting on a turtle while the other rests on a snake. On the wall to the left of Ong Bac De, about 4m off the ground, is Thien Loi, the God of Lightning, who slays evil people. Below Thien Loi are the military commanders of Ong Bac De (on the lower step) and Thien Loi's guardians (on the upper step). At the top of the two carved pillars that separate the three alcoves are the Goddess of the Moon (on the left) and God of the Sun (on the right).

Out the door on the left-hand side of the Jade Emperor's chamber is another room. The semi-enclosed area to the right (as you enter) is presided over by Thanh Hoang, the Chief of Hell; to the left is his red horse. Of the six figures lining the walls, the two closest to Thanh Hoang are Am Quan, the God of Yin (on the left), and Duong Quan, the God of Yang (on the right). The other four figures, the Thuong Thien Phat Ac, are gods who dispense punishments for evil acts and rewards for good deeds. Thanh Hoang faces in the direction of the famous Hall of the Ten Hells. The carved wooden panels lining

## Quan Am Thi Kinh

Quan Am Thi Kinh was a woman unjustly turned out of her home by her husband. She disguised herself as a monk and went to live in a pagoda, where a young woman accused her of fathering her child. She accepted the blame – and the responsibility that went along with it – and again found herself out on the streets, this time with her 'son'. Much later, about to die, she returned to the monastery to confess her secret. When the emperor of China heard of her story, he declared her the Guardian Spirit of Mother and Child.

It is believed that she has the power to bestow male offspring on those who fervently believe in her and as such is extremely popular with childless couples.

Banana boats at Ho Chi Minh City's Thi Nghe Market

The bustling market in Cholon, Ho Chi Minh City

Meditating monks at the Cao Dai Great Temple in Tay Ninh, north of Ho Chi Minh City

Notre Dame Cathedral, Ho Chi Minh City

Modern architecture in Ho Chi Minh City

Inside Ho Chi Minh City's Central Post Office

the walls graphically depict the varied torments awaiting evil people in each of the Ten Regions of Hell. At the top of each panel is one of the Judges of the 10 Regions examining a book in which the deeds of the deceased are inscribed.

On the wall opposite Thanh Hoang is a bas-relief wood panel depicting Quan Am Thi Kinh standing on a lotus blossom. On the panel, Quan Am Thi Kinh is shown holding her 'son'. To her left is Long Nu, a very young Buddha who is her protector. To her right is Thien Tai, her guardian spirit, who knew the real story all along (see the boxed text 'Quan Am Thi Kinh'). Above her left shoulder is a bird bearing prayer beads.

To the right of the panel of Quan Am Thi Kinh is a panel depicting Dia Tang Vuong Bo Tat, the King of Hell.

On the other side of the wall is a fascinating little room in which the ceramic figures of 12 women, overrun with children and wearing colourful clothes, sit in two rows of six. Each of the women exemplifies a human characteristic, either good or bad (as in the case of the woman drinking alcohol from a jug). Each figure represents one year in the 12-year Chinese calendar. Presiding over the room is Kim Hoa Thanh Mau, the Chief of All Women.

Off to the right of the main chamber, stairs lead to a 2nd-floor sanctuary and balcony.

The Jade Emperor Pagoda is in a part of the city known as Da Kao (or Da Cao). To get there, go to 20 Đ Dien Bien Phu and walk half a block in a northwest direction.

**Dai Giac Pagoda** This Vietnamese Buddhist pagoda *(112 Đ Nguyen Van Troi)* is built in a style characteristic of pagodas constructed during the 1960s. In the courtyard, under the unfinished 10-level, red-and-pink tower inlaid with porcelain shards, is an artificial cave of volcanic rocks in which there is a gilded statue of the Goddess of Mercy. In the main sanctuary, the 2.5m-high gilt Buddha has a green neon halo, while below, a smaller white reclining Buddha (in a glass case) has a blue neon halo. Dai Giac Pagoda is 1.5km towards the city centre from the gate to the airport.

**Vinh Nghiem Pagoda** Inaugurated in 1971, this pagoda *(open 7.30am-11.30am & 2pm-6pm daily)* is noteworthy for its vast sanctuary and eight-storey tower, each level of which contains a statue of the Buddha. It was built with help from the Japan-Vietnam Friendship Association, which explains the presence of Japanese elements in its architecture. At the base of the tower (only open on holidays) is a shop selling Buddhist ritual objects. Behind the sanctuary is a three-storey tower, which serves as a repository for carefully labelled ceramic urns containing the ashes of people who have been cremated. The pagoda is just off Đ Nguyen Van Troi in District 3.

**Le Van Duyet Temple** Dedicated to Marshal Le Van Duyet (1763–1831), this temple is also the burial place of him and his wife. The marshal was a South Vietnamese general and viceroy who helped put down the Tay Son Rebellion and reunify Vietnam. When the Nguyen dynasty came to power in 1802, he was elevated by Emperor Gia Long to the rank of marshal. Le Van Duyet fell into disfavour with Gia Long's successor, Minh Mang, who tried him posthumously and desecrated his grave. Emperor Thieu Tri, who succeeded Minh Mang, restored the tomb, thus fulfilling a prophesy of its destruction and restoration. Le Van Duyet was considered a national hero in the South before 1975, but is disliked by the communists because of his involvement in the expansion of French influence.

The temple itself was renovated in 1937 and has a distinctly modern feel to it, though since 1975 the government has done little to keep it from becoming dilapidated. Among the items on display are a portrait of Le Van Duyet, some of his personal effects (including European-style crystal goblets) and other antiques. There are two wonderful life-size horses statues on either side of the entrance to the third and last chamber, which is kept locked.

During celebrations of Tet and the 30th day of the seventh lunar month (the anniversary of Le Van Duyet's death), the tomb is thronged with pilgrims. Vietnamese used to come here to take oaths of good faith if they could not afford the services of a court of justice.

There are tropical fish on sale for visitors. The caged birds that are for sale are bought by pilgrims and freed to earn merit. The birds are often recaptured (and liberated again).

The temple is reached by heading north from the city centre on Đ Dien Tien Hoang, all the way to ĐL Phan Dang Luu; it's easy to spot from the southeast corner.

**Tran Hung Dao Temple** This small temple *(36 Đ Vo Thi Sau; open 6am-11am & 2pm-6pm Mon-Fri)* is dedicated to Tran Hung Dao, a national hero, who vanquished an invasion force in 1287. The force, said to have numbered 300,000 men, had been dispatched by the Mongol emperor Kublai Khan. The temple is a block northeast of the telecommunication dishes that are between Đ Dien Bien Phu and Đ Vo Thi Sau.

The public park between the dishes and ĐL Hai Ba Trung was built in 1983 on the site of the **Massiges Cemetery**, a burial ground for French soldiers and settlers. The remains of French military personnel were exhumed and repatriated to France. The tomb of the 18th-century French missionary and diplomat Pigneau de Béhaine, Bishop of Adran, which was completely destroyed after reunification, was also here.

**Cho Quan Church** Built by the French about 100 years ago, Cho Quan Church *(133 Đ Tran Binh Trong; open 4am-7am & 3pm-6pm Mon-Sat, 4am-9am & 1.30pm-6pm Sun)* is one of the largest churches in HCMC. It's the only church we've seen in the city where the figure of Jesus on the altar has a neon halo. The view from the belfry is worth the steep climb. The church is between ĐL Tran Hung Dao and Đ Nguyen Trai. Sunday masses are held at 5am, 6.30am, 8.30am, 4.30pm and 6pm.

## Central Ho Chi Minh City

**Notre Dame Cathedral** Built between 1877 and 1883, Notre Dame Cathedral *(Dong Khoi Area map; Đ Han Thuyen)* is set in the heart of HCMC's government quarter.

The cathedral faces Đ Dong Khoi. It is neo-Romanesque with two 40m-high square towers, tipped with iron spires, which dominate the city's skyline. In front of the cathedral (in the centre of the square bounded by the main post office) is a statue of the Virgin Mary. If the front gates are locked, try the door on the side of the building that faces Reunification Palace.

Unusually, this cathedral has no stained-glass windows: the glass was a casualty of fighting during WWII. A number of foreign travellers worship here and the priests are allowed to add a short sermon in French or English to their longer presentations in Vietnamese. The 9.30am Sunday mass might be the best one for tourists to attend.

**Xa Loi Pagoda** Built in 1956, Xa Loi Pagoda *(89 Đ Ba Huyen Thanh Quan; open 7am-11am & 2pm-5pm daily)* is famed as the repository of a sacred relic of the Buddha. In August 1963, truckloads of armed men under the command of President Ngo Dinh Diem's brother, Ngo Dinh Nhu, attacked Xa Loi Pagoda, which had become a centre of opposition to the Diem government. The pagoda was ransacked and 400 monks and nuns, including the country's 80-year-old Buddhist patriarch, were arrested. This raid and others elsewhere helped solidify opposition among Buddhists to the Diem regime, a crucial factor in the US decision to support the coup against Diem. This pagoda was also the site of several self-immolations by monks protesting against the Diem regime and the American War.

Women enter the main hall of Xa Loi Pagoda by the staircase on the right as you come in the gate; men use the stairs on the left. The walls of the sanctuary are adorned with paintings depicting the Buddha's life.

Xa Loi Pagoda is in District 3 at, near Đ Dien Bien Phu. A monk preaches every Sunday from 8am to 10am. On days of the full moon and new moon, special prayers are held from 7am to 9am and 7pm to 8pm.

**Phung Son Tu Pagoda** Built by the Fujian congregation in the mid-1940s, Phung Son Tu Pagoda, *(338 Đ Cong Tru)* is more typical of HCMC's Chinese pagodas. The interior is often hung with huge incense spirals that burn for hours. Worshippers include both the ethnic Chinese and ethnic Vietnamese. Phung Son Tu is dedicated to Ong Bon, Guardian Spirit of Happiness and Virtue, whose statue is behind the main altar in the sanctuary. On the right-hand side of the main hall is the multi-armed Buddhist Goddess of Mercy. This pagoda is only 1km from the city centre.

**Mariamman Hindu Temple** This is the only Hindu temple (*Chua Ba Mariamman; 45 Đ Truong Dinh; open 7am-7pm daily*) still in use in HCMC, and is a little piece of south-ern India in the centre of town. Though there are only 50 to 60 Hindus in HCMC – all of them Tamils – this temple is also considered sacred by many ethnic Vietnamese and eth-nic Chinese. Indeed, it is reputed to have miraculous powers. The temple was built at the end of the 19th century and dedicated to the Hindu goddess Mariamman.

The lion to the left of the entrance used to be carried around the city in a street proces-sion every autumn. In the shrine in the mid-dle of the temple is Mariamman, flanked by her guardians Maduraiveeran (to her left) and Pechiamman (to her right). In front of the Mariamman figure are two lingas. Favourite offerings placed nearby often include joss sticks, jasmine, lilies and gladioli. The wood-en stairs, on the left as you enter the building, lead to the roof, where you'll find two colour-ful towers covered with innumerable figures of lions, goddesses and guardians.

After reunification, the government took over the temple and turned part of it into a factory for joss sticks. Another section was occupied by a company producing seafood for export – the seafood was dried on the roof in the sun. The whole temple is to be returned to the local Hindu community.

Mariamman Temple is only three blocks west of Ben Thanh Market. Take off your shoes before stepping onto the slightly raised platform.

**Saigon Central Mosque** Built by South Indian Muslims in 1935 on the site of an

earlier mosque, the Saigon Central Mosque (*Dong Khoi Area map; 66 Đ Dong Du*) is an immaculately clean and well-kept island of calm in the middle of the bustling Dong Khoi area. In front of the sparkling white-and-blue structure, with its four nonfunc-tional minarets, is a pool for ritual ablutions, required by Islamic law before prayers. Take off your shoes before entering the sanctuary.

The simplicity of the mosque is in marked contrast to the exuberance of Chinese temple decorations and the rows of figures, facing elaborate ritual objects, in Buddhist pago-das. Islamic law strictly forbids using human or animal figures for decoration.

Only half a dozen Indian Muslims remain in HCMC; most of the community fled in 1975. As a result, prayers – held five times a day – are sparsely attended, except on Friday, when several dozen worshippers (mainly non-Indian Muslims) are present.

There are 12 other mosques serving the 5000 or so Muslims in HCMC.

## Cholon
There is a slew of interesting Chinese-style temples in Cholon (District 5), and it's well worth heading over to Chinatown for a half-day or more to explore. Beside the temples and pagodas, there is some excellent Chi-nese and Vietnamese food to sample, plus a couple of water parks, if you get templed-out and feel like a swim.

While you're exploring, stroll over to the strip of **traditional herb shops** (*Đ Hai Thuong Lan Ong*) between Đ Luopong Nhu Hoc and Đ Trieu Quang Phuc for an olfac-tory experience you won't soon forget. Here the streets are filled with amazing sights, sounds, and, most of all rich herbal smells.

**An Quang Pagoda** This pagoda (*Đ Su Van Hanh*) gained some notoriety during the American War as the home of Thich Tri Quang, a powerful monk who led protests against the South Vietnamese government in 1963 and 1966. When the war ended, you would have expected the communists to be grateful. Instead, he was placed under house arrest and later thrown into solitary confine-ment for 16 months. Thich Tri Quang was eventually released and is said to be still living at An Quang Pagoda.

An Quang Pagoda is on Đ Su Van Hanh, near the intersection with Đ Ba Hat, in District 10.

**Tam Son Hoi Quan Pagoda** This pagoda (*Chua Ba Chua; 118 Đ Trieu Quang Phuc*) was built by the Fujian congregation in the 19th century and retains most of its original rich ornamentation. The pagoda is dedicated to Me Sanh, the Goddess of Fertility. Both men and women – but more of the latter – come here to pray for children.

To the right of the covered courtyard is the deified general Quan Cong, with his long black beard; on either side he is flanked by two guardians, the mandarin general Chau Xuong on the left (holding a weapon) and the administrative mandarin Quan Binh on the right. Next to Chau Xuong is Quan Cong's sacred red horse.

Behind the main altar (directly across the courtyard from the entrance) is Thien Hau, the Goddess of the Sea, who protects fishermen and sailors. To the right is an ornate case in which Me Sanh, in white, sits surrounded by her daughters. In the case to the left of Thien Hau is Ong Bon. In front of Thien Hau is Quan The Am Bo Tat, enclosed in glass.

Across the courtyard from Quan Cong is a small room containing ossuary jars and memorials in which the dead are represented by their photographs. Next to this chamber is a small room containing the papier-mache head of a dragon of the type used by the Fujian congregation for dragon dancing.

Tam Son Hoi Quan Pagoda is close to 370 ĐL Tran Hung Dao.

**Thien Hau Pagoda** This pagoda (*Ba Mieu, Pho Mieu or Chua Ba; 710 Đ Nguyen Trai; open 6am-5.30pm daily*) was built by the Cantonese congregation in the early 19th century. One of the most active in Cholon, it's dedicated to Thien Hau (also known as Tuc Goi La Ba). It is said that Thien Hau can travel over the oceans on a mat and ride the clouds to wherever she

pleases. Her mobility allows her to save people in trouble on the high seas.

Thien Hau is very popular in Hong Kong (where she's called Tin Hau) and in Taiwan (where her name is Matsu); this might explain why Thien Hau Pagoda is included on so many tour-group agendas.

Though there are guardians to either side of the entrance, it is said that the real protectors of the pagoda are the two land turtles that live here. There are intricate ceramic friezes above the roof line of the interior courtyard. Near the huge braziers are two miniature wooden structures in which a small figure of Thien Hau is paraded around on the 23rd day of the third lunar month. On the main dais are three figures of Thien Hau, one behind the other, all flanked by two servants or guardians. To the left of the dais is a bed for Thien Hau. To the right is a scale-model boat and on the far right is the Goddess Long Mau, Protector of Mothers and Newborns.

**Nghia An Hoi Quan Pagoda** Built by the Chaozhou Chinese congregation, Nghia An Hoi Quan Pagoda (*678 Đ Nguyen Trai; open 4am-6pm*), is noteworthy for its gilded woodwork. There is a carved wooden boat over the entrance and, inside to the left of the doorway, is an enormous representation of Quan Cong's red horse with its groom. To the right of the entrance is an elaborate altar in which a bearded Ong Bon stands holding a stick. Behind the main altar are three glass cases. In the centre is Quan Cong and to either side are his assistants, Chau Xuong (on the left) and Quan Binh (on the right). To the right of Quan Binh is an especially elaborate case holding Thien Hau.

Nghia An Hoi Quan Pagoda is not far from Thien Hau Pagoda.

**Cholon Mosque** The clean lines and lack of ornamentation of the Cholon Mosque (*641 Đ Nguyen Trai; open daily*) are in stark contrast to nearby Chinese and Vietnamese Buddhist pagodas. In the courtyard is a pool for ritual ablutions. Note the tiled niche in the wall (*mihrab*) indicating the direction of prayer, which is towards Mecca. The mosque was built by Tamil Muslims in 1932. Since 1975, it has served the Malaysian and Indonesian Muslim communities.

**Quan Am Pagoda** Founded by the Fujian congregation, Quan Am Pagoda *(12 Đ Lao Tu)* was built in 1816. The temple is named for Quan The Am Bo Tat, the Goddess of Mercy.

This is the most active pagoda in Cholon and the Chinese influence is obvious. The roof is decorated with fantastic scenes, rendered in ceramic, from traditional Chinese plays and stories. The tableaux include ships, houses, people and several ferocious dragons. The front doors are decorated with very old gold-and-lacquer panels. On the walls of the porch are murals, in slight relief, of scenes from China around the time of Quan Cong. There are elaborate woodcarvings on roof supports above the porch.

Behind the main altar is A Pho, the Holy Mother Celestial Empress, gilded and in rich raiment. In front of her, in a glass case, are three painted statues of Thich Ca Buddha, a standing gold Quan The Am Bo Tat, a seated laughing Ameda and, to the far left, a gold figure of Dia Tang Vuong Bo Tat (King of Hell).

In the courtyard behind the main sanctuary, in the pink-tiled altar, is another figure of A Pho. Quan The Am Bo Tat, dressed in white embroidered robes, stands nearby. To the left of the altar is her richly ornamented bed. To the right of the altar is Quan Cong, flanked by his guardians. To the far right, in front of another pink altar, is the black-faced judge Bao Cong.

**Phuoc An Hoi Quan Pagoda** Built in 1902 by the Fujian congregation, Phuoc An Hoi Quan Pagoda *(184 Đ Hung Vuong)* is one of the most beautifully ornamented pagodas in HCMC. Of special interest are the many small porcelain figures, the elaborate brass ritual objects and the fine woodcarvings on the altars, walls, columns and hanging lanterns. From outside the building you can see the ceramic scenes, each containing innumerable small figurines, which decorate the roof.

To the left of the entrance is a life-size figure of the sacred horse of Quan Cong. Before leaving on a journey, people make offerings to the horse. They then stroke the horse's mane and ring the bell around its neck. Behind the main altar, with its stone and brass incense braziers, is Quan Cong, to whom the pagoda is dedicated. Behind the altar to the left is Ong Bon and two servants. The altar to the right is occupied by representations of Buddhist (rather than Taoist) personages. In the glass case are a plaster Thich Ca Buddha and two figures of the Goddess of Mercy, one made of porcelain and the other cast in brass.

**Ong Bon Pagoda** Built by the Fujian congregation, Ong Bon Pagoda *(Chua Ong Bon & Nhi Phu Hoi Quan; 264 ĐL Hai Thuong Lai Ong; open 5am-5pm)* is dedicated to Ong Bon, Guardian Spirit of Happiness and Virtue. The wooden altar is intricately carved and gilded.

As you enter the pagoda, there is a room to the right of the open-air courtyard. In it, behind the table, is a figure of Quan The Am Bo Tat in a glass case. Above the case is the head of a Thich Ca Buddha.

Directly across the courtyard from the pagoda entrance, against the wall, is Ong Bon, to whom people come to pray for general happiness and relief from financial difficulties. He faces a fine, carved wooden altar. On the walls of this chamber are rather indistinct murals of five tigers (to the left) and two dragons (to the right).

In the area on the other side of the wall with the mural of the dragons is a furnace for burning paper representations of the wealth that people wish to bestow upon their deceased family members. Diagonally opposite is Quan Cong flanked by his guardians Chau Xuong (to his right) and Quan Binh (to his left).

ĐL Hai Thuong Lan Ong runs parallel to ĐL Tran Hung Dao.

**Ha Chuong Hoi Quan Pagoda** This typical Fujian pagoda *(802 Đ Nguyen Trai)* is dedicated to Thien Hau, who was born in Fujian. The four carved stone pillars, wrapped in painted dragons, were made in China and brought to Vietnam by boat. There are interesting murals to either side of the main altar. Note the ceramic relief scenes on the roof.

The pagoda becomes extremely active during the Lantern Festival, a Chinese holiday held on the 15th day of the first lunar month (the first full moon of the new lunar year).

**Cha Tam Church** It was in Cha Tam Church *(25 Đ Hoc Lac)* that President Ngo Dinh Diem and his brother Ngo Dinh Nhu took refuge on 2 November 1963, after fleeing the Presidential Palace during a coup attempt. When their efforts to contact loyal military officers (of whom there were almost none) failed, Diem and Nhu agreed to surrender unconditionally and reveal where they were hiding.

The coup leaders sent an M-113 armoured personnel carrier to the church and the two were taken into custody. However before the vehicle reached central Saigon, the soldiers had killed Diem and Nhu by shooting them at point-blank range and then repeatedly stabbing their bodies.

When news of the deaths was broadcast on radio, Saigon exploded with rejoicing. Portraits of the two were torn up and political prisoners, many of whom had been tortured, were set free. The city's nightclubs, which had closed because of the Ngos' conservative Catholic beliefs, were reopened. Three weeks later the US president, John F Kennedy, was assassinated. As his administration had supported the coup against Diem, some conspiracy theorists have speculated that Kennedy was killed by Diem's family in retaliation.

Cha Tam Church, built around the turn of the 19th century, is an attractive white and pastel-yellow structure. The statue in the tower is of François Xavier Tam Assou (1855–1934), a Chinese-born vicar apostolic (delegate of the pope) of Saigon. Today, the church has a very active congregation of 3000 ethnic Vietnamese and 2000 ethnic Chinese.

Masses are held daily. Cha Tam Church is at the western end of ĐL Tran Hung Dao.

**Khanh Van Nam Vien Pagoda** Built between 1939 and 1942, by the Cantonese congregation, Khanh Van Nam Vien Pagoda *(46/5 Đ Lo Sieu; open 6.30am-5.30pm daily)* is said to be the only Taoist pagoda in Vietnam. The number of true Taoists in HCMC is said to number only 4000, though most Chinese practice a mixture of Taoism and Buddhism.

A few metres from the door is a statue of Hoang Linh Quan, chief guardian of the pagoda. There is a Yin-and-Yang symbol on the platform on which the incense braziers sit. Behind the main altar are four figures: Quan Cong (on the right) and Lu Tung Pan (on the left) represent Taoism; between them is Van Xuong representing Confucianism; and behind Van Xuong is Quan The Am Bo Tat.

In front of these figures is a glass case containing seven gods and one goddess, all of whom are made of porcelain. In the altars to either side of the four figures are Hoa De (on the left), a famous doctor during the Han dynasty, and Huynh Dai Tien (on the right), a disciple of Laotse (Thai Thuong Lao Quan in Vietnamese).

Upstairs is a 150cm-high statue of Laotse. Behind his head is a halo consisting of a round mirror with fluorescent lighting around the edge of it.

Off to the left of Laotse are two stone plaques with instructions for inhalation and exhalation exercises. A schematic drawing represents the human organs as a scene from rural China. The diaphragm, agent of inhalation, is at the bottom. The stomach is represented by a peasant ploughing with a water buffalo. The kidney is marked by four Yin-and-Yang symbols, the liver is shown as a grove of trees and the heart is represented by a circle with a peasant standing in it, above which is a constellation. The tall pagoda represents the throat and the broken rainbow is the mouth. At the top are mountains and a seated figure that represents the brain and the imagination, respectively.

The pagoda operates a home for 30 elderly people who have no families. Each of the old folk, most of whom are women, have their own wood stove made of brick and can cook for themselves. Next door, also run by the pagoda, is a free medical clinic, which offers Chinese herbal medicines and acupuncture treatments to the community. If you would like to support this worthy venture, you can leave a donation with the monks.

Prayers are held daily from 8am to 9am. To reach the pagoda, turn off Đ Nguyen Thi Nho, which runs perpendicular to Đ Hung Vuong, between Nos 269B and 271B.

**Phung Son Pagoda** This pagoda (*Greater HCMC map; Phung Son Tu & Chua Go; 1408 ĐL 3/2; open 5am-7pm*) is extremely rich in statuary made of bronze, wood, ceramic and hammered copper. Some statues are gilded while other beautifully carved ones are painted. This Vietnamese Buddhist pagoda was built between 1802 and 1820 on the site of structures from the Oc-Eo (Funan) period, contemporaneous with early centuries of Christianity. The foundations of Funanese buildings have been discovered here.

Once upon a time, it was decided that Phung Son Pagoda should be moved to a different site. The pagoda's ritual objects – bells, drums, statues – were loaded onto the back of a white elephant, but the elephant slipped because of the great weight, and all the precious objects fell into a nearby pond. This event was interpreted as an omen that the pagoda should remain at its original location. All the articles were retrieved except for the bell, which locals say was heard ringing until about a century ago, whenever there was a full or new moon.

The main dais, with its many levels, is dominated by a gilded A Di Da Buddha seated under a canopy flanked by long mobiles resembling human forms without heads. A Di Da is flanked by Quan The Am Bo Tat (on the left), and Dai The Chi Bo Tat (on the right). To the left of the main dais is an altar with a statue of Bodhidharma, who brought Buddhism from India to China. The statue, which is made of Chinese ceramic, has a face with Indian features.

As you walk from the main sanctuary to the room with the open-air courtyard in the middle, you come to an altar with four statues on it, including a standing bronze, Thich Ca Buddha, of Thai origin. To the right is an altar with a glass case containing a statue made of sandalwood, and claimed to be Long Vuong (Dragon King), who brings rain. Around the pagoda building are a number of interesting monks' tombs.

Phung Son Pagoda is in District 11. Prayers are held three times a day from 4am to 5am, 4pm to 5pm and 6pm to 7pm. The main entrances are locked most of the time because of problems with theft, but the side entrance (to the left as you approach the building) is open during the listed hours.

## PARKS
### Cong Vien Van Hoa Park
Next to the old Cercle Sportif, which was an elite sporting club during the French-colonial period, the bench-lined walks of Cong Vien Van Hoa Park are shaded with avenues of enormous tropical trees.

This place still has an active sports club, although now you don't have to be French to visit. There are 11 tennis courts, a swimming pool and a clubhouse, all of which have a grand colonial feel about them. There are Roman-style baths, and a coffee shop overlooks the colonnaded pool.

The tennis courts are available for hire at a reasonable fee. Hourly tickets are on sale for use of the pool and you can even buy a bathing costume, if you don't have one. The antique dressing rooms are quaint, but there are no lockers. Other facilities include a gymnasium, table tennis, weights, wrestling mats, and ballroom-dancing classes.

In the morning, you can often see people here practising the art of *thai cuc quyen*, or slow-motion shadow boxing. Within the park is also a small-scale model of Nha Trang's most famous Cham towers.

Cong Vien Van Hoa Park is adjacent to Reunification Palace. There are entrances across from 115 Đ Nguyen Du and on Đ Nguyen Thi Minh Khai.

### Ho Ky Hoa Park
This park (*Greater HCMC map; open 7am-9.30pm daily*), whose name means 'Lake and Gardens', is a children's amusement

park in District 10, just off ĐL 3 Thang 2. It is behind Vietnam Quoc Tu Pagoda. There are paddle, rowing and sailing boats for hire. Fishing is allowed in the lakes and a small swimming pool is open to the public for part of the year. The cafés are open year round. Ho Ky Hoa Park is most crowded on Sundays.

## BINH SOUP SHOP

It might seem strange to introduce a noodle-soup restaurant as a sight, but there is more to this shop (Greater HCMC map; ☎ 848 3775; 7 Đ Ly Chinh Thang, District 3; noodle soup 15,000d) than just the soup. The Binh Soup Shop was the secret headquarters of the VC in Saigon. It was from here that the VC planned its attack on the US embassy and other places in Saigon during the Tet Offensive of 1968. One has to wonder how many US soldiers ate here, completely unaware that the staff were all VC infiltrators. By the way, the pho isn't bad here.

## BINH QUOI TOURIST VILLAGE

Built on a small peninsula in the Saigon River, the Binh Quoi Tourist Village (Lang Du Lich Binh Quoi; ☎ 899 1831, ☎ 899 4103; 1147 Đ Xo Viet Nghe Tinh; bungalows US$8-10) is a slick tourist trap operated by Saigon Tourist. Backpackers are few, but upmarket tourists get carted out here by the busload and some city-weary locals also seem to like it.

The village is essentially a park featuring boat rides, water puppets, a restaurant, a swimming pool, tennis courts, a camping ground, a guesthouse, bungalows and other amusements for the kids. The park puts in a plug for Vietnam's ethnic minorities by staging their traditional weddings accompanied by music. There are some alligators in an enclosure for viewing. River cruises can be fun – the smaller cruise boats have 16 seats and the larger ones have 100 seats.

Next door to the water-puppet theatre, you can make bookings for the local nightlife, including dinner cruises and shows.

The bungalows are one of the better-value places to stay here. Built on stilts above the water, the bungalows give you a taste of traditional river life in the Mekong Delta, but with air-con and tennis courts. It's worth asking for a room with good views of the river.

Binh Quoi Tourist Village is 8km north of central HCMC in the Binh Thanh district. You can get there by cyclo, motorbike or taxi. A much-slower alternative is to charter a boat from the Bach Dang pier area on the Saigon River.

## FITNESS CLUBS & POOLS

If you don't make it to Saigon Water Park or one of its recent clones, there are several fine swimming pools at plush tourist hotels. You needn't stay at these hotels to use the facilities, but you must pay an admission fee of US$5 to US$10 per day. Hotels offering access to their pools include the Omni, Metropole, Palace and Rex.

There are a number of less-expensive public pools and some of the newer ones are in very good condition. These pools charge by the hour and this works out to be very cheap, if you're staying only a short time. Lam Son Pool (Greater HCMC map; ☎ 835 8028; 342 Đ Tran Binh Trong, District 5; admission 5000d per hr, 6000d after 5pm; open 8am-8pm daily) is one such place and has an Olympic-sized pool. Or you can visit the pool at the Workers' Club (Central HCMC map; ☎ 930 1819; 55B Đ Nguyen Thi Minh Khai, District 3; admission 10,000d per hour).

The International Club (Greater HCMC map; ☎ 865 7695; 285B Đ Cach Mang Thang Tam, District 10; admission 25,000d; open 9am-midnight daily) also has a mid-sized outdoor swimming pool, as well as a sauna and steam rooms, an exercise gym and beauty salon inside. There is also a massage service, and a 120,000d ticket entitles you to a 50-minute rub-down and all-day use of the club's facilities. However there are definitely better places for a massage in town, notably Spa Tropic (see the Massage & Spas section).

If you're interested in martial arts, the best place to see (or try) thai cuc quyen is at Cong Vien Van Hoa Park or the Cholon district where there is a large ethnic-Chinese population.

## WATER PARKS

In the past several years a slew of water parks have appeared in and around HCMC. They're the perfect antidote for anyone who needs to cool down from an overdose of pagodas and museums. Anyone with kids and a half-day to spare will quickly come to appreciate these wet and wonderful playgrounds on a sweltering day. Bring a waterproof camera. The best time to avoid the crowds is between 11am and 2pm on weekdays (most Vietnamese prefer to stay out of the midday sun) – but this is also the best time of day to get sunburnt.

**Saigon Water Park** (☎ 897 0456; Đ Kha Van Can; adult/child 60,000/35,000d, swim-only ticket 35,000d; open 9am-5pm Mon-Fri, 9am-8pm Sat, 8am-8pm Sun & public holidays) is a giant oasis in the suburbs. This refreshing complex on the banks of the Saigon River is chock-full of pools and water rides, including loop-the-loop slides, a children's wading pool and even a 'wave pool'. There is also a restaurant here with fine views over the river. Saigon Water Park is in the Thu Duc District (near Go Dua Bridge). It's too far for cyclos, but you can take a meter taxi for about 50,000d, or catch a shuttle bus (once every half-hour) from Ben Thanh Market for 5000d.

**Shark Waterland** (Cholon map; ☎ 853 7867; Đ Ham Tu, District 5; admission 20,000-45,000d; open 8am-9pm daily) may not be the most clever name to call a swimming venue, but it's a good spot if you happen and be in Cholon. They have both pools and slides. A bit further afield is the **Dam Sen Water Park**, and if all these aren't enough **Vietnam Water World** is way out of town, in the eastern suburbs.

## Massage & Spas

One of the best and cheapest rub-downs in town can be had at the **Vietnamese Traditional Massage Institute** (Pham Ngu Lao Area map; ☎ 839 6697; 185 Đ Cong Quynh; open 9am-9am daily). Here you can enjoy a no-nonsense massage performed by a well-trained blind masseur from the Ho Chi Minh City Association for the Blind. The cost is just 25,000d per hour (air-con comfort will set you back an extra 10,000d). There is also

a sauna room available for 20,000d per hour. There are 18 masseurs on call, so reservations are not necessary.

One place to spoil yourself on a top-notch 'proper' massage is **Spa Tropic** (Central HCMC map; ☎ 822 8895; e info@ spatropic.com; 187B Hai Ba Trung, District 3; open 10am-8pm daily). This Zen-like beauty spa offers an array of aromatherapy facial treatments (US$28), body treatments (US$20-35) and therapeutic massage (from US$18), from Swedish and deep-tissue to shiatsu. Spa Tropic can be found in the same quiet alley as Tib Restaurant. Call ahead for reservations.

Most upmarket hotels offer some kind of massage service, some more legitimate than others.

## BOWLING

The **Diamond Superbowl** (Dong Khoi Area map; ☎ 825 7778; 4th floor, Diamond Plaza, 34 ĐL Le Duan; open 10am-1am daily) is a state-of-the-art, 32-lane bowling alley smack dab in the centre of town. It's very popular with locals, and is notable for having fluorescent bowling balls and computerised scoring. Attached is a large amusement centre with billiards, a video-game arcade and shops. Bowling rates depend on the time of day, and whether it's a weekday or weekend. Lanes cost from 100,000d to 200,000d per hour, and per game charges are from 20,000d to 40,000d. Shoe rental costs 5000d.

## GOLF

The **Vietnam Golf and Country Club** (Cau Lac Bo Golf Quoc Te Viet Nam; ☎ 733 0124, fax 733 0127; 40-42 Đ Nguyen Trai, Ap Gian Dan, District 2) was the first in Vietnam to provide night golfing under floodlights. The club is in Lam Vien Park, about 15km east of central HCMC. Membership starts at a cool US$41,000, but paying visitors are welcome. Use of the driving range costs US$10, or you can play a full round for US$82. Other facilities include tennis courts and a swimming pool.

The **Rach Chiec Driving Range** (☎ 896 0756; open 6am-10pm daily) is a good place to practise your swing. A bucket of 50 balls costs 40,000d. Clubs, shoes and instructors can be hired. It's in An Phu village, a 20-minute drive north along National Hwy 1 from central HCMC.

If you're serious about golfing, there are top-notch courses in both Phan Thiet (see the South-Central Coast chapter) and Dalat (see the Central Highlands chapter).

Visit w www.vietnamgolfresorts.com for more information on the courses and reasonably priced golf package tours.

## COOKING COURSES
The **Vietnam Cookery Center** offers an array of Vietnamese cooking courses in HCMC; basic courses are five hours in duration. For more information, contact **Expat Services** (☎ 823 5872, fax 823 5873; e vietnam cookery@hcm.vnn.vn; 177 Đ Dien Bien Phu, District 3).

## LANGUAGE COURSES
The vast majority of foreign-language students enrol at **Teacher Training University** (Dai Hoc Su Pham; ☎ 835 5100; e ciec er@hcm.vnn.vn; 280 An Duong Vuong, District 5) at Ho Chi Minh City University. Private classes cost US$4 per hour, or US$2.50 per hour for group classes.

Another option is the **University of Social Sciences & Humanities** (Dai Hoc Khoa Hoc Xa Hoi Va Nhan Van; ☎ 822 5009; 12 Dinh Tien Hoang, District 1). Here group classes run on a term schedule and cost US$2.80 per hour.

## PLACES TO STAY
Each different category of traveller has staked out its own turf in this city. Budget travellers tend to congregate around the Pham Ngu Lao area at the western end of District 1; this area has by far the widest availability of cheap accommodation. Travellers with a little more cash to spare prefer the more upmarket hotels concentrated around Đ Dong Khoi, on the eastern side of District 1. French travellers seem to have an affinity for District 3, while Cholon attracts plenty of visitors from Hong Kong and Taiwan.

## PLACES TO STAY – BUDGET
If you don't really know where you want to stay, but are limited by budget, it's not a bad idea to take a meter taxi into Pham Ngu Lao and proceed on foot. If you don't want to lug your bags around, which also makes you a prime target for touts, consider dropping your gear at one of the travellers cafés and setting out on foot. Most won't mind keeping an eye on it for you and they'll be happy to show you the tour programmes they have on offer. One simple solution is to email or fax ahead for reservations – most hotels will fetch you at the airport for around US$5.

### Pham Ngu Lao Area
Đ Pham Ngu Lao, Đ De Tham and Đ Bui Vien form the heart of the budget-traveller haven. These streets and the adjoining alleys, collectively known as 'Pham Ngu Lao', contain a treasure-trove of cheap accommodation, restaurants, bars, cafés and travel agents, most catering to the budget end of the market.

At last count there were well over a hundred places to stay in the area, so finding a room is *never* a problem here. Finding the right one is another story. A few places here have dorms (US$3), and there are countless cheap 'minihotels' (US$6 to US$10). In the US$10 to US$20 range, newer (and higher standard) minihotels offer amenities such as fridges, baths, telephones and satellite TV.

---

### Your Friendly Taxi Driver

A minor warning – some airport taxi drivers like to play a little game when it comes to taking you to a hotel. They want the hotel to pay them a commission and they know which hotels pay commissions and which don't. If you want to go to a hotel which does not pay commissions then don't be surprised if the driver claims that place is very dirty, unsafe, expensive or even out of business.

The bottom line is don't *always* believe what your driver tells you. The same thing applies also to drivers of cyclos, motorbikes and taxis that are parked at the train station.

About 100m south of Đ Pham Ngu Lao is Đ Bui Vien, which is rapidly being transformed into a solid string of guesthouses and minihotels. **'Minihotel alley'**, flanked by (and addressed as an extension of) Đ Bui Vien and Đ Pham Ngu Lao, has more than a dozen virtually identical places. Most are family-run and range from US$6 to US$10 for fan rooms and US$10 to US$15 for bigger air-con rooms (some with balconies).

**Bich Thuy Guesthouse** *(Friendly Guesthouse;* ☎ *836 9953;* e *phucgreyhair@hotmail.com; 5 Đ Do Quang Dau; dorm beds US$3, rooms with fan/air-con from US$5/7)* is a very low-budget place run by friendly Mr Phuc, a veteran tourist driver. Breakfast is complimentary, and if you're in need of a cheap sprucing, there is a hair salon in the lobby!

**Tan Thanh Thanh Hotel** *(*☎ *837 3595, fax 836 7027;* e *tanthanhthanh@hcm.fpt.vn; 205 Đ Pham Ngu Lao; dorm beds from US$3, rooms US$5-10)* was the first place in this neighbourhood to offer dormitory accommodation. Guests here are also served a complimentary breakfast.

Other cheap places nearby include **Hotel 265** *(*☎ *836 7512, fax 836 1883;* e *hotelduy@hotmail.com; 265 Đ De Tham; dorm beds US$3, air-con rooms from US$10/12)*, **Vinh Guesthouse** *(*☎ *836 8585, fax 836 8787;* e *lelehotel@hcm.fpt.vn; 269 Đ De Tham; air-con rooms US$10)* and **Peace Hotel** *(*☎ *837 2025, fax 836 8824;* e *hasanvnn@hcm.vnn.vn; 272 Đ De Tham; singles/doubles with fan US$7/8, singles/doubles with air-con US$9/10)*.

**Giang Son Guesthouse** *(*☎ *837 7547, fax 837 7548;* e *giangson_guesthouse@hotmail.com; 283/14 Đ Pham Ngu Lao; US$8-12)* is a new place tucked into an alley off the noisy main street.

**Ha Vy Hotel** *(*☎ *836 9123;* e *havy@saigonnet.vn; 16-18 Đ Do Quang Dau; fan room US$7, air-con room US$10)* is a large new family-run hotel that has been receiving good reports.

The Pham Ngu Lao area boasts an excellent selection of slightly upmarket minihotels in the US$12 to US$25 range. A selection of these are described here.

It's worth checking out the trio of superb family-run hotels run by warm-hearted Madam Cuc, a local personality who knows how to make her guests feel safe and at home. All three places feature spotless rooms that are well-appointed (fridges, air-con, satellite TV, bathtubs etc) and the staff provide a most welcoming reception. Virtually identical in size and style, they all share the same email address and fax number. They are **Hotel 127** *(*☎ *836 8761, fax 836 0658;* e *madamcuc@hcm.vnn.vn; 127 Đ Cong Quynh; rooms US$12-20)*, **Hotel 64** *(64 Đ Bui Vien; rooms US$10-20)* and **MC Hotel** *(184 Đ Cong Quynh; rooms US$14-20)*.

If all of these are full, you might try **Hotel 70** *(*☎ *836 5649, fax 836 9569; 70 Đ Bui Vien)*, a couple of doors down from Hotel 64. It also maintains a high standard and charges around the same prices.

**Duna Hotel** *(*☎ *837 3699, fax 837 6606;* e *dunahotelvn@hcm.vnn.vn; 265 Đ Pham Ngu Lao; rooms US$10-20)* is one of the newest minihotels in the area. It has an elevator and a small in-house restaurant.

**Spring House Hotel** *(*☎ *837 8312, fax 837 8311;* e *hanhhoahotel@hcm.vnn.vn; rooms US$15-20)* is another good-looking new place with an elevator.

**Hanh Hoa Hotel** *(*☎ *836 0245, fax 836 1482;* e *hanhhoahotel@hcm.vnn.vn; 237 Đ Pham Ngu Lao; rooms US$12-25)* is the older sister hotel of the Spring House Hotel.

**Southern Hotel** *(*☎ *837 0922, fax 836 9105;* e *southernhotel@hcm.vnn.vn; 216 Đ De Tham; rooms US$10-30)* is a friendly place. The 'special room' (US$30) has its own private garden terrace.

**Le Le Hotel** *(*☎ *836 8686, fax 836 8787;* e *lelehotel@hcm.fpt.vn; 171 Đ Pham Ngu Lao; rooms US$12-40)* is another hotel with an elevator and satellite TV.

**Giant Dragon Hotel** *(*☎ *836 1935, fax 836 7279;* e *gd-hotel@hcm.vnn.vn; 173 Đ Pham Ngu Lao; rooms/suites US$18/23)* has fairly plush rooms with satellite TV.

**Mai Phai Hotel** *(*☎ *836 5868, fax 837 1575;* e *maiphaihotel@saigonnet.vn; 209 Đ Pham Ngu Lao; rooms US$10-15)* gets good reports from travellers. Rates include breakfast.

**Hotel 211** (☎ 836 7353, fax 836 1883; ⓔ hotelduy@hotmail.com; 211 Đ Pham Ngu Lao; fan rooms US$7-8, air-con rooms US$9-12), next door to Mai Phai, is a large budget place. All rooms have private bath with hot water, and rates include breakfast.

**Coco Loco Guesthouse** (☎ 837 2647; 373/2 Pham Ngu Lao; air-con rooms US$10) is an older place down a tiny alley behind the Thai Binh Market.

**Quyen Thanh Hotel** (☎ 836 8570, fax 836 9946; ⓔ quyenthanhhotel@hcm.vnn.vn; 212 Đ De Tham; fan/air-con rooms from US$8/10) has basic rooms and some larger fully equipped rooms. There is an excellent **souvenir shop** on the ground floor, a good place to look for locally made lacquerware, snake wine and various other trinkets.

## Other Areas

An alternative, about 10 minutes' walk south from the Pham Ngu Lao area, is a string of fine guesthouses in the quiet alley connecting Đ Co Giang and Đ Co Bac.

**Miss Loi's Guesthouse** (Central HCMC map; ☎/fax 836 7973; 178/20 Đ Co Giang; ⓔ missloi@hcm.fpt.vn; fan rooms US$8-10, air-con rooms US$12-15) was the first hotel to appear here, and is probably still the best. Zany Miss Loi throws in breakfast free and even has her own in-house beauty salon! There's also a pool table in the lobby. Many of her neighbours are jumping into this business and the area is rapidly developing into another backpackers haven. To reach the guesthouses walk southwest on Đ Co Bac and turn left after you pass the nuoc mam shops.

**Tan Hai Long Hotel** (Central HCMC map; ☎ 08-927 2738, fax 825 6012; 14 Đ Le Lai; ⓔ tanhailonghotel@hcm.vnn.vn; rooms US$15-30) is a tall minihotel with a prime central location near the Ben Thanh Market. There are great views (and plenty of noise) from the upper-floor balconies.

**Bat Dat Hotel II** (Cholon map; ☎ 855 5902; 41 Đ Ngo Quyen; twins with air-con 150,000d) is the cheap cousin of the nearby (and pricier) Bat Dat Hotel. It's old, but has a certain derelict charm. The bright blue trim on the exterior makes it easy to spot.

## PLACES TO STAY – MID-RANGE
### Pham Ngu Lao Area

With the incredible deals you get for under US$20 it's not really worth upgrading. But if you prefer a larger, business hotel, there are a few places to consider in the area.

**Liberty 4 Hotel** (☎ 836 5822, fax 836 5435; 265 Đ Pham Ngu Lao; rooms US$25-60) has nice rooms, but it's questionable as to whether they're worth the price. The hotel offers excellent views from its 9th-floor restaurant.

**Vien Dong Hotel** (☎ 836 8098, fax 836 8812; ⓔ viendonghotel@hcm.fpt.vn; 275A Đ Pham Ngu Lao; single rooms US$25-55, twins US$30-60) is another large state-run place. Amenities include a rooftop **restaurant** and a nightclub.

**Metropole Hotel** (Central HCMC map; ☎ 832 2021, fax 832 2019; 148 ĐL Tran Hung Dao; rooms US$35-70) is a fancy Saigon Tourist place with a swimming pool.

**Windsor Saigon Hotel** (☎ 836 7848, fax 836 7889; ⓔ reservations@windsorsaigon hotel.com; 193 ĐL Tran Hung Dao; singles/doubles from US$90/95), a short walk south of Đ Bui Vien, has all amenities – including a white stretch Cadillac limo parked out front! There's a pleasant rooftop garden **café**, and an excellent in-house **bakery-deli** offering pastries, fine wine, cheese and sausages.

### Dong Khoi Area

If you want to base yourself in the city centre, there's a good number of well-appointed hotels along Đ Dong Khoi or near the Saigon River. All of them offer amenities such as air-con and satellite TV.

**Thang Long Hotel** (☎ 822 2595, fax 824 5220; ⓔ thanglonghotel@hcm.fpt.vn; 48 Đ Mac Thi Buoi; singles/doubles from US$16/20, suites US$35/40) is a minihotel with a distinctively Chinese feel to it. The same goes for the **Dong Do Hotel**, just across the street.

**Kim Long Hotel** (Golden Dragon Hotel; ☎ 822 8558, fax 822 5024; ⓔ kimlong hotel@hcm.vnn.vn; 58 Đ Mac Thi Buoi; singles/doubles US$20/25) is another nice minihotel on the same street. Front rooms have large balconies.

**Bach Dang Hotel** (☎ 825 1501, fax 823 0587; 33 Đ Mac Thi Buoi; rooms US$39-45) is a bright and airy place. Some rooms offer views of the Saigon River.

**Kim Do Hotel** (☎ 822 5914, fax 822 5915; 133 ĐL Nguyen Huế; rooms US$40-100) is a fancy place brought to you by Saigon Tourist.

**Asian Hotel** (☎ 829 6979, fax 829 7433; e asianhotel@hcn.fpt.vn; 150 Đ Dong Khoi; rooms from US$35) is a contemporary hotel right in the centre of town. It's notable for its in-house **restaurant**.

**Bong Sen Hotel** (Lotus Hotel; ☎ 829 1516, fax 829 8076; 117-123 Đ Dong Khoi; twins with air-con US$50-180), affectionately called 'The BS' by travellers, is popular with business people.

**Bong Sen Annexe** (☎ 823 5818, fax 823 5816; 61-63 ĐL Hai Ba Trung; singles/ doubles US$45/56, with city views US$50/ 65, junior suites US$70/85) is an attractive choice offering slightly more reasonable rates than Bong Sen.

**Spring Hotel** (☎ 829 7362, fax 822 1383; 44-46 Đ Le Thanh Ton; doubles US$25-59) is a tidy place with a subtle Japanese feel to it. Breakfast is complimentary.

**Orchid Hotel** (☎ 823 1809, fax 829 2245; 29A Đ Don Dat; singles US$25-40, doubles US$30-50), on the corner of Đ Thai Van Lung, is another good place, with an array of amenities including karaoke and 24-hour room service.

## District 3
This district (see Central HCMC map) attracts a large number of French travellers, possibly because of its architecture.

**Chancery Saigon Hotel** (☎ 930 4088, fax 930 3988; e chancery@hcm.vnn.vn; 196 Đ Nguyen Thi Minh Khai; rooms US$40-60), near the Saigon Star, is a modern luxurious all-suite hotel brought to you by the US Best Western chain.

**Saigon Star Hotel** (☎ 823 0260, fax 823 0255; 204 Đ Nguyen Thi Minh Khai; rooms US$45-85++), next door, is also nice and features satellite TV, two **restaurants**

and a **coffee shop**, a karaoke club and a business centre. Rates include breakfast.

**International Hotel** (☎ 930 4009, fax 930 4566; e international-ht@hcm.vnn.vn; 19 Đ Vo Van Tan; rooms US$30-50++) maintains plush standards for the price. Rooms are fitted with all the usual amenities (satellite TV, minibar, IDD phones and safety-deposit boxes).

## District 5 (Cholon)
**Bat Dat Hotel** (☎ 855 1662; 238-244 ĐL Tran Hung Dao; twins with air-con US$30-45) is the snazzier cousin of the nearby Bat Dat Hotel II.

**Caesar Hotel** (☎ 835 0677, fax 835 0106; 34-36 ĐL An Duong Vuong; twins US$26-40), right inside the bustling Andong Market, is an easy place to find. This place is usually full of Taiwanese businessmen.

**Arc En Ciel Hotel** (Rainbow Hotel; ☎ 855 4435, fax 855 2424; 52-56 Đ Tan Da; singles/ doubles from US$20/30) is another popular venue for tour groups from Hong Kong and Taiwan, and includes the Rainbow Disco Karaoke. The hotel is on the corner of ĐL Tran Hung Dao.

## Tan Binh & Phu Nhuan Districts
These are the areas out towards the airport in the northern part of the city (see the Greater HCMC map).

**Novotel** (☎ 842 1111, fax 842 4363; e rsvn -gpnovotel@hcm.vnn.vn; 309B Đ Nguyen Van Troi; rooms US$64-110++) is certainly one of the nicest hotels near the airport. Nonguests can use the hotel pool for US$8.

**Omni Hotel** (☎ 844 9222, fax 844 9200; e rsvns@omnisaigonhotel.com; 251 Đ Nguyen Van Troi; rooms US$63-185++) provides the poshest accommodation in the area. This place has everything from room safes to a florist to a health club.

**Chains First Hotel** (☎ 844 1199, fax 844 4282; e first.hotel@hcm.vnn.vn; 18 Đ Hoang Viet; rooms from US$40-60++) boasts a coffee shop, a gift shop, tennis courts, a sauna, massage services, three **restaurants**, a swimming pool, a business centre and a free airport shuttle service. Rates include breakfast and a basket of fruit.

HO CHI MINH CITY

## PLACES TO STAY – TOP END

Nearly all of HCMC's top hotels are concentrated in District 1, most of them in the Dong Khoi area. Don't be scared off by the published rates; hefty discounts can often be negotiated. Just send an email and ask for the current 'promotional' rates.

**Continental Hotel** (☎ 829 9201, fax 824 1772; e continental@hcm.vnn.vn; 132-134 Đ Dong Khoi; rooms US$55-130), one of the city's most historic lodgings, was the setting for much of the action that aoccured in Graham Greene's well-known novel *The Quiet American*. The hotel dates from the turn of the 19th century and received its last renovation in 1989, unfortunately at the hands of its current owner, Saigon Tourist.

**Rex Hotel** (☎ 829 6043, fax 829 6536; e rexhotel@hcm.vnn.vn; 141 ĐL Nguyen Hué; twins & suites US$70-550), a giant place, is another classic central hotel. Its ambience of mellowed kitsch dates from the time it put up US army officers. Amenities include a large gift shop, a tailor, a beauty parlour, massage, acupuncture and a small swimming pool on the 6th floor. There are great views from the rooftop veranda, which is decorated with caged birds and potted bonsai bushes shaped like animals.

**Caravelle Hotel** (☎ 823 4999, fax 824 3999; e hotel@caravellehotel.vnn.vn; 19 Lam Son Square; rooms US$160-980++) is an enormous posh place that sits on a prime piece of real estate, once occupied by the Catholic Diocese of Saigon. It's hands-down one of the most luxurious hotels in HCMC. Nonguests can swim in the hotel pool for US$10.

**Majestic Hotel** (☎ 829 5514, fax 822 9744; e fomajestic@sgt.vnn.vn; 1 Đ Dong Khoi; rooms US$70-130, suites US$150-220) dates back to 1925. It is right on the Saigon River and following major renovations it can truly reclaim its title as one of the city's most majestic hotels. As one guest wrote: 'The Majestic wins hands-down for class and bygone-days atmosphere'.

**Grand Hotel** (☎ 823 0163, fax 823 5781; e grand-hotel@fmail.vnn.vn; 12 Đ Ngo Duc Ke; rooms US$45-220), on the corner of Đ Dong Khoi, is aptly named. This renovated landmark building is notable for its spacious suites with 4.5m-high ceilings and French windows. There is an indoor swimming pool and good massage service.

**Saigon Prince Hotel** (☎ 822 2999, fax 822 5888; 63 ĐL Nguyen Hué; twins US$80-200++) has glittering, luxury rooms. Local expats say it has the best massage service in town. Its US$14 massage-sauna-Jacuzzi package (Monday to Friday) is decent value.

**Norfolk Hotel** (☎ 829 5368, fax 829 3415; e norfolk@bdvn.vnd.vet; 117 Đ Le Thanh Ton; singles US$85-125++, twins US$100-140++) is an Australian joint venture and is popular with business travellers. All rooms boast satellite TV and a minibar. Rates include breakfast.

**New World Hotel** (☎ 822 8888, fax 835 0446; e bcnwhs@hcm.vnn.vn; 76 Đ Le Lai; rooms from US$70, presidential suite US$850) is an enormous luxury tower near the Pham Ngu Lao district. The clientele tends to be mainly Chinese-speaking tour groups from Hong Kong and Taiwan, but anyone with hard currency is welcome.

**Riverside Hotel** (☎ 822 4038, fax 825 1417; e hotelriversidesg@hcm.vnn.vn; 18 Đ Ton Duc Thang; doubles US$40-120), very close to the Saigon River, is an old colonial building that has been renovated and now features a good **restaurant** and bar.

**Renaissance Riverside Hotel** (☎ 822 0033, fax 823 5666; e bc.rrhs@hcm.vnn.vn; 8-15 Đ Ton Duc Thang; rooms US$90-155) is a new glitzy skyscraper. Don't confuse it with the Riverside Hotel, which, as the name suggests, also overlooks the river. Nonguests can use the pool here for US$10.

**Hotel Sofitel Plaza Saigon** (☎ 824 1555, fax 824 1666; e sofsgn-resa@hcmc.net nam.vn; 17 ĐL Le Duan; rooms from US$150, presidential suite US$1450) has 291 rooms and is among the sleekest of HCMC's posh hotels. There are two fine in-house **restaurants**, and L'Elysee Bar features live jazz and a delightful terrace. Nonguests can use the rooftop swimming pool for US$12.

## PLACES TO STAY – RENTAL

It's estimated that there are some 15,000 expats living in HCMC.

The budget market is served chiefly by the minihotels scattered all around town. Discounts can be negotiated for long-term rentals at almost any hotel; expect to pay somewhere between US$200 and US$300 per month for a decent air-con room. If you've got a big budget, but don't need a large space, even the big luxury hotels offer steep discounts to long-termers. The name of the game is negotiation.

Expats who enjoy a liberal budget have two basic options – villas or specially-built luxury flats. Small villas in the city centre rent for around US$250 to US$500 a month. Serviced apartments typically range from US$1000 to US$2000 a month.

## PLACES TO EAT

Both Vietnamese and Western food are widely available in HCMC and English menus are common. Cholon's speciality is Chinese food. If you are feeling spring-rolled out, don't fret; there is plenty of superb international food around.

### Vietnamese

**Central Area** It is a bit difficult to find, but **Nam Giao** (Central HCMC map; ☎ 825 0261; 136/15 Le Thanh Ton; mains 6000-10,000d; open 8am-9pm daily) is worth the quest. Tucked away in an alley of cosmetic shops, behind Ben Thanh Market, it's cheap, delicious and always packed with locals. The food here is Hué-style and superb. There's a simple photo menu, but if you can't choose, try the combo platter (thap cam) for 10,000d.

**Bo Tung Xeo** (Dong Khoi Area map; ☎ 825 1330; 31 Đ Ly Tu Trong) is a popular indoor-outdoor eatery in the city centre and it serves amazingly cheap and tasty Vietnamese barbecued food. The house speciality is tender marinated beef (30,000d a portion, including a salad) which you grill over charcoal right at your table. There are also good seafood dishes on the menu, and the cheerful staff speak English.

Along Đ Ngo Duc Ke, near the river in District 1, there's a strip of excellent restaurants serving good, cheap Vietnamese food.

**Restaurant 19** (Dong Khoi Area map; ☎ 829 8882; 19 Đ Ngo Duc Ke) serves a very

tasty variation on Hanoi's fish cakes (cha ca) and good Thai dishes as well.

**Restaurant 13** (Dong Khoi Area map; 13 Đ Ngo Duc Ke) is highly popular with locals and expats alike, and is near Restaurant 19.

**Thy 4 Two** (Dong Khoi Area map; ☎ 827 2737; 20 Đ Thi Sach; lunch 70,000d; open lunch & dinner), pronounced 'tea for two', is a cosy little bistro doing Vietnamese fare. The lunch sets are very reasonable.

**Tib Restaurant** (Dong Khoi Area map; ☎ 829 7242; 187 ĐL Hai Ba Trung, District 3; mains 45,000-55,000d, open 11am-10pm daily) is housed in a Sino-French villa, down a quiet alleyway. They do good Hué-style dishes, and a mean jackfruit salad with grilled sesame.

Other popular places with traditional decor and fine food in the Dong Khoi area include **Tan Nam Restaurant** (☎ 829 8634; 60-62 Đ Dong Du) and **Cool** (Kinh Bac; ☎ 829 1364; 30 Đ Dong Khoi), where there is an ethnic feel and plenty of plant life to enrich the air.

**Nam An** (☎ 822 0246; between Đ Nguyen Hué & Đ Dong Khoi; open 7am-11pm daily) is a popular indoor-outdoor place modelled on a Buddhist temple. The menu selection is vast and varied, and prices are fair.

**Pham Ngu Lao Area** Located right in the centre of backpacker land, **Nam Bo** (☎ 837 8616; 199A Pham Ngu Lao; mains 10,000-15,000d; open 5am-midnight) is a remarkable outdoor eatery. Here a wide variety of traditional Vietnamese dishes can be ordered from a long line of clean Vietnamese food stalls.

**Lac Thien** (☎ 837 1621; 28/25 Đ Bui Vien; mains 10,000-20,000d; open 7am-midnight) was cloned straight from the trio of travellers restaurants, run by deaf people, up in Hué. The food is excellent (especially their Hué-style dishes) and cheap.

**Pho Bo** (96 Đ Bui Vien) is a classic little hole in the wall that whips up tasty bowls of beef noodle soup.

### Gourmet Vietnamese

Compared to what you would pay for fine Vietnamese food abroad, HCMC's better

Vietnamese restaurants are a bargain. It's possible to eat like a king in a fancy upmarket restaurant for around US$10 or US$20 per person. Aspiring interior designers will enjoy checking out the ethnic decor at many of the better places.

All of the following can be found on the Dong Khoi Area map.

**Lemon Grass** (☎ 822 0496; 4 Ð Nguyen Thiep; open 11am-2pm & 5pm-10pm daily) is one of the best Vietnamese restaurants in the city centre. You'd be hard-pressed to find anything bad on the menu, so if you can't decide what to order just pick something at random. Two women in traditional costume play musical instruments while you eat.

**Mandarine** (☎ 822 9783; 11A Ð Ngo Van Nam) offers a fine selection of traditional dishes drawing from southern, central and northern cooking styles. The food is superb, and the pleasant decor and traditional-music performances make it an all-round good bet. A house speciality worth trying is the Hanoi-style *cha ca*.

**Hoi An** (☎ 823 1049; 11 Ð Le Thanh Ton), just down the street (and run by the same people as Mandarine) is a lovely, Chinese-style place decorated in a classical, antique motif. Here they specialise in central Vietnamese and imperial Hué-style dishes, and also have the heaviest wooden chairs in Vietnam!

## Other Asian

**Central Area** Indian is the dominant cuisine here, but keep an eye out for others.

**Encore Angkor** (Dong Khoi Area map; ☎ 822 6278; 5 Ð Nguyen Thiep) may be the only restaurant in Vietnam specialising in Cambodian-inspired Khmer cuisine. This stylish little bistro is run by Daniel Hung, a French photographer born to Khmer-Vietnamese parents. He serves beautifully presented, traditional Khmer dishes at very reasonable prices.

**Chao Thai** (Dong Khoi Area map; ☎ 824 1457; 16 Ð Thai Van Lung; lunch set 80,000d, meals from 50,000d) is one of Vietnam's best Thai restaurants. The lunch sets here are good value. Recommended dishes include the prawn cakes, Chiang Mai sausages and

winged-bean salad. **Sawadee** is another Thai choice on nearby Ð Thi Sach.

**Hakata** (Dong Khoi Area map; ☎ 824116; 2 Ð Le Thanh Ton) serves some of the best Japanese fare in town, and good sushi.

**Urvashi** (Dong Khoi Area map; ☎ 821 3102; 27 Ð Hai Trieu; lunch set US$3-4) has some of the best Indian food in District 1. It prepares a variety of Indian cooking styles and the thali lunch set is a guaranteed filler.

**Indian Heritage** (Dong Khoi Area map; ☎ 823 4687; 26A Ð Le Thanh Ton; lunch buffet US$5), also central, serves an excellent lunch buffet.

**Ashoka** (Dong Khoi Area map; ☎ 823 1372; 17A/10 Ð Le Thanh Ton), across the street from Indian Heritage, is another moderately priced Indian restaurant with a lunch buffet and halal food.

**Tandoor** (Central HCMC map; ☎ 824 4839; 103 Ð Vo Van Tan, District 3) can also be recommended for North Indian dishes.

For really cheap Indian food, you have to go the atmospheric, cult-like **canteen** (66 Ð Dong Du), behind the Saigon Central Mosque. The fish curry (21,000d) is lovely. Meals come with all-you-can-eat-rice, plus free ice tea and bananas.

**Cholon** District 5 is the place to eat Chinese food. All of the following places can be found on the Cholon map.

**My Huong** (☎ 856 3586; 131 Ð Nguyen Tri Phuong) is a highly popular indoor-outdoor restaurant serving up all kinds of good food, including superb noodle soup with duck.

**Tiem An Nam Long** (cnr ÐL Hau Giang & Ð Pham Dinh Ho; most dishes under US$2), near the Binh Tay Market, is noteworthy for tasty wok-fried dishes and sidewalk seating. There is an English menu with no prices, but everything is cheap.

**Tiem Com Chay Phat Huu Duyen** (☎ 857 7919; 527 Ð Nguyen Trai; open 7.30am-10pm) is a tiny but very popular Chinese vegetarian restaurant near the southern end of Ð Phuoc Hung.

**Hong Phat** (206 Ð Hai Thuong Lai Ong) serves cheap and delicious noodle soup with pork.

**Dong Nguyen** (89-91 Đ Chau Van Liem) specialises in tasty roast chicken with rice (com ga).

## French Restaurants

HCMC has an astounding selection of great French restaurants, from the inexpensive and casual bistro to the exquisite top-notch restaurant. Unless stated otherwise, all of the following can be found on the Dong Khoi Area map.

**Bibi's** (☎ 829 5783; 8A/8D2 Đ Thai Van Lung) is a great place in the city for casual French bistro fare. The bright Mediterranean decor creates a pleasant atmosphere.

**Augustin** (☎ 829 2941; 10 Đ Nguyen Thiep; most mains 50,000d) is another popular spot serving great bistro-style food. Many consider it the city's best cheap French restaurant.

**La Fourchette** (☎ 836 9816; 9 Đ Ngo Duc Ke) is another excellent choice, right in the city centre, for authentic but inexpensive French food.

**Le Jardin** (☎ 825 8465; 31 Đ Thai Van Lung; mains 35,000-55,000d; open 7.30pm-10.30pm daily) is a charming little bistro attached to the **Institute of Cultural Exchange with France** (Idecaf; cnr Đ Thai Van Lung & Đ Le Thanh Ton). The shaded terrace café in the front garden is a popular hangout for local French expats.

**L'Etoile** (Central HCMC map; ☎ 829 7939; 180 ĐL Hai Ba Trung; all-day set meals 15,000d) serves terrific, if a bit expensive, French food. Their all-day 'fast food' menu, however, is a good value. A set meal could be roast chicken with a choice of five sauces, a mini salad and baguette.

**Camargue** (☎ 824 3148; 16 Đ Cao Ba Quat) is housed in a stunning restored villa with an open-air terrace. The menu includes a variety of gourmet dishes complimented by a well-appointed wine list. Camargue, also home to trendy **Vasco's Bar**, is a short walk from the Municipal Theatre.

**Le Caprice** (☎ 822 8337; 5B Đ Ton Duc Thang), for those who prefer a fancy French restaurant, is a very high-class place on the top floor of the Landmark building; the views are stunning and so are the prices.

**Au Manoir du Khai** (☎ 823 8873; 251 Đ Dien Bien Phu) is Vietnam's first attempt at five-star Continental dining. Ironically, it was opened by a local Vietnamese fashion guru named Khai (the brains behind Khai Silk and a handful of other superb restaurants and hotels in Vietnam). Well, at least the chef is French. This lavish villa sits in a high-walled enclosure in District 3.

## Other European

**Central Area** Unless stated otherwise, all of the following places to eat can be found on the Dong Khoi Area map.

**Skewers** (☎ 829 2216; 8A/1/D2 Đ Thai Van Lung; mains 25,000-50,000d; open 11.30am-2pm & 6pm-11.30pm Mon-Sat, 6pm-11.30pm Sun) specialises in Mediterranean cuisine, notably barbecued skewered meat. There's a nice atmosphere and an open kitchen so you can watch the cooks at work.

**Annie's Pizza** (☎ 839 2577; 45 Đ Mac Thi Buoi; pizzas 40,000-70,000d) does a good pepperoni and mozzarella, and if you don't feel like trekking over there, just phone from your hotel for a free delivery.

**Givral** (☎ 829 2747; 169 Đ Dong Khoi) is a long-standing restaurant across the street from the Continental Hotel. It has a good selection of cakes, home-made ice cream and yoghurt. There's also French, Chinese, Vietnamese and Russian cuisine on the menu.

**Brodard Café** (☎ 822 3966; 131 Đ Dong Khoi) is an oldie but goodie restored into a Parisian-style café. This place is known for good café food and its prices are OK. It's across Đ Dong Khoi from the Caravelle Hotel, on the corner of Đ Nguyen Thiep.

**Why Not?** (☎ 822 6138; 24 Đ Thai Van Lung) is a French-run place worth checking out for good European food, or a game of darts.

**Santa Lucia** (☎ 822 6562; 14 ĐL Nguyen Hué) has some of the best authentic Italian food in town.

**Gartenstadt** (☎ 822 3623; 34 Đ Dong Khoi) is a popular expat lunch spot, in the same area as Santa Lucia, with good German fare.

**Mogambo's Cafe** (☎ 825 1311; 20 Đ Thi Sach) is noted for its Polynesian decor and juicy burgers. This place is a restaurant, pub and hotel.

**Globo Cafe** (☎ 822 8855; 6 Đ Nguyen Thiep), one of the trendier bar-restaurants in the Dong Khoi area, does good French and Italian dishes, including praiseworthy pizza.

**Cafe Latin** (☎ 822 6363; 25 Đ Dong Du) is Vietnam's first tapas bar. It has a superb wine collection and fresh bread that's baked daily. The attached **Billabong Restaurant** is notable for Aussie and international cuisine.

**Paloma Cafe** (☎ 829 5813; 26 Đ Dong Khoi) is a stylish place with wooden tables, white tablecloths, polished silverware and aggressive air-con. It's very popular with young, fashion-conscious Vietnamese.

**Hoa Vien** (Central HCMC map; ☎ 825 8605; 30 Đ Mac Dinh Chi) is HCMC's only Czech restaurant. The big drawcard is the draught Pilsner Urquell beer.

**ABC Restaurant** (Central HCMC map; ☎ 823 0388; 172H Đ Nguyen Dinh Chieu, District 3; mains 25,000-50,000d; open till 3am), a trendy joint for cheap and tasty late-night chow, has indoor and outdoor seating and an extensive menu – from noodle soup and fresh seafood to juicy steaks.

**Maxim's Dinner Theatre** (☎ 829 6676; 15 Đ Dong Khoi; open 11am-11pm), a Saigon institution next to the Majestic Hotel, is very much what the name implies – a restaurant with **music performances**. The menu includes Chinese and French food. The sea slug and duck web has disappointed a few travellers, but the creme caramel and vanilla soufflé should not be missed. Maxim's is usually empty until dinner, even though it's open for lunch. Reservations are recommended on weekends.

**Pham Ngu Lao Area** Đ Pham Ngu Lao and Đ De Tham form the axis of HCMC's budget-eatery haven. Western backpackers easily outnumber the Vietnamese here, and indeed the locals have trouble figuring out the menus (banana muesli does not translate well into Vietnamese).

Don't let the name fool you. **Good Morning Vietnam** (☎ 837 1894; 197 Đ De Tham; pasta 30,000-50,000d, pizza 35,000-80,000d; open 8am-10pm) is the best of Pham Ngu Lao's Italian eateries. It serves authentic northern Italian dishes (pasta is served with freshly grated parmesan cheese) and great home-made ice cream.

**Kim Cafe** (☎ 836 8122; e cafekim@ hcm.vnn.vn; 266 Đ De Tham), a long-running hang-out for budget travellers, is a good place to eat and meet people.

**Sinh Cafe** (☎ 836 7338, fax 836 9322; e sinhcafevietnam@hcm.vnn.vn; 246-248 Đ De Tham), near Kim Cafe, is a nearly identical setup.

**Saigon Cafe** (195 Đ Pham Ngu Lao), on the corner of Đ De Tham, is worthy of a plug and, along with **Cafe 333** (also on Đ De Tham), is where the largest numbers of expats congregate.

**Linh Cafe** (291 Đ Pham Ngu Lao) is another travellers café run by friendly people. You can also book tours here.

**Café Duy Linh** (Đ Pham Ngu Lao) nearby is a cosy little café serving great sandwiches and light meals. It is one of the few places in the neighbourhood with any form of attractive decor.

## Seafood
**Miss Saigon** (Dong Khoi Area map; ☎ 823 8174; 86 Đ Le Thanh Ton; mains 35,000-50,000d; open 10.30am-11pm), a stone's throw from the Rex Hotel, serves respectable seafood and Vietnamese dishes. You can dine in air-con comfort or outside, surrounded by views of past and present – on one side an army tank and on the other a row of tennis courts, where HCMC's nouveaux riches swat at fuzzy yellow balls in the heat.

## Vegetarian
On the first and 15th days of the lunar month, **food stalls** around the city – especially in the markets – serve vegetarian versions of meaty Vietnamese dishes. While these stalls are quick in serving customers, a little patience is required – the cooking takes time, but it's worth the wait.

The largest concentration of vegetarian restaurants is in and around the Pham Ngu Lao area.

**Bodhi Tree** (☎ 837 1910; 174/6 Đ Pham Ngu Lao) is in a narrow alley, two streets east of Đ De Tham. The food is excellent and very cheap. One neighbour has cleverly opened up a place with the exact same name.

The owners of **Tin Nghia** (☎ 821 2538; 9 ĐL Tran Hung Dao; open 7am-8.30pm; mains 7000-10,000d) are strict Buddhists. This simple establishment is about 200m from Ben Thanh Market. It serves an assortment of cheap and delicious traditional Vietnamese food prepared with tofu, mushrooms and other vegetables.

**Dinh Y** (☎ 836 7715; 171B Đ Cong Quynh; mains 5000-10,000d), just across the road from Thai Binh Market, is run by a Cao Dai family. It serves very inexpensive and delicious vegie fare, and has an English menu.

## Cafés, Coffee Shops & Ice Cream

All of the following establishments are in the Dong Khoi area.

**Dong Du Cafe** (☎ 823 2414; 31 Đ Dong Du) is a stylish place in the city centre that does great coffee and home-made ice cream.

**Paris Deli** (☎ 829 7533; 31 Đ Dong Khoi • ☎ 821 6127; Saigon Centre, 65 ĐL Le Loi) is the place to head for freshly baked pastries and bread. Both branches do eat-in, take-away and deliveries.

**Chi Lang Cafe** (cnr Đ Dong Khoi & Đ Le Thanh Ton) is a long-running coffee shop in the Dong Khoi area in a park-like setting and indoor-outdoor seating.

**Kem Bach Dang** (☎ 829 2707; 28 & 28 ĐL Le Loi) serves some of the best ice cream (kem) in Vietnam. The twin branches are located across Đ Pasteur from each other and have very reasonable prices. A speciality is ice cream served in a baby coconut with candied fruit on top (kem trai dua).

**Fanny** (☎ 821 1633; 29/31 Đ Ton That Thiep; ice-cream scoop 6000-15,000d; open 8am-11pm) serves up excellent Franco-Vietnamese ice cream, including many tropical fruit flavours. It's just east of Đ Pasteur, in the same French villa as the popular Temple Club.

## Food Stalls

Noodle soup is available all day long at **street stalls** everywhere. A large bowl of delicious beef-noodle soup usually costs between 7000d and 15,000d. Just look for the signs that say 'pho'.

**Pho 2000** (Central HCMC map; ☎ 822 2788; 1-3 Đ Phan Chu Trinh; pho 14,000d; open 6am-2am daily), near the Ben Thanh Market, is a good place to sample your first bowl of pho – it was good enough for the former US president, Bill Clinton, to stop in and slurp down a bowl.

**Pho Hoa** (Central HCMC map; ☎ 829 7943; 260C Đ Pasteur; soup 15,000d; open 5am-midnight) is another popular place with foreigners in District 3.

Markets always have a side selection of food items, often on the ground floor or in the basement. Clusters of food stalls can be found in Thai Binh, Ben Thanh and Andong Markets.

> The best noodle soup that I had was in the Ben Thanh Market itself. The food stalls inside the market were clean, the food fresh and the soup very tasty. It's also a fun place to eat because you quickly become the centre of attention.
> **John Lumley-Holmes**

Sandwiches with a French look and a very Vietnamese taste are sold by street vendors. Fresh baguettes are stuffed with something resembling pâté (don't ask) and cucumbers seasoned with soy sauce. A sandwich costs between 5000d and 15,000d, depending on what it's filled with. Sandwiches filled with imported French cheese cost a little more. A la carte baguettes usually cost between 500d and 2000d.

## Self-Catering

Simple meals can easily be assembled from fruit, vegetables, French bread, croissants, cheese and other delectables sold in the city's markets and at street stalls. But avoid the unrefrigerated chocolate bars – they taste like they were left behind by the Americans in 1975.

There are plenty of places in the city centre to shop for food and drinks, including supermarkets, shopping malls and small import shops. Two good supermarkets near the Pham Ngu Lao area are **Hanoi Mart** and

**Co-op Mart** on Đ Cong Quynh (see the Central HCMC map).

**Chez Guido** (☎ 840 4448, ☎ 898 3747; fax 803 5101; mains 30,000-50,000d open 9.30am-11pm) is a hugely popular home-delivery service, the perfect place to call when you just don't feel like going out to eat. It has an extensive menu with everything from pizza and pasta to burgers, plus a full range of Vietnamese dishes. Call and ask for a menu to be faxed over to your hotel.

## ENTERTAINMENT

War-time Saigon was known for its riotous nightlife. Liberation in 1975 put a real dampener on evening activities, but the pubs and discos have recently staged a comeback. However, periodic 'crack-down, clean-up' campaigns – allegedly to control drugs, prostitution and excessive noise – continue to keep the city's nightlife on the quiet side.

### Pubs & Bars

**Central Area** HCMC's widest and wildest variety of nightlife choices is in the central area, notably around Đ Dong Khoi. In 2001 local authorities, as part of their war against 'social evils,' required all bars and clubs to close by midnight. Enforcement varies from day to day, but you can always depend on the pubs in the Pham Ngu Lao area to stay open till the wee hours.

**AQ Cafe** (Central HCMC map; ☎ 829 8344; 39 Đ Mac Dinh Chi; open 7am-midnight) is housed in a 100 year-old wooden house across the street from Hoa Vien. This dimly-lit, indoor-outdoor café features a spacious garden and cool jazz music. Coffee (8000d) and beer (15,000d) are served here.

**No 5 Ly Tu Trong** (Central HCMC map; ☎ 825 6300; 5 Đ Ly Tu Trong) is a stylish place that's run by a long-term Swiss expat named Heinz. The decor of this restored French-colonial villa is stylish and sleek. Good music, tasty food and beer, pool and friendly staff all contribute to the pleasant atmosphere.

**Underground** (Dong Khoi Area map; ☎ 829 9079; 69 Đ Dong Khoi; open 10am-midnight daily), located in the basement of the Lucky Plaza building, is another popular gathering spot for expats and travellers alike. This spacious London tube–theme bar has a good happy hour and excellent pizza.

**Sheridan's Irish House** (Dong Khoi Area map; ☎ 823 0973; 17/13 Đ Le Thanh Ton; open 11am-late daily) is a traditional Irish pub beamed straight from the backstreets of Dublin.

The legendary imitation **Hard Rock Cafe** (Dong Khoi Area map; 24 Đ Mac Thi Buoi) has been around for years. The real Hard Rock had plans to open in town a few years back, but perhaps these guys scared 'em off? You're not likely to spot any music celebrities here, but if you're looking for a 'Hard Rock Cafe – Saigon' T-shirt, this is the place to get it.

**Chu** (Dong Khoi Area map; ☎ 822 3907; 158 Đ Dong Kho), near the Notre Dame Cathedral, may be the only bar in the world advertising 'wine, noodles and cigars'. And that's what they've got: respectable wine; an interesting twist on Vietnamese noodle soup, pho bo with sirloin; and a climate-controlled stock of Cuban cigars. There's live music Monday to Saturday from 9pm.

---

### Sunday Night Live

The Dong Khoi area is the place to be on Sunday and holiday nights (and lately Saturday nights as well). The streets are jam-packed with young people cruising (di troi) on bicycles and motorbikes. Everyone is dressed in their fashionable best (often with the price tag still attached). The mass of slow-moving humanity is so thick on Đ Dong Khoi that you may have to wait until dawn to get across the street. It is utter chaos at intersections, where eight, 10 or more lanes of two-wheeled vehicles intersect without the benefit of traffic lights, safety helmets or sanity.

Near the Municipal Theatre, fashionably dressed young people take a break from cruising to watch the endless procession, lining up along the street next to their cycles. The air is electric with the glances of lovers and animated conversations among friends. Everyone is out to see and be seen – it's a sight you shouldn't miss.

**Blue Gecko Bar** *(Dong Khoi Area map; ☎ 824 3483; 31 Đ Ly Tu Trong; open 5pm-late)* is a major Aussie hang-out with the coldest beer in town. The music is good – if you like Australian music – and you can shoot pool or watch sport on the half-dozen or so TVs.

**Wild West Saloon** *(☎ 829 5127; 33 ĐL Hai Ba Trung)* and the **Wild Horse Bar** *(Đ Thai Van Lung)* are two places, both in the Dong Khoi area, done up in a full-blown cowboy motif. In a similar vein, **Tex-Mex Cantina** *(Dong Khoi Area map; ☎ 829 5950; 24 Đ Le Thanh Ton)*, notable for its pool table, also features Mexican food with a Texan twist.

**Q Bar** *(Dong Khoi Area map; ☎ 823 3479; 7 Lam Son Square; open 6pm-midnight)* attracts a far more sophisticated clientele for drinks (20,000d to 50,000d). This is where HCMC's fashion-conscious, alternative crowd hangs out. The stylish decor is cool and minimalist, and the music is hip. Q Bar is on the side of the Municipal Theatre, directly across from the Caravelle Hotel.

**Temple Club** *(Dong Khoi Area map; ☎ 829 9244; 29 Đ Ton That Thiep; mains 40,000-70,000d)* is another chic spot with brick walls and a Chinese atmosphere. There is a comfy lounge area in the back and a restaurant in the front. Like the decor? You can take some of it home with you – all of the furniture here is for sale! Drinks are priced between 25,000d and 70,000d.

**Saigon Saigon,** in the Caravelle Hotel, is a fancy bar with the best views in the city centre.

**Pham Ngu Lao Area** When it comes to nightlife, the Pham Ngu Lao area has several hot spots, in addition to the always hoppin' travellers-café scene.

**Allez Boo Bar** *(☎ 837 2505; 187 Đ Pham Ngu Lao; beer from 12,000d; mains from 20,000d; open 7pm-late)*, on the corner of Đ De Tham, is a dimly lit, bamboo-decorated place that's always packed with backpackers and always blaring music.

**Sahara Music Cafe** *(☎ 837 8084; 277 Đ Pham Ngu Lao; open 9am-late)* is more pool-bar than restaurant, but it also serves good Western food (soups, salads, burgers and sandwiches). It is definitely one of the more stylish places in the neighbourhood.

**Long Phi Bar** *(☎ 836 9319; 163 Đ Pham Ngu Lao; open 11am-6am)* is one of the longest-running in Pham Ngu Lao's dark and decadent pub scene.

**Bar Rolling Stones** *(177 Đ Pham Ngu Lao)*, **Backpacker Bar** *(169 Đ Pham Ngu Lao)*, also known as Lost in Saigon, and **Guns & Roses Bar** *(207 Đ Pham Ngu Lao)* are virtual clones of the Long Phi Bar. All are known for their pool tables, *very* late hours (some never close!) and party atmosphere.

## Nightclubs

The following dance clubs can be found on the Dong Khoi Area map.

Dance places in Vietnam have a tendency to change with the wind, but **Apocalypse Now** *(☎ 824 1463; 2C Đ Thi Sach)* is one exception to the rule. It's been around forever and leads the pack for those seeking a naughtier edge. The music is loud, and the patrons are from all walks of life and apocalyptically rowdy.

**Shark** *(☎ 825 7783; 5-15 Đ Ho Huan Nghiep; cover charge US$4)* is one of the hottest dance spots in the city centre, and well-located near the river – the cover charge entitles you to one free drink.

**Maya** *(☎ 829 5180; 6 Đ Cao Ba Quat; mains from 25,000d; open 5pm-late)* is the place for Latin dancing, and salsa lessons are held. It can also be recommended for serving respectable South American food and tapas, and the decor is chic.

**Sam Son** *(☎ 829 1219; 28A ĐL Le Loi)* is a routine Vietnamese disco five nights a week, but on Tuesday and Friday nights it has long been a gathering place for HCMC's gay men.

## Cinemas

There are plenty of cinemas *(rap)* in the city centre, the problem for foreigners is that very few films are shown in languages other than Vietnamese. One notable exception is the **Diamond Cinema** *(163 Đ Dong Khoi)* in the Diamond Plaza building.

French films are screened at the French cultural centre **Idecaf** *(☎ 822 4577; 31 Đ*

*Thai Van Lung)* on Tuesday at 8pm. You can also rent and watch French-language movies and videos here for under US$1.

## Water Puppets

This art really comes from the north, but in recent years has been introduced to the south because it has been such a hit with tourists. There are two venues to see water puppets in HCMC. At the **War Remnants Museum** (☎ 829 0325; 28 Đ Vo Van Tan) and **History Museum** (☎ 829 8146) schedules vary, but shows tend to start when a group of five or more customers has assembled.

## Municipal Theatre

Municipal Theatre *(Nha Hat Thanh Pho; ☎ 829 9976; Đ Dong Khoi)* is between the Continental and Caravelle Hotels. Each week it offers a different programme, which may be Eastern European–style gymnastics, classical music or traditional Vietnamese theatre. There is typically some kind of performance at 8pm; inquire at the theatre, or ask at your hotel.

If there's nothing happening when you're in town, you can at least pop into the modish **Q Bar**, around the side of the building, for a drink.

## Conservatory of Music

Performances of both traditional Vietnamese and Western classical music are held at the Conservatory of Music *(Nhac Vien Thanh Pho Ho Chi Minh; ☎ 824 3774; 112 Đ Nguyen Du; performances at 7.30pm Mon-Fri Mar-May & Oct-Dec)* near Reunification Palace. Students aged seven to 16 attend the conservatory, which performs all the functions of a public school in addition to providing instruction in music. The music teachers here were trained in France, Britain and the USA, as well as the former Eastern Bloc. The school is free, but most of the students come from well-off families, who can afford to purchase the prerequisite musical instruments.

## Saigon Race Track

When South Vietnam was liberated in 1975, one of the Hanoi government's policies was to ban debauched, capitalistic pastimes such as gambling. Horse-racing tracks – mostly found in the Saigon area – were shut down. However, the government's need for hard cash has caused a rethink.

Dating from around 1900, Saigon Race Track *(Cau Lac Bo The Thao Phu To; ☎ 855 1205; 2 Đ Le Dai Hanh, District 11; open 12.30pm-4.30pm Sat & Sun)* reopened in 1989. Like the state lottery, the race track is extremely lucrative. But grumbling about just where the money is going has been coupled with widespread allegations about the drugging of horses. The minimum legal age for jockeys is 14 years; most look like they are about 10.

The overwhelming majority of gamblers are Vietnamese though there is no rule prohibiting foreigners from joining in the fun of risking your dong. The minimum legal bet is 2000d and, for the high rollers hoping to become a dong billionaire, the sky's the limit. For the cheapskates, there is an entry fee of 1000d.

Plans to introduce off-track betting have so far not materialised. However, illegal book-making (bets can be placed in gold!) does offer one form of competition to the government-owned monopoly.

## SHOPPING
## Arts & Crafts

In the last few years the free market in tourist junk has been booming – you can pick up a useful item such as a lacquered turtle with a clock in its stomach or a ceramic Buddha that whistles the national anthem. And even if you're not the sort of person who needs a wind-up mechanical monkey that plays the cymbals, there is sure to be something that catches your eye.

It is actually amazing what people do with soda cans: cutting them up and moulding them into cyclos, helicopters, aircraft carriers, you name it!

The Dong Khoi area has a reputation as the centre for handicrafts, but most shop owners drive a hard bargain. The Pham Ngu Lao area also has good pickings.

**Nguyen Freres** *(☎ 822 9654; 2A ĐL Le Duan; open 9am-7pm)* is a sprawling antique shop across from the Sofitel Plaza Saigon. It specialises in furniture, and silk.

**Oriental Home** (☎ 910 0194; w www .madeinvietnamcollection.com; 2A ĐL Le Duan; 9am-7.30pm) is in the same building and sells furniture, statues, ceramics, lamps and lanterns, and stone carvings.

**Indochine House** (29 Đ Dong Du), smack dab in the city centre, is worth checking out for both antiques and reproduction furniture.

**Authentique Interiors** (Đ Dong Khoi) this an interesting place to look for locally made home furnishings.

## Galleries
HCMC is brimming with art galleries. Both **Blue Space Gallery** (☎ 821 3695; 1A Đ Le Thi Hong Gam; open 9am-6pm daily), inside the Fine Arts Museum and **Vinh Loi Gallery** (☎ 930 5006, fax 930 3154; 41 Đ Ba Huyen Thanh Quan, District 3; open 9am-6pm daily) are top-end galleries and can be found on the Central HCMC map.

## Carved Seals
No bureaucracy, communist or otherwise, can exist without the official stamps and seals that provide the raison d'être for legions of clerks. This need is well-catered to by the numerous shops strung out along the street just north of the New World Hotel (opposite side of ĐL Ham Nghi and just west of Ben Thanh Market). In Cholon, you can find shops making these seals along Đ Hai Thuong Lai Ong.

Most Vietnamese also own carved seals bearing their name (an old tradition borrowed from China). You can have one made too, but ask a local to help translate your name into Vietnamese. You might want to get your seal carved in Cholon using Chinese characters; these are certainly more artistic (though less practical) than the Romanised script used by the Vietnamese today.

## Clothing
At the budget end of the scale, T-shirts are available from vendors along ĐL Nguyen Hué in the city centre, or Đ De Tham in the Pham Ngu Lao area. Expect to pay about

US$2 for a printed T-shirt, or US$3 to US$5 for an embroidered one.

There are numerous tailors in District 1 and also in Cholon; several upmarket hotels have in-house tailors.

Women's ao dai, the flowing silk blouse (with a slit up the sides) and trousers (see the boxed text 'Camau Saves the Ao Dai' in the Mekong Delta chapter), are tailored at shops in and around Ben Thanh Market and around the Rex and Continental Hotels. There are also male ao dai available – these are a looser fit and come with a silk-covered head wrap to match the top of the outfit.

**Ao Dai Si Hoang** (☎ 829 9156; e siho ang@hcm.vnn.vn; 36 Ly Tu Trong • ☎ 822 5271; 260 Đ Pasteur, District 3) has two locations that are nice and reliable, if slightly expensive, places to have ao dai made.

## Coffee
Vietnamese coffee is prime stuff and is amazingly cheap, if you know where to buy it. The best grades are from Buon Ma Thuot and the beans are roasted in butter. Obviously, price varies according to the quality and also with the seasons. You can buy whole beans or have them ground for no extra charge.

The city's major markets have the best prices and widest selection. We scored some top-grade caffeine in Ben Thanh Market, also the best place to find the peculiar coffee-drippers used by the Vietnamese. Get a stainless-steel one, which are easier to use than the cheaper aluminium ones. Also look in the market for a coffee grinder if you're buying whole beans.

## Stamps & Coins
Immediately to your right, as you enter the **main post office** (2 Cong Xa Paris), is a counter selling stationery and some decent stamp collections. Also as you face the entrance from the outside, to your right are a few stalls that have stamp collections and other goods such as foreign coins and banknotes. You can even find stuff from the former South Vietnamese regime. Prices are variable: about 30,000d will get you a respectable set of late-model stamps already

mounted in a book, but the older and rarer collections cost more.

Many **bookshops** and **antique shops** along Đ Dong Khoi sell overpriced French Indochinese coins and banknotes as well as packets of Vietnamese stamps.

## Markets

The **street market** that runs along Đ Huynh Thuc Khang and Đ Ton That Dam in the Dong Khoi area sells everything. The area used to be known as the 'electronics black market', until early 1989, when it was legalised. It's now generally called **Huynh Thuc Khang Street Market**, although it doesn't have an official name.

You can still buy electronic goods of all sorts – from mosquito zappers to video cassette recorders – but the market has expanded enormously to include clothing, washing detergent, lacquerware, condoms, pirated cassettes, posters of Ho Chi Minh, Michael Jackson and Mickey Mouse, smuggled bottles of Johnny Walker, Chinese-made 'Swiss' army knives and just about everything to satisfy your material needs.

**Ben Thanh Market** HCMC has a number of huge indoor markets selling all manner of goods. These are some of the best places to pick up conical hats and *ao dai*. The most central of these is the recently renovated Ben Thanh Market *(Cho Ben Thanh; cnr ĐL Le Loi, ĐL Ham Nghi, ĐL Tran Hung Dao & Đ Le Lai)*. The market and surrounding streets make up one of the city's liveliest areas. Everything that's commonly eaten, worn or used by the Saigonese is available here: vegetables, fruits, meat, spices, biscuits, sweets, tobacco, clothing, hats, household items, hardware and so forth. The legendary slogan of US country stores applies equally well here: 'If we don't have it, you don't need it.'

Known to the French as Les Halles Centrales, it was built in 1914 from reinforced concrete; the central cupola is 28m in diameter. The main entrance, with its belfry and clock, has become a symbol of HCMC.

Opposite the belfry, in the centre of the traffic roundabout, is an equestrian statue of Tran Nguyen Hai, the first person in Vietnam to use carrier pigeons. At the base of it, on a pillar, is a small white bust of Quach Thi Trang, a Buddhist woman killed during antigovernment protests in 1963.

Nearby, food stalls sell inexpensive meals, and consequently there are also two notable restaurants very near the market that are worth looking for: **Pho 2000** for noodle soup, and **Nam Giao** for Hué-style dishes – see Places to Eat for the low-down. Ben Thanh Market is 700m southwest of the Rex Hotel.

**The Old Market** Despite the name, this is not the place to find antiques. Nor is it the place to look for electronics or machinery (go to Dan Sinh Market for these). Rather, the Old Market is where you can most easily buy imported (or black-market?) food, wine, shaving cream, shampoo etc. However, if its Vietnamese name, Cho Cu, is written or pronounced without the correct tones it means 'penis'; your cyclo driver will no doubt be much amused if you say that this is what you're looking for. Perhaps directions would be better – the Old Market is on the north side of ĐL Ham Nghi between Đ Ton That Dam and Đ Ho Tung Mau.

**Dan Sinh Market** Also known as the War Surplus Market, this is the place to shop for a chic pair of combat boots or rusty dog tags. It's also the best market for electronics and other types of imported machinery – you could easily renovate a whole villa from the goods on sale.

The market *(Central HCMC map; 104 Đ Yersin)* is next to Phung Son Tu Pagoda. The front part is filled with stalls selling automobiles and motorbikes, but directly behind the pagoda building you can find reproductions of what seems to be second-hand military gear.

Stall after stall sells everything from handy gas masks and field stretchers to rain gear and mosquito nets. You can also find canteens, duffel bags, ponchos and boots. Anyone planning on spending time in Rwanda or New York City should consider picking up a second-hand flak jacket (prices are good).

**Binh Tay Market** Cholon's main market is Binh Tay Market (Cho Binh Tay; ĐL Hau Giang), an architectural masterpiece that's Chinese in style, with a great clock tower in the centre. Much of the business here is wholesale. Binh Tay Market is about 1km southwest of Đ Chau Van Liem, although on the Cholon map it's technically about one block outside of Cholon in District 6.

**Andong Market** Cholon's other indoor market, Andong (Greater HCMC map), is very close to the intersection of ĐL Tran Phu and ĐL An Duong Vuong. This market is four storeys high and is packed with shops. The 1st floor has heaps of clothing, including imported designer jeans from Hong Kong, the latest pumps from Paris and ao dai. The basement is a gourmet's delight of small restaurants – a perfect place to pig out 'on a shoestring'.

## GETTING THERE & AWAY
### Air
The following list of HCMC's Asia-region airline offices, are all found in District 1. To locate other international airlines, check the listings in the Guide or Time Out.

**Cathay Pacific Airways** (☎ 822 3203, fax 825 8276) 58 Đ Dong Khoi

**Japan Airlines** (☎ 821 9099, fax 821 9097) 115 Đ Nguyen Hué

**Korean Air** (☎ 824 2878, fax 824 2877) 34 Đ Le Duan

**Lao Aviation** (☎ 822 6990, fax 822 6990) 181 Đ Hai Ba Trung

**Malaysia Airlines** (☎ 824 2885, fax 824 2884) 132-134 Đ Dong Khoi

**Pacific Airlines** (☎ 823 1285, fax 822 8130) 2 Đ Dong Khoi

**Singapore Airlines** (☎ 823 1588, fax 823 1554) Saigon Tower, 29 ĐL Le Duan

**Thai Airways International** (☎ 829 2809, fax 822 3465) 65 Đ Nguyen Du

**Vietnam Airlines** (☎ 829 2118, fax 823 0273) 116 ĐL Nguyen Hué

Tan Son Nhat Airport was one of the three busiest airports in the world during the late 1960s. The runways are still lined with lichen-covered, mortar-proof aircraft retaining walls, hangars and other military structures.

You must reconfirm all reservations for flights out of the country. For more details on international air travel see the Getting There & Away chapter.

Nearly all domestic flights are operated by Vietnam Airlines. Pacific Airlines also flies the HCMC–Hanoi and HCMC–Danang route. See the Getting Around chapter for details on routes and schedules.

### Bus
Intercity buses depart from and arrive at a variety of stations around HCMC. **Cholon bus station** is the most convenient place to get buses to Mytho and other Mekong Delta towns. It's on Đ Le Quang Sung, one street north of the sprawling Binh Tay Market.

Less convenient than Cholon bus station, **Mien Tay station** (Ben Xe Mien Tay; ☎ 825 5955) nevertheless has even more buses to areas south of HCMC (basically the Mekong Delta). This huge station is about 10km west of HCMC in An Lac, a part of Binh Chanh district (Huyen Binh Chanh). Buses and minibuses from Mien Tay serve most towns in the Mekong Delta.

Buses to points north of HCMC leave from **Mien Dong bus station** (Ben Xe Mien Dong; ☎ 829 4056), in Binh Thanh district about 5km from central HCMC on National Hwy 13 (Quoc Lo 13), the continuation of Đ Xo Viet Nghe Tinh.

The station is just under 2km north of the intersection of Đ Xo Viet Nghe Tinh and Đ Dien Bien Phu.

There are services from Mien Dong to Buon Ma Thuot (15 hours), Danang (26 hours), Haiphong (53 hours), Nha Trang (11 hours), Hanoi (49 hours), Hué (29 hours), Pleiku (22 hours), Vinh (42 hours), Quang Ngai (24 hours), Qui Nhon (17 hours), Nam Dinh (47 hours) and Tuy Hoa (12 hours). Most buses leave daily from 5am to 5.30am.

Buses to Tay Ninh, Cu Chi and points northeast of HCMC depart from the **Tay Ninh bus station** (Ben Xe Tay Ninh; ☎ 849 5935), in Tan Binh district west of the centre. To get there, head all the way out on Đ Cach Mang Thang Tam. The station is about 1km past where Đ Cach Mang Thang Tam merges with Đ Le Dai Hanh.

## Train

**Saigon train station** (*Ga Sai Gon;* ☎ *823 0105; 1 Đ Nguyen Thong; ticket office open 7.15am-11am & 1pm-3pm daily*) is in District 3. Trains from here serve cities along the coast north of HCMC.

Train tickets can be purchased from the **Saigon Railways Tourist Services** (☎ *08-836 7640, fax 836 9031; 275C Đ Pham Ngu Lao*) or from most travel agents.

For details on the *Reunification Express* service see the Getting Around chapter.

## Car

Inquire at almost any tourist café, travel agent or your hotel to arrange car rental. The agencies in the Pham Ngu Lao area generally offer the lowest prices.

## Boat

There is regular hydrofoil service to Vung Tao (1¼ hours, adult/child US$10/5) from the **Bach Dang jetty** on Đ Ton Duc Thang. For more information contact **Vina Express** (☎ *821 5609*) at the jetty.

In Vung Tao you board the hydrofoil at **Cau Da pier**, opposite the Hai Au Hotel. **Vina Express** (☎ *856530*) has a Vung Tao office by the pier.

Cargo ferries to the Mekong Delta depart from the **dock** (☎ *829 7892*) at the river end of ĐL Ham Nghi. There is a daily service to the provinces of An Giang and Vinh Long and to the towns of Ben Tre (8 hours), Camau (30 hours; once every 4 days), Mytho (6 hours; departs 11am) and Tan Chau. Buy your tickets on the boat. Simple food may be available on board. Be aware that these ancient vessels lack the most elementary safety gear, such as life jackets.

## Organised Tours

There are surprisingly few day tours of HCMC itself available, though any local travel agent can come up with something in exchange for a fee. Hiring a cyclo for a half-day or full day of sightseeing is another interesting option, but be sure to agree on the price before setting out (most drivers charge around US$1 per hour).

There are heaps of tours to the outlying areas such as the Cu Chi Tunnels, Tay Ninh and the Mekong Delta. Some tours are day trips and other are overnighters. The cheapest tours by far are available from cafés and agencies in the Pham Ngu Lao area (see Travel Agencies earlier in this chapter).

## GETTING AROUND
### To/From the Airport
**Tan Son Nhat Airport** is 7km from central HCMC. Metered taxis are your best bet and cost around 60,000d (US$4) between the airport and the city centre. You'll be enthusiastically greeted by a group of taxi drivers after you exit the terminal; most are OK, but make sure that: the driver agrees to use the meter and it is switched on after you get in the car. The final fare shouldn't go much over 60,000d to get to the city centre.

Be aware that taxi drivers will probably recommend a 'good and cheap' hotel, and deliver you to a hotel for a commission; if you don't know where you are going, this is not a bad system per se. Problems arise, however, when you ask a taxi driver to take you to a place that doesn't pay commission. The driver may tell you the hotel is closed, burned down, is dirty and dangerous, or anything to steer you somewhere else.

If you're travelling solo and without much baggage, a motorbike taxi is an option for getting to/from the airport. Drivers hang out near the airport car park and typically ask around US$3 to go to the city centre. If you take a motorbike taxi to Tan Son Nhat, you may have to walk the short distance from the airport gate to the terminal. Private cars can bring you into the airport, but must drop you off at the domestic terminal, only a minute's walk from the international terminal.

To get to the airport you can call a taxi (see the Taxi section). Some cafés in the Pham Ngu Lao area do runs to the airport – these places even have sign-up sheets, where you can book share taxis for US$2 per person.

Also see the boxed text 'Your Friendly Taxi Driver' earlier in this chapter.

## Bus

Few tourists make use of the city buses; they are safer than cyclos, though less aesthetic. Now that HCMC's People's Committee has resolved to phase out cyclos, some money is finally being put into the badly neglected public-transport system.

At present, there are only a few bus routes, though more undoubtedly will be added. No decent bus map is available and bus stops are mostly unmarked, so it's worth summarising the main bus lines.

Saigon–Cholon buses depart from **Me Linh Square** (by the Saigon River) and continue along ĐL Tran Hung Dao to Binh Tay Market in Cholon, then return along the same route. The buses running this route have air-con and video movies and the driver is well dressed! All this for 3000d. Buy your ticket on board from the attendant.

Mien Dong–Mien Tay buses depart from **Mien Dong bus station** (northeast HCMC), pass through Cholon and terminate at **Mien Tay bus station** on the western edge of town. The fare is 5000d.

## Car & Motorbike

Travel agencies, hotels and cafés are all in the car rental business. Most vehicles are relatively recent Japanese- or Korean-made machines – everything from subcompacts to minibuses. However, it's occasionally possible to enjoy a ride in a vintage vehicle from the 1950s or '60s. Not long ago, classic American cars (complete with tail fins and impressive chrome fenders) were popular as 'wedding taxis'. Prestige these days, however, means a white Toyota. Nevertheless, some of the old vehicles can be hired for excursions in and around HCMC. You'll also see the occasional French-built Renault or Citroën. The former Soviet Union chips in with Ladas, Moskviches and Volgas.

If you're brave, you can rent a motorbike and really earn your 'I Survived Saigon' T-shirt. Many say this is the fastest and easiest way to get around the city and that's probably true as long as you don't crash into anything.

Motorbike rentals are ubiquitous in places where tourists tend to congregate – the

Pham Ngu Lao area is as good as any. Ask at the cafés.

A 50cc motorbike can be rented for US$5 to US$8 per day. Before renting one make sure it's rideable, and if you're wise you'll wear a helmet.

**Saigon Scooter Centre** (☎ 0903-845819, fax 511 3491; e ssc@hcm.vnn.vn, w www .saigonscootercentre.com; 174 Đ Bui Thi Xuan, Tan Binh district) offers rentals of classic Vespa and Lambretta scooters, and a range of other well-maintained bikes. Daily rental rates start from US$10 and discounts are offered for longer rentals. For an extra fee, it'll provide a one-way service, with a pick-up of the bikes anywhere in Vietnam.

## Taxi

Metered taxis cruises the streets, but it's often easier to phone for one. Several companies in HCMC offer metered taxis and they charge almost exactly the same rates. The flagfall is from 8000d to 12,000d for the first kilometre. Most rides in the city centre cost less than 25,000d.

The following contact details are for HCMC's main taxi companies.

| | |
|---|---|
| Ben Thanh Taxi | ☎ 842 2422 |
| Mai Linh Taxi | ☎ 822 6666 |
| Red Taxi | ☎ 844 6677 |
| Saigon Taxi | ☎ 842 4242 |
| Vina Taxi | ☎ 811 1111 |

## Motorbike Taxi

A quick (if precarious) way around town is to ride on the back of a *xe om* (sometimes called a *honda om*). You can either try to flag someone down or ask a Vietnamese to help find one for you. *Xe om* drivers usually hang out on street corners, looking for passengers. The accepted rate is comparable to cyclos.

## Cyclo

You can hail a cyclo along major thoroughfares almost any time of the day or night. In HCMC, many of the drivers are former South Vietnamese army soldiers and quite a few know at least basic English, while others are quite fluent. Each driver has a story of war, 're-education', persecution and poverty to tell (see the boxed text 'Life on the Streets').

In an effort to control HCMC's rapidly growing traffic problems, there are presently 51 streets on which cyclos are prohibited to ride. As a result, your driver must often take a circuitous route to avoid these trouble spots; the police will not hesitate to fine him. For the same reason, the driver may not be able to drop you off at the exact address you want, but will bring you to the nearest side street. Try to have some sympathy since it is not the driver's fault. Perhaps the authorities would have served the city better by allowing the quiet and atmospheric cyclos carte blanche and forcing the smoke-spewing cars to take an alternative route.

Short hops around the city centre should cost around 5000d, and definitely no more than 10,000d; District 1 to central Cholon costs about 20,000d. Overcharging tourists is the norm, so negotiate a price beforehand and

## Life on the Streets

Through the smoke and pollution, groups of battered old men lean against their cyclos – three-wheeled rickshaws, operated by pedal-power, with a seat attached to the front. Win, a veteran cyclo driver recently explained, 'It's hard to earn one's living. You have to bend in order to pedal and earn a little money.'

Before the American War many cyclo drivers were doctors, teachers or journalists, but like many of their friends they were punished for siding with the Americans. After the cease-fire, tens of thousands of them were stripped of their citizenship and sent to re-education camps for seven years or more. Over 20 years later, it is still impossible for them to return to the jobs they are qualified to do and, as most do not have an official residence permit (which means they cannot own property or a business), it's technically illegal for them to be in the city. Many of these men have never had families because they could not afford (or were not permitted by the government) a home to live in.

Around the restaurants, hotels, nightclubs and karaoke bars of central Ho Chi Minh City (HCMC), it's hard to miss them in their worn clothes and tar-stained sandals (from years of being caught in the jagged chains of the cyclos). The comings and goings at hotels are a constant form of entertainment (and business) for HCMC's cyclo drivers. Nothing misses their sharp eyes. Their courteous propositions hide their desire to establish your first name and claim you as 'their property' while you're in town. Once known, cries of your name across crowded streets will hound you as the determined drivers compete for your business.

Cyclo drivers are, however, excellent city guides – they know every corner of the city and can give you a potted history of the key sites. Also, the front seat of a cyclo really is one of the best ways to see HCMC – but it does take some getting used to. In heavy traffic it's like riding a roller coaster at a fairground; the traffic races towards you from every direction at startling speeds and, just when you think you are surely going to die, your cyclo driver slips into a gap that magically appears in the traffic, while you thank the gods that you are still in one piece.

Tourists love to reverse roles and have a go in the saddle, mistakenly thinking that it is easy to spend one's day cycling from place to place, but their opinions quickly change. In most cases they find the cyclos too hard to peddle and, if they advance at all, they don't get very far on the uneven, potholed roads.

The drivers' homes are usually a street corner, which are made colourful and interesting by using wooden tables and small, multicoloured, plastic footstools, which support them only inches off the ground. Their floor is broken up bits of pavement slabs and their 'drinks cabinet' (a street stall or two) nestles just behind them.

After a day's sightseeing, they might invite you to join them for either a whisky in a Coke bottle or the local beer Ba, Ba, Ba – pronounce it 'baa-baa-baa' slowly because in Vietnamese it can also sound like you are saying 'three old women'!. An evening with these guys is always worthwhile.

**Juliet Coombe**

have the exact change ready. You can rent a cyclo for around US$1 per hour, a fine idea if you will be doing a lot of touring; most cyclo drivers around the Pham Ngu Lao area can produce a sample tour programme.

Enjoy cyclos while you can, as the municipal government intends to phase them out.

### Xe Lam

Tiny three-wheeled vehicles, *xe lam* (otherwise known as Lambrettas) connect the various bus stations. There is a useful *xe lam* stop on the northwest corner of Ð Pham Ngu Lao and Ð Nguyen Thai Hoc (see the Pham Ngu Lao Area map), where you can catch a ride to the Mien Tay bus station for the Mekong Delta.

### Bicycle

A bicycle is a great, if slow, way to get around the city and see things. Bikes can be rented from a number of places – many hotels, cafés and travel agencies can help you.

A good place to buy a decent (ie, imported) bicycle is at the shops near the New World Hotel on Ð Le Thanh Ton, a short walk from the Pham Ngu Lao area (see the Central HCMC map). For cheap (and poorly assembled) domestic bicycles and parts, try the ground floor of the **Tax Department Store** (*Dong Khoi Area map; cnr ÐL Nguyen Hué & ÐL Le Loi*).

For on-the-spot bicycle repairs, look for an upturned army helmet and a hand pump sitting next to the curb.

Bicycle parking lots are usually just roped-off sections of pavement. For about 1000d you can safely leave your bicycle (theft is a big problem). Your bicycle will have a number written on the seat in chalk or stapled to the handlebars and you'll be given a reclaim chit – don't lose it! If you come

back and your bicycle is gone, the parking lot is supposedly required to replace it.

### Boat

It's easy to hire a motorised 5m-long boat to tour the Saigon River. There's always someone hanging around looking to charter a boat. Ask them to bring it to you (they can easily do this), rather than you going to the boat.

The price should be around US$5 per hour for a small boat or US$10 to US$15 for a larger, faster craft. Interesting destinations for short trips include Cholon (along Ben Nghe Channel) and the zoo (along Thi Nghe Channel). Note that both channels are fascinating, but filthy – raw sewage is discharged into the water. Tourists regard the channels as a major attraction, but the government considers them an eyesore and has already launched a programme to move residents out. The channels will eventually be filled in and the water diverted into underground sewerage pipes.

For longer trips up the Saigon River, it is worth chartering a fast speedboat from Saigon Tourist. Although these cost US$20 per hour, you'll save money as a cheap boat takes at least five times longer for the same journey. Splitting the cost between a small group of travellers makes sense and it can be more fun boating with others. Although cruising the Saigon River can be interesting, it pales in comparison with the splendour of the canals in the Mekong Delta (see the Mekong Delta chapter for details.

Since you hire boats by the hour, some will go slowly because they know the meter is running. You might want to set a time limit at the start.

Ferries across the Saigon River leave from the **dock** at the foot of ÐL Ham Nghi and run every half-hour or so (4.30am to 10.30pm).

# Around Ho Chi Minh City

## CU CHI TUNNELS

☎ 08

The town of Cu Chi has now become a district of greater Ho Chi Minh City (HCMC), and has a population of about 200,000 (it had about 80,000 residents during the American War). At first glance, there is little evidence here to indicate the intense fighting, bombing and destruction that went on in Cu Chi during the war. To see what went on, you have to dig deeper – underground.

The tunnel network of Cu Chi became legendary during the 1960s for its role in facilitating Viet Cong (VC) control of a large rural area only 30km to 40km from HCMC. At its height, the tunnel system stretched from the South Vietnamese capital to the Cambodian border; in the district of Cu Chi alone, there were more than 250km of tunnels. The network, parts of which were several storeys deep, included innumerable trap doors, specially constructed living areas, storage facilities, weapons factories, field hospitals, command centres and kitchens.

The tunnels made possible communication and coordination between the VC-controlled enclaves, isolated from each other by South Vietnamese and American land and air operations. They also allowed the VC to mount surprise attacks wherever the tunnels went – even within the perimeters of the US military base at Dong Du – and to disappear into hidden trapdoors without a trace. After ground operations against the tunnels claimed large numbers of US casualties and proved ineffective, the Americans resorted to massive firepower, eventually turning Cu Chi's 420 sq km into what the authors of *The Tunnels of Cu Chi* (Tom Mangold & John Penycate) have called 'the most bombed, shelled, gassed, defoliated and generally devastated area in the history of warfare'.

Cu Chi has become a place of pilgrimage for Vietnamese school children and communist-party cadres. Parts of this remarkable tunnel network (which are enlarged and upgraded versions of the real thing) are open

### Highlights

- Crawl through the network of narrow tunnels dug by the Viet Cong at Cu Chi
- Observe one of the serene daily worship services at the colourful Caodai temple in Tay Ninh
- Get off the beaten track and into the wilds of Cat Tien National Park, a bird-watcher's paradise
- Make the journey to the remote Con Dao Islands, where prison history meets a natural paradise

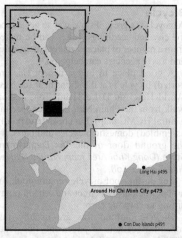

Long Hai p495

Around Ho Chi Minh City p479

Con Dao Islands p491

to the public. The unadulterated tunnels, though not actually closed to tourists, are hard to get to and are rarely visited.

There are numerous war cemeteries all around Cu Chi.

### History

The tunnels of Cu Chi were built over a period of 25 years, which began some time in the late 1940s. They were the improvised response of a poorly equipped peasant army to its enemy's high-tech ordnance, helicopters, artillery, bombers and chemical weapons.

The Viet Minh built the first dugouts and tunnels in the hard, red earth of Cu Chi (the area is ideal for the construction of tunnels) during the war against the French. The excavations were used mostly for communication between villages and to evade French army sweeps of the area.

When the VC's National Liberation Front (NLF) insurgency began in earnest around 1960, the old Viet Minh tunnels were repaired and new extensions were excavated. Within a few years the tunnel system assumed enormous strategic importance, and most of Cu Chi district and the nearby area came under firm VC control. In addition, Cu Chi was used as a base for infiltrating intelligence agents and sabotage teams into Saigon. The stunning attacks in the South Vietnamese capital during the 1968 Tet Offensive were planned and launched from Cu Chi.

In early 1963, the Diem government implemented the botched Strategic Hamlets Program, under which fortified encampments, surrounded by many rows of sharp bamboo spikes, were built to house people 'relocated' from communist-controlled areas. The first strategic hamlet was in Ben Cat district, next to Cu Chi. Not only was the programme carried out with incredible incompetence, alienating the peasantry, but the VC launched a major effort to defeat it; the VC was able to tunnel into the hamlets and control them from within. By the end of 1963, the first showpiece hamlet had been overrun.

The series of setbacks and defeats suffered by the South Vietnamese forces in the Cu Chi area rendered a complete VC victory by the end of 1965 a distinct possibility. In the early months of that year, the guerrillas boldly held a victory parade in the middle of Cu Chi town. VC strength in and around Cu Chi was one of the reasons the Johnson

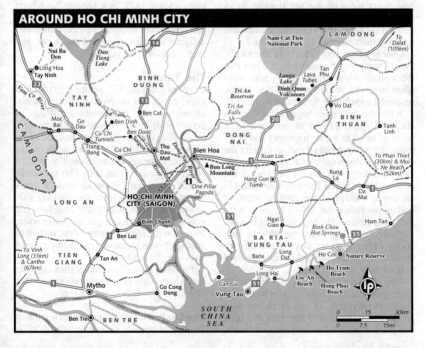

**AROUND HO CHI MINH CITY**

administration decided to involve US troops in the war.

To deal with the threat posed by VC control of an area so near the South Vietnamese capital, one of the USA's first actions was to establish a large base camp in Cu Chi district. Unknowingly, they built it right on top of an existing tunnel network. It took months for the 25th Division to figure out why they kept getting shot at in their tents at night.

The US and Australian troops tried a variety of methods to 'pacify' the area around Cu Chi, which came to be known as the Iron Triangle. They launched large-scale ground operations involving tens of thousands of troops, but failed to locate the tunnels. To deny the VC cover and supplies, rice paddies were defoliated, huge swathes of jungle bulldozed, and villages evacuated and razed. The Americans also sprayed chemical defoliants on the area from the air and then, a few months later, ignited the tinder-dry vegetation with gasoline and napalm. But the intense heat interacted with the wet tropical air in such a way as to create cloudbursts that extinguished the fires. The VC remained safe and sound in their tunnels.

Unable to win this battle with chemicals, the US army began sending men down into the tunnels. These 'tunnel rats', who were often involved in underground fire fights, sustained appallingly high casualty rates.

When the Americans began using German shepherd dogs, trained to use their keen sense of smell to locate trapdoors and guerrillas, the VC put out pepper to distract the dogs. They also began washing with American toilet soap, which gave off a scent the canines identified as friendly. Captured US uniforms, which had the familiar smell of bodies nourished on US-style food, were put out to confuse the dogs further. Most importantly, the dogs were not able to spot booby traps. So many dogs were killed or maimed that their horrified handlers refused to send them into the tunnels.

The USA declared Cu Chi a free-strike zone: minimal authorisation was needed to shoot at anything in the area, random artillery was fired into the area at night, and pilots were told to drop unused bombs

and napalm there before returning to base. But the VC stayed put. Finally, in the late 1960s, American B-52s carpet-bombed the whole area, destroying most of the tunnels along with everything else around. The gesture was militarily useless by then because the USA was already on its way out of the war. The tunnels had served their purpose.

The VC guerrillas serving in the tunnels lived in extremely difficult conditions and suffered horrific casualties. Only about 6000 of the 16,000 cadres who fought in the tunnels survived the war. In addition, thousands of civilians in the area were killed. Their tenacity was extraordinary considering the bombings, the pressures of living underground for weeks or months at a time, and the deaths of countless friends and comrades.

The villages of Cu Chi have since been presented with numerous honorific awards, decorations and citations by the government, and many have been declared 'heroic villages'. Since 1975, new hamlets have been established and the population of the area has more than doubled; however chemical defoliants remain in the soil and water, and crop yields are still poor.

## The Tunnels

Over the years the VC, learning by trial and error, developed simple but effective techniques to make their tunnels difficult to detect or disable. Wooden trapdoors were camouflaged with earth and branches; some were booby-trapped. Hidden underwater entrances from rivers were constructed. To cook, they used 'Dien Bien Phu kitchens', which exhausted the smoke through vents many metres away from the cooking site. Trapdoors were installed throughout the network to prevent tear gas, smoke or water from moving from one part of the system to another. Some sections were even equipped with electric lighting.

Presently, two of the tunnel sites are open to visitors. One is near the village of Ben Dinh and the other is at Ben Duoc.

**Ben Dinh** This small, renovated section of the tunnel system *(admission 65,000d)* is

Long Xuyen's floating market

Women working in rice paddies, An Giang province

Rice crops in rural Vietnam, An Giang province

Naked rice terraces after the harvest

JOHN BANAGAN

Women of the Mekong Delta wearing traditional *ao dai*

CRAIG PERSHOUSE

A woman on the crocodile-infested Hau Giang River, Mekong Delta

JOHN ELK III

Herding ducks in Chau Doc

near the village of Ben Dinh, 50km from HCMC. In one of the classrooms at the visitors centre, a large map shows the extent of the network (the area shown is in the northwestern corner of greater HCMC). The tunnels are marked in red, VC bases are shown in light grey and the light blue lines are rivers (the Saigon River is at the top). Fortified villages held by South Vietnamese and American forces are marked in grey, while blue dots represent the American and South Vietnamese military posts that were supposed to ensure the security of nearby villages. The dark blue area in the centre is the base of the American 25th Infantry Division. Most prearranged tours do not take you to this former base, but it is not off limits and you can arrange a visit if you have your own guide and driver.

To the right of the large map are two cross-section diagrams of the tunnels. The bottom diagram is a reproduction of one used by General William Westmoreland, the commander of American forces in Vietnam (1964–8). For once, the Americans seemed to have had their intelligence information right (though the tunnels did not pass under rivers, nor did the guerrillas wear headgear underground).

The section of the tunnel system presently open to visitors is a few hundred metres south of the visitors centre. It snakes up and down through various chambers along its 50m length. The unlit tunnels are about 1.2m high and 80cm across. A knocked-out M-41 tank and a bomb crater are near the exit, which is in a reforested eucalyptus grove.

**Ben Duoc** These are not the genuine tunnels, but a full reconstruction (admission 65,000d) for the benefit of visitors. The emphasis here is more on the fun fair (tourists are given the chance to imagine what it was like to be a guerrilla) and attracts far more Vietnamese than foreigner visitors.

## Cu Chi War History Museum

This museum is not actually at the tunnel sites, it's just off the main highway in the central area of the town of Cu Chi. Sadly, the Cu Chi War History Museum (Nha Truyen Thong Huyen Cu Chi; admission US$1) is rather disappointing and gets few visitors (most day tours from HCMC do not make a stop here).

It's a small museum and almost all explanations are in Vietnamese. One English explanation attached to a canoe reads:

Mr Nguyen Van Tranh's boat. He now is living in hamlet Mui Con, Phuoc Hiep village. During the wars against the French colonialists and the American imperialists, he was using this boat for transporting food and weapons, as well as carrying revolutionary cadres to and fro.

There is a collection of some gruesome photos showing civilians who were severely wounded or killed after being attacked by American bombs or burned with napalm. A painting on the wall shows American soldiers armed with rifles being attacked by Vietnamese peasants armed only with sticks. A sign near the photos formerly read (in

---

## Shoot!

Ever wondered what it feels like to fire an AK-47? Well, if you visit the Cu Chi Tunnels, you'll have a chance to find out.

There are target shooting ranges at both the Ben Dinh and Ben Duoc tunnel sites, where tourists line up in droves to handle the military big guns. You can choose from an array of weapons: the M-1, M-3, M-4, M-14, M-16, M-30 and M-60, and the ever-popular Russian AK-47 rifle. If rifles aren't your cup of tea, there are plenty of handguns (including Colt 45s for you Clint Eastwood wannabes), 30-60 machine guns and shot guns to boot.

Hearing protection is mandatory and the congenial, fatigues-clad firearm staff will provide you with a good pair of DJ-style headphones to wear. Still, if you have a set with you, we recommend you wear a pair of earplugs underneath – these guns are loud!

The cost of US$1 per bullet is a relative bargain, considering it's the only opportunity most people will ever get.

Vietnamese) 'American conquest and crimes', but this was changed in 1995 to read 'Enemy conquest and crimes'. Apparently, some effort is being made to tone down the rhetoric in anticipation of receiving more US visitors.

One wall of the museum contains a long list of names, all VC guerrillas killed in the Cu Chi area. An adjacent room of the museum displays recent photos of prosperous farms and factories, an effort to show the benefits of Vietnam's economic reforms. There is also an odd collection of pottery and lacquerware with no explanations attached. In the lobby, near the entrance, is a statue of Ho Chi Minh with his right arm raised, waving hello.

### Getting There & Away

Cu Chi district covers a large area, parts of which are as close as 30km to central HCMC. The Cu Chi War History Museum is closest to the city, while the Ben Dinh and Ben Duoc tunnels are about 50km and 70km respectively from central HCMC by highway. There is a back road that reduces the distance significantly, though it means driving on bumpy dirt roads.

**Organised Tours** An organised tour is the easiest way to visit the Cu Chi tunnels and is not at all expensive. Most of the cafés on Đ Pham Ngu Lao in HCMC run combined full-day tours to the Cu Chi tunnels and Caodai Great Temple (see Caodai Holy See in the Tay Ninh section) for around US$4.

**Bus** The buses going to Tay Ninh pass though Cu Chi, but getting from the town of Cu Chi to the tunnels by public transport is impossible – it's 15km, so you'll have to hire a motorbike. (See Getting There & Away section in the Tay Ninh section for details.)

**Taxi** Hiring a taxi in HCMC and driving out to Cu Chi is not all that expensive, especially if the cost is split by several people. For details on hiring a car or taxi, see Getting Around in the Ho Chi Minh City chapter.

A visit to the Cu Chi tunnel complex can easily be combined with a stop at the headquarters of the Caodai sect in Tay Ninh. A taxi for an all-day excursion to both should cost about US$40.

## TAY NINH

☎ 066 • pop 41,300

Tay Ninh town, the capital of Tay Ninh province, serves as the headquarters of one of Vietnam's most interesting indigenous religions, Caodaism. The Caodai Great Temple at the sect's Holy See is one of the most striking structures in all of Asia. Built between 1933 and 1955, the temple is a rococo extravaganza combining the conflicting architectural idiosyncrasies of a French church, a Chinese pagoda, Hong Kong's Tiger Balm Gardens and Madame Tussaud's Wax Museum.

Tay Ninh province, northwest of HCMC, is bordered by Cambodia on three sides. The area's dominant geographic feature is Nui Ba Den (Black Lady Mountain), which towers above the surrounding plains. Tay Ninh province's eastern border is formed by the Saigon River. The Vam Co River flows from Cambodia through the western part of the province.

Because of the once-vaunted political and military power of the Caodai, this region was the scene of prolonged and heavy fighting during the Franco–Viet Minh War. Tay Ninh province served as a major terminus of the Ho Chi Minh Trail during the American War, and in 1969 the VC captured Tay Ninh town and held it for several days.

During the period of tension between Cambodia and Vietnam in the late 1970s, the Khmer Rouge launched a number of cross-border raids into Tay Ninh province, and committed atrocities against civilians. Several cemeteries around Tay Ninh are stark reminders of these events.

### Information

**Tay Ninh Tourist** (☎ 822 376, fax 822470; e tanitour@hcm.vnn.vn; 210 Đ 30/4) is located in the Hoa Binh Hotel.

### Caodaism

Caodaism (Dai Dao Tam Ky Pho Do) is the outcome of an attempt to create the ideal religion through the fusion of the secular and religious philosophies of the East and West. The result is a potpourri that includes bits and pieces of most of the religious philosophies known in Vietnam during the early 20th century: Buddhism, Confucianism, Taoism, native Vietnamese spiritualism, Christianity and Islam.

The term Caodai (meaning high tower or palace) is a euphemism for God. The hierarchy of the sect, whose priesthood is non-professional, is partly based on the structure of the Roman Catholic Church.

**History** Caodaism was founded by the mystic Ngo Minh Chieu (also known as Ngo Van Chieu and born 1878), a civil servant who once served as district chief of Phu Quoc Island. He was widely read in Eastern and Western religious works and became active in seances, at which his presence was said to greatly improve the quality of communication with the spirits. Around 1919 he began to receive a series of revelations from Caodai in which the tenets of Caodai doctrine were set forth.

Caodaism was officially founded as a religion in a ceremony held in 1926. Within a year, the group had 26,000 followers. Many of the sect's early followers were Vietnamese members of the French-colonial administration. By the mid-1950s, one in eight southern Vietnamese was a Caodai and the sect was famous worldwide for its imaginative garishness. The Caodai had established a virtually independent feudal state in Tay Ninh province and retained enormous influence over its affairs for the next two decades. But in 1954, British author Graham Greene, who had once considered converting to Caodaism, wrote in the *Times* of London: 'What on my first two visits has seemed gay and bizarre (is) now like a game that has gone on too long.'

The Caodai also played a significant political and military role in South Vietnam from 1926 to 1956, when most of the 25,000-strong Caodai army, which had been given support by the Japanese and later the French, was incorporated into the South Vietnamese Army. During the Franco–Viet Minh War,

Caodai munitions factories specialised in making mortar tubes out of automobile exhaust pipes.

Because they refused to support the VC during the American War – and despite the fact that they had been barely tolerated by the Saigon government – the Caodai feared the worst after Reunification. Indeed, all Caodai lands were confiscated by the new communist government and four members of the sect were executed in 1979. However, in 1985 the Holy See and some 400 temples were returned to Caodai control.

Caodaism is strongest in Tay Ninh province and the Mekong Delta, but Caodai temples can be found throughout southern and central Vietnam. Today, there are an estimated three million followers of Caodaism, most of them concentrated in the Mekong Delta region. Vietnamese who fled abroad after the communists came to power have spread the Caodai religion to Western countries, though their numbers are not large.

**Philosophy** Much of Caodai doctrine is drawn from Mahayana Buddhism, mixed with Taoist and Confucian elements (Vietnam's 'Triple Religion'). Caodai ethics are based on the Buddhist ideal of 'the good person', but incorporate traditional Vietnamese taboos and sanctions as well.

The ultimate goal of the disciple of Caodaism is to escape the cycle of reincarnation. This can only be achieved by the performance of certain human duties, including first and foremost following the prohibitions against killing, lying, luxurious living, sensuality and stealing.

The main tenets of Caodaism include believing in one god, the existence of the soul and the use of mediums to communicate with the spiritual world. Some of the Caodai practices include priestly celibacy, vegetarianism, communication with spirits through seances, reverence for the dead, maintenance of the cult of ancestors, fervent proselytising and sessions of meditative self-cultivation.

Following the Chinese duality of Yin and Yang, there are two principal deities, the female Mother Goddess and the male God (a duality that somewhat complicates the belief in 'one god'). There is a debate among the Caodai as to which deity was the primary source of creation.

According to Caodaism, history is divided into three major periods of divine revelation. During the first period, God's truth was revealed to humanity through Laotse (Laozi) and figures associated with Buddhism, Confucianism and Taoism. The human agents of revelation during the second period were Buddha (Sakyamuni), Mohammed, Confucius, Jesus and Moses. The Caodai believe that their messages were corrupted because of the human frailty of the messengers and their disciples. They also believe that these revelations were limited in scope, intended to be applicable only during a specific age to the people of the area in which the messengers lived.

Caodaism sees itself as the product of the 'Third Alliance Between God and Man', the third and final revelation. Disciples believe that Caodaism avoids the failures of the first two periods because it is based on divine truth as communicated through the spirits that serve as messengers of salvation and instructors of doctrine. Spirits who have been in touch with the Caodai include deceased Caodai leaders, patriots, heroes, philosophers, poets, political leaders and warriors, as well as ordinary people. Among the contacted spirits who lived as Westerners are Joan of Arc, René Descartes, William Shakespeare (who hasn't been heard from since 1935), Victor Hugo, Louis Pasteur and Vladimir Ilyich Lenin. Because of his frequent appearances to Caodai mediums at the Phnom Penh mission, Victor Hugo was posthumously named the chief spirit of foreign missionary works.

Communication with the spirits is done in Vietnamese, Chinese, French and English and the methods of receiving messages from the spirits illustrate the influence of both East Asian and Western spiritualism. Sometimes, a medium holds a pen or Chinese calligraphy brush. In the 1920s, a 66cm-long wooden staff known as a *corbeille à bec* was used; mediums held one end while a crayon attached to the other wrote out the spirits' messages. The Caodai also use what is known as *pneumatographie*, in which a blank slip of paper is sealed in an envelope and hung above the altar; when the envelope is taken down, there is a message on the paper.

Most of the sacred literature of Caodaism consists of messages communicated to its leaders during seances held between 1925 and 1929. From 1927 to 1975, only official seances held at Tay Ninh were considered reliable and divinely ordained by the Caodai hierarchy, though dissident groups continued to hold seances that produced communications contradicting accepted doctrine.

The Caodai consider vegetarianism to be of service to humanity because it does not involve harming fellow beings during the process of their spiritual evolution. They also see vegetarianism as a form of self-purification and several different vegetarian regimens are followed by Caodai disciples. The least rigorous diet involves eating vegetarian food six days a month, but priests must be full-time vegetarians.

The clergy is open to both men and women (but women are prevented from reaching the highest levels), although when male and female officials of equal rank are serving in the same area, male clergy are in charge. Female officials wear white robes and are addressed with the title *huong*, which means perfume; male clergy are addressed as *thanh*, meaning pure. Caodai temples are constructed so that male and female disciples enter on opposite sides; women worship on the left, men on the right.

All Caodai temples observe four daily ceremonies, which are held at 6am, noon, 6pm and midnight. These rituals, during which dignitaries wear ceremonial dress and hats, include offerings of incense, tea, alcohol, fruit and flowers. All Caodai altars have the 'divine eye' above them, which became the religion's official symbol after Ngo Minh Chieu saw it in a vision he had, while on Phu Quoc Island.

## Caodai Holy See

The Caodai Holy See, which was founded in 1926, is 4km east of Tay Ninh, in the village of Long Hoa.

The complex includes the Caodai Great Temple (Thanh That Cao Dai), administrative offices, residences for officials and adepts, and a hospital of traditional Vietnamese herbal medicine, which people from all over the south travel to for treatment. After reunification, the government 'borrowed' parts of the complex for its own use (and perhaps to keep an eye on the sect).

Prayers are conducted four times daily in the Great Temple, though they may be suspended during Tet. It's worth visiting during prayer sessions (the one at noon is most popular with tour groups from HCMC), but take care not to disturb the worshippers. Only a few hundred priests participate in weekday prayers, but during festivals, several thousand priests, dressed in special white garments, may attend. The Caodai clergy has no objection to your photographing temple objects, but you cannot photograph people without their permission, which is seldom granted. However, you can photograph the prayer sessions from the upstairs balcony, an apparent concession to the troops of tourists who come here every day.

It is important that guests wear modest and respectful attire inside the temple; that means no shorts or sleeveless T-shirts, although sandals are OK since you have to take them off anyway before you enter.

Set above the front portico of the Great Temple is the 'divine eye'. Americans often comment that it looks as if it were copied from the back of a US$1 bill (raising the question of why a divine eye is on US currency). Lay women enter the Great Temple through a door at the base of the tower on the left. Once inside, they walk around the outside of the colonnaded hall in a clockwise direction. Men enter on the right and walk around the hall in an anticlockwise direction. Shoes and hats must be removed upon entering the building. The area in the centre of the sanctuary (between the pillars) is reserved for Caodai priests.

A mural in the front entry hall depicts the three signatories of the 'Third Alliance Between God and Man': the Chinese statesman and revolutionary leader Dr Sun Yatsen (1866–1925) holds an ink stone; while the Vietnamese poet Nguyen Binh Khiem (1492–1587) and French poet and author Victor Hugo (1802–85) write 'God and Humanity' and 'Love and Justice' in Chinese and French (Nguyen Binh Khiem writes with a brush; Victor Hugo uses a quill pen). Nearby signs in English, French and German each give a slightly different version of the fundamentals of Caodaism.

The Great Temple is built on nine levels, which represent the nine steps to heaven. Each level is marked by a pair of columns. At the far end of the sanctuary, eight plaster columns entwined with multicoloured dragons support a dome representing the heavens – as does the rest of the ceiling. Under the dome is a giant star-speckled blue globe with the 'divine eye' on it.

The largest of the seven chairs in front of the globe is reserved for the Caodai pope, a position that has remained unfilled since 1933. The next three chairs are for the three men responsible for the religion's law books. The remaining chairs are for the leaders of the three branches of Caodaism, represented by the colours yellow, blue and red.

On both sides of the area between the columns are two pulpits similar in design to *minbar,* found in mosques. During festivals, the pulpits are used by officials to address the assembled worshippers. The upstairs balconies are used if the crowd overflows.

Up near the altar are barely discernible portraits of six figures important to Caodaism: Sakyamuni (Siddhartha Guatama, the founder of Buddhism), Ly Thai Bach (Li Taibai, a fairy from Chinese mythology), Khuong Tu Nha (Jiang Taigong, a Chinese saint), Laozi (the founder of Taoism), Quan Cong (Guangong, Chinese God of War) and Quan Am (Guanyin, the Goddess of Mercy).

## Long Hoa Market

Long Hoa Market *(open 5am-6pm daily)* is several kilometres south of the Caodai Holy See complex. This large market sells meat, food staples, clothing and pretty much everything else you would expect to find in a rural marketplace. Before reunification, the Caodai sect had the right to collect taxes from the merchants here.

## Places to Stay & Eat

**Hoa Binh Hotel** (☎ 821315, fax 822345; 210 Đ 30 Thang 4; air-con rooms 220,000-310,000d), 5km from the Caodai Great Temple, is the main place in town where travellers can stay, though few spend the night (most sign up for day-trips). It's a classic Russian-style concrete slab, and rates include breakfast.

**Anh Dao Hotel** (☎ 827306; Đ 30 Thang 4; twins/doubles 170,000/250,000d), about 500m west of Hoa Binh Hotel, is old and rather nondescript, though the rates here also include a decent breakfast.

Both hotels have in-house **restaurants**, but there's cheaper and better Vietnamese food right next door to the Hoa Binh Hotel at **Thanh Thuy** (☎ 827606; Đ 30 Thang 40; dishes 25,000-45,000d). You won't find prices on the menu, but the cost is reasonable and portions are large.

If you're heading to Tay Ninh with your own wheels, one of the better restaurants to look for along National Hwy 22 is called **Kieu** (☎ 850357; 9/32 Hwy 22), around 5km from Caodai Temple towards HCMC. The food is cheap and good, and the brick kilns out back are interesting to poke around in after lunch.

## Getting There & Away

**Bus** There are buses from HCMC to Tay Ninh that leave from the **Tay Ninh bus station** (Ben Xe Tay Ninh) in Tan Binh district and **Mien Tay bus station** in An Lac.

Tay Ninh is situated on National Hwy 22 (Quoc Lo 22), 96km from HCMC. (The road passes through **Trang Bang**, the place where the famous photograph of a severely burnt young girl, screaming and running, was taken by a journalist during an American napalm attack, during the American War.) There are several **Caodai temples** along National Hwy 22, including one (which was under construction in 1975) that was heavily damaged by the VC.

**Taxi** An easy way to get to Tay Ninh is by chartered taxi, perhaps on a day trip that includes a stop in Cu Chi. An all-day return trip to both should cost about US$40.

## NUI BA DEN
☎ 066

Nui Ba Den (Black Lady Mountain; admission adults/children 6000/2000d) is 15km northeast of Tay Ninh. The mountain rises 850m above the rice paddies, corn, cassava (manioc) and rubber plantations of the surrounding countryside. Over the centuries, Nui Ba Den has served as a shrine for various peoples of the area, including the Khmer, Chams, Vietnamese and Chinese, and there are several **cave temples** on the mountain. The summits of Nui Ba Den are much cooler than the rest of Tay Ninh province, most of which is only a few dozen metres above sea level.

Nui Ba Den was used as a staging area by both the Viet Minh and the VC, and was the scene of fierce fighting during the French and American Wars. At one time there was a US Army firebase and relay station at the summit, which was later, ironically, defoliated and heavily bombed by US aircraft.

The name Black Lady Mountain is derived from the legend of Huong, a young woman who married her true love despite the advances of a wealthy mandarin. While her husband was away doing military service, she would visit a magical statue of Buddha at the mountain's summit. One day, Huong was attacked by kidnappers, but preferring death to dishonour, she threw herself off a cliff. She then reappeared in the visions of a monk who lived on the mountain, and he told her story.

The hike from the base of the mountain to the main temple complex and back takes about 1½ hours. Although steep in parts, it's not a difficult walk – plenty of old women in sandals make the journey to worship at the temple. Around the temple complex a few stands sell snacks and drinks.

If you'd like more exercise, a walk to the summit and back takes about six hours. The fastest (and easiest) way is via the **chair lift** (one-way/return adults 25,000/45,000d, children 10,000/20,000d) that shuttles the pilgrims up and down the hill.

At the base of the mountain there are lakes and manicured gardens, and as with many such sacred sites in Asia, a strange mix of religion and tacky amusement park–style attractions: paddle boats for hire; ceramic beaver trash bins; and a choo-choo tram car (tickets 1000d) to save the weary a bit of walking.

Very few foreign tourists make it to the mountain, but it's a very popular place for Vietnamese people. Owing to the crowds, visiting on Sunday or during a holiday or festival is a bad idea.

### Place to Stay & Eat
**Nha Nghi Thuy Dong** (☎ 624204, bungalows 120,000d), about 500m inside the main entrance gate, rents grotty A-frame bungalows on the lakeside. Each bungalow has a basic squat toilet, and showers are outside.

A cheaper alternative if you're planning to overnight is to camp. There are simple two-person A-frame **platform tents** (50,000d) with mat floors, a fan and a hammock strung below, as well as freestanding **camping tents** (70,000d) for rent near the bungalows. Shared toilets and cold showers are available for 500d or you can shower for free at the nearby Trung Pagoda, where the monks will prepare you traditional vegetarian meals with a day's advance notice (the food is free, but a contribution is suggested).

**Thuy Dong Restaurant** is attached to the bungalow complex and has nice views of the lake. There are also a few nearby **food stalls** and kiosks selling cold drinks and souvenirs. Outside the main gate in the parking area, look for the **stalls** selling locally produced dried fruit and sweets made from coconuts and sugar cane.

### Getting There & Away
There is no public transport to Nui Ba Den. If you're not travelling with your own wheels, the easiest way to reach the site is to take a *xe om* from Tay Ninh for around 50,000d.

## ONE PILLAR PAGODA
The official name of this interesting pagoda is Nam Thien Nhat Tru, but everyone calls it the One Pillar Pagoda of Thu Duc (*Chua Mot Cot Thu Duc;* ☎ 08-896 0780; 1/91 Đ *Nguyen Du).*

The One Pillar Pagoda of Thu Duc is modelled after Hanoi's One Pillar Pagoda, though the two structures are not identical. Hanoi's original pagoda was built in the 9th century, but was destroyed by the French and rebuilt by the Vietnamese in 1954; HCMC's version was constructed in 1958.

When Vietnam was partitioned in 1954, Buddhist monks and Catholic priests wisely fled south to avoid persecution and continued to practise their religion. One monk from Hanoi who travelled south in 1954 was Thich Tri Dung. Shortly after his arrival in Saigon, Thich petitioned the South Vietnamese government for permission to construct a replica of Hanoi's famous One Pillar Pagoda. However, President Ngo Dinh Diem was a Catholic with little tolerance for Buddhist clergy and denied permission. Nevertheless, Thich and his supporters raised the funds and built the pagoda in defiance of the president's orders. At one point, the Diem government ordered the monks to tear down the temple, but they refused even though they were threatened with imprisonment for not complying. Faced with significant opposition, the government's dispute with the monks reached a standoff. However, the president's attempts to harass and intimidate the monks in a country that was 90% Buddhist did not go down well at all and ultimately contributed to Diem's assassination by his own troops in 1963.

During the war, the One Pillar Pagoda of Thu Duc was in possession of an extremely valuable plaque said to weigh 612kg. After liberation, the government took it for 'safekeeping' and brought it to Hanoi. However, none of the monks alive today could say just where it is.

The pagoda is in the Thu Duc district, about 15km northeast of central HCMC. Tours to it are rare, so you'll have to visit by rented motorbike or car.

## CAN GIO
☎ 08
The only beach within the municipality of HCMC is at Can Gio, a low-lying palm-fringed island, where the Saigon River

meets the sea. The island was created by silt washing downstream, so the beach is hard-packed mud rather than the fine white sand that sun worshippers crave. Furthermore, the beach is in a rather exposed position and is lashed by strong winds. For these reasons, Can Gio gets few visitors and the beach remains entirely undeveloped.

But before you scratch Can Gio off your list of places to visit, it's worth noting that the island does have a wild beauty, plus some good fresh seafood to sample. And, unlike the rest of HCMC, overpopulation is hardly a problem here (chiefly because the island lacks a fresh water supply).

The land here is only about 2m above sea level and the island is basically one big mangrove forest. The salty mud makes most forms of agriculture impossible, but aquaculture is another matter and the most profitable business here is shrimp farming. The hard-packed mud beach also teems with clams and other sea life, which island residents dig up to eat or sell. There is also a small salt industry – sea water is diverted into shallow ponds and is left to evaporate until a white layer of salt can be harvested. Can Gio has a small port where fishing boats can dock, but the shallow water prevents any large ships from dropping anchor here.

From about 1945 to 1954, Can Gio was controlled by Bay Vien, a general who also controlled a casino in Cholon. He was something of an independent warlord and gangster, but former President Ngo Dinh Diem persuaded Bay Vien to join forces with the South Vietnamese government. Not long thereafter, Bay Vien was murdered by an unknown assailant.

## Can Gio Mangrove Park

Can Gio Mangrove Park (*Lam Vien Can Gio;* ☎ 874 3069, fax 874 3068; admission 7000d) is a 70,000-hectare mangrove forest formed by sediment deposits from the Dong Nai and Long Tau Rivers. The **Can Gio Museum**, also in the park, has displays on flora and fauna of the area, as well as exhibits relating to local war history. Near the museum is an area where hundreds of monkeys live. Feeding the monkeys is popular with tourists, but

be *very* careful with your belongings; the monkeys here are well practised at swiping bags, pens, and sunglasses, and the chances of retrieval are next to none. These critters are more skilled than the 'motorbike cowboy' thieves in HCMC!

## Caodai Temple

Though much smaller than the Caodai Great Temple at Tay Ninh, Can Gio boasts a Caodai Temple of its own. It's near the market and is easy to find.

## Can Gio Market

Can Gio has a large market, which is made very conspicuous by some rather powerful odours. Seafood and salt are definitely the local specialities. The vegetables, rice and fruit are all imported by boat from HCMC.

## War Memorial & Cemetery

Adjacent to the local shrimp hatchery, is a large and conspicuous cemetery and war memorial (Nghia Trang Liet Si Rung Sac), 2km from Can Gio Market. Like all such sites in Vietnam, the praise for bravery and patriotism goes entirely to the winning side and there is nothing said about the losers. Indeed, all of the former war cemeteries containing remains of South Vietnamese soldiers were bulldozed after liberation – a fact that still causes much bitterness.

## The Beach

The southern side of the island faces the sea, creating a beachfront nearly 10km long. Unfortunately, a good deal of it is inaccessible because it's been fenced off by shrimp farmers and clam diggers. Nevertheless, there is a point, about 4km west of the market, where a dirt road leads off the main highway to HCMC, and heads towards the beach. The road is easily distinguished by the telephone poles and wires running alongside it. At the beach, you'll find a handful of stalls selling food and drinks.

The surface of the beach is as hard as concrete and it is possible to ride a motorbike on it; however, this is not recommended because it damages the local ecology. While the beach may seem dead at first glance, it swarms with life just below the surface, as the breathing holes in the mud suggest, and you can hear the crunch of tiny clam shells as you stroll along the surface. The water here is extremely shallow and you can walk far from shore, but take care – there is a good deal of inhospitable and well-armed sea life in these shallow waters. Stingrays, stonefish and sea urchins are just some of the local residents who can and will retaliate if you step on them.

The hills of the Vung Tau Peninsula are easily visible on a clear day.

### Places to Stay & Eat
Most visitors do Can Gio as a day trip, and for good reason – the hotels in town are total dumps. Moreover, they are often full so call ahead if you intend to stay.

**Guesthouse 30/4** (☎ 874 3022; rooms with fan/air-con 150,000/250,000d) is a very basic place, but at least it's near the beach.

**Filao Restaurant** (☎ 874 3164), near Guesthouse 30/4, is a good place to sample local seafood. Ditto for the **restaurant** (☎ 874 3150) attached to Guesthouse 30/4.

There are a few stalls around the **market** near the fishing port, and a couple of solitary **food and drink stalls** next to the beach. All they serve is Coca-Cola, snacks and instant noodles, but it beats starving. It might be prudent to bring some food and bottled water with you on the odd chance that the food stalls are closed.

### Getting There & Away
Can Gio is about 60km southeast of central HCMC, and the fastest way to make the journey is by car or motorbike. Travel time is approximately two hours.

There is a **ferry crossing** (motorbike/car 2000/10,000d) 15km from HCMC at Binh Khanh (Cat Lai), a former US naval base. The road is paved all the way from HCMC to Can Gio. Once you get past the ferry, there is very little traffic and both sides of the road are lined with lush mangrove forests.

## BUU LONG MOUNTAIN
Since various tourist pamphlets will tell you that Buu Long Mountain (admission 5000d)

is the 'Halong Bay of the south', you would be forgiven for thinking that it must be nothing short of stunningly beautiful. In truth it's no Halong Bay, but it could be worth a day trip to Buu Long Mountain to escape the crowds of HCMC. Since the recent opening of water parks in and around the city, the crowds have diminished and it's once again a peaceful place to visit.

The summit is 60m above the car park, and there are several good walking trails. The top of the mountain is marked by a pagoda, from where you can look down and clearly see **Long An** (Dragon Lake). There is some lovely countryside scenery, good bird-watching and sweeping views of the rural farms along the Dong Nai River.

There are a few **refreshment shops** where you can buy cold drinks and noodles, but we recommend trying out the food at the small **vegetarian restaurant** at the top of the mountain.

Buu Long Mountain is 32km from central HCMC, and is best reached by car or motorbike. It's 2km off the main highway after crossing the bridge that marks the border between HCMC municipality and Dong Nai province.

**Action Max** (☎ 0913-929137; e action-max@hcm.vnn.vn) is a tour outfit in HCMC that organises enjoyable outdoor adventure trips to Buu Long Mountain.

## LONG AN
The shoreline along Long An (Dragon Lake; admission 3000d) is dressed up with a few pavilions and decorative souvenir stands. To reach the lake, you have to descend Buu Long Mountain and pass through another gate, where you pay the admission fee. And for a small extra charge, you can paddle a boat around the slimy green waters in pursuit of the dragon that is said to live at the bottom of the lake. Although we didn't spot the dragon, we did find the boat ride an excellent way to escape the lottery-ticket and postcard vendors.

## TRI AN FALLS
Tri An Falls form an 8m-high and 30m-wide cascade on the Song Be (Be River).

The falls are awesome in the late autumn, when the river's flow is at its greatest. Tri An Falls are in Dong Nai province, 36km from Bien Hoa and 68km northeast of HCMC (via Thu Dau Mot).

Further upstream is Tri An Reservoir (Ho Tri An), a large artificial lake, fed from the forest highlands around Dalat and created by the Tri An Dam. Completed in the early 1980s with Soviet assistance, the dam and its adjoining hydroelectric station supplies the bulk of HCMC's electric power.

## VUNG TAU
☎ 064 • pop 161,300

Vung Tau, known under the French as Cap St Jacques (and so-named by Portuguese mariners in honour of their patron saint), is a heavily commercialised beach resort on the South China Sea, about 128km southeast of HCMC.

Vung Tau's beaches are easily reached from HCMC and have thus been a favourite of that city's residents since French colonists first began coming here around 1890. However, they are none too clean and not Vietnam's nicest by any stretch of the imagination: offshore drilling and sewerage flowing downriver from HCMC are a considerable source of pollution. Beachgoers looking for an escape from HCMC would do much better making the two-hour drive to Long Hai or, better yet, the three-hour trip to beautiful Mui Ne Beach (see the South-Central Coast chapter).

Visitors can cycle around, or climb up, Vung Tau Peninsula's two mountains. There are also a number of **religious sites** around town, including several pagodas and a huge standing figure of Jesus blessing the South China Sea. The 360-degree view from the 1910 lighthouse *(hai dang)* atop Small Mountain is spectacular, especially at sunset.

Vung Tau became briefly famous to the world in 1973, when the last US troops in Vietnam left here by ship. However, a small contingent of American advisers, diplomats and Central Intelligence Agency (CIA) agents remained in Vietnam for another two years – their moment on the world's centre stage came in 1975 during the rooftop helicopter evacuation of the US embassy in Saigon.

Vung Tau has long competed with HCMC to attract foreign sex tours to Vietnam – massage parlours are ubiquitous. However,

---

### Love for Sale

The number of Vietnamese women who have, especially in recent years, married foreign men is astounding. Whether for their beauty, their grace or their nature, Vietnamese women are increasingly being swept off their feet by foreigners, and in many cases, swept away from their homeland to live with their husbands.

Plenty of such women have gone to live in Western countries, but there are a legion of Vietnamese brides around Asia as well. Perhaps the largest number of Vietnamese wives outside of Vietnam is in Taiwan. In contrast with the thousands who've married Taiwanese men, at least until recently, the number of Vietnamese men married to Taiwanese women you could probably have counted on one hand. But that has all changed now, thanks to an entrepreneurial trend in Baria province.

According to local news reports there is a growing number of overweight Taiwanese women, many of whom are considered 'unmarriageable' at home in face-conscious Taiwan, marrying Vietnamese men. So what's the catch? Why would a slender Vietnamese guy want to marry a woman three times his weight, with whom he probably cannot communicate anyhow? The answer: money.

Matchmakers have turned this development into big business, and bridal brokers are making the deals – brace yourself – based on the actual size and weight of the prospective brides! Currently the going rate the family of the Taiwanese bride pays to the family of the Vietnamese groom is in the range of 1.2 to 1.8 million dong per kilo, and incredibly the number of such marriages is on the increase. So much for the old adage: this is one case where size *does* matter!

the AIDS epidemic has caused some soul-searching and there has been a half-hearted crackdown on this lucrative industry.

Theft has also increased in the area. Watch out for kids who may try to pick your pockets or snatch a bag. There are also HCMC-style motorbike cowboys.

All that said, nowadays perhaps the best reason to visit Vung Tau would be to board a ferry or helicopter to the Con Dao Islands (see the following section), one of the most off-the-beaten-track places in Vietnam.

During weekends and holidays, Vung Tau's hundred or so hotels can get heavily booked, but usually you can find a room.

### Getting There & Away

The best way to reach Vung Tau is by the hydrofoil (adult/child US$10/5, about 1¼ hours) that leaves frequently from the **Bach Dang Jetty** in HCMC. In Vung Tao you board the hydrofoil at **Cau Da pier**, opposite the Hai Au Hotel. **Vina Express** (☎ 856530) has a Vung Tao office by the pier.

Convenient minibuses to Vung Tau also depart from in front of the Saigon Hotel, on Ð Dong Du near the Saigon Central Mosque.

The best way to get around the Vung Tau Peninsula is by rental bicycle or motorbike. There are also plenty of meter taxis.

### CON DAO ISLANDS

☎ 064 • pop 1,650

The Con Dao Archipelago is a remarkable group of 15 islands and islets, 180km (97 nautical miles) south of Vung Tau in the South China Sea.

The largest island in the group, with a total land area of 20 sq km, is the partly forested Con Son Island, which is ringed with bays, bathing beaches and coral reefs. Con Son Island is also known by its Europeanised Malay name, Iles Poulo Condore (Pulau Kun-dur), which means 'Island of the Squashes'. Local products include teak and pine wood, fruit (grapes, coconuts and mangoes), cashews, pearls, sea turtles, lobster and coral.

Occupied at various times by the Khmer, Malays and Vietnamese, Con Son also served as an early base for European commercial ventures in the region. The first recorded European arrival was a ship of Portuguese mariners in 1560. The British East India Company maintained a fortified trading post here from 1702 to 1705 – an experiment that ended when the English on the island were massacred in a revolt by the Macassar soldiers they had recruited on the Indonesian island of Sulawesi.

Con Son Island has a strong political and cultural history, and an all-star line-up of Vietnamese revolutionary heroes (many streets are named after them) were incarcerated here. Under the French, Con Son was used as a major prison for opponents of French colonialism, earning a fearsome reputation for the routine mistreatment and torture of prisoners. In 1954 the island was taken over by the South Vietnamese government, which continued to take advantage of its remoteness to hold opponents of the government (including students) in horrifying conditions. During the American War,

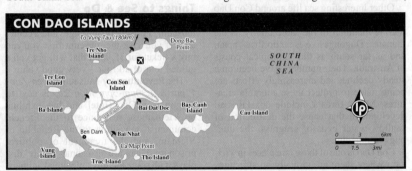

the South Vietnamese were joined here by US forces.

For the intrepid traveller, Con Dao offers a rich (if tragic) history, as well as ample pursuits for nature lovers and beach bums. Roughly 80% of the land area in the island chain is part of **Con Dao National Park**, and there are plenty of great hiking opportunities, as well as deserted beaches.

The park headquarters is a good place to get information, and the staff can direct you to the hikes (some trails have interpretive signage in English and Vietnamese). From March to November there's a beautiful and leisurely two-hour trek starting from the airport runway (no access on mornings with helicopter flights!). The walk leads through thick forest and mangroves, and past a hilltop stream to **Bamboo Lagoon** (Dam Tre). You'll definitely need a local guide to find your way, but once there it's stunning and there's good snorkelling in the bay. You could even consider arranging for a boat to come and pick you up. Also at park headquarters, is an exhibition hall with well-presented displays on the diversity of local forest and marine life, threats to the local environment, and local conservation activities.

Con Dao is Vietnam's most important **sea-turtle** nesting ground and since 1995 the Worldwide Fund for Nature (WWF) has been working with local park rangers on a long-term monitoring programme. During nesting season (March to September) the park sets up six ranger stations to rescue threatened nests and move them to the safe haven of hatcheries.

Other interesting sea life around Con Dao includes the **dugong**, a rare and seldom-seen marine mammal in the same family as the manatee. Dugongs live as far north as Japan, and as far south as the subtropical coasts of Australia. Their numbers have been on a steady decline, and increasingly efforts are being made to protect these adorable creatures. Major threats include coastal road development that cause the destruction of shallow-water beds of seagrass, the dugongs' staple diet.

Con Dao is one of those rare places in Vietnam where there are virtually no structures over two storeys, and where the traveller's experience is almost hassle-free. There's even no need to bargain at the local market! Owing to the relative cost and inaccessibility, mass tourism has thankfully been kept to a minimum.

These days most visitors to Con Son are package-tour groups of former VC soldiers, who were imprisoned on the island. The Vietnamese government generously subsidises these jaunts as a show of gratitude for their sacrifice. It's safe to say that foreign tourists are few and far between, but as the infrastructure and access improves, this is bound to change. Those who make the effort to go now are not likely to regret it.

Con Son town is a sleepy seafront spot that would make a perfect location for a period film. All three of the town's hotels are along Đ Ton Duc Thang, along a strip of forlorn single-storey French villas (most are abandoned and in disrepair, but nonetheless photogenic). Nearby is the local **market**, which is busiest between 7am and 8am.

The best time to visit Con Dao is from November to February. The rainy season lasts from June to September, but there are also northeast and southwest monsoons in autumn that can bring heavy winds. In November 1997 typhoon Linda did a number here: 300 fishing boats were lost, reefs were wiped out and the forests flattened. September and October are the hottest months, though even then the cool island breezes make Con Dao relatively comfortable when compared with HCMC or Vung Tau.

## Things to See & Do

The main sights on Con Son Island are a museum, a prison, prison cages and a cemetery. If you visit the museum first you can buy a ticket for 35,000d that will get you a guided tour of all four – very good value.

The **Revolutionary Museum** *(open 7am-11pm & 1.30pm-5pm Mon-Sat)* is next to Saigon Con Dao Hotel and has exhibits on Vietnamese resistance to the French, communist opposition to the Republic of Vietnam, and the treatment of political prisoners. There are also some 'nature' displays with some awfully embalmed animals.

The most bizarre is a monkey sitting with his legs crossed and smoking a cigarette.

**Phu Hai Prison**, a short walk from the museum, is the largest of the 11 prisons on the island. Built in 1862, the prison houses several enormous detention buildings, one with about 100 shackled and emaciated mannequins that are all too lifelike. Equally eerie are the empty solitary cells with ankle shackles (the decree written on the walls in Vietnamese means 'no killing fleas') prisoners were not allowed to dirty the walls.

The notorious **Tiger Cages** were built by the French in 1940s. From 1957 to 1961 nearly 2000 political prisoners were confined in these tiny cells. Here there are 120 chambers with ceiling bars, where guards could watch down on the prisoners like tigers in a zoo, and another 60 solariums with no roof at all.

Over the course of four decades of war, some 20,000 people were killed on Con Son and 1994 of their graves can be seen at **Hang Duong Cemetery**. Sadly, only 700 of these graves bear the name of the victims. Vietnam's most famous heroine, Vo Thi Sau (1933–1952), was the first woman executed (by a firing squad) on Con Son, on 23 January 1952. Today's pilgrims come to burn incense at her tomb, and make offerings of mirrors and combs (symbolic because she died so young). In the distance behind the cemetery you'll see a huge **monument** symbolising three giant sticks of incense.

**Phu Binh Camp** is not part of the main tour, but is another prison camp that can be visited on Con Son. Built in 1971 by the Americans, this one has 384 chambers and was known as Camp 7 until 1973, when it closed following evidence of torture. After the Paris Agreements in 1973, the name was changed to Phu Binh Camp.

## Beaches & Islands
On Con Son there are several good beaches worth finding. Inquire at the hotels about snorkelling gear rental for about 50,000d per day.

**Bai Dat Doc** is one nice beach with beds of seagrass and the possibility of sighting dugongs.

**Bai Nho** is a quiet and secluded beach, but getting there involves trekking over (or around) some large boulders.

**Bai Nhat** is small and very nice, though it's exposed only during low tide.

**Bai An Hai** looks nice, but there are a good number of fishing boats moored nearby, and a few too many sandflies.

**Bai Loi Voi** is OK as well, and shallow, but there can be a fair bit of rubbish and lots of sea shells.

The best beaches of all are on the islands, such as the beautiful white-sand beach on **Tre Lon**.

Perhaps the best all-round island to visit is **Bay Canh**, which has lovely beaches, old-growth forest, mangroves, coral reefs (good snorkelling at low tide) and sea turtles (seasonal). There is a fantastic two-hour walk to a functioning French-built **lighthouse**.

## Places to Stay
**ATC** (☎ 830666, fax 830111; e atccd@vol .vnn.vn; 16B Đ Ton Duc Thang; singles/ doubles in villa US$18/20, rooms in stilt house US$25) is a family-run inn set in a lovely four-room French villa built in 1929. It's decorated with rattan furniture and the landscaping features stone walkways through manicured gardens. In addition to the villa, there are two attractive hill-tribe stilt houses on site, both relocated here from Hoa Binh in the north. Rates include breakfast, and the lunches and dinner fare can also be recommended here.

**Saigon Con Dao Hotel** (☎ 830366, fax 830567; 18 Đ Ton Duc Thang; singles US$20 doubles US$25-30), run by Saigon Tourist, is just up the street from ATC and is also built around a few old French villas. Inquire at the Saigon Tourist office on Đ Le Thanh Ton in HCMC, which usually offers reasonably priced package tours to the island.

**Phi Yen Hotel** (☎ 830168, fax 830428; singles/doubles with air-con 180,000/ 222,000d) is a basic minihotel. The more expensive rooms have sea views, sort of.

## Getting There & Away
**Air** The only way to fly to Con Son Island is on an 18- or 24-seat Russian helicopter

operated by Vietnam Airlines (US$75 one way). The hardest part is getting a reservation: there's always a chance of being bumped if one of the top brass needs your seat. Flights in both directions are on Tuesday and Saturday only, so book as far in advance as possible. Plans are in the works to upgrade the airport and extend the runway for fixed-wing aircraft, but for now helicopter is the only choice.

**Boat** The 180km route between Vung Tau and Con Dao takes anywhere from 12 to 15 hours on a ship operated by the Vietnamese navy. Civilians can get permission to do this boat journey provided there is a reasonably large group making the trip. Inquire at the **Oil Service Company & Tourism** (☎ 852012, fax 852834; 2 ĐL Le Loi, Vung Tau).

## Getting Around

**To/From the Airport** The tiny Con Son airport is about 15km from the town centre, so it's advisable to book your hotel ahead and arrange to be met at the airport. Otherwise, try a motorbike taxi or a shared taxi.

**Bicycle** Several of the main sites on Con Son, such as the Revolution Museum and Phu Hai Prison, are within walking distance of town, but to get further afield a bicycle is ideal. If you can't bring your own (recommended), all of the hotels rent bikes for about US$2 per day. There are excellent coastal cycling routes (such as from town to Bai Nhat Beach and onto Ben Dam), some nice gradual ups and downs, and thankfully very little motor traffic.

**Boat** If you want to explore the islands by boat, hire one from the national-park office. A 12-person boat costs around 1,000,000d per day, which means short of gathering some fellow travellers to share the cost, it's not cheap. Hopefully with time there will be some cheaper options available.

## LONG HAI
☎ 064

Mass tourism has turned Vung Tau into something of a circus, and many travellers

crave a less-commercialised seaside retreat within a couple of hours' drive of HCMC. Long Hai, 30km northeast of Vung Tau, is one such place, but can really only be recommended if you can afford to stay at the mid-range or top-end accommodation choices.

Backpacker cafés in HCMC can organise trips here, and it is also easy enough to travel to independently, but because of the standard of the cheaper accommodation, you'd probably be better off making the three-hour drive from HCMC to Mui Ne Beach (see the South-Central Coast chapter).

The western end of the beach is where fishing boats moor and is therefore none-too-clean. However, the eastern end is attractive, with a reasonable amount of white sand and palm trees. Some of the nicest municipal beach is in front of the Military Guesthouse. You can rent beach chairs here for 10,000d.

After the Tet holiday (roughly from the 10th to 12th day of the second lunar month), Long Hai hosts an annual major **fishermen's pilgrimage festival**, where hundreds of boats come from afar to worship at Mo Co Temple.

Apart from the beaches, there are several sites in the area well worth exploring. At Minh Dam, 5km from Long Hai, there are **caves** with historical connections to the Franco–Viet Minh and American Wars. Nearby there is a **mountain-top temple** with great panoramic views of the coastline.

Another 20km away at Dia Dao there are **underground tunnels** (similar, but on a smaller scale, to those at Cu Chi) dating from the American War.

**Chua Phap Hoa** is a peaceful pagoda set in a forest with lots of wild monkeys. There are some good trails here for short hikes.

If you are heading to/from National Hwy 1, north of Long Hai, a less-travelled route is via the **hot springs** at Binh Chau, just 60km away from Long Hai. There are also plenty of other beaches to seek out as you make your way north or south along the coastal Rte 55.

## Places to Stay – Budget

**Dong Nai Guesthouse** (☎ 868421; rooms with fan/air-con 100,000/150,000d) is a friendly place that looks good. Facilities include a tennis court and a swimming pool.

**Huong Bien Hotel** (☎ 868430; rooms with fan/air-con 120,000/150,000d) offers beach bungalows hidden among the palm and pine trees. There are five bungalows with two rooms in each. Most rooms have fan and cold bath, and some have air-con.

The **Military Guesthouse** (Nha Nghi Quan Doi; ☎ 868316; fan rooms 80,000d, air-con rooms 120,000-160,000d) is run by the navy, which may help explain its prime beach-front location. There are fan rooms in the main building and two better-situated beach houses are also available.

**Rang Dong Hotel** (☎ 868356; air-con rooms 180,000d) is a Soviet-style place that's memorable chiefly for the karaoke, which cranks up the decibels from about 6am until midnight. The foul sounds are enhanced by the cavernous concrete building's echo-chamber acoustics.

## Places to Stay – Mid-Range
**Thuy Duong Tourist Resort** (☎ 886215, fax 886180; beach bungalows US$15-20, hotel rooms US$30-80) is a large complex in Phuoc Hai village, about 4km from Long Hai. The vast resort sprawls out on both sides of the road, and there are eight types of rooms to choose from, including bungalows, cottages and suites. Day use of the clean, attractive beach costs 15,000d.

## Places to Stay – Top End
**Anoasis Beach Resort** (☎ 868227, fax 868228; e anoasisresort@hcm.vnn.vn, w www.anoasisresort.com.vn; bungalows US$104++, family bungalows US$126++, villas US$248++) is one of Vietnam's most splendid beachside retreats. This stylish boutique resort is the brainchild of French-Vietnamese helicopter pilot Anoa Dussol-Perran (see the boxed text 'Anoa Dussol-Perran'), who along with her husband created this little slice of paradise. Anoasis boasts cosy wooden cottages spread out over a landscape of green lawn, plants and flowers.

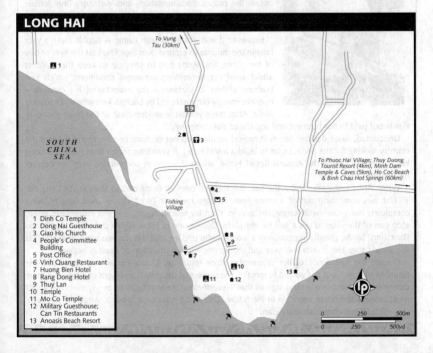

**LONG HAI**

*To Vung Tau (30km)*

*SOUTH CHINA SEA*

*Fishing Village*

*To Phuoc Hai Village; Thuy Duong Tourist Resort (4km), Minh Dam Temple & Caves (5km), Ho Coc Beach & Binh Chau Hot Springs (60km)*

1  Dinh Co Temple
2  Dong Nai Guesthouse
3  Giao Ho Church
4  People's Committee Building
5  Post Office
6  Vinh Quang Restaurant
7  Huong Bien Hotel
8  Rang Dong Hotel
9  Thuy Lan
10  Temple
11  Mo Co Temple
12  Military Guesthouse; Can Tin Restaurants
13  Anoasis Beach Resort

0      250      500m
0      250      500yd

There is a swimming pool, a private beach and a fine **restaurant**. Recreational opportunities include cycling, fishing, tennis and, of course, massage.

There is a choice of 'cottage bungalows', two-bedroom 'family bungalows' (accommodating up to four guests), or the palatial, two-bedroom 'ocean villa' with kitchenette,

## Anoa Dussol-Perran

Since the late 1980s, thousands of overseas Vietnamese have returned to their homeland. Many have surmounted innumerable challenges, returning after so many years abroad to what is still an insular and largely conservative society. One of the most fascinating stories is that of Anoa Dussol-Perran, a gutsy French national who was born in Vietnam but left at the age of four with her adoptive French parents.

A multitalented woman with a flair for getting the most out of life, Dussol-Perran developed a passion for flying helicopters, which she indulged whenever she could get away from her work in real estate. Although she had lived most of her life in France, she also was keenly aware of her Vietnamese heritage and in 1993 she made a momentous decision to return…in style.

She left Paris by helicopter in June, and three weeks and 41 stops later, landed at Hanoi airport,

where she announced that she was going to set up a helicopter charter service. The local authorities were not impressed. They impounded her chopper and she was summoned to explain her actions in front of a none-too-sympathetic committee of government officials.

After nine months of legal wrangles, and cutting her way through miles of red tape, Dussol-Perran was finally able to obtain the proper documentation, and Vietnam's only female helicopter pilot set up the country's only privately run charter company.

However, it was not all smooth flying. A terrible crash a year later in the mountains around Dien Bien Phu cost the lives of two of her pilots, and Anoa had to struggle to keep the business afloat amid ever-worsening economic conditions, which saw business visitors to Vietnam – the mainstay of her clientele – overwhelmingly outnumbered by backpackers who stuck to *terra firma*. After three years, the sudden crash of the Asian economy finally put paid to her business and she closed the company.

Undaunted, Anoa decided her next project would keep her on *terra firma* and she scoured the country looking for the perfect spot to build a resort hotel. A year-long search brought her to Long Hai, today the site of the Anoasis Resort Hotel, which she runs in conjunction with her hotelier husband Ricardo.

When Anoa first came across the site, the tattered ruins of Emperor Bao Dai's lavish Long Hai villa, it was something out of a scene from *Indiana Jones* or *Tomb Raider*. And despite being completely overgrown with jungle, she braved it out for several nights, sleeping rough (and alone) atop one of the villas to get a feel for the place. During one of these nights she was visited (or so she claims) by the ghostly apparition of a woman who told her that this site was her home, and that she should stay. Her search was over and six months later construction of Anoasis began.

Despite the turbulence of her experiences since returning, Dussol-Perran has committed her future to Vietnam and has vowed to remain. The success of the resort, and signs of expansion there during our last visit, are a clear sign of this. Nevertheless, Anoa refuses to be pigeonholed about what projects she might entertain in the future. One thing is for sure, though, whatever she does, she will do it with her customary élan.

terrace and Jacuzzi; all rates include a full continental breakfast. Weekend rates are slightly higher than the weekday rates listed above. Special discounts are offered for stays of two nights or more. Day use of the private beach and swimming pool is available for nonguests (adults/kids US$10/5).

## Places to Eat

There is a cluster of good beachside restaurants called **Can Tin 1, 2 and 3** near the Military Guesthouse.

Across from the Palace Hotel, **Thuy Lan** is also good (and clean), as is the seaside **Vinh Quang**, near the Huong Bien Hotel.

## Getting There & Away

Long Hai is 124km from HCMC and takes about two hours to reach by car. There are some Long Hai–HCMC buses (30,000d, 3 hours), though not many. Getting from Vung Tau to Long Hai is more difficult – you may have to rent a motorbike and drive yourself.

## Getting Around

Motorbike-taxi drivers hang around all the likely tourist spots in the area.

## LOC AN BEACH
☎ 064

Heading northeast along the coast from Long Hai to Binh Chau, there's a turn-off onto Rte 328. It takes 10km to get from the turn-off to **Ho Tram Beach**. This beach itself is disappointing, but about half-way along, there's a right-hand turn. Take this road as it leads to a beautiful and seldom-visited beach at **Ben Cat-Loc An**.

## Places to Stay & Eat

If you follow the road a few kilometres to the beach, you will eventually reach a fork with signs posted for the lone accommodation choice in the area.

**Thuy Hoang** (☎ 874223; bungalows with air-con 250,000d) consists of small A-frame beach bungalows, and has an indoor-outdoor **restaurant** that serves good locally caught seafood and cold beer.

## HO COC BEACH
☎ 064

About 45km northeast of Long Hai is the remote and beautiful Ho Coc Beach. It's still a very undeveloped area, though the weekends bring crowds of Vietnamese tourists.

The area surrounding the beach is part of an 11,000-hectare rainforest that was designated a nature reserve in 1975. Most of the larger wildlife was exterminated or else relocated for safety reasons (most of the elephants were sent to Thailand under a government programme), but plenty of birds and monkeys can be spotted in the forest. Guides for the walking trails can be hired for about 50,000d a day. Inquire at **Hang Duong Ho Coc** (☎ 878145, fax 873878).

## Places to Stay & Eat

There are only two accommodation choices and they are right at the beach.

**Khu Du Lich Bien Ho Coc** (☎ 878175, fax 871130; bungalows 120,000d) consists of five little wooden A-frame bungalows, each with an attached bath with cold water only. The adjoining **restaurant** serves good seafood.

**Hang Duong Ho Coc** (☎ 878145, fax 873878; rooms 120,000-150,000d) is about 50m south down the beach from Khu Du Lich Bien. These cosy wooden cottages are set back about 100m from the beach. Rooms have fans and an attached bath (cold water only). There is also one larger cottage on the beach, which has a five-person room, or a single room upstairs.

## Getting There & Away

Public transport can be a little difficult, mainly because there isn't any. Some of the budget cafés in HCMC offer appealing day and overnight trips to Ho Coc. This also makes for a good (but very long) day trip on a motorbike. The 10km unsealed road to Ho Coc takes you through the forest of the local nature reserve.

## BINH CHAU HOT SPRINGS
☎ 064

About 140km from HCMC, and 60km northeast of Long Hai, is Binh Chau Hot

Springs (*Suoi Khoang Nong Binh Chau;* ☎/fax 871130; admission 15,000d). There is a pleasant resort here and, for the most part, tacky commercialisation is blessedly absent.

The main drawcard is the outdoor hot-spring baths. All private baths are for rent and each bath is on its own covered wooden platform, complete with a small changing room. The baths range from 37°C to 40°C, and the minerals in the water are said to be beneficial to your bones, muscles and skin, and are also said to improve blood circulation and mental disorders!

The baths come in different sizes and prices. A 3-sq-metre bath for two people costs 60,000d, a 5-sq-metre bath for up to five people costs 100,000d and a 10-sq-metre bath for a party of 10 will set you back 160,000d. A dip in a large, shared swimming pool costs 6000d per person, or 3000d for kids.

After your bath, the touristy thing to do is take a ride in an ox-drawn cart around the resort. Until recently there was wildlife in the area, including tigers and elephants, but it seems humans have nearly won the area over. In 1994, six elephants were captured near the springs, but after a few months of keeping them as pets they were turned over to the zoo in HCMC (seems the owners of the resort were unaware of how much it costs to feed six elephants). Nowadays, the only wildlife you are likely to spot are ceramic lions, cheetahs and panthers, which decorate the marshes around the springs.

To get to the hot springs, you have to walk down a wooden path. Be sure that you don't stray from the paths, as the earthen crust is thin here and you could conceivably fall through into an underground pool of scalding water! The hottest spring reaches 82°C, which is hot enough to boil an egg in 10 to 15 minutes. The locals like to boil eggs in the cauldrons set aside for this purpose; you'll find a couple of small springs where bamboo baskets have been laid aside for just this purpose. Raw eggs are on sale for 2000d each.

Despite what you might hear, you should not drink the water here. However, at the time of writing, the management was planning to import a special European water filtration

## Spratly Spat

The **Paracel Islands** (Quan Dao Hoang Sa), 300km east of Danang, and the **Spratly Islands** (Quan Dao Truong Sa), 475km southeast of Nha Trang, seem likely to be the source of future conflict between all the nations surrounding the South China Sea.

Several of the Paracel Islands, which historically have been only sporadically occupied, were seized by China in 1951. In the 1960s, a few islands were occupied by the South Vietnamese, who were driven out by Chinese forces in 1964, an action protested by both the Saigon and Hanoi governments.

The Spratlys, which consist of hundreds of tiny islets, are closer to Borneo than Vietnam. They have been claimed by virtually every country in the vicinity, including the Philippines, Malaysia, Indonesia, China, Taiwan and Vietnam. In 1988 Vietnam lost two ships and 70 sailors in a clash with China over the Spratlys. In mid-1992 Chinese military patrol boats reportedly opened fire several times on Vietnamese cargo vessels that were leaving Hong Kong, bringing trade between Vietnam and Hong Kong to a near halt. The explanation given was that China was trying to prevent smuggling.

Both archipelagos have little intrinsic value, but the country that has sovereignty over them can claim huge areas of the South China Sea – reported to hold vast oil reserves – as its territorial waters. China pushed tensions to a new high in 1992 by occupying one of the islets claimed by Vietnam, and by signing contracts with a US company (Crestone Corporation) to search for oil in the disputed areas. Vietnam returned the favour in 1996, by signing an oil exploration contract with a competing American company, Conoco. Also in 1996, the Philippine navy destroyed a small Chinese-built radar base on Mischief Reef in the Spratlys. The sovereignty of the islands remains unresolved.

system to filter and distribute bottled spring water across Vietnam.

The resort has a **hotel** and an adjoining **restaurant**, and massage and acupuncture are also on offer.

### Places to Stay

**Hotel Cumi** (☎ 871131; air-con rooms 300,000-450,000d) is a bit expensive, but at least breakfast is included.

### Getting There & Away

The resort is in a compound 6km north of the village of Binh Chau. The road connecting Rte 55 to Binh Chau used to be primarily mud and potholes. This changed in the early 1990s when the Australian government donated funds to build a new road. While you might question why Binh Chau was so favoured – do Canberra officials have an irresistible urge to visit hot springs? – you can't complain about the smooth ride.

Good highway or not, there is no public transport. You'll need a motorbike or car; if you choose the latter, perhaps you can find some travellers to share the expense.

The sealed road continuing north from the Binh Chau turn-off to Ham Tan peters out after about 2km, from where it's back to an unsealed but smooth surface.

### HAM TAN

Ham Tan is a pleasantly secluded **beach** 30km northeast of Binh Chau Hot Springs. It's safe to say that visitors of any sort are infrequent. From Ham Tan, it's only about another 30km north to National Hwy 1.

### CAT TIEN NATIONAL PARK

☎ 061 • elevation 700m

Straddling the border of three provinces, Lam Dong, Dong Nai and Binh Phuoc, Cat Tien National Park (☎/fax 791228; admission 20,000d) is just 150km from HCMC and 40km from Buon Ma Thuot. In the 2nd century AD, the Cat Tien area was a religious centre of the Funan empire, and ancient Oc-Eo cultural relics have been discovered in the park.

Cat Tien was hit hard with defoliants during the American War, but the large old-growth trees survived and the smaller plants have recovered. Just as importantly, the wildlife has made a comeback and in 2002 Unesco added Cat Tien National Park to its list of biosphere reserves.

The 73,878-hectare park is home to 77 mammal species, 133 freshwater fish species, 40 reptile species, 14 amphibian species, plus an incredible array of insects, including 457 species of butterfly. Many of these creatures are listed as rare and endangered, but none of them more than the Javan rhinoceros. Considered one of the rarest mammals in the world, this unusual rhino exists only in Cat Tien (there are said to be seven or eight living in the park) and a few other locations scattered throughout Southeast Asia. Leopards are also believed to live in the park, while another rare creature found here is a type of wild ox called a gaur.

The jungles of Cat Tien support an astounding variety of **bird life** (326 species), and avid bird-watchers flock here from around the world. Rare birds in the park include the orange-necked partridge, green peafowl and Siamese fireback. There is also a very healthy population of monkeys. Leeches are another less-desirable member of the local fauna so come prepared, especially during the wet season.

Elephants also roam the park, but their presence has caused some controversy. In the early 1990s, a herd of 10 hungry elephants fell into a bomb crater, created during the American War just outside of Cat Tien. Local villagers took pity on the elephants and dug out a ramp to rescue them. Tragically, since then 28 villagers have been killed by rampaging elephants. Theoretically, the problem could have been 'solved' by shooting the elephants, but the Vietnamese government wasn't willing to risk the wrath of international environmental groups. However, none of these organisations has come up with the funds for relocating the elephants, some of which were finally removed to zoos. In the longer term, such conflicts are likely to be repeated because of the increasing competition between Vietnam's wildlife and its growing population for the same living space.

Cat Tien also boasts a wide range of evergreen, semideciduous and bamboo forests; some 1800 species of plants thrive in the park.

Cat Tien National Park can be explored on foot, by mountain bike, by jeep and also by boat along the Dong Nai River. There are several well-established hiking trails in the park. Jeeps can be rented for shorter trips (120,000d) and also to visit **Crocodile Swamp** (Bau Sau, 160,000d). The latter is a 9km drive from the park headquarters and you have to trek the last 4km to the swamp; the walk takes about three hours round-trip. It may be possible for smaller groups (four or less) to spend the night at the ranger's post here. It's a good place to view the wildlife that comes to drink in the swamp.

Hiring a guide in the national park costs 50,000/100,000d per half/full day, or 160,000d to overnight in the jungle.

## Places to Stay & Eat

There are **bungalows** (*☎/fax 791228; triples with fan/air-con 80,000/100,000d*) near the park headquarters. There is also a small **restaurant** nearby.

## Getting There & Away

The most common approach to the park is from National Hwy 20, which connects Dalat with HCMC. To reach the park, you have to follow a narrow 24km road which branches west from National Hwy 20 at Talai Junction (Nga Ban Talai), 125km north of HCMC and 175km south of Dalat. The road to the park is signposted at the junction. With your own wheels getting to the park is easy and arrangements can be made with the rangers once you arrive.

Another approach to the park is by boat across Langa Lake and then on foot from there. **Dalat Holidays** (*☎ 829422, fax 821122; e langbian@hcm.vnn.vn*) or **Phat Tire Ventures** (*☎ 829422; e kim@phattireventures .com, w www.phattireventures.com*), reputable ecotour operators in Dalat are a good place to inquire about this and other access options from the Central Highlands (including mountain biking to the park from Dalat).

If you're interested in arranging a customised trip to Cat Tien National Park, a good place in HCMC to inquire at is **Sinhbalo Adventures** (*☎ 08-837 6766, ☎/fax 836 7682; w www.sinhbalo.com; 283/20 Đ Pham Ngu Lao*).

# Mekong Delta

Pancake flat but lusciously green and beautiful, the Mekong Delta is the southernmost region of Vietnam. It was formed by sediment deposited by the Mekong River, a process which continues today; silt deposits extend the delta's shoreline at the mouth of the river by as much as 79m per year. The river is so large that it has two daily tides. At low tide in the dry season, boats cannot even move through the shallow canals.

The land of the Mekong Delta is renowned for its richness, and almost half of it is under cultivation. The area is known as Vietnam's 'bread basket', though 'rice basket' would be more appropriate. The Mekong Delta produces enough rice to feed the entire country, with a sizable surplus.

When the government introduced collective farming to the delta in 1975, production fell significantly and there were food shortages in Saigon (although farmers in the delta easily grew enough to feed themselves). People from Saigon would head down to the delta to buy sacks of black-market rice, but the police set up checkpoints and confiscated rice from anyone carrying more than 10kg, with the aim of preventing 'profiteering'. All this ended in 1986, and farmers in this region have since propelled Vietnam forward to become the world's second largest rice exporter after Thailand (see also the boxed text 'Rice Production').

Other products from the delta region include coconut, sugar cane, fruit and fish. Although the area is primarily rural, it is one of the most densely populated regions and nearly every hectare is intensively farmed. The only exceptions are the sparsely inhabited mangrove swamps around Camau province, where the land is not as productive.

The Mekong River is one of the world's great rivers, and its delta is one of the world's largest. The Mekong originates high in the Tibetan plateau, flowing 4500km through China, between Myanmar and Laos, through Laos, along the Laos-Thailand border, and through Cambodia and Vietnam

## Highlights

- Take a boat trip through the countless canals that splinter near the end of the mighty Mekong River
- Explore the delta's bustling floating markets near Cantho or Vinh Long
- Discuss Buddhism with monks at elaborate Khmer pagodas
- Homestay on one of the island fruit orchards around Vinh Long
- Explore the sites around Chau Doc on your way to or from Cambodia via boat along the Mekong River
- Relax on the powdery white-sand beaches of remote Phu Quoc Island

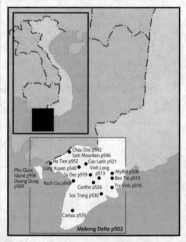

on its way to the South China Sea. At Phnom Penh (Cambodia), the Mekong River splits into two main branches: the Hau Giang (Lower River, also called the Bassac River), which flows via Chau Doc, Long Xuyen and Cantho to the sea; and the Tien Giang (Upper River), which splits into several branches at Vinh Long and empties into the sea at five points. The numerous branches of the river explain the Vietnamese name for the Mekong: Song Cuu Long (River of Nine Dragons).

The water flow in the Mekong begins to rise around the end of May and reaches its highest point in September; it ranges from 1900 to 38,000 cubic metres per second depending on the season. A tributary of the river that empties into the Mekong at Phnom Penh drains Cambodia's Tonlé Sap Lake. When the Mekong is at flood stage, this tributary reverses its flow and drains into Tonlé Sap, thereby somewhat reducing

the danger of serious flooding in the Mekong Delta. Unfortunately, deforestation in Cambodia is disturbing this delicate balancing act, resulting in more flooding in Vietnam's portion of the Mekong River basin.

In recent years seasonal flooding has claimed the lives of hundreds and forced tens of thousands of the region's residents to evacuate from their homes. In some areas, inhabitants are not able to return to their homes until the waters fully recede several months later. Floods cause hundreds of millions of dollars in damage and have a

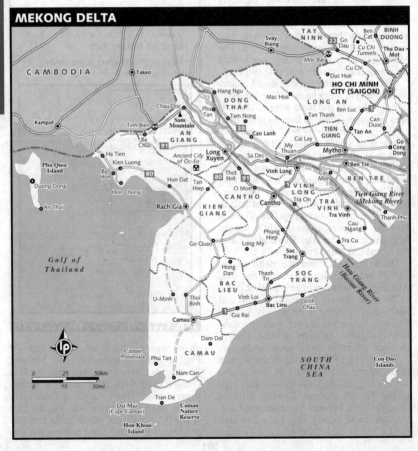

catastrophic effect on regional rice and coffee crops.

Living on a flood plain presents some technical challenges. Lacking any high ground to escape flooding, many delta residents build their houses on bamboo stilts to avoid the rising waters. Many roads are submerged or turn to muck during floods; all-weather roads have to be built on raised embankments, but this is expensive. The traditional solution has been to build canals and travel by boat. There are thousands of canals in the Mekong Delta – keeping them properly dredged and navigable is a constant but essential chore.

A further challenge is keeping the canals clean. The normal practice of dumping all garbage and sewage directly into the waterways behind the houses that line them is taking its toll. Many of the more populated areas in the Mekong Delta are showing signs of unpleasant waste build-up. One can only hope the government will take stronger measures to curb this pollution.

Estuarine crocodiles are found in the southern parts of the delta rivers, particularly in the Hau Giang River. These creatures can be very dangerous and travellers are advised to keep a healthy distance from them at all times.

The Mekong Delta was once part of the Khmer kingdom, and was the last region of modern-day Vietnam to be annexed and settled by the Vietnamese. Cambodians, mindful that they controlled the area until the 18th century, still call the delta 'Lower Cambodia'. The Khmer Rouge tried to follow up on this claim by raiding Vietnamese villages and massacring the inhabitants. This led the Vietnamese army to invade Cambodia in 1979 and oust the Khmer Rouge from power. Most of the current inhabitants of the Mekong Delta are ethnic Vietnamese, but there are also significant populations of ethnic Chinese and Khmer as well as a few Chams.

A major activity in the Mekong Delta is **boating**. Indeed, the only way you're really going to get a close look at the delta is to tour the canals by boat. However, several provincial governments in the Mekong Delta, such as those in Mytho and Vinh Long, have essentially banned private entrepreneurs from renting boats to foreigners. Not every provincial government is so restrictive though – there are several places in the delta, Cantho and Ben Tre for example, where you can simply rent a boat and go where you like.

It is worth mentioning that if you want to visit one of the amazing **floating markets**, it is nearly impossible do to so on a one-day trip from Ho Chi Minh City (HCMC). These markets are at their bustling best early in the morning and usually finish before noon, so you should plan to spend at least one night someplace in the delta; Cantho is as good a place as any to do this, and there are several floating markets in the vicinity.

## Getting There & Away

Most travellers head to the Mekong Delta on an organised tour. With all of the cheap and easy-to-book delta tours available now, few choose to travel independently, particularly those with limited time in Vietnam. The tours are indeed a temptation, and can usually save you a good deal of time, as well as money. But those who do decide to do it on their own will have all the more access to areas that are off the beaten track, with many less-visited places to discover.

Travel by public bus is cheap, but can be hair-raising and rough. Express minibuses are nearly as cheap, but faster and far more comfortable. The ultimate way to see the delta, however, is by private car, bicycle or rented motorbike. Two-wheeling around the delta is good fun, especially getting lost among the maze of country roads! Real hardcores might investigate hopping a cargo boat from HCMC – a slow but fascinating way to head into the delta.

Wherever you go in the delta (except for Mytho), be prepared for ferry crossings. By regulation at many ferry crossings, only drivers can ride onto the ferry in their vehicles; others must walk on and off, and this can include a wait in the baking Mekong sun. Fruit, soft drinks and other food are sold in the waiting area. Oh yes, and lottery tickets! With the completion of the Australian-engineered

## Rice Production

The ancient Indian word for rice, *dhanya*, meaning 'sustainer of the human race', is apt when describing the importance of rice to the Vietnamese.

A Vietnamese fable tells of a time when rice did not need to be harvested. Instead it would be summoned through prayer and arrive in each home from the heavens, in the form of a large ball. One day, a man ordered his wife to sweep the floor in preparation for the coming of the rice, but she was still sweeping when the huge ball arrived and struck it by accident causing it to shatter into many pieces. Since then, Vietnamese have had to toil to produce rice by hand.

Rural Vietnam today is in many ways similar to what it would have been centuries ago: women in conical hats *(non bai tho)* irrigating fields by hand, farmers stooping to plant the flooded paddies, and water buffalo ploughing seedbeds with harrows.

Despite the labour-intensive production process, rice is the single most important crop in Vietnam, involving 70% of the working population. While always playing an important role in the Vietnamese economy, its production intensified considerably as a result of economic reforms, known as *doi moi*, or 'renovation', in 1986. The reforms shifted agricultural production away from subsistence towards cash cropping, transforming Vietnam from a rice importer to exporter in 1989. In 1997 Vietnam exported over 3.5 million tonnes of rice; for the first time in its history, northern Vietnam had excess rice for export, contributing about 270,000 tonnes. In 1999 rice exports rose to a record 4.5 million tonnes. Since then the yearly average has been hovering around 3.5 million tonnes.

Half of the production and the majority of rice exports from Vietnam come from the Mekong Delta. The Red River Delta is the main rice supplier for the north, although supplies often need to be supplemented by the south. Rice produced in the highlands is an important crop for ethnic minorities, although their output is relatively small compared with the rest of the country. Ironically, it's powerful rural cartels, which set their own prices for seeds, fertilisers and pesticides, that reap the rewards.

The importance of rice in the diet of the Vietnamese is evident in the many rice dishes available, including rice omelette *(banh xeo)*, rice porridge *(chao)* and extremely potent rice wine *(ruou gao)*, to name a few. Vietnam's ubiquitous *com pho* restaurants serve white rice *(com)* with a variety of cooked meat and vegetables, as well as noodle soup *(pho)*.

In Vietnam, the dominant rice growing system is 'irrigated lowland'. Despite advances in rice production, such as the introduction of new plant varieties and increased use of fertilisers, much of the work involved with growing the plant itself is still carried out without modern machinery. Fields are ploughed and harrowed with the assistance of water buffaloes, seeds are planted by hand, and when the seedlings reach a certain age they have to be individually uprooted and transplanted (again manually) to another field, to avoid root rot. This painstaking process is mostly undertaken by women. Irrigation is typically carried out by two workers using woven baskets on rope to transfer water from canals to the fields. When the water level is high enough, fish can be raised in the paddies.

Rice plants take three to six months to grow, depending on the type and the environment. In Vietnam, the three major cropping seasons are winter-spring, summer-autumn and the wet season. When ready to harvest, the plants are thigh high and in about 30cm water. The grains grow in drooping fronds and are cut by hand, then transported by wheelbarrows to thrashing machines that separate the husk from the plant. Other machines are used to 'dehusk' the rice (for brown rice) or 'polish' it (for white rice). A familiar sight at this stage is brown carpets of rice spread along roads to dry before milling. While rice continues to grow in Vietnam, the intensification of production since the start of the 1990s has led to problems such as salinity. In addition there has been a growing infestation of rice-field rats caused by the hunting of snakes (which hunt the rats). Unabated environmental degradation and high population growth are placing further pressure on Vietnam's staple grain supply. This, together with the increasing warnings against high fertilisation, may mean the long-term future of rice production in Vietnam is not guaranteed.

My Thuan suspension bridge back in 2000, one less ferry ride is necessary to reach the Mekong River from HCMC, and travel time has thankfully been slashed by around an hour.

Since the opening of the river border crossing between Vietnam and Cambodia at Vinh Xuong (near Chau Doc), more and more travellers are choosing this route over the land border at Moc Bai. Don't forget, however, that visas for entering Vietnam or Cambodia must be arranged *before* heading to the border.

**Organised Tours** Plenty of inexpensive minibus tours can be booked at travel agents in HCMC. The cheapest ones are sold around the Pham Ngu Lao area. However, before you book, make some comparisons. Cheapest is not always best – remember that you usually get what you pay for. This is not to say that you need to book a pricey tour, but sometimes 'rock bottom' means all you will get is a brief glance at the delta region. The cost largely depends on how far from HCMC the tour goes. The standard of accommodation, transport, food and the size of the group will be other determining factors.

Refer to the Travel Agencies section in the Ho Chi Minh City chapter for a list of tour operators. Lately budget travellers have had good things to say about **Delta Adventure Tours** (☎ 08-836-8542; ⓔ sgnkim cafe@hotmail.com, ⓦ www.deltaadventure tours.com; 187A Pham Ngu Lao), including their trips to/from Cambodia via Chau Doc. For private customised tours of the Mekong Delta (on two or four wheels), HCMC's **Sinhbalo Adventures** (ⓦ www.sinhbalo .com) cannot be beat.

## MYTHO
☎ 074 • pop 169,300
Mytho, the quiet capital city of Tien Giang province, is the closest city in the Mekong Delta to HCMC, and visitors on whirlwind 10-day Vietnam tours come here for day trips to catch a glimpse of the famous river. In order to visit floating markets, however, you'll need to continue on to Cantho (see the Around Cantho section later).

Being located so close to booming HCMC, one would expect Mytho to have profited handsomely from the country's economic reforms. Sadly, this is not the case – Mytho is one of the poorest cities in the Mekong Delta, though it is said to have the richest government and one of the strictest police forces.

Mytho was founded in the 1680s by Chinese refugees fleeing Taiwan for political reasons. The Chinese have virtually all gone now, having been driven out in the late 1970s when their property was seized by the government. The economy – or what's left of it – is based on tourism, fishing and the cultivation of rice, coconuts, bananas, mangoes, longans and citrus fruit.

## Orientation
Mytho, which sprawls along the bank of the northernmost branch of the Mekong River, is laid out in a fairly regular grid pattern.

The bus station is several kilometres west of town. Coming from the bus station, you enter Mytho on Đ Ap Bac, which turns into Đ Nguyen Trai (oriented west-east).

Parallel to the Mekong River is Đ 30 Thang 4 (also written as Đ 30/4), named for Saigon Liberation Day.

## Information
**Tien Giang Tourist** (*Cong Ty Du Lich Tien Giang;* ☎ 872154, fax 873578; ⓦ www .mekotours.com; open 7am-5pm daily) is the official tourism authority for Tien Giang province. Mekong River boat tours can be booked at the main river-front **tourist office** (☎ 873184; 8 Đ 30 Thang 4), or at a smaller **branch office** (☎ 875189; 25 Đ Nam Ky Khoi Nghia) just up the street.

## Boat Tours
Boat trips are the highlight of a visit to Mytho. The small wooden vessels can navigate the mighty Mekong (barely), but the target for most trips is cruising past pleasant rural villages through the maze of small canals. Depending on what you book, destinations usually include a coconut-candy workshop, a honey-bee farm (try the banana wine!) and an orchid garden.

MEKONG DELTA

The Mytho People's Committee almost has a monopoly on boat travel and their prices are so high that you need to be in a large group to make it economical. If you try to rent a boat on your own, you'll pay at least US$25 for a two- to three-hour tour. If you sign up with a tour group in HCMC, it could be as cheap as US$7 per person, including transportation between HCMC and Mytho. When comparing prices, check to see what you are actually getting – the tours can last anywhere from one to four hours (not including HCMC–Mytho travel time). When you add up the cost, it would be impossible

to do it any cheaper on your own, though many prefer to do it that way.

Several private boat operators in Mytho defy the authorities by peddling their own boat trips. They are indeed cheaper than the 'official' rates (at around 50,000d per hour), but they are also illegal and there's a small chance your boat may be 'pulled over' and you (or more likely your driver) fined by the river cops. The best place to look for these freelancers is around Cuu Long restaurant or, ironically, just outside the doors of the Tien Giang Tourist office. But they'll probably find you first.

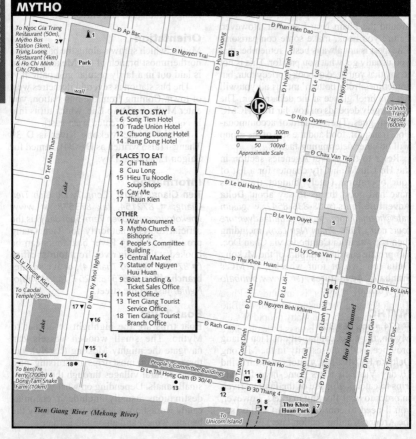

**MYTHO**

To Ngoc Gia Trang Restaurant (50m), Mytho Bus Station (3km), Trung Luong Restaurant (4km) & Ho Chi Minh City (70km)

Đ Ap Bac
Đ Phan Hien Dao
Đ Nguyen Trai
Đ Hung Vuong
Đ Huynh Tinh Cua
Đ Le Loi
Đ Nguyen Hue
Đ Ngo Quyen
Đ Chau Van Tiep
Đ Le Dai Hanh
Đ Le Van Duyet
Đ Ly Cong Van
Đ Thu Khoa Huan
Đ Do Huu
Đ Le Loi
Đ Nguyen Binh Khiem
Đ Lanh Binh Can
Đ Dinh Bo Linh
Đ Rach Gam
Đ Thien Ho
Đ Huyen Toai
Đ Trung Trac
Đ Phan Thanh Gian
Đ Trinh Hoai Duc
Đ Le Thi Hong Gam (Đ 30/4)
Đ 30 Thang 4
Đ Truong Cong Dinh

Park
wall
Lake
Lake
Bao Dinh Channel
Tien Giang River (Mekong River)
To Unicorn Island

To Caodai Temple (50m)
Đ Ly Thuong Kiet
Đ Tet Mau Than
Đ Nam Ky Khoi Nghia
To Ben Tre Ferry (700m) & Dong Tam Snake Farm (10km)

To Vinh Trang Pagoda (600m)

Thu Khoa Huan Park

People's Committee Buildings

Approximate Scale
0    50    100m
0    50    100yd

**PLACES TO STAY**
6   Song Tien Hotel
10  Trade Union Hotel
12  Chuong Duong Hotel
14  Rang Dong Hotel

**PLACES TO EAT**
2   Chi Thanh
8   Cuu Long
15  Hieu Tu Noodle Soup Shops
16  Cay Me
17  Thaun Kien

**OTHER**
1   War Monument
3   Mytho Church & Bishopric
4   People's Committee Building
5   Central Market
7   Statue of Nguyen Huu Huan
9   Boat Landing & Ticket Sales Office
11  Post Office
13  Tien Giang Tourist Service Office
18  Tien Giang Tourist Branch Office

## Nearby Islands

See Around Mytho for information about trips to nearby Dragon, Tortoise and Unicorn Islands. (Trips to Phoenix Island are covered in the Around Ben Tre section.)

## Mytho Church & Bishopric

Mytho Church (32 Đ Hung Vuong), a solid pastel-yellow building at the corner of Đ Nguyen Trai, was built about a century ago. The stone plaques set in the church walls express thanks to Fatima and other figures.

Today, two priests, two nuns and several assistants minister to most of Mytho's 7000 Catholics. Masses are held at 5am and 5pm on Monday to Saturday and at 5am, 7am and 5pm on Sunday, with catechism classes in the late afternoon.

## Caodai Temple

If you missed the one in Tay Ninh, Mytho has its own smaller Caodai Temple (Đ Ly Thuong Kiet), which is worth a look. It's between Đ Dong Da and Đ Tran Hung Dao.

## Mytho Central Market

This market is an area of town along Đ Trung Trac and Đ Nguyen Hue that is closed to traffic. The streets are filled with stalls selling everything from fresh food and bulk tobacco to boat propellers. In an attempt to clear these streets, the local government has built a three-storey concrete monstrosity on the riverside, intending to relocate vendors inside. With the high rent and taxes, however, there have been very few takers, and the top two floors of the building remain empty.

## Chinese District

The Chinese district is around Đ Phan Thanh Gian on the eastern bank of the Bao Dinh Channel. Though many people of Chinese descent remain, there is little else here to suggest that you're in Chinatown.

## Vinh Trang Pagoda

Vinh Trang Pagoda (60A Đ Nguyen Trung Truc) is a beautiful and well-maintained sanctuary. The charitable monks here provide a home for orphans, disabled and other needy children.

The pagoda is about 1km from the city centre. To get there, take the bridge east across the river on Đ Nguyen Trai, and after 400m turn left. The entrance to the sanctuary is about 200m from the turn-off, on the right-hand side of the building as you approach it from the ornate gate.

## Places to Stay

Rang Dong Hotel (☎ 874400; 25 Đ 30 Thang 4; air-con rooms with cold bath US$8, with hot bath US$10-12) is privately run and one of the better cheap places in town. It's popular with budget travellers.

Both of the following government-run hotels are definitely showing their age.

Trade Union Hotel (Khach San Cong Doan; ☎ 874324, fax 878857; e congdoan tourist@hcm.vnn.vn; 61 Đ 30 Thang 4; rooms with fan/air-con 100,000/150,000d) is a large place with river views from some of the rooms. The air-con rooms come with a fridge.

Song Tien Hotel (☎ 872009, fax 884745; 101 Đ Trung Trac; fan rooms 100,000-120,000d, air-con rooms 150,000-250,000d) is another large place of a similar standard.

Chuong Duong Hotel (☎ 870875, fax 874250; 10 Đ 30 Thang 4; rooms/suites US$20/30) is Mytho's most luxurious accommodation offering. This spacious and attractive building boasts a prime riverside location and the food served at the in-house restaurant is respectable. All of the rooms overlook the Mekong River, making the rates rather reasonable for what you get.

Another possible option to consider is staying overnight in a bungalow on Unicorn Island (Thoi Son); inquire at Tien Giang Tourist. There are other homestay options around Vinh Long and Ben Tre.

## Places to Eat

Chi Thanh (☎ 873756; 279 Đ Tet Mau Than; soups 10,000d, mains 15,000-30,000d; open 10am-10pm daily) is a tidy spot for delicious and inexpensive Vietnamese fare.

Thuan Kien (47 Đ Nam Ky Khoi Nghia; mains 10,000-20,000d; open 5am-9pm) and Cay Me (60 Đ Nam Ky Khoi Nghia; mains 10,000-15,000d; open 7am-9pm) are two more good local spots, but they are definitely on the messier side.

**Cuu Long** (☎ 870779; Đ 30 Thang 4; mains 20,000-30,000d; open 7am-9pm) has the advantage of being right on the shore of the Mekong River, but the food and decor leave something to be desired.

Mytho is known for a special vermicelli soup, *hu tieu my tho*, which is richly garnished with fresh and dried seafood, pork, chicken and fresh herbs. It is served either with broth or dry (with broth on the side), and can also be made vegetarian. Although it is found at almost any eatery in town, there are a handful of *hu tieu* speciality restaurants (open mornings only). Carnivores will enjoy **Hu Tieu 44** (44 Đ Nam Ky Khoi Nghia; soups 6000d; open 5am-noon), while vegetarians should look for **Hu Tieu Chay 24** (24 Đ Nam Ky Khoi Nghia; soups 3000d; open 6am-9am).

Group tours tend to congregate in larger restaurants on the outskirts of town; the following are two of the better ones to look out for.

**Ngoc Gia Trang** (☎ 872742; 196 Đ Ap Bac; set meals US$4-12), on the road entering Mytho from HCMC, is a pleasant place. It's a bit pricey compared with the restaurants in town, but it has a lovely courtyard atmosphere and good set meals.

**Trung Luong** (☎ 855441), a few kilometres out of town, is near the gate marking the entry point to Mytho. Here too there is a nice garden, and the tour groups that stop here appreciate the clean toilets. The caged monkey, birds and python, however, do not necessarily add to the charm.

## Getting There & Away

**Bus** Mytho is served by buses leaving HCMC from **Mien Tay bus station** in An Lac, and also from the bus station in Cholon (10,000d). Buses from Cholon have the added advantage of dropping passengers right in Mytho, as opposed to the bus station outside of town.

The **Mytho bus station** (Ben Xe Khach Tien Giang; open 4am-5pm) is several kilometres west of town. To get there from the city centre, take Đ Ap Bac westward and continue on to National Hwy 1 (Quoc Lo 1).

Buses to HCMC (2 hours) leave when full from the early morning until about 5pm. There are also daily bus services to most points in the Mekong Delta.

**Car & Motorbike** The drive from HCMC to Mytho along National Hwy 1, by car or motorbike, takes about two hours.

Road distances from Mytho are 16km to Ben Tre, 104km to Cantho, 70km to HCMC and 66km to Vinh Long.

**Boat** The car ferry to Ben Tre province leaves from **Ben Pha Rach Mieu station** about 1km west of Mytho city centre, near 2/10A Đ Le Thi Hong Gam (the continuation west of Đ 30 Thang 4). The ferry operates between 4am and 10pm and runs at least once an hour. Ten-person trucks shuttle passengers between the ferry terminal and the bus station.

## Getting Around

**Bicycle** You can rent a bicycle from Tien Giang Tourist.

## AROUND MYTHO
## Dragon Island

A walk through the well-known longan orchards of Dragon Island (Con Tan Long) is pleasant. The lush, palm-fringed shores of the island are lined with wooden fishing boats; some of the residents of the island are shipwrights. There is a small **restaurant** on the island. Dragon Island is a five-minute boat trip from the dock at the southern end of Đ Le Loi.

## Other Islands

The other two islands in the vicinity are Tortoise Island (Con Qui) and Unicorn Island (Thoi Son). For booking a trip to these islands or any of the others, it's cheapest to arrange a day tour from HCMC.

## Dong Tam Snake Farm

The snake farm (admission 15,000d) at Dong Tam, about 10km from Mytho towards Vinh Long. Most of the snakes raised here are pythons and cobras. The snakes are bred for eating, for their skins and for producing antivenin. The king cobras are raised only for exhibit – they are extremely aggressive and are even capable of spitting poison; do not get too close to their cages. The regular cobras are kept in an open pit and will generally ignore you if you ignore them, but will strike if provoked. On the other hand, the pythons are docile enough to be taken out of their cages and 'played with' if you dare, but be warned the larger ones are capable of strangling a human.

Dong Tam also has a collection of mutant turtles and fish on display. The cause of their genetic deformities is almost certainly the spraying of Agent Orange during the American War, which was particularly intensive in the forested parts of the Mekong Delta.

Other creatures exhibited here include sea turtles, deer, monkeys, bears, crocdiles, owls, canaries and other birds. (All the names and explanations of the creatures are written in Vietnamese only.)

The snake farm is operated by the Vietnamese military for profit. It's open to the public and taking photos is encouraged. At your request, the staff will drape you with a large python to create that perfect photo for the loved ones back home. The **restaurant** at the snake farm includes cobra on the menu, and there is also a shop here where you can stock up on cobra antivenin.

The farm was formerly run by a retired Viet Cong (VC) colonel named Tu Duoc. He ran the place very efficiently, but after he died in 1990 facilities have gone steadily downhill. The cages look dirty, the animals neglected and the employees dispirited. It's certainly a sharp contrast to Bangkok's slick Snake Institute.

You'll need your own transport to get to Dong Tam Snake Farm. Coming from HCMC, continue for 3km beyond the turnoff to Mytho and turn left at the Dong Tam Junction (signposted). From the junction, follow the dirt road for 4km, turn right and continue for 1km until you reach the snake farm. To get there from Mytho, follow Đ Le Thi Hong Gam west along the river for around 7km and just beyond the Binh Duc post office turn right and follow the dirt road for 3km to the farm.

## One in Every Country

One of the world's commonalities, something shared by urbanites of all different nationalities in their own language, is a somewhat derogatory term for rural folk. English speakers call them country bumpkins, red necks or hicks, while the Japanese, for example, say *inaka mon*.

In Vietnam, however, the word for countryside is *nha que*, and this is the term they use in the north. But in the 'rice basket' of the Mekong Delta, the regional articulation of choice is *hai lua*. Literally 'second rice', *hai lua* refers to when the customarily not-so-clever second son of a large rice farming family (the guy with no street savvy) visits the big city. Remember *Crocodile Dundee*?

*Hai lua*, pronounced high loo-ah, can be a handy phrase to learn before heading into the Mekong Delta. Now, we're not suggesting here that you attempt to go around insulting the locals. Rather, using this expression in a self-deprecating way, or perhaps aiming the slur at your travel companion, will surely get a rise out of the locals. It would be like saying, 'Please forgive the stupidity of my feeble-witted friend.' Just remember not to use it towards people you don't know!

## BEN TRE
☎ 075 • pop 111,800

The picturesque little province of Ben Tre, just south of Mytho, consists of several large islands in the mouth of the Mekong River. The area gets few visitors because it's off the main highways. The provincial capital is also called Ben Tre, and is a friendly sort of place with a few old buildings near the banks of the Mekong.

Ben Tre is a good place for boat trips and, unlike Mytho, Vinh Long and Cantho, the People's Committee doesn't have a monopoly on the boat tour business, so prices have remained low.

Ben Tre is famous for coconut candy (*keo dua*). Many local women work in small factories making coconut sweets, spending their days boiling large cauldrons of sticky mixture, before rolling it out and cutting sections off into squares and wrapping them into paper for sale.

**Ben Tre Tourist** (☎ 829618, fax 822440; 65 Đ Dong Khoi) also has a branch office adjacent to the Dong Khoi Hotel.

Ben Tre has two **Internet cafés**, one on Đ Hung Vuong and the other on Đ Tran Quoc Tuan.

### Vien Minh Pagoda

Right in the centre of Ben Tre, this is the head office of the Buddhist Association of Ben Tre province. Though the history of the pagoda is vague, the local monks say it is over 100 years old. The original structure was made of wood, but it was torn down to make way for the present building. Reconstruction took place from 1951 to 1958, using bricks and concrete.

An interesting feature of Vien Minh Pagoda is a large white statue of Quan The Am Bo Tat (Goddess of Mercy) set in the front courtyard. The Chinese calligraphy that adorns the pagoda was performed by an old monk. None of the current monks at the pagoda can read Chinese, though some of the local worshippers can.

### Truc Giang Lake

Truc Giang Lake, a small but pleasant lake fronting the Dong Khoi Hotel, is a place to play around in paddle boats. The surrounding park is too small for much strolling.

### Places to Stay

**Phuong Hoang Hotel** (☎ 821385; 28 Hai Ba Trung; rooms 120,000-140,000đ) is a 10-room minihotel that's decent value.

**Trade Union Hotel** (☎ 825082; 50 Đ Hai Ba Trung; air-con rooms 130,000-150,000đ) is a bit worse for wear, but it's one of the cheapest places in town.

**Hung Vuong Hotel** (☎ 822408; 166 Đ Hung Vuong; old-wing rooms US$10, new-wing rooms US$15-37) was recently renovated and looks nice. All rooms here have air-con, but those in the old wing have cold water only. It also has a big **restaurant**.

**Ben Tre Hotel** (☎ 822223; 8/2 Đ Tran Quoc Tuan; air-con rooms US$13-23) is one of the better places in town, and all rooms have hot water. There's an Internet café nearby.

**Dong Khoi Hotel** (☎ 822240; 16 Đ Hai Ba Trung; doubles with air-con US$20-35) is Ben Tre's plushest accommodation. Take a

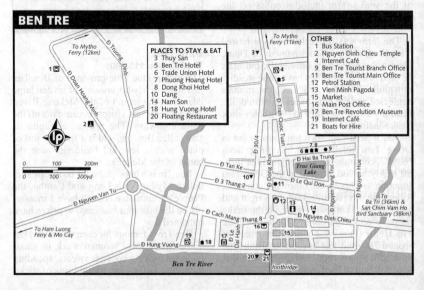

**BEN TRE**

To Mytho Ferry (12km)
To Mytho Ferry (11km)

Đ Truong Dinh
Đ Doan Hoang Minh
Đ Tran Quoc Tuan
Đ 30/4
Đ Dong Khoi
Đ Hai Ba Trung
Đ Nguyen Trung Truc
Đ Nguyen Hue
Đ Tan Ke
Đ Le Qui Don
Đ 3 Thang 2
Đ Nguyen Van Tu
Đ Cach Mang Thang 8
Đ Nguyen Dinh Chieu
Đ Hung Vuong
Đ Le Dai Hanh

Truc Giang Lake

Ben Tre River

footbridge

To Ham Luong Ferry & Mo Cay

To Ba Tri (36km) & San Chim Vam Ho Bird Sanctuary (38km)

**PLACES TO STAY & EAT**
3 Thuy San
5 Ben Tre Hotel
6 Trade Union Hotel
7 Phuong Hoang Hotel
8 Dong Khoi Hotel
10 Dang
14 Nam Son
18 Hung Vuong Hotel
20 Floating Restaurant

**OTHER**
1 Bus Station
2 Nguyen Dinh Chieu Temple
4 Internet Café
9 Ben Tre Tourist Branch Office
11 Ben Tre Tourist Main Office
12 Petrol Station
13 Vien Minh Pagoda
15 Market
16 Main Post Office
17 Ben Tre Revolution Museum
19 Internet Café
21 Boats for Hire

0    100    200m
0    100    200yd

## Monkey Bridges – An Endangered Species

One of the most endearing sights in the Mekong Delta is a person making their way across one of the fascinating 'monkey bridges' (cau khi). These simple, arch-shaped footbridges are usually built of uneven logs about 30cm to 80cm wide and have only a simple bamboo railing. They are suspended anywhere from 2m to 10m above the canals, and connect tiny villages throughout the region to main roads.

At first glance the bridges look more like makeshift scaffolding than a bridge to cross. It's amazing to watch the locals traverse these narrow catwalks with bicycles and heavy loads balanced between their shoulders on bamboo poles. A fall from one of these tightrope bridges could result in serious injury, but the Vietnamese just glide across with ease (and smiles on their faces).

In 1998 the government initiated a programme to begin replacing the region's monkey bridges with safer, 1m-wide wood plank overpasses. Later, in 2000, the plan was amended with a new and improved agenda to do away with all of the delta's monkey bridges once and for all, and to replace them with more durable concrete bridges. While the move no doubt is a victory in terms of improvement to the local infrastructure throughout the Mekong Delta, giving local people easier and safer access across the canals, sadly the traditional landscape is suffering an aesthetic loss. The days of seeing these charming bridges everywhere are numbered, but still, with literally thousands of bridges to dismantle and replace, you can rest assured that there will always be some left to find.

peek at the hotel's gift shop – the souvenir spoons, chopsticks and coconut-wood ashtrays are certainly beautiful. This hotel has the most upmarket restaurant in town. On Saturday night a band entertains the guests.

### Places to Eat
Nam Son (☎ 822888, 40 Đ Phan Ngoc Tong; mains 15,000-30,000d) is popular for Vietnamese fare and usually packed with locals eating roast chicken and drinking draft beer.

Dang and Thuy San, both on Đ 30 Thang 4 as you enter town, are two other places to consider for Vietnamese fare, fresh river fish and seafood.

There is a floating restaurant anchored on the south side of town near the market. The food and decor is unremarkable, but you can't beat the location.

If you're travelling on the cheap, just head over to the market, which has plenty of food stalls where you can fill up for peanuts.

### Getting There & Away
As this is an island province, crossing the Mekong River is a prerequisite for reaching Ben Tre. Slow as it is (about 45 minutes each way), the Mytho–Ben Tre crossing is the fastest option. There are other possible ferry crossings further south but these are so

slow and unreliable that you shouldn't count on them. Ferry crossings are much quicker if you're travelling by motorbike (as opposed to car) since there are numerous small boats that can take you across the river.

Public buses stop at the bus station east of the town centre on Đ Doan Hoang Minh. Private minibuses also make the Ben Tre–HCMC run daily. They operate on no fixed schedule, so you'll need to inquire locally. Try asking around the market, or by the petrol station on Đ Dong Khoi (where some vans leave from).

### Getting Around
Ben Tre Tourist has a high-speed boat for rent, though it's not cheap at US$35 per hour. It can hold about eight people. Slower and larger boats can also be rented here, but other bargains can be negotiated at the public pier near the market. Here you can figure on about 25,000d per hour, with a minimum of two hours cruising the local canals. Check with the boat drivers who hang around near the end of the footbridge.

## AROUND BEN TRE
### Phoenix Island
Until his imprisonment by the communists for his antigovernment activities and the

consequent dispersion of his flock, the Coconut Monk (Ong Dao Dua) led a small community on Phoenix Island (Con Phung), a few kilometres from Mytho. In its heyday, the island was dominated by a fantastic open-air sanctuary *(admission 10,000d)* that looked a bit like a cross between a cheaply built copy of Disneyland and the Tiger Balm Gardens of Singapore. The dragon-enwrapped columns and the multi-platformed tower, with its huge metal globe, must have once been brightly painted, but these days the whole place is faded, rickety and silent. Nevertheless, it's good kitsch – check out the model of the Apollo rocket set among the Buddhist statues! With a bit of imagination, though, you can picture how it all must have appeared as the Coconut Monk presided over his congregation, flanked by elephant tusks and seated on a richly ornamented throne.

The Coconut Monk was so named, it is said, because he once ate only coconuts for three years; others claim he only drank coconut juice and ate fresh young corn. Whatever the story, he was born Nguyen Thanh Nam (though he later adopted Western name order, preferring to be called Nam Nguyen Thanh) in 1909, in what is now Ben Tre province. He studied chemistry and physics in France at Lyon, Caen and Rouen from 1928 until 1935, when he returned to Vietnam, got married and had a daughter.

In 1945 the Coconut Monk left his family in order to pursue a monastic life. For three years he sat on a stone slab under a flagpole and meditated day and night. He was repeatedly imprisoned by successive South Vietnamese governments, which were infuriated by his philosophy of achieving reunification through peaceful means. He died in 1990.

The Coconut Monk founded a religion, Tinh Do Cu Si, which was a mixture of Buddhism and Christianity. Representations of Jesus and the Buddha appeared together, as did the Virgin Mary and eminent Buddhist women. He employed both the cross and Buddhist symbols. The plaques on the 3.5m-high porcelain jar (created in 1972) tell all about him.

The Coconut Monk's complex is visible from the car ferry that runs from near Mytho to Ben Tre province.

It would be nice to think that money from admission tickets is going to maintain the place. But, apparently, this is not the case – the island's adornments are falling apart and the place is becoming increasingly dilapidated. As one traveller lamented:

The island is a great disappointment. It has faded almost into nothing. Beware of the cunning old chap claiming to be an ex-monk who drags you around the few sights at high speed and then demands you buy him an extortionate beer at the kiosk.

**Sue Grossey**

The Mytho police will not permit you to visit this island using a private boat, so you would have to hire a government one for at least US$25 in order to get here from Mytho. However, you can hire a private boat from Ben Tre province, which is just across the river.

## Nguyen Dinh Chieu Temple

This temple is dedicated to Nguyen Dinh Chieu, a local scholar. It's in the Ba Tri district, about a 30-minute drive (36km) from Ben Tre. It's a very charming temple, excellent for photography.

## Bird Sanctuary

The locals make much of the storks that nest at the local bird sanctuary, **San Chim Vam Ho** (☎ 858669; *admission 10,000d*), which is 38km from Ben Tre town. Ben Tre Tourist has speedboats that can make the round trip in about two hours, or slow boats that take about five hours. You can check the going rates at Ben Tre Tourist and compare them with what the freelance boat operators are charging.

To get there overland, follow Đ Nguyen Dinh Chieu east out of town for 20km to Giong Tram. Turn left onto the windy, rural dirt road leading to Trai Tu K-20 (Prison K-20); you'll reach the prison after travelling 11km (you may see hundreds of prisoners out tilling the fields), and then turn right and drive the final 7km to Vam Ho.

## VINH LONG

☎ 070 • pop 124,600

Vinh Long, the capital of Vinh Long province, is a medium-sized town along the banks of the Mekong River, about midway between Mytho and Cantho.

**Cuu Long Tourist** (☎ 823616, fax 823357; Đ 1 Thang 5) is one of the more capable state-run tour outfits in the Mekong Delta. There is also a small **booking office** near the Phuong Thuy restaurant, which rents out bicycles (US$2 per day) and motorbikes (US$8).

Cuu Long Tourist offers a variety of boat tours ranging from three to five hours in length, as well as overnight excursions. Tour destinations include small canals, fruit orchards, brick kilns, a conical palm hat workshop and the Cai Be Floating Market. Homestays at the one of the orchards can also be arranged (see the boxed text 'A Home Away from Home').

As is the case in most of the Mekong Delta, if you're travelling independently you will need to organise at least a few people to go with you in order to make the prices of these tours reasonable.

Internet access can be found at **La Huy** (37 Đ Trung Nu). The rate charged there is 100d per minute.

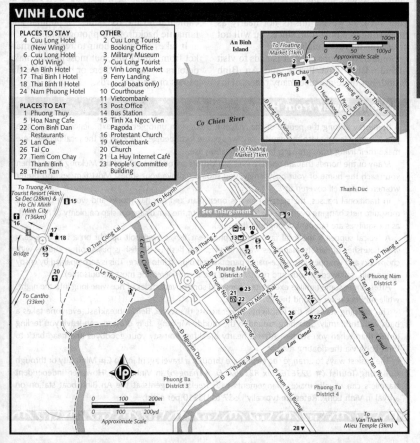

**VINH LONG**

**PLACES TO STAY**
4 Cuu Long Hotel (New Wing)
6 Cuu Long Hotel (Old Wing)
12 An Binh Hotel
17 Thai Binh I Hotel
18 Thai Binh II Hotel
24 Nam Phuong Hotel

**PLACES TO EAT**
1 Phuong Thuy
5 Hoa Nang Cafe
22 Com Binh Dan Restaurants
25 Lan Que
26 Tai Co
27 Tiem Com Chay Thanh Binh
28 Thien Tan

**OTHER**
2 Cuu Long Tourist Booking Office
3 Military Museum
7 Cuu Long Tourist
8 Vinh Long Market
9 Ferry Landing (local boats only)
10 Courthouse
11 Vietcombank
13 Post Office
14 Bus Station
15 Tinh Xa Ngoc Vien Pagoda
16 Protestant Church
19 Vietcombank
20 Church
21 La Huy Internet Café
23 People's Committee Building

## Mekong River Islands

What makes a trip to Vinh Long worthwhile is not the town itself but the beautiful small islands in the river. The islands are totally given over to agriculture, especially the growing of tropical fruit, which are shipped to markets in HCMC.

To visit the islands you have to charter a boat through Cuu Long Tourist. Small boats cost around US$25 per person for a three-hour journey (minimum of three people). However, you may be able to negotiate a better deal. The tours include an English- or French-speaking Vietnamese guide.

One way to bypass the government monopoly is to take the public ferry (3000d) to one of the islands and then walk around on your own; however, this is not nearly as interesting as a boat tour, since you will not cruise the narrow canals.

Some of the more popular islands to visit include Binh Hoa Phuoc and An Binh Island, but there are also many others. This low-lying region is as much water as land, and houses are generally built on stilts. Bring plenty of film because there are photo opportunities in every direction you look.

## Cai Be Floating Market

This bustling river market (open 5am-5pm) is worth including on a boat tour from Vinh Long. It is best to go early in the morning. Wholesalers on big boats moor here, each specialising in one or a few types of fruit or vegetables. Customers cruise the market in smaller boats and can easily find what they're looking for, as the larger boats hang samples of their goods from tall wooden poles.

One interesting thing you won't see at other floating markets is the huge Catholic cathedral on the riverside – a popular and fantastic backdrop for photographs.

It takes about an hour to reach the market from Vinh Long, but most people make detours on the way there or back to see the canals or visit orchards.

### A Home Away from Home

A homestay among the people of the Mekong Delta is an unforgettable experience and can give you a unique insight into the day-to-day lives of the local people. The bulk of the local people here make their living from growing fruit or cultivating rice.

Many of the homes that are open to Western visitors are on the banks of the Mekong River. When you reach the home of your host family, you should remove your shoes. Most families also prefer women to be well covered up.

In traditional houses, the sleeping area is open plan and has hammocks and wooden beds with mosquito nets hanging overhead (before the last rays of the sun disappear slap on plenty of repellent, as mosquitoes are rampant throughout the area).

A typical supper is the local favourite, elephant-ear fish, served bolt upright on a bed of greens with flourishes of carrots shaped as water flowers. The flesh of the fish is pulled off in chunks with chopsticks and wrapped into a rice-paper pancake and dipped into sauce. This is accompanied by crispy spring rolls, followed by soup and rice (Mekong rice is considered the most flavoursome).

After dinner some families exchange stories and songs over bottles of rice wine long into the night, while others cluster around the TV.

The morning starts as the first lights flicker across the water. Before breakfast, everyone takes a bath with the family. Splashing around in the muddy Mekong, fully dressed, can leave you feeling dirtier than when you started! After a hearty breakfast you say your goodbyes and head back to Vinh Long via the floating market.

The easiest ways to arrange such a visit are through a travel agent in Ho Chi Minh City or through **Cuu Long Tourist** (☎ 823616, fax 823357; Đ 1 Thang 5) in Vinh Long. However, independent travellers can usually make arrangements with freelance agents at the An Binh boat station on arrival in Vinh Long. Rates are typically US$7 to US$10 per night.

## Military Museum

It might not be up to the standard of the military museums in HCMC and Hanoi, but there is a military museum *(Bao Tang Quan Su; open 8am-10am & 7pm-9pm Sat & Sun)* close to the Cuu Long Hotel.

## Van Thanh Mieu Temple

A big surprise in Vinh Long is the large and beautiful Van Thanh Mieu Temple *(Phan Thanh Gian Temple; Đ Tran Phu)* by the river. It's unusual as far as Vietnamese temples go. To begin with, it's a Confucian temple, which is very rare in southern Vietnam. Another oddity is that while the rear hall is dedicated to Confucius, the front hall was built in honour of the local hero Phan Thanh Gian. A plaque outside the temple entrance briefly tells his story – Phan Thanh Gian led an uprising in 1930 against the French colonists. When it became obvious that his revolt was doomed, Phan killed himself rather than be captured by the colonial army. No-one is quite certain exactly when the hall honouring Phan was built, but it seems as if it must have been some time after 1975.

The rear hall, built in 1866, has a portrait of Confucius above the altar. The building was designed in the Confucian style and looks like it was lifted straight out of China.

Van Thanh Mieu Temple is several kilometres southeast of town. Don't confuse it with the much smaller Quoc Cong Pagoda on Đ Tran Phu, which you will pass along the way.

## Places to Stay

**Cuu Long Hotel** *(☎ 823656, fax 823357; 501 Đ 1 Thang 5; old-wing rooms with fan/air-con US$20/30, new-wing rooms US$35-45)* has two branches right on the river front. The old wing address is given here. All air-con rooms have satellite TV, and rates include breakfast.

**An Binh Hotel** *(☎ 823190; 3 Đ Hoang Thai Hieu; air-con rooms 130,000-160,000d)* is nice enough, but not favoured by travellers because it's away from the scenic river front. Facilities here include tennis courts and a massage service.

**Nam Phuong Hotel** is well situated near the river and market.

**Thai Binh I Hotel** and **Thai Binh II Hotel** are two cheap options on the outskirts of town. Fan rooms are US$7, air-con rooms are US$10.

**Truong An Tourist Resort** *(☎ 823161; rooms US$25)* is midway on the 8km stretch of road between Vinh Long and the My Thuan bridge. It's a quiet place to stay if you don't mind being away from town. There are cottages here, but not much else to do except sit by the river and enjoy the park-like surroundings.

Cuu Long Tourist can arrange for you to spend the night at one of four **island farmhouses** (see the boxed text 'A Home Away from Home'). Options include staying in a brick house, a colonial-style house or a cottage in a large bonsai garden. Perhaps the most interesting choice is the house built on stilts above the river in the traditional Mekong Delta style. All of these places are certainly peaceful, but they are isolated – commuting to town involves a boat trip. The overnight cost is about US$34 per person, including the boat trip, guide, meals and a stop at the Cai Be floating market.

## Places to Eat

**Thien Tan** *(☎ 824001; 56/1 Đ Pham Thai Buong; mains 40,000-50,000d; open 8am-10pm)* specialises in barbecued dishes and is considered to be the best eatery in town. Recommended is the fish cooked in bamboo *(ca loc nuong tre)* and chicken cooked in clay *(ga nuong dat set)*. If you're feeling brave, consider the roasted rice-field rat *(chout quay)*.

**Tiem Com Chay Thanh Binh** *(☎ 825530; 487 Đ 2 Thang 9; mains 4000-6000d; open 6am-8pm)* dishes up incredibly cheap and delicious vegie fare.

**Phuong Thuy**, right on the river front, has OK food, but what really makes the place is the fine view.

**Hoa Nang Café** is another place for good river views and reasonable meals and is near Phuong Thuy.

**Lan Que** *(☎ 823262; Đ 2 Thang 9)* is a popular local joint that serves up genuine

Vietnamese food, including good turtle and frog dishes.

**Tai Co** has Chinese fare and very good hotpot *(lau)*. It's just down the street from Lan Que.

There are a string of local point-and-eat **com binh dan restaurants** along Đ Nguyen Thi Minh Khai that are worth checking out.

If great food at cheap prices is more important than scenery, check out the **Vinh Long Market**. This is also a great place to find delicious fruit, such as bananas, mangoes and papayas.

### Getting There & Away

**Bus** There are buses between Vinh Long and HCMC (3 hours), which leave HCMC from **Cholon bus station** in District 5, and from **Mien Tay bus station** in An Lac. You can also get to Vinh Long by bus from Mytho, Tra Vinh, Cantho, Chau Doc and other points in the Mekong Delta.

**Car & Motorbike** Vinh Long is just off National Hwy 1, 66km from Mytho, 33km from Cantho and 136km from HCMC.

**Boat** It may also be possible to travel by cargo boat from Vinh Long all the way to Chau Doc (near the Cambodian border), but you'll probably need a Vietnamese person to help you decide if you want to attempt this.

### TRA VINH
☎ 074 • pop 70,000

Bordered by the Tien and Hau branches of the Mekong, Tra Vinh's location on a peninsula makes it somewhat isolated. Getting there is a straight up and back trip, because no car ferries cross the rivers here (motorbikes can be ferried by small boats). Western tourists are few, though there are several very worthwhile things to see here.

There are about 300,000 ethnic Khmer living in Tra Vinh province. At first glance, they might seem to be an invisible minority since they all speak fluent Vietnamese and there is nothing outwardly distinguishing about their clothing or lifestyle. However, digging a little deeper quickly reveals that Khmer culture is alive and well in this part

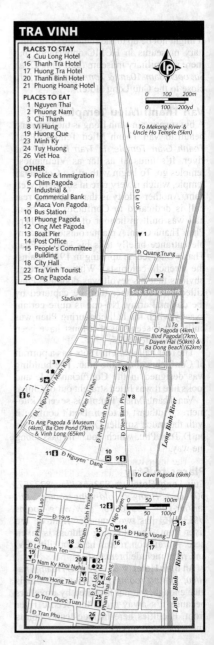

**TRA VINH**

PLACES TO STAY
4 Cuu Long Hotel
16 Thanh Tra Hotel
17 Huong Tra Hotel
20 Thanh Binh Hotel
21 Phuong Hoang Hotel

PLACES TO EAT
1 Nguyen Thai
2 Phuong Nam
3 Chi Thanh
8 Vi Hung
19 Huong Que
23 Minh Ky
24 Tuy Huong
26 Viet Hoa

OTHER
5 Police & Immigration
6 Chim Pagoda
7 Industrial & Commercial Bank
9 Maca Von Pagoda
10 Bus Station
11 Phuong Pagoda
12 Ong Met Pagoda
13 Boat Pier
14 Post Office
15 People's Committee Building
18 City Hall
22 Tra Vinh Tourist
25 Ong Pagoda

To Mekong River & Uncle Ho Temple (5km)

Đ Le Loi

Đ Quang Trung

Stadium

See Enlargement

To O Pagoda (4km),
Bird Pagoda (7km),
Duyen Hai (50km) &
Ba Dong Beach (62km)

Đ Nguyen Thi Minh Khai
Đ Kien Thi Nhan
Đ Dien Bien Phu
Đ Pham Dinh Phung

Long Binh River

To Ang Pagoda & Museum
(4km), Ba Om Pond (7km)
& Vinh Long (65km)

Đ Nguyen Dang

To Cave Pagoda (6km)

Đ Pham Ngu Lao
Đ Pham Dinh Phung
Đ Ngo Quyen
Đ 19/5
Đ Hung Vuong
Đ Le Thanh Ton
Đ Nam Ky Khoi Nghia
Đ Pham Hong Thai
Đ Le Loi
Đ Pham Thai Buong
Đ Tran Quoc Tuan
Đ Tran Phu

Long Binh River

of Vietnam. There are over 140 Khmer pagodas in Tra Vinh province, compared with 50 Vietnamese and five Chinese pagodas. The pagodas have schools to teach the Khmer language – most of the locals in Tra Vinh can read and write Khmer at least as well as Vietnamese.

Vietnam's Khmer minority are almost all followers of Theravada Buddhism. If you've visited monasteries in Cambodia, you may have observed that Khmer monks are not involved in growing food and rely on donations from the strictly religious locals. Here in Tra Vinh, Vietnamese guides will proudly point out the monks' rice harvest as one of the accomplishments of liberation. To the Vietnamese government, nonworking monks were parasites. The Khmers don't necessarily see it the same way, and they continue to donate funds to the monasteries surreptitiously.

Between the ages of 15 and 20, most boys set aside a few months or years to live as monks (they decide themselves on the length of service). Khmer monks can eat meat, though they cannot kill animals.

There is also a small but active Chinese community in Tra Vinh, one of the few remaining in the Mekong Delta region.

## Information
**Tra Vinh Tourist** (☎ 862559, fax 866768; 64-6 Đ Le Loi) has a monopoly here. The staff can book various trips to sites around the province, though the boat trips prove to be the most interesting.

The **Industrial & Commercial Bank** (15A Đ Dien Bien Phu) can exchange foreign currencies and it also handles Visa cash advances.

## Ong Pagoda
The Ong Pagoda (Chua Ong & Chua Tau; cnr Đ Pham Thai Buong & Đ Tran Quoc Tuan) is a very ornate, brightly painted building. Rare for the Mekong Delta region, this is a 100% Chinese pagoda and is still a very active place of worship. The red-faced god on the altar is deified general Quan Cong (in Chinese, Guangong, Guandi or Guanyu). Quan Cong is believed to offer protection against war and is based on an historical figure, a soldier of the 3rd century. You can read more about him in the Chinese classic The Romance of the Three Kingdoms.

The Ong Pagoda was founded in 1556 by the Fujian Chinese Congregation, but has been rebuilt a number of times. Recent visitors from Taiwan and Hong Kong have contributed money for the pagoda's restoration, which is why it is in such fine shape.

## Ong Met Pagoda
The chief reason for visiting this large Khmer pagoda is that it's the most accessible, being right in the centre of town. The monks at Ong Met Pagoda (Chua Ong Met) are friendly and happy to show you around the interior.

## Chim Pagoda
An interesting monastery, Chim Pagoda (Chua Chim) sees few visitors because you have to wind your way along dirt roads to find it. It's actually just 1km off the main highway to Vinh Long in the southwest part of town. Probably the best way to get there, if you don't have your own wheels, is to get a local to take you on a motorbike.

The friendly monks here claim that the pagoda was built 500 years ago, though the present structure is obviously much newer. There are about 20 monks in residence here.

## Ba Om Pond & Ang Pagoda
Known as Ao Ba Om (Square Lake), this is a spiritual site for the Khmers and a picnic and drinking spot for local Vietnamese. The square-shaped pond is surrounded by tall trees and is pleasant if not spectacular.

More interesting is the nearby Ang Pagoda (Chua An in Vietnamese; Angkor Rek Borei in Khmer), a beautiful and venerable Khmer-style pagoda. There is also an interesting **Khmer Minority People's Museum** (Bao Tang Van Hoa Dan Tac; admission free) of Khmer culture on the far side of the lake, though little is labelled in English. Opening hours are irregular.

Ba Om Pond is 7km southwest from Tra Vinh along the highway towards Vinh Long.

## Uncle Ho Temple

Sometimes Vietnam throws something totally unexpected at you. Tra Vinh chips in with the Uncle Ho Temple (Den Tho Bac), dedicated, of course, to the late president Ho Chi Minh. Perhaps Tra Vinh's enterprising People's Committee was looking for a way to distinguish its fine town and put it on the tourist circuit. If so, it may have succeeded – although no monks have taken up residence, 'worshippers' continue to flock here (Communist Party brass arrive regularly in their chauffeur-driven limousines). A local tourist pamphlet calls the temple the 'pride of Tra Vinh's inhabitants'. Ho himself would no doubt be horrified.

The Uncle Ho Temple is located within the Long Duc commune, 5km north of Tra Vinh town.

## Boat Tours

The narrow Long Binh River meanders southward from Tra Vinh town for over 10km before reaching a spillway, which was built to prevent sea water from intruding at high tide. Otherwise, the salt would contaminate the river and kill the crops.

It is possible to hire boats from the pier on the east side of town to take you downstream to the spillway. Of course, Tra Vinh Tourist can also book you onto these trips, which typically take about 1½ hours by speedboat, longer for a slower boat.

Tours can also be arranged to Oyster Island (Con Ngao), an offshore mud flat that supports a small contingent of oyster farmers (of limited interest for most). Tra Vinh Tourist offers trips for US$100 per boat regardless of group size, though you should be able to negotiate something cheaper with boat drivers at the pier.

## Places to Stay

**Huong Tra Hotel** (☎ 853182; 67 Đ Ly Thuong Kiet; rooms with fan & shared toilet 40,000d, with air-con & attached bath 70,000-80,000d is Tra Vinh's dingiest budget place. It's fair to say you get what you pay for.

**Thanh Binh Hotel** (☎ 858906; 1 Đ Le Thanh Ton; rooms with fan/air-con US$4/8)

is slightly better than Huong Tra, though still seedy.

**Phuong Hoang Hotel** (☎ 852270; 1 Đ Le Thanh Ton; singles with fan US$3-5, doubles with air-con US$7-12) is a decent-looking place. All rooms have private bath.

**Thanh Tra Hotel** (☎ 853621, fax 853769; 1 Đ Pham Thai Buong; rooms US$8-27) is where most of the tour groups are put up for the night.

**Cuu Long Hotel** (☎ 862615; 999 Đ Nguyen Thi Minh Khai) was under reconstruction at the time of writing.

## Places to Eat

**Nguyen Thai** (☎ 852145; 88 Đ Le Loi) is a good choice for Vietnamese and seafood – there is a wide variety of choice.

**Phuong Nam** (☎ 853511; Đ Chau Van Tiep) prepares excellent barbecued and clay-pot dishes.

**Vi Hung** (Đ Dien Bien Phu) is a very cheap place doing simple rice dishes.

**Viet Hoa** (☎ 836046; 80 Đ Tran Phu), run by a friendly Chinese family, is one of the best places to eat in town.

**Tuy Huong** (8 Đ Dien Bien Phu) is another good place to sample local Vietnamese fare. Ditto for **Chi Thanh** (105 Đ Nguyen Thi Minh Khai), **Huong Que** (16 Đ Nam Ky Khoi Nghia) and **Minh Ky** (9 Đ Nam Ky Khoi Nghia), nearby.

## Getting There & Away

Tra Vinh is 65km from Vinh Long and 205km from HCMC. Either Vinh Long or Cantho would be logical places to catch buses to Tra Vinh.

## AROUND TRA VINH
## Chua Co

Chua Co is a particularly interesting Khmer monastery because the grounds form a bird sanctuary. Several types of stork and ibis arrive here in large numbers just before sunset to spend the night. Of course, there are many nests here and you must take care not to disturb them.

Chua Co is 43km from Tra Vinh. Travel 36km to Tra Cu, and then follow the sandy road for 7km to the monastery.

## Luu Cu

Some ancient ruins are to be found at Luu
Cu, south of Tra Vinh near the shores of the
Hau Giang River. The ruins include brick
foundations similar to those found at Cham
temples. There have been a series of archaeological digs here and the site is now
protected. Luu Cu attracts a large number of
French tourists. The site is 10km from the
town of Tra Cu (36km from Tra Vinh).

## Ba Dong Beach

This yellow-sand beach is not bad compared with other 'beaches' in the Mekong
Delta, but the main attraction here is the
peace and quiet (it sees very few visitors).
**Tra Vinh Tourist** (☎ 862559) runs a **restaurant** and some simple **bungalows** by the
beach – it is possible to stay overnight for
around US$5.

To get to Ba Dong Beach from Tra Vinh,
head 50km along the paved road to Duyen
Hai and follow the bumpy dirt road for
12km until you reach the beach.

## SA DEC

☎ 067 • pop 101,800

The former capital of Dong Thap province,
Sa Dec gained some small fame as the setting
for *The Lover*, a film based on the novel by
Marguerite Duras. Two of the classic French
villas used in the film can be seen across the
river from the outdoor market area.

Sa Dec is famous for its many nurseries
that cultivate flowers and bonsai trees. The
flowers are picked almost daily and transported fresh to shops in HCMC. These
nurseries are a major sightseeing attraction
for domestic tourists, especially around the
Tet festival holiday.

Groups doing a whirlwind tour of the
Mekong Delta often make a lunch stop here
and drop in on the nurseries.

There's an **Internet service** next door to
the post office.

## Huong Tu Pagoda

The Huong Tu Pagoda (Chua Co Huong Tu)
is of classic Chinese design. A bright white
statue of Quan The Am Bo Tat standing
on a pedestal adorns the grounds. Don't

confuse this place with the adjacent Buu
Quang Pagoda, which is somewhat less
glamorous.

## Nurseries

The nurseries *(vuon hoa)* operate year-round,
though they are practically stripped bare of
their flowers just before Tet. You're welcome
to have a look around, but don't pick any
flowers unless you plan on buying them.
Photography is permitted – indeed, the flower
farmers are quite used to it.

The nurseries don't belong to one person.
There are many small operators here, each

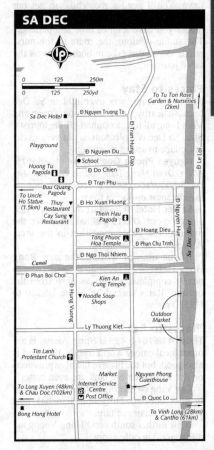

with a different speciality. The most famous garden is called the Tu Ton Rose Garden (Vuon Hong Tu Ton), which has over 500 different kinds of roses in 50 different shades and colours.

## Uncle Ho Statue

We're not being facetious – they really do call it 'Uncle Ho Statue' (Tuong Bac Ho) in Vietnamese. Ho Chi Minh didn't live in Sa Dec, but his father did. To commemorate this bit of historical consequence, a large statue of Ho Chi Minh (but not his father!) has been erected a few kilometres west of town. You'll need a motorbike to get out there, as it's probably too far for a cyclo, unless you have a lot of time and patience. The statue is along the route to the nurseries, so you can take in both sights on the same journey.

## Places to Stay

Not many foreigners overnight in Sa Dec because nearby Cao Lanh, Long Xuyen and Vinh Long all tend to siphon off the tourists. Still, Sa Dec is a pleasant, if not very exciting, place to spend an evening.

**Nguyen Phong Guesthouse** (☎ 866515; A10 Đ Tran Hung Dao; rooms with fan/air-con 80,000/100,000d) is very basic, but it's the cheapest option in town.

**Sa Dec Hotel** (☎ 861430; fan rooms US$8, air-con rooms US$15-18) has long been the main tourist accommodation in the area. All rooms have bathtubs.

At the time of writing, the new **Bong Hong Hotel** (☎ 861301; 80 Đ Quoc Lo) was nearly complete, and looks posh from the outside. Rates should be in the US$20 to US$30 range.

## Places to Eat

**Thuy** (☎ 861644; 439 Đ Hung Vuong) is another local eatery worth trying. The food is also good, but the bizarre facial expressions on the fish in the big tank are even better!

**Cay Sung** (☎ 861749; 437 Đ Hung Vuong) is next door to Thuy and also has respectable Vietnamese fare.

A bit further south on Đ Hung Vuong are a few good noodle shops

## Getting There & Away

Sa Dec, located in Dong Thap province midway between Vinh Long and Long Xuyen, is accessible by bus, minibus and car.

## CAO LANH

☎ 067 • pop 139,100

Cao Lanh is a new town carved from the jungles and swamps of the Mekong Delta region. Its up-and-coming status has much to do with its designation as the provincial capital of Dong Thap province. Boat tours of the bird sanctuaries and Rung Tram Forest are major attractions in this region.

## Information

**Dong Thap Tourist** (☎ 852136, fax 855637; 2 Đ Doc Binh Kieu) deserves kudos for being so helpful. This is the best place to inquire about boat tours of the surrounding area. There is a boat-station **branch office** (☎ 821054) that handles boat tours from a landing in My Hiep village.

Public **Internet access** is available at the Xuan Mai Hotel.

## War Memorial

The War Memorial (Dai Liet Si; admission free), located on the eastern edge of town off Hwy 30, is Cao Lanh's most prominent landmark. This masterpiece of socialist-style sculpture boasts a clamshell-shaped building displaying a large Vietnamese star alongside a hammer and sickle. In front of this are several large concrete statues of victorious peasants and soldiers with upraised fists and brandishing weapons. The surrounding grounds are decked out with the graves of over 3000 VC who died while fighting in the American War.

Construction of the War Memorial began in 1977 and finished in 1984.

## Nguyen Sinh Sac Grave Site

Another significant tomb is that of Nguyen Sinh Sac (1862–1929). Nguyen's main contribution to Vietnamese history was being the father of Ho Chi Minh. His large tomb (Lang Cu Nguyen Sinh Sac) occupies one hectare, about 1km southwest of central Cao Lanh.

Although there are various plaques (in Vietnamese) and tourist pamphlets extolling Nguyen Sinh Sac as a great revolutionary, there is little evidence to suggest that he was involved in the anticolonial struggle against the French.

## Places to Stay

**Cao Lanh Hotel** (☎ 851061; *72 Đ Nguyen Hue; rooms with fan & cold bath 50,000d, with air-con & hot bath 90,000d*) is considerably older and grottier than the others; a definite candidate for renovations.

**Binh Minh Hotel** (☎ 853423; *147 Đ Hung Vuong; rooms with fan/air-con US$3/8*), one of the cheapest places in town, is recommended. The owner is a friendly local school teacher.

**Thien An Hotel** (☎ 853041; *air-con rooms US$10-12*) is about 500m from the War Memorial. This new place is decent value and a couple of the rooms have river views. All rooms have attached hot bath.

**Xuan Mai Hotel** (☎ 852852, fax 853058; *2 Đ Le Qui Don; doubles with air-con US$16-20*) is a recently renovated place behind the post office. All the rooms here are equipped with air-con, hot water and even baths, and Internet access is also available here.

**Hoa Binh Hotel** (☎ 851469, fax 851218; *air-con rooms US$18-25*) is located on the eastern side of town on Hwy 30, opposite the War Memorial. It is the city's most up-market hotel, and rooms have satellite TV. Try to book a room in the pleasant villa at the rear – it's conveniently located near the in-house **beer garden**!

**Song Tra Hotel** (☎ 852504, fax 852623; *178 Đ Nguyen Hue; rooms US$14-20*) also features satellite TV.

## Places to Eat

Cao Lanh is famous for rice-field rats *(chuot dong)*, and it's a good a place as any to sample the local delicacy!

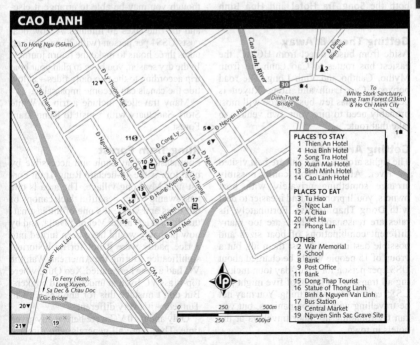

## CAO LANH

To Hong Ngu (56km)

Cao Lanh River

Đ Dien Bien Phu

30

Dinh Trung Bridge

To White Stork Sanctuary, Rung Tram Forest (23km) & Ho Chi Minh City

Đ 30 Thang 4

Đ Ly Thuong Kiet

Đ Nguyen Dinh Chieu

Đ Le Qui Don

Đ Cong Ly

Đ Nguyen Hue

Đ Ly Tu Trong

Đ Nguyen Trai

Đ Hung Vuong

Đ Nguyen Du

Đ Doc Binh Kieu

Đ Thap Moi

Đ Pham Huu Lau

Đ CM-18

To Ferry (4km), Long Xuyen, Sa Dec & Chau Doc

Duc Bridge

0        250        500m
0        250        500yd

**PLACES TO STAY**
1   Thien An Hotel
4   Hoa Binh Hotel
7   Song Tra Hotel
10  Xuan Mai Hotel
13  Binh Minh Hotel
14  Cao Lanh Hotel

**PLACES TO EAT**
3   Tu Hao
6   Ngoc Lan
12  A Chau
20  Viet Ha
21  Phong Lan

**OTHER**
2   War Memorial
5   School
8   Bank
9   Post Office
11  Bank
15  Dong Thap Tourist
16  Statue of Thong Lanh Binh & Nguyen Van Linh
18  Central Market
19  Nguyen Sinh Sac Grave Site

**A Chau** *(☎ 852202; 105B Đ Ly Thuong Kiet; mains 15,000-40,000d; open 8am-9pm)* specialises in fried pancakes *(banh xeo)* that you roll up and dip in fish sauce. The goat hotpot *(lau de)* is also yummy.

**Tu Hao** *(☎ 852589; Đ Dien Bicn Phu, mains 25,000-45,000d; open 10am-9pm)* is one of the best eateries in town. They serve all kinds of barbecued food, including rice-field rats and the snakes who like to eat them! The house special are the fresh spring rolls *(cuon banh trang)*.

**Ngoc Lan** *(208 Đ Nguyen Hue)* is worth a try if you're after something local. We recommend the shredded frog, or better yet, the 'raw dish bowel'.

**Viet Ha** *(☎ 851639)*, serving good Vietnamese food, is on the road to/from the ferry, just south of the Duc Bridge.

**Phong Lan** (Orchid Garden), near Viet Ha, is a tastier but slightly more expensive option.

In a pinch, there are decent restaurants in both the **Song Tra Hotel** and **Hoa Binh Hotel**.

### Getting There & Away
Aside from buses direct from HCMC, the easiest bus routes to Cao Lanh are from Mytho, Cantho and Vinh Long. The road between Cao Lanh and Long Xuyen is beautiful but has few buses – you will most probably need to hire your own vehicle to take that route.

### Getting Around
The sights around Cao Lanh are best visited by river. Although you could possibly arrange something privately with boat owners, you'll probably find it easier to deal with **Dong Thap Tourist**. Fortunately, its rates are reasonable. There are too many different combinations of boat sizes and possible destinations to list them all, but a group of 15 people would be charged about US$2 per person for a half-day tour, including all transport. A group of five might pay US$5 each for the same thing. You may not be travelling with 14 companions, but you can try rounding up other travellers at the hotels in town.

## AROUND CAO LANH
### White Stork Sanctuary
To the northeast of Cao Lanh is a bird sanctuary (Vuon Co Thap Muoi) for white storks. A white stork standing on the back of a water buffalo is the symbol of the Mekong Delta, and you probably have more chance of seeing a stork here than anywhere else. The sanctuary only covers two hectares, but the birds seem mostly undisturbed by the nearby farmers (who have been sternly warned not to hunt them).

The storks have grown accustomed to people and are fairly easy to spot, as they feed in the mangrove and bamboo forests in the area. They live in pairs and don't migrate with the seasons, so you can see them at any time of the year. The birds live on fresh-water crabs and other titbits that they catch in the canals.

There are no roads as such to the bird sanctuary, so getting there requires a trip by boat. Dong Thap Tourist can arrange this, though you may be able to arrange it elsewhere. A speedboat costs US$25 per hour, and the ride takes 50 minutes. A slow boat costs US$4 per person (with 20 people) and takes three hours to make the return journey. In the dry season, you have to plan your boat trip according to the two daily tides – at low tide the canals can become impassable.

Many travellers include a trip to White Stork Sanctuary with a visit to Rung Tram Forest.

### Rung Tram Forest
Southeast of Cao Lanh and accessible by boat tour is the 46-hectare Rung Tram Forest near My Long village. The area is one vast swamp with a beautiful thick canopy of tall trees and vines. It's one of the last natural forests left in the Mekong Delta, and by now probably would have been turned into a rice paddy were it not for its historical significance. During the American War, the VC had a base here called Xeo Quit where top-brass VC lived in underground bunkers. But don't mistake this for another Cu Chi Tunnels – it's very different.

Only about 10 VC were here at any given time. They were all generals who directed the war from here, just 2km from a US military base. The Americans never realised that the VC generals were living right under their noses. Of course, they were suspicious about that patch of forest, and periodically dropped some bombs on it just to reassure themselves, but the VC remained safe in their underground bunkers.

The location of the base was so secret that the wives of the generals didn't even know it. They did occasionally pay their husbands conjugal visits, but this had to be arranged at another special bunker.

When the US military departed from Vietnam in 1973, the VC grew bolder and put the base above ground. Attempts by the South Vietnamese military to dislodge the VC were thwarted – while the South was running out of funding and ammunition, the VC were able to build up their forces in the Mekong Delta and openly challenge the Saigon regime.

Access to the area is most popular by boat, and many visitors combine a visit with a trip to White Stork Sanctuary. A speedboat from Cao Lanh to Rung Tram Forest takes only a few minutes, but a slow boat takes around 30 minutes (depending on the tides). It is also possible now to reach the forest by road if you are travelling by car or motorbike.

Beware of the exceedingly mean red ants here: they are huge, fast and very aggressive.

## Tram Chim Nature Reserve

Due north of Cao Lanh in Tam Nong (Dong Thap province) is Tram Chim National Wetland Reserve (Tram Chim Tam Nong), notable for its eastern sarus cranes (*Grus antigone sharpii*). Over 220 species of birds have been identified within the reserve, but ornithologists will be most interested in the rare red-headed **cranes**, which grow to over 1.5m high. The birds nest here from about December to June. From July to November, they go on holiday to Cambodia, so you must schedule your visit to coordinate with the birds' travel itinerary, if you want to see them. Also, the birds are early risers – early morning is the best time to see them, though you might get a glimpse when they return home in the evening. During the day, the birds are of course engaged in the important matter of eating.

Seeing these birds requires a considerable commitment (time, effort and money), so it's really a special-interest tour. Because you'll need to be up at the crack of dawn, staying in Cao Lanh doesn't work out too well – you would have to head out at 4.30am and travel in the dark over an unlit dirt road. This is not advisable, so you really need to stay at the government guesthouse in Tam Nong, which is much closer to where the birds are.

**Tam Nong** is a sleepy town 45km from Cao Lanh. The one-way drive takes 1½ hours by car, though this may be reduced to an hour when the currently abysmal road is resurfaced. It is also possible to get there by boat. A speedboat takes only one hour, but costs US$25 per hour to rent. A slow boat (US$4 per person) can be arranged from Dong Thap Tourist, but the one-way journey takes four hours and requires 20 people to make it economically viable. From the guesthouse in Tam Nong, it takes another hour by small boat (US$15 per hour) to reach the area where the red-headed cranes live and another hour to return. To this, add whatever time you spend (perhaps an hour) staring at your feathered friends through binoculars (you need to take your own), and then the requisite one to four hours to return to Cao Lanh, depending on your mode of transport.

The state-run **guesthouse** (*fan rooms US$10*) in Tam Nong is just before you cross the bridge heading into the town centre. We found the guesthouse deplorable; not only were the rooms filthy, the place was overrun with thousands of bugs and the staff had no insecticide. If you're going to stay here, you may want to stock up on toxic chemicals in Cao Lanh, or try to score a can of bug killer in town.

Tam Nong shuts down early – if you want to eat dinner in town, make arrangements before 5pm.

**Phuong Chi** (*☎ 827230; 537 Thi Tran Tram Chim*) is a good restaurant close to the market in the town centre. Meals can be served later if you book in advance, but you will have to pay extra.

MEKONG DELTA

There are heaps of mosquitoes in Tam Nong in the evening, so come prepared with insect repellent.

## CANTHO

☎ 071 • pop 330,100

Cantho, capital of Cantho province, is the political, economic, cultural and transportation centre of the Mekong Delta, as well as the largest city in the region. Rice-husking mills provide a major local industry.

This friendly, bustling city is connected to most other population centres in the Mekong Delta by a system of rivers and canals. These waterways and the colourful 'floating markets' around the city are the major tourist drawcard in Cantho – travellers come here to do economical boat trips.

## Information

**Money** Foreign-currency exchange can be done at **Vietcombank** (Ngan Hang Ngoai Thuong Viet Nam; ☎ 820445; 7 ĐL Hoa Binh), as well as at **Indovina Bank** (cnr Đ 30 Thang 4 & Đ Chau Van Liem).

**Travel Agencies** The provincial tourism authority is **Cantho Tourist** (☎ 821852, fax 822719; 18-20 Đ Hai Ba Trung). The staff here are pleasant, speak English, French and Japanese, and are well equipped to serve tourists. This is one of the only Vietnamese tourist offices we've found that can actually provide a map of its own city!

**Vietnam Airlines** (☎ 824088) has a booking desk inside the office.

**Emergency** Try the local **hospital** (cnr Đ Chau Van Liem & ĐL Hoa Binh) for any medical emergencies.

## Munirangsyaram Pagoda

The ornamentation of Munirangsyaram Pagoda (36 ĐL Hoa Binh) is typical of Khmer Hinayana Buddhist pagodas: it doesn't have any of the multiple Bodhisattvas and Taoist spirits common in Vietnamese Mahayana pagodas. In the upstairs sanctuary, a 1.5m-high representation of Siddhartha Gautama, the historical Buddha, sits serenely under a Bodhi tree.

Built in 1946, the Munirangsyaram Pagoda serves the Khmer community of Cantho, which numbers about 2000. The Khmer monks hold daily prayers here.

## Cantonese Congregation Pagoda

This small Chinese pagoda (Quan Cong Hoi Quan; Đ Hai Ba Trung) was built by the Cantonese Congregation. The original one was constructed on a different site about 70 years ago. The current pagoda was built with funds donated by overseas Chinese more recently. Cantho used to have a large ethnic-Chinese population, but most of them fled after the anti-Chinese persecutions (1978–79).

The pagoda occupies a splendid location facing the Cantho River.

## Central Market

This market is strung out along Đ Hai Ba Trung. Many local farmers and wholesalers arrive here by boat to buy and sell. The fruit section, near the intersection of Đ Hai Ba Trung and Đ Ngo Quyen, is particularly colourful and stays open until late evening.

## Ho Chi Minh Museum

This is the only museum (☎ 814764; 6 ĐL Hoa Binh; admission free; open 8am-11am & 2pm-4.30pm Tues-Sat) in the Mekong Delta devoted to Ho Chi Minh, and it's a bit of a mystery as to why it was built here as Ho Chi Minh never lived in Cantho. If you are willing to overlook that small sticking point, there is no reason not to visit this large museum. It's inside a gated courtyard near the main post office.

## Cantho Museum

The enormous Cantho Museum (☎ 813890; 6 Đ Phan Dinh Phuong) is easy to spot – it's located opposite the main post office.

## Boat Tours

The most interesting thing to do in Cantho is take a boat ride through the canals and visit a floating market. The cost for this varies but is around US$3 per hour for a small paddle boat, which can carry two or three passengers. You won't have to look hard for the boats – they will be looking for you. Just wander by the riverside near the market and you'll have plenty of offers. There is of course the option of booking through Cantho Tourist, but this leaves little room for negotiation. Most of the boats are operated by women.

Bring your camera, but keep it in a plastic bag when it's not in use because it's easy to get splashed by the wake of motorised boats. The paddle boats only go on the smaller canals (which are actually more interesting), because the current is weaker.

Larger motor boats can go further afield, and it's worth considering hiring one to make a tour of the Mekong River itself. Check the going rates at Cantho Tourist, and then see what's on offer at the pier by the Ninh Kieu Hotel. For a three-hour tour of the canals and Cai Rang floating market expect to pay around 120,000d for a small boat (one to four people), or 150,000d for a larger one (five to 12 people). The cost of a five-hour boat trip to the Phong Dien floating market (one to 10 people) is around 200,000d. The name of the game is negotiate.

For more on the area's floating markets, see the Around Cantho section.

## Places to Stay

Cantho boasts the best range of accommodation in the Mekong Delta.

### Places to Stay – Budget

**Hien Guesthouse** (☎ 812718; e hien_gh@ yahoo.com; 118/10 Đ Phan Dinh Phung; singles/doubles with fan US$4/5, doubles with air-con US$8) is a bona fide travellers' place. Family-run and friendly, it's tucked down a narrow (and quiet) alley a few minutes' walk from the city centre. The owner is a local school teacher and an excellent source of local travel information. Dependable motorbikes can be rented here for around US$5 a day. Basic but clean rooms come with floor-level mattresses, though proper beds were planned for the new rooms under construction when we last visited.

**Huy Hoang Hotel** (☎ 825833; 35 Đ Ngo Duc Ke; rooms with fan/air-con 80,000/ 130,000d) is another trendy spot for the backpacker crowd.

**Hotel-Restaurant 31** (☎ 825287; 31 Đ Ngo Duc Ke; twins with fan 70,000d, doubles with air-con 120,000d), also popular, is near Huy Hoang. The **restaurant** here is recommended, especially their beef dishes.

**Phan Trung Hotel** (☎ 824477; 9 Đ Le Thanh Ton; fan rooms without bath 50,000d, air-con rooms 110,000-150,000d) is another choice in the budget realm.

**Phong Nha Hotel** (☎ 821615; 75 Đ Chau Van Liem; rooms with fan/air-con 60,000/ 150,000d) is cheap and there is a photoprocessing shop right next door, but it is on a noisy street with many motorbikes.

**Ngan Ha Hotel** (☎ 821024, fax 823396; 39-41 Đ Ngo Quyen; rooms US$10-14) is a private hotel in a convenient but noisy location. All rooms have air-con and hot bath, and rates include breakfast.

### Places to Stay – Mid-Range

**Doan 30 Cantho Hotel** (☎ 823623; 80A Đ Nguyen Trai; rooms with fan/air-con US$10/ 18, deluxe rooms US$20-30) is an army-owned place at the northern end of town. It has some rooms with balconies and river views. There is an outdoor **café** on the riverside, and the hotel's private boat landing is convenient for boat trips. Rates include a simple breakfast.

**Asia Hotel** (Khach San Chau A; ☎ 812800, fax 812779; e asiahotel@hcm.vnn.vn; 91 Đ Chau Van Liem; rooms US$20-35) is a nice place with large balconies. Rates are inclusive of breakfast. There is a similar standard at the nearby **Cantho Hotel**.

**Tay Do Hotel** (☎ 827009, fax 827008; 61 Đ Chau Van Liem; air-con rooms US$27-35) is a recently restored place with amenities like satellite TV. The rooms at the back are quieter, and cheaper.

**Quoc Te Hotel** (International Hotel; ☎ 822079, fax 821039; e ksquocte-ct@hcm .vnn.vn; 12 Đ Hai Ba Trung; rooms US$22-46) is starting to show its age, but it has the advantage of being on the river. The expensive suites have an excellent view of the river, but the budget rooms are pretty bleak and not really worth the price.

**Saigon-Cantho Hotel** (☎ 825831, fax 823288; 55 Đ Phan Dinh Phung; singles

MEKONG DELTA

# CANTHO

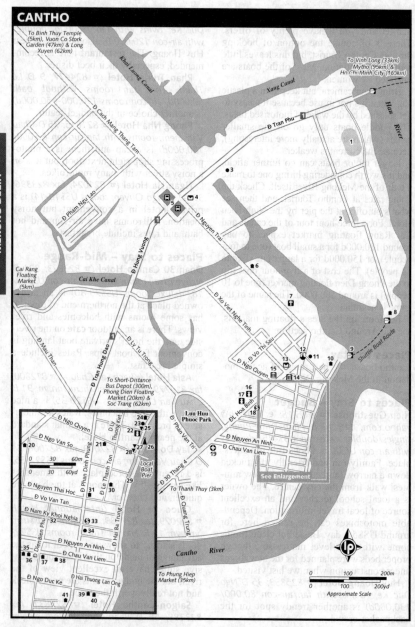

To Binh Thuy Temple
(5km), Vuon Co Stork
Garden (47km) & Long
Xuyen (62km)

Khai Luong Canal

Xang Canal

To Vinh Long (33km)
Mytho (95km) &
Ho Chi Minh City (165km)

Hau River

Đ Cach Mang Thang Tam

Đ Tran Phu

Đ Pham Ngu Lao

Đ Hung Vuong

Đ Nguyen Trai

Cai Rang Floating
Market
(5km)

Cai Khe Canal

Đ Mau Than

Đ Tran Hung Dao

Đ Ly Tu Trong

Đ Xo Viet Nghe Tinh

Đ Vo Thi Sau

Đ Ngo Quyen

Shuttle Boat Route

To Short-Distance
Bus Depot (300m),
Phong Dien Floating
Market (20km) &
Soc Trang (62km)

Luu Huu
Phuoc Park

Đ Phan Van Tri

DL Hoa Binh

Đ Nguyen An Ninh

Đ Chau Van Liem

See Enlargement

Đ Ngo Quyen

Đ Ngo Van So

Đ Ly
Thuong Kiet

Đ Phan Dinh Phung

Đ Le Thanh Ton

Đ Nguyen Thai Hoc

Đ Vo Van Tan

Đ Nam Ky Khoi Nghia

Điện Biên Phu

Đ Nguyen An Ninh

Đ Chau Van Liem

Đ Ngo Duc Ke

Đ Hai Ba Trung

Đ Hai Thuong Lan Ong

Local Boat
Pier

Đ 30 Thang 4

To Thanh Thuy (3km)

Đ Quang Trung

To Phung Hiep
Market (35km)

Cantho River

0      30      60m
0      30      60yd

0        100        200m
0        100        200yd
Approximate Scale

## CANTHO

| PLACES TO STAY | | PLACES TO EAT | | 13 | Main Post Office |
|---|---|---|---|---|---|
| 6 | Doan 30 Cantho Hotel | 2 | Local Cafés | 14 | Cantho Museum |
| 8 | Victoria Cantho Hotel | 25 | Thien Hoa | 15 | Ho Chi Minh Museum |
| 10 | Golf Hotel Cantho | 27 | Mekong; Phuong Nam | 16 | Vietnamese Pagoda |
| 20 | Hoa Binh Hotel | 28 | Nam Bo | 17 | Munirangsyaram |
| 21 | Ngan Ha Hotel | 32 | Restaurant Alley | | Pagoda |
| 24 | Quoc Te Hotel | | | 18 | Vietcombank |
| 30 | Phan Trung Hotel; Fountain | OTHER | | 19 | Hospital |
| 31 | Saigon-Cantho Hotel | 1 | Stadium | 22 | Cantonese Congregation |
| 35 | Asia Hotel | 3 | Cai Khe Market | | Pagoda |
| 36 | Phong Nha Hotel; | 4 | Cai Khe Post Office | 23 | Cantho Tourist |
| | Photo-processing Shop | 5 | Cantho Bus Station | | & Vietnam Airlines |
| 37 | Tay Do Hotel | 7 | Church | 26 | Ho Chi Minh Statue |
| 38 | Cantho Hotel | 9 | Hydrofoil Boat Landing | 29 | Central Market |
| 39 | Huy Hoang Hotel | 11 | Provincial People's | 33 | Indovina Bank |
| 40 | Hotel-Restaurant 31 | | Committee Building | 34 | Local People's |
| 41 | Hien Guesthouse | 12 | Fountain | | Committee Building |

US$30-40, doubles US$39-49) is a three-star place with an in-house **restaurant**, a massage service, a sauna and karaoke. Rates include breakfast.

**Hoa Binh Hotel** (☎ 820059, fax 810217; e hoabinhct@hcm.vnn.vn; 5 ĐL Hoa Binh; rooms US$18-31, suites US$52) was renovated back in 1999 and sort of earns its three stars. Rooms have air-con, IDD phones and satellite TV.

### Places to Stay – Top End

**Victoria Cantho Hotel** (☎ 810111, fax 829259; e victoriact@hcm.vnn.vn, w www .victoriahotels-asia.com; rooms US$110-190, Internet room rates US$80-140), a lovely place, is Cantho's *creme de la creme* and is located right on the river front. There are rooms with garden or river views and eight spacious suites; rates include tax and service. Facilities include two fine **restaurants**, an open-air bar, tennis courts and a swimming pool; even if you're not staying at the resort, it is worth coughing up US$5 for day use of the pool. The shuttle boat across the river is free. The hotel offers high-priced boat trips which link the Victoria Cantho and Chau Doc resorts in 2½ hours (US$55 per person); stopovers can be arranged en route.

**Golf Hotel Cantho** (☎ 812210, fax 812282; e golf4@hcm.vnn.vn; w www .vietnamgolfhotel.com; 2 Đ Hai Ba Trung; rooms US$60-70, suites US$130-180) is an enormous and glitzy new riverside high rise near the Ninh Kieu pier. Tastefully decorated rooms are furnished to a 'T' and there are incredible views from the upper-floor balconies. Hotel facilities include a swimming pool, a health club and a beauty salon, and room rates include tax and service.

### Places to Eat

Along the Cantho River waterfront there are several café-restaurants, most serving Mekong specialities such as fish, frog and turtle, as well as standard backpacker fare.

**Nam Bo** (☎ 823908; 50 Đ Hai Ba Trung; mains 25,000-50,000d; open 9am-11pm) offers excellent European and Vietnamese cuisine in a delightful atmosphere. It is housed in a thoughtfully restored, classic French villa, and the view of the local fruit market from the 2nd-storey terrace can't be beat. If you can't decide what to order, the pizzas are recommended.

You'll find several other popular eateries along the river-front strip, across from the huge silver Uncle Ho statue (which, incidentally, bears a curious resemblance to the Tin Man in *The Wizard of Oz*).

Always packed are **Mekong** (☎ 821646; 38 Đ Hai Ba Trung; mains 15,000-25,000d; open 6am-2am) and **Phuong Nam** (☎ 812077; 48 Đ Hai Ba Trung; most mains 25,000d; open 9am-11pm), both of which serve good Vietnamese food.

The speciality of the house at **Thien Hoa** (☎ 821942; 26 Đ Hai Ba Trung; mains 15,000-25,000d; open 9am-11pm) are delicious Hué-style spring rolls *(dac biet cha gio re)*.

**Restaurant Alley** *(Đ Nam Ky Khoi Nghia)* is an appropriate name for this place, a good spot to escape the tourist scene on the river front. Situated in an alley between Đ Dien Bien Phu and Đ Phan Dinh Phung, there are about a dozen **local restaurants** scattered on both sides of the street.

**Thanh Thuy** *(☎ 840207; 149 Đ 30 Thang 4; mains 20,000-40,000d; open 10am-10pm)* is a goat-meat speciality restaurant run by a Frenchman named Christian – formerly a chef in Toulouse. Try the curried goat, or if you're feeling brave, the goat-scrotum hot-pot. They also do good standard Vietnamese fare. The restaurant is a few kilometres out of town, just beyond the local university. Look for the sign on your left, just beyond the junction with Đ Tran Hoang Na. You can easily reach it by bicycle or on a *xe loi* (see Getting Around in this section) for about 5000d per person.

## Getting There & Away

**Air** Vietnam Airlines has had on-again off-again flights between Cantho and HCMC. At the time of writing, flights were off again.

**Bus** There are buses leaving HCMC from Mien Tay bus station in An Lac (5 hours). Express minibuses make the same trip in about the same time.

The **main bus station** in Cantho is about a kilometre north of town at the intersection of Đ Nguyen Trai and Đ Tran Phu. There is another **short-haul bus depot** about 300m south of the intersection of Đ 30 Thang 4 and Đ Mau Than, which is good for getting to/from Soc Trang and the Phung Hiep floating market.

**Car & Motorbike** Whether you travel by car or motorbike, the ride from HCMC to Cantho along National Hwy 1 takes about four hours. There is one ferry crossing at Binh Minh (in Cantho). The Cantho ferry runs from 4am to 2am.

To get from ĐL Hoa Binh in Cantho to the ferry crossing, go along Đ Nguyen Trai to the main bus station and turn right onto Đ Tran Phu.

## Getting Around

**Xe Loi** Unique to the Mekong Delta, these makeshift vehicles are the main form of transport around Cantho. A *xe loi* is essentially a two-wheeled wagon attached to the rear of a motorbike, creating what resembles

---

### It Could Be You

Asians love to gamble, and the Vietnamese are no exception. Lottery madness has swept Vietnam, particularly in the south (the rage has yet to consume hill tribes in the northern provinces), with tickets being issued in some 40 different provincial areas. While Vietnam's lottery is a legitimate, government-sanctioned cash cow, frequently reported ticket forgeries, as well as occasional printing mistakes, add a whole other element to the game.

Tickets come in three basic varieties, each costing 2000d. The most popular style is roughly fashioned on paper currency and features chic 1970s motifs like cherry-red sports cars, flowers or voluptuous Vietnamese supermodels. Less popular are instant tickets, sealed in a perforated paper packet and checked on the spot with the vendors who hold the day's winning numbers. Finally there are instant win scratch cards, which are most popular in the central provinces and typically decorated with exotic African wildlife.

Tickets are primarily pedalled on the street by young children and the elderly, who clear a 10% commission on each ticket sold (less than US1¢). Daily winning numbers, announced each afternoon, can be checked with the vendors (earning you the unspoken obligation to buy another one) or in local newspapers the following day. Cash prizes, determined by winning numbers sequentially matching the six-digit number on your ticket, max out at 50 million dong, about US$350. Winners have one month to make claims.

a motorised cyclo, but with four wheels touching the ground rather than two. Fares around town should be about 3000d per person (they can carry two, or sometimes more), a bit higher for trips to outlying areas.

## AROUND CANTHO

Perhaps the biggest drawcard of the delta is its colourful **floating markets**. Unlike the floating markets you may have seen in Thailand, where small wooden boats thread narrow canals, most floating markets here are on the banks of wide stretches of river. Most open early to avoid the daytime heat, so try to visit between 6am and 8am. The tides, however, are also a factor as bigger boats must often wait until the water is high enough for them to navigate.

Today, a number of the smaller, rural floating markets are disappearing, largely due to improved roads and access to private and public transport. Many of the larger markets near urban areas, however, are still going strong.

Rural areas of Cantho province, renowned for their durian, mangosteen and orange orchards, can easily be reached from Cantho by boat or bicycle.

### Cai Rang Floating Market

Just 6km from Cantho in the direction of Soc Trang is Cai Rang, the biggest floating market in the Mekong Delta. There is a bridge here that serves as a great vantage point for photography. The market is best before 9am, and though some vendors hang out until noon, it's less lively by then.

Cai Rang can be seen from the road, but it is far more interesting to reach by boat. From the market area in Cantho, it takes about an hour by river, or you can drive to the Cau Dau Sau boat landing (by the Dau Sau Bridge), from where it only takes about 10 minutes to reach the market.

### Phong Dien Floating Market

This is perhaps the best floating market in the Mekong Delta, as there are fewer motorised craft here and more stand-up rowing boats. It's less crowded than Cai Rang, and there are far fewer tourists. The market is

at its bustling best between 6am and 8am. Phong Dien is 20km southwest of Cantho, and most get there by road.

It is theoretically possible to do a whirlwind boat trip here, visiting the small canals on the way and finishing back at the Cai Rang floating market. This journey should take approximately five hours return from Cantho.

### Phung Hiep Market

Until recently, the small town of Phung Hiep was notable for its eerie snake market. In 1998, however, a new national law banned the capture and sale of snakes in an effort to control the rapidly multiplying rat population (due to a relative absence of snakes) which had been devastating rice crops. Snake sellers throughout the country are now forced to operate underground.

These days the snake cages that used to swell with cobras and pythons are empty, and Phung Hiep is back to being a regular (yet interesting) market. There is a small-scale floating market under the bridge and boats can be hired here for a tour along the river.

Phung Hiep is right on National Hwy 1, and is 35km from Cantho in the direction of Soc Trang.

### Stork Garden

Vuon Co (admission 2000d) is a 1.3-hectare stork sanctuary on the road between Cantho and Long Xuyen. It is a popular stop for group tours, who come to view the thousands of storks that reside here. There is a tall wooden viewing platform, and the best times of day to see the birds are from 5am to 6am, and again between 4pm and 6pm.

Vuon Co is in the Thot Not district, about 15km southeast of Long Xuyen. Look for a sign in the hamlet of Thoi An: 'Ap Von Hoa'; coming from Cantho the sign is on the west side of the road, immediately after a small bridge. It is a few kilometres off the main highway. Walk to it in about 30 minutes, or hire a motorbike taxi for about 5000d.

## SOC TRANG

☎ 079 • pop 110,800

Soc Trang is the capital of Soc Trang province. Khmer people make up about 28%

population. The town itself isn't much, but the Khmers have built some very impressive temples in the area. Furthermore, there is a very colourful annual festival (usually in December), and if you're in the vicinity at the right time, it's very much worth your while to catch it.

**Soc Trang Tourist** (☎ 821498, ☎ 822015, fax 821993; 131 Đ Nguyen Chi Thanh) is adjacent to the Phong Lan 2 Hotel. The staff are friendly enough, but speak little English and are not all that accustomed to walk-in tourists.

### Kh'leng Pagoda

This stunning pagoda (Chua Kh'leng) looks like it's been transported straight from Cambodia. Originally built from bamboo in 1533, it had a complete rebuild in 1905 (this time using concrete). There are seven religious festivals held here every year that are worth seeing – people come from outlying areas of the province for these events. Even at outside of festival times, Khmer people drop in regularly to bring donations and pray.

At the time of writing, 10 monks were residing in the pagoda. This place also serves as a base for over 150 student monks who come from around the Mekong Delta to study at Soc Trang's College of Buddhist Education across the street. The monks are friendly, and happy to show you around the pagoda and discuss Buddhism.

### Khmer Museum

This museum is dedicated to the history and culture of Vietnam's Khmer minority. Indeed, it serves as a sort of cultural centre, and traditional dance and music shows are periodically staged here. You'll have to make inquiries about performances because there is no regular schedule; however, there's no doubt that something could be arranged for a group provided a little advance notice is given.

The Khmer Museum, opposite Kh'leng Pagoda, is officially closed on weekends, but even during the week you may have to roust someone to let you in.

### Clay Pagoda

Buu Son Tu (Precious Mountain Temple) was founded over 200 years ago by a Chinese family named Ngo. Today the temple is better known as Chua Dat Set (Đ Mau Than 68; admission free) or Clay Pagoda.

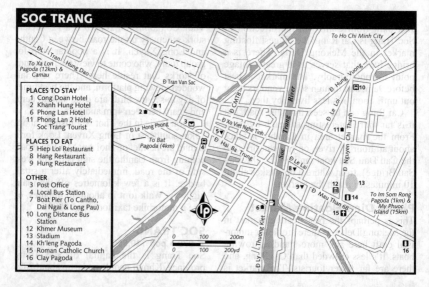

## SOC TRANG

To Ho Chi Minh City

ĐL Tran Hung Dao

To Xa Lon Pagoda (12km) & Camau

Đ Tran Van Sac

**PLACES TO STAY**
1 Cong Doan Hotel
2 Khanh Hung Hotel
6 Phong Lan Hotel
11 Phong Lan 2 Hotel; Soc Trang Tourist

**PLACES TO EAT**
5 Hiep Loi Restaurant
8 Hang Restaurant
9 Hung Restaurant

**OTHER**
3 Post Office
4 Local Bus Station
7 Boat Pier (To Cantho, Dai Ngai & Long Pau)
10 Long Distance Bus Station
12 Khmer Museum
13 Stadium
14 Kh'leng Pagoda
15 Roman Catholic Church
16 Clay Pagoda

Đ Hung Vuong

Đ Le Hong Phong

Đ Xo Viet Nghe Tinh

Đ Le Loi

Soc Trang River

Đ Nguyen Chi Thanh

To Bat Pagoda (4km)

Đ Hai Ba Trung

Đ Le Lai

Đ Mau Than 68

Đ Ly Thuong Kiet

To Im Som Rong Pagoda (1km) & My Phuoc Island (15km)

0    100    200m
0    100    200yd

Unassuming from the outside, this pagoda is highly unusual in that nearly everything inside is made entirely of clay. These objects were hand-sculpted by the monk Ngo Kim Tong. From age 20 until his death at 62, Tong, a genius artisan, dedicated his life to decorating the pagoda. He made the hundreds of statues and sculptures that adorn the interior today.

Entering the pagoda, visitors are greeted by one of Ngo's greatest creations – a six-tusked clay elephant (which is said to have appeared in a dream of Buddha's mother). Behind this is the centre altar, which alone was built from over five tonnes of clay. In the altar are a thousand Buddhas seated on lotus petals. Other highlights include a 13-storey Chinese-style tower over 4m tall. The tower features 208 cubbyholes, each with a mini-Buddha figure inside, and is decorated with 156 dragons.

Two giant candles have been burning unceasingly since the clay artist died in 1970. To get an idea of how big these were to begin with (200kg and 260cm tall), there is another pair waiting to be lit when the current ones (expected to burn until 2005) are spent.

Though some of the stuff here is bordering on kitsch (our favourites are the lions with red light bulbs for eyeballs), the pagoda was not intended to be a Dalatesque tacky tourist theme park. It is an active place of worship, and totally different from the Khmer and Vietnamese Buddhist pagodas found elsewhere in Soc Trang. The resident monk, Ngo Kim Giang, is the younger brother of the artist and a delightful old man to chat with about the pagoda. He speaks excellent French, but unfortunately very little English.

The Clay Pagoda is within walking distance of the town centre. Needless to say, the clay objects in the pagoda are highly fragile – do not touch.

## Im Som Rong Pagoda

This large, beautiful Khmer pagoda was built in 1961 and is notable for its well-kept gardens. A plaque on the grounds honours the man who donated the funds to build the pagoda. There are many monks in residence here, most of whom are very friendly and happy to chat.

Im Som Rong Pagoda is over 1km east of Soc Trang on the road to My Phuoc Island. When you reach the main gate it's a 300m walk along a dirt track to the pagoda itself.

## Oc Bom Boc Festival

This is a Khmer name so don't bother trying to look it up in your Vietnamese dictionary. Once a year, the Khmer community turns out for longboat races on the Soc Trang River, an event that attracts visitors from all over Vietnam and even Cambodia. First prize is over US$1000, so it's not difficult to see why competition is so fierce.

The races are held according to the lunar calendar on the 15th day of the 10th moon, which roughly means December. The races start at noon, but things get jumping in Soc Trang the evening before. Not surprisingly, hotel space is at a premium during the festival, and travellers without a prepaid hotel reservation will probably have to sleep in a car or minibus.

## Places to Stay

**Phong Lan 2 Hotel** (☎ 821757; 133 Đ Nguyen Chi Thanh; doubles with fan US$8, with air-con US$10-16), though run-down, is still an OK place to stay and notable for its massage and sauna service.

**Khanh Hung Hotel** (☎ 821027, fax 820099; 15 ĐL Tran Hung Dao; fan rooms US$5, air-con rooms US$9-12) boasts a large indoor-outdoor café. There is satellite TV, but it only shows Indian soap operas and movies.

**Cong Doan Hotel** (☎ 825614; 4 Đ Tran Van Sac), nearly opposite the Khanh Hung, is a state-run hotel that was under reconstruction at the time of writing.

**Phong Lan Hotel** (☎ 821619; 124 Đ Dong Khoi; fan rooms US$16, air-con rooms US$21-23), near the river, is a bit pricey by local standards. If you're with a group, the hotel can arrange a traditional Khmer music and dance show.

## Places to Eat

Most restaurants in Soc Trang do not have English menus, nor are meal prices written

MEKONG DELTA

anywhere, so you will have to work it out in this town like the Vietnamese do.

**Hung** (☎ 822268; 74-6 Đ Mau Than 68) is one of the best places in town. It's open from breakfast until late into the evening and always seems to be busy.

**Hang** (☎ 822416; 2 Đ Le Lai) and **Hiep Loi** (☎ 821301; 11 Đ CMT8; open 5.30am-10.30pm) are two other popular local spots worth trying for Vietnamese food.

## AROUND SOC TRANG
### Bat Pagoda
This is one of the Mekong Delta's most unusual sights, and it has now become a favourite stopoff for both foreign and domestic tourists. The Bat Pagoda (Chua Doi) is a large monastery compound. You enter through an archway and almost immediately hear the eerie screeching of the large colony of fruit bats that resides here. There are literally thousands of these creatures hanging from the fruit trees. The largest bats weigh about 1kg and have a wing span of about 1.5m.

Fruit bats make plenty of noise – in the morning the din is incredible, and likewise the smell. The bats are not toilet trained, so watch out when standing under a tree or bring an umbrella. In the evening, the bats spread their wings and fly out to invade orchards all over the Mekong Delta, much to the consternation of farmers, who are known to trap the bats and eat them. Inside the monastery the creatures are protected, and the bats seem to know this – no doubt this is why they stay.

Locals tend to show excessive zeal in shaking the trees to make the bats fly around so that tourists can take photos but it's better to leave the poor things in peace. You can easily get a photo of the bats hanging off a branch if you have a good telephoto lens. The best times for visiting are early morning and at least an hour before sunset, when the bats are most active. Around dusk, hundreds of bats swoop out of the trees to go hunting.

The monks are very friendly and don't ask for money, though it doesn't hurt to leave a donation. The pagoda is decorated

with gilt Buddhas, and murals paid for by overseas-Vietnamese contributors. In one room there's a life-size statue of the monk who was the former head of the complex. There is also a beautifully painted Khmer longboat here of the type used at the Oc Bom Boc Festival.

Behind the pagoda is a bizarre tomb painted with the image of a pig. It was erected in memory of a pig with five toenails (usually pigs have only four toenails). It died in 1996, but two other rare pigs with five toenails have survived and are being raised by the monks. These pigs are not for eating – they are pets.

Little kids hang around the front gate and beg from the tourists, but they aren't allowed inside the monastery grounds. We didn't give money but handed over a packet of biscuits – the kids devoured them as if they hadn't eaten in over a week. Perhaps they hadn't.

There is a **restaurant** just opposite the Bat Pagoda, but it does not serve bat meat.

The Bat Pagoda is about 4km west of Soc Trang. You can catch a motorbike taxi here, or easily walk there in under an hour. About 3km out of town towards the pagoda the road splits into two – take the right fork and continue for 1km.

### Xa Lon (Sa Lon) Pagoda
This magnificent, classic Khmer pagoda is 12km from Soc Trang, towards Camau, on National Hwy 1. The original structure was built over 200 years ago from wooden materials. In 1923 it was completely rebuilt, but proved to be too small. From 1969 to 1985, the present-day large pagoda was slowly built as funds trickled in from donations. The ceramic tiles on the exterior of the pagoda are particularly stunning.

As at other pagodas, the monks lead an austere life. They eat breakfast at 6am and beg for contributions until 11am, when they hold a one-hour worship. They eat again at noon and study in the afternoon – they do not eat dinner.

At present, around 25 monks reside here. The pagoda also operates a school for the study of Buddhism and Sanskrit. The reason for studying Sanskrit, as the monks explained, is that all original books about Buddhism were written in this ancient language.

## My Phuoc Island

A 15km journey east of Soc Trang brings you to the Hau River. From there it's a short boat ride to My Phuoc Island. It's an isolated spot very suitable for growing fruit. The local government tourist agency likes to bring foreigners here for tours of the orchards. You can do it yourself, though this is a little complicated since you'll need a motorbike to get to the river.

## BAC LIEU

☎ 0781 • pop 129,300

Bac Lieu, the capital of southern Bac Lieu province, is 280km from HCMC. Of the 800,000 people living in the province, about 8% are of Chinese or Cambodian origin.

The town has a few elegant but forlorn French colonial buildings, like the impressive **Fop House** (now used as a community sports centre), but not much else.

Farming is a difficult occupation here because of saltwater intrusion, which means that the town has remained fairly poor. The province is, however, known for its healthy longan orchards. In addition to this, the enterprising locals eke out a living from fishing, oyster collection and shrimp farming, as well as salt production (obtained from evaporating saltwater ponds that form immense salt flats).

For the Vietnamese people, Bac Lieu's main claim to fame is the grave site of Cao Van Lau (1892–1976), famed composer of 'Dai Coa Hoai Long' ('Night Song of the Missing Husband'; see the boxed text.)

Most foreigners give the tomb a miss, and instead use Bac Lieu as a springboard to reach the outstanding bird sanctuary out of town. However if you're keen on seeing it, head out on Đ Cao Van Lau towards the bird sanctuary for about 1km, turn right and follow the dirt road for 150m to the grave.

The sleepy **Bac Lieu tourist office** (☎ 822623, fax 823655) is next to the Bac Lieu Hotel.

---

### Dai Coa Hoai Lang

Since my husband
Carried a sword and set off
I have been waiting for news of him
At night in my dreams
I look forward to receiving his news
And my heart aches
Though you live far away
You should not be unfaithful
Every night I long for news of you

In the daytime I am like a stone
Looking for my husband
Do you know, darling
That every night I am troubled with worries
When will we be reunited?
Don't let our love fade
My only wish is for your good health
And that one day you will return home
So we can live again as one

---

## Places to Stay & Eat

Most hotels in town are near the roundabout where the roads fork off to Soc Trang and Camau.

**Bac Lieu Guest House** (☎ 823815; 8 Đ Ly Tu Trong; doubles with fan & shared toilet US$4, with air-con & toilet US$6-7) is a real budget special.

**Bac Lieu Hotel** (☎ 822437, fax 823655; 4-6 Đ Hoang Van Thu; air-con rooms US$15-25) is a fancier place.

**Hoang Cung Hotel** (☎ 823362; 1B/5 Đ Tran Phu; fan rooms 100,000d, air-con 150,000-250,000d), about 1km from the roundabout (in the direction of Soc Trang), has clean rooms.

There is an OK **restaurant** in the Bac Lieu Hotel, but you're better off looking outside for local **seafood restaurants**.

## AROUND BAC LIEU
### Bac Lieu Bird Sanctuary

Five kilometres from town, Bac Lieu Bird Sanctuary (Vuon Chim Bac Lieu; ☎ 835991; admission 10,000d) is most notable for its 50-odd species of birds, including a large population of graceful white herons. This is one of the most interesting sights in the

MEKONG DELTA

Mekong Delta, and is surprisingly popular with Vietnamese tourists. Foreign visitors are rare, probably because Bac Lieu is in such an out-of-the-way place.

Whether or not you get to see any birds depends on what time of year you visit. Bird populations are at their peak in the rainy season – approximately May to October. The birds hang around to nest until about January, then fly off in search of greener pastures. There are basically no birds from February until the rainy season begins again.

Because of flooding, most travellers try to avoid the Mekong Delta during the rainy season, so it's better to aim for a December visit.

Although the drive is only 5km, the road is in bad shape. The rest of the trek is through dense jungle. Bring plenty of repellent as there are lots of mosquitoes. There is some mud to slog through so don't wear your expensive Italian shoes and white socks. You should also bring bottled drinking water, binoculars, film and a camera (with a powerful telephoto lens, if you have one).

Pay the admission fee when you reach the entrance of the bird sanctuary. You can (and should) hire a guide here – you'll probably get lost without one. Actually, the guides aren't supposed to take any money, so give them a tip (US$2 is enough) discreetly. Most guides do not speak English. Transport and guides can also be arranged at the Bac Lieu tourist office, but hiring a guide here will cost you around US$8.

### Xiem Can Khmer Pagoda

Following the same road that takes you to the Bac Lieu Bird Sanctuary, drive 7km from Bac Lieu to reach this pagoda. As Khmer pagodas go, it's OK, but you can definitely see better ones in Tra Vinh or Soc Trang (not to mention Cambodia).

### Bac Lieu Beach

The same road leading to the Bac Lieu Bird Sanctuary and Xiem Can Khmer Pagoda eventually terminates 10km from Bac Lieu at this beach (Bai Bien Bac Lieu). Don't expect any white sand – it's hard-packed Mekong Delta mud. Quite a few shellfish and

other slimy (and probably poisonous) things crawl around where the muck meets the sea. Tidal pool enthusiasts might be impressed. Locals may be willing to take you for a walk on the tidal flats where they harvest oysters.

### Moi Hoa Binh Pagoda

This Khmer pagoda (Chua Moi Hoa Binh or Se Rey Vongsa) is 13km south of Bac Lieu along National Hwy 1 (look to your left while driving to Camau).

The pagoda is uniquely designed, and chances are good that the monastery's enormous tower will catch your eye even if you're not looking for it. As pagodas in Vietnam go, it's relatively new, having first been built in 1952. The tower was added in 1990 and is used to store the bones of the deceased. There is a large and impressive meeting hall in front of the tower.

Most Khmer people in the area head for monastery schools in Soc Trang to receive a Khmer education. Apart from the small contingent of student monks, very few students study at the Moi Hoa Binh Pagoda.

## CAMAU
☎ 0780 • pop 173,300

Built on the swampy shores of the Ganh Hao River, Camau is the capital and largest city in Camau province, which has a total population of 1.7 million, and occupies the southern tip of the Mekong Delta. A wasteland for centuries, the area was first cultivated in the late 17th century.

Camau lies in the middle of Vietnam's largest swamp. The area is known for mosquitoes the size of hummingbirds – during the rainy season you might need a shotgun to keep them at bay. The mosquitoes come out in force just after dark and some travellers find they need to sit under a mosquito net just to eat dinner. The population of Camau includes many ethnic Khmers. Due to the boggy terrain, this area has the lowest population density in southern Vietnam.

Camau has developed rapidly in recent years, but the town itself is rather dull. We recommend treading softly around the local police force. The main attractions here are the nearby swamps and forests, which can be explored by boat. Bird-watchers and aspiring botanists are reportedly enthralled with the area. Unfortunately, high hotel prices, the long distance from HCMC and the vampire mosquitoes all conspire to keep the number of foreigners to a minimum. Still, the local tourist literature tries hard: 'Camau – people and nature still remain innocent, generous and of specialty fit stature.'

## Information

**Travel Agencies** Interesting boat trips (two days and two nights to Nam Can, Dat Mui (Cape Camau), the Da Bac Islands and the U-Minh Forest) can be organised at **Camau Tourist** (Cong Ty Du Lich Minh Hai; ☎ 831828; 1 Đ Ly Bon). Other services available here include foreign-currency exchange, boat rentals and visa extensions.

**Money** Near the post office, **Incombank**, does foreign-currency exchange and cash advances for Visa and MasterCard.

## Zoo

Officially labelled the 19th May Forest Park, Camau's zoo 'shelters' a poorly maintained collection of miserable animals.

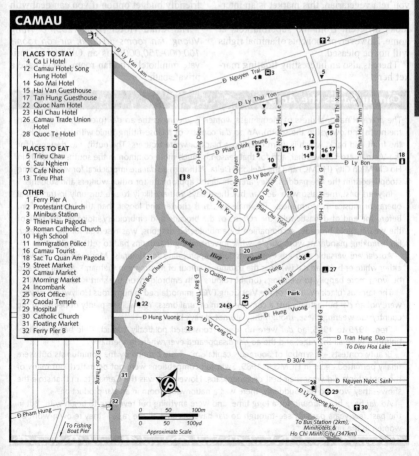

**CAMAU**

PLACES TO STAY
4  Ca Li Hotel
12 Camau Hotel; Song Hung Hotel
14 Sao Mai Hotel
15 Hai Van Guesthouse
17 Tan Hung Guesthouse
22 Quoc Nam Hotel
23 Hai Chau Hotel
26 Camau Trade Union Hotel
28 Quoc Te Hotel

PLACES TO EAT
5  Trieu Chau
6  Sau Nghiem
7  Cafe Nhon
13 Trieu Phat

OTHER
1  Ferry Pier A
2  Protestant Church
3  Minibus Station
8  Thien Hau Pagoda
9  Roman Catholic Church
10 High School
11 Immigration Police
16 Camau Tourist
18 Sac Tu Quan Am Pagoda
19 Street Market
20 Camau Market
21 Morning Market
24 Incombank
25 Post Office
27 Caodai Temple
29 Hospital
30 Catholic Church
31 Floating Market
32 Ferry Pier B

0    50    100m
0    50    100yd
Approximate Scale

To Fishing Boat Pier

To Bus Station (2km), Minihotels & Ho Chi Minh City (347km)

To Dieu Hoa Lake

**MEKONG DELTA**

In the grounds of the zoo, along with a few noisy **cafés**, is a 'botanic garden', which looks rather like a half-acre patch of weeds. In short, there is nothing particularly inviting to see or do here.

## Camau Market

Try not to get this place confused with the zoo. This is actually a wholesale market, and not really a place for people to do their shopping. The animal life that's on display here, including heaps of fish and turtles, is cleaned, packed into crates, frozen and shipped off to HCMC by truck. Even if you're a vegetarian, this market is an interesting place to wander around – it certainly looks different from the supermarkets at home. However, proponents of animal rights will not be pleased.

There is also an interesting **floating market** here.

## Caodai Temple

Though not as large as the one in Tay Ninh, the Caodai Temple (Đ Phan Ngoc Hien) is still an impressive place, and it's staffed by friendly monks. The temple was built in 1966 and seems to be fairly active.

## Places to Stay

By the standards of most other Mekong Delta cities, Camau's hotels tend to be a bit pricey for what you get.

**Hai Van Guesthouse** (Nha Nghi Thanh Son; ☎ 832897; 18 Đ Phan Dinh Phung; rooms with fan & shared bath 40,000d) is a friendly budget option if you can deal with a little dirt.

**Hai Chau Hotel** (☎ 831255; Đ Hung Vuong; fan rooms 50,000d, air-con rooms 100,000-150,000d) is an OK-looking private minihotel. The fan rooms don't have a private bath.

---

### Camau Saves the *Ao Dai*

The graceful national dress of Vietnamese women is known as the *ao dai* (pronounced ow-zai in the north and ow-yai in the south). An *ao dai* consists of a close-fitting tunic with long panels at the front and back, which is worn over loose black or white trousers. The outfit was designed for the Vietnamese hot weather, and for that reason is much more common in the south, especially in Ho Chi Minh City (HCMC) and the Mekong Delta. Although *ao dai* are impractical for women doing stoop labour in the rice paddies, they are considered appropriate for office workers and students.

In years past, men also wore *ao dai*, but these days you are likely to see this only in traditional operas or musical performances. The male *ao dai* is shorter and looser than the female version. Before the end of dynastic rule, the colours of the brocade and embroidery indicated the rank of the wearer; gold brocade, accompanied by embroidered dragons, was reserved for the emperor. High-ranking mandarins wore purple, while lower-ranking mandarins had to settle for blue.

*Ao dai* are versatile and are even considered appropriate for funerals. Mourners usually wear either white or black *ao dai* (white is the traditional colour of mourning in Vietnam). *Ao dai* can also be worn more happily to weddings (bright colours with embroidery on the shirt is appropriate).

The famous 'black pyjamas' of the Viet Cong (VC), immortalised in numerous Hollywood movies, were not *ao dai* but actually just a common form of rural dress. You will see plenty of people in the countryside wearing these, though they are not always black.

From 1975 to 1985, *ao dai* were no longer considered politically correct. Chic baggy military uniforms were all the rage, and the *ao dai* disappeared everywhere in Vietnam.

Beauty contests – a symbol of bourgeois capitalism – were banned by the communists but were finally permitted again in HCMC in 1989. Swimsuit competitions were not permitted, but many of the contestants did wear their best designer jeans. However, it was the Camau team that stole the show – they wore *ao dai*. Suddenly, there was a nationwide boom in *ao dai* production.

*Ao dai* have been around for a long time, and were anything but revealing to begin with. But in the past few years partially see-through *ao dai* have become all the rage – they're even worn by women in the north.

**Tan Hung Guesthouse** (☎ 831622; 11 Đ Ly Bon; beds 60,000d) is a budget option with squalid rooms with fan and shared bath, but it's cheap.

**Sao Mai Hotel** (☎ 831035, 834913; 38-40 Đ Phan Ngoc Hien; fan rooms 40,000-60,000d, air-con rooms 70,000-140,000d) looks better on the outside than the inside, but it's also cheap.

**Camau Trade Union Hotel** (☎ 833245; 9 Đ Luu Tan Tai; rooms with fan/air-con 60,000/135,000d), almost opposite the Cao-dai Temple, is a bit worse for wear, but reasonably priced.

**Quoc Te Hotel** (☎ 826745, fax 834470; 179 Đ Phan Ngoc Hien; fan rooms 70,000d, air-con rooms 100,000-300,000d) is a rec-ommendable new place with clean and comfortable rooms.

**Quoc Nam Hotel** (☎ 827281; 23 Đ Pham Boi Chau; fan rooms 80,000-120,000d, air-con rooms 150,000-180,000d) is another good private hotel. There's a pleasant **café** on top floor with great views.

**Ca Li Hotel** (☎ 829405; 121 Đ Nguyen Trai; air-con rooms 180,000-250,000d) is a nice new minihotel conveniently located near the minibus station.

**Camau Hotel** (☎ 831165, fax 835075; 20 Đ Phan Ngoc Hien; air-con rooms 120,000-220,000d) has better conditions than at Sao Mai, and rates include breakfast. Ditto for the **Song Hung Hotel** (☎ 822822, fax 822824; 28 Đ Phan Ngoc Hien; air-con rooms 140,000-220,000d).

## Places to Eat

Camau's speciality is shrimp, which are raised in ponds and mangrove swamps.

Decent spots for local seafood include **Trieu Chau** (243 Đ Ly Thai Ton), the newer **Sau Nghiem** (☎ 832913; 42 Đ Ly Thai Ton) and **Trieu Phat**, between the Camau Hotel and Sao Mai Hotel.

There is a cluster of small **roadside restaurants** on Đ Ly Bon, at the entrance to the street market. They are very cheap and the food is OK. The friendly **outdoor restaurant** in the Camau Trade Union Hotel is not bad, and certainly more aesthetically pleasing than eating in the market.

**Cafe Nhon** (Đ Nguyen Huu Le) is a nice place for coffee and watching the street life.

## Getting There & Away

**Bus** The buses from HCMC to Camau leave from **Mien Tay bus station** in An Lac. The trip takes 11 hours by regular bus and eight hours by express bus. There are sev-eral daily express buses to HCMC leaving between 5am and 10.30am.

The **Camau bus station** is 2.5km from the centre of town, along National Hwy 1 towards HCMC.

A faster and more comfortable option to get back to HCMC is by express minibus (60,000d). These leave from the **minibus station** (121 Đ Nguyen Trai).

**Car & Motorbike** Camau is the end of the line for National Hwy 1; it's the southern-most point in Vietnam that's accessible by car and bus. Drivers who boldly attempt to drive on the 'highway' south of Camau will soon find their vehicles sinking into a quagmire of mud and mangroves.

Camau is 178km from Cantho (3 hours) and 347km from HCMC (8 hours).

**Boat** Approximately once every four days, cargo boats run between Camau and HCMC. The trip takes 30 hours and is certainly not comfortable.

Of more interest is the boat from Camau north to Rach Gia (the boat docks in Rach Soi, about 10km from Rach Gia). This departs **Ferry Pier B** daily at around 5.15am (20,000d, 10 hours). Bicycles/motorbikes can be taken on board for 10,000/15,000d. Hammocks can be rented for 5000d. Ferry Pier B is also the spot where you can catch the speedboats heading south to Ngoc Hien.

Also popular are the boats to U-Minh Forest. These depart from **Ferry Pier A**. You'll have to do some negotiating to arrange a tour here. It's also worth asking staff at the hotels as they may be able to arrange a whole group.

## Getting Around

There are plenty of water taxis along the canal at the back of Camau Market. For longer trips upriver, larger longboats collect at the cluster of jetties just outside the market area. You can either join the throngs of passengers going downriver or hire the whole boat for about 50,000d an hour.

## AROUND CAMAU
### U-Minh Forest

The town of Camau borders the U-Minh Forest, a huge mangrove swamp covering 1000 sq km of Camau and Kien Giang provinces. Local people use certain species of mangrove as a source of timber, charcoal, thatch and tannin.When the mangroves flower, bees feed on the blossoms, providing both honey and wax. The area is an important habitat for waterfowl.

The U-Minh Forest, which is the largest mangrove swamp in the world outside of the Amazon basin, was a favourite hideout for the VC during the American War. US patrol boats were frequently ambushed here and the VC regularly planted mines in the canals. The Americans responded with chemical defoliation, which made their enemy more visible at the same time as doing enormous damage to the forests. Replanting efforts at first failed because the soil was so toxic, but gradually the heavy rainfall has washed the dioxin out to sea (where it no doubt poisons fish) and the forest is returning. Many eucalyptus trees have also been planted here because they have proved to be relatively resistant to dioxin.

Unfortunately the mangrove forests are being further damaged by clearing for shrimp-raising ponds, charcoal production and woodchipping. The government has tried to limit these activities, but the conflict between nature and humans continues. The conflict will probably get worse before it gets better, because Vietnam's population is still growing rapidly.

The area is known for its birdlife, but these creatures have also taken a beating. Nevertheless, ornithologists will derive much joy from taking boat trips around Camau. Don't expect to find the swarms of birds to be nearly as ubiquitous as the swarms of mosquitoes.

Camau Tourist offers all-day tours of the forest by boat. It costs US$135 per boat (maximum 10 people), though bargaining is possible. You can also talk to the locals down at Ferry Pier A to see if you can find a better deal.

### Bird Sanctuary

The Bird Sanctuary (Vuon Chim) is about 45km southeast of Camau. Storks are the largest and most easily seen birds here, though smaller feathered creatures also make their nests in the tall trees. Remember however that birds will be birds – they don't particularly like humans to get close to them, and they leave their nests early in the morning in search of food. Thus, your chances of getting up close and have one of them hop onto your finger for a photo session are rather slim.

Camau Tourist offers a full-day tour by boat to the sanctuary for US$120 (one to 10 people).

## NAM CAN
☎ 0780

Except for a minuscule fishing hamlet (Tran De) and an offshore island (Hon Khoai), Nam Can stakes its claim as the southernmost town in Vietnam. Few tourists come to this isolated community, which survives mainly from the shrimp industry.

At the very southern tip of the delta is the **Camau Nature Reserve**, sometimes referred to as the Ngoc Hien Bird Sanctuary. It's one of the least developed and most protected parts of the Mekong Delta region. In this area, shrimp farming is prohibited. Access is only by boat.

At the southern end of the reserve is the tiny fishing village of Tran De. A public ferry connects Tran De to Nam Can. If you are obsessed with reaching Vietnam's southern tip, you'll have to take a boat from Tran De to Hon Khoai Island.

If you're looking to visit another remote spot, you can hire a boat to take you to Dat Mui (Cape Camau), the southwestern tip of Vietnam. However, few people find this worthwhile.

## Places to Stay

**Nam Can Hotel** (☎ *877039; air-con rooms US$16*) is the only decent accommodation option in Nam Can, so you'll have little choice unless you plan on camping.

## Getting There & Away

A road connecting Camau to Nam Can is shown on most maps of Vietnam, but it's little more than wishful thinking. Basically, it's a muddy track that is underwater most of the time, though some have attempted it by motorbike.

The trip to Nam Can from Camau is best done by speedboat. These boats are readily available in Camau and they take about four hours to do the journey.

From Nam Can south to Tran De takes another four hours.

## HON KHOAI ISLAND

This island, 25km south of the southern tip of the Mekong Delta, is the southernmost point in Vietnam. Unlike the delta, which is pancake flat and intensively cultivated, Hon Khoai Island is rocky, hilly and forested. Unfortunately, getting there is fraught with hassles and few people bother. To begin with, the island is a military base, so travel permits are needed. To get these, apply in Camau at either the police station or Camau Tourist. More than likely, the police will refuse you anyway and you'll be referred to Camau Tourist. There is a small charge for this service.

The only accommodation that's available on Hon Khoai Island is at the **military guesthouse**.

## Getting There & Away

To get to Hon Khoai Island from Camau, you will first need to get yourself to Nam Can. From there you have to change boats for Tran De and then from Tran De, you have to catch a fishing boat to Hon Khoai Island.

## LONG XUYEN

☎ 076 • pop 238,100

Long Xuyen, the capital of An Giang province, was once a stronghold of the Hoa Hao sect, founded in 1939. The sect empha-

sises simplicity in worship and it does not believe in temples or intermediaries between humans and the Supreme Being. Until 1956, the Hoa Hao had an army and constituted a major military force in this region.

The town's big claim to fame is being the birthplace of Vietnam's second president, Ton Duc Thang. There is a museum in town dedicated to Bac Ton (Uncle Ton), as well as a large statue bearing his likeness.

Today, Long Xuyen is a moderately prosperous town, and the surrounding area does a good trade in agriculture, fish processing and cashew nuts. There are a few sights to see around town, but for travellers its value is mainly as a transit point with good food, accommodation and a foreign-exchange bank (change travellers cheques here if you're heading to Chau Doc; there is no place in Chau Doc to do so). The market along the riverside is colourful and lively, and boats can be hired here for about 50,000d per hour.

## Information

**An Giang Tourist** (☎ *841036, fax 847785;* e *angiangtour@ham.vnn.vn; 17 Đ Nguyen Van Cung; open 7am-11am & 1pm-5pm daily*) is beside the Long Xuyen Hotel. The staff can speak some English, and are courteous enough, but beyond selling tours they are of little use to visitors.

**Vietnam Airlines** (☎ *320320; open 7am-9pm Mon-Sat, 7am-3pm Sun*) has a booking office in the Cuu Long Hotel.

## Long Xuyen Catholic Church

One of the largest churches in the Mekong Delta, Long Xuyen Catholic Church is an impressive modern structure with a 50m-high bell tower. It was constructed between 1966 and 1973, and can seat 1000 worshippers. Masses are held daily.

## An Giang Museum

This sleepy little museum (*Bao Tang An Giang;* ☎ *841251; 77 Đ Thoai Ngoc Hau; admission free; open 7.30am-10.30am Tues, Thur, Sat & Sun, 2pm-4.30pm Sat & Sun*) is a proud highlight of An Giang province, featuring photographs and the personal

MEKONG DELTA

effects of the former president, Ton Duc Thang. There are also some artefacts from the Oc-Eo site near Rach Gia (see Around Rach Gia later in this chapter) and displays that detail the history of this region from the 1930s to the present day.

## Long Xuyen Protestant Church

This Protestant church (4 Đ Hung Vuong) is a small, modern structure. Prayers are held on Sunday from 10am to noon.

## Cho Moi District

Across the river from Long Xuyen, Cho Moi district is known for its rich groves of fruit such as bananas, durians, guava, jackfruit, longans, mangoes, mangosteens and plums.

The women here are said to be the most beautiful in the Mekong Delta.

Cho Moi district can be reached by boat from the ferry terminal at the foot of Đ Nguyen Hue.

## Places to Stay

**Thai Binh Hotel II** (☎ 847078; 4-8 Đ Nguyen Hue A; fan rooms with cold bath 70,000d, with hot water 120,000-220,000d) is an older place, but it's privately run, the staff are friendly and it's reasonably priced.

**Long Xuyen Hotel** (☎ 841927, fax 842483; e longxuyenhotel@hcm.vnn.vn; 19 Đ Nguyen Van Cung; fan rooms US$7, air-con rooms US$9-16) has rooms with baths. Optional life insurance is sold at reception for US11¢ per day!

**Cuu Long Hotel** (☎ 841365, fax 843176; 15 Đ Nguyen Van Cung; rooms without windows US$12, with windows US$14-19) has air-con and hot water in all rooms, and rates include breakfast.

**Dong Xuyen Hotel** (☎ 942260, fax 942268; e longxuyenhotel@hcm.vnn.vn; Đ 9A Luong Van Cu; doubles/suites 300,000 /450,000d), Long Xuyen's newest and fanciest accommodation offering, is right in the centre of town. The rooms are well

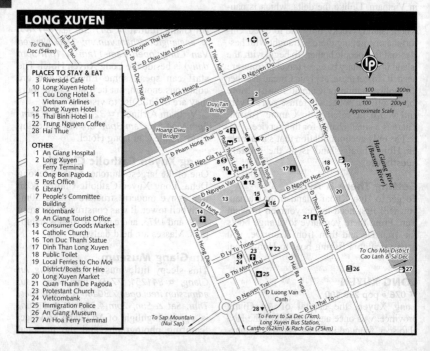

## LONG XUYEN

To Chau Doc (54km)

**PLACES TO STAY & EAT**
3 Riverside Café
10 Long Xuyen Hotel
11 Cuu Long Hotel & Vietnam Airlines
12 Dong Xuyen Hotel
15 Thai Binh Hotel II
22 Trung Nguyen Coffee
28 Hai Thue

**OTHER**
1 An Giang Hospital
2 Long Xuyen Ferry Terminal
4 Ong Bon Pagoda
5 Post Office
6 Library
7 People's Committee Building
8 Incombank
9 An Giang Tourist Office
13 Consumer Goods Market
14 Catholic Church
16 Ton Duc Thanh Statue
17 Dinh Than Long Xuyen
18 Public Toilet
19 Local Ferries to Cho Moi District/Boats for Hire
20 Long Xuyen Market
21 Quan Thanh De Pagoda
23 Protestant Church
24 Vietcombank
25 Immigration Police
26 An Giang Museum
27 An Hoa Ferry Terminal

Hau Giang River (Bassac River)

Duy Tan Bridge
Hoang Dieu Bridge

0   100   200m
0   100   200yd
Approximate Scale

To Cho Moi District Cao Lanh & Sa Dec

To Sap Mountain (Nui Sap)

To Ferry to Sa Dec (7km), Long Xuyen Bus Station, Cantho (62km) & Rach Gia (75km)

appointed (satellite TV, minibar etc) and facilities and services include massage, sauna and steam bath and a Jacuzzi.

## Places to Eat
Besides the hotel restaurants, it's slim pickings for decent places to eat in Long Xuyen.

**Hai Thue** (☎ 842432; 328/4 Đ Hung Vuong) serves up excellent and cheap Vietnamese food.

There is good coffee at **Trung Nguyen** (Đ Pham Thang Long), and a happening scene at the **riverside cafés** on Đ Pham Hong Thai.

## Getting There & Away
**Bus** The buses heading from HCMC to Long Xuyen leave from the **Mien Tay bus station** in An Lac.

**Long Xuyen bus station** (Ben Xe Long Xuyen; ☎ 852125; opposite 96/3B Đ Tran Hung Dao) is at the southern end of town. Buses from Long Xuyen to Camau, Cantho, Chau Doc, Ha Tien, HCMC and Rach Gia leave from here.

**Car & Motorbike** Long Xuyen is 62km from Cantho, 126km from Mytho and 189km from HCMC.

**Boat** To get to the **Long Xuyen ferry dock** from Đ Pham Hong Thai, cross Duy Tan Bridge and turn right. Passenger ferries leave from here to Cho Vam, Dong Tien, Hong Ngu, Kien Luong, Lai Vung, Rach Gia, Sa Dec and Tan Chau. Boats going to Rach Gia (15,000d) take about nine hours, and leave at 6.30am and/or 8am. You can also catch boats from here to Sa Dec at noon, taking about four hours and costing 10,000d.

From the An Hoa ferry terminal you can also catch boats to Cao Lanh and Sa Dec.

## Getting Around
The best way to get around Long Xuyen is to take a cyclo, *xe dap loi* (a two-wheeled wagon pulled by a bicycle) or a *xe loi*.

Car ferries from Long Xuyen to Cho Moi district (across the river) leave from the **ferry terminal** near the market every half-hour between 4am and 6.30pm.

# CHAU DOC
☎ 076 ● pop 100,000
Perched on the banks of the Bassac River, Chau Doc is a pleasant little town near the Cambodian border. Chau Doc has quite sizable Chinese, Cham and Khmer communities, each of which has built distinctive temples that are worth a visit. The city was once known for its dugout-canoe races.

Since the opening of the nearby Vinh Xuong and Tinh Bien borders between Vietnam and Cambodia, more and more travellers are finding their way to Chau Doc. Those who are not rushing in one direction or another will discover it's a nice place to chill out for a few days. There are a good many places to explore, especially in the outlying areas of town (see the Around Chau Doc section).

Be aware that there is no place to change travellers cheques or get cash advances in Chau Doc; you should take care of exchanging money before you arrive (nearby Long Xuyen is a popular place to do this).

## Chau Phu Temple
Chau Phu Temple (Dinh Than Chau Phu; cnr Đ Nguyen Van Thoai & Đ Gia Long) was built in 1926 to worship the Nguyen dynasty official Thoai Ngoc Hau, who is buried at Sam Mountain (see the Around Chau Doc section). The structure is decorated with both Vietnamese and Chinese motifs. Inside are funeral tablets bearing the names of the deceased and some biographical information about them.

## Chau Doc Church
This small Catholic church, constructed in 1920, is across the street from 459 Đ Lien Tinh Lo 10 and is not far from Phu Hiep ferry landing. There are Masses daily.

## Mosques
Domed and arched **Chau Giang Mosque** serves the local Cham Muslims and is in the hamlet of Chau Giang. To get there, take the car ferry from Chau Giang ferry landing in Chau Doc across the Hau Giang River. From the ferry landing, walk away from the river for 30m, turn left and walk 50m.

MEKONG DELTA

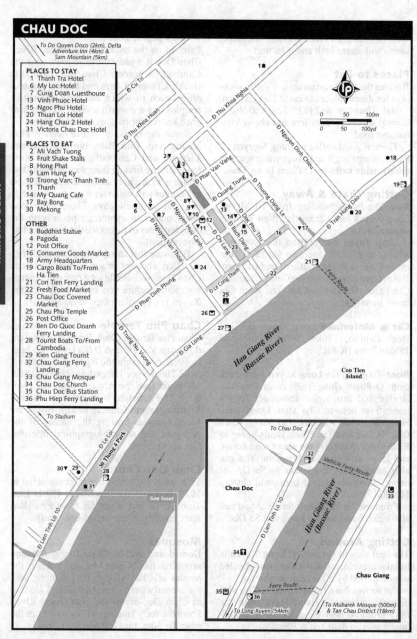

# CHAU DOC

To Do Quyen Disco (2km), Delta
Adventure Inn (4km) &
Sam Mountain (5km)

**PLACES TO STAY**
1  Thanh Tra Hotel
6  My Loc Hotel
7  Cung Doan Guesthouse
13 Vinh Phuoc Hotel
15 Ngoc Phu Hotel
20 Thuan Loi Hotel
24 Hung Chau 2 Hotel
31 Victoria Chau Doc Hotel

**PLACES TO EAT**
2  Mi Vach Tuong
5  Fruit Shake Stalls
8  Hong Phat
9  Lam Hung Ky
10 Truong Van; Thanh Tinh
11 Thanh
14 My Quang Cafe
17 Bay Bong
30 Mekong

**OTHER**
3  Buddhist Statue
4  Pagoda
12 Post Office
16 Consumer Goods Market
18 Army Headquarters
19 Cargo Boats To/From
   Ha Tien
21 Con Tien Ferry Landing
22 Fresh Food Market
23 Chau Doc Covered
   Market
25 Chau Phu Temple
26 Post Office
27 Ben Do Quoc Doanh
   Ferry Landing
28 Tourist Boats To/From
   Cambodia
29 Kien Giang Tourist
32 Chau Giang Ferry
   Landing
33 Chau Giang Mosque
34 Chau Doc Church
35 Chau Doc Bus Station
36 Phu Hiep Ferry Landing

To Stadium

D Cu Tri
D Thu Khoa Nghia
D Nguyen Dinh Chieu
D Thu Khoa Huan
D Phan Van Vang
D Quang Trung
D Thuong Dang Le
D Tran Hung Dao
D Nguyen Huu Canh
D Doc Phu Thu
D Bach Dang
D Chi Lang
D Nguyen Van Thoai
D Le Cong Thanh
D Phan Dinh Phung
D Trung Nu Vuong
D Gia Long
D Le Loi
30 Thang 4 Park
D Lien Tinh Lo 10

Hau Giang River
(Bassac River)

Con Tien
Island

0    50    100m
0    50    100yd

See Inset

To Chau Doc

Chau Doc

Chau Giang

Vehicle Ferry Route

Ferry Route

Hau Giang River
(Bassac River)

D Lien Tinh Lo 10

To Long Xuyen (54km)

To Mubarek Mosque (500m)
& Tan Chau District (18km)

MEKONG DELTA

The **Mubarak Mosque** (Thanh Duong Hoi Giao), where children study the Koran in Arabic script, is also on the river bank opposite Chau Doc. Visitors are permitted, but you should avoid entering during the calls to prayer (five times daily) unless you are a Muslim.

There are other small mosques in the Chau Doc area. These are accessible by boat, but you'll probably need a local guide to find them all.

### Floating Houses

These houses, whose floats consist of empty metal drums, are both a place to live and a livelihood for their residents. Under each house, fish are raised in suspended metal nets: the fish flourish in their natural river habitat; the family can feed them whatever scraps it has handy; and catching the fish requires less exertion than fishing. You can find these houses floating all around the Chau Doc area, and get a close-up by hiring a boat (please be respectful of their privacy though). To learn more about the workings of these fish cages, see the boxed text 'Fish Farming'.

### Places to Stay – Budget & Mid-Range

**Cong Doan Guesthouse** (☎ 866477; doubles 40,000d) is a real cheapie, but it's grimy, loud and has no air-con or private toilets.

**My Loc Hotel** (☎ 866455; 51B Đ Nguyen Van Thoai; doubles with fan 60,000d, with air-con 100,000-200,000d) is a popular yet ageing place. Fan rooms have cold bath only.

**Vinh Phuoc Hotel** (☎ 866242; 12-14 Đ Quang Trung; singles with fan/air-con US$6/8, doubles with air-con US$10) is a good-looking minihotel right in the town centre.

**Thuan Loi Hotel** (☎ 866134, ☎ 865380; 18 Đ Tran Hung Dao; doubles with fan US$6, with air-con US$10-12) is a pleasant place that commands a good location on the riverside. The 3rd-floor terrace is a great place to watch life on the river go by.

**Ngoc Phu Hotel** (☎ 866484; 17 Đ Doc Phu Thu; fan rooms 100,000d, doubles/triples with air-con 150,000/ 250,000d) is a large,

livable place. A similar standard prevails at the **Hang Chau 2 Hotel** (Đ Nguyen Van Thoai; air-con rooms 120,000-300,000d).

**Thanh Tra Hotel** (☎ 866788; 77 Đ Thu Khoa Nghia; twins with fan & cold bath 70,000d, with air-con 120,000d) is a quiet and friendly place, but it's often full with tour groups.

**Delta Adventure Inn** (Nha Khach Long Chau; ☎ 861249; e deltaadventureinn@hot mail.com; beds in a fan hut US$2; air-con rooms US$8-15), our personal favourite, is a cosy little travellers haven set amid the beautiful rice paddies about 4km from Chau Doc (see the Sam Mountain map). Cheap beds can be rented in a rustic thatched hut, while the nicer air-con rooms are in pleasant little duplex cottages. The views of Sam Mountain are lovely from the internal moat around the property. At night the central **café-restaurant** is fitted with a giant mosquito net that transforms it into a Mongolian yurt! Free shuttle wagons take guests in and out of town from 6am to 10pm.

### Places to Stay – Top End

**Victoria Chau Doc Hotel** (☎ 865010, fax 865020; e victoriachaudoc@hcm.vnn.vn, w www.victoriahotels-asia.com; 32 Đ Le Loi; rooms US$90-180++, Internet rates US$70-115++), set right on the riverside, is by far the fanciest place in town. The **Bassac Restaurant** (see Places to Eat) here is superb, and the top-floor massage salon offers the best river views in town. Nonguests can indulge themselves with day use of the swimming pool and fitness centre for US$5, or have a sauna and massage for US$8. The hotel offers high-priced boat trips linking the Victoria Cantho and Chau Doc resorts (US$55 per person, 2½ hours); stopovers can be arranged en route. Victoria boats also cruise between Chau Doc and Phnom Penh, Cambodia (US$85 per person).

### Places to Eat

Chau Doc has some truly excellent restaurants to offer.

**Bay Bong** (☎ 867271; 22 Đ Thuong Dang Le), among the town's excellent restaurants, specialises in hotpots and soups, as well

## Fish Farming

Fish farming constitutes some 15% of Vietnam's total seafood output and is widely practised in An Giang province, in the region near the Cambodian border. The highest concentration of 'floating houses' with fish cages can be observed on the banks of the Bassac River in Chau Doc, near its confluence with the mighty Mekong.

The primary fish farmed here are two species of Pangasiidae (a member of the Asian catfish family), *Pangasius bocourti* and *P. hypophthalmus*. It is interesting to note that even with two tides a day here, there is no salt water in the river. Around 15,000 tonnes of fish are exported annually, primarily to European and American markets (about 5% makes it to Australia and Japan), in the form of frozen white fish fillets.

The two-step production cycle starts with capturing fish eggs from the wild, followed by raising the fish to a marketable size – usually about 1kg. Fish are fed on a kind of dough made by the farmers from cereal, vegetables and fish scraps. The largest cage measures 2000 cu metres and can produce up to 400 tonnes of raw fish in each 10-month production cycle.

Since 1994 the French Institute for International Agronomic Research and Development (Cirad) has  been carrying out a project to develop an artificial reproduction method for the two *Pangasiidae* species. The first successful attempt was in 1995, and by 2000 production was up to 700 million larvae for each species. Further research is being conducted in Chau Doc on the nutrition and reproduction of the fish.

as fresh fish dishes. Try the stewed fish in a clay pot *(ca kho to)*, or sweet-and-sour soup *(canh chua)*.

**Mekong**, just across the road from the Victoria Chau Doc Hotel, is another place worthy of a plug. Set outdoors in front of a classic old French villa, it's a lovely place for lunch or dinner.

**Lam Hung Ky** *(71 Đ Chi Lang)* serves up some good Chinese and Vietnamese food, as does the neighbouring restaurant, **Hong Phat** *(79 Đ Chi Lang)*.

Other options nearby are the **Thanh** *(42 Đ Quang Trung)*, **Truong Van** *(15 Đ Quang Trung)* and the vegetarian **Thanh Tinh** *(13 Đ Quang Trung)* – the name of the latter means 'to calm the body down'.

**My Quang Cafe** *(25 Đ Doc Phu Thu)* is another popular eatery that is well known for its friendly service.

If you'd like to sample what's considered the best fruit shakes *(sinh to)* in town, look out for the **stalls** that are located on the corner of Đ Phan Van Vang and Đ Nguyen Van Thoai.

**Mi Vach Tuong** *(Đ Thu Khoa Nghia)*, literally meaning noodles along the wall, is a great breakfast noodle joint beside the local basketball court.

**Chau Doc Covered Market** has excellent, cheap Vietnamese food. The market is spread out along Đ Bach Dang.

**Bassic Restaurant** in the Victoria Chau Doc Hotel can't be beaten for fine dining. It also has good snack food such as burgers, sandwiches, spicy chicken wings and pizza at the hotel's poolside **Bamboo Bar**.

### Entertainment

Chau Doc is a fairly sleepy town and tends to shut down early.

The **Lobby Bar** in the Victoria Chau Doc Hotel is a nice, 'civilised' place for a drink or a game of pool.

**Do Quyen** *(☎ 865565; 7 Đ Truong Dua; open 8.30pm-11pm Sat)* is an interesting little local disco about 2km from Chau Doc on the way to Sam Mountain. At the time of writing, it was only open on Saturday, so you might inquire before heading out there.

## Getting There & Away

**Bus** The buses from HCMC to Chau Doc leave from the Mien Tay bus station in An Lac; the express bus can make the run in six hours.

The **Chau Doc bus station** (Ben Xe Chau Doc) is located southwest of town towards Long Xuyen. Buses from Chau Doc leave here for Camau, Cantho, Ha Tien, Long Xuyen, Mytho, HCMC, Soc Trang and Tra Vinh.

**Car & Motorbike** By road, Chau Doc is approximately 117km from Cantho, 181km from Mytho and 245km from HCMC.

The Chau Doc–Ha Tien road is 100km in length and is now in decent shape. As you approach Ha Tien, the land turns into a mangrove swamp that is infertile and almost uninhabited. This area is a bit scary, especially with Cambodia just a few kilometres away. It's considered reasonably safe during the day, but it's not advisable to be out here after dark. The drive takes about three hours, and it's possible to visit Ba Chuc and Tup Duc en route. If you don't plan to drive yourself, *xe om* drivers typically charge about US$5.

**Boat** There are daily boat services (via the Mekong River) between Chau Doc and Phnom Penh (Cambodia), a fascinating way to enter or exit this part of Vietnam. Departures in either direction are at around 8am and the trip takes the better part of a day. Most local guesthouses and hotels can organise tickets (US$10-15 one way). Be aware that you must arrange your Vietnamese or Cambodian visa beforehand (visas cannot be issued at the border but can easily be arranged, usually within a few days, in Phnom Penh or HCMC). The Victoria Hotel also runs a fancier (and more expensive) boat along the same route.

No-frills cargo boats run daily between Chau Doc and Ha Tien via the Vinh Te Canal (US$5); it's an interesting 95km trip. The canal, which straddles the Cambodian border, is named after Vinh Te, the wife of Thoai Ngoc Hau, who built it. Departures are at 4am (13 hours).

There are also cargo boats that go to/from Vinh Long.

## Getting Around

*Xe loi* can be hired around town for a few thousand dong.

Boats to Chau Giang district (across the Hau Giang River) leave from two docks: vehicle ferries depart from **Chau Giang ferry landing** (Ben Pha Chau Giang; opposite 419 Đ Le Loi); smaller, more frequent boats leave from **Phu Hiep ferry landing** (Ben Pha FB Phu Hiep), a little further south.

Vehicle ferries to Con Tien Island depart from the **Con Tien ferry landing** (Ben Pha Con Tien) at the river end of Đ Thuong Dang Le; you can catch boats to Chau Giang and Tan Chau from the **Ben Do Quoc Doanh ferry landing** (Đ Gia Long), opposite the post office.

Private boats (rowed standing up) can be hired from either of these spots (10,000d per hour), and are highly recommended for seeing the floating houses and visiting nearby Cham minority villages and mosques.

Prices for all of the public ferries (500d) are doubled at night; bicycles or motorbikes require their own ticket (1000d).

## AROUND CHAU DOC
☎ 076

### Tan Chau District

Tan Chau district is famous all over southern Vietnam for its traditional industry, silk making.

The market in Tan Chau has a selection of competitively priced Thai and Cambodian goods.

To get to Tan Chau district from Chau Doc, take a boat across the Hau Giang River from the Phu Hiep ferry landing, and then catch a ride on the back of a *xe om* (about 10,000d) for the 18km trip to Tan Chau district.

### Sam Mountain

There are dozens of pagodas and temples, many of them set in caves, around Sam Mountain (Nui Sam), which is about 6km southwest of Chau Doc out on Đ Bao Ho Thoai. The Chinese influence is obvious,

**MEKONG DELTA**

and Sam Mountain is a favourite spot for ethnic Chinese (both pilgrims from HCMC and tourists from Hong Kong and Taiwan).

Climbing the peak is, of course, the highlight of a visit to Sam Mountain. The views from the top are spectacular (weather permitting) and you can easily look out over Cambodia. There is a military outpost on the summit, a legacy of the days when the Khmer Rouge made cross-border raids and massacred Vietnamese civilians. The outpost is still functional, and the soldiers are quite used to tourists taking photos now; however, you should ask permission and perhaps ply the soldiers with cigarettes before taking photos of them or anything that could be considered militarily sensitive.

Walking down is easier than walking up, so if you want to cheat, have a motorbike take you to the summit. The road to the top is on the east side of the mountain. You can walk down along a peaceful, traffic-free trail on the north side which will bring you to the main temple area. The summit road has been decorated with amusement-park ceramic dinosaurs and the like, perhaps a sign of the abominations to come. But there are also some small shrines and pavilions,

which add a bit of charm and also remind you that this is indeed Vietnam and not Disneyland.

**Tay An Pagoda** This pagoda (Chua Tay An) is renowned for the fine carving of its hundreds of religious figures, most of which are made of wood. Aspects of the building's architecture reflect Hindu and Islamic influences. The first chief monk of Tay An Pagoda (founded in 1847) came from Giac Lam Pagoda in Saigon. Tay An was last rebuilt in 1958.

The main gate is of traditional Vietnamese design. Above the bi-level roof are figures of lions and two dragons fighting for possession of pearls, chrysanthemums, apricot trees and lotus blossoms. Nearby is a statue of Quan Am Thi Kinh, the Guardian Spirit of Mother and Child (see the boxed text 'Quan Am Thi Kinh' in the Ho Chi Minh City chapter).

In front of the pagoda are statues of a black elephant with two tusks and a white elephant with six tusks. Around the pagoda are monks' tombs. Inside are Buddha statues adorned with psychedelic disco lights.

**Temple of Lady Chua Xu** Founded in the 1820s, the Temple of Lady Chua Xu (Mieu Ba Chua Xu) stands facing Sam Mountain, not far from Tay An Pagoda. The first building here was made of bamboo and leaves; the last reconstruction took place in 1972.

According to legend, the statue of Lady Chua Xu used to stand at the summit of Sam Mountain. In the early 19th century, Siamese troops invaded the area and, impressed with the statue, decided to take it back to Thailand. But as they carried the statue down the hill, it became heavier and heavier, and they were forced to abandon it by the side of the path.

One day some villagers who were cutting wood came upon the statue and decided to bring it back to their village in order to build a temple for it; but it weighed too much for them to budge. Suddenly, there appeared a girl who, possessed by a spirit, declared herself to be Lady Chua Xu. She announced to them that 40 virgins were to

SAM MOUNTAIN

To Chau Doc (6km)
Delta Adventure Inn

Bong Diep Restaurant
Temple of Lady Chua Xu
Station for Transport to Chau Doc
Vinh Te Temple
Post Office Hotel
Tomb of Thoai Ngoc Hau
Tay An Pagoda
Restaurants

260m

Cavern Pagoda (Chua Hang)
Victoria Nui Sam Hotel (under construction)

Ben Da Market

0    0.5    1km
0  0.25  0.5mi
Approximate Scale

To Tri Ton, Ba Chuc, Cam Mountain & Tinh Border Crossing (22km)

be brought and that they would be able to transport the statue down the mountainside. The 40 virgins were then summoned and carried the statue down the slope, but when they reached the plain, it became too heavy and they had to set it down. The people concluded that the site where the virgins halted had been selected by Lady Chua Xu for the temple construction, and it's here that the Temple of Lady Chua Xu stands to this day.

Another story claims that the wife of Thoai Ngoc Hau, builder of the Vinh Te Canal, swore to erect a temple when the canal, whose construction had claimed many lives, was completed. She died before being able to carry out her oath, but Thoai Ngoc Hau implemented her plans by building the Temple of Lady Chua Xu.

Offerings of roast whole pigs are frequently made here, providing an interesting photo opportunity. The temple's most important festival is held from the 23rd to the 26th day of the fourth lunar month. During this time, pilgrims flock here, sleeping on mats in the large rooms of the two-storey resthouse next to the temple.

**Tomb of Thoai Ngoc Hau** A high-ranking official, Thoai Ngoc Hau (1761–1829) served the Nguyen lords and, later, the Nguyen dynasty. In early 1829, Thoai Ngoc Hau ordered that a tomb be constructed for himself at the foot of Sam Mountain. The site he chose is not far from Tay An Pagoda.

The steps are made of red 'beehive' stone *(da ong)* brought from the southeastern part of Vietnam. In the middle of the platform is the tomb of Thoai Ngoc Hau and those of his wives, Chau Thi Te and Truong Thi Miet. Nearby are several dozen other tombs where officials who served under Thoai Ngoc Hau are buried.

**Cavern Pagoda** The Cavern Pagoda (Chua Hang, also known as Phuoc Dien Tu) is about halfway up the western side of Sam Mountain. The lower part of the pagoda includes monks' quarters and two hexagonal tombs in which the founder of the pagoda, a female tailor named Le Thi Tho, and a former head monk, Thich Hue Thien, are buried.

The upper section consists of two parts: the main sanctuary, in which there are statues of A Di Da (the Buddha of the Past) and Thich Ca Buddha (Sakyamuni, the Historical Buddha); and the cavern. At the back of the cave behind the sanctuary building is a shrine dedicated to Quan The Am Bo Tat.

According to legend, Le Thi Tho came from Tay An Pagoda to this site half a century ago to lead a quiet, meditative life. When she arrived, she found two enormous snakes, one white and the other dark green. Le Thi Tho soon converted the snakes, who thereafter led pious lives. Upon her death, the snakes disappeared.

## Places to Stay & Eat

For details on the excellent **Delta Adventure Inn** (between Chau Doc and Sam Mountain), see Places to Stay in the Chau Doc section earlier.

**Post Office Hotel** *(Nui Sam Hotel; ☎ 861666, fax 861600; doubles/quads with air-con US$20/25)* is a decent hotel across the road from the Tay An Pagoda. It shares the building with the local post office, and you can take care of any philatelic needs in the lobby. Rooms are clean and rates include breakfast.

**Victoria Nui Sam Hotel**, under construction at the time of writing, features attractive stone cottages with red-tiled roofs. It's on the road leading to the summit of Sam Mountain, situated on a bluff with expansive views overlooking the plains into Cambodia.

## BA CHUC

Close to the Cambodian border, just inside Vietnam, is Ba Chuc, otherwise known as the Bone Pagoda. The pagoda stands as a grisly reminder of the horrors perpetrated by the Khmer Rouge. Between 1975 and 1978, Khmer Rouge guerrillas regularly crossed the border into Vietnam and slaughtered civilians. And this is to say nothing of the million or so Cambodians who were also killed.

Between 12 April and 30 April 1978, the Khmer Rouge killed 3157 people at Ba Chuc. Only two people are known to have survived. Many of the victims were tortured to death.

The Vietnamese government might have had other motives for invading Cambodia at the end of 1978, but certainly outrage at the Ba Chuc massacre was a major reason.

Two other notable pagodas at Ba Chuc are Chua Tam Buu and Chua Phi Lai. The 'bone' pagoda has a common tomb housing the skulls and bones of over 1100 victims. This resembles Cambodia's Choeung Ek killing fields, where thousands of skulls of Khmer Rouge victims are on display. Near the skull collection is a temple that displays gruesome photos taken shortly after the massacre. The display is both fascinating and horrifying – you do need a strong stomach to visit.

To reach Ba Chuc, follow the unpaved road that runs along the canal from Chau Doc to Ha Tien. You then need to turn off this main road onto Hwy 3T and follow it for 4km.

## TUC DUP HILL
**elevation 216m**

During the American War Tuc Dup Hill served as a strategic base of operations, favoured for its network of connecting caves. *Tuc dup* is Khmer for 'water runs at night', and it is also known locally as the 'two-million-dollar hill'. Tuc Dup is 35km from Chau Doc and 64km from Long Xuyen.

## RACH GIA
☎ 077 • pop 172,400

Rach Gia, the capital of Kien Giang province, is a booming port city on the Gulf of Thailand. The population includes significant numbers of both ethnic Chinese and ethnic Khmers.

Fishing and agriculture have made the town reasonably prosperous. Easy access to the sea and the proximity of Cambodia and Thailand have also made smuggling a profitable business here. The Rach Gia area was once famous for the large feathers used to make ceremonial fans for the Imperial Court, but this is one industry that has little chance of being revived, despite economic liberalisation.

Visitors' main interest in Rach Gia is to catch the ferry to Phu Quoc Island.

## Information
**Travel Agencies** The provincial tourism authority is **Kien Giang Tourist** (*Cong Ty Du Lich Kien Giang;* ☎ 862081, fax 862111; 12 Đ Ly Tu Trong).

**Money** Rach Gia is the last place to exchange money before Ha Tien or Phu Quoc Island. **Vietcombank** (☎ 863427) is near the west end of Đ Hem Nguyen Trai.

## Pagodas & Temples
**Nguyen Trung Truc Temple** This temple (*18 Đ Nguyen Cong Tru*) is dedicated to Nguyen Trung Truc, a leader of the resistance campaign of the 1860s against the newly arrived French. Among other exploits, he led the raid that resulted in the burning of the French warship *Espérance*. Despite repeated attempts to capture him, Nguyen Trung Truc continued to fight until 1868, when the French took his mother and a number of civilians hostage and threatened to kill them if he did not surrender. Nguyen Trung Truc turned himself in and was executed by the French in the marketplace of Rach Gia on 27 October 1868.

The first temple structure was a simple building with a thatched roof; over the years it has been enlarged and rebuilt several times. The last reconstruction took place between 1964 and 1970. In the centre of the main hall there is a portrait of Nguyen Trung Truc on an altar.

**Phat Lon Pagoda** This large Cambodian Hinayana Buddhist pagoda, whose name means Big Buddha, was founded about two centuries ago. Though all of the three dozen monks who live here are ethnic Khmers, ethnic Vietnamese also frequent the pagoda.

Inside the sanctuary (*vihara*), figures of the Thich Ca Buddha wear Cambodian- and Thai-style pointed hats. Around the exterior of the main hall are eight small altars.

The two towers near the main entrance are used to cremate the bodies of deceased monks. Near the pagoda are the tombs of about two dozen monks.

Prayers are held here daily from 4am to 6am and 5pm to 7pm. The pagoda, off Đ

Quang Trung, is officially open during the seventh, eighth and ninth lunar months (summer season), but guests are welcome all year round.

**Ong Bac De Pagoda** In the centre of town, Ong Bac De Pagoda *(14 Đ Nguyen Du)* was built by Rach Gia's Chinese community about a century ago. On the central altar there is a statue of Ong Bac De, who is considered a reincarnation of the Jade Emperor. To the left is Ong Bon, Guardian Spirit of Happiness and Virtue; and to the right is Quan Cong.

**Pho Minh Pagoda** Only a handful of Buddhist nuns live at Pho Minh Pagoda, *(cnr Đ Co Bac & Đ Nguyen Van Cu; open 6am-10pm)*. This small pagoda was built in 1967 and contains a large Thai-style Thich Ca Buddha that was donated by a Buddhist organisation based in Thailand. Near the Thai-style Buddha there is a Vietnamese-style Thich Ca Buddha. The nuns living here reside in a building that's behind the main hall.

The pagoda is open to visitors and prayers are held every day from 3.30am to 4.30am and 6.30pm to 7.30pm.

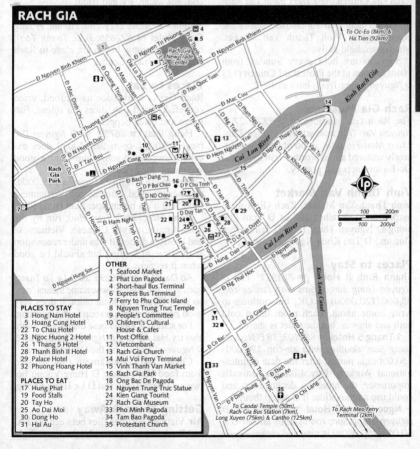

RACH GIA

To Oc-Eo (8km) & Ha Tien (92km)

Rach Gia New Trade Center

Kinh Rach Gia

Rach Gia Park

Cai Lon River

Cai Lon River

Kinh Xung Canal

To Caodai Temple (50m), Rach Gia Bus Station (7km), Long Xuyen (75km) & Cantho (125km)

To Rach Meo Ferry Terminal (2km)

**OTHER**
1  Seafood Market
2  Phat Lon Pagoda
4  Short-haul Bus Terminal
6  Express Bus Terminal
7  Ferry to Phu Quoc Island
8  Nguyen Trung Truc Temple
9  People's Committee
10 Children's Cultural House & Cafes
11 Post Office
12 Vietcombank
13 Rach Gia Church
14 Mui Voi Ferry Terminal
15 Vinh Thanh Van Market
16 Rach Gia Park
18 Ong Bac De Pagoda
21 Nguyen Trung Truc Statue
24 Kien Giang Tourist
27 Rach Gia Museum
33 Pho Minh Pagoda
34 Tam Bao Pagoda
35 Protestant Church

**PLACES TO STAY**
3  Hong Nam Hotel
5  Hoang Cung Hotel
22 To Chau Hotel
23 Ngoc Huong 2 Hotel
26 1 Thang 5 Hotel
28 Thanh Binh II Hotel
29 Palace Hotel
32 Phuong Hoang Hotel

**PLACES TO EAT**
17 Hung Phat
19 Food Stalls
20 Tay Ho
25 Ao Dai Moi
30 Dong Ho
31 Hai Au

0    100    200m
0    100    200yd

**Tam Bao Pagoda** This pagoda *(open 6am-8pm)*, which dates from the early 19th century, is near the corner of Đ Thich Thien An and Đ Ngo Quyen; it was last rebuilt in 1913. The garden contains numerous trees sculpted as dragons, deer and other animals.

Prayers are held from 4.30am to 5.30am and 5.30pm to 6.30pm.

**Caodai Temple** This is a small Caodai Temple *(189 Đ Nguyen Trung Truc)* constructed in 1969.

### Churches

**Rach Gia Church** *(Nha Tho Chanh Toa Rach Gia)*, a red-brick structure built in 1918, is in Vinh Thanh Van subdistrict, across the channel from Vinh Thanh Van Market. Masses are held daily.

Services are held every Sunday from 10am to noon at the **Protestant Church** *(133 Đ Nguyen Trung Truc)*, built in 1972.

### Rach Gia Museum

The Rach Gia Museum *(☎ 863727; 27 Đ Nguyen Van Troi; admission free; open 7am-11am Mon-Fri, or by appointment)* was recently restored and is worth a visit to see the Oc-Eo artefacts and pottery.

### Vinh Thanh Van Market

Vinh Thanh Van Market, Rach Gia's main market area, stretches east of Đ Tran Phu along Đ Nguyen Thoai Hau, Đ Trinh Hoai Duc and Đ Thu Khoa Nghia.

### Places to Stay

**Thanh Binh II Hotel** *(☎ 861921; 119 Đ Nguyen Hung Son; rooms with fan/air-con 45,000/120,000d)* is OK, but nothing to write home about. Each room has a cold bath and shower, but the toilet is shared.

**1 Thang 5 Hotel** *(☎ 862103; 38 Đ Nguyen Hung Son; doubles with air-con 120,000-150,000d)* is named after the date of International Workers' Day. Like the festival's importance, the hotel has declined too and could use a renovation. It is cheap though.

**Ngoc Huong 2 Hotel** *(☎ 863499; 150 Đ Nguyen Hung Son; rooms with fan/air-con 50,000/150,000d)* is new and clean.

**To Chau Hotel** *(☎ 863718; 16 Đ Le Loi; rooms with hot water from 140,000d)* has bath and air-con in all rooms and also has a garage.

**Palace Hotel** *(☎ 863049; 243 Đ Tran Phu; rooms with fan US$7, with air-con & hot bath US$18-23)* is a good place but starting to show it's age. Surprisingly, the cheapest rooms (on the top floor) are the ones with balconies.

**Phuong Hoang Hotel** *(☎ 866525; 6 Đ Nguyen Trung Truc; rooms 160,000-250,000d)* is one of a handful of private minihotels in town. All rooms here have air-con, hot water, TV and fridge.

A similar standard prevails at **Hong Nam Hotel** *(☎ 873090; Đ Ly Thai To)* and **Hoang Cung Hotel** *(☎ 872655; Đ Le Thanh Ton)*; both of these new hotels are close to Rach Gia's New Trade Centre.

### Places to Eat

Rach Gia is known for its seafood, dried cuttlefish, dried fish slices *(ca thieu)*, fish sauce and black pepper.

**Hung Phat** *(☎ 86759; 97 Đ Nguyen Du; meals 25,000d; open 9am-10pm)* does excellent sweet-and-sour soups and a good vegetarian fried rice.

**Tay Ho** *(16 Đ Nguyen Du; meals 15,000d)* also serves good Chinese and Vietnamese food, and it's a bit cheaper than Hung Phat.

**Dong Ho** *(124 Đ Tran Phu)*, run by the same family, serves Chinese, Vietnamese and Western dishes. It was under renovation at the time of writing but should be good when it reopens.

**Ao Dai Moi** *(☎ 866295; 26 Đ Ly Tu Trong; open 7.30am-9pm)*, whose name means 'new *ao dai*', is run by a local tailor. It does very good *pho* and won ton soup in the morning.

For standard Vietnamese dishes you might also try **Hai Au** *(cnr Đ Nguyen Trung Truc & Đ Nguyen Van Cu)*, by the Cai Lon River.

Cheap, tasty Vietnamese food is sold from **food stalls** along Đ Hung Vuong between Đ Bach Dang and Đ Le Hong Phong.

### Getting There & Away

**Air** Vietnam Airlines flies between HCMC and Rach Gia twice weekly; the same flight carries on to Phu Quoc Island (see Phu Quoc Island later in this chapter).

**Bus** Buses from HCMC to Rach Gia leave from the Mien Tay bus station in An Lac; the express bus takes six to seven hours. Night buses leave Rach Gia for HCMC between 7pm and 11pm.

The **main Rach Gia bus station** (Ben Xe Rach Soi; 78 Đ Nguyen Trung Truc) is 7km south of the city (towards Long Xuyen and Cantho). Buses link Rach Gia with Cantho, Dong Thap, Ha Tien, Long Xuyen and HCMC.

There is a **minibus terminal** (Ben Xe Ha Tien; Đ Tran Quoc Toan) closer to town that offers daily express services to Long Xuyen, Sa Dec and HCMC.

Yet a third bus terminal, this one next to Rach Gia New Trade Centre, is where you can catch buses to Hon Chong and Ha Tien.

**Car & Motorbike** Rach Gia is 92km from Ha Tien, 125km from Cantho and 248km from HCMC.

**Boat** At the western end of Đ Nguyen Cong Tru is **Rach Gia Park,** where you catch the ferries across to Phu Quoc Island (see Phu Quoc Island later in this chapter).

**Mui Voi ferry terminal** (*mui* means nose and *voi* means elephant – so named because of the shape of the island) is at the northeastern end of Đ Nguyen Thoai Hau. Cargo boats running from here make daily trips leaving at 8am to Long Xuyen (15,000d, nine hours).

Boats for Camau leave at 5am from the **Rach Meo ferry terminal** (☎ 811306; 747 Đ Ngo Quyen), about 2km south of town.

## AROUND RACH GIA
### Ancient City of Oc-Eo
Oc-Eo was a major trading city during the 1st to 6th centuries AD, when this area (along with the rest of southern Vietnam, much of southern Cambodia and the Malay peninsula) was ruled by Funan, the Indian-influenced empire. Much of what is known about the Funan empire, which reached its height during the 5th century AD, comes from contemporary Chinese sources and

the archaeological excavations at Oc-Eo. The excavations have uncovered evidence of significant contact between Oc-Eo and what is now Thailand, Malaysia and Indonesia, as well as Persia and even the Roman Empire.

An elaborate system of canals around Oc-Eo was once used for both irrigation and transportation, prompting Chinese travellers of the time to write about 'sailing across Funan' on their way to the Malay peninsula. Most of the buildings of Oc-Eo were built on piles, and pieces of these structures indicate the high degree of refinement achieved by Funanese civilisation. Artefacts found at Oc-Eo are on display in HCMC at the History and Fine Arts Museums, in Hanoi at the History Museum and in Long Xuyen at the An Giang Museum.

Though there is in fact very little to see here, the remains of Oc-Eo are not far from Rach Gia. The nearest site is Cau Chau, a hill 11km inland that is littered with potsherds and shells. It's near the village of Vong The, which can be reached by 4WD, bicycle or motorbike (about 8km away). Head 3km towards Ha Tien, cross on the local ferry and continue for 5km more. Oc-Eo is most accessible during the dry season. Special permission may be required to visit; for more information, contact Kien Giang Tourist. You might also inquire at the Hong Nam Hotel; ask for Mr Duong Quang, a local English teacher who may be able to guide you to Oc-Eo.

## HA TIEN
☎ 077 • pop 90,100
Ha Tien is on the Gulf of Thailand 8km from the Cambodian border. The area is known for its production of seafood, black pepper and items made from the shells of sea turtles. All around the area are lovely, towering limestone formations that give this place a very different appearance from the rest of the Mekong Delta. The rock formations support a network of caves, many of which have been turned into cave temples. Plantations of pepper trees cling to the hillsides. On a clear day, Phu Quoc Island is easily visible to the west.

Ha Tien was a province of Cambodia until 1708. However, in the face of attacks by the Thais, the Khmer-appointed governor, a Chinese immigrant named Mac Cuu, turned to the Vietnamese for protection and assistance. Mac Cuu thereafter governed this area as a fiefdom under the protection of the Nguyen Lords. He was succeeded as ruler by his son, Mac Thien Tu. During the 18th century, the area was invaded and pillaged several times by the Thais. Rach Gia and the southern tip of the Mekong Delta came under direct Nguyen rule in 1798.

During the Khmer Rouge regime, their forces repeatedly attacked the Vietnamese territory and massacred thousands of civilians here. The entire populations of Ha Tien and nearby villages (in fact, tens of thousands of people) fled their homes. Also during this period, areas north of Ha Tien (along the Cambodian border) were sown with mines and booby traps, which have yet to be cleared.

Though the government has designated Ha Tien a 'frontier economic zone', the border crossing here is not yet open to tourists. Rumours are circulating, however, that it is just a matter of time. Check with travel agencies and the local English-language magazines.

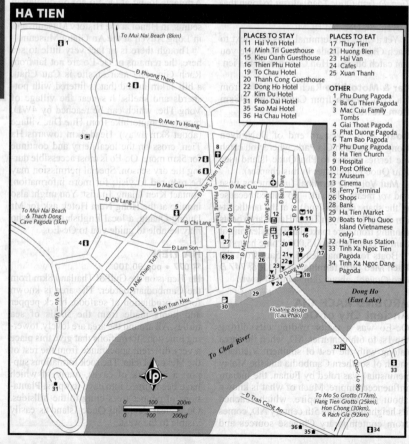

**HA TIEN**

To Mui Nai Beach (8km)

Đ Phuong Thanh

Đ Mac Tu Hoang

Đ Mac Cuu

Đ Chi Lang

To Mui Nai Beach & Thach Dong Cave Pagoda (3km)

Đ Chi Lang

Đ Lam Son

Đ Mac Thien Tich

Đ Vo Van

Đ Ben Tran Hau

Phuong Thanh

Đ Dong Da

Đ Mac Cong Du

Đ Tham Tuong Sanh

Đ Bach Dang

Đ To Chau

Floating Bridge (Cau Phao)

To Chau River

Quoc Lo 80

*Dong Ho (East Lake)*

Đ Tran Cong An

To Mo So Grotto (17km), Hang Tien Grotto (25km), Hon Chong (30km), & Rach Gia (92km)

0    100    200m
0    100    200yd

**PLACES TO STAY**
11 Hai Yen Hotel
14 Minh Tri Guesthouse
15 Kieu Oanh Guesthouse
16 Thien Phu Hotel
19 To Chau Hotel
20 Thanh Cong Guesthouse
22 Dong Ho Hotel
27 Kim Du Hotel
31 Phao Dai Hotel
35 Sao Mai Hotel
36 Ha Chau Hotel

**PLACES TO EAT**
17 Thuy Tien
21 Huong Bien
23 Hai Van
24 Cafes
25 Xuan Thanh

**OTHER**
1 Phu Dung Pagoda
2 Ba Cu Thien Pagoda
3 Mac Cuu Family Tombs
4 Giai Thoat Pagoda
5 Phat Duong Pagoda
6 Tam Bao Pagoda
7 Phu Dung Pagoda
8 Ha Tien Church
9 Hospital
10 Post Office
12 Museum
13 Cinema
18 Ferry Terminal
26 Shops
28 Bank
29 Ha Tien Market
30 Boats to Phu Quoc Island (Vietnamese only)
32 Ha Tien Bus Station
33 Tinh Xa Ngoc Tien Pagoda
34 Tinh Xa Ngoc Dang Pagoda

## Pagodas & Tombs

**Mac Cuu Family Tombs** The tombs (Lang Mac Cuu) are on a low ridge not far from town. They are known locally as Nui Lang, the Hill of the Tombs. Several dozen relatives of Mac Cuu are buried here in traditional Chinese tombs decorated with figures of dragons, phoenixes, lions and guardians.

The largest tomb is that of Mac Cuu himself; it was constructed in 1809 on the orders of Emperor Gia Long and is decorated with finely carved figures of Thanh Long (Green Dragon) and Bach Ho (White Tiger). The tomb of Mac Cuu's first wife is flanked by dragons and phoenixes. At the bottom of the ridge is a shrine dedicated to the Mac family.

**Tam Bao Pagoda** This pagoda *(Sac Tu Tam Bao Tu; 328 Đ Phuong Thanh; open 7am-9pm daily)* was founded by Mac Cuu in 1730. It is now home to several Buddhist nuns. In front of the pagoda is a statue of Quan The Am Bo Tat standing on a lotus blossom in the middle of a pond. Inside the sanctuary, the largest statue on the dais is of A Di Da, the Buddha of the Past. It is made of bronze, but has been painted. Outside, the building are the tombs of 16 monks.

Near Tam Bao Pagoda is a section of the city wall dating from the early 18th century. Prayers are held from 8am to 9am and 2pm to 3pm. From the 15th day of the fourth lunar month to the 15th day of the seventh lunar month (roughly from May to August) prayers are held six times a day.

**Phu Dung Pagoda** This pagoda *(Phu Cu Am Tu; open 6am-10pm daily)* was founded in the mid-18th century by Mac Thien Tich's wife, Nguyen Thi Xuan. It is now home to one monk.

In the middle of the main hall is a peculiar statue of nine dragons embracing a newly born Thich Ca Buddha. The most interesting statue on the main dais is a bronze Thich Ca Buddha brought from China, which is kept in a glass case. On the hillside behind the main hall are the tombs of Nguyen Thi Xuan and one of her female servants; nearby are four monks' tombs.

Behind the main hall is a small temple, Dien Ngoc Hoang, dedicated to the Taoist Jade Emperor. The figures inside are of Ngoc Hoang flanked by Nam Tao, the Taoist God of the Southern Polar Star and the God of Happiness (on the right), and Bac Dao, the Taoist God of the Northern Polar Star and the God of Longevity (on the left). The statues are made of papier-mache moulded over bamboo frames.

Prayers are held from 4am to 5am and 7pm to 8pm. To get to Phu Dung Pagoda, turn off Đ Phuong Thanh at No 374.

**Thach Dong Cave Pagoda** Also known as Chua Thanh Van, this is a subterranean Buddhist temple 4km from town.

To the left of the entrance is the Stele of Hatred (Bia Cam Thu), which commemorates the massacre by the Khmer Rouge of 130 people here on 14 March 1978.

Several of the chambers contain funerary tablets and altars to Ngoc Hoang, Quan The Am Bo Tat and the two Buddhist monks who founded the temples of this pagoda. The wind here creates extraordinary sounds as it blows through the grotto's passageways. Openings in several branches of the cave afford views of nearby Cambodia.

## Dong Ho

Dong Ho (East Lake) is not a lake at all but an inlet of the sea. The 'lake' is just east of Ha Tien, and bounded to the east by a chain of granite hills known as the Ngu Ho (Five Tigers) and to the west by the hills, To Chan. Dong Ho is said to be most beautiful on nights when there is a full or almost-full moon. According to legend, on such nights fairies dance here in the moonlight.

**MEKONG DELTA**

### Warning!

Ha Tien itself is considered safe day or night; however, the rural areas northwest of town along the Cambodian border can be dangerous at night. In particular, this includes Mui Nai Beach. Khmer gangsters have on occasion slipped across the border at night to commit robberies or kidnap people for ransom.

## Ha Tien Market

Ha Tien has an excellent market along the To Chau River. It's well worth your while to stop here – many of the goods are from Thailand and Cambodia, and prices are lower than in HCMC. Cigarette smuggling is particularly big business.

## Places to Stay

Ha Tien's budget accommodation is very basic. Guesthouses charge around 12,000d to sleep on a straw mat on a cement floor. These places include **Thanh Cong Guesthouse**, on Đ To Chau.

**Minh Tri Guesthouse** (☎ 852724; 22 Đ To Chau; rooms with fan/air-con 70,000/ 120,000d) is a slightly better option than the latter.

**Kieu Oanh Guesthouse** (☎ 852748; 20 Đ To Chau; rooms with fan/air-con 80,000/ 120,000d), next door to Minh Tri, has a similar standard.

**Thien Phu Hotel** (☎ 851144; 684 Đ Chi Lang; rooms with fan US$5, 6-person room US$14), moving upmarket, is a clean place. There is a three-bed room that can sleep six people.

**Kim Du Hotel** (☎ 851929, fax 852119; 14 Đ Phuong Thanh; rooms with air-con 140,000-230,000d) is a new, pleasant place, and the in-house **restaurant** is good. Rates include breakfast.

**Hai Yen Hotel** (☎ 851580; 15 Đ To Chau; small/large air-con rooms 200,000/250,000d) is another private hotel that is worth considering. All rooms have hot water and a fridge.

**To Chau Hotel** (☎ 852148; Đ To Chau; fan rooms US$5, with air-con US$8-10) is a decent-looking state-owned hotel.

**Dong Ho Hotel** (☎ 852141) is another decent choice in the same price range, but it's closer to the river. Rooms have air-con, TV and fridge.

**Sao Mai Hotel** (☎ 852740; Đ Tran Cong An; rooms with fan 80,000d, singles/doubles with air-con 120,000/150,000d) is a nice friendly place south of the floating bridge.

**Ha Chau Hotel** (☎ 852553; fan rooms 80,000d, air-con rooms US$8-10), next door to Sao Mai, is of a similar standard.

**Phao Dai Hotel** (☎ 851849; fan rooms 80,000d, air-con 120,000-140,000d), in the far southwest of town, is a relatively quiet place.

## Places to Eat

Ha Tien's speciality is an unusual variety of coconut that can only be found in Cambodia and this part of Vietnam. These coconuts contain no milk, but the delicate flesh is delicious. Restaurants all around the Ha Tien area serve the coconut flesh in a glass with ice and sugar. The Cambodians have long claimed that any place which has these coconuts is part of Cambodia (hence the Khmer Rouge's justification for their attacks on this part of Vietnam).

**Hai Van** (☎ 850344; 4 Đ Ben Tran Hau; mains 25,000-40,000d) is a new place dishing up Vietnamese, Chinese and Western meals.

**Xuan Thanh** (cnr Đ Ben Tran Hau & Đ Tham Tuong Sanh), a friendly place, serves some of the best grub in Ha Tien. Opposite the market, it has tasty food and the most salubrious surroundings in town.

**Huong Bien** (Đ To Chau) is also an excellent place to eat.

**Thuy Tien** (Đ Dong Ho) has decent food, but most go for the scenic lakeside location.

## Getting There & Away

**Bus** Buses from HCMC to Ha Tien leave from the Mien Tay bus station in An Lac; the trip takes nine to 10 hours.

**Ha Tien bus station** (Ben Xe Ha Tien) is on the other side of the floating toll bridge from the centre of town. Buses leave from here to An Giang province, Cantho (5.50am and 9.10am), Vinh Long province, HCMC (2am) and Rach Gia (5 hours, five times a day).

**Car & Motorbike** Ha Tien is 92km from Rach Gia, 95km from Chau Doc, 206km from Cantho and 338km from HCMC.

**Boat** Passenger ferries dock at the **ferry terminal**, which is not far from the To Chau Hotel near the floating bridge. Daily ferries depart for Chau Doc (3 hours) at 6am. You can travel by boat all the way from HCMC to Ha Tien with a change of boats in Chau Doc, but it's a very long journey and the boats are anything but luxurious.

## AROUND HA TIEN

There are numerous other islands off the coast between Rach Gia and the Cambodian border. Some local people make a living gathering precious swiftlet nests (the most important ingredient of that famous Chinese delicacy bird's-nest soup), on the islands' rocky cliffs.

### Beaches

The beaches in this part of Vietnam face the Gulf of Thailand. The water is incredibly warm and calm here, like a placid lake. The beaches are OK for bathing and diving, but hopeless for surfing.

Mui Nai (Stag's Head Peninsula) is 8km west of Ha Tien; it is said to resemble the head of a stag with its mouth pointing upward. On top is a lighthouse, and there are sand beaches on both sides of the peninsula. Mui Nai is accessible by road from both Ha Tien and from Thach Dong Cave Pagoda.

No Beach (Bai No), lined with coconut palms, is several kilometres west of Ha Tien near a fishing village.

Bang Beach (Bai Bang) is a long stretch of dark sand shaded by *bang* trees.

### Mo So Grotto

About 17km towards Rach Gia from Ha Tien, and 3km from the road, Mo So Grotto consists of three large rooms and a labyrinth of tunnels. Sadly, the local Morning Star cement factory has carted away a substantial amount of limestone and managed to cause irreparable damage to the grotto. The cave is accessible on foot during the dry season and by small boat during the wet season. Visitors should take torches (flashlights) and a local guide.

### Hang Tien Grotto

Hang Tien Grotto, 25km towards Rach Gia from Ha Tien, served as a hideout for Nguyen Anh (later Emperor Gia Long) in 1784, when he was being pursued by the Tay Son Rebels. His fighters found zinc coins buried here, a discovery that gave the cave its name, Coin Grotto. Hang Tien Grotto is accessible by boat.

## Hon Giang Island

Hon Giang Island, which is about 15km from Ha Tien and can be reached by small boat, has a lovely, secluded beach.

## HON CHONG

☎ 077

This small and secluded village beach resort has the most scenic stretch of coastline on the Mekong Delta mainland. It is a peaceful place (most of the year) and worth chilling out in for a few days. Hon Chong (also called Binh An) is seldom visited by foreign travellers.

The big attractions here are Chua Hang Grotto, Duong Beach and Nghe Island. Though a far cry from the stunning 3000-plus islands and grottoes of Halong Bay (see the Northeast Vietnam chapter), the stone formations are indeed photogenic. Aside from the three gargantuan eyesore cement factories that spew out smoke along the road from Ha Tien, the coastal drive there boasts some beautiful landscape.

### Chua Hang Grotto

The grotto is entered through a Buddhist temple set against the base of a hill. The temple is called Hai Son Tu (Sea Mountain Temple). Visitors light incense and offer prayers here before entering the grotto itself, whose entrance is behind the altar. Inside is a plaster statue of Quan The Am Bo Tat. The thick stalactites are hollow and resonate like bells when tapped.

### Duong Beach

This beach (also known as Bai Duong) runs north from Chua Hang Grotto and is named for its long-needled pine trees *(duong)*. The southern area can get busy with Vietnamese tourists (and their beloved karaoke), but otherwise the 3km stretch of coast is quite tranquil.

Although this is easily the prettiest beach in the Mekong Delta, don't expect any white sand. The waters around the delta contain heavy concentrations of silt (and recently, cement dust), so the beach sand tends to be hard while in the water it's muddy. Still, the water is reasonably clear here and this is the only beach south of HCMC (excluding those on Phu Quoc Island) that looks appealing to swimmers. The beach is known for its spectacular sunsets.

From the busy southern end of the beach (near Chua Hang Grotto), you can see Father and Son Isle (Hon Phu Tu) several hundred metres offshore; it is said to be shaped like a father embracing his son. The island, a column of stone, is perched on a 'foot' worn away by the pounding of the waves; the foot is almost fully exposed at low tide. Boats can be hired at the shore to row out for a closer look.

### Nghe Island

This is the most beautiful island in the area, and is a favourite pilgrimage spot for Buddhists. The island contains a **cave temple** (Chua Hang) next to a large statue of Quan The Am Bo Tat, which faces the sea. The area where you'll find the cave temple and statue is called Doc Lau Chuong.

Finding a boat to the island is not too difficult, though it is much cheaper if you round up a group. Inquire at the Hon Trem Guesthouse; a full-day, three-island boat trip costs around US$60, and the boat can hold 15 people. The boat ride to the island usually takes about one to two hours. There is also a speedboat for hire at the waterside **Doi Xanh restaurant**, 4.5km from the Chua Hang Grotto back towards Ha Tien. The owner charges US$50/100 for a half-/full day of island hopping. The boat can carry around 20 people.

At the time of writing, tourists were not permitted to stay on the island.

### Places to Stay

A word of warning: the hotels are completely packed out when Buddhists arrive to worship 15 days before and one month after Tet. Another worship deluge occurs in March and April.

**Green House Guesthouse** (☎ 854369; air-con rooms US$16-20) is the first place

you will see as you arrive in Hon Chong. It is a family-run guesthouse, with nice clean rooms, perched on a knoll overlooking Duong Beach. Meals can be arranged.

**Phuong Thao Hotel** (☎ 854357; rooms with fan/air-con 80,000/130,000d) is 200m beyond the Green House Guesthouse and has bungalow-style rooms.

**Hon Trem Guesthouse** (☎/fax 854331; air-con rooms from 130,000d) is a state-owned place near the bend in the road, about 1km before the beach gate. It features rooms in a large cottage, or in the main building. The hotel can prepare meals on request. New hill-top bungalows were under construction at the time of writing.

**Huong Bien Guesthouse** (dorm beds US$2, doubles with fan US$4) is near the entrance gate to the Chua Hang Grotto and therefore rather noisy.

**Binh An Hotel** (☎ 854332, fax 854533; fan rooms US$4, air-con rooms 140,000-160,000d) is 1km towards Chua Hang Grotto on the same road as the Phuong Thao Hotel, and is a fine place. It's in a large quiet compound surrounded by a wall with gardens. All rooms have a private bath. The old-wing fan rooms are grotty but cheap, while rooms in the new wing feature air-con and are much nicer.

**My Lan Hotel** (☎ 759044, fax 759040; fan rooms 110,000d, air-con rooms 180,000-210,000d) is a recommendable hotel that was invested in by overseas Vietnamese from Milan, Italy (hence its name My Lan). Rooms are nondescript, but clean.

**Hai Son Tourist Resort** (☎ 759226) was under construction next to My Lan Hotel when we last visited. It promises to be nice, and rooms with fan/air-con should be around 120,000/170,000d.

### Places to Eat

Aside from special orders prepared at your hotel, there are **food stalls** just near the entrance of Chua Hang Grotto. For only a few dollars, you can point to one of the live chickens, which will be summarily executed and barbecued for you.

**Hong Ngoc,** just near the entrance gate to the Chua Hang Grotto, is a good place to sample delicious Ha Tien coconuts. The owner speaks French.

## Getting There & Away

Chua Hang Grotto and Duong Beach are 32km from Ha Tien towards Rach Gia. The access road branches off the Rach Gia–Ha Tien highway at the small town of Ba Hon, which is just west of the cement factory at Kien Luong. Buses can drop you off at Ba Hon, from where you can hire a motorbike.

There's also a direct bus service from Rach Gia to Hon Chong (15,000d, 4 hours). It departs from the **Ben Xe Ha Tien bus station** (Ð 30 Thang 4) in Rach Gia at 10am, and leaves again from Hon Chong (outside Huong Bien Guesthouse) to Rach Gia at 4am.

## PHU QUOC ISLAND

☎ 077 • pop 52,700

Mountainous and forested Phu Quoc Island is in the Gulf of Thailand, 45km west of Ha Tien, and 15km south of the coast of Cambodia. This tear-shaped island, which is 48km long and has an area of 1320 sq km, is ringed with some of the most beautiful beaches in Vietnam. There are fantastic views of marine life through transparent blue-green waters (though unfortunately there are no scuba diving operators on the island – yet).

Phu Quoc is claimed by Cambodia; its Khmer name is usually rendered Ko Tral. Needless to say, the Vietnamese view it very differently, and to this end have built a substantial military base covering much of the northern end of the island. Phu Quoc is governed as a district of Kien Giang province.

Phu Quoc Island served as a base for the French missionary Pigneau de Behaine during the 1760s and 1780s. Prince Nguyen Anh, who later became Emperor Gia Long, was sheltered here by Behaine when he was being hunted by the Tay Son Rebels.

During the American War there was a little fighting here, but Phu Quoc Island was mainly useful to the Americans as a prison for captured VC.

Phu Quoc is not really part of the Mekong Delta, and doesn't share the delta's extraordinary ability to produce rice. The most valuable crop is black pepper, but the islanders have traditionally earned their living from the sea. Phu Quoc is also famous in Vietnam for its production of high-quality nuoc mam.

The island is also known for Phu Quoc hunting dogs. The dogs have been a great success – with their help, the islanders have decimated most of the island's wildlife. These dogs are said to be able to pick up the scent of their master from over 1km away.

Phu Quoc has tremendous tourism potential, which is so far mostly unrealised. Transport difficulties, not to mention some of the best beaches being occupied by military bases, have contributed to keeping the visitors away. But since it became a national park in 2001, the island is gaining more attention. **Phu Quoc National Park** covers close to 70% of the island, an area of 31,422 hectares.

Phu Quoc's rainy season is from July to November. The peak season for tourism is mid-winter, when the sky is blue and the sea is calm; however, when it's not raining, it's stinking hot (at least when the sun is up). Bring sunglasses and plenty of sun block and be prepared to spend the afternoons at the beach or in the shade. Don't set out to explore the island unless you've got at least 2L of water in your day-pack or else you'll dehydrate.

## Information

**Travel Agencies** The local tourism authority, **Phu Quoc Tourist** (☎ 846318, fax 847125), has a sleepy office in central Duong Dong. The staff here sell pricey minibus and boat tours, but otherwise they don't do much that couldn't be accomplished through your hotel.

Most travellers get around the island by hired motorbike. There are a handful of English-speaking motorbike guides on the island, the most notorious of whom is **Tony** (☎ 077-846144). Raised by a US military family, Tony speaks a distinctive breed of Al Pacino English that could easily land him a role in the next sequel to The Godfather. He is easy to find (more likely he'll find you) or can be faxed if you want to book ahead.

MEKONG DELTA

MEKONG DELTA

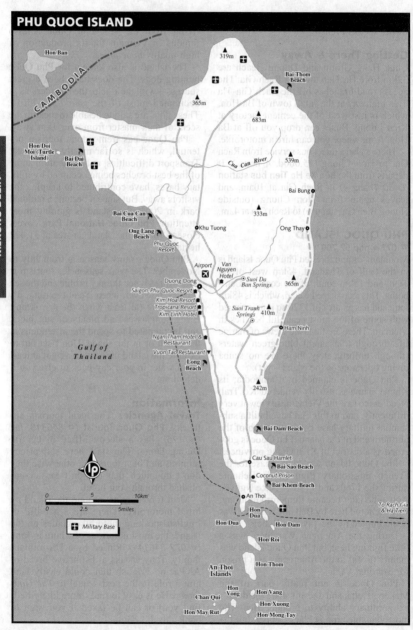

# PHU QUOC ISLAND

Hon Ban

CAMBODIA

319m

Bai Thom Beach

365m

683m

Hon Doi Moi (Turtle Island)

Bai Dai Beach

539m

Cua Can River

Bai Bung

Bai Cua Can Beach

333m

Ong Thay

Khu Tuong

Ong Lang Beach

Phu Quoc Resort

Airport

Van Nguyen Hotel

Duong Dong

Suoi Da Ban Springs

365m

Saigon-Phu Quoc Resort
Kim Hoa Resort
Tropicana Resort
Kim Linh Hotel

Suoi Tranh Springs

410m

Ham Ninh

Ngan Tham Hotel & Restaurant

Vuon Tao Restaurant

Long Beach

Gulf of Thailand

242m

Bai Dam Beach

Cau Sau Hamlet

Bai Sao Beach

Coconut Prison

Bai Khem Beach

An Thoi

To Rach Gia & Ha Tien

Hon Dua

Hon Dam

Hon Roi

Hon Thom

An Thoi Islands

Hon Vong

Hon Vang

Chan Qui

Hon Xuong

Hon May Rut

Hon Mong Tay

0     5     10km
0   2.5   5miles

Military Base

**Money** There is no place on the island to cash travellers cheques and the rate for changing dollars at the Agricultural Bank in Duong Dong is rotten. In other words, take care of all your money changing before you arrive. You can, of course, pay for almost anything with US dollars.

## Duong Dong

The island's chief fishing port is Duong Dong, a town on the central west coast. The airport and most of the hotels are here.

The town is not that exciting, though the markets are mildly interesting. The bridge nearby is a good vantage point to photograph the island's fishing fleet – you'll notice that this tiny harbour is anything but clean.

According to tourist brochures, the town's main attraction is **Cau Castle** (Dinh Cau). In fact, it's not so much a castle as a combination temple and lighthouse. It was built in 1937 to honour Thien Hau (Goddess of the Sea), who protects sailors and fishermen. The castle is worth a quick look, and it does give you a good view of the entrance to the harbour.

## Fish Sauce Factory

OK, OK, so it's not your average sightseeing attraction, but more than a few have enjoyed a visit to the distillery of Nuoc Mam Hung Thanh, the largest of Phu Quoc's fish-sauce makers. At first glance, the giant wooden vats may make you think you've arrived for a wine tasting, but one sniff of the festering *nuoc mam* essence brings you right back to reality (it's actually not so bad after a few minutes).

Most of the sauce produced is exported to the mainland for domestic consumption, though a surprising amount finds its way abroad to kitchens in Japan, the USA, Canada and France.

The factory is a short walk from the markets in Duong Dong. There is no charge to visit, though you'd be best off taking a guide along, unless you speak Vietnamese. Should you feel compelled to take a bottle of the stuff home to your loved ones as a souvenir, try the Hung Thanh retail shop, near the bridge in town.

## An Thoi

The main shipping port is An Thoi at the southern tip of the island. This town is not blessed with scenic sights, though the market here is definitely worth a quick look. This is the embarkation point for Ha Tien and Rach Gia, or for day trips to the An Thoi Islands.

## Beaches

**Bai Dai & Bai Thom** These are both remote beaches: Bai Dai is in the far northwest and Bai Thom is on the northeastern coast. You will require a motorbike ride of at least an hour over very bad roads. You can rest assured that neither beach is crowded. Bai Thom was closed to the public at the time of writing.

Both are in military areas – the military usually opens these beaches to civilians on Sunday but you must leave your passport with the military receptionist while you're on the base. This is problematic since most hotels insist on taking your passport until you check out. In any event, do not try to sneak onto the beaches: make local inquiries and obey the rules.

**Bai Cua Can** This is the most accessible beach in the northwest. Bai Cua Can is 11km from Duong Dong, though it's a rather long dusty trip by motorbike.

**Long Beach** This beach (Bai Truong) is one long spectacular stretch of sand from Duong Dong southward along the west coast, almost to An Thoi port (20km). The southern end of the beach is known as Tau Ru Bay (Khoe Tau Ru). The water is crystal clear and the beach is lined with coconut palms.

Long Beach is easily accessible on foot (just walk south from Duong Dong's Cau Castle), but you will need a motorbike or bicycle to reach some of the remote stretches towards the southern end of the island. The beach around the Kim Linh Hotel is a particularly popular spot. There are a few bamboo huts where you can buy drinks, but bring water if you're planning a long hike along this beach.

**Bai Khem** The most beautiful white-sand beach of all is Bai Khem (Bai Kem), meaning 'cream beach'. The name is inspired by the creamy white sand, which resembles powdered chalk. Its only shortcoming is that it lacks shade – there are no trees here.

The beach is in a cove on the southeastern side of the island. This place is totally undeveloped because it's a military area, but civilians are permitted to enter. Turn off the main highway by the English sign saying 'Restricted Area – No Trespassing'. It's 28km from Duong Dong and 2km from An Thoi, so you'll almost certainly have to go there by motorbike. You should lock the motorbike securely since you won't be able to watch it; however, theft is not a big problem in this remote spot.

**Bai Sao & Bai Dam** Along the southeast part of the island just north of Bai Khem there are two other beaches, Bai Sao and Bai Dam.

## Suoi Da Ban

Compared with the waterlogged Mekong Delta, Phu Quoc has very little surface moisture; however, there are several springs that originate in the hills. The most accessible of these is Suoi Da Ban (Stony Surface Stream). Basically, it's a white-water creek tumbling across some attractive large granite boulders. There are deep pools and it's pleasant enough for a swim. Don't forget to bring plenty of mosquito repellent.

The stream is in the south-central part of the island. There is no admission charge, though there is a 4000d fee for parking a motorbike.

## Forest Reserves

Phu Quoc's poor soil and lack of surface water have disappointed farmers for generations, although their grief has been the island's environmental salvation. About 90% of the island is forested, and the trees now enjoy official protection. Indeed, this is

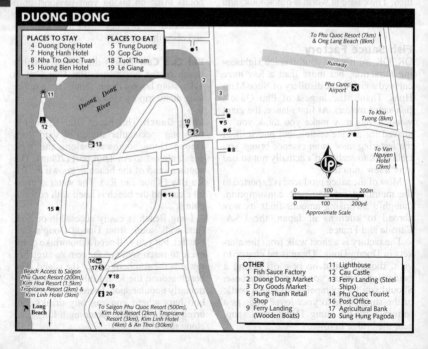

## DUONG DONG

**PLACES TO STAY**
4 Duong Dong Hotel
7 Hong Hanh Hotel
8 Nha Tro Quoc Tuan
15 Huong Bien Hotel

**PLACES TO EAT**
5 Trung Duong
10 Gop Gio
18 Tuoi Tham
19 Le Giang

To Phu Quoc Resort (7km) & Ong Lang Beach (8km)

Runway

Duong Dong River

Phu Quoc Airport

To Khu Tuong (8km)

To Van Nguyen Hotel (2km)

0    100    200m
0    100    200yd
Approximate Scale

Beach Access to Saigon Phu Quoc Resort (200m), Kim Hoa Resort (1.5km) Tropicana Resort (2km) & Kim Linh Hotel (3km)

Long Beach

To Saigon Phu Quoc Resort (500m), Kim Hoa Resort (2km), Tropicana Resort (3km), Kim Linh Hotel (4km) & An Thoi (30km)

**OTHER**
1 Fish Sauce Factory
2 Duong Dong Market
3 Dry Goods Market
6 Hung Thanh Retail Shop
9 Ferry Landing (Wooden Boats)
11 Lighthouse
12 Cau Castle
13 Ferry Landing (Steel Ships)
14 Phu Quoc Tourist
16 Post Office
17 Agricultural Bank
20 Sung Hung Pagoda

the last large stand of forest in southern Vietnam.

The forest is most dense in the mountainous northern half of the island. This area has been declared a forest reserve (Khu Rung Nguyen Sinh). You'll need a motorbike or mountain bike to get into the reserve. There are a few primitive dirt roads, but no real hiking trails.

## An Thoi Islands

Off the southern tip of Phu Quoc are the tiny An Thoi Islands (Quan Dao An Thoi). These 15 islands and islets can be visited by chartered boat, and it's a fine area for sightseeing, fishing, swimming and snorkelling. Hon Thom (Pineapple Island) is about 3km in length and is the largest island in the group. Other islands here include Hon Dua (Coconut Island), Hon Roi (Lamp Island), Hon Vang (Echo Island), Hon May Rut (Cold Cloud Island), Hon Dam (Shadow Island), Chan Qui (Yellow Tortoise) and Hon Mong Tay (Short Gun Island).

Most boats depart from An Thoi on Phu Quoc, but you can make arrangements through hotels in Duong Dong. The Tropicana Resort has a large boat for charter that can make the trip directly from Long Beach. The Kim Linh also has two boats for day hire, one that can carry eight to 10 passengers (US$35) and a larger one that can carry 15 to 20 people (US$65). Boat charters are seasonal and generally do not run during the rainy season.

## Coconut Prison

Being an island and a economically marginal area of Vietnam, Phu Quoc was useful to the French-colonial administration – chiefly as a prison. The Americans took over where the French left off, and as a consequence Phu Quoc was used to house about 40,000 VC prisoners.

The island's main penal colony was known as the Coconut Prison (Nha Lao Cay Dua) and is near An Thoi town. Though it's considered an historic site and plans are under way to open a museum here, it's still used as a prison. Not too surprisingly, few visitors come to check it out.

## Places to Stay

Depending on the tourist load, prices for Phu Quoc's hotels and resorts are very much negotiable.

**Long Beach** Near the beach and cheap, **Kim Linh Hotel** (☎ 846611, fax 846144; e quochoapq@yahoo.com; fan rooms 100,000 -120,000d) is an ageing place with concrete buildings, but it remains the favourite of backpackers. It's often full, but the management tries to accommodate any overflow by renting out tents on the beach or allowing people to sleep in hammocks in the restaurant after it closes.

**Tropicana Resort** (☎ 847127; e vn@yahoo .com; rooms US$15-30), a few hundred metres north, is a nicer resort. Rooms are in bungalows, and windsurfers and boats are for hire. Credit cards are accepted, and rates include breakfast and airport pick-up. There is a veranda **restaurant** for watching sunsets. Staff speak French and English.

**Kim Hoa Resort** (☎ 847039, fax 848261; rooms US$10, bungalows US$15-20), a short walk from the Tropicana, is a friendly place near the beach. Here too there is a pleasant terrace **restaurant**. As a footnote, the proprietor of the resort also owns a local nuoc mam factory and sometimes offers tours to interested parties.

**Saigon-Phu Quoc Resort** (☎ 846510, fax 847163; e sgphuquocresort@hcm.vnn.vn, w www.scphuquocresort.com.vn; rooms US$34-97++, family house US$234++) is a snazzy place that rents rooms in villa-type houses. The cheaper rooms are offered in a four-bedroom villa, while the more expensive rate is for a villa with two rooms. The rooms are attractive, and have a good vantage point overlooking the beautiful beach. There is a swimming pool and a large restaurant on the property.

**Ong Lang Beach** Ong Lang Beach, 7km north of Duong Dong near the hamlet of Ong Lang, is rockier and less beautiful than Long Beach, but is unquestionably less crowded and quieter.

**Phu Quoc Resort** (Khach San Thang Loi; ☎ 091-919891, fax 846144; rooms

US$10-20) is a lovely resort that has 10 wooden bungalows set in a vast open garden setting, under the shade of cashew nut, palm and mango trees. The staff are friendly and the restaurant is cosy. Room rates vary depending on the size. The resort is also known locally as Ong Lang (named after the beach).

**Duong Dong** Most travellers prefer to put up at the beach, though there are several options in the town, if you're not set on staying by the sea.

**Duong Dong Hotel** (☎ 846106; fan rooms without bath 50,000d), close to Duong Dong Market, has rooms that are dark boxes, but the management is friendly.

**Nha Tro Quoc Tuan** (☎ 847552; fan rooms with toilet 70,000d), slightly better than Duong Dong Hotel, is nearby.

**Hong Hanh Hotel** (☎ 847187; doubles with fan/air-con 100,000/180,000d), directly across from the airport, is a basic minihotel with clean rooms.

**Huong Bien Hotel** (☎ 846113, fax 847065; fan rooms 120,000d, air-con rooms 160,000-290,000d) is a large government-run hotel on the west side of Duong Dong. It's right on Long Beach, but unfortunately not the nicer part. The hotel's name means 'fragrant sea', possibly a reference to the sewerage discharged from the nearby Duong Dong fishing harbour.

**An Thoi** Although few travellers care to stay in the township of An Thoi , it's worth considering if you arrive late on the ferry or will be taking the ferry early the next morning.

**Thanh Dat Guesthouse** (Nha Khach Phuong Tham; ☎ 844022; fan rooms 50,000-80,000d) is the only place to stay in town.

## Places to Eat
**Gop Gio**, near the ferry landing in Duong Dong, is a casual eatery that wins hands down for the freshest (and cheapest) seafood in town. Also worth a try in town is **Trung Duong**.

**Tuoi Tham** and **Le Giang** are two more local places on the way from Duong Dong to Long Beach.

For atmosphere and fine food, check out the seafront terrace restaurants at the **Tropicana Resort** and the **Kim Hoa Resort**.

For something a bit more local (and loud), try the outdoor **beachside restaurants** near the Kim Linh Hotel.

There are heaps of cheap **food stalls** all around the market area in Duong Dong.

## Getting There & Away
**Air** Vietnam Airlines has four flights weekly between HCMC and Duong Dong, Phu Quoc's main town. Some flights make a stop en route at Rach Gia, on the mainland.

A popular round trip between HCMC and Phu Quoc is to travel overland through the Mekong Delta, taking a ferry to the island (or a flight for 430,000d from Rach Gia, and when you're finally tanned and rested, taking the short one-hour flight (670,000d) back to HCMC.

**Boat** For information about the upmarket cruises between Bangkok (Thailand) and Phu Quoc Island, you should contact **Star Cruises** (ⓦ www.starcruises. com).

All passenger ferries departing and arriving at Phu Quoc use the port of An Thoi on the southern tip of the island.

There are **ferries** (☎ 863242) every morning between Rach Gia and Phu Quoc (140km). Departures are at 9am, but may vary depending on the tides and passenger load. In any case, it's best to be there early, not only to be assured passage, but also to stake out a good spot to sit or lie down on. On the smaller ferry boats, avoid the cosy-looking platform over the engine unless you fancy being slow-roasted during the trip! Be sure to stock up on snacks and water in town, or at the docks.

None of the boats in the fleet (three vintage steel vessels and five wooden fishing boats) are very comfortable. They are usually packed with too many passengers (who string hammocks across every possible nook and cranny) and cargo (including noisy fighting cocks and other exotic animals). Although we haven't heard of any mishaps, concerned parties might consider flying. Boats cannot dock at Rach Gia when the tide is low – passengers and cargo have to be ferried offshore in a small shuttle boat.

The fare is 66,000d and the ride to An Thoi takes about eight hours. Most travellers jump off here and catch a motorbike to Duong Dong. However, if you're not in a rush to reach your hotel by sundown, it's possible to pay an extra 15,000d (when you buy your ticket) and stay on board right up to Duong Dong. This takes another 1½ hours, plus about an hour waiting while the ferry unloads cargo in An Thoi, but you're likely to appreciate a moonlit cruise up the coast.

There are on-again off-again boats between Ham Tinh (on the east coast of Phu Quoc) and Ha Tien on the mainland, but these are considered to be dangerous and not worth the risk.

## Getting Around

**To/From the Airport** Phu Quoc's airport is almost in central Duong Dong. Unless your luggage is really heavy, you can easily walk the few hundred metres to the centre of town. If you're heading for one of the hotels on Long Beach, just walk down the beach from the Huong Bien Hotel.

The motorbike drivers at the airport will charge you about US$1 to most hotels, but are notorious for trying to cart people off to where they can collect a commission. If you know where you want to go, tell them you've already got a reservation.

**Bus** There is a skeletal bus service between An Thoi and Duong Dong. Buses run perhaps once every hour or two. There is a bus waiting for the ferry at An Thoi to take passengers to Duong Dong (10,000d).

**Motorbike** You'll hardly have to look for the motorbike taxis – they'll be looking for you. Some polite bargaining may be necessary. For most short runs within the town itself, 5000d should be sufficient. Otherwise, figure on around 10,000d for about 5km. From Duong Dong to An Thoi should cost you about 30,000d.

Motorbike can be hired for US$10 per day. Add another US$5 if you want a driver as well. This should be sufficient to get you anywhere on the island. If interested, just ask at your hotel.

There are no paved roads on the island, and after a day of motorbike riding you can expect to be covered from head to toe with dust.

**Bicycle** If you can ride a bicycle in the tropical heat over these dusty, bumpy roads, more power to you. Bicycle rentals are available through most hotels for about US$1 per day.

# Language

## LANGUAGES IN VIETNAM

Vietnamese is the official language of Vietnam, and it is spoken throughout the country. Dialectical differences are marked between the north, central and southern regions. There are also dozens of different languages spoken by the various ethnic minorities, particularly in the Central Highlands and the far north of the country. Khmer, the Cambodian language, is spoken in parts of the Mekong Delta, and in addition Laotian and various Chinese dialects can be heard in spots along their respective borders.

The Vietnamese people's knowledge of foreign languages reflects their country's relationship with foreign powers – cordial or otherwise – in recent history.

Much of Vietnam's elder generation still speak French, while many middle-aged Vietnamese speak Russian and other Eastern European languages – many of these people spent time in countries like Russia, Bulgaria and the former East Germany during the Cold War (at least until it thawed in the late 1980s). Today, however, Vietnam's youth has fully embraced the English language. A fair number of young people also study Japanese, French and other Western European languages.

From around 1980 to about 1987, anyone caught studying English was liable to be arrested. This was part of a general crackdown against people wanting to flee to the West. That attitude has changed and today the study of English is being pursued with a passion. The most widely spoken foreign languages in Vietnam are Chinese (Cantonese and Mandarin), English and French, more or less in that order. People in their 50s and older (who grew up during the colonial period) are much more likely to understand some French than southerners of the successive generation, for whom English was indispensable for professional and commercial contacts with the Americans.

## Alexandre de Rhodes

One of the most illustrious of the early missionaries was the brilliant French Jesuit scholar Alexandre de Rhodes (1591–1660). De Rhodes first preached in Vietnamese only six months after arriving in the country in 1627, and he is most recognised for his work in devising *quoc ngu*, the Latin-based phonetic alphabet in which Vietnamese is written to this day. By replacing Chinese characters with quoc ngu, de Rhodes facilitated the propagation of the gospel to a wide audience.

Over the course of his long career, de Rhodes flitted back and forth between Hanoi, Macau, Rome and Paris, seeking support and funding for his missionary activities and battling both Portuguese colonial opposition and the intractable Vatican bureaucracy. In 1645, he was sentenced to death for illegally entering Vietnam to proselytise, but was expelled instead; two of the priests with him were beheaded.

For his contributions, Alexandre de Rhodes gained the highest respect from the Vietnamese (in the south, anyway), who called him *cha caả* (father). A memorial statue of de Rhodes stands in central Saigon.

Some southern Vietnamese men – former combat interpreters – speak a quaint form of English peppered with all sorts of charming southern-American expressions such as 'y'all come back' and 'it ain't worth didley squat', pronounced with a perceptible drawl. Apparently, they worked with Americans from the deep south, carefully studied their pronunciation and diligently learned every nuance.

Many of the Vietnamese who speak English – especially former South Vietnamese soldiers and officials – learned it while working with the Americans during the war. After reunification, almost all of them spent periods of time ranging from a few months to 15 years in 're-education camps'. Many of these former South Vietnamese soldiers and officials will be delighted to renew contact with Americans, with whose compatriots they spent so much time, often in very difficult circumstances, half a lifetime ago. Former long-term prisoners often have friends and acquaintances all over the country (you meet an awful lot of people in 10 or more years), constituting an 'old boys' network' of sorts.

These days, almost everyone has a desire to learn English. If you're looking to make contacts with English students, the best place is at the basic food stalls in university areas. But at times you might find yourself looking to avoid such contacts, as one foreigner commented:

At a sightseeing spot I was approached by a group studying English in evening classes. They go in their spare time to tourist areas hoping to get a chance to talk with foreigners. Sometimes it gets a bit tiresome to cope with enthusiastic students with a very limited vocabulary, but I believe it is a must to be polite and never to be arrogant or rude. I observed that foreigners are often disrespectful towards Vietnamese, and that really annoyed me. Often the locals told me that foreigners are reluctant, evasive and also insulting when approached by Vietnamese students. I tried to explain to my counterparts that some travellers might be afraid when approached and surrounded by a group of strangers. I explained to them the paranoia caused by crime in the West, which they found surprising – they simply weren't aware of the problems of Western societies. When I

told them openly of the negative aspects of my country, they immediately opened up to me too, telling off-the-record facts. Silly small talk is not what they are interested in, only the language barrier reduces conversations to that level. Better be prepared for questions about capitalist societies: economics, law, the parliamentary system and so on.

Spoken Chinese (both Cantonese and Mandarin) is making a definite comeback after years of being supressed. The large number of free-spending tourists and investors from Taiwan and Hong Kong provides the chief motivation for studying Chinese. In addition, cross-border trade with mainland China has been increasing rapidly and those who can speak Chinese are well positioned to profit from it.

After reunification, the teaching of Russian was stressed all over the country. With the collapse of the USSR in 1991, all interest in studying Russian has ground to a screeching halt. Most Vietnamese who bothered to learn the language have either forgotten it or are in the process of forgetting it now.

## VIETNAMESE

The Vietnamese language (Kinh) is a fusion of Mon-Khmer, Tai and Chinese elements. Vietnamese derived a significant percentage of its basic words from the non-tonal Mon-Khmer languages. From the Tai languages, it adopted certain grammatical elements and tonality. Chinese gave Vietnamese most of its philosophical, literary, technical and governmental vocabulary, as well as its traditional writing system.

### Written Vietnamese

For centuries, the Vietnamese language was written in standard Chinese characters (chu nho). Around the 13th century, the Vietnamese devised their own system of writing (chu nom or just nom), which was created by combining Chinese characters or using them for their phonetic significance only. Both writing systems were used simultaneously until the 20th century – official business and scholarship was conducted in chu nho, while chu nom was used for popular literature. The Latin-based *quoc ngu* script, widely used since WWI, was developed in the 17th century by Alexandre de Rhodes (see the aside earlier in this chapter). The use of quoc ngu served to undermine the position of Mandarin officials, whose power was based on traditional scholarship written in chu nho and chu nom, scripts largely inaccessible to the masses.

The Vietnamese treat every syllable as an independent word, so 'Saigon' is spelt 'Sai Gon' and 'Vietnam' is written as 'Viet Nam'. Foreigners aren't too comfortable with this system – we prefer to read 'London' rather than 'Lon Don'. This leads to the notion that Vietnamese is a 'monosyllabic language', where every syllable represents an independent word. This idea appears to be a hangover from the Chinese writing system, where every syllable is represented by an independent character and each character is treated as a meaningful word. In reality, Vietnamese appears to be polysyllabic, like English. However, writing systems do influence people's perceptions of their own language, so the Vietnamese themselves will insist that their language is monosyllabic – it's a debate probably not worth pursuing.

## Pronunciation

Most of the names of the letters of the quoc ngu alphabet are pronounced like the letters of the French alphabet. Dictionaries are alphabetised as in English except that each vowel/tone combination is treated as a different letter. The consonants of the Romanised Vietnamese alphabet are pronounced more or less as they are in English with a few exceptions, and Vietnamese makes no use of the Roman letters 'f', 'j', 'w' and 'z'.

| | |
|---|---|
| c | as an unaspirated 'k' |
| đ | (with crossbar) a hard 'd' as in 'do' |
| d | (without crossbar) as the 'z' in 'zoo' (north); as the 'y' in 'yes' (south) |
| gi- | as a 'z' (north); as 'y' (south) |
| kh- | as the 'ch' in German *buch* |
| ng- | as the '-nga-' sound in 'long ago' |
| nh- | as the 'ni' in 'onion' |
| ph- | as the 'f' in 'far' |
| r | as 'z' (north); as 'r' (south) |
| s | as 's' (north); as 'sh' (south) |
| tr- | as 'ch' (north); as 'tr' (south) |
| th- | a strongly aspirated 't' |
| x | like an 's' |
| -ch | like a 'k' |
| -ng | as the 'ng' in 'long' but with the lips closed |
| -nh | as the 'ng' in 'sing' |

## Tones

The hardest part of studying Vietnamese for westerners is learning to differentiate between the tones. There are six tones in spoken Vietnamese. Thus, every syllable in Vietnamese can be pronounced six different ways. For example, depending on the tones, the word *ma* can be read to mean 'phantom', 'but', 'mother', 'rice seedling', 'tomb' or 'horse'.

The six tones of spoken Vietnamese are indicated with five diacritical marks in written form (the first tone is left unmarked). These should not be confused with the four other diacritical marks used to indicate special consonants and vowels, such as the crossbar in đ.

The following examples show the six different tone representations:

| Tone Name | Example | |
|---|---|---|
| *dấu ngang* | *ma* | 'ghost' |
| *dấu sắc* | *má* | 'mother' |
| *dấu huyền* | *mà* | 'which' |
| *dấu nặng* | *mạ* | 'rice seedling' |
| *dấu hỏi* | *mả* | 'tomb' |
| *dấu ngã* | *mã* | 'horse' |

A visual representation looks something like this:

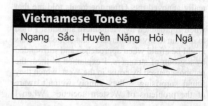

**Vietnamese Tones**

Ngang  Sắc  Huyền  Nặng  Hỏi  Ngã

## Grammar

Vietnamese grammar is fairly straight-forward, with a wide variety of possible sentence structures. Nouns have no masculine/feminine or plural forms and verbs have only one form regardless of gender, person or tense. Instead, tool words and classifiers are used to show a word's relationship to its neighbours. For example, in the expression *con mèo (của) tôi* (my cat), *con* is the classifier, *mèo* is the noun, *của* means 'of/belong to' (and can be omitted), and *tôi* is the personal pronoun 'I'.

Questions are asked in the negative, as with *n'est-ce pas?* in French. When the Vietnamese ask 'Is it OK?' they say 'It's OK, isn't it?'. The answer 'no' means 'Not OK it isn't,' which is the double negative form of 'Yes, it's OK'. The answer 'yes', on the other hand, means 'Yes, it isn't OK' or as we would say in English, 'No, it isn't OK'. The result is that when negative questions ('It's not OK, is it?') are posed to Vietnamese, great confusion often ensues.

## Proper Names

Most Vietnamese names consist of a family name, a middle name and a given name, in that order. Thus, if Henry David Thoreau had been Vietnamese, he would have been named Thoreau David Henry and would have been addressed as Mr Henry – people are called by their given name, but to do this without using the title Mr, Mrs or Miss is considered as expressing either great intimacy or arrogance of the sort a superior would use with his or her inferior.

In Vietnamese, Mr is *Ông* if the man is of your grandparents' generation, *Bác* if he is of your parents' age, *Chú* if he is younger than your parents and *Anh* if he is in his teens or early 20s. Mrs is *Bà* if the woman is of your grandparents' age and *Bác* if she is of your parents' generation or younger. Miss is *Chị* or *Em* unless the woman is very young, in which case *Cô* might be more appropriate. Other titles of respect are *Thầy* (Buddhist monk or male teacher), *Bà* (Buddhist nun), *Cha* (Catholic priest) and *Cô* (Catholic nun).

There are 300 or so family names in use in Vietnam, the most common of which is Nguyen (which is pronounced something like 'nwee-en'). About half of all Vietnamese have the surname Nguyen! When women marry, they usually (but not always) take their husband's family name. The middle name may be purely ornamental, may indicate the sex of its bearer or may be used by all the male members of a given family. A person's given name is carefully chosen to form a harmonious and meaningful ensemble with their family and middle names and with the names of other family members.

For a more comprehensive guide to the language, get a copy of Lonely Planet's *Vietnamese phrasebook*. The following list of words and phrases will help get you started. Some variation exists between the Vietnamese of the north and the south – this is indicated in this chapter by (N) and (S) respectively.

## Pronouns

| | |
|---|---|
| I | *tôi* |
| you | *ông* (to an older man) |
| | *bà* (to an older woman) |
| | *anh* (to a man your own age) |
| | *chị* (to a woman your own age) |
| he | *cậu ấy/anh ấy* (N) |
| | *cậu đó/anh đó* (S) |
| she | *chị ấy/cô ấy* (N) |
| | *chị đó/anh đó* (S) |
| we | *chúng tôi* |
| they | *họ* |

## Greetings & Civilities

| | |
|---|---|
| Hello. | *Xin chào.* |
| How are you? | *Có khỏe không?* |
| Fine, thank you. | *Khỏe, cám ơn.* |
| Good night. | *Chúc ngủ ngon.* |
| Excuse me. (often used before questions) | *Xin lỗi.* |
| Thank you. | *Cảm ơn.* |
| Thank you very much. | *Cảm ơn rất nhiều.* |
| What's your name? | *Tên là gì?* |
| My name is ... | *Tên tôi là ...* |

**LANGUAGE**

## Useful Words & Phrases

| | |
|---|---|
| Yes. | *Vâng.* (N) |
| | *Dạ.* (S) |
| No. | *Không.* |
| I don't understand. | *Tôi không hiểu.* |
| I need ... | *Tôi cần ...* |
| I like ... | *Tôi thích ...* |
| I don't like ... | *Tôi không thích ...* |
| I want ... | *Tôi muốn ...* |
| I don't want ... | *Tôi không muốn ...* |
| change money | *đổi tiền* |
| come | *đến* |
| give | *cho* |
| fast | *nhanh* (N) |
| | *mau* (S) |
| slow | *chậm* |
| man | *nam* |
| woman | *nữ* |
| understand | *hiểu* |

## Getting Around

| | |
|---|---|
| What time does the first bus depart? | *Chuyến xe buýt sớm nhất chạy lúc mấy giờ?* |
| What time does the last bus depart? | *Chuyến xe buýt cuối cùng sẽ chạy lúc mấy giờ?* |
| How many kilo-metres to ...? | *Cách xa bao nhiêu ki-lô-mét ...?* |
| How long does the journey take? | *Chuyến đi sẽ mất bao lâu?* |
| I want to go to ... | *Tôi muốn đi ...* |
| What time does it arrive? | *Mấy giờ đến?* |
| Go. | *Đi.* |
| hire a car | *thuê xe hơi* (N) |
| | *muớn xe hơi* (S) |
| bus | *xe buýt* |
| bus station | *bến xe* |
| cyclo (pedicab) | *xe xích lô* |
| map | *bản đồ* |
| railway station | *ga xe lửa* |
| sleeping berth | *giường ngủ* |
| timetable | *thời biểu* |
| train | *xe lửa* |

## Around Town

| | |
|---|---|
| office | *văn phòng* |
| post office | *bưu điện* |
| restaurant | *nhà hàng* |
| telephone | *điện thoại* |

| | |
|---|---|
| boulevard | *đại lộ* |
| bridge | *cầu* |
| highway | *xa lộ* |
| island | *đảo* |
| mountain | *núi* |
| National Highway 1 | *Quốc Lộ 1* |
| river | *sông* |
| square (in a city) | *công viên* |
| street | *phố/đường* (N/S) |
| north | *bắc* |
| south | *nam* |
| east | *đông* |
| west | *tây* |

## Accommodation

| | |
|---|---|
| hotel | *khách sạn* |
| guesthouse | *nhà khách* |
| Where is there a (cheap) hotel? | *Ở đâu có khách sạn (rẻ tiền)?* |
| How much does a room cost? | *Giá một phòng là bao nhiêu?* |
| I'd like a cheap room. | *Tôi thích một phòng loại rẻ.* |
| I need to leave at ... o'clock (tomorrow morning). | *Tôi phải đi lúc ... giờ (sáng mai).* |
| air-conditioning | *máy lạnh* |
| bathroom | *phòng tắm* |
| blanket | *mền* |
| fan | *quạt máy* |
| hot water | *nước nóng* |
| laundry | *giặt ủi* |
| mosquito net | *màng* |
| reception | *tiếp tân* |
| room | *phòng* |
| room key | *chìa khóa phòng* |
| 1st class room | *phòng loại 1* |
| 2nd class room | *phòng loại 2* |
| sheet | *ra trải giường* |
| toilet | *nhà vệ sinh* |
| toilet paper | *giấy vệ sinh* |
| towel | *khăn tắm* |

## Shopping

| | |
|---|---|
| I'd like to buy ... | *Tôi muốn mua ...* |
| How much is this? | *Cái này giá bao nhiêu?* |
| I want to pay in dong. | *Tôi muốn trả bằng tiền Việt Nam.* |